U.S. Military Operations

U.S. Military Operations

LAW, POLICY, AND PRACTICE

Edited by Geoffrey S. Corn
Rachel E. VanLandingham
and
Shane R. Reeves

Foreword by General Stanley A. McChrystal
U.S. ARMY, RETIRED

OXFORD
UNIVERSITY PRESS

OXFORD
UNIVERSITY PRESS

Oxford University Press is a department of the University of Oxford. It furthers the University's objective of excellence in research, scholarship, and education by publishing worldwide.

Oxford New York
Auckland Cape Town Dar es Salaam Hong Kong Karachi Kuala Lumpur Madrid
Melbourne Mexico City Nairobi New Delhi Shanghai Taipei Toronto

With offices in
Argentina Austria Brazil Chile Czech Republic France Greece Guatemala Hungary
Italy Japan Poland Portugal Singapore South Korea Switzerland Thailand
Turkey Ukraine Vietnam

Published in the United States of America by
Oxford University Press
198 Madison Avenue, New York, NY 10016

Library of Congress Cataloging-in-Publication Data

U.S. military operations : law, policy, and practice / edited by Geoffrey S. Corn,
Rachel E. VanLandingham, Shane R. Reeves ; foreword by General Stanley A. McChrystal,
U.S. Army, retired.
pages cm
Includes bibliographical references and index.
ISBN 978-0-19-932857-4 (hardback : alk. paper)—ISBN 978-0-19-045663-4 (pbk. : alk. paper)
1. Military law—United States. 2. War (International law) I. Corn, Geoffrey S., editor.
II. VanLandingham, Rachel E., editor. III. Reeves, Shane R., editor. IV. Title: United States military operations.
KF7209.U17 2015
343.73'01—dc23

2015017146

9 8 7 6 5 4 3 2 1

Printed in the United States of America on acid-free paper

Note to Readers

This publication is designed to provide accurate and authoritative information in regard to the subject matter covered. It is based upon sources believed to be accurate and reliable and is intended to be current as of the time it was written. It is sold with the understanding that the publisher is not engaged in rendering legal, accounting, or other professional services. If legal advice or other expert assistance is required, the services of a competent professional person should be sought. Also, to confirm that the information has not been affected or changed by recent developments, traditional legal research techniques should be used, including checking primary sources where appropriate.

(Based on the Declaration of Principles jointly adopted by a Committee of the American Bar Association and a Committee of Publishers and Associations.)

DISCLAIMER

The views expressed herein are the personal views of the respective chapter authors, and nothing herein reflects the official policy or position of any government, governmental agency, or nongovernmental agency.

As legal advisers, we dedicate this book to the courageous U.S. service members who tirelessly implement and protect the law in dangerous situations around the globe.

CONTENTS

FOREWORD

General Stanley A. McChrystal (U.S. Army, retired)

General Stanley A. McChrystal (ret.) was called "one of America's greatest warriors" by Secretary of Defense Robert Gates. He is the former commander of U.S. and International Security Assistance Forces (ISAF) Afghanistan and the former commander of the nation's premier military counterterrorism force, Joint Special Operations Command (JSOC). He is best known for developing and implementing the counterinsurgency strategy in Afghanistan, and for creating a comprehensive counterterrorism organization that revolutionized the interagency operating culture. General McChrystal is a graduate of West Point and the U.S. Naval War College. He also completed fellowships at Harvard's John F. Kennedy School of Government in 1997 and the Council on Foreign Relations in 2000. Throughout his military career, General McChrystal held several leadership and staff positions, including commanding the 75th Ranger Regiment. After 9/11 until his retirement in 2010, General McChrystal spent more than seven years deployed to combat in a variety of leadership positions. General McChrystal's memoir, "My Share of the Task," *was a* "New York Times" *bestseller in 2013. He is currently a senior fellow at Yale University's Jackson Institute for Global Affairs and cofounder of the McChrystal Group, a leadership consulting firm.*

In my early military career, a commander's military lawyer—a Judge Advocate, or JAG—was probably most useful for administrative actions, or in explicitly disciplinary matters. As with so many other aspects of war that have transformed since then, advances in technology, the media, and the battlefield have irrevocably changed the role of the JAG: today, every aspect of military operations requires competent, ethical, and timely legal advice.

Modern military actions run the gamut from defensive cyber maneuvers, detention operations, state capacity building, and missions to kill or capture al Qaida leaders during operations in Afghanistan and Iraq. Although military lawyers have always been important in contemporary military operations, today they are critical to mission success. Our nation's Judge Advocates provide legal, and at times, policy advice that is integrated into every aspect of military operations.

This is an inevitable consequence of the complexity of the twenty-first-century military environment. Contemporary technology has only made the law more relevant on the battlefield, as it permits a more nuanced approach to the use of armed force. The increasing ability to be precise, to amass vast amounts of intelligence through reconnaissance and surveillance, and to use amazing stand-off capabilities, demand experienced legal operators. Judge Advocates contribute to strategic, operational, and tactical successes by ensuring commanders understand and integrate applicable law and policy into each stage and aspect of an operation. In today's fast-paced, often fluid operating environments, this is vital.

It is therefore easy to write an introduction to a book that vividly describes how military commanders navigate and operationalize today's sometimes arcane and complicated web of legal rules. Military attorneys are the lynchpin in that process, and their first-hand accounts make this book both highly credible and useful. My own former legal advisor, Brigadier General Rich Gross, one of this book's contributors and currently the top operational attorney in the Department of Defense, epitomizes today's warrior lawyer. The support he and his JAG colleagues provided to my commands during our long association was indispensable to our units' successes. Although numerous experts on "military law" exist in academia and think tanks, the contributors to this book have lived and breathed the law amid the fast, often confusing flow of war. They have personally experienced how the legal rubber meets the road, and have taken on the responsibility of advising, knowing that the law serves as both a brake on—as well as a green light for—commanders' decisions.

I would encourage the many academics, politicians, policymakers, students, and others interested in the law of military operations to read this book. By doing so, they will gain a greater understanding for how the law is integrated into operations (for example, how proportionality is actually assessed and implemented) and for the role of the military legal advisor. The authors of this book, military law practitioners from all the services, possess a remarkable range and breadth of expertise. They not only succinctly relay the legal framework of their respective chapter topics, but more importantly, if they describe how the "black-letter law" actually manifests itself outside of books and treaties, in real military operations.

In my view, such a work is long overdue. This book should be considered an essential resource for anyone genuinely interested in understanding the law of military operations. No true understanding of the exercise of U.S. military power can be attained without a solid appreciation for how the law shapes military missions and their outcomes. This book contributes to that appreciation, and it does so with a nuanced sophistication I have come to expect from the remarkable ranks of attorney warfighters who are the United States' JAGs.

CONTRIBUTORS

LTC Jim Barkei is an active duty Army Judge Advocate. LTC Barkei deployed in support of the 1st Infantry Division, International Security Assistance Force (ISAF) and United States Forces-Afghanistan in Iraq and Afghanistan, respectively.

Anthony W. Bell III a Lieutenant Colonel in the Air Force Judge Advocate General's Corps. He previously worked as an Assistant Professor of Law at the United States Air Force Academy where he taught Cyber Law, National Security Law, and Introduction to Law.

Colonel Jeffrey Bovarnick is a U.S. Army judge advocate. COL Bovarnick's prior assignments include: Chief, International and Operational Law, Combined Joint Task Force-180, Bagram, Afghanistan; Chief, Investigative Judge Team, Law and Order Task Force, Forward Operating Base Shield, Iraq; Chair, International and Operational Law Department.

Gary D. Brown Colonel, USAF (ret.) was the first Staff Judge Advocate at U.S. Cyber Command. He served as the senior legal advisor to America's cyber command from 2009 to 2012.

Colonel Gary P. Corn is a Judge Advocate, United States Army. His most recent assignment is as the Staff Judge Advocate/principal legal advisor for the Commander of U.S. Cyber Command.

Geoffrey S. Corn is The Presidential Research Professor of Law at South Texas College of Law in Houston Texas, who retired in 2004 from the U.S. Army as a Lieutenant Colonel.

Colonel James H. Dapper is an active duty Air Force Judge Advocate. Currently, Col Dapper serves as the senior legal adviser for the Air Force's Air Mobility Command.

Renn Gade Colonel, U.S. Army (ret.), is currently the Senior Legal Counsel at the National Counterterrorism Center. While in the military he served as the Staff Judge Advocate to a number of joint and Army commands, including: U.S. Special Operations Command, Multinational Force-Iraq, Multinational Corps-Iraq, XVIII Airborne Corps, and the 82nd Airborne Division.

Kevin H. Govern is an Associate Professor of Law at Ave Maria School of Law, and Executive Board Member at the University of Pennsylvania Law School's Center for Ethics and the Rule of Law.

Matthew R. Grant is Colonel, U.S. Air Force, Judge Advocate General's Corps; Director of Legal Services, U.S. Air Forces in Europe—United Kingdom.

Richard C. "Rich" Gross Brigadier General, U.S. Army. He is currently serving as the Legal Counsel to the Chairman of the Joint Chiefs of Staff, the Pentagon, Washington, DC.

Ian Henderson is Group Captain for the Royal Australian Air Force.

Sandra L. Hodgkinson is currently a Captain in the Navy JAG reserves. She is a former member of the Senior Executive Service in the U.S. government. She has taught National Security Law at Catholic University Columbus School of Law since 2007.

Todd C. Huntley is Captain, Judge Advocate General's Corps, U.S. Navy; Head, National Security Law Department, International and Operational Law Division, Office of the Navy Judge Advocate General and Adjunct Professor, Georgetown University Law Center.

Chris Jenks is Assistant Professor of Law and Criminal Justice Clinic Director, SMU Dedman School of Law, Lieutenant Colonel (retired), U.S. Army.

Stanley A. McChrystal General, United States Army (retired).

Mark P. Nevitt Commander (CDR), United States Navy is an active duty Navy Judge Advocate. A former Naval Flight Officer who has flown missions from aircraft carriers, CDR Nevitt is currently assigned as the Regional Environmental Counsel for the Mid-Atlantic Region in Norfolk, VA.

Charles N. Pede Brigadier General, Commander, United States Army Legal Services Agency and Chief Judge, U.S. Army Court of Criminal Appeals.

Todd W. Pennington Lieutenant Colonel, United States Air Force, is an active duty Air Force Judge Advocate.

Jody M. Prescott Senior Fellow, West Point Center for the Rule of Law; adjunct professor, Department of Political Science, University of Vermont.

Shane R. Reeves is a Lieutenant Colonel in the United States Army and an Associate Professor at the United States Military Academy, West Point.

Stephanie M. Smart is a retired Navy Judge Advocate and currently Associate Deputy General Counsel (Intelligence), Department of Defense. While on active duty, Stephanie commanded Naval Legal Service Office Southeast, served as Deputy Legal Counsel to the Chairman of the Joint Chiefs of Staff, and Fleet Judge Advocate to Commander, U.S. Seventh Fleet in Yokosuka, Japan.

Rachel E. VanLandingham is an Associate Professor of Law at Southwestern Law School. She served as an active-duty Judge Advocate and retired as a Lieutenant Colonel in the U.S. Air Force. While an active duty Air Force Judge Advocate, Professor VanLandingham served in the position of Chief, International Law at

U.S. Central Command from 2006 to 2010 and as U.S. Central Command Liaison to the International Committee of the Red Cross.

Jack Vrett is a former U.S. Army Judge Advocate who served as the Chief of International & Operational Law for the 101st Airborne Division while on active duty and currently practices law in Chicago, IL.

Paul Walker a Commander in the Navy Judge Advocate General's Corps, is currently assigned as the Director of the Navy Judge Advocate General's Cyber, Information Operations and Intelligence Law Division.

Dave Wallace is a Colonel in the United States Army and a Professor and the Deputy Head, Department of Law at the United States Military Academy, West Point.

Marc Warren is a senior counsel in the Aviation and Administrative Law & Regulatory practice groups in Crowell & Moring's Washington, DC, office. Prior to joining Crowell & Moring, Marc served as acting chief counsel of the Federal Aviation Administration.

Richard M. Whitaker serves as the Director of Sensitive Activities Oversight, United States Special Operations Command (USSOCOM). Additionally, he is a retired Colonel, United States Army.

Major Winston Williams U.S. Army, is a Judge Advocate currently serving as an Academy Professor in the Department of Law at the United States Military Academy, West Point.

1 }

The U.S. Judge Advocate in Contemporary Military Operations

COUNSEL, CONSCIENCE, ADVOCATE, CONSIGLIERE, OR ALL OF THE ABOVE?

Renn Gade*

I. Introduction

In July 1775, at the insistence of General George Washington and a full year before finalizing the Declaration of Independence, the Continental Congress appointed a lawyer to help with the many courts-martial (criminal trials) in the ragtag Continental Army. The Army, a patriotic but fierce bunch, needed a lawyer to help the command instill discipline into the force through the use of military justice. Thus was born the U.S. Army Judge Advocate General's Corps.[1] Since this time, military legal practice has changed dramatically. Uniformed military attorneys, called Judge Advocates or Judge Advocates General (JAs or JAGs), in all military branches play a key role in contemporary military operations, advising on issues well beyond their original mandate of military discipline.[2]

---

* Colonel Renn Gade, U.S. Army (ret.), is currently the Senior Legal Counsel at the National Counterterrorism Center. While in the military he served as the Staff Judge Advocate to a number of joint and Army commands, including: U.S. Special Operations Command, Multinational Force-Iraq, Multinational Corps-Iraq, XVIII Airborne Corps, and the 82nd Airborne Division. He also served as the Military Assistant to the Department of Defense General Counsel, Deputy Legal Counsel to the Chairman of the Joint Chiefs of Staff, and Chief, International and Operational Law, Office of the Judge Advocate General. He is a graduate of Drake University and Drake University Law School. He also holds a LLM from the U.S. Army Judge Advocate General's Legal Center and School, and a MS in National Security Strategy from the National War College. The views expressed here are his own.

[1] *See* Army Judge Advocate Corps home page, http://www.goarmy.com/jag/about/history.html (last visited Apr. 26, 2013).

[2] Judge Advocates are members of their military service JAG Corps, or JAGC. The JAGC are legal branches within the U.S. military and Commonwealth countries. An officer serving in a JAGC is typically called a "Judge Advocate," or less accurately a "JAG"; more colloquially in the Army and U.S. Marine Corps they are sometimes referred to as "Judge" (regardless whether the officer is

An Army brigade commander in a recent operation remarked that he "always traveled with his lawyer and public affairs officer."[3] This acknowledgment of the criticality of the command legal officer and his or her advice typifies the culmination of years of hard work and dedication by individual Judge Advocates. The transition from the Judge Advocate's historical peacetime (or garrison) mission to a military legal practice that encompasses all domestic and international law affecting the conduct of military operations was a lengthy one. Military lawyers' integral role in the planning and conduct of today's U.S. military operations came about with the evolution of operational law as a legal discipline. In other words, Judge Advocates today do not limit their practice to military justice, but serve across the spectrum of military operations. They advise commanders and staffs on a wide variety of operational law issues, including the law of armed conflict, rules of engagement, lethal and nonlethal targeting, detainee operations, fiscal law, foreign claims, contingency contracting, investigations, and rule of law.

The integration of legal services into every facet of modern U.S. military operations is a relatively recent phenomena, and one that is not likely to erode in today's legalistic world. This chapter focuses on the role military attorneys play in military operations, based on the assumption that an understanding of who Judge Advocates are and how they perform their mission supporting the U.S. warfighter is essential to understanding U.S. military operations in general.[4] This chapter briefly describes the evolution of operational law, or "op law" as those in the Army call it; touches upon the structure of the provision of legal services in each military branch; explains military culture; and identifies particular roles for Judge Advocates. The chapter concludes with the author's recommended "Rules of the Road" for Judge Advocates in the twenty-first century. Although various military organizational structures and doctrines evolve and change, much of the following will continue to ring true, though perhaps altered a bit to fit new paradigms.

---

currently serving as a military judge). Per Department of Defense regulation, all U.S. JAs are graduates of law schools recognized by the American Bar Association. In operational units, JAs serve primarily as legal advisors to the command to which they are assigned.

[3] Unless otherwise noted, quotations in this chapter from military officers reflect personal communications to the author.

[4] The U.S. military services are informally, and functionally, roughly bifurcated into operational and institutional elements. The operational units conduct full-spectrum operations around the world. The institutional portion of the military service supports the operational elements. Institutional organizations provide the infrastructure necessary to raise, train, equip, deploy, and ensure the readiness of the operational forces. The training component provides military skills and professional education to service members, and allows for quick expansion in time of war. Military installations provide the power-projection platforms required to deploy land forces promptly to support combatant commanders. Once those forces are deployed, the institutional elements provide the logistics needed to support them. Without the institutional side, the operational units cannot function. Without the operational units, the institutional part of the service has no purpose. The focus of this chapter is on the operational, or non-train and equip side, and its commanders and their JAs.

II. Judge Advocate Evolution

The statutory edicts in today's federal Uniformed Code of Military Justice (UCMJ), the important role that Judge Advocates play in providing advice and assistance to commanders, and the part they play in the regulation of military discipline has not changed dramatically since 1775.[5] The various service JAG Corps' almost sole focus on military justice and discipline remained constant until World War II, when prolonged postwar nation-building required military lawyers' expertise to expand into contracts, claims, real estate law, and legal assistance to service members. Providing legal services in the areas of military justice, claims, legal assistance, and administrative law from the confines of non-battlefield military installations generally became the "garrison" or peacetime prime areas of practice for the various JAG Corps. This changed due to an evolution in military legal practice beginning in the 1960s.

This evolution started as U.S. Army Judge Advocates in Vietnam participated in determining the status of captured enemy personnel, reporting and investigating war crimes, adjudicating foreign claims, and assisting South Vietnamese authorities with what is today called "rule of law" missions. As U.S. troop levels rose in Vietnam, Judge Advocates also pushed forward to provide legal assistance and military justice to division headquarters, brigade headquarters, and at smaller firebases as a forerunner to what would later become common practice.[6] However, this field of "operational law" developed even more significantly in the post-Vietnam era. In 1974, in response to the findings of the Peers Commission Report on the My Lai killings, the Department of Defense established the DoD Law of War Program.[7] This program required (and continues to do so), inter alia, that a Judge Advocate review all operational plans, policies, and directives, in all the services, for compliance with the Law of War (LOW).[8] In short, no plan was

---

[5] The UCMJ is the foundation of military law in the United States. It was established by Congress in accordance with the authority given by the Constitution in Article I, Section 8, Clause 14, which provides that "The Congress shall have Power . . . To make Rules for the Government and Regulation of the land and naval forces." U.S. CONST. art I, § 8. The UCMJ is found in Title 10, Subtitle A, Part II, Chapter 47 of the United States Code. The UCMJ was passed by Congress and became effective on May 31, 1951, though it has been subject to numerous piecemeal revisions since. The UCMJ traces its origin to the Second Continental Congress and the establishment of the Articles of War to govern the conduct of the Continental Army. The UCMJ, the Rules of Court Martial (the military analogue to the Federal Rules of Criminal Procedure), and the Military Rules of Evidence (the analogue to the Federal Rules of Evidence) have continually evolved since implementation.

[6] *See generally* FREDERIC L. BORCH III, JUDGE ADVOCATES IN COMBAT: ARMY LAWYERS IN MILITARY OPERATIONS FROM VIETNAM TO HAITI (2001) (providing an excellent history of the evolution of the Army JAGC). *See also* PATRICIA A. KERNS, THE FIRST 50 YEARS: U.S. AIR FORCE JUDGE ADVOCATE GENERAL'S DEPARTMENT (JAG) (2004) for a history of the USAF JAGC 1939–1999.

[7] *See* Borch, *supra* note 6, at 30, 51; U.S. DEP'T OF DEF., DIR. 2311.01E, DOD LAW OF WAR PROGRAM (May 9, 2006) (incorporating Change 1, November 15, 2010, replacing U.S. DEP'T OF DEF., DIR. 5100.77) (hereinafter DoDD 2311.01E). *See also* CHAIRMAN JOINT CHIEFS OF STAFF INSTRUCTION (CJCSI) 5810.01B, IMPLEMENTATION OF THE DOD LAW OF WAR PROGRAM (Mar. 25, 2002).

[8] *See* DoDD 2311.01E, *supra* note 7, ¶ 5.7.3.

complete without first checking with a military lawyer. As a consequence, Judge Advocates became closely involved in the planning and execution of military operations at all levels of unit command, and were thus drawn further into the military command and staff structure.[9]

This new LOW Program requirement of military attorney review set the stage for additional developments in the law of armed conflict.[10] During the negotiation and drafting of the Additional Protocols to the Geneva Conventions in 1974–1977, the United States promoted the newly conceived Article 82 of Additional Protocol 1, with which it was already in substantial compliance.[11] Article 82 demonstrated the international community's recognition of the complexity of the LOW and concomitantly expanded the role of Judge Advocates by requiring that "legal advisors are [*sic*] available, when necessary, to advise military commanders at the appropriate level on [the law of war] and on the appropriate instruction to be given to the armed forces on this subject."[12]

Within some U.S. Army units, Judge Advocates had already moved into positions on the headquarters staff that better enabled them to advise commanders on the LOW.[13] In 1983, this transition, at least in the Army, was tested by

---

[9] Commanders, assisted by their staffs, integrate numerous processes and activities within the headquarters and across the force as they exercise mission command. The framework within which this happens is the operations process. The operations process consists of the major mission command activities performed during operations: planning, preparing, executing, and continuously assessing the operation. *See* Army Tactics, Techniques, and Procedures (ATTP) 5-0.1, Commander and Staff Officer Guide, 1-2, Sept. 14, 2011. *See infra* note 13 for additional information on the military staff.

[10] The terms "law of armed conflict" (LOAC), "law of war," and "international humanitarian law" (IHL) are generally considered synonymous. The term "armed conflict" and LOAC is preferred to "war" in the U.S. military legal community. *See* Int'l & Operational Law Dep't, The Judge Advocate General's Legal Ctr. & Sch., U.S. Army, Operational Law Handbook 11 (2011) [hereinafter Handbook].

[11] *See* Protocol Additional to the Geneva Conventions of 12 August 1949, and relating to the Protection of Victims of International Armed Conflicts (AP I), art. 82, June 8, 1977, 1125 U.N.T.S. 3 (hereinafter AP I). The United States signed but never ratified AP1. Nonetheless, certain provisions of AP1 are recognized as customary international law by the U.S. *See, e.g.*, remarks by Michael Matheson, U.S. Department of State, at the *Sixth Annual American Red Cross-Washington College of Law Conference on International Humanitarian Law: A Workshop on Customary International Law and the 1977 Protocols Additional to the 1949 Geneva Conventions*, 2 Am. U. Int'l L. Rev. (Issue 2, 1987).

[12] Matthew E. Winter, *Finding the Law—The Values, Identity, and Function of the International Law Adviser*, 128 Mil. Law Rev. 1, 5, 16–18 (1990). A commander is the uniformed military officer in command of a military formation, unit, or operation. Command is the authority that a commander in the armed forces lawfully exercises over subordinates by virtue of rank or assignment. Command includes the authority and responsibility for effectively using available resources and for planning the employment of, organizing, directing, coordinating, and controlling military forces for the accomplishment of assigned missions. It also includes responsibility for health, welfare, morale, and discipline of assigned personnel. Joint Chiefs of Staff, Joint Pub. (JP) 1-02, Department of Defense Dictionary of Military and Associated Terms, 45 (Nov. 8, 2010) (as amended through Nov. 15, 2012).

[13] A military staff is a group of officers and enlisted personnel who are responsible for the administrative, operational, and logistical needs of a unit. The staff supports commanders, assists subordinate units, and informs units and organizations outside the headquarters. Staffs support the

Operation Urgent Fury in Grenada, when Judge Advocates from the Army's 82d Airborne Division and XVIII Airborne Corps participated in the lead elements of that operation.[14] The consequent demand for "forward-deployed" Judge Advocates (those located "down-range" in hostile or other areas designated as combat zones) to advise commanders changed the practice of military law, at least in the U.S. Army. The lessons learned from these operations led to the adoption of the term "operational law," which then resulted in the creation of operational law curricula, full-time operational law instructors, and the creation in 1986 of the Center for Law and Military Operations (CLAMO) at the Army Judge Advocate General's Legal Center and School in Charlottesville, Virginia.[15]

---

commander in understanding situations, making and implementing decisions, controlling operations, and assessing progress. Commanders often personally disseminate their intent and planning guidance, but they rely on the staff to communicate the majority of it in the form of plans and orders. Each staff section provides control over its area of expertise within the commander's intent. Although commanders make key decisions, trained and trusted staff members are given decision-making authority based on the commander's intent, thus freeing the commander from routine decisions. Most Western militaries have adopted the general staff system in structuring their militaries' staff functions. In this system, each staff position in a headquarters or unit is assigned a letter-prefix corresponding to the formation's element and one or more numbers specifying a role. The staff numbers are not hierarchical, but are traceable back to Napoleonic practice:

- 1, for personnel
- 2, for intelligence
- 3, for operations
- 4, for logistics
- 5, for plans
- 6, for signal (i.e., communications or information technology)
- 7, for training
- 8, for finance and contracts
- 9, for civil military operations.

The staff functions are prefixed with a letter. This practice is derived from the Prussian General Staff system in which the staff function was initiated with a "G." The increasing complexity of modern armies, and the spread of the staff concept to service elements and multilateral operations, has demanded the addition of new prefixes. These element prefixes include:

- A, for Air Force headquarters
- C, for Combined headquarters (multiple nations) headquarters
- G, for Army or Marines headquarters division level and above
- J, for Joint (multiple services) headquarters
- N, for Navy headquarters
- S, for staff roles within headquarters of organizations commanded by an officer with the rank of lieutenant colonel or below.

For example, the Operations Officer for an Army division would be the G3, the Plans Officer for an Air Force wing would be the A5, and the Intelligence Officer for a unified combatant command would be a J2. *See generally* ARMY DOCTRINE PUBLICATION (ADP) 5-0 (FM 5-0), THE OPERATIONS PROCESS (May 17, 2012); ARMY DOCTRINE PUBLICATION (ADP) 6-0 (FM 6-0), MISSION COMMAND (May 17, 2012); ARMY TACTICS, TECHNIQUES, AND PROCEDURES (ATTP) 5-0.1 COMMANDER AND STAFF OFFICER GUIDE (Sept. 14, 2011).

[14] Borch, *supra* note 6, at X, 6, 69, 81.

[15] Operational law is the body of domestic, foreign, and international law that directly affects the conduct of military operations. *See* U.S. DEP'T OF THE ARMY, FIELD MANUAL 1-04 (FM 1-04), LEGAL SUPPORT TO THE OPERATIONAL ARMY ¶ 5-14 (Jan. 26, 2012). *See also* Borch, *supra* note 6, at 81;

Army and other service Judge Advocates took part in lead elements and played a number of important roles in Operation Just Cause (1989, Panama) and Operations Desert Shield/Desert Storm (1990–1991).[16] In the 1990s, following the collapse of the Soviet Union, legal support became even more important in the politically sensitive contingency operations generically called Military Operations Other than War (MOOTW).[17] Judge Advocates subsequently deployed their diverse set of evolving skills in support of operations in Somalia, Haiti, the Balkans, and Southwest Asia.[18] During this time, the Army injected legally oriented events (e.g., rules of engagement dilemmas, property damage claims, and civilians on the battlefield) into the training scenarios at the combat training centers in order to increase training realism. Since the mid-1990s, Army Judge Advocates have been assigned as evaluators (called observer/controllers) at all Army combat training centers.[19]

The years of constant military operations following the terrorist attacks of September 11, 2001 (9/11), have continued a general trend in all the military services toward even greater Judge Advocate involvement in combat operations. Judge Advocates have deployed at every level of command in support of operations in Afghanistan, Iraq, the Horn of Africa, and elsewhere. The complex nature of these high-intensity combat, counterterrorism, and counterinsurgency operations have placed a premium on Judge Advocate support, while refining the practice of international and operational law into an essential element of U.S. mission command.[20] A cursory understanding of the operational portion of the U.S. armed forces is necessary to further appreciate the development of this

---

Marc Warren, *Operational Law—A Concept Matures*, 152 MIL. L. REV. 33 (1996); David E. Graham, *Operational Law—A Concept Comes of Age*, ARMY LAWYER 9–10 (July 9, 1987). All three of these works provide an excellent narrative history of this military and legal evolution.

[16] *See* Borch, *supra* note 6, at 91, 123, 166–70.

[17] The Army defined MOOTW (pronounced "mootwah") as "military activities during peacetime and conflict that do not necessarily involve armed clashes between two organized forces." U.S. DEP'T OF THE ARMY, FIELD MANUAL 100-5 (FM 100-5), OPERATIONS, 13-1 (June 14, 1993) (obsolete). MOOTW was coined by the United States military during the post–Cold War 1990s, and focused on deterring war, resolving conflict, promoting peace, and supporting civil authorities in response to domestic crises. It encompassed peacekeeping, peacemaking, peace enforcement, and peace building. The concept and acronym has since largely fallen out of usage.

[18] FM 1-04, *supra* note 15, ¶ 1-1 to 1-2.

[19] The combat training centers (CTCs) were created in the 1980s; they are found at the Joint Readiness Training Center (JRTC) at Fort Polk, Louisiana; the National Training Center (NTC) at Fort Irwin, California; the Joint Multinational Readiness Center (JMRC) at Hohenfels, Germany; and the Mission Command Training Program at (MCTP) Fort Leavenworth, Kansas. The first three concentrate on the training of maneuver battalions and brigades fighting against a realistic opposing force, while MCTP serves as a deployable training center that sends teams to support commanders as they train their brigade, division, corps, and joint task force staffs, generally with simulations linked to the National Simulation Center. The observer/controllers serve as evaluators, coaches, and mentors to the force being trained, and provide after-action reviews during and after the training exercise. Other services and the joint staff conduct individual or unit training exercises. There is often JA involvement in the scenario design, and legal issues are commonly part of the exercise.

[20] *See, e.g.*, FM 1-04, *supra* note 15, ¶ 1-2.

so-called operational law, as is a rudimentary understanding of the supporting JAGC structure and personnel of the various services.

III. U.S. Military Operational Forces

A. OPERATIONAL COMMAND AUTHORITY

The fundamental purpose of U.S. military power is to deter or wage war in support of national policy. In these capacities, military power is a coercive instrument, designed to achieve by force or the threat of force what other means have not.[21] Of course, military forces may also be employed in more benign ways for a variety of important national policy reasons, such as disaster relief, noncombatant evacuations, or training of indigenous forces.

The Department of Defense primarily employs its forces through joint operations. "Joint" connotes activities, operations, and organizations in which elements of two or more military departments participate.[22] In joint operations forces from all services (Army, Navy, Marines, and Air Force) are meant to work in a coordinated, complementary manner rather than planning and executing military operations independently.[23] Joint warfare is team warfare.

Nearly thirty years after the Goldwater-Nichols Department of Defense (DoD) Reorganization Act (Goldwater-Nichols) removed the institutional barriers to "jointness," the United States military is a joint team (though the various JAG Corps are not, and are exempted from mandatory joint assignments under the statute).[24] Under Goldwater-Nichols, military *advice* was centralized in the Chairman of the Joint Chiefs (CJCS) as opposed to the military service chiefs. The CJCS was designated as the principal military adviser to the President, National Security Council, and Secretary of Defense. The act increased the ability of the CJCS to devise and direct overall military *strategy*, but concomitantly provided greater *operational command* authority to "unified" and "specified" field commanders. According to the act, the CJCS *may not exercise military command over the Joint Chiefs of Staff or any of the armed forces*. Section 162(b) of the act prescribes that "unless otherwise directed by the President, the chain of command to a unified or specified combatant command runs—(1) from the President to the Secretary of Defense;" and "(2) from the Secretary of Defense to the commander of the combatant command."[25] The CJCS is advised by a one-star Legal

---

[21] *See* Joint Chiefs of Staff, Joint Pub. (JP) 3-0, Joint Operations, I-1 (Aug. 11, 2011).

[22] Joint Chiefs of Staff, Joint Pub. (JP) 1, Doctrine for the Armed Forces of the United States, I-1 (Mar. 25, 2013).

[23] Joint operations are distinct from combined operations, the latter consisting of military operations conducted by armed forces from two or more allied countries. JP 1-02, *supra* note 12, at 45.

[24] *See* Goldwater-Nicholls DOD Reorganization Act of 1986 (Pub.L. 99–433), 10 U.S.C. §§ 151–155 (2012).

[25] 10 U.S.C. § 162b (2012).

Counsel (LC) and is supported by a staff of approximately eight to ten JAs from all the services.[26]

Accordingly, directions for military operations emanate from the National Command Authority, a term used to collectively describe the President and the Secretary of Defense. The President, as commander in chief of the armed forces, is the ultimate authority under Article 2 of the Constitution.[27] The Secretary of Defense, combatant commander, a subordinate unified commander, or an existing joint task force (JTF) commander may establish JTFs. Combatant commanders have responsibility for a geographic area of responsibility (AOR) or a particular function (e.g., Special Operations Forces) assigned through the Unified Command Plan, which is approved by the President.[28] A colonel or equivalent Staff Judge Advocate (SJA) and an office of approximately eight to ten JAs from all services advise the combatant commanders and serve as members of their combatant commanders' personal staffs. The primary warfighting combatant commands, such as U.S. Central Command, have various sub-commands, including those broken out per service, such as U.S. Air Forces Central Command or CENTAF (the Air Force command that reports both to the Air Force chain of command and to the joint Central Command chain of command, and provides Air Force assets to the Central Command commander).

The chain of command for purposes other than the operational direction of combatant commands—that is, for equipping, supporting, and training requirements—runs from the President to the Secretary of Defense to the secretaries of the military departments to the chiefs of the services. The military departments are separately organized, each under respective civilian secretaries, and are primarily responsible for the training and equipping of their personnel to perform joint warfighting, peacekeeping, and humanitarian/disaster assistance tasks.[29] Each

---

[26] 10 U.S.C. § 156 (2012). Since the terrorist attacks of September 11, 2001, the Legal Counsel to the Chairman of the Joint Chiefs of Staff office and some of the combatant command legal offices have been augmented on a continuing basis with several reserve JAs. The one-star "Chairman's Legal," as he or she is informally known, rotates among the services and is chosen via a board process.

[27] "The President shall be Commander in Chief of the Army and Navy of the United States, and of the Militia of the several States, when called into the actual Service of the United States. . . ." U.S. CONST. art. II, § 2, cl. 1.

[28] A combatant command is a unified or specified command with a broad continuing mission under a single commander established and designated by the President, through the Secretary of Defense and with the advice and assistance of the Chairman of the Joint Chiefs of Staff. Combatant commands typically have geographic or functional responsibilities. *See* JP 1-02, *supra* note 12, 41; JOINT CHIEFS OF STAFF, JOINT PUB. (JP) 5-0, JOINT OPERATION PLANNING, II-6 (Aug. 11, 2011). There are currently nine combatant commands: U.S. Africa Command (AFRICOM), U.S. Central Command (U.S. CENTCOM), U.S. European Command (EUCOM), U.S. Northern Command (NORTHCOM), U.S. Pacific Command (PACOM), U.S. Southern Command (SOUTHCOM), U.S. Special Operations Command (SOCOM), U.S. Strategic Command (STRATCOM), and U.S. Transportation Command (TRANSCOM). *See* Defense Freedom of Information Policy Office, *available at* http://www.dod.mil/pubs/foi/dfoipo/combatant_command.html (last visited June 20, 2014).

[29] *See* 10 U.S.C. § 101(a)(8) (2012); Dept. of Defense Directive 5100.01, Functions of the Department of Defense and Its Major Components, 3 (Dec. 21, 2010); JP 1–02, *supra* note 12, at 171.

department and service generally operates in a separate domain, for example, Navy on the seas and Air Force in the air and space. It is important to emphasize that the services do not conduct combat operations; they provide trained and equipped forces to combatant commanders who subsequently conduct combat operations.

B. OPERATIONAL JUDGE ADVOCATES BY SERVICE

Army Judge Advocates serve as legal advisors at every level of operational command, as well as occasionally deploying with battalion task forces.[30] As a former The Judge Advocate General for the United States Army (TJAG) stated repeatedly, "We are Soldiers who happen to be lawyers."[31] Brigade legal sections provide legal services across the core legal disciplines: military justice, international and operational law, administrative and civil law, contract and fiscal law, claims, and legal assistance. A brigade legal section includes two JAs (a Brigade Judge Advocate (BJA) is usually a major, with a captain as a trial counsel), a brigade senior paralegal non-commissioned officer (NCO) (usually a sergeant first class), and paralegal soldiers (usually a mix of privates and junior sergeants) are assigned to subordinate battalions. During deployments, a brigade legal section may also be augmented with an additional JA, usually a captain. The BJA is the

---

[30] Military organizations are hierarchical structures, and military legal offices are typically located at higher levels of the hierarchy in all of the services. In the Army, the ascending unit formation is typically: squad, platoon, company, battalion, brigade, division, corps, and numbered army. As noted, JAs are typically assigned beginning at the battalion level, and Army paralegals are assigned to battalions. A battalion has three hundred to a thousand soldiers, consists of three to five companies, and is normally commanded by a lieutenant colonel. A battalion is capable of independent operations of limited duration and scope. An armored or air cavalry unit of equivalent size is called a squadron. A brigade has 1,500–3,200 soldiers, and is normally commanded by a colonel. During the recent conflicts, the Army transitioned from a traditional, division-based force into a brigade-based force in order to address the challenges of waging war and conducting extended stabilization operations. Some important capabilities that were formerly part of a division were made organic to the brigade combat team (BCT) organization. This "Modular Force" structure put a larger portion of the Army's combat power on an expeditionary setting in what's been described as a "plug and play" manner. Essentially, BCTs are *task organized as a standardized, interchangeable, and self-contained unit. See* The Army Homepage, *available at* http://www.army.mil/info/organization/ (last visited Apr. 26, 2013). A BCT headquarters commands the tactical operation of two to five organic or attached combat battalions. Armored Cavalry, Ranger, and Special Forces (SF) units of similar size are categorized as regiments or SF groups. *See* Field Manual 3-0, Operations, C-1–C-13 (Feb. 27, 2008) (superseded by Army Doctrine Publication 3-0, Unified Land Operations (Oct. 10, 2011), but still providing sound explanatory information on Army organization).

[31] The Judge Advocate General (TJAG) is the senior Judge Advocate of the service, and per statute is a Lieutenant General or Vice Admiral, though the senior JA of the Marine Corps is a two-star general and is called the Staff Judge Advocate to the Commandant of the Marine Corps (SJA to CMC). The statutory authority of The Judge Advocates General is found at 10 U.S.C. § 3072, *et seq.* (Army): 10 U.S.C. § 5148 *et seq.* (Navy); 10 U.S.C. § 5046 (SJA to Commandant to the Marine Corps); and 10 U.S.C. § 8037 *et seq.* (Air Force). Major General Michael Nardotti, TJAG, U.S. Army, from 1993 to 1997, provided visionary leadership that brought about much of the transformative changes regarding the practice of international and operational law within the Army.

primary legal advisor to the brigade commander, and serves as a member of the commander's personal and special staff. All military legal personnel in the brigade work under the direction and control of the BJA.

An Office of the Staff Judge Advocate (OSJA), led by a SJA, provides legal support to the commander, staff, and soldiers at division, corps, and echelons above corps.[32] A division SJA is typically a colonel, and a corps SJA is a colonel.[33] A division OSJA might have 15–25 JAs of varying rank assigned, while corps OSJAs may have up to 45 JAss or nearly 100 total personnel assigned. The Army JAGC has approximately 1,850 active duty officers.[34]

In an increasingly decentralized modular force, JAs from all the services understand the importance of maintaining positive working relationships with the military attorneys above and below their unit. This is accomplished by means of the "technical chain" of supervision, that is, the major at the brigade level can and should seek out the SJA at the division level, and the SJA at the division level can and should seek out the SJA at the corps level for support and assistance on professional areas of interest. Unlike the formal chain of command applicable to everyone in every unit, the technical chain seeks to facilitate assistance among the JAs in the unit hierarchy. The nature of the legal profession often requires a stronger technical chain of supervision along JAGC channels than in other branches or communities of interest. Service TJAGs have a statutory obligation to "direct

---

[32] The SJA is the field representative of TJAG for the services, and of the SJA to the Commandant in the Marine Corps. As TJAG's assigned representative, the SJA has the responsibility to deliver legal services within a particular unit or command. The SJA is also responsible for his or her office of legal cadre, or the Office of the Staff Judge Advocate. This officer is responsible for planning and resourcing legal support, as well as conducting training, assignments, and the professional development of JAGC personnel assigned to the command and its subordinate units. In accordance with Article 6 of the UCMJ, the SJA is authorized to communicate directly with his or her respective TJAG and other supervisory JAs of superior or subordinate commands as necessary. The SJA serves as the primary legal advisor to the commander exercising General Court Martial Convening Authority (GCMCA) as prescribed by UCMJ and the *Manual for Courts-Martial*. The SJA is a member of the commander's personal and special staff. In accordance with Article 6 of the UCMJ, at all times the commander and the SJA shall communicate directly on matters relating to the administration of military justice, including, but not limited to, all legal matters affecting the morale, good order, and discipline of the command. The SJA provides legal advice and support to the staff and coordinates actions with other staff sections to ensure the timely and accurate delivery of legal services throughout the command. *See* FM 1-04, *supra* note 15, ¶¶ 4-21 to 4-22.

[33] A division has ten thousand to eighteen thousand soldiers, and normally has four assigned BCTs. A division is commanded by a major general, and divisions are numbered and categorized by one of five types: light infantry, mechanized infantry, armored, airborne, and air assault (e.g., 1st Armored Division or 82d Airborne Division). The division is the Army's primary tactical warfighting headquarters, and it can conduct sustained engagements, as well as serve as a joint task force. A corps has multiple divisions, twenty to forty thousand soldiers, and is typically commanded by a lieutenant general. The corps can be a joint task force and provide the framework for multinational operations. At echelons above corps, the Army has Theater Army Headquarters. The theater army is the primary vehicle for Army support to joint and multinational forces (e.g., Third Army/U.S. Army Central under U.S. Central Command). *See* FIELD MANUAL 3-0, OPERATIONS, *supra* note 30.

[34] Interview with Lieutenant Colonel Joseph B. Berger III, Personnel, Plans & Training Office, Office of The Judge Advocate General (Apr. 25, 2013).

the members of the JAGC in the performance of their duties."[35] Furthermore, all JAs are attorneys subject to civilian rules of professional conduct, continuing legal education requirements, and professional discipline from their licensing organization, which requires enhanced technical supervision along JAGC channels. Finally, by statute, the SJA or legal officer of any command is entitled to communicate directly with the SJA or legal officer of a superior or subordinate command, as well as with the service TJAG.[36]

Like the Army, the sister services are organized in a hierarchical manner. The 2013 end strength for the Air Force was 328,900 active personnel.[37] The active duty Air Force JAGC has approximately 1288 officers.[38] Air Force JAs are assigned to every Air Force base, which usually constitutes a wing, providing administrative and military justice support to the wing commander and subordinate group and squadron commanders. Judge Advocates are also assigned to the various higher headquarter levels of the Air Force, which typically consist of Numbered Air Forces and Major Commands. Regarding operations, Air Force units typically deploy as wings or as individual squadrons, and have individual JAs deployed with each to provide both operational and nonoperational support. The Air Force maintains a robust legal presence at all air operations centers, ensuring that air commanders have twenty-four-hour operational legal advice regarding the entire spectrum of air operations.[39]

The U.S. Navy's operating forces include fleets that play dual roles and serve a dual chain of command. As a service component, the fleets provide, train, and equip naval forces and report administratively to the Chief of Naval Operations. Operationally, these commands report to Unified Combatant Commanders and conduct operations as the combatant commander directs. The 2013 end strength for the Navy was 322,700 active personnel.[40] The active duty Navy JAGC has approximately 855 officers.[41] Legal offices at strategic commands, such as United States Naval Forces Europe, are manned by two to five JAs and are led by a Navy commander or captain. Navy JAs of varying ranks and varying office size configurations are also assigned to tactical units, including Carrier Strike Groups, Expeditionary Strike Groups, Amphibious Readiness Groups, and various special operations commands. The primary focus of the JAs assigned to Navy operational commands is advice to the commander and the staff. When individual

---

[35] 10 U.S.C. § 307 (2012).

[36] 10 U.S.C. § 806(b) (2012).

[37] White House budget (Apr. 26, 2013), *available at* http://www.whitehouse.gov/sites/default/files/omb/budget/fy2013/assets/mil.pdf.

[38] Air Force Judge Advocate General's Corps, Office of Professional Development, AF/JAX (May 3, 2013).

[39] Air Force Instruction 38-101, Air Force Organization, Mar. 16, 2011, change Sept. 28, 2012, 8–24.

[40] Cong. Research Serv., R42651, FY2013 National Defense Authorization Act: Selected Military Personnel Policy Issues (Jan. 16, 2013), *available at* http://www.fas.org /sgp/crs/natsec/R42651.pdf. (last visited June 8, 2015) .

[41] Navy JAG Annual Report to the American Bar Association (Apr. 8, 2013), *available at* http://www.jag.navy.mil/library/jag_references.htm.

sailors require complex personal legal assistance, Navy Region Legal Service Offices provide this advice.[42]

The U.S. Marine Corps is a separate service branch within the Department of the Navy. The civilian branch of the Department of Defense is tasked with overseeing both the Navy and Marine Corps. The Marine Corps was founded to serve as an infantry unit aboard naval vessels, and the Marines have always capitalized on the Navy's global mobility. The two branches have their own separate and distinct chain of command. The Secretary of the Navy oversees the two, but the Navy is led by the Chief of Naval Operations, while the Marines are led by the Commandant of the Marine Corps. The 2013 end strength for the Marine Corps was 197,300 active duty personnel.[43]

There are currently 566 active duty Marine JAs.[44] Unlike the other services, there is no United States Marine Corps (USMC) JAG Corps; rather they are managed like every other Marine "line" officer. The Headquarters, USMC manages Marine JA assignments with the recommendation of the Staff Judge Advocate to the Commandant of the Marine Corps (SJA to CMC). While deployed (i.e., assigned to a combatant commander to perform combat missions or in preparation of such assignment), Marine JAs are commonly assigned to Marine Expeditionary Forces (MEF), divisions, wings, logistic groups, regiments, and battalions.[45] A MEF SJA is a colonel who has a staff of assigned Marine JAs. A Marine division SJA is a lieutenant colonel or major who has a cadre of several Marine JAs. The subordinate battalions also have a Marine JA assigned, usually in the rank of captain. While in garrison, however, the majority of Marine JAs

---

[42] *See* JAG Billets Requiring Special or Detailed Knowledge of the Law of Armed Conflict and Training Objectives for Navy Judge Advocates in Such Billets, JAGINST 3300.1A CH-3, *available at* http://www.jag.navy.mil/library/instructions/3300_1a_ch3.pdf (detailing the Chief of Naval Operations' requirement for certain Navy Judge Advocates with international and operational law training); http://usnavyjagcorps.wordpress.com/2012/12/20/navy-announces-legal-services-change/ (explains the organization of Navy legal service offices) (last visited July 25, 2014).

[43] *See* White House budget, *supra* note 37.

[44] Interview with Major Joseph Galvin, USMC, International and Operational Law (JAO), Judge Advocate Division, HQ, USMC, Washington DC (Mar. 11, 2013).

[45] Marine Corps operational units are organized as teams, squads, platoons, companies (or batteries, if artillery), battalions, regiments, and divisions. The Marine Air-Ground Task Force (MAGTF, pronounced "magtaf") is a term used for all operational missions. The MAGTF structure integrates a ground element, an aviation element, and a logistics element under a command element. The basic structure of the MAGTF never varies, though the number, size, and type of units comprising each of its four elements are mission dependent. There are three types of MAGTFs: the Marine Expeditionary Force (MEF), the Marine Expeditionary Brigade (MEB), and the Marine Expeditionary Unit (MEU). A MEF is commanded by a lieutenant general and is comprised of a division, an air wing, and a logistics group. The MEB is constructed around an infantry regiment, a composite air group, and a logistics regiment. The MEB, commanded by a brigadier or major general, can function independently as the lead echelon of the MEF, or as part of a joint task force. A MEU is the smallest type of MAGTF and is built around an infantry battalion, a composite aircraft squadron, and a logistics battalion. A MEU has approximately 2,200 Marines, is usually commanded by a colonel, and is deployed from an amphibious assault ship. U.S. Marine Corps homepage at http://www.marines.com/operating-forces/structure (last visited July 25, 2014).

are assigned to and work in the Legal Services Support Sections (LSSS) within the Marine Corps installation commands. There are four LSSSs geographically located, and each is led by a colonel as the Officer-in-Charge. The LSSS solely provides legal services, but the advice to the command and staff of a unit is provided by the unit SJA. When needed for deployments, Marine JAs are assigned to the deploying units based on the mission analysis.[46]

Although there are significant variations among the services regarding where and to which echelon of command legal advisors are assigned and provide advice, the common feature is that there are more JAs and they are more forward-deployed (actively working and living outside of the continental United States, in direct support of combat operations) than their predecessors of just a few decades ago.[47] This fifty-year evolution in military and legal affairs of the increased utility of JAs coincides with increased globalization, the growing importance of law internationally and domestically, and not coincidentally, the enormous influence of global and immediate information (and, of course, since 9/11 the longest period of continuous combat the United States has ever experienced). Numerous commentators have noted these phenomena and the concomitant rise in what has come to be known as "lawfare."[48] This strategy of using or misusing law as a substitute for traditional military means in order to achieve an operational or strategic objective further amplifies the drive for more JAs as contemporary military operations are complex, legally intensive events. Compliance with the law is more than an ethical responsibility; adherence to the law has been transformed into a strategy that helps to serve the purpose of the warfighter.

C. MILITARY CULTURE

The military's distinct way of life and values generate a culture of respect for the law; this culture is relevant to understanding how military attorneys function. The U.S. military is commonly viewed as a homogenous entity. Although the services do share certain common characteristics, the Army, Navy, Marines, and the Air Force have notably divergent attributes reflective of their respective domains in war and warfighting doctrine. Two prominent military commentators suggested

---

[46] *See* http://www.marines.com/being-a-marine/roles-in-the-corps/command-element/judge-advocate (last visited July 25, 2014).

[47] *See, e.g.*, Panel: More Judge Advocates Needed, MARINE CORPS TIMES (Jan. 15, 2011), *available at* http://www.marinecorpstimes.com/article/20110115/NEWS/101150312/Panel-More-judge-advocates-needed (last visited July 25, 2014) (the article notes that a congressionally mandated panel found that current and future operational demands required additional Navy and Marine Judge Advocates to support military operations); Charles J. Dunlap Jr., *It Ain't No TV Show: JAGs and Modern Military Operations*, 4(2) CHI. J. OF INTERNATIONAL LAW 479–80 (2003).

[48] *See, e.g.*, Charles J. Dunlap Jr., *Lawfare Today: A Perspective*, YALE J. OF INT'L AFFAIRS 146, 146 (Winter 2008). Maj. Gen. (ret.) Dunlap first used the term in this context in 2001. *See also* Charles J. Dunlap Jr., *Lawfare: A Decisive Element of 21st Century Conflicts?*, 54 JOINT FORCES QUARTERLY 34, 35 (2009).

that broad depictions for the self-perceived general culture of the military services include:

- Army: Obedient servant, emphasis on people.
- Air Force: Victory through technology.
- Navy: Independent exercise of sovereignty.
- Marine Corps: The nation's force of choice.[49]

Of course within the military services there are distinct subcultures within the various branches, communities of interest, and occupational specialties.[50] The warrior subculture is dominant in each of the services. Whether it is the infantry or fighter pilots, those who actually do the killing are at the tip of the metaphorical spear.[51] Those farther down the shaft of the spear provide intelligence, communications, and other support to the combatants. Still farther down the spear shaft are combat service supporters who provide logistical, medical. and transportation support more closely aligned with civilian occupations. Not surprisingly, those at the tip of the spear or closer to the tip of the spear most closely identify themselves as part of the time-honored profession of arms.[52]

One aspect of military culture that is often overlooked and misunderstood is rank structure. The military services are divided into officer, non-commissioned officer, and enlisted ranks, each with its own subculture.[53] The officer subculture is dominant by statutory design, but it is also the officer corps in each service that develops and upholds the distinctive foundations of the profession that permits high professional status within our society.[54]

---

[49] Michael J. Meese & Isaiah Wilson III, The Military Culture: Forging a Joint Warrior Culture, The National Security Enterprise: Navigating the Labyrinth 127–29 (2011).

[50] The reserve forces have their own unique subculture, especially the National Guard with its roots in the militia tradition.

[51] *See generally* Dick Couch, A Tactical Ethic: Moral Conduct in the Insurgent Battlespace 17–18, 26–27 (2010).

[52] Don M. Snider, *The Future of American Military Culture: An Uninformed Debate on Military Culture*, Orbis 20–22 (Winter 1999).

[53] The officer corps has commissioned officers and warrant officers. Commissioned officers are appointed by the President, with the approval of the Senate. Warrant officers are rated as an officer above the senior-most enlisted ranks, but below the commissioned officer grades. Warrant officers are highly skilled specialty officers (e.g., helicopter pilots and legal administrators), and each branch of service manages and uses warrant officers differently, or not at all. For appointment to warrant officer one, a warrant is approved by the Secretary of the military service. For chief warrant officer ranks, warrant officers are commissioned by the President and take the same oath as commissioned officers. Warrant officers can command units, vessels, and aircraft; however, the warrant officer's primary task as a leader is to serve as a technical expert. Only officers command; non-commissioned officers in positions of authority can be said to have control or charge rather than command. Army Regulation 600-20, Army Command Policy, 1–5, Sept. 20, 2012.

[54] All elected or appointed officers, including military commissioned officers, take the same oath office (the President's oath is unique). 5 U.S.C. § 3331(2015). The oath of office for enlisted and NCOs is different. The notable difference between the officer and enlisted oaths is that the oath taken by officers does not include any provision to obey orders (only the Constitution), while enlisted personnel are bound by the Uniform Code of Military Justice to obey "the orders of the officers appointed over me, according to regulations and the Uniform Code of Military Justice." 10 U.S.C. § 502(2006).

Samuel Huntington, the noted Harvard political scientist, authored *The Soldier and the State* more than a half century ago, and it remains one of the most influential books on the military.[55] Huntington's theory of civil-military relations holds that during wartime, civilian leaders determine the policy goals of the war, then stand aside to let the professional military conduct the war. Huntington's core theory is: (1) there is a meaningful difference between the civilian and military roles, (2) the key to civilian control is military *professionalism*, and (3) the key to military professionalism is military autonomy.[56] Huntington's theory addresses the central problem of civil-military relations: the relationship of the military as an institution to civilian society. The theory provides useful insights into the civilian-military distinction, the idea of military subordination as essential to democratic theory, and the importance of military professionalism. The U.S. military has generally endorsed many of Huntington's conclusions, and it has made this work and his arguments central to their education on civil-military relations. Therefore, it may also be the single best source for describing the military value set and military culture.[57]

Huntington posited that "the modern officer corps is a professional body and the modern officer a professional man. . . . Professionalism distinguishes the military officer of today from the warriors of previous ages."[58] Professional status implies a unique and socially useful expertise, "the management of violence."[59] Professionalism also means the acceptance of the social obligation and acknowledgement of a moral responsibility to provide and use that expertise on behalf of society, and a shared sense of organic unity and consciousness among military officers as a group apart from laymen.[60]

The elements of the military profession fall within the domain of officers. Officers receive a commission from the nation to act on its behalf to protect the nation by managing violence, and society in turn expects individual accountability in large and small matters by those officers.[61] Officers theorize about strategy,

---

Snider, *supra* note 52, at 22-25 notes and explains the reasons for the cultural dominance of the officer corps.

[55] *See generally* Samuel P. Huntington, The Soldier and the State (1957).

[56] Huntington asserts that the distinguishing characteristics of a profession are its expertise, responsibility, and corporateness. He further states that the "specialized expertise of the military officer" is "best summed up by the phrase 'the management of violence.'" *Id.* at 11.

[57] Huntington's theory has been challenged over the decades, but it remains the preeminent theory of civil-military relations. For more recent theories on civil-military relations, see also Morris Janowitz, The Professional Soldier (1960); Peter D. Feavor, Armed Servants: Agency, Oversight, and Civil-Military Relations (2003); Mackubin T. Owens, U.S. Civil-Military Relations after 9/11 (2011).

[58] Huntington, *supra* note 55, at 7.

[59] *Id.* at 11–13.

[60] *Id.* at 10, 14–18.

[61] For examples of this societal contract, see, e.g., Paul Yingling, *A Failure in Generalship*, Armed Forces Journal 2 (May 2007); Mark Thompson, *The Military's New Surge in Accountability*, Time (Feb. 17, 2010), *available at* http://www.time.com/time/nation/article/0,8599,1964052,00.html#ixzz2N5nN09bc; Thomas Ricks, The Generals: American Military Command from World War II to Today (2012).

reflect on war and conflict, write doctrine, compose campaign plans, create the requirements for industry to build the instruments of war, develop the personnel systems that support the profession, and adjudicate the military justice system. In short, all actions in the military are accomplished over the signature of either a commanding officer or a staff officer. Last, officers, especially commanding officers, shape the organizational climate of their unit, every day, and in every way. The officer corps of the military services shares this ethos, and that may be the most important element of the military culture.[62]

Another element of military culture is discipline. The Judge Advocate Generals Corps' primary statutory mission is to assist the command in the preservation of "good order and discipline" and the military justice system is one of the tools available to commanders.[63] The purpose of discipline is to minimize confusion in an uncertain and chaotic operational environment, and to "ritualize the violence of war."[64] Following disciplined actions and reactions sustains soldiers in combat and helps to define when and how they may violate normal societal prohibitions against violence and killing. The need to control behavior lies in the military's unique place among professions as an American institution sanctioned to kill in pursuit of national objectives. Because of the potential threat inherent in this distinctive function, societal norms and laws govern how and when the task is to be performed. The U.S. expects its service members to fight with courage and proficiency, and to do so honorably. Service members are expected to show compassion for civilians and those out of combat, as well as maintain an active awareness of political sensibilities and the potential repercussions of their actions. While military justice and administrative actions are tools for the commander to instill discipline, internalized values, traditions, trust, and member commitment are more powerful means of achieving control over those engaged in potentially lethal societal services that are not easily monitored.

A third element of military culture is esprit de corps and cohesion, both of which measure an operational unit's willingness to fight. Cohesion is that feeling of identity and comradeship that holds small organizational elements together. "Esprit de corps" refers to the commitment and pride that unit members feel for the largest military establishment, whether it be their division or their service. It is popularly believed that unit cohesion is the key factor in motivating soldiers to fight, rather than abstract ideology or love of nation. Simply put, soldiers fight primarily for one another. Popular movies such as *Saving Private Ryan*[65] and

---

[62] *See* Snider, *supra* note 52, at 11, 23. Huntington summarized the military mind and military professional ethic as "conservative realism.... It exalts obedience as the highest virtue of military men. The military ethic is thus pessimistic, collectivist, historically inclined, power-oriented, nationalistic, militaristic, pacificist, and instrumentalist in its view of the military profession." Huntington *supra* note 55, at 79.

[63] 10 U.S.C. § 934(2015), UCMJ Art. 134, General Article (2012).

[64] Snider, *supra* note 52, at 15.

[65] *Saving Private Ryan*. Dir. Steven Speilberg. Paramount Pictures, 1998.

Black Hawk Down[66] recognize the group cohesion thesis. The "band of brothers" phenomenon, a name taken from the St. Crispin's Day speech in Shakespeare's *Henry V*, envisions soldiers as united by their common experiences and sacrifices.[67] Samuel Stouffer's "The American Soldier" studies chronicled the attitudes of U.S. soldiers who served in World War II soldier's attitudes toward battle.[68] Stouffer argued that ideology, patriotism, or fighting for the cause were not major factors in combat motivation; rather "primary group cohesion" was the motivator. Stouffer's conclusions supported S.L.A. Marshall's work *Men against Fire*, which defined the motivation to fight simply as "the presence or presumed presence of a comrade."[69] A more recent paper by Dr. Leonard Wong, of the Army War College, validated the popular belief that unit cohesion is a key issue in motivating soldiers to fight.[70]

Surprisingly, however, many soldiers in Iraq were motivated by patriotic ideals. Wong credits today's volunteer Army with having more educated soldiers with a better understanding of the overall mission. He further asserts that this "truly professional army" has an unmatched level of trust between the soldiers and the leaders who have competently trained their units.[71] Of course, this does not mean that all cohesive units are effective in combat. Cohesiveness and esprit de corps, along with competency, materiel sufficiency, sound strategy, and trust in the chain of command are the coins for success.

The final element of military culture is ritual. The ceremonial traditions and military etiquette displayed in military life are historical habits and customs used to manage anxiety and affirm members' solidarity with one another, with the larger military establishment, and with the nation. Military induction, salutes, uniforms, uniform insignia, promotion ceremonies, change of command, reviews,

---

[66] *Black Hawk Down*. Dir. Ridly Scott. Columbia Pictures, 2001.

[67] William Shakespeare, *Henry V* (1599) Act IV, Scene 3, which depicts Henry V before the Battle of Agincourt. Of course, the popular miniseries *Band of Brothers*, based on the Stephen Ambrose 1992 book of the same name, and which fictionalized the history of Easy Company, 506th Parachute Infantry Regiment, 101st Airborne Division, falls into this same mold. *Band of Brothers*, Dir. Phil Alden Robinson, et al. Producers Steven Speilberg and Tom Hanks. Home Box Office, 2001.

[68] Samuel A. Stouffer, Edward A. Suchman, Leland C. DeVinney, Shirley A. Star & Robin M. Williams Jr., Studies in Social Psychology in World War II, The American Soldier 125 (1949).

[69] S.L.A. Marshall, Men against Fire: The Problem of Battle Command 42 (1947); *but see* Roger J. Spiller, *S.L.A. Marshall and the Ratio of Fire*, The RUSI Journal 63–71 (Winter 1988) (discrediting Marshall's "ratio of fire" thesis).

[70] Leonard Wong et al., *Why They Fight: Combat Motivation in the Iraq War*, Strategic Studies Institute, Carlislie, PA (2003), *available at* http://www.strategicstudiesinstitute.army.mil/pdffiles/pub179.pdf.

[71] *Id.* at 17–20. Because the demands that battle places on soldiers have changed over time, it is possible that the depiction of the factors that drive soldiers in battle is due for re-evaluation. The recent controversy over the creation of a new medal to honor the exploits of those military personnel who remotely pilot aerial vehicles is a concrete reminder of change. *See* Andrew Tilghman, *Pentagon's New High-Tech Warfare Medal Draws Backlash*, USA Today (Feb. 14, 2013), http://www.usatoday.com/story/news/nation/2013/02/14/new-medal-draws-backlash/1921413.

award presentations, weddings, retirements, and funerals represent the military life cycle. These rituals serve to forge and communicate a common identity and group affiliation, as well as motivation and reaffirmation for continued sacrifice in service to the country.[72]

Huntington's theory was developed in the zeitgeist of the Cold War, nuclear confrontation, and a conscript army. Today's military is smaller, older, more diverse, and more likely to be married than the force that served a generation or two ago.[73] A larger proportion of minorities and women serve as officers and enlisted personnel than during the Cold War.[74] Proportionately fewer high school dropouts and more college graduates fill the enlisted ranks. Since the advent of the All-Volunteer Force in 1973, educational standards for NCOs have improved tremendously. More of America's fighting forces are husbands or wives, and a growing proportion is married to someone else who serves in the military.[75] At the same time, America's wars are being fought by a dwindling share of its population. The 9/11 attacks ushered in the longest period of sustained conflict in the nation's history, yet during this period the military participation rate fell below 0.5 percent.[76] Not since the peacetime years between World War I and World War II has a smaller share of Americans served in the armed forces.[77] In the past thirty years, we have also witnessed a revolution in military affairs, with advances in weapons and information technology that allow for pinpoint, standoff kinetic strikes and the capacity for offensive operations in the cyber domain.[78] After all this change, whether Huntington's theory still merits the general approval of the officer corps and America at large merits much empirical research and objective analysis.[79]

---

[72] Perhaps the most distinctive aspect of military service is that in a society that extols self-absorbed individualism, the soldier is committed to unlimited personal liability on behalf of the nation.

[73] *The Military-Civilian Gap: War and Sacrifice in the Post-9/11 Era*, Pew Research Center, 73, Oct. 5, 2011.

[74] *Id.*

[75] *Id.*

[76] *Id.*

[77] *Id.*

[78] The "Revolution in Military Affairs" (RMA) is a theory about the future of warfare, first popularized after the swift U.S. military victory in Desert Shield/Storm. The concept is often connected to technological advances in weaponry and communications and organizational changes in the United States and other militaries. For elaboration and history on RMA, see Williamson Murray, *Thinking about Revolutions in Military Affairs*, Joint Forces Q. 69–71 (Summer 1997); Scott Stephenson, *The Revolution of Military Affairs: 12 Observations on an Out-of-Fashion Idea*, Military Rev. 38 (May–June 2010).

[79] *See, e.g.*, Leonard Wong, *Generations Apart: Xers and Boomers in the Officer Corps*, Strategic Studies Institute, Carlisle, PA (2000) as an example of the type of exhaustive research needed after this period of Long War and societal change.

IV. The Law's Strategic Role and the U.S. Military

Regardless whether Huntington's views have changed in small or gross measure, the military culture as noted above, as exemplified by actions as varied as an individual service member's actions or a unit commander's mission focus, reinforces the value of adherence to the law.[80] Accordingly, there are certain frequently unstated core assumptions that underlie all military missions:

- Law contributes to national security.
- Law reflects the ethics and values of the nation.
- Adherence to the law promotes the Rule of Law abroad.
- The strategic consequences of transgressions can be fatal.

Law is "a process of authoritative decision . . . a social and political process of decision making . . . the legal process establishes the framework and source of legitimacy for the bodies which, in turn, make lawful decisions in accordance with its standards."[81] In the realm of national security, the law provides the President, U.S. leaders, and military commanders with the instruments of power to enable national security, and regulates the employment of those instruments. It creates a legal framework and implementation process to ensure that the actions of a military command reflect the values of the nation. However, although the law related to national security is today seemingly ubiquitous, it is not all encompassing. It is not a codal touchstone for a universe of unknowns. Thus, the law will provide the boundaries for the formal decision-making process by a military staff, but it is the informal discussions within a command and staff that demonstrate the intersection of law, policy, ethics, values, and command instinct, which results in a course of action.

In the international context, law regulates the methods and means to achieve national security objectives. Law is the cement in the relations between nation-states. Treaties and agreements between and among states govern trade, commerce, diplomacy, and nearly every aspect of this digital era in the post-Westphalian system.[82] Likewise, in times of crisis, the law provides consistency, predictability, continuity through a common understanding, and a source of authority for international and multilateral organizations to orchestrate, to arbitrate, and to intervene in when necessary.

---

[80] Of course, My Lai, Haditha, Abu Ghraib, and other notable instances of egregious misconduct by both junior service members and senior leaders belie this assertion. Stress on the force, lowered enlistment standards, inferior leadership, or other causative factors can have deleterious impact on military values, but that topic is beyond the scope of this chapter.

[81] John Norton Moore, Frederick S. Tipson & Robert F. Turner, National Security Law 25 (1990).

[82] *Id.* at 27 (quoting Professor Richard Falk, *A New Paradigm for International Legal Studies: Prospects and Proposals*, 84 Yale L.J. 99–100 (1975)).

For expeditionary armed forces,[83] law protects the U.S. service member abroad with negotiated legal protections, such as providing them with combatant immunity for otherwise-criminal acts of violence undertaken in armed conflict.[84] Just as important, the law reflects and projects American values of democracy and liberty. The U.S. military justice system simultaneously provides protection for the military accused, as well as justice for any victim of law of war or criminal violations. Similarly, adherence to the Department of Defense Law of War program, conformity with customary legal obligations concerning the conduct of hostilities, and compliance with the regulatory and legal guidance found in Field Manual 2-22.3 in interrogations are all concrete expressions of the U.S. national ethos.[85]

Although seemingly a tautology, respect for the law promotes the rule of law.[86] As noted elsewhere, al Qaida and its extremist progeny fail because they offer little or nothing in the way of programs or policies for governance save brutality and misogyny.[87] The rule of law is the alternative to terrorism and violence.[88] The rule of law embodied in the Western tradition provides structure for competition, an impartial administration of criminal justice, and an opportunity for all, regardless of gender, ethnicity, or religious beliefs. As one U.S. general officer remarked amid the chaos of postwar-reconstruction Iraq, "I never thought I'd hear myself say this, but I love bureaucrats. In their absence, I've really come to appreciate the structure they provide."[89]

The strategic consequences of failing to adhere to the law can be tactically, operationally, and strategically catastrophic. The depraved acts of a few poorly led soldiers at Abu Ghraib prison, which occurred within an environment

---

[83] Each of the services uses and applies the term "expeditionary" in some manner. Generally, expeditionary means an armed force organized to accomplish a specific objective in a foreign country. An expeditionary military force is one that can conduct military operations abroad on short notice in response to crises, with forces tailored to achieve limited and clearly stated objectives. *See* JP 1-02, *supra* note 12, at 92.

[84] Lawful combatants bear no criminal responsibility for killing or injuring enemy military personnel or civilians taking an active part in hostilities, or for causing damage or destruction to property, provided his or her acts are in lawful compliance with the law of armed conflict. *See* HANDBOOK, *supra* note 10, at 16.

[85] *See, e.g.*, DoDD 2311.01, *supra* note 7; JOINT CHIEFS OF STAFF, INSTR. 3121.01B, THE STANDING RULES OF ENGAGEMENT/STANDING RULES FOR THE USE OF FORCES (June 13, 2005); U.S. DEP'T OF THE ARMY, FIELD MANUAL 2-22.3 (FM 2-22.3), HUMAN INTELLIGENCE COLLECTOR OPERATIONS (Sept. 6, 2006).

[86] *See generally*, Couch, *supra* note 51, at 10–11, 26–27 (arguing that ethical and moral conduct on the battlefield is a force multiplier, and that "moral/ethos training" must complement all professional combat skill training).

[87] *See* JAMES E. BAKER, IN THE COMMON DEFENSE: NATIONAL SECURITY LAW FOR PERILOUS TIMES 308 (2007) (citing LAWRENCE WRIGHT, THE LOOMING TOWER 261 (2007)); *see also* Thomas R. McCabe, *The Strategic Failures of al Qaeda*, PARAMETERS 60 (Spring 2010).

[88] Military doctrine explicitly recognizes the value and importance of rule-of-law activities in support of the core military mission of stability operations. *See* FM 1-04, *supra* note 15, at App. F; *see also* THE JUDGE ADVOCATE GEN.'S LEGAL CTR. & SCH., U.S. ARMY, RULE OF LAW HANDBOOK: A PRACTITIONERS GUIDE FOR JUDGE ADVOCATES 11–12 (2011).

[89] Lieutenant General John R. Vines, Aug. 2005, notes on file with the author.

of extralegal maneuvers orchestrated and sanctioned at the highest levels of the Defense Department and administration at the time, has been described as "non-biodegradable" and as a "strategic defeat" by the United States.[90] Misconceived decisions or policies by leaders complicit or abetted by poor legal advice produce not only a corrosive effect on lawyers and the legal profession, but, more important, on the nation.[91] The costs of decisions and policies gone awry can injure the reputation, credibility, and perceived legitimacy of the nation for generations.[92]

Of course, adherence to and respect for legal obligations does not guarantee success or any particular result. Fear of violating the law, and its attendant consequences, does motivate some types of behavior, but the law does not compel a soldier to move while under fire or a JA to speak the truth to a physically domineering and charismatic leader in a meeting. Those acts all require varying degrees of leadership, technical skill, and perhaps most important, the type of physical and moral courage inherent in the lawyer's ethical and moral obligation as a servant to the nation as his or her ultimate client. In short, the human element cannot be divorced from grand strategy and willful compliance to the law.

A. ROLES OF THE JUDGE ADVOCATE

The clarity of representational obligations for military lawyers is in many cases clearly defined and easily identified (although nonetheless challenging in execution), for example, advising a soldier on a family law issue or the command on an environmental, contract, or fiscal law issue; or representing a soldier accused of criminal misconduct. In contrast, military lawyers embedded within an operational "battle staff," such as the JA embedded in the J3 Plans section providing legal advice to that headquarters element, confront a far more complex and less-defined representational environment.[93] These lawyers, like corporate

---

[90] General David Petraeus on *Meet the Press*, Feb. 21, 2010 ("Abu Ghraib and other situations like that are non-biodegradable. They don't go away. The enemy continues to beat with them like a stick...") (quoted in HUFFINGTON POST, http://www.huffingtonpost.com/2010/02/21/petraeus-takes-on-cheneyi_n_470608.html) (last visited July 25, 2014). *See also The Professor of War*, VANITY FAIR, May 2010 ("There is no doubt that Abu Ghraib was a stain on our national character, and reminded us yet again of the power of our actions. The incidents there likely inspired many men and women to fight against us, and they still do, as a matter of fact."); *see also Interview with Admiral Mike Mullen*, 54 ARMED FORCES J. 8 (2009); *see also* Douglas A. Pryer, *At What Cost Intelligence? A Case Study of the Consequences of Ethical (and Unethical) Leadership*, MILITARY REV. 16 (May–June, 2010).

[91] *See, e.g.*, Raffi Khatchadourian, "*The Kill Company*," THE NEW YORKER 43 (July 6, 2009) (suggesting that an Army brigade commander's overly aggressive and unchecked actions and rhetoric in Iraq led to civilian murders).

[92] For a good exegesis of decisions made at the strategic level and their consequent impact, see generally JACK GOLDSMITH, THE TERROR PRESIDENCY: LAW AND JUDGMENT INSIDE THE BUSH ADMINISTRATION (2009).

[93] The staff structure is generally described *supra* in note 13. The personal and special staff groups are part of the larger headquarters staff. Personal staff officers work under the immediate control of, and have direct access to, the commander. By law or regulation, personal staff officers have a

counsel, must constantly bear in mind that their ethical obligation is to represent the interest of the client, which is the command and the nation, and avoid the temptation to reflexively equate the interest of the commander with that of the client. Although in most situations there will be no inconsistency between these interests, the ultimate duty to the nation as the client necessitates that the JA maintain a level of objectivity toward the supported command unlike that of any other member of the staff. This tension can be especially acute for the senior military lawyer on the staff—the SJA—who has the broadest legal portfolio, and who is often seen as the commander's and senior staff officer's personal lawyer.

In professional literature, there are many constructs for the duty of the lawyer devoted to military or national security legal issues: advocate, judicial, advisory, and public interest model.[94] One writer has stated that the JA who serves as an operational law advisor essentially plays the following roles: advocate, judge, counselor, and "the conscience."[95] These four roles may be performed separately or in various admixtures depending on the issue and the stage of the military operation.

Advocate: the advocate is more commonly associated with the "hired gun" in the civil or criminal context. Advisors in the operational law environment must be aware of the risk associated with becoming an advocate in the decision-making process. Unlike the adversarial contest, there is no independent trier of fact in the operational law setting, and the JA who plays the advocate during the decision-making process may become a tool for legitimizing legally

---

unique relationship with the commander. The commander establishes guidelines or gives guidance on when a personal staff officer informs or coordinates with the chief of staff (or executive officer, "XO") or other staff members. Some personal staff officers have responsibilities as special staff officers and work with a coordinating staff officer. The personal staff includes, for example, the Aide-de-Camp, Chaplain, Command Sergeant Major, Command Surgeon, and SJA. All staff officers having duties at a headquarters and not included in the general staff (G or coordinating staff) or in the personal staff are part of the special staff. The special staff includes certain technical specialists and heads of services (e.g., antiaircraft officer, transportation officer). The number of special staff officers and their responsibilities vary with authorizations, the desires of the commander, and the size of the command. The chief of staff exercises coordinating staff responsibility over special staff officers. *See* ATTP 5-01, *supra* note 9, ¶¶ 2-76, 2-105-114. The SJA and the Office of the SJA are members of the commander's personal staff and special staff. FM 1-04, *supra* note 15, ¶ 4-22.

[94] *See, e.g.*, American Bar Association Model Rules of Professional Conduct, Preamble and Scope, (2012) ¶ 2, *available at* http://www.americanbar.org/groups/professional_responsibility/publications/model_rules_of_professional_conduct/model_rules_of_professional_conduct_preamble_scope.html [hereinafter ABA Model Rules]. Paragraph 2 is quoted in full here.

> As a representative of clients, a lawyer performs various functions. As advisor, a lawyer provides a client with an informed understanding of the client's legal rights and obligations and explains their practical implications. As advocate, a lawyer zealously asserts the client's position under the rules of the adversary system. As negotiator, a lawyer seeks a result advantageous to the client but consistent with requirements of honest dealings with others. As an evaluator, a lawyer acts by examining a client's legal affairs and reporting about them to the client or to others.

Id.

[95] Winter, *supra* note 12, at 14.

problematic decisions. In that circumstance, "the advocate" role becomes "the cheerleader" who follows the charismatic leader and applauds his client-leader all the way into deep trouble. The "cheerleader" stands in contrast to the JA who provides independent, objective advice to the command throughout the operational decision-making process, and who then might assume an advocacy role after the commander makes a defensible decision.[96] Of course the JA often must utilize his or her advocacy skills to convince a commander and/or the staff that a particular course of action is the most advisable—in this sense, JAs truly live their "Advocate" name.

Judge: the JA is the authority on the law and is frequently asked to provide a legal opinion on a proposed action, for example, the use of certain weapon systems, the legality of certain proposed targets, or the status of civilians taking part in hostilities. In these circumstances, the JA must incorporate military considerations into the decision-making process. In order to provide competent advice, the JA must understand military tactics, strategy, and weapons systems.[97] The JA may advise the commander on the applicable LOAC principle, but must be careful to not become "Solomon" by invading the purview of the commander by making decisions reserved for the commander. The oft-repeated adage is certainly true here: lawyers advise and commanders decide.

Counselor: the counselor is a "facilitator who enables the commander to accomplish his or her goals within the law."[98] This role assumes that the JA knows and understands the intent of the commander, and that the JA proposes alternatives in compliance with the law. The archetypal counselor is instrumentally involved throughout the military decision-making process and provides input during the development of the plan, rather than reviewing the plan in isolation as it nears completion and either acting akin to the judicial role or meeting the calculation of some by simply being the "rubber stamp" for the plan.[99]

Conscience: the JA is often explicitly directed to serve as the "conscience of the command" (along with the Chaplain and Inspector General), and in this role the JA in the operational environment reminds commanders that the LOAC includes humanitarian principles that may not be sacrificed for military necessity.[100] Of course, the danger in that role is that the JA may be considered too idealistic, and perceived as "Dr. No" from whom no action is ever positively reviewed and who is consequently ignored by the command and staff; hence the JA must provide acceptable alternatives and be able to clearly outline what the law requires and accepts.

---

[96] *Id.* at 22–26.

[97] *See generally,* Charles A. Dunlap, *Some Reflections on the Intersection of Law and Ethics in Cyber War,* Air & Space Power J. 36 (Jan.–Feb. 2013) ("the virtue of competence").

[98] Winter, *supra* note 12, at 30.

[99] *See* FM 1-04, *supra* note 15, ch. 6 (explaining the role that Judge Advocates should play in the military planning process).

[100] Lisa L. Turner, *The Detainee Interrogation Debate and the Legal-Policy Process,* 54 Armed Forces J. 42 (2009). (Commanders described Judge Advocates as "the red light on the commander's desk," or "the conscience of the Service").

1. Amalgam: The Consigliere Model

Many successful JAs have adopted the "consigliere" model as the amalgam of these roles. Although this may hint of Robert Duvall's dispassionate, too loyal, and criminally complicit character Tom Hagen in *The Godfather*,[101] the term as used here refers to JAs who are close, trusted colleagues, and serve as a confidant and senior statesman for the commander and the organization. Ideally, these JAs are devoid of personal ambition and dispense disinterested and sometimes tough advice for the advancement of the mission, the command, and the nation.

The consigliere model can accommodate the multiple roles expected of the JA, and the model can lead to success for the policy and the client in the legally intensive twenty-first century. Thankfully, in the U.S. system, the JA and the commander or leader she advises are both sworn to support and defend the Constitution. That common affirmation provides some real and concrete guidance for both the lawyer and the client, and helps the JA avoid becoming the Tom Hagen character. It also means that depending on the decision and the status of the decision in the staff action process, the JA can carry out the duties of each of these roles or models by shifting seamlessly from one to the next.

There are certain institutional risks associated with the consigliere model. Unlike their civilian counterparts, government and military lawyers do not compete in the marketplace, but they do compete for the "power, prestige, and influence" that comes with the ability to advise and influence leaders.[102] The willingness of the lawyer to tell the leader what the lawyer believes the leader wants, or to subtlety shade the answer to tough questions, may lead to greater access to the leader, enhanced personnel evaluations, more prestigious assignments, advancement in rank, and ultimately greater influence over decisions and policy. This trend has also been described, with good reason, as the "race to the bottom," which is one of the trappings of a too-comfortable consigliere model.[103]

I. CAUTIONARY TALE

Although involving lawyers at the highest level of the U.S. government, the Department of Justice, Office of Professional Responsibility (OPR) "Report into the Office of Legal Counsel's Memoranda concerning Issues Relating to the Central Intelligence Agency's Use of 'Enhanced Interrogation Techniques' on Suspected Terrorists" is equally instructive to the JAs at the tactical and operational levels of the military.[104] The OPR report examined in great detail the facts, circumstances,

---

[101] *The Godfather*. Dir. Francis Ford Coppola. Paramount Pictures, 1972.

[102] *See* Peter Margulies, *When to Push the Envelope: Legal Ethics, the Rule of Law, and National Security Strategy*, 30 FORDHAM INT'L L.J. 644 (2006).

[103] *Id. See also* John C. Dehn, *Institutional Advocacy, Constitutional Obligations, and Professional Responsibilities: Arguments for Government Lawyering without Glasses*, 110 COLUMBIA L. REV. 73–88 (2010) (providing an analysis of institutional advocacy by government lawyers and the risk of client over-identification).

[104] Dep't of Justice, Office of Prof'l Responsibility (OPR) *Report into the Office of Legal Counsel's Memoranda concerning Issues Relating to the Central Intelligence Agency's Use of "Enhanced Interrogation Techniques" on Suspected Terrorists* (July 29, 2009), *available at* http://cdm16064.contentdm.oclc.org/cdm/ref/collection/p266901coll4/id/2317 [hereinafter OPR Report].

research, and writing of key Office of Legal Counsel (OLC) opinions and concluded that the legal work "fell short of the standards of thoroughness, objectivity, and candor that apply to Department of Justice (DoJ) lawyers."[105] The OPR report further concluded, inter alia, that the prime author for the opinions "knowingly failed to provide a thorough, objective, and candid interpretation of the law."[106] The author did this by knowingly providing incomplete and one-sided advice in his analysis, not conveying any of the uncertainty or ambiguity of this complex area of the law, failing to modify his memorandum when confronted with contrary facts, and misrepresenting the strength of an earlier OLC opinion that he had largely written.[107] The DoJ concluded further that the author "put his desire to accommodate the client above his obligation to provide thorough, objective, and candid legal advice, and that he therefore committed intentional professional misconduct."[108] While recognizing that fear and uncertainty followed the attacks of September 11, 2001, the report stated, "situations of great stress, danger and fear do not relieve Department attorneys of their duty to provide thorough, objective, and candid legal advice, even if that advice is not what the client wants to hear."[109]

The OLC opinions examined in the OPR report served to advance the administration's post-9/11 antiterrorism efforts, boosted the ideological views of the author and like-minded people in the White House, and gave the author of the opinions "extraordinary influence in the administration."[110] In the end, the reputations of the lawyers involved, the OLC, and the nation were tarnished at home and abroad. Moreover, the ideological views advanced by the authors of the OLC opinions and others were harmed as the authority of the presidency was diminished rather than amplified. The nation remains engaged in litigation and a debate on the efficacy and propriety of interrogation techniques.[111] Lawyers at the tactical-to-strategic level of government are susceptible to this "race to the bottom," and the cautionary tale of the OLC opinions mandates steadfast objectivity.

Mindful that the organization, unit, or department—not the leader—is the client, and that the lawyer cannot counsel the client in conduct that the lawyer knows is criminal, fraudulent, or contrary to the interests of the organization and/or the nation, the lawyer can still be placed in an awkward position with the leader.[112] The

---

[105] *Id.* at 251.

[106] *Id.*

[107] *Id.* at 252.

[108] *Id.* at 254.

[109] *Id.*

[110] Goldsmith, *supra* note 92, at 22–24.

[111] OPR Report, *supra* note 104, at 228–30. *See, e.g.*, Massimo Calibresi, *The Truth about Torture*, Time, Dec. 14, 2012; "Statement to Employees from Acting Director Michael Morell about the SSCI Report on Past Agency Program," Dec. 14, 2012, https://www.cia.gov/news-information/press-releases-statements/2012-press-releasese-statements/message-from-adcia-about-ssci-report.html; *see also* Leonard Pitts Jr, *Does Torture Work?*, Chi. Trib., Jan. 16, 2013, http://articles.chicagotribune.com/2013-01-16/news/sns-201301151800--tms--lpittsctnwl-a20130116-20130116_1_torture-bush-era-defenders.

[112] *See, e.g.*, Army Regulation (AR) 27-26, Rules of Professional Conduct for Lawyers (May 1, 1992); 28 U.S.C. § 530B (2012), 28 CFR 77 for statutory and codal provisions for government lawyers; *see also* ABA Model Rules, *supra* note 94, at Rule 1.2(d).

equilibrium between achieving the leader's intent and the lawyer's obligation to uphold her ethical obligations and the integrity of the governmental system can be difficult to achieve, especially in a situation of perceived national security extremis. So, while seeking the proximity and access required to understand the leader's intent and the command's situational context, the lawyer cannot be so close to the client or the problem that she loses the objectivity and independence so essential to the exercise of sound legal judgment. This problem becomes particularly acute when the leader possesses a powerful, charismatic personality to which people—including the lawyer—may be drawn for virtuous, public-minded purposes. The best legal advisors should share a common goal with the leader of timely, unvarnished, tough advice that is without the perturbation of private gain, ideology, or career advancement. Unvarnished advice is what the leader deserves and what the lawyer's duty requires—not providing advice that ultimately harms the leader, the institution, and the public weal.

B. QUALITIES OF THE JUDGE ADVOCATE

This potential tension between core ethical obligations, and the demands of the operational advisory context highlight desirable and durable qualities in the best JAs. This short (but non-exhaustive) list of relevant qualities are normally associated with excellence in the practice of operational law:

- Having the ability to rapidly identify issues, review and research the issues (time permitting), and provide a cogent recommendation in a timely manner.
- Having the intuitive knowledge that success is the mission, not the legal work that supports the mission.
- Having the ability to compartmentalize—certainly classified matters, but the ability to move quickly from one issue to the next as well.
- Being broadly schooled in many legal disciplines, history, economics, and life, but being an expert in international and domestic law and policy that impacts military operations (operational law).
- Being proficient in the tools and technologies associated with the art of war.
- Being expert in whatever staff action processes the command or organization uses.
- Being a leader who inspires others and demonstrates concern for, and empathy with, subordinates.

These qualities provide the foundation for the tremendous success that has defined all the services' JAG organizations as the demand for operational legal advice has increased exponentially during the past two decades. This trend has also produced a population of senior military commanders increasingly accustomed to timely and comprehensive legal support to military operations.

V. Rules of the Road: Advice for Dispensing Military Operational Legal Advice

What follows is a compilation of guidance this author refers to as "Rules of the Road," dispensed by an all-star team of general officer and flag officer commanders to their SJAs.[113] These recommendations for the best ways to function as a JA have been compiled and distilled by the author over his military career.[114] The all-star team of senior officers is not otherwise identified in this chapter, but they own decades of service to the nation, and their statements represent the sentiment and wisdom of their peer leaders. These "rules" frame the vital relationship between lawyer and commander, as well as define the commander's expectations for successfully executing the legal advisory function. A portion of the relationship between the commander and the JA is found in the law—particularly the UCMJ, as stated above—while other aspects of that foundation are framed by informal rules, especially those that have developed over the last several decades.[115] Combining these rules with the traits above provides a veritable roadmap for the successful operational legal advisor. Dissecting these rules also offers valuable insight into the functions and roles of the JA in the operational context. These rules include the following: move away from the desk; this is a people business; you SME, not me; you are not all-knowing; tell me what it means; bring solutions, then bring coffee; and no surprises, please.

A. RULE 1. MOVE AWAY FROM THE DESK

- Judge Advocates must build knowledge and competency by getting involved in operations and participating in planning
- Judge Advocates must know how and where information flows

"Perhaps the most fundamental legal skill consists of determining what kind of legal problems a situation may involve, a skill that necessarily transcends any particular specialized knowledge. A lawyer can provide adequate representation

---

[113] Rules of the Road are often confused with traffic laws, yet the two are supremely different. Traffic laws regulate vehicles. On the other hand, Rules of the Road cover motor vehicles, as well as other conveyances, and encompass informal rules for orderly movement and are intended to facilitate growth and change in the dynamic area of transportation. The combination of these informal rules and prescribed laws are all-encompassing. Likewise, these Rules of the Road for JAs combine the statutory grounding with the informal rules of practical and successful practice.

[114] The author served as the Staff Judge Advocate for division, corps, joint and combined corps units, and joint and combined theater headquarters in peacetime and during armed conflict. The author also served as the Staff Judge Advocate for a unified combatant command, as deputy legal counsel to the Chairman of the Joint Chiefs of Staff, and as Chief, International and Operational Law for the Army Judge Advocate General.

[115] *See, e.g.*, Title 10 U.S.C. Chap. 47, the Uniform Code of Military Justice, which generally details the authority of the commander, the rights of the service member, and the duties of the military lawyer in military justice matters.

in a wholly novel field through necessary study."[116] In order to render truly "competent" legal advice, JAs must have a comprehensive understanding of not only the law, but also the means by which the commander conducts the military business. Judge Advocates cannot maximize their understanding of the military arts and the national security process by simply taking up shop behind a desk. Stasis is poison to the good JA. Legal advisors need to get out and understand the means and methods used in the military enterprise. This understanding is also a matter of competency and trust. A commander told a JA who wished to attend an advanced parachuting operations course: "You know you don't get paid to jump out of airplanes [not true], you get paid to give me advice. But, every leader in this outfit has had to complete this course in order to lead, so attending and graduating will help you build credibility on the street." If military competency is demonstrated by the JA, the leader places greater trust and confidence in the legal advice rendered, and this trust is compounded by the JA's inclusion in all aspects of the decision-making process.

This competency begins with the service legal "basic courses" of two-to-four months in length. These courses augment law school education by concentrating on military legal foundations, and build upon the military training the attorneys receive from their commissioning source. The various service JA organizations utilize a mix of commissioning sources: direct commission, Reserve Officer Training Corps. (ROTC), and to a small extent, the military academies (U.S. Military Academy at West Point, U.S. Naval Academy in Annapolis, and the U.S. Air Force Academy in Colorado Springs). The intent behind the JA's military training and education is to produce a broadly skilled officer capable of accomplishing today's mission and succeeding in an uncertain future. Additional training and education in core legal disciplines, varied assignments, diverse duties, professional military education (e.g., airborne, air assault, staff schools), advanced civilian or military legal education, and self-development accomplish the goal of the broadly skilled JA.

Once assigned to an operational unit, the JA's learning and understanding really begins. Curiosity and humility are two key ingredients in this learning process. Generally, people are proud of the work they do, and simply inquiring about the function they perform and how their equipment operates will bring volumes of information. Judge Advocates are expected to master the staff action process in the organization, and in order to do that, the attorney needs to know the people who do this—the teammates who receive the cables, messages, or information in the message center; the analysts who sort through the traffic; the translators who interpret the intercept; the executive assistants who control their boss's schedule and the aides and chief of staff who control the flow of information to the boss and other senior leaders. If the JA knows the people in the

[116] *See* ABA Model Rules, *supra* note 94, at Rule 1.1 ("A lawyer shall provide competent representation to a client. Competent representation requires the legal knowledge, skill, thoroughness and preparation reasonably necessary for the representation").

organization, she will know how information flows in the organization, and if needed, how to get actions completed thoroughly yet quickly.

Getting out from behind the desk is more than following Rule 2 ("This Is a People Business"): this edict is about understanding the systems, the processes, and the people who run them. If advising a commander on a lethal strike, the JA must understand targeting doctrine, the targeting cycle, the weapon systems that may be used, and the tools used to assist in deducing the collateral damage assessment, in order to render advice on the LOAC principles of military necessity, distinction, and proportionality. Getting out on a foot patrol, becoming familiar with the communication devices, and sitting with the analyst helps the JA understand what he is opining on. The JA should spend a great deal of time in planning sessions and getting involved in the inner workings of operations, and this is true whether it is legal advice on targeting issues, contracts, or intelligence issues. This is also true whether operating at the tactical or national and strategic level—indeed understanding the tactical level will make for better advice at the strategic level because the JA will better understand the limits and capabilities of the systems and the humans involved. Being visible in the organization, becoming part of the organization, and perceiving the issues and solutions will make for an improved JA and enhance one's credibility with the commander and the rest of the organization.

B. RULE 2. THIS IS A PEOPLE BUSINESS

- Judge Advocates must know the staff.
- Judge Advocates are leaders.
- Judge Advocates must be available and discreet.

Formal lines of coordination are often explicitly drawn in the law, and there is even more likely to be a formalized or express statement on how a military staff is supposed to function, whether by way of regulation or standard operating procedures. However, personal relationships really matter and are often more important to effectiveness as a JA than the prescribed rules. The best thing anyone ever said to the officer new to the staff was to "get to know everyone else as soon as possible." In daily operations, but especially in time-stressed situations, knowing the person to turn to on the staff for answers or action may mean the difference between success and failure.

As one boss said about a mistaken and misguided staff officer, "I've learned that it's best to extend a presumption of goodness to everyone. That officer is not a communist. He comes with a different skill set; a different background and my job as the commander is to harness all these disparate talents into a cohesive and efficient team."[117] That commander was a tough taskmaster, but firmly believed that using the "scorched earth view of human relations" did not work, and that

[117] This aphorism is rather similar to "Hanlon's Razor," which is generally known as "Never attribute to malice that which is adequately explained by stupidity."

more could be accomplished by "praising up." Extending a presumption of goodness to fellow workers means they will be more willing to bring their skills and abilities to the problem.

That same boss considered everyone a leader, regardless of the person's position in the command and staff. The fundamentals of leadership—taking care of others, having an inspiring vision of success, using excellent verbal and written communication, and exercising superior judgment—apply equally to all. For that commander, the admonition was especially true for the JA; "I will lead; I expect you to be a leader." In the commander's view "The Judge" often had a subtly greater effect on the staff than was otherwise indicated by the JA's position on the organizational chart because fellow staff officers respected the JA's counsel, and most knew that the leader also sought out their JA's legal and common-sense-type advice.

Another commander told his SJA in his initial office call that

> I will be inclusive. You are welcome and encouraged to attend any meeting in the headquarters that you wish. I may ask whether your time is best used at some meeting, but assuming you are read-into that program (and as my lawyer you should be read-into all or nearly every program that we have), I won't kick you out of a meeting and no one else on staff will either. I will expect you to understand the context of problems and decisions, and you can't do that unless you have a seat at the table or attend the meeting. In fact, I'll affirm you and your value in public. That said, I expect that you will add value to the process, and not bog down the process at the last moment with nitpick English grammar comments (although sometimes excellent writing skills will come in handy for the process).[118]

Another commander said, "You won't hear me making lawyer jokes or otherwise denigrate you or anyone else. I learned that a 'joke' about someone other than myself often has a larger and unintended consequence elsewhere, especially on other parts of the staff that may misread my intent or may be less-knowledgeable about the value that The Judge brings to a staff."

The commander in the first office call also said,

> I will be hard on you. There are many talented lawyers and I expect you to be around and available—all the time. You have to actually read the read-ahead material and attend the meetings in order to hear that golden nugget of information that is key to the policy or decision. I won't go to you only when I have problems. Sometimes leaders want their lawyer around only if they get close to the edge of the envelope, or in a crisis, and think that bringing in the lawyer at the last moment will provide CYA. In my experience, that type

[118] The process of being "read into" a program generally entails being approved for access to particularly sensitive and restricted information about a classified program, receiving a briefing about the program, and formally acknowledging the briefing, usually by signing a non-disclosure agreement.

of relationship is not good and it will quickly become adversarial—that's not what I need. This will require physical and mental endurance on your part. Whether by design or bad luck, requests for legal chops[119] will come in at 1700, or on a weekend, and you will have to act. If there are complex legal issues to be dealt with, it's a lot easier to deal with them when you've prepped me with the problem before that call from the Headquarters or OSD Cables at 0200 on a Thursday night.

Finally, the commander expected the lawyer to be discreet: "I am not asking you to look the other way if anything illegal or inappropriate occurs. No, I expect you to apprise me if anything like that ever happens. I fully expect and ask that you share that information up your technical chain of influence or command. I do, however, expect that you will be discreet about anything that I share with you about other people, my intentions, or my personal thoughts."

C. RULE 3. YOU SME, NOT ME

- Judge Advocates are the staff legal experts.
- Judge Advocates provide policy advice only when clearly labeled.

Among the many lessons learned in the past decade of war is the certainty that we exist in an exceedingly complex, often ambiguous, constantly evolving world. It is clearly a new world, brave or otherwise. Military legal issues faced at even the lowest tactical level demand precise, nuanced answers. Incorrect responses can have unforgiving consequences. There are no shortcuts to the mastery of military and national security issues: study, research, networking, and experience. On the positive side of the professional ledger, those involved in national security and military affairs do not labor in a dull environment. It is deeply rewarding because there is no governmental interest "more compelling than the security of the Nation,"[120] and lawyers have assumed an extensive role in these complex, legally intensive national security affairs.[121]

Many commanders, though not all, will know a great deal about the law. Their decades of education, training, and experience in the art of war make them

---

[119] In the staff action process, the various portions of the staff must review, edit, coordinate, and approve the various staff communications or efforts. That coordination process is often memorialized with the signature or initials of the staff officer on the staff action processing document, referred to as "the chop."

[120] Haig v. Agee, 453 U.S. 280 (1981).

[121] *See, e.g.*, Goldsmith, *supra* note 92, at 129–30; Alex Richard, *Jeh Johnson: The Role of Lawyers in National Security Policy-Making*, The Stanford Rev. (Oct. 11, 2012), http://stanfordreview.org/article/jeh-johnson-the-role-of-lawyers-in-national-security-policy-making/; *see also* Defense Secretary Leon Panetta, "One thing I've learned is every time I turn around, I face a group of lawyers. . . .Lawyers basically have to review these issues to make sure they feel comfortable that we have the legal basis for what we're being requested to do. And I understand the need for that." Anne Gearan & Craig Whitlock, *Panetta "Confident" US Will Approve Aiding French Mission*, Wash. Post, Jan. 16, 2013, at A1.

highly knowledgeable, but as one general officer said, "You SME,[122] not me."[123] This is not to say that the JA's word will go unchallenged. Some commanders and some on the staff may challenge the JA's legal opinions. This may occur when the commander, key staff members, or the JA are new to the position. The savvy legal advisor will anticipate this and will be prepared to provide in-depth substantive support for recommendations and advice. Every unit and organization has its own legal and policy authorities, history, culture, mission, and trends. Understanding the "special sauce" of the organization is the key to success. Once the JA's unit is mastered, it is prudent to study and understand the units or agencies above and below, as well as others that are regularly dealt with. Supervisory Judge Advocates lead by educating those who work for them, in a patient, persistent, and thoughtful manner.

The consigliere JA will be asked or have the opportunity to provide advice on many issues. This is a particularly nettlesome area, as the consigliere JA, by dint of trust, education, and wide-ranging expertise, may provide cogent advice on legal and all manner of issues. Judge Advocates are members of the bar and constrained by their states' legal ethics standards.[124] The service TJAGs also establish their own JAGC ethics rules.[125] Judge Advocates must comply with service credentialing and ethics rules or face disciplinary action, including courts-martial.[126] Judge Advocates are required to provide their clients with "candid advice" based on their "independent professional judgment."[127] This obligation is so important that Congress enacted legislation that expressly licensed "the ability of officers of the [service] who are designated as judge advocates assigned or attached to, or performing duty with, military units to give independent legal advice to commanders."[128] In exercising independent professional judgment and rendering candid advice, JAs may refer "not only to the law but to other considerations such as moral, economic, social and political factors, that may be relevant. . ."[129] Moreover, JAs are bound to discuss "the legal and moral consequences of any proposed course of conduct with a client to make a good faith effort to determine the validity, scope, meaning, or application of the law."[130] Finally, commanders often *expect* the consigliere JA to discuss non-legal factors along with technical legal advice.

---

[122] "Subject Matter Expert (SME), pronounced "smee."

[123] It is not uncommon for generals or admirals to have spent up to ten years of their military career at various types of military and civilian schools. Meese, *supra* note 49, at 125.

[124] *See* FM 1-04, *supra* note 15, ¶ 4-35.

[125] *See, e.g.*, AR 27-26, *supra* note 112, at i, 1.

[126] *See* Sam Lagrone, *Disbarred JAG Convicted at Trial*, Air Force Times (Apr.1, 2008), http://www.airforcetimes .com/news/2010/02/airforce_murphy_retirement_022210w/ (last visited Apr. 26, 2013).

[127] *See, e.g.*, AR 27-26, *supra* note 112, Rule 2.1; the service rules hew closely to the ABA Model Rules.

[128] 10 U.S.C. § 3037(e)(2)(2015) (Army); §5046(d)(2)(2015) (Marines); §5148(e)(2)(2015) (Navy); §8037(f)(2)(2015) (Air Force).

[129] AR 27-26, *supra* note 112, Rule 2.1.

[130] *Id.* Rule 1.2.

Military decisions, especially those impacting strategic issues and the proclivity of small decisions to become large issues, frequently blur the distinction between law and policy. Although this difference is difficult to divine at times, and some JAs have fallen sway to the allure of power in policy decisions, the key is awareness of the specter of subjectivity and avoiding intrusion into the leader's province of decision-making.[131] If the JA does provide policy *advice*, then it is essential for her credibility with the leader to demarcate clearly the legal opinion from the policy advice. The JA can never dress up policy advice as legal opinion without adversely affecting the integrity of that opinion and all future legal opinions.

One may occasionally hear that commanders and staff officers are relying on their "gut" to make a decision or course of action. Gut feelings or gut reactions are instinctive feelings or intuitive reactions. "Gut instinct" is learned behavior, and it might serve the leader well at times, but not so well on other occasions. This dynamic is the product of that person's experience, knowledge, and training, and is often reflective of the person's general worldview. Military commanders have decades of training, education, and experience, and their "gut feeling" is often a finely tuned and very sophisticated apparatus. However, when leaders says they are going with their "gut" in a targeting decision, for example, it is worthwhile to consider the amount and type of experience, training, and education in targeting by the particular leader. If the leader lacks that requisite knowledge, and the leader's worldview is shaped exclusively by reading *The New York Times* and other media, which may be helpful to understanding larger political issues, then it is incumbent upon the JA to quietly assist in the training and instruction for that leader. Similarly, JAs might rely on their gut instinct when rendering an opinion, but that gut instinct must be formed by legal knowledge, impartial facts, and years of worldly experience—garnered personally or by consultation with more experienced mentors.

D. RULE 4. YOU ARE NOT ALL-KNOWING

- Judge Advocates are not expected to know everything about the law.
- Judge Advocate have the tools to get the answer.
- Judge Advocates must network with other legal experts.

Lawyers are generally smart and have met with considerable academic success in their lives, so it occasionally comes as a surprise to JAs that commanders and fellow staff are bright, well read, and equally intelligent (if not more so). As one leader said, "Lawyers don't know it all. I don't expect every lawyer to know every aspect of the law. I do expect some humility and courage—don't be afraid to ask questions of me, others in this organization, or your talented subordinates. I expect that you will provide your best advice in a manner commensurate with

[131] *See* William J. Dunn, *Going Forward: Improving the Legal Advice of National Security Lawyers*, 32 B.C. Int'l Int'l & Comp. L. Rev. 241 (2009) (providing an excellent discussion on this point).

the situation. I do expect you to come prepared." Each of the services has "reach back" tools available to operational JAs for use in helping to address novel, time sensitive, or particularly complex issues. The service international and operational law sections have uniformed and civilian attorneys who have developed an expertise in many international law fields, and the same can be said for the combatant commander OSJAs and Chairman's Legal offices. The Army's Center for Army Lessons Learned and the Center for Law and Military Operations compiles and publishes useful experiences from operations, and also serves to provide answers to JAs in the field.[132]

Another boss related that he "expected staff officers of every stripe to come with and develop relationships with senior mentors. Every person needs knowledgeable, trustworthy people for reach back—time permitting—on issue analysis and as a simple sounding board." In the armed forces context, those mentors should understand the military arts—history, ethics, doctrine, theory, intelligence and communications platforms, weapons systems, and cultures—as well as the context of the operations.

E. RULE 5. TELL ME WHAT IT MEANS

- Judge Advocates cannot simply recite the law, policy, regulation, or executive order.
- The Judge Advocate's acme is in relating any operational impact.
- Judge Advocates must be succinct.

A senior leader's most important commodity is time. There is often little time for lengthy legal opinions with a recitation of every statute or a detailed legal analysis. As others have said about staff officers in general, and as applicable to legal advisors—be prompt, be fast, be brief, be gone! Commanders expect JAs to answer four questions on any action:

- Is it legal?
- Is it advisable?
- If it is not legal or if not advisable, then what are the alternatives?
- What is the recommended course of action?[133]

The JA must be able to succinctly relate what the statute, executive order, regulation, or policy says, and then tell the commander how it impacts operations or the decision contemplated. An inability to transform complex legal analysis into a "bottom line" breeds dissatisfaction and risks marginalization of the JA. For example, an operator at an intelligence headquarters was overheard having said, "Damn lawyers, if I wanted to know everything about the law, I'd have gone to

---

[132] *See* CALL home page, http://usacac.army.mil/CAC2/call/ (last visited Apr. 27, 2013); *see also* CLAMO home page, http://www.loc.gov/rr/frd/Military_Law/CLAMO.html (last visited Apr. 27, 2013) (providing a listing of CLAMO lessons-learned publications and practitioners' guides).

[133] Turner, *supra* note 100, at 42.

law school. Just tell me what it means and whether I can do it." This view might be a bit simplistic, but it expresses the occasional frustration of senior leaders. Commanders understand that a 3/4-page bulletized memo may not adequately explain the significant legal nuances of a policy or decision, but they also expect the JA to devise an information strategy that provides the commander with a fuller picture by way of a read-ahead memo, contemporaneous explanation, or follow-up brief.

F. RULE 6. BRING SOLUTIONS, THEN BRING COFFEE

- Judge Advocates are skilled at issue identification.
- Judge Advocates provide legal risks, mitigation strategies, possible solutions, and courses of action.
- Judge Advocates must remain objective.

This is certainly linked to the previous rule, but leaders generally expect staff officers to not only identify the problem, but also to bring solutions. In law, as in life, those who can also identify solutions will find endless success. Problem identification is fundamental to the profession, but great JAs isolate the problem and chart, or help to chart, the solution. It is this problem-solving capability that leverages the ultimate value of the JA: sound judgment.

This presumption is not a simple incantation of the overused maxim "how to get to yes." Every commander knows there are times when the JA may say no because some contemplated action is unlawful or otherwise contrary to regulation or policy. Every commander expects loyalty from the JA, but also understands that the commander is not the ultimate client; rather the unit, the service, the nation is ultimately the client. Like fellow staff officers, the JA serves in the commander's chain, but unlike fellow staff officers, the JA also reports to a supervisory technical chain of other JAs from higher headquarters that eventually ends with the most senior uniformed lawyer in that service. Indeed, "the staff judge advocate or legal officer of any command is entitled to communicate directly with the staff judge advocate or legal officer of a superior or subordinate command, or with the Judge Advocate General."[134] Although every officer has the duty to elevate an issue over the commander's head if she is convinced the commander intends to act illegally (or else the officer is arguably derelict in the performance of her duties), the JA has the unique stovepipe of the technical chain that allows him or her to raise the issue without going through the very mechanism that may be at fault—the formal chain of command.

Commanders do not set out to create new legal precedents, and therefore most JAs are not expected to author the legal opinion that attempts to set that new standard. Although leaders do not often set out to create new precedent, there are occasions when the law does not appear to facilitate decisive action

---

[134] 10 U.S.C. § 806 (2012).

that aligns with threats, capabilities, or needs.[135] Judge Advocates who counsel leaders to push to or over the edge of the envelope on operational issues risk being labeled an accomplice, and the unilateral, studied disregard for the law has its own collateral consequences for the JA, commander, and nation. There is an established process of vetting legal issues up the JA's technical chain, and a JA must do this when he concludes that the law fundamentally undermines a vital operational objective. More important, national leaders and senior military leaders have the ability to readily advance changes in law and policy; legal advisors can identify those gaps in the law, and even assist in developing those legislative and policy fixes.

Every leader understands and accepts this environment, but there is also an expectation that there are usually lawful, creative solutions. Identifying the problem is a fine first step, but JAs provide sound counsel by setting out and balancing the relative costs and benefits of a decision. The baseline legal cost/benefit analysis starts with the oft-told parable: just because it is legal, does not mean it is right, but if it is illegal, then it is always wrong. Sound counsel must also point out not only the benefits if a proposed action is successful, but also the risk of error in estimating the likelihood of success. Included in this legal risk analysis must also be the consequences of not taking action—the "do nothing" option. Once legal risk is identified, prudent counsel must recommend steps to mitigate that risk, and recommend other possible courses of action. The rules stated above mean that the JA knows and understands the bureaucratic procedures well enough to apply the legal grease to the process in order to assist in bringing it to a conclusion. Again, JAs in the operational context must be especially diligent not only in enforcing their own objectivity, but also in identifying institutional error or bias.

A vignette might illustrate the various roles of the JA in a dynamic operational environment. An American ground unit suffered a number of casualties from an improvised explosive device (IED) that struck a vehicle returning to a forward operating base. It appeared that the IED was command-detonated and that the combatants that planted and set off the device had drawn back into the safety of their urban setting. A unmanned aerial vehicle flying overhead at the time of the explosion picked up with its overhead cameras two individuals, who may have been armed. The individuals moved away from the area immediately afterward and entered a densely packed series of one-to-four-story buildings. Human intelligence identified the specific building the two individuals ran toward after the bombing. Intelligence was sparse, but the best estimate was that the two combatants might be in the building, which may have been a house, and may also have a number of civilians inside. The combatants were believed to be foot soldiers,

---

[135] Ethics rules do permit legal advisors to seek good faith modifications to existing domestic law by determining the "validity, scope, meaning, or application of the law" by such means as litigation or in international law by means of detecting and expanding emerging international norms in tribunals, courts, and state practice. *See* ABA Model Rules, *supra* note 94, at 1.2, 8.4; *see also* Margulies, *supra* note 102, at 666 (arguing when certain conditions are met, a national security lawyer at the strategic level can advise a leader to push the edge of the envelope on a national security decision).

not mid- or upper-level leaders. The entire unit was justifiably angry at the loss of comrades, and some planners suggested a raid into the area to secure and clear the building. The commander asked if he could seek an air strike on the house. The JA should have advised the commander that a building containing combatants engaged in an IED strike may be a legitimate military objective, but it appeared that the IED strike was over, and hence distinction may be an issue. Furthermore, the presence of an unknown number of civilians would pose problems under the principle of proportionality, particularly given the combatants' low rank.[136] Intelligence also suggests that the enemy's unit was gradually leaving the area, within the space of the next day or so. The JA might suggest, as an alternative to an immediate air strike, that the unit wait for the combatants to exit the building and seek transport in a vehicle that could be targeted without placing civilians at risk. The JA could also ask whether the unit could deploy a sniper to target the armed occupants of the building with less risk to the civilians inside.[137]

Though assigned to the unit the JA in the above scenario did not fall prey to an emotional urge for revenge, but rather was engaged throughout the decision-making process in providing advice and offering alternative courses of action. As demonstrated in the vignette, the value of intelligence in national security matters is paramount. Although JAs are not intelligence analysts, JAs by means of their training and education can be sophisticated consumers of intelligence, and can provide valuable contributions to the decisional process by leveraging the analytical skills central to the practice of law, and through a lawyer's sixth sense: healthy skepticism.[138] Similarly, astute JAs must be aware of systemic

---

[136] According to the principle of proportionality, the anticipated loss of life and damage to property incidental to attacks must not be excessive in relation to the concrete and direct military advantage expected to be gained. Proportionality provides a means by which military commanders can balance military necessity and unnecessary suffering in circumstances when an attack may cause incidental damage to civilian personnel or property. AP I, *supra* note 11, at art. 51(5)(b); art. 57(2)(b) (similarly directs that "an attack shall be cancelled or suspended if it becomes apparent that he objective is not a military one or . . . that the attack may be expected to cause incidental loss of human life, injury to civilians, damage to civilian objects, or a combination thereof, which would be excessive in relation to the concrete and direct military advantage anticipated."). *See also* U.S. Dep't of the Army, Field Manual 27-10 (FM 27-10), The Law of Land Warfare, (July 18, 1956) ¶ 41.

[137] Furthermore, if the targets are not known to be members of an enemy armed group, the law requires an assumption that they are civilians who had directly participated in hostilities, and they cannot be targeted unless so engaged in such hostilities, which typically includes immediate preparation for and egress from the hostile action. *See generally* International Committee of the Red Cross, Interpretive Guidance on the Notion of Direct Participation in Hostilities under International Humanitarian Law (Nils Melzer ed., 2009), *available at* http://www.icrc.org/eng/assets /files/other/icrc-002-0990.pdf; *see also* AP I, *supra* note 11, art. 51(3) (a civilian only "enjoy[s] the protections afforded" by the Law of Armed Conflict "unless and for such time as they take a direct part in hostilities.").

[138] *See* James B. Comey, *Intelligence under the Law*, The Green Bag, 439 (2007); *see also* Robert S. Litt, General Counsel, Office of Dir. of Nat'l Intelligence, Comments at Georgetown Univ. Law School, Nat'l Security L. Section conference (Oct. 25, 2012) (noting that evidence-based training, the speed and pressure involved in trial work, and an emphasis on succinct oral and written communication skills can help to prepare an attorney for national security law work.) *But see* Dunn, *supra* note 132, at 256.

bias in the operational arena that compels speed and action. There are certainly many issues and problems that necessitate quick advice and immediate decisions, but as supported by history and brutal hindsight, not all operational decisions have demanded hasty decisions, and some could have benefitted from further factual development and cool reason.[139]

Judge Advocates will know how and when to "slow decisional velocities" in order to assist the commander and staff in the decision-making process.[140] Likewise, the experienced and attuned JA will know when to move purposefully. Without being obstructionist or risk averse, it is the JA's responsibility in delivering sound legal advice to gather all available facts, determine the amount of time available, explore options, and carve out the maximum available time for deliberation and decision by the commander.

G. RULE 7. NO SURPRISES, PLEASE

- It is all about information sharing.
- Judge Advocates must keep the commander and the technical chain informed.

Surprises are unavoidable in military operations, and commanders and their staffs live by the mantra that "no plan survives first contact with the enemy." That said, commanders do not like to be surprised. The best JAs know the best way to avoid surprise is to share information early and often; as the old adage goes, "unlike fine wine, bad news does not get better with time." On a large staff the channels of communication can be long and difficult, so it is best to share information to the maximum extent possible, consistent with security classifications. It is exceptionally important to stay abreast of what is happening globally, read the daily intelligence reports, and attend staff meetings in order to hear that "golden nugget" of information. At bottom, avoiding or minimizing surprise is all about information sharing. Although it is essential to keep the boss informed, it is also important to keep the next higher in the JA's technical chain informed of events and initiatives.[141] The boss should expect and want the JA to keep the

---

[139] *See* Couch, *supra* note 51, at xviii ("Quite simply, the care and restraint with which we use military force on the insurgent battlefield, and especially how we treat noncombatants, is a vital part of the mission").

[140] *See generally* Dunn, *supra* note 51, at 246; Charles J. Dunlap Jr., *Ethical Issues of the Practice of National Security Law: Some Observations*, 38 Ohio N. Univ. L. Rev. 1057, 1076 (2012).

[141] The rules applicable to the uniformed services, similar to ABA Model Rule 1.13(b), provide that Judge Advocates may seek "guidance from higher authoirty in the technical chain of supervision, including, if warranted by the seriousness of the matter, referral to the Army lawyer assigned to the staff of the acting official's next superior in the chain of command." AR 27-26, *supra* note 112, Rule 1.13(c)(5). The access to guidance from senior military attorneys is protected by law. The Uniform Code of Military Justice states that JAs are "entitled to communicate directly with the staff judge advocate or legal officer of a superior or subordinate command, or with the Judge Advocate General." *See* 10 U.S.C. § 806 (2011).

technical chain informed, but it is prudent for the JA to apprise the boss of those occasions when the JA talks up the chain.

VI. Conclusion

The role of JAs in U.S. military operations has evolved from World War II, through Vietnam, Panama and Grenada, to Iraq and Afghanistan. This evolution has been greatly accelerated in the post-9/11 era of persistent conflict. In contemporary military operations, JAs certainly play a large and helpful role as key advisors to the command and staff. Whether at home or abroad, the JA's primary mission continues to be to provide assistance to the commander and the staff regarding military justice matters. It is no accident that the preamble to the Manual for Courts-Martial stresses the importance of military justice: "The purpose of military law is to promote justice, to assist in maintaining good order and discipline in the armed forces, to promote efficiency and effectiveness in the military establishment, and thereby to strengthen the national security of the United States."[142] Commanders also expect JAs to have mastered other core competencies: international and operational law, administrative and civil law, contract and fiscal law, claims, and legal assistance. Similarly, when deployed, JAs must be fully competent in a variety of subjects ranging from detainee operations and foreign claims to inter-agency collaboration in support of Rule of Law operations.

Judge Advocates uniquely sit as both special staff and personal staff officers. This ready access to the commander and staff often allows for close personal and professional relationships with key leaders. The JA must be able to effortlessly shift among the roles of Judge, Advocate, Counselor, and Conscience. The consigliere JA model sums up these various roles and maximizes the JA's skill, education, training, and experience in advising the command. There may be an expectation that the close, personal, trusted relationship between the commander and "the Judge" will provide for service to the commander in any and all circumstances. However, the JA's unique professional supervision along the legal technical chain reflects the imperative that the nation, not the commander, is the ultimate client. The primary function of those engaged in the military enterprise is to defend the nation. Judge Advocates must have the skill, courage, and judgment to be able to advise "no" when under time-constrained pressure and "yes" when faced with true military exigencies. Commanders and JAs are solemnly advised to follow the Rules of the Road in an effort to balance the national interests of liberty and security.

---

[142] Manual for Courts-Martial, United States, Preamble, pt. I-1, (2012).

2 }

Modern Weapons and the Law of Armed Conflict

Dave Wallace and Shane R. Reeves*

I. Introduction

The lightning-fast pace of contemporary scientific and technological advancement is breathtaking, with some calling it "innovation on steroids" or "innovation at warp speed."[1] In the past few decades alone, the world has witnessed rapid and dramatic developments such as the proliferation of the Internet, advances in artificial intelligence, groundbreaking HIV drugs, genome sequencers, agricultural genetics, nanotechnology, and biofuels, to name just a few. Not surprisingly, these high-tech advancements have altered the means and methods of warfare[2] and are shaping how armed conflicts can and will be fought on the land, sea, air, and cyber battlefields of today and tomorrow.[3]

---

* Shane Reeves is a Lieutenant Colonel in the United States Army. He is a Professor and the Deputy Head, Department of Law at the United States Military Academy, West Point. Dave Wallace is a Colonel in the United States Army. He is a Professor and the Head, Department of Law at the United States Military Academy, West Point, New York. The views expressed here are their personal ones and do not necessarily reflect those of the Department of Defense, the United States Army, the United States Military Academy, or any other department or agency of the U.S. government. The analysis presented here stems from their academic research of publicly available sources, not from protected operational information.

[1] *See, e.g.*, Erik Brynjolfsson & Michael Schrage, *The New, Faster Face of Innovation*, WALL ST. J., Aug. 17, 2009, *available at* http://online.wsj.com/news/articles/SB10001424052970204830304574130820184260340.

[2] The "means" of warfare refers to the weapons that are used to fight. The "methods" of warfare refers to the tactics of fighting. It is important that an operational lawyer understand not only what may be legally targeted but how to target. *See* INT'L & OPERATIONAL LAW DEP'T, THE JUDGE ADVOCATE GENERAL'S LEGAL CTR. & SCH., U.S. ARMY, LAW OF WAR DESKBOOK 137 (2013) [hereinafter LAW OF WAR DESKBOOK].

[3] *See* Michael N. Schmitt, *War, Technology and the Law of Armed Conflict*, 82 INT'L L. STUDIES 137, 138 (Anthony M. Helm ed. 2006).

Military-related cutting edge technologies revolutionizing and fundamentally altering warfare is not a new phenomenon. One need only consider the invention of the chariot, crossbow, gun powder, machine guns, tanks, airplanes, submarines, nuclear weapons, missiles, satellites, and computers, among many others.[4] At the beginning of the twenty-first century, similar patterns have emerged regarding modern weapons. Cyber and space weapons, robots, armed drones, and even bio-smart weapons are no longer found only in science fiction. Many of these weapons and associated technologies have already been used in present-day armed conflicts.[5] Whether it is the ability to attack remotely, the lack of attribution associated with the use of force, the potential consequences in terms of the scope and magnitude of a strike, or even potentially not having a human actor in the kill chain, there are undeniably some emerging tools and techniques of warfare that are transformational.

The meta-question provoked by the military and humanitarian consequences associated with these existing and emerging technologies[6] is whether the normative framework comprising the law of armed conflict is adequate to regulate these ever-advancing means of warfare. Does the law of armed conflict provide sufficient guidance and stricture for states and other battlefield actors as they develop and use these revolutionary technologies?[7] Answering this question is not simply an academic exercise, as it is weapons that determine how warfare is executed and often won. It is therefore critical for those involved in military operations to understand the legal regulatory framework for approving new weapons and munitions.

This chapter begins with a brief discussion of the history of efforts to regulate permissible weapons and munitions. As the increasingly sophisticated nature of weapons law is inextricably linked to this history, Part II provides important context for understanding this component of the law of armed conflict. The framework of the law of weaponry, the principles for regulating the means of warfare, and the process for determining whether a weapon is lawful in military operations are all considered in Part III. Part IV concludes that, notwithstanding the claims of some critics,[8] weapons law is sufficiently robust and pliable to regulate current and emerging means of war.

---

[4] *See, e.g.*, Paul A. Robblee Jr., *The Legitimacy of Modern Weaponry: A Thesis Presented to the Judge Advocate General's School, United States Army* 6 (1975) (*citing* C. Fenwick, International Law 667 (4th ed. 1965)) (noting attempts in the twelfth century to ban the use of the crossbow as a violation of chivalric code); Shane R. Reeves & Bill J. Johnson, *Autonomous Weapons: Are You Sure These Are Killer Robots? Can We Talk About It?*, The Army Lawyer 25, 27–30 (Apr. 2014) (discussing the dramatic changes to warfare caused by aerial bombardment).

[5] *See generally* P.W. Singer, Wired for War (2009) (noting the increasing use of drones and robots on the modern battlefield).

[6] The LOAC is "predicated on a subtle equilibrium between the two diametrically opposed stimulants of military necessity and humanitarian considerations." Yoram Dinstein, The Conduct of Hostilities under the Law of International Armed Conflict 5 (2d ed. 2010).

[7] For a broad discussion on the topic, see generally Christopher Greenwood, *The Law of Weaponry at the Start of a New Millennium*, 71 Int'l L. Studies 185–231 (Michael N. Schmitt & Leslie C. Green eds., 1998).

[8] *See, e.g.*, Hum. Rhts. Watch, Losing Humanity: The Case against Killer Robots (Nov. 2012), http://www.hrw.org/reports/2012/11/19/losing-humanity-0 [hereinafter Losing Humanity] (arguing for a preemptive and absolute ban on autonomous weapons absent a thorough LOAC analysis).

II. A Brief History of Regulating Weapons of War

Limitations on the use of certain weapons and munitions in warfare have their roots in antiquity,[9] with prohibitions dating back many centuries.[10] The Greek, Roman,[11] and Hindu traditions all banned the use of poisons as a weapon of war.[12] The Second Lateran Council in 1139 A.D. under Innocent II prohibited the use of the crossbow as deadly and odious to God.[13] It was Hugo Grotius in his 1625 book, *De jure belli ac pacis* [14] who demonstrated the necessity of *temperamenta belli*—imposing limitations or restrictions on the destructive power of weapons to be used on the battlefield.[15]

In more recent centuries, the law of armed conflict (LOAC) has increasingly prohibited or limited a number of weapons by treaty or custom. Unquestionably, one of the most important set of rules governing warfare emerged from the American Civil War in April 1863. General Orders No. 100, *Instructions for the Government of Armies of the United States in the Field*,[16] widely known as the "Lieber Code,"[17] marked the first attempt to compile existing laws and customs of war into one document, and to impose them on an army engaged in an armed conflict. Among its many contributions, the Lieber Code discussed what should be permissible, and conversely impermissible, in warfare by defining and developing the overarching core principle of military necessity.[18] Additionally, the Lieber Code reflected an early formulation of the prohibition on superfluous

---

[9] *See* Geoffrey Best, War & Law since 1945, 293 (1994).

[10] *See generally* Christopher Greenwood, *The Law of Weaponry at the Start of the New Millennium*, *in* The Conduct of Hostilities in International Humanitarian Law, Vol. II, The Library of Essays in International Humanitarian Law 186 (Michael N. Schmitt & Wolff Heintschel von Heinegg eds., 2012) [hereinafter *The Law of Weaponry*].

[11] *See* Adam Roberts & Richard Guelff, Documents on the Laws of War 53 (3d ed. 2003).

[12] *See* Christopher Greenwood, *Historical Development and Legal Basis*, *in* The Handbook of International Humanitarian Law 17 (Dieter Fleck ed., 2d ed. 2008) (noting that the Hindu Code of Manu, written circa 200 A.D. banned the use of poison arrows).

[13] Gary D. Solis, The Law of Armed Conflict: International Humanitarian Law in War 5 (2010).

[14] The English translation is "On the Law of War and Peace" and is an early discussion on the legal status of warfare.

[15] *See* Jean-Marie Henckaerts & Louise Doswald-Beck, Customary International Humanitarian Law, Vol I: Rules 390 (2005) [hereinafter Rules].

[16] U.S. War Dep't, Instructions for the Government of Armies of the United States in the Field, General Orders, No. 100 (Apr. 24, 1863) [hereinafter Lieber Code], *reprinted in* The Laws of Armed Conflicts 3 (Dietrich Schindler & Jiri Toman eds., 3d rev. ed. 1988).

[17] The code was written by Francis Lieber (1798–1872) who was a German-American legal and political science scholar who taught Jurisprudence at Columbia University. *See* Paul Finkelman, *Francis Lieber and the Law of War*, N.Y. Times, Mar. 2, 2013, *available at* http://opinionator.blogs.nytimes.com/2013/03/02/francis-lieber-and-the-law-of-war/?_php=true&_type=blogs&_r=0.

[18] *See* William H. Boothby, Weapons and the Law of Armed Conflict 72 (2009) (*citing* Lieber Code, *supra* note 16, art. 14) ("Military necessity, as understood by modern civilized nations, consists in the necessity of those measures which are indispensable for securing the ends of the war, and which are lawful according to the modern law and usages of war."). This definition of military necessity has remained mostly intact in current U.S. doctrine. *See, e.g.*, U.S. Dep't of the Army, Field Manual 27–10, The Law of Land Warfare para. 3.a. Change 1, 1976) [hereinafter FM 27-10] (defining military

injury and unnecessary suffering,[19] and it reinforced the well-established prohibition on poisons.[20] Finally, and in some sense most important, the Lieber Code not only regulated Union forces during the Civil War, but acted as a blueprint for use by many other countries for regulating warfare.[21]

Although the Lieber Code began the contemporary trend of limiting the means and methods of warfare, it is the 1868 St. Petersburg Declaration[22] that is regarded as the first major international treaty prohibiting the use of a particular weapon during armed conflict.[23] The treaty renounced the employment of any projectile of a weight below 400 grams, which is either explosive or charged with fulminating or inflammable substances.[24] Beyond the St. Petersburg Declaration, the First Hague Peace Conference in 1899 addressed, among other issues, asphyxiating gases[25] and expanding bullets.[26] Of particular significance, the so-called Martens

---

necessity as "those measures not forbidden by international law which are indispensable for securing the complete submission of the enemy as soon as possible.").

For a more detailed discussion on the principle of military necessity, see generally Brian J. Bill, *The Rendulic "Rule": Military Necessity, Commander's Knowledge, and Methods of Warfare*, *in* 12 YEARBOOK OF INTERNATIONAL HUMANITARIAN LAW 119–31(2009); Shane R. Reeves & David Lai, *A Broad Overview of the Law of Armed Conflict in the Age of Terror*, *in* THE FUNDAMENTALS OF COUNTERTERRORISM LAW 147–49 (Lynne Zusman ed., 2014) (stating that military necessity is "discounted in the rules" that comprise the LOAC with the particular provisions of the law either allowing for violence and destruction or forbidding such conduct out of deference to humanitarian considerations); Michael N. Schmitt, *Military Necessity and Humanity in International Humanitarian Law: Preserving the Delicate Balance*, 50 VA. J.INT'L L., 795, 799 (2010).

[19] *See* BOOTHBY, *supra* note 18, at 88 (noting that "military necessity does not permit the infliction of suffering for its own sake").

[20] *See id.* The Lieber Code specifically states that "[m]ilitary necessity does not admit of cruelty . . . It does not admit of the use of poison in any way, nor the wanton devastation of a district." Lieber Code, *supra* note 16, art. 16.

[21] *See* R.R. BAXTER, *Conventional Weapons under Legal Prohibitions*, *in* THE CONDUCT OF HOSTILITIES IN INTERNATIONAL HUMANITARIAN LAW, VOL. II, THE LIBRARY OF ESSAYS IN INTERNATIONAL HUMANITARIAN LAW 51 (Michael N. Schmitt & Wolff Heintschel von Heinegg eds., 2012).

[22] 1868 St. Petersburg Declaration Renouncing the Use, in Times of War, of Explosive Projectiles under 400 Grammes Weight [hereinafter 1868 St. Petersburg Declaration].

[23] *See* ROBERTS & GUELFF, *supra* note 11, at 53.

[24] Declaration Renouncing the Use, in Time of War, of Certain Explosive Projectiles under 400 Grammes Weight pmbl., Nov. 29, 1868, 18 Martens Nouveau Recueil (ser. 1) 474, 138 Consol. T.S. 297. By way of background on the agreement:

> The prohibition followed the development of a bullet which exploded upon contact with a hard surface. In 1863 the bullet was introduced into the Imperial Russian Army to be used for blowing up ammunition wagons. In 1864 the Imperial War Minister considered it to be improper to use such a bullet against troops and its use was therefore strictly controlled. However, in 1867, a modification of the bullet was developed, which enabled it to explode on contact with even a soft surface. Moreover, unlike previous projectiles, the new bullet shattered upon explosion. . . . Tsar Alexander II invited states to attend an International Military Commission in St. Petersburg to consider the matter.

ROBERTS & GUELFF, *supra* note 11 at 53.

[25] *See* Hague Declaration (IV, 2) concerning the Prohibition of the Use of Projectiles Diffusing Asphyxiating Gases, July 29, 1899, 26 Martens Nouveau Recueil (ser. 2) 998, 187 Consol. T.S. 453.

[26] *See* Hague Declaration (IV, 3) concerning the Prohibition of the Use of Expanding Bullets, July 29, 1899, 26 Martens Nouveau Recueil (ser. 2) 1002, 187 Consol. T.S. 459 (prohibiting "the use

Clause, perhaps the most well-known provision of the LOAC, first appeared in the Preamble to the 1899 Hague Convention II on land warfare.[27] The purpose of the Martens Clause was, in part, to assure certain states that the regulations could not be viewed as setting forth the only rules that would be applicable during an armed conflict.[28] Friedrich von Martens (1845–1909), delegate and legal advisor of Tsar Nicholas II at the Hague Peace Conferences and the Livonian Professor at the University of St. Petersburg, is credited with the contribution of the clause.[29] The magisterial words of the Martens Clause have found expression in many LOAC treaties since 1899. It provided as follows:

> Until a more complete code of the laws of war has been issued, the High Contracting Parties deem it expedient to declare that, in cases not included in the regulations adopted by them, the inhabitants and the belligerents remain under the protection and the rule of the principles of the law of nations, as they result from the usages established among civilized peoples, from the laws of humanity, and the dictates of the public conscience.[30]

The Martens Clause therefore overlays a general regulation on weapons and munitions so that even when no specific prohibition or limitation is applicable to a particular weapon, broader principles still must be adhered to by the parties to a conflict.[31] Accordingly, the underlying principles contained in the Martens Clause are particularly relevant to emerging technology not regulated by specific treaties in the law of armed conflict.[32]

---

of bullets which expand or flatten easily in the human body, such as bullets with a hard envelope which does not entirely cover the core or is pierced with incisions."). Although the United States is not a signatory to the treaty, it does adhere to the prohibition. *See* W. Hayes Parks, *Memorandum of Law—Sniper Use of Open-Tip Ammunition*, The Army Lawyer 86, 87 (Feb. 1991). For an excellent discussion on whether this provision remains relevant on the modern battlefield, see Joshua F. Berry, *Hollow Point Bullets: How History Has Hijacked Their Use in Combat and Why It Is Time to Reexamine the 1899 Hague Declaration concerning Expanding Bullets*, 206 Mil. L. Rev. 88–156 (2010).

[27] *See* Solis, *supra* note 13, at 53. The Martens Clause emerged in the context of a debate about the legal status under the LOAC of armed conflict of resistance fighters during an occupation. *See* Emily Crawford, *The Modern Relevance of the Martens Clause* 1, 1 (2011), *available at* http://papers.ssrn.com/sol3/papers.cfm?abstract_id=1810177 (last visited August 11, 2013).

[28] *See* Geoffrey S. Corn, Victor Hansen, Richard B. Jackson, Chris Jenks, Eric Talbot Jensen & James A. Schoettler Jr., The Law of Armed Conflict: An Operational Approach 56 (2012) [hereinafter The Law of Armed Conflict: An Operational Approach].

[29] *See The Law of Weaponry, supra* note 10, at 34. Martens was also a conference organizer and humanist, who in 1902 received the ICRC's Distinguished Service Award. *See* Solis, *supra* note 13, at 53.

[30] Hague Convention II with Respect to the Laws and Customs of War on Land and its annex: Regulations concerning the Laws and Customs of War on Land, pembl. 29 July 1899, 32 Stat. 1803, 1 Bevans 247, 26 Martens Nouveau Recueil (ser. 2) 949, 197 Consol. T.S. 429.

[31] *See* Boothby, *supra* note 18, at 67.

[32] The Martens Clause is the subject of a great deal of controversy, with some arguing that it represents an enforceable legal principle and others arguing the clause is more general guidance. *See infra* notes 189–98 and accompanying text.

A second peace conference was convened in The Hague in 1907.[33] That international gathering was quite successful in considering weapons and rules of war,[34] with its most notable contribution being the *Convention (IV) respecting the Laws and Customs of War on Land and its annex: Regulations concerning the Laws and Customs of War on Land* (commonly referred to as "Hague Regulation IV").[35] Hague Regulation IV's important principles became central to understanding and applying the law of armed conflict to weapons. First among these principles is the important expression that the right of belligerents to adopt means of injuring the enemy is not unlimited.[36] It also prohibits the use of means and methods of warfare of a nature to cause superfluous injury or unnecessary suffering.[37]

The horrors caused by certain classes of weapons in World War I resulted in more specific international prohibitions. In particular, states endeavored to ban the use of chemical and biological weapons with the landmark *1925 Geneva Gas Protocol for the Prohibition of the Use in War of Asphyxiating, Poisonous or other Gases, and of Bacteriological Methods of Warfare*.[38] The treaty was reinforced and strengthened with subsequent instruments in 1972 (on biological weapons)[39] and 1993 (on chemical weapons)[40] by prohibiting the development, stockpiling, and transfer of weapons of mass destruction. As an important side note, the 1972 Biological Weapons Convention is arguably the first treaty that prohibits an entire category of weapons.[41]

The international community's interest in prohibiting and limiting conventional weapons increased toward the end of the twentieth and beginning of the twenty-first centuries. For example, the Convention on Certain Conventional Weapons, or "CCW,"[42] addressed such weapons and munitions

---

[33] THE HAGUE PEACE CONFERENCES OF 1899 AND 1907 AND INTERNATIONAL ARBITRATION: REPORTS AND DOCUMENTS xix (Shabtai Rosenne ed., 2001).

[34] *See* SOLIS, *supra* note 13, at 53.

[35] Hague Convention No. IV, Respecting the Laws and Customs of War on Land, Oct. 18, 1907, 36 Stat. 2227, and Annex, 36 Stat. 2295 [hereinafter Hague Regulation IV].

[36] *Id.* at Art. 22.

[37] *Id.* at Art. 23.

[38] *See generally* Protocol for the Prohibition of the Use in War of Asphyxiating, Poisonous or Other Gases, and of Bacteriological Methods of Warfare, Geneva, June 17, 1925, 26 U.S.T. 571, 94 L.N.T.S. 65.

[39] *See generally* Convention on the Prohibition of the Development, Production and Stockpiling of Bacteriological (Biological) and Toxin Weapons and on Their Destruction, Apr. 10, 1972, 1015 U.N.T.S. 163 [hereinafter Biological Weapons Convention].

[40] *See generally* Convention on the Prohibition of the Development, Production, Stockpiling and Use of Chemical Weapons and on Their Destruction, Jan. 13, 1993, 1974 U.N.T.S. 317.

[41] *See* BOOTHBY, *supra* note 18, at 126 (noting that comprehensive and specific prohibitions apply in relation to biological/bacteriological weapons.); LAW OF WAR DESKBOOK, *supra* note 2, at 165 ("The U.S. renounced all use of biological and toxin weapons.").

[42] *See generally* Convention on Prohibitions or Restrictions on the Use of Certain Conventional Weapons Which May Be Deemed to Be Excessively Injurious or to Have Indiscriminate Effects,

as land mines,[43] incendiary weapons,[44] and blinding lasers.[45] The prohibitions memorialized in the CCW reinforced general principles of the law of armed conflict such as the prohibition on indiscriminate weapons and the obligation of participants to avoid use of weapons designed to cause, or of a nature to cause, superfluous injury or unnecessary suffering.[46] In addition to the CCW, more recent, and controversial, agreements such as the Ottawa Treaty on anti-personnel mines[47] and the Convention on Cluster Munitions,[48] attempt to ban or otherwise restrict specific conventional weapons or munitions.

This brief historical synopsis highlights some of the more significant milestones in the formation of the law of weaponry. From an operational perspective, understanding the restrictions and limitations on specific weapons is critical for the planning and execution of military operations. Although some weapon restrictions will have only a de minimis affect on a military operation, others may fundamentally alter a commander's actions. As mentioned previously, the fundamental maxim of the law of armed conflict provides that the right of belligerents to adopt means of injuring the enemy is not unlimited.[49] Obviously, if one were to renounce this foundational maxim, one would enter into a realm of arbitrary conduct on battlefields.[50]

Oct 10, 1980, 1342 U.N.T.S. 137, 19 I.L.M. 1523 [hereinafter CCW]. The original Convention on Conventional Weapons, with three protocols, was adopted on October 10, 1980, and opened for signature for one year from April 10, 1981. At present, 117 states are parties to the Convention on Conventional Weapons. *See* United Nations Office at Geneva (UNOG), *available at* http://www.unog.ch/80256EE600585943/%28httpPages%29/3CE7CFC0AA4A7548C12571C00039CB0C?OpenDocument (last visited Aug. 17, 2014).

[43] *See generally* Protocol on Prohibitions or Restrictions on the Use of Mines, Booby-Traps and Other Devices (Protocol II), as amended May 3, 1996, 2048 U.N.T.S. 133 [hereinafter CCW Protocol II].

[44] *See generally* Protocol on Prohibitions or Restrictions on the Use of Incendiary Weapons (Protocol III), Oct. 10, 1980, 1342 U.N.T.S. 171, 19 I.L.M. 1534 [hereinafter CCW Protocol III].

[45] *See generally* Protocol on Blinding Laser Weapons (Protocol IV), Oct. 13, 1995, 35 I.L.M. 1218.

[46] *See* CCW, *supra* note 42, at Preamble.

[47] Convention on the Prohibition of the Use, Stockpiling, Production and Transfer of Anti-Personnel Mines and on Their Destruction (Ottawa Convention), 1 March 1999, 36 I.L.M. 1507. Whereas weapons treaties historically were proposed by state actors, the catalyst for the Ottawa Convention was nongovernmental organizations (NGOs). Some have argued that this "democratizing" has significantly changed how international law will be developed in the future. *See generally* Kenneth Anderson, *The Ottawa Convention Banning Landmines, the Role of International Non-governmental Organizations and the Idea of International Civil Society*, 11 EJIL 91–120 (2000). However, these NGO-initiated treaties are often rejected by state actors who are active manufacturers or users of these munitions and weapons, thus raising questions about the viability of a process that circumvents state actors in the development of weapons treaties. *See* Law of War Deskbook, *supra* note 2, at 161.

[48] *See generally* Convention on Cluster Munitions, 3 Dec. 2008, 48 I.L.M. 357.

[49] Hague Regulation IV, *supra* note 35, at Art. 22.

[50] *See* Morris Greenspan, The Modern Law of Land Warfare 391 (1959).

III. The Legal Parameters of Regulating Weapons

A. THE FOUNDATIONS OF THE LAW OF WEAPONRY

Before we delve into the paradigmatic structure of the laws related to weapons, it is important to provide some background and context. The laws related to weaponry are best conceptualized as a subset of the law of armed conflict.[51] Therefore, the principles that control the formation and interpretation of weapons law are the same as those of the law of armed conflict (LOAC).[52]

The underlying objective of both the laws related to weaponry and the wider law of armed conflict is to strike a grand, and at times delicate, equilibrium.[53] That is, the LOAC norms represent a balance between two diametrically opposed impulses: military necessity and humanitarian considerations.[54] Whereas military necessity is best understood as a broad "attempt to realize the purpose of armed conflict, gaining military advantage," humanitarian considerations are intent on "minimizing human suffering and physical destruction" in warfare.[55] The LOAC, both in treaty and custom, is infused with these competing meta-principles[56] "thereby ensuring that force is applied on the battlefield in a manner allowing for the accomplishment of the mission while simultaneously taking appropriate humanitarian considerations into account."[57]

This equilibrium is certainly not new to the law of armed conflict or the law of weaponry.[58] Accordingly, when considering the means and methods of warfare, "the law of armed conflict has never been about ensuring a 'fair fight'; rather, it comprises prohibitions, restrictions, and obligations designed to balance a state's interest in effectively prosecuting the war (military necessity) with its interest in minimizing harm to those involved in a conflict."[59] Any question regarding the

---

[51] *See* BOOTHBY, *supra* note 18, at 22.

[52] *Id.*

[53] *See The Law of Weaponry, supra* note 10, at 7.

[54] *See* Kjetil Mujezinovic Larsen, Camilla Guldahl Cooper & Gro Nystuen, *Introduction by the Editors: Is There a "Principle of Humanity" in International Humanitarian Law?, in* SEARCHING FOR A "PRINCIPLE OF HUMANITY" IN INTERNATIONAL HUMANITARIAN LAW 9 (Kjetil Mujezinovic Larsen, Camilla Guldahl Cooper & Gro Nystuen eds., 2012) [hereinafter SEARCHING FOR A "PRINCIPLE OF HUMANITY" IN INTERNATIONAL HUMANITARIAN LAW].

[55] SOLIS, *supra* note 13, at 260.

[56] *See* Bill, *supra* note 18, at 119 ("Military necessity is a meta-principle of the law of war . . . in the sense that it justifies destruction in war. It permeates all subsidiary rules."); DINSTEIN, *supra* note 6, at 16.

[57] Shane R. Reeves & Jeffrey S. Thurhner, *Are We Reaching a Tipping Point? How Contemporary Challenges Are Affecting the Military Necessity-Humanity Balance*, HARV. NAT. SEC. J. FEATURES ONLINE 1(June 2013), *available at* http://harvardnsj.org/2013/06/ are-we-reaching-a-tipping-point-how-contemporary-challenges-are-affecting-the-military-necessity-humanity-balance/.

[58] *See* Christopher Greenwood, *Humanitarian Requirements and Military Necessity, in* THE HANDBOOK OF INTERNATIONAL HUMANITARIAN LAW 37–38 (Dieter Fleck ed., 2d ed. 2008) (discussing generally how the principles of military necessity and humanity check and balance each other throughout the LOAC).

[59] Michael N. Schmitt & Jeffrey S. Thurnher, *"Out of the Loop": Autonomous Weapon Systems and the Law of Armed Conflict*, 4 HARV. NAT. SEC. J. 231, 232 (2013).

legality of a weapon per se or how that weapon is used in an armed conflict must be viewed through the prism of that grand balance. Put in a slightly different manner, the law of armed conflict is fundamentally concerned, to the maximum extent possible, with maintaining important humanitarian values during warfare.[60] As stated by Professor Christopher Greenwood:

> [t]he principal objective of the law of weaponry is the protection of these values. Thus, the prohibition of indiscriminate weapons and methods of warfare is designed to serve the objective of distinguishing between civilians and civilian objects, on the one hand, and combatants and military objectives, on the other, and protecting the former. Similarly, the principle that belligerents may not employ weapons or methods of warfare of a nature to cause unnecessary suffering serves the objective of protecting even combatants from suffering and death, which is not necessary for the achievement of legitimate military goals.[61]

Given the above, it is fair to state that combatants may be lawfully killed or wounded during combat by any weapon except those that violate the LOAC.[62]

B. REGULATING WEAPONS IN ARMED CONFLICT

So what weapons or munitions violate the LOAC? There are three distinct categories of regulations or restrictions on the means of warfare. Each will be discussed below.

1. Per Se Unlawful Weapons

The first category focuses on the legality of the weapon itself.[63] That is, there are certain weapons that are unlawful per se because they are either designed or of a nature to cause unnecessary suffering to combatants,[64] or they are indiscriminate.[65] A weapon or munition will cause unnecessary suffering "if it inevitably or in its normal use has a particular effect, and the injury caused thereby" is disproportionate to the "military advantage to be gained from use."[66] This principle embodies the humanitarian interest in eliminating useless and senseless suffering on the battlefield.[67] Thus, a weapon is not per se unlawful because it causes severe suffering or injury to a combatant, but only if during its normal use it would cause disproportionate suffering or injury to a combatant.

---

[60] *The Law of Weaponry*, *supra* note 10, at 7.

[61] *See id.* at 8.

[62] *See* GREENSPAN, *supra* note 50, at 316.

[63] *Id.* at 243.

[64] *See id.* at 244.

[65] *See* BOOTHBY, *supra* note 18, at 69 ("the prohibition of weapons, methods, or means of warfare of a nature to cause superfluous injury or unnecessary suffering is the first great principle of weapons law, its second is the principle of discrimination.").

[66] LAW OF WAR DESKBOOK, *supra* note 2, at 154.

[67] *See* BOOTHBY, *supra* note 18, at 55.

This balancing test acknowledges "that necessary suffering to combatants is lawful in armed conflict, and may include severe injury or loss of life" if justified by military necessity.[68] However, the test also explicitly recognizes that "those means and methods of warfare that unnecessarily aggravate the suffering of combatants, that is, which cause suffering serving no military purpose" are expressly prohibited.[69] This prohibition is well established in the law of armed conflict and is binding on all state actors as it is a reflection of customary international law.[70]

There are a number of weapons that violate the principle of unnecessary suffering and are illegal per se under the law of armed conflict.[71] As discussed in Part II the prohibition on poison or poisoned weapons is a long-standing and universally recognized ban under the law of armed conflict.[72] Other examples of unlawful weapons include: lasers specifically designed, as their sole combat function or as one of their combat functions, to cause permanent blindness;[73] lances with barbed heads; and projectiles filled with glass.[74] This small sampling of weapons prohibited by international law illustrates the important maxim that belligerents are "especially forbidden . . . to employ arms, projectiles or material calculated to cause unnecessary suffering."[75]

Similar to a weapon that causes unnecessary suffering, a means of warfare that by its nature is indiscriminate is also per se illegal.[76] As parties to a conflict "shall at all times distinguish between the civilian population and combatants and between civilian objects and military objectives"[77] using an indiscriminate weapon violates this international legal obligation.[78] It is inarguable that the

---

[68] *Id.*

[69] Michael N. Schmitt, *Autonomous Weapon Systems and International Humanitarian Law: A Reply to the Critics*, HARV. NAT'L SEC. J. FEATURES 9 (2013), http://harvardnsj.org/wp-content/uploads/2013/02/Schmitt-Autonomous-Weapon-Systems-and-IHL-Final.pdf.

[70] *Id.* at 8–9 (*citing* Protocol Additional to the Geneva Conventions of 12 August 1949, and Relating to the Protection of Victims of International Armed Conflict (Protocol I) art. 35(2), June 8, 1977, 1125 U.N.T.S. 3 [hereinafter AP I]) ("Article 35(2) of Additional Protocol I to the 1949 Geneva Conventions affirms the prohibition and irrefutably reflects customary international law" and therefore the "norm binds even States that are not Party to the Protocol, such as the United States.").

It is important to note that, unlike the Hague and Geneva Conventions, the United States has not ratified AP I or AP II, but finds many portions of the protocol customary international law. *See generally* Michael J. Matheson, *Remarks on the United States Position on the Relation of Customary International Law to the 1977 Protocols Additional to the 1949 Geneva Conventions*, 2 AM. U.J. INT'L L. & POL'Y 419 (1987).

[71] *Id.* at 245 (Rule 71).

[72] *See supra* text and accompanying notes 12; RULES, *supra* note 15, at 251 (Rule 72).

[73] *Id.* at 292 (Rule 86).

[74] *See* FM 27–10, *supra* note 18, at para. 34.

[75] Hague Regulation IV, *supra* note 35, at art. 23(e).

[76] *See* GREENSPAN, *supra* note 50, at 245.

[77] AP I, *supra* note 70, at art. 48.

[78] *See* COMMENTARY ON THE ADDITIONAL PROTOCOLS OF 8 JUNE 1977 TO THE GENEVA CONVENTIONS OF 12 AUG. 1949, 598 (para. 1863) (Yves Sandoz et. al. eds., 1987) [hereinafter Commentaries] ("It is the foundation on which the codification of the laws and customs of war rests: the civilian population and civilian objects must be respected and protected . . . The entire system established in The Hague in 1899 and 1907 and in Geneva from 1864 to 1977 is founded on this rule.").

distinction principle is a norm of customary international[79] law and its codification is found in Additional Protocol I.[80] Whereas those weapons that cause unnecessary suffering are per se illegal due to their impact upon combatants,[81] the use of weapons that are by nature indiscriminate is prohibited[82] based upon the humanitarian concern for the civilian population.[83]

A per se illegal indiscriminate means of warfare may include either a weapon incapable of being directed at a specific military object or a weapon with uncontrollable effects. The V2 rocket used by Germany against England at the end of the Second World War, which was unable to be aimed or directed, is a classic example of an indiscriminate weapon.[84] However, it is important to note that there is a difference between per se illegal indiscriminate weapons and a weapon that is used in an indiscriminate manner.[85] The rule does not prohibit imprecise means of warfare but extends to only those that are "shots in the dark."[86] Thus, a weapon is only unlawful per se based on it being indiscriminate when it is "of a nature to strike combatants, military objectives, civilians, and civilian objects without distinction."[87]

Additional Protocol I clarifies what constitutes a weapon incapable of discriminating by giving the following illustration. An indiscriminate attack includes a "bombardment by any methods or means which treats as a single military objective a number of clearly separated and distinct military objectives located in a

---

[79] *See* RULES, *supra* note 15, at 25, 40 (Rule 7, 12); Schmitt, *supra* note 68, at 10.

[80] *See, e.g.*, AP I, *supra* note 70, at art. 48.

[81] *See id.* ("In that it is otherwise unlawful to attack civilians, this norm applies only to suffering or injury experienced by combatants.").

[82] RULES, *supra* note 15, at 244 (Rule 71).

[83] *See* BOOTHBY, *supra* note 18, at 69 ("The law of armed conflict has as one of its central underlying themes, the continuing protection of civilians from attacks, and their effects").

[84] Commentaries, *supra* note 78, at 620 (para. 1958).

[85] *See* Schmitt, *supra* note 69, at 10. Professor Schmitt states:

> The prohibition on weapon systems that are indiscriminate because they cannot be aimed at a lawful target is often confused with the ban on use of discriminate weapons in an indiscriminate fashion. The classic case is that of the SCUD missiles launched by Iraq during the 1990–91 Gulf War. While it is true that the missiles were inaccurate, they were not unlawful per se because situations existed in which they could be employed discriminately. In particular, the missiles were capable of use against troops in open areas such as the desert, and they actually struck very large military installations without seriously endangering the civilian population. However, when launched in the direction of cities, as repeatedly occurred during the conflict, their use was undeniably unlawful. Even though the cities contained military objectives, the missiles were insufficiently accurate to reliably strike any of them.

Id. (citation omitted). Where the line is between a per se indiscriminate weapon and an inaccurate weapon is unclear. One alternative argument is that no weapon should be considered per se indiscriminate due to accuracy as theoretically there is always a possible situation where only combatants or military objectives are targeted.

[86] TALLINN MANUAL ON THE INTERNATIONAL LAW APPLICABLE TO CYBER WARFARE 145 (Rule 43 and commentary) (Michael Schmitt ed., 2013) [hereinafter TALLINN MANUAL].

[87] *Id.*

city, town, village or other area containing a similar concentration of civilians or civilian objects."[88] Reading this provision in conjunction with Additional Protocol I, Article 51(4)(b)[89] "it would seem clear that weapons must be capable of direction at individual military objectives and that this requirement must be understood in the context of the attack."[90] Based upon this guidance parties to a conflict knows they may not "use weapons that are incapable of distinguishing between civilian and military targets."[91]

An indiscriminate weapon also includes means of warfare "incapable of afflicting only combatants" and whose effects are difficult to control.[92] Biological weapons serve as an excellent example as their effects cannot be limited, or even reasonably predicted, as required by the principle of distinction.[93] In contrast to a weapon incapable of being aimed at a military objective, a biological weapon is fully capable of being directed at a specific object. However, it is the biological weapon's unpredictable effects, coupled with a reasonable expectation that it will adversely affect the health or survival of the population, which makes it impossible to use in a discriminate manner.[94] Biological weapons are therefore, as a class of weapons, unlawful per se.[95] The 1972 Biological Weapons Convention memorializes the absolute prohibition on this entire category of weapons.[96] Commenting on the legality of biological weapons, the International Committee of the Red Cross's study of customary international law specifically noted that "[i]t can be concluded from the drive to eliminate biological weapons over the last three decades that states believe that these weapons should not exist and therefore must not be used in any circumstances, including non-international armed conflicts."[97]

Similarly, a cyber weapon that would trigger an uncontrollable chain of events resulting in physical damage would be an indiscriminate weapon.[98] For example, using malware to attack dual-use cyber infrastructure will likely disable the military target but also spread into the civilian network.[99] If the damage caused by

---

[88] *See* AP I, *supra* note 70, at art. 51(5)(a).

[89] Stating, in part, "indiscriminate attacks are . . . those which employ a method or means of combat which cannot be directed at a specific military objective." *Id.* at art. 51(4)(b).

[90] Boothby, *supra* note 18, at 78.

[91] Advisory Opinion, Legality of the Threat or Use of Nuclear Weapons, 1996 I.C.J. 226, 257 (July 8).

[92] Boothby, *supra* note 18, at 84 (*citing* Michael N. Schmitt, *War, Technology and International Humanitarian Law*, Harv. Univ. Occasional Paper Series 10 (Summer 2005)).

[93] *See* AP I, *supra* note 70, at art. 51(4)(c).

[94] *See* Schmitt, *supra* note 69, at 14 (using a "biological contagion used to infect combatants" whose subsequent spread is uncontrollable" as an example of a per se illegal indiscriminate weapon.).

[95] *See* Greenspan, *supra* note 50, at 243. *See also* Biological Weapons Convention, *supra* note 39; Rules, *supra* note 15, at 256 (Rule 73).

[96] *See generally* Biological Weapons Convention, *supra* note 39; Stefan Oeter, *Methods and Means of Combat, in* The Handbook of International Humanitarian Law 174 (Dieter Fleck ed., 2d ed. 2008).

[97] Rules, *supra* note 15, at 257 (Rule 73).

[98] *See* Tallinn Manual, *supra* note 86, at 144–46 (Rule 43 and commentary).

[99] Schmitt, *supra* note 69, at 14.

the uncontrollable effects is such that injury or physical damage results, the cyber weapon is considered an indiscriminate, and therefore per se illegal, weapon.[100]

Obviously the protection of civilians is one of the main goals of the law of armed conflict,[101] and it is for this reason that indiscriminate weapons are prohibited. The *United Kingdom's Manual on the Law of Armed Conflict* captures the illegality of both categories of indiscriminate weapons by expressly stating "[i]t is prohibited to employ weapons which cannot be directed at a specific military objective or the effects which cannot be limited as required by Additional Protocol I and consequently are of a nature to strike military objectives and civilians or civilian objects without distinction."[102] This legal prohibition is absolute, but generally coincides with the contemporary military interest of "seeking to ensure that weapons direct their destructive effect as accurately and reliably as possible at the military capability of the enemy."[103] With the advent of asymmetric warfare and the complexity of the contemporary battlefield,[104] the employment of indiscriminate weapons is less likely as the humanitarian reasons for their prohibition is increasingly converging with the military interest of those in armed conflicts.[105]

2. The Misuse of Otherwise Lawful Weapons

The second category of regulations or restrictions focuses on the unlawful use of an otherwise lawful weapon. This set of controls is sometimes referred to as the "conduct of hostilities rules" and "applies to a weapon system's use irrespective of whether or not the weapon system is lawful per se."[106] These rules explain "the technical limits at which the necessities of war ought to yield to the requirements of humanity" in regards to weapon usage.[107] Again, it is considerations of military necessity and humanity that "constitute guiding principles for the

---

[100] *See* TALLINN MANUAL, *supra* note 86, at 146 (Rule 43 and commentary) (stating that the harm caused by the cyber weapon cannot simply be annoying but must rise to that which would be considered collateral damage).

[101] *See* Nils Melzer, *Foreword to Interpretive Guidance on the Notion of Direct Participation in Hostilities under International Humanitarian Law* 4, ICRC (May 2009) [hereinafter ICRC INTERPRETIVE GUIDANCE], *available at* http://www.icrc.org/eng/assets /files/other/icrc-002-0990.pdf.

[102] *United Kingdom Ministry of Defence*, THE MANUAL ON THE LAW OF ARMED CONFLICT para. 6.4 (2004).

[103] BOOTHBY, *supra* note 18, at 69 (discussing how success in contemporary armed conflicts is increasingly reliant upon accurate and proportionate weapons). *See also* U.S. DEP'T OF ARMY, FIELD MANUAL 3-24/U.S. MARINE CORPS WARFIGHTING PUBLICATION 3-33.5, COUNTERINSURGENCY, 1–24 (Dec. 15, 2006) (discussing how counterinsurgency efforts are undermined by law of war violations).

[104] *See* David Wallace & Shane R. Reeves, *The Law of Armed Conflict's "Wicked" Problem: Levee en Masse in Cyber Warfare*, 89 INT'L L. STUD. 646, 646–47 (2013) (discussing the increasingly complicated modern battlefield and the trend toward hybrid armed conflicts).

[105] BOOTHBY, *supra* note 18, at 69.

[106] Schmitt, *supra* note 69, at 8.

[107] 1868 St. Petersburg Declaration, *supra* note 22, at prmbl. "The 1868 St. Petersburg Declaration, for example, explicitly recognized the need to strike such a balance." Schmitt, *Military Necessity and Humanity*, *supra* note 18, at 799.

interpretation of the rights and duties of belligerents" in warfare, including their use of a weapons.[108]

The balance between military necessity and humanity that permeates throughout the LOAC establishes the foundation for the conduct of hostilities rules. The rules, never overlooking military requirements while simultaneously never losing sight of humanitarian considerations,[109] provide the broad framework for determining the legality of using a weapon.[110] The LOAC's four core principle are of primary importance to this framework.[111] The four principles of military necessity, distinction, proportionality, and unnecessary suffering limit how warfare is conducted, and by extension, regulate the means that may be employed by the parties to a conflict.[112] Without question, the core principles are widely accepted and regarded as customary, and the relevance of each to the law of weaponry will be briefly discussed below.[113]

A. MILITARY NECESSITY

Francis Lieber, in arguably his "greatest theoretical contribution to the modern law of war,"[114] stated that "[m]ilitary necessity, as understood by modern civilized nations, consists in the necessity of those measures that are indispensable for securing the ends of the war, and that are lawful according to the modern law and uses of war."[115] Lieber's statement echoed Napoleon, who said "[m]y great maxim has always been, in politics and war alike, every injury done to the enemy, even though permitted by the rules, is excusable only so far as it is absolutely necessary; everything beyond that is criminal."[116] Although military necessity is mentioned in all four of the 1949 Geneva Conventions and in both 1977 Additional Protocols it is not specifically defined in these foundational LOAC treaties.[117]

Yet thinking of military necessity as a stand-alone principle with regard to regulating weapons is unhelpful.[118] Any weapon arguably has some military

---

[108] ICRC INTERPRETIVE GUIDANCE, *supra* note 101, at 78–79.

[109] DINSTEIN, *supra* note 6, at 17.

[110] Schmitt, *supra* note 69, at 14 (stating that the rules act as a safeguard against misuse of a weapon system).

[111] SOLIS, *supra* note 13, at 251 (noting that all conduct in armed conflict is examined "in the light of the core concepts, the four of which are closely intertwined.").

[112] *See* GREENSPAN, *supra* note 50, at 313. *See also* THE LAW OF ARMED CONFLICT: AN OPERATIONAL APPROACH, *supra* note 28, at 114 (explaining that the four core principles originated from the combat experiences of warriors over the centuries, thereby facilitating the ability of belligerents to accomplish their battlefield objectives on the one hand while incorporating important humanitarian considerations on the other).

[113] *See* Bill Boothby, *The Law of Weaponry—Is It Adequate?*, *in* INTERNATIONAL LAW AND ARMED CONFLICT: EXPLORING THE FAULT LINES 297 (Michael Schmitt & Jelena Pejic eds., 2007).

[114] Burris M. Carnahan, *Lincoln, Lieber and the Laws of War: The Origin and Limits of the Principles of Military Necessity*, 2 AMER. J. INT'L LAW, 213, 213 (1998).

[115] Lieber Code, *supra* note 16, at art. 14.

[116] BEST, *supra* note 9, at 242 (*citing* MAX HUBER, ZEITSCHRIFT FUR VOLKERRECHT 353 (1913)).

[117] *See* SOLIS, *supra* note 13, at 259.

[118] *See, e.g.*, Bill, *supra* note 18, at 134 ("But in this broad discipline of means and methods of war, what has not yet been addressed to which might military necessity have some applicability? There is very little. In the area of weapons, various treaties address and regulate specific weapons and their

value, and its use can easily be defended as necessary.[119] Further, the prohibition described by Lieber—that the weapon must be lawful—is "discounted" throughout the rules that comprise the LOAC.[120] The definition of military objective serves as an example. "The condition that military objectives yield some military advantage" makes "any separate requirement for military necessity superfluous."[121] Similarly, in a proportionality analysis, if a weapon is used that lacks military advantage but causes incidental loss of civilian life or property the principle is violated.[122] "Taking these observations together" it is clear that military necessity has "no independent valence when assessing" the legality of a weapon.[123]

As mentioned previously, military necessity "proscribes, indirectly, what might otherwise constitute lawful acts of warfare."[124] It should not be characterized as a distinct rule of the LOAC, "but rather as a foundational principle that undergirds the entire body of law."[125] Military necessity as a principle has more general applicability in that it pervades "the entirety of the Law of Armed Conflict" and "is continually addressed in subsidiary positive law."[126] "[I]t can be stated categorically that no part" of the LOAC "overlooks military requirements, just as no part . . . loses sight of humanitarian considerations," with every legal norm crafted with these two principles in mind.[127] Thus, with regard to regulating weapons, military necessity is best understood not as a stand-alone principle but rather as a broad attempt to ensure that the need to gain military advantage over the enemy is counterbalanced by the humanitarian consideration of "minimizing human suffering and physical destruction" in warfare.[128]

---

employment . . ." with "the rules either recogniz[ing] military necessity or state their prohibition in absolute terms.").

[119] For example, using a glass bullet has military value. It is extraordinarily difficult to locate remnants of the bullets in a body. Thus, glass bullets would cause a party to a conflict to expend extreme amounts of resources on medical care while simultaneously decreasing their armed forces' will to fight.

[120] *See* Bill, *supra* note 18, at 131.

[121] Schmitt, *supra* note 69, at 22 (*citing* AP I, *supra* note 70, at art. 52(2)). This provision specifically states:

> Attacks shall be limited strictly to military objectives. In so far as objects are concerned, military objectives are limited to those objects which by their nature, location, purpose, or use make an effective contribution to military action and whose total or partial destruction, capture or neutralization, in the circumstances ruling at the time, offers a definite military advantage.

Id.

[122] *See* AP I, *supra* note 70, at art. 51(5)(b).

[123] Schmitt, *supra* note 69, at 22.

[124] *See* Jasmine Moussa, *Can the* Jus ad Bellum *Override the* Jus in Bello? *Reaffirming the Separation of the Two Bodies of Law*, 90 Int'l Rev. of the Red Cross 963, 981 (Dec. 2008). *See also* Dinstein, *supra* note 6, at 18.

[125] Schmitt, *supra* note 69, at 22. *See also* Schmitt, *Military Necessity and Humanity*, *supra* note 18, 795–839.

[126] Reeves & Lai, *supra* note 18, at 147–48.

[127] Dinstein, *supra* note 6, at 17.

[128] Solis, *supra* note 13, at 260.

B. DISTINCTION

The principle of distinction, at times characterized as fundamental or "intransgressible,"[129] is the most important rule a combatant must observe.[130] In terms of the distinction between civilians and combatants, the parties to an armed conflict must at all times distinguish between civilians and combatants, directing attacks only against combatants and not against civilians.[131] Similarly, the parties must distinguish between civilian objects and military objectives.[132] The principle of distinction is universally recognized in both customary practice and treaty law as inviolable.[133]

Again, it is important to reiterate that there is a difference between an indiscriminate per se illegal weapon and the use of a weapon in an indiscriminate manner.[134] For those weapons not per se unlawful, discriminate use is required as distinction "serves as the fount" for the LOAC rules that "seek to safeguard civilians, civilian objects, and other protected persons and places during the conduct of hostilities."[135] Discriminate use clearly includes not using a weapon to directly target a civilian or civilian object.[136] Further, a weapon should be capable of adequate control in terms of the place of impact and the nature and extent of its effects.[137]

The rules concerning precautions in an attack are also germane to deciding whether a weapon is used in a discriminate manner. Those conducting an attack are obligated to take "all feasible precautions in the choice of means and methods of attack with a view to avoiding, and in any event to minimizing, incidental loss of civilian life, injury to civilians and damage to civilian objects."[138] "Feasible" is defined as that which is "practicable or practically possible, taking into account all circumstances ruling at the time, including humanitarian and military considerations."[139] For those choosing to use a weapon, this obligation requires taking "precautions using the equipment, and in particular the weapons, available

---

[129] Legality of the Threat or Use of Nuclear Weapons, *supra* note 91, at 257.

[130] *Id.* at 251.

[131] RULES, *supra* note 15, at 3 (Rule 1) (stating that hostilities "may only be directed against combatants… [but] must not be directed against civilians."). *See also* AP I, *supra* note 70, at art. 48; Protocol Additional to the Geneva Conventions of August 1949, and Relating to the Protection of Victims of Non-international Armed Conflict (Protocol II) art. 13(1), June 8, 1977, 1125 U.N.T.S. 609 [hereinafter AP II] ("[t]he civilian population and individual civilians shall enjoy general protections against the dangers arising from military operations.").

[132] RULES, *supra* note 15, at 25 (Rule 7). *See also* AP I, *supra* note 70, at art. 48; AP II, *supra* note 131, at art. 13(1).

[133] SOLIS, *supra* note 13, at 251–52.

[134] *See generally supra* notes 76–105 and accompanying text.

[135] Schmitt, *supra* note 69, at 15.

[136] *Id.*

[137] Again, where the line is drawn between being an indiscriminate weapon and a weapon capable of discriminate use is unclear. For a more extensive discussion, see generally BOOTHBY, *supra* note 18, at Ch. 6.

[138] AP I, *supra* note 70, at art. 57(2)(a)(ii).

[139] CCW, Protocol II, *supra* note 43, at art. 3(4).

to them"[140] to ensure that the means chosen will "cause the least harm to civilians and civilian objects without sacrificing military advantage."[141] Although this "assessment as to the compliance of the weapon as such with the discrimination principle will be based on whether it can be directed, and whether its effects can be limited," the appropriate use of the weapon will depend on the "likelihood that the weapon will be capable of lawful employment" in the existing circumstances.[142]

C. PROPORTIONALITY

Civilian casualties, or damage to civilian property, do not necessarily indicate a violation of the principle of distinction, as incidental loss of civilian life may lawfully occur during military operations.[143] Pursuant to the principle of proportionality, launching an attack that may be expected to cause incidental loss of civilian life, injury to civilians, or damage to civilian objects is prohibited if the death, injury, or damage to civilian life and property is excessive in relation to the direct and concrete military advantaged gained.[144] The principle of proportionality is primarily concerned with minimizing collateral damage in an armed conflict,[145] and thus the rule is "applicable to the *use* of weapons and is not, as such, a rule that will determine the legality of a weapon."[146]

When deciding whether to use a particular weapon system, careful consideration must be given to the (expected or anticipated) military advantage, alternative means of accomplishing the same result, and the expected loss to civilians in terms of life, injury, and property.[147] Commanders have significant discretion in making these determinations as the military advantage gained is circumstance-specific and the incidental loss to civilian life and property can usually only be estimated.[148] The decision to use a certain means of warfare will therefore be dependent upon these determinations, the weapon's particular capabilities, and the environment in which it will operate.[149]

D. UNNECESSARY SUFFERING

The principle of unnecessary suffering or superfluous injury has been set forth in a number of treaties, including the St. Petersburg Declaration and The Hague

---

[140] *See* BOOTHBY, *supra* note 18, at 79.

[141] Schmitt, *supra* note 69, at 24.

[142] *See* BOOTHBY, *supra* note 18, at 80.

[143] *See* AP I, *supra* note 70, at art. 51(5)(b). Civilians may also forfeit their protection from attack, by directly participating in hostilities, see *id.* at art. 51(3), or by acting as voluntary human shields. *See id.* at art. 51(7).

[144] *Id.* at art. 51(5)(b); 57(2)(a)(iii).

[145] DINSTEIN, *supra* note 6, at 74.

[146] *See* BOOTHBY, *supra* note 18, at 44.

[147] *See* ROBERT KOLB & RICHARD HYDE, AN INTRODUCTION TO THE INTERNATIONAL LAW OF ARMED CONFLICTS 48 (2008).

[148] *See* Schmitt, *supra* note 69, at 24 (stating that the proportionality analysis is contextual).

[149] *See id.*

Declarations and Regulations.[150] More recently, Additional Protocol I, Art. 35(2) stated that "[i]t is prohibited to employ weapons, projectiles, and materials and methods of warfare of a nature to cause superfluous injury or unnecessary suffering."[151] The prohibition specifically refers to the effect of a weapon on combatants as the objective of warfare is to disarm the enemy. Accordingly, it is prohibited to use any means or methods of warfare that exceed what is necessary to render the enemy hors de combat, meaning that the parties are not free to inflict injury or damage in an unlimited manner.[152] This prohibition on unnecessary suffering or superfluous injury is exceptionally important in regards to weaponry.[153] As noted by Professor Yoram Dinstein,

> [a] weapon is not banned on the ground of unnecessary suffering merely because it causes "great" or even "horrendous" suffering or injury. The effects of certain weapons may be appalling, but this is not, in and of itself, enough to render these weapons illegal. A weapon is proscribed only if it causes injury or suffering that can be avoided, given the military constraints of the situation.[154]

Thus, a weapon's "normal use" is important for determining whether it violates the principle of unnecessary suffering per se.[155] If the military advantage gained by a weapon's normal use outweighs the injury caused, it is not per se unlawful;[156] however, the weapon may still violate the principle of unnecessary suffering if it is used outside of its intended purpose or is altered in order to exacerbate suffering.[157] For example, the Long Range Acoustic Device (LRAD) allows military personnel to communicate over long distances in order to ascertain an approaching vehicle's intent.[158] Although the LRAD is primarily a communication device it can also act, if used outside of its intended purpose, as a non-lethal acoustic energy weapon.[159] A 2007 legal review found that "[s]hould the LRAD be employed with the intent to cause discomfort to the listener, it would be considered a non-lethal weapon, but because the discomfort is well short of permanent damage to the ear, it does not violate the legal threshold of 'superfluous injury or

---

[150] *See* RULES, *supra* note 15, at 237 (Rule 70).

[151] AP I, *supra* note 70, at art. 35(2).

[152] Commentaries, *supra* note 78, at 400 (para. 1411).

[153] *See* Yoram Dinstein, *The Principle of Proportionality*, *in* SEARCHING FOR A "PRINCIPLE OF HUMANITY" IN INTERNATIONAL HUMANITARIAN LAW, *supra* note 54, at 79.

[154] *Id.* Professor Dinstein notes that making the determination of whether a weapon causes superfluous or unnecessary suffering requires a comparison between the weapon and other options. That is, does an alternative weapon that is otherwise available cause less injury or suffering? Additionally, are the effects produced by the alternative weapon effective? *See id.*

[155] *See supra* notes 63–75 and accompanying text for discussion on what makes a weapon per se unlawful for violating the principle of unnecessary suffering.

[156] LAW OF WAR DESKBOOK, *supra* note 2, at 154.

[157] *See* TALLINN MANUAL, *supra* note 86, at 144.

[158] *See* Joe Schrantz, *The Long Range Acoustic Device: Don't Call It a Weapon—Them's Fightin' Words*, THE ARMY LAWYER 53, 54 (Aug. 2010).

[159] *Id.*

unnecessary suffering.' "[160] The approval of the LRAD as a non-lethal weapon was clearly based on the temporary and mild nature of its effects. However, the LRAD could very easily violate the principle of unnecessary suffering if the acoustic output of the device was dramatically increased with the sole intent of causing intense pain and permanent ear damage.

It is also possible for an otherwise lawful weapon to violate the principle of unnecessary suffering if it is misused. Employing incendiary weapons against enemy combatants in the open serves as an example, albeit a controversial one. The International Committee of the Red Cross's (ICRC) Customary International Humanitarian Law study states that "the anti-personnel use of incendiary weapons is prohibited, unless it is not feasible to use a less harmful weapon to render a person *hors de combat*."[161] Although the ICRC's position is far from universally accepted as it is contrary to the language of Protocol III of the CCW, it serves as a good illustration of an otherwise lawful weapon being misused.[162]

"All weapons are capable of misuse in a variety of ways," and therefore it is important to identify "the pattern of injury and suffering to be expected as a result" of the weapon's "normal, intended use."[163] Deviating from the "normal, intended" use places the weapon user at risk of causing superfluous injury. Further, the principle of unnecessary suffering "extends to the use of otherwise lawful means of warfare" that are "altered in order to exacerbate suffering or injury."[164] For these reasons it is critical that a presumptively lawful weapon be left unaltered and properly employed as to do otherwise may violate the principle of unnecessary suffering.

E. THE ENVIRONMENT

Aside from the four core principles of the law of armed conflict, various other legal limitations must be considered when employing a weapon. These range from obligations to protect cultural property to avoiding works and installations containing dangerous forces.[165] Although these considerations are more relevant to a discussion on targeting, which is outside of this chapter's scope, it is important to highlight the prohibition on using a weapon that causes extensive damage to the natural environment.

---

[160] Memorandum from the Office of The Judge Advocate General, U.S. Army, to Program Executive Office, Ground Combat Sys., Subject: Full-Spectrum Effects Platform/Sheriff; Final Legal Review (Jan. 22, 2007).

[161] RULES, *supra* note 15, at 289 (Rule 85).

[162] Protocol III of the CCW simply requires that military objectives be clearly separated from concentrations of civilians before use of an incendiary weapon. *See* CCW Protocol III, *supra* note 44, art. 2(3). The question becomes whether combatants are considered within the definition of a "military objective." *Compare* DINSTEIN, *supra* note 6, at 85 (arguing that the definition includes enemy military personnel) *and* Commentaries, *supra* note 80, at 635 (para. 2017) ("it is clear that members of the armed forces are military objectives") *with* Bill, *supra* note 18, at 135 (presenting arguments for not including combatants within the definition of military objective).

[163] BOOTHBY, *supra* note 18, at 63.

[164] TALLINN MANUAL, *supra* note 86, at 144.

[165] *See generally* AP I, *supra* note 70, at art. 52–58.

Additional Protocol I, Article 35(3) states that "it is prohibited to employ methods or means of warfare which are intended, or may be expected, to cause widespread, long-term and severe damage to the natural environment."[166] Article 55 expressly notes that parties to a conflict are obligated to take care

> in warfare to protect the natural environment against widespread, long-term and severe damage. This protection includes a prohibition of the use of methods or means of warfare which are intended or may be expected to cause such damage to the natural environment and thereby prejudice the health or survival of the population.[167]

While Article 35(3) protects the environment at large, article 55 is interpreted as "only appl[ying] in the limited circumstances" where civilians or civilian objects on land are affected.[168] The United Kingdom, reiterating this interpretation, notes that Article 35(3) "relates to all methods of warfare on land, sea, or in the air and irrespective of where in the world they are utilized" while Article 55 "only relates to environmental damage on the territory or in the territorial sea of a state party to the conflict."[169]

Although an adverse impact on the environment is a natural consequence of warfare, only a certain amount of damage is lawful. For this reason certain weapons that are particularly harsh on the natural environment are prohibited. However, which weapons cause "widespread, long-term and severe damage" is unclear.[170] States are conservative in their interpretation of this prohibition, ensuring that environmentally sensitive military weapons, such as chemical agents or herbicides, are not automatically precluded from use.[171] Rather than relying upon a traditional "balancing of military necessity against the quantum of expected destruction," most states see the combined elements found in Articles 35(3) and 55 as establishing "an absolute ceiling of permissible destruction" to the environment allowed by a weapon.[172] Therefore, only those weapons that exceed the maximum level of allowable damage to the environment, such as those that affect the "survival or health of the population," are proscribed.[173]

---

[166] *Id.* at art. 35(3).

[167] *Id.* at art. 55.

[168] BOOTHBY, *supra* note 18, at 95 (*citing* APV ROGERS, LAW ON THE BATTLEFIELD 166 (2004)).

[169] *Id.* (*citing* THE MANUAL ON THE LAW OF ARMED CONFLICT, *supra* note 102, at para. 5.29.1).

[170] *See, e.g.*, INT'L & OPERATIONAL LAW DEP'T, THE JUDGE ADVOCATE GENERAL'S LEGAL CTR. & SCH., U.S. ARMY, OPERATIONAL LAW HANDBOOK 235 (2006) [hereinafter HANDBOOK] ("The individual meanings of the terms 'widespread,' 'long-term' and 'severe' damage have been debated at length").

[171] *See* THE MANUAL ON THE LAW OF ARMED CONFLICT, *supra* note 102, at para. 5.29.3. The Manual states:

> these provisions do not automatically prevent certain types of military objectives such as nuclear submarines or super tankers from being legitimate targets nor do they automatically prevent the use of certain means of warfare such as herbicides or chemical agents.

Id.

[172] *See* HANDBOOK, *supra* note 170, at 235.

[173] BOOTHBY, *supra* note 18, at 96.

Although this threshold is extremely high,[174] a commander must remain cognizant of his legal obligation to take into account how his use of a weapon may impact the environment.[175]

3. By Agreement or Specific Treaty

The third distinct category of regulating or restricting the means of warfare is by agreement or through a specific treaty. This is often not considered a separate category[176] as the regulations or restrictions on the means of warfare found in treaties or agreements remain exclusively based upon either the per se illegality or misuse of a weapon.[177] However, agreements and treaties are emerging as a truly independent form of regulating weapons. Modern treaties proposing restrictions on weapons often no longer rely solely on established legal arguments as reason for ratification but now also rely on more novel justifications.

The most recent example is the campaign to ban autonomous weapons. A number of groups are campaigning[178] for a state-sanctioned agreement that prohibits research, development, and deployment of this means of warfare.[179] This coalition argues for a preemptive ban on autonomous weapons, believing the technology violates "dictates of public conscience"[180] and "may further the indiscriminate and disproportionate use of force" in warfare.[181] Combining a

---

[174] *See* HANDBOOK, *supra* note 170, at 235. In explaining the limitations of the general protections found in AP I 35(3) and 55 the authors state that "there is little doubt that the majority of the carnage caused during World Wars I and II (with the possible exception of the two nuclear devices exploded over Japan) would not have met this threshold requirement." *Id.*

[175] This area of weapon's law is in flux as environmental protection is increasingly drawing the attention of state actors. If this trend continues it "is foreseeable that acceptable standards in war will be more restrictively expressed in [the] future and that weapons design will need to take that factor increasingly into account." BOOTHBY, *supra* note 18, at 105.

[176] Most legal scholars believe that there are two distinct categories of illegal weapons: per se illegal, and those improperly used. *See, e.g.*, GREENSPAN, *supra* note 50, at 243; BOOTHBY, *supra* note 18, at 69. *But see* LAW OF WAR DESKBOOK, *supra* note 2, at 165 (recognizing this third category and stating that weapons may be found illegal by agreement or specific treaty prohibition).

[177] For example, the various protocols of the 1980 Convention on Prohibitions or Restrictions on the Use of Certain Conventional Weapons (CCW) regulate weapons such as land mines, booby traps, and non-detectable fragments. When one reads the preamble to the CCW, the treaty specifically notes that the parties are reminded that the treaty is based, in part, upon the principle of unnecessary suffering, general protections of civilians, and obligations toward the environment. *See* CCW, *supra* note 42, at Prmbl.

[178] The most prominent group to oppose autonomous weapons is Human Rights Watch. *See generally* LOSING HUMANITY, *supra* note 8.

[179] *See, e.g.*, Campaign to Stop Killer Robots, http://www.stopkillerrobots.org/2014/01/infographicaoav/ (last visited Feb. 7, 2014) (stating "[f]ully autonomous weapons-or killer robots-are weapons that can, without human control, detect, select and engage targets. They do not yet exist, but the rapid developments in robotics and autonomous technology, indicate that it is only a matter of time before fully autonomous weapons become an inhumane reality."); LOSING HUMANITY, *supra* note 8; Berlin Statement, International Committee for Robot Arms Control (Oct. 2010), http://icrac.net/statements/ [hereinafter Berlin Statement].

[180] Q & A on Autonomous Weapons, HUMAN RIGHTS WATCH, Oct. 21, 2013, http://www.hrw.org/news/2013/10/21/ qa-fully-autonomous-weapons.

[181] Berlin Statement, *supra* note 179.

variety of legal arguments these anti-autonomous weapon advocates are vehemently working to prevent any possibility of a future with "autonomous robot weapons."[182]

The established legal arguments relied upon by the anti-autonomous weapon coalition, such as their concerns about the core four principles of the LOAC, are not surprising or unusual.[183] However, their parallel argument for banning autonomous weapons is more unusual. Believing fully autonomous weapons violate the "dictates of public conscience"[184] due to a lack of human discretion in making lethal decisions,[185] the proponents of a preemptive treaty root their secondary line of reasoning in the Martens Clause.[186]

As discussed earlier in the chapter,[187] the Martens Clause has formed an important part of the LOAC since it first appeared in the Preamble to the 1899 Hague Convention II on land warfare.[188] The words of the Martens Clause have found expression in most LOAC treaties since 1899, with the Clause being integrated into the preambles of early treaties such as the 1899 and 1907 Hague Conventions.[189] In other conventions, such as Additional Protocol I, the Martens Clause has an elevated status and is included in the main text of the treaty.[190]

The Martens Clause, capturing the humanitarian dimension of the LOAC,[191] recognizes that the positive LOAC is incomplete. As a result the clause notes that "until a more complete code of the laws of war has been issued" and in cases "not included in the Regulations" those affected by warfare "remain under the protection and the rule of the principles of the law of nations, as they result from the usages established among civilized peoples, from the laws of humanity, and the dictates of the public conscience."[192] However, there is no universally agreed

---

[182] Campaign to Stop Killer Robots, *supra* note 179 (statement of Professor Noel Sharkey, Chair of the International Committee for Robot Arms Control). *See also* Angela Kane, United Nations High Representative for Disarmament Affairs, *Killer Robots and the Rule of Law*, The World Post, July 7, 2013, http://www.huffingtonpost.com/A-View-from-the-United-Nations-/killer-robots-and-the-rul_b_3599657.html (last visited Feb. 13, 2014) (stating "we need not wait for a weapon system to emerge fully before appropriate action can be taken to understand its implications and mitigate and eliminate unacceptable risks.").

[183] *See, e.g.*, Losing Humanity, *supra* note 8, at 37–42 (asserting that fully autonomous weapons will be unable to comply with fundamental principles of the Law of Armed Conflict). *See also* Schmitt, *supra* note 69, at 8–26 (outlining the legal arguments presented by the anti-autonomous weapon groups and ultimately dismissing their claims); Reeves & Johnson, *supra* note 4, at 26–30 (arguing that the LOAC is not violated by autonomous weapons).

[184] *See* Schmitt, *supra* note 69, at 6 (discussing the sensitivity of the human interface issue).

[185] *But see id.* at 4 ("Of course, a fully autonomous system is never completely human-free. Either the system designer or an operator would at least have to program the system to function pursuant to specified parameters.").

[186] *See* Losing Humanity, *supra* note 8, at 30 ("[a]n initial evaluation of fully autonomous weapons shows . . . such robots . . . might contravene the Martens Clause.").

[187] *See supra* notes 27–31 and accompanying text.

[188] *See* Solis, *supra* note 13, at 53.

[189] *See, e.g.*, Hague Regulation IV, *supra* note 35, at prmbl.

[190] *See* AP I, *supra* note 70, at art. 1.

[191] *See* Searching for a "Principle of Humanity" in International Humanitarian Law, *supra* note 54, at 3–8 (discussing the Martens Clause in reference to humanitarian aims).

[192] Rene Provost, International Human Rights and Humanitarian Law 5 (2002).

upon interpretation of the Martens Clause, with the topic being the subject of a long-standing debate.[193] The lack of clarity concerning the Clause has left it

> subject to a variety of interpretations, both narrow and expansive. At its most restricted, the Clause serves as a reminder that customary international law continues to apply after the adoption of a treaty norm. A wider interpretation is that, as few international treaties relating to the laws of armed conflict are ever complete, the Clause provides that something which is not explicitly prohibited by a treaty is not ipso facto permitted. The widest interpretation is that conduct in armed conflicts is not only judged according to treaties and custom but also to the principles of international law referred to by the Clause.[194]

The ambiguity of the Martens Clause's language coupled with the absence of a universally accepted interpretation offers an alternative argument for regulating or restricting weapons. For those uncomfortable with the lack of human control of fully autonomous weapons, an expansive reading of the Martens Clause provides a legal foundation for a prohibitory treaty even if these weapons are not per se unlawful or being misused in a traditional sense. The Martens Clause is simply one example where proponents of prohibiting a weapon have found a novel theory to support a proposed treaty. Concern about the lack of transparency with cyber weapons,[195] moral objections to the immense devastation caused by nuclear weapons,[196] or some other independent justification may in the future influence the development of weapons law.

C. THE PROCESS OF REGULATING WEAPONS

The linchpin between the legal principles and the effective restrictions on weapons lies in an express obligation of parties, and a corresponding review mechanism, to determine whether new weapons comply with the LOAC.[197] That obligation is memorialized in Article 36 to Additional Protocol I, which provides:

> In the study, development, acquisition, or adoption of a new weapon, means or method of warfare, a High Contracting Party is under an obligation to

---

[193] *See* Rupert Ticehurst, *The Martens Clause and the Laws of Armed Conflict*, 317 Int'l Rev. of the Red Cross, 125, 125–34 (Apr. 30, 1997); Searching for a "Principle of Humanity" in International Humanitarian Law, *supra* note 54, at 6.

[194] *Id.* at 125.

[195] *See* Tallinn Manual, *supra* note 86, at 141 (defining a cyber weapon). The Stuxnet worm is an example of a cyber weapon that is "invisible, anonymous, and devastating." *See* Michael Joseph Gross, *A Declaration of Cyber War*, Vanity Fair, Apr. 2011, *available at* http://www.vanityfair.com/culture/features/2011/04/stuxnet-201104.

[196] *See* Ticehurst, *supra* note 193, at 132–33 ("Proponents of the illegality of nuclear weapons emphasized the importance of natural law . . . [t]he Martens Clause supports this position as it indicates that the laws of armed conflict do not simply provide a positive legal code, they also provide a moral code.").

[197] Commentaries, *supra* note 78, at 421–22 (1987).

> determine whether its employment would, in some or all circumstances, be prohibited by this protocol or by any other rule of international law applicable to the High Contracting Party.[198]

This obligation is an accurate reflection of customary international law[199] and applies equally to the state that manufactures weapons as well as to the state that purchases new weapons.[200] Notwithstanding this clear legal obligation, few states currently undertake this obligatory examination before employing a new means of warfare.[201]

In contrast, the United States views the language of Article 36 as compulsory, and was among the first states to establish a formal examination for new weapons.[202] This examination includes a legal review[203] to ensure compliance with the LOAC for every type of munition and weapon fielded by the United States.[204] An attorney appointed by one of the armed services or the Department of Defense (DoD)[205] conducts the review to make certain that "[t]he acquisition and procurement of DoD weapons and weapon systems shall be consistent with all applicable domestic law and treaties and international agreements . . ., customary international law, and the law of armed conflict . . . "[206] These "reviews occur as early as possible before the award of the engineering and manufacturing development contract and again before award of the initial production contract."[207]

The legal review specifically analyzes "[w]hether there is a specific rule of law, whether by treaty obligation of the United States or accepted by the United States as customary international law, prohibiting or restricting the use of the weapon or cyber capability in question."[208] If no prohibition or restriction exists, the legal review determines "[w]hether the weapon or cyber capability is calculated to cause superfluous injury" or is "capable of being directed against a specific

---

[198] AP I, *supra* note 70, at art. 36.

[199] *See* Harvard Program on Humanitarian Policy and Conflict Research, Manual on International Law Applicable to Air and Missile Warfare with Commentary Rule 6 (2010).

[200] *See* Commentaries, *supra* note 78, at 426.

[201] Marie Jacobsson, *Article 36 of Additional Protocol I*, *in* 82 Int'l L. Studies 183, 184 (Anthony M. Helm ed., 2006); Michael Bothe, Karl Josef Partsch & Waldemar A. Solf, New Rules for Victims of Armed Conflicts: Commentary on the Two 1977 Protocols Additional to the Geneva Conventions of 1949, 200 (para. 2.3) (1982) ("The obligations of this article require a thorough national review.").

[202] *See id.*

[203] *See* Boothby, *The Law of Weaponry—Is It Adequate?*, *supra* note 113, at 302 (noting that all state actors must receive legal advice before employing a new weapon).

[204] *See* The Law of Armed Conflict: An Operational Approach, *supra* note 28, at 203.

[205] Law of War Deskbook, *supra* note 2, at 154 ("all U.S. weapons must be reviewed by the Service TJAG for legality under the law of armed conflict.") (*citing* Dep't of Def., Directive 3000.3, Policy for Non-lethal Weapons, ¶ 5.6.2 (July 9, 1996); Dep't of Def., Directive 5000.1, The Defense Acquisition System, ¶ E1.1.15(May 12, 2003)).

[206] Dep't of Def., Directive 5000.1, *supra* note 205, at ¶ E1.1.15.

[207] Law of War Deskbook, *supra* note 2, at 154.

[208] U.S. Air Force, Instruction 51-402, Legal Review of Weapons and Cyber Capabilities ¶ 3.1.1 (July 27, 2011).

military objective and, if not, is of a nature to cause an effect on military objectives and civilians or civilian objects without distinction."[209] The focus of these legal reviews is therefore on determining whether the proposed weapon will violate an existing legal obligation or is per se unlawful.

However, it is important to note that these legal reviews "examine only the legality of a weapon system" and do not generally consider the use of a weapon, "since [this would be] contextual in nature."[210] A proportionality analysis, for example, is not part of the legal review, as compliance with the principle "depends on the situational risk to civilians and civilian objects and the anticipated military advantage in the attendant circumstances."[211] As any weapon is capable of misuse, it is not feasible for a legal review to anticipate and address every employment possibility for a particular means of warfare.[212] Whether the weapon is used properly is instead based upon the particular circumstances in which it is employed.[213]

Some argue that the legal review should also ensure the weapon is in compliance with the Martens Clause.[214] Again, this remains a point of debate and is dependent upon how the Martens Clause is interpreted. Proponents of a narrow interpretation argue that the Martens Clause only applies in the absence of treaty law and is "a failsafe mechanism meant to address *lacunae* in the law; it does not act as an overarching principle that must be considered in every case."[215] As a result the likelihood that a future weapon system "would not violate applicable treaty and customary law, but be unlawful based on the Martens Clause" is exceptionally low.[216] The United States currently does not require the legal review to include a Martens Clause compliance assessment for a new weapon.[217]

If the legal review finds that the proposed means of warfare violates the LOAC, the weapon may not be deployed.[218] On the other hand, if the review is complete and finds the weapon legally sufficient, then commanders and all other personnel

---

[209] *Id.* at ¶ 3.1.2. Professor Schmitt notes that the Air Forces guidance's "extension of its substantive requirements to cyber capabilities" is noteworthy as it "illustrates the principle that the rules of international humanitarian law regarding the legality of weapon systems apply fully to weapons that did not exist at the time a particular treaty norm was crafted or customary law crystallized." *See* Schmitt, *supra* note 69, at 31.

[210] *See* Schmitt, *supra* note 69, at 30.

[211] *Id.*

[212] *See* Bothe et al., *supra* note 201, at 200–01 (noting that it is impractical for a legal review to analyze all use issues).

[213] Schmitt, *supra* note 69, at 32.

[214] *See, e.g.*, ICRC, *A Guide to the Legal Review of New Weapons, Means and Methods of Warfare: Measures to Implement Article 36 of Additional Protocol I of 1977*, ¶ 1.2.2.3 (2006).

[215] Schmitt, *supra* note 69, at 32.

[216] *Id.*

[217] *See generally* Air Force, Instruction 51–402, *supra* note 208.

[218] *See* Dinstein, *supra* note 6, at 80. Any significant modification to an existing weapon system will require a new legal review. *See* Schmitt, *supra* note 68, at 29.

are entitled to assume the weapon is lawful.[219] This assumption is dependent on the weapon being used for its normal, expected purpose.

In the process of regulating weapons, the legal review is critically important. The review clarifies whether the use of a new weapon developed or acquired by a state is in compliance with the LOAC.[220] Yet the legal review is not the sole component of the regulatory process, as the circumstances in which a lawful weapon is used remain limited by the conduct of hostilities rules. More specifically, those employing a weapon remain responsible for ensuring it is properly used despite the existence of a legal review.[221] Whether a weapon is allowed in a military operation is therefore dependent upon both the finding of legal sufficiency in the review combined with a state actor's compliance with the universal obligation to not misuse an otherwise lawful weapon.

IV. Conclusion

It is naïve to believe that the LOAC, like international law in general, holds together much better on paper than in practice.[222] Similarly, it would be a mistake not to believe that modern technologies such as drones, cyber weapons, bio-smart and fully autonomous weapons raise many interesting questions for the development and application of the LOAC. However, the emergence of new and novel weapons is expected and anticipated within the law. The law of weaponry has repeatedly developed in such a way as to successfully regulate new means of warfare.[223] As discussed in this chapter, weapons law provides a dynamic and fluid regulatory framework capable of addressing the myriad of challenges presented by new weapons.

Admittedly, the general principles and specific provisions of the law of weaponry can at times be confusing in application. Yet weapons law, although less than perfect, remains a vibrant and evolving legal regime that clearly cannot be "disregarded as an anachronism."[224] Of course this remains true only as long as this body of law continues to balance a state's ability to defend itself when necessary "while minimizing the suffering that is caused to participants in the conflict and those unhappily affected by it."[225] By ensuring these countervailing principles are in equilibrium, the law regulating and restricting weapons will remain "relevant to the conduct of military operations."[226]

---

[219] Int'l & Operational Law Dep't, The Judge Advocate General's Legal Ctr. & Sch., U.S. Army, Operational Law Handbook 26 (2014).

[220] Bothe et al., *supra* note 201, at 199.

[221] *See* Schmitt, *supra* note 69, at 30 ("reviews examine only the legality of a weapon system as such, not its use in any particular circumstance.").

[222] Best, *supra* note 9, at 5.

[223] Greenwood, *supra* note 7, at 219.

[224] *Id.*

[225] Boothby, *supra* note 18, at 386–87.

[226] *Id.* at 388.

3}

Legal Classification of Military Operations

Geoffrey S. Corn*

I. Introduction

Military operations do not occur in a legal vacuum. Indeed, law is a pervasive aspect of planning and executing such operations. To a certain extent, this has always been true, although never before has the role of law been so central to the perception and reality of strategic, operational, and tactical success. Today, law can be its own line of operation: the "rule of law" is now used as a verb to denote the nexus of political/military efforts in the context of a particular operation.[1]

There is no correlation, however, between the importance of law as a ubiquitous component of planning and execution, and the clarity of what law applies to a given operation. Identifying applicable law, when the law applies, and how that law interacts with other sources of law is therefore a critical aspect of mission planning and execution. The complexity associated with this analysis is the result of several realities. First, military operations rarely fall within neat boxes of legal characterization, but instead range across a spectrum of factual situations implicating different sources of domestic and international law. Second, because this continuum potentially implicates both international and domestic law (and within each of these categories of law, involves different branches or sources of obligation) law applicability analysis will often require reconciliation of these different sources. Third, military operations are often launched and sometimes fully executed without a clear indication of the applicable sources of law. Fourth,

* Presidential Professor of Law at South Texas College of Law, Lieutenant Colonel (ret), U.S. Army. Former Special Assistant to the U.S. Army Judge Advocate General for Law of War Matters, and Chief of the Law of War Branch, U.S. Army Office of the Judge Advocate General International and Operational Law Division.

[1] *See* The National Security Strategy of the United States 1, 3 (2002), *available at* http://www.state.gov/documents/organization/63562.pdf. (The 2002 National Security Strategy (NSS) mentioned the term "rule of law" nine times. "America must stand firmly for the nonnegotiable demands of human dignity: the rule of law; limits on the absolute power of the state; free speech; freedom of worship; equal justice; respect for women; religious and ethnic tolerance; and respect for private property.").

policy-based compliance with core principles of the law of armed conflict (LOAC) frequently dilute any urgency to provide clarity on the controlling legal framework and the deconfliction of different sources of law—that is, legal ambiguity often provides greater room to maneuver for policymakers, creating a perceived advantage they may seek to preserve. Military and civilian lawyers supporting the planning and execution of operations will, nonetheless, seek to identify with as much clarity as possible, controlling legal authorities.

In his 1996 Army Lawyer essay titled "*Civilian Protection Law,*" then Major Richard Whitaker addressed the complexity of seeking to provide legal clarity in an inherently complex and uncertain operational environment, noting:

> In the last decade, however, the most frequent application of United States power occurred in diverse operations that repeatedly defied the application of the traditional law of armed conflict. During the course of each of these operations, military lawyers have experienced substantial difficulty finding the overall regime or structure of laws that provides answers for the complex legal issues generated by these "new age and nuanced operations."
>
> . . .
>
> The operational planners for recent OOTW (Operations Other Than War, the then in vogue term for military operations below the threshold of armed conflict) have reinforced the need for solutions by documenting the essential role that operational lawyers play in both the planning and execution of OOTW. Both the judge advocate and his client understand that OOTW are high stake affairs, which frequently enjoy less than universal international or domestic support. They further understand that OOTW are placed in jeopardy by anything less than consistently exceptional legal support. This vulnerability is magnified by nearly every element of OOTW that require the application of rules and law that are not yet found in (or not yet understood as) conventional doctrine.[2]

Whitaker proceeded to offer a generalized framework for blending a variety of legal regimes in order to clarify the issue of dealing with civilians in the operational environment. His focus was non-conflict military operations, the type of operation that dominated the pre-September 11th strategic military environment. However, in one respect, Whitaker was prescient in his recognition that contrary to the simplicity suggested in texts, manuals, and the military classroom, identifying what law applies to complex military operations will often be the first critical challenge military legal advisors must confront.

Whitaker could not however, have predicted the exponential increase in the complexity, and with it the significance of, law implicated by the range of U.S. military operations initiated following the terrorist attacks of September 11, 2001. However, Whitaker could not have predicted the exponential increase in

---

[2] Major Richard M. Whitaker, *Civilian Protection Law in Military Operations: An Essay*, ARMY LAWYER 3, 5 (Nov. 1996).

the complexity—and with it the significance—of law implicated by the range of U.S. military operations initiated following the terrorist attacks of September 11, 2001. His assumption that it would be relatively clear what law applied during an armed conflict (as opposed to non-conflict missions, such as peacekeeping operations) failed to appreciate the complexity of this emerging operational situations. For example, simply concluding that the Geneva Conventions apply during international armed conflicts failed to predict the law applicability complexities of the post-9/11 operational reality. This assumption was understandable based on Whitaker's personal experience in the first Gulf War, but does not withstand the realities of what might legitimately be characterized as a new generation of American military operations. Instead, what the former Commandant of the Marine Corps labeled the "three block war" with high intensity conflict on one block, humanitarian assistance on another block, and constabulary operations on a third block, all in the context of the same military operation, in many ways defines this new era.[3] Nonetheless, Whitaker's recognition that law applicability analysis is at the same time complex and strategically essential has never had more relevance than today, and now holds true in armed conflict as well as in operations not reaching that intensity.

Part II of this chapter will provide an overview of the relationship between the nature of military operations and controlling legal authorities. Part III is an overview of the law applicability continuum in the context of operations that qualify as armed conflict. Part IV will then explain common approaches used by the U.S. armed forces to work through these challenges, to include extension of principles derived from the LOAC to guide operational execution in contexts of legal uncertainty.

II. Conflict Classification and Law Applicability

War is a highly regulated endeavor. From the inception of organized hostilities, societies imposed constraints on the conduct of belligerents. Today, respect for these constraints is central to the legitimacy of military operations, which itself is a core strategic principle for operational success:

> Legitimacy, which can be a decisive factor in operations, is based on the actual and perceived legality, morality, and rightness of the actions from the various perspectives of interested audiences. These audiences will include our national leadership and domestic population, governments, and civilian populations in the operational area, and nations and organizations around the world.[4]

---

[3] Joseph J. Collins, *Afghanistan: Winning a Three Block War*, The Journal of Conflict Studies (2004), *available at* http://journals.hil.unb.ca/index.php/JCS/article/viewArticle/204/361.

[4] Joint Chiefs of Staff, Joint Publication 3-0, Joint Operations A-4 (Aug. 11, 2011), *available at* http://www.dtic.mil/doctrine/new_pubs/jp3_0.pdf.

Although it may be axiomatic that armed hostilities must be conducted pursuant to legal regulation, the determination of when the law of conflict regulation comes into force is more complex. Accordingly, the first step in this regulatory process is understanding the situations and conditions that trigger applicability of the LOAC, the contemporary term for the antecedent laws and customs of war. This analytical process is known colloquially as conflict classification and is an aspect of all U.S. military operations.

Contemporary conflict classification analysis is based on the post–World War II revisions to the Geneva Conventions. At that time, the assembled national delegations responded to the unfortunate reality that comprehensive treaty provisions developed to protect war victims meant very little unless the conditions of treaty applicability were made binding on states involved in hostilities. To achieve this imperative, each of the four Geneva Conventions that emerged from that drafting conference included, for the first time, articles dictating conditions of applicability; that is, when their protective provisions came into force. This "law trigger" concept took the form of an identical article 2 and 3 in each treaty, known today as common articles 2 and 3 (CA2 and CA3). Although originally applicable only to the LOAC treaties in which they were included (the four Geneva Conventions) the CA2/3 law applicability standard evolved rapidly to apply to the full corpus of the LOAC, not only the Geneva Conventions.

CA2 defines the point at which a dispute between states triggers applicability of the LOAC, a situation known as international armed conflict, or IAC.[5] CA3, in contrast, required compliance with a more limited body of humanitarian regulation. CA3 calls for the humane treatment of individuals not actively participating in hostilities during "conflicts not of an international character occurring within the territory of a High Contracting Party" [a party state]; such conflicts are known more commonly as non-international armed conflicts (NIAC).[6] Like CA2, CA3 did not

---

[5] *See* Geneva Convention for the Amelioration of the Condition of the Wounded and Sick in Armed Forces in the Field, Aug. 12, 1949, T.I.A.S. 3362, art. 2 [hereinafter GC I]; Geneva Convention for the Amelioration of the Condition of Wounded, Sick, and Shipwrecked Members at Sea, Aug. 12, 1949, T.I.A.S. 3363, art. 2 [hereinafter GC II]; Geneva Convention Relative to the Treatment of Prisoners of War, Aug. 12, 1949, T.I.A.S. 3364 art. 2 [hereinafter GC III]; Geneva Convention Relative to the Treatment of Civilian Persons in Time of War, August 12, 1949, T.I.A.S. 3365, art. 2 [hereinafter GC IV]. Each of these Conventions includes the following identical article:

> In addition to the provisions which shall be implemented in peacetime, the present Convention shall apply to all cases of declared war or of any other armed conflict which may arise between two or more of the High Contracting Parties, even if the state of war is not recognized by one of them. The Convention shall also apply to all cases of partial or total occupation of the territory of a High Contracting Party, even if the said occupation meets with no armed resistance.

[6] *See* GC I, *supra* note 5, at art. 3; GC II, *supra* note 5, at art. 3; GC III, *supra* note 5, at art. 3; GC IV, *supra* note 5, at art. 3. Each of these Conventions includes the following identical article:

> In the case of armed conflict not of an international character occurring in the territory of one of the High Contracting Parties, each Party to the conflict shall be bound to apply, as a minimum, the following provisions:

purport to trigger any law beyond its organic humane treatment mandate; and like CA2, this NIAC law trigger also evolved into the standard for assessing applicability of an ever-growing corpus of customary international law to this category of armed conflicts.[7]

In U.S. practice, the IAC/NIAC law triggering standards embedded in CA2 and CA3 are considered definitive. As a result, applicability of LOAC regulation as a matter of law (as opposed to policy-based application, which will be discussed in greater detail below) is contingent on two fundamental factors: (1) the existence of armed conflict, and (2) the nature of the armed conflict.[8] Both of these factors involve a certain degree of analytical complexity and result in an accordant law applicability uncertainty, uncertainty that has traditionally been mitigated by policy-based extension of LOAC principles to all military operations.

War, as a colloquial term, is routinely used to describe situations of armed hostilities. War is not, however, the defining condition that results in application of international legal conflict regulation. The trigger for applicability of this law is armed conflict, an international legal term development to mitigate the risk[9] that this law might be avoided by characterizing situations of hostilities as something other than war. Thus, the 1949 Geneva Conventions utilized the term "armed

---

> (1) Persons taking no active part in the hostilities, including members of armed forces who have laid down their arms and those placed "hors de combat" by sickness, wounds, detention, or any other cause, shall in all circumstances be treated humanely, without any adverse distinction founded on race, colour, religion or faith, sex, birth or wealth, or any other similar criteria.

[7] *See* Int'l & Operational Law Dep't, The Judge Advocate General's Legal Ctr. & Sch., U.S. Army, Law of War Deskbook Ch. 3 (2000) [hereinafter Law of War Deskbook]. *See also* UK Ministry of Defense, The Manual for the Law of Armed Conflict, ¶ 3.1 (2004) [hereinafter UK Manual]; International Committee of the Red Cross, *What Is International Humanitarian Law*, Advisory Service on International Humanitarian Law (July 2004), *available at* http://www.icrc.org/eng/assets/files/other/what_is_ihl.pdf. This fact sheet clearly reflects the international/internal evolution of the triggering paradigm:

> International humanitarian law distinguishes between international and non-international armed conflict. **International armed conflicts** are those in which at least two States are involved. They are subject to a wide range of rules, including those set out in the four Geneva Conventions and Additional Protocol I. **Non-international armed conflicts** are those restricted to the territory of a single State, involving either regular armed forces fighting groups of armed dissidents, or armed groups fighting each other. A more limited range of rules apply to internal armed conflicts and are laid down in Article 3 common to the four Geneva Conventions as well as in Additional Protocol II. *Id.*

[8] *See* Int'l & Operational Law Dep't, The Judge Advocate General's Legal Ctr. & Sch., U.S. Army, Law of Armed Conflict Deskbook 39–40, 69–71 (2010), *available at* http://www.fas.org/irp/doddir/army /deskbook.pdf.

[9] *See generally* Leslie Green, *What Is—Why Is There—the Law of War, in The Law of Armed Conflict: Into the Next Millennium*, 71 Naval War College 141 (1998). *See also* Laurie Blank & Geoffrey S. Corn, *The Laws of War: Regulating the Use of Force, in* National Security Law in the News: A Guide for Journalists, Scholars, and Policymaker (ABA 2012); *supra* note 6 and accompanying text.

conflict" to characterize situations triggering the humanitarian protections provided by the treaties, a deliberate response to the regulatory avoidance inherent in the disconnect between a legal state of war and situations involving de facto armed hostilities.[10] The treaty drafters believed this would provide a much more pragmatic standard for bringing into force international humanitarian protections, a standard based not on legal technicalities but on the de facto existence of hostilities. Hence, what prior to 1949 was known as the law of war is today commonly referred to as the LOAC or international humanitarian law (IHL), each term indicating a deliberate decoupling of conflict regulation from the formal existence of a state of war.[11]

It is therefore obvious why identifying a situation of armed conflict is the first step in determining LOAC applicability. However, there is no definitive definition of this term. In U.S. practice (and international practice in general), the meaning of this term is based in large measure on the guidance offered by the Commentaries to the four Geneva Conventions published by the International Committee of the Red Cross (ICRC), an extremely persuasive source of insight into the intent of the treaty drafters.[12] The Commentary proposes a number of factors to be assessed, in a totality-of-circumstances approach, to determine what situations qualify as armed conflicts.

Assessing the existence of armed conflict is easiest when the armed forces of states engage in hostilities against each other in response to an inter-state dispute. According to the Commentary to CA2, neither duration nor intensity of

---

[10] *See generally* Int'l Committee of the Red Cross, *How Is the Term "Armed Conflict" Defined in International Humanitarian Law?*, Opinion Paper (Mar. 2008), *available at* http://www.icrc.org/eng/assets/files/other/opinion-paper-armed-conflict.pdf.

[11] *See, e.g.*, Int'l Comm. of the Red Cross Commentary, III Geneva Convention Relative to the Treatment of Prisoners of War 23 (Jean S. Pictet et al. eds., 1960) [hereinafter Commentary, GC III] (using the broad term "armed conflict" in lieu of the more restrictive term "war," and stating that "the occurrence of de facto hostilities is sufficient" to satisfy the conditions established in Common Article 2). However, it is also important to note that any conflict that qualifies as a war within the meaning of international law, specifically in the odd event two or more nations declare war in the future, will also qualify as an international armed conflict within the meaning of Common Article 2.

[12] *See* Int'l Comm. of the Red Cross Commentary, I Geneva Convention for the Amelioration of the Condition of the Wounded and Sick in Armed Forces in the Field 19–23 (Jean S. Pictet et al. ed., 1960) [hereinafter Commentary, GC I]. A similar Commentary was published for each of the four Geneva Conventions. However, because Articles 2 and 3 are identical—or *common*—to each Convention, the Commentary for these articles is also identical in each of the four Commentaries. *See also* Law of War Deskbook, *supra* note 7, at ch. 3.

> The International Criminal Tribunal for the Former Yugoslavia, while not explicitly relying on these criteria, nonetheless followed the general logic reflected therein when it determined in the first opinion addressing the jurisdiction of the Tribunal that "an armed conflict exists whenever there is a resort to armed force between States or protracted armed violence between governmental authorities and organized armed groups or between such groups within a State."

Id.; Prosecutor v. Tadic, Case No. IT-94-1-AR72, Appeal on Jurisdiction ¶ 70 (Oct. 2, 1995), *reprinted in* 35 I.L.M. 32 (1996).

such hostilities is relevant to the determination: any fighting between armed forces qualifies as an armed conflict. In fact, the Commentary emphasizes that the adoption of the term "armed conflict" was intended in part to prevent states from disavowing humanitarian obligations in such situations, based on a lack of duration or intensity of hostilities:[13] factors that might legitimately exclude the situation from the legal definition of war.[14] Armed conflict is accordingly a de facto situation, deliberately distinct from de jure war.[15] De facto hostilities between state armed forces, even if brief, are armed conflicts.[16]

Determining the meaning of armed conflict in the non-international context is far more complex. The key analytical focus in doing so has historically been to identify the line between internal civil disturbances (situations falling below the threshold of armed conflict), and internal hostilities of sufficient magnitude to require application of international legal conflict regulation.[17] Prior to 1949, internal struggles between a government and opposition forces were largely beyond the reach of international law. Hence this regulatory extension has been an evolving concept, influenced substantially by state practice. The recent events in Syria illustrate the challenge, with widespread disagreement on whether that situation qualifies as an armed conflict subject to the LOAC, or is in the alternative a breakdown of civil authority subject to domestic law, and to a lesser degree the international law of human rights.[18] Although an expansive application of humanitarian principles may

---

[13] *See* COMMENTARY, GC I, *supra* note 12, at 32 ("It makes no difference how long the conflict lasts, or how much slaughter takes place. The respect due to human personality is not measured by the number of victims.").

[14] *Id.*

[15] *Id.*

[16] An example of this application concept was the capture of U.S. Army personnel by Serbia after they had strayed across the Macedonia/Serbia border while participating in a United Nations authorized peacekeeping mission in Macedonia. Although neither the United States nor Serbia asserted a state of war existed, and although the confrontation between the U.S. forces and Serbian armed forces was brief and involved very little violence, the United States asserted the three soldiers were prisoners of war by operation of the Geneva Convention Relative to the Protection of Prisoners of War, because the confrontation in which they were captured qualified as an international armed conflict. *See* Geoffrey S. Corn, *To Be or Not To Be, That Is the Question: Contemporary Military Operations and the Status of Captured Personnel*, ARMY LAWYER 1, 17 (June 1999) (*cited in* JENNIFER K. ELSEA, CONG. RESEARCH SERV., PL 31367, TREATMENT OF "BATTLEFIELD DETAINEES" IN THE WAR ON TERRORISM (Jan. 23, 2007).

[17] *See* COMMENTARY, GC I, *supra* note 12, at 49–50.

[18] *See, e.g.*, THE JUDGE ADVOCATE GEN.'S LEGAL CTR. & SCH., U.S. ARMY, RULE OF LAW HANDBOOK; A PRACTITIONERS GUIDE FOR JUDGE ADVOCATES 1, 79–80 (2009), *available at* http://www.loc.gov/rr/frd/Military_Law/pdf/rule-of-law_2009.pdf. According to the commentary:

> Where international law generally governs relationships between states, human rights law (although a form of international law) regulates relationships between states and individuals.
>
> Human rights law can be applicable to Judge Advocates engaged in rule of law operations in two ways: through the application of customary international human rights law to their activities or through the application of the host nation's human rights obligations. If engaged in combat operations, however, the U.S. regards the law of war as an exclusive legal regime or a lex specialis. Under this view, the law of war operates to the exclusion of competing legal frameworks such as human rights law. *Id.* at 79–80.

seem logical, it is equally logical that states would resist the armed conflict characterization when seeking to avoid the perception of having lost control of an internal situation.

As the Commentary to CA3 emphasized, no single factor establishes this demarcation line. Instead, a totality-of-circumstances approach must be utilized to assess the existence of internal armed conflicts, relying on an array of factors.[19] Of the numerous factors suggested in the Commentary, perhaps the most instructive was the focus on the state response to the threat: resort to the use of regular (and by "regular," it is fair to presume that the Commentary refers to combat as opposed to constabulary) armed forces, is a significant indicator that the situation has most likely crossed the threshold into the realm of armed conflict.[20]

The analytical methodology proposed by the ICRC Commentary criteria proved remarkably effective in practice and, remains to be a focal point for the professional military education of U.S. military lawyers (JAGs). For example, short-duration/small-scale hostilities between states have been characterized as armed conflicts, such as when the U.S. Naval pilot Lieutenant Bobby Goodman was shot down by Syrian forces while flying a mission in relation to the U.S. peacekeeping presence in Lebanon in 1982, or when three U.S. Army soldiers were ambushed by Serbian military forces on the border between Serbia and Macedonia.[21] In neither of these cases did the United States assert it was in a war with the opponent state, or that a widespread armed conflict existed. Instead, these isolated engagements were characterized as sufficient to trigger the applicability of LOAC humanitarian obligations vis-à-vis the captured U.S. personnel.[22] As for the non-international context, the use of regular armed forces for sustained operations against internal dissident groups that cannot be suppressed with law enforcement capabilities only makes it difficult for a state to credibly disavow the existence of armed conflict.

Once the existence of armed conflict is determined, it is then necessary to assess whether the armed conflict should be characterized as international or non-international. This characterization dictates the bundle of LOAC rules that apply to the conflict as a matter of law. As noted above, pursuant to the structure of the Geneva Conventions, international armed conflicts within the meaning of CA2 trigger the full corpus of LOAC regulation.[23] In contrast, non-international

---

[19] COMMENTARY, GC I, *supra* note 12, at 49–50 (listing criteria that "are useful as a means of distinguishing a genuine armed conflict from a mere act of banditry or an unorganized and short-lived insurrection.").

[20] *Id.*

[21] Interview with W. Hays Parks, a senior attorney for the Defense Department and recognized expert on the law of armed conflict (Apr. 23, 1999). Parks was personally involved in developing the U.S. position on the status of Lieutenant Goodman, and indicated during the interview that the United States asserted prisoner-of-war status for Goodman as a matter of law, due to the existence of an "armed conflict" between the United States and Syria within the meaning of Common Article 2.

[22] *Id.*

[23] *See, e.g.*, UK MANUAL, *supra* note 7, at ¶ 2.1; LAW OF WAR DESKBOOK, *supra* note 7, at ch. 3.

armed conflicts trigger a less comprehensive, although expanding, body of regulation: the humane treatment mandate of Common Article 3, in certain situations the rules of the 1977 Additional Protocol II to the Geneva Conventions (a treaty that supplemented the very limited content of CA3), and customary LOAC rules applicable to all armed conflicts.[24] Today, because many of the rules originally developed or applied to IAC are considered equally applicable to NIAC by operation of customary international law, the regulatory distinction between these two categories of armed conflict is much less significant than it was in 1949.

Nonetheless, important differences remain, not the least of which is the uncertainty associated with the content of treaty rules extended from one category of armed conflict to another in the form of customary principles, and questions about enforceability of those principles. More fundamentally, because certain core regulatory concepts remain applicable exclusively in the context of IAC—such as the entitlement to prisoner-of-war status and the accordant lawful combatant's privilege, and international legal rules related to obligations of neutral states—distinguishing IAC from NIAC remains an important aspect of defining operational legal obligations.

Neither CA2 nor CA3 defined the meaning of "international" or "non-international." This has resulted in some uncertainty in distinguishing between these two categories of armed conflict.[25] However, this uncertainty has not been especially substantial. Consistent with the proposal of the ICRC Commentary, the existence of a dispute between two or more states is generally understood as the sine qua non of characterizing an armed conflict as international.[26] Nonetheless, this has not eliminated all uncertainty in U.S. practice when armed force is used by one state in the territory of another state. Such uncertainty has emerged when the situation suggests that the intervention was not the result of an inter-state dispute, even if the intervention is not the result of consent of the state where the operations occur.[27]

The 1989 U.S. intervention in Panama exemplifies this armed conflict without dispute-between-states theory of conflict classification. Specifically, the United States launched the attack to remove General Manuel Noriega from power in Panama and destroy the Panamanian Defense Force, the regular armed forces

---

[24] *See* Leslie C. Green, The Contemporary Law of Armed Conflict 59–61 (2d ed. 2000); *see also* Int'l & Operational Law Dep't, The Judge Advocate General's Legal Ctr. & Sch., U.S. Army, Law of War Deskbook ch. 3 (2007).

[25] *See generally* Adam Roberts, *Counter Terrorism, Armed Forces and the Laws of War*, 44 Survival (quarterly journal of IISS, London) 1 (Spring 2002). *See also* Jennifer K. Elsea, Cong. Research Serv., RL 31191, Terrorism and the Laws of War: Trying Terrorists as War Criminals before Military Commissions CRS 10–14 (Dec. 11, 2001) [hereinafter Elsea] (analyzing whether the attacks of September 11, 2001, triggered the law of war).

[26] *See* Commentary, GC I, *supra* note 12, at 32.

[27] *See, e.g.*, United States v. Noriega, 808 F. Supp. 791, 794 (S.D. Fla. 1992) (addressing and rejecting the U.S. assertion that the intervention in Panama to topple General Noriega did not qualify as an international armed conflict because the United States had been invited to intervene by Guillermo Endara, the democratically elected president of Panama).

of Panama.[28] Operation Just Cause involved the use of more than twenty thousand U.S. forces who engaged in intense combat with the Panamanian Defense Forces.[29] Nonetheless, the United States considered the conflict non-international. The basis for this characterization was that General Noriega was not the legitimate leader of Panama; therefore the U.S. dispute with him did not qualify as a dispute with Panama.[30] Although the U.S. federal district court that adjudicated Noriega's claim to prisoner-of-war status ultimately rejected this characterization and concluded the armed conflict was international,[31] it is not the only example of asserting a lack of a dispute between states as a basis for classifying an invasion of another state's territory as non-international.[32] Other situations that implicated this uncertainty include the 1992 U.S. military intervention in Somalia, and the 2001 U.S. intervention in Afghanistan. In both these situations, the United States characterized the object of intervention as failed states, thereby eliminating the "dispute" element of international armed conflict (although in the case of Afghanistan this position was subsequently reversed).[33] Although not a widely endorsed theory of conflict characterization, these examples nonetheless indicate that CA2 did not eliminate all potential uncertainty in relation to military action against the de facto armed forces of another state.

The 1949 extension of international humanitarian regulation into the realm of non-international armed conflicts[34] was unquestionably a landmark development

---

[28] *See generally* THOMAS DONNELLY, MARGARET ROTH & CALEB BAKER, OPERATION JUST CAUSE: THE STORMING OF PANAMA (1991).

[29] *Id.*

[30] *See Noriega*, 808 F. Supp. at 794.

[31] *Id.*

[32] A similar rationale was relied upon to conclude that combat operations conducted by U.S. forces in Somalia during Operation Provide Comfort did not result in an international armed conflict. *See generally* CTR. FOR LAW & MILITARY OPERATIONS (CLAMO) & THE JUDGE ADVOCATE GEN.'S SCH., CLAMO REPORT: THE MARINES HAVE LANDED AT CLAMO (1998).

[33] *See generally* Jay S. Bybee, Memorandum for Alberto R. Gonzales, Counsel to the President, and William J. Haynes II, General Counsel of the DoD Re: Application of Treaties and Laws to al Qaeda and Taliban Detainees (Jan. 22, 2002), *available at* http://www.washingtonpost.com/wp-srv/nation/documents/012202bybee.pdf.

[34] *See* COMMENTARY, GC I, *supra* note 12, at 38. According to the Commentary:

> This Article is common to all four of the Geneva Conventions of 1949, and is one of their most important Articles. It marks a new step forward in the unceasing development of the idea on which the Red Cross is based, and in the embodiment of that idea in the form of international obligations. It is an almost unhoped for extension of Article 2 above. Born on the battlefield, the Red Cross called into being the First Geneva Convention to protect wounded or sick military personnel. Extending its solicitude little by little to other categories of war victims, in logical application of its fundamental principle, it pointed the way, first to the revision of the original Convention, and then to the extension of legal protection in turn to prisoners of war and civilians. The same logical process could not fail to lead to the idea of applying the principle to all cases of armed conflicts, including those of an internal character.

Id.

in humanitarian regulation.[35] In contrast to inter-state action, it would therefore seem obvious that hostilities between a state and nonstate organized armed opponents would fall into the category of non-international armed conflict. Responsive primarily to the brutal civil wars that ravaged Spain, Russia, and other states during the years between the two world wars,[36] this term, however, was originally understood to denote only hostilities occurring within the territory of the state. As a result, the advent of what is sometimes characterized as transnational armed conflicts, or "internationalized" non-international armed conflicts (hostilities between state and nonstate groups occurring outside the territory of the state), has been the most significant source of contemporary conflict classification uncertainty.

During the five-plus decades between 1949 and 2001, the internal (akin to civil wars) meaning of the term "non-international" solidified, and became almost axiomatic. However, this purely internal scope of application did not account for combat operations launched by a state using regular armed forces against a transnational nonstate opponent outside its borders, therefore producing a regulatory lacuna. Such operations would fail to satisfy the requisite inter-state dispute element of CA2, and, based on the traditional internal interpretation of NIAC, would also fail to trigger the law of NIAC. However, CA3 itself does not expressly use "internal" as the indicator of the type of armed conflict triggering its humanitarian mandate. Instead, it expressly indicates that its substantive protections apply during all conflicts "not of an international character."[37] This ostensibly more expansive terminology would become the basis for the assertion that extraterritorial military operations may legitimately be characterized as NIACs, and are not automatically IACs.

By characterizing its struggle against al Qaeda as an armed conflict, the U.S. military response to the September 11th terrorist attacks exposed this regulatory gap.[38] Although this strain has produced international and national

---

[35] *See* INT'L COMM. OF THE RED CROSS, COMMENTARY ON THE ADDITIONAL PROTOCOLS OF 8 JUNE 1977 TO THE GENEVA CONVENTIONS OF 12 AUGUST 1949, 1330 (Yves Sandoz et al. eds., 1987) [hereinafter AP I COMMENTARY] ("In 1971 the possibility of creating a single protocol relating to the protection of the civilian population in all types of conflict was still envisaged. As the majority of experts expressed a preference for maintaining the distinction between international armed conflict and non-international armed conflict because of the characteristic features of each of these cases, the ICRC abandoned the idea of a single protocol on this point and introduced into the draft of Protocol II a part on the protection of the civilian population, following the example of draft Protocol I. A definition of the civilian population was proposed, together with the general principle of protection and rules of conduct to be applied during hostilities. Finally, it was provided that objects indispensable to survival should be protected and safeguarded.").

[36] *See, e.g.*, UK MANUAL, *supra* note 7, at ¶ 2.1; LAW OF WAR DESKBOOK, *supra* note 7, at ch. 3.

[37] *See* GC I, *supra* note 5, at art. 3; GC II, *supra* note 5, at art. 3; GC III, *supra* note 5, at art. 3; GC IV, *supra* note 5, at art. 3.

[38] *See* Kenneth Watkin, *Controlling the Use of Force: A Role for Human Rights Norms in Contemporary Armed Conflict*, 98 AM. J. INT'L L. 1, 2–8 (2004) (discussing the complex challenge of conflict categorization-related military operations conducted against highly organized nonstate groups with transnational reach). *See also* Kirby Abott, *Terrorists: Combatants, Criminals, or…?*; The Measures of International Law: Effectiveness, Fairness, and Validity, Published Proceedings of the 31st Annual Conference of the Canadian Council on International Law Oct. 24–26, 2002; *see also*

uncertainty as to the law applicable to these hostilities, it has contributed substantially to a reassessment of this assumed internal qualifier.[39] In the lower court judgment in *Hamdan v. Rumsfeld*, Judge Stephen F. Williams, in his concurring opinion, articulated the logic motivating this reassessment.[40] In that opinion, he responded to the majority conclusion that CA3's humanitarian protections did not apply to armed conflict with al Qaeda because the President has determined that this conflict is one of international scope, and therefore not internal:

> Non-State actors cannot sign an international treaty. Nor is such an actor even a "Power" that would be eligible under Article 2 (¶ 3) to secure protection by complying with the Convention's requirements. Common Article 3 fills the gap, providing some minimal protection for such non-eligibles in an "armed conflict not of an international character occurring in the territory of one of the High Contracting Parties." The gap being filled is the non-eligible party's failure to be a nation. Thus the words "not of an international character" are sensibly understood to refer to a conflict between a signatory nation and a non-State actor. The most obvious form of such a conflict is a civil war. But given the Convention's structure, the logical reading of "international character" is one that matches the basic derivation of the word "international," i.e., *between nations*. Thus, I think the context compels the view that a conflict between a signatory and a non-State actor is a conflict "not of an international character." In such a conflict, the signatory is bound to Common Article 3's modest requirements of "humane" treatment and "the judicial guarantees which are recognized as indispensable by civilized peoples."[41]

As Judge Williams recognized, it is fundamentally inconsistent with the logic of the LOAC to detach the applicability of regulation from de facto hostilities, situations necessitating conflict regulation and the legally mandated respect for fundamental humanitarian protections. What was needed was a pragmatic reconciliation of these two considerations. Although he was unable to persuade his peers on the D.C. Circuit to adopt this logic, his instinct was later validated by a majority of the Supreme Court in *Hamdan v. Rumsfeld*.[42] Relying on the plain text of CA3, the Supreme Court held that CA3's humanitarian protections were in fact applicable to the armed conflict with al Qaeda.[43] According to the

---

ELSEA, *supra* note 25, at CRS 10–14 (analyzing whether the attacks of September 11, 2001, triggered the law of war).

[39] *See generally* Human Rights Council, *Report of the Commission of Inquiry on Lebanon*, U.N. Doc. A/HRC/3/2 (Nov. 23, 2006), *available at* http://www2.ohchr.org/english/bodies/hrcouncil/docs/specialsession/A.HRC.3.2.pdf; Text of Order Signed by President Bush on Feb. 7, 2002, outlining treatment of al Qaida and Taliban detainees, http://www.lawofwar.org/Bush_torture_memo.htm.

[40] *See* Hamdan v. Rumsfeld, 415 F.3d 33, 44 (2005).

[41] *Id.* (Williams, J., concurring).

[42] Hamdan v. Rumsfeld, 548 U.S. 557, 628–33 (2006).

[43] *Id.* at 631–32.

opinion, the term "non-international" must be understood in "contradistinction" from "international" within the meaning of CA2.[44] Thus, any armed conflict that does not qualify as inter-state must be non-international within the meaning of CA3. In so holding, the Court not only closed the regulatory gap that enabled the United States to deny CA3 protections to al Qaeda detainees, but it contributed to what many believe is an important revision to the understanding of what qualifies as a CA3 NIAC.

Characterization of counterterror operations as an armed conflict, even non-international, continues to generate substantial controversy. However, this controversy is today focused more on the issue of whether such operations qualify as armed conflict rather than on whether transnational military operations may qualify as non-international within the meaning of CA3. Critics of this U.S. LOAC interpretation assert that these operations are insufficient in duration and intensity to rise above the law enforcement threshold, and point especially to al Qaeda's lack of military organization and the absence of sustained combat between al Qaeda and U.S. forces. An International Law Association committee report on the meaning of armed conflict illustrates this criticism.[45] According to the report:

> In May 2005, the Executive Committee of the International Law Association (ILA) approved a mandate for the Use of Force Committee to produce a report on the meaning of war or armed conflict in international law. The report was motivated by the United States' position following the attacks of 11 September 2001 that it was involved in a "global war on terror." In other words, the U.S. has claimed the right to exercise belligerent privileges applicable only during armed conflict anywhere in the world where members of terrorist groups are found. The U.S. position was contrary to a trend by states attempting to avoid acknowledging involvement in wars or armed conflicts.
>
> . . .
>
> . . . Plainly, the existence of armed conflict is a significant fact in the international legal system, and, yet, the Committee found no widely accepted definition of armed conflict in any treaty. It did, however, discover significant evidence in the sources of international law that the international community embraces a common understanding of armed conflict. *All armed conflict* has certain minimal, defining characteristics that distinguish it from situations of non-armed conflict or peace. In the absence of these characteristics, states may not, consistently with international law, simply declare that a situation is or is not armed conflict based on policy preferences. The Committee confirmed that at least two characteristics are found with respect to all armed conflict:
>
> 1.) The existence of organized armed groups

[44] *Id.* at 630–31.

[45] *See* Commentary, GC III, *supra* note 11, at 19–27.

> 2.) *Engaged in fighting of some intensity*
>
> In addition to these minimum criteria respecting all armed conflict, [International Humanitarian Law (IHL)] includes additional criteria so as to classify conflicts as either international or non-international in nature.
>
> . . .
>
> . . . The Committee, however, found little evidence to support the view that the Conventions apply in the absence of fighting of some intensity . . .[46]

Requiring a certain level of intensity may seem logically linked to excluding from the scope of LOAC applicability the type of low-level internal disturbances the ICRC Commentary indicated would not trigger CA3. For the United States, however, it seems clear that extending this criterion to the contemporary threat environment undermines the original purpose of the armed conflict concept: synchronization of conflict regulation with de facto situations of armed hostilities.[47] How the intensity, duration, and organization concept will impact conflict characterization in an era of evolving transnational nonstate threats is a chapter of international law still being written. It does not, however, seem likely that the United States will step back from its current expansive interpretation of NIAC.

III. Conflict Classification in Practice: Mitigating Uncertainty and Preserving Flexibility

Conflict classification uncertainty does not result exclusively from debates over the meaning of international legal terminology. Policy plays a significant role in the classification equation, and it is simply error to ignore the fact that situations involving the use of U.S. armed forces that may appear objectively unambiguous may very well not be viewed with such clarity from a policy perspective. Ideally, legal analysis should always drive policy positions. But at the strategic level of decision-making, history suggests this is not always the case. As a result, the strategic decision to employ U.S. military force may often be made without first articulating a clear position on the legal character of the operation vis à vis LOAC applicability. Although such articulations will often inevitably emerge in relation to long-term military commitments, such as the Iraq and Afghanistan conflicts, other short-duration operations have been conducted without ever reaching this point of legal and policy clarity.

This uncertainty obviously poses substantial risk at the operational and tactical levels of command. As noted in the introduction to this chapter, military operations cannot be permitted to occur in a regulatory vacuum. In recognition of these two potentially disparate realities (that operations may be initiated

---

[46] *Id.* at 1–2 (emphasis added).

[47] *See* COMMENTARY, GC III, *supra* note 11, at 19–27.

without a clearly articulated legal characterization, but that such operations must be conducted within a regulatory framework), the Department of Defense has long embraced the policy-based extension of LOAC regulation to *all* military operations. Understanding the scope and rationale for this policy, and how this policy often necessitates an issue-by-issue approach to law applicability analysis, is essential for appreciating the intersection of conflict classification law and policy in U.S. practice.

A. OPERATIONAL REALITY, CLASSIFICATION UNCERTAINTY, AND THE POLICY SOLUTION

In response to the conflict classification uncertainty associated with the U.S. role in Vietnam, and the perceived need to enhance LOAC training and war crimes investigations, the Department of Defense (DoD) implemented a policy titled *The Law of War Program*.[48] This policy included a clear and direct mandate for all U.S. armed forces: comply with the law of war during all armed conflicts, and the principles of the law of war during all other military operations.[49] Although the DoD has never explicitly articulated what LOAC principles are implicated by the policy, or a controlling definition of these principles,[50] this term is generally understood to refer to the core LOAC norms such as military necessity, humanity, distinction, and proportionality.[51] The recently revised U.K. Ministry of Defense *Manual for the Law of Armed Conflict* provides a useful definition of these principles, one that is consistent with U.S. practice:

> Despite the codification of much customary law into treaty form during the last one hundred years, four fundamental principles still underlie the law of armed conflict. These are military necessity, humanity, distinction, and proportionality. The law of armed conflict is consistent with the economic and efficient use of force. It is intended to minimize the suffering caused by armed conflict rather than impede military efficiency.[52]

---

[48] *See generally* U.S. Dep't of Def., Dir. 2311.01E, DoD Law of War Program (May 9, 2006) [hereinafter Law of War Program].

[49] *Id.* at ¶ 4.1. The actual language from the Department of Defense Policy reads as follows: "Members of the DoD Components comply with the law of war during all armed conflicts, however such conflicts are characterized, and in all other military operations." *Id.*

[50] *Id.* The purported justification for this omission is that each subordinate service is then able to define the content of this term for purposes of its forces. Leaving definition of these principles to individual services creates obvious concerns of inconsistent practice. This concern is unacceptable in the contemporary environment of joint operations. It is likely, however, that a joint standard will be established by the Department of Defense in a Department of Defense Law of War Manual, which is currently under development.

[51] *See, e.g.*, UK Manual, *supra* note 7, at ¶ 2.1 ("Despite the codification of much customary law into treaty form during the last one hundred years, four fundamental principles still underlie the law of armed conflict. These are military necessity, humanity, distinction, and proportionality.").

[52] *Id.*

Although it seems almost axiomatic that the policy implicates these core principles, it also suggests that contextual analysis warrants extending more precise LOAC rules to military operations when an issue arises implicating such rules—for example, in relation to the collection and care of the wounded and sick, or the temporary seizure of civilian property.

Ultimately, the DoD policy is intended to ensure that even when the legal characterization of a military operation is uncertain, U.S. forces follow rules providing for a legitimate balance between military necessity and humanity concepts (the obligation to mitigate the suffering associated with armed conflict), which provide the foundation for the more detailed treaty rules that have evolved to implement these principles.[53] The relationship between these core LOAC principles and these LOAC treaties developed during the past century is explained as follows by the distinguished LOAC scholar, Professor Adam Roberts:

> Although some of the law is immensely detailed, its foundational principles are simple: the wounded and sick, POWs and civilians are to be protected; military targets must be attacked in such a manner as to keep civilian casualties and damage to a minimum; humanitarian and peacekeeping personnel must be respected; neutral or non-belligerent states have certain rights and duties; and the use of certain weapons (including chemical weapons) is prohibited, as also are other means and methods of warfare that cause unnecessary suffering.[54]

The motivation for the initial implementation and continued applicability of this important policy is twofold. First, it provides a common baseline standard of LOAC compliance, a standard essential for both consistency in training and operational compliance during the planning and execution of military operations that span the wide range from peacekeeping to full-scale conflict.[55] Second, it responds to the reality that such operations are often initiated prior to a clear conflict classification determination.[56] By providing for consistency in training

---

[53] Rod Powers, *Law of Armed Conflict (LOAC): Rules of War*, About.com, http://usmilitary.about.com/cs/wars/a/loac.htm (last visited July 11, 2014).

[54] Roberts, *supra* note 25, at 7–8.

[55] Interview with W. Hays Parks, Special Assistant to the Judge Advocate General of the Army for Law of War Matters, Office of the Judge Advocate General, in Rosslyn, VA (Apr. 23, 1999). Parks is the Chair of the Department of Defense Law of War Working Group, is a recognized expert on the law of armed conflict, and is one of the original proponents of the Law of War Program.

[56] For example, the uncertainty related to the application of the laws of war to Operation Just Cause in Panama is reflected in the following excerpt from a submission related to judicial determination of General Noriega's status: "[T]he United States has made no formal decision with regard to whether or not General Noriega and former members of the PDF charged with pre-capture offenses are prisoners of war, but has stated that each will be provided all prisoner of war protections afforded by the law of war." *See* U.S. Dep't of the Army, Memorandum of Law (1990) (quoted in United States v. Noriega, 808 F. Supp. 791, 794 n24 (S.D. Fla. 1992)). In Somalia, although U.S. forces engaged in intense combat operations against nonstate organized armed militia groups (*see* Mark Bowden, Black Hawk Down: A Story of Modern War 3 (1999)), there was never a formal determination of the status of the conflict. *See* Maj. Geoffrey S. Corn & Maj. Michael L. Smidt, *To Be or Not to Be,*

and operational regulation, the policy contributed substantially to disciplined military operations, and enhanced the clarity of lines of permissible conduct for U.S. forces.

Because of the proverbial fog of war, ensuring such regulatory clarity has always been and remains a critically important aspect of disciplined and credible military operations. This consideration is perhaps undervalued in contemporary conflict classification discourse, especially when the product of that discourse is increased regulatory uncertainty. Interestingly, one of the most important precursors to the many LOAC treaties developed during the twentieth century, the *Oxford Manual of the Laws of War on Land*, emphasized the value of such consistency:

> By [codifying the rules of war derived from state practice], it believes it is rendering a service to military men themselves . . . . A positive set of rules, on the contrary, if they are judicious, serves the interests of belligerents and is far from hindering them, since by preventing the unchaining of passion and savage instincts—which battle always awakens, as much as it awakens courage and many virtues—it strengthens the discipline which is the strength of armies; it also ennobles their patriotic mission in the eyes of the soldiers by keeping them within the limits of respect due to the rights of humanity.[57]

While the DoD policy unquestionably serves an important purpose, it is not a talisman for the resolution of every operational legal issue in the midst of conflict classification uncertainty. One weakness in this approach, exposed during the first years of the U.S. conflict against al Qaeda, is that policy, unlike legal obligation, is always malleable. If and when the Secretary of Defense determines deviation from the mandate is necessary, or is instructed by higher authority to deviate from this policy, there is no basis to prevent such action. This reality is reflected in the February 7, 2002, policy established by President Bush regarding the treatment of captured Taliban and al Qaeda personnel.[58] After accepting the Department of Justice conclusion that the humane treatment provision of CA3 did not apply to al Qaeda detainees (for reasons explained above), the President directed that "[a]s a matter of policy, the United States Armed Forces shall continue to treat detainees humanely and, to the extent appropriate and consistent with military necessity, in a manner consistent with the principles of Geneva."[59] The military necessity qualifier to this humane treatment policy

---

That Is the Question: Contemporary Military Operations and the Status of Captured Personnel, ARMY LAW. 5–6 (June 1999).

[57] *See* Int'l Comm. of the Red Cross, *The Laws of War on Land* 1 (1880) [hereinafter Oxford Manual of the Laws of War on Land], *available at* http://www.icrc.org/applic/ihl/ihl.nsf/INTRO/140?OpenDocument.

[58] *See generally* ICRC Customary IHL, *United States of America Practice Relating to Rule 87. Humane Treatment*, *available at* http://www.icrc.org/customary-ihl/eng/docs/v2_cou_us_rule87 [hereinafter *Humane Treatment*] (text of order signed by President Bush on Feb. 7, 2002, outlining and regarding the humane treatment of al-Qaida and Taliban detainees) (last visited Feb. 9, 2013).

[59] *Id.*

mandate indicates a limitation to the protection that would be inconsistent with application of a legally mandated variant of this protection. Although such deviations have been rare in practice, this nonetheless exposes one significant limit of a policy extension of LOAC principles.

B. RULES OF ENGAGEMENT: LINKING STRATEGIC POLICY TO TACTICAL EXECUTION

In practice, the policy-based application of LOAC principles is effectuated primarily through rules of engagement (ROE). United States' military doctrine defines ROE as "directives issued by competent military authority that delineate the circumstances and limitations under which United States forces will initiate and/or continue combat engagement with other forces encountered."[60] As a mechanism to provide operational and tactical military commands greater control over the execution of combat operations, ROE are utilized in all U.S. military operations. In fact, the impact of ROE is so ubiquitous that for many members of the armed forces they are viewed as synonymous with the LOAC.[61] This perception is understandable, as ROE are utilized to implement LOAC obligations. However, it is also inaccurate, because although ROE must be consistent with the LOAC (in other words, ROE may not authorize conduct prohibited by the LOAC), it is quite common for ROE to impose limitations on operational conduct more restrictive than what is required by the LOAC.

The primary purpose of ROE is to regulate the use of combat power (the use of force). Rules of engagement are issued pursuant to an instruction by the Chairman of the Joint Chiefs of Staff, CJCSI 3121.01B: Standing Rules of Engagement/Rules for the Use of Force (SROE).[62] This instruction defines the purpose of the SROE as:

> The purpose of these SROE is to provide implementation guidance on the application of force for mission accomplishment and the exercise of the inherent right and obligation of self-defense. In the absence of superseding guidance, the SROE establish fundamental policies and procedures governing the actions to be taken by US force commanders in the event of military attack against the United States and during all military operations, contingencies, terrorist attacks, or prolonged conflicts outside the territorial jurisdiction of the United States, including the Commonwealths of Puerto

---

[60] Joint Chiefs of Staff, Joint Pub. 1-02, Department of Defense Dictionary of Military and Associated Terms 230 (Nov. 8, 2013), *available at* http://www.dtic.mil/doctrine/new_pubs/jp1_02.pdf.

[61] Geoffrey S. Corn & Lt. Col. Gary P. Corn, *The Law of Operational Targeting: Viewing the LOAC through an Operational Lens*, 47 Tex. Int'l L.J. 337, 352 (2012) (discussing that although the ROE are not law, their limitations must be consistent with that of the LOAC, and the ROE "serves as an additional source of authority defining guidelines for permissible combat actions.").

[62] Joint Chiefs of Staff, Instr. 3121.01B, The Standing Rules of Engagement/Standing Rules for the Use of Force for U.S. Forces encl. A, ¶ 1d (June 13, 2005)[hereinafter SROE].

> Rico and Northern Marianas, US possessions, and US territories. To provide uniform training and planning capabilities, this document is authorized for distribution to commanders at all levels and is to be used as fundamental guidance for training and directing their forces.[63]

All ROE for U.S. operations are issued pursuant to the procedures established in the instruction, and when subordinate commands believe that mission accomplishment necessitates modification to the ROE issued by higher command, the instruction provides a mechanism whereby modifications may be requested and issued.[64] Although the primary focus of ROE is the regulation of combat power, ROE are also used routinely to emphasize other obligations derived from LOAC principles. In fact, the unclassified base ROE instruction reiterates the mandate of the DoD Law of War Program Directive by providing:

> US forces will comply with the Law of War during military operations involving armed conflict, no matter how the conflict may be characterized under international law, and will comply with its principles and spirit during all other operations.[65]

ROE will be addressed more extensively in subsequent chapters of this book. However, what is important here is to note that the principal mechanism for providing operational forces with mission accomplishment authority, the ROE, incorporates the obligation to comply with LOAC principles during all military operations.[66] In so doing, the national-level policy mandate is translated into "soldier's rules" that apply to every member of the force participating in a given military operation.[67] Accordingly, ROE cards issued to individual members of the unit not only provide guidance on when employment of force is authorized, but include other rules such as the prohibition against looting, the obligation to

---

[63] *Id.* at encl. A, ¶ 1a.

[64] Lt. Col. Marc L. Warren, *Operational Law—A Concept Matures*, 152 Mil. L. Rev. 33, 56 (1996) (stating rules may be modified in or supplemented during an actual operation; "[s]oldiers must be alert and responsive to, and trained to anticipate, changes in ROE. Changes in the application of the ROE may occur because of changes in mission or threat."). *See also* Int'l & Operational Law Dep't, The Judge Advocate General's Legal Ctr. & Sch., U.S. Army, Operational Law Handbook ch. 5 (2012) ("The ROE process must anticipate changes in the operational environment and modify supplemental measures to support the assigned mission. Commanders and their staffs must continuously analyze ROE and recommend modifications to meet changing operational parameters.").

[65] SROE, *supra* note 62, at encl. A, ¶ 1g.

[66] Warren, *supra* note 64, at 52–53 (the JCS SROE contain numerous improvements over the JCS PROE, such as governing the use of force in not only self- defense, but in mission accomplishment).

[67] *Id.* at 64 (there are nine minimum principles, which every soldier should know and obey: (1) Soldiers fight only enemy combatants; (2) Soldiers do not harm enemies who surrender. Disarm them and turn them over to your superiors; (3) Soldiers do not kill or torture enemy prisoners of war; (4) Soldiers collect and care for the wounded, whether friend or foe; (5) Soldiers do not attack medical personnel, facilities, or equipment; (6) Soldiers destroy no more than the mission requires; (7) Soldiers treat all civilians humanely; (8) Soldiers do not steal. Soldiers respect private property and possessions; (9) Soldiers should do their best to prevent violations of the law of war.

collect and care for the wounded and sick, the obligation to respect civilians and civilian property, and the obligation to refrain from inflicting unnecessary suffering on an opponent.[68]

Taken as a whole, the combined effect of policy-based regulation implemented through training and ROE guidance continues to provide an essential "default setting" for the regulation of military operations falling outside the context of accepted legal triggers for LOAC application, or during periods of conflict classification uncertainty. Although an incomplete substitute for definitive conflict classification, this DoD policy plays a vital role in operational regulation. Because modification may only be made at the highest levels of national command, military commanders and the military lawyers who provide them with operational law counsel must presume that all operations will be conducted in accordance with LOAC principles. This approach will normally provide a workable framework for resolving even complex operational issues. When, however, the general nature of this policy mandate results in its own operational uncertainty, an issue-by-issue legal analysis will often be utilized to provide for the resolution of such issues.

C. ISSUE-BASED ANALYSIS AND PRESERVATION OF FLEXIBILITY

One consequence of conflict classification uncertainty has been the need to address legal issues on a case-by-case basis.[69] This process normally begins at the operational level of command, the level where forces are executing military operations to achieve national strategic objectives. As legal questions arise, military lawyers—judge advocates, or JAGs—at that level seek to provide commanders and their supporting staffs with responsive advice. In many cases, controlling policies, including the DoD Law of War Program and existing ROE, will provide sufficient authority to resolve these questions. At times, however, guidance from superior levels of command is requested to clarify legal and/or operational uncertainties.

It should be noted that this process is not unique to situations of uncertain conflict classification. Even when there is a clear U.S. position on the nature of an armed conflict and the applicable law, issues will arise requiring definitive interpretations of this law. In practice, what JAGs refer to as the technical chain of command, the line of JAGs supporting commanders up through the operational chain of command, is utilized to seek these legal interpretations.[70] At each

---

[68] *Humane Treatment, supra* note 58.

[69] *See generally* Int'l Committee of the Red Cross, *International Humanitarian Law and the Challenges of Contemporary Armed Conflicts*, Reports and Documents (Sept. 2007), *available at* http://www.icrc.org/eng/assets/files/other/irrc-867-ihl-challenges.pdf.

[70] *See generally* Joint Chiefs of Staff, Joint Publication 1-04, Legal Support to Military Operations (Aug. 17, 2011), http://www.dtic.mil/doctrine/new_pubs/jp1_04.pdf (comprehensive list of joint force staff judge advocate's responsibilities and duties) [hereinafter Legal Support to Military Operations].

ascending level of command, the issue will be assessed, and if possible addressed. When an issue is of a nature that is perceived to require assessment from the next higher command, it will be pushed up the technical chain.

For LOAC issues, the pinnacle of this process is the General Counsel (GC) for the Department of Defense. As the lawyer for the Secretary of Defense, the DoD GC is the senior legal advisor in the operational chain of command. This might come as a surprise to many outside observers, particularly because the GC is a politically appointed civilian attorney and not a uniformed military lawyer. However, this corresponds with the overall concept of civilian control of the military. As noted in an earlier chapter, the senior military lawyers for each service are not included in the operational chain of command, but instead provide legal resources and advice to their respective Service Chiefs.[71]

This is not to suggest that they do not provide input into this issue-resolution process. On the contrary, they, or more specifically their representatives, play an integral role in this process. This normally occurs in the Department of Defense Law of War Working Group (LOWWG), an ad hoc committee of LOAC experts from all the military service Judge Advocate offices, the Chairman of the Joint Chiefs of Staff Legal Advisors office, and in many cases representatives from the Department of State and the Department of Justice.[72] The DoD GC's representative chairs the LOWWG; this is usually the attorney assigned the LOAC portfolio within the GC's office. The LOWWG functions to vet operational legal issues and to make recommendations to the GC on their resolution. The Group also seeks to identify potential issues on the horizon so as to prepare legal positions in advance in order to mitigate uncertainty if and when the issues arise.[73]

In many ways, this issue-by-issue approach provides potential strategic-level advantages, especially when combined with the Law of War Program policy. That policy-based compliance with LOAC principles will normally be effective to provide operational clarity on most legal issues. When issues require further analysis, the issue-by-issue approach allows national-level command the opportunity to craft policies determined consistent with controlling domestic

---

[71] *Id.* The Joint Publication notes:

> The GCs of the Military Departments, the judge advocates general (TJAGs), and judge advocates general (JAGs) of the Services provide advice to the Secretaries of the Military Departments and Chiefs of the Services as they carry out their Title 10, USC, responsibilities for organizing, training, and equipping US military forces. Although the Military Departments are not part of the operational chain of command for joint US military operations, their GCs and TJAG/JAGs can provide joint force SJAs with significant reachback capabilities and expertise in international and operational law. TJAG/JAGs also have statutory authority to supervise the administration of military justice within the Services. *Id.*

[72] *See generally* LAW OF WAR PROGRAM, *supra* note 48 (discussing the purpose, scope, policy, and responsibilities of the DoD Law of War Program).

[73] *See generally Summary of Legal Issues Relevant to Terrorism Incidents of 11 Sept. 01* (Oct. 21, 2001), *available at* http://www.higginsctc.org/terrorism/TerrorismLegalIssuesSummary.pdf. The use of this group to address current operational issues is ad hoc as well, and often personality-driven.

and international legal obligations. This is often possible even in the absence of an overall conflict classification determination. Why would this be perceived as strategically beneficial? Because it allows for issue resolution without committing to more extensive obligations that may later be determined inconsistent with the nature of the mission or the strategic imperative.

Two examples illustrate this methodology. The first is Operation Just Cause, the 1989 U.S. invasion of Panama.[74] When the operation was launched, there was no enunciation of the nature of the armed conflict. As noted above, although it certainly seemed to satisfy the CA2 international armed conflict criteria, the request for intervention by Guillermo Endara, the candidate the United States considered the lawfully elected president of Panama, created uncertainty as to whether the operation fell within the scope of CA2 as a matter of law. Nonetheless, U.S. forces executed the operation in accordance with IAC principles and rules, to include application of the prisoner-of-war provisions of the Third Geneva Convention (GPW). In fact, the United States conducted dozens of Article 5 Tribunals, hearings based on Article 5 of the GPW utilized to determine prisoner-of-war (POW) status, when it is uncertain that a detainee qualifies for that legal status.[75]

However, the United States did not definitively acknowledge the invasion qualified as an IAC. Other issues were addressed on an ad hoc basis, resulting in decisions based on the apparent conclusion the conflict was in fact a NIAC. First, the United States never acknowledged obligations as an occupying power. In retrospect, this may have been a strategic blunder, for it set the conditions for several days of lawlessness and widespread looting in major population centers as the result of the destruction of the Panamanian security apparatus. Although the United States did rapidly reconstitute a Panamanian police force and assist that force with U.S. military assets, it never assumed full responsibility for governing Panamanian territory subject to U.S. military control. Such an assertion of authority would obviously have been inconsistent with the strategic foundation for the intervention: assistance to the democratically elected government of Panama. It may have also proven a strategic liability, as it might confirm suspicions that the United States was treating a Latin American neighbor as a banana republic.

General Noriega's post-capture treatment involved a much more controversial decision indicating the rejection of an IAC characterization.[76] Noriega had been

---

[74] *See generally* United States v. Noriega, 808 F. Supp. 791, 794 (S.D. Fla. 1992).

[75] *See generally* U.S. Dep't of Army, Reg. 190-8, Enemy Prisoners of War, Retained Personnel, Civilian Internees and Other Detainees (Oct. 1, 1997) (Army Regulation 190-8 is a multi-service publication that discusses policies and planning guidance for the treatment, care, accountability, legal status, and administrative procedures for enemy civilian internees, prisoners of war, and retained persons and is designated as OPNAVINST 3461.6 (Navy), AFJI31-304 (Air Force), and MCO 3461.1 (Marine Corps)).

[76] Geoffrey S. Corn & Sharon G. Finegan, *America's Longest Held Prisoner of War: Lessons Learned from the Capture, Prosecution, and Extradition of General Manuel Noriega*, 71 La. L. Rev. 1111, 1112 (2011). ("General Noriega was ignominiously transported to the U.S. by military aircraft,

indicted for violation of federal law prior to the invasion, and was brought to Miami for trial on those indictments immediately following his capture. Noriega demanded POW status (in a failed effort to avoid answering for these charges).[77] The U.S. government responded by asserting that because Endara had requested U.S. assistance, the armed conflict in Panama had not been international within the meaning of CA2.[78] Although the government assured the court that Noriega would be treated consistently with the GPW pursuant to DoD policy, it rejected his request for legal POW status. Noriega ultimately prevailed in his status claim when the trial court ruled that the invasion qualified as an IAC pursuant to CA2, and Noriega remained a POW for the duration of his criminal incarceration.[79] However, the episode illustrates the interaction between the Law of War policy and case-by-case resolution of particular issues.

United States' personnel involved in the initial invasion of Afghanistan in 2001–2002 experienced a similar situation. When they began detaining captured personnel (and personnel handed over by the Northern Alliance), there was no clear indication of the character of the armed conflict. Accordingly, the JAGs supporting the mission advised commanders that detainees should be treated consistent with the principles of the GPW, although they should not be formally designated POWs.[80] The actual legal status of these detainees became a significant issue at the strategic level of command, where it was ultimately decided that they did not qualify for any protected status pursuant to the Geneva Conventions.[81] Although this decision proved controversial, and the designation of these detainees as unprivileged enemy belligerents remains controversial to this day, the process of relying on the LOAC principles default position until supplemented by a more formal legal determination of the issue illustrates the interaction of law and policy in operational execution.

---

turned over to federal authorities, and subsequently tried and convicted in the United States District Court for the Southern District of Florida.")

[77] *Id.; see also* United States v. Noriega, 117 F.3d 1206, 1210 (11th Cir. 1997).

[78] *See* Geoffrey S. Corn, Hamdan, *Lebanon, and the Regulation of Hostilities: The Need to Recognize a Hybrid Category of Armed Conflict*, 40 VAND. J. TRANSNAT'L L. 295, 323–25, 329 (2007) (noting how both President Bush and the Supreme Court relied on Common Articles 2 and 3 to reach opposite conclusions about the applicability of Geneva Conventions to post-9/11 conflict).

[79] *See, e.g.*, United States v. Noriega, 808 F. Supp. 791 (S.D. Fla. 1992) (addressing and rejecting the U.S. assertion that the intervention in Panama to topple General Noriega did not qualify as an international armed conflict because the United States had been invited to intervene by Guillermo Endara, the democratically elected president of Panama).

[80] Letter from William Taft to Jim Haynes (March 22, 2002), *in* THE TORTURE DEBATE IN AMERICA 283, 284 (Karen J. Greenberg ed., 2005). President Bush decided that neither the al Qaeda terrorists nor the Taliban qualify for prisoner-of-war status under the GPW. However, he decided that he wanted all detainees treated humanely, consistent with the general principles of the GPW.

[81] Srividhya Ragavan & Michael S. Mireles Jr., *The Status of Detainees from the Iraq and Afghanistan Conflicts*, UTAH L. REV. 619, 621–22 (2005) (discussing the Bush administration's classification of al Qaeda and the Taliban prisoners as unlawful combatants, therefore not eligible for protection under the Geneva Conventions, meaning unrestricted means could be used to obtain information from them).

The relative legitimacy and/or wisdom of this methodology are beyond the scope of this chapter, and there are many experts who believe that it is imperative to articulate a clear conflict classification position prior to initiating any military operation. However, understanding the impact of law on U.S. military operations necessitates an appreciation of this very common process, a process unlikely to change significantly in the future.

IV. Conclusion

Determining the international legal framework applicable to military operations is a complex process that highlights the intersection of law and national security policy. Although many scholars consider this process quite simple, U.S. practice indicates that this is not the case, even if the complexity is the result of initial reticence to assert a firm position on the nature of an operation. However, operational legal classification is also critically important, as it impacts virtually every aspect of mission execution.

Because U.S. armed forces are called upon to conduct missions across a wide range of operational situations, it is essential that certain core regulatory principles be applied as a proverbial default position. This imperative is satisfied through national military policy, which requires U.S. armed forces to comply with the LOAC during all armed conflicts, and with the principles of the LOAC during any other military operation. Although history has demonstrated that this approach is not a talisman for resolving all operational issues, the same history demonstrates that this is a feasible method to mitigate operational legal uncertainty.

The rules governing armed conflict, whether international or non-international, will inevitably evolve as the nature of conflict itself evolves. The U.S. armed forces will almost certainly be at the focal point of that evolution, and how such terms are applied to their operations will continue to impact strategic, operational, and tactical decisions. The core imperative of conducting military operations pursuant to logical and effective norms remains a constant aspect of credible mission execution. Whether applied as a matter of law or national policy, the LOAC has and will continue to provide that regulatory framework.

4 }

The *Jus ad Bellum*

Geoffrey S. Corn*

I face the world as it is, and cannot stand idle in the face of threats to the American people. For make no mistake: evil does exist in the world. A non-violent movement could not have halted Hitler's armies. Negotiations cannot convince al Qa'ida's leaders to lay down their arms. To say that force is sometimes necessary is not a call to cynicism—it is a recognition of history; the imperfections of man and the limits of reason.[1]

I. Introduction

No employment of U.S. military power occurs without an assessment of domestic and international legal authority. In U.S. practice, this assessment occurs at the strategic level, normally involving interagency coordination. Although military lawyers are most commonly associated with assessments of legal issues related to the execution of military operations (the principal focus of this text), it would be error to suggest that they are neither concerned with nor involved in decisions as to the legal basis for these operations. At the strategic level of command, military lawyers participate in the assessment of these issues, offering their reasoned judgments on domestic and international legal authorities applicable to proposed operational courses of action.

Unlike many other chapters in this text, this one will not focus on the process for these assessments, or the "nuts and bolts" integration of military legal advisors in this process. It is sufficient to note that both the Secretary of Defense and the Chairman of the Joint Chiefs of Staff—two essential players in the interagency

* Presidential Professor of Law at South Texas College of Law, Lieutenant Colonel (Retired), U.S. Army. Former Special Assistant to the U.S. Army Judge Advocate General for Law of War Matters, and Chief of the Law of War Branch, U.S. Army Office of the Judge Advocate General International and Operational Law Division.

[1] President Barack Obama, Nobel Peace Prize Acceptance Speech (Dec.10, 2009) [hereinafter President Obama].

decision-making process related to military operations—receive advice from their respective legal advisors. In the case of the Secretary of Defense, this advice is provided by the General Counsel to the Department of Defense, the senior civilian attorney in the Department.[2] In contrast, the Chairman is advised by the Legal Counsel to the Chairman, a judge advocate in the rank of brigadier general or rear admiral (lower half).[3] Each of these legal advisors is supported by a staff of military and civilian lawyers of the highest level of expertise. Every military action planned and/or executed by the U.S. armed forces will therefore be subject to a formal legal opinion by each of these advisors indicating the legal basis for the operation.

Instead, this chapter will explain the U.S. interpretation of the international legal basis for the conduct of these operations (the *jus ad bellum*). This interpretation provides the critical foundation for projecting U.S. military power to reach identified terrorist targets. It also reflects an unquestioned international legal framework that defines when states may legitimately resort to force to achieve their national or multinational strategic objectives. Although this framework may be unquestioned, its application in the context of counterterror operations is anything but.

One need only consider the mission executed against Osama bin Laden in 2011 to understand the complexity of the legal issues surrounding the use of military force as a counterterrorism tool. Because of the transnational character of the terrorist threat, even prior to September 11, 2001, the United States considered it necessary to project military power into the sovereign territory of other states to target terrorist capabilities. This practice became significantly more common following the September 11th attacks, and triggered widespread controversy in the international legal and policy community. What right did the United States have to violate the sovereignty of other states in order to achieve its national counterterrorism objectives? Was the United States obligated to rely on the efforts of these states to neutralize terrorist operatives identified within their borders? If not, did international law require the United States to obtain the consent of the state prior to launching a military attack against those terrorists? Was acting without such consent or cooperation illegal aggression against a fellow member of the international community?

These questions remain as complex today as they were on September 12, 2001. They can only be answered through the prism of international law, or more specifically the branch of international law that defines the authority and limitations on the use of military force by states: the *jus ad bellum*. Indeed, no treatment of the relationship between counterterror military operations and international law is complete without considering the international legal basis to employ force at the outset. From an operational perspective, readers might be surprised to learn that every plan for the conduct of U.S. military action is subject to legal review.

---

[2] 10 U.S.C. § 140 (2013).

[3] 10 U.S.C. § 156 (2013).

This review includes an assessment of both the international and domestic legal bases for the operation.

International law delimits state legal authority to use military force externally to achieve national security objectives. Known as the *jus ad bellum*,[4] loosely translated this term refers to the legality of war. The contemporary legal framework establishing state authority to use of force was in large measure responsive to the carnage of World War II. Responding to the acknowledged failure of international law to prevent that war, the victorious Allies set about to remedy the deficiencies in the post–World War I effort to prohibit the use of force as a means of resolving international disputes. That initial effort was defined by a treaty prohibiting war as a means to resolving international disputes (the Kellogg-Briand Pact) and the creation of an international organization intended, inter alia, to provide a collective international security mechanism (the League of Nations). The post–World War II objective of improving upon these initial but failed efforts to limit resort to military force between states produced the use-of-force framework enshrined in the Charter of the United Nations (U.N. Charter), which has since evolved to become a universally accepted use-of-force standard.[5]

The foundation of this so-called "U.N. Charter paradigm" is Article 2(4) of the U.N. Charter, obligating all states to respect the territorial sovereignty of other states, and prohibiting the use of force or the threat of force among states.[6] Implicit in this prohibition is the absence of legal authority for any such use of force by one state against another; the result is the qualification of such use as an act of unlawful aggression. The prohibition against the aggressive use of military force did not, however, originate with the Charter. The origins of this prohibition predated World War II when war was prohibited in the Pact of Paris (Kellogg-Briand Pact). Although obviously ineffective in preventing the greatest military conflict in human history, this international legal prohibition of war remains an important precursor to the contemporary legality equation. Building upon this prohibition, the U.N. Charter reflects the recognition that the efficacy of this prohibition would turn on both a meaningful international enforcement mechanism and the authority for states to come to the aid of other states subjected to acts of aggression.[7]

This understanding, and the two means of achieving an effective prohibition against aggression, came to define the U.N. Charter use-of-force paradigm. First, the prohibition against aggressive use of force was reaffirmed in Article 2(4) of the Charter.[8] Second, the Charter vested the U.N. Security Council with the

---

[4] *See generally* Giuliano Enriques, *Considerazioni sulla teoria della guerra nel diritto internazionale* [Considerations on the Theory of War in International Law], 7 Rivista Di Diritto Internazionale [J. Int'l L.] 172 (1928) (this was the first use of the words "*jus ad bellum*").

[5] *See* Yoram Dinstein, War, Aggression, and Self Defense 87–94 (5th ed. 2011) (describing the function of Article 2(4) of the Charter and how this advances the goal of addressing the shortcomings of the Kellogg-Briand Pact).

[6] U.N. Charter art. 2, ¶ 4.

[7] *Id.* at art 42; 51 (stating that the use of force is authorized only for the purposes of collective or individual self-defense or pursuant to a resolution by the Security Council).

[8] *See id.* at art. 2, ¶ 4.

responsibility to respond to violations of Article 2(4) (acts of aggression, breaches of the peace, and threats to international peace and security) by any necessary means to include authorizing use of military force by member states to restore international peace and security.[9] Such uses of force, because authorized by the community of nations through the Security Council, would be lawful precisely because they would be conducted for the purpose of restoring international peace and security. Finally, the Charter acknowledged the inherent right of states to use force for individual and collective self-defense in response to acts of aggression.[10] This right, enshrined in Article 51 of the Charter, has been interpreted to apply not only to actual acts of aggression, but also to imminent threats of aggressive attack.[11]

Accordingly, the framework for assessing the international legality to use military force establishes a presumptive prohibition against such use. This presumption is rebutted by one of three conditions. First, the use of force is requested by the state where the use occurred. Such consent-based military intervention in another state is consistent with Article 2(4) because it is not directed against the sovereign interests of another state.[12] Second, the use of force is authorized by the Security Council exercising its power to authorize military action in response to a breach of international law, for the purpose of restoring international peace and security. Third, the use of force is conducted in response to an act of aggression or an imminent threat of aggression pursuant to the inherent state authority to act in individual or collective self-defense.

With the exception of consent-based uses of force, determining what constitutes unlawful aggression or an imminent threat of unlawful aggression is obviously a critical aspect of assessing the legality of using military force. When a state is actually attacked by another state, such as when Iraq invaded Kuwait in 1989, aggression is relatively self-evident. However, a threat to international peace and security triggering the individual and collective right of self-defense has always been complex.[13] In 1974, the United Nations General Assembly sought to provide greater clarity of what triggers this in General Assembly Resolution 3314, defining aggression.[14] Although General Assembly Resolutions do not bind member states, this definition is regarded by distinguished *jus belli* scholars[15]

---

[9] *Id.* at art. 39.

[10] *See id.* at art. 42, 51.

[11] U.N. Secretary-General, *In Larger Freedom: Towards Development, Security and Human Rights for All*, ¶ 124, U.N. Doc. A/59/2005 (May 21, 2005), *available at* http://www2.ohchr.org/english/bodies/hrcouncil/docs/gaA.59.2005_En.pdf.

[12] For a different view on the role of consent in the legality of military force, see Int'l & Operational Law Dep't, The Judge Advocate General's Legal Ctr. & Sch., U.S. Army, Law of Armed Conflict Deskbook 31 (2010) ("Consent is not a separate exception to Article 2(4). If a state is using force with the consent of host state, then there is no violation of the host state's territorial integrity or political independence; thus, there is no need for an exception to the rule.").

[13] *See* Dinstein, *supra* note 5, at 187–241 (describing the history of self-defense and its application in international law).

[14] G.A. Res. 3314 (XXIX), annex, U.N. Doc. A/9631 (Dec. 14, 1974).

[15] *See, e.g.* Dinstein, *supra* note 5, at 136–40.

as generally authoritative, and has been relied on by the International Court of Justice.[16] Resolution 3314 lists six situations that qualify as aggression:

(a) The invasion or attack by the armed forces of a State of the territory of another State, or any military occupation, however temporary, resulting from such invasion or attack, or any annexation by the use of force of the territory of another State or part thereof,
(b) Bombardment by the armed forces of a State against the territory of another State, or the use of any weapons by a State against the territory of another State;
(c) The blockade of the ports or coasts of a State by the armed forces of another State;
(d) An attack by the armed forces of a State on the land, sea or air forces, or marine and air fleets of another State;
(e) The use of armed forces of one State which are within the territory of another State with the agreement of the receiving State, in contravention of the conditions provided for in the agreement or any extension of their presence in such territory beyond the termination of the agreement;
(f) The action of a State in allowing its territory, which it has placed at the disposal of another State, to be used by that other State for perpetrating an act of aggression against a third State;
(g) The sending by or on behalf of a State of armed bands, groups, irregulars or mercenaries, which carry out acts of armed force against another State of such gravity as to amount to the acts listed above, or its substantial involvement therein.[17]

How, if at all, this definition impacts the invocation of individual or collective self-defense in response to threats or acts of terrorism is an extremely complex question.[18] This complexity is the result of several considerations. First, the

---

[16] *See* Case concerning Military and Paramilitary Activities in and against Nicaragua (Nicar. v. U.S.), 1986 I.C.J. 14, 195 (June 27) [hereinafter Nicaragua] (indicating that the definition of aggression annexed to the Resolution "may be taken to reflect customary international law").

[17] G.A. Res. 3314 (XXIX), *supra* note 14.

[18] *See* Resolution RC/Res.6, The Crime of Aggression, Adopted at the 13th plenary meeting, on 11 June 2010, by consensus (June 28, 2010), *available at* http://www.icc-cpi.int/iccdocs/asp_docs/Resolutions/RC-Res.6-ENG.pdf.

The recent adoption of a definition of aggression by the Review Conference of the Rome Statute of the International Criminal Court (held in Kampala, Uganda between May 31 and June 11, 2010) adds a potentially new dimension to this analysis. The amendment to Article 8 of the Rome Statute defines aggression as follows:

1. For the purpose of this Statute, "crime of aggression" means the planning, preparation, initiation or execution, by a person in a position effectively to exercise control over or to direct the political or military action of a State, of an act of aggression which, by its character, gravity and scale, constitutes a manifest violation of the Charter of the United Nations.

primary focus of the General Assembly Resolution is state action, and not the actions of transnational nonstate terrorist groups. In fact, it is highly unlikely that the drafters of the Resolution (or more precisely the definition of aggression annexed to the Resolution) seriously contemplated individual or collective response to transnational terrorist threats (much less the other emerging nonstate threats to states, such as organized criminal syndicates, cyber threats, and widespread piracy). Second, the Resolution itself indicates that the list is non-exhaustive, and that the Security Council may determine that other acts constitute aggression. How this impacts the right of individual states to also make such determinations is unclear, although it does seem to indicate that such a right may exist. Third, the acts listed *presumptively* but not *conclusively* qualify as aggression. None of these acts fall into that definition when committed pursuant to the inherent right of individual or collective self-defense, or pursuant to Security Council authorization. Because the United States engages in such conduct only pursuant to an assertion of such lawful authority, the validity of these assertions is central to assessing whether military action producing effects referenced in the Resolution are legally justified or beyond the scope of international legal authority.

Adding to this complexity is the simple reality that the terrorist attacks of September 11, 2001, created an entirely new category of controversy surrounding

---

> 2. For the purpose of paragraph 1, "act of aggression" means the use of armed force by a State against the sovereignty, territorial integrity or political independence of another State, or in any other manner inconsistent with the Charter of the United Nations. Any of the following acts, regardless of a declaration of war, shall, in accordance with United Nations General Assembly resolution 3314 (XXIX) of December 14, 1974 . . .

The Resolution then incorporates the list of acts constituting aggression contained in General Assembly Resolution 3341. *See id.* Assuming the amendment is ratified by the member states, it will not take effect until 2017. Furthermore, the Security Council will play a significant role in any prosecutorial effort. First, the Security Council retains primacy in determining when a state has been the victim of aggression, and may (as in the case of any other crime defined by the Statute) refer the matter to the ICC. However, the ICC prosecutor is vested with authority to initiate an investigation into an allegation of aggression either on her own initiative or in response to a request by a state party. In such situations, if the Security Council has not determined that the alleged incident qualifies as an act of aggression in a period of six months from the time of the request to initiate an investigation, the prosecutor must obtain authorization from the Court to proceed. The Security Council is authorized to block such an investigation, but doing so requires a Resolution (and therefore the agreement of all permanent members), which must be renewed annually. *Personam* jurisdiction extends only to nationals of a state party that has not opted out of the aggression amendment. *See* Julia Martínez Vivancos, *Questions & Answers on the Crime of Aggression Amendment Adopted at the ICC Review Conference in Kampala, Uganda*, The American Non-Governmental Organizations Coalition for the International Criminal Court (July 22, 2010), *available at* http://www.amicc.org/docs/AggressionQA.pdf.

The potential impact of this amendment on U.S. officials responsible for ordering the execution of counterterror military operations in the future seems too speculative to assess at this point. Even assuming the United States accedes to the treaty and therefore becomes subject to the jurisdiction of the Court, how the Security Council and/or prosecutor would interpret such operations is impossible to predict. Nonetheless, the incorporation by the amendment of the Resolution 3314 definition is an important endorsement of the significance of that definition.

the definition of aggression, the exercise of individual and collective self-defense, and the Security Council's power to authorize collective military action in response to the threat of transnational terrorism. How this controversy is impacted by the *jus ad bellum* is critical to the legitimacy and efficacy of the struggle against terrorism.

II. The U.N. Charter and the Right of Self-Defense

As noted above, the U.N. Charter established a per se prohibition against use of force as a means of achieving a national objective.[19] Article 2(4) of the Charter of the United Nations provides: "All Members shall refrain in their international relations from the threat or use of force against the territorial integrity or political independence of any state, or in any other manner inconsistent with the purposes of the United Nations."[20] Uses of force are, however, lawful when they fall into any of three exceptions to this per se prohibition. The first is consent from the state in which the military action occurs. The second exception is a collective security action authorized by the Security Council pursuant to Chapter VII of the Charter.[21] The third—recognized in Article 51 of the Charter—is use of force as an act of individual or collective self-defense.[22]

---

[19] For an excellent summary of the U.N. Charter's use-of-force legal framework, see INT'L & OPERATIONAL LAW DEP'T, THE JUDGE ADVOCATE GENERAL'S LEGAL CTR. & SCH., U.S. ARMY, OPERATIONAL LAW HANDBOOK ch. 1 (2007) [hereinafter HANDBOOK] (Legal Basis for the Use of Force); *see also* DINSTEIN, *supra* note 5 at 87–94.

[20] *See* U.N Charter art. 2, ¶ 4.

[21] Article 42 provides:

> Should the Security Council consider that measures provided for in Article 41 would be inadequate or have proved to be inadequate, it may take such action by air, sea, or land forces as may be necessary to maintain or restore international peace and security. Such action may include demonstrations, blockade, and other operations by air, sea, or land forces of Members of the United Nations.

Id. at art. 42.

[22] Article 51 provides:

> Nothing in the present Charter shall impair the inherent right of individual or collective self-defense if an armed attack occurs against a Member of the United Nations, until the Security Council has taken measures necessary to maintain international peace and security. Measures taken by Members in the exercise of this right of self-defense shall be immediately reported to the Security Council and shall not in any way affect the authority and responsibility of the Security Council under the present Charter to take at any time such action as it deems necessary in order to maintain or restore international peace and security.

Id. at art. 51.

A. CONSENT

Consent is a commonly utilized exception, and presents little definitional uncertainty. Since 1945, it has been common for states confronting internal and/or external threats to call upon other states to provide military support to their cause. Although less common, states have also consented to the armed intervention in their territory by a neighboring state responding to a nonstate threat emanating from the territory of the consenting state. For example, the United States conducted a punitive raid into Mexico in 1916 with the consent of the Carranza government in response to cross-border attacks by Pancho Villa's insurgent forces. In either situation, state consent renders the intervention consistent with Article 2(4) because it nullifies any assertion that the intervening state used military force "against" the intervened state's sovereignty.

Can consent be implied from lack of opposition to such an intervention? This issue was raised when Israel conducted a military intervention into Lebanon in 2006 for the purpose of degrading Hezbollah military capabilities. Neither Israel nor Lebanon characterized the intervention as an armed conflict between the two states, which created uncertainty as to whether the operation amounted to an act of aggression by Israel. From Israel's perspective, the failure of Lebanon to prevent attacks against Israel by Hezbollah justified a self-help military action pursuant to the inherent right of self-defense. However, it is easy to understand why other states might consider the intervention an impermissible act of aggression. In such a situation, how should the lack of opposition by the state in whose territory the intervention occurs factor into the analysis? Although it may be plausible to conclude that this is evidence of tacit recognition that the action is justified as an act of self-defense, it is difficult to reconcile a unilateral decision by one state to engage in combat operations in the territory of another state with valid implied consent. Nonetheless, the consequence of failing to object to such an action, either directly between the states or by seeking condemnation from the U.N. Security Council, may result in de facto, if not de jure consent.

Another complex issue related to a consent-based intervention is assessing the permissible scope of the intervening state's military action. In the domestic context, the scope of consent is either dictated by the consenting party or implied from the objective of the intrusion. Should an analogous approach be applied to consent-based interventions? It would seem that the ideal means of determining scope would take the form of an express agreement between the two states, with the consenting state defining the scope at the time of consent. However, this might not be a realistic expectation, especially because there may be significant political and diplomatic considerations that make the two states averse to any formal or explicit indication of consent. Ultimately, whether the actions of the intervening state are consistent with the consent granted by the territorial state will be a diplomatic matter between the two states.

B. SELF-DEFENSE AND THE USE OF FORCE AGAINST TERRORIST THREATS

Inter-state relations—or perhaps more precisely stated as inter-state disputes—have been the historic focal point of law and practice related to state uses of force outside their own territory. The text and drafting history of the Charter reflect this focus.[23] Accordingly, prior to September 11, 2001, state-generated threats to international peace and security dominated use-of-force legality analysis. However, over time nonstate threats have become increasingly relevant to this analysis. Today, these nonstate threats are considered, at least certainly by the United States, sufficient to justify invoking one of the Charter's two exceptions to the presumptive prohibition against the use of force.[24] Mass exodus of refugees across borders, internal armed conflicts, internal acts of genocide, crimes against humanity, and even impunity for violations of international law have provided the basis for Security Council invocation of collective action. Of equal significance, states affected by the threat of transnational terrorism and other external nonstate threats have increasingly asserted the inherent right of self-defense as a legal justification for military action directed against these threats.

This trend reflects the responsiveness of the *jus ad bellum* to the evolving perception of what constitutes a threat to international peace and stability. In the view of many experts, the right of self-defense and the authority for the Security Council to authorize collective security actions now extend to the threat to international peace and security resulting from transnational nonstate entities such as organized terrorist groups.[25] For the United States, this interpretation of the international legal authority to employ force in self-defense lies at the very foundation of the military component of ongoing U.S. military operations directed against transnational terrorists. This theory is reflected not only in the statements of both Presidents George W. Bush and Barack Obama, but also in congressional action—most notably, the Joint Resolution Authorizing the Use of Military Force enacted immediately after the terrorist attacks of September 11, 2001. In this Resolution, Congress noted:

> Whereas, on September 11, 2001, acts of treacherous violence were committed against the United States and its citizens; and
>
> Whereas, such acts render it both necessary and appropriate that the United States exercise its rights to self-defense and to protect United States citizens both at home and abroad; and
>
> Whereas, in light of the threat to the national security and foreign policy of the United States posed by these grave acts of violence; and

---

[23] *See History of the United Nations: Moscow and Teheran Conferences*, United Nations, http://www.un.org/en/aboutun /history/moscowteheran.shtml (last visited June 18, 2014).

[24] *See* President Obama, *supra* note 1.

[25] *See* Jeremy P. Sharp, Cong. Research Serv., RS21324, Congressional Action on Iraq 1990–2002 (2003).

> Whereas, such acts continue to pose an unusual and extraordinary threat to the national security and foreign policy of the United States; and
>
> Whereas, the President has authority under the Constitution to take action to deter and prevent acts of international terrorism against the United States.[26]

Unaltered since the date of enactment, the continuing reliance on this authorization by President Obama, and by the courts reviewing the legality of the government's exercise of wartime powers, is a clear indication that self-defense remains at the core of the U.S. counterterror policy. The Resolution, commonly referred to as the Authorization for Use of Military Force (AUMF), also provides the domestic legal basis for many of the U.S. counterterror operations.

A more complex question is whether there is widespread international support for this interpretation, and especially whether that support has been manifested at the U.N. Security Council. As noted above, the authority to use military force in pursuit of collective security may only be invoked pursuant to Chapter VII of the U.N. Charter. Article 41 of the Charter mandates as a predicate to such authorization a Security Council determination that there has been a breach of the peace, act of aggression, or threat to international peace and security.[27] Prior to the terror attacks of 9/11, the Security Council had expanded the range of international crises that fell within the scope of Article 41 (for example, humanitarian crises such as those that occurred in Kosovo and Somalia, or mass migrations such as was ongoing in Haiti in 1992). However, the threat of transnational terrorism had not up to that point been classified as a threat within the meaning of Article 41. It was therefore unclear in the wake of those attacks whether the Security Council would endorse military action under the umbrella of collective security, thereby providing authority to use force against the transnational terrorist threat consistently with the Charter's presumptive prohibition.

Many experts believe this uncertainty was eliminated when, on September 12, 2001, the Security Council passed Resolution 1368, which ostensibly reflected a Security Council determination that international terrorism qualified as a threat to international peace and security.[28] The Resolution emphasized member state intent "to combat by all means threats to international peace and security caused by terrorist acts."[29] It also recognized the right of individual and collective self-defense in response to acts of international terrorism, and expressed on behalf of the Security Council, "its readiness to take all necessary steps to respond to the terrorist attacks of 11 September 2001, and to combat all forms of terrorism."[30]

---

[26] S.J. Res. 23, 107th Cong. (2001) (enacted), *available at* http://www.gpo.gov/fdsys/pkg/PLAW-107publ243/html/PLAW-107publ243.htm.

[27] U.N. Charter art. 41.

[28] *See generally* S.C. Res. 1368, U.N. Doc. S/RES/1368 (Sept. 12, 2001).

[29] *Id.*

[30] *Id.* ¶ 5.

UNSCR 1368 did not, however, include the language historically associated with authorizations to use military force in response to a threat to international peace and security: that members states are authorized to use "all necessary means" to restore international peace and security. As a result, it is uncertain whether Resolution 1368 is properly interpreted as authorizing a collective military response to international terrorism.[31] However, the United States clearly viewed the Resolution as an endorsement of its assertion that the terrorist groups responsible for the September 11th attacks presented an ongoing threat to international peace and security justifying a collective military response. Furthermore, even conceding some uncertainty as to the overall meaning of this Resolution, there is no uncertainty that it indicated the attacks triggered the inherent right of individual and collective self-defense.

This latter conclusion was manifested in a number of ways. First, the United States was quite instrumental in bringing Resolution 1368 before the Security Council and in securing its adoption. More important, on October 7, 2001, Ambassador Negroponte, the U.S. Permanent Representative to the Security Council, submitted a letter to the Council President indicating that:[32]

> In accordance with Article 51 of the Charter of the United Nations, I wish, on behalf of my Government, to report that the United States of America, together with other States, has initiated actions in the exercise of its inherent right of individual and collective self-defense following armed attacks that were carried out against the United States on September 11, 2001.[33]

Negroponte also placed the Security Council on notice as to the use-of-force authority invoked by the United States derived from Article 51's right of individual and collective self-defense:

> In response to these attacks, and in accordance with the inherent right of individual and collective self-defense, United States armed forces have initiated actions designed to prevent and deter further attacks on the United States. These actions include measures against Al-Qaeda terrorist training camps and military installations of the Taliban regime in Afghanistan.[34]

The United States provided this notice in accordance with Article 51 of the Charter, which requires member states invoking the inherent right of self-defense to inform the Security Council of their action and the justification.[35] This notice was a clear and unambiguous assertion by the United States of the legal basis for

---

[31] *See* William Michael Reisman, *In Defense of World Public Order*, 95 Am. J. Int'l L. 833, xxx (2001).

[32] *See* Letter from John D. Negroponte to UN Security Council President (Oct. 7, 2001), *available at* http://www.bits.de/public/documents/US_Terrorist_Attacks/negroponte.htm.

[33] *Id.*

[34] *Id.*

[35] This requirement ostensibly enables the Security Council to effectively assume responsibility for the situation in an effort to restore international peace and security.

the forthcoming use of military force against the transnational terrorist threat.[36] Furthermore, no action to limit the exercise of self-defense or to assume responsibility for the military response followed this notification. Accordingly, not only does this letter clearly indicate the U.S. interpretation of its right to act in self-defense in response to the terror attacks of September 11th, it also suggests that other members of the Security Council accepted this interpretation (at least tacitly).

This is not to suggest that invoking the right of self-defense in response to international terrorism is without controversy. From the inception of the U.S. "War on Terror," many experts argued that the threat of international terrorism is insufficient to trigger a use of force pursuant to Article 51;[37] or that if terrorism is a threat to international peace and security, only the Security Council is authorized to address that threat. These positions reflect the traditional state-centric focus of self-defense, and the traditional military threats associated with that focus. International terrorist groups rarely conduct the type of sustained combat operations normally associated with state armed forces, or even organized insurgent groups.[38] According to many experts, this calls into question the validity of invoking military response authority normally justified only when confronting such a sustained military threat. Under this view, international terrorism has been and remains a form of international criminal activity to be addressed through cooperative law enforcement, and where necessary military support to law enforcement.

Even if we assume terrorism is a threat sufficient to justify resort to self-defense, another complicating factor related to the exercise of that right is assessing when a terrorist threat reaches a sufficient level of intensity. Article 51 does not define that trigger point with precision. However, because the article indicates that the right is triggered in response to an "armed attack," to resort to armed force self-defense has always been understood to require a situation of absolute self-help or of strict necessity. Even that language, however, has never been understood to require a state to wait until it has become an actual victim of an attack in order to act in self-defense. If the state is attacked, the right to respond in self-defense to prevent continuing or potentially future attacks is relatively clear. What has always been more difficult is determining at what point a state may act to preempt an imminent attack before it occurs.

The controversy surrounding preemptive self-defense certainly predates the threat of international terrorism. As a general proposition, the existence of an imminent threat has always marked the outer limit of self-defense authority.[39]

---

[36] U.N. Charter art. 51.

[37] Mary Ellen O'Connell, *The Myth of Pre-emptive Self-Defense*, ASIL Task Force on Terrorism (Aug. 2002), *available at* http://www.youscribe.com/catalogue/presentations/actualite-et-debat-de-societe/the-myth-of-preemptive-self-defense-358784

[38] *Id.*

[39] *See* Anthony C. Arend, *International Law and the Preemptive Use of Military Force*, 26 Wash. Q. 89, 91 (2003); Mark L. Rockefeller, *The "Iminent Threat" Requirement for the Use of Preemptive Military Force: Is It Time for a Non-temporal Standard?*, 33 Deny J. Int'l L. & Pol'y 131, 131 (2004).

The imminence requirement has also been understood to limit the legitimate invocation of self-defense authority so that it is consistent with the U.N. Charter's presumptive prohibition against using force. Accordingly, although preemptive self-defense has, and remains, an accepted principle in the use-of-force equation, extending self-defense beyond preemption into the realm of prevention has always been perceived as overbroad and legally invalid because it decouples self-defense from an imminence trigger.

The concept of imminence as it relates to the contemporary debate over the legitimate scope of self-defense is derived from a centuries-old incident involving a response by Canadian forces loyal to the British Crown against dissident forces seeking to achieve independence.[40] In 1837, dissident forces took refuge on an island in the Niagara River straddling the border between the United States and Canada. Canadian forces loyal to the Crown launched a raid against the dissident forces, captured a ship called the *Caroline* from them, and towed it back to a Canadian port where it was burned. The attack triggered a diplomatic dispute between the United States and the United Kingdom over the legality of the action.

The diplomatic dispute was ultimately resolved peacefully. The significance of the *Caroline* incident lies in the correspondence that provided the foundation for the resolution. In that correspondence, U.S. Secretary of State Daniel Webster articulated a series of elements justifying resort to anticipatory self-defense, elements that evolved to define the concept of imminent threat.[41] According to Webster, employing force for the purpose of self-defense in anticipation of an act of aggression is justified only when the threat is considered "instant, overwhelming, and leaving no choice of means, and no moment for deliberation."[42] This imminence framework has been almost universally accepted as the appropriate criteria for determining when anticipatory self-defense is legally permissible.

It was this line between preemption and prevention that proved increasingly controversial in the wake of the September 11th terrorist attacks, and continues to generate controversy to this day. Responding to an asserted new type of threat to the nation, President Bush began to articulate what later came to be characterized as the Bush doctrine of preemption.[43] As articulated in the 2002 U.S. National Security Strategy, the combination of terrorist capability and access to weapons of mass destruction necessitated a much more expansive conception of individual and collective self-defense. The United States asserted that the imperative of eliminating such threats, even when they might be in their nascent stage, was justified as an act of self-defense precisely because the opportunity to do so

---

[40] *See* Terence Taylor, *The End of Imminence?*, 27 Wash. Q. 57 (2004).

[41] Christopher Greenwood, *International Law and the Pre-emptive Use of Force: Afghanistan, Al-Qaeda, and Iraq*, San Diego Int'l L. J. 7, 12–13 (2003) (*quoting* letter from Daniel Webster to Henry S. Fox [British ambassador] of April 24, 1842).

[42] *Id.*

[43] President Bush spoke of "preemption" in a speech on combating terrorism given at West Point in May 2002. *See* Mike Allen & Karen DeYoung, *Bush: U.S. Will Strike First at Enemies; In West Point Speech, President Lays Out Broader U.S. Policy*, Wash. Post, June 2, 2002, at A01.

when the threat becomes imminent may be elusive or nonexistent.[44] Accordingly, the United States would invoke the inherent right of self-defense to justify resorting to military force to disable terrorist capabilities even before those capabilities manifested themselves in the form of an imminent attack.[45]

It is clear that the response to the terror attacks of September 11th, and what came to be known as the Bush doctrine of preemption, went beyond the *Caroline* imminence principles and called into question U.S. commitment to those principles. Many critics argued that this was nothing more than a subterfuge to provide legal sanction for preventive military action, an exercise of authority unjustified by the inherent right of self-defense and inconsistent with the U.N. Charter.[46] Others, including the Bush administration, took the position that the nature of the threat of terrorism required a more expansive interpretation of the concept of imminence.

President Obama appears to have adopted the view that the meaning of imminence must be contextually adjusted to deal with the threat of transnational terrorism. Although there is no use of the term "prevention," it is clear that President Obama has not abandoned the use of military force to attack terrorist operatives outside of the theater of active combat operations in Afghanistan and Iraq. In fact, it is well documented that his administration has significantly increased the number of such attacks, relying tactically on unmanned aerial vehicles (Predator drones) to execute these missions, and legally on the inherent right of self-defense in justification.[47] Whether characterized as preemption or prevention, the outcome seems consistent with the policies of President Bush: the United States will continue to invoke the right of self-defense to justify resort to military force to attack transnational terrorist targets.

President Obama's administration has, in fact, clarified the full scope of the authority asserted by the United States to use military force against the al Qaida threat. In a critically important speech on this subject, John O. Brennan, the Assistant to the President for Homeland Security and Counter Terrorism, explained that not only did the United States consider operations directed against al Qaida legally justified as acts of self-defense, but that these operations need not

---

[44] *See* President George W. Bush, *The National Security Strategy of the United States* (Sept. 2002), *available at* http://georgewbush-whitehouse.archives.gov/nsc/nss/2002/nss3.html.

[45] *Id.* This apparent modification of the trigger for exercising self-defense was widely condemned as invalid. Critics asserted that expanding the scope of self-defense to include preemptive action would open the door to acts of aggression cloaked in a disingenuous legal characterization. *See generally*, O'Connell, *supra* note 37; Lawrence J. Lee et al., *The Legality and Constitutionality of the President's Authority to Initiate an Invasion of Iraq*, 41 Colum. J. Transnat'l L. 15, 19 (2002). The degree of criticism generated by the Bush doctrine calls into question whether it significantly altered the traditional imminence requirement for resort to military force in self-defense or whether it will be treated as an aberration and not legally influential.

[46] *See* generally Mary Ellen O'Connell, *The Power & Purpose of International Law* (2008), at 146 (critiquing the doctrine of preemption).

[47] *See* Kenneth Anderson, *Predators over Pakistan*, The Weekly Standard, Mar. 8, 2010, *available at* http://www.weeklystandard.com/print/articles/predators-over-pakistan; *see also* Jane Mayer, *The Predator War*, The New Yorker, Oct. 26, 2009, *available at* http://www.newyorker.com/reporting/2009/10/26/091026fa_fact_mayer.

be confined to active operational zones. Brennan began the speech by emphasizing the continuing justification for self-defense action:

> Obviously, the death of Usama Bin Laden marked a strategic milestone in our effort to defeat al-Qa'ida. Unfortunately, Bin Laden's death, and the death and capture of many other al-Qa'ida leaders and operatives, does not mark the end of that terrorist organization or its efforts to attack the United States and other countries. Indeed, al-Qa'ida, its affiliates and its adherents remain the preeminent security threat to our nation.[48]

Brennan then addressed the scope and duration of self-defense action:

> First, our definition of the conflict. As the President has said many times, we are at war with al-Qa'ida. In an indisputable act of aggression, al-Qa'ida attacked our nation and killed nearly 3,000 innocent people. And as we were reminded just last weekend, al-Qa'ida seeks to attack us again. Our ongoing armed conflict with al-Qa'ida stems from our right—recognized under international law—to self-defense.
>
> An area in which there is some disagreement is the geographic scope of the conflict. The United States does not view our authority to use military force against al-Qa'ida as being restricted solely to "hot" battlefields like Afghanistan. Because we are engaged in an armed conflict with al-Qa'ida, the United States takes the legal position that—in accordance with international law—we have the authority to take action against al-Qa'ida and its associated forces without doing a separate self-defense analysis each time. And as President Obama has stated on numerous occasions, we reserve the right to take unilateral action if or when other governments are unwilling or unable to take the necessary actions themselves. [49]

Finally, Brennan emphasized that although these operations may appear to be a continuing manifestation of what was characterized during the Bush era as preventive war, what they in fact indicate is an evolving and contextual definition of imminence:

> We are finding increasing recognition in the international community that a more flexible understanding of "imminence" may be appropriate when dealing with terrorist groups, in part because threats posed by non-state actors do not present themselves in the ways that evidenced imminence in more traditional conflicts. After all, al-Qa'ida does not follow a traditional command structure, wear uniforms, carry its arms openly, or mass its troops at

---

[48] John O. Brennan, Assistant to the President for Homeland Security and Counterterrorism, Remarks at Harvard Law School Program on Law and Security, Strengthening Our Security by Adhering to Our Values and Laws (Sept. 16, 2011), *available at* http://www.whitehouse.gov/the-press-office/2011/09/16/remarks-john-o-brennan-strengthening-our-security-adhering-our-values-an [hereinafter Brennan Remarks at Harvard].

[49] *Id.*

> the borders of the nations it attacks. Nonetheless, it possesses the demonstrated capability to strike with little notice and cause significant civilian or military casualties. Over time, an increasing number of our international counterterrorism partners have begun to recognize that the traditional conception of what constitutes an "imminent" attack should be broadened in light of the modern-day capabilities, techniques, and technological innovations of terrorist organizations.[50]

As Brennan noted, the United States is not alone in its interpretation that terrorism is a threat of sufficient magnitude to trigger the right to self-defense, although as Brennan acknowledged in his speech, there is little consensus on the legitimate scope of self-defense authority:

> Others in the international community—including some of our closest allies and partners—take a different view of the geographic scope of the conflict, limiting it only to the "hot" battlefields. As such, they argue that, outside of these two active theatres, the United States can only act in self-defense against al-Qa'ida when they are planning, engaging in, or threatening an armed attack against U.S. interests if it amounts to an "imminent" threat. [51]

Although Brennan is indeed correct that there remains significant division on the permissible scope of counterterror military operations, it has become increasingly accepted that in at least some situations transnational terrorism does trigger the right of self-defense. Indeed, the first indication of broad consensus on this interpretation emerged immediately following the September 11th attacks. NATO's collective response to the attacks provides a particularly significant indication of this support. On September 12, 2001, the North Atlantic Council invoked, for the first time in its history, Article 5 of the NATO treaty, authorizing member states to act in the collective self-defense of the United States.[52] There can be little doubt that this invocation was based on a consensus among the alliance members that the terror attacks qualified as an act of aggression, the sole trigger for invoking Article 5.[53]

---

[50] *Id.*

[51] *Id.*

[52] *See Collective Defense*, NATO, http://www.nato.int/cps/en/SID-85648058-8934EDC9/natolive/topics_59378.htm (last visited Sept. 19, 2012).

[53] Article 5 states:

> The Parties agree that an armed attack against one or more of them in Europe or North America shall be considered an attack against them all and consequently they agree that, if such an armed attack occurs, each of them, in exercise of the right of individual or collective self-defence recognized by Article 51 of the Charter of the United Nations, will assist the Party or Parties so attacked by taking forthwith, individually and in concert with the other Parties, such action as it deems necessary, including the use of armed force, to restore and maintain the security of the North Atlantic area. Any such armed attack and all measures taken as a result thereof shall immediately be reported to the Security Council. Such measures shall be terminated when the Security Council has taken the measures necessary to restore and maintain international peace and security.

The North Atlantic Treaty, art. 5 (Apr. 4, 1949), *available at* http://www.nato.int/cps/en/natolive/official_texts_17120.htm.

It is possible that at the time of this invocation the NATO member states assumed the attacks were executed by a state, thereby diluting the significance of this action in terms of the relationship among terrorism, aggression, and self-defense. This, however, seems unlikely. Even on that early date, it was widely assumed the United States was the victim of terrorist attacks. Even conceding that such uncertainty existed on September 12th, the fact remains that NATO made no effort to repeal or modify its invocation as transnational terrorist responsibility for the attacks became clear in the days and weeks that followed. Accordingly, NATO's action stands as an important milestone not only in the history of the alliance, but also in the evolution of the *jus ad bellum*.

Nor have the two post-September 11th Presidents been solely responsible for this invocation of the inherent right of self-defense. In the 2001 Authorization for the Use of Military Force, a Joint Resolution overwhelmingly passed by Congress and a law that remains in effect to this day, Congress noted that the terrorist attacks of September 11th "render it both necessary and appropriate that the United States exercise its rights to self-defense. . . ."[54] The Resolution also provides:

> That the President is authorized to use all necessary and appropriate force against those nations, organizations, or persons he determines planned, authorized, committed, or aided the terrorist attacks that occurred on September 11, 2001, or harbored such organizations or persons, in order to prevent any future acts of international terrorism against the United States by such nations, organizations or persons.[55]

This Resolution leaves absolutely no doubt about the interpretation of international law at the core of the U.S. struggle against transnational terrorism. Congress, the President who signed the Resolution into law, and his successor who continues to rely on it to justify targeting, detaining, and trying terrorist operatives, all believe transnational terrorism justifies a legal right to use military force in self-defense.

All of this indicates one indisputable fact: for U.S. armed forces, the inherent right of self-defense has been central to the ongoing use of combat power to disable or destroy al Qaida terrorist networks, whether in Afghanistan or other countries. Furthermore, the scope of these operations, which have been ongoing for more than a decade, demonstrate the theory articulated by Brennan: that the very nature of terrorism requires a contextual modification to the concept of imminence.[56] The long-term impact on international law of this U.S. interpretation of the right of self-defense is unclear. It does seem clear, however, that as states

---

[54] Authorization for the Use of Military Force, Pub. L. 107–40, 115 Stat. 224 (2001) [hereinafter AUMF].

[55] *Id.*

[56] *See* Brennan Remarks at Harvard, *supra* note 48.

continue to invoke self-defense in response to transnational terrorism, it will be increasingly difficult to condemn such actions as violations of international law.

C. THE "UNABLE OR UNWILLING" FACTOR

Once the United States characterized the struggle against transnational terrorism as an armed conflict, it raised the prospect of identifying, and neutralizing, terrorist operatives in locations not experiencing ongoing ground combat operations: Somalia, for example versus Afghanistan, or Iraq prior to cessation of combat activities the end of 2011 in the latter. In the decade following September 11th, and especially during President Obama's tenure, this extension of combat operations outside of combat zones became more frequent.[57] Combined with the capability provided by remotely piloted aircraft (drones), this resulted in an increasingly common practice of attacking these operatives in the territory of states not engaged in armed conflict with the United States, even when there was no indication of consent for the attacks.

The Obama administration's position is that these attacks are justified as an exercise of the inherent right of self-defense, a position not unlike that of the Bush administration. However, President Obama added another element to the legal analysis for these attacks: the "unable or unwilling" test: even absent consent, the United States may act in self-defense when a terrorist threat is identified in the territory of another state and that state is unable or unwilling to address the threat. This position was emphasized by Attorney General Eric Holder:

> International legal principles, including respect for another nation's sovereignty, constrain our ability to act unilaterally. But the use of force in foreign territory would be consistent with these international legal principles if conducted, for example, with the consent of the nation involved—or after a determination that the nation is unable or unwilling to deal effectively with a threat to the United States.[58]

A number of international legal experts contest the validity of this use-of-force theory, asserting that absent consent, actions such as the raid that killed bin Laden violate international law. There is now, however, clear evidence that the United States rejects such a reading of international law, and has and will continue to assert the legal authority to act in self-defense against nonstate threats located in the territory of another sovereign. Harvard Professor Jack Goldsmith, the former Director of the Office of Legal Counsel in the Department of Justice credited with reversing many of the overreaching legal opinions that first emerged from that

---

[57] Mark V. Vlasic, *Assassination & Targeted Killing—A Historical and Post-Bin Laden Legal Analysis*, 43 Geo. J. Int'l L. 259, 291 (2012).

[58] Attorney General Eric Holder, Remarks at Northwestern University School of Law (Mar. 5, 2012), [hereinafter General Holder], *available at* http://www.justice.gov/iso/opa/ag/speeches/2012/ag-speech-1203051.html.

office following September 11th, emphasized this point in 2012. According to his editorial on law and targeting terrorists, targeted killings:

> are consistent with the U.N. Charter's ban on using force "against the territorial integrity or political independence of any state" only if the targeted nation consents or the United States properly acts in self-defense. There are reports that Yemen consented to the strike on Awlaki. But even if it did not, the strike would still have been consistent with the Charter to the extent that Yemen was "unwilling or unable" to suppress the threat he posed. This standard is not settled in international law, but it is sufficiently grounded in law and practice that no American president charged with keeping the country safe could refuse to exercise international self-defense rights when presented with a concrete security threat in this situation. The "unwilling or unable" standard was almost certainly the one the United States relied on in the Osama bin Laden raid inside Pakistan.[59]

How the "unable or unwilling" assessment is made remains unclear.[60] The most that can be derived from the statements of the Obama administration is that this is an executive branch determination related to all uses of force in the territory of another sovereign.[61]

Objections to this theory of legality are understandable. Allowing one state to decide that another state is unable to prevent a threat from materializing from its territory is an exercise of self-help that seems inconsistent with the U.N. Charter principle that states "resolve disputes peacefully."[62] If a state, such as the United States, believes another state is unable or unwilling to prevent its territory from being used as a staging base for terrorist attacks, one solution would be to bring the matter to the attention of the Security Council. Should the Council agree with such an assertion, it would certainly qualify as a threat to international peace and security, thus triggering the Council's collective security powers. In the alternative, if the threatened state concludes the threat is imminent, requiring

---

[59] Jack Goldsmith, *Fire When Ready*, Foreign Policy (Mar. 19, 2012), http://www.foreignpolicy.com/articles/2012/03/19/fire_when_ready.

[60] Ashley S. Deeks, *"Unwilling or Unable": Toward a Normative Framework for Extraterritorial Self-Defense*, 52 Va. J. Int'l L. 483, 486–88 (2012). This theory of legal justification for using military force in the territory of another state was relied on in earlier contexts, such as the 1970 U.S. military incursion into Cambodia in response to North Vietnamese use of that nation's territory as a base of operations. In a 1989 speech at the U.S. Army Judge Advocate General's School, this theory was cited as a legal basis to conduct military operations in the territory of another nation in response to an imminent or ongoing threat of terrorist attacks. *See* Abraham Sofaer, *Terrorism, the Law, and National Self-Defense*, 126 Mil. L. Rev. 86, 106–09 (1989).

[61] There is an ongoing debate concerning the obligation of the Executive to disclose their methodology for making this determination. *See, e.g.*, Am. Civil Liberties Union v. Dep't of Justice, 808 F. Supp. 2d 280 (D.D.C. 2011), *overruled by* Am. Civil Liberties Union v. Cent. Intelligence Agency, 710 F.3d 422 (D.C. Cir. 2013) (holding that the CIA was not required to disclose information pursuant to a FOIA request pertaining to drone strikes because it fell within the exemption for information subject to executive order to be kept secret in the interest of national defense or foreign policy).

[62] U.N. Charter art. 33.

immediate self-help action, it could attribute responsibility for the terrorist activity to the locus state.

Both of these approaches, however, present negative consequences. Referring a matter to the Security Council would indeed avert a unilateral exercise of self-help. In reality, such a referral might compromise the operational effectiveness of action against the terrorist target by either tipping off the target and/or providing time to react to the exposure to attack. For the United States, it appears the ability to exploit a window of opportunity is viewed as too valuable to forgo in the interest of collective security response. Attributing the terrorist threat to the locus state as an alternative is diplomatically charged. In some cases, this might be justified by the totality of the intelligence related to the threat. This was clearly the foundation for U.S. and Coalition action against the Taliban in 2001.[63] However, in many other cases, the United States (or other states) will likely conclude that the terrorist group is exploiting the territory of another state without indication of state sponsorship. Attributing the terrorist presence to that state could therefore be perceived as inconsistent with objective facts and with diplomatic interests.

III. What Type of Response Is Proportional?

Once the right of self-defense is invoked, ensuring the military response to the threat is proportional is an important element of the legitimate exercise of that right.[64] States resorting to military force in response to an actual or imminent threat are obligated to use only the amount of force required to restore the status quo of peace and security.[65] The purpose of this proportionality requirement is clear: to prevent states from transforming a legitimate self-defense response into an act of aggression by exceeding the protective objective of the response.

Like the imminence requirement, there has never been a clear consensus on how to define the proportionality element of a valid exercise of self-defense. The responding state or states are responsible for balancing their legitimate self-defense need with the limited lawful purpose of the action. If the use of force system operates ideally, the U.N. Security Council will intervene promptly to assume responsibility for restoring international peace and security. However, in practice this has rarely been the pattern regarding self-defense actions. Instead, states have been left to assess the permissible scope of military action and resolve disputes related to exceeding that scope diplomatically. Each exercise of self-defense since 1945 has accordingly contributed to a body of practice that adds substance to the parameters of the proportionality element.

---

[63] *See U.S. Focus in Afghanistan is on al Qaeda, Negropante Says*, U.S. EMBASSY—ISRAEL (July 19, 2002), http://www.usembassy-israel.org.il/publish/peace/archives/2002/july/072004.html.

[64] *See* DINSTEIN, *supra* note 5, at 192–208.

[65] *Id.* at 208–12.

The response to transnational terrorism adds a new layer of complexity to self-defense proportionality analysis. For example, some experts question the proportionality of the invasion of Afghanistan to oust the Taliban regime in response to the September 11th attacks. However, the fact that a substantial number of nations committed forces in support of this objective provides significant evidence in support of the conclusion that this military response was widely considered to be consistent with the proportionality requirement.[66] The use of military strikes against terrorist operatives outside of Afghanistan (especially drone attacks) raises a far more complicated issue of proportionality. However, the primary debate surrounding these attacks relates to the predicate issue of whether invocation of the right of self-defense can even extend to such operatives.[67]

IV. When is the Right to Self-Defense Exhausted?

Another particularly difficult issue in relation to self-defense action is determining when that authority terminates. Article 51 of the U.N. Charter suggests that resort to self-defense, either individual or collective, should be understood as a temporary expedient pending intervention of the Security Council exercising its primary responsibility to maintain international peace and security.[68] Unfortunately, as noted above, practice is rarely consistent with this ideal distribution of authority over the use of military force. Instead, exercises of the right of self-defense have often been met by Security Council inaction, leaving the responding state or states to make their own determination of when the status quo ante has been restored and the authority of self-defense has terminated.

Determining the expiration date of a self-defense action has never been simple. Furthermore, determining the point at which an aggressive threat has been neutralized has always been easier when dealing with the conventional state threat then when dealing with unconventional nonstate threats. Characterizing transnational terror networks as armed groups triggering the inherent right of self-defense has made this determination even more complicated. The U.S. self-proclaimed "War on Terror" is now the longest war in the nation's history, with no clear end in sight. Indeed, the U.S. Supreme Court in its *Boumediene* decision suggested that individuals captured during the course of this conflict face a genuine prospect of "generational" detention.[69]

Identifying the point in time when the authority to take military action based on the inherent right of self-defense terminates is obviously critical in relation to the legal rights and obligations triggered by that authority. In the absence of Security Council action to assume responsibility for responding to the threat

---

[66] *See* U.N. Charter art. 51; *see also* Dinstein, *supra* note 5 at 192–208.
[67] *See* O'Connell, *supra* note 37, at 9–11.
[68] *See* U.N. Charter art. 51.
[69] Boumediene v. Bush, 553 U.S. 723 (2008).

that triggered the individual or collective self-defense response, it seems difficult to avoid the reality that the responding state is ultimately entrusted with the responsibility to determine when that authority terminates. This in fact may be one of the reasons there is such widespread hostility to the notion of treating transnational terrorism as a threat justifying resort to self-defense; unlike more traditional military threats, the difficulty in determining when the threat has been neutralized produces an almost inevitable indefinite source of authority to use military force.

The right of self-defense is not, however, an indefinite source of authority. The underlying premise justifying resort to military force as a measure of self-defense is one based on pure necessity.[70] Doing so operates to restore an environment of international peace and security. Accordingly, the use of force employed pursuant to this authority is justified only so long as it is necessary to protect the state from the triggering threat; once that threat is neutralized, the state is obligated to cease military action.

Of course, this raises the difficult question of how a state is to judge when the threat of a highly dispersed transnational terrorist group has been defeated or degraded sufficiently to terminate the necessity for using military force. There is no clear answer to this question. To date, states such as the United States and Israel appear to be treating the threat of transnational terrorism as an ongoing one, with no viable end state or termination point. Indeed, the inability of the state to determine with any degree of precision when its actions have eliminated the threat of terrorism is a significant factor relied on by critics of characterizing terrorism as a trigger for the right of self-defense.[71] For these critics the very nature of terrorism falls outside this triggering category precisely because terrorism defies the traditional methods by which armed opponents are brought into submission. Nonetheless, so long as states continue to invoke the inherent right of self-defense in response to the threat of terrorism, the question of when action in self-defense is no longer justified by virtue of the disabling effect of their military response will remain critical.

V. Collective Security in Response to the Threat of Transnational Terrorism

Security Council Authorization pursuant to Chapter VII of the United Nations Charter could provide an alternate legal basis to use force against the threat of international terrorism.[72] Should the Security Council determine that a terrorist entity constituted a threat to international peace and security, and that peaceful

---

[70] U.N. Charter art. 51.

[71] *See* O'Connell, *supra* note 37, at 9–11 (explaining that self-defense may be used if there is clear and convincing evidence that the enemy will attack again).

[72] *See* U.N. Charter art. 39.

measures would be ineffective in responding to such threat, the Council could authorize member states to employ military force for the purpose of defeating the threat for the purpose of restoring international peace and security.[73] Although the collective security mechanism of the U.N. Charter was originally conceived to respond to threats to international peace and security resulting from the actions of states, it is today a reality that threats created by nonstate entities are considered sufficient to trigger this Security Council authority.

Although the Security Council routinely condemns international terrorism, and has authorized peaceful means (such as asset seizures) to combat terrorism, it has not to date authorized collective military action in response to an international terrorism threat. The Security Council Resolution passed immediately following the terrorist attacks of September 11, 2001, although acknowledging the inherent right of self-defense in response to those attacks, did not authorize collective action against al Qaida or any other terrorist entity.[74] In fact, at least one distinguished scholar has challenged the interpretation that this Resolution authorized any type of military response to terrorism.[75] Indeed, it is difficult to conclude with certainty that even the acknowledgment of the Article 51 right of self-defense contained within that Resolution permitted military action against transnational terrorist organizations. Instead, it is plausible that the reference to the inherent right of self-defense was focused not on such nonstate threats, but instead on the state (Afghanistan) that harbored and sponsored this terrorist threat.[76]

---

[73] *Id.* at arts. 40–41.

[74] *See* S.C. Res.1368, U.N. Doc. S/RES/1368 (Sept. 12, 2001).

[75] *See, e.g.*, William Michael Reisman, *International Legal Responses to Terrorism*, 22 Hous. J. Int'l L. 3, 51–54 (1999).

[76] Security Council Resolution 1368 states:

> *The Security Council,*
>
> *Reaffirming* the principles and purposes of the Charter of the United Nations,
>
> *Determined* to combat by all means threats to international peace and security caused by terrorist acts,
>
> *Recognizing* the inherent right of individual or collective self-defense in accordance with the Charter,
>
> 1. *Unequivocally condemns* in the strongest terms the horrifying terrorist attacks which took place on September 11, 2001 in New York, Washington, D.C. and Pennsylvania and *regards* such acts, like any act of international terrorism, as a threat to international peace and security;
> 2. *Expresses* its deepest sympathy and condolences to the victims and their families and to the people and Government of the United States of America;
> 3. *Calls* on all States to work together urgently to bring to justice the perpetrators, organizers and sponsors of these terrorist attacks and *stresses* that those responsible for aiding, supporting or harbouring the perpetrators, organizers and sponsors of these acts will be held accountable;
> 4. *Calls also* on the international community to redouble their efforts to prevent and suppress terrorist acts including by increased cooperation and full implementation of the relevant international anti-terrorist conventions and Security Council resolutions, in particular resolution 1269 (1999) of 19 October 1999;

Confining either collective security efforts or the exercise of state self-defense to those states responsible for providing safe haven or sponsorship to transnational terrorist organizations is certainly less controversial than applying both of those authorities to the terrorist organizations themselves. Consistent with well-established principles of state responsibility, terrorist attacks emanating from the state of sponsorship can appropriately be attributed to the sponsoring state for purposes of both collective security and inherent self-defense. The United States did not, however, view UNSCR 1368 in such limited terms. Nonetheless, even an expansive or liberal reading of that resolution does not support the conclusion that it represented a Chapter VII authorization for collective security action by the community of nations.

Although the Security Council has yet to invoke the collective security mechanism of the Charter to authorize military action in response to transnational terrorism, doing so might offer certain advantages over simply acknowledging the inherent right of self-defense. By submitting the response authority to the judgment of the Security Council, the members of the Council would be in a position not only to determine when the terrorist threat justified resort to military action, but also the legitimate scope and duration of such action. This remains, however, an unlikely course of action, precisely because of the uncertainty created by the nature of the transnational terrorist threat, and whether such a threat is properly considered the object of collective security military action.

Can the actions of transnational terrorist groups qualify as aggression within the meaning of international law? This is a vexing question, and one with no clear consensus. From the U.S. perspective, the answer is clearly yes, although this is not a view that garners widespread international support, at least not overt support. From an international legal perspective, two sources of authority are particularly relevant to such assessment: the decision by the International Court of Justice (ICJ) in the case of *Nicaragua v. United States*, and the U.N. General Assembly Resolution defining aggression. Although neither of these sources are binding on states or on the U.N. Security Council, the analytical methodology they reflect are widely regarded as authoritative on assessing aggression and the accordant legitimacy of a self-defense response, and therefore serve as important guideposts.

The ICJ's *Nicaragua* opinion arose out of Nicaragua's allegation that the United States had, inter alia, engaged in illegal aggression by mining Nicaraguan harbors, conducting sabotage missions against Nicaraguan ports, oil installations, and a naval base; and provided ongoing support to the Contras, an internal dissident group challenging the Sandanista government.[77] The United States

---

5. *Expresses* its readiness to take all necessary steps to respond to the terrorist attacks of September 11, 2001, and to combat all forms of terrorism, in accordance with its responsibilities under the Charter of the United Nations;
6. *Decides* to remain seized of the matter.

S.C. Res.1368, U.N. Doc. S/RES/1368 (Sept. 12, 2001).

[77] Nicaragua, *supra* note 16, at ¶ 114

challenged the jurisdiction of the Court to hear the case brought against it by Nicaragua. When the Court rejected this challenge, the United States terminated participation in the proceedings. Prior to doing so, however, the United States asserted its conduct in Nicaragua was legally justified as an act of collective self-defense in support of El Salvador.[78] This theory was premised on an assertion that Nicaragua's support for the leftist insurgents in El Salvador amounted to unlawful aggression against that neighboring state, and therefore pursuant to Article 51 of the U.N. Charter, the United States acted legally when it engaged in conduct directed against Nicaragua for the purpose of assisting in the defense of El Salvador.[79]

After determining that the United States was in fact responsible for laying mines and the alleged acts of sabotage, the ICJ ruled that these actions did amount to aggression in violation of customary international law.[80] However, what is more significant in relation to assessing the impact of nonstate terrorist actions directed against state interests was the Court's analysis of the relationship between state sponsorship of nonstate dissident forces (in this case the Contra insurgents sponsored by the United States) and the definition of aggression triggering the right of individual and collective self-defense. First, the Court concluded that:

> [i]t may be considered to be agreed that an armed attack must be understood as including not merely action by regular armed forces across an international border, but also "sending by or on behalf of a State of armed bands, groups, irregulars or mercenaries, which carry out acts of armed force against another State of such gravity as to amount to (*inter alia*) an actual armed attack conducted by regular forces, 'or substantial involvement therein.'"[81]

Accordingly, the decision supports the invocation of the inherent right of self-defense in response to an act of aggression by both regular armed forces of another state *and* paramilitary forces acting as an agent or on behalf of a state.[82] Extending this concept to the United States and Coalition attack against Afghanistan following the September 11th attacks therefore supports the conclusion that this action qualified as legitimate self-defense, as Afghanistan bore state responsibility for the conduct of the al Qaida. Furthermore, although the decision did not address the relationship between nonstate paramilitary activities and the inherent right of self-defense, the fact that the Court concluded military action by paramilitary forces can qualify as aggression bolsters the U.S. theory of self-defense in response to the attacks of September 11th.[83]

---

[78] *Id.* at ¶ 229. *See also* Leslie Rose, *U.S. Bombing of Afghanistan Not Justified as Self-Defense under International Law*, 59 Guild Prac. 65, 66–67 (2002).

[79] *See* Nicaragua, *supra* note 16, at ¶ 210.

[80] *Id.* ¶ 211, 227.

[81] *Id.* ¶ 195.

[82] *Id.* ¶ 176, 195–199.

[83] *Id.* ¶ 242.

The Court also addressed the level of state sponsorship of paramilitary activities necessary for the attribution of those activities to the state. This issue was relevant to both the assertion that the United States had committed acts of aggression against Nicaragua (by supporting the Contras), and the assertion that armed activities against Nicaragua directed or supported by the United States were justified as collective self-defense in response to Nicaraguan aggression toward El Salvador (by supporting the Farabundo Martí National Liberation Front (FMLN) leftist insurgents in El Salvador). The Court concluded that it:

> . . . does not believe that the concept of "armed attack" includes not only acts by armed bands where such acts occur on a significant scale but also assistance to rebels in the form of the provision of weapons or logistical or other support. Such assistance may be regarded as a threat or use of force, or amount to intervention in the internal or external affairs of other States.[84]

Thus, the Court drew a demarcation line between the use of paramilitary (or irregular) forces as a state proxy, with their hostilities effectively directed by the state, and the provision of logistical (including military logistics such as weapons and ammunition) to such forces. According to the Court, only the former category qualified as aggression triggering the inherent right of individual and collective self-defense.[85]

Based on this demarcation, the Court ruled that U.S. support for the Contras rose to the level of aggression, because this support included "organizing or encouraging the organization of irregular forces or armed bands . . . for incursion into the territory of another state."[86] In contrast, the Court rejected the assertion that Nicaraguan support for the FMLN in El Salvador qualified as an act of aggression because it was instead logistical.[87] Specifically, the Court found that:

> . . . between July 1979 and the early months of 1981, an intermittent flow of arms was routed via the territory of Nicaragua to the armed opposition in that country. The Court was not however satisfied that assistance has reached the Salvadorian armed opposition, on a scale of any significance, since the early months of 1981, or that the Government of Nicaragua was responsible for any flow of arms at either period. Even assuming that the supply of arms to the opposition in El Salvador could be treated as imputable to the Government of Nicaragua, to justify invocation of the right of collective self-defence in customary international law, it would have to be equated with an armed attack by Nicaragua on El Salvador.[88]

The ICJ's analysis focused exclusively on state sponsorship of paramilitary or irregular forces and how that sponsorship triggers the right of self-defense.

---

[84] *Id.* ¶ 195.
[85] Nicaragua, *supra* note 16, ¶ 195.
[86] *Id.* ¶ 228.
[87] *Id.* ¶ 230.
[88] *Id.* ¶ 230.

However, it must be considered instructive on the response to acts of violence by transnational terrorist groups. The Court's decision arguably establishes a criterion for determining what level of state sponsorship and support justifies attribution of terrorist violence to the state. If this is true, any state invoking the inherent right of self-defense to use force against another state based on a sponsorship theory—such as the international use of force against Afghanistan based on al Qaida sponsorship—must establish support more analogous to command and control than simply logistics. This is obviously a significant consideration for states such as Israel that face a continuing threat of terrorist violence facilitated by support from other states, such as Iran. What is less certain is how the nature of the support provided, and/or the organization supported, should impact this analysis. Specifically, would the provision of such support qualify as aggression if the weapons provided the capability to inflict mass destruction? Although the ICJ's opinion did not include any such qualifier, because those facts were not before the Court, such distinctions provide states facing such threats with a legitimate basis to distinguish state sponsorship of terrorism from other types of threats.

The *Nicaragua* decision also has potential significance in relation to the contemporary U.S. practice of drone attacks directed against suspected terrorist operatives outside of an area of traditional combat operations. The decision provides a useful template for assessing when terrorist actions are belligerent in nature, thereby providing a basis for asserting the right of self-defense to engage in such attacks.[89] The distinction between general logistical support and operational command and control of irregular forces arguably bolsters the U.S. view that attacking individuals in the operational chain of command is justified because they qualify as belligerent operatives. The significance of this command and control role in the legality analysis related to a decision to attack terrorist operatives with deadly force outside the area of traditional combat operations was emphasized by Attorney General Holder:

> Let me be clear: an operation using lethal force in a foreign country, targeted against a U.S. citizen who is a senior operational leader of al Qa'ida or associated forces, and who is actively engaged in planning to kill Americans, would be lawful at least in the following circumstances: First, the U.S. government has determined, after a thorough and careful review, that the individual poses an imminent threat of violent attack against the United States; second, capture is not feasible; and third, the operation would be conducted in a manner consistent with applicable law of war principles.[90]

Although this analysis related specifically to an attack against a U.S. citizen, the emphasis on the operational command and control function seems consistent with the ICJ's view of conduct that qualifies as aggression. However, it also calls

---

[89] *Id* ¶ 195.

[90] *See* General Holder, *supra* note 58.

into serious question the legality of directing such attacks against individuals providing logistical support to terrorist operatives, such as financiers and terrorist recruiters. Although not directly on point, the line between logistics and command and control—what Major General Charles Dunlap called "the kill chain"—seems an important factor for both assessing when activities of nonstate groups qualify as aggression and when individuals associated with such groups are lawfully subject to deliberate attack, particularly outside of an armed conflict.[91]

Another aspect of the *Nicaragua* decision with potential significance for future U.S. counterterror efforts was the Court's response to the U.S. invocation of the right of collective self-defense. Although the Court acknowledged that customary international law recognizes the right of collective self-defense, it rejected the U.S. invocation of that right. This rejection was based not only on the determination that Nicaraguan support for the FMLN did not rise to the level of aggression, but also on its conclusion that El Salvador had never itself invoked the right of self-defense against Nicaragua. In essence, the Court concluded that a state cannot assert collective self-defense unless and until the protected victim state invokes that right itself.[92]

This limitation on invoking the right of collective self-defense could become significant if, in the future, the United States believes a terrorist group is threatening the stability of another state. In such a situation, it would be difficult to sustain a claim of collective self-defense to use force against that group unless the state being assisted requested that assistance. Of course, such a request would operate as consent for the military intervention, which would render irrelevant any concerns implicated by this aspect of the *Nicaragua* decision. However, it is also plausible that the United States will view the destabilizing terrorist activity as a threat not only to the state where the group is located, but also to the United States itself. In such a situation, the intersection of collective self-defense and U.S. national self-defense presents one of the most complex use-of-force legality dilemmas in contemporary practice.

VI. The *Wall* and *Uganda* Decisions: The International Court of Justice's Rejection of Terrorism as a Self-Defense Trigger

Although it is clear that the United States, as well as a number of other states impacted by the threat of transnational terrorism, consider this threat sufficient to trigger the inherent right of self-defense, the ICJ seems to have rejected this interpretation of Article 51.[93] In its decision on the legality of Israel's construction

---

[91] Brigadier General Charles J. Dunlap Jr., *The Role of the Lawyer in War: It Ain't No TV Show: JAGs and Modern Military Operations*, 4 Chi. J. Int'l L. 479, 483 (2003).

[92] *See* Nicaragua 1986 I.C.J. at ¶¶ 222–223.

[93] Barry A. Feinstein & Justus Reid Weiner, *Israel's Security Barrier: An International Comparative Analysis and Legal Evaluation*, 37 Geo. Wash. Int'l L. Rev. 309, 384–88 (2005) (discussing the United States' perspective of Israel's security barrier. Also discussing numerous

of a barrier wall between Israel and Palestinian-populated areas of the West Bank, the ICJ considered and rejected Israel's assertion that the wall was a justified measure of self-defense in response to widespread terrorist attacks launched from the occupied territories.[94] The Israeli High Court of Justice had already considered this same issue and concluded that the wall was in fact a legitimate exercise of the inherent right of self-defense, and a necessary and proportional response to the nonstate terrorist threat plaguing Israel.[95] The ICJ reached a radically different conclusion.

The ICJ never reached the issues of necessity or proportionality because it rejected the predicate invocation of the right of self-defense. According to the Court, a state could invoke this right only in response to an external threat: a threat emanating from another state.[96] Because the nonstate threat of terrorist activity asserted by Israel as the justification for its self-defense action emanated from within its occupied territories, the Court concluded Israel had no international legal right for this action.[97]

One dissenting justice criticized the Court's judgment because it failed to adequately consider the impact of state practice when analyzing the meaning of Article 51.[98] According to this justice, it defied judicial logic to ignore the reality that numerous specially affected states, as well as international organizations such as NATO and even the Security Council, had adopted interpretations of the Article 51 right of self-defense consistent with Israel's invocation of that right.[99] Because self-defense is a fundamentally state-focused right, the impact of this state practice was, in his view, critical to assessing the contemporary meaning of that right.

The ICJ reached a similar, if not more expansive rejection of the right of self-defense in response to nonstate threats in its Uganda/DRC opinion.[100] In

---

examples of walls/barriers comparative to that of Israel and the lack of criticism received on those barriers); Legal Consequences of the Construction of a Wall in the Occupied Palestinian Territory, Advisory Opinion, I.C.J. 136 (July 9, 2004) [hereinafter ICJ Wall Advisory Opinion].

[94] ICJ Wall Advisory Opinion, supra note 93, at 138.

[95] H.C.J 2056/04 *Beit Sourik Village Council v. The Government of Israel* PD 1, 45–46 (2004) (Isr.), *available at* http://elyon1.court.gov.il/files_eng/04/560/020/a28/04020560.a28.pdf. (The Israeli High Court of Justice was aware of the killing and destruction brought by the terror attacks against the state and its citizens. The court held that Israel had a right to erect a "fence" for security reasons on territory it considers "disputed." The court also held that the fence was a proportionate response to the terror attacks, but ordered a specific segment moved to alleviate the hardship of Palestinian villagers).

[96] *See* ICJ Wall Advisory Opinion, *supra* note 93, at 142.

[97] *Id.*

[98] *Id.* at 240–41.

[99] *Id.* at 242–43.

[100] Armed Activities on the Territory of the Congo (*Democratic Republic of the Congo v. Uganda*), I.C.J. Judgement 168, 169 (Dec. 19, 2005) [hereinafter Uganda Case 2005] (stating: The Court finds that, "Uganda violated the principles of non-use of force in international relations and of non-intervention; that it violated its obligations under international human rights law and international humanitarian law; and that it violated other obligations owed to the Democratic Republic of the Congo." The Court also finds that "the Democratic Republic of the Congo violated obligations owed to Uganda under the Vienna Convention on Diplomatic Relations of 1961").

that case, Uganda claimed the right to invoke self-defense in response to nonstate rebel groups attacking its territory from the Democratic Republic of the Congo.[101] Although these attacks, unlike the *Wall* case, did emanate from the territory of another state, the ICJ nonetheless rejected the invocation of the right of self-defense due to the nonstate nature of the rebel groups. According to the decision:

> It is further to be noted that, while Uganda claimed to have acted in self-defence, it did not ever claim that it had been subjected to an armed attack by the armed forces of the DRC. The "armed attacks" to which reference was made came rather from the ADF. The Court has found above (paragraphs 131–135) that there is no satisfactory proof of the involvement in these attacks, direct or indirect, of the Government of the DRC. The attacks did not emanate from armed bands or irregulars sent by the DRC or on behalf of the DRC, within the sense of Article 3 *(g)* of General Assembly resolution 3314 (XXIX) on the definition of aggression, adopted on 14 December 1974. The Court is of the view that, on the evidence before it, even if this series of deplorable attacks could be regarded as cumulative in character, they still remained non-attributable to the DRC.
>
> For all these reasons, the Court finds that the legal and factual circumstances for the exercise of a right of self-defence by Uganda against the DRC were not present. Accordingly, the Court has no need to respond to the contentions of the Parties as to whether and under what conditions contemporary international law provides for a right of self-defence against large-scale attacks by irregular forces. Equally, since the preconditions for the exercise of self-defence do not exist in the circumstances of the present case, the Court has no need to enquire whether such an entitlement to self-defence was in fact exercised in circumstances of necessity and in a manner that was proportionate.[102]

Therefore for the ICJ, apparently, the nature or gravity of the threat is not the essential predicate for triggering the inherent right of self-defense. Instead, only a state-sponsored threat satisfies that triggering requirement.[103]

The combined impact of these two decisions on the use of military force against transnational terrorist threats is potentially profound. If this requirement for state action as a necessary element to trigger the inherent right of self-defense is an accurate interpretation of international law, it essentially undermines the entire U.S. military response to terrorism.[104] However, the impact of these decisions is difficult to assess. Unsurprisingly, proponents of a pragmatic interpretation of the inherent right of self-defense have been critical of the decision,

---

[101] *Id.* at 172–73.

[102] Noam Lubbell, Extraterritorial Use of Force against Non-State Actors 33 (2010).

[103] *See* Uganda Case, *supra* note 100, at 219.

[104] Feinstein & Weiner, *supra* note 93, at 522.

focusing on the same flaw as the dissenting justice.[105] Furthermore, it is clear that it has had little impact on the continued assertion of this right by states such as the United States and Israel in response to the threat of transnational terrorism. Nonetheless, it is impossible to ignore the fact that the ICJ categorically rejected these assertions. Ultimately, how state practice continues to evolve regarding this issue should indicate whether this decision will be viewed as an aberration, or will gain traction as an indication of a much more limited right than that asserted by the United States.

VII. Conclusion

Characterizing terrorism as an armed attack has profound legal consequences. The first is that the victim state may consider the act of terrorism a legitimate trigger for the inherent right of individual or collective self-defense. When a state conducts military action pursuant to this theory of legal authority, the action will trigger a law of armed conflict-based regulatory framework, one fundamentally distinct from that associated with a law enforcement response. As a result, invoking the right of self-defense in response to a transnational terrorist threat will involve an exercise of state power that would normally be considered legally prohibited, resulting in deprivations of life, liberty, and property inconsistent with peacetime legal authorities. The U.S. response to the terror attacks of September 11th provide the quintessential example of this effect for both the state actors engaged in response and the individuals they encounter during their counter-terror military operations. It is therefore unsurprising that such an approach to the threat of terrorism has, and will continue, to generate substantial criticism and legal opposition. Nonetheless, it seems impossible to ignore the reality that for at least some states and the international community, invoking the right of self-defense in response to the threat of transnational terrorism will remain an important option for protecting national security.

[105] The ICJ could have addressed the question of self-defense and prolonged occupations in far more detail, as the law is not entirely clear in this area. Grappling with this issue, probably one of the most controversial areas in international law, may have given the opinion more credibility. The ICJ could have also provided more of an analysis as to why the construction of the wall along its current route is unreasonable, justifying its decisions by legal argument. *See* Victor Kattan, *The Legality of the West Bank Wall: Israel's High Court of Justice v. the International Court of Justice*, 40 Vand. J. Transnat'l L. 1425, 1514–16 (2007). *See also* Michael Reisman, *Holding the Center of the Law of Armed Conflict*, 100 Am. J. Int'l L. 852, 856 (2006). *See also* Derek Jinks, *The Changing Laws of War: Do We Need a New Legal Regime after September 11?: Protective Parity and the Laws of War*, 79 Notre Dame L. Rev. 1493, 1497 (2004) ("the protection of noncombatants from attack is predicated on a clear distinction between combatants and noncombatants. If attacking forces cannot distinguish between enemy soldiers and civilians, this type of rule cannot work well .... It is the goal of protecting innocent civilians that requires a sharp line between combatants and noncombatants").

5}

Military Cyberspace Operations

Gary D. Brown,* Paul Walker,** and Anthony W. Bell III***

I. Introduction

On August 7, 2008, Russia invaded the country of Georgia in order to support the breakaway provinces of South Ossetia and Abkhazia, Georgia.[1] The invasion was precipitated by the Georgian government's attempt to use force to subdue the breakaway republics and bring them back under its rule.[2] Russian "peacekeeping" troops, stationed in South Ossetia, responded to the attacks and requested support from Russia.[3] According to news reports, Georgia experienced the effects of cyberspace operations starting at least twenty-four hours, and possibly up to three weeks, before the Russian military invasion began.[4] The cyberspace operations affected websites

---

* Gary D. Brown, Colonel, USAF (ret.) was the first Staff Judge Advocate at U.S. Cyber Command. He served as the senior legal advisor to America's cyber command from 2009 to 2012. He holds an LLM in international law from Cambridge University. The views expressed here are his own.

** Paul Walker, a Commander in the Navy Judge Advocate General's Corps, is currently assigned as the Director of the Navy Judge Advocate General's Cyber, Information Operations and Intelligence Law Division. Commander Walker previously served as an Operational Law Attorney at United States Cyber Command, where he served as legal adviser to multiple Operational Planning Teams and as the lead targeting attorney. Commander Walker has an LLM in National Security and Foreign Relations Law from George Washington University School of Law, where his writing focused on cyberspace operations. The views expressed here are Commander Walker's personal opinion and do not necessarily represent the views of the Department of Defense, the Department of the Navy, or United States Cyber Command.

*** Anthony Bell, a Lieutenant Colonel in the Air Force Judge Advocate General's Corps, has an LLM in National Security and Foreign Relations Law with an emphasis in cyber operations from George Washington University School of Law. He previously worked as an Assistant Professor of Law at the United States Air Force Academy where he taught Cyber Law, National Security Law, and Introduction to Law. The views expressed here are his own.

[1] Michael Schwirtz, Anne Barnard & C.J. Shivers, *Russia and Georgia Clash over Separatist Region*, N.Y. Times, Aug. 8, 2008, http://www.nytimes.com/2008/08/09/world/europe/09georgia.html?pagewanted=all&_r=0.

[2] *Id.*

[3] *Id.*

[4] David Hollis, *Cyber War Case Study: Georgia 2008*, Small Wars J. (Jan. 6, 2011), http://smallwarsjournal.com /blog/journal/docs-temp/639-hollis.pdf.

related to "communications, finance and government" services.[5] The Russian invasion of Georgia was the first publicly recorded instance where cyberspace operations were combined with air, sea, and land military operations.[6] Russia denied conducting these cyberspace operations as part of its invasion of Georgia; however, the cyberspace operations appeared to be coordinated with the ground assault, and it is widely believed that they were either carried out by the Russian government or by groups sympathetic to Russia with operational knowledge of its military plans.[7] The fact that cyber operations (regardless of who carried them out) were used in conjunction with, and in support of, traditional military operations demonstrates that cyberspace is a new operational domain, one in which the United States needs to be prepared to defend against attacks and to exploit available opportunities against adversaries.

The Russo-Georgia conflict raises a number of legal issues under both international and domestic law. Some of the questions raised include: (1) What are the domestic authorities for the United States military to carry out similar cyberspace operations, cyber-attacks,[8] or other cyber disruptions[9] in support of its assigned mission?; (2) Are government, finance, and communications websites and command and control facilities appropriate military targets under International Humanitarian Law (IHL)?;[10] and (3) Can cyberspace operations be attributed to a source with sufficient certainty to enable a response to such attacks, either in self-defense or using the international legal doctrine of countermeasures?[11] This chapter provides insight into how the U.S. government is structured to defend, exploit, and attack in cyberspace, as well as the operational authorities that allow the military to conduct such operations. Additionally, this chapter provides insight, guidance, and discussion regarding the current state of international humanitarian and domestic law and how those sources of law impact cyberspace operations, such as the one described above. It also provides perspective regarding future legal challenges, and how legal advisers to national decision-makers, including military and national security attorneys, can help shape international law in this emerging field.

---

[5] *Id.* at 2.

[6] *Id.*

[7] *Id. See also* Noah Shachtman, *Top Georgian Official: Moscow Cyber Attacked Us—We Just Can't Prove It*, Wired Mag. (Mar. 11, 2009), *available at* http://www.wired.com/dangerroom/2009/03/georgia-blames/.

[8] The term "cyber-attack" will be used to describe the level of force typically ascribed to physical armed attack: an act of violence that causes significant property damage, injury, or death.

[9] The term "cyber disruption" (or just "disruption") will be used in this chapter to describe actions that do not rise to the level of an armed attack for self-defense purposes, or do not rise to an act of violence for targeting purposes under *jus in bello* principles.

[10] International Humanitarian Law (IHL) provisions can be found in the Geneva Conventions and their Additional Protocols.

[11] This is by no means a complete list of the questions raised by the above scenario, but these questions and more will be addressed in the following pages.

II. Cyber Command and Its Operational Authorities

The National Security Act of 1947 created the National Military Establishment, which was renamed two years later as the Department of Defense (DoD).[12] The Secretary of Defense has the authority to manage the affairs of the DoD as well as the various military departments: the Navy, Army, Air Force, and at times the Coast Guard.[13]

Several years of increasing adversarial efforts against U.S. national security information systems culminated in a serious penetration of a DoD classified computer network in 2008. The DoD's response to this penetration, referred to as Operation Buckshot Yankee, was a critical motivation for Secretary Robert M. Gates's 2008 memorandum creating U.S. Cyber Command.[14] The Command was established as a subordinate unified command reporting to U.S. Strategic Command.[15] U.S. Cyber Command is responsible for "planning, coordinating, integrating, synchronizing, and directing activities to operate and defend the Department of Defense information networks and when directed, conducts full-spectrum military cyberspace operations . . . in order to ensure U.S. and allied freedom of action in cyberspace, while denying the same to our adversaries."[16]

U.S. Cyber Command

> [C]entralizes command of cyberspace operations, strengthens DOD cyberspace capabilities, and integrates and bolsters the DOD's cyber expertise. U.S. Cyber Command's efforts support the Armed Services' ability to confidently conduct high-tempo, effective operations as well as protect command and control systems and the cyberspace infrastructure supporting weapons system platforms from disruptions, intrusions and attacks.[17]

In order to understand U.S. Cyber Command's functions, it is important to define a number of key terms. Currently, the DoD defines "cyberspace" as "a global domain within the information environment consisting of the interdependent network of information technology infrastructures, including the Internet,

---

[12] *About the Department of Defense*, *available at* http://www.defense.gov/about/ (last visited May 11, 2014).

[13] 10 U.S.C. § 101(A)(8) (2013); 14 U.S.C. §§ 1–4 (2013). The Coast Guard can be transferred from the Department of Homeland Security to the Department of the Navy by a Congressional Declaration of War or by Presidential Executive Order.

[14] Ellen Nakashima, *Defense Officials Discloses Cyberattack*, Wash. Post (Aug. 24, 2010), *available at* http://www.washingtonpost.com/wp-dyn/content/article/2010/08/24/AR2010082406495.html).

[15] William J. Lynn III, *Defending a New Domain*, Foreign Affairs (Sept./Oct. 2010). *See also* Sec. of Def. Memo, *Establishment of a Subordinate Unified U.S. Cyber Command under U.S. Strategic Command for Military Cyberspace Operations* (June 23, 2009), *available at* http://info.publicintelligence.net/OSD05914.pdf.

[16] U.S. Cyber Command Fact Sheet, *available at* http://www.defense.gov/home/features/2010/0410_cybersec/docs/CYberFactSheet%20UPDATED%20replaces%20May%2021%20Fact%20Sheet.pdf (last visited May 5, 2014).

[17] Air Force Doctrine Document 3-12, Cyberspace Operations 23 (July 15, 2010).

telecommunications networks, computer systems, and embedded processors and controllers."[18] "Cyberspace operations" are defined as the "employment of cyberspace capabilities where the primary purpose is to achieve objectives in or through cyberspace."[19] "Cyberspace superiority" is defined as "the degree of dominance in cyberspace by one force that permits the secure, reliable conduct of operations by that force, and its related land, air, maritime, and space forces at a given time and place without prohibitive interference by an adversary."[20] "Defensive cyberspace operations" (DCO) are defined as the "passive and active cyberspace operations intended to preserve the ability to utilize friendly cyberspace capabilities and protect data, networks, net-centric capabilities, and other designated systems."[21] "Offensive cyberspace operations" (OCO) are defined as "cyberspace operations intended to project power by the application of force in or through cyberspace."[22] "Defensive cyberspace operation response action" (DCO-RA) is defined as the "deliberate, authorized defensive measures or activities taken outside of the defended network to protect and defend Department of Defense cyberspace capabilities or other designated systems."[23]

As mentioned above, U.S. Cyber Command is a sub-unified command of the United States Strategic Command, which is one of nine Combatant Commands,[24] and one of its roles is to provide warfighters with a cyberspace operations capability. The term "cyberspace operations" can be used to describe a broad range of possible activities. Cyberspace operations can be as innocuous as exploiting computer information to determine the location, size, and capability of an enemy army. or as disruptive as a distributed denial of service (DDoS)[25] action against a nation's communication facilities, such as what occurred in the case of the Russo-Georgia conflict of 2008. Cyberspace operations might also be used to execute actions as aggressive as kinetic military activities, such as manipulating computerized sensors to cause military fuel tanks to overpressure and explode, or interfering with a computer control system in order to render a nation's air defense systems inoperable for a period of time.

---

[18] Joint Chiefs of Staff, Joint Publication 1-02, Dep't of Def. Dictionary of Military and Associated Terms (Nov. 8, 2010) [hereinafter JP 1-02].

[19] *Id.*

[20] *Id.*

[21] *Id.*

[22] *Id.*

[23] *Id.*

[24] 10 U.S.C. § 164 (2014). Combatant Commanders are responsible for the performance of missions assigned to that command by the President, or by the Secretary of Defense with the approval of the President. Combatant Commanders use forces from at least two of the military services, and are assigned ongoing missions that are usually defined by geography and in a limited scope by function.

[25] Denial of Service attack is accomplished technologically—the primary goal of an attack is to deny the victim(s) access to a particular resource. It is an explicit attempt by a hacker to prevent legitimate users of a computer-related service from using that service. *See* Allen Householder et al., *Managing the Threat of Denial-of-Service Attacks*, CERT Coordination Center 2 (Oct. 2001).

The military departments support U.S. Cyber Command by providing it with military forces and capability.[26] As an example, the United States Air Force has established a subordinate unit devoted to cyberspace operations.[27] The 24th Air Force is comprised of three cyber wings[28] including the 688th Information Operations Wing, the 67th Network Warfare Wing, and the 689th Combat Communications Wing. These Wings, through the 24th Air Force, provide the U.S. Cyber Command with operational capability in the form of trained personnel, cyber tools, and capabilities. The other military departments are also structured to provide similar operational capability to the U.S. Cyber Command.

The United States is not alone in developing cyberspace options in support of national security. A few other nations are quite proficient, and many states have nascent military capabilities for cyberspace.[29] In fact, the establishment of the U.S. Cyber Command appears to have motivated other nations to develop similar commands and capabilities,[30] as have specific cyber threats.[31] The Russo-Georgian conflict demonstrated that cyberspace is, and will be for the foreseeable future, a part of military conflict. The larger question remains: What rules, if any, apply to military cyberspace operations? The treaties governing military conflict were agreed to prior to the advent of the Internet, so there is some question whether they apply to this new realm of military operations. If they do apply, exactly how do cyberspace operations fit under rules written with only kinetic operations in

---

[26] *See generally* U.S. DEP'T OF DEF., DIRECTIVE 5100.1, FUNCTIONS OF THE DEP'T OF DEF. AND ITS MAJOR COMPONENTS (Dec. 21, 2010). Each service is organized as a sub-department to the Department of Defense. The Military Departments are responsible for organizing, training, supplying, and equipping forces for assignment to the Unified Combatant Commands. *See id.*

[27] *See* AIR FORCE INSTRUCTION 38-101 para. 3.2 (2012). A Numbered Air Force (NAF) is a type of organization in the United States Air Force that is subordinate to a Major Command (MAJCOM). It has assigned to it operational units such as wings, squadrons, and groups. It prepares forces for deployment and employment.

[28] *Id.* at para. 3.3. The standard wing generates and employs combat capability. One commander has the authority and responsibility to command the wing. The standard operational wing structure is a wing with four dependent groups (operations, maintenance, mission support, and medical), with related functions and disciplines aligned under the appropriate group.

[29] RICHARD A. CLARKE & ROBERT K. KNAKE, CYBER WAR: THE NEXT THREAT TO NATIONAL SECURITY AND WHAT TO DO ABOUT IT 46 (2010). The authors estimate that between twenty and thirty nations have established offensive cyber units.

[30] China, India, and Russia are examples. *See* Tania Branigan, *Chinese Army to Target Cyber War Threat*, THE GUARDIAN, July 22, 2010, *available at* http://www.guardian.co.uk/world/2010/jul/22/chinese-army-cyber-war-department; Harish Gupta, *India Setting Up Cyber Command*, MSN NEWS, May 15, 2011, *available at* http://news.in.msn.com/national/article.aspx?cp-documentid=5160226#page=1; *Vice Prime Minister Rogozin Pledges to Set Up Cyber Command in Russia*, CNEWS, Mar. 22, 2012, *available at* http://eng.cnews.ru/news/top/indexEn.shtml?2012/03/22/482544.

[31] For example, South Korea is confronted with significant cyber activity from North Korea, which has served as an impetus for the creation of their military cyber unit, Jung Sung Ki, *Cyber Warfare Command to Be Launched in January*, THE KOREA TIMES, Dec. 1, 2009, *available at* http://www.koreatimes.co.kr/www/news/nation/2009/12/205_56502.html; and Iran was victimized by the Stuxnet virus, *Iran to Launch First Cyber Command*, PRESSTV, Mar. 25, 2012, *available at* http://presstv.com/detail/184774.html.

mind? The next section analyzes International Humanitarian Law (IHL)[32] plus relevant domestic law and their application to cyberspace operations.

III. International Law and Military Cyberspace Operations

The United States takes the position that IHL applies in cyberspace.[33] There appears to be an emerging consensus on this point, at least among Western nations. This is perhaps best evidenced by the publication of the *Tallinn Manual*.[34]

NATO's Cooperative Cyber Defence Centre of Excellence (CCD COE) sponsored the *Tallinn Manual on the International Law Applicable to Cyber Warfare*, published in 2013. The *Manual* is the product of twenty world-class academics, legal practitioners, and technical experts who, during a three-year project sponsored by CCD COE, examined the international law issues surrounding cyber warfare. The *Manual* consists of rules these experts unanimously agreed reflect customary international law. The rules are supported by commentary that discusses the issues in more precise detail, especially with regard to setting out the differences of opinion among the experts about the state of the law. The *Manual* is not law, or even government policy, but it does represent the studied reflections of an auspicious group of Western international law experts. As such, it is critical evidence in making the case that international law, and in particular IHL, applies to cyber warfare, and an important first step in determining more precisely *how* law might govern conduct in cyberspace.[35]

The International Committee of the Red Cross (ICRC), an authoritative voice on matters of IHL, participated in the Tallinn process as an observer, and concurs that IHL is applicable to cyber warfare.[36] The views of China and Russia, two states with significant capability in the cyber domain, are less clear. Both China and Russia have argued for a new treaty regime to govern cyberspace. Though this could be seen as indicating Chinese and Russian rejection of IHL's application to cyberspace, it may simply be that as a matter of negotiating tactics the

---

[32] The IHL is composed of both treaty and customary international law and is also termed the Law of Armed Conflict (LOAC) or the Law of War (LOW).

[33] Harold Hongju Koh, *International Law in Cyberspace*, Keynote Address at the U.S. Cyber Command Inter-Agency Legal Conference (Sept. 18, 2012) (stating that the laws of armed conflict apply "to regulate the use of cyber tools in hostilities, just as it does other tools"), *available at* http://www.state.gov/s/l/releases/remarks/197924.htm.

[34] *See* TALLINN MANUAL ON THE INTERNATIONAL LAW APPLICABLE TO CYBER WARFARE, 30 (Michael Schmitt ed., 2013) [hereinafter TALLINN MANUAL].

[35] *See generally* Michael N. Schmitt, *International Law in Cyberspace: The Koh Speech and* Tallinn Manual *Juxtaposed*, 52 HARV. INT'L. L. J. 13 (Dec. 2012); Dieter Fleck, *Searching for International Rules Applicable to Cyber Warfare—A Critical First Assessment of the New* Tallinn Manual, 18 J. OF CONFLICT AND SEC. L. 331 (2013); Colonel Kirby Abbott, Assistant Legal Adviser, NATO Supreme Headquarters Allied Powers Europe, Address at Chatham House (Mar. 15, 2013), http://www.chathamhouse.org/events/view/189465.

[36] *See* Cordula Droege, *Get Off My Cloud: Cyber Warfare, International Humanitarian Law, and the Protection of Civilians*, 94 INT'L REV. RED CROSS 1, 9 (2013).

two states have not yet publicly accepted the premise that IHL would apply to the cyberspace portion of an armed conflict. Russian and Chinese positions in United Nations's (U.N.) cyber-security discussions appear to seek concessions on the right of states to control information, potentially in an attempt to impose controls on freedom of speech.[37] In any event, both countries seem to be softening their positions, including supporting U.N. declarations that international law in general applies in cyberspace.[38]

Long-standing DoD policy is to apply IHL in all U.S. military operations.[39] However, implementing this DoD policy is not always easy, particularly given the difficulty of equating any given cyberspace operation with a historical kinetic equivalent. All cyber analogies break down sooner or later; usually sooner. As a result, through an excess of caution (and DoD policy), unnecessary and novel applications of IHL have crept into U.S. cyberspace operations. These creative applications have the troubling potential to restrict cyberspace operations that could serve humanitarian ends. This issue will be explored in greater detail in the following sections.

A. "ATTACKS" IN CYBERSPACE OPERATIONS

Cyberspace is ubiquitous; it is anywhere and everywhere. That, at least, is the claim of those who argue for cyberspace exceptionalism, the idea that the nature of cyberspace is so unusual that traditional laws, rules, and regulations may not apply.[40] But the banality of cyberspace is also grounded in the cold, hard reality of hardware, such as servers, computers, routers, and switches, along with wires,

---

[37] Tim Maurer, *Cyber Norm Emergence at the United Nations—An Analysis of the UN's Activities regarding Cyber-Security?* 20–22 (Belfer Center for Science and International Affairs, Harvard Kennedy School, Cambridge, MA, Discussion Paper No. 2011-11, Sept. 2011); Jason Healey, *Breakthrough or Just Broken? China and Russia's UNGA Proposal on Cyber Norms*, New Atlanticist Pol'y & Analysis Blog (Sept. 21, 2011), *available at* http://www.acus.org/new_atlanticist/breakthrough-or-just-broken-china-and-russias-unga-proposal-cyber-norms (discussing differences between Russian and Chinese formulations of "information security" and U.S. formulation of "cyber security," as well as indicating that the United States and the United Kingdom have "pledged" to be bound by laws of armed conflict, while Russia and China state that further study is needed).

[38] *See* Detlev Wolter, *The UN Takes a Big Step Forward on Cyber Security*, Arms Control Today (Sept. 2013), *available at* https://www.armscontrol.org/act/2013_09/The-UN-Takes-a-Big-Step-Forward-on-Cybersecurity (stating that all of the five permanent members of the Security Council and ten other regional leaders in cyber recognized that international law, including principles of state responsibility, apply to state behavior in cyberspace, though clarifying that although Russia further concurred that international humanitarian law applied in cyberspace, the Chinese repeatedly stated that such an explicit confirmation was too soon and did not commit to the latter principle).

[39] *See* Dep't of Defense Directive 2311.01E, DoD Law of War Program, para. 4.1 (Sept. 5, 2006) [hereinafter DODD 2310.01E].

[40] "This report describes cyberspace as terra nullius, currently beyond the reach of mature political discourse." Paul Cornish, David Livingstone, Dave Clemente & Claire Yorke, On Cyber Warfare (Nov. 2010), *available at* https://www.chathamhouse.org/sites/default/files/public/Research/International%20Security/r1110_cyberwarfare.pdf.

cables, and all the other paraphernalia used to connect one network to another to another, ad infinitum (almost), to create the Internet. In some cases, the components are connected to stand-alone networks that are physically separated, or "air gapped,"[41] from other, supposedly more vulnerable networks, but the principle is the same. All of these items are owned by someone, whether a company, a government, or a private individual, and each has a physical presence somewhere in, or above in orbit, the world.

"Achiev[ing] objectives in or through cyberspace" may be seen, observed, or felt, at least until the equipment is turned off or disconnected from the Internet.[42] This is a unique situation that occurs in no other historical warfighting domain. A lawyer reviewing military cyberspace operations must ensure she has a thorough understanding and grasp of the concept of operations for each cyberspace operation under review. This understanding must include detailed knowledge of how cyber capabilities will be applied, what effects will occur from the use of cyber capabilities, and where those intended effects will occur. The "where" must include not just the virtual location of the Internet Protocol (IP) address or the media access control (MAC) address,[43] but also the physical location of the equipment. This is necessary because in the U.S. policy and interagency environment, geography still matters.

The substantial difference between cyberspace operations and other, more traditional types of military operations creates special challenges. In order to achieve a particular cyberspace objective, it may be necessary to have effects (i.e., to have an aim point for the operation) in an entirely different part of cyberspace. To further complicate matters, the objective and the aim point are often geographically distinct, perhaps widely separated, quite possibly hosted on physical infrastructure in two or more countries. Although this aspect of cyberspace operations has any number of potential international legal implications, a lawyer reviewing such a geographically dispersed operation must first identify those portions of the cyberspace operation confined to areas of ongoing armed conflict. For those portions of the cyberspace operation that may have effects outside such an area, the lawyer must appreciate and provide clear advice regarding when these warfighting effects amount to a prohibited use of force. The following discussion tackles these questions in order, moving from the rules regulating warfare, or the *jus in bello*, to those regulating the legality of resort to war, the *jus ad bellum*.[44]

---

[41] An "air gap" is the "separation of two networks so that there is 'nothing but air' between them." Harry Newton, Newton's Telecom Dictionary (23rd ed. 2007). The idea of an air gapped network is that it is less vulnerable to Internet-based attacks because it is not connected to the Internet, although this idea has been debunked, both by the opinion of experts and by one highly publicized example—Stuxnet. *See infra* notes 53–56.

[42] *See* JP 1-02, *supra* note 18, at 64 (defining "cyberspace operations").

[43] "A MAC address is the hardware address of a device that is designed to be connected to a shared network medium." Newton, *supra* note 41, at 574–75.

[44] These are separate and distinct areas for legal examination, and great care must be taken to not conflate the legal issues arising under each. *See* Cordula Droege, *Get Off My Cloud: Cyber Warfare, International Humanitarian Law, and the Protection of Civilians*, 94(886) Int'l. Rev. Red

During an armed conflict, attacks against military objectives, including military objectives that may serve both military and civilian ends, often referred to as dual-use objects, are permitted.[45] Kinetic attacks are usually readily and easily identifiable as such, because people are injured or killed and property is damaged or destroyed. However, there is great confusion regarding what is an attack in cyberspace, because of the unending use of the word "attack" by hackers, techies, talking heads, the popular media, bloggers, tweeters, and the technical press, not to mention numerous public figures, including senior military officials and politicians. This overuse has caused confusion over the legal significance of slight electronic affronts, such as the mere intrusion or scan of a network or computer system, and more significant actions, such as the destruction of critical data or hardware.

Article 49 of Additional Protocol I to the Geneva Conventions, accepted as customary international law,[46] defines "attacks" as "acts of violence ... whether in offence or defence."[47] Though early scholarship on military cyberspace operations focused heavily on what constituted a use of force under Article 2(4) of the U.N. Charter, recent scholarship has addressed interpretation of Article 49 in the cyber context,[48] culminating in Rule 30 of the *Tallinn Manual*. That rule defines a cyber attack as "a cyber operation, whether offensive or defensive, that is reasonably expected to cause injury or death to persons or damage or destruction to objects."[49] On its face, this is an eminently reasonable interpretation that ensures consistency in applying IHL to military operations, whether they are kinetic or occurring in or through cyberspace. Such a consequence-based approach ensures military operations not traditionally subject to the targeting principles of IHL,

---

CROSS 545 (Summer 2012) ("Under *jus ad bellum*, the question is whether and when cyber operations amount to a use of force within the meaning of Article 2(4) of the UN Charter and/or to an armed attack with the meaning of Article 51 of the UN Charter, and under what circumstances they trigger a right to self-defence. Whatever the views in this *jus ad bellum* discussion, it should be recalled that the objects of regulation of *jus ad bellum* and *jus in bello* are entirely distinct: while *jus ad bellum* specifically regulates inter-state relations and the requirements for the lawful resort to force between states, *jus in bello* regulates the behavior of parties to the conflict and its object and purpose is to protect the military and civilian victims of war.").

[45] *See* Protocol Additional to the Geneva Conventions of 12 August 1949, and Relating to the Protection of Victims of International Armed Conflicts (Protocol I), 8 June 1977, 1125 UNTS 3, art. 52(2) [hereinafter *Additional Protocol I*]; JEAN-MARIE HENCKAERTS & LOUISE DOSWALD-BECK, CUSTOMARY INTERNATIONAL HUMANITARIAN LAW VOLUME I: RULES 32 (2005) [hereinafter Rules].

[46] *See, e.g.*, PROGRAM ON HUMANITARIAN POLICY AND CONFLICT RESEARCH, MANUAL ON INTERNATIONAL LAW APPLICABLE TO AIR AND MISSILE WARFARE 1 (2009) [hereinafter *Air and Missile Warfare Manual*] (stating that attack "means an act of violence, whether in offence or in defence."); SAN REMO MANUAL ON INTERNATIONAL LAW APPLICABLE TO ARMED CONFLICTS AT SEA 5 (Louise Doswald-Beck ed., 1995) ("most of its provisions are considered to state the law which is currently applicable") [hereinafter *San Remo Manual*]; Louise Doswald-Beck, *The* San Remo Manual on International Law Applicable to Armed Conflicts at Sea, 89 AM. J. INT'L L. 192, 192 (1995) (stating that the *Manual* contains "international law currently applicable to armed conflicts at sea").

[47] *Additional Protocol I*, *supra* note 45, art. 49.

[48] *See, e.g.*, Schmitt, *supra* note 35, at 94; Paul A. Walker, *Rethinking Computer Network "Attack": Implications for Law and U.S. Doctrine*, 1 NAT'L SEC. L. BRIEF 33, 47 (2010).

[49] TALLINN MANUAL, *supra* note 34, at 92.

such as psychological operations[50] and cyber espionage, are treated consistently in the cyber domain. In other words, cyberspace operations that do not result in Rule 30's stated consequences, but are merely disruptive in nature, causing "inconvenience, irritation, stress or fear," such as psychological operations, are also not subject to IHL; therefore, the principles of distinction or proportionality are not applicable.[51]

The Commentary to the *Tallinn Manual's* Rule 30 provides an interesting discussion on cyber operations that result in the loss of an object's functionality. The majority of the Group of Experts took the position that an operation causing loss of functionality requiring the replacement of system components was an attack. However, with regard to cyberspace operations that do not require physical replacement of components, but do necessitate an operating system or other data to be restored for the system to function again, the Group of Experts was unable to agree whether such should be considered an attack. To add additional complexity to this issue, these subtle differences may be difficult to distinguish. For instance, in the Shamoon actions against Saudi Arabia's ARAMCO oil company that occurred in 2012,[52] it is unclear whether the company replaced thirty thousand hard drives because they no longer worked or because it was simply easier to do so rather than reinstalling the operating systems. This uncertainty makes it difficult to assess whether Shamoon, had it occurred during an armed conflict, would based on this type of functionality loss have qualified as an "attack." Conversely, it seems that Shamoon would not qualify as an attack based on the stricter, higher standard requiring physical damage or destruction of an object if the hard drives remained operable.

Stuxnet provides a clearer example of an actual scenario that, had it occurred during the course of an armed conflict, would be considered an attack subject to the core principles of military necessity, distinction, avoidance of unnecessary suffering, and proportionality.[53] Stuxnet came to the world's attention in 2010 when it was discovered by an Eastern European antivirus firm on computers in Iran. Infections of this malware occurred predominantly within Iran, though other Middle Eastern and even some European countries also found Stuxnet

---

[50] Now called "Military Information Support Operations" in U.S. doctrine. *See* JP 1-02, *supra* note 18, at 171. *See also* Michael N. Schmitt, *Wired Warfare: Computer Network Attack and* Jus in Bello, INT'L REV. RED CROSS 365, 373, 378 (2002).

[51] TALLINN MANUAL, *supra* note 34, at 160 ¶ 5 of Commentary to Rule 51. This is not to say, of course, that IHL does not apply to cyberspace operations not amounting to an attack; the perfidy rules may well apply to military information support operations and military deception operations carried out by cyberspace operations.

[52] Byron Acohido, *Why the Shamoon Virus Looms as a Destructive Threat*, USA TODAY, May 16, 2013, *available at* http://www.usatoday.com/story/cybertruth/2013/05/16/shamoon-cyber-warfare-hackers-anti-american/2166147/.

[53] An excellent technical analysis of Stuxnet and its characteristics was published by Symantec. *See* Nicolas Falliere, Liam O Murchu & Eric Chien, *W32.Stuxnet Dossier, ver. 1.4* (Feb. 2011), *available at* http://www.symantec.com/content/en/us/enterprise/media/security_response/whitepapers/w32_stuxnet_dossier.pdf. Technical details about Stuxnet in this chapter are drawn from this report.

on their computer networks. Kaspersky Laboratories and Symantec conducted detailed forensic analysis of Stuxnet and were able to determine that Stuxnet used a minimum of four zero-day exploits[54] to establish either an initial foothold in a computer system or network, or to propagate further within the network. Once on a system, Stuxnet examined the system setup, looking for a particular configuration of devices, including specific programmable logic controllers (PLCs). If that configuration was not found, then Stuxnet had no effect on the system or network. If, however, the correct configuration was identified, Stuxnet proceeded to issue instructions to the PLCs designed to slow down or speed up the operation of the equipment controlled by the PLCs. In the case of Stuxnet, it was determined that the configuration it was looking for was one matching the configuration of Siemens equipment controlling the operations of centrifuges at the Iranian uranium enrichment plant located at Natanz, Iran.

One of the most novel characteristics of Stuxnet was its ability to cause the equipment readings available to plant operators to seem to be within normal limits.[55] Based on footage from video cameras installed by the International Atomic Energy Agency as part of its monitoring efforts, it was later determined that close to a thousand centrifuges at Natanz were replaced during or just after the time period that Stuxnet was operating undetected.[56] In the case of Stuxnet, the damage caused to nearly a thousand nuclear centrifuges was not only reasonably foreseeable, but very likely the intended result of Stuxnet's introduction into the Iranian systems. Unlike the Russo-Georgia DDoS example that opened this chapter, Stuxnet is an example of a stand-alone cyberspace operation that, if it occurred during the course of an armed conflict, would be subject to the law of armed conflict's targeting principles, because it caused physical damage to the facilities equipment.

Of course, Stuxnet did not occur during the course of an armed conflict, which raises even more interesting questions about its status as a possible use of force in cyberspace. Unsurprisingly, the question of whether a cyberspace operation constitutes a use of force is becoming increasingly important for both lawyers and policymakers to understand. The nexus between virtual technology and warfighting grows on an almost daily basis, and senior decision-makers and

---

[54] A "zero-day exploit" is a security, software, or system vulnerability that is not known to the equipment manufacturer; this means that a patch or other fix for the vulnerability has not yet been developed and published to the users of the equipment or software.

[55] For an excellent summation of the forensic activity leading to the discovery of Stuxnet and facts such as this one, *see* Kim Zetter, *How Digital Detectives Deciphered Stuxnet, the Most Menacing Malware in History*, WIRED (July 7, 2011), *available at* http://www.wired.com/threatlevel/2011/07/how-digital-detectives-deciphered-stuxnet/all/.

[56] *See* Joby Warrick, *Iran's Natanz Nuclear Facility Recovered Quickly from Stuxnet Cyberattack*, WASH. POST (Feb. 16, 2011), *available at* http://www.washingtonpost.com/wp-dyn/content/article/2011/02/15/AR2011021505395.html (describing how video cameras captured details as Iran replaced more than 10 percent of the nine thousand centrifuges in use at the Natanz uranium enrichment plant). *See also* David Albright, Paul Brannan & Christina Walrond, *Stuxnet Malware and Natanz: Update of ISIS December 22, 2010 Report*, ISIS Report (Feb. 15, 2011).

their lawyers must keep pace with the legal and policy issues that emerge. For example, cyber capabilities that support military deception and information support operations often occur without regard to precise geographic boundaries[57] and require astute legal analysis. In cases short of armed conflict, lawyers should be aware that cyberspace operations can rise to a use-of-force level prohibited by the United Nations Charter. If this threshold is to be crossed, it should be done advisedly.

B. USE OF FORCE AND ARMED ATTACK IN CYBERSPACE: TRIGGERING SELF-DEFENSE

In 2011, the United States issued its *International Strategy for Cyberspace*, in which it stated, "[W]hen warranted, the United States will respond to hostile acts in cyberspace as we would to any other threat to our country."[58] However, until a year later it provided no detail regarding what would constitute a hostile act. In a speech to the United States Cyber Command legal conference in September 2012, State Department Legal Adviser Harold Koh for the first time provided an official U.S. government position on what constitutes a use of force in cyberspace: "[c]yber activities that proximately result in death, injury or significant destruction would likely be viewed as a use of force."[59] Less than a month later, Secretary of Defense Leon Panetta used a similar statement in a speech to business executives in describing what would constitute "an imminent threat of attack" possibly requiring the Department of Defense to take action to defend the nation.[60] Koh also provided three specific examples of cyber activity that the United States would consider a use of force: "(1) operations that trigger a nuclear plant meltdown; (2) operations that open a dam above a populated area causing destruction; or (3) operations that disable air traffic control resulting in airplane crashes."[61] In the first two examples, the type of damage or destruction caused is equivalent to the type of physical damage that would result from dropping a bomb on the respective target. The result of the third example is the type of outcome that would otherwise require a missile to achieve.

Article 2(4) of the United Nations Charter states that member states "shall refrain in their international relations from the threat or use of force" against

---

[57] *See infra* section III.E. for a more detailed discussion on cyber support to such operations.

[58] Office of the Pres. of the United States, *International Strategy for Cyberspace: Prosperity, Security, and Openness in a Networked World* (May 2011), *available at* http://www.whitehouse.gov/sites/default/files/rss_viewer/international_strategy_for_cyberspace.pdf.

[59] Koh address, *supra* note 33, at 6.

[60] Secretary Panetta specifically stated that "If we detect an imminent threat of attack that will cause significant, physical destruction in the United States or kill American citizens, we need to have the option to take action against those who would attack us to defend this nation when directed by the president." Leon E. Panetta, U.S. Sec'y of Defense, Remarks on Cybersecurity to the Business Executives for National Security, New York City (Oct 11, 2012), http://www.defense.gov/transcripts/transcript.aspx?transcriptid=5136.

[61] Koh address, *supra* note 33, at 3.

other states. In the Koh speech, the United States became the first nation to provide a degree of specificity to the term "threat or use of force" as applied to cyberspace. The announcement of the U.S. position on use of force in cyberspace came close on the heels of the online publication of the *Tallinn Manual*, whose description of "unambiguous" uses of force is very similar to the U.S. position. The *Manual* states that "[a]cts that injure or kill persons or damage or destroy objects are unambiguously uses of force." The *Manual* also addresses "less clear" cases by using an assessment based on the following factors: severity, immediacy, directness, invasiveness, measurability of effects, military character, state involvement, and presumptive legality.[62] Though less nuanced, the U.S. position is also less ambiguous, providing not only a clearer indication of the line that military cyberspace operations should not cross in the absence of armed conflict, but also a clear situational threshold at which the United States will consider using force in self-defense, regardless of whether the self-defense action will be accomplished via cyberspace or other means. Of course, although clearer, the U.S. position is also potentially self-serving: it allows the United States to engage in uses of cyber force while claiming that such uses are not armed attacks, as it limits such attacks to those causing *significant* destruction or death, and not the seemingly lower *Tallin Manual* threshold of simply damage, destruction, or death.

This U.S. definition of an illegal use of force in cyberspace also serves as a trigger for self-defense because of the unique legal position of the United States regarding the relationship between "use of force" and "armed attack." Under Article 51 of the U.N. Charter, states retain an inherent right to self-defense against an armed attack. Most states and legal scholars view the use of two distinct terms, "use of force" and "armed attack," as embodying distinct levels of activity, each with different legal results.[63] Succinctly put, under this view, states can respond with a use of force in self-defense to an armed attack, but may not respond with force against activity that is a mere use of force.[64] In other words,

---

[62] This approach is usually identified with the *Manual*'s General Editor, Professor Michael Schmitt, who first presented it in 1999. *See* Michael N. Schmitt, *Computer Network Attack and the Use of Force in International Law: Thoughts on a Normative Framework*, 37 Colum. J. Transnat'l L. 885 (1999).

[63] *See* Case Concerning Military and Paramilitary Activities in and Against Nicaragua (Nicar. v. U.S.), 1986 I.C.J. 14, para. 195 (June 27) [hereinafter Nicaragua] *See also* Tom Ruys, "Armed Attack" and Article 51 of the UN Charter: Evolutions in Customary Law 146–47 (2010).

[64] *See* Tallinn Manual, *supra* note 34, at 47 stating:

> The International Group of Experts acknowledged a contrary view whereby the distinction between the two concepts is either so narrow as to be insignificant or non-existent. This position, articulated by the United States after the Nicaragua judgment, asserts that any illegal use of force can qualify as an armed attack triggering the right of self-defence; . . . [O]n this view, no gap exists between an unlawful use of force and an armed attack, although the principles of necessity and proportionality that apply to actions in self-defence may limit the responses available to a State that has been attacked.

Id. See also Schmitt, *supra* note 35, at 21–22 (describing the U.S. position on this point and stating that "No member of the International Group of Experts agreed that an armed attack was nothing more than a use of force, *sans plus*.").

there is a response gap between activity that is a use of force and the greater amount of force that is an armed attack, in both consequences and effects.

For at least twenty-five years, the United States has not recognized the existence of such a response gap.[65] Instead, as Koh reiterated in his September 2012, speech to the Cyber Command Legal Conference: "the United States has for a long time taken the position that the inherent right of self-defense potentially applies against *any* illegal use of force."[66] Koh recognized that although other states may distinguish between the two terms discussed above, such that there is a higher threshold for armed attacks than for uses of force, he explicitly rejected the use of such a threshold in U.S. practice, regardless of domain.[67]

Given this difference in legal positions, it is worth examining whether there is a resulting substantive difference in the trigger for self-defense, at least pertaining to cyber operations, as announced by the United States. Again, the best available basis for comparison is the *Tallinn Manual*. The *Manual* utilizes the "scale and effects" test to determine whether a cyber operation rises to the level of an armed attack. That test is drawn from the International Court of Justice decision in its well-known *Nicaragua* case.[68] In applying the "scale and effects" test to cyberspace operations, the *Manual* draws a clear distinction between the types of consequences (deaths, injuries, and damage or destruction of property) that are implicated in the U.S. formulation of illegal use of force/armed attack, and cyberspace actions that "do not result in injury, death, damage, or destruction, but which otherwise have extensive negative effects."[69]

For the latter case, the *Manual*'s drafters could not achieve a consensus. Using the "classic scenario" of a "cyber incident directed against the New York Stock Exchange that causes the market to crash," the *Manual* described the differences between those who do not see it as an armed attack because there was no "condition precedent" of harm to persons or physical damage, and those who focus on the "catastrophic effects" and would label it as an armed attack.[70] The former viewpoint is very much in keeping with the tenor of Koh's remarks, in which all of the examples he used involved injuries to persons or physical damage or destruction.[71] At a minimum,

---

[65] *See* Abraham D. Sofaer, *International Law and the Use of Force*, 82 Am. Soc. of Int'l L. Proceedings 420, 422 (1988).

[66] Koh address, *supra* note 33.

[67] *Id.*

[68] Tallinn Manual, *supra* note 34, at 55 (Rule 13(5)) (citing Nicaragua, *supra* note 63, para. 195). The discussion in the *Tallinn Manual*, drawn from the International Court of Justice's opinion in U.S. v. Nicaragua, notes that the "scale and effects" of an intervention were more important in determining whether a state's actions constituted an armed attack than whether the forces employed were regular armed forces or some form of paramilitary force.

[69] *Id.* at 56 ¶ 9 of Commentary to Rule 13. *See also id.* at 55 ¶ 6 of Commentary to Rule 13 ("The International Group of Experts agreed that any use of force that injures or kills persons or damages or destroys property would satisfy the scale and effects requirement [of an armed attack].").

[70] *Id.* at 56, ¶ 9 of Commentary to Rule 13.

[71] Koh, *supra* note 33, at 3 ("Commonly cited examples of cyber activity that would constitute a use of force include, for example: (1) operations that trigger a nuclear plant meltdown; (2) operations

then, given the disagreement between the *Manual*'s experts, the common point of agreement between the *Manual* and the U.S. position is the requirement for harm to persons or damage or destruction of property.[72] In this sense, there is very little practical difference, if any, between the U.S. views on an illegal use of force/armed attack in the cyber arena and the *Manual*'s definition of an armed attack.[73] In responding in self-defense to an armed attack outside of a traditional armed conflict, a state's reaction is constrained by the principles of necessity and proportionality, regardless whether the armed attack is directly kinetic or results from cyber operations.[74] Proportionality in the *jus ad bellum* legal regime is not the same as proportionality as it is used in international humanitarian law, or the *jus in bello* (the laws applying during conflicts). During armed conflicts, proportionality requires that the military advantage to be gained from an attack outweighs the reasonably foreseeable deaths or injuries to civilians and damage to civilian property from an attack.[75] In the *jus ad bellum* Article 51 self-defense setting, it means that a state's response must be proportionate to the threat that is presented during the armed attack against the state.[76] In that sense, the state is not limited to responding "in kind" to the attack, but may take the steps it deems necessary to eliminate the threat confronting it. It may be

---

that open a dam above a populated area causing destruction; or (3) operations that disable air traffic control resulting in airplane crashes.")

[72] *Accord* Schmitt, *supra* note 35, at 13, 21 ("The Experts and the US Government agree that cyber operations that kill or seriously injure individuals or cause serious damage to objects qualify as armed attacks."). With respect to the *Manual*'s "classic scenario" of the cyber incident against the NYSE that was not among Koh's examples, it appears that the current U.S. view, as articulated by Koh, tends to side with those in the *Manual*'s International Group of Experts who require harm to persons or damage to objects as a condition precedent to an armed attack determination. After providing the examples quoted *supra* note 61 and accompanying text, he states "[o]nly a moment's reflection makes you realize that this is common sense: if the physical consequences of a cyber attack work the kind of physical damage that dropping a bomb or firing a missile would, that cyber attack should equally be considered a use of force." Koh, *supra* note 33, at 3.

[73] At first blush, one possible difference might be Koh's use of "significant" as a modifier to describe, ostensibly, a quantum of property damage or destruction required. Although the *Manual*'s Rule 13 on armed attack uses the rather ambiguous "scale and effects" formulation, its subsequent discussion focuses on "the most grave" uses of force as described in the International Court of Justice's Nicaragua (Merits) opinion. *See* Tallinn Manual, *supra* note 34, at 55 ¶ 6 to Commentary to Rule 13 (*quoting* Nicaragua, *supra* note 63, para. 191). Although the Commentary to Rule 13 does not describe the difference between a use of force and armed attack using the word, in the *Manual*'s discussion of use of force in Rule 11, the drafters acknowledge that the phraseology they use to describe a use of force ("[a]cts that injure or kill persons or damage or destroy objects") is "analogous" to the conclusion they draw in the Commentary to Rule 13. Commentary to Rule 13 concerning armed attacks explains that "the harm [is required] to be 'significant.'" Tallinn Manual, *supra* note 35, at 47, 48 ¶ 8 to Commentary to Rule 11.

[74] Tallinn Manual, *supra* note 35, at 61 Rule 14.

[75] *Additional Protocol* I, *supra* note 45, Art. 57 provides a working definition of proportionality under the heading of under a rule establishing precautions in the attack noting combatants should "refrain from deciding to launch any attack which may be expected to cause incidental loss of civilian life, injury to civilians, damage to civilian objects, or a combination thereof, which would be excessive in relation to the concrete and direct military advantage anticipated."

[76] *See* Nicaragua, *supra* note 63, para. 194.

difficult, however, to ascertain the nature and extent of that threat when the armed attack occurs via cyberspace operations.

As is often noted, the nature of cyberspace lends itself to anonymity and operations carried out in a clandestine manner. As a result, attribution of cyberspace operations has historically been difficult. Recent years, though, have seen any number of examples of forensic examinations leading to attribution in fairly short order, often by using the increasingly useful technique of crowdsourcing.[77] Particularly when a piece of malware enters a network that is not connected to the Internet (known as "air gapped" systems), the nature of the threat is very hard to determine. The receiving state may not know whether the malware's entry vector was based on vulnerability in its own system or occurred from placement by witting or unwitting hands. When the malware just shows up on an air gapped system, with no obvious entry vector or connection to the outside world, framing a response to the threat presented by the malware becomes extremely difficult. Stuxnet's entry into an "air gapped" industrial control system at Iran's Natanz nuclear facility is an example.[78]

Stuxnet is the closest example of an armed attack occurring in cyberspace to date, but even it may not have crossed the armed conflict threshold. The victim state, Iran, never characterized Stuxnet as an armed attack,[79] even though it met the significant physical damage requirement of the *Tallinn Manual* and the U.S. government's recently stated position. This fact illustrates an important aspect of the *jus ad bellum* framework: while the characterization of use of force as an armed attack is supposed to be a de facto one, the actual characterization by the nation-states involved is often a political decision that differs from the facts.

Once Stuxnet is set aside as a candidate, the drop-off to the next possible candidate for an armed attack is steep and rapid. The conclusion reached by the *Tallinn Manual*'s International Group of Experts is concise: "No international cyber incidents have, as of 2012, been unambiguously and publicly characterized by the international community as reaching the threshold of an armed attack."[80] Despite the lack of acknowledgment of a cyber event rising to the level of an armed attack, there remains a substantial amount of cyberspace activity presenting significant threats to the national interests of states. Whether these threats

[77] *See, e.g.*, Zetter, *supra* note 55 (describing the twenty-four hour, round-the-clock and round-the-world efforts by Symantec researchers on Stuxnet); Kim Zetter, *DuQu Mystery Language Solved with the Help of Crowdsourcing*, WIRED (Mar. 19, 2012) (describing efforts of security research firm Kaspersky to get public assistance from the Internet "crowd" to diagnose the coding language used in malware suspected to be related to Stuxnet).

[78] Paul K. Kerr, *The Stuxnet Computer Worm: Harbinger of an Emerging Warfare Capability*, CRS 1 (Dec. 9, 2010). The theory that air gapping protects systems, or even exists, is losing support, partly because of incidents such as Stuxnet. Eric Byres, *Air Gaps a True Myth*, INDUSTRIAL SAFETY & SECURITY SOURCE (July 5, 2012), *available at* http://www.isssource.com/air-gaps-a-true-myth/.

[79] For a discussion on the possible reasons Iran never claimed Stuxnet as an armed attack, see Gary D. Brown, *Why Iran Didn't Admit Stuxnet Was an Attack*, 63 JOINT FORCES Q. 70 (4th Quarter 2011).

[80] TALLINN MANUAL, *supra* note 34, at 57, 58 ¶ 13 of Commentary to Rule 13.

are in the nature of espionage, system access efforts, or disruption, the question arises as to what can be done about such threats when self-defense measures are not an option. The next section discusses the international law concept of countermeasures, the potential use of that concept as a legal rationale justifying non-forcible response measures, and the circumstances under which such response measures could be undertaken by a state.

C. COUNTERMEASURES IN CYBERSPACE

When a state is the victim of an international wrong committed by another state, one of the available responses for the victim state under international law is to initiate one or more countermeasures, to include retorsion.[81] Hence if an unlawful use of cyber force against a victim state falls below the Article 51 threshold of armed attack, hence not providing the victim state with a right to self-defense, the victim state can nonetheless lawfully resort to countermeasures in response. Countermeasures must be non-forcible in nature and are subject to strict conditions of execution. In addition, their execution carries a certain degree of risk for states that err in their use. This section identifies the requirements necessary for a state to consider the use of countermeasures, identifies the conditions and limitations that international law places on the use of countermeasures by a state, and then applies those requirements, conditions, and limitations to a real-world example in order to demonstrate the possible utility of countermeasures in defensive cyberspace operations. This section is not intended to be an exhaustive treatment of the application of countermeasures in cyberspace operations. The intent, instead, is to introduce the reader to a concept that is anticipated to receive increasing attention as states experience increased levels of state-sponsored cyber activity posing threats to their national security interests, but without rising to the level of an armed attack (or without rising to the level of an unlawful use of force, if one uses the U.S. interpretation, which seems to define "use of force" as an armed attack, per the discussion *supra*).

For a state to consider the use of a non-forcible countermeasure, it must be responding to an internationally wrongful act committed by another state.[82]

---

[81] Countermeasures are, by traditional definition, unlawful actions rendered lawful because they are undertaken as countermeasures. Draft Articles on Responsibility of States for Internationally Wrongful Acts, International Law Commission, Art. 22 (2001) [hereinafter *Draft Articles*] ("The wrongfulness of an act of a State not in conformity with an international obligation towards another State is precluded if and to the extent that the act constitutes a countermeasure taken against the latter State . . ."). A more accurate, albeit less well-known international law concept, is retorsion. Retorsion is simply the imposition of harsh, though not necessarily illegal, measures undertaken as a specific and comparable response to harsh measures undertaken by the victim of the retorsion. *Id.* at 128 (describing retorsion as "'unfriendly' conduct which is not inconsistent with any international obligation of the State engaging in it even though it may be a response to an internationally wrongful act."). Cyberspace complicates the division between countermeasures and retorsion because there is not universal agreement on precisely which actions are unlawful. Because of that ambiguity, this chapter uses "countermeasures" as a generic term to cover both situations.

[82] *Id.* at 129.

There are two key aspects of this overarching requirement. First, the receiving state must determine that the activity in question is, in fact, an internationally wrongful act.[83] Such a determination can be based on the sending state's failure to abide by an obligation that it has under international law.[84] The obligation does not have to be based on a treaty obligation, but may be based in customary international law applicable to all states.[85] Most particular to cyberspace operations, for example, may be actions occurring in or through cyberspace that violate a state's sovereignty or the prohibition on intervening in the internal affairs of other states (the non-intervention principle). Actions violating either of these principles could be construed as an internationally wrongful act.

The second aspect of this requirement (that a state commit an international wrong) is the need for the conduct to be attributed to the sending state.[86] There are a number of key methods for attributing conduct to a state. In the easiest case, conduct by an organ of the state is attributable to the state, without regard to how the organ is characterized (executive, legislative, or judicial, or any other function).[87] There are other permutations, such as whether a person or entity exercises elements of government authority, particularly the authority responsible for the international wrong,[88] and the instance when state organs are placed at the disposal of a state by another state.[89]

If we move beyond organs or entities directly associated with a state, a state can be held responsible for conduct committed by a person or group when that conduct is committed under the state's direction or control or when the person or group are acting on the state's instructions. There are a great many issues and complications with this approach, not least of which is the quantum and type of evidence necessary to demonstrate the degree of direction and control or instructions necessary to invoke state responsibility for the international wrong.

---

[83] *Id.* at 130 stating:

> A State taking countermeasures acts at its peril, if its view of the question of wrongfulness turns out not to be well founded. A State which resorts to countermeasures based on its unilateral assessment of the situation does so at its own risk and may incur responsibility for its own wrongful conduct in the event of an incorrect assessment.

[84] *Id.* ("Countermeasures may only be taken by an injured State in order to induce the responsible State to comply with its obligations under Part Two, namely, to cease the internationally wrongful conduct . . . .").

[85] *Id.* at 55 ("International obligations may be established by a customary rule of international law, by a treaty or by a general principle applicable within the international legal order.").

[86] *Id.* at 130 (stating in the Commentary that "countermeasures may only be adopted against a State which is the author of the internationally wrongful act").

[87] *Id.* at 40, Article 4 ("The conduct of any State organ shall be considered an act of that State under international law, whether the organ exercises legislative, executive, judicial or any other function . . . .").

[88] *Id.* at 42, Article 5 (stating that states are responsible for the conduct of persons or entities that are not organs of the state, but who are "empowered by the law of that State to exercise elements of the governmental authority . . . .").

[89] *Id.* at 43, Article 6 ("The conduct of an organ placed at the disposal of a State by another State shall be considered an act of the former State under international law . . . .").

Instances of direction and control attribution often arise when a state entity, such as an intelligence agency, recruits individuals or a group to act as proxies. In his September 2012 speech on the application of international law to cyberspace operations, U.S. State Department Legal Adviser Koh confirmed that the U.S. view was in accord with the Draft Articles on State Responsibility: "States are legally responsible for activities undertaken through 'proxy actors,' who act on the state's instructions or under its direction or control."[90] It is important to note, however, that a state will not be held responsible for all the actions of a group to which the state is providing general support.[91] Instead, the state will only be held responsible for the specific operations that it directed or controlled.[92] Obviously, this requirement complicates the evidentiary problem immeasurably.

Once a state has determined the existence of an international wrong committed against it by another state, the state must comply with very specific conditions before it can execute countermeasures. First and foremost, the countermeasure may only be taken against the state that is committing the international wrong.[93] That is not to say, however, that the effects of a countermeasure may only legally impact the offending state or the offending state's citizens. As the Commentary to the Draft Articles on State Responsibility make clear, countermeasures may have "incidental" effects on a third state or third parties located outside the offending state.[94] Such indirect effects may even go so far as to cause substantial economic disruptions in businesses located outside the offending state.[95] Second, a countermeasure may only be taken against an *ongoing* international wrong, because the object of the countermeasure is to persuade the offending state to abide by its international law obligations and cease the activity that constitutes the wrong.[96] A third corollary condition to this last point is that the countermeasure must not be permanent in nature.[97] Once the offending state initiates compliance with its international obligations, the countermeasure must be halted so that the respective states may resume their international obligations.[98] As a final condition to the execution of countermeasures,

---

[90] Koh, *supra* note 33, at 4.

[91] *See Draft Articles*, *supra* note 81, at 47 (Commentary to Art. 8) (characterizing the International Court of Justice's decision in *Nicaragua* as holding the United States responsible "for its own support for the contras" while "only in certain individual instances were the acts of the contras themselves held attributable to it, based upon actual participation of and directions given by that State.").

[92] *Id.*

[93] *Id.* at 129 (Article 49(1)) ("An injured State may only take countermeasures against a State which is responsible for an internationally wrongful act in order to induce that State to comply with its obligations under Part Two.").

[94] *Id.* at 130.

[95] *Id.* at 130–31 (Commentary to Art. 49) (using an example of suspension of a trade agreement with the responsible state causing "one or more companies [to] lose business or even go bankrupt").

[96] *Id.* (stating that the purpose of countermeasures is to "induce [the offending] State to comply with its obligations of cessation and reparation.").

[97] *Id.* at 130 (stating that the phrase "for the time being" in paragraph 2 of Article 49 "indicates the temporary or provisional character of countermeasures," whose object is the "restoration of a condition of legality" between the states); *id.* at 131 (stating that paragraph 3 of Article 49 imposes a duty on states to "as far as possible choose countermeasures that are reversible").

[98] *Id.* at 137 (Article 53) ("Countermeasures shall be terminated as soon as the responsible State has complied with its obligations under Part Two in relation to the internationally wrongful act.").

the state desiring to exercise countermeasures must first call upon the responsible state to comply with its obligations under international law and, failing that, provide notice to the responsible state of its intent to take countermeasures and offer to negotiate with the offending state.[99] Of these two notice requirements—notice of international wrong and notice of intent to take countermeasures—only the second does not need to occur if there is a need to take "urgent countermeasures" in order for a state to "preserve its rights."[100]

There are also important limitations on the execution of countermeasures. Chief among them is that the countermeasure must be "commensurate with the injury suffered."[101] This proportionality concept for countermeasures is not the same as that for the exercise of self-defense, where the response must be proportionate (commensurate) to the threat, which allows for a response that is much wider in scope, because "threats" may be varied and multiple in scope.[102] Likewise, this limitation is not the same as the proportionality principle in the laws of armed conflict, because the countermeasures limitation is about limiting the response to the nature of the harm imposed by the international wrong, and does not involve a balancing of military necessity with foreseeable death, injury, or damage.[103] As previously mentioned, countermeasures may not involve the use of force. Other limitations are that countermeasures must observe protections for fundamental human rights, they may not be taken as reprisal for the international wrong suffered, and, in addition to the peremptory norm against the use of force, a countermeasure may not violate any other peremptory norm of general international law.[104]

Although there are no examples of states using countermeasures in the cyber domain, it is possible to examine the potential application of the countermeasures doctrine to activity in cyberspace by using a real-world example of suspected state-backed cyberspace activity. In September 2012, a number of U.S. banking websites were subjected to distributed denial of service (DDoS) actions that caused those sites to be unavailable to bank customers for short periods of time.[105] Banks affected included Bank of America, Citigroup, Wells Fargo,

---

[99] *Id.* at 135 (Article 52) ("Before taking countermeasures, an injured State shall: (a) call upon the responsible State, in accordance with article 43, to fulfill its obligations under Part Two; (b) notify the responsible State of any decision to take countermeasures and offer to negotiate with that State.").

[100] *Id.* at 135 (Art. 52(2)).

[101] *Id.* at 134, Art. 51 ("Countermeasures must be commensurate with the injury suffered . . .").

[102] *See* TALLINN MANUAL, *supra* note 34, at 62 ¶ 5 of Commentary to Rule 13 (describing self-defense proportionality as "the scale, scope, duration, and intensity of the defending response to that required to *end the situation that has given rise to the right to act in self-defense*") (emphasis added).

[103] *Compare id.* (focusing proportionality in countermeasures on the "injury suffered") *with Additional Protocol* I, *supra* note 45, Art. 51(5)(b) (stating that attacks may not cause "incidental loss of civilian life, injury to civilians, damage to civilian objects, . . . which would be excessive in relation to the concrete and direct military advantage anticipated").

[104] *See Draft Articles*, *supra* note 81, at 131(Art. 50).

[105] *See generally* Nicole Perlroth & Quentin Hardy, *Bank Hacks Were Work of Iranians, Officials Say*, N.Y. TIMES, Jan. 9, 2013, at B1.

U.S. Bancorp, PNC, Capital One, Fifth Third Bank, BB&T, and HSBC.[106] Unlike previous historical DDoS actions, though, these DDoS disruptions involved unprecedented levels of bandwidth, up to 70 Gigabits per second (Gbps), which complicated the banks' efforts at mitigation.[107] The DDoS actions also introduced the novelty of using the banks' encryption processes against them by flooding the bank sites with encryption requests.[108] This method provides the ability to slow the site's performance with fewer overall requests.[109] An Iranian hacker group, Izz ad-Din al-Qassam Cyber Fighters, has taken responsibility for the DDoS actions, claiming they were retaliation for an anti-Islam video that made fun of Muhammad.[110] James A. Lewis, a cyber security expert with the Center for Strategic and International Studies and a former official with the Departments of State and Commerce, attributed the DDoS actions to the Iranian government: "There is no doubt within the U.S. government that Iran is behind these attacks."[111] Anonymous U.S. government sources also provided the same assessment in press reporting.[112] Iran, however, denied any responsibility for the DDoS actions against the banking websites.[113]

Before the United States could use countermeasures against Iran, it would have to determine that the DDoS actions constituted an international wrong. In this case, if committed by a state, the actions interfere with the ability of U.S. citizens to use banking services provided by U.S. banks hosted on servers located in the United States. Although there is no physical violation of U.S. territory, the DDoS action has disruptive effects on U.S. territory and U.S. citizens. Accordingly, it is a violation of sovereignty, and also likely a violation of the non-intervention principle. Of course, both determinations hinge upon the other requirement that the wrong be attributed to a state actor, which is difficult to meet given the current public record. Anonymous assertions will not support the attribution required under international law.[114] Even if the U.S. government were to go on the record with the claim that the DDoS actions were undertaken at the direction and under the control of the Iranian government, some quantum of evidence would be necessary to support such an assertion before the international community.[115] Such

---

[106] *Id.*

[107] *Id.*

[108] *Id.*

[109] *Id.*

[110] *Id.*

[111] *Id.*

[112] *Id.*

[113] *Id.* If Iran did accept responsibility, it might argue that the activity was a countermeasure undertaken in response to the unlawful U.S.-Israeli Stuxnet attack against it.

[114] *See Draft Articles, supra* note 81, at 35 ("In this as in other respects the attribution of conduct to the State is necessarily a normative operation. *What is crucial is that a given event is sufficiently connected to conduct (whether an act or omission) which is attributable to the State* under one or other of the Rules set out in chapter II.") (emphasis added).

[115] For instance, although a disaster of substance, then-Secretary of State Colin Powell's speech to the United Nations in advance of the U.S. invasion of Iraq in 2003 is an example of a state putting forth an intelligence-based case in front of the international community to justify a state action. *See,*

instances usually involve revealing information collected during the course of a state's intelligence operations, and thus risk exposing sources and methods, so states are often reluctant to make such assertions or provide extensive factual support when they are made. A full exploration of how such an assertion would be supported under international law is beyond the scope of this discussion. Suffice to say that under the present circumstances, there is insufficient attribution to Iran to support the use of countermeasures as a response to what are arguably simply actions by an Iranian "hacktivist" group.

Assuming *arguendo* that the United States could and would sufficiently support a claim that the DDoS actions were attributable to the Iranian government, how would the conditions and limitations of countermeasures play out in the DDoS scenario? First, any action that would violate international law, but for the doctrine of countermeasures, could only be taken against Iran. This has particular importance in the DDoS scenario as the computer, servers, and networks that are networked together into the "BOTNET" used to conduct the DDoS are generally spread among many countries.[116] Even the command and control servers used to control the DDoS actions are often located in other countries. If the individuals who are sending commands to the servers to control the BOTNET are located in Iran, it may be possible to take an action through cyberspace on the systems they are using, in order to stop the DDoS from continuing. If it is necessary to take action on the elements of the BOTNET that are located outside Iran, such action could only be taken in a manner that does not violate the sovereignty of the third state. This could be done by seeking the consent and cooperation of the third state or by taking an action that is so *de minimus* as to not itself constitute a violation of the third state's sovereignty.[117]

The present example also presents a question relative to the rule that restricts the use of countermeasures to the time frame wherein the international wrong is ongoing. The DDoS actions in question have continued intermittently from September 2012.[118] According to one report, the heaviest instances occur on Tuesdays, Wednesdays, and Thursdays.[119] The interesting question that arises under the countermeasures doctrine for this scenario is whether a countermeasure can only be taken during a period of active DDoS activity in order to stop that activity (clearly permissible), or in order to prevent that activity from reoccurring may also be taken during a period of consistent or near-consistent

---

e.g., Steven R. Weisman, *Powell Calls His U.N. Speech a Lasting Blot on His Record*, NY Times (Sept. 9, 2005), http://www.nytimes.com/2005/09/politics/09powell.html.

[116] A botnet is a network of "bots" or programs that work on an automated basis. The network of bots may consist of thousands of machines that have been infected with computer viruses so that they may be put to work for some purpose, often criminal. Newton, *supra* note 41, at 175.

[117] Paul A. Walker, *Law of the Horse or Law of the Submarine: The Future of State Behavior in Cyberspace*, Noontime Lecture at the Army War College (Nov. 26, 2013).

[118] Danielle Walker, *Hacktivists Plan to Resume DDoS Campaign against U.S. Banks*, SC Mag. (Mar. 8, 2013), *available at* http://www.scmagazine.com/hacktivists-plan-to-resume-ddos-campaign-against-us-banks/article/283474/#.

[119] *Id.*

episodic activity. The question may assume greater importance if the effectiveness of available countermeasures is impacted by the timing of their employment. This is a very dynamic but unsettled area of the law, particularly with respect to activity in cyberspace that will likely develop further as a result of state practice.

The third requirement of countermeasures is that they must be reversible, or temporary in nature.[120] This is relatively easy to accomplish in cyberspace operations, which can be precisely tailored to achieve specific effects. For instance, DDoS actions will often affect only a specific website or a specific category of websites.[121] Finally, in the Iranian DDoS example, prior to using countermeasures, the United States would be obligated to call upon the Iranian government to cease the alleged international wrong, in this case the DDoS actions against U.S. banks.[122] There is no requirement that this be done in a public manner that alerts the entirety of the international community, but, at a minimum, must occur on a government-to-government basis.[123] Of course, the requesting state would maintain the record of this interaction to help justify at a later date its actions in using countermeasures. This notification requirement must occur prior to the use of countermeasures, though it could also occur contemporaneously with the countermeasures if a state determined that the need to act was so urgent as to excuse or waive the additional requirement to warn a state in advance.[124] The difficulty in the present example is that there has been an ongoing pattern of activity constituting an international wrong over an extended period of time without any apparent effort to address the wrong via countermeasures or any other mechanism. As a result, for purposes of the present example, the United States would also have to warn Iran of the intent to use countermeasures, as there would appear to be no urgent need to take such measures without the required warning.

At the same time, any U.S. response to these alleged Iranian DDoS actions would be limited to measures not involving the use of force, which, as previously discussed, would allow a fairly broad spectrum of action in cyberspace under the U.S. definition of illegal use of force.[125] Also, the U.S. responsive countermeasure must be proportionate to the harm or injury caused.[126] For example, the countermeasure could not disable Internet access across the entire country of Iran as a measure to stop these nuisance actions on a small number of websites in the banking sector. A more proportionate measure would be to affect the computers of those conducting the DDoS actions, by corrupting files or programs used to

---

[120] *See supra* note 97.

[121] *See supra* note 25.

[122] *See supra* notes 99–100.

[123] *Id.*

[124] *Id.*

[125] *Draft Articles, supra* note 81, at 131 (Art. 50) ("Countermeasures shall not affect: (a) the obligation to refrain from the threat or use of force as embodied in the Charter of the United Nations; . . .").

[126] *Id.*

send commands to the BOTNET via the command and control servers or causing those computers to reboot or shutdown.

As the example of the alleged Iranian DDoS actions illustrates, the application of countermeasures in the context of cyberspace is a complicated affair, involving matters of public diplomacy, as well as highly technical and precise cyberspace operations. A high degree of expertise is required to carry out such operations in accordance with international law. For countries in possession of the required infrastructure and skilled personnel, countermeasures present a viable legal rationale for responding to international wrongs in cyberspace not amounting to an armed attack.[127] At the same time, it may prove difficult to implement countermeasures with the type of "net speed" needed to respond to cyber threats and still meet all the requirements, conditions, and limitations under international law. Given that no state has yet acknowledged attempts to respond directly to threats in cyberspace, much less attempted to justify its actions under international law, whether as self-defense or countermeasures, future state practice with accompanying *opinio juris* will have a dramatic impact on the evolution of law in this area.

D. OFFENSIVE CYBERSPACE OPERATIONS

Military forces conducting armed attacks using cyberspace operations—that is, actions causing death, injuries, or damage or destruction of property—trigger the law of armed conflict (LOAC), also known as international humanitarian law (IHL).[128] Specifically, the principles of military necessity, distinction, unnecessary suffering, and proportionality must be applied to targeting decisions and the execution of such operations.[129] This is the clearly established U.S. position, as well as the position of the International Group of Experts that drafted the *Tallinn Manual*.[130] As discussed previously, though, not all states have adopted this position—at least publicly—at this point in the evolution of cyberspace operations.[131]

Prior to our discussing the three key principles in detail, it bears repeating that cyberspace operations that are only disruptive in nature, causing irritation

---

[127] *See* Tallinn Manual, *supra* note 33, at 36 (discussing application of countermeasures in cyberspace Rule 9 "Counter Measures").

[128] "It is DoD policy that . . . [m]embers of the DoD Components comply with the law of war during all armed conflicts, however such conflicts are characterized, and in all other military operations." DODD 2310.01E, *supra* note 39, para. 4.

[129] The principle of unnecessary suffering would also theoretically apply to cyberspace operations, but pertinent instances are rare and speculative, at best. *See* Tallinn Manual, *supra* note 34, at 144 ("Means and methods of cyber warfare will only in rare cases violate [Rule 42 on "Superfluous Injury or Unnecessary Suffering"]."). As such, an extended treatment of unnecessary suffering is best left for another day.

[130] International Strategy for Cyberspace: Prosperity, Security and Openness in a Networked World 9 (2011), The U.S. Presidential Strategy for Cyberspace can be found at: http://www.whitehouse.gov/sites/default/files/rss_viewer/international_strategy_for_cyberspace.pdf (last visited date June 8, 2015) *See also* Tallinn Manual, *supra* note 34, at 5.

[131] *Supra* note 38.

or inconvenience, do not trigger IHL and hence are not subject to the principles of distinction and proportionality.[132] In other words, there is no requirement in IHL for the objects of disruptive cyberspace operations to undergo the rigorous vetting and validation inherent in the U.S. targeting process. That process is designed to ensure that the principles of distinction and proportionality, as well as military necessity, are properly accounted for in the development of targets and the planning of military strike operations. The pace of operations, in the fastest-paced domain of all, would be substantially slowed down and impeded by any requirement to undertake the same type of extensive target development required by traditional targeting analysis. An expedited kinetic targeting cycle in traditional military operations is targeting that occurs within twenty-four hours.[133] Even a nuclear attack from Russia would be detected in time to give the U.S. President twelve minutes to assess and determine a response.[134] By contrast, a cyber-attack could arrive without warning, because of the speed at which packets of information travel across the Internet.[135]

Applying the IHL principles during the use of cyberspace operations that are only disruptive in nature might lead to decisions against the use of such operations when that use could actually serve humanitarian ends.[136] Although IHL application in such situations is not required by law or policy, its principles are, per the authors' experiences, occasionally utilized and result in the misapplication of the IHL principles, which in turn results in undue weight being given to effects that are ancillary in nature, and are neither harmful nor destructive. The sections below focus on the issues generated by the application of these principles within the cyberspace domain.

1. Military Necessity

As in kinetic operations, the military necessity of striking a target in and through cyberspace derives largely from the commander's objectives. The U.S. operational

---

[132] *See* Tallinn Manual, *supra* note 33, at 106–13 Rules 30–32 and accompanying text (discussing the definition of "attack" and the application of the principles of distinction and proportionality to cyberspace actions that cause death, injuries, or destruction).

[133] *See* Joint Chiefs of Staff, Joint Publication 3-60: Joint Targeting, x (Jan. 31, 2013) [hereinafter JP 3-60].

[134] *See* Global Zero, Global Zero U.S. Nuclear Policy Commission Report: Modernizing U.S. Nuclear Strategy, Force Structure and Posture 5 (2012), *available at* http://www.globalzero.org/files/gz_us_nuclear_policy_commission_report.pdf.

[135] For example, information can travel on an undersea cable between Boston and Dublin in sixty-three milliseconds, which means the trip could occur six and a half times in the blink of an eye. *See Hibernia Atlantic Trans-Atlantic Cable System*, *available at* http://www.hiberniaatlantic.com/pdf/hibernia_Brochure.pdf (last visited May 17, 2014); Steve Lohr, *For Impatient Web Users, an Eye Blink Is Just Too Long to Wait*, N.Y. Times (Feb. 29, 2013), *available at* http://www.nytimes.com/2012/03/01/technology/impatient-web-users-flee-slow-loading-sites.html?pagewanted=all&_r=0.

[136] *See* Walker, *supra* note 118, at 52 (comparing effectiveness and lack of collateral damage of DDoS in Georgia in 2008 with NATO bombing of Serbian television station during the Kosovo conflict, leading to sixteen deaths and the station being off-air for six hours).

planning process is premised on starting with an understanding of what the military commander wants to achieve through military operations.[137] With that understanding, targets are developed to accomplish those objectives. How a specific target assists in achieving the military commander's objectives is, in essence, the military necessity for striking that target.[138] Using this process, the objectives drive decisions relative to each target. Then, once the target is selected, the appropriate weapon system is paired against that target in order to achieve the effect against that target required to meet the commander's objective. This simple description of a complex planning process is familiar to U.S. military planners of operations large and small, from nuclear strikes to precision special operations missions. Military cyberspace operations must be planned and executed using the same process to ensure that military necessity for cyber targets is properly identified and integrated into the decision-making process.

The real risk in conducting military cyberspace operations is that shortcuts will lead to changes to the planning process that introduce the possibility of decoupling targets from the commander's objectives.[139] Such an outcome might, then, call into question the military necessity of striking a particular target. Put another way, military planners and lawyers must guard against a tendency in cyberspace operations for target access to drive planning, rather than the other way around. Similarly, beginning the planning process with a "target" already paired with a cyber weapon to generate a specific effect is putting the cart before the horse. As an example, State A and State B are in an armed conflict. During the course of that conflict, one of State A's military commanders wants to use cyber means to affect State B's integrated air defense system as part of a planned attack. Rather than develop direct access to State B's air defense system, State A's cyber planners decide to use an existing access to State B's electrical power system to indirectly affect the air defense system. However, by using this method, State A's cyber planners cannot tell the military commander precisely when the air defense system will be degraded. As a result, the State A military commander decides to use a kinetic strike instead of cyber means to achieve his objective.[140] As this example illustrates, the desired effect of a proposed cyber action should be based on the commander's objectives rather than achieving an effect simply because the possibility exists to achieve the effect.

A proper understanding of the necessity of striking a particular target is also necessary to correctly apply the principles of distinction and proportionality. Although Additional Protocol I does not contain a description of military

---

[137] *See* JP 3-60, *supra* note 133, at xi ("Understanding the military end state and the commander's intent, centers of gravity, objectives, desired effects, and required tasks developed during operational planning provides the impetus for the targeting process.").

[138] *See* Joint Chiefs of Staff, Joint Publication 1-04: Legal Support to Military Operations, II-2 (Aug. 17, 2011) (stating that "the principle of military necessity justifies those measures not forbidden by international law that are indispensable for securing the complete submission of the enemy as soon as possible," and that it is applied with all the other law of war principles).

[139] Paul A. Walker, Address to Cyber Elective Course, Army War College (May 2, 2014).

[140] *Id.*

necessity, the description of "military objective" contained in Article 52(2) is reflective of customary international law: "those objects which by their nature, location, purpose or use make an effective contribution to military action and whose total or partial destruction, capture or neutralization, in the circumstances ruling at the time, offers a definite military advantage."[141] In many respects, military necessity is this description applied to specific targets based on the commander's objectives. The interaction between military necessity and distinction occurs at the point of distinguishing these military objectives, including dual-use objects that meet the above definition, from civilian objectives.[142] Similarly, the "definite military advantage" of striking a target helps form the necessity of striking that target, which is then weighed against the consequences of an attack in the proportionality discussion.[143]

2. Distinction

"The principle of distinction applies to cyber activities that amount to an attack in the context of an armed conflict, and it requires that the intended effect of the attack must be to harm a legitimate *military* target."[144] Civilian objects may not be the object of cyber activity amounting to an attack, but cyberspace presents particular difficulties in differentiating between wholly civilian objects and military objects, which are frequently of a dual-use nature in cyberspace. It is worth understanding, then, what factors turn an ostensibly civilian object in cyberspace into one that can also be considered a legitimate military target for attack.

Although the term "dual-use" does not appear in any treaty or compilation of customary international law, the concept is widely recognized in international law, including by the International Committee of the Red Cross.[145] The term stems from the application of the criteria contained in Additional Protocol I Article 52(2) ("objects which by their nature, location, purpose or use make an effective contribution to military action") to objects that are not inherently military in nature. Civilian objects that make an "effective contribution" to military action are valid military targets for attack.[146] In cyberspace, the swath of infrastructure potentially implicated by this standard is vast. Any military communication system that makes use of the Internet places at least some portions of the Internet infrastructure at risk of attack by an adversary. The Internet was created to be a survivable communications system, and it has retained this character to the present.[147] Internet "packets" of information traverse widely and use multiple paths

---

[141] *Additional Protocol* I, *supra* note 45, Art. 52(2).

[142] *Id.*

[143] The term "direct military advantage" is the equivalent used in Article 51's discussion of proportionality. *Id.*, Art. 51(5)(b).

[144] Koh, *supra* note 33, at 3.

[145] *Additional Protocol* I, *supra* note 45, art. 52(2); Rules, *supra* note 48, at 32.

[146] *Additional Protocol* I, *supra* note 45, art. 52(2).

[147] *See e.g.*, BBC News, *Internet Pioneer Paul Baran Passes Away* (Mar. 28, 2011), *available at* http://www.bbc.co.uk/news/technology-12879908.

to reach their intended destinations. Given the size and extent of the Internet, it appears to have reached the goal of being the ultimate backup communications system. Though it would be ineffective for a combatant to launch cyberspace operations against the vastness of the Internet, it is possible to impact an adversary's Internet communications by targeting in a focused manner. Such operations may consist of targeting specific military networks, which are often linked to the broader Internet through specific, often limited, Internet access points. These "chokepoints" are not only much more effective targets from an operational standpoint, but from a legal perspective they are usually closer and more pertinent to the military end user, resulting in better distinction between military and civilian objectives.

Beyond dedicated military networks, there may be a great deal of latitude to conduct attacks via military cyberspace operations against networks that serve both civilian and military purposes. For instance, the *Tallinn Manual* provides an example of a network being used for military and civilian purposes where it is impossible for the attacker to know with certainty which portion of the network is being used by distinctly military transmissions, as opposed to civilian ones.[148] In fact, as discussed above, the design of the Internet is such that military and civilian transmissions are using all portions of that network at the same time. In such circumstances, the *Manual* states that "the entire network . . . qualifies as a military objective," with the scant qualifier that "those aspects [of the network] in which transmission is reasonably likely."[149] That determination in some respects is already undermined at the outset of the example with the statement that it might be impossible to know which parts of the network are being used for military transmissions.[150]

At the same time, for reasons of both legality and practicality, the *Manual* cautions against targeting broad swathes of the Internet. The *Manual* concludes that "virtually any attack against the Internet would have to be limited to discrete segments."[151] Given the earlier discussion, such discrete segments could be an entire network connected to, or comprising part of, the Internet. This discussion highlights the often-difficult question of exactly what is or is not a "network," given that most of the networks that comprise the Internet share common connection points. Major Internet Service Providers (ISPs) also have their corporate backbone networks that are used to carry traffic between networks, often including military networks. According to the *Manual*, an attack causing destruction of part of such a backbone network would comply with the principle of distinction because the backbone network is properly considered a military object.[152] The same analysis would apply to attacks against the undersea cable systems that carry communications traffic, including highly secure and encrypted military

---

[148] TALLINN MANUAL, *supra* note 34, at 135 ¶ 3 of Commentary to Rule 39.

[149] *Id.*

[150] *Id.*

[151] *Id. at* 136, ¶ 6 of Commentary to Rule 39.

[152] *Id.*

communications, between continents. The *Manual* does provide, though, that the principle of proportionality would apply to deaths, injuries, damage, or destruction resulting from the disruption of emergency, civil defense, disaster relief, and law enforcement services resulting from the destruction of the backbone network or cable system.[153]

Importantly, when the disruption of the network or communication system does not involve destruction or damage of civilian property, or reasonably foreseeable civilian deaths or injuries, there is much greater latitude in conducting military cyberspace operations.[154] The principle of proportionality does not apply in those circumstances. Instead, such operations may be subject to the more amorphous, less easily defined standard of minimizing harm to civilian objects or the exhortations of the Martens Clause.[155] Enforcement of these less-certain terms is difficult. Given the lack of state practice in this area, it is unclear how such concerns will manifest themselves in actual state-sponsored cyberspace operations.

Military cyberspace operations must also comply with that portion of the distinction principle that prohibits indiscriminate attacks.[156] A state must be capable of directing its cyberspace operations only at military objectives. In the past, cyberspace operations have been criticized for an inability to comply with this requirement.[157] To the extent that such analyses were overly reliant on examples of cyberspace activity conducted by nonstate actors, such as criminals and hacktivists, such concerns were largely misplaced. Recent examples of cyberspace activity, some of which may or may not be state-sponsored, illustrate the precision that is possible in the conduct of cyberspace operations. A prime example is Stuxnet, which was apparently designed in such a way as to only affect a very specific industrial control system configuration.[158] According to the

---

[153] *Id.*

[154] *Id. at* 106–13 Rules 30–32 and accompanying text (discussing the definition of "attack" and the application of the principles of distinction and proportionality to cyberspace actions that cause death, injuries, or destruction).

[155] The Martens Clause is named for its author, Fyodor Fyodorovich Martens, the head of the Russian delegation to The Hague Peace Conferences of 1899. "In cases not covered by this Protocol or by other international agreements, civilians and combatants remain under the protection and authority of the principles of international law derived from established custom, from the principles of humanity and from the dictates of public conscience." Hague Convention No. II, Respecting the Laws and Customs of War on Land, Preamble, July 29, 1899. The Clause was repeated in the Laws and Customs of War on Land (Hague IV) in 1907 and provides the spirit behind paragraph 2 of Article 1 of Additional Protocol I to the Geneva Conventions. *See* Hague Convention No. IV, Respecting the Laws and Customs of War on Land, Preamble, Oct. 18, 1907, 36 Stat. 2227, and Annex, 36 Stat. 2295; *Additional Protocol* I, *supra* note 45, art.1.

[156] *Additional Protocol* I, *supra* note 45, art. 51(4).

[157] *See, e.g.*, Duncan B. Hollis, *Why States Need an International Law for Information Operations*, 11 Lewis & Clark L. Rev. 1023, 1042–44 (2007); Davis Brown, *A Proposal for an International Convention to Regulate the Use of Information Systems in Armed Conflict*, 47 Harv. Int'l L.J. 179, 193–97 (2006); Mark R. Shulman, Note, *Discrimination in the Laws of Information Warfare*, 37 Colum. J. Transnat'l L. 939, 953–57 (1999).

[158] Falliere, Murchu & Chien, *supra* note 53, at 2 (stating, in the Executive Summary, that "Stuxnet is a threat targeting a specific industrial control system likely in Iran.").

forensics examinations, that configuration was only located at the Natanz uranium enrichment facility in Iran.[159] Although the Stuxnet malware did manage to get transferred to computer systems outside Natanz and far beyond the borders of Iran, it apparently had no effects in those other locations.[160] In the context of those other locations it became just another piece of inert software sitting on a computer or server.

Other examples of precise potential cyberspace operations abound. For instance, it is possible to target information flowing to and from specific websites through the use of techniques such as Domain Name System (DNS) hijacking. In these cases, only the traffic to specific websites is affected and sometimes redirected to other websites, either for commercial advantage or to deliver a hacktivist information support operations. Even the most notorious blunt cyber instrument, the DDoS action, not considered an attack under IHL, can be used in a manner that can potentially discriminate between military and civilian objects (websites). There are several examples of this. The 2008 Russo-Georgian conflict included DDoS activity against government websites, many of which appear to have been specifically targeted due to their information dissemination capabilities.[161] The alleged Iranian-backed DDoS attacks occurring against U.S. banks were focused on specific websites, with no bleed-over into other sectors.[162] Finally, the hacking collective known as Anonymous also has conducted DDoS activity against single, or point targets, such as PayPal.[163] Though none of these examples were "military objects," they are illustrative of the type of precise DDoS effects that can be delivered based on the use of specific techniques.

Military cyberspace operations can be carried out in a manner that fully comports with and respects the principle of distinction. Military objects, including those known colloquially as "dual-use," can be readily determined and targeted for attack via cyberspace operations in a discriminate manner. As with any other type of military attack, even the most precise action may involve damage to civilian objects, and civilian injuries or even deaths. In such cases, the attack that occurs in or through cyberspace must also comply with the principle of proportionality.

3. Proportionality

In U.S. military practice, the principle of proportionality is put into operational practice through the use of the collateral damage estimate (CDE). The CDE accounts for the deaths, injuries, or damage to civilian objects that results

---

[159] *Id.*

[160] *Id.*

[161] *See* John Bumgarner & Scott Borg, *Overview by the US-CCU of the Cyber Campaign against Georgia in August of 2008*, A US-CCU Special Report, 6 (Aug. 2009), at 6 [hereinafter US-CCU Overview]; Jeffrey Carr, Inside Cyber Warfare 15–19 (2012).

[162] *See* Perlroth & Hardy, *supra* note 105, at B1.

[163] *See* Alex Hamilton, *13 Plead Guilty to Anonymous Hack on Paypal*, techradar.pro (Dec. 12, 2013), http://www.techradar.com/news/internet/thirteen-plead-guilty-to-anonymous-hack-on-paypal/.

incidentally from attacks conducted against military objects.[164] Koh described the principle with respect to cyberspace operations, noting "proportionality prohibits attacks that may be expected to cause incidental loss to civilian life, injury to civilians, or damage to civilian objects that would be excessive in relation to the concrete and direct military advantage anticipated."[165] Decision-makers must therefore weigh any expected collateral injury and damage against the military advantage expected to be gained from the attack, and determine whether the requirement of proportionality is met.

For kinetic operations, there is an established methodology for estimating the collateral damage that will result from a particular type of strike. The methodology examines the characteristics of the chosen weapon, considers the aim point used for the particular strike, and analyzes known factors such as blast radius versus the strength characteristics of the target's construction in combination with surrounding objects.[166] There is substantial discussion in military circles regarding the methodologies for calculating the CDE for attacks occurring during the course of cyberspace operations. As long as the analysis focuses on the appropriate consequences (deaths, injuries, and damage/destruction of property), there is a strong argument that the current CDE methodology is sufficient to account for cyberspace operations. The key is having an accurate understanding of the cyberspace attack's expected outcome, not only in cyberspace, but the effect that is expected to manifest itself, if any, in the physical world. This is not to suggest that the current CDE methodology will apply to every attack in cyberspace, but that it is the proper starting point given the wealth of information developed over the years and used in that model. Two examples serve to illustrate this point.

A common example of an attack in cyberspace is some type of cyberspace activity that shuts down an electrical power system. Speaking in such broad terms, however, masks the fact that any given electrical power system is made up of individual components, with those components having individual elements. As with a kinetic strike, it is these components and elements, whether transformers, generators, power stations, substations, control systems, etc., that will be affected by a given cyber attack. Once that information is known, it is a relatively easy task to analyze how the loss of that component or element will affect the operations of a given electrical power system. Proper application of the CDE methodology will require an understanding of how the cyber capability will operate and what real world effect will be generated. For instance, if the component or element will be damaged due to loss of functionality, there may not

---

[164] *See generally* Gregory S. McNeal, *The U.S. Practice of Collateral Damage Estimation and Mitigation* (Working Paper Series), *available at* http://papers.ssrn.com/sol3/papers.cfm?abstract_id=1819583 (last visited Feb. 17, 2012) (discussing the technical methodology employed by the United States for preplanned targeting and its overarching goal of minimizing civilian casualties).

[165] Koh, *supra* note 33 (source not paginated).

[166] *See* McNeal, *supra* note 164.

be a need to account for possible loss of life such as would occur if the intent is to cause the power generator to explode.[167]

A more difficult example involves injecting false information into an air traffic control system in such a way that it is either intended (or foreseeable) to cause civilian aircraft to crash into each other. In such cases, the current CDE methodology may be of little use when the intent is to cause destruction that, by its desired terms, has a great degree of collateral damage. The example also raises issues related to targeting and military necessity. Is the target the air traffic control system (possibly with the intent to undermine confidence in the system), with the destroyed airliner and civilian occupants being collateral damage? Or is the target the two airliners, and the cyber-attack against the air traffic control system is simply the means to accomplish the operation? It may well be too much of a stretch in order to reach the latter conclusion to determine that two civilian airliners are military objects, but it would not be so farfetched if the two aircraft intended to be involved were both part of the adversary's military, or were otherwise carrying a valid object of attack, such as a senior military leader. Note that in this latter modification, although the individual military leader might supply the military necessity or advantage, the advantage gained would need to be weighed against the civilian loss of life that might also result when the aircraft crashed.

All offensive operations are necessarily dependent on timely and accurate intelligence to understand the target, its military significance, and the expected consequences of the attack. This intelligence requirement is particularly critical in the case of attacks occurring in and through cyberspace, where a great deal more information about the target environment, such as what is connected to that specific element of cyberspace and where it is connected, is necessary in order to accurately understand and assess the impact of a given cyber operation. As with kinetic operations, perfect intelligence is not required prior to conducting operations.[168] However, in the case where a cyberspace operation is going to result in deaths, injuries, and damage to or destruction of property, reasonable steps must be taken by the attacker to ensure she understands the extent of that damage and its characterization as either direct or incidental (collateral).[169]

---

[167] An example often given in public speeches by the Commander of U.S. Cyber Command, General Keith B. Alexander, is that of the Sayano-Shushenskaya hydroelectric plant in Russia. Remote direction was given to bring a turbine online, and the turbine's resulting failure caused seventy-five deaths. Although the direction was properly authorized in this instance, General Alexander uses the example in order to illustrate what could happen if someone gained access to a power plant's system and was able to send an order that either appeared to be properly authorized or appeared to come from proper authority. *See* THOMAS RID, CYBER WAR WILL NOT TAKE PLACE 38 (2013).

[168] The general principle is expressed in Art. 28(a) of the Rome Statute. *See* 1998 Rome Statute of the International Criminal Court, art. 28(a), July 17, 1998, 2187 UNTS 90/37 ILM 1002. Several states, including the United Kingdom and Canada, made this application of the rules explicit in statements accompanying their signing of Add'l. Protocol 1. *See* ICRC, *Treaties and State Parties to Such Treaties*, http://www.icrc.org/applic/ihl/ihl.nsf/States.xsp?xp_viewStates=XPages_NORMStatesParties&xp_treatySelected=470, (last visited May 18, 2014).

[169] *See* TALLINN MANUAL, *supra* note 34, at 159 (Rule 51).

The proportionality analysis for cyberspace operations, including attacks, should not be any different or more expansive than currently exist for kinetic attack operations, but this may be easier in theory than in practice. First, the principle of proportionality applies only to actions meeting the definition of attack, which currently seems to cover only operations resulting in kinetic damage or injury.[170] Under this view, few cyber operations, at least those contemplated today, are required by IHL to be proportionate (although policy considerations and other bodies of law may also constrain the activities of nations). Second, when considering the issue of proportionality, lawyers and policymakers must be aware that collateral effects such as irritation, inconvenience, or network access disruption caused to civilians by attacks occurring in cyberspace do not appear to be appropriate for consideration as collateral damage. The inclusion of such effects risks diluting and negating the importance of the proportionality principle. Moreover, such an expansive view is not likely to survive state practice, primarily because of the foregoing logic, and because of fear that such a view of collateral effects will bleed over into the analysis for the effects of kinetic strikes.

E. TRADITIONAL MILITARY ACTIVITIES

Up to this point in the chapter, the discussion has centered on applying the international law prior to hostilities (*jus ad bellum*), and the international laws applicable during armed conflict (*jus in bello*) to military cyberspace operations. It is also necessary to highlight a number of key domestic law issues. Given the clandestine nature (at least at this point in time) of cyberspace operations, it is necessary to review the Covert Action Statute.[171] Familiarity with the requirements of 50 U.S.C. § 3093 is necessary to ensure that military cyberspace operations are conducted as traditional military activities, and thereby are not considered as covert actions, which are subject to significant restrictions.[172]

50 U.S.C. § 3093 defines "covert action" as "activities of the United States Government to influence political, economic, or military conditions abroad, where it is intended that the role of the United States Government will not be apparent or acknowledged publicly . . . ."[173] The statute mandates a number of procedural steps that must occur as part of the authorization of such activity. Notably, the statute generally[174] requires written Presidential "findings" prior to

---

[170] There are emerging contrary views. *See, e.g.*, Droege, *supra* note 44, at 571–76; Michael N. Schmitt, *The Law of Cyber Warfare: Quo Vadis?*, 25 Stan. L. & Pol'y Rev. 269 (2014).

[171] 50 U.S.C. § 3093 (2014).

[172] The importance of the distinction between traditional military activities and covert actions is that activities that are not covert actions are not subjected to the substantial congressionally imposed requirements for the conduct of covert action.

[173] 50 U.S.C. § 3093(2014).

[174] Under certain circumstances, requiring "immediate action," the written finding may be delayed up to forty-eight hours. *See id.* § 3093(a)(1)(2014).

the execution of covert action and reporting to the House and Senate intelligence committees, among other equally onerous prerequisites.[175]

The use of the phrase "influence political, economic, or military conditions abroad" in the covert action definition is a broad formulation that could potentially implicate a wide range of clandestine military activity, which may be either operational or intelligence-related in nature. Importantly, the statute exempts from its procedural requirements "traditional military activity."[176] Though the term is not defined in the statutory language, it is explained in some detail in the legislative history:

> It is the intent of the conferees that "traditional military activities" include activities by military personnel under the direction and control of a United States military commander (whether or not the U.S. sponsorship of such activities is apparent or later to be acknowledged) preceding and related to hostilities which are either anticipated (meaning approval has been given by the National Command Authorities for the activities and for operational planning for hostilities) to involve U.S. military forces, or where such hostilities involving United States military forces are ongoing, and, where the fact of the U.S. role in the overall operation is apparent or to be acknowledged publicly.[177]

First and foremost, to be a "traditional military activity" it must be under the "direction and control of a United States military commander."[178] Second, the activity must be related to ongoing or anticipated hostilities, with "anticipated" simply meaning, "approval has been given by the National Command Authorities for the activities and for operational planning for hostilities."[179] Here, either the Secretary of Defense or the President (or both) must approve both the specific activity to be carried out in anticipation of hostilities and the operational planning that such activity supports. Critically, when the fact of U.S. participation in the overall operation is apparent, or, in the case of anticipated hostilities, will be apparent or acknowledged publicly, then there is no requirement that U.S. government sponsorship of specific military operations must be apparent or acknowledged.[180] Such operations are still "traditional military activities" even

---

[175] For a full examination of the statute and its implications for military cyberspace operations, see Paul A. Walker, *Traditional Military Activities in Cyberspace: Preparing for "Netwar,"* 22 FLA. J. INT'L L. 333 (2010).

[176] One of the statute's listed exceptions is for "traditional diplomatic or military activities or routine support to such activities." 50 U.S.C. § 3093(e)(2)(2014).

[177] H.R. REP. NO. 102–66, at 24 (1991) (Conf. Rep.), *reprinted in* 1991 U.S.C.C.A.N. 243, 252 [hereinafter Conf. Rep].

[178] *Id.* The legislative history goes so far as to even state the obverse, in that "[a]ctivities that are not under the direction and control of a military commander should not be considered as 'traditional military activities.'" *Id.*

[179] *Id.*

[180] *Id.* This conclusion stems from the parenthetical language in the Conference Report's description of traditional military activity: "(whether or not the U.S. sponsorship of such activities is apparent or later to be acknowledged)." *Id.* The Senate Report was even more explicit on this point, stating:

> [t]he possibility exists, however, that military elements who are not identifiable to the United States could be used to carry out an operation to achieve a military or political

though they are conducted clandestinely (i.e., it is not apparent who is behind the activity) and may never be acknowledged.

Another requirement is that the activity in question must be the type of activity that the military has historically carried out. This requirement stems not only from the use of "traditional" in the exception's description, but also from expressed legislative intent. The Conference Report states "that in defining for the first time in statute the term 'covert action' they do not intend that the new definition exclude any activity which heretofore has been understood to be a covert action, nor to include any activity not heretofore understood to be a covert action."[181] If the activity in question is part of a continuing and evolving pattern of historic military activity, particularly if that pattern of activity predates passage of the 1991 Intelligence Authorization Act,[182] then it may be characterized as "traditional" in nature. Such a determination is agnostic as to the means and methods of warfare used, which allows for technological change and evolution in the means and methods used to carry out traditional ends. As an example, disruption of enemy communications or lines of communication is an ancient and historical practice of militaries, from intercepting and capturing battlefield runners to cutting telegraph lines in the Civil War to the use of electronic warfare to jam radar, radio, and other battlefield communications. In this respect, the use of cyberspace operations to disrupt computer- and network-based communications is simply a new way of conducting old business between opposing militaries.

At the same time, there is nothing in the legislative history of the Covert Action Statute that restricts traditional military activity to any particular geographic boundary or particular area of ongoing hostilities. As long as the activity meets the criteria discussed above and relates to ongoing or anticipated hostilities, then it is properly categorized as a traditional military activity. This is particularly true in the area of Military Information Support Operations (MISO). These operations are generally focused in such a way that the activity occurs in a narrow manner that is either responsive to adversary activity or is disseminated in such a way that it reaches a particular audience.[183] This is so

---

> objective abroad where there is no intent to acknowledge the involvement or sponsorship of the United States. Indeed, such operation need not be in support of U.S. military forces. The Committee does not view this potential use of military forces as a "traditional military activity" under subsection (e)(2).

S. Rep. No. 102–85 (1991).

[181] Conf. Rep, *supra* note 177, at 24.

[182] Intelligence Authorization Act, Fiscal Year 1991, codified in part at 50 U.S.C. § 3093.

[183] *See* Joint Chiefs of Staff, Joint Publication 3-13: Information Operations, II-9 (Nov. 27, 2012) ("MISO are planned operations to convey selected information and indicators to foreign audiences to influence their emotions, motives, objective reasoning, and ultimately the behavior of foreign governments, organizations, groups, and individuals . . . its [Target Audience] includes not just potential and actual adversaries, but also friendly and neutral populations.").

regardless of whether the MISO activities occur in an area of ongoing hostilities or on Internet websites and chat forums that are used to disseminate adversary propaganda.

An argument can be made that for military activity to be considered "traditional," the activity in question must comply with international law, specifically the international body of law known as the law of armed conflict, but also, arguably, all of international law. Under this view, military activity that violates international laws, such as state sovereignty or the nonintervention principle, would not constitute traditional military activity. Under U.S. domestic law, according to this view, such activities would have to comply with the procedural and congressional reporting requirements of 50 U.S.C. § 3093, even if carried out by the armed forces under the direction and control of a military commander. With respect to cyberspace operations, uncertainty surrounding the application of international law principles such as sovereignty, neutrality, and the non-intervention principle, to name but a few, make this analysis a challenge. The challenges posed by the international law compliance requirements inherent to the traditional military activity analysis is discussed in more detail in the final section of this chapter.

IV. Contemporary Challenges and How Military Lawyers Are Influencing the Law

The possibility of cyber warfare has presented a number of new challenges for practitioners, ranging from the basic (such as exactly what is cyber warfare), to the complex (such as how do we distinguish crime, espionage, and acts of international aggression in a low-attribution environment, while still maintaining respect for privacy and freedom of speech). Examples of these challenges are set out below.

One fundamental problem that must be overcome in order to analyze cyber warfare is the difficulty in defining the battle space. Although DoD doctrine asserts that cyberspace is an independent operations domain, on par with land, sea, air, and space,[184] there has been little actual application of this principle to operations. Most approaches to the issue have looked at the effects of cyber operations in physical space, rather than the specific effects of cyber operations in cyberspace. The more interesting issues arise when considering what goes on in cyberspace, wherever and whenever that might be. Put this way, the issue raises unprecedented questions with regard to the difference between domestic and international action, the distinction between military and civilian objects, the role of private citizens and corporations in defending the nation, the issues of sovereignty and neutrality, and more.

---

[184] U.S. Dep't of Def. Quadrennial Defense Review Report 37, Feb. 2010 [hereinafter QDR] ("Cyberspace, defined as a global domain within the information environment that encompasses the interdependent networks of information technology infrastructures, including the Internet and telecommunication networks.").

Legal issues surrounding the classification of armed conflict are similarly challenging. The nuances between the laws governing the resort to armed conflict and the laws governing behavior during an armed conflict tend to blur to an even greater extent for cyberspace operations for two reasons. One is that there is no international consensus on what cyber activity rises to the level of triggering an armed conflict. The second is that the United States has stated it is in an ongoing global armed conflict against al Qaeda and associated forces that justifies the extraterritorial application of armed force against enemy combatants in that conflict.[185] Certainly, this worldview would permit the use of cyber techniques anywhere in the world to advance gains in the conflict, although such operations might be limited by other considerations.

A. CYBER GEOGRAPHY

Cyberspace does not map well to physical geography. Certainly servers, routers, cables, and all the other physical equipment that enables the Internet to exist can be located on the planet or in orbit around the planet. The location of the individual bits of hardware, however, fails to convey the nature of cyberspace. It is not as simple as locating a particular hard drive containing data, and determining whether the country within whose physical boundaries that hard drive is located may properly be targeted. It is easiest to explain the degree of complexity through an example.

Country A and Country X are engaged in an armed conflict. Country X has obtained the secret locations of Country A's military leaders and plans to target them. The geographical coordinates are recorded in an electronic file. Clearly, this file is targetable as military information. If there is but a single copy of the file, determining its physical location may be straightforward. More than likely, however, there are multiple copies of the file located on servers in different places. Still, if all the servers are located in Country X, the geography question is not all that interesting.

To make the situation more realistic, let us say Country A is engaged in an armed conflict with Armed Group X, with members located in many countries around the globe. In this case, X might use the Internet as its primary command, control, and communications system (C3). The Internet is, after all, free, robust, and ubiquitous. Other than the lack of security, though there is a measure of that provided just by virtue of the huge volume of traffic, the Internet is the perfect C3 system. Using its shared C3 system, X stores the file as an attachment to a draft email in a popular email system, and backs it up onto a cloud server provided by a public company. To X, it might appear that there are only two copies of the file, but in reality there are likely several, because both the email and the cloud

---

[185] *See, e.g.*, Jeh Johnson, General Counsel of the U.S. Dep't of Defense, The Conflict against al Qaeda and Its Affiliates: How Will It End?, Address at the Oxford Union, Oxford University (Nov. 30, 2012).

server will be backed up on numerous occasions by the operators of the services. Further, X will not know where the servers containing the backups, or even the originals, of the file are located. For example, the leader of Group X might be in Country Y, saving the electronic file using the Internet services. Both of the services might be headquartered in Country A, but use servers located in countries B, C, D, and Z. In this case, when Country A wants to delete or modify the targetable file, exactly where is the action occurring? Some might argue, although it would be a minority position, that "destroying" the file would constitute a use of force that would be unlawful if carried out in a country in a neutral status. Most would probably conclude the action fell short of a use of force, but might still be in violation of the sovereignty of a neutral country.

Regardless of what legal regime might apply to the activity, destruction and modification of files both seem more like military action than like the collection of intelligence. Consequently, both appear to be appropriate military operations of a non-intelligence variety. On the other hand, the above example could be characterized as an intelligence operation rather than a military operation. Intelligence is critically important to military operations; it has been said that the Allies won WWII through intelligence, specifically through the ULTRA program that cracked Germany's Enigma code.[186] Even in more traditional situations, it can be quite difficult to determine just where intelligence gathering ends and military operations begin. For instance, if special operations forces are stealthily inserted into enemy territory as part of the preparation for hostilities, even if they are only present for the purpose of collecting intelligence, if they damage equipment or injure enemies during the mission, it might be difficult to determine exactly when the "intelligence" mission ended and the "operations" mission began. The same difficulty exists in cyber operations, but just to make it clear that the same issues exist when cyber operations have more direct physical effects, let us examine a cyberspace operation that aims to create a kinetic effect.

Using the same actors set out above, let us say Group X has a piece of malware that is capable of infecting the control system for major oil pipelines, causing overpressure in the pipelines that will lead to breaks, major oil spills, and interruption of strategic oil supplies. The malware is saved to a dozen free file upload servers, from where it will be downloaded by several dozen hacker members of Group X who will deploy it immediately thereafter. Country A's decision to delete copies of this malware will include consideration of whether such an action will violate the sovereignty of the countries where the targeted servers are located. This malware is objectively a bad thing, and it is tempting to think that the host countries would be responsible for its deployment. As details above establish, it is not as simple as it might first appear. It is difficult to determine exactly whose territory is hosting the malware. Even if that is possible, pinning responsibility on the sovereign would require determining the sovereign was aware of the existence

[186] *See A Byte out of History* (Oct. 6, 2011), *available at* (http://www.fbi.gov/news/stories/2011/october/intelligence_100611/intelligence_100611).

of the malicious software on its territory and made a conscious decision not to take steps to prevent its distribution.[187]

B. CYBER SPEED

At speeds that make deliberation impossible, and algorithms that defy any logic outside the Internet, using geography to explain what goes on just does not work very well. Internet packets make the round trip between the United States and Europe in about sixty-five milliseconds.[188] When the weapons of cyber warfare can move back and forth between continents fifteen times each second, it is only the artificial application of traditional rules to the situation that make it appear the weapons exist at one location exclusively.[189] Considered at the speed at which humans interact with the world, the packets, or weapons, exist in both places simultaneously. This is just one more aspect of the difficulty in applying traditional notions of geography to cyberspace.

C. ATTRIBUTION AND IDENTITY

Despite the assurances of former Defense Secretary Leon Panetta in his October 2012 speech on cyberspace, attribution will continue to remain an incredibly complex issue for cyberspace operations.[190] In traditional kinetic operations, attribution is usually not a problem. It was pretty clear, for example, who invaded Poland in 1939. The 1983 bombing of the U.S. Marine barracks in Beirut marked the beginning of a new era in warfare. Unattributed, or loosely attributed, bombings (often suicide bombings), of targets valuable to strategically powerful nations leaves those nations often unable to respond. This asymmetric and unlawful type of warfare makes it challenging for nations to strike back.[191] Cyber operations continue along the same line, although so far with no directly lethal results. When banks are hacked or utilities' systems penetrated, responsibility and attribution for the hack is often difficult for the victim state to establish. Without such attribution, it is difficult for states to mount a response.

Complicating matters further, even when an action is attributed to an individual, in some cases during the Russo-Georgian conflict in 2008, the standing of the individual may be unclear.[192] An individual hacker may be acting based on a criminal

---

[187] *See generally* Ashley S. Deeks, *Pakistan's Sovereignty and the Killing of Osama Bin Laden*, American Society of International Law Insights, http://www.asil.org/insights110505.cfm (last visited May 5, 2011).

[188] *See* http://www.internettrafficreport.com/.

[189] There is significant debate about what qualifies as a weapon in cyberspace. Some of the debate can be found at Duncan Blake & Joseph S. Imburgia, *"Bloodless Weapons"? The Need to Conduct Legal Review of Certain Capabilities and the Implications of Defining Them as "Weapons,"* 66 Air Force L. Rev. 157 (2010); Thomas Rid & Peter McBurney, *Cyber-Weapons*, 157 Rusi J. 6 (Mar. 2012).

[190] *See* Panetta, *supra* note 60.

[191] QDR, *supra* note 184, at 37.

[192] Evgeny Morozov, *An Army of Ones and Zeros: How I Became a Soldier in the Georgia-Russia Cyberwar*, Slate, Aug. 14, 2008, http://www.slate.com/id/2197514 (describing his effort to "enlist" in

motivation, or may merely be mischievous. Or the hacker may be acting out of a sense of patriotism (as a "hacktivist"), may be loosely guided by a national government (as a sort of modern privateer), or may be directly employed by a government as an intelligence or military asset. There are an endless number of motivations that may be driving the behavior. The most important thing to note is that finding out who was sitting at the keyboard, even in cases where that is possible, does not tell the whole story.

V. Overlapping Authorities and Equities

To date the United States has been indecisive, at least in public, regarding which U.S. government entity is responsible for defending the nation's cyberspace and cyber infrastructure. On paper, DoD is responsible for defending DoD's cyber assets.[193] DHS is responsible for protecting the nation's other cyber infrastructure, including nonmilitary government networks and private sector assets.[194] The familial struggle continues, however, despite the written guidance.

DHS asserts its primacy in the area of cyber security, leaving cyber defense to DoD.[195] DoDn wants U.S. Cyber Command to be co-located with the nation's largest intelligence agency (the National Security Agency, or NSA) in order to operate; based on this, DoD asserts its willingness to handle cyber defense for the whole nation. Yet the public is uncomfortable with NSA "reading its email"[196] while the United States has also publicly condemned China for stealing the intellectual property of U.S. companies.[197] This makes it appear that the United States

---

the cyberwar in order to illustrate the media fallacy describing the hand of Russia behind the action, and relating his experience of, within an hour, finding three separate methods that could be used against Georgia, two of them fairly simple to use and at least one from a Russian hacker website); Carr, *supra* note 161, at 89–90.

[193] *See* U.S. Cyber Command mission statement, http://www.stratcom.mil/factsheets/Cyber_Command/ (last visited June 8, 2015).

[194] *See* Department of Homeland Security mission statement, http://www.dhs.gov/national-cyber-security-division (last updated Dec. 17, 2012).

[195] It is a DHS mission to "safeguard and secure cyberspace." *See* http://www.dhs.gov/safeguard-and-secure-cyberspace (last updated Oct. 2, 2012).

[196] *See, e.g.,* Adam Clark Estes, *Prepare to Have Your Email Read by NSA*, The Atlantic Wire, June 17, 2011, http://www.theatlanticwire.com/technology/2011/06/prepare-have-your-email-read-nsa/38931/.

[197] *See, e.g., China's Cyber-Intrusions off Concern, Says Hillary Clinton*, Reuters, May 4, 2012, http://www.huffingtonpost.com/2012/05/04/china-cyber-intrusions_n_1476865.html;

Office of the National Counterintelligence Executive, *Foreign Spies Stealing U.S. Economic Secrets in Cyberspace: Report to Congress on Foreign Economic Collection and Industrial Espionage, 2009-2011* (Oct., 2011), http://www.ncix.gov/publications/reports/ fecie_all/Foreign_Economic_Collection_2011.pdf; Mark Landler, Clinton Urges Global Response to Internet Attacks, N.Y. Times, Jan. 21, 2010, http://www.nytimes.com/2010/01/22/world/asia/22diplo.html.

is condemning spying, except that it agrees with the rest of the world that espionage is not prohibited under international law.[198]

Meanwhile, the FBI's ability to help private companies with cyber security from the inside is limited, because companies fear inviting the FBI in will result, among other ills, in expansive investigations and loss of reputation, and consequent loss of stock value.[199] Congress says something must be done regarding cyber security, and legislators have said DHS cannot get the job done, but Congress has been unable to pass a cyber-security bill for twelve years.[200] The White House has threatened to issue an executive order to avoid the congressional impasse. In conclusion, confusion reigns supreme.

Related to the issue of who in government should be primarily responsible for cyber security is the issue of who will be in charge of cyber forces. Command and control (C2) is one of the most important, and certainly the most mundane, of the issues confronting those who operate in this area. Because of the loose (to nonexistent) connection between cyber operations and physical geography, there is no immediately identifiable correct answer to the question "Who ought to be in charge of this planned operation?" A few specific challenges in this area are set out below.

As noted *supra*, cyber operations intended to have an effect in a given location will almost certainly occur on some cyber infrastructure located somewhere else. For example, forces operating in Afghanistan may rely on the Internet as a communications platform . . . and why not? It is free, robust, and ubiquitous. If International Safety Assistant Forces wished to prevent access to a web page known to be used by the enemy, it could do so by affecting access on the user's end, perhaps by intercepting traffic at a router. The router might be located in a neighboring country. ISAF might also conduct the operation by disrupting the web page on the hosting server, which almost certainly would be located somewhere outside Afghanistan. This simple example illustrates how any cyber operation is likely to cross national boundaries. This can create real conflicts in determining who is in charge, because national boundaries are how states organize their militaries and foreign affairs.

For most nations, the question of who should run an operation in a given geographic region typically assumes that the national leadership has decided which agency should be in charge. In U.S. cyber operations, the choices are many. The FBI, NSA, CIA, DoD, DoS, and DHS, among others, all have publicly declared

---

[198] *See* Heather Harrison Dinnis, Cyber Warfare and the Laws of War 157 (2012) ("espionage in time of war is not a violation of the laws of armed conflict (as evidenced by Article 24 of the Hague Regulations above), or indeed any other international law. . . .").

[199] *See* James B. Comey, Director, Federal Bureau of Investigation, Address at RSA Conference, San Francisco (Feb. 26, 2014), *available at* http://www.fbi.gov/news/speeches/the-fbi-and-the-private-sector-closing-the-gap-in-cyber-security.

[200] *See* Benjamin Wittes, Lawfare (Feb. 14, 2013, 7:48 AM), http://www.lawfareblog.com/2013/02/allan-friedman-on-why-the-executive-order-on-cyber/ (quoting Allan Friedman, and noting, among other things, that Congress has failed to pass a cyber security bill since 2002).

cyber capabilities. With cyber adversaries operating in the nether region among military operations, terrorism, and criminal activity, the challenge becomes obvious.

Further complicating matters is that cyberspace may be thought of as a man-made domain. Cyberspace is facilitated by the Internet, which is largely privately owned. This means civilians will be involved in any cyber action. Involving civilians in any military action can be legally challenging, but the cyber subspecies of military actions are even more complex. Most civilians involved in military operations, whether at the leadership or action level, are government employees, or at least government contractors. In cyberspace, operations will, almost by definition, involve nongovernment civilians.

One unprecedented challenge in cyber warfare is that, in many ways, private industry is better equipped to handle the threat than the military, because the private sector has years of experience dealing with said threat. Most cyber warfare is conducted over the Internet; the traffic is controlled by private entities that are in the best position to see and counter threats. In fact, even if a government ultimately takes action, it would rely on reporting by industry, as well as industry's facilitation of government action—unless the government takes over the provision of Internet services. This may be different in China, where the government has a much more invasive role in Internet services, largely through the "Great Firewall," a collection of computer security measures managed by as many as fifty thousand civil servants to control and monitor its citizens' access to information on the Internet.[201]

A final challenge for those involved in this area has involved crafting useful doctrine applicable to cyber operations. Cyber doctrine may be unique in military history, in that other doctrine has been codified over time, and after significant practice of the type of warfare at issue. Whether one considers military doctrine to have started with Sun Tzu 2,500 years ago or with Western military manuals in the early twentieth century, it has previously been a collection of what might be referred to as "best practices" in warfare.[202] There was plenty of land and sea warfare practice to study before the military manuals were written, and airpower doctrine did not begin to develop until after the strategic bombing and other air exchanges of World War II.[203]

Cyber doctrine has been different. DoD struggled mightily over cyber doctrine, even taking the unusual step of issuing a Joint Test Publication when it could not achieve consensus on cyber doctrine after years of debate.[204] There have

---

[201] *See* Lulu Yilun Chin, *Breaking Through China's Great Firewall*, BLOOMBERG BUSINESSWEEK, Mar. 20, 2014, *available at* http://www.businessweek.com/articles/2014-03-20/secretive-web-activists-give-chinese-a-way-around-censorship. *See also* http://www.greatfirewallofchina.org/ (last visited May 18, 2014).

[202] Dennis Drew & Don Snow, *Military Doctrine from Making Strategy: An Introduction to National Security Processes and Problems* (Aug. 1988), *available at* http://www.au.af.mil/au/awc/awcgate/readings/drew1.htm.

[203] *Id.*

[204] *See* John T. Bennett, *GAO: Conflicting Orders Have Led to Confusion over DOD's Cyber Strategy*, THE HILL, Aug. 30, 2011, http://thehill.com/news-by-subject/defense-homeland-security/178795-gao-analysts-conflicting-orders-have-led-to-confusion-over-dods-cyber-strategy.

been protracted efforts to write national cyber doctrine, apparently culminating in a classified Presidential Policy Directive, as reported by the media. However, Presidential directives are high-level documents and do not typically address the nuts and bolts of military practice.[205] At the core of the problem is the lack of cyber operations available for study. Without some sampling of what has or has not worked in cyber operations, the crafting of cyber doctrine would be based primarily upon speculation, and this would rob it of effectiveness. In the absence of evidence, the creation of doctrine has degenerated into another interagency battle over manpower and resources.[206]

With all this in the background, military lawyers can help by ensuring that whenever cyber operations are conducted, the law and policy supporting them is carefully captured for future reference. It is particularly important for lawyers in this area to follow the guidance given, and, in cases where the rationale is not perfectly obvious, to record how and why they reached their legal conclusions. If the words of orders and policies are simply ignored, they will remain a barrier to future operations and may serve as the basis for future, unworkable doctrine. On the other hand, if the operational legal adviser provides carefully reasoned, written opinions, they might serve as important building blocks for establishing better guidance for future operations.

VI. Conclusion

When cyber operations were used during the Russo-Georgia conflict of 2008, a seemingly new era of armed conflict began. Thereafter, the United States took a number of actions to embrace cyberspace as a new operational domain, to include the very significant step of creating U.S. military command dedicated to cyber space. The military departments created and assigned units to support this new sub-unified command. Clarity in law and policy is needed to support this new capability. Speed, geography, and attribution are three of the major factors that make cyberspace operations problematic from a command and control standpoint. What are the rules of engagement that allow a cyber operator, a junior officer or enlisted member, to know if she can employ a countermeasure or conduct a cyber operation in response to an intrusion or an attack? Does the military have the authority to defend civilian networks inside the United States? The advent of

---

[205] *See, e.g.*, Ellen Nakashima, *Obama Signs Secret Directive to Help Thwart Cyberattacks*, WASH. POST, Nov. 14, 2012, http://articles.washingtonpost.com/2012-11-14/world/35505871_1_networks-cyberattacks-defense.

[206] The *Department of Defense Strategy for Operating in Cyberspace* (July 2011). As the title suggests, the document was proposed to clarify DoD's cyberspace strategy, but did little more than generally articulate the threat and propose information sharing and cooperation across a myriad of federal and international agencies. It was not helpful in setting out cyber doctrine. For a more detailed discussion, see David Fulghum, Paul McLeary & Bill Sweetman, *Cyber Planning Runs Into Bureaucratic Roadblocks*, AVIATION WEEK, Aug. 1, 2011, *available at* http://aviationweek.com/awin/cyber-planning-runs-bureaucratic-roadblocks.

this new domain in warfare raises a number of legal questions. These questions are largely considered ones of domestic law and policy.

As the potential has increased for nations to deliver kinetic effects directed at adversaries through cyberspace, numerous legal questions have arisen to include: What type of law applies, and if traditional IHL applies, to what type of activities does it attach? In response to these questions, the early consensus among Western nations is that IHL does generally apply to cyberspace operations. For example, the United States has stated publicly that IHL applies to cyberspace operations.[207] However, just because a consensus has emerged does not mean that the debates are over, as IHL fails to answer all of the challenges created by cyberspace. Sending troops, aircraft, or weapons over a neutral nation's land or airspace would be a clear violation of that nation's neutrality. However, that same clear understanding is missing when sending 1's and 0's over that same state's telecommunications infrastructure. Is the latter likewise a violation of either a nation's neutrality or its sovereignty? This new domain in warfare has the potential to not only do great harm to interconnected nation-states, much like the advent of the bomber did to the cities of Europe during WWII, but also to advance international humanitarian law in mitigation of catastrophic outcomes related to cyber warfare.

---

[207] *See* Koh, *supra* note 33 (source not paginated).

6 }

Targeting and the Law of Armed Conflict

Gary P. Corn*, James H. Dapper**, and Winston Williams***

Those skilled in war cultivate the Tao (the way of humanity and justice) and preserve the laws and are therefore able to formulate victorious policies.[1]

---

* Colonel Gary P. Corn is a Judge Advocate, United States Army. His most recent assignment is as the Staff Judge Advocate/principal legal advisor for the Commander of US Cyber Command. Other assignments include Chief, Operational Law Branch, International and Operational Law Division, Office of the Judge Advocate General of the Army, Deputy Legal Counsel, Office of the Legal Counsel to the Chairman of the Joint Chiefs of Staff, Staff Judge Advocate, United States Army South, Fort Sam Houston, Texas, and Chief, International Law, Combined Forces Command-Afghanistan, Kabul, Afghanistan. Colonel Corn is a graduate of The Judge Advocate General's School, United States Army (LLM with Honors); George Washington University National Law Center (with Honors); Bucknell University; United States Army War College (MA in National Security Studies, Distinguished Graduate); and the Escola de Comando e Estado Maior do Exército do Brasil (Command and General Staff College of the Brazilian Army), Rio de Janeiro, Brazil.

** Colonel James H. Dapper is an active duty Air Force judge advocate. He obtained his JD at the University of Texas; an MS in strategic studies from the National War College; an MS in electrical engineering from California State University, Long Beach; and a BS in electrical engineering from the University of Texas. Prior to entering the legal profession, Colonel Dapper worked as a developmental engineer on several military satellite programs. He has served as a legal advisor in support of combat air operations, counterterrorism operations, the Joint Staff, and a geographic combatant command. Currently, Colonel Dapper serves as the senior legal adviser for the Air Force's Air Mobility Command. He thanks Colonel Gary Corn for the invitation to contribute to this project, and Professors Geoffrey Corn and Rachel VanLandingham for shepherding it through to completion.

*** Major Winston Williams, U.S. Army, is a Judge Advocate currently serving as an Academy Professor in the Department of Law at the United States Military Academy, West Point, New York. Major Williams has served in a number of legal positions including Trial Counsel for 3rd Brigade, 82nd Airborne Division, Tikrit, Iraq; Senior Trial Counsel, 82nd Airborne Division, Fort Bragg, North Carolina; Senior Operational Law Observer/Controller at the Joint Readiness Training Center, Fort Polk, Louisiana; and Professor of International and Operational Law at the Judge Advocate General's Legal Center and School in Charlottesville, Virginia. Major Williams holds a LLM in Military Law from the Judge Advocate General's School, and a JD from the University of Tennessee College of Law. The positions and opinions in this chapter are those of the authors and do not represent the official views of the Department of Defense or the United States Air Force or Army.

[1] Sun Tzu, The Art of War 88 (Samuel B. Griffith, trans., 1963).

I. Introduction

In the predawn hours of February 14, 1991, two United States Air Force F-117 Nighthawk Stealth Fighters dropped two 2,000-pound GBU-27 laser-guided "Bunker-Buster" bombs[2] on the Al-Firdus district bomb shelter in downtown Baghdad, also known as the Amiriyah shelter.[3] United States Central Command placed the bunker on the Master Attack Plan (MAP)[4] based on an intelligence assessment that, although it was known to have been originally constructed as a bomb shelter, it had been modified to serve as part of the Iraqi national command, control, and communications (C3) network and that senior Iraqi military officials were actively using it to command and control Iraqi forces in the field.[5] The attack resulted in the deaths of several hundred civilians who had been sheltering inside, prompting international outrage and allegations that the attack was a war crime.[6]

Much has been written analyzing the legality of the attack on the Al Firdus bunker.[7] The point here is not to re-litigate the various arguments for and against the attack. What the debate highlights, however, is that the decision to employ lethal combat power[8] in armed conflict is never made in a legal vacuum, no matter how operationally sound the decision might appear to be on its face. Every

---

[2] *See* Andreas Parch, Directory of U.S. Military Rockets and Missiles Appendix 5: Guiding Bombs, Paveway III, Raytheon (Texas Instruments) Paveway III, *available at* http://www.designation-systems.net/dusrm/app5/paveway-3.html (last updated Aug 21, 2008).

[3] Dep't of Defense, Final Report to Congress, Conduct of the Persian Gulf War 194, app. O, at 704 (1992), *available at* http://www.tjsl.edu/slomansonb/9.7_Conduct_PGW_I.pdf [hereinafter Gulf War Final Report]; Rick Atkinson, Crusade: The Untold Story of the Persian Gulf War 284–85 (1993).

[4] Gulf War Final Report, *supra* note 3, at 155. The current U.S. doctrinal term for the target list is the Joint Integrated Prioritized Target List (JIPTL). Joint Chiefs of Staff, Joint Publication 1-02, Department of Defense Dictionary of Military and Associated Terms 150 (Nov. 8, 2010, amended through Aug. 15, 2013) [hereinafter JP 1-02].

[5] Gulf War Final Report, *supra* note 3, at 194. According to the DoD, the bunker displayed other physical indicia of having been converted to a military C3 node, such as having camouflage on the roof, and being surrounded by barbed wire with Iraqi soldiers controlling access. Further, intelligence indicated there were no civilians located in the facility. *Id.*

[6] *See, e.g.*, Dilip Hiro, Desert Shield to Desert Storm: The Second Gulf War 361 (2003); Human Rights Watch, *Needless Deaths in the Gulf War: Civilian Casualties during the Air Campaign and Violations of the Laws of War*, ch. 3, § D (1991), *available at* http://www.hrw.org/reports/1991/gulfwar/CHAP3.htm (asserting that the United States failed to provide required warnings prior to the attack).

[7] *See, e.g.*, Geoffrey S. Corn, Hamdan, *Lebanon, and the Regulation of Hostilities: The Need to Recognize a Hybrid Category of Armed Conflict*, 40 Vand. J. Transnat'l L. 295, 352 (2007); Michael W. Lewis, *The Law of Aerial Bombardment in the 1991Gulf War*, 97 Am. J. Int'l L. 481, 504 (2003) (asserting that the U.S. military correctly assessed the bunker as a legitimate target).

[8] "The total means of destructive and/or disruptive force which a military unit/formation can apply against the opponent at a given time." JP 1-02, *supra* note 4, at 46.

decision to employ lethal, destructive force is grounded in, and bounded by, the authority and proscriptions contained in the law of armed conflict (LOAC).[9]

Disrupting and degrading enemy command and control capabilities makes perfect operational sense, and is a common focus of targeting in armed conflict.[10] Yet in the case of the bombing of the Al Firdus bunker, the decision whether to attack required the commander to consider and render determinations on a series of difficult questions, with limited or imperfect information available at the time.[11] The commander had to ensure not only that the anticipated effects would advance operational objectives, but that the action would be both lawful and consistent with any operational or policy restraints or constraints that had been imposed at higher levels of command.[12]

---

[9] The law of armed conflict, also referred to as the law of war or international humanitarian law, "is that part of [customary and treaty] international law that regulates the conduct of armed hostilities." *Id.* at 164.

[10] *See* U. S. Dep't of Army, Field Manual 3–0, Operations, 7–38 (2008, with Change 1, Feb. 22, 2011) [hereinafter FM 3-0] ("*Disintegrate* means to disrupt the enemy's command and control system, degrading the ability to conduct operations while leading to a rapid collapse of the enemy's capabilities or will to fight."); U.S. Dep't of Army, Field Manual 3–60, The Targeting Process 1–3 (Nov. 26, 2010) ("Attacking command and control nodes may force the enemy to use less capable, less secure backup communications systems that can be more easily exploited by friendly force.") [hereinafter FM 3-60].

[11] Although military commanders often make, and are ultimately responsible for, the decision to conduct specific attacks, more commonly the commander's subordinates make attack decisions based on specified or implied delegations of the commander's authority. The term "commander" is used throughout this chapter to refer to anyone exercising the authority to conduct an attack. *See, e.g.*, Chairman of the Joint Chiefs of Staff Instruction 3160.01A, No-Strike and Collateral Damage Estimation Methodology (Oct. 12, 2012), Encl. D. Although unclassified, this is a controlled publication not available to the general public. The general contours of the No-Strike and CDM can be derived from the superseded version of the instruction, *Chairman of the Joint Chiefs of Staff Instruction 3160.01, No-Strike and Collateral Damage Estimation Methodology* (Feb. 13, 2009), which was released to the American Civil Liberties Union (ACLU) through the Freedom of Information Act, *available at* https://www.aclu.org/files/dronefoia/dod/drone_dod_3160_01.pdf [hereinafter CJCSI 3160.01].

[12] A constraint is "a requirement placed on the command by a higher command that dictates an action, thus restricting freedom of action." JP 1–02, *supra* note 4, at 55. A restraint is "a requirement placed on the command by a higher command that prohibits an action, thus restricting freedom of action." *Id.* at 238. Constraints and restraints are usually contained in mission orders and accompanying Rules of Engagement (ROE). United States' doctrine defines ROE as "directives issued by competent military authority that delineate the circumstances and limitations under which U.S. forces will initiate and/or continue combat engagement with other forces encountered." JP 1–02, *supra* note 4, at 224. Rules of engagement provide a framework that encompasses national policy goals, mission requirements, and the rule of law. Although the doctrines of various armed forces differ, ROE generally tend to perform three basic functions: to act as a control mechanism for the transition from peacetime to combat operations (armed conflict), to provide standing force protection authority and guidance to unit commanders and individual soldiers in the form of self-defense rules, and to provide a command and control mechanism for national command authorities and military commanders to ensure the use of military force complies with strategic political and military aims. *See* Int'l & Operational Law Dep't, The Judge Advocate Gen.'s Legal Ctr & Sch., U.S. Army, Operational Law Handbook 79 (2014) [hereinafter Operational Law Handbook].

For example, did the bunker qualify as a lawful target by virtue of its nature, location, purpose, or use as a lawful military objective? Did the fact that it was originally constructed as a bomb shelter afford it some special status or degree of protection against attack? If so, had the Iraqi military failed to properly identify it as such, or had they used it in such a manner as to divest it of its protected status? Were civilians (commonly referred to as noncombatants[13]) present in the bunker or within the range of the lethal effects of the attack? If so, were they participating directly in hostilities? If not, would the expected incidental harm to them be excessive in relation to the concrete and direct military advantage anticipated from the attack? Were means other than attacking with the two GBU-27s available to achieve the same effect at less risk to non-combatants? Was the United States required to issue a warning prior to effecting the attack? Did the commander have a duty to develop additional intelligence to better answer any or all of the preceding questions prior to authorizing the strike?

Before use of lethal combat force the LOAC compels commanders and soldiers at every echelon of operations to answer predicate legal questions such as those listed above. Whether it is an infantryman training his individual weapon on suspected enemy soldiers, or a brigade operations officer authorizing the use of indirect fires against an unidentified individual observed through grainy video feed digging a hole in a road at night, both must make a good faith judgment, at a minimum, that the intended object of attack is a legitimate military target whose engagement is not anticipated to inflict unreasonable collateral damage. Although as noted below, some targets are selected and approved through a deliberate process with the luxury of time, the reality of combat is usually quite different; combatants[14] are frequently required to make these life-or-death judgments with only seconds to deliberate.

Use of well-trained military lawyers to assist commanders and other operational decision- makers with LOAC application might be ideal, and is in fact an increasing reality in many militaries around the world.[15] But it is unrealistic to think that military lawyers will always be available to advise on the legality of employing deadly combat power, and an error to think their advice should ever

---

[13] Technically, non-combatants are defined as members of the armed forces who are hors de combat (out of combat) because they are wounded, sick, shipwrecked, or prisoners of war, or fulfill certain non-combat functions such as chaplains and medical personnel. *See* Operational Law Handbook, *supra* note 12, at 16; Int'l & Operational Law Dep't, The Judge Advocate Gen.'s Legal Ctr. & Sch., Law of War Deskbook 135–37 (2011) [hereinafter Law of War Deskbook]. The term is used here in its more colloquial sense of those persons not participating directly in hostilities.

[14] Unless otherwise indicated, the term "combatants" is used in the broad sense of belligerents, that is, persons engaged in hostilities in an armed conflict on behalf of a party to the conflict. *See, e.g.*, UK Ministry of Defence, The Manual of the Law of Armed Conflict 37–38 (2004) [hereinafter UK Manual]; Law of War Deskbook, *supra* note 13, at 95–97, 134.

[15] *See* Protocol Additional to the Geneva Conventions of 12 August 1949, and Relating to the Protection of Victims of International Armed Conflicts art. 82, June 8, 1977, 1125 U.N.T.S. 3 [hereinafter AP I] ("The High Contracting Parties at all times . . . shall ensure that legal advisors are available, when necessary. . . .").

substitute for the operator's decision-making obligation. As the adage goes, military lawyers advise, commanders decide.

Thus, although training all combatants on the core principles of the LOAC is both legally required and operationally sound,[16] experience has shown that the development and employment of rigorous, disciplined targeting systems and procedures is a vital—perhaps even the most predictably effective—means for ensuring maximum LOAC compliance in relation to the use of combat power. Commanders, their staffs, and the soldiers, sailors, airmen, and marines who execute military operations depend on simplified systems that make routine the integration of law into operational planning and execution. These systems—all of which seek to effectuate, among other things, the synchronization of law and operations—transform the complex rules and principles of the LOAC into digestible, understandable, trainable, and easily applicable concepts.

Targeting involves a delicate and fluid balance of military art and science, the science serving only as an aid to the art of military decision-making.[17] The availability and efficacy of the science will vary depending on the dynamics of the operational environment, to include the time, available information, and level at which the decision is being made. Generally, the disciplined, repeatable processes employed in well-developed targeting systems such as the U.S. Joint Targeting Process are only practicable for selecting and engaging deliberate, or preplanned, targets; this type and method of target selection usually occurs at the operational or strategic level.[18] At the tactical level, where target engagement is typically much more fluid and time-constrained, the art of targeting predominates. But although operational exigencies may not allow for application of all the specific procedures of the Joint Targeting Process, the underlying principles are the same, and are applied to the maximum extent feasible to guide every targeting decision. Experience also teaches that, when possible, these systems and procedures are most successful when they integrate military legal experts into the decision-making process.

It is said that these systems and procedures "operationalize" the LOAC, which is the subject of this chapter. Before addressing the targeting process itself,

---

[16] States are explicitly required to "include the study [of the law of armed conflict] in their programmes of military . . . instruction, so that the principles thereof may become known to all their armed forces." Geneva Convention for the Amelioration of the Condition of the Wounded and Sick in Armed Forces in the Field art. 47, Aug. 12, 1949, 75 U.N.T.S. 31 [hereinafter GC I]; Geneva Convention for the Amelioration of the Condition of Wounded, Sick, and Shipwrecked Members, art. 48, Aug. 12, 1949, 75 U.N.T.S. 85 [hereinafter GC II]; Geneva Convention, Relative to the Treatment of Prisoners of War, art. 127, Aug. 12, 1949, 75 U.N.T.S. 135 [hereinafter GC III]; Geneva Convention Relative to the Protection of Civilian Persons in Time of War, art. 144, Aug. 12, 1949, 75 U.N.T.S. 287 [hereinafter GC IV]. *See also* DEP'T OF DEFENSE DIRECTIVE 2311.01E, DOD LAW OF WAR PROGRAM, para. 5.7.2 (May 9, 2006) (certified current as of Feb. 22, 2011) (mandating the implementation of effective programs to prevent violations of the law of war, including law of war training and dissemination).

[17] *See* CJCSI 3160.01, *supra* note 11, at D-1 to D-2.

[18] *See infra*, notes 110 to 111 and accompanying text.

however, the chapter turns first to a review of the core LOAC principles governing the means and methods of employing combat power.

II. The Law of Targeting

Those most familiar with war understand that it "is a *violent clash* of competing interests between or among organized groups, each attempting to impose their will on the opposition."[19] War, and its modern analog of armed conflict, is without question the single most violent and destructive endeavor upon which humans embark. And although warfare itself is not per se unlawful,[20] it is universally recognized that during *any* armed conflict, the warring parties' discretion to employ violence is not legally unfettered. The international community has, since the mid-to-late nineteenth century, accepted that belligerents must "refrain from employing any kind or degree of violence which is not actually necessary for military purposes."[21] Its correlative foundational maxim, found in the "Regulations concerning the Laws and Customs of War on Land, annexed to Hague Convention IV Respecting the Laws and Customs of War on Land" (Hague IV), is that "[t]he right of belligerents to adopt means of injuring the enemy is not unlimited."[22]

The limitations on the right of belligerents referred to in Article 22 of the Fourth Hague Convention are found in the body of positive and customary norms that comprise the LOAC, developed within two broad but overlapping frameworks: the *Hague Tradition* of regulating the means and methods of warfare, and the *Geneva Tradition* of respecting and protecting the victims of warfare.[23] The former, derived primarily from Articles 22 through 41 of the annex to Hague IV, as well as several treaties regulating specific aspects of warfare such as the 1993 Chemical Weapons Convention, generally regulates tactics, stratagems, and weapons. Of the two traditions, the Hague Law is generally considered as providing the more relevant normative framework for assessing targeting decisions.[24]

---

[19] Strategic Landpower Task Force, *Strategic Landpower: Winning the Clash of Wills*, 2 (2013), *available at* http://www.arcic.army.mil/app_Documents/Strategic-Landpower-White-Paper-28OCT2013.pdf.

[20] For a discussion of the body of international law governing the legal basis for states to use force against one another, referred to as the *jus ad bellum*, see Operational Law Handbook, *supra* note 12, at 1–8; Law of War Deskbook, *supra* note 13, at 25–35.

[21] Dep't of the Army, Field Manual 27-10, The Law of Land Warfare, par. 3 (July 18, 1956, with Change 1, July 15, 1977) [hereinafter FM 27-10].

[22] Regulations concerning the Laws and Customs of War on Land, annexed to Hague Convention IV Respecting the Laws and Customs of War on Land, Oct. 18, 1907, 36 Stat. 2277, art. 22 [hereinafter Hague IV]; AP I, *supra* note 15, art. 35(1) ("In any armed conflict, the right of the Parties to the conflict to choose methods or means of warfare is not unlimited.").

[23] *See, e.g.*, Law of War Deskbook, *supra* note 13, at 17–19.

[24] However, this distinction (between Hague and Geneva law) lost significant meaning in 1977 when the two traditions were effectively merged in Additional Protocols I and II to the 1949 Geneva Conventions. Although the United States is not a signatory to either of the Additional Protocols,

United States Army commanders are instructed that:

> Those who plan or decide upon an attack . . . must take all reasonable steps to ensure not only that the objectives are identified as military objectives or defended places . . . but also that these objectives may be attacked without probable losses in lives and damage to property disproportionate to the military advantage anticipated.[25]

This brief, but important directive reflects the base principles of conflict regulation that lie at the heart of the LOAC and that define the legal boundaries of the targeting process. These four fundamental LOAC principles are assayed below.

A. THE FOUR FUNDAMENTAL PRINCIPLES

The LOAC is not intended to outlaw war or impede the parties' ability to effectively wage hostilities. So long as the parties to a conflict wage hostilities within the borders of the LOAC, "they may be pursued fiercely and relentlessly."[26] It instead reflects a delicate balance between the necessity, and hence the authority in warfare to use sufficient force to destroy an enemy's warfighting capabilities, and the humanitarian maxims that the unnecessary suffering of combatants should be prevented, and civilians should be spared the harmful effects of military operations to the maximum extent possible.[27] As such, the law of targeting "requires that all reasonable precautions . . . be taken to ensure that only military objectives are targeted so that non-combatants, civilians, and civilian objects are spared as much as possible from the ravages of war."[28] The four fundamental principles of military necessity, distinction, proportionality, and humanity that underlie the LOAC provide the basis for the rules governing targeting decisions.

---

it considers as reflective of customary international law most of the Protocols' provisions relevant to targeting. *See Remarks in Session One: The United States Position on the Relation of Customary International Law to the 1977 Protocols Additional to the 1949 Geneva Conventions*, in *The Sixth Annual American Red Cross -Washington College of Law Conference on International Humanitarian Law*, 2 AM. U.J. INT'L L. & POL'Y 419 (1987). Customary international law (CIL) is that law resulting from the general and consistent practice of states followed from a sense of legal obligation or *opinio juris*, and is binding on the United States. *See* RESTATEMENT (THIRD) OF FOREIGN RELATIONS LAW OF THE UNITED STATES, Vol. I, §§ 102, 111 (AM. LAW INST. 1987); *see also* The Paquete Habana, 175 U.S. 677 (1900); *see also* LAW OF WAR DESKBOOK, *supra* note 13, at 3.

[25] FM 27-10, *supra* note 21, at para. 41.

[26] YORAM DINSTEIN, THE CONDUCT OF HOSTILITIES UNDER THE LAW OF INTERNATIONAL ARMED CONFLICT 2 (2d ed. 2010).

[27] *Id.* at 4–6 ("[LOAC] must be predicated on an equilibrium between the two diametrically opposed stimulants of military necessity and humanitarian considerations.").

[28] DEP'T OF THE NAVY, NAVAL WARFARE PUBLICATION 1-14M, THE COMMANDER'S HANDBOOK ON THE LAW OF NAVAL OPERATIONS 8.1 (July 2007) [hereinafter LAW OF NAVAL OPERATIONS].

1. Military Necessity

First codified in the Lieber Code in 1863,[29] the principle of military necessity justifies only those measures in warfare, not otherwise prohibited by international law, which are indispensible for securing the complete or partial submission of the enemy as soon as possible with the minimum expenditure of life and resources.[30] Although the principle of military necessity is a reflection of the underlying authority of belligerents to employ lethal, destructive force against enemy personnel and property, it is simultaneously recognition that that authority is not without limit.[31]

"The principle of military necessity recognizes that force resulting in death and destruction will have to be applied to achieve military objectives, but its goal is to limit suffering and destruction to that which is necessary to achieve a valid military objective."[32] Before attacking any target, a military commander or decision-maker must make a predicate determination that the intended attack is militarily necessary. Application of overwhelming force against the enemy's military capabilities is then permitted so long as it does not employ an otherwise prohibited means or method of warfare, and is consistent with the principles of distinction, proportionality, and humanity, as discussed below.

2. Distinction

Of the four LOAC principles the most critical to the targeting process is that of distinction. Characterized as a "cardinal principle" of the law by the International Court of Justice,[33] distinction is central to the limitation of destruction associated with warfare and to the protection of the civilian population from the harmful effects of war.[34] The essence of the principle is that civilians should be spared, to the maximum extent feasible, from the effects of military operations. As such, military attacks (understood to be any acts of violence against the enemy, whether in offense or defense),[35] should be directed only against military targets, including combatants, and not at civilians, civilian objects, or non-combatants.

---

[29] Instructions for the Government of Armies of the United States in the Field (Lieber Code), 24 April 1863, art. 14.

[30] FM 27-10, *supra* note 21, para. 3; UK MANUAL, *supra* note 14, at 21–22.

[31] As evidenced by the rejection of the German plea of "Kreigsraison" at Nuremburg. *See* United States v. List (The Hostage Case), reprinted in 11 TRIALS OF WAR CRIMINALS BEFORE THE NUREMBURG MILITARY TRIBUNALS UNDER CONTROL COUNCIL LAW NO. 10, at 1230 (1950). Military necessity is available as a defense only with respect to those LOAC norms that specifically include it as an exception to a general proscription, such as Article 23(g) of Hague IV. *See* DINSTEIN, *supra* note 26, at 6–7.

[32] *See* LAW OF NAVAL OPERATIONS, *supra* note 28, at 5.3.1.

[33] *Advisory Opinion on the Legality of the Threat or Use of Nuclear Weapons*, 1996 ICJ Rep. 226, 257.

[34] *See* LAW OF WAR DESKBOOK, *supra* note 13, at 141 ("The principle of distinction . . . forms the foundation for much of the Geneva tradition of the law of war").

[35] AP I, *supra* note 15, art. 49.

This requirement thereby serves as the prima facie means of shielding civilians from the effects of combat by essentially immunizing them from attack.

Although firmly rooted in the customs and usages of war, it was not until 1977 that international will finally coalesced around a codified definition of the principle of distinction.[36] This definition was established in Protocol I Additional to the Four Geneva Conventions of 1949 (AP I), along with numerous rules intended to implement the principle. Taken together, these provisions provide the framework for assessing the legality of proposed targets. Article 48 of AP I provides:

> In order to ensure respect for and protection of the civilian population and civilian objects, the Parties to the conflict shall at all times distinguish between the civilian population and combatants and between civilian objects and military objectives and accordingly shall direct their operations only against military objectives.[37]

The application of this principle during armed conflict is so central to the regulation of warfare that it transcends treaty obligations, and applies to all armed conflicts as a matter of customary international law.[38] According to the International Committee of the Red Cross Commentary to AP I, distinguishing between lawful and unlawful targets is at the very foundation of virtually every provision of the contemporary law of armed conflict.[39]

The first, and perhaps the most important provision implementing Article 48's basic rule of distinction, is the rule of military objective.[40] In order to implement the distinction obligation, military operations must be directed only at those

---

[36] *See* Commentary on the Additional Protocols of 8 June 1977 to the Geneva Conventions of 12 August 1949, 615 (Yves Sandoz et al. eds., 1987)[hereinafter AP I Commentary] (indicating that the rule related to the protection of civilians from the harmful effects of hostilities "explicitly confirms the customary rule that innocent civilians must be kept outside hostilities as far as possible and enjoy general protection against danger arising from hostilities.").

[37] AP I, *supra* note 15, art. 48.

[38] Eritrea—Ethiopia Claims Commission, Partial Award, Western Front, Aerial Bombardment and Related Claims, 45 ILM 396, 417, 425 (2006).

[39] *See* AP I Commentary, *supra* note 36, at 586:

> [The rule of distinction] is the foundation on which the codification of the laws and customs of war rests: the civilian population and civilian objects must be respected and protected in armed conflict, and for this purpose they must be distinguished from combatants and military objectives. The entire system established in The Hague in 1899 and 1907 (1) and in Geneva from 1864 to 1977 (2) is founded on this rule of customary law.

Other sources of authority support this proposition. As noted above, the International Court of Justice emphasized the customary nature of this principle in the Advisory Opinion on the Legality of the Threat or Use of Nuclear Weapons. *Advisory Opinion on the Legality of the Threat or Use of Nuclear Weapons*, 1996 ICJ Rep. 226, 257. *See also* Richard I. Miller, The Law of War 17–27 (1975) ("Although it was never officially contained in an international treaty, the principle of *protection* and of *distinction* forms the basis of the entire regulation of war . . . .").

[40] *See* AP I Commentary, *supra* note 36, at 630 ("[I]n order to apply the basic rule contained in Article 48, it is necessary to know what constitutes civilian objects, on the one hand, and military objectives, on the other.").

persons, places, or things that qualify as lawful military objectives. Article 52(2) of AP I defines military objective as "those objects which by their nature, location, purpose or use make an effective contribution to military action and whose total or partial destruction, capture, or neutralization, in the circumstances ruling at the time, offers a definite military advantage."[41] All other persons, places, and things are, by definition, civilians or civilian objects that "shall not be made the object of attack."[42]

The rule of military objective has two components: persons and objects.[43] With respect to the former, it is generally understood that members of the enemy armed forces, referred to as combatants or belligerents, are considered lawful military objectives, unless hors de combat.[44] However, the exact meaning of "enemy armed forces" is subject to substantial debate. Much of this debate is driven by AP I's seemingly strict dichotomy between combatants and civilians: Article 50 defines civilians in the negative, as anyone who does not qualify as a combatant under Article 4 of the Third Geneva Convention and Article 43 of AP I.[45] Thus, AP I would seem to suggest that one is either a (lawful) combatant *or* a civilian, at least in armed conflicts characterized as international. However, this interpretation may be at odds with the U.S. concept of unprivileged enemy belligerents.

Neither the Geneva Conventions nor AP I specifically identify or define a separate category of "unlawful" combatants or belligerents, leading some to conclude that, at least with respect to international armed conflicts, no such category exists.[46] The United States, however, considers that members of organized armed groups, whether privileged to engage in hostilities or not, are distinct from civilians.[47] For the purposes of targeting, such individuals qualify as

---

[41] AP I, *supra* note 15, art. 52(2). For a discussion of the evolution of the rule of military objective, see Horace B. Robertson Jr., *The Principle of the Military Objective in the Law of Armed Conflict*, *in* THE LAW OF MILITARY OPERATIONS 197 (Michael N. Schmitt ed., 1998). The rule of military objective is also closely associated with, and often described as a component of the principle of military necessity. *See, e.g.*, LAW OF WAR DESKBOOK, *supra* note 13, at 133; LAW OF NAVAL OPERATIONS, *supra* note 28, at 5.3.1.

[42] AP I, *supra* note 15, art. 51(2); 52(1).

[43] Although Article 52(2) refers only to objects, it is understood to include enemy personnel within its meaning. *See, e.g.*, UK MANUAL, *supra* note 14, at 54; DINSTEIN, *supra* note 26, at 89. According to the ICRC's Official Commentary to the rule, "[i]t should be noted that the definition is limited to objects but it is clear that members of the armed forces are military objectives . . . ."). AP I Commentary, *supra* note 36, at 635 (quoting the Preamble of the Declaration of St. Petersburg).

[44] For a discussion of the rules regarding those persons hors de combat, see LAW OF WAR DESKBOOK, *supra* note 13, at 135–36.

[45] Article 4 of GC III and 43 of AP I define combatants as: "Members of the armed forces of parties to the conflict; members of militias and organized resistance movements belonging to a Party to the conflict; members of regular armed forces belonging to governments not recognized by the Detaining Power; and members of a levee en masse—inhabitants of non-occupied territory who spontaneously take up arms to resist invading forces." GC III, *supra* 16, art. 4; AP I, *supra* note 14, art. 43.

[46] *See* LAW OF WAR DESKBOOK, *supra* note 13, at 96 (citing Pub. Comm. Against Torture in Israel v. Gov't of Israel, HCJ 769/02 (2005)).

[47] *Id.* at 96–97. This issue is further clouded in the case of non-international armed conflicts, where the LOAC provides less regulation or definitional guidance. *See id.* at 100–01. For a discussion of the issue of civilians and belligerents in non-international armed conflicts, see NILS

legitimate military objectives on the same basis as GC III and AP I combatants. As such, they may be targeted at any time during the pendency of the conflict. As noted, however, not all countries recognize the concept or category of unlawful or unprivileged belligerents, and thus consider all individuals not meeting the GC III/AP I definition of combatants to be civilians protected from attack unless and only while they participate directly in hostilities.

Applying the rule of military objective to individuals is further complicated by the unsettled concept of direct participation in hostilities (DPH). This rule, expressed in Articles 51 and 13 of AP I and II respectively, provides simply that "[c]ivilians shall enjoy the protection afforded by this [section/part] unless and for such time as they take a direct part in hostilities."[48] On its face, this rule may seem straightforward. Civilians who take up arms and commit hostile acts against a party to the conflict forfeit their protected status under the LOAC and "may be attacked in the same manner as identified members of an opposing armed force."[49] However, the exact contours of the DPH exception, both as to the specific meaning of direct participation and the temporal parameters of the rule, have been and remain the subject of intense debate.[50] Applying this rule on the contemporary battlefield, where belligerents (combatants) frequently fail to distinguish themselves from the civilian population, and civilians often participate sporadically in hostilities to varying degrees, has proved exceptionally difficult.[51]

As noted, Article 52 of AP I also protects civilian objects from attack or reprisal, limiting attacks strictly to military objectives: objects that "make an effective contribution to military action and whose total or partial destruction, capture or neutralization, in the circumstances ruling at the time, offers a definite military

---

MELZER, INT'L COMM. OF THE RED CROSS, INTERPRETIVE GUIDANCE ON THE NOTION OF DIRECT PARTICIPATION IN HOSTILITIES UNDER INTERNATIONAL HUMANITARIAN LAW 26–32 (2009), *available at* http://www.icrc.org/web/eng/siteengo.nsf/html/p0990.

[48] AP I, *supra* note 15, art. 51(3); Protocol Additional to the Geneva Conventions of 12 August 1949, and Relating to the Protection of Victims of Non-international Armed Conflicts, art. 13.

[49] OPERATIONAL LAW HANDBOOK, *supra* note 12, at 21.

[50] The intensity of this debate is reflected in the strong opposition expressed to the International Committee for the Red Cross 2009 *Interpretative Guidance on the Notion of Direct Participation in Hostilities under International Humanitarian Law*, to include many of the experts who participated in the six-year project to produce the guidance; many withdrew their names from the final product because of this issue. *Compare* NILS MELZER, INT'L COMM. OF THE RED CROSS, INTERPRETIVE GUIDANCE ON THE NOTION OF DIRECT PARTICIPATION IN HOSTILITIES UNDER INTERNATIONAL HUMANITARIAN LAW 78 (2009), *available at* http://www.icrc.org/web/eng/siteengo.nsf/html/p0990 *with* Michael N. Schmitt, *The Interpretive Guidance on the Notion of Direct Participation in Hostilities: A Critical Analysis*, 1 HARV. NAT'L SEC'Y J. 5 (2010); W. Hays Parks, *Part IX of the ICRC "Direct Participation in Hostilities" Study: No Mandate, No Expertise, and Legally Incorrect*, 42 INT'L L. & POL. 769, 778–80 (2010); Kenneth Watkin, *Opportunity Lost: Organized Armed Groups and the ICRC "Direct Participation in Hostilities" Interpretive Guidance*, 42 N.Y.U. J. INT'L L. & POL. 641 (2010).

[51] *See, e.g.*, OPERATIONAL LAW HANDBOOK, *supra* note 12, at 21. *See generally* Rachel VanLandingham, *Meaningful Membership: Making War a Bit More Criminal*, 35 CARDOZO L. REV. 79 (2013) (analyzing and proposing legal criteria for determining membership in nonstate armed groups, for purposes of lethal targeting as combatants during armed conflict, in the absence of such criteria in extant LOAC).

advantage" to the attacking party.[52] All objects "used directly by the armed forces," such as weapons, tanks, transports, command and control systems, etc., are by their nature military objectives and subject to attack.[53] Locations may be considered military objectives if they are "militarily important because they must be captured or denied an enemy, or because the enemy must be made to retreat from them."[54] A bridge, for example, may qualify as a military objective based on its importance to friendly or enemy maneuver. "Purpose," as used in Article 52, refers to the future intended or possible use of an object,[55] whereas "use" is "concerned with [the object's] present function."[56] Thus, a civilian runway built to military specifications so it can be used for military aircraft in time of conflict may qualify as a military objective, as will a school presently occupied by enemy troops.

It should be noted, however, that those who plan or decide on attacking an object are under a duty to do everything feasible to verify that it is in fact a military objective.[57] Further, in the case of doubt whether objects normally dedicated to civilian purposes have been converted to military objectives, the attacking force must presume that they have not, and refrain from attacking them.[58]

3. Proportionality

The principle of distinction, as implemented by the rule of military objective, is the starting point for any legal analysis of a targeting decision, for it imposes on the commander an obligation to refrain from intentionally targeting civilians or civilian objects. But, as evidenced by the example of the Al Firdus bunker, the intermingling of military objectives and protected civilians is a ubiquitous fact of modern warfare. As such, inherent in the principle of distinction is the

---

[52] AP I, *supra* note 15, art. 52.

[53] AP I Commentary, *supra* note 36, at 636 ("A closer look at the various criteria used reveals that the first refers to objects which, by their 'nature,' make an effective contribution to military action. This category comprises all objects directly used by the armed forces: weapons, equipment, transports, fortifications, depots, buildings occupied by armed forces, staff headquarters, communications centres etc.").

[54] OPERATIONAL LAW HANDBOOK *supra* note 12, at 20. According to the AP I Commentary:

> Clearly, there are objects which by their nature have no military function but which, by virtue of their location, make an effective contribution to military action. This may be, for example, a bridge or other construction, or it could also be, as mentioned above, a site which is of special importance for military operations in view of its location, either because it is a site that must be seized or because it is important to prevent the enemy from seizing it, or otherwise because it is a matter of forcing the enemy to retreat from it.

AP I Commentary, *supra* note 33, at 636.

[55] OPERATIONAL LAW HANDBOOK *supra* note 12, at 23; LAW OF WAR DESKBOOK, *supra* note 13, at 133.

[56] AP I Commentary, *supra* note 33, at 636 ("The criterion of 'purpose' is concerned with the intended future use of an object, while that of 'use' is concerned with its present function.").

[57] AP I, *supra* note 15, art. 57(2).

[58] *Id.* arts. 52(1), (3). For a discussion of special protections and requirements for certain civilian property such as cultural property, see *infra* notes 83–94 and accompanying text.

attendant obligation to minimize *unintended* harm to civilians to the maximum extent feasible during operations. Although properly directed at a lawful military objective, an attack may be of such a scale or nature as to, in essence, rise to the level of an intentional attack on civilians. The prohibition against such attacks is captured in the LOAC rules implementing the principle of proportionality.

Although civilians "shall enjoy general protection against dangers arising from military operations,"[59] it is not per se unlawful to cause incidental injury to civilians or to damage civilian objects, generally referred to as collateral damage, during an attack against a lawful military objective.[60] The LOAC clearly prohibits making civilians the deliberate object of attack, but also accepts as a reality that "armed conflicts entail dangers for the civilian population."[61] Thus the law admits of the fact that "civilians may be victims of mistaken target identification or of unintended but inevitable side effects of an attack on a legitimate target in their vicinity."[62] The LOAC rules contained in Articles 51 and 57 of AP I reflect a balance of these competing realities and interests, one that limits *unintentionally* inflicted harm to civilians during hostilities when the extent of that harm is so significant that it is tantamount to intentional harm.

Although there is no substitute for turning to these provisions when analyzing a targeting decision, their understanding can be facilitated by thinking in terms of three primary sub-components:

1. The absolute prohibition on indiscriminate attacks;
2. The obligation to take certain precautions to protect civilians and non-combatants;
3. The obligation to refrain from any attack that "may be expected to cause incidental injury to civilians, damage to civilian objects, or a combination thereof, which would be excessive in relation to the concrete and direct military advantage anticipated,"[63] commonly referred to as the proportionality test.

Each of these sub-components shares the same objective, but achieves it differently. Of the three, the absolute prohibition against indiscriminate attacks is most obviously related to the principle of distinction. No member of the military profession should object to the absolute prohibition against intentionally indiscriminate attacks. It is the extension of this prohibition to the unintentional

---

[59] *Id.* art. 51.

[60] Law of Naval Operations, *supra* note 28, at 8.3.1.

[61] AP I Commentary, *supra* note 36, at 617.

[62] Jean-Francois Queguiner, *Precautions under the Law Governing the Conduct of Hostilities*, 88 Int'l Rev. of the Red Cross 793, 794 (Dec. 2006).

[63] Although this proportionality test is used in Protocol I to define the meaning of an indiscriminate attack, see AP I, *supra* note 15, art. 51(5)(b), and as a component of the Article 57 precautions in the attack obligations, see id. art. 57(2)(a) and (b), it is a stand-alone provision in Field Manual 27–10, which, in paragraph 41, indicates that "loss of life and damage to property incidental to attacks must not be excessive in relation to the concrete and direct military advantage to be gained." FM 27–10, *supra* note 21, at 5.

violation of the distinction between lawful and unlawful targets that poses the greatest dilemma in application.

In order to achieve this extension, Protocol I defines "indiscriminate attacks" as:

> (a) those which are not directed at a specific military objective;
> (b) those which employ a method or means of combat which cannot be directed at a specific military objective;
> (c) those which employ a method or means of combat the effects of which cannot be limited as required by this Protocol;

and consequently, in each such case, are of a nature to strike military objectives and civilians or civilian objects without distinction.[64]

Article 51(4) does not mean that the mere presence of civilians or civilian objects makes any planned attack "indiscriminate." Instead, it reinforces the principle of distinction by capturing within the definition means and methods of attack that by their nature cannot distinguish between military objectives and the civilian population.[65] As with virtually all the LOAC provisions related to targeting decisions, application of this rule is fact-intensive. The law of war is designed to provide general guidance to combatants, and commanders retain a great deal of flexibility when analyzing the legality of targeting decisions. "Article 51 should not be read to categorically prohibit any employment of non- precision-guided munitions," which are frequently not available to use.[66] But it does prohibit the employment of such weapons in an arbitrary manner, such as Iraq's random firing of ballistic missiles with rudimentary guidance systems (the notorious Scuds) into Israel and Saudi Arabia during the First Gulf War.

Article 51 also defines as indiscriminate attacks:

> by bombardment by any methods or means which treats as a single military objective a number of clearly separated and distinct military objectives located in a city, town, village or other area containing a similar concentration of civilians or civilian objects . . . [67]

---

[64] AP I, *supra* note 15, art. 51(4) (emphasis added).

[65] The Official Commentary reinforces this conclusion: "The provision begins with a general prohibition on indiscriminate attacks, i.e., attacks in which no distinction is made. Some may think that this general rule should have sufficed, but the Conference considered that it should define the three types of attack covered by the general expression 'indiscriminate attacks.'" AP I Commentary, *supra* note 36, at 620.

[66] International and Operational Law Division, The Judge Advocate General's School, *Practice Note: Principle 3—Endeavor to Prevent or Minimize Harm to Civilians*, ARMY LAW. 58 (Oct. 1998). *See also* Prosecutor v. Gotovina, Case No. IT-06-90-A, Appeals Chamber Judgment, paras. 52–69 (Nov. 16, 2012), http://www.icty.org/x/cases/gotovina/acjug/en/121116_judgement.pdf (rejecting Trial Chambers conclusion that artillery rounds impacting beyond 200 meters of legitimate military targets in a populated area were per se evidence of indiscriminate attacks).

[67] AP I, *supra* note 15, art. 51(5).

According to the Official Commentary, this provision was a direct response to the devastation caused by the type of area or "carpet" bombing frequently employed in the Second World War.[68] Accordingly, although the devastation caused by such bombing may in no way be intended, it is nonetheless considered an indiscriminate employment of a method of warfare, and therefore prohibited.

The most commonly understood expression of the principle of proportionality is set out in Article 51(5)(b) of AP I, which considers attacks indiscriminate if they:

> may be expected to cause incidental loss of civilian life, injury to civilians, damage to civilian objects, or a combination thereof, which would be excessive in relation to the concrete and direct military advantage anticipated.[69]

Although a subcomponent of Article 51 (and Article 57),[70] it is commonly treated as a stand-alone "test" for analyzing the legality of targeting decisions.[71]

In today's operations, the proportionality rule may be the most challenging aspect of the law related to employment of means and methods of warfare. The LOAC does not define the key terms of the rule: "excessive" and "military advantage."[72] The rule requires the application of professional military judgment when balancing these competing interests, based on the information reasonably available to the decision-maker under the circumstances prevailing at the time an attack is authorized.[73] According to the Official Commentary to AP I, there was a great deal of debate related to these provisions, with much criticism aimed at the imprecise nature of the language used in the "test."[74] This test, however, is based on a presumption that the basic rule of minimizing civilian harm should always be a guide for military planners,[75] that the rule will be applied in good faith by

---

[68] "It is characteristic of such bombing that it destroys all life in a specific area and razes to the ground all buildings situated there. There were many examples of such bombing during the Second World War, and also during some more recent conflicts . . . ." AP I Commentary, *supra* note 36, at 624.

[69] AP I, *supra* note 14, art. 51(5)(b).

[70] *Id.* art. 57(2)(a)(iii).

[71] Article 51's proportionality test echoes nearly identical language incorporated into U.S. military manuals prior to 1977. For example, Field Manual 27–10 has long stated:

> [L]oss of life and damage to property incidental to attacks must not be excessive in relation to the concrete and direct military advantage expected to be gained. Those who plan or decide upon an attack, therefore, must take all reasonable steps to ensure . . . that these objectives may be attacked without probable losses in lives and damage to property disproportionate to the military advantage anticipated.

FM 27-10, *supra* note 21, para. 41.

[72] It should be noted, however, that military advantage is not restricted to tactical gains, nor to each target in isolation. It is intended to refer to the advantage anticipated from the attack considered as a whole, within the context of overall campaign objectives. *See* Operational Law Handbook, *supra* note 12, at 13.

[73] All too often the prevailing circumstances involve combat in urban environments and comingling of civilians and military objectives.

[74] AP I Commentary, *supra* note 36, at 625.

[75] *See id.*

military commanders cognizant of this imperative,[76] and that it is the last step in an analytical process intended to ensure the destructive effects of combat are minimized.

The Official Commentary to AP I attests to the fact that the "proportionality" test is only one aspect of a larger analytical process intended to protect civilians. In response to the argument that the "proportionality" rule of AP I legalizes *any* attack, so long as the loss of civilian life or damage to civilian property is not excessive in relation to the concrete and direct military advantage gained, the Commentary states:

> This theory is manifestly incorrect. In order to comply with the conditions, the attack must be directed against a military objective with means which are not disproportionate in relation to the objective, but are suited to destroying only that objective, and the effects of the attacks must be limited in the way required by the Protocol; *moreover*, even after those conditions are fulfilled, the incidental civilian losses and damages must not be excessive.[77]

Thus, although imprecise, the proportionality rule embodied in Articles 51 and Article 57 of AP I can be viewed as the critical "last line of defense" against inflicting unintended civilian harm on such a scale that is tantamount to being indiscriminate.

4. Unnecessary Suffering

Often referred to as the principle of humanity, this principle obliges military forces to avoid causing gratuitous injury to the enemy, and is reflected in the 1907 Hague Convention prohibition against employing "arms, projectiles or material calculated to cause unnecessary suffering."[78] Different than the other three fundamental principles, the primary focus of the principle of unnecessary suffering is not on civilians, but on limiting the suffering of combatants themselves. It is a principle targeted at weaponry, prohibiting those weapons that are per se calculated to cause unnecessary suffering, as well as the employment of otherwise lawful means or methods in a manner that causes unnecessary suffering.[79] Implicit in the prohibition is the recognition that necessary suffering to combatants is lawful, and may include severe injury or death. That is, the rule is not a restriction on the parties' right to attack enemy personnel with lethal force. The rule operates to restrict the use of weapons whose employment is specifically intended to

---

[76] *See* William J. Fenrick, *The Rule of Proportionality and Protocol I in Conventional Warfare*, 98 Mil. L. Rev. 91 (Fall 1982).

[77] AP I Commentary, *supra* note 36, at 625–26.

[78] Hague IV, *supra* note 22, art. 23(e). *See also* Operational Law Handbook, *supra* note 12, at 14. It should be noted that, although frequently used as a synonym for the principle of unnecessary suffering, the principle of humanity is an overarching principle undergirding the entire LOAC.

[79] Law of War Deskbook, *supra* note 13, at 143; Operational Law Handbook, *supra* note 12, at 13.

cause a specific effect considered by governments to be manifestly disproportionate to the military advantage to be gained by its use.[80]

Generally, the principle of unnecessary suffering is less relevant to targeting decisions than the others in that the law requires weapons to be reviewed for compliance prior to their fielding and employment.[81] However, otherwise lawful means may at times be employed in novel ways, requiring commanders and their supporting legal advisors to be vigilant and cognizant of the rule.[82]

B. SPECIFIC PROHIBITIONS

1. Hors de Combat

In addition to the four customary principles and their implementing rules discussed above, the LOAC protects a number of specific categories of places and objects that must be accounted for in the targeting process. For example, as mentioned above, members of an enemy's armed forces who serve as chaplains, medical personnel exclusively engaged in medical duties, administrative staffs of medical units,[83] wounded and sick in the field and at sea,[84] and prisoners of war[85] are all considered hors de combat and not targetable. Similarly, undefended places,[86] cultural property,[87] medical units and establishments[88] and transports,[89] hospitals,[90] potentially objects deemed indispensable to the survival of the

---

[80] OPERATIONAL LAW HANDBOOK, *supra* note 12, at 13.

[81] *See* AP I, *supra* note 15, art. 36. *See also* DEP'T OF DEF. DIRECTIVE 5000.1, THE DEFENSE ACQUISITION SYSTEM (May, 2003); U.S. DEP'T OF ARMY, ARMY REGULATION 27-53, REVIEW OF LEGALITY OF WEAPONS UNDER INTERNATIONAL LAW (Jan. 1979); U.S. DEP'T OF AIR FORCE, AIR FORCE INSTRUCTION 51-402, WEAPONS REVIEW (May 1994); U.S. DEP'T OF NAVY, SEC'Y OF THE NAVY INSTR. 5000 2D, IMPLEMENTATION AND OPERATION OF THE DEFENSE ACQUISITION SYSTEM AND THE JOINT CAPABILITIES INTEGRATION AND DEVELOPMENT SYSTEM (Oct. 2008).

[82] For example, when the 1st Infantry Division of the U.S. Army conducted the initial breach of Iraq's front lines in the Gulf War, it used M1-A1 Abrams tanks retrofitted with plows, and combat earthmovers to bury hundreds of Iraqi soldiers in their trenches. *See* Patrick J. Sloyan, *Army Said to Plow Under Possibly Thousands of Iraqi Soldiers in Trenches*, WASH. POST, Sept. 12, 1991, at 11.

[83] GC I, *supra* note 16, art. 24; LAW OF WAR DESKBOOK, *supra* note 13, at 136–37.

[84] GC I, *supra* note 16, art. 12; GC II, *supra* note 16, art. 12; LAW OF WAR DESKBOOK, *supra* note 13, at 135–36.

[85] GC III, *supra* note 16, art. 4; Hague IV, *supra* note 22, art. 23 (c), (d); LAW OF WAR DESKBOOK, *supra* note 13, at 135–36.

[86] Hague IV, *supra* note 22, art. 25. Undefended places include towns, villages, dwellings, or buildings. *Id. See also* LAW OF WAR DESKBOOK, *supra* note 13, at 138; FM 27-10, *supra* note 21, para. 39b.

[87] *See generally* Convention for the Protection of Cultural Property in the Event of Armed Conflict, May 14, 1954, 249 U.N.T.S. 240. *See also* Hague IV, *supra* note 22, art. 27; AP I, *supra* note 15, art. 53; FM 27-10, *supra* note 21, paras. 45, 47; LAW OF WAR DESKBOOK, *supra* note 13, at 139–40.

[88] GC I, *supra* note 16, art. 19; FM 27-10, *supra* note 21, paras. 257, 258; LAW OF WAR DESKBOOK, *supra* note 13, at 138–39.

[89] GC I, *supra* note 16, art. 35 (ground transports); AP I, *supra* note 15, arts. 25–27 (air transports); LAW OF WAR DESKBOOK, *supra* note 13, at 139.

[90] GC I, *supra* note 16, art. 19; GC IV, *supra* note 16, arts. 18 & 19; FM 27-10, *supra* note 21, paras. 257–58; LAW OF WAR DESKBOOK, *supra* note 13, at 138.

civilian population,[91] and works and installations containing dangerous forces,[92] benefit from special protections and may not be made the object of attack except under very narrow circumstances. In nearly every case, misuse by the enemy of protected property or places can convert them into legitimate military objectives that may be attacked, subject to the rules of proportionality and unnecessary suffering discussed above.[93]

2. The Precautions Rule

In order to ensure adherence to, and effective application of, the foregoing principles and rules, the LOAC has long placed an obligation of due-diligence and good faith on combatants when selecting and engaging targets. Prior to 1977, this general customary obligation[94] to take precautions in the attack was derived from a broad interpretation of the 1899 and 1907 Hague Conventions and the 1949 Geneva Conventions, as well from more explicit provisions contained in a number of treaties regulating the use of specific weapons.[95] The regime set out in Article 57 of Protocol I provides the most comprehensive expression of the "Precautions in Attack" rule.[96]

Article 57 establishes the general rule, applicable to *both* the attacking and defending force, that "[i]n the conduct of military operations, constant care shall be taken to spare the civilian population, civilians, and civilian objects."[97] The following summary illustrates the nature of the specific provisions of Article 57 intended to implement this general rule with respect to attacks:

- the parties to the conflict must do everything feasible to verify that targets of attack are valid military objectives;
- the parties to the conflict must do everything feasible to choose means and methods of combat which will avoid or minimize harm to civilians and/or their property;

---

[91] AP I, *supra* note 15, art. 54 (prohibiting attacks against objects or places such as foodstuffs, crops, livestock, water installations, and irrigation works); LAW OF WAR DESKBOOK, *supra* note 13, at 140.

[92] AP I, art. 56; AP II, art. 15. The United States does not consider these provisions of the Protocols as reflective of customary international law, but factors them into targeting decisions due to the pervasive international acceptance of AP I and II. LAW OF WAR DESKBOOK, *supra* note 13, at 140.

[93] *See, e.g.*, LAW OF NAVAL OPERATIONS, *supra* note 28, § 8.10.2 ("[M]isuse of protected places and objects for military purposes renders them subject to legitimate attack during the period of misuse."). The general rule that misuse can subject protected places and objects to attack is derived from certain specific treaty references, and is considered a rule of CIL. *See* Int. Comm. of the Red Cross, *Customary International Humanitarian Law Database*, Rule 10, *available at* http://www.icrc.org/customary-ihl/eng/docs/v1_rul_rule10 (last visited June 8, 2015). ("Civilian objects are protected against attack, unless and for such time as they are military objectives.").

[94] *See id.*, Rule 15 and commentary thereto, *available at* https://www.icrc.org/customary-ihl/eng/docs/v1_cha_chapter5_rule15#Fn_38_9 (last visited June 8, 2015).

[95] Queguiner, *supra* note 62, at 795.

[96] AP I, *supra* note 15, at art. 57.

[97] *Id.* The general rule is broader than just attacks; commanders must consider the effect on the civilian population of any operation under consideration and take steps to reduce the potential negative effects as much as possible. UK MANUAL, *supra* note 14, at 81–82.

- when circumstances permit, the parties to the conflict must provide advance warnings for attacks which may affect the civilian population;
- when choosing among several military objectives for obtaining a similar military advantage, the parties to the conflict must select the objective with the least likelihood of causing civilian casualties;
- the parties to the conflict must refrain from launching, cancel, or suspend any attack which may be expected to cause incidental harm to civilians or their property which would be excessive in relation to the concrete and direct military advantage anticipated;
- effective advance warning shall be given of attacks which may affect the civilian population, unless circumstances do not permit.[98]

Article 57 also imposes an obligation, when considering among several objectives each of which offers "a similar military advantage," to select the one the attack on which may be expected to cause the least danger to civilian lives and objects.[99] This rule raises difficult interpretive questions, not the least of which is: What constitutes a "similar military advantage"? A review of the Official Commentary to Article 57 indicates the focus of the rule is on civilian objects used to support the enemy war effort, such as transportation facilities and economic targets.[100] Like many targeting decisions, assessing the relative weight of different objectives will be committed to the good faith judgment of the military officer, based on overall mission imperatives and the information reasonably available at the time.

This last point warrants further elaboration. Warfare is a highly chaotic human endeavor—the fog of war being very real.[101] Combatants are often operating in time- and resource-constrained environments, under extreme stress, and with imperfect information available to make targeting judgments. It is natural that they will make mistakes. Targeting mistakes can occur for a variety of reasons, such as: weapons malfunctions causing munitions to hit the wrong target; misidentification of an objective due to flawed intelligence; and intelligence, surveillance, and reconnaissance (ISR) operations failing to identify the presence of civilians on or near the objective. The fact that mistakes are made does not, ipso facto, mean that LOAC violations have occurred.

The inclusion of the expressions "everything feasible" or "all feasible" throughout Article 57 is recognition that, when taking precautions in attack, combatants

---

[98] *Id.* This is a paraphrase of the actual language used in Article 57.

[99] AP I, *supra* note 2, art. 57(3).

[100] The Commentary, *supra* note 7, at 687 ("Instead of attacking railway stations, which are usually located in towns, the railway lines were hit at crucial points, but away from inhabited areas; the same action was taken with respect to roads."). *See also* Queguiner, *supra* note 62, at 805.

[101] As the famed Carl Von Clausewitz noted, "War is an area of uncertainty; three quarters of the factors on which action in war is based are wrapped in a fog of greater or lesser uncertainty." CARL VON CLAUSEWITZ, ON WAR 101 (1984) (Michael Howard & Peter Paret eds. and trans., 1984).

"cannot be required to do the objectively impossible . . . ."[102] Feasible precautions are not those that "are practically impossible,"[103] but rather should be understood to be those "which are practicable or practically possible taking into account *all circumstances ruling at the time*, including humanitarian *and* military considerations."[104]

Thus, the precautions rule does not impose an absolute duty, but rather "a duty to act in good faith to take practicable measures, and persons acting in good faith may make mistakes."[105] What measures are practicable must be assessed on a case-by-case basis, considering the operational circumstances prevailing at the time, such as the relative availability of ISR capabilities,[106] the time available to collect additional intelligence, the availability of precision- guided munitions, the nature of the target to be engaged (i.e., is it a hardened target requiring employment of more destructive munitions), and the degree of risk to friendly forces that would be involved in employing means or methods that might mitigate risk of collateral damage to some degree.[107] It is critically important to emphasize that any post-attack review of a decision to attack an objective must be judged not based on hindsight, but on the information actually available to the decision-maker at the time the attack was ordered.[108]

The foregoing discussion has offered just a brief overview of the core LOAC principles and specific provisions relevant to the targeting process. Like the doctrinal principle of restraint—the purpose of which is to limit collateral damage and prevent the unnecessary use of force[109]—these rules and principles seek to advance the basic humanitarian imperative that all combatants should endeavor to minimize civilian suffering. The targeting process provides the means to operationalize this imperative and the complex and nuanced rules that implement it.

---

[102] Queguiner, *supra* note 62, at 809.

[103] Dinstein, *supra* note 26, at 139 (quoting Eritrea-Ethiopia Claims Commission, Partial Award, Central Front, Ethiopia's Claim 2 (2004), 43 ILM 1275, 1295 (2004)).

[104] UK Manual, *supra* note 14, § 5.32, fn. 191.

[105] William J. Fenrick, *Targeting and Proportionality during the NATO Bombing Campaign against Yugoslavia*, 12(3) EJIL 501 (2001).

[106] Official Commentary at 680:

> Finally, one delegation remarked that the identification of objectives depended to a large extent on the technical means of detection available to the belligerents. This remark seems to be correct. For example, some belligerents might have information owing to a modern reconnaissance device, while other belligerents might not have this type of equipment.

[107] *See* Fenrick, *supra* note 105, at 501 (recognizing the difficulty of the question of risk to friendly forces, but acknowledging that commanders have a duty to limit casualties to their own forces). *See also* Official Commentary at 608 (acknowledging that "the circumstances of combat and the control of airspace may render it more difficult" to employ the most precise weapon or munitions with the potential for the smallest collateral effects.). *See also* UK Manual, *supra* note 13, at 82–84.

[108] Dinstein, *supra* note 26, at 139. *See also* Brian J. Bill, *The Rendulic "Rule": Military Necessity, Commander's Knowledge, and Methods of Warfare*, *in* 12 Yearbook of International Humanitarian law 119, 128 (2009).

[109] Joint Chiefs of Staff, Joint Pub. 3-0, Joint Operations, at A-3 (Aug. 11, 2011) [hereinafter JP 3-0].

III. The Targeting Process

At its most basic level, targeting is the process by which a military decision-maker, whether an individual soldier, sailor, airmen, or marine, or high-level commander, decides who or what to engage with combat power, and when, where, why, and how he or she will do so.[110] "Targeting systematically analyzes and prioritizes targets and matches appropriate lethal and nonlethal actions to those targets to create specific desired effects" in support of overall operational objectives.[111] First, a discussion of the operational definition of target.

A. TARGETS DEFINED

Understanding the targeting process and how it integrates LOAC considerations starts with the operational and legal definition of a target. In common parlance, a target is understood as something or someone fired at or marked for attack.[112] For the United States, the doctrinal definition is more specific: "A target is an entity (person, place or thing) considered for possible engagement or action to alter or neutralize the function it performs for the adversary." [113] These entities may "include the wide array of mobile and stationary forces, equipment, capabilities, and functions that an enemy commander can use to conduct operations."[114] Generally, the relative importance of a specific target "derives from its potential contribution to achieving a commander's objective(s) or otherwise accomplishing assigned tasks."[115]

Targets "should be logically and causally" related to objectives at all levels of war: strategic, operational, and tactical.[116] Whether a target is selected through a deliberate planning process, or identified as an emergent opportunity, it should

---

[110] Frequently, commanders use Rules of Engagement (ROE) as a primary tool to regulate these decisions on the use of armed force in the context of applicable political and military policy, and domestic and international law. JOINT CHIEFS OF STAFF, JOINT PUB. 3–60, JOINT TARGETING, at A-1 (Jan. 31, 2013) [hereinafter JP 3-60]. Defined in U.S. doctrine as "directives issued by competent military authority that delineate the circumstances and limitations under which U.S. forces will initiate and/or continue combat engagement with other forces encountered," ROE provide a framework that encompasses national policy goals, mission requirements, and the rule of law. JP 1-02, *supra* note 4, at 224. Although the doctrines of various armed forces differ, ROE generally tend to perform three basic functions: to act as a control mechanism for the transition from peacetime to combat operations (armed conflict), to provide standing force protection authority and guidance to unit commanders and individual soldiers in the form of self-defense rules, and to provide a command and control mechanism for national command authorities and military commanders to ensure the use of military force complies with strategic political and military aims. OPERATIONAL LAW HANDBOOK, *supra* note 12, at 73.

[111] JP 3-60, *supra* note 110, at vii.

[112] MERRIAM-WEBSTER'S COLLEGIATE DICTIONARY 1278 (11th ed. 2003).

[113] JP 3-60, *supra* note 110, at vii (Target defined).

[114] FM 3-60, *supra* note 10, at 1–1.

[115] JP 3-60, *supra* note 110, at I-1.

[116] *Id.* at I-2.

be selected and engaged only if it supports the commander's objectives, guidance, and intent. However, even if an entity meets these criteria, it must first qualify as a lawful military objective as defined in the LOAC.[117]

B. TARGET TYPES AND CATEGORIES

Every target has unique characteristics that will impact not only its relative importance to achieving overall objectives, but may also present increased risks of undesired or unintended effects if attacked. Consider, for example, the Al Firdus bunker that opened this chapter. Its putative status as a hardened air-raid shelter presented distinct risks of unwanted collateral effects, while at the same time limiting the means available to effectively disrupt its use (or misuse) as a command and control (C2) node. The fact that intelligence identified it as a suddenly active C2 node for senior Iraqi leadership prompted its elevation in priority and short-notice addition to the air tasking order (ATO).[118]

To account for some of the more operationally important differences in target characteristics, as well as the fluid and unpredictable nature of combat, the targeting process and targets are generally separated into distinct categories. Targeting is categorized as either deliberate (planned) or dynamic targeting (targets of opportunity). Individual targets are categorized as sensitive, time-sensitive (TST), high-value (HVT), and high-payoff targets (HPT).[119]

Planned, or deliberate, targets "are known to exist in the operational environment with engagement actions scheduled against them."[120] These targets are generally identified with sufficient time (usually at least twenty-four hours from execution) for a thorough analysis and placement on detailed target lists.[121] They may be either scheduled for prosecution at a specific time, or for on-call execution (actions planned but not scheduled). In contrast, dynamic targeting focuses on targets of opportunity, those that "meet the criteria to achieve objectives" but that are identified too late for selection or inclusion as a planned target.[122] Targets of opportunity are either unplanned—known to exist in the operational environment but that are not detected or located in time to be scheduled for preplanned attack, or unanticipated—unknown, or not expected to exist in the operational environment.[123]

The potential effects, intended or unanticipated, of attacking some targets may warrant special care or caution in treatment. For example, key enemy anti-aircraft capabilities may be located in close proximity to a protected place such as

---

[117] AP I, *supra* note 14, art. 52(2). *See supra* notes 40–43 and accompanying text for discussion on military objective.

[118] GULF WAR FINAL REPORT, *supra* note 3, at 194.

[119] JP 3-60, *supra* note 110, at I-9, II-1 to II-3.

[120] *Id.* at II-1 to II-2; FM 3-60, *supra* note 10, at 1–5.

[121] JP 3-60, *supra* note 101, at II-19.

[122] *Id.* at II-1 to II-2; FM 3-60, *supra* note 10, at 1–5.

[123] JP 3-60, *supra* note 110, at II-1 to II-2; FM 3-60, *supra* note 10, at 1–5.

a hospital or a school,[124] or the target may contain weapons of mass destruction (WMD) or other materials that, if released, might pose undue risk to the civilian population or the environment. In such cases, the target is designated as sensitive, and strike approval authority is withheld to very senior levels in the chain of command, even to the highest levels of national military command, such as the Secretary of Defense or the President in the case of the United States.[125] Sensitive targets include those that exceed certain thresholds generally established at the national level, "such as high collateral damage or collateral effect . . .; adverse political or diplomatic ramifications . . .; environmental harm/hazard . . .; or adverse public sentiment (local or international)."[126] For U.S. forces, the criteria for establishing sensitive targets are generally set out in classified contingency plans or execute orders, including rules of engagement (ROE).[127] Targets meeting these criteria are subject to a special review and approval process.[128]

Not to be confused with a sensitive target, a "time-sensitive target," or TST, is one that "rises to such a level that it poses (or will soon pose) a [significant strategic or operational threat] to friendly forces, or presents a highly lucrative, fleeting opportunity of tactical advantage" so as to require immediate engagement if located.[129] For example, certain long-range, WMD-capable weapons platforms, or key enemy commanders, might be designated as TSTs. Because TSTs require significant commitment of intelligence resources and attack assets—the employment of which will likely be disruptive of preplanned operations—the authority to designate them is generally withheld to high levels of command.

Another type of especially important target is one that the enemy commander requires for the successful completion of his or her mission. The loss of these high-value targets (HVT) would be expected to seriously degrade important enemy functions. When the loss of an HVT would be expected to significantly contribute to the success of the friendly commander's course of action, it is designated as a high-payoff target (HPT).[130]

The different categories and target designations discussed above are designed to facilitate the linkage between targeting decisions and operational necessities. From a LOAC perspective, they also often reflect the direct and concrete military advantage that may be gained by an attack, as well as the limits on time and information that may be available to the commander. The targeting process needs to be disciplined but flexible enough to account for the exigencies inherent in finding, fixing, tracking, targeting, and engaging enemy targets in complex combat environments.

---

[124] *See infra* notes 84–91 and accompanying text discussing protected places.

[125] JP 3-60, *supra* note 110, at I-8.

[126] *Id.*; FM 3-60, *supra* note 10, at 1–5.

[127] JP 3-60, *supra* note 110 at I-8.

[128] *Id.* (referring to Chairman of the Joint Chiefs of Staff Instruction (CJCSI) 3122.06C, Sensitive Target Approval and Review (STAR) Process (Aug. 28, 2009) (classified publication)).

[129] *Id.* at I-8 to I-9; FM 3-60, *supra* note 10, at 1–5.

[130] JP 3-60, *supra* note 110, at I-9.

C. THE TARGETING PROCESS

Targeting, as opposed to target, is "the process of selecting and prioritizing targets and matching the appropriate response to them, considering operational requirements and capabilities."[131] The targeting process:

> defines what targets are to be engaged, by which assets, using which method and in which priority order. It also specifies targets that are restricted or may not be engaged at all. Above all, the process aims to ensure all involved are entirely clear about their targeting and coordination responsibilities and constraints, in time and space.[132]

At its most developed level, targeting is a complex, multidisciplinary process that seeks to coordinate and synchronize efforts across the staff, friendly and coalition units, and the six warfighting functions.[133] The goal of the process it to identify, acquire, and attack those "resources (targets) the enemy can least afford to lose or that provide him with the greatest advantage."[134]

Although doctrine and terminology may differ among militaries, certain core concepts are common to all. Whether at the strategic, operational, or tactical level of warfare, the ultimate objective of any military commander is to employ his or her available capabilities in a synchronized manner to successfully achieve a defined end state as efficiently and effectively as possible. In warfare, this involves leveraging available assets to generate combat power to achieve a desired effect at the selected time and place. With today's enhanced weapons technologies, commanders will frequently seek to generate these effects with long-range, highly destructive stand-off weapons systems. The nature of these systems and the attendant risks inherent in their employment further necessitate a highly disciplined and analytical targeting process.

To assist commanders with integrating, synchronizing, and directing operations, U.S. doctrine organizes all available capabilities into six basic operational functions: command and control, intelligence, fires, movement and maneuver, protection, and sustainment.[135] Commanders generate and apply combat power through the correct application of each of these six functions. Although the relative weight of each function may vary according to each mission, the fires function is often critical to executing the commander's overall concept of operations. This is true regardless of whether fires are employed to enhance the overall effect

---

[131] *Id.* at I-1.

[132] NATO Standardization Agency, Allied Joint Publication 3(B): Allied Joint Doctrine for the Conduct of Operations para. 0448 (2011).

[133] *See infra* note 135 and accompanying text.

[134] FM 3-60, *supra* note 10, at 1–1.

[135] JP 3-0, *supra* note 109, at III-1. U.S. Army doctrine now substitutes mission command for command and control, and describes these six "elements of combat power" collectively as the warfighting functions. FM 3-0, *supra* note 10, at 4–1; U.S. Dep't of Army, Army Doctrine Reference Publication, Unified Land Operations, 4–1 (May 16, 2012).

of the other functions (such as maneuver and movement), or to create and preserve conditions for the success of the operation itself.

Fires are defined as the use of weapon systems to create specific lethal or non-lethal effects on a target.[136] As a warfighting function, fires consist of the related tasks and systems that provide the coordinated use of surface-to-surface indirect fires, air-to-surface fires, naval surface fires, and command and control of these capabilities through the targeting process.[137] It includes tasks associated with integrating and synchronizing the effects of these types of fires, as well as command and control warfare, plus those effects of other warfighting functions.[138] As part of the commander's integrated plan, fires can be employed for a variety of purposes.[139] Commanders ensure the effective integration and synchronization of fires into their plans through the use of standard target selection and execution processes that seek to link intelligence, plans, and operations across all levels of command.

Targeting is a cyclical and iterative process requiring constant flexibility and adaptability in order to respond to the dynamic nature of operations. At the most basic level, it involves planning, execution, and assessment of the efficacy of each engagement or attack. The targeting cycle can be further broken down into six phases, represented in the figure below.[140]

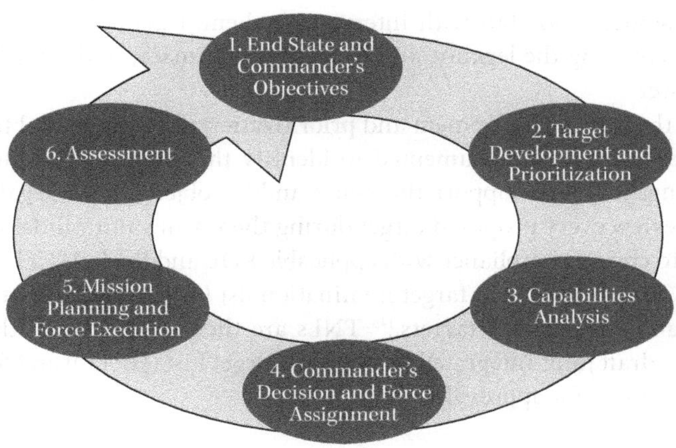

[136] JP 1-02, *supra* note 4, at 102.

[137] FM 3-60, *supra* note 10, at 1–1 to 1-2.

[138] *See* JP 3-0, *supra* note 109, at III-1 ("The joint functions reinforce and complement one another, and *integration across the functions is essential to mission accomplishment.*") (emphasis in original).

[139] Such as to: provide fire support to assist air, land, maritime, and special operations forces to move, maneuver, and control territory, populations, airspace, and key waters; interdict enemy capabilities to divert, disrupt, delay, or destroy the enemy's military potential before it can be used effectively against friendly forces; attack strategic objectives and centers of gravity; and to counter air and missile threats.

[140] JP 3-0, *supra* note 109, at II-3 to II-4.

Targeting involves multiple processes, "all linked and logically guided by the joint targeting cycle, that continuously seek to analyze, identify, develop, validate, assess and prioritize targets for engagement in order to create the effects needed to help achieve the commander's objectives."[141] The intersection of mission imperatives, policy considerations, and the law are constantly at play during all six phases of the targeting cycle. Commanders, planners, and to the extent possible, legal advisors, must be cognizant of these factors at all times. The legal analysis begins with the identification of the commander's end state and objectives, and carries through the entire process to the assessment and related recommendations for re-engagement. There are certain points in the process, however, where a thorough legal analysis is most critical to the commander's decision-making.

A thorough understanding of the military end state and the commander's intent, objectives, desired effects, and required tasks drives the entire targeting process. If the end state and objectives are in any way tainted with an improper or illegal purpose, or if they are premised on a misinterpretation of the authorities underlying the overall operation, then the engagement of every target is at risk of legal infirmity. Accordingly, it is at this critical stage that legal considerations inform the development of combat force initiation procedures as well as employment-restraints or constraints such as ROE.[142] Whether advising the commander establishing the end state and objectives, or assisting subordinate commanders and staff with interpreting them, legal advisors play a crucial role in ensuring the legality, and hence the legitimacy, of the application of combat power.

During the target development and prioritization phase, potential targets are analyzed, assessed, and documented to identify those targets that, when successfully engaged, will support the commander's objectives.[143] Legal advisors normally review every proposed target during the vetting and validation step of this phase to ensure compliance with applicable ROE and the LOAC.[144] Validated targets are documented on a target nomination list (TNL), which contains both restricted and unrestricted targets.[145] TNLs are then consolidated (the United States uses a draft Joint Integrated Prioritized Target List (JIPTL)) and forwarded to the commander for approval.

---

[141] JP 3-60, *supra* note 110, at I-6.

[142] The LOAC sets the legal limits for defining and engaging lawful targets, while ROE serve as an additional source of authority delineating the circumstances and limitations under which forces can employ combat power. Accordingly, ROE limitations must be consistent with law, but are technically not law. Instead, they are constraints or restraints based on mission imperatives and policy considerations, under which forces may initiate or continue combat engagement. *See* OPERATIONAL LAW HANDBOOK, *supra* note 12, ch. 5.

[143] JP 3-60, *supra* note 110, at II-5.

[144] *Id.* at II-11.

[145] A restricted target is a valid target that has specific restrictions placed on it due to operational considerations and requires coordination and approval from the headquarters imposing the restrictions. *Id.* at II-13.

Once the TNLs are compiled, each nominated target is evaluated against available capabilities to determine the most efficient and effective means of engagement "while minimizing collateral damage and waste of resources."[146] It is at this stage that the commander and staff engage in the detailed analysis of available capabilities in relation to desired effects.[147] This process of target identification, force allocation, and "weaponeering"[148] is heavily impacted by the LOAC principle of proportionality.[149] The commander and planners seek to mitigate the risk of collateral damage by selecting weapons and tactics that will, to the greatest feasible extent, produce the desired effect while minimizing collateral damage. For U.S. forces, the "collateral damage estimation process is a critical component of the effects estimate step in the joint targeting process . . . ."[150]

D. NO-STRIKE LISTS, RESTRICTED TARGET LISTS, AND THE COLLATERAL DAMAGE ESTIMATE METHODOLOGY

Recall the obligations of the precautions in attack rule. Commanders must do everything feasible to, among other things, verify the object of attack is a lawful military objective; choose a means or method of attack with a view to avoiding, or at least minimizing, collateral damage; and refrain from launching an attack reasonably expected to cause collateral damage disproportionate to the concrete and direct military advantage anticipated.[151] To meet these obligations, the U.S. incorporates a process within a process—embedding a collateral damage estimation (CDE) methodology (CDM) within the broader Joint Targeting Process.

The CDM, outlined in *Chairman of the Joint Chiefs of Staff Instruction 3160.01A, No-Strike and Collateral Damage Estimation Methodology*,[152] provides the tools for a commander to estimate potential collateral effects prior to approving an attack, and "mitigate unintended or incidental damage or injury to civilian or noncombatant persons or property or the environment."[153] It assists commanders in reasonably identifying lawful military objectives, determining those that qualify as sensitive, and weighing the risks of attack against military necessity. "In short, the CDM is a means for a commander to adhere to the [LOAC]."[154]

---

146 *Id.*

147 *Id.* at II-10 to II-11.

148 Weaponeering is "the process of determining the quantity of a specific type of lethal or nonlethal means required to create a desired effect on a given target." JP 1-02, *supra* note 4, at 300.

149 United States Joint Forces Command, Joint Fires and Targeting Handbook III-69 to II-79 (2007) [hereinafter Joint Fires and Targeting Handbook] (discussing weaponeering and the Collateral Damage Estimation process).

150 JP 3-60, *supra* note 110, at II-16.

151 AP I, *supra* note 14, art. 57; FM 27-10, *supra* note 18, para. 41.

152 *See* CJCSI 3160.01, *supra* note 11.

153 *Id.* at D-1.

154 *Id.*

The CDM is a process based both on science and military art, with the aiding, but not substituting for, the latter. It is derived from sophisticated, physics-based computer modeling backed up by weapons testing data and direct combat observations that "provides commanders with an understanding of weapon effects, incidental consequences, and mitigation techniques, enabling more balanced, comprehensive judgments."[155]

The science employed in the CDM is not, however, exact or infallible, and is not a substitute for the sound military judgment of the commander. The CDM produces "an estimate to assist a commander in the decision making process relying on informed data and sound judgment."[156] In addition to the CDE, the commander must weigh a number of other factors such as operational objectives, end-state considerations, other LOAC and ROE considerations, target characteristics, risk to friendly forces, and strategic risk, which together or alone may outweigh the value of the CDM input.[157] But as the instruction admonishes, potential collateral damage can, depending on the operational environment, be an overriding issue. And of course, when a commander believes that a proposed attack option will result in collateral damage that will be excessive in relation to the concrete and direct military advantage anticipated, he must either find a means or method to mitigate the risk down, or abandon the attack.

Before turning to the estimation methodology, a few words are in order on the obligation to do everything feasible to verify that the intended object of attack is a lawful military objective. *CJCSI 3160.01* addresses this obligation through two primary means: the concept of positive identification (PID) and the No-Strike List (NSL).

Positive identification is defined as "the reasonable certainty that a functionally and geospatially defined object of attack is a legitimate military target in accordance with the [LOAC] and applicable ROE."[158] Establishing PID is a mandatory condition precedent to engaging any target.[159] Reasonable certainty can be established through a variety of technical and sensory means, either individually or in combination,[160] and in certain circumstances mission orders or ROE may specify the type and number of means required.

An NSL is a "list of objects or entities characterized as protected from the effects of military operations under international law and/or rules of engagement" such as medical, educational, diplomatic, cultural, religious, and historical

---

[155] *Id.* at D-2. *See also* Powerpoint Presentation, *Joint Targeting Cycle and Collateral Damage Estimation Methodology (CDM)*, slide 20 (Nov. 10, 2009), *available at* http://www.aclu.org/files/dronefoia/dod/drone_dod_ACLU_DRONES_JOINT_STAFF_SLIDES_1–47.pdf.

[156] CJCSI 3160.01, *supra* note 11, at D-2.

[157] *Id.*

[158] *Id.* at A-6.

[159] *Id.* at D-A-8, D-B-1.

[160] *See* JP 1-02, *supra* note 4, at 218 ("An identification derived from observation and analysis of target characteristics including visual recognition, electronic support systems, noncooperative target recognition techniques, identification friend or foe systems, or other physics-based identification techniques.").

sites.[161] No-strike entities are those designated by an appropriate authority (in the case of the United States, usually a Combatant Commander) "upon which kinetic or non-kinetic operations are prohibited to avoid violating international law, conventions, or agreements, or damaging relations with coalition partners and indigenous populations."[162] Once an object has been placed on the NSL, it cannot be removed except by the designating authority or higher.

Proximity of lawful military targets to No-Strike entities does not preclude engagement, but any anticipated damage to the object must be factored into the proportionality analysis. If the enemy improperly uses a No-Strike entity, it may lose its protected status, either temporarily or permanently, and be subject to attack.[163] Generally, it must first be removed from the NSL before it can be attacked, except in cases "where the need to strike is time sensitive (whereupon it is nominated as a time sensitive target (TST)), and/or . . . troops are in contact and taking hostile fire from [the entity]."[164]

The NSL should not be confused with a restricted target list (RTL). Restricted targets are otherwise valid military targets that the commander (or higher command) have placed engagement restrictions on "for operational, political, intelligence gain/loss, environmental, collateral damage, and/or ROE considerations."[165] Unlike No-Strike entities, restricted targets may be attacked in accordance with the imposed restrictions.

Once an object is positively identified and verified against the NSL, the framework of the CDM is used to assess whether attacking the intended target will risk collateral damage. If the answer is yes, the CDM addresses whether the risk can be mitigated below established thresholds through weaponeering without unacceptably increasing risk to the mission or friendly forces. It is a complex framework built around five mutually dependent CDE Levels. Each level is based on a progressively refined analysis of available intelligence, weapon type and effect, the physical environment, target characteristics, and delivery scenarios with risk thresholds established in specific mission orders or ROE for each of the five CDE levels.[166]

If, within each level, the estimated collateral damage cannot be mitigated below the established threshold, the target must be analyzed applying the more exacting mitigation (weaponeering) criteria at each progressive CDE level. Generally, the higher the analysis progresses up through the CDE levels, the higher the strike approval authority will be. Those targets assessed to involve risk of collateral damage exceeding the noncombatant and civilian casualty cutoff

---

[161] *Id.* at 198.

[162] CJCSI 3160.01, *supra* note 11, at C-1.

[163] *See supra* note 93 and accompanying text.

[164] *Id.* at C-B-5. Although misuse by the enemy is itself a violation of the LOAC and may subject the place or object to attack, oftentimes it will remain on the NSL for overriding operational or policy reasons.

[165] *Id.* at C-B-5; JP 3-60, *supra* note 101, at II-13.

[166] *Id.* at D-A-1.

value (NCV),[167] or meeting other designated criteria, must be processed through the linked Sensitive Target and Assessment Review (STAR) Process for approval at the national level.[168]

In the final analysis, the CDM is a process designed to assist the commander with five basic questions that must be answered before engaging any target:

- Can I positively identify the object I want to affect?
- Are there protected or collateral objects, civilian or noncombatant personnel, involuntary human shields, or significant environmental concerns within the effects range of the weapon I would like to use to attack the target?
- Can I mitigate damage to those collateral concerns by attacking the target with a different weapon or with a different method of engagement, yet still accomplish the mission?
- If not, how many civilians and noncombatants do I think will be injured or killed by the attack?
- Are the collateral effects of my attack excessive in relation to the expected military advantage gained and do I need to elevate this decision to the next level of command to attack the target based on the ROE or STAR policy in effect?[169]

Integrating these CDM questions into the targeting process is the means to operationalize the precautions in the attack rule.

The CDM is unprecedented in the rigor and thoroughness it incorporates into applying the precautions in attack rule. But the CDM has limits. It must be understood that it does not predict the actual outcome of weapon employment. "The operational environment, weapon's reliability, and fidelity of intelligence data are primary factors that account for a CDE output differing from actual combat employment."[170] It generates an estimate to aid the commander's decision-making and to calibrate delegations of strike authority with operational risk. In the end, nothing substitutes for the commander's sound military judgment.

The CDM is also limited in its application. It does not apply to surface-to-surface direct fire weapon systems or rotary or fixed wing air-to-surface direct fire weapon systems less than 105mm, due to operational practicality.[171] This does not relieve combatants of their obligation to comply with the LOAC when

---

[167] The NCV is "The casualty threshold for any anticipated effects, which if exceeded, would require the combatant commander to forward a target to the [Secretary of Defense] or President for national-level review as a sensitive target unless delegated otherwise according to the established ROE." *Id.* at GL-7.

[168] *Id.* at D-4; JP 3-60, *supra* note 10, at II-16. The STAR process is governed by *Chairman of the Joint Chiefs of Staff Instruction 3122.06C, Sensitive Target Assessment and Review (STAR) Process* (Dec. 12, 2007) (classified publication).

[169] CJCSI 3160.01, *supra* note 11, at D-A-6 to D-A-7.

[170] *Id.* at C-1.

[171] *Id.* at D-4.

targeting with these weapon systems—just the need to conduct the formal CDM process. The CDM does not account for weapon malfunctions, operational delivery errors, or altered delivery tactics based on operator judgment, or for unknown transient civilian or noncombatant personnel or equipment in the vicinity of a target area.[172] Commanders remain responsible to account for these factors, mindful of the obligation to cancel or suspend an attack if it becomes apparent that the objective is not a lawful target, or that it will result in unreasonable collateral damage.[173] Finally, the CDM is "not intended to deny a commander the ability to respond to time-sensitive targeting events and should not be used as the sole justification to impede or delay fires for time-sensitive targeting."[174] The process is flexible and must be adjusted to account for operational exigencies, especially with respect to dynamic targeting.

E. FIND, FIX, TRACK, TARGET, ENGAGE, ASSESS

The first three steps of the iterative process applicable to deliberate targeting are outlined above: identification of the commander's objectives and end state, target development and prioritization, and a capabilities analysis. At this stage, the nominated targets normally move into the current operations cycle, and the processes for deliberate and dynamic targets begin to merge. Once proposed targets have been vetted and validated in the capabilities analysis phase, targeteers work with planners to develop an execution plan that allocates available forces, sensors, and weapons systems against the targets on the JIPTL to achieve operational objectives. The information, to include the CDE, is then presented to the relevant commander for approval.[175]

Once approved, the approving headquarters issues tasking orders to the assigned units, and the targets move into the mission planning and force execution phase. Applying the Find, Fix, Track, Target, Engage, Assess (F2T2EA) process, the executing unit locates the target, establishes positive identification (PID), and confirms that all targeting criteria are met, to include information related to the presence of civilians or civilian objects.[176] Necessary adjustments are made if circumstances warrant (such as the unexpected presence of civilians), including cancellation of the attack. Targets of opportunity and TSTs are prosecuted using the same F2T2EA process, applying the guidance developed and issued through the deliberate targeting cycle.[177]

Whether emergent or preplanned, once a target is found, fixed, and tracked, the executing unit makes the final engagement decision. The target engagement authority reconfirms that the target meets the commander's objectives

---

[172] *Id.*

[173] AP I, *supra* note 14, art. 57(2)(b).

[174] CJCSI 3160.01, *supra* note 11, at D-3.

[175] JP 3-60, *supra* note 110, at II-16 to II-17.

[176] *Id.* at II-20 to II-30.

[177] *Id.*

and criteria, and re-validates the target itself, the CDE, and compliance with the LOAC and ROE.[178] The commander or his delegee transmits approval to engage the target along with any additional guidance or restrictions, and the target is attacked. The effects are assessed, and the cycle begins again.

Frequently, especially with respect to emergent targets located by a platform capable of attack, the F2T2EA proceeds at an extremely condensed pace, with several steps occurring nearly simultaneously. "These targets still require confirmation, verification, validation, and authorization, but in a shorter timeframe than the deliberate targeting process allows."[179] The dynamic, time-sensitive nature of such engagements requires flexibility in the application of the targeting process, and factors in heavily when assessing the reasonableness of targeting decisions. Well-developed and exercised battle drills, especially those that incorporate operational legal advice, reduce the likelihood of mistakes being made.

Below are two unique perspectives on the targeting process and the integration of LOAC.

F. A VIEW FROM ABOVE

Lawful use of military force from aerial vehicles requires extraordinary efforts to distinguish targets from non-targets. How does one discern between friend and foe at Mach speed? How does one balance, in a few seconds, whether collateral damage will be proportionally acceptable in light of the military necessity of striking the target? What effects does the military strategy require: damage or destroy? To answer these questions, military lawyers have worked over the years to integrate the LOAC into air-to-air and air-to-ground engagement decisions, leveraging where possible available sensor and weapon technology. In addition, the process of planning and executing bombing missions has grown in sophistication. This section presents recent experience on how the LOAC affects the delivery of combat effects from the air. It is essentially an iterative process that in the end produces specialized aerial ROE.

Similarly, execution of aerial attacks increasingly incorporates support from trained operators and decision-makers monitoring the situation from outside the cockpit. Unlike the pilot, they often have the greater luxury of time and myriad sources of data, and are not burdened with simultaneously flying and navigating the aircraft. Consider the following scenarios with two essential elements in mind: a command and control center and a pilot in the cockpit of a fixed-wing aircraft. In each case, the targeting dynamics and decision cycles vary greatly.

The command and control center has multiple trained operators assessing real-time feeds of information describing the state of play on the battlefield. They convert this information into real-time priorities. They assess newly discovered targeting opportunities while accomplishing the commander's integrated plan

---

[178] *Id.* at II-27 to II-29; FM 3-60, *supra* note 10, at A-4.

[179] FM 27-10, *supra* note 10, at A-1.

for striking deliberate targets. A significant challenge for the command and control center is deciding when to re-mission airborne assets onto newly discovered targeting opportunities. At the other end of this effort, the pilot faces separate challenges. She travels swiftly over the battlefield, which may contain surface-to-air threats, and in an airspace that may contain air-to-air threats. The pilot flies a machine with finite time-on-target or loiter capability and has an on-board suite of sensors, including human vision that paints, in some sense, a more complete picture of a small portion of the battlefield.

1. Scenario One

An unarmed or lightly armed, remotely piloted aircraft (RPA) detects a heavy equipment truck hauling an adversary's tank through a residential city landscape. By virtue of markings or other outward indicators, the truck and its load are identifiable as valid military targets, but because of the truck's location, the risk of collateral damage appears to be high. The problem is really one of physics. The critical question is: When will the truck emerge onto a stretch of road that matches the timing of an aircraft loaded with a weapon that will not produce collateral damage disproportional to the expected military gain in destroying both the truck and the tank? So long as the RPA is able to keep tabs on the target, this problem is largely an issue for those manning the command and control center to resolve. Are there aircraft currently airborne with the right weapons on board? Do potentially available aircraft have higher priority targets for the weapons and fuel they have aboard? When is it expected that the target will appear in an area where the risk of collateral damage is sufficiently diminished or eliminated? Does that match the timing of available airborne assets? What degree of collateral damage is deemed both legally and operationally acceptable? With what degree of confidence can the target be attacked within the limits of legally and operationally acceptable collateral damage? For attack of mobile ground targets, this can be difficult to determine.

If we return to the Joint Targeting Process described above, this scenario presents a clear example of dynamic targeting. The emergent nature of the target and the compressed pace of the F2T2EA process present particularly difficult challenges to the decision-maker, whether in a distant operations center or the cockpit of the attacking aircraft. Although the process for executing dynamic targets must be flexible enough to meet operational requirements, operators must adhere to the basic LOAC principles. The military art of target decision-making, honed by training, battle drills, and legally sound and understandable ROE, is at its zenith in such dynamic targeting scenarios.

2. Scenario Two

After an attack on a deliberate target, a pilot whose aircraft is armed with two 500-pound bombs begins her flight back to base. The pilot receives a call from her command and control center indicating that friendly "troops-in-contact" (troops engaging the enemy) need help. The firefight is occurring in a village. The pilot acknowledges this call for fires and indicates a fuel level that would support delivery of her ordnance on adversary positions. Because of the proximity between the clashing ground forces she will need the help of an on-the-ground spotter.

Before releasing the bombs, the pilot must first establish positive identification. She must make a reasonable determination, with the limited and fast-moving information available, that the objects of her intended attack are legitimate military targets. She must then determine whether she can reasonably deliver her ordnance with sufficient precision to achieve the desired effects. Further, she must assess, in light of the information available, whether the attack would be likely to cause impermissible collateral damage—that is, collateral damage that would be excessive in relation to the direct and concrete military advantage to be gained.

Viewed purely from the basis of attacking enemy troops lodged in a populated neighborhood, the risk of disproportionate collateral damage would appear high. But the fact that the enemy troops are presently engaging friendly forces, and those forces have signaled a need for assistance, factors heavily into assessing the direct and concrete advantage of attacking the enemy with close air support. From this perspective, the ground commander or the pilot would have to quickly—at times within minutes—process a number of difficult questions, such as whether the friendly ground forces can retreat to a defensible position with acceptable risk.

The ultimate decision is one of military judgment, and often must be made with imperfect information. If not, then an aerial attack using 500-pound bombs in a residential area raises the question of whether risks of collateral damage can be significantly mitigated by adjusting the bombing run vector and fusing of the weapon. A significant problem is balancing the unknown risk of collateral damage and measures taken to mitigate that risk with the requirement that it produce enough destruction to enemy forces to offer friendly forces an opportunity to retreat or move to a defensible position.

Further complicating this scenario is the issue of the interplay between the LOAC and principles of self-defense. Differing views exist on the importance of collateral damage when force is used in unit self-defense.[180] Some nations take the view that, even in self-defense, the LOAC principal of proportionality must have a moderating effect. Other nations oppose this view, positing that in matters of unit self defense, all necessary means may be employed without regard to collateral damage and/or proportionality.

3. Scenario Three

A pilot is enforcing a United Nations (UN)-sanctioned no-fly zone over Country A. Country A sits next to Country Z. Country Z is hostile to the UN mission, the pilot's country, and Country A. Since the no-fly zone was established, Country

---

[180] *See, e.g.*, Major Eric C. Husby, *A Balancing Act: In Pursuit of Proportionality in Self-Defense for On-Scene Commanders*, ARMY LAW 11 (May 2012).

Z has positioned significant military forces on the border of Country A, held maneuvers along the border, and issued a steady stream of vitriol in the media. While the UN pilot is on patrol, he spots (or is alerted by a C2 asset) a fast-moving jet flying toward his four-o-clock position from the direction of the border with Country Z, but it has not yet crossed the border. Country Z is known to fly fourth-generation fighter aircraft armed with air-to-air missiles that have what is known as "beyond visual" range. Because of the geometry including altitudes, fuel state, distances, and speed, the UN pilot has about fifteen seconds to make a decision. Is he observing actions that indicate intent to attack him—in ROE parlance, a demonstration of hostile intent?[181] Should he stick around to investigate?

He can call for help from his command and control center, but even if they are simultaneously tracking the situation, it will take too long for them to add much information. Fifteen seconds is not enough time to hold a discussion that determines what the most prudent and acceptable course of action should be in light of the overall mission, commander's intent, and geopolitical factors. And yet, the pilot must decide whether to turn toward a potential adversary and engage in combat or attempt to evade and maneuver to a place of safety.

Because of the limited time required to make such decisions, it is imperative that ROE and special instructions for aircrews address likely air-to-air scenarios such as the one above. A fighter pilot needs to know with as much specificity as possible whether he has the authority to engage enemy aircraft, what means are acceptable to reasonably identify aircraft as legitimate targets, or otherwise how to discern whether the aircraft presents an imminent threat of death or grievous bodily harm to the pilot or others such that he may take action in self-defense. Nations do not all agree on what those triggers should be, hence complicating ROE in a coalition setting. Regardless, imaginative aircrews and legal advisors should take the time to work through scenarios, produce practical ROE, and ensure aircrews are well-trained prior to facing such decisions. Similarly, those serving in command and control centers must have a similar understanding of the ROE and be ready to offer helpful advice or to issue clear orders to a pilot facing this type of challenge.

G. A VIEW FROM BELOW

1. Scenario

A battalion is deployed to Country B in support of a contingency operation. The battalion operations center receives a report that one of its squads operating in an urban area is pinned down by enemy fire from a multiple-story building. The squad

---

[181] The United States defines "Hostile Intent" in its Standing Rules of Engagement as "[t]he threat of imminent use of force against the United States, U.S. forces or other designated persons or property. It also includes the threat of force to preclude or impede the mission and/or duties of U.S. forces, including the recovery of U.S. personnel or vital USG property." *Chairman of the Joint Chiefs of Staff Instruction (CJCSI) 3121.01B, Standing Rules of Engagement/Standing Rules for the Use of Force for US Forces* (June 13, 2005), A-3.

is trapped in an alley and cannot maneuver due to enemy fire. The squad leader requests close air support to eliminate the enemy threat. The squad leader does not know if there are any civilians in the building, but the squad leader informs the operations center that the squad will be out of ammunition in roughly fifteen minutes. The battalion commander, who is located in the operations center, must decide how best to support this squad with some form of air-delivered munitions while minimizing potential collateral damage. The commander checks with the Air Liaison Officer (ALO) to see what air assets are available. The ALO informs the commander that the only air assets available do not have Precision-Guided Munitions (PGMs). Furthermore, the battalion commander does not have direct legal support in the operations center—the legal advisor is located in the brigade operations center. Thus, the battalion commander has to make a critical decision with limited information, little time, and less-than-optimal assets.

This scenario is a routine dilemma for commanders operating in today's complex tactical environment. Commanders of tactical units rely on the delivery of combat effects from the air to support their ground forces. For these reasons, targeting at the tactical level presents many unique challenges for commanders and legal advisors serving at the brigade and battalion level. In the United States Army, the brigade combat team (BCT) is the close combat force in major military operations for a division or joint task force.[182]

The BCT is the primary land force used to attack deliberate targets proposed by higher levels of command. In addition to deliberate targets, the BCT conducts unplanned targeting engagements to support targets of opportunity and troops-in-contact.[183] The challenges associated with unplanned targeting engagements are magnified by the limited assets available at the tactical level. Although most BCTs contain over 3,500 soldiers, these units have limited organic targeting assets outside of indirect fire capabilities.[184] Thus, the BCTs rely on other units to provide aerial direct-fire assets such as fixed-wing and rotary-wing aircraft.[185] Limited organic assets and short time windows pose significant challenges for legal advisors serving at the tactical level. To overcome these challenges, the legal advisor has to know how the unit conducts deliberate targeting and responds to troops-in-contact situations.

The legal advisor supporting the tactical fight must understand the unit's deliberate targeting process in order to provide timely and effective legal support. In addition, the legal advisor must ensure that the commander and staff are able

---

[182] U. S. Dep't of Army, Field Manual 3–90.6, The Brigade Combat Team, 1–1 (Sept. 20, 2010) [hereinafter FM 3-90.6].

[183] Troops-in-contact (TIC) is "an unplanned engagement occurring when US or NATO ground forces unexpectedly come into contact with insurgent forces." Marc Garlasco, *Troops in Contact*, *in* Human Rights Watch 29, 30 (Brad Adams et al. eds., Sept. 2008). These situations often involve attacks or imminent attacks on U.S. forces, which justify the use of force in self-defense. The scenario at the beginning of this section is an example of troops-in-contact.

[184] FM 3-90.6, *supra* note 182, at 1–1.

[185] The BCT only has indirect fire capabilities provided by the organic fires battalion. Rotary or fixed-wing aerial support comes from outside the BCT on a mission-specific basis. *Id.* at 1–7.

to respond within the legal parameters during unanticipated engagements with the enemy. Legal advisors can achieve the necessary efficacy by (1) knowing their role in the targeting process, (2) being proactive during the unit's targeting meetings, and (3) assisting the unit with responding to troops-in-contact situations.

The legal advisor's role in the targeting process is to provide the decision-maker and the staff with analysis and contemporaneous legal advice during the early planning phases.[186] Most BCTs use the Decide, Detect, Deliver, and Assess (D3A) methodology for deliberate targeting.[187] In the decide function, the commander along with the staff determines which targets to attack and when and where the targets are likely to be found. The decide function produces a high payoff target list (HPTL), the target selection standards, and the attack guidance matrix.[188] These products allow the staff to prioritize the targets, establish the level of accuracy for attack, and decide how and when the BCT will engage the targets.[189] Legal advisors should assist the staff in developing and analyzing these products to ensure that the HPTL contains legitimate military objectives, and that the standards for acquiring the targets and engaging them comply with the principle of distinction.[190]

The next step in the D3A methodology is the detect function, which involves locating the high payoff target (HPT) accurately enough to engage it. During this step, the operations and intelligence sections leverage various assets to locate the targets to the acceptable level of accuracy.[191] These are the same standards established by the staff and approved by the commander in the decide function. The legal advisor, however, still has to ensure that the unit has positively identified the target.[192] In order to do this, the legal advisor should continuously review the information gathered from the various intelligence collection assets during the detect function. Proactive participation by the legal advisor during this phase will assist the staff's compliance with the rules of engagement and help prevent having their plan derailed during the deliver function.

The deliver function is a critical phase for the legal advisor because the unit decides to engage the target with lethal force.[193] The unit will determine which assets are available to engage the target and develop the collateral damage estimate

---

[186] U. S. Dep't of Army, Field Manual 1-04, Legal Support to the Operational Army, 6–1 (Jan. 26, 2012) [hereinafter FM 1-04].

[187] FM 3-90.6, *supra* note 182, at 7–5; FM 3-60, *supra* note 10, at 1–1.

[188] FM 3-90.6, *supra* note 182, at 7-6. The target selection standards "focus on accuracy to establish criteria for deciding when targets are located accurately enough to attack." The attack guidance matrix "addresses the targets or target sets to attack, how and when they will be attacked, and the desired effects that attacking the target will generate."

[189] *Id.* at 6–1.

[190] The legal advisor reviews the target selection standards and the attack guidance matrix to get early visibility on the unit's plan for engaging targets. This will allow the legal advisor to anticipate legal issues and provide effective input throughout the rest of the targeting process.

[191] *Id.* at 7–8.

[192] The standard for positive identification for deliberate targeting at the tactical level is the same as the standard for aerial engagements.

[193] *Id.*

(CDE).[194] In this phase, the legal advisor has two main legal concerns: distinction and proportionality. First, the legal advisor has to ensure that the unit complies with the principle of distinction by establishing and maintaining positive identification of the target throughout the deliver function. Second, the legal advisor reviews the collateral damage estimate from the fires cell. This estimate will provide the legal advisor with situational awareness of potential issues related to the principle of proportionality. In addition, the estimate may require the unit to seek higher-level approval for this mission in accordance with the rules of engagement.

The final phase of the targeting process is the assess function. During this phase the unit examines the outcome of the engagement and conducts a battle damage assessment.[195] This assessment is significant for the legal advisor to provide consequence management advice to the commander. Lethal engagements often result in collateral damage in the form of civilian deaths, injuries, or property damage. Consequently, the commander needs advice from the legal advisor on how to respond to this incidental loss of life and damage.

The role of the legal advisor in the targeting process may seem daunting in light of the fast-paced tactical environment. For this reason, the legal advisor is often co-located with the fires cell to provide legal reviews of targeting plans and orders.[196] Also, there are two best practices that can assist with remaining proactive and informed throughout this process. First, attending the various targeting meetings and working groups is vital to maintaining situational awareness and training the staff.[197] Second, being a part of the targeting board will ensure that the commander does not approve targets for lethal engagement without the legal advisor's review.[198]

The targeting cycle affords multiple opportunities for the legal advisor to provide input on proposed targets and gain situational awareness on future target engagements. Although BCTs approach targeting in unique ways, each of these units has a targeting working group meeting and a targeting board during their targeting cycle. The targeting working group[199] provides the legal advisor with an opportunity to provide input on targets that are within a thirty-six-hour window.[200] This working group focuses on synchronizing the BCT's assets to find,

---

[194] *See supra* note 142. The collateral damage estimate is based on "processes for a commander to conduct collateral damage estimation and mitigate unintended or incidental damage or injury to civilian or noncombatant persons or property. It assists commanders in weighing risk against military necessity and in assessing proportionality within the framework of the military decision-making process." U. S. Dep't of Army, Army Technical Publication 3-60.1, Dynamic Targeting, 137 (May 7, 2012).

[195] *Id.* at 7–9.

[196] FM 3-90.6, *supra* note 182, at 7–2.

[197] FM 1-04, *supra* note 186, at 5–5.

[198] FM 3-60, *supra* note 10, at 4–10.

[199] The number of working groups the BCT uses is unique to that particular unit. Therefore, the legal advisor has to know how his or her BCT conducts the targeting meetings.

[200] FM 3-60, *supra* note 10, at 4–3.

track, attack, and assess HPTs.[201] The targeting working group will provide the legal advisor with the methods for collecting information on HPTs and the means of engaging these targets. The legal advisor will be able to reinforce the legal standards for engaging each of the HPTs that are within the thirty-six-hour window.

The targeting board provides the legal advisor an opportunity to participate in the commander's decision-making process as it relates to targeting recommendations for command approval. The targeting board is a "temporary grouping of select staff with delegated decision authority to provide targeting decision recommendations for command approval."[202] This meeting is more formal than the working group, and requires input from each of the members in order to make recommendations to the commander. The legal advisor is often a member of the select staff included in this meeting, and is required to provide a legal review for the commander. Most commanders will not approve the board's recommendations without input from the legal advisor.

Many BCTs conduct the targeting working group and the targeting board meeting daily or weekly depending on the pace of the operational environment. This frequency provides the legal advisor with multiple opportunities to enhance the staff's understanding of the ROE and the LOAC principles of distinction and proportionality. The staff's proficiency with applying these in the operational environment will alleviate, but not eliminate, the challenges associated with deliberate targeting. In addition to deliberate targeting, the commander and the staff will often have to make quick decisions, sometimes without the assistance of the legal advisor, during unplanned targeting engagements related to troops-in-contact situations similar to the scenario at the beginning of this section.

As unplanned enemy engagements, troops-in-contact situations trigger the right of self-defense under the rules of engagement.[203] When a subordinate unit encounters the enemy, the unit will respond in self-defense. The BCT commander has the right and obligation to defend the forces assigned to the brigade; hence the staff will direct and/or redirect assets to support the unit engaging the enemy.[204] These assets include indirect fire assets along with aviation and close air support. Because of the hasty nature of troops-in-contact, a formal collateral damage estimate is not possible. The staff, however, still conducts an estimate for engaging targets in these situations. In addition, the legal advisor may not be present to provide support to this unplanned targeting event. Thus, the staff has to employ force in a manner consistent with the ROE and LOAC principles without direct legal support. In light of this dilemma, how does the legal advisor ensure that their commanders make legally sound and timely decisions in troops-in-contact situations outside the legal advisor's presence?

---

[201] *Id.* at 4–4.

[202] *Id.* at 4–5.

[203] Chairman of the Joint Chiefs of Staff, Instruction 3121.01B, Standing Rules of Engagement/Standing Rules for the Use of Force for U.S. Forces, A-1 (June 13, 2005) [hereinafter CJCSI 3121.01B]; Garlasco, *supra* note 183, at 30.

[204] CJCSI 3121.01B, *supra* note 203, at A-1.

The legal advisor can assist the commander and the staff with making sound decisions in the absence of direct legal support by conducting cyclic ROE training and updating the battle drills. The legal advisor routinely provides ROE training prior to deployment to a contingency operation. A fast-paced operational environment may render this training obsolete; therefore, the legal advisor should update the ROE training to match the operational tempo.[205] The updated training will be based on enemy tactics and lessons learned from the targeting cycles, and will aid the staff in adapting to the current enemy situation while complying with the applicable ROE.

Although such cyclic training is helpful, the staff still needs to have battle drills[206] that reflect the compliance with the ROE. Each unit has a set of drills they use to respond to various events. One of those events is troops-in-contact. The legal advisor should review these battle drills to ensure compliance with the ROE prior to deployment to a contingency operation. During the deployment, the assess phase of the D3A targeting methodology provides the legal advisor with a cyclic opportunity to review the battle drills and to make the required changes. Solid battle drills can mitigate the challenges related to the staff's ability to comply with the ROE; however, collateral damage during troops-in-contact situations is unavoidable in many instances.[207]

There are a number of reasons for higher civilian casualties and property damage during troops–in-contact targeting engagements. First, the BCT responds using the assets available, which may not be as accurate as those used during deliberate targeting. Second, the staff often cannot conduct a formal CDE, hence denying the staff the ability to mitigate the effects of the munitions. Third, effective communication with the unit in contact is difficult; therefore the staff may not have all the information needed to anticipate and hastily mitigate collateral damage. For these reasons, the legal advisor should ensure that consequence management is included in the troops-in-contact battle drill to assess the damage and respond to immediate inquiries.

Legal advisors at the tactical level, working closely with their units, can alleviate many of the challenges of tactical-level targeting. Commanders at this level play a significant role in the targeting process. These leaders are the critical decision-makers who link the air component to the ground force. Consequently, the legal advisor's support to the commander's decision-making process can

---

[205] Major Winston S. Williams Jr., *Training the Rules of Engagement for the Counterinsurgency Fight*, Army Law. 42, 47 (Jan. 2012).

[206] A battle drill is

> a collective action, executed by a platoon or smaller element, without the application of a deliberate decision-making process. The action is vital to success in combat or critical to preserve life. The drill is initiated on a cue, such as an enemy action or your leader's order, and is a trained response to that stimulus.

U. S. Dep't of Army, Field Manual 3–21.75, The Warrior Ethos and Soldier Combat Skills paras. 1–7 (Jan. 28, 2008).

[207] *See* Garlasco, *supra* note 183, at 30.

ensure that the unit's process of nominating, tracking, and engaging targets complies with the principles of distinction and proportionality. The legal advisor's ability to integrate with the staff, provide training, and update the battle drills will directly impact the unit's compliance with LOAC and ROE.

IV. Conclusion

Targeting is one of the most fundamentally important components of modern combat operations. The processes employed to ensure the right targets are engaged with means and methods best suited to achieving operational ends is dynamic and complex. The LOAC is a critical aspect of that process. Its effective integration and synchronization requires far more than just a basic familiarity with the applicable treaty and customary norms. The LOAC is an elaborate set of rules developed from a desire among civilized nations to prevent unnecessary suffering and destruction in warfare. At the same time, the LOAC recognizes that under certain circumstances, states have the need to wage war, and therefore seeks to strike a balance between humanitarian protections and the legitimate imperatives of warfare. Understanding this balance and the complex interaction among law, policy, and military doctrine on the battlefield is critical to the effective integration of legal advice into the targeting process, and to LOAC compliance.

7}

Developing Rules of Engagement

OPERATIONALIZING LAW, POLICY, AND MILITARY IMPERATIVES AT THE STRATEGIC LEVEL

Gary P. Corn*

I. Introduction

In June 1863, General Robert E. Lee, determined to capitalize on his recent victory over the Army of the Potomac at the Battle of Chancellorsville, led his Army of Northern Virginia northward through the Shenandoah Valley into Pennsylvania. Lee's strategic objective was to strike a decisive blow against Northern forces and effectively threaten Philadelphia, Baltimore, and Washington in order to strengthen the growing peace movement in the North and possibly gain needed foreign recognition of the Confederacy.[1] By late June, Lee's three Army Corps were spread out over a wide area of south central Pennsylvania, and Lee had issued them strict orders not to become decisively engaged with Union forces until the Confederate Army was concentrated at a place of Lee's choosing.[2]

* Colonel Gary P. Corn is a Judge Advocate, United States Army. His most recent assignment is as the Staff Judge Advocate/principal legal advisor for the Commander of US Cyber Command. Other assignments include Chief, Operational Law Branch, International and Operational Law Division, Office of the Judge Advocate General of the Army, Deputy Legal Counsel, Office of the Legal Counsel to the Chairman of the Joint Chiefs of Staff, Staff Judge Advocate, United States Army South, Fort Sam Houston, Texas, and Chief, International Law, Combined Forces Command-Afghanistan, Kabul, Afghanistan. Colonel Corn is a graduate of The Judge Advocate General's School, United States Army (LLM. with Honors); George Washington University National Law Center (with Honors); Bucknell University; United States Army War College, (MA in National Security Studies, Distinguished Graduate); and the Escola de Comando e Estado Maior do Exército do Brasil (Command and General Staff College of the Brazilian Army), Rio de Janeiro, Brazil. The positions and opinions in this chapter are those of the author and do not represent the official views of the Department of Defense or the United States Army.

[1] James M. McPhereson, Battle Cry of Freedom: The Civil War Era 647 (1988).

[2] *Id.* at 653–54.

On June 30, the lead elements of Lieutenant General A.P. Hill's Third Corps approached the small town of Gettysburg, intending to enter the town to confiscate what was reported as a large supply of shoes. Noticing the presence of an undetermined number of Union troops, the brigade commander withdrew and returned to confer with Hill. Despite General Lee's order, Hill directed Major General Henry Heth, one of his division commanders, to conduct a reconnaissance in force the following morning to determine the size and strength of the Union force and "to get those shoes."[3] Around 5 am on Wednesday, July 1, two brigades of Heth's division advanced to Gettysburg. Instead of finding shoes, however, the Confederate troops ran head-on into two brigades of Union cavalry that had arrived the day before and realized the strategic importance of the town. Rather than breaking contact, Hill attacked in force. What ensued over the next three days was the climactic battle of the American Civil War; a decisive, bloody defeat of Lee's Army and the turning point in favor of the North's ultimate victory over the South.

The point of the foregoing is not to provide a brief history on the Battle of Gettysburg; much has been written on the subject. It is to highlight that military commanders have been placing boundaries on the time, place, and manner in which their forces apply combat power since long before the advent of the term "rules of engagement,"[4] and for reasons beyond seeking to ensure their operations complied with applicable law. They have done so based on the acute understanding that unrestrained, undisciplined, and uncoordinated use of force in military operations generally leads to disastrous results at all levels: tactical, operational, and strategic.[5] General Lee understood very well the principles of war,[6] especially the principle of mass.[7] He issued what was in effect a rule of engagement—to not become decisively engaged with the enemy until such time as his force was sufficiently concentrated—in order to apply that principle. It was clear operational guidance that his subordinate commander ignored. The tactical and operational engagement into which Major General Heth's division pulled the remainder of Lee's Army violated both this core principle and Lee's stated command intent. The rest is history.[8]

---

[3] *Id.*

[4] The term "Rules of Engagement" was first introduced into military lexicon in the 1950s. *See infra*, notes 23–26 and accompanying text.

[5] Commonly referred to in doctrine as the three "Levels of War," they "model the relationship between national objectives and tactical actions." JOINT CHIEFS OF STAFF, JOINT PUBLICATION 3-0, JOINT OPERATIONS I-12 (Aug. 20, 2011) [hereinafter JP 3-0].

[6] United States' doctrine has traditionally recognized nine Principles of War—objective, offensive, mass, economy of force, maneuver, unity of command, security, surprise, and simplicity—which "represent the most important nonphysical factors that affect the conduct of operations at the strategic, operational, and tactical levels." U.S. DEP'T OF ARMY, FIELD MANUAL 3-0, OPERATIONS, App. A-1 (Feb. 27, 2008) (with Change 1, Feb. 22, 2011).

[7] "The purpose of mass is to concentrate the effects of combat power at the most advantageous place and time to produce decisive results." JP 3-0, *supra* note 5, at A-2.

[8] To be fair, once engaged, Lee reversed himself and committed to the battle. And some argue that his intent was to fight at Gettysburg all along. GENERAL EDWARD J. STACKPOLE, THEY MET AT

Juxtapose the previous example with that of the Battle of Naco in the fall of 1914. At the time, Naco was a heavily contested battleground between Mexican federal and rebel forces that threatened to spill over the border into the United States.[9] In response, the 9th and 10th Cavalry Regiments were deployed from nearby Fort Huachuca, Arizona, to protect the U.S. border and to ensure U.S. neutrality was not violated.[10] To make certain the overall strategic objective was achieved, the cavalry regiments were issued strict tactical orders not to return fire across the border, despite the fact that they were routinely fired upon and "[t]he provocation to return the fire was very great."[11] In this case, the U.S. forces maintained tactical discipline, thereby ensuring strategic success—the border was protected, neutrality guaranteed, and a wider conflict between the United States and the Mexican factions was averted. For their "splendid conduct and efficient service" the President and the Chief of Staff of the Army specifically commended the men of the 9th and 10th Cavalry.[12]

The foregoing are examples of traditional political and military aims operating to shape or constrain military operations. In today's world, the law, especially the Law of Armed Conflict (LOAC), is an additional factor that pervades nearly every aspect of operations, starting with the application of combat power, to the point where U.S. doctrine has elevated adherence to law to the pantheon of the Principles of War.[13] The primary doctrinal tool developed to operationalize governing legal precepts is the guidance contained in the rules of engagement (ROE).

Rules of engagement are generally defined as rules, either in the form of guidance or directives, issued by competent authority, which delineate the circumstances and limitations under which military forces may initiate and/or continue using force against other forces, individuals, or objects encountered.[14] They are addressed differently in the military doctrines of those armed forces that employ

---

GETTYSBURG 104–05 (1956). But there is general agreement that he issued the order not to engage, and history would seem to tell us that his initial instinct was correct.

[9] James P. Finley, *Buffalo Soldiers at Huachuca: The Battle of Naco*, 1 HUACHUCA ILLUSTRATED (1993), *available at* http://net.lib.byu.edu/estu/wwi/comment/huachuca/HI1-10.htm.

[10] *Id.*

[11] *Id.* (quoting Colonel William C. Brown).

[12] *Id.* (*citing* FRANK TOMPKINS, CHASING VILLA: THE LAST CAMPAIGN OF THE U.S. CAVALRY 37–38 (1934)).

[13] Joint doctrine adds the principles of legitimacy, restraint, and perseverance to the traditional nine principles. JP 3-0, *supra*, note 5, at A-4.

[14] The United States defines ROE as "directives issued by competent military authority that delineate the circumstances and limitations under which U.S. forces will initiate and/or continue combat engagement with other forces encountered . . . ." JOINT CHIEFS OF STAFF, JOINT PUBLICATION 1-02: DEPARTMENT OF DEFENSE DICTIONARY OF MILITARY AND ASSOCIATED TERMS 270 (Nov. 8, 2010, as amended through Aug. 15, 2012) [hereinafter JP 1-02]. The International Institute of Humanitarian Law's RULES OF ENGAGEMENT HANDBOOK defines ROE as directives or guidance "issued by competent authorities [that] assist in the delineation of the circumstances and limitations within which military forces may be employed to achieve their objectives." INTERNATIONAL INSTITUTE OF HUMANITARIAN LAW, RULES OF ENGAGEMENT HANDBOOK 1 (Nov. 2009) [hereinafter SAN REMO HANDBOOK].

them, often appearing in execute orders, deployment orders, operational plans and orders, and stand-alone directives.

Rules of engagement are often broader than the definition above would indicate. Although ROE may, as in the examples above, serve a single purpose, more frequently they reflect the confluence of operational requirements, policy imperatives, and law, translated into parameters on how commanders employ force and conduct all types of military operations. In addition to providing authorization for and/or placing limits on the use of force, to include clarifying the different levels of force that can be used in different circumstances, ROE often also address the positioning and posturing of forces, the employment of specific capabilities, the handling and disposition of captured or detained persons, and any delegations or withholdings of authorities to approve any of the foregoing.[15] In the final analysis, ROE are in essence a critical command and control tool. They are designed to give military and political leadership greater control over the execution of operations, both combat and noncombat, by subordinate forces.

Although originally developed in the United States,[16] ROE have become a key component of military planning and operations, and are utilized with ever-greater frequency and sophistication by a number of states and international organizations. In today's information environment, it is rare that reports investigating or challenging a particular military's use of force will not make reference to, and often turn on, compliance with applicable ROE. They have become ubiquitous, and experience has proved that poorly calibrated and drafted ROE, coupled with a lack of effective training to ensure the forces understand the ROE governing mission execution, can quickly translate into strategic mission failure. As such, military commanders and planners, civilian leadership, and the lawyers who advise them must have a thorough and grounded understanding of ROE principles and doctrine.

Developing and implementing effective ROE is central to the success of modern military operations. They form a principal component of operational planning and execution at all levels of command, and must be consonant with and support national policy objectives, governing legal principles, and the operational concept. As operational direction and guidance, ROE are the responsibility of the commander and his or her operations staff element—usually the G/J-3. However, operational legal advisors play a crucial supporting role in the analysis, drafting, promulgation, and training of ROE.[17]

---

[15] San Remo Handbook, *supra* note 14, at 1; United Nations, Dep't of Peacekeeping Operations, United Nations Peacekeeping Operations Principles and Guidelines 25 (2008) [hereinafter, UNPKO Principles and Guidelines].

[16] Currently, U.S. ROE guidance is contained in *Chairman of the Joint Chiefs of Staff Instruction (CJCSI) 3121.01B, Standing Rules of Engagement/Standing Rules for the Use of Force for US Forces* (June 13, 2005) [hereinafter SROE/SRUF].

[17] *See* U.S. Dep't of Army, Field Manual 1-04, Legal Support to the Operational Army, 5-4 and App. C (Jan. 26, 2012) [hereinafter FM 1-04]; *see generally* Joint Chiefs of Staff, Joint Publication 1-04, Legal Support to Military Operations (Aug. 17, 2011).

Whether in the form of standing rules or rules developed for specific missions, ROE are nearly always promulgated first at the strategic level and disseminated down the chain of command, where they are incorporated into operational planning and training at each echelon as part of the normal operations order process. And although operational and tactical level commanders are generally empowered to issue additional ROE, they are rarely permitted to issue measures more permissive than those set at higher levels. Strategic ROE can therefore have a profound impact on the execution of military operations all the way down to the individual soldiers on the ground. Getting strategic ROE right is critical, and starts with a review of the history, purposes, and processes of ROE.

II. History

In the broadest sense of the term, ROE are as old as military operations themselves. Although not specifically denominated as such, from the moment that the human activity called warfare morphed into organized battle, likely in Mesopotamia between four and two thousand B.C.,[18] military commanders have sought to strictly control and synchronize the application of force to maximize combat power and achieve specified objectives. From the famed Greek Phalanx to the shock formations of the German Blitzkrieg to contemporary Joint Operations doctrine, the evolution of warfare has involved an ever-increasing level of sophistication designed to both maximize combat power and ensure its employment furthers, but does not undermine or transgress, nationally defined policies and goals. Developments in areas such as weapons technology, force structures, and battlefield tactics relate to the former purpose. Rules of engagement are a more recent iteration of this broader evolutionary process devised to achieve the latter.

One of the most frequently cited examples of an early ROE is the famous order issued at the Battle of Bunker Hill in 1775, "Don't one of you shoot until you see the whites of their eyes."[19] Although historians differ over who in fact gave the order, it was plainly issued as a tactical control measure to maximize the effect of American forces' firepower in the face of a superior British foe.[20] Although some might consider this order to be more correctly categorized as a fire-control measure,[21] it certainly "delineated the circumstances and limitations under which"

---

[18] *See, e.g.*, JOHN KEEGAN, A HISTORY OF WARFARE 126–36 (1993).

[19] JOHN E. LEWIS, THE MAMMOTH BOOK OF HOW IT HAPPENED 179 (1998). Historians differ over whether this order was issued by General Israel Putnam or Colonel William Prescott.

[20] Geoffrey S. Corn & Lieutenant Colonel Gary P. Corn, *The Law of Operational Targeting: Viewing the LOAC through an Operational Lens*, 47 TEX. INT'L L.J. 337, 354 (2012).

[21] *See* Center for Law and Military Operations and Headquarters Marine Corps, *Rules of Engagement: What Are They and Where Do They Come From?*, MARINE CORPS GAZETTE 59 (Apr. 2002) [hereinafter CLAMO and HQMC]. Fire-control measures are "the means by which commanders or subordinate leaders control fires, in order to help the unit acquire the enemy, focus fires on him, distribute the effects of the fires, and prevent fratricide." DEP'T OF ARMY FIELD MANUAL 3–21.10, THE INFANTRY RIFLE COMPANY, 9–19 (July 27, 2006) [hereinafter FM 3-21.10]. They include, inter alia, engagement criteria, engagement priorities, sectors of fire, and target reference points.

the colonial forces were to engage their British adversaries, and is thus better understood as a progenitor to current tactical ROE under the broad definitions prevailing today.[22]

Rules of engagement both as a term and a recognized concept emerged in the 1950s in the form of special instructions issued to govern U.S. air operations.[23] During the Korean War, "General Douglas McArthur received orders from Washington that American bomber aircraft were neither to enter Chinese airspace nor destroy the Shuiho Dam on the North Korean side of the Yalu River"—orders that were clearly aimed at reducing the risk of direct Chinese intervention in the conflict and possible nuclear escalation.[24] In 1954, the Joint Chiefs of Staff (JCS)[25] issued "Intercept and

---

Dep't of Army Field Manual 3–90, Tactics, 2–64 (July 1, 2001). Interestingly, U.S. Army doctrine lists ROE as a "Threat-Based Fire-Control Measure." FM 3-21.10, at 9–9, 9–17. The term has been dropped from U.S. joint doctrine in favor of "fire support coordination measure": "[a] measure employed by commanders to facilitate the rapid engagement of targets and simultaneously provide safeguards for friendly forces." JP 1–02, *supra* note 14, at 116; Joint Chiefs of Staff, Joint Publication 3–09, Joint Fires Support, iii (June 3, 2010).

[22] *See* CLAMO and HQMC, *supra* note 21, at 59. Prior to the infamous "shot heard round the world" and the commencement of active hostilities in the American Revolution, the Second Continental Congress several times issued instructions, particularly to the militias of Boston and New York, to engage British troops only as a matter of self-defense, stating that the residents of those cities should "act on the defensive so long as may be consistent with their safety and security," to "repel force by force" and take other measures essential "for protecting the inhabitants from insult and injury." Jack Rove, Revolutionaries: A History of the Invention of America 88 (2010). This restraining direction was aimed squarely at controlling the nature and circumstances of any potential hostilities in order to maintain the upper hand strategically. The same restraint was exercised up until the very commencement of hostilities at Lexington, Massachusetts, on April 19, 1775, when Captain Jonas Parker ordered his militia, "Stand your ground men. Don't fire unless fired upon; but if they mean to have a war, let it begin here." Robert Debs Heinl Jr., Dictionary of Military and Naval Quotations 272 (1996).

[23] *See* Major Mark S. Martins, *Rules of Engagement for Land Forces: A Matter of Training, Not Lawyering*, 143 Mil. L. Rev. 1, 35 (1994).

[24] *Id.* McArthur's failure to obey this direction contributed to his eventual relief from command.

[25] In 1954 the Joint Chiefs of Staff (JCS) was the senior-most military body in the national chain of command that provided overall operational direction and control of the armed forces. Based on a structure originally implemented during the Second World War, it was formally established by the National Security Act of 1947, Pub.L. 80–253, 61 Stat. 495, codified at 50 U.S.C. ch.15. Joint Chiefs of Staff, Origin of Joint Concepts, http://www.jcs.mil/page.aspx?id=12 (last visited Nov. 17, 2012). It consisted of a Chairman, the Chief of Staff of the Army, the Chief of Staff of the Air Force (which was established as a separate service by the same act), and the Chief of Naval Operations. The Commandant of the Marine Corps was to be consulted on matters concerning the Corps, but was not a regular member until 1979 when the law was amended. As a result of the 1986 Department of Defense Reorganization Act, commonly known as the Goldwater-Nichols Act, the Chairman and the JCS no longer have operational executive or command authority over the armed forces, as the chain of command runs from the President to the Secretary of Defense, and from the Secretary of Defense to the Commanders of the Combatant Commands. 10 U.S.C. § 162(b)(2000). The JCS now serve as military advisers, with the Chairman serving as the principal military adviser to the President, the National Security Council, the Homeland Security Council, and the Secretary of Defense. 10 U.S.C. § 151(1986). However, owing to his statutory responsibilities and functions, and the fact that the President may direct that the combatant commands communicate with the President and the Secretary of Defense through him, the Chairman still exercises considerable

Engagement Instructions" to the Air Force, and in 1958 officially adopted the sobriquet "rules of engagement."[26]

Although employed with greater frequency during the 1960s and 1970s, ROE lacked any degree of standardization and, with minor exceptions, did not focus on tactical land force operations.[27] It was not until 1981, with the JCS's issuance of The Worldwide Peacetime Rules of Engagement for Seaborne Forces, and their expansion in 1986 in the JCS Peacetime ROE for all U.S. Forces (PROE), that U.S. ROE began to take on the shape of a standardized set of guidance evidencing "a clear statement of national views on self-defense in peacetime that also could smooth the transition to hostilities."[28] These nascent ROE were the result of a study directed by Admiral Thomas B. Hayward in 1979 intended not only to achieve greater standardization, but to also "bring together in a single document [the] various references while also providing a list of supplemental measures from which a force commander could select when he felt it necessary to clarify force authority beyond basic self-defense statements."[29]

As the name of the 1981 ROE implies, they, and the 1986 PROE, were heavily focused on naval operations. This was understandable given the state of tensions with the Soviet Union at the time.[30] United States and Soviet naval forces routinely shadowed each other in a delicate game of strategic chess, and thus it was important to prevent a local commander from overreacting to a minor insult or probe, as this could result in an outbreak of a conflict that could quickly escalate into World War III.[31] In addition to extending the applicability of the ROE to all U.S. forces, the most significant development in the 1986 iteration of the ROE was the adoption of standing authority, approved by the Secretary of Defense, for naval forces to respond not just to actual attacks, but to apply "an accelerated sequence up the scale of force" in anticipation of an imminent attack—that is, an authority to exercise anticipatory self-defense.[32]

---

influence over current military planning and operations and has the authority to issue, on behalf of the Secretary of Defense, important operational guidance and direction to the armed forces. *See* 10 U.S.C. §§ 153, 163(1986). *See also* Joint Chiefs of Staff, About the Joint Chiefs of Staff, http://www.jcs.mil/About.aspx (last visited June 9, 2015). The Chairman's issuance of the SROE/SRUF is a prime example.

[26] Trevor Findlay, The Use of Force in UN Peace Operations 14, n.26 (2002); Gary D. Solis, The Law of Armed Conflict, International Humanitarian Law in War 492 (2010).

[27] Some ROE were issued to ground forces during Vietnam, but were generally considered unhelpful and an inadequate substitute for training. *See* Solis, *supra* note 26, at 492–93.

[28] W. Hays Parks, *Righting the Rules of Engagement*, U.S. Naval Institute Proceedings, May 1989, at 83–84. *See also* Martins, *supra* note 23, at 42.

[29] Parks, *supra* note 28, at 83–84.

[30] W. Hays Parks, *Deadly Force Is Authorized*, U.S. Naval Institute Proceedings, Jan. 2001, at 32 (noting that "the primary purpose [of the ROE] being to protect carrier battle groups from a preemptive strike by the Soviet Navy").

[31] Corn & Corn, *supra* note 20, at 355. *See also* International Law Note, *"Land Forces" Rules of Engagement Symposium: The CLAMO Revises the Peacetime Rules of Engagement*, Army Law. 48, 48–49 (Dec. 1993) [hereinafter *ROE Symposium*].

[32] Solis, *supra* note 26, at 492; Parks, *supra* note 30, at 33. As we shall see later in this chapter, the inherent right of anticipatory self-defense is at the core of the current U.S. SROE.

On October 26, 1988, the JCS modified the PROE primarily to reflect lessons learned from the inconsistent application of the new self-defense authorities in the USS *Stark* and *Vincennes* incidents.[33] Although the 1988 PROE were applicable to all military operations, they were still heavily focused on naval operations, applied only to operations short of actual war or prolonged conflict, and were Cold War oriented. After the 1989 fall of the Berlin Wall, however, it became increasingly clear that U.S. ground forces would be deployed and employed in "nebulous situations resulting from peacekeeping and peace-enforcement missions, as well as humanitarian interventions"—uncertain situations similar to those the Navy had historically faced requiring "rules to guide their engagements with potentially hostile forces."[34] To address the deficiencies in the 1988 PROE, the U.S. Army Deputy Chief of Staff for Operations tasked a group of eighteen senior line officers and military lawyers to develop recommendations for the JCS on how to improve the land forces portion of the PROE. The group's recommendations were far more comprehensive than the original tasking called for, urging needed revisions to the entire document to reflect its applicability to the full spectrum of joint operations.[35] The recommendations eventually led to the publication in 1994 of the *Chairman of the Joint Chiefs of Staff Instruction 3121.01, Standing Rules of Engagement for U.S. Forces.*[36]

The 1994 Standing Rules of Engagement (SROE) have been revised twice and are currently undergoing a third revision, but the basic structure remains.[37] As

[33] *ROE Symposium, supra* note 31, at 48; Parks, *supra* note 30, at 33. On May 17, 1987, thirty-seven sailors were killed when an Iraqi Mirage jet fired two Exocet missiles at the USS *Stark* erroneously believing it was a commercial vessel bound for an Iranian port. The *Stark* was patrolling in the Persian Gulf for what have been described as ambiguous purposes during the "Tanker War" phase of the Iran-Iraq War. Stephen Andrew Kelley, *Better Lucky than Good: Operation Earnest Will as Gunboat Diplomacy*, Naval Postgraduate School 35–42 (June 2007), *available at* http://www.nps.edu/Academics/Centers/CCC/research/StudentTheses/kelley07.pdf. The official investigation into the *Stark* incident deemed the existing rules of engagement (ROE) to have been sufficient "to enable Stark to properly warn the Iraqi aircraft" and "to defend herself against hostile intent without absorbing the first hit." *Id.* at 41 (citing Grant Sharp, Investigation Report: Formal Investigation into the Circumstances surrounding the Attack on USS Stark (FFG-31) on May 17, 1987, at 32 (Washington: Department of Defense, 1987)). However, not all agreed, evidenced by subsequent modifications granting more robust self-defense authorities. *Id. See also ROE Symposium, supra* note 31, at 48. The attack on the *Stark* also contributed to the initiation of Operation Earnest Will—the U.S. protection of reflagged Kuwaiti Tankers, and the more direct U.S. involvement that eventually led to the *Vincennes* incident, another tragic event on the opposite end of the ROE self-defense spectrum. On July 3, 1988, the U.S.S. *Vincennes*, also on duty in the Persian Gulf, erroneously identified an Iranian commercial airliner, Iran Air Flight 655, as an inbound hostile aircraft and shot it down, killing 290 civilians. Kelley at 81; *ROE Symposium, supra* note 31, at 48.

[34] *ROE Symposium, supra* note 31, at 48.

[35] *Id.* at 49.

[36] Parks, *supra* note 28, at 83–84.

[37] The current version of the SROE is contained in the 2005 SROE/SRUF, *supra* note 16. The author served as a principal action officer for the pending draft revision of CJCSI 3121.01B. *See also* Int'l & Operational Dep't, The Judge Advocate Gen.'s Legal Ctr. & Sch., U.S. Army, Operational Law Handbook 74 (2010) [hereinafter Operational Law Handbook].

discussed more fully below, the SROE contain both standing self-defense authorities applicable to U.S. armed forces during all military operations, with amplifying guidance specific to the various domains in which U.S. forces operate (air, maritime, land, space, etc.), and for certain specific mission sets (counterdrug support, noncombatant evacuation operations). Additionally, the SROE includes an enclosure containing enumerated supplemental ROE measures that may be authorized at different levels of command for specific contingencies or operations.[38] This basic structure is designed to ensure, in a standardized form, the inherent right and obligation of units and individuals to exercise self-defense at all times, while providing a process for the rapid development of mission-specific ROE, which will always depend on the legal, policy, and military circumstances prevailing at the time.

The U.S. SROE is probably the most recognized, developed, and tested ROE system in existence, but by no means is it the only one. The North Atlantic Treaty Organization (NATO) has adopted a standardized ROE system,[39] as have many of the individual alliance members, as well as other countries. The United Nations, through the Department of Peacekeeping Operations (DPKO),[40] has developed model ROE for the peacekeeping missions it oversees,[41] recognizing that "[i]n the volatile and potentially dangerous environments into which contemporary peacekeeping operations are often deployed ... ROE ... should be sufficiently robust to ensure that a United Nations peacekeeping operation retains its credibility and freedom of action to implement its mandate."[42] Additionally, a number of regional and independent organizations have produced forms of model ROE over the last several years.[43] In each case, the different ROE systems and processes are grounded on a number of central shared principles discussed below.

---

[38] Although the majority of the SROE is classified Secret, the base portions are unclassified and reprinted in chapter 5 of the *Operational Law Handbook*. *See* OPERATIONAL LAW HANDBOOK, *supra* 37, at 82–96.

[39] NORTH ATLANTIC TREATY ORGANIZATION, NATO MC 362/1, NATO RULES OF ENGAGEMENT [hereinafter NATO ROE].

[40] DPKO provides political and executive direction to UN peacekeeping operations around the world and maintains contact with the Security Council, troop and financial contributors, and parties to the conflict in the implementation of Security Council mandates. United Nations, Dep't of Peacekeeping Operations, https://www.un.org/en/peacekeeping/about/dpko/ (last visited June 9, 2015.

[41] UNITED NATIONS, DEP'T OF PEACEKEEPING OPERATIONS, DEP'T OF FIELD SUPPORT, UNITED NATIONS INFANTRY BATTALION, VOL. II, Ann. C (Aug. 2012) [hereinafter UN Model ROE].

[42] UNPKO PRINCIPLES AND GUIDELINES, *supra* note 15, at 25.

[43] *See, e.g.*, SAN REMO HANDBOOK, *supra* note 14; CONFERENCE OF AMERICAN ARMIES, GUIDE FOR THE FORMULATION AND INTERPRETATION OF THE RULES OF ENGAGEMENT FOR PEACEKEEPING OPERATIONS (2011), *available at* http://www.redcea.org/en-US/PublicManuals/CAA_ROE_ENG.pdf[hereinafter CAA ROE HANDBOOK].

III. The "Ingredients" of ROE

For a growing number of militaries today, ROE have become the primary doctrinal tool for regulating the use of force during military operations. Since the end of World War II, lessons learned, and relearned, have shown that the success of any military operation depends heavily on the appropriate and disciplined use of force. Undisciplined and overly aggressive use of force undermines legitimacy.[44] Overly constricting ROE can degrade commanders' and soldiers' ability to defend themselves and accomplish the mission.[45] Both of these countervailing risks can lead to strategic failure. The convergence of a number of historical factors over the last half century have brought these risks into sharper focus and demonstrated a heightened need to more tightly "harness military action to political ends."[46] Effective ROE simply "are critical to mission accomplishment."[47]

The risks inherent in the overly precipitous and perhaps indiscriminate, or, conversely, overly tentative, uses of force have been hyper-exposed in the age of an instantaneous news cycle and aggressive information warfare. The impact of the proverbial "Strategic Corporal"—a term coined to describe the strategic impact that the actions an individual soldier, sailor, airman, or marine can have—is, by now, obvious.[48] The difficult and inherent challenges in calibrating the use of force identified during the heyday of "Military Operations Other Than War," or MOOTW, pale in comparison to the complexities encountered in the politically and legally amorphous operational environments of counterinsurgency, counterterror, and stability operations in places such as Iraq and Afghanistan, where the traditional Wartime/Peacetime ROE dichotomy quickly evaporates. Self-defense and offensive mission accomplishment authorities often operate simultaneously in the same battle space, and sometimes seemingly at cross-purposes.

Striking the delicate balance between achieving the legitimate and necessary application of force, and the risk of inhibiting military initiative and creating hesitancy of the military force to protect and defend itself, begins with drafting ROE at the strategic level that "are versatile, understandable, easily executable,

---

[44] For example, the infamous Mai Lai massacre and subsequent cover-up are widely recognized as significant contributing factors to the loss of public support for the Vietnam War. *See, e.g.*, History, Mai Lai Massacre, http://www.history.com/topics/my-lai-massacre (last visited Dec. 30, 2012).

[45] Such as in the case of the devastating car-bomb attack on the U.S. Marine compound at the Beirut International Airport on October 23, 1983, which killed 241 U.S. service members. *See* Report of the DoD Commission on Beirut International Airport Terrorist Act, Oct. 23, 1983, at 47–51, *available at* https://www.fas.org/irp/threat/beirut-1983.pdf (addressing the ROE and concluding that "the mission statement, the original ROE, and the implementation in May 1983 of dual "Blue Card–White Card" ROE contributed to a mindset that detracted from the readiness of the [United States contingent of the Multinational Force] to respond to the terrorist threat which materialized on 23 October 1983.").

[46] Martins, *supra* note 23, at 34.

[47] Center for Law and Military Operations, Rules of Engagement (ROE) Handbook for Judge Advocates 1-1 (2000) [hereinafter ROE Handbook].

[48] Gen. Charles C. Krulak, *The Strategic Corporal: Leadership in the Three Block War*, Marines Mag., Jan. 1999.

and legally and [strategically, operationally] and tactically sound."[49] The process starts with drafters fully informed of the policy, legal, and mission imperatives that ROE effect.[50]

A. THE PURPOSES OF ROE

Although the doctrines of various armed forces differ, ROE generally tend to perform three basic functions: to serve as a control mechanism for the transition from peacetime to combat operations (armed conflict), to provide standing force protection authority and guidance to unit commanders and individual soldiers in the form of self-defense rules, and to provide a command and control mechanism for national command authorities and military commanders to ensure the use of military force complies with strategic political and military aims.[51] Well-developed ROE doctrine, systems, and procedures also serve as a key planning tool and provide the foundation for general and mission-specific use-of-force training.

Rules of engagement are based on the three pillars of national policy, operational requirements, and law.[52] These purposes, discussed more fully below, frequently overlap, necessitating use-of-force guidance to convey this area of convergence. The interplay of these three pillars, or purposes of ROE, is typically depicted by the diagram in Figure 7.1 below.[53]

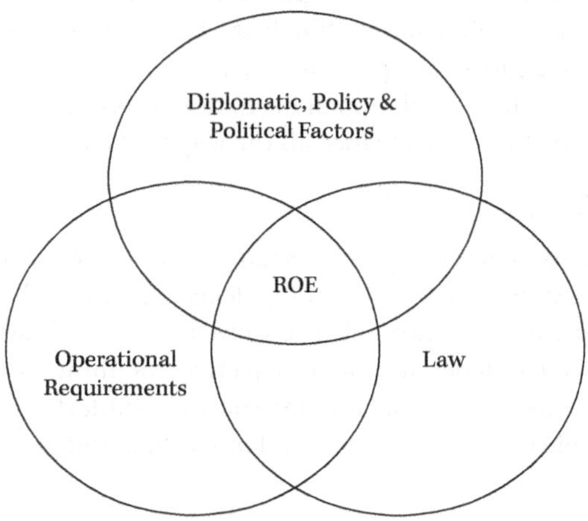

FIGURE 7.1 Influencing ROE development.

[49] OPERATIONAL LAW HANDBOOK, *supra* note 37, at 73.

[50] *Id.*

[51] *See id.*

[52] Richard J. Grunawalt, *The JCS Standing Rules of Engagement: A Judge Advocate's Primer*, 42 A.F. L. REV. 245, 247 (1997).

[53] Then-Captain Ashley Roach first introduced this Venn diagram in 1983. Captain Ashley J. Roach, *Rules of Engagement*, NAVAL WAR COLLEGE REV. 46, 48 (Jan./Feb. 1983).

1. Political Purposes

The days of total warfare in which belligerents engaged in the complete mobilization of fully available resources and population, with little or no differentiation between combatants and civilians, are seemingly a vestige of the past. There is no question that in the nearly seventy years since the Second World War, militaries have been employed with increasing frequency in operations short of armed conflict, and the conflicts that have occurred have been generally constrained in scope and objectives. Whether these instances involve humanitarian assistance, peacekeeping, peace enforcement, or actual armed conflict, modern military operations are marked by complex policy constraints and restraints[54] aimed at, inter alia, controlling the escalation of hostilities, influencing domestic and international public opinion, achieving strategic aims, and respecting the sovereignty and interests of coalition partners or neutral third parties. Rules of engagement serve as the operational means to "assure that national policy will be followed in wartime or in sudden emergencies which do not allow time for communications between [national political leadership] and [commanders in] the field."[55]

An example of a policy-based ROE would be a rule restricting or prohibiting U.S. forces from using riot control agents (RCA), given that the United States does not interpret international law as prohibiting use of RCAs in all circumstances;[56] another would be a rule prohibiting the introduction of ground troops into an area of armed conflict, as in the case of the U.S. intervention in Libya in March 2011.[57] A classic example of the strategic consequences of failing to adhere to what was at the time a policy-based ROE is the broadening of the Korean War in 1950. Escalation in the form of open Chinese intervention resulted from General Douglas McArthur's direct violation of his national command authority's orders (by authorizing U.S. forces to advance all the way to the Chinese border).[58]

2. Military Purposes

Consider again this chapter's opening example of General Lee's order prior to the Battle of Gettysburg to avoid becoming decisively engaged with Union forces until Lee's Army was concentrated. Lee's order bore no relation to governing legal principles or Confederate policy objectives or limitations; it was purely intended to guarantee operational mission success. Similarly, commanders today often limit or enable subordinate units' and individual soldiers' freedom of action

---

[54] A constraint and a restraint are requirements placed on a command by a higher command that either dictate or prohibit an action, respectively, thus restricting freedom of action. JP 1-02, *supra* note 14, at 61, 267.

[55] Roach, *supra* note 53, at 47.

[56] For a discussion of the U.S. position on the use of riot control agents and herbicides, see Operational Law Handbook, *supra* note 37, at 19. *See also* Martins, *supra* note 23, at 24 & fn. 70.

[57] *See infra* notes 156–258 and 184–289 and accompanying text.

[58] General McArthur's actions contributed to his ultimate relief of command. Michael D. Pearlman, Truman and MacArthur: Policy, Politics, and the Hunger for Honor and Renown 134–98 (2008).

through ROE. Commanders may withhold the authority to use particular weapons systems or tactics in order to conserve resources or avoid premature engagement with enemy forces. For example, during an armed conflict, a commander may limit forces operating in his rear security area to only self-defensive force, both to conserve combat resources as well as to reduce the likelihood of unwanted, though lawful, civilian casualties.[59]

3. Legal Purposes and the Relationship of ROE to the Law

In addition to the traditional nine principles of war, U.S. joint doctrine now recognizes three additional principles of operations, to include legitimacy and restraint. The purpose of the principle of legitimacy is to maintain legal and moral authority in the conduct of operations.[60] The purpose of restraint is to limit collateral damage and prevent the unnecessary use of force.[61] The adoption of these principles is a clear recognition of the decisive importance that legally and morally correct actions, both actual and perceived, can have on contemporary military operations. Rules of engagement have evolved into a primary command and control means for applying these principles of legitimacy and restraint; ROE operationalize such applicable legal principles during military operations.

Although ROE should typically avoid simply restating the law, they may serve to reinforce and operationalize certain legal obligations of particular relevance to the mission, such as a rule prohibiting attacks on protected places (hospitals, churches, shrines, schools, museums, etc.) except in self-defense or in cases where they lose their protection due to enemy misuse. More commonly, ROE will transmit permissions to use force otherwise authorized by law, such as an ROE declaring forces hostile in armed conflict,[62] or impose restrictions designed to better ensure compliance with the LOAC, such as a rule prohibiting the use of indirect fires in populated areas without the use of direct observation.[63] Rules of engagement "are a major tool for

---

[59] Because the premise of the example is a situation of armed conflict, the use of offensive targeting would not be unlawful, nor would civilian casualties so long as the attacking forces comply with the rule of proportionality and precautions in the attack. *See* Protocol Additional to the Geneva Conventions of 12 Aug. 1949, and Relating to the Protection of Victims of International Armed Conflicts (Protocol I), arts. 52.2, 57, June 8, 1977, 1125 U.N.T.S. 3, *available at* http://www.icrc.org/ihl.nsf/FULL/470?OpenDocument [hereinafter AP I]; Int'l and Operational Law Dep't, The Judge Advocate General's Legal Center and School, Law of War Deskbook 139–57 (2011); Geoffrey Corn, *Mixing Apples and Hand Grenades: The Logical Limit of Applying Human Rights Norms to Armed Conflict*, 1 J. Int'l Humanitarian Legal Studies 52, 74–76, 84–85 (2010).

[60] JP 3–0, *supra* note 5, at A-4.

[61] *Id.* at A-3.

[62] Once a force is declared hostile, the basis for using force against it or its individual members shifts from conduct to status. That is, units or members of the declared hostile force may be engaged regardless of whether they are committing hostile acts or demonstrating hostile intent. Operational Law Handbook, *supra* note 37, at 75.

[63] Indirect fire is "[f]ire delivered on a target that is not itself used as a point of aim for the weapons or the director." JP 1-02, *supra* note 14, at 169. Use of unobserved indirect fire in populated areas is not prohibited per se by the LOAC. *See* Prosecutor v. Gotovina, ICTY Case No. IT-06-90-A, Judgment in the Appeals Chamber at 8–34 (Nov. 16, 2012). An ROE requiring direct observation would improve accuracy in target identification, engagement, and collateral damage estimation, thereby diminishing the likelihood of LOAC violations or other undesired effects.

ensuring that a commander's actions stay within the bounds of national and international law."[64]

The sources of law relevant to ROE development are varied. International law, especially LOAC rules regulating the conduct of hostilities, will nearly always impact on military operations.[65] Critically, the *ad bellum* prong of the LOAC also cannot be ignored. Nor can International Human Rights Law (IHRL), which may apply to aspects of certain operations.[66] The domestic law of both the state conducting operations and of the state in whose territory the operations are being conducted may also impact ROE.[67]

Rules of engagement are *not*, however, themselves international law, and should not be conflated with legal obligations.[68] Rules of engagement and the LOAC, for example, are two distinct sources of operational regulation. Although ROE will often incorporate LOAC obligations and authorities, they are not synonymous. It is particularly important to note that although ROE are not coterminous with the LOAC, they must be completely consistent with this and any other applicable body of law. Rules of engagement often impose restrictions far narrower than those required by law, but can never relieve commanders of underlying legal obligations. Thus, although there are provisions of the LOAC that do not affect a mission's ROE, all ROE must comply with the LOAC.

This is illustrated by the Venn diagram in Figure 7.1 above, which reflects the common situation where the authority provided by the ROE is more restrictive than the applicable law. In order to provide greater protection against collateral injury to civilians, the ROE may require that the engagement of a clearly defined military objective in a populated area be authorized only when the target is under direct observation, or may withhold the authority to engage those targets to higher levels when the expected collateral damage exceeds preestablished values.[69] This

---

[64] Roach, *supra* note 53, at 49.

[65] As a matter of policy, U.S. armed forces "comply with the law of war during all armed conflicts, however such conflicts are characterized, and in all other military operations." U.S. DEP'T OF DEF., DIR. 2311.01E, DOD LAW OF WAR PROGRAM para. 4.1 (May 9, 2006) (certified current as of Feb. 22, 2011).

[66] *See, e.g.*, Corn, *supra* note 59; OPLAW HANDBOOK, *supra* note 37, at 44.

[67] *See* SAN REMO HANDBOOK, *supra* note 14, at 2.

[68] ROE may achieve the status of enforceable domestic law, usually in the form of a lawful military order, but this will depend on the law of each state. *See* SAN REMO HANDBOOK, *supra* note 14, at 1. For the United States, ROE are generally considered lawful military orders, the violation of which may form the basis of military criminal liability as a failure to obey or a dereliction. *See* Uniform Code of Military Justice, art. 92, 10 U.S.C. § 892(2012).

[69] For example, U.S. ROE issued during armed conflict will normally establish what is called the Noncombatant and Civilian Casualty Cutoff Value, or NCV. The NCV is defined as "the casualty threshold for any anticipated effects, which if exceeded, would require the combatant commander to forward a target to the [Secretary of Defense] or President for national-level review as a sensitive target unless delegated otherwise according to the established ROE." CHAIRMAN, JOINT CHIEFS OF STAFF INSTRUCTION 3160.01, NO-STRIKE AND THE COLLATERAL DAMAGE ESTIMATION METHODOLOGY, GL-7 (Feb. 13, 2009) (the cited version of this instruction was released to the American Civil Liberties Union pursuant to a Freedom of Information Act request, and is available at http://www.aclu.org/drone-foia-department-defense-documents) [hereinafter CJCSI 3160.01]. All

relationship with applicable law, which always sets the outermost limits on the legitimate uses of force, is fundamental to the proper formation and application of ROE.[70]

To illustrate this interaction between ROE and the LOAC, consider an ROE provision that allows a soldier to kill an enemy. Although this provision is completely appropriate, it does not give the soldier the authority to kill an enemy who is surrendering, because such conduct would violate the LOAC.[71] Similarly, if the ROE allow a pilot to destroy a bridge with a bomb, that does not relieve the pilot of the responsibility to do a proportionality analysis and be reasonably certain that any expected incidental civilian deaths or damage to civilian property would not be "excessive in relation to the concrete and direct military advantage"[72] to be gained by the destruction of the bridge. In this way, ROE ensures compliance with the laws of war by reinforcing the requirement to abide by the LOAC.

B. THE CONVERGENCE OF LAW, POLICY, AND MILITARY PURPOSES

Any one of the three pillars described above might form the basis for an ROE measure. An ROE withholding the authority to employ certain weapons systems, such as nuclear or chemical weapons, or to engage certain specified targets, may serve the sole purpose of avoiding conflict escalation—an established national policy imperative. More frequently, these imperatives converge, and ROE are drafted to capture and implement the confluence of these multiple purposes. The issue of direct participation in hostilities (DPH) is a good example of such confluence.

It is well established in customary and treaty law that, during an armed conflict, civilians may not be made the object of attack, "unless and for such time as he or she takes a direct part in hostilities."[73] At first blush, this rule may seem simple enough. Civilians who take up arms and commit hostile acts against a party to the conflict forfeit their protected status under the LOAC and "may be targeted in the same manner as the identified members of an opposing armed force."[74] However, the exact contours of the DPH exception, both as to the specific

---

targets, whether above or below the NCV established for the operation, are still subject to the rules of military objective, proportionality, and precautions in the attack. The NCV effects operational and policy imperatives for more centralized decision-making.

[70] *See* SROE/SRUF, *supra* note 16, at encl. A, para. 1d ("U.S. forces will comply with the Law of Armed Conflict during military operations involving armed conflict, no matter how the conflict is characterized under international law, and will comply with the principles and spirit of the Law of Armed Conflict during all other operations.").

[71] Susan L. Turley, *Keeping the Peace: Do the Laws of War Apply?*, 73 Tex. L. Rev. 139, (1994).

[72] AP I, *supra* note 59, art. 57.2b.

[73] *Id.* arts. 50, 51; Protocol Additional to the Geneva Conventions of 12 Aug. 1949, and Relating to the Protection of Victims of Non-international Armed Conflicts (Protocol II), art. 13, June 8, 1977, *available at* http://www.icrc.org/ihl.nsf/FULL/475?OpenDocument.

[74] Operational Law Handbook, *supra* note 37, at 30.

meaning of "direct participation" and the temporal parameters of the rule, have been and remain the subject of intense debate.[75]

States are required to train their armed forces on the LOAC;[76] such training would presumably include instruction on DPH. Hence informing soldiers in combat that they are authorized to engage civilians directly participating in hostilities consistent with the LOAC would not, on its face, be legally objectionable.[77] However, the lack of clarity and consensus on the exact meaning of DPH, coupled with the risks attendant to an overly robust application of the rule, especially in counterinsurgency and NIAC (non-international armed conflict) environments, militate against providing such broad authority, absent, at a minimum, some additional definitional precision. Definitional guidance or policy-based restrictions on the exercise of DPH targeting authority would be properly cast in ROE.

Another available policy option might be the promulgation of ROE limiting forces to engaging hostile civilians only in the exercise of immediate self-defense. Limiting tactical targeting in this way would serve the multiple purposes of safely confining the use of force within more generally accepted parameters of the DPH rule, of adhering to operational military objectives to minimize civilian engagements, and of positively shaping domestic and international public opinion while preserving national policy flexibility with respect to establishing *opino juris* on the provision's meaning.[78]

---

[75] The intensity of this debate is reflected in the strong opposition expressed to the International Committee for the Red Cross' 2009 *Interpretative Guidance on the Notion of Direct Participation in Hostilities under International Humanitarian Law*, to include many of the experts who participated in the six-year project to produce the guidance and the withdrawal of their names from the final product. *See, e.g.*, Nils Melzer, Int'l Comm. of the Red Cross, Interpretive Guidance on the Notion of Direct Participation in Hostilities under International Humanitarian Law 78 (2009), *available at* http://www.icrc.org/web/eng/siteengo.nsf/html/p0990; Michael N. Schmitt, *The Interpretive Guidance on the Notion of Direct Participation in Hostilities: A Critical Analysis*, 1 Harv. Nat'l Sec'y J. 5 (2010); W. Hays Parks, *Part IX of the ICRC "Direct Participation in Hostilities" Study: No Mandate, No Expertise, and Legally Incorrect*, 42 Int'l L. & Pol. 769, 778–80 (2010); Kenneth Watkin, *Opportunity Lost: Organized Armed Groups and the ICRC "Direct Participation in Hostilities" Interpretive Guidance*, 42 N.Y.U. J. Int'l L. & Pol. 641 (2010).

[76] Under the Geneva Conventions, states are explicitly required to "include the study [of the law of armed conflict] in their programmes of military . . . instruction, so that the principles thereof may become known to all their armed forces." Geneva Convention for the Amelioration of the Condition of the Wounded and Sick in Armed Forces in the Field art. 47, Aug. 12, 1949, 75 U.N.T.S. 31; Geneva Convention for the Amelioration of the Condition of Wounded, Sick, and Shipwrecked Members, art. 48, Aug. 12, 1949, 75 U.N.T.S. 85; Geneva Convention, Relative to the Treatment of Prisoners of War, art. 127, Aug. 12, 1949, 75 U.N.T.S. 135; Geneva Convention Relative to the Protection of Civilian Persons in Time of War, art. 144, Aug. 12, 1949, 75 U.N.T.S. 287. *See also* DoD Law of War Program, *supra* note 65, para. 5.7.2 (mandating the implementation of effective programs to prevent violations of the law of war, including law-of-war training and dissemination.).

[77] *See* San Remo Handbook, *supra* note 14, at 5, 38.

[78] Any such limitation would of course have to be weighed carefully against its potential to increase risk to forces and mission accomplishment.

IV. Operationalizing the Underlying Legal Paradigm

As noted, one of the primary purposes of any set of ROE is to ensure the use of force during military operations is grounded in and consistent with applicable law. This is especially true at the level of translating national policy objectives into strategic military direction and guidance. Strategic-level ROE set parameters within which the entire armed force will operate, whether in peacetime or in war; such overarching guidance will also limit the nesting ROE issued at each subordinate level of command, down to the tactical commander and the soldiers on the ground. Rules of engagement drafting, especially at the strategic level, therefore should start with an identification and understanding of the legal paradigm within which the anticipated operations will take place.[79]

Not all nations have the capacity or capability to unilaterally project military power beyond their borders. The U.S. military does. It is organized, trained, and equipped for sustained, large-scale combat operations anywhere in the world, and the capabilities it possesses to conduct these missions also enable a wide variety of other operations as well. Whether conducted unilaterally or multinationally, modern military operations "vary in scope, purpose, and conflict intensity across a range that extends from military engagement, security cooperation, and deterrence activities to crisis response and limited contingency operations and, if necessary, to major operations."[80] The nature of the strategic security environment may require American or other forces to engage in several types of joint or multinational operations simultaneously across the range of military operations—such as civil support, humanitarian assistance, peacekeeping or peace enforcement, counter-drug, and low-, mid-, and high-intensity armed conflict to name a few—across what is referred to as the "conflict continuum."[81] Understanding and identifying the unique legal framework within which each of these types of operations will be conducted at any point along the conflict continuum is vital to establishing strategically, operationally, and tactically sound use of force rules, or ROE.

Even the most benign employment of the military, such as in a humanitarian assistance mission, will always involve some degree of risk to the executing forces from hostile groups or individuals. There is simply no civilian analog to military forces conducting humanitarian assistance, disaster relief, or peacekeeping operations, which will have unique tasks, organization, weapons, and missions, plus will involve an open and recognizable national presence in a foreign territory.[82] Without legally sound and effective use-of-force guidance, at least two

---

[79] For example, the transition from conduct-based defensive use-of-force authorities to status-based offensive use-of-force authorities is permissible only within the context of armed conflict. *See* Corn, *supra* note 59 at 74–76.

[80] JP 3-0, *supra* note 5, at V-1.

[81] *Id.* at V-1, 3–5.

[82] *See* Lieutenant Colonel Mark S. Martins, *Deadly Force Is Authorized, But Also Trained*, ARMY LAW. 1 (Oct. 2001) (responding to W. Hays Parks, *Deadly Force Is Authorized*, U.S. NAVAL INST. PROC., Jan. 2001, at 32–37). *See also* UNPKO PRINCIPLES AND GUIDELINES, *supra* note 15, at 35.

dangers to even the most routine military missions will be risked. The first danger is that troops "will respond tentatively to an attack, thereby permitting harm to themselves, to fellow soldiers, or to some mission essential facility. The second, opposite, danger is that troops will strike out too aggressively, thereby harming innocents" and jeopardizing legitimacy and mission success.[83] Lessons from the complex operational environments of Iraq and Afghanistan, among others, have shown that these same risks are omnipresent even in the context of armed conflict, where forces may legally operate under the broadest use-of-force authorities.

How forces respond to anticipated and unanticipated threats, and how they employ force to achieve their assigned missions, is primarily a function of training and discipline.[84] But training can only be as effective as the standards on which it is based. Legally suspect standards will inexorably lead to legally suspect actions. This is true whether the ROE are intended to be standing orders or applicable only to a specific mission. For example, the transition from conduct-based use-of-force authorities to status-based offensive use-of-force authorities is permissible only within the context of armed conflict. Any set of ROE that provides standing authorities to make this transition, or authorizes offensive uses of force for specific missions, must account for this and other legal precepts. The U.S. SROE "provide implementation guidance on the application of force for [both] mission accomplishment and the exercise of self-defense" for this very reason.[85]

A. SELF-DEFENSE AND STANDING RULES OF ENGAGEMENT

Owing to its expeditionary nature and history and its significant ongoing presence around the globe, the United States has issued standing ROE guidance to all U.S. armed forces operating outside of the United States since 1986.[86] The actual standing rules of the SROE (as opposed to the mission-specific supplemental measures also contained in the instruction) focus primarily on providing implementation guidance on the exercise of self-defense.[87] In addition to the general, unclassified self-defense guidance in Enclosure A, the SROE provide standing guidance and authorities tailored to specific operational domains and missions, which are contained in seven appendices. These are: Maritime Operations, Air Operations, Land Operations, Space Operations, Information Operations, Noncombatant Evacuation Operations, and Counterdrug Support Operations Outside U.S. Territory. The starting point

---

[83] Martins, *supra* note 23, at 5.

[84] *See generally* Martins, *supra* note 82.

[85] SROE/SRUF, *supra* note 16, at A-1.

[86] *See supra* notes 27–29 and accompanying text. The current SROE "establish fundamental policies and procedures governing the actions to be taken by U.S. commanders and their forces during all military operations and contingencies and routine Military Department functions occurring outside U.S. territory (which includes the 50 states, the commonwealths of Puerto Rico and Northern Marianas, U.S. possessions, protectorates and territories) and outside U.S. territorial seas." SROE/SRUF, *supra* note 16, at 1.

[87] SROE/SRUF, *supra* note 16, at A-1.

for a review of these authorities is the "inherent right and obligation of unit commanders to exercise unit self-defense in response to a hostile act or demonstrated hostile intent."[88]

1. The Law of Individual Self-Defense and Defense of Others

The nucleus of most sets of ROE consists of the rules regulating the circumstances in which forces and individual soldiers can use force to defend themselves and others while conducting operations across the spectrum of peace and conflict. Peacetime ROE are premised on the right of self-defense and the attendant requirement that force may only be used to respond to or thwart an actual or imminent unlawful first use of force.[89] Mission accomplishment ROE build on this baseline of self-defense, tailoring the more robust use-of-force authorities that become available as operations move across the continuum from peace to war.[90]

The basic right of individuals, civilian or otherwise, to use deadly force to counter immediate threats of death or grievous bodily harm is an ancient and universal principal recognized in the domestic law of all nations.[91] Normally expressed in terms of an excuse or justification to a criminal charge of homicide, this right generally permits a nonaggressor to use proportionate force, up to and including deadly force, upon another if he reasonably believes that such force is necessary to protect himself or a third party from the imminent use of unlawful deadly force (which includes the threat of grievous bodily harm) by the other person.[92] It is this basic construction that forms the foundation for measuring the legality of state security forces' uses of deadly force within the general human rights framework and its prohibition against the arbitrary deprivation of life.[93]

2. The Right of National Self-Defense

Similarly, the right of nations to defend themselves against armed attacks is universally recognized and enshrined in the United Nations Charter.[94] A number of

---

[88] *Id.* at 3, A-2.

[89] Roach, *supra* note 53, at 49.

[90] For example, the status-based targeting authority applicable in armed conflict, or other unique use-of-force authorities applicable to specific mission sets such as counter-piracy operations. *See infra* Section III.B.

[91] *See* Schlomit Wallerstein, *Justifying the Right of Self-Defense: A Theory of Forced Consequences*, 91 Va. L. Rev. 999, 999 (2005) ("the right to self-defense is recognized in all jurisdictions"); Major John J. Merriam, *Natural Law and Self-Defense*, 206 Mil. L. Rev. 43, 46 (2010). As noted, the law of personal self-defense, although universal, is nearly exclusively a matter of domestic law. As an affirmative defense, however, it is included in the Rome Statute and has been recognized by the ad hoc war crimes tribunals. Rome Statute of the International Criminal Court, art. 31(c), July 1, 2002, 2187 U.N.T.S. 90.

[92] *See, e.g.*, Model Penal Code, secs. 3.05, 8.01, 8.02; Manual for Courts-Martial, United States, R.C.M. 916(e)(1)(2012).

[93] International Covenant on Civil and Political Rights, art. 2, Dec. 16, 1966, 999 U.N.T.S. 171.

[94] UN Charter, Art. 51.

> Nothing in the present Charter shall impair the inherent right of individual or collective self-defence if an armed attack occurs against a Member of the United Nations, until the Security Council has taken measures necessary to maintain international peace and

states understand this right to extend beyond actual attack to allow the legitimate exercise of self-defense in the face of an imminent armed attack.[95] Further still, the right of units and individual soldiers to exercise self-defense, either as a right derivative of Article 51 or based on the more general principles of law described above, is also broadly recognized.[96] Promulgation of self-defense ROE will vary according to the issuing authority's views of the source and substance of each of these types of self-defense.

3. Levels of Self-Defense

Rules of engagement generally distinguish between three levels, or types, of self-defense: national, unit, and individual. The International Institute of Humanitarian Law's *Rules of Engagement Handbook* describes each level as follows:

> *National Self-Defence.* As recognized in Article 51 of the United Nations Charter, refers to the right of a nation to defend itself against armed attack, and for most nations, the threat of imminent armed attack.
>
> *Unit Self-Defence.* Unit commanders have the right to defend their unit and other units from their nation in the face of attack or imminent attack. For some nations, the concept of *unit self-defence* is both a right and an obligation; whereas for some others the concept is only a right.
>
> *Individual Self-Defence.* This refers to the right of an individual to defend himself or herself (and in some cases other individuals) from an *attack* or imminent *attack*.[97]

The U.S. SROE similarly addresses all three levels of self-defense. *National Self-Defense* is defined as the "[d]efense of the United States, U.S. forces, and in certain circumstances, U.S. persons and their property, and/or U.S. commercial

---

> security. Measures taken by Members in the exercise of this right of self-defence shall be immediately reported to the Security Council and shall not in any way affect the authority and responsibility of the Security Council under the present Charter to take at any time such action as it deems necessary in order to maintain or restore international peace and security.

Id.

[95] Operational Law Handbook, *supra* note 37, at 6–7; Chatam House, International Law, *Principles of International Law on the Use of Force by States in Self-Defence*, at 7, n.12 (Oct. 2005); Yoram Dinstein, War Aggression and Self-Defence 187–92 (2005) (although Dinstein rejects the theory of anticipatory self-defense, his description of *interceptive self-defense* bears little difference in substance).

[96] San Remo Handbook, *supra* note 14, at 4; NATO ROE, *supra* note 39 at; SROE/SRUF, *supra* note 16, at A-2 (describing the right of self-defense as inherent); UN Model ROE, *supra* note 41, at Ann. ("[n]othing in these ROE negates a Commander's right and obligation to take all necessary and appropriate action for self-defence. All personnel may exercise the inherent right of self-defence."); CAA ROE Handbook, *supra* note 43, at 28–31 (stating "every [set of] ROE must have rules regarding legitimate self defense . . . ." and providing model rules for individual and unit self-defense.).

[97] San Remo Handbook, *supra* note 14, at 3.

assets from a hostile act or demonstration of hostile intent."[98] With respect to unit and individual self-defense, the SROE provide:

> Unit commanders always retain the inherent right and obligation to exercise unit self-defense in response to a hostile act or demonstrated hostile intent. Unless otherwise directed by a unit commander as detailed below, military members may exercise individual self-defense in response to a hostile act or demonstrated hostile intent. When individuals are assigned and acting as part of a unit, individual self-defense should be considered a subset of unit self-defense. As such, unit commanders may limit individual self-defense by members of their unit. Both unit and individual self-defense includes defense of other U.S. military forces in the vicinity.[99]

Some states' ROE do not include authorities or guidance with respect to national self-defense, preferring to retain the decision on whether national self-defense will be invoked to the highest levels of governmental authority. Others, such as the United States, owing to the significant presence of its military forces around the globe, opt for empowering commanders with some delegated authority to act in the immediate defense of the nation.[100] How any such delegations and authorities are scoped is of paramount importance to one of the central purposes of ROE—to act as a control mechanism for the transition from peace to war—and must be framed within the issuing state's domestic war powers legal framework.

But although the right of states to defend themselves against armed attacks is not disputed, the scope of this right has always been a source of significant disagreement. Not all states agree that the right of national self-defense encompasses the right of a state to use force to repel an attack before it actually occurs—so called "anticipatory self-defense."[101] Nor is there agreement over exactly what acts

---

[98] SROE/SRUF, *supra* note 16, at A-3.

[99] *Id.* at A-2. Previous versions of the SROE addressed each level of self-defense separately, similar to the San Remo Handbook. For example, the 2000 version provides:

> *National Self-Defense.* Defense of the United States, U.S. forces, and in certain circumstances, U.S. persons and their property, and/or U.S. commercial assets from a hostile act or demonstration of hostile intent.
>
> *Unit Self-Defense.* The act of defending a particular U.S. force element, including individual personnel thereof, and other U.S. forces in the vicinity, against a hostile act or demonstrated hostile intent.
>
> *Individual Self-Defense.* The inherent right to use all necessary means available and to take all appropriate actions to defend oneself and US forces in one's vicinity from a hostile act or demonstrated hostile intent is a unit of self-defense. Commanders have the obligation to ensure that individuals within their respective units understand and are trained on when and how to use force in self-defense.

ROE Handbook, *supra* note 47, at A-11.

[100] The actual authorizations and guidance to unit commanders is classified. *See* SROE/SRUF, *supra* note 16, at A-3.

[101] *See* Operational Law Handbook, *supra* note 37, at 6–7 (discussing the concept of anticipatory self-defense). *See also* Dinstein, *supra* note 95, at 182–87.

would constitute an armed attack or a use of force sufficient to trigger Article 51 rights, anticipatorily or otherwise.[102] Also, states differ on the source and scope of the different types of self-defense, and for some states, self-defense is not governed by ROE at all.[103] Whether the right—individual, unit, or national—is inherent, extends to the defense of property or to third parties, and whether it can be exercised anticipatorily and under what conditions are all matters of debate that should be accounted for in any set of self-defense ROE. Despite these important differences, most self-defense ROE do share some common elements.

4. Basic Principles of Self-Defense

The modern *jus ad bellum* is reflected in the United Nations Charter and essentially provides two bases for a state to lawfully resort to the use of force: pursuant to a Security Council authorization under Chapter VII of the Charter, or in the legitimate exercise of self-defense pursuant to Article 51. With respect to the latter, which traces its roots to the *Caroline* doctrine[104] and customary international law, three principles are generally accepted as governing national self-defense actions: necessity, proportionality, and timeliness.[105]

Necessity is a threshold criterion fundamental to the law of self-defense.[106] It exists when resort to force is the only means by which a state can end or avert an unlawful attack against it. As such, the principle imposes on states an absolute requirement to exhaust all available peaceful means of ending or preventing the attack; "there should be no practical non-military alternative to the proposed course of action that would be likely to be effective in averting the threat or bringing an end to an attack."[107] The SROE reinforces the requirement of necessity

---

[102] *See* Dinstein, *supra* note 95, at 193–96 (discussing, inter alia, *Case concerning Military and Paramilitary Activities in and against Nicaragua* 1986 I.C.J. 14 (June 27) and *Case concerning Oil Platforms*, 42 I.L.M. 1334 (2003)). The debate over what actions rise to the level of an armed attack has taken on renewed vigor of late in relation to cyber operations. *See, e.g.*, Tallinin Manual on International Law Applicable to Cyberwarfare 45–53 (Michael N. Schmitt et al. eds., 2013), *available at* https://www.ccdcoe.org/249.html [hereinafter Tallinin Manual]; Nils Melzer, Cyber Warfare and International Law 13–16 (2011), *available at* http://unidir.org/pdf/activites/pdf2-act649.pdf.

[103] San Remo Handbook, *supra* note 14, at 3.

[104] In 1837, British troops set fire to a steamer, the *Caroline*, on the U.S. side of the Niagra River, alleging self-defense in that the *Caroline* had been used to transport Canadian rebels across the border to attack British forces. U.S. Secretary of State Daniel Webster filed a strong objection to the British action and justification, stating "[i]t will be for . . . [Her Majesty's] Government to show a necessity of self-defence, instant, overwhelming, leaving no choice of means, and no moment of deliberation" and the action must not be "unreasonable or excessive, since the act, justified by the necessity of self-defense, must be limited by that necessity, and kept clearly within it." Chatam House, *supra* note 95, at 7, n.12. *See also* Martin A. Rogoff & Edward Collins Jr., *The* Caroline *Incident and the Development of International Law*, 16 Brook. J. Int'l L. 493 (1990).

[105] Dinstein, *supra* note 95, at 237–43; Operational Law Handbook, *supra* note 37, at 5.

[106] Chatam House, *supra* note 95, at 7.

[107] *Id. See also* Operational Law Handbook, *supra* note 37, at 4–5; Geoffrey S. Corn et al., The Law of Armed Conflict: An Operational Approach 19–22 (2012) [hereinafter The Law of Armed Conflict].

through the principle of de-escalation, which states that, time and circumstances permitting, a force threatening attack should be given a warning and given the opportunity to withdraw or cease threatening actions prior to the use of defensive counter-force.[108]

Proportionality bounds the level of force employed in self-defense, limiting it in scope, intensity, and duration to that which is reasonably necessary to counter an attack or imminent threat thereof. Stated differently, "the force used, taken as a whole, must not be excessive in relation to the need to avert or bring the attack to an end."[109] Although the force may not be excessive, it "should be sufficient to respond decisively" to the threat, and "may exceed the means and intensity" of the threat so long as the "nature, duration and scope of force used [do not] exceed what is required."[110]

Timeliness requires that the responsive use of force must happen within some reasonable proximity in time to the hostile act. Undue delay in response to an attack or threatened attack attenuates the immediacy and necessity to use force in self-defense.[111]

Most ROE today operationalize the principle of necessity through the concepts of hostile act and hostile intent, which are generally defined as an attack, or the threat of an imminent attack, respectively.[112] The linkage of these concepts to Article 51 is apparent. The U.S. SROE defines each more broadly:

> *Hostile Act.* An attack or other use of force against the United States, U.S. forces or other designated persons or property. It also includes force used directly to preclude or impede the mission and/or duties of U.S. forces, including the recovery of U.S. personnel or vital USG property.
>
> *Hostile Intent.* The threat of imminent use of force against the United States, U.S. forces or other designated persons or property. It also includes the threat of force to preclude or impede the mission and/or duties of U.S. forces, including the recovery of U.S. personnel or vital USG property.[113]

---

108 SROE/SRUF, *supra* note 16, at A-3.

109 Chatam House, *supra* note 95, at 10. The principle of proportionality in self-defense must be distinguished from the LOAC principle that bears the same name. SROE/SRUF, *supra* note 16, at A-3. The *in bello* rule of proportionality, reflected in article 57 of AP I, prohibits the attack of an otherwise legitimate military objective if the expected level of collateral damage "would be excessive in relation to the concrete and direct military advantage anticipated" from the attack. In contrast to self-defense proportionality, the *in bello* rule is designed to protect non-targetable third parties, not the object of the attack itself.

110 SROE/SRUF, *supra* note 16, at A-3.

111 Operational Law Handbook, *supra* note 37, at 5; The Law of Armed Conflict, *supra* note 107, at 20.

112 *See* SROE/SRUF, *supra* note 16, at A-3 (Necessity "[e]xists when a hostile act occurs or a when a force demonstrates hostile intent."); San Remo Handbook, *supra* note 14, at 3, 22; Operational Law Handbook, *supra* note 37, at 75. Some states and organizations decline to use these terms in favor of simply acknowledging the right of self-defense in response to an attack or imminent attack. *See, e.g.*, NATO ROE, *supra* note 39, paras. 7–9.

113 SROE/SRUF, *supra* note 16, at A-3.

Notable in these two definitions are the synonymous treatment of the terms "attack" and "use of force," the inclusion of the protection of property as within the scope of self-defense, and the authorization for U.S. forces to use force against those threatening or actually impeding or precluding mission accomplishment.

The authority to respond in self-defense in the face of demonstrated hostile intent reflects the concept of anticipatory self-defense, and like necessity and proportionality, traces its roots to the *Caroline* doctrine's requirement that a threatened attack must be "instant, overwhelming, leaving no choice of means, and no moment of deliberation."[114] The majority of states accept that they need not absorb a first strike before they can resort to the use of force in self-defense. Consensus is lacking, however, on the degree of immediacy that must be present before this self-help remedy is available in international law.

The U.S. position on this question is well documented and clearly expressed in operational terms in the SROE. Not only does the United States consider the right of national self-defense to include the right to act peremptorily in anticipation of an imminent attack, it considers the right to be triggered by actual or threatened "uses of force," evidencing a view of the synonymous meaning of "attack" and "use of force" in Articles 2(4) and 51 of the Charter.[115] These positions are captured in the definitions of "hostile act" and "hostile intent" described above, as well as in the guidance set out in the SROE on imminence. "The determination of whether the use of force against U.S. forces is imminent will be based on an assessment of all facts and circumstances known to U.S. forces at the time and may be made at any level. *Imminent does not necessarily mean immediate or instantaneous.*"[116]

Contrast this SROE guidance with NATO's, which defines "imminence" in terms of the *Caroline* doctrine as meaning "that the need to defend is manifest, instant, and overwhelming."[117] This divergence is reflective of competing views on the basic elements of the international law of self-defense.[118] These divergent views are further complicated by a lack of clarity as to the underlying source of legal authority to exercise self-defense below the national level.

---

[114] Chatam House, *supra* note 95, at 5 fn. 5, (quoting Exchange of letters between US Secretary of State Daniel Webster and Lord Ashburton, Foreign Secretary of Great Britain, relating to the case of the SS *Caroline*, 1837; 29 BFSP 1137–1138; 30 BFSP 195–196).

[115] *See, e.g.*, Remarks by Harold Hongju Koh, Legal Adviser, U.S. Department of State, International Law in Cyberspace, U.S. Cyber Command Inter-Agency Legal Conference (Sept. 18, 2012), *available at* http://opiniojuris.org/2012/09/19/harold-koh-on-international-law-in-cyberspace.

[116] SROE/SRUF, *supra* note 16, at A-3 (emphasis added).

[117] NATO ROE, *supra* note 39, para. 7.

[118] Prior versions of the SROE did not contain a definition of imminence. *See* ROE Handbook, *supra* note 47, at App. A. Its inclusion in 2005 likely reflects the Bush administration's expanded view of self-defense, first articulated in the 2002 National Security Strategy. *See* Operational Law Handbook, *supra* note 37, at 6–7. For a broader discussion of the implications of this expanded definition, see Colonel Gary P. Corn, *Should the Best Offense Ever Be a Good Defense*, Strategy Research Project (Carlisle Barracks, PA: U.S. Army War College, Apr. 15, 2014); Merriam, *supra* note 91.

As noted, not all states include national self-defense authorities in their ROE, and in the case of U.N. ROE for peacekeeping missions, national self-defense is inapplicable. But ROE nearly always address individual, if not unit self-defense. With the exception of providing the *Standing Rules for the Use of Force* (SRUF), discussed below, the SROE effectively apply a unitary standard across all levels of self-defense—a standard derived from the *jus ad bellum* principles discussed above. The content of the base guidance in the SROE is the same, with any possible modifications left to mission-specific ROE, which is usually promulgated at the operational level and below.[119] Subordinate commanders are permitted to restrict, but not broaden, Secretary of Defense-approved ROE, and any such restrictions must be consistent with unit commanders' "inherent right and obligation to exercise unit self-defense."[120] As regards individual self-defense, the SROE incorporated a change in 2005 clarifying that for individuals assigned and acting as part of a unit, their right of self-defense is a subset of unit self-defense, and the unit commander can therefore limit their right.[121]

The U.S. approach of applying a unitary standard across all levels of self-defense is a remnant of the maritime origins of the SROE, and reflects a view that individual and unit self-defense rights are derivative of the inherent right of national self-defense. This view is not, however, uniformly accepted. For some states, such as Great Britain, the right of individual soldiers to exercise self-defense stems from, and is coextensive with, their domestic penal law.[122] For some, self-defense must be exercised consistent with IHRL. A third view would seem to indicate the existence of an independent customary international law right of individual self-defense. In each of these cases, serious questions arise as to whether traditional ROE principles developed to implement *ad bellum* national self-defense precepts provide legally sound guidance for individual and unit self-defense.[123] Operational legal advisors must understand their respective states' legal and policy positions on these important questions when drafting, interpreting, and advising on self-defense ROE.

5. ROE versus RUF

Consider, for example, the relatively recent use-of-force dichotomy between ROE and Rules for The Use of Force (RUF) applicable to U.S. forces. The RUF, which provide theoretically distinct use of force rules primarily applicable to domestic military operations, were developed and incorporated into *CJCSI 3121.01B* in 2005. This change was the direct result of a tragic, deadly incident on the Texas side of the U.S.-Mexico border during a counterdrug operation in support of law

---

[119] *See* ROE Handbook, *supra* note 47, at Ann. B (providing multiple examples of mission-specific ROE annexes).

[120] SROE/SRUF, *supra* note 16, at 2.

[121] *Id.* at A-2. For those who view self-defense as an inherent, natural-law right, this change has proved controversial. *See* Corn, *supra* note 118, 14–17.

[122] R v Clegg [1995] 1 AC 482. *Cf.* Dinstein, *supra* note 95, at 220 ("It must be grasped that, from the standpoint of international law, all self-defence is national self-defence.")

[123] *See generally* Corn, *supra* note 118.

enforcement, and the realization that the ROE did not sufficiently reflect governing constitutional norms on the reasonable use of force.[124] The primary reason for this critical point was that, unlike U.S. military operations abroad, which are governed by international law, domestic operations are subject to domestic law, starting with, and principally, the Fourth Amendment to the Constitution.[125]

Basically, the SRUF apply when U.S. forces conduct civil support operations and routine Military Department functions within U.S. territory or territorial seas.[126] Under the SRUF, unit commanders and, unless otherwise restricted, individual service members, always retain the inherent right and obligation to exercise self-defense in response to a hostile act or demonstrated hostile intent, both of which are defined identically to the SROE.[127] Unlike the SROE, however, the SRUF refines the general hostile act/hostile intent construct to align its application with domestic constitutional law, starting with a description of the governing RUF principles:

> US federal law provides the legal basis for the use of force under the SRUF. US courts have long recognized the federal government's authority to use force,

---

[124] Center for Law and Military Operations (CLAMO), "ROE v. RUF," *Marine Corps Gazette* (Mar. 2006); Maj. Daniel J. Sennott, *Interpreting Recent Changes to the Standing Rules for the Use of Force*, Army Law. 52 (Nov. 2007). The precipitating event occurred on May 20, 1997, when four Marines conducting ground reconnaissance as part of a Department of Defense counterdrug support mission shot and killed Esequiel Hernandez, the eighteen-year-old goat herder and son of a local rancher, at a crossing of the Rio Grande River near Redford, Texas. A subsequent investigation determined, inter alia, that the Marines believed Hernandez fit the description of an armed scout for Mexican drug traffickers, that Hernandez fired his .22 caliber rifle in the direction of the Marines several times before they maneuvered on him and returned fire, and that the Marines had acted consistent with the mission ROE. *See* Major General John T. Coyne, United States Marine Corps, Investigation to Inquire Into the Circumstances Surrounding the Joint Task Force-6 (Jtf-6) Shooting Incident That Occurred on 20 May 1997 near the Border between the United States and Mexico, 07 APR 98, *available at* http://shapleigh.org/system/reporting_document/file/142/focus_documents142.pdf [hereinafter Coyne Report]. More important for the purposes of this discussion, however, the investigations also determined that the ROE for the mission "may [have been] legally correct for the purposes for which [they] were intended, but [they were] an inappropriate set of terms of reference for military support to domestic law enforcement operations . . . ." *Id.* para. 762 (*citing* Col. W.H. Parks report to Maj. Gen. J.T. Coyne; Subj.: "Request for Expert Opinion concerning Compliance with Rules of Engagement" (Nov. 15, 1997)).

[125] The U.S. Supreme Court has ruled that the Fourth Amendment to the U. S. Constitution prohibits the use of deadly force to effect an arrest or prevent the escape of a suspect unless the police officer reasonably believes that the suspect committed or attempted to commit crimes involving the infliction or threatened infliction of serious physical injury and a warning of the intent to use deadly physical force was given, whenever feasible. Tennessee v. Garner, 471 U.S. 1 (1985). The Court has said that the test of reasonableness under the Fourth Amendment is not capable of "precise definition" or "mechanical application." "[T]he reasonableness of a particular use of force must be viewed from the perspective of a reasonable officer at the scene, rather than with 20/20 vision of hindsight . . . ." Moreover, "allowance must be made for the fact that officers are often forced to make split-second judgments in circumstances that are tense, uncertain, and rapidly evolving about the amount of force that is necessary in a particular situation." The question is whether the officers' actions are "objectively reasonable" in light of the facts and circumstances confronting them." Graham v. Connor, 490 U.S. 396, 397 (1989).

[126] SROE/SRUF, *supra* note 16, at M-1.

[127] *Id.*

> including deadly force, in the performance of federal duties. The use of force by an Executive agency of the federal government is balanced against the civil rights of US citizens afforded by the Bill of Rights. The Constitutional standard is whether the use of force violates the Fourth Amendment's prohibition against unreasonable searches and seizures. In applying this standard, the primary focus is the reasonableness of a particular use of force, which is an objective measurement based on all the facts and circumstances known to the service member at the time of the use of force. The concept of reasonableness pervades the use of force rules under the SRUF, and should not be confused with the LOAC principles that form the legal basis of the SROE.[128]

The SRUF implements these principles in specific rules governing the use of both non-deadly and deadly force. Deadly force is allowed in defense of DoD personnel or third parties reasonably believed to be under imminent threat of death or seriously bodily harm. However, the force used must be the minimum necessary, and is only allowed as a matter of last resort.[129] Further, consistent with *Tennesse v. Garner*, the SRUF provide authority to use deadly force to prevent the escape of a fleeing prisoner, but only under very limited circumstances.[130] This pursuit authority is more limited than the general pursuit authority of the SROE, which allows U.S. forces to pursue and engage forces that have committed a hostile act or demonstrated hostile intent so long as those forces continue to commit or demonstrate hostility, and the pursuit is reasonably continuous and uninterrupted.[131]

Under the British view of individual self-defense, the SROE/SRUF use-of-force dichotomy would likely be unsustainable. Applying that view would require individual self-defense rules (and perhaps unit self-defense rules) distinct from those for national self-defense, reflecting the constitutional standards set forth in *Tennessee v. Garner*, *Graham v. Connor*, and their progeny. The point here is not to dissect, let alone resolve the debates over the contours of the international law of self-defense—a matter beyond the scope of this chapter. The issues are presented merely to highlight the need at the strategic level to ensure that whatever self-defense authorities are included in ROE, they are consonant with the issuing state's *opinio juris* (or the issuing organization's interpretation of law) and policy views on the issue of national, unit, and individual self-defense.

The operational impact of correctly identifying and conveying strategic guidance on self-defense authorities cannot be understated. For operations short of armed conflict, self-defense ROE will nearly always provide the outer limit of deadly force authority. For U.S. commanders, they not only have a right, but an

---

[128] *Id.* at M-2-3.

[129] *Id.* at M-5.

[130] *Id.* at M-6.

[131] *Id.* at A-6. Self-defense pursuit should be distinguished from the concept of "hot pursuit," which applies only in a maritime law enforcement context. *See* San Remo Handbook, *supra* note 14, at 4.

obligation to exercise unit self-defense at all times.[132] They, along with their staff planners and operators at all levels must have a thorough understanding of their standing self-defense and use-of-force authorities in order to properly train for and execute their missions.

B. BEYOND SELF-DEFENSE

Whatever uncertainties may exist regarding the finer points of self-defense, one aspect is beyond dispute—the authority to use force in self-defense is conduct-dependent. That is, the legal authority to use force in self-defense exists only when an individual soldier, unit commander, or national leader reasonably assesses that the conduct of the supposed-aggressor rises to a threshold level of threatened or actual unlawful force. This proposition, prevalent in peacetime, is stood on its head in the context of armed conflict. Once a nation transitions from peace to a state of armed conflict, its individual soldiers and commanders are legally sanctioned to use maximum deadly force against any member of the enemy belligerent force, not otherwise protected under the law, based solely on that individual's status.

There are a number of situations that military forces are likely to encounter during their myriad operations that will fall somewhere between this bright conduct-versus-status-based use- of-force paradigm.[133] For example, under certain circumstances, states may employ proportionate "countermeasures," short of uses of force as embodied in the UN Charter, against another state that is responsible for an internationally wrongful act, in order to induce that state to comply with its obligations under international law.[134] For another example, unique law enforcement authorities may permit limited uses of force beyond self-defense during law- enforcement-related military operations. By virtue of the nature and/or frequency with which these operations occur, they often lend themselves to the promulgation of additional standing guidance. Again, ROE developed for these unique missions must be grounded in and adhere to the specialized legal regimes governing them. Two examples illustrate this point: noncombatant evacuation and maritime operations.

---

[132] SROE/SRUF, *supra* note 16, at 2, A-2. The exact meaning of this obligation, and the potential consequence for failing to adequately meet it, are unclear. The inclusion of the commander's obligation in the SROE implies a military duty, the failure of which might form the basis of disciplinary action. *See* 10 U.S.C. § 892 (2010) (defining the punitive offense of dereliction of duty in the Uniform Code of Military Justice).

[133] San Remo Handbook, *supra* note 14, at 4.

[134] *See Case concerning Military and Paramilitary Activities in and against Nicaragua* 1986 I.C.J. 14 (June 27) and *Case concerning Oil Platforms*, 42 I.L.M. 1334 (2003) (Simma, J. dissenting); United Nations, International Law Commission, Responsibility of States for Internationally Wrongful Acts, Chpt. II (2001). *See also* Tallinin Manual, *supra* note 102, at 40–44 (discussing countermeasures in the context of cyber operations). Because of the unsettled nature of the law in this area, policy-based limitations on standing operational authorities would be particularly appropriate.

1. NEOS

On June 2, 1990, the United States deployed elements of the 22nd Marine Expeditionary Unit into Liberia to evacuate U.S. citizens and others caught in the crossfire of the Liberian Civil War and under direct threat of attack from rebel forces.[135] Nearly three thousand U.S. and non-U.S. citizens were evacuated.[136] Similarly, on July 19, 2006, the Government of Canada commenced the evacuation of approximately fourteen thousand of its citizens from Lebanon in the midst of an armed conflict between Israel and Hezbollah.[137] These are but two of many examples of what have come to be known doctrinally as noncombatant evacuation operations, or NEOs.[138]

The NEOs are generally conducted in support of the rescuing state's ministry or department responsible for foreign affairs, often arise with little or no notice, and "usually involve swift insertion of a force, temporary occupation of an objective, and a planned withdrawal upon completion of the mission."[139] The NEOs may be conducted with the consent of the state from which the evacuees will be taken, but frequently, conditions dictate that NEOs be conducted in non-permissive (where the host country will not permit evacuation) or uncertain environments.[140] Accordingly, the legal basis for each operation varies considerably.

The NEOs, certainly of the non-permissive and uncertain categories, raise significant legal questions because of their use-of-force implications. At a minimum, the evacuation force will likely have to physically enter the sovereign territory of the state from which the NEO will be conducted, and at most may need to use actual combat force to effect entry, protect itself and the evacuees, and otherwise accomplish its assigned mission.[141]

Absent host-nation consent, there is no international consensus on the legal basis to conduct a NEO. A number of states view NEOs as encapsulated within the "protection of nationals abroad" doctrine, a long-standing legal justification for military assistance to a state's own citizens outside of its borders.[142] Whether understood as a legitimate exercise of a state's right of self-defense or an action not rising to the level of an Article 2(4) use of force, there is general agreement that non-consensual NEOs should be limited in scope and duration, and available

---

[135] Michael R. Gordon, *U.S. Forces Evacuate 74 after Threats in Liberia*, N.Y. Times, Aug. 6, 1990, *available at* http://www.nytimes.com/1990/08/06/world/us-forces-evacuate-74-after-threats-in-liberia.html; Andrew W.R. Thomson, *Doctrine of the Protection of Nationals Abroad: Rise of the Non-combatant Evacuation Operation*, 11 Wash. U. Global Studies L. Rev. 627, 657 (2012).

[136] Another 2,444 people would be evacuated from Liberia six years later in Operation Assured Response. Joint Chiefs of Staff, Joint Pub. 3–68, Non-combatant Evacuation Operations, at III-8 (Dec. 23, 2010) [hereinafter JP 3–68].

[137] http://www.parl.gc.ca/Content/SEN/Committee/391/fore/rep/rep12may07-e.pdf.

[138] *See* Thomson, *supra* note 135, at 654–58; JP 3-68, *supra* note 136, at I-1.

[139] JP 3-68, *supra* note 136, at I-2.

[140] Operational Law Handbook, *supra* note 37, at 137.

[141] *See* JP 3-68, *supra* note 136, at I-3; Operational Law Handbook, *supra* note 37, at 151–52.

[142] Thomson, *supra* note 135, at 630–33; Dinstein, *supra* note 95, at 231–34.

to a state only under the following three conditions: (1) an imminent threat of injury to nationals abroad, (2) a failure or inability on the part of the territorial sovereign to protect them, and (3) measures of protection strictly confined to the object of protecting them against injury.[143] Thus, even under the majority view that NEOs are legally justified as matters of self-defense, the "principle of proportionality requires that any incursion of this nature be terminated as soon as possible, with a minimal encroachment on the sovereignty of the local State."[144]

The NEOs, and the ROE supporting them, must also account for issues such as the rescuing state's domestic legal and policy construct for NEOs;[145] the sovereignty and neutrality of states in the vicinity of the NEO operation; the status of evacuated personnel; the authority to search evacuees; and the amount of force that the executing units may employ in immediate self-defense, defense of the evacuees and possibly other third parties, and more broadly to accomplish the evacuation mission. Ideally, ROE addressing these issues should be promulgated for each specific NEO as part of the crisis action planning process. Due to the nature of NEOs, however, some level of standing guidance serves as an appropriate and useful operational tool for units called on to execute on little or no notice.

2. Maritime Operations

Naval forces operate in a unique geophysical and political domain, subject to shifting, evolving, and competing claims of sovereignty and jurisdiction over the world's oceans, other large bodies of water, and adjacent land masses. The traditional classification of the world's oceans into internal waters, territorial seas, and high seas has been challenged over the last century by the development of concepts such as exclusive economic zones, archipelagic waters, and aggressive assertions of state sovereignty. Disputes over conflicting territorial and sovereignty claims are frequently points of friction and potential hostilities among states.[146] Add to this confusing mix the proliferation in recent years of piracy, illicit trafficking of narcotics and weapons, terrorism, and other threats in the maritime domain, and it becomes clear that naval forces will likely face a variety of complex use-of-force scenarios on a routine basis.

Not surprisingly, the domestic and international laws governing naval operations are complex, and a subject well beyond the scope of this chapter.[147] Suffice

---

[143] Dinstein, *supra* note 95, at 231 (*citing* Sir Humphrey Waldock, *The Regulation of the Use of Force by Individual States in International Law*, 81 Receuil Des Cours 455, 467 (1952)); Thomson, *supra* note 135, at 628–29.

[144] Dinstein, note 95, at 232.

[145] For example, Executive Order 12656 assigns primary responsibility for the protection or evacuation of U.S. citizens and nationals abroad to the Department of State, with the Department of Defense acting in a supporting role. Exec. Order 12656, §§ 502(2), 1301(f), 53 Fed. Reg. 47491 (Nov. 18, 1988) (amended by Exec. Order No. 13,074, 63 Fed. Reg. 7277 (Feb. 12, 1998)).

[146] Peter Apps, *Geopolitics, Resources Put Maritime Disputes Back on Map*, Reuters, Oct. 1, 2012, http://www.reuters.com/article/2012/10/01/us-maritime-disputes-idUSBRE8900BG20121001.

[147] *See, e.g.*, Dep't of the Navy, Navy Warfare Publication 1-14M, The Commander's Handbook on the Law of Naval Operations (July 2007) [hereinafter NWP 1-14M].

it to say that both the international Law of the Sea and, in the case of the United States, domestic constitutional and statutory law, provide the legal basis in certain situations for naval forces to use varying degrees of force short of offensive, status-based targeting, but beyond pure self-defense rules.

For example, international law has long recognized a general duty of all nations to cooperate in the repression of piracy on the high seas.[148] This general duty is also reflected in the U.S. Constitution and statutes,[149]as well as in a number of Security Council resolutions.[150] Pursuant to this body of law, U.S. warships and aircraft "have an obligation to repress piracy on or over international waters against any vessel or aircraft, whether U.S. or foreign flagged," which may include, among other things, the seizure of pirate vessels.[151] Similarly, naval forces may be directed to conduct Maritime Interception Operations (MIO) in order to protect defined national security interests. These operations "may range from querying the master of the vessel to stopping, boarding, inspecting, searching, and potentially even seizing the cargo or the vessel," all of which involve varying degrees of force.[152] Also, U.S. naval forces routinely engage in Freedom of Navigation (FON) operations to assert and exercise navigation rights and freedoms under international law in regions with maritime sovereignty claims the U.S. considers unlawful. These operations involve naval units transiting disputed areas to avoid setting the precedent that the international community has accepted these unlawful claims, and obviously involve the risk of conflict and engagement. Promulgation of standing use-of-force guidance and authorities to address the unique and complex realm of routine maritime operations helps ensure they are conducted consistent with law and national policy objectives, and in a manner that does not place the executing units at undue risk.

Thus far, this chapter has focused on the legal issues and operational considerations that factor into the promulgation of strategic level standing ROE. Standing ROE establish a baseline against which, in the absence of specific orders or guidance, a state's armed forces can train and operate consistent with nationally established thresholds for initiating and/or continuing combat engagements or otherwise using force. But every military operation is unique, and a common practice is to issue ROE that build on this baseline and provide rules specifically tailored to the particular exigencies of the mission or operation to be executed.

---

148 This customary international law principle is codified in the 1958 Convention on the High Seas and the 1982 Law of the Sea Convention.

149 U.S. Const. art. I, § 8; 18 U.S.C. § 1651 *et seq.* (2010); *see* NWP 1-14M, *supra* note 147, at 3–5.

150 *See, e.g.*, S.C. Res. 2020, U.N. Doc. S/RES/2020 (2011) (piracy off the coast of Somalia); United Nations, Division of Oceans and Law of the Sea, United Nations Documents on Piracy, http://www.un.org/Depts/los/piracy/piracy_documents.htm.

151 SROE/SRUF, *supra* note 16, at A-4; NWP 1-14M, *supra* note 147, at 3–5.

152 NWP 1-14M, *supra* note 147, at 4–6.

C. MISSION ACCOMPLISHMENT ROE, ROE DEVELOPMENT, AND THE MILITARY PLANNING PROCESS

On March 19, 2011, a coalition led by the United States, France, and Great Britain[153] directly intervened in the Libyan civil war to stop the widespread and systematic attacks by regime forces against the civilian population.[154] This unprecedented action quickly transitioned from a U.S.-led coalition—Operation Odyssey Dawn—to a full-scale NATO-led operation—Operation Unified Protector—which included a No-Fly Zone, an arms embargo, and sustained air-to-ground combat engagements and a naval blockade to protect civilians and civilian population centers under attack or threat of attack.[155] Between March 31 and October 31, 2011, when Unified Protector officially ended, NATO flew over 26,500 sorties over Libya, including over 9,700 strike sorties, and destroyed over 5,900 military targets.[156] NATO did so without introducing ground combat forces into Libya, and under narrowly tailored ROE that effectively imposed a "zero expectation" of civilian casualties.[157]

The underlying legal basis for Operations Odyssey Dawn, and later Unified Protector, was clearly not self-defense: neither NATO, the broader coalition, nor any of the individual member states ever came under attack or threat of attack from Libya prior to March 19, 2011. Yet they initiated and engaged in sustained hostilities with the Gaddafi regime and its armed forces until rebel factions succeeded in deposing the regime in October 2011. None of the participants could have conducted these offensive combat operations under standing self-defense ROE or principles, such as the SROE. Mission-specific ROE tailored to the unique nature of the conflict were necessary.

Operation Unified Protector provides a unique and paradigmatic example of strategic, tailored ROE promulgated to promote operational adherence to policy objectives, military priorities, and the rule of law. Unlike Operation Enduring Freedom—the U.S. operation against Afghanistan and al Qaeda that began in 2001[158]—Odyssey Dawn and Unified Protector were legally grounded in, and bounded by, U.N. Security Council Resolution (UNSCR) 1973.[159] The limited scope of UNSCR 1973 had a marked impact on the planning and execution of

---

[153] The initial coalition consisted of Belgium, Canada, Denmark, France, Italy, Norway, Qatar, Spain, the United Kingdom, and the United States.

[154] *Libya: US, UK and France Attack Gaddafi Forces*, BBC News Africa, Mar. 20, 2011, http://www.bbc.co.uk/news/world-africa-12796972.

[155] NATO assumed lead responsibility for operations on March 31, 2011.

[156] NATO Fact Sheet, Operation Unified Protector Final Mission Stats (Nov. 2, 2011), http://www.nato.int/nato_static/assets/pdf/pdf_2011_11/20111108_111107-factsheet_up_factsfigures_en.pdf.

[157] Letter from Peter Olson, Legal Adviser to NATO, to the International Commission of Inquiry on Libya (Jan. 23, 2012) [hereinafter Olson Letter].

[158] *See* Sec. Council Res. 1368 (2001) (recognizing the United States' inherent right of self-defense under Article 51 against the perpetrators of the 9/11 attacks); Operational Law Handbook, *supra* note 37, at 4.

[159] Sec. Council Res. 1973, ¶¶ 4–16 (2011).

Libyan operations, which will be discussed after an outline of the basic facets of "mission accomplishment" ROE.

1. Mission Accomplishment ROE

No two military operations or missions are ever the same. The circumstances, objectives, bases, and conditions will always vary and evolve during the course of any given operation; so too must the ROE if they are to be operationally relevant and effective. "Developing and implementing ROE is a dynamic process that must be flexible enough to meet changes in the operational setting."[160]

As the name implies, and in contradistinction to standing ROE, mission accomplishment ROE are narrowly tailored rules issued for specific missions or operations. They generally take the form of a series of individual measures used to define the limits on or to grant authority for the use of force. In SROE parlance, these "supplemental measures" are intended to:

a) provide enough of the framework underlying the policy and military guidance to enable the commanders to appropriately address unforeseen situations when immediate decisions and reactions are required;
b) provide clear and tactically realistic military policy and guidance to commanders on the circumstances in which force can be used to accomplish the mission; and
c) enable subordinate commanders to request additional measures needed to carry out their mission.[161]

"The goal in formulating ROE is to ensure they allow maximum flexibility for mission accomplishment while providing clear, unambiguous guidance to the forces affected."[162]

A. PERMISSIVE VERSUS RESTRICTIVE ROE

Different than the approach taken by some countries or international organizations, the SROE are fundamentally permissive in nature. That is, when assigned a mission, commanders are authorized to use any lawful weapon or tactic available to accomplish that mission, unless specifically restricted by a supplemental measure issued by competent higher authority.[163] An important caveat to this general proposition is that certain weapons and tactics specifically require prior approval of the Secretary of Defense before subordinate commanders can employ them.[164] This distinction is reflected in the general organization of Enclosure I of the SROE. The first ninety-nine listed measures are those that specify actions

---

[160] SROE/SRUF, *supra* note 16, at I-1.

[161] *Id.* at I-1-2.

[162] *Id.* at I-1.

[163] *Id.*; Operational Law Handbook, *supra* note 37, at 76. It is important to note here that what weapons or tactics are lawfully available hinges directly on the underlying legal basis for the operation.

[164] SROE/SRUF, *supra* note 16, at I-1.

requiring Secretary of Defense approval. The remaining five hundred or so are measures that allow commanders at lower levels to place limits on the use of force during the conduct of certain actions.[165]

The permissive nature of the SROE is of particular operational significance when considered in connection with the central ROE concept of a declared hostile force (DHF). The SROE defines a DHF simply as "Any civilian, paramilitary or military force or terrorist(s) that has been declared hostile by appropriate U.S. authority."[166] The legal and operational implications of this ROE designation cannot be understated. Once a force is declared hostile, the basis for engaging that force or any member thereof shifts from conduct to status; that is, the authority of U.S. forces to employ deadly force are not limited to countering a hostile act or demonstration of hostile intent.[167] Subject to the LOAC rules of proportionality and precautions in the attack, any positively identified (PID)[168] member of the DHF may be made the object of lethal force, at any time, so long as he is not otherwise protected from attack.[169]

The policy and procedures regarding the authority to declare forces hostile under the SROE are understandably classified.[170] As the underlying legal basis for issuing this extraordinary ROE measure is the rule of military objective[171]—which is available only in the circumstance of armed conflict—this would seem to counsel against an overly broad or decentralized delegation. For U.S. forces being ordered into hostilities, the DHF ROE measure is the cornerstone on which all other combat ROE are built.[172] Although the declaration does not relieve soldiers of the burden of reasonably identifying members of the DHF or otherwise complying with the LOAC, it provides them with clear and unambiguous operational guidance, reducing to a minimum the risk of hesitancy in the application of combat power.

---

[165] *Id.* at 2. The authority to issue a limited number of these supplemental measures is retained to the combatant commanders. Commanders will often issue supplemental measures to authorize specific actions or uses of force in order to provide operational clarity to subordinates, such as authorizing the use of certain weapons systems *viz.* crew-served weapons.

[166] *Id.* at A-3. *See* San Remo Handbook, *supra* note 14, at 82 ("any civilian, paramilitary, or military force or terrorist organization that has been declared hostile by appropriate authority.").

[167] SROE/SRUF, *supra* note 16, at A-2; Operational Law Handbook, *supra* note 37, at 75.

[168] Positive identification, or PID, is not defined in the SROE. It is now nearly always included in mission-specific ROE as a required condition to attacking a target, and defined as a reasonable certainty that the proposed target is a legitimate target in accordance with the Law of War. *See* Operational Law Handbook at 102 (reprint of the MNC-I ROE Card in effect in Iraq in March 2007); CJCSI 3160.01, *supra* note 69, at A-6.

[169] Noncombatants and those who have surrendered or been placed hors de combat. Operational Law Handbook, *supra* note 37, at 75.

[170] SROE/SRUF, *supra* note 37, at A-2-3.

[171] *See* AP I, *supra* note 59, art. 52(2) (defining military objectives); Prosecutor v. Tadic, ICTY Case No. IT-94-1, Opinion and Judgment, para. 607 (May 7, 1997) (explaining that the rule of "military objective" applies to all armed conflicts as a matter of customary international law).

[172] See, for example, the unclassified tactical ROE card issued to individual soldiers prior to the invasion of Iraq in March 2003, reprinted in the *Operational Law Handbook*. Operational Law Handbook, *supra* note 37 at 101.

It is rare, however, that even combat ROE will be so open-ended as to simply declare relevant forces hostile and thereby allow commanders and their forces to use all lawful weapons and tactics to accomplish the mission. The ROE governing the initial invasion of Iraq in 2003 serve as an example. Among other restrictions, U.S. forces were directed not to target enemy infrastructure unless necessary in self-defense or if ordered to by their commander.[173] This restriction on combat use of force was not directly compelled by the LOAC, but instead served distinct military and policy purposes to limit the scope of the conflict and preserve the country's vital infrastructure for post-conflict stability.

Further, the lessons of recent conflicts demonstrate that probably the single most difficult challenge on the modern battlefield is compliance with the LOAC rule of distinction.[174] The asymmetric tactic of insurgents to deliberately blend with the civilian populace rather than distinguish themselves by uniforms or some other recognizable symbol strains nearly to the breaking point the operational utility and suitability of declaring forces hostile, at least with respect to tactical, hasty engagements. Additional ROE measures are nearly always necessary to attend to this and other policy, military, and legal requirements.

B. THE RELATIONSHIP BETWEEN MISSION ACCOMPLISHMENT ROE AND SELF-DEFENSE

The relationship between mission accomplishment and self-defense ROE—unfortunately not a model of clarity—can have significant operational impacts, especially in the context of combat operations. The prevailing interpretation of the SROE's statement that commanders always retain the inherent right and obligation to exercise unit self-defense is that political, military, or legal limitations effected through mission accomplishment ROE have "*no* impact on a commander's" inherent self-defense right and obligation.[175] This view is hard to reconcile with the view that unit self-defense is derivative of national self-defense, as a state is never *required* to, but *may* respond in self-defense under the right circumstances. Certainly commanders up the chain of command, and especially national command authorities, can withhold from subordinate commanders access or permissions to employ certain weapons systems or tactics that might otherwise be available to them. It would seem that the more accurate view is that the SROE establishes a presumption that mission accomplishment ROE should not restrict commanders' inherent right and obligation to exercise unit self-defense.

In the context of combat operations, the line between actions that constitute pure self-defense, such as a unit responding to a hostile band of civilians, and a unit performing the doctrinal military mission of conducting a hasty defense

---

173 *Id.*

174 AP I, *supra* note 59, art. 48 ("Parties to the conflict shall at all times distinguish between the civilian population and combatants and between civilian objects and military objectives and accordingly shall direct their operations only against military objectives.").

175 OPERATIONAL LAW HANDBOOK, *supra* note 37, at 75 (emphasis in original).

against a belligerent attack, is often blurred. Any use of combat power in the latter circumstance would constitute an "attack" as defined in the LOAC[176] and be subject to the normal LOAC targeting rules, and so to presumably targeting ROE, which could conceivably limit response options.[177] This tension has been highlighted in recent years in the frequent debates over the tactical directives issued in Afghanistan.[178]

In the final analysis, what is clear is that where mission accomplishment ROE are intended to impact or restrict the means available to commanders to exercise self-defense, they should be absolutely clear on that point. Otherwise, the general presumption in favor of self-defense should attach.

2. ROE Development and Mission Planning

The promulgation of mission-specific ROE is part of the normal military decision-making and planning process, and starts with the mission analysis.[179] For the United States, this process begins at the national strategic level with the military's receipt of the key policy direction and guidance from the President, and the related identification of the underlying legal basis for the assigned operation or mission. For both deliberate and crisis action planning (CAP),[180] this initial phase involves intense coordination among the National Security Staff, the Office of Secretary of Defense, the Joint Staff, and the relevant Combatant Commands. The President's direction and guidance is ultimately translated into the mission and intent transmitted to the Combatant Commands through the Chairman of the Joint Chiefs of Staff via a Secretary of Defense Execute Order (EXORD). It is generally in the EXORD that the Secretary will promulgate the mission specific ROE.

"Operations planning and ROE development are parallel and collaborative processes that require extensive integration."[181] This collaborative process

---

[176] AP I, *supra* note 59, art. 49(1) ("'Attacks' means acts of violence against the adversary, whether in offence or in defence.").

[177] *See* Major Eric C. Husby, *A Balancing Act: In Pursuit of Proportionality in Self-Defense for On-Scene Commanders*, ARMY LAW. 6–14 (May 2012).

[178] *E.g.*, Rajiv Chandrasekaran, *Petraeus Reviews Directive Meant to Limit Afghan Civilian Deaths*, WASH. POST, July 9, 2010, *available at* http://www.washingtonpost.com/wp-dyn/content/article/2010/07/08/AR2010070806219.html. For the most recent unclassified version of the Afghanistan tactical directives, see Memorandum from General John R. Allen, Commander, International Security and Assistance Force/United States Forces-Afghanistan, subject: COMISAF's Tactical Directive (Nov. 30, 2011), *available at* http://www.isaf.nato.int/images/docs/20111105%20nuc%20tactical%20directive%20revision%204%20(releaseable%20version)%20r.pdf.

[179] *See generally* CHAIRMAN OF THE JOINT CHIEFS OF STAFF PUBLICATION 5-0, JOINT OPERATION PLANNING (Aug. 11, 2011) [hereinafter JP 5-0]; ROE HANBOOK, *supra* note 47, ch. 1.

[180] "Deliberate planning" is defined as "The Adaptive Planning and Execution system process involving the development of joint operation plans for contingencies identified in joint strategic planning documents." JP 1-02, *supra* note 14, at 85. "Crisis action" planning is defined as The Adaptive Planning and Execution system process involving the time-sensitive development of joint operation plans and operation orders for the deployment, employment, and sustainment of assigned and allocated forces and resources in response to an imminent crisis." *Id.* at 74.

[181] SROE/SRUF, *supra* note 16, at J-1.

occurs both horizontally and vertically across and among the commands and staffs involved. That is, upon receipt of a warning order or initial planning direction, the supported Combatant Command will begin to analyze the mission and develop recommended supplemental ROE measures it assesses as needed to support the operation. These recommendations will in turn be integrated into the Joint Staff and OSD's planning and EXORD development and further refined before being presented to the Secretary of Defense for approval. Once an EXORD is published, this process is repeated down the chain of command, with each subordinate level of command factoring into its mission analysis, planning, and operations orders the ROE received from its higher headquarters.

As an operational function, ROE development is the responsibility of the operational planners on the commander's staff, normally the Director of Operations, or J-3.[182] Throughout this process military and civilian operational lawyers work closely with the J-3 to provide expertise on the legal principles applicable to the operation and to facilitate the drafting of clear, "plain language" ROE that support the mission, operational construct, and desired end state.[183] Further, the ROE process is not static. During the course of operations, commanders at any level can either issue additional ROE, or request modification or supplementation of the issued ROE.[184]

Consider again Operation Unified Protector. Responding to the "escalation of violence, and the heavy civilian casualties" being inflicted by Gaddafi regime forces in what were viewed as likely crimes against humanity, the Security Council determined that the situation constituted a threat to international peace and security, and enacted Resolution 1973 authorizing member states to, inter alia, impose a no-fly zone and an arms embargo, and "to take all necessary measures . . . to protect civilians and civilian populated areas under threat of attack in the Libyan Arab Jamahiriya, including Benghazi, while excluding a foreign occupation force of any form on any part of Libyan territory . . . ."[185]

On March 18, 2011, President Obama made a public statement with respect to the situation in Libya and UNSCR 1973 that provides valuable insight into the policy objectives of the United States and its coalition partners. In his remarks, the President made it clear that the goal of any U.S. military intervention would be to protect innocent civilians in Libya, that it would do so by providing unique capabilities to enable coalition operations, and importantly, that it would not deploy ground troops into Libya and would not use force to go beyond the

---

[182] *Id.* For deliberate planning, the Director for Strategic Plans and Policies, or J-5, will play a large role. *Id.*

[183] *Id.* at J-1 ("As an expert in the law of military operations and international law, the Staff Judge Advocate (SJA) plays a significant role, with the J-3 and J-5, in developing and integrating ROE into operational planning."). Often this legal support is provided through integrating military lawyers into the Joint Planning Group and/or an ROE Planning Cell. *See id.* at J-4; ROE HANDBOOK, *supra* note 47, at 1-31-32; *see generally* JP 5-0, *supra* note 179.

[184] OPERATIONAL LAW HANDBOOK, *supra* note 37, at 78.

[185] Sec. Council Res. 1973, ¶¶ 4-16 (2011).

well-defined goal of protecting Libyan civilians from attack.[186] NATO's policy position on Libya was in line with the U.S. objectives.[187]

From the perspective of developing ROE to support Libyan operations, these policy statements and the circumscribed use-of-force authorization contained in the operative paragraph of UNSCR 1973 are particularly significant. Despite the fact that the U.S. coalition and NATO clearly entered into armed conflict against the Libyan regime forces, declaring those forces hostile and engaging in pure status-based targeting would have been suspect from both a legal and policy perspective. And although the ROE for Libyan operations remain classified, it appears from NATO's response to the International Commission of Inquiry on Libya that they were properly scoped to reflect what was in essence a conduct-based use-of-force authority in UNSCR 1973.[188] The central policy objective of protecting Libyan civilians also militated heavily in favor of establishing a NCV[189] of zero, which is exactly what NATO apparently did.[190]

The specific ROE issued for Odyssey Dawn and later for Unified Protector were obviously more detailed than simply addressing the targeting status of Libyan regime forces. Based on the policy statements cited above, the inclusion of a restriction on introducing ground forces into Libya, as well as ROE addressing a host of other aspects of the operations such as the rules governing the conduct of the naval blockade and the no-fly zone, rules restricting the targeting of Libyan command and control infrastructure, and the conduct of information operations, among others, would seem appropriate. Across the board, whatever ROE were actually promulgated had to reflect the controlling legal and policy requirement to protect civilians and civilian-populated areas under threat of attack.

C. MULTINATIONAL ROE

No discussion of ROE would be complete without commenting on the particular challenges involved with managing ROE in a multinational setting. The U.S. default rule is that subject to Secretary of Defense authorization, U.S. forces assigned to the operational or tactical control of a multinational force will follow the ROE of the multinational force for mission accomplishment, but will retain the inherent right of self-defense as set forth in the SROE.[191] When operating under U.S. operational control in conjunction with a multinational force,

[186] President Barack Obama, Remarks by the President on the Situation in Libya, Mar. 18, 2011, *available at* http://www.whitehouse.gov/the-press-office/2011/03/18/remarks-president-situation-libya.

[187] *See* NATO, Remarks on Libya Following the Working Lunch of NATO Ministers of Foreign Affairs with Non-NATO Contributors to Operation Unified Protector, Apr. 14, 2011, *available at* http://www.nato.int/cps/en/natolive/official_texts_72544.htm; Olson Letter, *supra* note 157.

[188] *See* Olson Letter, *supra* note 157, at 2.

[189] *See supra* note 69.

[190] Olson Letter, *supra* note 157, at 2.

[191] SROE/SRUF, *supra* note 16, at A-1.

U.S. forces will follow U.S. ROE for both self-defense and mission accomplishment, but should make reasonable efforts to develop common ROE.[192]

In practice, multinational ROE are never as simple as the SROE rules would seem to imply. Each nation comes to coalition operations with different policy objectives, interpretations of governing law—starting with the underlying legal basis for the operation itself,[193] treaty obligations and operational capabilities. Synchronizing and deconflicting multiple sets of ROE or the different caveats that each state's forces take to a common set of ROE can present real operational difficulties.

Although much of the heavy lifting of ROE synchronization occurs at the operational and tactical level of command, strategic level planners and commanders can and should anticipate many of the challenges and issues normally present in coalition operations, and, to the maximum extent possible, draft ROE accordingly. For example, one consistently identified problem is the inability to share and coordinate ROE among coalition partners due to overly restrictive classification of each country's ROE.[194] Publication of unclassified ROE, to the extent possible, will alleviate this problem. Similarly, coordination, especially between the legal advisors to the different force-contributing states, can identify and perhaps avoid differences in terminology, meaning, and drafting styles that can also create obstacles to interoperability.[195]

It is not possible to anticipate every ROE issue that will arise in coalition operations, nor to completely solve all of those that are identified. But the synchronization challenges that the tactical and operational level commanders will inevitably be left to address can be substantially lessened through well-thought-out strategic level ROE.

VI. Conclusion

Today's military operations, especially combat operations, are immensely complex and fluid endeavors demanding precise regulation. Nowhere is that precision more important than in the application of combat power. Overly aggressive, or even worse, unlawful uses of force will quickly undermine the legitimacy of military operations and risk strategic failure. On the other hand, commanders and soldiers who are overly tentative and hesitant in the face of deadly threats can quickly lead to unnecessary casualties and mission failure. Use-of-force guidance

---

[192] *Id.*

[193] For example, a number of states contributing forces to NATO's International Security and Assistance Force (ISAF) in Afghanistan did not view the situation as one amounting to armed conflict, and therefore restricted their forces' authority to use force accordingly. *See* Center for Law and Military Operations, The Judge Advocate General's Legal Center & School, Forged in the Fire: Legal Lessons Learned during Military Operations 1994–2008, 343 (2008).

[194] *Id.* at 344.

[195] *Id.* at 345.

must be properly calibrated to the circumstances on the ground while consonant with law, policy, and military imperatives. Rules of engagement have evolved as the primary command and control tool to regulate the use of force during military operations and to ensure it is applied in support of national strategic aims and mission accomplishment.

Whether in the form of standing ROE issued to regulate operations during peacetime and to control the transition to combat, or ROE specifically tailored to particular operations, effective ROE at the tactical level start with sound ROE developed at the strategic level. As this chapter has illustrated, strategic-level ROE reflect the confluence of a number of independent but overlapping pillars, to include, perhaps most importantly, applicable law. As such, it is incumbent on military planners and commanders, guided by the sound analysis and advice of their operational legal advisors, to identify the law applicable to, and underlying, each and every military operation. It is through this understanding of the law that the operationalization of these principles can be promulgated into understandable, memorable, trainable, and relevant ROE.

8}

Tactical Implementation of Rules of Engagement in a Multinational Force Reality

Jody M. Prescott*

I. Introduction

The operationalization of law and policy in the form of restrictions and permissions as to the proper use of armed force has been known in Western culture since at least the time of the Roman Empire. Even gladiatorial engagement in Roman arenas was subject to a number of rules regarding the use of lethal force that were linked to imperial edicts, professional ethics, and the expectations of the masses to maintain an affordable program of entertainment and diversion.[1] Today, "rules of engagement" (ROE) is a generic term used to describe the latitude afforded different military decision-makers at the strategic, operational, and tactical levels as to the means and methods they might use to conduct their operations. From a strategic perspective as a civilian commander in chief, for example, Margaret Thatcher in the Falklands War understood ROE to be

> the means by which the politicians authorize the framework within which the military can be left to make the operational decisions. They have to satisfy the operational objectives for which a particular military operation is undertaken. They must also give the man on the spot reasonable freedom to react as is required and to make his decisions knowing that they will be supported by the politicians.[2]

---

* Jody M. Prescott, Senior Fellow, West Point Center for the Rule of Law; adjunct professor, Dep't of Political Science, University of Vermont. The opinions expressed by the author in this chapter are his alone, and do not represent the views of any government agency.

[1] *See generally* M.J. Carter, *Gladiatorial Combat: The Rules of Engagement*, 102 THE CLASSICAL J. 97 (Dec. 2006–Jan. 2007) (contrary to popular belief, combat to the death among gladiators was not common after the time of Augustus unless imperial permission was granted to make this a condition of the match, and the existence of professional norms among gladiators, the use of referees, and the high cost to the match-holders were a professional gladiator leased from a gladiator service provider to die, mitigated in favor of allowing beaten opponents to surrender).

[2] MARGARET THATCHER, THE DOWNING STREET YEARS: 1979–1990, 201 (1993).

Down at the tactical level, however, ROE may in fact be very directive and provide the individual combatant with little discretion regarding the use of force, such as Colonel William Prescott's perhaps apocryphal command of "Don't fire until you see the whites of their eyes!" to his militia troops on Breed's Hill in 1775.

As important as the operationalization of law, policy, and military objectives into ROE is, it often tends to obscure the complicated flip side of that process: the operationalization of the ROE themselves. This is particularly true in the context of multinational operations, the networked character of which presents complexities not ordinarily found in purely national operations, or at least not to the same degree. Judging by recent military operations in Iraq, Afghanistan, and Libya, multinational operations appear to be the model favored by developed nations to execute their military activities. Multinational operations provide important political, operational, and logistical advantages to the Troop Contributing Nations (TCNs) that participate,[3] and in the current era of austere resources, likely budgetary advantages as well. These benefits are not without cost, however, and ROE are an area in which the operational complexity of an operation might significantly increase because of its multinational character.

To properly understand the nature and scope of this complexity, it is not enough to look merely at what ROE have been agreed upon by the TCNs and published to their respective headquarters and units deployed in support of an operation. Particularly as today's wars appear to have become in the words of General Sir Rupert Smith, "wars amongst the people,"[4] the domestic and international agendas of the TCNs involved in the operation, as well as the political and operational realities of the nations within which these wars are fought, have significant impacts on the manner in which armed force is actually applied. To more fully explain the practical challenges of operationalizing ROE in multinational operations, this chapter will first briefly examine the dynamic relationship between ROE and understandings of the law of armed conflict (LOAC). Second, the doctrinal treatment of U.S. ROE and NATO ROE will be explored as an example of the significant differences that can exist between national and multinational use of armed force guidance, even when militaries are partnered in long-standing alliances. Third, certain practical issues with the training of commanders, staffs, and soldiers will be described, followed by a discussion of the impact of ROE upon command and control of multinational operations. Next, issues regarding the use of ROE in multinational operations will be discussed, and finally, the importance of analysis and modification of ROE, and the role played by investigations in the understanding and application of multinational force ROE will be highlighted.

---

[3] Joint Chiefs of Staff, Joint Publication 3-16, Multinational Operations ix–x (2013), *available at* www.fas.org/irp/doddir/dod/jp3-16.pdf (last visited June 30, 2014).

[4] Toni Pfanner, *Interview with General Sir Rupert Smith*, 88 Int'l Rev. Red Cross 719, 719–22 (2006).

II. The Relationship between ROE and Understandings of LOAC

At one level, the relationship between ROE and understandings of LOAC would not appear to be dynamic at all. LOAC is the law, and it must be followed upon pain of criminal prosecution for violating it as an individual combatant, or as a military or civilian commander.[5] LOAC, in the form of the Geneva Conventions of 1949,[6] the Additional Protocols of 1977,[7] and the customary international law that have developed from them and other treaties governing the use of armed force,[8] enjoy widespread, and in some cases, universal acceptance by the international community. ROE, although they may reflect individual nations' views on international law, domestic law, and policy, must nonetheless be consistent with LOAC. ROE would appear, therefore, to be in a dependent and subordinate relationship to LOAC at this level, not a dynamic one in which they influence understandings of LOAC. When it comes to the operationalization of ROE, however, a closer examination reveals that in practical terms the relationship is not so one-sided.

The dynamic nature of this relationship tends to be underappreciated by those without significant practical experience in actually training and then applying ROE. An example of this is perhaps the International Committee of the Red Cross' INTERPRETIVE GUIDANCE ON THE DIRECT PARTICIPATION IN HOSTILITIES.[9] The rule that otherwise-protected civilians do not lose their immunity from targeting by opposing military forces unless they are taking a direct part in hostilities[10] effects a fundamental LOAC principle, that of distinction between combatants and civilians.[11] As the recent conflicts in Afghanistan, Iraq, and Libya, have

---

[5] *See, e.g.*, Rome Statute of the International Criminal Court art. 8, July 1, 2002, 2187 U.N.T.S. 90 (military and civilian commanders may be tried for war crimes).

[6] Geneva Convention for the Amelioration of the Condition of the Wounded and Sick in Armed Forces in the Field, Aug. 12, 1949, 6 U.S.T. 3114, 75 U.N.T.S. 31; Geneva Convention for the Amelioration of the Condition of Wounded, Sick and Shipwrecked Members of Armed Forces at Sea, Aug. 12, 1949, 6 U.S.T. 3217, 75 U.N.T.S. 85; Geneva Convention Relative to the Treatment of Prisoners of War, Aug. 12, 1949, 6 U.S.T. 3316, 75 U.N.T.S.135; Geneva Convention Relative to the Protection of Civilian Persons in Time of War, Aug. 12, 1949, 6 U.S.T. 3516, 75 U.N.T.S. 287.

[7] Protocol Additional to the Geneva Conventions of Aug. 12, 1949, and Relating to the Protection of Victims of International Armed Conflicts, June 8, 1977, 1125 U.N.T.S. 3 [hereinafter *AP I*]; Protocol Additional to the Geneva Conventions of Aug. 12, 1949, and Relating to the Protection of Victims of Non-International Armed Conflict, June 8, 1977, 1125 U.N.T.S. 609.

[8] *See generally* JEAN-MARIE HENCKAERTS & LOUISE DOSWALD-BECK, CUSTOMARY INTERNATIONAL HUMANITARIAN LAW: RULES (2005).

[9] INTERNATIONAL COMMITTEE OF THE RED CROSS, INTERPRETIVE GUIDANCE ON THE NOTION OF DIRECT PARTICIPATION IN HOSTILITIES UNDER INTERNATIONAL HUMANITARIAN LAW 7 (Nils Melzer ed., 2009), *available at* http://www.icrc.org/ eng/assets /files/other/icrc-002-0990.pdf [hereinafter ICRC INTERPRETIVE GUIDANCE].

[10] "Civilians shall enjoy the protection afforded by this Section, unless and for such time as they take a direct part in hostilities." *AP I, supra* note 7, art. 50.3.

[11] The International Court of Justice has held that distinction is one of the "intransgressible principles of customary international law," and that it "must be observed by all States whether or not they have ratified the conventions that contain them." Legality of the Threat or Use of Nuclear Weapons, Advisory Opinion, 1996 I.C.J. 226, 257 (July 8, 1996).

shown, however, making this distinction in the course of a war amongst the people can be very difficult. The intent of the INTERPRETIVE GUIDANCE was to help refine the legal parameters and the application of the norm of direct participation in hostilities, so as to achieve the very laudable goal of greater protection of civilians in the course of armed conflict. There was apparently a great deal of consensus among the international group of experts who worked on the INTERPRETIVE GUIDANCE as to the basic parts of the concept. For example, it was apparently generally agreed that for engagement with armed force to be allowed under LOAC, a certain threshold of harm must be crossed because of the individual's actions; that the harm was directly caused by the individual; and that a nexus existed between the individual's actions and a conflict.[12]

However, because of the significant disagreement among the experts as to the application of the norm in actual operations, and concern that the interpretation favored by the ICRC and others was too restrictive, the subsequent publication of the INTERPRETIVE GUIDANCE was controversial. The scope of the controversy is well-detailed elsewhere,[13] and it is not necessary to examine it thoroughly for purposes of this chapter. From a practical perspective, the INTERPRETIVE GUIDANCE does not work well in wars amongst the people because it is in effect structured along the assumption that LOAC is the driver of targeting processes. In seeking to maximize the protection of civilians, it forgets that in balancing compliance with LOAC and achieving legitimate military objectives, military operations are intelligence-driven, that intelligence itself is often of markedly uneven granularity, and that military operators are accustomed to making lawful decisions in this context under the LOAC standard of reasonable certainty.[14] Military operators, mindful of their ROE and advised by legal experts, will often rely upon reasonable inferences based upon their experiences and available intelligence in making their targeting decisions. ROE are applied to targets as a result of the target validation process and during the actual engagement, however deliberate or expedited these events might be. Targets are not identified on the basis of their conformance with precise legal guidelines and perfect situational awareness and then recommended for engagement. In practice, this makes an enormous difference, and it means that the relationship between the ROE and the understandings of LOAC is actually much more dynamic than it might first appear.

As will be discussed in the following section on ROE and doctrine, the concept of "hostile intent" as the basis upon which to engage an apparent adversary

---

[12] ICRC INTERPRETIVE GUIDANCE, *supra* note 9, at 47, 52, 58.

[13] *See, e.g.*, Damien Van Der Toorn, *"Direct Participation in Hostilities": A Legal and Practical Road Test of the International Committee of the Red Cross's Guidance through Afghanistan*, 17 AUS. INT'L L. J. 7, 17–28 (2010) (thorough synopsis of criticisms of the Interpretive Guidance coupled with pragmatic suggestions for improving it).

[14] The INTERPRETIVE GUIDANCE recognizes that reasonable certainty under the prevailing circumstances is the standard that military operators will apply in targeting decisions, *supra* note 8, at 76, but it fails to realize the practical import of applying this standard in an intelligence-driven targeting process.

with armed force is central to an understanding of the practical application of ROE in the modern multinational force setting. In an operational theater such as Afghanistan, for example, where insurgents hide among the people, dressing like them and even carrying out the ordinary activities of everyday life, it can be very difficult to distinguish them from civilians, often until they actually begin shooting.[15] The insurgents are not wearing uniforms, carrying their weapons in the open, or even moving in recognizable military formations. To determine whether they are in fact enemy combatants in the context of their ROE, opposing soldiers must therefore rely upon less obvious indicators of the insurgents' warlike disposition.

The INTERPRETIVE GUIDANCE, however, assesses "hostile intent" as being too bound up with ROE to be useful in determining the legal contours of the norm of direct participation in hostilities. Viewing hostile intent as a technical ROE term, and ROE as national political and command guidance on the use of armed force that do "not necessarily reflect the precise content of" LOAC, the INTERPRETIVE GUIDANCE found it to be "unhelpful, confusing or even dangerous to refer to hostile intent for the purpose of defining direct participation in hostilities."[16] Although it is true that understandings of "hostile intent" may vary according to different national interpretations of ROE, the definition of hostile intent is completely relevant to a discussion of the definition of direct participation in hostilities, because in many ways it sets the lowest threshold for activity that can be seen as justifying a lethal response from an opposing armed force in armed conflict involving unfriendly actors who do not necessarily identify themselves as being members of an organized armed force. Given this operational reality, one of the most significant challenges militaries face is how to properly account for it in their use-of-force doctrines.

III. Doctrine

Doctrine is the basis for training and education in military organizations, and a tool to ensure both the uniformity of performance of military tasks and their efficacy in reliably achieving military objectives. In terms of doctrine, however, different military organizations define the term "ROE" quite differently. To highlight these differences and their significance to training and operations, this section will compare a national ROE doctrine, that of the United States, with a multinational doctrine, that of NATO, an organization of which the United States is an integral part.

[15] Gilles Dorronsoro, *The Afghanistan Problem*, L.A. TIMES, Oct. 20, 2009, *available at* http://articles. latimes.com/2009/oct/20/opinion/oe-dorronsoro20?pg=3.

[16] ICRC INTERPRETIVE GUIDANCE, *supra* note 9, at 59 n.151.

A. U.S. ROE DOCTRINE

The United States defines "ROE" quite simply as "directives issued by competent military authority that delineate the circumstances and limitations under which U.S. forces will initiate and/or continue combat engagement with other forces encountered."[17] It also recognizes a conceptual distinction between ROE, which deal with mission accomplishment, and measures geared towards self-defense.[18] In practice, however, as will be discussed *infra*, this distinction might not be so crisp. When U.S. forces are operating as part of a multinational force, the multinational force ROE will apply for mission accomplishment purposes if so authorized by the Secretary of Defense, but otherwise U.S. forces will operate under the U.S. SROE.[19] In terms of self-defense under the SROE, U.S. forces always "retain the inherent right and obligation to exercise unit self-defense in response to a hostile act or demonstrated hostile intent."[20]

The U.S. SROE define in some detail different categories of types of self-defense that would authorize U.S. forces to respond with up-to-lethal force, including inherent (unit and individual), national, and collective self-defense.[21] Interestingly, unlike many of its NATO allies, the legal basis for the use of inherent self-defense by U.S. forces is not specifically set out in domestic law. United Kingdom soldiers, for example, find that their authority to respond to a situation in self-defense is governed by British common and statutory law, which requires that the use of lethal force to prevent an act likely to endanger life must be reasonable, and a last resort.[22]

Some writers argue that the U.S. legal basis may be derived from notions of national self-defense as found in international law, but one writer cogently argues that it is instead an acknowledged right itself under customary international law and separate from the concept of national self-defense.[23] The practical significance of this is shown by the U.S. SROE allowing U.S. forces to respond with lethal force to acts they perceive to be hostile in fact or in intent. "Hostile acts" are defined broadly as "attack[s] or other use[s] of force against the [U.S.], U.S. Forces, or other designated persons or property."[24] The examples provided to illustrate the scope of acts considered hostile confirm this broad application, and

---

[17] Joint Chiefs of Staff, Joint Publication 1-02, Department of Defense Dictionary of Military and Associated Terms 317 (Jan. 31, 2011).

[18] Int'l & Operational Law Dep't, The Judge Advocate General's Legal Ctr. & Sch., U.S. Army, Operational Law Handbook 87 (2010) [hereinafter Operational Law Handbook].

[19] Joint Chiefs of Staff, Instr. 3121.01B, The Standing Rules of Engagement/Standing Rules for the Use of Force for U.S. Forces encl. A, A-1 (June 13, 2005) [hereinafter *U.S. SROE*].

[20] *Id.* at A-2. Collective self-defense includes protecting those who are not U.S. nationals. *Id.*

[21] *Id.*, Enclosure A, A-2 to A-3.

[22] *See* Peter Rowe, *The United Nations Rules of Engagement and the British Soldier in Bosnia*, 43 Int'l & Comp. L. Quart. 946, 948, 951 (1994) (discussing the relationship between mission rules of engagement and controlling British law).

[23] Charles P. Trumbull IV, *The Basis of Unit Self-Defense and Implications for the Use of Force*, 23 Duke J. Comp. & Int'l L. 121, 126–48 (2012).

[24] *U.S. SROE, supra* note 19, Enclosure A, A-3.

"include[s] force used directly to preclude or impede the mission and/or duties of U.S. personnel or vital [U.S. government] property." "Hostile intent" in the U.S. SROE is defined just as broadly, as "the threat of imminent use of force against the United States, U.S. forces or other designated persons or property. It includes the threat of force to preclude or impede the mission and/or duties of U.S. forces . . ."[25] and as will be discussed *infra*, both U.S. definitions are less restrictive than their NATO ROE counterparts.[26] This broader U.S. definition is also coupled with a more expansive definition of the term "imminent." For the United States.,

> The determination of whether the use of force against U.S. forces is imminent will be based on an assessment of all the facts and circumstances known to U.S. forces at the time and may be made at any level. Imminent does not mean immediate or instantaneous.[27]

When forces are "declared hostile," no specific demonstration of hostile intent or a hostile act is required prior to engaging them with armed force.[28]

B. NATO ROE

Deployed NATO forces operate under ROE approved by the North Atlantic Council (NAC).[29] These ROE are formulated in accordance with a NATO Military Committee document, MC 362/1, which provides both interpretive guidance and a menu of potential ROE from which the actual rules may be selected or modified.[30] NATO views ROE as "directives to military forces (including individuals) that define the circumstances, conditions, degree, and manner in which force, or actions which might be construed as provocative, may be applied."[31] As a fundamental distinction, then, one trained in the U.S. understanding of ROE would not necessarily understand that under NATO ROE matters that would not concern the use of armed force in a kinetic sense either in delivery or effect

---

[25] *Id.*, Enclosure A, ¶ f, A-3.

[26] *See* North Atlantic Treaty Organization, Military Committee, MC 362/1, NATO Rules of Engagement, ¶¶ 3–5, App.1, Annex 1 (June 30, 2003) [hereinafter *NATO ROE*].

[27] *U.S. SROE, supra* note 19, Enclosure A, A-3. One writer has recommended that the U.S. military should return to the use of "imminent" as understood in the 2000 version of the U.S. SROE, arguing that the current definition is not only different from the traditional understanding of "imminent" in the context of national self-defense, but also inconsistent with the understanding of imminent in the military criminal justice concept of self-defense, and likely to cause misunderstandings among local national civilians in a theater of operations as to how their otherwise innocent activities could be construed by U.S. personnel as manifestations of hostile intent or hostile acts. *See* Major John J. Merriam, *Natural Law and Self-Defense*, 206 MIL. L. REV. 43, 73–87 (2010).

[28] *U.S. SROE, supra* note 19, Enclosure A, Appendix A, ¶ 3.

[29] The NAC is NATO's executive body, and it "brings together representatives of all the Allies at the level of ambassadors, ministers or heads of State and government." NATO PUBLIC POLICY DIVISION, NATO HANDBOOK 15 (2006).

[30] *See* Colonel Osman Aytac, *Laws and Rules for Soldiers in Armed Conflicts, Crises and Counter-terrorism*, 47 LEGAL ASPECTS OF COMBATING TERRORISM 77, 85–88 (2008).

[31] *NATO ROE, supra* note 26, at 2.

could be restrained by particular ROE if deemed provocative. For example, as the author experienced during the course of a NATO headquarters exercise, the training audience's chief of information operations refused to respond to an exercise scenario that had prompted the commander to order the broadcast of certain messages to the population of a notional adversary because he deemed them as provocative, and such broadcasts had not been authorized in the ROE developed by the headquarters for the exercise.[32]

NATO ROE define self-defense as the "use of such necessary and proportional force, including deadly force, by NATO/NATO-led forces and personnel to defend themselves against attack or an imminent attack."[33] "Imminent" in this context means "that the need to defend is manifest, instant, and overwhelming."[34] NATO ROE recognize that the various NATO member nations will have different interpretations of the right to engage in self-defense,[35] and to cross-level these inconsistencies ROE are provided for mission accomplishment that include the authority to respond to manifestations of hostile intent and hostile acts.[36] For example, NATO Rule 421 provides that "[a]ttack against [designated] force(s) or [designated] target(s) demonstrating hostile intent (not constituting an imminent attack) against NATO/NATO-led forces is authorized."[37] The NATO ROE define "hostile intent" as having two elements: the "capability and preparedness of individuals, groups of personnel or units which pose a threat to inflict damage," and "evidence, including intelligence, which indicates an intention to attack or otherwise inflict damage."[38] In illustrating this definition, the NATO ROE look in part to objective, physical indicators of ill intent, such as "maneuvering into weapons launch positions," and non-tactical events such as the "increased movements of ammunition and the requisition of transport."[39] This definition also sets a threshold of harm to be used to help determine whether hostile intent is present, noting "[i] solated acts of harassment, without intelligence or other information indicating an intention to attack or otherwise inflict damage, will not normally be considered hostile intent."[40] In the NATO ROE, Rule 429, an "[a]ttack on [designated] force(s) in [designated] circumstances is authorised,"[41] which is similar to the U.S. SROE concept of "declared hostile" forces to a degree, but obviously more constrained.[42]

---

[32] In fact, information operations have a separate appendix in the NATO ROE. *Id., Information Operations (Info Ops)*, Appendix 2, Annex A, A-2-1 to A-2-2.

[33] *Id.* at ¶ 7.

[34] *Id.* at ¶ 7.c.

[35] *Id.* at 3–4.

[36] *Id.* at ¶ 2, App. 1, Annex A.

[37] *NATO ROE, supra* note 26, at A-19.

[38] *Id.* at ¶ 3, App. 1, Annex A.

[39] *Id.* at ¶ 4, App. 1, Annex A.

[40] *Id.*

[41] *Id.* at A-19.

[42] *Id.*

The different legal bases used by NATO nations in defining the scope of self-defense has the effect of lowering the threshold for U.S. forces to respond with up to lethal force in self-defense as compared to many of its NATO allies, and this could result in inconsistent applications of the use of armed force in operations. Suppose a U.S. unit on patrol in a NATO operation receives information acquired by an unmanned aerial vehicle (UAV) that two hillsides away, out of visual and small arms engagement range, a group of apparent insurgents appear to be gathering. The U.S. commander recognizes the potential danger posed to the U.S. unit, and believes that the apparent insurgents have demonstrated hostile intent. The U.S. commander informs his chain of command that he has a self-defense situation, and requests that air assets engage the apparent insurgents. Suppose further that the air asset assigned to support the U.S. unit belongs to a TCN that applies a restrictive concept of self-defense that would require actual or imminent attack as a trigger for engaging adversaries. Suppose also that this interpretation of self-defense informs the TCN's understanding of the NATO hostile intent and hostile act ROE under which it operates, and when the pilot makes her own assessment prior to engagement, she determines that attacking the gathering of apparent insurgents falls neither within the definition of self-defense that she must apply, nor the definitions of the applicable use of force ROE dealing with hostile intent or hostile act. Even if offensive attack were an option under the ROE consistent with NATO Rule 429, she cannot positively identify the gathering as "designated" insurgents under that rule. Accordingly, she does not believe that she has authority to engage, and does not attack.

The reverse situation is also possible. Assume, hypothetically, that the NATO TCN to which the pilot belonged is in command of a certain area of operations in the same country. Accordingly, this nation furnishes the headquarters commander, many of the troops, and important for purposes of this example, the legal advisor. United States' personnel are assigned to the headquarters staff, but the senior U.S. officer is not in command. Suppose the headquarters has been made aware that a local national civilian has been seen routinely observing the traffic in and out of the headquarters compound from a nearby hillside, and apparently talking on a cellular telephone as he watches. When the NATO TCN commander asks his legal advisor whether the observer could be properly engaged as a matter of self-defense or under the applicable NATO attack ROE, the legal advisor concludes the person cannot, and advises against attack. In the legal advisor's view, there is no indication of an imminent attack, nor is there the sort of demonstration of hostile intent or hostile act that would allow application of the NATO ROE on this basis. Finally, offensive attack under Rule 429 would not be allowed, because the observer cannot be identified as a designated insurgent. The senior U.S. officer, however, perceives hostile intent under the U.S. SROE, and concerned that there might be an attack on her U.S. headquarters element, requests an air strike. Aside from the obvious command and control issues were this to happen, from the TCN's perspective it would also potentially put the TCN commander in the awkward position of being responsible for a subordinate who had committed an act not allowed under TCN self-defense and NATO

ROE, which resulted in the death of an ostensible civilian. Both hypothetical scenarios illustrate the nature of the operational problems that could occur in a multinational setting in which different TCN forces not only use different rules of self-defense, but also find that the understandings of these rules color and inform the understandings of the mission-accomplishment ROE.

IV. Training

United States' doctrine recognizes the importance of regular ROE training for commanders and soldiers, and the complementary nature of such training with LOAC training.[43] United States' doctrine sets out a tiered approach, which begins with classroom instruction to familiarize the training audience with basic ROE concepts, using vignettes of ROE situations, followed by individual training, and then collective training that will take small units at the company level and below through situational training exercises (STXs) to test their application of ROE principles in the field.[44] For commanders and staff, U.S. doctrine recommends the additional steps of command post exercises and larger-scale field training exercises.[45]

Because LOAC training is often incorporated in ROE training, it is not surprising that soldiers sometimes conflate the two. For example, if soldiers are not training for a specific mission that has its own established ROE, they might train with generic ROE cards that in part reiterate essential LOAC concepts, but which then are perhaps viewed in the understanding of the individual soldier as ROE. Care must taken to carefully craft generic training ROE cards to help minimize this misunderstanding.[46] United States' doctrine also emphasizes the importance of integrating ROE training with other task training so that it will be more effective, such as inserting an ROE vignette into a patrolling STX,[47] and including legal advisors in the actual design of scenarios to ensure fidelity with the ROE training objective during the STX.[48] The use of role-players in STXs can be particularly useful in increasing the realism and dynamism of the STX play.[49]

---

[43] Ctr. for Law & Military Operations (CLAMO) & The Judge Advocate Gen.'s Sch., Rules of Engagement (ROE) Handbook for Judge Advocates 2–2 (2000) [hereinafter ROE Handbook].

[44] *Id.* at 2-2 to 2-3.

[45] ROE Handbook, *supra* note 43, at 2–2; Operational Law Handbook, *supra* note 18, at 93.

[46] *See, e.g.*, ROE Handbook, *supra* note 43, Appendix C, C-50 (generic forced entry ROE card that focuses on specific actions rather than LOAC principles).

[47] *Id.* at 2–3.

[48] *Id.* at 2–8.

[49] *Id.* at 2–9; Operational Law Handbook, *supra* note 18, 92. The proper training of role players so that they remain within their assigned roles as they interact with the soldiers can itself present many challenges, and requires careful planning, and, interestingly, training on the ROE for the event. Lieutenant Colonel Jody M. Prescott & Captain Jerry Dunlap, *Law of War and Rules of Engagement Training for the Objective Force: A Proposed Methodology for Training Role-Players*, Army Lawyer 43, 45–47 (Sept. 2000).

To help bridge the gap between U.S. national training and multinational operations, one U.S. writer has recognized the need for U.S. pre-deployment training for multinational missions to account for the different doctrinal definitions that might be used by multinational partners, and to "develop SOPs that are easy to understand and address multinational procedures" and that are sufficiently "flexible to account for changes to multinational assets and their national caveats."[50] This understanding of multinational terminology and procedures can then be incorporated into scenario-driven exercises for both staff and soldiers.[51]

In multinational military organizations such as NATO, LOAC training is foremost a national responsibility. Organizations such as NATO cannot be party to the different international treaties and agreements that make up such a significant part of LOAC,[52] and there is some question whether such an organization that is not a nation-state could be legally bound by customary LOAC.[53] This is perhaps even more the case when an established organization such as NATO forms the core of a temporary headquarters, such as ISAF, which includes many non-NATO partners. Importantly, however, all the NATO nations have ratified the 1949 Geneva Conventions, and all but two have ratified Additional Protocols I and II,[54] and they are of course all bound by customary LOAC. Further, many TCNs choose to implement LOAC in part or in whole in military operations as a matter of policy, regardless of whether the operation occurs within the context of an international armed conflict.[55]

Because LOAC training is a national obligation, each nation implements its own training strategy to meet national requirements.[56] Therefore, even TCN forces that habitually train and operate together might have received their national LOAC and ROE training in different ways, and might therefore have different perspectives on the implementation of LOAC and ROE in the field.[57] To help ensure that NATO commanders receive forces trained to the most common standard possible, NATO has issued STANDARDIZATION AGREEMENT (STANAG) 2449, TRAINING IN THE LAW OF ARMED CONFLICT. STANAG 2449 recognizes as a matter of NATO policy that its forces will follow the spirit and principles of LOAC even in operations not considered part of armed conflicts.[58] It also outlines broad training principles, such as the need for regular LOAC training, and training before deployments and during operations, and the need to incorporate LOAC into training exercises.[59] The STANAG sets out training objectives

---

[50] Maj. Winston S. Williams, Jr., *Multinational Rules of Engagement: Caveats and Friction*, ARMY LAWYER, 24, 27 (Jan. 2013).

[51] *Id.*

[52] Jody M. Prescott, *Training in the Law of Armed Conflict—A NATO Perspective*, 7 J. MIL. ETHICS 66 (2008).

[53] *Id.* at 67.

[54] *Id.*

[55] *Id.* at 68.

[56] *See id.* at 68–69.

[57] *Id.* at 67.

[58] Prescott, *supra* note 52, at 69.

[59] *Id.* at 68.

designed to ensure consistent LOAC application in actual operations, recommends the incorporation of conflict situations in exercises, and requires commanders and staffs to consider LOAC factors in the planning and execution of operations.[60] The STANAG further provides outlines for the different content of LOAC training that should be given to different personnel depending upon their ranks and levels of responsibility, and specifically identifies certain topics that are pertinent to multinational force operations, such as working with ROE.[61] The most recent NATO publication on LOAC training, however, is likely of only modest usefulness from a training perspective, because it merely reiterates the body of LOAC in a series of unhelpful slides without prioritizing the information or meaningfully addressing LOAC's important functional linkages to ROE.[62]

Most NATO ROE training is conducted during regular static headquarters exercises facilitated by the Joint Warfare Centre (JWC) in Norway,[63] or in mission rehearsal exercises for deploying headquarters units facilitated by the JWC or the Joint Force Training Centre (JFTC) in Poland.[64] These training events routinely use military and civilian subject matter experts to give specialized briefings to the training audiences and to serve as role players.[65] When possible, staff officers are brought back from deployed locations to enhance the currency and realism of the training, and training officers from the JWC and the JFTC often visit a theater of operations to acquire the most current operational information and SOPs for incorporation into scenarios during scenario development and vetting.[66]

Additional training if the ROE change while deployed presents many challenges to both TCN units and headquarters, such as security, logistics, and simply being able to find a time when units and personnel are not engaged, so that they can receive the training.[67] The training becomes potentially more complex when a multinational force headquarters clarifies a subtle point in ROE that is not immediately obvious to soldiers,[68] or issues tactical guidance, for example, that

---

[60] *Id.* at 69.

[61] *Id.* at 71.

[62] NATO Standardization Agency, NATO Standard, ATrainP-2, Training in the Law of Armed Conflict (ed. A, ver. 1, Mar. 2013).

[63] *Exercises and Training, ISAF*, JWC webpage, http://www.jwc.nato.int/isaf (last visited July 23, 2015).

[64] *See generally Conceptual Approach to Mission Specific Training*, 3 Training through Transformation (Mar. 2013), http://www.jftc.nato.int/JFTC%20Magazine3/index.html (the magazine of the Joint Force Training Centre).

[65] Carol Saynisch, A *Real Cast of Characters: How Deployed Grey Cell Role Players Create "Teachable Moments,"* 17 The Three Swords 47–50 (May 10, 2010), http://www.jwc.nato.int/images/stories/threeswords/THREE_SWORDS_17.pdf.

[66] Lieutenant Colonel Bob Taylor, *Training for Operations: ISAF Mission Rehearsal Training*, 14 The Three Swords 17, 18–20 (Nov. 3, 2008), http://www.jwc.nato.int/images/stories/threeswords/THREE_SWORDS_14.pdf.

[67] *See* Maj. R. Aubrey Davis III, *From the Courtroom to the CAOC: Operational Litigation and NATO in Libya*, 39 The Reporter 41, 42–43 (2012), for a description of the challenges faced in orienting attack squadron personnel to the new NATO ROE when the United States-led Operation Odyssey Dawn transitioned to the NATO-led Operation Unified Protector for Libya.

[68] ROE Handbook, *supra* note 43, at 2–11.

addresses related use of force concepts that impact ROE and self-defense considerations rather than LOAC itself (as that is a national responsibility).[69] Multinational headquarters' guidance must not be contrary to its different forces' understanding of how their respective nations want them to implement their ROE, and therefore may be purposefully vague in certain areas. For the forces of most TCNs, use-of-force guidance is likely trained in an integrated fashion with LOAC and military tasks prior to deployment; in-theater training on changes of ROE directed by a multinational force headquarters will not likely have the same degree of integration.

The regular static NATO headquarters exercises and the operation-oriented mission rehearsal exercises are invaluable in moving a multinational headquarters staff toward a common shared understanding of ROE, as well as the meaning and use of the SOPs that implement them. This shared understanding makes the operation of the deployed headquarters more efficient upon arrival in theater. Perhaps as important in this age of instant media coverage and the review of operations by international and nongovernmental organizations (NGOs), a common shared understanding of how different national perspectives of LOAC and ROE are reconciled and accommodated in the multinational operation leads to clarity in discussing and explaining operations to the public.

V. Command and Control

Unity of command is understood by all militaries as an essential element of successful operations. Within a multinational military organization, however, understandings of ROE both at the general level and as to specific rules themselves, and the SOPs intended to implement them, might cause a degree of functional disunity. Further, the legal status of the multinational force in the receiving state, and the presence of other international forces can also add wrinkles of complexity to the understanding of the ROE. The situation in Afghanistan, for example, was complicated in certain ways from an ROE perspective because there were two concurrent multinational operations, each with different ROE and different missions, but often involving the same core NATO TCNs. The initial U.S. invasion itself continued as a multinational counterterrorism mission, and was regulated for many years by an exchange of letters between the United States and Afghanistan.[70] The International Security Assistance Force (ISAF), on the other hand, had a security assistance mission in furtherance of annually

[69] *See, e.g.*, Headquarters, Int'l Sec. Assistance Force, Tactical Dir. (July 6, 2009) (unclassified version), *available at* http://www.nato.int/isaf/docu/official_texts/Tactical_Directive_090706.pdf (last visited June 4, 2015).

[70] Embassy of the United States of America, Diplomatic Note No. 202, entered into force May 28, 2003, 2002 U.S.T. LEXIS 100.

approved U.N. Security Council resolutions,[71] and had a status-of-forces agreement in place reflecting the more limited scope of that mission.[72]

The impact of such legal limitations is perhaps best shown by the request of an NGO for ISAF support in northern Afghanistan. As a result of the successful U.S. campaign in Afghanistan against the Taliban and al Qaeda in late 2001 and early 2002, certain Afghan allies of the United States captured large numbers of Taliban prisoners. One of these commanders, General Abdul Rashid Dostum, was alleged to have allowed Taliban prisoners to be packed into trucks; denied food, water, and medical care; and then shot.[73] The bodies were then said to have been buried in mass graves in Northern Afghanistan.[74] An NGO, Physicians for Human Rights, requested ISAF assistance in investigating and providing security for these mass graves,[75] but ISAF found the request to be outside the scope of its mission and a matter for the Afghan government to investigate if it wished. ISAF could assist the Afghan government in investigative efforts, but could not undertake independent action. President Obama directed that allegations that U.S. government officials had obstructed an investigation into these potential war crimes be enquired into.[76]

Within NATO, understandings of mission limitations and the use of force mean that it is not necessarily a given that all commands issued by a superior commander from one TCN will be followed by a subordinate commander from another TCN, even if the order does not violate LOAC or the specific ROE. In the 1999 Kosovo campaign, for example, British General Sir Michael Jackson rejected an order from the NATO force commander to use his forces to seize the Pristina airfield because he thought it would lead to a senseless escalation of hostilities with Russian forces.[77] This could be described as being in keeping

---

[71] S.C. Res. 1386, U.N. Doc. S/RES/1386 (Dec. 20, 2001), http://daccess-dds-ny.un.org/doc/UNDOC/GEN/N01/708/55/pdf/N0170855.pdf, was the first authorization of ISAF. Under Chapter VII, ISAF was authorized to take all necessary measures to assist "in the maintenance of security in Kabul and its surrounding areas." *Id.* Although the geographical scope of ISAF was later expanded to cover all of Afghanistan by S.C. Res. 1510, U.N. Doc. S/RES/1510 (Oct. 13, 2003), http://www.nato.int/ISAF/topics/mandate/UNSCR/resolution_1510.pdf, the substance of its mission was not changed.

[72] Military Technical Agreement between the International Security Assistance Force (ISAF) and the Interim Administration of Afghanistan (Interim Administration), Jan. 4, 2002, *available at* http://www.operations.mod.uk/fingal/isafmta.pdf.

[73] James Risen, *U.S. Inaction Seen after Taliban P.O.W.'s Died*, N.Y. Times, July 10, 2009, *available at* http://www.nytimes.com/2009/07/11/world/asia/11afghan.html.

[74] *Id.*

[75] *Forensic Investigations, Chronology of PHR Activities and Investigations concerning the Mass Graves at Dasht-e-Laile near Sherbergan, Afghanistan*, Physicians for Human Rights website, http://physiciansforhumanrights.org/library/chronology-of-phr-actions-and.html, last visited Feb. 5, 2010 [hereinafter *PHR*].

[76] *Obama Orders Review of Alleged Slayings of Taliban in Bush Era*, CNN, July 13, 2009, *available at* http://edition.cnn.com/2009/POLITICS/07/12/obama.afghan.killings.

[77] *Confrontation over Pristina Airport*, BBC News, Mar. 9, 2000, *available at* http://news.bbc.co.uk/2/hi/671495.stm. In contrast, the refusal of German General Ramms in 2008 to order ISAF to attack narcotics traffickers despite the NATO force commander's guidance to do so is perhaps better described as the rejection of a perceived illegal order. Matthias Gebauer & Susanne Kölbl, *Order*

with the NATO ROE concern regarding actions deemed to be provocative, and is referred to colloquially as "showing the national red card." It could happen at any level within a multinational force.[78] For NATO-backed operations, non-NATO TCNs ordinarily sign a participation agreement with NATO setting out the conditions under which their forces will participate in the multinational force operation.[79] It is understood, however, that even when a TCN's military forces, NATO or non-NATO, transfer under operational control of the multinational force commander, the TCN will still retain the final say as to how its forces will be employed. Often, such conditions will be set out in advance. Although the actual ROE for the mission will be established by the NAC in accordance with MC 362/1 prior to deployment, many nations will issue so-called declared caveats to these rules, which reflect specific national understandings as to implementation of the rules, consistent with national domestic and international legal obligations and political considerations.[80] Caveats are also used to limit the operational uses that may be made of a TCN's forces, and these limitations may reflect either actual training or equipment capability issues, or political decisions limiting risk to units.[81] Although even declared caveats will come with unpublished national guidance that might further restrict the use of force, what are perhaps even more problematic for the multinational force commander are the so-called "undeclared caveats," which are national restrictions on the use of force that have not been published at all. This particularly complicates responses to emergent situations, as well as planning for deliberate operations.[82]

In addition to common ROE, command and control over multinational forces will also be affected through the use of multinational force headquarters SOPs that are related to ROE.[83] Although SOPs are intended to make operations more efficient, there are often problems in terms of their actual implementation. First, within a multinational force there may be one designated language to ensure consistent communications. Not all members of the multinational force

---

to Kill Angers German Politicians, Der Spiegel, Jan. 29, 2009, *available at* http://www.spiegel.de/international/world/0,1518,604430,00.html.

[78] In the CAOC responsible for conducting the NATO air operations in Libya, for example, "there were a large number of senior national representatives that served as their nations' 'red-card holders' . . . along with their national Legal Advisors." Davis, *supra* note 67, at 42.

[79] Security in Afghanistan: The International Security Assistance Force (ISAF), Peace Operations Backgrounder, The Henry L. Stimson Center, June 2002, at 2, *available at* http://www.stimson.org/images/uploads/research-pdfs/ISAFbackgrounder.pdf (last visited June 4, 2015).

[80] Vincent Morelli & Paul Belkin, Cong. Research Serv., RL 33627, NATO in Afghanistan: A Test of the Transatlantic Alliance 10 (Dec. 3, 2009); *Germany's Non-combat Caveats to Be Reviewed by NATO*, Deutsche Welle, Nov. 28, 2006, *available at* https://www.fas.org/sgp/crs/row/RL33627.pdf.

[81] Morelli & Belkin, *supra* note 80.

[82] Frank Cook, NATO Parliamentary Assembly Committee Report, NATO Operations: Current Priorities and Lessons Learned (2008).

[83] *See, e.g.*, Colonel Jody M. Prescott, *Fall 2008—ISAF LEGAD and Targeting Conference*, 17 NATO Legal Gazette 7, 8 (Nov. 10, 2008), http://www.ismllw.org/NATO%20LEGAL%20GAZETTE/Legal%20GazetteIssueNo%2017.pdf [hereinafter "*LEGAD Conference*"].

headquarters staff, to say nothing of the subordinate TCN units in the field, may actually be as fluent in the common language as desired. This can lead to difficulties in determining precisely what the SOP means regarding the use of force, even in something as seemingly routine as checkpoint procedures. Further, it is not uncommon for a multinational force headquarters to rely upon a specific functional TCN headquarters unit to provide high value resources such as reconnaissance UAVs and strike aircraft. For example, a CAOC primarily staffed by U.S. personnel, but also including allied staff, located in the Middle East provides these services to ISAF.[84] Despite the fact that the personnel at both the CAOC and the supported ISAF headquarters share a common mother tongue and are in large part from the same TCNs, because the functional headquarters is a TCN element using TCN SOPs and the supported headquarters element uses multinational force SOPs, hypothetically there could be subtle, but significant, differences between them. Their respective SOPs for striking a target might use the same words and similar concepts and processes, but have different definitions and structures.

For example, in modern air operations, the LOAC principle of proportionality is usually addressed through collateral damage estimates (CDEs) performed by a targeting cell, and are typically conducted according to SOPs based on doctrine.[85] Different levels of weapons release authority might be assigned on the basis of the extent of expected collateral damage resulting from the CDE. Multinational force CDEs might result from a hybridization of different doctrines from various nations, accreted through numerous rotations of personnel during the deployment. Although not listed in the ROE approved for the multinational mission by the controlling civilian authority, such as NATO's NAC, weapons release authority levels would be in essence ROE themselves, embedded in an SOP that few officers in the multinational headquarters would ever likely become aware of.

Further, it is quite possible that TCN forces could find themselves working with receiving state forces in combined operations, such as ISAF with the Afghan National Army in Afghanistan. Depending upon the situation, unless the forces have had the opportunity to train with each other at the soldier level, and plan the operation together at the commander and staff level, the lines of command and control could become blurred. This could become complicated by different understandings of ROE. In addressing this possibility, the Commander of International Security Assistance Force Joint Command has noted, "The Afghan forces in the field are full partners. Each commander has a red card, and he can stop the operation if needed," "[b]ut when we work together, we find that we agree on 90% of things . . ."[86] To further this cooperation, "Afghan officers are in

---

[84] Thom Shanker, *Civilian Risks Curbing Strikes in Afghan War*, N.Y. Times, July 23, 2008, *available at* http://www.nytimes.com/2008/07/23/world/asia/23military.html.

[85] Davis, *supra* note 67, at 46.

[86] ISAF: NATO Forces in Afghanistan: General Wants Troops Ready for "Complex Human Terrain" in Afghanistan, Dec. 14, 2009, http://www.facebook.com/note.php?note_id=203462739839 (last visited Feb. 4, 2010).

the ISAF operations center, and ISAF liaisons are in Afghan operations centers. NATO trainers work with Afghan forces to train them, and once the Afghan forces are in the field, NATO forces partner with them."[87] This degree of cooperation and coordination would undoubtedly work to avoid issues resulting from different understandings of ROE and SOPs, but only a mission as long-lasting as ISAF's is likely to provide the opportunity to identify enough receiving state officers sufficiently qualified to serve effectively in such liaison roles.

VI. Operations

Earlier sections of this chapter addressed certain examples of ROE implementation issues in multinational operations, such as the difficulty of distinguishing insurgents from the civilian population, the potential impacts of different national understandings of self-defense and the concepts of hostile intent and hostile act, and the use of the national red card. This section will examine operational issues in the context of civilian casualties.

The majority of civilian casualties resulting from ISAF air strikes were caused not by deliberate attacks, but when available air assets were immediately tasked with providing air support to ISAF and associated Afghan forces in self-defense, or Troops in Contact (TIC) situations.[88] Beginning with General David D. McKiernan's first "tactical directive" issued in 2008[89] shortly after the conclusion of the investigation into the civilian casualties caused by air strikes near Azizabad, Afghanistan,[90] successive ISAF commanders have worked hard to find ways to minimize civilian casualties and damage to civilian property while engaging insurgent forces in Afghanistan.[91] Statistics regarding civilian casualties in Afghanistan suggest that these directives had a positive impact in reducing civilian deaths and injuries, although the tempo of combat had increased significantly over the time during which they had been in effect.[92] Although

---

[87] *Id.*

[88] Human Rights Watch, "*Troops in Contact*"—*Airstrikes and Civilian Deaths in Afghanistan* 29–33 (Sept. 8, 2008) [hereinafter *TIC*].

[89] Headquarters, Int'l Sec. Assistance Force, Tactical Dir. (Dec. 30, 2008), *available at* www.nato.int/isaf/docu/official_texts/Tactical_Directive_090114.pdf.

[90] *See, e.g.*, Brigadier Gen. Michael Callan, Executive Summary of AR 15–6 Investigation into the New Information Relative to Civilian Casualties from Engagement by US and Afghan Forces on Aug. 21–22, 2008 in Azizabad, Shindand District, Herat Province, Afghanistan, U.S. Central Command (2008) (United States concludes 33 civilians killed in airstrike, other sources claim 90) (copy on file with author).

[91] ISAF Headquarters Press Release, General Petraeus Issues Updated Tactical Directive: Emphasizes "Disciplined Use of Force," Aug. 4, 2010, http://smallwarsjournal.com/documents/isafnewsrelease2.pdf; ISAF HQ Memorandum, Subject: Tactical Directive, July. 6, 2009, www.nato.int/isaf/docu/official_texts/Tactical_Directive_090706.pdf; ISAF HQ Memorandum, Subject: Tactical Directive, Dec. 30, 2008, at www.nato.int/isaf/docu/official_texts/Tactical_Directive_090114.pdf.

[92] Jason Motlagh, *Petraeus Toughens Afghan Rules of Engagement*, Time, Aug. 6, 2010, *available at* www.time.com/time/printout/0,8816,2008863,00.html.

successive ISAF commanders gradually adjusted the tactical directives, they were criticized as being costly in terms of second-guessing use-of-force decisions made by junior officers, who ostensibly attempted to comply with the guidance and then felt penalized for their misapplication.[93]

General McKiernan was also deeply concerned about the high numbers of civilian casualties resulting from ISAF soldiers responding in self-defense to perceived attacks at vehicle checkpoints, and directed his staff to develop a new vehicle checkpoint SOP applicable to all ISAF forces.[94] Importantly for purposes of operationalizing ROE, the new SOP relied upon the use of a standard checkpoint setup and equipment pack, including signs, safety cones, and speed bumps to slow Afghan vehicles transiting the checkpoints.[95] The new checkpoint SOP afforded ISAF soldiers more time to go through escalation of force measures to assess whether motorists were actually intending to attack them. In essence, the vehicle checkpoint SOP then became part of the ISAF ROE. One writer argued that with military functions that are not strictly military in nature but also have a significant law and order component, such as vehicle checkpoints, ensuring compliance with the procedures to be followed by motorists might actually require that the applicable ROE be published to motorists so that "they are less likely to be killed or injured by taking actions which soldiers may mistakenly perceive as posing a combat risk."[96] Although the ISAF Combined Joint Psychological Operations Task Force (CJPOTF) did in fact create newsprint, radio, and television commercials explaining to Afghan civilians what they could expect at vehicle checkpoints,[97] reducing civilian casualties from incidents at checkpoints still proved challenging.[98] Further, new equipment, even if commercially available, costs money, as does the fielding of it, important points to consider in the process of operationalizing ROE changes.

The vehicle checkpoint example also demonstrates how feedback loops can exist between the application of force under ROE on the basis of the perception of direct participation in hostilities in one setting and another seemingly unrelated functional area, such as detention. For example, during the time the United States was in control of the Parwan Detention Facility outside Bagram

---

[93] *See, e.g.*, Andrew Tilghman, *Shifting Guidelines Prompt Calls for ROE Reform*, Army Times, Apr. 23, 2012, http://www.armytimes.com/article/20120423/NEWS/204230316/Shifting-guidelines-prompt-calls-ROE-reform (U.S. Marine Corps company commander relieved of command following disputed compliance with Tactical Directive in ordering continued small arms engagement).

[94] *See LEGAD Conference*, *supra* note 83, at 7–8.

[95] John Stevens, A *Vignette: Coalition Casualties, Vehicle Control Points/Cordons & CIVCAS*, 1 COIN Common Sense 6 (Feb. 2010), *available at* http://www.isaf.nato.int/COIN-publication/feb10.pdf.

[96] Peter Rowe, *The Rules of Engagement in Occupied Territory: Should They Be Published?*, 8 Melbourne J. Int'l L. 327, 332 (2007).

[97] Between 2008 and 2009, the ISAF Chief Legal Advisor participated in reviews of CJPOTF products prior to distribution to the Afghan public (author's notes).

[98] Richard A. Oppel Jr, *Tighter Rules Fail to Stem Deaths of Innocent Afghans at Checkpoints*, N.Y. Times, Mar. 26, 2010, *available at* www.nytimes.com/2010/03/27/world/asia/27afghan.html.

Air Field, Afghanistan, many of the detainees had reported that they became involved in the insurgency because someone they knew had been shot, presumably by Afghan National Army or ISAF soldiers. The U.S. Army recognized that the unacceptably high rate of Afghan deaths resulting from checkpoint incidents in which ISAF soldiers had opened fire because they believed they were being attacked, but in fact were not, contributed to this impetus to join the insurgency, that is, decide to take a direct part in hostilities.[99]

Even in a theater of operations in which the need to respond to self-defense situations is obviated because there are no NATO troops on the ground, the NATO air operations in Libya showed how challenging it can be to execute a multinational military operation with strict ROE that call for no civilian casualties as collateral damage.[100] First, otherwise valid military targets that are contributing to the attacks on the civilian population cannot be prosecuted.[101] Second, even with sophisticated targeting technology and methods, targeteers cannot know for an absolute certainty that there are not protected civilians present,[102] an unfortunate lesson long since learned in Afghanistan.[103] Third, military organizations and soldiers quickly learn to adapt to new patterns in the use of force against them. Libyan forces loyal to Colonel Qaddafi discontinued using obvious military equipment and formations and donned civilian clothing instead to make it harder for NATO aircraft to target them.[104] Further, in some cases Libyan rebels had taken over captured government equipment,[105] and this may have in part been responsible for NATO airstrikes that actually engaged rebel forces by mistake, ironically killing a number of people they were seeking to protect under the restrictive ROE.[106]

Another potential ROE problem that could occur is when authorization to engage on the basis of hostile intent or a hostile act, which is conduct-based,

---

[99] *Id.*

[100] Human Rights Watch, Unacknowledged Deaths—Civilian Casualties in NATO's Air Campaign in Libya, Letter to Phillipe Kirsch from NATO legal advisor Peter Olson, Jan. 23, 2012, Annex II (2012), *available at* http://www.hrw.org/sites/default/files/reports/libya0512webwcover.pdf.

[101] *Canadian Pilots Abort Bombing over Risk to Civilians*, CTV NEWS, May 19, 2011, www.ctv.ca/CTVNews//20110322/canadian-cf-18s-operation-odyssey-dawn-libya-110322.

[102] Lin Noueihed, *Gaddafi's Son Buried as NATO Air-Strike Support Continues*, THE SCOTSMAN, May 2, 2011, *available at* http://news.scotsman.com/libya/Gaddafi39s-son-buried-as-Nato.6761458.jp.

[103] David S. Cloud, *Predator Drones: High-Tech Tools and Human Errors*, STARS AND STRIPES, April 11, 2011, *available at* www.stripes.com/news/predator-drones-high-tech-tools-and-human-errors-1.140744.

[104] Ben Farmer, *Libya: Gaddafi Forces Disguised as Civilians*, THE TELEGRAPH, Mar. 31, 2011, *available at* www.telegraph.co.uk/news/worldnews/africaandindianocean/libya/8419832/Libya-Gaddafi-forces-disguised-as-civilians.html.

[105] David Wood, *Libya Air War: Pilots Struggle to Avoid Civilian Casualties*, HUFFINGTON POST, May 25, 2011, www.huffingtonpost.com/2011/03/21/libya-air-war-pilots-civilians_n_838733.html.

[106] Hadeed Al-Shalchi, *Heavy Clashes in Libya's Rebel-Held Misrata*, THE SAN DIEGO UNION-TRIBUNE, Apr. 8, 2011, *available at* www.utsandiego.com/news/2011/apr/08/heavy-clashes-in-libyas-rebel-held-misrata.

morphs into a status-based understanding. For example, suppose ROE state that an individual who is involved in a particular type of activity, such as handling a particular type of weapon, may be engaged in self-defense because the handling of the weapon is per se a demonstration of hostile intent. In the perception of a soldier, that person who might otherwise be a protected civilian now becomes labeled as a "weapon handler." Suppose also that the handling of the weapon, because of its nature, might be mistaken for other non-hostile activities—for example, the cleaning of an irrigation ditch next to the road could be perceived as the emplacement of an improvised explosive device (IED) along the roadbed. In the soldier's mind, the person might then functionally be seen as having the status of an identified enemy combatant who could be engaged at will on the basis of being an "IED Emplacer," rather than a possible civilian engaged in a peaceful activity that must be objectively assessed for manifestations of hostile intent or hostile acts.

VII. Analysis, Investigation, and Modification

National and multinational military organizations continuously evaluate their operations and procedures to determine whether improvements in the way they conduct their activities might be made, and if so, how such changes might be accomplished. Rules of engagement are assessed in this manner as well, and particularly in the case of multinational operations, external inputs into this analysis through different formal investigations into uses of armed force become very significant. Modification of ROE in a multinational operation can be politically challenging once the operation is underway. Both U.S. and NATO doctrine recognize that changes to ROE might be necessary, however, and each sets out a process to effect modification.

A. ANALYSIS

The first problem a multinational headquarters might face in conducting rigorous analysis of its ROE is simply acquiring the pertinent data. Collecting real-time information about how operations are proceeding has become technologically possible on a scale that could only be imagined a generation ago. Even for the most technologically sophisticated military force, however, this flood of information could present significant problems in terms of timely processing it into useful intelligence.[107] Because of classification concerns, not all commanders and staff officers within a multinational force structure necessarily get to see all the information and the analysis conducted upon it by certain TCNs. So, within this deluge of data, the pertinent information made available might have

---

[107] Christopher Drew, *Military Is Awash in Data from Drones*, N.Y. TIMES, Jan. 10, 2010, *available at* http://www.nytimes.com/2010/01/11/business/11drone.html?ref=world.

been significantly redacted to address security and classification concerns.[108] Additionally, information and analysis collected by the TCNs regarding operations their respective national forces conducted might not be releasable because of domestic legislation or policy concerns. For example, different TCNs will investigate potentially improper uses of force using their own procedures. Some TCNs may conduct quick assessments,[109] while others may need to work their way through both military and domestic civilian legal procedures before a determination can be made as to whether the use of force was proper.[110]

For a multinational force headquarters attempting to track such incidents and to analyze them to see whether there are improvements to be made to existing ROE, SOPs, or other guidance concerning the use of force, these different TCN procedures may mean that months pass before any information is received regarding specific incidents. Ultimately, the information received might not be very detailed, and therefore not very useful. Further, given the pace of operations in a typical multinational force area of operations, a delay of a few months means that the focus of the command and staff has likely long since moved on to other matters, and they may have in fact already corrected any deficiencies in the directives governing the use of force.

Once the TCN data and incident-specific analysis are obtained, they should be appropriately contextualized and synthesized to develop a sound analytical basis for recommending an ROE modification. This could require establishing specialized analysis structures working according to their own SOPs. As an example of this, ISAF set up a Civilian Casualty Tracking Cell, which both oversaw investigations into civilian casualty incidents and liaisoned with human rights groups engaged in protection of the civilian population.[111] Importantly, the ISAF Legal Office was included in the analysis process and therefore was able to make recommendations from both the legal and the ROE perspectives in instances of civilian casualties. Complementing this effort at the NAC level, guidance was then issued to better standardize the methods by which civilian casualties were tracked and counted.[112] This high-level effort was complemented

---

[108] *See, e.g.*, USCENTCOM's *Unclassified Executive Summary, U.S. Central Command Investigation into Civilian Casualties in Farah Province, Afghanistan on 4 May 2009*, 1 no. 1, June 18, 2009, *available at* www.hsdl.org/?view&did=35748 ("The full report of the investigation is classified is [sic] currently protected in accordance with law and regulation pertaining to national security.") (last visited June 30, 2014).

[109] U.K. forces for example conduct "Shooting Incident Reviews," which are ordinarily both thoroughly and quickly conducted. *See, e.g.*, *Afghan Shooting Incident Review, Defence in the Media: Monday 16 July 2007*, Official News Blog of the UK Ministry of Defence, http://www.blogs.mod.uk/defence_news/2007/07/defence-in-th-2.html (last visited Aug. 28, 2013).

[110] *See infra* text accompanying footnotes 122–128.

[111] *See ISAF Press Release, Ask ISAF: Civilian Casualty Tracking Cell Manager Answers Your Questions*, ISAF webpage, May 24, 2009, www.nato.int/isaf/docu/mediaadvisory/2009/05-may/ma090524-035.html (last visited June 30, 2014).

[112] NATO Press Release, NATO Nations Approve Civilian Casualty Guidelines, NATO webpage, Aug. 6, 2010, http://www.nato.int/cps/en/natolive/official_texts_65114.htm?selectedLocale=en (last visited June 30, 2014).

by subordinate command initiatives to analyze incidents in which civilian casualties have occurred to determine, in a systematic fashion, whether modifications to tactics used by NATO forces might result in fewer incidental losses among non.-combatants. Such a system[113] was used in 2010 by a subordinate ISAF headquarters in Kandahar, and was apparently successful not just in identifying beneficial changes in tactics, but also in increasing the transparency of the process by including the UN, the International Committee of the Red Cross, and human rights groups as participants.[114]

B. INVESTIGATION

The criteria used by a multinational force headquarters structure in tracking potentially improper uses of force may still be geared toward the use of information too highly classified to be easily released. This presents potential problems when the multinational force attempts to reconcile its analysis and statistics with those kept by other IOs [115]and NGOs promoting transparency and accountability.[116] Further, because the IOs and NGOs conduct their own investigations,[117] and might even have better access to incident sites than the military, the sources of information each uses will often be quite different; however, there may be no practicable way to test the veracity of the sources as the parties try to find consensus on how events transpired or how many casualties were involved. This could be further complicated by the likelihood that the protocols used by each to collect information and analyze are not similar, and that each makes different assumptions regarding the relative veracity of the different sources from which they collect.

Investigating potential ROE violations in areas where fighting is still occurring presents significant logistical and security challenges for investigators. In

---

[113] *See generally* Ewan Cameron et al., *Tracking Civilian Casualties in Combat Zones Using Civilian Battle Damage Assessment Ratios*, 147 British Army Rev. 87–93 (2009).

[114] Bruce Spencer, *Interview with Ewan Cameron, Health Care Advisor, Regional Command South*, audio file, Association of Military Surgeons of the United States webpage, *available at* www.amsus.org/index.php/podcast-list (last visited Aug. 28, 2013).

[115] An example would be the United Nations Commission on Human Rights.

[116] *See* UN Assistance Mission in Afghanistan, Annual Report on Protection of Civilians in Armed Conflict, 2009, 6–7 (2010). *See also* Gordon Rayner et al., *Army Colonel Arrested over Alleged Leaks to Human Rights Researcher*, The Telegraph, Feb. 4, 2009, *available at* http://www.telegraph.co.uk/news/newstopics/politics/defence/4513991/Army-Colonel-arrested-over-alleged-leaks-to-human-rights-researcher.html.

[117] *See, e.g., TIC, supra* note 88, which was

> based on field research in Afghanistan, interviews with US, NATO and Afghan officials, and the creation of a detailed database of every reported airstrike in Afghanistan between November 2005 and July 2008. To quantify civilian deaths we have used various sources, including the Afghan NGO Security Office (ANSO), United Nations Assistance Mission in Afghanistan (UNAMA), the Afghan Independent Human Rights Commission, various media outlets, and hospitals where available.

Id. at 8.

modern combat, and particularly in combating an insurgency, there really is no secure rear area. Further, the contested areas in which combat tends to occur might be beyond the areas in which either side can feasibly provide security and logistical support. Even for skilled investigators, conducting a thorough investigation to the standard required to generate reliable information for ROE analysis under these conditions could be difficult. In Afghanistan, for example, even if sufficient logistical and security support could have been provided to an investigation, potential contamination of the investigation site before the investigation begins,[118] difficulty in obtaining detailed information about the actions of insurgent forces and the number of civilians present,[119] the lack of forensic evidence, the cultural norms mandating the quick burial of bodies[120] and discouraging exhumation, and the highly politicized nature of the conflict made it difficult to gather reliable evidence.

As noted earlier, issues of classification could likely hamper the collection of information and evidence by an investigating team from either a TCN or a multinational force headquarters.[121] Even if classification is not an issue, political and sovereignty concerns regarding the safekeeping and chain of custody of collected information and items, and possible forensic tests that might be conducted upon items, could become problematic. Also, TCNs might choose not to make their personnel available for questioning by investigative teams from other nations or the multinational headquarters.[122] Further, there could conceivably be multiple investigations into a particular incident, each using it own protocols and methods for obtaining evidence and information. The receiving state, IOs and NGOs, and even private companies who may have had contractors involved in a particular situation all might conduct independent investigations into use-of-force incidents. For example, in September 2009 an air strike requested by German ISAF personnel upon fuel tankers that had been captured by insurgents resulted in a significant (but disputed) number of civilian casualties.[123] This case was investigated by ISAF when it first occurred;[124] by a German military

---

[118] Risen, *supra* note 73.

[119] *TIC*, *supra* note 88, at 15.

[120] *Islamic Funeral Rites*, About.com, http://islam.about.com/cs/elderly/a/funerals.htm (last visited Feb. 5, 2010).

[121] *Final Report to the Prosecutor by the Committee Established to Review the NATO Bombing Campaign against the Federal Republic of Yugoslavia*, ICTY webpage, http://www.icty.org/sid/10052 (last visited June 30, 2014). For example, the Committee noted that NATO's reply had been "couched in general terms," and had not answered "specific questions about specific incidents." The Committee did assume however "the NATO and NATO countries' press statements are generally reliable and that explanations have been honestly given." *Id.* at 90.

[122] In a multinational military headquarters such as NATO, criminal jurisdiction over soldiers remains with the TCN.

[123] ISAF News Release, ISAF *Commander Appoints Board to Lead Investigation into Kunduz Air Strike*, ISAF Webpage, ISAF News Release #2009-681, Sept. 8, 2009, http://www.nato.int/isaf/docu/pressreleases/2009/09/pr090908-681.html (last visited Feb. 4, 2010) [hereinafter *Kunduz*].

[124] *Id.*

police investigation;[125] by an official joint ISAF team including a U.S. Air Force officer, a German officer, and a legal advisor;[126] by an Afghan team appointed by President Karzai;[127] and by a civilian prosecutor in Germany,[128] and then during an official parliamentary investigation in Germany.[129] It would also appear that the ICRC looked into the incident.[130] Multiple investigations could tend to muddy the investigative waters, and depending upon translations, for example, could result in witnesses providing inconsistent information.

C. MODIFICATION

Although ROE are typically established prior to the commencement of an operation, and ordinarily promulgated at the strategic level and then pushed down through subordinate levels of command,[131] analysis and investigation of circumstances on the ground might demonstrate that they need to be modified so that military operations can be more effective. United States' doctrine recognizes that the legal advisor has an important part to play in the military decision- making process used by staffs to develop courses of action for the commander to conduct military operations. The steps of this process in which the legal advisor is particularly useful include working with the staff to identify changes to the ROE that will be necessary to accomplish the mission, drafting an ROE annex to the eventual operations order, and potentially creating an ROE card to be distributed to the troops.[132] United States' doctrine also positions an ROE cell under the control of the J-3 (operations) section consisting of J-2 (intelligence), operations, and J-5 (plans) staff officers and a legal advisor as providing for these functions.[133] Commanders at any level are authorized to request additional ROE, and the SROE provide a template for drafting an ROE request.[134] In distributing ROE to subordinate headquarters, a superior commander may tailor the ROE

---

[125] N. Blome et al, *German KSK Special Forces Involved in Deadly Bombing*, Das Bild, Dec. 11, 2009, *available at* http://www.bild.de/BILD/news/bild-english/world-news/2009/12/10/kunduz-air-strike-new.

[126] *Kunduz*, *supra* note 123.

[127] *Id.*

[128] Ulf Gartzke, *German General: NATO Exonerates Bundeswehr in Kunduz Tanker Air Strike*, WeeklyStandard.com, Nov. 1, 2009, http://www.weeklystandard.com/weblogs/TWSFP/2009/11/german_general_nato_exonerate.

[129] *Kunduz Airstrike Inquiry Begins in Berlin*, Deutsche Welle, Jan. 21, 2010, *available at* http://www.dw.com/en/kunduz-airstrike-inquiry-begins-in-berlin/a-5152057.

[130] *Afghanistan: No Respite for Civilians as Violence Continues*, ICRC Afghanistan webpage, Oct. 15, 2009, http://www.icrc.org/web/eng/siteengo.nsf/html/afghanistan-update-151009 (last visited Feb. 4, 2010).

[131] Operational Law Handbook, *supra* note 18, at 90. Legal advisors are cautioned that although there might be circumstances requiring such a change, such as when the current mission of the unit could not have been foreseen by the ROE planners originally, such circumstances "will be relatively rare." *Id.*

[132] *U.S. SROE*, *supra* note 26, Enclosure J, J-2 to J-3; ROE Handbook, *supra* note 43, at 1–30.

[133] *U.S. SROE*, *supra* note 26, Enclosure J, J-1, J-4; ROE Handbook, *supra* note 43, 1–31.

[134] Operational Law Handbook, *supra* note 18, at 90.

and withhold authority to conduct certain actions from subordinate commanders, but such restrictions must be reported to the Secretary of Defense.[135]

NATO's ROE development and modification process is no less complex. Upon request of a strategic-level NATO commander, NATO ROE are issued to the NATO forces by the NAC, and they include a Political Policy Statement (PPS), which "frame the authorised ROE in the proper context for the mission."[136] Interestingly, the PPS is accompanied by Political Policy Indicators, which tell the NATO force commander the NAC's assessment whether NATO efforts are intended to de-escalate the situation, leave it largely unchanged, or perhaps even accept some risk of escalation.[137] The NAC may also pre-approve other ROE that do not become effective unless certain contingencies occur or certain operational milestones are met. These are called dormant ROE, and the strategic commander must notify the NAC when they become effective.[138]

After receipt of the NAC ROE authorization, the strategic-level commander will issue a tailored ROE implementation message to subordinate headquarters, informing them of the NAC decision and potentially withholding certain ROE at the strategic level.[139] Withholding ROE is a completely appropriate way for the superior commander to limit the use of force by subordinate units, but requesting and tracking delegations of withheld ROE can become very time-consuming and frustrating for subordinate commanders. Importantly, although English and French are the two official NATO languages, TCNs "may translate the ROE into their own language to facilitate understanding."[140]

Although NATO ROE doctrine recognizes that a NATO force might decide that its current ROE seem insufficient given the situation on the ground, it encourages military headquarters to first seek "further political direction and guidance from the NAC . . . if required, or issuing appropriate operational and tactical direction and guidance through the chain of command," rather than submitting a request for ROE change.[141] In the event that an ROE modification is required, however, commanders at any level are able to forward ROE requests through their chains of commands for consideration.[142] Although as a matter of practice static NATO headquarters in Europe assigned specific operations officers the duty of tracking ROE, there was no such officer in the ISAF headquarters in Kabul in 2008 through 2009.[143] Efficiency in ROE matters is promoted in a

---

[135] *Id.* at 91.

[136] *NATO ROE*, *supra* note 26, at ¶ 14, 7.

[137] *Id.*

[138] *Id.* at ¶ 24, 9.

[139] *Id.* at ¶¶ 22, 25, 9. Amplification lines are used by way of clarification for the separate rules as necessary. *Id.* at Annex E, E-2.

[140] *Id.* at ¶ 26, 9.

[141] *Id.* at ¶ 12, 6. The Tactical Directives issued by successive ISAF commanders are examples of compliance with this guidance.

[142] *Id.* at Annex E, E-1 to E-2.

[143] Author's notes.

multinational headquarters when such an officer is assigned, because writing an ROE request, for example, requires a high degree of familiarity with the ROE, the request process, and LOAC.

VIII. Conclusion

The operationalization of ROE in the activities of a large multinational force, particularly when the fighting is occurring in large part among the people, is complex. The same considerations of law, policy, and military necessity that were balanced and crystallized to yield the ROE under which the multinational force operates continue to exert powerful and sometimes contradictory influences upon the manner in which those ROE are actually applied. Subtle differences between the national ROE of the TCNs that are part of the operation, and between the TCNs and the multinational force itself, might be significant operationally, but impossible to remediate politically. The impacts of these differences can be minimized, however. First, the lessons identified in operationalizing multinational force ROE need to be recognized as a specific category within which to collect information for analysis and archiving. Second, on this basis, education and training of commanders, staff, and soldiers should familiarize them with practical measures to bridge the gaps in terminology and understandings of different ROE. Third, a holistic understanding of the flow and interplay of use-of-force guidance and its application in operations should be cultivated within a dedicated cell in the operations staff section. An ad hoc cell that ordinarily only comes together during the military decision-making process is not likely to have the same continuity of focus required to manage ROE in modern multinational operations. Finally, a multinational force must give thought to its interactions with IOs, NGOs, and the public regarding use-of-force issues and civilian casualties, and it might need to create new staff infrastructure and SOPs not only to provide credibility in its management of information and analysis regarding ROE, but to expand the scope of possible pertinent inputs into decisions whether to modify the ROE as well.

9}

Detention Operations

A STRATEGIC VIEW

Sandra L. Hodgkinson*

I. Introduction

Military detention operations are one of the principal ways to remove enemy fighters from the battlefield during war, and certainly are a humane alternative to killing them. At the end of hostilities, the detainees are released, presumably to return to normal lives where they may be recognized for their sacrifices. Through the principle of reciprocity, honorable soldiers maintain the highest standards of detention, so that if they are captured, they will be treated well in return.[1] To

* Sandra L. Hodgkinson is a former member of the Senior Executive Service in the U.S. government who served in the following positions: The Special Assistant to the Deputy Secretary of Defense; Deputy Assistant Secretary of Defense for Detainee Affairs; Distinguished Visiting Research Fellow at National Defense University; Deputy to the Ambassador-at-Large for War Crimes Issues; Director for International Justice at the National Security Council, The White House; and Senior Advisor on Human Rights for the Coalition Provisional Authority (CPA) in Baghdad, and as a Foreign Affairs Officer at the Department of State's Bureau of Democracy, Human Rights and Labor. She began her career as an attorney in the Navy Judge Advocate General's Corps (JAG) Corps, and is currently a Captain in the Navy JAG reserves. She has taught National Security Law at Catholic University Columbus School of Law since 2007, and also at National Defense University last year. She has published more than fifteen articles and two book chapters on international law. She is currently Vice President and Chief of Staff at DRS Technologies, a mid-sized defense firm owned by Finmeccanica of Italy.

[1] William H. Forman Jr., *The U.S. POW Experience since World War II*, *available at* http://www.isanet.ccit.arizona.edu/noarchive/forman.htm (last visited Jan. 11, 2013) (quoting General Eisenhower's response to a Russian general who asked him about why the United States treated German POWs so well). General Eisenhower stated:

> in the first place my country was required to do so by the terms of the Geneva Convention. In the second place, the Germans had some thousands of American and British prisoners and I did not want to give Hitler the excuse or justification for treating our prisoners more harshly than he was already doing.

Id. It is important to note that the notion of reciprocal treatment is a moral aspiration, versus a legally binding defense. Accordingly, treatment in violation of the law of war is not a valid defense

date, the United States has, unfortunately, rarely met an enemy that reciprocates the high standards of detention required under international law.[2] Further, while the United States' has made great efforts to to adhere to the detention regime outlined in international law, for the past decade its practices have been under attack.

Criminal law, in contrast, is often considered the gold standard for detention. It uses detention to punish unlawful behavior, deter future criminal conduct, and protect society. Through due process of law, individuals who are jailed for alleged unlawful conduct are generally afforded certain rights before they are imprisoned, and will usually not be incarcerated absent a guilty conviction by a court of law or other judicial determination that detention is warranted for safety, security, or flight reasons. Criminal law detention fits into what is called a "law enforcement" paradigm, meaning that the purpose of the detention is to enforce criminal laws, not to win wars.

In the current post-September 11, 2001 (9/11) context, military battlefield detention and law enforcement detention have become inextricably linked. Today's principal military conflict between the United States and a nonstate actor, al Qaeda, blurs the lines between the law of war and the law enforcement paradigm in several ways. First, al Qaeda as an organization is hierarchical and carries out military-style operations on the battlefield with a clear rank structure and the goal of military defeat of the United States and its other enemies.[3] It led

---

for reciprocal treatment in violation of the law of war. The U.S. Naval Handbook states, "The concept of reciprocity is not applicable to humanitarian rules of law that protect the victims of armed conflict." COMMANDER'S HANDBOOK ON THE LAW OF NAVAL OPERATIONS NWP 1-14M PG 6-5 (July 2007) [hereinafter NWP 1-14M]. As Eisenhower reasons, one argument for treating forces well in times of armed conflict is to encourage them to do the same to our forces.

[2] Of the 28,570 Japanese-held U.S. Army POWs during World War II, only about 60 percent returned to the United States at the end of the war, many with countless stories of torture and abuse; there was also ample support of rampant torture and abuse of U.S. POWs by the North Koreans during the Korean War, the North Vietnamese during the Vietnam War, and the Iraqis during the Persian Gulf War. *See generally* Forman, *supra* note 1. The only military enemy who treated U.S. POWs well were the Germans in World War II out of respect for the Geneva Convention. *Id.*

[3] The initial armed conflict against Afghanistan following 9/11 was in response to a view that al Qaeda had engaged in an "armed attack" against the United States, which went beyond merely criminal and was instead an act of war. *See* Military Order on Detention, Treatment, and Trial of Certain of Certain Non-citizens in the War against Terrorism, 66 Fed. Reg. 57833 (Nov. 13, 2001) [hereinafter Nov. 13, 2001 Military Order] (indicating that the terrorist activities of al Qaeda resulted in and "armed conflict" with the United States). *See also* Hamdan v. Rumsfeld, 126 S. Ct. 2749 (2006) (holding that an armed conflict existed between the United States and al Qaeda); Geoffrey S. Corn, Hamdan, *Lebanon, and the Regulation of Armed Hostilities: The Need to Recognize a Hybrid Category of Armed Conflict*, 40 VAND. J. TRANSNAT'L L 295 (2006); Derek Jinks, *The Applicability of the Geneva Conventions to the "Global War on Terrorism,"* 46 VA. J. INT'L L. 165 (2005); Jordan J. Paust, *Post-9/11 Overreaction and Fallacies regarding War and Defense, Guantanamo, the Status of Persons, Treatment, Judicial Review of Detention, and Due Process in Military Commissions*, 79 NOTRE DAME L. REV. 1335 (2004); Jennifer Elsea, *Terrorism and the Laws of War: Trying Terrorists as War Criminals before Military Commissions*, CONG. RESEARCH SERV., RL31191, (Dec. 11, 2001) (analyzing whether the attacks of September 11, 2001 triggered the law of war); *Principles of Military Organization*, THE AL QAEDA MANUAL, UK/BM-12 Translation, *available at* http://www.fas.org/irp/world/para/manualpart1_1.pdf (last visited Mar. 14, 2013) (describing the Principles, Requirements

multiple attacks on the United States, including the World Trade bombing of 1992, the East African bombings in Kenya and Tanzania in 1998, the attack on the USS *Cole* in 2000, and the 9/11 attacks.[4] Although al Qaeda largely operates like a regular military armed force, declared war on the United States, and is currently engaged in military operations against the United States and al Qaeda's perceived enemies in Afghanistan, Pakistan, the Horn of Africa, Yemen, and elsewhere, it does not actually report to a state.[5] It is a nonstate actor, quite different from a classic military enemy.

The U.S. position is that battlefield detention is entirely appropriate for the duration of hostilities to keep members of al Qaeda off of the battlefield,[6] and that members of al Qaeda can also be prosecuted as war criminals for violations of the Geneva Conventions for the way they fight, either during or after the war.[7] They can also be prosecuted by U.S. or foreign courts with adequate jurisdiction for any acts of terrorism they may commit.[8] Given the roles of both armed conflict and law enforcement in this conflict with al Qaeda, it is therefore not surprising that there has been some confusion about the applicability of battlefield detention under the laws of war versus a traditional law enforcement regime. Other current examples of overlapping armed conflict regimes with traditional law enforcement regimes can be found in places such as Colombia, where the government has used both military and law enforcement measures to address the activities of the Revolutionary Armed Force of Columbia (FARC),[9] and Iraq, where a classic state-on-state conflict morphed into a non-international armed conflict fueled by an insurgency after the Iraqi government reclaimed its sovereignty in 2004.[10] All

---

and Missions required of al Qaeda's Military Organization, principally "[t]he overthrow of the godless regimes and their replacement with an Islamic regime"). The Al Qaida Manual was found in Manchester, England by British police during the search of an al Qaida member's home; this translation was used as evidence in federal court in New York City as Government Exhibit 1677-T in an embassy bombing trial.

[4] *See Al Qaida Timeline: Plots and Attacks, Hunt for Al-Qaida*, MSNBC News, http://www.msnbc.msn.com/id/4677978/ns/world_news-hunt_for_al_qaida/t/al-qaida-timeline-plots-attacks/#.UPBZr_F5mSM (last visited Jan. 11, 2011).

[5] *See* John B. Bellinger III, Legal Adviser for the U.S. Department of State and National Security Council, *Legal Issues in the War on Terrorism*, Comments at the London School of Economics, Oct. 31, 2006, *available at* http://www.state.gov/s/l/2006/98861.htm (describing why "War Is an Appropriate Paradigm for the Conflict").

[6] *See generally* Jordan J. Paust, *Self-Defense Targetings of Non-state Actors and Permissibility of U.S. Use of Drones in Pakistan*, 19 J. Transnat'l L. &. P. 237, 238 (arguing the case that self-defense is allowed against an armed attack by a nonstate actor).

[7] *See generally* Nov. 13, 2001 Military Order, *supra* note 1.

[8] Zacarias Moussaoui is a good example of a 9/11 co-conspirator who was prosecuted in a U.S. Article III court after he was arrested in Minnesota before 9/11; he was convicted and sentenced to life in prison. *See, e.g.* "Zacarias Moussaoui Fast Facts," June 5, 20140, *available at* http://www.cnn.com/2013/04/03/us/zacarias-moussaoui-fast-facts/index.html.

[9] *See* Robert Valencia, *Colombia and FARC: Will the Internal Conflict Reach an End?*, Yale J. Int'l Aff. (July 3, 2012), *available at* http://yalejournal.org/2012/07/Colombia-and-farc-will-the-internal-conflict-reach-an-end/ (last visited Feb. 17, 2013).

[10] *See generally* Sandra Hodgkinson, *The Legacy of Iraq: Impact on International Law*, ASIL Proceedings (Mar. 2008).

of these cases demonstrate the difficult line that can exist between armed conflict and law enforcement.

This chapter will begin with a broad overview of the U.S. position on the international legal authority to detain captured personnel in the course of military operations across the spectrum of military operations, including state-versus-state conflict (such as the initial phase of the Iraq War), state-versus-nonstate-actor conflict (such as the current U.S. conflict with al Qaeda), and conflicts involving insurgent or rebel groups (such as post-sovereignty Iraq, Colombia, and the Democratic Republic of the Congo). It will then provide specifics on U.S. domestic law, which has also had a significant effect on U.S. detention operations. The chapter will next discuss the labyrinth of developing and coordinating detention policies at the strategic level: this is an inter-agency process laden with competing interests and heavily influenced by external actors, including the media, as well as battlefield exigencies. It will then describe how these policies are shaped and promulgated down through the various military components to the battlefield. To illustrate how this process works, the chapter will look at some specific strategic-level issues, including whether the character of the conflict is international or non-international, which rules to apply to varying categories of combatants, where to physically detain combatants, and whether to seek legislative changes to detention authority. The chapter concludes with a strategic view of the future of detention operations for the United States, arguing that battlefield detention remains as important to U.S. warfighters as ever before, and must remain a key weapon in the U.S. military arsenal for the future. Throughout this chapter, the U.S. conflict with al Qaeda will emerge as the backbone for its existing strategic choices, and as a stunning example of how international perceptions and foreign policy concerns can have a significant impact on an area that was once just a concern of military lawyers abroad on a battlefield.

II. The International Legal Authority to Detain Captured Personnel in Armed Conflict

The customary international law of war has long recognized battlefield detention as a necessary component of war.[11] Several international treaties and agreements have codified this by developing specific rules governing the conduct of forces who are detaining captured personnel, including: the Hague Conventions of 1899 and

[11] *See, e.g.*, 1 JEAN-MARIE HENCKAERTS & LOUISE DOSWALD-BECK, CUSTOMARY INTERNATIONAL HUMANITARIAN LAW: RULES, RULE 99 [hereinafter RULES] International Committee of the Red Cross (ICRC), Customary International Humanitarian Law, Rule 99, Deprivation of Liberty, http://www.icrc.org/customary-ihl/eng/docs/v1_cha_chapter32-rule99#FN-38-4 (last visited June 4, 2015) ("the Third Geneva Convention in based on the long-standing custom that POWs may be interned for the duration of active hostilities").

1907;[12] the Geneva Conventions of 1929;[13] and the principal treaties governing battlefield detention today, the Geneva Conventions of 1949 (Geneva Conventions),[14] and their Additional Protocols of 1977.[15] The Third Geneva Convention on Prisoners of War (Third Geneva Convention) specifically addresses the modern core rules relative to the treatment of prisoners of war (POWs).[16] According to the Third Geneva Convention, in a state-on-state conflict, a captured detainee will be classified as a POW if the detainee is a regular member of a High Contracting Party's military force, or if the detainee is a member of an irregular armed force that falls under a responsible chain of command, wears a uniform or other distinctive insignia, carries weapons openly, and follows the law of armed conflict.[17] When a detainee's status under this Convention is in doubt, the detainee is to be considered a POW until a neutral decision-maker convenes a competent tribunal.[18] These tribunals have come to be known as "Article 5 tribunals," taking the name of the relevant article in the Third Geneva Convention, and are generally comprised of three military officers who make a battlefield assessment of the status of the individual.[19] If a detainee meets the status determination of POW, then the full panoply of rights under the Third Geneva Convention applies, and specific rules regarding conditions of confinement, treatment, and daily life are clearly delineated. After the United States initiated the Iraq War in 2003, for example, Saddam Hussein and all members of his military leadership were considered upon capture to be POWs, and were afforded the protections set forth in

---

[12] Convention (II) with Respect to the Laws and Customs of War on Land and its annex: Regulations concerning the Laws and Customs of War on Land, The Hague, July 29, 1899, 32 Stat. 1803, and Annex, Convention (IV) respecting the Laws and Customs of War on Land and its annex: Regulations concerning the Laws and Customs of War on Land, The Hague, Oct. 18, 1907, 36 Stat. 2227, and Annex, 36 Stat. 2295.

[13] Geneva Convention Relative to the Treatment of Prisoners of War, Geneva July 27, 1929, 47 Stat. 2021. The Geneva Conventions of 1929 were the preceding documents to the full Geneva Conventions of 1949, and provided a minimal set of rules on detention of captured forces.

[14] Geneva Convention for the Amelioration of the Condition of the Wounded and Sick in Armed Forces in the Field, Aug. 12, 1949, T.I.A.S. 3363; Geneva Convention for the Amelioration of the Condition of Wounded, Sick, and Shipwrecked Members of Sea, Aug. 12, 1949, T.I.A.S. 3363; Geneva Convention Relative to the Treatment of Prisoners of War, Aug. 12, 1949, T.I.A.S. 3364 [hereinafter *Geneva Convention III*]; Geneva Convention Relative to the Treatment of Civilian Persons in Time of War, Aug. 12, 1949, T.I.A.S. 3365 [hereinafter *Geneva Convention IV*].

[15] Protocol Additional to the Geneva Conventions of August 12, 1949, and Relating to the Protection of Victims of International Armed Conflicts (Additional Protocol I), June 8, 1977, 1125 U.N.T.S. 3 [hereinafter *Additional Protocol I*]; Protocol Additional to the Geneva Conventions of August 12, 1949, and Relating to the Protection of Victims of Non-international Armed Conflicts (Additional Protocol II), June 8, 1977, 1125 U.N.T.S. 609 [hereinafter *Additional Protocol II*]. The United States is not party to either Additional Protocol I or II, but does recognize significant aspects of these two treaties as customary international law. Most key U.S. allies are states party to these two treaties, and therefore consider all of the provisions of the treaties as binding upon the state's troops when engaged in hostilities.

[16] *See generally Geneva Convention III, supra* note 14.

[17] *Id.* art. 4.

[18] *Id.* art. 5.

[19] *Id.*

the Geneva Conventions.[20] However, when a captured individual does not meet the requirements for POW status, because, for example, he was not wearing anything to distinguish himself from the civilian population, or failed to carry his weapons openly or follow the laws of war,[21] then the Geneva Conventions do not provide nearly as much guidance on the conditions of detention and how he is to be treated.

For guidance on treatment falling outside of POW status, Common Article 3, which is an article common to all four of the Geneva Conventions of 1949, is to be applied in "conflicts not of an international character" such as guerilla wars.[22] For states party to Additional Protocol II of the Geneva Conventions, there are also rules for organized military forces, which are under a responsible chain of command and exercise control over part of their territory so that they can carry out sustained and concerted military operations.[23] Many countries, though not the United States, have determined that Common Article 3 is customary international law[24] in every type of conflict, from state-on-state to internal conflicts, and therefore apply all of its provisions as a baseline minimum standard of treatment.[25]

Although the Bush administration did not agree that Common Article 3 was legally applicable to its conflict with al Qaeda as a matter of law in the early years of the war against al Qaeda, it focused on ways to apply the principles of Common Article 3 as a matter of policy.[26] The U.S. Supreme Court later determined that the U.S. fight with al Qaeda was indeed governed by Common Article 3 as a conflict "not of an international character" because al Qaeda, as a nonstate actor, was not a "High Contracting Party" to the Geneva Conventions and therefore was ineligible for the full protections of the Geneva Conventions.[27] Accordingly, the Supreme Court determined that Common Article 3 *legally applied to this non-international armed conflict* and governed the treatment of captured members of al Qaeda.[28] The Supreme Court did not make a determination as to whether Common Article 3 legally applied to the Taliban, which was the fighting

---

[20] *See, e.g., Saddam a Prisoner of War,* One News, Jan. 10, 2004, http://tvnz.co.nz/content/247731/425822/article.html.

[21] *Geneva Convention III, supra* note 14, art. 4.

[22] *Id.*, art 3.

[23] *See Additional Protocol II, supra* note 15, art. 1.

[24] Customary International Law is law that has developed through a consistent and regular practice of states over time, based upon a view that the custom is in fact the law.

[25] *See* M. Gandhi, *Common Article 3 of the Geneva Conventions, 1949 in the Era of International Criminal Tribunals*, Notes and Comments, *in* ISIL Year Book of International and Humanitarian Refugee Law, *available at* http://www.worldiii.org/int/journals/ISILYBIHRL/2001/11/html(last visited June 4, 2015).

[26] *See* DoD Internal Memorandum from Deputy Secretary Gordon England to Secretary Rumsfeld, OSD 18148-05, *Treatment for All Detainees* (Sept. 6, 2005) (on file with author)(laying out pros and cons for applying Common Article 3 as a matter of policy, versus establishing a new minimum standard of treatment).

[27] Hamdan v. Rumsfeld, 548 U.S. 557, 633–34 (2006).

[28] *Id.*

force for the Afghan government (which the United States did not recognize) at the time the war began. The Department of Defense (DoD) nonetheless immediately passed DoD Directive 2310.01E, which made Common Article 3 applicable to all detention operations.[29] Common Article 3 specifically requires that all detainees be treated humanely; that they not be subjected to cruel and degrading treatment, hostage taking, or torture; and that in criminal cases they be subjected to a regularly constituted court providing judicial guarantees.[30]

In addition to the prohibitions found in Common Article 3, for states party to Additional Protocol I of the Geneva Conventions, Article 75 provides additional fundamental guarantees for detainees, including the right to be informed of the reason for any arrest, a host of judicial procedures applicable to the criminal justice system, and separate quarters for women.[31] Similar to Common Article 3, many countries and the International Committee of the Red Cross (ICRC) also believe that Additional Protocol I (AP I) is customary international law and therefore applicable to all international armed conflicts.[32] The United States has had a mixed opinion on this matter. In 1987, State Department Deputy Legal Advisor Mike Matheson stated that the United States did view Article 75 of Additional Protocol I as customary international law.[33] This position was subsequently refuted during the early years of the War on Terror[34] but later quasi-reinstated in 2011. At this time, the State Department issued a letter indicating that the United States would follow Article 75 as a matter of law, but that it had not reached the level of consensus necessary to actually be customary international law.[35] It is

---

[29] *See* U.S. DEP'T OF DEF. DIR. 2311.01E, DOD LAW OF WAR PROGRAM ¶ 4.2 (Sept. 5, 2006) [hereinafter DOD LAW OF WAR PROGRAM]. The Directive specifically states "It is DoD policy that:[a]ll detainees shall be treated humanely and in accordance with U.S. law, the law of war, and applicable U.S. policy." *Id.* ¶ 4.1. It goes on to state that "all persons subject to this Directive shall observe the requirements of the law of war, and shall apply, without regard to a detainee's legal status, at a minimum the standards articulated in Common Article 3 to Geneva Conventions of 1949 . . . *Id.* ¶ 4.2. *Id.*

[30] *Geneva Conventions III, supra* note 14, art. 3.

[31] *Additional Protocol I, supra* note 15, art. 75. The United States is not party to Additional Protocol I but considers many of its provisions to be binding as customary international law. *See* Michael J. Matheson, *Session One: The United States Position on the Relation of Customary International Law to the 1977 Protocols Additional to the 1949 Geneva Conventions*, 2 AM. U. J. INT'L. L. & POL'Y, 419, 422, 428 n.39 (Fall 1987).

[32] *See, e.g.,* John Cerone, *Status of Detainees in International Armed Conflict, and Their Protection in the Course of Criminal Proceedings*, ASIL INSIGHTS, Jan. 2002 ("All those who do not benefit from greater protection under the Third or Fourth Conventions are entitled to the protection of Article 75 of Protocol I to the extent its provisions embody customary law."); *see also* 2 CUSTOMARY INTERNATIONAL HUMANITARIAN LAW: PRACTICE, Part II (Jean-Marie Henckaerts & Louise Doswald-Beck eds., 2005) [hereinafter PRACTICE].

[33] *See* Matheson, *supra* note 31.

[34] John B. Bellinger III, *For Obama, Vexing Detainee Decisions Loom*, Apr. 14, 2010, at http://www.cfr.org/human-rights/Obama-vexing-detainee-decisions-loom/p21895 (stating that disagreement within the excecutive branch had not produced a position on this issue); Julian E. Barnes, *Internal Critics Seek a Softer Line, Bush Administration Moderates Push to Change Detention and Interrogation Policies before Their Time's Up*, L.A. TIMES, Nov. 12, 2008, at A20.

[35] *See* John B. Bellinger III, *Obama's Announcements on International Law*, LAWFARE (Mar. 8, 2011, 8:33 PM), *available at* http://www.lawfareblog.com/2011/03/obamas-announcements-on-

important to note that this statement restricted the U.S. application of Article 75 to international armed conflicts only—important particularly because this administration has repeatedly stated that it considers, in agreement with the Supreme Court, the conflict against al Qaeda to be a non-international one.[36] However, the White House also confirmed in its March 2011 release that its military practice was already compliant with the Protocol's provisions, thereby implying that Article 75 also was applicable to al Qaeda, though seemingly more as a matter of policy. That is, the United States did not state that it considered application of Article 75 to those detained in a non-international armed conflict—such as al Qaeda—to be required by law, but it specifically highlighted the fact that its current practices were already consistent with it. Perhaps this makes sense given that Articles 4–6 of Additional Protocol II, which the United States has not yet ratified, are analogous to Article 75, AP I, and would, if the Reagan administration position is taken, apply to all non-international armed conflicts if ratified.[37]

The original purpose for the United States issuing a statement on the legal applicability of Article 75, which was first discussed under the Bush administration, was to link this article's provisions to the conflict with al Qaeda; that was unfortunately not achieved. Linking Article 75 to the conflict with al Qaeda would have provided a more robust *legal framework* applicable to the conflict, rather than relying on policy. Nonetheless, at least as a matter of policy, Article 75 currently supplements Common Article 3 as applicable to anyone the United States currently detains or will detain in the current conflict, and is moving in the direction of becoming customary international law in all conflicts.

As stated above, regarding non-international armed conflict in general, Additional Protocol II of the Geneva Conventions has provisions for fundamental guarantees: Articles 4–6, which are similar to Common Article 3 but a bit

---

international-law/. Bellinger argues that in the memo of March 7, 2011, the Obama administration committed to Article 75 of Additional Protocol I when it stated it "cho[o]se out of a sense of legal obligation to treat the principles set forth in Article 75 as applicable to any individual detained in an international armed conflict, and expects all other nations to adhere to these principles as well." *Id.* In Bellinger's view, this is a statement indicating that the Obama administration is attempting to create customary international law, implying that the administration shared the position of the prior administration that it was not yet a matter of customary international law.

[36] *See Al-Aulaqi v. Obama et al.*, Opposition to Plaintiff's Motion for Preliminary Injunction and Memorandum in Support of Defendants' Motion to Dismiss, U.S. District Court for the District of Columbia, p. 1, Sept. 24, 2010, http://static1.firedoglake.com/28/files/2010/09/100925-Al-Aulaqi-USG-PI-Opp-MTD-Brief-FILED.pdf (last visited Mar. 26, 2013) (stating that the United States is in a non-international armed conflict against al Qaida); *see also* Harold Hongju Koh, Legal Adviser, Dep't of State, Keynote Address at the Naval War College: International Law and Armed Conflict in the Obama Administration (June 22, 2011), *available at* http://www.usnwc.edu/getattachment/f53eec9c-1e22-48bb-8fb2-85f6f70b9c9b/The-Honorable-Harold-Koh-slideshow.pdf) (discussing specific U.S. positions regarding non-international armed conflict against al Qaida and associated forces).

[37] *See* John Bellinger III, *Further Thoughts on the White House Statement about Article 75*, LAWFARE (Mar. 13, 2011, 7:56 PM), http://www.lawfareblog.com/2011/03/further-thoughts-on-the-white-house-statement-about-article-75.

smaller than Article 75 of Additional Protocol I.[38] The United States is not party to Additional Protocol II either; however this provision provides legal guidance for detentions carried out under Additional Protocol II for states party to the Protocol, including in places such as Colombia and the Democratic Republic of the Congo.[39]

Although this section has focused primarily on the classification of detained individuals and the treatment they receive in accordance therewith, it is also worth referencing the targeting discussion elsewhere in this book, which describes in detail targeting decisions related to members of Organized Armed Groups, and civilians taking "direct participation in hostilities" (DPH).[40] It is essential that decisions related to who is targetable in a given conflict be fully aligned with who is detainable. That is, if an individual is targetable, that person should meet detention criteria as well. However, the inverse is not true: the detention universe is much larger than the targeting one, given that civilians can be temporarily detained (interned) for reasons of security during an armed conflict but cannot be targeted, unless (and during) an act of DPH.[41] Additionally, there are individuals who are hors de combat via surrender or wounds who may be detainable yet remain immune from direct targeting.[42]

III. U.S. Domestic Legal Authorities Related to Detention

In addition to the international legal authorities, there are also domestic legal authorities that provide guidance to military detentions. The U.S. Constitution provides Congress with the authority to make laws regarding captures on land and water.[43] Accordingly, Congress makes detention rules that govern the conduct of the U.S. armed forces when it determines appropriate. In areas where Congress is silent, the President, as Commander in Chief, is presumed to have the legal authority to make rules that govern the conduct of our armed forces in general and during specific operations, which he or she may delegate to the Secretary

---

[38] *Additional Protocol II, supra* note 15, art. 4. The United States is not a party to Additional Protocol II; see *id.* for a discussion of the Obama administration's efforts to have Additional Protocol II ratified by the Senate. However, article 4 does apply to other states party to Additional Protocol II, including many U.S. key allies.

[39] *See* List of States Party, Protocol Additional to the Geneva Conventions of August 12, 1949, and Relating to the Protection of Victims of Non-international Armed Conflicts (Protocol II), 9 June 1977, *available at* http://www.icrc.org/ihl.nsf/WebSign?ReadForm &id-475&ps=P (last visited Feb. 17, 2013).

[40] *See* Chapter 6 of this volume (discussing the law of targeting).

[41] *See generally Geneva Conventions IV, supra* note 14, art. 42, 43 (Article 78 governs internment of protected persons, civilians, during occupation whereas Articles 42 and 43 apply to non-occupation armed conflict situations).

[42] These are individuals who can be detained in conflict, but the use of lethal force against is prohibited. *See generally, Geneva Conventions III, supra* note 14, arts. 33 and 47.

[43] U.S. Const., art. I, § 8, cl. 11 ("make Rules concerning Captures on Land and Water").

of Defense.[44] Congress, which approves the Manual for Courts-Martial, does not address the rules for detention in this document, but nonetheless in the Preamble asserts that military commissions, which may be prescribed by the President or by another authority subject to international law, are to be "guided" by the rules for courts-martial.[45] Beyond these general rules in the Manual, the Department of Defense establishes more specific guidelines and procedures for detention that comply with both international law and the domestic laws passed by Congress.

The most frequently cited Department of Defense guidelines on military detention are translations of the Geneva Conventions into U.S. policies and practices for detention in a soldier-friendly way. As a result, the Army Field Manual, which has been revised several times since its original version in 1956, reflects the provisions of the Third Geneva Convention applicable for Prisoners of War, which generally apply in any traditional armed conflict between states.[46] Service-specific and theater-specific orders and procedures often incorporate the Army Field Manual and other Department of Defense Directives, orders, and policies on detention into current procedures. Specific military operations can have additional, operation-specific guidelines or rules of engagement (ROE) that supersede the generic guidance. There has been significant public debate about some of the reported additional guidance provided to U.S. service members for handling detainees captured during the conflict with al Qaeda.[47]

At the beginning of most armed conflicts involving the United States that could require military detention, Congress authorizes the President to use military force with an "Authorization for Use of Military Force" (AUMF). The AUMF of 2002, for the Iraq War, authorized President Bush to use force "as he determine[d] to be necessary and appropriate .... [to] defend the national security of the United States against the continuing threat posed by Iraq; and enforce all relevant United Nations Security Council Resolutions regarding Iraq."[48] From the invasion on March 20, 2003, until June 28, 2004, when the U.S. government passed sovereignty back to an interim Iraqi government, the AUMF in Iraq provided this U.S. domestic legal basis for military operations and detention.

---

[44] U.S. CONST. art. II. *See also* Youngstown Sheet & Tube Co. v. Sawyer, 343 U.S. 579 (1952) (for Justice Jackson's concurrence stating that the President's authority is at his greatest when the Congress gives him express authority).

[45] *See generally* MANUAL FOR COURTS-MARTIAL, UNITED STATES, Preamble (2012 ed.).

[46] U.S. DEP'T OF ARMY, FIELD MANUAL 27–10, LAW OF LAND WARFARE 1–2, 2–34a, 2–36 (July 18, 1956); *see also* U.S. DEPT'T OF ARMY, REG. 190–8, ENEMY PRISONERS OF WAR, RETAINED PERSONNEL, CIVILIAN INTERNEES AND OTHER DETAINEES (Oct. 1, 1997). *See also* Geneva Convention III, *supra* note 14.

[47] *See Rumsfeld, Mistake to End Enhanced Interrogation*, CBS NEWS· (Aug. 5, 2011), http://www.cbs.news.com/..../rumsfeld-mistake-to-end-enhanced-interrogation (last visited Feb. 27, 2013); *Donald Rumsfeld's Ugly Suits—In these Times*, (Sept. 23, 2011), *available at* http://www.inthesetimes.com/article/11966/donald_rumsfeld's_ugly_suits (last visited Feb. 27, 2013) (both articles describe the use of enhanced guidance to our military forces on the handling of detainees during the War on Terror).

[48] Authorization for the Use of Military Force against Iraq Resolution of 2002, H.J. Res. 114, 107th Cong. (2002) [hereinafter *AUMF for Iraq*].

The 2001 AUMF, which has formed the basis of the conflict with al Qaeda, however, stands out as the most significant AUMF in terms of the detention authority it provided. This AUMF was passed in September 2001 shortly following the 9/11 attacks. Because al Qaeda had been training in Afghanistan with the support of the Taliban and its forces, the U.S.-led military operations against Afghanistan were based in international law under Article 51 of the U.N. Charter as self-defense.[49] The congressionally passed AUMF for this operation, however, provided specific authority as to who the military was at war with and where. It stated:

> That the President is authorized to use all necessary and appropriate force against those nations, organizations, or persons he determines planned, authorized, committed, or aided the terrorist attacks that occurred on September 11, 2001, or harbored such organizations or persons, in order to prevent any future acts of international terrorism against the United States by such nations, organizations or persons.[50]

This AUMF did not make any geographic reference to Afghanistan, Pakistan, or any other country, leaving in place an authority that could presumably be used anywhere. By authorizing the use of force against the groups that "planned, authorized, committed or aided" the 9/11 attacks, the AUMF laid out fairly broad grounds for the executive branch and military to follow.[51] In the years since the conflict began, this AUMF has remained unchanged, and has continued to provide domestic legal authority for the detention of all captured individuals fitting into this category.[52] Federal judges hearing habeas corpus petitions filed by detainees captured under this authority have applied this standard as the basis for detention, and the executive branch has had to demonstrate that detained individuals are lawfully being held pursuant to the authority set out in this AUMF.[53] It is of interest to note that during the latter part of the Obama administration, habeas judges have generally deferred to the President and determined that the government was lawfully detaining individuals pursuant to this authority.[54]

Beyond the AUMF, Congress has legislated in a number of areas related to detention in the years since 9/11. The first and most significant one was the passage of the Detainee Treatment Act of 2005, which guaranteed that no detainee would be subjected to "cruel, inhuman, or degrading treatment or punishment"

---

[49] *See* Chapter 4 of this volume explaining the *jus ad bellum*.

[50] Authorization for the Use of Military Force, S.J. Res. 23, 170th Cong. Sec. 2 (2001) (enacted) [hereinafter *AUMF*].

[51] *Id.*

[52] Graham Cronogue, *A New AUMF: Defining Combatants in the War on Terror*, 22 Duke J. Comp. & Int'l L. 377, 378, 402 (2012) (arguing for a revision of the ten-year-old AUMF).

[53] *Id.*

[54] *Id.* at 383. *See also* Andy Worthington, *Guantanamo Habeas Results: The Definitive List* (2012), *available at* http://www.andyworthington.co.uk/guantanamo-habeas-results-the-definitive-list/ (last visited Mar. 12, 2013) (describing how the last eleven habeas corpus provisions had been won by the government, as well as six recent appeals).

(CIDT), and stripped statutory habeas corpus from applying to the detainees at Guantanamo Bay.[55] Congress also passed the Military Commissions Act of 2006,[56] after the Supreme Court determined in the *Hamdan v. Rumsfeld* decision that the Bush administration's Military Commissions Act was not a "regularly constituted court,"[57] among other concerns, in accordance with Common Article 3 of the Geneva Conventions. Congress also passed a revised Military Commissions Act of 2009 to further improve procedures under the Obama administration, to address concerns related to the prior Military Commissions Act.[58] Over the past several years, Congress has played a significant constraining role on the Obama administration's desires to close Guantanamo Bay. In 2012, for example, language in the defense budget placed restrictions on both the administration's ability to transfer detainees from Guantanamo Bay to their home countries, and to prevent the administration from either releasing or bringing these detainees into the United States.[59] Although this is far from an exhaustive list of legislation related to detainee issues, it represents a growing involvement of Congress and U.S. domestic law in military detention, albeit primarily aimed at detention at Guantanamo Bay, Cuba, a de facto U.S. sovereign territory far from the battlefield.

IV. The Process for Developing Detention Policies at the Strategic Level of Command

Consistent with a growing trend toward centralization of decision-making at the strategic level across the spectrum of military operations, detention operations has been an area where decision-making has become increasingly centralized and standardized.[60] The international and domestic legal attention paid

---

[55] Detainee Treatment Act of 2005, 42 U.S.C. § 2000dd (2006) (prohibiting the "cruel, inhuman or degrading treatment or punishment" of detainees and eliminating federal court jurisdiction over detainees from Guantanamo Bay challenging the legality of their detention in court). This provision ensured that the provisions in Article 16 of the Convention Against Torture (CAT) were legally applicable to detainees at Guantanamo Bay (which had been questioned by members of the Bush administration). *See id.* The provision stripping the habeas corpus statute's applicability to Guantanamo Bay was added to gain bipartisan support for this legislation by addressing the Supreme Court's 2004 ruling in *Hamdi v. Rumsfeld*, 542 U.S. 507, 509 (2004) (the Court ruled that the habeas corpus statute applied). Later, in the *Boumedienne v. Bush* decision, 553 U.S. 723 (2008), the Supreme Court reinstated habeas corpus at Guantanamo Bay with their holding that the Constitution's habeas corpus provision (not just the statute) applied to Guantanamo Bay.

[56] Military Commissions Act of 2006, 10 U.S.C. §§ 948a–950w (2006).

[57] Hamdan v. Rumsfeld, 548 U.S. 557, 628–29, 632 (2006).

[58] *See* Military Commission Act of 2009, 10 U.S.C. §§ 948a–950t (2009).

[59] *See* 2012 National Defense Authorization Act (NDAA), P.L. 112–81 (2012) (regulates status determinations and periodic review proceedings, and restricts transfers of detainees from Guantanamo to foreign countries or the United States).

[60] *See* Milan N. Vego, *Operational Command and Control in the Information Age*, 35 Joint Forces Q. (Dec. 2004), *available at* http://www.dtic.mil/dtic/tr/fulltext/u2/a524597.pdf

(providing a broader discussion on the centralization of decision-making at operational and strategic levels).

to detention operations over the past decade have contributed to this centralization. In addition, the intense domestic and international media scrutiny of U.S. detention operations at Guantanamo Bay and the abuse at Abu Ghraib prison in Iraq placed the U.S. military and government in a defensive posture with respect to anything related to detention in recent years.[61] As a result, the incentive for local commanders to act on their own with respect to detention operations decreased, while the penalties for missteps increased drastically. During the 2004–2005 period alone, several significant detainee investigations were conducted into DoD detention operations, including Vice Admiral Albert T. Church's high profile "Church Report" regarding abuse allegations at Guantanamo Bay,[62] and Major General George Fay and CIA Inspector General Major Antonio General Taguba's investigations of Abu Ghraib.[63] As a result of these investigations, several senior officials and detention personnel were recommended for disciplinary action and passed over for all future promotions related to their time in detention facilities.[64] This had the natural effect of elevating to the highest possible level those questions related to detention, while at the same time, senior Washington leadership, tired of the negative media stories and constant criticism from key battlefield allies, was urging the Pentagon to control detention operations at the highest level as well. The bottom-up and top-down interests were therefore aligned, and resulted in a significant strategic level interest in all matters related to detention.

---

[61] *See* Neil A. Lewis, *Red Cross Finds Detainee Abuse in Guantanamo*, N.Y. TIMES, Nov. 30, 2004, *available at* http://www.nytimes.come/2004/11/30/politicis/30gitmo.html?-r=0; Scott Higham & Joe Stephens, *New Details of Prison Abuse Emerge, Abu Ghraib Detainees' Statements Describe Sexual Humiliation and Savage Beatings*, WASH. POST, May 21, 2004, at A01; Adam Zagorin, *Pattern of Abuse*, TIME, Sept. 23, 2005 (reporting on a new Army investigation into new allegations of abuse in Iraq and Afghanistan).

[62] *See* ARMY REGULATION 15-6: FINAL REPORT, INVESTIGATION INTO FBI ALLEGATIONS OF DETAINEE ABUSE AT GUANTANAMO BAY, CUBA DETENTION FACILITY, Apr. 1, 2005, as amended June 9, 2005, *available at* http://www.defense.gov/news/Jul2005/d20050714 report.pdf [hereinafter *Church Report*] (describing in general the conclusions of the investigations team into a series of alleged detainee abuse events at Guantanamo Bay in the 2002–2003 time frame, and twenty-seven recommendations for changes).

[63] *See* LTG Anthony R. Jones, AR 15-6 Investigation of the Abu Ghraib Prison and 205th Military Intelligence Brigade, and MG George R. Fay, AR 15-6 Investigation of the Abu Ghraib Detention Facility and 205th Military Intelligence Brigade, with Executive Summary, *available at* https://www.thetorturedatabase.org/document/fay-report-investigation-205th-military-intelligence-brigades-activites-abu-ghraib (last visited June 4, 2015) [hereinafter *Fay Report*]; and AR 15-6 Investigation of the 800th Military Police Brigade, certified copy of May 27, 2004, *available at* http://www.aclu.org/torturefoia/released/TR3.pdf [hereinafter *Taguba Report*]; Thomas R. Eddlem, *CIA Torture Investigation Declassified*, NEW AMERICAN, Aug. 26, 2009, *available at* http://www.thenewamerican.com/usnews/crime/item/ 5839-cia-torture-investigation-declassified.

[64] *See Taguba Report, supra* note 63 (recommending action against BG Janis Karpinski, Colonel Pappas, and twelve other individuals); *Church Report, supra* note 62; Tom Squitieri, *Pentagon Report on Prisoner Abuse Met with Skepticism*, USA TODAY, Mar. 10, 2005, *available at* http://www.usatoday30.usatoday.com/news/washington/2005-03-10-prison-abuse_x.htm (raising concerns that only low-level leadership was held responsible for the abuse at Guantanamo Bay).

Today's centralized, interagency process for developing policy, doctrine, and law for detention operations developed in the 2004–2005 time period, and has remained relatively constant throughout the Bush and Obama administrations. There are multiple entities involved at various levels making decisions regarding detention law and policy within the executive branch. At the most senior level, the National Security Council has played both a strategic and tactical role in setting detainee policies over the past several years.[65] The National Security Act of 1947 created the National Security Council (NSC) to improve coordination between the military services and the other branches of government handling national security matters, such as the intelligence community.[66] Today, it continues to play this role, and has expanded its mandate to cover broader issues, including detention. The NSC staffing process is made up of three levels of decision-making authority.[67] During both the Bush and Obama administrations, the interagency coordination process was used to tackle the detainee issue.[68] Under the Bush administration, starting in 2004, there was a Detainee Policy Coordinating Committee (PCC),[69] which was renamed an Interagency Policy Committee (IPC) in the Obama administration, but played principally the same role.[70] These PCC/IPC meetings have focused entirely on detainee issues, and have served as an interagency coordinating and consensus-building body for new policy changes and changes in implementation of existing policies related to detainee issues across the interagency. The PCC/IPC is made up of representatives from the National Security Council staff; the Defense, State, Justice and Homeland Security Departments; and the Intelligence Community; it met weekly during

---

[65] Alan G. Whittaker, Shannon A. Brown, Frederick C. Smith & Ambassador Elizabeth McKune, The National Security Policy Process: The National Security Council and Interagency System, Annual Update, Aug. 15, 2011, at 18 (stating that Detainees is a key area for the IPC/DC process); *Leaving Guantanamo, Politics, Pressures, and Detainees Returning to the Fight*, Subcommittee on Oversight and Investigations of the Committee on Armed Services, HASC Comm. Print 112-4, Jan. 2012 (describing the role of the Detainee PCC under the Bush administration and the Detainee IPC under the Obama administration). *See also* Joe Palazzolo, *NSC Picks Up Where Gitmo Task Force Left Off*, MAIN JUSTICE, POLITICS, POLICY AND THE LAW (Jan. 22, 2010), *available at* http://www.mainjustice.com/2010/22/nsc-picks-up-where- gitmo-task-force-left-off/.

[66] *See* National Security Act of 1947, Pub. L. 110–53, 61 Stat. 496, 50 U.S.C. Sec. 401 (1947). *See also* Office of the Historian, Department of State, National Security Act of 1947, *Milestones: 1945–1952*, http://history.state.gov/milestones/1945-1952/NationalSecurityAct (last visited Sept. 30, 2012).

[67] *See* National Security Presidential Directive 1, Organization of the National Security Council System, Feb. 13, 2001 [hereinafter *NSPD-1*]; Presidential Policy Directive 1, Organization of the National Security Council System, Feb. 13, 2009 [hereinafter *PPD-1*] (Presidents Bush and Obama both set forth the same three-level staffing process that has been in place since 1989, although in 2010, President Obama renamed the "National Security Council" staff the "National Security Staff.") *See* Lauren Rozen, *Introducing the National Security Staff*, POLITICAL (Jan. 4, 2010), *available at* http://www.political.com/blogs/laurenrozen/0110/Introducting-the-National-Security-Staff.html.

[68] During the Bush administration, the NSPD-1 established six PCCs, and originally the detainee issue was formed under the Democracy, Human Rights and International Operations PCC, although it later became the Detainee PCC. *See NSPD-1, supra* note 67, for the list of established PCCs.

[69] *See NSPD-1, supra* note 67 (stating that "[t]he NSC/PCCs shall be the main fora for international coordination of national security policy").

[70] *PPD-1, supra* note 67.

its heyday at the Assistant Secretary or Deputy Assistant Secretary-level at the White House.[71] The PCC/IPC participants generally provide their recommendations to the Deputies Committee (DC) level, the next level up in the National Security Staffing process, comprised of delegated Deputy or Under Secretaries of the Departments and/or General Counsel.[72] The DC considers recommendations made by the PCC/ICC level, and either approves them, requests further work to be done, or sends them up to the next level, the Principals Committee (PC), which is comprised of Cabinet Secretaries or their designees.

Ultimately, the full National Security Council, to include the President, could be used to make a significant decision on detainee issues.[73] At all levels of the NSC staffing process, different Departments bring different views on detainee issues to the table, which require either consensus building, or a decision as to which course of action to take. For example, multiple PCC, DC, and PC meetings over the year have examined the issue of whether to close Guantanamo Bay or keep it open, whether to continue military commissions, and whether to reform U.S. law and policy on detention, and what level of process should be afforded to detainees captured on battlefields such as Iraq or Afghanistan.[74] The Detainee PCC under the Bush administration was heavily involved in decisions that would more traditionally fall to tactical commanders, such as which detainees from Guantanamo, Iraq, or Afghanistan could be transferred back to third or home countries, or released. The Obama administration continued the same degree of tactical decision-making, although it retooled the detainee review process slightly when it established the interagency Executive Order Task Force (EOTF).[75] Although many operational commanders could easily argue that it makes no sense to have a Washington, DC-based interagency group reviewing tactical decisions such as who to keep in detention, and who to release or transfer, the reality is that the detainee issue became so politicized that even senior

---

[71] *See NSPD-1, supra* note 67.

[72] *See id.* ("[The NSC DC] shall review and monitor the work of the interagency process . . .").

[73] National Security Council (NSC), The White House Website, President Barack Obama, http://www.whitehouse.gov/administration/eop.gov (last visited Oct. 1, 2012).

[74] *See generally* Sarah Mendelson, *Closing Guantanamo: From Bumper Sticker to Blueprint* (Ctr. for Strategic Int'l. Stud., Draft Rep't, July 15, 2008), *available at* http://csis.org/files/media/csis/pubs/080715_draft_csis_wg_gtmo.pdf (describing the various options available to the Obama administration in moving forward on Guantanamo); and Eric Schmitt, *U.S. to Expand Detainee Review in Afghan Prison*, N.Y. Times, Sept. 12, 2009, http://www.nytimes.com/2009/09/13/world/asia/13detain.html?_r0 (describing Obama administration policy changes to the detention operations at Bagram).

[75] *See* Exec. Order #13492, Review and Disposition of Individuals Detained at the Guantanamo Bay Naval Base and Closure of Detention Facilities, Jan. 22, 2009 (stating that the detention facilities would be closed within a year); Exec. Order No. 13567, Periodic Review of Individuals Detained at Guantanamo Bay Naval Station, Pursuant to the Authorization for Use of Military Force, Mar. 7, 2011 (establishing a new Periodic Review Board, which provided an interagency review of a detainee's status that differed slightly from the Administrative Review Board used during the Bush administration).

military leadership at the Pentagon in strategic level positions have sought guidance and approval for actions from an interagency body.

The advantage of this process is that a combination of the best intelligence from the intelligence community, the most comprehensive tactical/operational information from the warfighter, and the most reliable information from the State Department regarding third-country intentions, best positions the U.S. government to make good decisions. The downside of the process is that these decisions, even on tactical battlefield detention issues, can take significant time to make, and when done away from the immediate context of the battlefield, can be wrong. In some cases, the interagency coordination process resulted in a far better overall position, such as the establishment of the administrative review processes, and the adoption of Common Article 3 throughout all of DoD detention policy, whereas in other cases, it just slowed down the process and did not contribute meaningfully to the war effort in real time.

There were also external influences on the interagency decision-making process from U.S. allies and from the media. Key U.S. allies fighting alongside it in both Iraq and Afghanistan raised concerns regarding U.S. detention practices in both wars. In Afghanistan, there were differing views as to whether the allies were actually at war,[76] and accordingly, whether detainees were entitled to a higher level of due process that would be more consistent with a law enforcement-based model of detention.[77] The ICRC, long considered the protecting power of detainees during armed conflict, took the position early on that there were enhanced procedural safeguards needed for the detainees held by the United States during the War on Terror in Afghanistan and Guantanamo Bay.[78] Beyond even the closest U.S. allies with troops in Afghanistan, other key partners criticized U.S. detention practices when those practices involved their own nationals; and considering that Guantanamo Bay originally held detainees from more than forty countries,[79] this was a big group. Criticisms of U.S. detention practices were

---

[76] *See* Bellinger, *supra* note 5 (defending U.S. position on the fact that the United States was in a state of war with al Qaida).

[77] In fairness to U.S. allies, they did not suffer an armed attack on 9/11 the way that the United States did, and accordingly, the domestic parliamentary approval processes in their countries may have only authorized them to engage in missions that would support the Afghan government's efforts to stabilize Afghanistan. Accordingly, their own basis for military intervention may not have stemmed from the same self-defense posture as the U.S. armed action unless they determined that the purpose of their military action in Afghanistan was in the collective self-defense of the United States. A more law-enforcement-based model of detention would be consistent with a more traditional peace-building type of mission. *See e.g.*, DW, Bundeswahr, *Debate on Germany's Status in Afghanistan Opens Up*, (July 7, 2009), http://www.dw.de/debate-on-germanys-status-in-afghanistan-opens-up/a-4868657-1 (describing the internal struggle in Germany over whether German troops in ISAF were "at war" in Afghanistan).

[78] Fisnik Abrashi, *Red Cross: Change Needed at US Prison*, USA TODAY, Apr. 14, 2008, *available at* http://usatoday30.usatoday.com/news/topstories/2008-04-14-638379388_x.htm (ICRC spokesperson stating that the ICRC has talked with the U.S. authorities "about the absence of a clear legal framework and sufficient procedural safeguards with regard to Guantanamo").

[79] *See* CCR Justice, *Breakdown of Guantanamo Detainees by Nationality as of January 8, 2010*, http://ccrjustice.org/files/Breakdown_of_GTMO_Population_by_Nationality_2010-01-08.pdf.

also made by countries whose troops participated in reconstruction efforts or were making other contributions. Numerous senior level diplomatic discussions or dialogues on these matters ended up focusing on U.S. detainee policies. These routine diplomatic bilateral and multilateral meetings ensured continued senior level attention in the U.S. government to addressing detainee policy in the right way. Several of the U.S. key allies worked together with the United States behind the scenes to develop an acceptable and durable legal framework,[80] given the scant amount of detail provided in Common Article 3 of the Geneva Conventions, and even Article 75 of Additional Protocol I and Article 4 of Additional Protocol II. These dialogues informed the Washington senior leadership, and in many cases helped to shape the U.S. detention policies going forward. In addition, the continuous dialogue with the ICRC at the strategic level in Washington, DC, has produced recommendations for the interagency process to consider.[81]

The media and broader nongovernmental organization community have also weighed in heavily on the detainee debate. The media has consistently reported on the detainee issue since the initial captures in Afghanistan, ranging in topics from Guantanamo Bay, military commissions, the U.S. government's internal discussions on the future of detention operations, detainee abuse, and due process rights for detainees in the U.S., Afghan, or Iraqi justice systems.[82] The focused attention on detainee abuse at Abu Ghraib and Guantanamo Bay were top headlines for years on a regular basis in the major news networks, and left the impression with readers that detainee abuse was rampant and was in most cases government-directed, a fact that is often disputed.

Human rights groups, such as Human Rights Watch and Amnesty International, among others, have also written extensive reports about U.S. detention policies and lobbied senior government officials for changes over the past decade.[83] Furthermore, United Nations treaty-reporting bodies, which oversee state implementation of treaty obligations under the Convention Against Torture (CAT) and the International Convention on Civil and Political Rights (ICCPR)

---

[80] *See* Bellinger, *supra* note 5; Michael Peel & Guy Dinmore, *U.S. Needs "Advice Not Criticism,"* Financial Times, *available at* http://www.ft.com/cms/s/0/89990310-48db-a996-0000779c2340.html#axzz2Mrfcgz4v (last visited Sept. 21, 2006)(describing U.S. engagement with international allies on treatment of terrorist suspects.).

[81] *See e.g.*, ICRC News Release 12/62, United States: ICRC President Completes Visit to Washington, Mar. 30, 2012, http://www.icrc.org/eng/resources/news-release/2012/united-states-news-2012-03-30.htm.

[82] *See. e.g.*, *Red Cross Monitors Barred from Guantanamo*, N.Y. Times (Nov. 16. 2007), http://www.nytimes.com/2007/11/16/washington/16gitmo.html; *BREAKING—New Abu Ghraib Photos Release (W/MORE IMAGES)*, Daily KOS (Feb. 14, 2006), http://www.dailykos.com/story/2006/02/14/187178/-BREAKING-New-Abu-Ghraib-Photos-Released-W-MORE-IMAGES.

[83] *See* Human Rights Web website, US Foreign Policy section for examples of the detailed and routine reporting on detainee issues that has occurred since the beginning of the Bush adminstration's actions in the War on Terror; *and* Human Rights Watch Report, *Human Rights Watch: US Should Act on Pledge to Close Guantanamo, Indefinite Detention Nine Years Later with No End in Sight*, Jan. 10, 2011 (one example of hundreds of reports and news articles authored by human rights organizations criticizing U.S. detainee policy in the past ten years).

body, have held hearings to address U.S. treaty compliance on a variety of issues, to include detainee affairs. These oversight bodies have issued recommendations after their review of the U.S. periodic report submissions and oral presentations provided by the U.S. delegation.[84] There is no question that myriad recommendations have been made to senior U.S. government leadership over the past ten years on detainee policy, which have resulted in significant changes to our detainee policy directed by the most senior levels of the U.S. government.

Beyond the senior level Washington interagency coordination process, which has been heavily influenced by external actors, there have also been varying levels of Department of Defense engagement on detainee issues from the Office of the Secretary and Deputy Secretary of Defense on down to the battlefield. The Deputy Secretary of Defense (DSD), under both the Bush and Obama administrations, has played the senior detainee coordinating role for the Department within the interagency, attending all of the DC meetings, and some of the PC meetings, and serving as the final decision-making authority on transfers and releases of detainees in U.S. control.[85] The OSD staff, including primarily the General Counsel and the Under-Secretary of Defense for Policy (USD-P) have the primary roles in oversight and policy guidance for the law of war program as a whole,[86] while USD-P has the primary responsibility to "[r]eview, ensure coordination of, and approve all implementing policy or guidance developed pursuant to" the DoD Directive on the Detainee Program and serve as the principal interlocutor with the ICRC.[87] Within the office of USD-P, the position of Deputy Assistant Secretary of Defense (DASD) for Detainee Affairs was created in 2005. The DASD played the principal role in coordinating all views on detainee policy, and making recommendations to the DSD for approval of changes or transfers and releases. The Joint Staff and the General Counsel make recommendations as well, but the DASD for Detainee Affairs plays the central clearinghouse role. As a result, OSD-Policy often promulgates detainee policy guidance, which flows downrange to deployed military, generally through the Combatant Command bureaucracy (CENTCOM for Iraq and Afghanistan and SOUTHCOM for Guantanamo Bay).

---

[84] *See* Second Periodic Report of the United States to the Committee against Torture, May 6, 2005, http://www.state.gov/j/drl/rls/c14907.htm; Second and Third Periodic Reports of the United States of America to the UN Committee on Human Rights concerning the International Covenant on Civil and Political Rights, Oct. 21, 2005, http://www.state.gov/j/drl/rls/55504.htm; *and* Fourth Periodic Report of the United States of America to the UN Committee on Human Rights concerning the International Covenant on Civil and Political Rights, Dec. 30, 2011, http://www.state.gov/j/drl/rls/179781.htm.

[85] Under the Bush administration, Deputy Secretary of Defense Gordon England played an extremely active role in making changes to DoD detention policy related to operations in Iraq, Afghanistan, and Guantanamo, and reviewing the detention of each captured individual being held at Guantanamo Bay. Deputy Secretary of Defense William J. Lynn, under the Obama administration continued this role, serving as the senior official to approve detainee transfers and releases, and to represent the DoD view in all interagency meetings at the DC and PC level.

[86] *See* DoD Law of War Program, *supra* note 29, ¶¶ 5.1–5.2.

[87] *Id.* ¶ 5.1.

The Joint Staff also has a Detainee Affairs Division, which serves as the Joint Staff office for the DoD Detainee Affairs Program, to liaise with the DASD Detainee Affairs, OSD, Combatant Commands, and State Department, and to represent Joint Staff views, assist with congressional inquiries, and receive ICRC reports.[88] Because OSD-Policy and the Joint Staff have held differing opinions on a variety of detainee-related issues, these are generally adjudicated at the DSD-level. When they cannot be resolved, they are elevated to the Secretary of Defense, who will hear views from the Chairman of the Joint Chiefs of Staff, the DSD, and the Under Secretary of Defense for Policy before arriving at a decision. The fact that the Secretary of Defense has been personally involved in a variety of detainee issues over the past decade is astounding, but a reflection of the reality of this complex issue. To complicate matters, the Secretary of Defense has often arrived at a position yet still felt compelled to bring it to the interagency PC for final approval before promulgation.

At the operational level, there is also an extremely robust grouping of military personnel dedicated to detainee issues, starting first at the Combatant Commands (COCOMs), and principally at CENTCOM and SOUTHCOM, who between them cover all of the current military operations stemming from the conflicts in Afghanistan and Iraq, and Guantanamo Bay, Cuba. Lawyers within the Staff Judge Advocate (SJA) Office at CENTCOM play a key role in advising the Combatant Commander on the law of war and the existing U.S. legal interpretations, and where on the ground there may be a need for additional guidance or assistance to ensure that these operations are being performed consistently and in accordance with the various levels of guidance available. At SOUTHCOM, the SJA Office provides the SOUTHCOM Combatant Commander with guidance and oversight of the detention facilities at Guantanamo Bay. When the ICRC provides a report on any of the detention facilities under the purview of a Combatant Commander, it is the expectation that these lawyers will brief the Combatant Commanders and make recommendations regarding any possible corrective measures needed.[89]

In theaters of active war, there are varying levels of personnel dedicated to detention operations, to include the SJA assigned to the Commander of U.S. Forces in-theater, as well as lawyers embedded with each of the operational units actively engaging in combat hostilities. In both Iraq and Afghanistan, embedded lawyers with the operational units have provided local advice and guidance on detainee issues and coordinated it with the in-country and COCOM SJAs. From the moment of capture, a detainee is initially screened at a battlefield location to ensure that this individual actually is an enemy fighter. This has become all the more complicated in recent wars given the enemy combatants are generally not wearing uniforms or other instinctive insignia, whereas it was a much more

---

[88] *See* Chairman of the Joint Chiefs of Staff Instruction, CJCSI 3290.01B, Program for Detainee Operations ¶ 5(e) (Feb. 9, 2007).

[89] *See* Chapter 12 of this volume for a more detailed discussion on DoD relations with the ICRC.

perfunctory role in state-on-state conflict where practically everyone detained was in enemy uniform. During this initial screening, some tactical information from the detainee may be necessary to clarify his role within the rank and file of enemy force. This information can also be helpful to ongoing operations that may be imminent, which is a collateral benefit of the battlefield screening process.

Once an individual is classified a prisoner of war (POW) through an Article 5 tribunal (there were many POWs in the first fifteen months of the Iraq War), or an Enemy Combatant (EC) who does not meet the Article 5 criteria, the person is removed to a Theater Internment Facility (TIF), where the person is housed with all of the other detainees of the same type. Camp Bucca, the largest TIF in Iraq, swelled to more than twenty-five thousand detainees at the height of the Iraq War, and then consistent with the international laws of war, was drawn down by the U.S. forces in an orderly fashion at the end of the war when all detainees were released, prosecuted by the Iraqi government, or otherwise turned over to the Iraqi government for their disposition.[90] Third-country nationals fighting in Iraq who had been detained were returned to their host nations. As the drawdown in Afghanistan is currently underway, there is a plan to similarly drawdown all of the detention facilities in Afghanistan, and transition the existing Detention Facility at Parwan over to the Afghan government as well.[91] Furthermore, there have been significant efforts to develop the criminal justice system in Afghanistan to prosecute those responsible for crimes they may have committed against the Afghan people, or for other acts of terrorism, which will assist the Afghan government in handling these individuals in the future.[92] At all of these facilities, and Guantanamo Bay, there exists today some of America's proudest and most dedicated military personnel. Developing this professional cadre over the past decade has taken significant effort through endless training and extensive oversight from military inspection teams, and through punishing individuals who have failed to meet the standards that the U.S. military expects.[93] At the end of the day, there is no finer force detaining enemy prisoners anywhere in the world, and the challenge for the U.S. government will be to maintain this level of readiness for future conflicts. The United States did not enter the new millennium in 2000 with adequate policy and other preparations (such as interrogator expertise, etc.) to detain thousands of enemy fighters, and it cannot afford to make that mistake again.

To assist these personnel to meet the standards that are set, there are numerous publications, and guidelines that are described in more depth earlier in this

---

[90] *See U.S. Detains Nearly 25,000 in Iraq*, http://rawstory.com/news/afp/us_detains_nearly_25000_ in _Iraq; *U.S. Military Closes Detention Camp in Iraq*, CNN News, Sept. 17, 2009, http://articles.cnncom/keyword/camp-bucca.

[91] *See* Rod Nordland, *U.S. and Afghanistan Agree on Prisoner Transfer as Part of Long-Term Agreement*, N.Y. Times, Mar. 9, 2012, *available at* http://www.nytimes.com/2012/03/10/world/asia/us-and-afghanistan-agree-prisoner-transfer-part-long-term-agreement.html.

[92] *See Corrections Programs in Afghanistan*, Fact Sheet, Bureau of International Narcotics and Law Enforcement Affairs, May 4, 2012, http://www.state.gov/j/inl/rls/fs/189319.htm.

[93] *See infra* notes 60–62 and accompanying text.

chapter that help to ensure uniformity in treatment and understanding of the requirements.[94] The Army Field Manual,[95] service-specific handbooks [96] and specific guidance that can come in many forms[97] help guide detainee personnel on a daily basis. Although there is often a desire at the Department of Defense to delegate authority down to the battlefield commanders, these same commanders often turn around and request "guidance" or "policy" from above to assist them in making decisions that will withstand the varying levels of scrutiny. Accordingly, there is a push-and-pull effect to the detainee policy guidance.

V. Strategic-Level Detention Issues

Whereas the prior section generally described the process for making strategic-level decisions within the U.S. government, this section will address some of the most significant strategic-level issues that have been, and will continue to be, under discussion at the highest levels of the U.S. government regarding detention operations.

A. CHARACTER OF THE CONFLICT

From the beginning of an operation, the first and most critical decision is how to characterize the conflict. Is it an inter-state conflict between High Contracting Parties of the Geneva Conventions, a military operation where the United States is supporting a nation in an internal struggle against insurgents or guerilla warriors, or a conflict against a transnational nonstate actor, such as that against al Qaeda? The initial determination as to whether the conflict is considered an international armed conflict or a non-international armed conflict has significant implications for the legal framework on detention, and the likely status of captured individuals. As the congressional AUMF for Afghanistan authorized the President to use "all necessary means" against those responsible for the 9/11 attacks and their conspirators and supporters, and military action began against Afghanistan's Taliban government who harbored them, the United States took the position that it was engaged in an international armed conflict against the Taliban and al Qaeda, a nonstate actor that behaved like a state actor due to its ability to wage war on a global scale.[98] The U.S. Supreme Court later ruled that the war with al Qaeda was instead a non-international armed conflict because al

---

[94] *See supra* note 46.

[95] *See generally Army Field Manual, supra* note 46.

[96] *See, e.g.*, NWP 1-14M, *supra* note 1, ch. 11 (setting forth the Navy's procedures for detainee operations in accordance with applicable DoD Instructions and Directions.).

[97] Specific guidance can come from the Secretary of Defense, Chairman of the Joint Chiefs of Staff or their delegees in various forms, including "policy guidance," "operational orders," or "fragmentary orders (FRAGOs)," as examples.

[98] *See supra* note 50.

Qaeda was not a High Contracting Party of the Geneva Conventions.[99] The difference between the international armed conflict and the non-international armed conflict legal regimes was significant in this case where neither al Qaeda nor the Taliban was determined by the Court to qualify for POW status. Accordingly, they fell outside of the principal protections in the Geneva Conventions. Given that the United States did not believe as a matter of law that Common Article 3 was applicable as a matter of customary law to all armed conflicts (rather than to non-international armed conflict alone, as it says on its face), this left the United States with a particularly scarce set of rules that it felt were legally binding on the treatment of our detainees.

The character of the conflict discussion was also significant in Iraq. As the initial phase of the Iraq war was principally a state-on-state conflict between two High Contracting Parties to the Geneva Conventions, the captured individuals who were part of the former Iraqi military and regime were considered to be POWs and afforded the full provisions of the Third Geneva Convention. On June 28, 2004, when sovereignty was restored for the interim Iraqi government,[100] arguably the character of the conflict changed as well, from an international armed conflict with Iraq to an operation where the United States was supporting an Iraqi government under attack from insurgents in its territory. Prime Minister Ayad Allawi requested ongoing support for security operations in Iraq until such time as his forces were capable of carrying out security operations.[101] Resolution 1546 provided the multinational force in Iraq the "authority to take all necessary measures to contribute to the maintenance of security and stability in Iraq," to which U.S. Secretary of State Colin Powell included "internment where ... necessary for imperative reasons of security."[102] The "imperative reasons of security" language in the Powell letter was taken from Article 78 of the Fourth Geneva Convention, which addresses the responsibilities of an Occupying Power when "it considers it necessary ... to take safety measures concerning protected persons."[103] Given that the Iraqi government would no longer be in a state of legal occupation after June 30, 2004, this use of the Fourth Geneva Convention's occupation language was an interesting choice, and perhaps the most analogous situation the administration could find to authorize continued use of security detention after the occupation ended. Were they civilians taking part in active hostilities against the Iraqi government who could be held under the laws of war, or were they more akin to regular criminals entitled to judicial due process of law in Iraqi courts? In this later non-international armed conflict

---

[99] *See generally* Hamdan v. Rumsfeld, 548 U.S. 557, 634 (2006).

[100] Sec. Res. 1546, SC/8117, June 8, 2004 (restoring Iraq sovereignty as of June 30, 2004).

[101] Letter of Ayad Allawi to the U.N. Security Council (June 5, 2004), *available at* http://www.un.org/Newa/Press/docs/2004/sc8117.doc.htm (stating "[u]ntil we are able to provide security for ourselves, including the defense of Iraq's land, sea, and air space, we ask for the support of the Security Council and the international community in this endeavor.").

[102] Letter of Secretary of State Colin Powell to the U.N. Security Council (June 5, 2004), *available at* http://www.un.org/Newa/Press/docs/2004/sc8117.doc.htm.

[103] *Geneva Convention IV, supra* note 14, art. 78.

regime, the rules for detention were different than those that existed during the POW phase of the Iraq war, and accordingly, there were strategic-level decisions on what level of process and protection to provide, and how involved to let Iraqi judges, magistrates, and courts be in the process. In the end, the United States ultimately settled on a hybrid approach that allowed for military detention and capture of Iraqi insurgents in military detention facilities, but also favored their prosecution in the Central Criminal Court of Iraq (CCCI) whenever possible for the crimes they committed, although these individuals were still referred to as security internees consistent with the Powell letter. As U.S. forces began to drawdown in Iraq, the Iraqi Strategic Framework Agreement (SFA) and its Security Agreement[104] set forth a process that required the United States to bring all new captures before an Iraqi magistrate within twenty-four hours of capture.[105] This blending of military capture with due process rights was driven by U.S. and Iraqi competing interests, but may well serve as a template in future operations.

B. CHANGES TO U.S. LEGAL FRAMEWORK

As discussed in some depth in the first section of this chapter, there are both international and domestic legal authorities that govern U.S. detention operations. Any decision to change an existing interpretation of the U.S. legal framework should be accomplished at the strategic level with full interagency coordination and an understanding of all of the implications. There are several areas, including Common Article 3 and Article 75 of Additional Protocol I, where there is a reasonable possibility of changing the U.S. position on legal applicability. For example, DoD Directive 2310.01E currently makes Common Article 3 applicable to all U.S. detention operations.[106] In a future classic inter-state conflict, the United States could determine that it no longer wants to set this as the baseline

[104] The Strategic Framework Agreement for a Relationship of Friendship and Cooperation between the United States of America and the Republic of Iraq, Global Security, http://www.globalsecurity.org/military/library/policy/national/iraq-strategic-framework-agreement.htm (last visited Feb. 10, 2013); Fact Sheet, *The Iraq Strategic Framework Agreement and the Security Agreement with Iraq*, http://georgebush-whitehouse/archives.gov/infocus/iraq (last visited Mar. 2, 2013). The Iraqi Strategic Framework Agreement (SFA) was the agreement between Iraq and the United States to govern the future overall political, economic, and security relationship between the United States and Iraq, while a separate Security Agreement was also reached with the Iraqi government to address the continued responsibilities and expectations of the parties for U.S. Forces remaining in Iraq, known as the Agreement between the United States of America and the Republic of Iraq on the Withdrawal of United States Forces from Iraq and the Organization of Their Activities during Their Temporary Presence in Iraq. This Security Agreement had many of the same categories as a traditional Status of Forces agreement (SOFA), but went beyond providing operational guidance as to what type of operations the military could engage in, which branch of the Iraqi government had to remain fully informed, and most important for this chapter, what process requirements would attach to Iraqi citizens captured by U.S. forces during military operations.

[105] SFA, *id.*, art. 22 (requiring all detentions to be in "accordance with Iraqi law" and to have all detained individuals brought before an Iraqi magistrate within twenty-four hours).

[106] DoD Law of War Program, *supra* note 29, ¶ 4.2.

standard for detention operations, and if the U.S. position at that time remains that Common Article 3 is not customary international law, this Directive could be rescinded. Because of the international implications of such a decision, it is clear that a strategic-level decision from the highest levels of the government would be warranted. In addition, if the Senate were to ratify Additional Protocol I, making it legally binding on the United States, there would be a need to review our current position on Article 75, which was established in 2011 to ensure it is fully compliant with the treaty. Further, any new law-of-war treaty with implications for detention practices, such as a Comprehensive Legal Framework Document on Detention, or an Additional Protocol 5 to the Geneva Conventions that addresses wars with a nonstate actor, would require strategic-level guidance.[107]

As for domestic legal authority, there are strategic-level decisions associated with almost all engagement by the Congress on specific detainee issues. Whether and how to engage Congress on pending legislation is an issue that must be coordinated within the interagency and the White House. Although all of the agencies have opposed current legislation regarding restrictions on transfers from Guantanamo Bay, the interagency still has to make a strategic-level decision about which issues they will take up with Congress, and which issues would cause the President to use a Presidential veto on a defense bill (which is rarely done, particularly in time of war.) Furthermore, the question as to whether to seek additional new legislation, or to modify legislation, is also a strategic-level decision. The DoD, for example, cannot make these decisions on their own, even during wartime when battlefield exigencies are arguably at their highest. The AUMF is a good example. There have been myriad debates over the past five years regarding the need to update the current AUMF applicable in the ongoing conflict with al Qaeda.[108] An AUMF that is linked to the 9/11 perpetrators and co-conspirators, who were carrying out operations in training camps in the Afghanistan and Pakistan region, becomes much more challenging to apply to a twenty-year-old who is captured fighting in the same region in 2012, or even removed in a place such as the Horn of Africa or Yemen. On 9/11, this fighter would have been about eight years old and therefore hardly able to conspire to commit 9/11. Furthermore, as the al Qaeda group structure continues to morph, organizations that were not part of al Qaeda on 9/11 might be now, and accordingly, an AUMF who is caught

---

[107] There has been a significant amount of discussion and debate over the utility of engaging in a process to develop an additional Geneva Convention, such as Additional Protocol 5 or otherwise, to address modern conflicts that do not fit as neatly into the existing Geneva Conventions. Although the window of opportunity to do so may be closing, it should not be ruled out that a process involving the key countries that do engage in armed conflict, and possibly even the ICRC, could help provide more clarity across the board on treatment for future captures.

[108] *See* Karl S. Chang, *Enemy Status and Military Detention in the War against al-Qaeda*, 47 Texas Int'l L.J. 1 (2012) (discussing who fits within the definition of an enemy under the AUMF); Glenn Greenwald, *Congress Endorsing Military Detention, a New AUMF*, Salon, Dec. 1, 2011, http://www.salon.com/2011/12/01/congress-endorsing-military-detention/ (describing legislation by Senators Carl Levin and John McCain that would expand AUMF language to individuals that "substantially supports" al Qaida, the Taliban, or "associated forces.").

in a different time frame and operational environment may not be as useful for U.S. detention operations today as a new one would be.

Last, on legal framework, there is an abundance of specific legal issues that have broad implications on U.S. detention operations as a whole, and accordingly, they take on a strategic significance. These issues are addressed throughout this book, but a few include the legal discussions with U.S. allies, the ICRC, and the broader external human rights community on the legal meaning of "direct participation in hostilities," and the definition of material support and how it applies in an armed conflict scenario, as examples.

C. WHEN MORE COULD BE LESS

Another key area for strategic-level decision-making is how far beyond minimum standards the United States should go in setting treatment standards. The humanitarian in most public servants will generally gravitate toward wanting to provide the highest standards of treatment possible, and for members of the U.S. military, it is harder to find a group that is more infused with a sense of doing what is right.[109] While previous sections of this chapter have hinted that there is a cost in the media and international community to doing less than what some believe the law requires, there may also be strategic costs for doing more than what the law requires. Specifically, through the ever-growing category of customary international law, there is a risk that a consistent pattern of treatment above the minimum standards required under international law will actually move the law to a new place. In fact, this may be a motivating factor for outside groups, which urge the United States to be the "beacon on the hill" and take the moral high ground on these detainee issues. If the United States raises the standard of treatment, others will likely follow, and over time customary international law may evolve to a point where the United States has in fact ceded some flexibility that might be necessary during times of war, even if it is not the preferred daily practice.

A good example of this might be the U.S. treatment of the Viet Cong during the Vietnam War. As a matter of law, the Vietcong were an irregular armed force that did not quality for POW status under the Geneva Conventions due to the fact that they did not wear uniforms or instinctive insignia, they did not carry their weapons openly (they attacked at night, and blended in during the day), and they did not follow the laws of war in their operations. As a matter of policy, the U.S. treated them as POWs, even though they were not legally entitled,

---

[109] This comment is in no way intended to reflect a view that individual service members have not engaged in both abhorrent and aberrant behavior while engaged in detainee operations. However, the vast majority of military service members are motivated by doing the right thing, and being respected by society for their actions. One will have a hard time finding a more dedicated and honorable group of military personnel than the guard force at Guantanamo Bay, who strive daily to find activities to stimulate the detainees, and to increase their contact with their family members around the world and their lawyers.

presumably because the United States felt a sense of moral duty because it was the right thing, and perhaps also under the mistaken belief that a high standard of treatment for the Vietcong would ensure that U.S. POWs held by the North Vietnamese forces would reciprocally be treated well.[110] This same strategic-level decision has surfaced with respect to Taliban and al Qaeda forces during the last ten years as well. Even though al Qaeda, and at least many Taliban forces,[111] have failed to meet the standards under the Geneva Conventions to be afforded POW status, there have been numerous recommendations to give them the higher level of treatment because the United States is an honorable nation. It is important to consider, however, whether or not all future irregular forces that do not follow the requirements of the Geneva Conventions should be eligible for POW status, which affords benefits that were originally designed to incentivize honorable military conduct. By removing one incentive for Geneva Conventions compliant behavior, we may be setting precedent or even establishing unintended customary international law in an area. Why would any irregular armed force ever be incentivized to distinguish themselves from the regular population again?

D. WHERE TO DETAIN INDIVIDUALS

While the Geneva Conventions require captured individuals to be detained in a safe area away from the immediate zone of danger of the battlefield,[112] the decision on where to house captured individuals was traditionally made within the theater of command to reflect the battlefield realities. In the post 9/11 world, however, where to detain captured individuals has been a strategic-level question. In the early days in Afghanistan, the United States captured detainees and held them aboard military vessels in transit to an actual detention site once the United States had established one.[113] Even after establishing an initial foothold in Afghanistan, a decision was made to remove nearly eight hundred individuals captured in Afghanistan and over the border in Pakistan by the Northern Alliance and to transfer them to Guantanamo Bay, Cuba. The original decision to use Guantanamo Bay was made in Washington, DC, at the highest levels of the U.S. government, presumably out of a belief that these captured individuals from

---

[110] *See* Forman, *supra* note 2.

[111] Because the Bush administration made a strategic-level decision that no member of al Qaida or the Taliban could be considered as POWs, Article 5 tribunals to determine status of a particular member of either organization were never conducted. *See* Jay S. Bybee, Office of Legal Counsel, Memorandum to Albert R. Gonzales, Memo 12, Feb. 7, 2002, *available at: The Torture Papers: The Road to Abu Ghraib*, http://www.american-buddha.com/911.memoforalbert2.7.02.htm. It is entirely plausible that an individual member of the Taliban who wore a distinctive insignia (headdress), carried a weapon openly, and followed the laws of war might have been eligible for POW status if an Article 5 tribunal had been conducted.

[112] *See Geneva Convention III, supra* note 14, art. 19.

[113] *British Group Alleges U.S. Used Ships as Prisons*, USA Today, June 2, 2008, http://www.usatoday30.usatoday.com/2008-06-02-britian-us_N.htm (advising of U.S. Navy statements that the United States had held small numbers of people for short periods of time on board the vessels).

more than forty countries were extremely dangerous, and were valuable targets for intelligence collection efforts in an area away from the field of battle.

Although reasonable minds do differ about the threat level of this early tranche of detainees that went to Guantanamo Bay, it is difficult to tell what real value the United States has gotten from taking them out of the theater of war. It has been alleged that the real reason for this move was to put the detainees into a "legal black hole"[114] where no real law applied so that they could be interrogated more harshly than they could have been in Afghanistan. This author does not believe the allegation; however, whatever original motivation existed to move detainees out of Afghanistan, it is clear that the overall strategic effect has been negative. Guantanamo Bay will likely go down in history as one of the U.S. government's largest stains on its human rights and justice record. Furthermore, transferring detainees out of Guantanamo Bay to their home countries or third countries has been extremely difficult diplomatically, and in certain circumstances impossible, and has cost the U.S. precious diplomatic capital that was needed during the Iraq and Afghanistan wars. And ultimately, the U.S. court system is now more integrally involved in the review of military detainees captured on foreign battlefields than ever before, an outcome that may have a negative ability on the executive branch's ability to fight future wars abroad without court interference at home.

Clearly, Guantanamo Bay failed to achieve the intended positive strategic effect. The strategic issue for current and future operations is how to prevent new captures from being transferred to Guantanamo Bay. Up until 2008, battlefield commanders were more than willing to send suspected high-level al Qaeda members to Guantanamo Bay and out of their theater. However, although the detainees sent out of theater may lessen the initial burden in-theater, they exponentially increased the burden on the rest of the U.S. government, which spends an inordinate amount of time negotiating for transfers or release, and defending the detainee cases in federal court. Accordingly, in future strategic choices regarding whether to keep detainees in theater or to send them somewhere else, strong consideration to the negative lessons of Guantanamo Bay should be considered.

VI. A Strategic View of the Future of Detention Operations

The past decade-plus since 9/11 has demonstrated that military detention in the modern era is complex and costly. Battlefield detention has come increasingly under attack from a due process standpoint, partly because no courts or judges are involved, partly because membership in a group (an armed force) can be sufficient to warrant detention, and perhaps in part because the military is not completely trusted, particularly when they are engaged in operations that cannot be fully transparent. Whatever the reasons, however, the single most important

---

[114] *See, e.g.*, Johan Steyn, *Guantanamo Bay: The Legal Black Hole*, Twenty-Seventh F.A. Mann Lecture, Nov. 25, 2003, http://www.statewatch.org/news/2003/nov/guantanamo.pdf.

strategic goal on detention is to ensure that legitimate, lawful, battlefield detention remain one of the key weapons the United States has in its arsenal to win future conflicts. The U.S. military cannot allow this authority to be taken away or even eroded, because keeping enemies off the battlefield remains one of the key cornerstones to any military offensive. In order to maintain this authority during these challenging times, the U.S. military will have to use detention authority appropriately, lawfully, and even judiciously. Battlefield detention is not indefinite in nature: it must end at the duration of hostilities, and accordingly, the United States must be prepared to release the remaining detainees at Guantanamo Bay when this conflict ends. Although some argue that this conflict will not end at any time soon, there are competing theories that would argue the United States is nearing a military victor against al Qaeda. As for the Taliban, if there is a peace agreement between the Afghan government and the Taliban, it would seem very odd for the United States to continue to hold Taliban detainees in connection with the conflict that began in Afghanistan. Some individuals the United States ultimately releases may even pose a continuing threat against the United States in the future, but battlefield detention does not allow the United States to hold them forever under law of armed conflict authority. Conversely, if these individuals have committed a crime, then they can be charged for the crimes they have committed, and if convicted, be incarcerated as convicted war criminals.

Along similar lines, the United States will need to maintain its current high level of adherence to the international laws of war governing detention operations. This will assist in maintaining legitimacy for battlefield detention. And last, the United States should continue to seek critical alliances with key allies to continue to press for rational and militarily useful interpretations of the law of armed conflict. Key U.S. allies have the same interests in preserving detention authority, and these strategic alliances have been critical to gaining acceptance for the notion that the United States is at war with a transnational nonstate actor. Pre-9/11, none of the U.S. key allies agreed with this principle; however, due to strategic engagement, there has been a steady and growing support for this proposition.[115]

Beyond some of the strategic-level issues raised above, the U.S. military should aim to normalize detention operations to the greatest extent possible into routine military operations, which are handled at the lowest level possible. With appropriate guidelines, and the existing manuals, publications, and level of training available on detainee issues, the U.S. military should get back into a mode where well-trained forces know how to best handle detainee matters locally. Taking decision-making out of the theater of war back to Washington, DC, is not a sustainable or desirable end state in future conflicts.

The next few years may bring some finality regarding the fate of Guantanamo Bay and inevitably, the remaining 140 or so detainees will be tried by military

---

[115] *See, e.g.*, Noah Lubbell, Extraterritorial Use of Force against Non-state Actors (2010); Hew Strachan & Sibulle Scheipers, The Changing Character of War (2011).

commission or released. There is a significant disparity in threat level among the remaining population, comprised of High-Value Detainees from the CIA detention program, as well as nearly a hundred Yemenis, who vary in threat but cannot return home due to the country's inability to mitigate their threat in any way, and another twenty or so detainees of varying threat levels who cannot be repatriated or transferred to third countries for other reasons.[116] The U.S. government would be smart to continue the current focus of the military commissions on the highest threats, and most criminalized subset of these detainees, including those responsible for the attack on the USS *Cole*, the U.S. Embassies in Kenya and Tanzania, and 9/11. The rest should be repatriated and/or released as this conflict draws down. This will leave the best legacy for U.S. detention operations as a whole, and for the military commissions that got off to a rocky and slow start.

As for new captures, it is highly unlikely that newly captured individuals will be sent to Guantanamo Bay, as President Obama has previously ruled that option out. Even in the event of a high-threat and high-value new capture, it would not make strategic sense to revisit this policy. Any detainee who goes to Guantanamo Bay is entitled to federal habeas corpus review of his or her detention.[117] Although the U.S. government's record of winning these federal habeas corpus hearings is very high for individuals captured back in the early days of the war in Afghanistan, it would be a much more challenging case to bring a 2013 or 2014 capture from outside of the "hot" battlefield of Afghanistan against the current AUMF, which is in essence frozen in time.[118] New captures in Afghanistan will likely go to the existing facility at Parwan until it is transferred to Afghan control, and beyond that the U.S. military should ensure that there are adequate detention facilities in any theater of operation for future military captures who are not going to be prosecuted. Detainees who will be prosecuted under regular U.S. law could be brought to the United States, rather than Guantanamo Bay, and there will likely be a handful of such cases in the upcoming years. Federal habeas review is required and necessary for the legacy Guantanamo Bay population, given their location, history, and time in detention. It should not, however, be the bedrock of future military detention. The U.S. military must ensure that it conducts appropriate Article 5 tribunals, and periodic reviews to ensure that military commanders continue to have the authority in theater to make determinations regarding who should be detained during military hostilities.

Future U.S. detention operations around the globe will have a much heavier due process element than in the past. In the early days of the conflicts in Afghanistan and Iraq, there was no attention paid to gathering "evidence" at the point of capture, or maintaining records that could ultimately be used in an

---

[116] Jennifer Daskal, *Don't Close Guantanamo*, N.Y. Times, Jan. 10, 2013, at Opinion Pages, http://www.nytimes.com2013/01/11/opinion/dont-close-guantanamo.html?_ro; Jonathan Karl, *"High-Value" Detainees Transferred to Guantanamo*, ABC News, *available at* http://abcnews.go.com/International/story?id=2400470 (last visited Sept. 6, 2006).

[117] Boumediene v. Bush, 553 U.S. 723 (2008).

[118] *See* Chang, *supra* note 108, at 1–6 (discussing the limits of the AUMF).

Afghan or Iraqi court. However, by 2008, this was commonplace in both theaters, and evidence was regularly being brought into the Afghan court system and the CCCI in Iraq. United States' forces will continue this trend moving forward, as prosecution at home or abroad is one key way to neutralize enemies, and in many circumstances, battlefield detention will not be possible. This trend toward criminalizing military operations has been relatively successful, and will likely continue, particularly as the conflict with al Qaeda begins to dissipate. Terrorists, whether behaving as an organized military force or not, may be prosecuted for their crimes, and this is the way most of the U.S. allies and third countries prefer to do it. If the United States wants them to play a role, then it may well need evidence.

Global terrorism is not going away, and the United States may need to increase its participation in international fora and dialogues with countries who routinely conduct military operations, to ensure that it has a seat at the table when countries decide to fill the gaps in existing laws. Staying outside the tent of international dialogues has never served the United States well, so this is an area where the United States can help to lead the debate and process. The rules for classic state-on-state conflict will probably change very little, although the United States may see fewer of these conflicts as compared to asymmetric, insurgent, or non-traditional forces joining the fight. In this light, the gap between the Additional Protocol I and Additional Protocol II States Party and the United States may grow wider. Although U.S. senior officials have complained that the Geneva Conventions do not provide specific enough guidance in a conflict with an organization such as al Qaeda,[119] other countries argue that the guidance is already there in the Additional Protocols. The United States would do well to revisit its position on this and make sure it is the right one for the future.

For other non-international armed conflicts, ongoing daily in places such as Colombia, the Democratic Republic of the Congo, and Syria among others, there will be a tension between some traditional romantic deference to "freedom fighters" and the growing fear of terrorists who are joining local insurgencies. If anything, there will be more efforts to clarify the rules in countries where this is a problem.

VII. Conclusion

The U.S. strategic goal for detention operations should be to preserve as much authority as possible for future conflicts and to exercise it wisely. By doing so,

---

[119] Vijay M. Padmanabhan & John B. Bellinger III, *Detention Operations in Contemporary Conflict: Four Challenges for the Geneva Conventions and Other Existing Law*, Social Science Research Network, Dec. 10, 2010, http://papers.ssrn.com/sol3/ papers.cfm?abstract-id=1734922; John B. Bellinger III, *Red Cross Conference Acknowledges "Gaps" in International Humanitarian Law Governing Detention*, LAWFARE (Dec. 3, 2011, 3:59 PM), http://wwwlawfareblog.com/2011/12/red-cross-conference-acknowledges-gaps-in-international-humanitarian -law-governing-detention/.

the United States is in the best position to utilize this humane alternative to killing on the battlefield, win its nation's wars quickly and decisively by removing threats early from the fight, and still remain the beacon on the hill for others to look up to and follow. There are many lessons from the past decade that can inform this administration and future decision-makers as they formulate detainee policy through the various Department of Defense and interagency processes. External players, such as the media, Congress, and ICRC will continue to play a crucial role. The United States should also continue to work with allies on the establishment of a broad-based acceptable international legal framework that permits law-of-war detention across the spectrum of conflict, even as it continues to whittle down the remaining Guantanamo Bay population. A solid U.S. law-of-war detainee program is a key component of the U.S. national defense and strategy now and in the future.

10 }

Detention Operations at the Tactical and Operational Levels

A PROCEDURAL APPROACH

Jeffrey Bovarnick* and Jack Vrett**

Detaining authorities should develop and implement standard operating procedures and other relevant guidance regarding the handling of detainees.[1]

I. Introduction

From the time military operations in Afghanistan moved from an international armed conflict to a non-international armed conflict over a decade ago,[2] detention

* Colonel Jeff Bovarnick is a U.S. Army judge advocate. He obtained his JD from New England Law, Boston and his LLM from the U.S. Army Judge Advocate General's School, Charlottesville, VA. Colonel Bovarnick's prior assignments include: Chief, International and Operational Law, Combined Joint Task Force-180, Bagram, Afghanistan; Chief, Investigative Judge Team, Law and Order Task Force, Forward Operating Base Shield, Iraq; Chair, International and Operational Law Department, The Judge Advocate General's Legal Center & School, Charlottesville; and Staff Judge Advocate, 101st Airborne Division (Air Assault), Fort Campbell, Kentucky, and Combined Joint Task Force–101, Bagram, Afghanistan. Colonel Bovarnick is currently assigned as a student at the U.S. Army War College, Carlisle, Pennsylvania. He would like to thank his coauthor for his expertise and input to this chapter and also Professor (LTC) Shane Reeves, USMA, for the edits of this book chapter, and Professors Geoffrey Corn and Rachel VanLandingham for the opportunity to write this chapter. The positions and opinions in this chapter are those of the author and do not represent the official views of the Department of Defense or the United States Army.

** Jack Vrett is a former U.S. Army Judge Advocate who served as the Chief of International & Operational Law for the 101st Airborne Division while on active duty and currently practices law in Chicago, IL.

1 Principle 5, The Copenhagen Process: Principles and Guidelines (Oct. 18–19, 2012), *available at* http://um.dk/en/~/media/UM/English-site/Documents/Politics-and-diplomacy/Copenhangen%20Process%20Principles%20and%20Guidelines.pdf. [hereinafter Copenhagen Principles].

2 *See generally* Michael N. Schmitt, *The War in Afghanistan: A Legal Analysis*, 85 INT'L L. STUD. (2009); GEOFFREY S. CORN, THE WAR ON TERROR AND THE LAW OF WAR: A MILITARY PERSPECTIVE (2009); Jeff Bovarnick, *Detainee Review Boards in Afghanistan: From Strategic Liability to Legitimacy*, ARMY LAW. 9 (June 2012). It is undisputed that Afghanistan was initially a Common Article 2 international armed conflict, thus triggering the full body of the law of war, including of course, GC III

operations have received intense scrutiny from all branches of the United States' government and the international community. While the President, Congress, and the courts executed, legislated, and litigated detention policy and laws at the strategic level, commanders and military lawyers at the operational and tactical levels worked within vague legal constructs for the handling of detainees between 2002 and 2009. However, since 2009 the United States has significantly enhanced the policies and procedures for all aspects of detention operations in Afghanistan.

Whereas the previous chapter provided an in-depth analysis and discussion of the strategic view of detention operations, this chapter provides an overview of detention operations at the operational and tactical levels, and examines the key legal principles and practical issues that military legal advisors must consider when advising commanders and operators at these levels.

Part II of this chapter discusses the numerous pre-capture considerations that impact detention operations. Part III then briefly reviews detention operations from 2002 to 2009 to highlight the evolution of the detainee review process during the prolonged conflict in Afghanistan. Finally, Part IV focuses on the efforts of commanders and operational lawyers to implement an improved detainee review process at U.S. detention facilities in Afghanistan.

II. Background

> The danger of al Qaeda is well known. . . . But we refuse to allow this enemy, with its contemptible tactics, to define the way in which we wage war. Our efforts remain grounded in the rule of law. In this unconventional conflict, we apply conventional legal principles . . . found in treaties and customary international law.[3]

Before planning for detention operations at the operational and tactical levels, military planners, including legal advisors and operators, must consider the nature of the military operation and the strategic objectives of the operation. Conflict classification, as described in detail in Chapter 2 of this volume, is essential in determining what sources of law apply. The nature of the conflict (international or non-international), along with the strategic objectives of the operations, will guide all policies and procedures that come afterward.

In many ways, the more traditional the conflict, the easier the legal equation becomes. When U.S. forces engage in international (inter-state) armed conflicts,

---

and its prisoner-of-war provisions. Exactly when the Common Article 2 conflict ended is a matter of debate (e.g., when the Taliban surrendered Kandahar, their seat of government, on December 9, 2001; when the Bonn Agreement was signed on December 20, 2001; or when President Hamid Karzai was elected on June 13, 2002); however, few dispute that after Karzai was appointed by the Loya Jirga in June 2002, the armed conflict clearly became an internal armed conflict.

[3] Jeh Charles Johnson, *The Conflict against Al Qaeda and Its Affiliates: How Will It End* (Nov. 30, 2012), *available at* http://www.lawfareblog.com/2012/11/jeh-johnson-speech-at-the-oxford-union/#_ftn24.

the Geneva Convention Relative to the Treatment of Prisoners of War[4] and the Geneva Convention Relative to the Protection of Civilian Persons in Time of War[5] provide the almost exclusive legal foundation for all detentions. At the most simplistic level, detainees captured in the context of such conflicts are either enemy prisoners of war (EPWs), or civilians interned (CIs) as a threat to the security of friendly forces. These two treaties provide the criteria for assessing which category an individual detainee falls into. They also indicate both the process that must be provided in the detention decision-making and continuation process, and the treatment obligations for these detainees.

This does not eliminate uncertainty as to a detainee's status, even during an international armed conflict. It is now clear that U.S. interpretation of the law of armed conflict (LOAC) allows for a third detainee classification: unprivileged enemy belligerent.[6] This detainee classification accounts for those enemy belligerent operatives who fail to satisfy the individual qualification requirements established by Article 4 of the GPW (carry arms openly, wear a fixed distinctive emblem recognizable at a distance, operate under responsible command, and conduct operations in accordance with the laws and customs of war)[7] and therefore are not considered a prisoner of war (POW). It was this failure that led President George W. Bush to conclude that captured Taliban personnel were not, as a matter of law, entitled to POW status.[8] Although this theory of "third category" detainees in international armed conflict is controversial and rejected by many U.S. allies, it also unquestionably influences the planning and execution of U.S. detainee operations.

Process and treatment requirements for EPWs and CIs is relatively straightforward. Army Regulation 190-8, which applies to all military services, implements the obligations of the GPW and the GC (Geneva Convention).[9] Most significantly, it provides procedural guidelines for use of an Article 5 Tribunal, a fact-finding hearing conducted in accordance with Article 5 of the GPW to resolve doubt as to whether a detainee qualifies for EPW status.[10] Although this process is relatively informal, the provisions of AR 190-8 provide important guidance to lawyers supporting POW operations and ensure a uniform process for

---

[4] *See generally* Geneva Convention Relative to the Treatment of Prisoners of War, Aug. 12, 1949, 6 U.S.T. 3316, 75 U.N.T.S. 135, art. 5[hereinafter GC III].

[5] *See generally* Geneva Convention Relative to the Protection of Civilian Persons in Time of War, Aug. 12, 1949, 6 U.S.T. 3516, 75 U.N.T.S. 287, art. 2 [hereinafter GC IV].

[6] *See* Shane R. Reeves & David Lai, *A Broad Overview of the Law of Armed Conflict in the Age of Terror*, *in* FUNDAMENTALS OF COUNTERTERRORISM LAW 146–47 (Lynn Zusman ed., 2014) (stating "The term unprivileged belligerent, also sometimes referred to as unlawful combatant, is not a distinct individual battlefield status . . . and is instead descriptive for those who unlawfully engage in combat activities by taking a part in hostilities "without being entitled to do so.") (citation omitted).

[7] GC IV, *supra* note 5, art. 4.

[8] Memorandum Op. for the Counsel to the President (Feb. 7, 2002), *available at* http://fas.org/irp/agency/doj/olc/taliban.pdf.

[9] *See generally* U.S. DEP'T OF ARMY, REG. 190–8, ENEMY PRISONERS OF WAR, RETAINED PERSONNEL, CIVILIAN INTERNEES AND OTHER DETAINEES (OCT. 1, 1997).

[10] *Id.* at 1.

the conduct of Article 5 Tribunals. It should be noted, however, that these tribunals are required only when doubt exists as to the status of a detainee.[11] For example, in the case of Taliban captives, President Bush determined that no such doubt existed as to their disqualification from EPW status; thus no such tribunals were ever conducted. AR 190-8 also provides guidance for the conduct of hearings to designate a civilian detainee as a CI, and for periodic review of that determination.[12]

For detainees who do not fall within one of these treaty-based categories, whether in an international armed conflict (the unprivileged enemy belligerent), a non-international armed conflict (because of the inapplicability of these treaty categories), or even during a non-conflict operation such as a peacekeeping mission, procedures must be adopted to ensure no one is subjected to an arbitrary deprivation of liberty. Unlike EPWs and CIs, however, the process provided to validate the asserted justification for detention must, by necessity, be implemented as a matter of policy. Although today there are ongoing efforts to develop internationally recognized best practices for such detention review procedures, the lack of international consensus on the procedural requirements related to such detentions, not to mention the substantive legal authority to detain such individuals, results in an absence of clear legal standards on the issue.

Even so, it is not permissible to subject captives not qualifying as EPWs or CIs to detention without process. It is relatively clear that such an action would be widely condemned as an arbitrary deprivation of liberty in violation of the most fundamental human rights and law of armed conflict principles.[13] Perhaps more important, subjecting individuals to detention with absolutely no process is tactically and operationally counterproductive. First, a simple reality of detention operations is that the necessity of detention is more aggressive at the point of capture when troops are still in harm's way than it is when facts are assessed from a more neutral and reasoned perspective. Establishing some procedure to assess detention justification therefore mitigates the risk of militarily unjustified detentions based on an initial, but perhaps misguided, assessment of necessity. Second, detention operations impose a significant logistical burden on friendly forces. It is counterproductive to bear this burden unnecessarily, and therefore implementing an efficient yet effective process to validate the necessity of detention serves the operational interests of U.S. forces. Finally, it is axiomatic that overzealous detention practices risk alienating the local population, which represents significant risk in most contemporary military operations.[14] Although no

---

[11] *Id.*

[12] *Id.*

[13] *See, e.g.*, Protocol Additional to the Geneva Conventions of 12 August 1949, and Relating to the Protection of Victims of International Armed Conflict (Protocol I) art. 75 June 8, 1977, 1125 U.N.T.S. 3 [hereinafter AP I] (noting that due process is a fundamental guarantee provided to those persons who are in the power of a Party to the conflict).

[14] *See, e.g.*, David Galula, Counterinsurgency Warfare: Theory and Practice 4 (Praeger Sec. Int'l 2006) (1964) (noting that the civilian population is the objective for both the insurgent and counterinsurgent); U.S. Dep't Of Army, Field Manual 3-24 /U.S. Marine Corpswarfighting Publication 3–33.5, Counterinsurgency 1–24 (Dec. 15, 2006) [hereinafter FM 3-24] ("Any human

process is likely to assuage all local and external critics of detention practices, this risk is mitigated by transparent and credible review procedures.

When the United States began detaining what it classified as unlawful enemy combatants (subsequently reclassified as unprivileged enemy belligerents) after initiating combat operations in response to the September 11th terrorist attacks, the significance, duration, and visibility of military detention practices rose to unprecedented significance. After what can only be described as initial stumbling that involved deviation from the procedural practices of the prior decade,[15] a process of developing and implementing detention procedures began, first at Guantanamo, then subsequently extended to Afghanistan.[16] Because the process developed and implemented for detention in Afghanistan has evolved as the doctrinal default standard minimally acceptable to justify the detention of captives who do not qualify as EPWs or CIs, it will be the focal point of this chapter.[17] The probability that this type of captive will continue to dominate U.S. military operations means understanding this process is essential.

In his September 2010 statement, Dr. Jakob Kellenberger, President of the International Committee of the Red Cross, acknowledged four areas in international humanitarian law that may have some legal gaps.[18] One of the highlighted areas included the protection of persons deprived of liberty, particularly in non-international armed conflict regulated only by Common Article 3.[19] A similar observation was provided by John B. Bellinger and Vijay M. Padmanabhan in an article that focused on the problems arising from the state's detention of nonstate actors falling outside the Common Article 2 paradigm.[20] Acknowledging that "a state is left without clear, comprehensive international rules to govern its detention operations,"[21] they posed four questions, two of which are relevant to the chapter: Which individuals are subject to detention? What legal process must the state provide to those detained?[22]

---

rights abuses or legal violations committed by U.S. forces quickly become known throughout the local populace and eventually around the world. Illegitimate actions undermine both long- and short-term COIN efforts.").

[15] *See* Bovarnick, *supra* note 2, at 9–10.

[16] As Iraq involved detention of EPWs and CIs, followed by detention pursuant to authority provided by the Iraqi government, there was never uncertainty as to the procedures required in that theater of operations, at least at some levels (uncertainty did exist in theater internment facilities such as Camp Bucca).

[17] This is the author's opinion based on experience.

[18] *See* Dr. Jakob Kellenberger, President of the International Committee of the Red Cross, Address on Strengthening Legal Protections for Victims of Armed Conflicts (Sept. 21, 2010), *available at* http://www.icrc.org/eng/resources/documents/statement/ihl-development-statement-210910.htm. The four areas discussed included: (1) protection for persons deprived of liberty; (2) repatriation for victims of violations; (3) protection of natural environment; and (4) protection of internally displaced persons. *Id.*

[19] *Id.* at 2.

[20] John B. Bellinger & Vijay M. Padmanabhan, *Detention Operations in Contemporary Conflicts: Four Challenges for the Geneva Conventions and Other Existing Law*, 105(2) AM. J. INT'L L. 201, 202 (Apr. 2011).

[21] *Id.*

[22] *Id.*

The U.S. armed forces have struggled to deal with this uncertainty since June 2002, when the armed conflict in Afghanistan morphed from international to non-international in character.[23] During the past decade, commanders and legal advisors operating in this complex legal environment gained experience and learned lessons in handling detainees—experience and lessons that are becoming increasingly incorporated into U.S. military doctrine. The use of hypothetical insurgents will help illustrate the complexity of planning and implementing military detention operations involving nonstate actors where it is difficult to distinguish between civilians and combatants.

A. THE INSURGENTS

Imagine U.S. forces are engaged in a non-international armed conflict (such as the one in Afghanistan) and, alongside host nation security forces, the United States is executing a counterinsurgency campaign aimed at separating the insurgent leaders from their base of support within the civilian population without alienating the people from their government. Insurgents have attacked government logistics centers, ambushed convoys, planted improvised explosive devices and land mines along roads, and engaged in sporadic acts of terror in populated centers.

Assume that during one such operation four suspected insurgents are temporarily detained. The mission of the military operation is to track the movement of a known insurgent cell leader, Insurgent A, to his bed down location in a small village. The partnered unit approaches the objective on foot, sets up a cordon, and conducts a methodical search for the cell leader. During the search, a lone gunman, Insurgent B, with a bolt-action rifle fires at the soldiers, and he is quickly overrun, disarmed, and captured by the security forces. The search continues and Insurgent A is captured. As interpreters explain the situation to the local village leader, the elder says he does not want any trouble, and in a show of goodwill, he points out Insurgent C, a newcomer to the village who is believed to make bombs and IEDs for the insurgents. Insurgent C is taken into custody along with his seventeen-year-old son, Insurgent D, who was caught trying to hide an automatic weapon, and whose hands field-tested positive for fertilizer and gunshot residue.

What were the planning considerations leading up to possible detention resulting from this operation? Is there legal authority for U.S. forces to detain these four insurgents? If so, what process should they be afforded in the detention process? The remainder of Part II will focus on the practical constraints and considerations in the detention operations system for legal advisors and operators at the tactical and operational levels.

---

[23] *See supra* note 2.

B. AUTHORITY TO DETAIN AND OPERATIONAL GUIDANCE

The first consideration in any military operation that may include taking detainees is determining the source of legal detention authority and ensuring this authority frames the planning and conduct of all detention operations. As described in detail in previous chapters, the authority to detain flows from both international and national sources. In the context of Common Article 2 or international armed conflicts, customary and treaty law authorizes parties to a conflict to detain those captured or retained on the battlefield.[24] In non-international armed conflicts, detention authority is found in customary international law, and implied from the terms of Common Article 3 to the four Geneva Conventions, and the 1977 Additional Protocol II supplementing these treaties.[25] Notwithstanding international law and how a conflict is characterized, U.S. military operations also require a positive grant of authority prior to the use of force, authority that provides the domestic legal basis for subjecting captured personnel to detention.[26] For example, U.S. military operations in Afghanistan after September 11, 2001, were authorized by Authorization for the Use of Military Force.[27] In Iraq, Congress authorized the use of force in the Iraq Resolution of 2002.[28] Even without such express congressional authorization, strategic-level legal advisors will identify the constitutional source of authority that permits subordinate commanders to engage in detention operations, such as the inherent authority of the

---

[24] *See generally* Geneva Convention for the Amelioration of the Condition of the Wounded and Sick in Armed Forces in the Field Aug. 12, 1949, 6 U.S.T. 3114, 75 U.N.T.S. 31 [hereinafter GC I]; Geneva Convention for the Amelioration of the Condition of Wounded, Sick and Shipwrecked Members of Armed Forces at Sea, Aug. 12, 1949, 6 U.S.T. 3217, 75 U.N.T.S. 85 [hereinafter GC II]; GC III, *supra* note 4; GC IV, *supra* note 5.

[25] In some circumstances the more strenuous standards of Additional Protocol I may apply to otherwise non-international armed conflicts in which "peoples are fighting against colonial domination and alien occupation and against racist regimes in the exercise of their right of self-determination." AP I, *supra* note 13, art. 1(4).

[26] *See generally*, The War Powers Resolution of 1973, 50 U.S.C. § 1541 et seq. (1973) (authorizing the President to employ U.S. military force abroad only with an authorization from Congress or in the case of a "national emergency created by an attack upon the United States, its territories or possessions, or its armed forces.").

[27] *See* Richard F. Grimmett, Cong. Research Serv., Authorization for Use of Force in Response to the 9/11 Attacks: Legislative History 1 (Jan. 16, 2007), *available at* http://fas.org/sgp/crs/natsec/RS22357.pdf. After the Senate passed Joint Resolution 23 on September 14, 2001, the President signed the legislation into law on Sept. 18, 2001. Pub. L. No. 107–40, 115 Stat. 224 (2001) [hereinafter Authorization for Use of Military Force (AUMF)]. Section 2(a) of the AUMF reads:

> That the President is authorized to use all necessary and appropriate force against those nations, organizations, or persons he determines planned, authorized, committed, or aided the terrorist attacks that occurred on September 11, 2001, or harbored such organizations or persons, in order to prevent any future acts of international terrorism against the United States by such nations, organizations or persons.

Id. at 6.

[28] Authorization for the Use of Military Force against Iraq Resolution of 2002, Public Law 107–243 (Oct. 16, 2002).

President to respond to a sudden attack, and the implied congressional support for military operations.[29]

Regardless of international and national law authority to detain individuals on the battlefield, field commanders may limit this authority in the form of operational orders, standing operating procedures, or rules of engagement.[30] At the operational and tactical levels, subordinate commanders may exercise their discretion to tailor detention authority to advance specific operational objectives. For example, commanders may determine that U.S. detention of an individual is counter to the establishment of a host nation national court system that enforces the rule of law. Depending on the tactical situation, a commander may indicate a preference for detention by a host nation's national security forces instead of U.S. military forces. Such constraints are dictated by policy and strategic objectives, not law

1. Kill versus Capture

As a predicate consideration, it is essential to recognize that although U.S. commanders frequently choose to prioritize capturing enemy belligerent operatives instead of attacking them with deadly combat power as a first resort, such decisions are always the result of tactical and operational judgments to forgo utilizing the full extent of lawful attack authority. Nonetheless, in recent years, a debate has emerged that in some scenarios, combat forces should be required to capture rather than use lethal force.[31] Commentators[32] have suggested that, when using force against civilians who are directly participating in hostilities,[33] the Law of Armed Conflict imposes a duty to capture rather than kill.[34]

---

[29] *See generally* Memorandum from John C. Yoo, Deputy Assistant Attorney Gen., U.S. Dep't of Justice, to the Deputy Counsel to the President (Sept. 25, 2001), *available at* http://www.lawfareblog.com/wp-content/uploads/2013/10/Memorandum-from-John-C-Yoo-Sept-25-2001.pdf; War Powers Resolution, Pub. L. No. 93-148, 87 Stat. 555 (1973), codified at 50 U.S.C. §§ 1541–1548, and in the Joint Resolution passed by Congress on September 14, 2001, Pub. L. No. 107-40, 115 Stat. 224 (2001).

[30] Rules of engagement are defined as "[d]irectives issued by competent military authority that delineate the circumstances and limitations under which United States forces will initiate and/or continue combat engagement with other forces encountered." Joint Chiefs of Staff, Joint Pub. 1–2, Dep't of Def. Dictionary of Military and Associated Terms 408–09 (Apr. 12, 2001). In particular, the ROE "establish fundamental policies and procedures governing the actions to be taken by US commanders" during a military operation. Joint Chiefs of Staff, Instr. 3121.01B, The Standing Rules of Engagement/Standing Rules for the Use of Force for U.S. Forces app. A-1 (June 13, 2005).

[31] *See* International Committee of the Red Cross, Interpretive Guidance on the Notion of Direct Participation in Hostilities under International Humanitarian Law 61 (Nils Melzer ed., 2009), *available at* http://www.icrc.org/eng/assets /files/other/icrc-002-0990.pdf [hereinafter ICRC Interpretive Guidance].

[32] *See generally id.*

[33] AP I, *supra* note 13, art. 51(3); *see* Protocol Additional to the Geneva Conventions of August 1949, and Relating to the Protection of Victims of Non-international Armed Conflict (Protocol II) art. 13(3), June 8, 1977, 1125 U.N.T.S. 609 [hereinafter AP II].

[34] *See, e.g.,* Richard S. Taylor, *The Capture versus Kill Debate: Is the Principle of Humanity Now Part of the Targeting Analysis When Attacking Civilians Who Are Directly Participating in Hostilities?*, Army Lawyer 103 (June 2010).

> [W]hile operating forces can hardly be required to take additional risks for themselves or the civilian population in order to capture an armed adversary alive, it would defy basic notions of humanity to kill an adversary or to refrain from giving him or her an opportunity to surrender where there manifestly is no necessity for the use of lethal force.[35]

The United States does not embrace this LOAC interpretation, and any obligation to use least harmful means to capture an enemy belligerent in any armed conflict will be imposed exclusively as a matter of policy. In a recently published article titled "Belligerent Targeting and the Invalidity of a Least Harmful Means Rule," a group of LOAC and military experts provide a comprehensive explanation for why attempting to impose such a rule, as a matter of law, in relation to enemy belligerent operatives is legally and operationally invalid.[36] Other distinguished LOAC scholars, such as Professor Michael Schmitt, echo this conclusion. As Schmitt notes, the law "already accounts for situations in which an opportunity to capture an enemy exists by prohibiting attacks on an individual who clearly expresses an intention to surrender."[37] He further states that the main issue is not whether the individual can feasibly be captured, but whether the person has clearly expressed an intent to surrender.[38] Commanders are within their authority to limit the rules of engagement to prioritize capturing rather than killing a target; however that decision is a tactical, not legal, decision.[39]

2. Deliberate versus Inadvertent Targets

Deliberate detention operations are carefully coordinated missions planned to capture a specific target or set of targets in a single or series of preplanned operations. In contrast, a majority of captives are detained through inadvertent capture in the context of conventional hostilities. Such inadvertent detention is, of course, an aspect of any military operation. However, current counterinsurgency and counterterror operations focus on deliberate detention as a common aspect of mission execution, often targeting key enemy leaders. Rather than focusing on low- level fighters who make up the vast majority of the insurgent forces, deliberate detention operations[40]

---

[35] ICRC Interpretive Guidance, *supra* note 31, at 82.

[36] Laurie R. Blank et al., *Belligerent Targeting and the Invalidity of a Least Harmful Means Rule*, 89 Int'l Law Studies 536, 610–13 (2013).

[37] Michael N. Schmitt, *The Interpretive Guidance on the Notion of Direct Participation in Hostilities: A Critical Analysis*, 1 Harv. Nat'l Sec. L.J. 1, 5 (2010) (internal quotations omitted).

[38] *Id. See also* Shane R. Reeves & Jeff S. Thurhner, *Are We Reaching a Tipping Point? How Contemporary Challenges Are Affecting the Military Necessity-Humanity Balance*, Harv. Nat. Sec. J. Features 1, 3–7 (2013) (discussing the "capture versus kill" debate and concluding that a capture requirement overemphasizes the principle of humanity upsetting the delicate balance between this meta-principle and that of military necessity).

[39] W. Hays Parks, *Part IX of the ICRC "Direct Participation in Hostilities" Study: No Mandate, No Expertise, and Legally Incorrect*, 42 Int'l Law & Politics 769, 809 (2010).

[40] Deliberate detention operation prioritizes quality over quantity, and the adjective "deliberate" signifies both the intentional element as well as the slow and methodical element.

target these key leaders and other essential nodes of the enemy's network to cripple its ability to carry out operations.

Intelligence reports are essential for deliberate detention operations. Detention operations planners, including JAGs, must review extensive reports to determine: (1) Who may be captured?; (2) What are the intelligence requirements for nominating a target?; (3) Is the information sufficient to justify the determination that an individual should be targeted for deliberate detention?; (4) Who approves the detention operation?; and (5) By what authority is the detention operation authorized?

In the hypothetical, as an insurgent cell leader Insurgent A was the target of a deliberate detention operation.[41] Insurgents B, C, and D could be considered inadvertent captures. Whether during deliberate targeting operations or other missions, persons will also fall within the custody of the military through inadvertent capture through one of two categories: (1) military personnel independently identify enemy activity (observe a hostile act or hostile intent), or (2) military personnel respond to reports of enemy activity (leaders must assess the facts and make an on-the- spot determination on detention). Insurgent B was captured after firing on U.S. forces (Category 1–hostile act). Insurgent C was detained after the village leader told the on-scene commander that Insurgent C was an IED maker (Category 2). Insurgent D was detained due to evidence suggesting insurgent activity (hybrid of both Category 1 and 2—U.S. soldiers observed the suspicious behavior, but he may not have been discovered without the village elder's report).

Regardless of the characterization, deliberate or inadvertent target, the detention decision is more complex in non-international armed conflict scenarios where the opposing force is not easily identified through uniforms or distinctive insignia. Commanders and legal advisors must assess intelligence and evidence in the context of the operating environment, oftentimes focusing on patterns of conduct to indicate belligerent status and accordant detainability. Accordingly, in counterinsurgency operations, these detention decisions can share many features of law enforcement detention decisions.[42] Although targets of deliberate detention operations are carefully vetted for accurate and reliable intelligence, targets of inadvertent detention often occur during the fog of war, and require difficult decisions by on scene commanders and equally difficult assessments of information after the fact to justify continued detention. This complexity is often exacerbated by the need to consider cultural sensitivities for any type of detention.[43] One example is a command-imposed requirement for female soldiers to guard

---

[41] As a cell leader, he was a member of an organized armed group and exercised a continuous combat function, and therefore met the test for lethal targeting under the law of armed conflict.

[42] *See* James Foley, *Troops Often Left to Decide Whether Suspicious Activity Warrants Detention*, Stars & Stripes (Feb. 2011), *available at* http://www.stripes.com/news/1.135430 (discussing the story of one company commander trying to decide whether to detain or not in an inadvertent capture situation in Afghanistan).

[43] *See generally* FM 3-24, *supra* note 14, at 2–16.

female detainees.[44] During partnered operations, the commander must be aware of ethnic tension if host nation troops are from a region that would aggravate distrust.[45] For example, in response to claims that night raids to capture insurgent leaders disrespected Afghan culture and honor,[46] the United States negotiated an agreement whereby only the Afghan government could approve night raids.[47] Although this agreement could be considered a strategic victory, the new limitations carried obvious tactical disadvantages for the operators tasked with carrying out missions during the day or sharing sensitive target information.

3. Point-of-Capture Issues: Duty to Protect, Custody, and Tactical Questioning

Once captured, the detaining authority must safeguard the detainee from further harm, rapidly transport the detainee to an area removed from combat action, and provide medical care without regard to friendly and enemy forces.[48] The U.S. armed forces implement these obligations by teaching all personnel the soldiers' rules called the "Five S's and T," the six fundamental steps of effective detainee handling: (1) Search, (2) Silence, (3) Safeguard, (4) Segregate, (5) Speed to the Rear, and (6) Tag.[49] Doing so transforms legal obligations related to the protection and respect of all detainees into a battle drill for the personnel most likely to capture them.

In partnered operations, U.S. forces must consider the tactical and strategic benefits and risks of host nation security forces taking custody of detainees. If both U.S. and partnered host nation security forces are present at the point of capture, the threshold question is which force has custody of the detainee. United States' commanders may perceive a legitimate interest in maintaining custody. However, when conducting partnered operations, there is often a more

---

44 *See, e.g.*, Janet Holliday, *Female Engagement Teams: The Need to Standardize Training and Employment*, 92(2) U.S. Military Rev. 90–91 (Mar.– Apr. 2012).

45 During the early years of the Soviet invasion and occupation of Afghanistan, the Soviet planners made a decision to pack the invasion force with reserve troops from largely Muslim Central Asian republic turned out to be a grave miscalculation. Instead of generating trust and reducing resistance among Afghans, it actually stoked millennia-old animosities between the country's dominant Pashtuns and its Tajiks, Uzbeks, and other Central Asian ethnic groups.

Gregory Feifer, The Great Gamble: The Soviet War in Afghanistan 105 (2009).

46 *See* Hamid Shalizi, *U.S. Reach Deal on Controversial Night Raids*, Reuters Wire Service News Report, Kabul, Afghanistan (Apr. 8, 2012), *available at* http://www.reuters.com/article/2012/04/08/us-afghanistan-nightraids-idUSBRE83703920120408.

47 International Security Assistance Force, Press Release 2012-04-CA-010, USFOR-A, *Afghanistan Sign Memorandum of Understanding on Special Operations* (Apr. 10, 2012); Memorandum of Understanding between the Islamic Republic of Afghanistan and the United States of America on Afghanization of Special Operations on Afghan Soil in Kabul Afghanistan (Apr. 8, 2012).

48 *See* Joint Chiefs of Staff, Joint Pub. 3-63, Detention Operations IV-1 (May 30, 2008) [hereinafter JP 3-63] ("Consistent with longstanding military practice, individuals captured or detained by U.S. forces must be evacuated expeditiously through transit points to reach an internment facility in a secure area.")

49 Dep't of the Army, Field Manual 2-22.3 Human Intelligence Collector Operations D-2-D-4 (Sept. 6, 2006) [hereinafter FM 2-22.3].

compelling perceived need to demonstrate the credibility and effectiveness of host nation forces. As they serve as the face of their government, allowing these forces to maintain custody of a captive bolsters their legitimacy and advances the goal of operating independently when they demonstrate sustained and lawful independent detention operations. Accordingly, commanders and legal advisors will ensure that detention rules and policies clearly specify the authority to detain and rules for transfer of custody in point-of-capture situations.[50]

Detainees will also frequently be questioned at the point of capture, and as a result treatment standards must be clearly understood by all friendly forces. More limited than interrogation, "tactical questioning is expedient initial questioning for information of immediate tactical value. Tactical questioning is generally performed by members of patrols, but can be done by any DOD personnel."[51] For example, Insurgent B may be asked why he engaged U.S. forces, whether he has other weapons, and whether other insurgents are in the area. Tactical questioning focuses on the current situation and force protection concerns, and it would be unrealistic to expect capturing forces to forgo this opportunity to gather potentially decisive information. Indeed, forces engaged in tactical operations will almost always be expected to gather and report such information to contribute to the intelligence development process. Because of this, it is an essential aspect of detention operations that *all* U.S. forces are trained in the humane treatment obligations applicable to all captives and detainees.[52] Leaders at all levels are accountable for the conduct of their subordinates, and these leaders ensure this training is effective and these obligations are implemented during operations.

Once the detainees have been moved from the point of capture to a safe collection point, conditions may support a more lengthy form of interrogation. The current policies for interrogation are clearly set forth in the publicly available U.S. Army Field Manual that U.S. law effectively adopts as the current standard for all wartime interrogations.[53] The Detainee Treatment Act provides that "[n]o person in the custody or under the effective control of the Department of Defense or under detention in a Department of Defense facility shall be subject to any treatment or technique of interrogation not authorized by and listed in the United States Army Field Manual on Intelligence Interrogation."[54] The interrogation methods incorporated into this manual fully comply with the most protective obligations of the Geneva Conventions. Accordingly, compliance with these sources of obligation ensures LOAC compliance.

1. Collection Points, Field Detention Sites, and Interrogation

Operational considerations require strategically placed, well-maintained collection points to temporarily house detainees captured during the course of tactical operations. As a practical matter, the fewer locations where detainees are

---

[50] JP 3-63, *supra* note 48 at IX, II-4.

[51] FM 2-22.3, *supra* note 49, at 1–7.

[52] *Id.* at vi–vii.

[53] The Detainee Treatment Act of 2005, 10 U.S.C.S. § 801, et seq. (2005).

[54] 10 U.S.C. § 1002 (2005).

being housed, the easier it is to maintain compliance with the legal requirements, such as the training and oversight of a guard force and interrogation operations. However, having only a limited number of approved collection and detention points may impose operational risk as commanders must secure and transport detainees longer distances from point of capture to the site. Joint Doctrine provides that collection points should "be located close to the area of actual operations for quick evacuation of detainees, but should also be situated in a location intended to provide for the safety and security of the detainees and the security force."[55]

2. Initial Verification, Transfer, Release, and Approval Authorities

During the interrogation process at a safe and secure collection point, a more complete picture of the asserted factual basis for detention will normally emerge. Interrogation should confirm or deny the detainee's level of involvement in enemy activity and/or knowledge of such activity.[56] The results of this initial interrogation process will be used to determine if further detention is warranted.

Commanders conduct initial reviews of the justification for continued detention at these initial collection points, utilizing thea process most feasible under the battlefield conditions at the time. Commands have used ad hoc working groups to review intelligence and evidence regarding newly captured detainees. This group is not intended to sit as a tribunal to definitively assess the detainee's status, but rather to serve as a preliminary review of the initial decision to detain. Operational lawyers often advise and/or participate in such working groups. However, even where a less formalized process is used for this assessment, commanders will invariably rely on JAG officers to offer recommendations as to the quality of information and justification for detention. Whether conducted by a working group or an individual reviewing authority, the end result will be a recommendation to a designated commander on whether the new detainee should be held for further interrogation, transferred to national partner forces, or released back to the point of capture.

At this initial stage, intelligence personnel confirm or deny the detainee's information and determine if there is a belligerent nexus sufficient to hold the detainee.[57] Even if a detainee has no connection to the insurgency, the commander may consider that the conduct that resulted in the capture justifies continued detention. If the conduct is not sufficient for continued U.S. detention but does indicate the detainee violated host-nation laws, there may be a policy to transfer the detainee to local authorities. The following hypothetical situations illustrate this continuum of potential detention outcomes:

---

[55] JP 3-63, *supra* note 48, at IV-2.

[56] FM 2-22.3, *supra* note 49, at 5–13.

[57] ICRC Interpretive Guidance, *supra* note 31, at 58–64 (belligerent nexus is an act that is specifically designed to directly cause the required threshold of harm in support of a party to the conflict and to the detriment of another).

Insurgent A was the target of a deliberate capture operation due to his role as an insurgent cell leader. Such operations tend to rely heavily on intelligence so the initial verification process will focus on confirming the identity of the detained person and his intelligence value. The commander may request additional time to interrogate at the initial detention point.

Insurgent B was detained after engaging U.S. forces, so an initial verification will seek to determine his level of involvement with armed insurgent groups. If the interrogation reveals only criminal conduct, law enforcement disposition may be more appropriate. If the detainee was an insurgent fighter, but is of low intelligence value, transfer to host-nation military authorities may be appropriate. Even after a thorough review of all facts and circumstances, such decisions are never clear-cut, and reasonable minds can differ on the appropriate disposition.

Insurgents C and D, father and son, each showed some degree of insurgent activity. The initial review following capture and interrogation may be more challenging. The evidence supporting their participation in an IED-making cell is subject to criticism. The village elder first identified Insurgent C as being new to the area, and the village elder's credibility may be in question. Was the on-scene commander able to corroborate any information? Insurgent D attempted to conceal a military-style automatic rifle, and the gunshot residue on his hands indicated recent use of a weapon. The fertilizer could indicate agricultural activity or bomb- making activity. Although many may question the strength of this evidence, the purpose of the initial review is to determine whether the detainees are sufficiently related to the armed conflict to warrant military detention.

For this hypothetical, the commander decides to detain Insurgents A and C for further interrogation. Insurgents B and D will be transferred to local authorities for military detention by host-nation security forces or criminal prosecution by the host-nation government.

A commander's decision to detain, transfer, or release a detainee may be subject to oversight and required approval from a higher headquarters. Policies and SOPs will designate the approval authorities for each step of the detention process. Before transferring a detainee to authorities of another country, even host-nation partner forces, commanders must consider the risk that the detainee will be subjected to maltreatment if transferred.[58] If the host nation has a history of abusing prisoners, the detaining commander must review that nation's detention procedures and practices to include inspecting host-nation detention sites to determine which locations respect detainee rights.[59] If a commander is inclined to refuse a request for transfer,

---

[58] 1984 Convention against Torture and Other Cruel, Inhuman or Degrading Treatment or Punishment, Art. 3, 1465 U.N.T.S. 85 (Dec. 10, 1984); *see also* the Geneva Convention Relating to the Status of Refugees, Art. 33, 189 U.N.T.S. 137 (July 28, 1951).

[59] ISAF detention operations in Afghanistan evolved to accommodate such safeguards after the release of a UN report that detailed widespread abuse of prisoners within the Afghan military. *See generally* United Nations Assistance Mission in Afghanistan (UNAMA), UN Office of the High Commissioner for Human Rights, *Treatment of Conflict Related Detainees in Afghan Custody* (Oct. 2011), available at http://www.refworld.org /docid/4e93ecb22.html. The principles of non-refoulement, therefore, prohibited ISAF nations from transferring detainees within their power into the custody of Afghan security forces when there were credible reports that the detainees would be abused. Accordingly, ISAF developed procedural checks to inspect and review Afghan

it is almost certain this issue will be raised to higher-level commands for coordination, to include legal review.

Another consideration for commanders when removing a person from the battlefield is notification to the family.[60] Sometimes the family will be present to witness the removal, but for persons captured away from their home, commanders must provide prompt notification through the ICRC, though the United States and the ICRC disagree as to what is considered prompt. In rare situations, the timing and/or detail of this notice may be influenced by imperative security concerns. When such concerns arise, JAG officers will normally vet the proposed modifications to ensure they are consistent with applicable international and domestic legal obligations, or at least approved at various higher levels of command. In this regard, it is important to note that even the third GC permits limiting a CI's external contact based on imperative security justification.[61]

Once this initial detention process has run its course, the detainee will enter a period of continued detention. The traditional armed conflict paradigm, featuring prisoners of war detained until the end of hostilities, breaks down in a conflict of indefinite, and potentially unending, duration, with actors not entitled to combatant status under international law.[62]

III. Detention Operations in Afghanistan: The U.S. Operational Detention Model

> *Internment without trial is so antithetical to the rule of law as understood in a democratic society that recourse to it requires to be carefully scrutinized by the courts of that society.*[63]

---

detention facilities, transferring detainees only to those locations and facilities that were abuse free. International Security Assistance Force, Press Release, 2011-10-CA-003, *ISAF Outlines Proactive Detainee Safeguards* (Oct. 10, 2011), *available at* http://www.isaf.nato.int/article/isaf-releases/isaf-outlines-proactive-detainee-safeguards.html.

[60] *See* Copenhagen Principles, *supra* note 1, at #11 (in non-international armed conflict and in a few other warranted situations, the detainee's family is to be notified of the deprivation of liberty, release, or transfer of the detainee).

[61] *See* GC III, *supra* note 4, art. 5. This article provides in relevant part:

> Where, in the territory of a Party to the conflict, the latter is satisfied that an individual protected person is definitely suspected of or engaged in activities hostile to the security of the State, such individual person shall not be entitled to claim such rights and privileges under the present Convention as would, if exercised in the favour of such individual person, be prejudicial to the security of such State.
>
> Where in occupied territory an individual protected person is detained as a spy or saboteur, or as a person under definite suspicion of activity hostile to the security of the Occupying Power, such person shall, in those cases where absolute military security so requires, be regarded as having forfeited rights of communication under the present Convention.

Id.

[62] *See* Bellinger & Padmanabhan, *supra* note 20, at 202.

[63] *Al-Jedda v. The United Kingdom*, No. 27021/08, European Court of Human Rights (quoting Lord Carswell), Strasbourg, fn 130 (July 7, 2011).

A. THE IMPLEMENTATION OF A COMPREHENSIVE DETAINEE REVIEW PROCESS FOR UNPRIVILEGED BELLIGERENTS

> *Time will tell whether these reforms will be implemented effectively and can resolve the underlying problems of arbitrary and indefinite detention, mistaken captures, and lack of evidence for legitimate prosecutions in Afghan courts.*[64]

From the inception of U.S. detention operations in Afghanistan through 2009, the density and efficacy of detention review process grew continuously.[65] This evolution culminated with the signature of three Executive Orders on January 22, 2009.[66] President Obama's goal in issuing these orders was very clear: correct past deficiencies in detainee operations, including one intended to specifically review detention policy options.[67] To this end, a Special Interagency Task Force was created to "identify lawful options for the disposition of individuals captured or apprehended in connection with armed conflicts and counterterrorism operations."[68] On March 13, 2009, in the *Guantanamo Bay Detainee Litigation* case before the D.C. District Court, documents submitted by the Attorney General's Office referenced this "forward-looking multi-agency effort ... to develop a comprehensive detention policy," and noted "the views of the Executive Branch may evolve as a result."[69] Perhaps the most significant information contained in the memorandum March 13, 2009, was the new definitional framework for who could be detained:

> The President has the authority to detain persons that the President determines planned, authorized, committed, or aided the terrorist attacks that occurred on September 11, 2001, and persons who harbored those responsible for those attacks.
>
> The President also has the authority to detain persons who were part of, or substantially supported, Taliban or al-Qaida forces or associated forces that

---

[64] *Fixing Bagram: Strengthening Detention Reforms to Align with U.S. Strategic Priorities*, Hum. Rts. First (Nov. 2009), *available at* http://www.therenditionproject.org.uk/pdf/PDF%2050%20[HRF-2009-11-REP%20Fixing%20Bagram].pdf.

[65] For a comprehensive discussion of the evolution of U.S. detention operations in Afghanistan, to include a candid assessment of policy failures, see Bovarnick, *supra* note 2, at 12–20.

[66] *See* Exec. Order 13,491 74 F.R. 4893 (2009) (Ensuring Lawful Interrogation); *See* Exec. Order 13,492 74 F.R. 4897 (2009) (Review and Disposition of Individuals Detained at the Guantanamo Bay Naval Base and Close of Detention Facitilies); *see* Exec. Order 13,493 74 F.R. 4901 (2009) (Review of Detention Policy Options).

[67] *See* Exec. Order 13,493, 74 C.F.R. 4901 (2010) (Review of Detention Policy Options).

[68] *Id.* § 1(a).

[69] *In re: Guantanamo Bay Detainee Litigation*, Respondent's Memorandum regarding the Government's Detention Authority Relative to the Detainees Held at Guantanamo Bay 2 (Mar. 13, 2009). One exhibit attached to the Respondent's Memorandum was the Declaration of Attorney General Eric Holder, which also emphasizes the ongoing work of the task force directed by the President. *See id.*

are engaged in hostilities against the United States or its coalition partners, including any person who has committed a belligerent act, or has directly supported hostilities, in aid of such enemy armed forces.[70]

These definitions provided the exclusive substantive legal basis to detain individuals captured in the context of military operations in Afghanistan. They also provided an important indication of the relationship between strategic mission and substantive detention authority. Although it is obviously impossible to predict how detention authority will be defined in future military operations, what this definition illustrates is that authority will always be derived from the nature of the mission and threat dynamics. Because national and international grants of mission authority, such as domestic authorizations for the use of force or UN Security Council resolutions will rarely include explicit grants of detention authority, subordinate commanders will often be responsible for defining the scope of this authority, and translating this authority into detention criteria for the force. In so doing, they must constantly tailor this scope to the genuine needs of military necessity and ensure consistency with international law.

In any military operation it is equally obvious that individuals may be captured or detained during tactical operations that, upon further assessment, do not fall within the established detention criteria. When this occurs, the military unit has no authority to detain, and must release those captured immediately. In Afghanistan, the criteria reproduced above provided the exclusive authority

---

[70] *Id.* at 2. It should also be noted that this definitional framework is essentially the same as the one used by the Bush administration, with one exception: the insertion of the word "substantially" with respect to the level of support to the Taliban, al Qaida, or associated forces. The prior definition just required "support," and not "substantial support." Although the authority to detain was established in the AUMF, the original definition for "enemy combatant" appeared in the Secretary of the Navy's July 2004 order establishing the CSRTs:

> For purposes of this Order, the term "enemy combatant" shall mean an individual who was part of or supporting Taliban or al-Qaida forces, or associated forces that are engaged in hostilities against the United States or its coalition partners. This includes any person who has committed a belligerent act or has directly supported hostilities in aid of such enemy armed forces.

Memorandum from Paul Wolfowitz to the Secretary of the Navy on Order Establishing Combatant Status Review Tribunal (July 7, 2004), *available at* http://www.defense.gov/news/jul2004/d20040707review.pdf. In the Military Commissions Act of 2006, the term "unlawful enemy combatant" was defined, in part, as "a person who has engaged in hostilities or who has purposefully and materially supported hostilities against the United States or its co-belligerents who is not a lawful enemy combatant (including a person who is part of the Taliban, al Qaeda, or associated forces)." Military Commissions Act of 2006, Pub. L. No. 109-366, §948a(1)(i), 120 Stat. 2600 (2006). The concept of substantial support, as described in the phrase "purposefully and materially supported," was carried through in the Military Commissions Act of 2009, which changed the term "unlawful enemy combatant" to "unprivileged enemy belligerent" and slightly altered the definition to: "an individual (other than a privileged belligerent) who—(A) has engaged in hostilities against the United States or its coalition partners; (B) has purposefully and materially supported hostilities against the United States or its coalition partners; or (C) was a part of al Qaeda at the time of the alleged offense under this chapter." *See* Military Commissions Act of 2009, Pub. L. No. 111-84, § 948a(7)(A–C), 123 Stat. 2474 (internal quotation marks omitted).

to detain post-March 2009, and were also utilized by the detainee review board established by the Secretary of Defense's July 2009 policy to assess the propriety of initial and continued detention. How this process is currently implemented in Afghanistan will be the focus of the remainder of this chapter.

B. FROM CAPTURE THROUGH A DETAINEE REVIEW BOARD (DRB)—AN OVERVIEW

When U.S. forces took an individual into custody in Afghanistan, it triggered a seventy-two-hour requirement that the unit commander, with advice of a judge advocate, validate that individual meets the criteria for continued internment and transfer to the Detention Facility in Parwan (DFIP) (this replaced the Bagram Theater Internment Facility, BTIF, also located at Bagram Airbase).[71] Because this determination often occured at the tactical level close to the point of capture, it did not benefit from the more robust review procedures that would apply at a more mature detention facility, and therefore it did not act as the ultimate judgment of detainability. However, it would result in continued detention pending further review. As a general rule, this subsequent review would occur at the DFIP, and under normal circumstances the detainee was required to be transferred to the DFIP within two weeks.

Once in the DFIP, the detainee was administratively segregated for the first fourteen days of his internment. This has been the process since 2002. After fourteen days at the DFIP, the detainee was assigned an Internment Serial Number (ISN), and the ICRC was usually provided access to the detainee. In this same time period, the detainee was notified of the DRB process and the date of the initial DRB, which must occur within sixty days of the detainee's arrival at the DFIP (these DRB procedures, as outlined here, were primarily implemented in 2009, replacing documentary proceedings that did not involve in-person hearings or advocate assistance). This notification is documented and later entered as an exhibit at the detainee's DRB hearing. Within thirty days of the detainee's arrival at the DFIP, a Personal Representative (PR) met with the detainee. This PR was a military officer (although normally not a Judge Advocate) who had undergone special training to prepare for performing the representational duties, a model derived from the GPW Article 5 tribunal process. The PR once again informed the detainee, normally through an interpreter, of the DRB process, and reviewed with the detainee the unclassified summary of specific facts supporting the detainee's initial detention and potential continued internment (this was also documented and later entered as an exhibit). During this initial meeting, the PR also hoped to gather enough information to be able to contact family members or

[71] This section is an excerpt from the author's previous published article titled "Detainee Review Boards in Afghanistan: From Strategic Liability to Legitimacy." *See* Bovarnick, *supra* note 2, at 22–24 (internal citations omitted). The article in its entirety is available at http://www.loc.gov/rr/frd/Military_Law/pdf/Bovarnick-Detainee.pdf.

others that may either appear in person, testify by telephone or video teleconference (VTC), or provide a statement on behalf of the detainee at the initial board. This is particularly critical in the case of mistaken identity.

Prior to the board, the PR typically meets with the detainee at least two more times to gather more witness leads and to prepare the detainee for his statement at the board. During this period, the PR will also access all databases, classified and unclassified, containing data on the detainee to assist in the PR's representation of the detainee at the board.

A day or two prior to the actual DRB hearing, the PR, recorder (the government representative, who is normally a Judge Advocate), analysts, and other DFIP personnel, as necessary, meet in a "pre-board" session to discuss each case scheduled before a DRB that week. During this session, the PR and recorder attempt to resolve disputes to minimize the adversarial nature of the case presented to the DRB. Although recorders must remain neutral, PRs must act in the best interest of the detainee. Regardless of areas of consensus, all information, including exculpatory evidence, must be presented to the DRB. The language on the "baseball card" (a one-to-three page synopsis of the facts surrounding the detainee's capture), the unclassified intelligence collected on the detainee prior to capture (if any), summaries of any interrogation reports, summaries of the detainee's activities in the DFIP, and a behavioral threat assessment are all distilled down to a few pages to be presented to the board to aid in its internment determination.

Like any complex administrative proceeding, prior coordination is essential for smooth, efficient, and professionally run boards. The administrative staff of the Legal Operations Directorate is responsible for notifying all parties, primarily the board members and DFIP personnel, to include the MPs, of the hearings scheduled. On the scheduled day, all parties know in advance how many cases a particular panel is going to hear that day. The DRB hearing room has seats for spectators, and all personnel with access to the DFIP are welcome to observe the proceedings.

The board members, recorder, PR, legal advisor, reporter, and interpreter gather in the DRB hearing room, and the president convenes the DRB and goes through the preliminary portion of the script, which includes the swearing of the parties. The first detainee is called, and the president continues through the script by informing the detainee of the purpose of the board and reminding the detainee of his rights at the board. The board president also discusses and admits the Detainee Notification Worksheet and Detainee Initial Interview Checklist as exhibits, thus confirming and adding to the record clear evidence that the detainee received prior notification and assistance prior to his hearing.

After the president's initial colloquy with the detainee, the recorder reads an unclassified summary of information, which includes the circumstances of capture and evidence against the detainee. Although the board president follows the script, the exact order of statements and questioning is left to the president's discretion. Regardless of the exact order, the detainee is provided the opportunity to make a statement to the board. The statement may be made in a question-and-answer format with the assistance of the PR, or the detainee may simply make a statement, which has been the primary practice in the past. Alternatively, the statement may combine both of these methods. In the end, the PR's determination of the most effective format should prevail.

After the detainee's statement, the board members and recorder may ask the detainees questions—as does the PR if he has not already done so. Again, although the recorder is neutral, he may question the detainee to ferret out additional information to assist the board in making its findings and recommendations. After the recorder's questions, board presidents generally allow the PR to follow up. The amount of back and forth (direct examination, cross-examination, re-direct, and re-cross) is left to the discretion of the president.

When witnesses or documents are presented during the open, unclassified portion of the hearing, the president controls the presentation of the evidence, to include the questioning of live witnesses. Capturing units, battle space owners, and other interested staff members may appear before a board or present documentary information in support of a particular position, so long as it is relevant to the board's determination. Testimony, for or against the detainee, may be presented live, via telephone or VTC, or in writing as a sworn or unsworn statement. Since March 2010, the inclusion of Afghan witness testimony has had a noticeable impact on the DRB process, not only in terms of logistics, but also in the frequency of releases for detainees supported by witness testimony. The considerable effort made to bring live witnesses to the DRBs, at least anecdotally, has also spread the word throughout Afghanistan that the DRB process is fair and legitimate and, perhaps more important in light of past missteps, that the treatment of the detainees in the new DFIP is exceptional.

The rules of evidence that apply in a criminal court do not apply at a DRB, which is considered an administrative hearing. The board may consider any information offered that it deems relevant and non-cumulative. Also, the board may consider hearsay evidence in the form of classified and unclassified reports, threat assessments, detainee transfer requests, targeting packets, disciplinary reports from the DFIP guards, observation reports from the behavior science assessment teams, photographs, videos, sound recordings, and all forms of sworn and unsworn statements and letters. Although admissibility is very broad, the board must still apply its judgment to determine the trustworthiness and appropriate weight of the information.

The rules described above apply equally to inculpatory and exculpatory information. For example, the concept of authentication is (or at least was) non-existent. If a detainee provides a cell phone number for a supporting witness, the witness is called and asked to identify himself. The witness is not sworn, and there is no way to verify the person's credentials; however, as PRs learn, the questioning of detainee-requested witnesses can backfire when the witnesses have not been interviewed prior to the hearing. The only other restriction, and perhaps the most important in the proceedings, is the prohibition on the use of any statement obtained by torture or through cruel, inhuman, or degrading treatment, except against a person accused of torture as evidence that the statement was made.

Once all of the unclassified evidence has been presented, the detainee is allowed a final opportunity to make another statement to the board. Here again, preparation in consultation with the PR is intended to make this opportunity meaningful, as the PR will assist the detainee in avoiding reiterating something said earlier or contradicting (perhaps indisputable) evidence the PR knows will be offered during the classified portion of the hearing (it should be noted, however, that the PR may not share any classified information with the detainee). When the detainee completes his statement, he is excused from the hearing room.

The recorder then opens the classified portion of the hearing by presenting documentary evidence or calling witnesses that possess classified information. The board members and PR can also question the witnesses. Once all of the classified information is presented, the recorder and PR may, at the board president's discretion, provide brief closing comments on the state of the evidence; however, they must refrain from making personal recommendations to the board. The PR can reiterate a detainee's request to be released.

After the president adjourns the board, the president and two other board members move to closed session deliberations to discuss the hearing, but they must include their individual findings and recommendations on the worksheet provided. The legal advisor collects the three sheets and records the majority vote on a consolidated worksheet, which the president must sign. Within seven days, a report of the proceedings, including a transcript and any exhibits admitted for a particular case, must be forwarded to the approval authority (the convening authority), and within fourteen days after that, the detainee must be notified in writing, in the detainee's language, of the approval authority's decision.

The increase in resources—primarily personnel—flowing into the Legal Operations Directorate has resulted in longer, more robust hearings. In September 2009, two recorders and one PR conducted twenty-six boards per day, once per week. The average time of a hearing was forty minutes, and no Afghan witnesses were called. Beginning in March 2010 the Legal Operations Directorate convened ten boards per day—split between two separate panels in two hearing rooms—five days per week. Hearing times have increased from an average of forty minutes to between ninety minutes and four hours per hearing, resulting in a more robust proceeding. The manning of this process therefore provides a useful template for future detention operations, although as noted earlier, mission and resources will almost always impact the extent of such manning. Due to the U.S. transfer of the DFIP to Afghan control in late 2014, this process is no longer extant.

C. STAFFING THE DETAINEE REVIEW BOARD PROCESS

In addition to a large administrative staff that contributes to the efficient operation of the DRBs, the personnel who actually participate in the DRBs include the recorder (the government representative), the detainee, the detainee's detailed

PR, the board members, the legal advisor, and the reporter.[72] The convening authority—the military officer empowered to order review and act on review board recommendations—also plays a critical role in appointing the board members, reviewing the proceedings and recommendations, and making the final determination on the detainee's status.

Each DRB is composed of three field grade officers, with the senior member acting as the board's president. The DRB members are selected from a pool of officers nominated for this duty by U.S Forces–Afghanistan and ISAF. The nominees are U.S. field grade officers (officers in the rank of Major–Colonel or equivalent naval rank). Similar to selection for duty as members of a court-martial, selection is based on consideration of certain qualifications such as "age, experience, and temperament, [and the ability] to exercise sound judgment and have a general understanding of combat operations and the current campaign plan to assess threats in theater and further the counterinsurgency mission [through] their participation on the board."[73] Additionally, to "ensure the neutrality of the review board, the convening authority shall ensure that none of its members was directly involved in the detainee's capture or transfer to the [DFIP]."[74]

The board president is responsible for managing the hearing, and utilizes an established script that ensures each proceeding includes all relevant process, to include informing the detainee of his rights once the proceedings begin. At the close of the hearing, each board member individually weighs the information presented, and once all of the information has been presented, the members deliberate in a closed session. Upon conclusion of deliberations, each member records his or her recommendations on a findings and recommendations worksheet. In a closed session, by a majority vote, using preponderance of the evidence as the burden of proof, the board must determine whether the detainee meets the criteria for internment and, if so, whether the threat posed by the detainee justifies continued internment. If a majority of the board determines the detainee *does not* meet the criteria for internment, the detainee must be released from Department of Defense custody as soon as practicable. This release decision is binding on the officer who convened the DRB, and under no circumstances may she override this order. If, in contrast, a majority of the board determines the detainee *does* meet the criteria for internment, then they must also make a

---

[72] This section is an excerpt from the author's previous published article titled "Detainee Review Boards in Afghanistan: From Strategic Liability to Legitimacy." *See* Bovarnick, *supra* note 2, at 28–32 (internal citations omitted). Direct quotes remain cited throughout this section. The article in its entirety is available at http://www.loc.gov/rr/frd/Military_Law/pdf/Bovarnick-Detainee.pdf.

[73] Memorandum from Vice Admiral Robert S. Harward, Commander, JTF 435 to U.S. Military Forces Conducting Detention Operations in Afghanistan (Feb. 1, 2010 unclassified draft) (on file with author).

[74] *See* Letter from Phillip Carter, Deputy Assistant Sec'y of Def. for Detainee Policy, to Senator Carl Levin, Chairman of the Senate Armed Servs. Comm. (July 14, 2010), *available at* http://www.wcl.american.edu/nimj/ documents/addendum.pdf?rd=1 (including Carter's two-page letter dated July 14, 2009, and the six-page July 2, 2009 Detainee Review Procedures enclosure [hereinafter Detainee Review Procedures]).

recommendation for an appropriate disposition to the convening authority. The possible recommendations include the following:

- Continued internment at the DFIP if necessary to mitigate the threat posed by the detainee.
- Transfer to Afghan authorities for criminal prosecution.
- Transfer to Afghan authorities for participation in a reconciliation program.
- Release without conditions.
- In the case of non-Afghans and non-U.S. third-country nationals, transfer to a third country for criminal prosecution, participation in a reconciliation program, or release.[75]

In contrast to a decision to release a detainee, the board's recommendation to detain or transfer is not binding on the convening authority. Accordingly, the convening authority is vested with plenary authority to order a more beneficial outcome for a detainee, but never a less beneficial outcome (a model adopted from the clemency power of a court-martial convening authority). For example, even if the board finds the detainee meets the criteria for internment, the convening authority may reject this finding and order release. Alternatively, the board could recommend continued internment in the DFIP, and the recommendation is similarly not binding on convening authority, who could decide to transfer the detainee to the host nation authorities.

The DRB recorder is a judge advocate officer; however, because the DRB is not an adversarial hearing, recorders must perform their role in a non-adversarial, neutral manner. Recorders are non-voting members that prepare the evidence packets for the voting board members. The impartiality obligation requires that they include within such packets all available exculpatory evidence. Finally, unlike the traditional function of a government representative, the recorder will not recommend or advocate for any particular finding, but instead provide relevant evidence and leave that decision to the member's discretion. However, recorders are expected to engage in adversarial testing of witnesses to ensure a full disclosure of relevant information for the members. Ultimately, the recorder is obligated to ensure all available relevant information comes before the board so the board can make the best possible determination in the case, even when that duty requires assisting and working with the PR to do so.

The PRs have perhaps the most challenging role in the DRB process. The PRs are non-lawyer, professional officers. According to the DRB directive, the PR "shall be a commissioned officer familiar with the detainee review procedures and authorized access to all reasonably available information (including classified information) relevant to the determination of whether the detainee meets the criteria for internment and whether the detainee's continued internment is

[75] Interview with Lieutenant Colonel Michael Devine, Deputy Dir., Legal Operations Directorate, JTF 435, in Bagram, Afghanistan (June 16, 2010).

necessary."[76] To facilitate execution of this duty, PRs participate in a one-week training course prepared and taught by instructors from the Judge Advocate General's Legal Center and School and other instructors. They also receive additional weekly training with other DRB personnel to hone their representational skills. With a few exceptions, the detainee may waive the appointment of a PR; however, to date, no detainee has waived his PR. More important, the PR:

> shall assist the detainee in gathering and presenting the information reasonably available in the light most favorable to the detainee. The [PR's] good faith efforts on behalf of the detainee shall not adversely affect his or her status as a military officer (e.g., evaluations, promotions, future assignments).[77]

Prior to the new DRBs, one of the primary complaints of the detainees (and the ICRC) was the lack of notice or information about the reasons for their detention and their ability to challenge their detention. Because the PRs have the task of explaining the process to the detainees, to include their own role as the detainee's representative, the basis for this complaint has been substantially ameliorated. Detainees are now apprised of when their board will convene, what to expect at the board, and the potential outcomes of the board. Additionally, the PR can assist a detainee to prepare a statement and answer questions at the board, as well as assist the detainee in gathering documents or arranging for a witness to speak on the detainee's behalf—all rights afforded to detainees by the new process. The PRs cannot disclose classified information to the detainee, and the detainee is excluded from the classified portion of the hearing, but the PR does have full access to classified information relevant to the case.

The legal advisor is a non-voting member who sits through the entire board and is available to advise board members on legal issues, a role based on the function of the legal advisor in military administrative separation boards. The board president can discuss any disputes over the criteria or admission of evidence, and other issues, with the legal advisor. The legal advisor also collects the findings and recommendations worksheets completed by the members and records the majority vote. The legal advisor typically reviews the hearing and the findings and recommendations of the board and provides a legal review of the proceedings. This review is facilitated by the requirement that a summarized transcript of the proceedings must be prepared within seven days. This transcript, along with any exhibits that were offered to the board and the findings and recommendations, become the record of the board that is presented to the convening authority for a decision on final disposition. In all cases, the legal advisor reviews the file for legal sufficiency, and a senior judge advocate will conduct a second legal review when continued internment is recommended. The detainee is then notified of the results within seven days of the sufficiency review.

---

[76] *Id.*

[77] *Id.*

As noted above, a decision to release the detainee is binding and non-reviewable. If, however, the detainee is subjected to continued internment pursuant to a DRB finding, a periodic review process is then triggered to ensure periodic validation of the necessity for continued detention. A review board composed of three officers conducts a "file" review every six months. The board applies a de novo standard of review, and its decision to order release (based on the conclusion that the detainee no longer represents a threat sufficient to justify continued detention), like that of the DRB, is binding.

D. A MODEL FOR FUTURE DETENTION OPERATIONS?

Building upon earlier efforts prompted at the Central Command level in coordination with the Office of the Secretary of Defense, and endorsed by President Obama's new team in 2009, JTF 435's enhancements to the detention review and validations process resulted in continued and significant improvements to the system. These enhancements have improved the fairness for detainees, reduced the number of unnecessarily detained individuals, rendered the review process more efficient by institutionalizing a review process, and improved the transparency and perception of legitimacy of this detention regime.[78] This is not to suggest that there are no longer critics of this process—far from it. The very notion of preventive detention for unconventional belligerents in a non-international armed conflict continues to generate substantial controversy. However, from a military operational perspective, such detention is an almost inevitable component of ground operations during any armed conflict (or even certain non-conflict military operations). Accordingly, adopting a similar approach to maximizing the efficiency and legitimacy of such operations is an essential aspect of strategic credibility and success in future operations.

How this evolution will impact future detainee operations is unclear. However, what does seem extremely unlikely is that the U.S. military would revert to the type of summary detention process that defined the early phases of detainee operations in Afghanistan and Guantanamo. Instead, this experience suggests recognition of two operational imperatives. First, all military operations may necessitate a detention operations component. Second, protecting individuals from arbitrary deprivations of liberty, and protecting the force from unnecessary allocation of resources, essentially mandates that all detention operations include a procedural review component. Although the extent of this process may evolve as operations become more mature, minimal standards must include notice of the basis of detention, an opportunity to be heard with the assistance of a personal representative, and a neutral decision-maker to rule on the validity of the detention.[79] The procedures developed in Afghanistan now provide a model for this process, which can then be tailored to the operational dynamics of any given operation.

---

[78] *See generally Detainee Review Boards*, *supra* note 2.

[79] *Detainee Review Boards*, *supra* note 2, at 30–31.

E. TREATMENT DURING DETENTION: AN ABSOLUTE TOUCHSTONE OF LEGITIMACY

Providing an effective process for the detention determination is only the first component to ensuring effective and legitimate detainee operations. Once detention is initiated, an equal if not more fundamental component is ensuring detainees are properly treated while in the custody of U.S. armed forces. For captives who qualify as POWs, Retained Persons, or Civilian Internees in the context of an international armed conflict, the comprehensive regulatory provisions of the relevant Geneva Conventions, incorporated into and implemented by military regulations, establish the legal and policy framework for ensuring proper treatment.[80] Although it is impossible to prevent all breaches of these obligations, the clear and legally established status of these detainees, coupled with the comprehensive nature of the treatment obligations triggered by such status, facilitates proper treatment by reducing uncertainty as to what standards are binding on U.S. forces.

The treatment obligations applicable to individuals detained during non-international armed conflicts (what the U.S. characterizes as unprivileged belligerents, formerly enemy combatants) are more general in nature. These detainees do not qualify for a defined status within the meaning of the Geneva Conventions.[81] This does not, however, suggest that these detainees fall outside the protection of international law, or are somehow less "worthy" of protection than their privileged belligerent counterparts. Instead, it is operationally and legally imperative that all U.S. personnel who come in contact with such detainees understand the necessity to respect and protect them as human beings who, by virtue of the conflict in which they were captured or detained, must be deprived of their liberty until they no longer represent a threat to friendly forces. Here, it must be emphasized that the detention of unprivileged belligerents is not intended for punitive purposes, nor an express or implied sanction, and they must be treated in accordance with fundamental legal obligations applicable to any person subjected to military custody and control during armed conflict.

It is axiomatic that treatment of detainees is a critical concern for any commander responsible for conducting detainee operations. Indeed, the maltreatment of individuals captured by the United States in the context of both the armed conflicts in Afghanistan and Iraq has been a major source of criticism against the United States and a major detriment to the effectiveness of U.S. operations.[82] Unfortunately, by originally defining the armed conflict with al Qaida

---

[80] GC III, *supra* note 4, art. 12–16.

[81] *See* Ex parte Quirin, 317 U.S. 1, 30–31 (1942) ("Lawful combatants are subject to capture and detention as prisoners of war" whereas "[u]nlawful combatants are likewise subject to capture and detention, but in addition they are subject to trial and punishment . . . .").

[82] *Detainee Review Boards, supra* note 2, at 13–14 (abuses at Abu Ghraib in Iraq as well as the deaths of prisoners at Bagram).

as falling into a seam between international and non-international armed conflicts, U.S. policymakers and their legal advisors asserted that no law operated to protect the interests of these wartime detainees, even while asserting the existence of armed conflict as the legal justification for their detention.[83] This episode illustrates why it is so essential to consistently emphasize the applicability of the humane treatment principle to all detainees, irrespective of the operational context in which they are captured. It is equally essential to ensure that detention policies and tactical operating procedures reflect commitment to compliance with this principle, and that implementation of such compliance is incorporated into training at all levels of command.

Humane treatment is a fundamental LOAC principle. It is derived from reference to numerous LOAC treaty provisions applicable across the spectrum of armed conflict,[84] and from the consistent practice of professional armed forces during military operations spanning from non-conflict operations to international armed conflict.[85] Because it provides the substantive content for Common Article 3 to the four Geneva Conventions, it is therefore a non-derogable obligation during all non-international armed conflicts. The centrality of the principle of humane treatment to the Geneva tradition of protecting victims of war is reflected in the ICRC Commentary to Common Article 3:

> Humane treatment. We find expressed here the fundamental principle underlying the four Geneva Conventions. It is most fortunate that it should have been set forth in this Article, in view of the decision to dispense with a Preamble. The value of the provision is not limited to the field dealt with in Article 3. Representing, as it does, the minimum which must be applied *in the least determinate of conflicts,* its terms must a fortiori be respected in the case of international conflicts proper, when all the provisions of the Convention are applicable.[86]

Humane treatment of detainees reflects the basic concept that all individuals, even those who actively oppose friendly armed forces, are entitled to respect and treatment as human beings when no longer capable of manifesting such opposition. This in turn is premised on a truism that animates the LOAC: the execution

---

[83] Geoffrey S. Corn & Eric Talbot Jensen, *Transnational Armed Conflict: A 'Principled' Approach to the Regulation of Counter-Terror Combat Operations*, 42 Isr. L. Rev. 46, 54 (2009) (the narrow meaning of "not an international character" has been reflected in Common Article 3 of the International Committee of the Red Cross commentary. Further, the Bush administration felt that the conflict against al Qaida fell into a "twilight zone" because al Qaida was a nonstate entity and therefore not "international," and because the conflict was global it could not be considered "non-international").

[84] *See* A.P.V. Rogers, Law on the Battlefield 29 (2006).

[85] *See* Geoffrey Corn, Hamdan, *Lebanon, and the Regulation of Armed Conflict: The Need to Recognize a Hybrid Category of Armed Conflict*, 40 Vand. J. Transnat'l L. 295, 315–20 (2007) (discussing policy-based application of LOAC principles during contemporary military operations).

[86] *See* Int'l Comm. of the Red Cross Commentary, I Geneva Convention for the Amelioration of the Condition of the Wounded and Sick in Armed Forces in the Field 52 (Jean S. Pictet et al. eds., 1960) [hereinafter Commentary, GC I] (emphasis added).

of military operations represents the implementation of national purpose, and is not motivated by personal interests, anger, or revenge.[87]

Although the humane treatment mandate for any person who is hors de combat is regarded as a sacrosanct part of the LOAC, it is much more difficult to comprehensively define the content of this principle. Military legal advisors must understand that this presents a genuine implementation challenge, and that commanders must understand the underlying objective of this obligation: restrain the instincts for revenge or gratuitous violence, and in so doing mitigate the suffering associated with armed conflict. Although an enemy is justifiably subject to attack with deadly combat power prior to submission, afterward no justification exists for treatment inconsistent with the broad concept of humanity. In some way, therefore, the definition of humane treatment is similar to the definition of pornography: "you know it when you see it."[88] Or perhaps it is more accurate to state that we know a violation when we see it. The most basic meaning of humane treatment is that an individual must be treated as a human being, and nothing less. However, the precise meaning of the term "humane" has always been elusive, and more susceptible to a negative than positive definition. This is clearly reflected in the substance of Common Article 3, which states the broad humane treatment mandate, but then uses a nonexclusive list of prohibited acts to define what violates this mandate.[89] This approach to giving meaning to the principle is emphasized in another excerpt from the ICRC Commentary:

> Lengthy definition of expressions such as "humane treatment" or "to treat humanely" is unnecessary, as they have entered sufficiently into current parlance to be understood. It would therefore be pointless and even dangerous to try to enumerate things with which a human being must be provided for his normal maintenance as distinct from that of an animal, or to lay down in detail the manner in which one must behave towards him in order to show that one is treating him "humanely", that is to say as a fellow human being and not as a beast or a thing. The details of such treatment may, moreover, vary according to circumstances—particularly the climate—and to what is feasible.
>
> On the other hand, there is less difficulty in enumerating things which are incompatible with humane treatment. That is the method followed in the Convention when it proclaims four absolute prohibitions. The wording adopted could not be more definite: "To this end, the following acts 'are' and 'shall remain prohibited at any time and in any place whatsoever.'" No possible loophole is left; there can be no excuse, no attenuating circumstances.[90]

---

[87] Corn & Jensen, *supra* note 83, at 25.

[88] Jacobellis v. Ohio, 378 U.S. 184, 197 (1964) (Justice Potter Stewart concurring) (Justice Stewart refuses to define hard-core pornography, but he concludes that he knows what it is when he sees it).

[89] Expert Report of Geoffrey S. Corn at 6, Al Shimari v. CACI Intern., Inc., 933 F. Supp. 2d 793 (2013) [hereinafter Expert Report of Geoffrey Corn], *available at* https://ccrjustice.org/files/AlShimari_Expert_Report_of_Geoffrey_S_Corn.pdf.

[90] Commentary, GC I, *supra* note 86, at 53.

Although the Commentary suggests the impracticability of a comprehensive definition of humane treatment, the reference to "treatment like a human being" has tremendous significance. This is particularly true with regard to captured enemy fighters.[91] Understanding the reality that mortal combat always presents a risk of evoking the darker side of human instinct—instinct that can and often has led to acts of revenge and retribution directed toward captured opponents—is essential to appreciate the significance of the premise that humane treatment means treating a former opponent as a human being. This mandate requires warriors restore to a status of human being opponents who may have been trying to kill the detaining forces only moments prior to capture. This does not necessarily become easier the more attenuated the detainee becomes from the immediate fight. Soldiers who have been trained to vilify the enemy are required to treat that enemy in a fundamentally different manner upon capture and during all phases of detention.[92]

When a belligerent opponent is captured, he becomes hors de combat, or "out of the fight."[93] Once detention of the enemy commences, conditions of detention become the critical elements of implementing the humane treatment obligation. However, it is important to analyze this obligation based on the differing levels of detention. Commentary to Common Article 3 indicates that "[T]he details of such treatment may, moreover, vary according to circumstances—particularly the climate—and to what is feasible."[94] Here, the list of expressed prohibitions contained in Common Article 3 becomes very significant, for they indicate that even at the point of capture, in the midst of intense combat, "circumstances" can never justify abusive treatment of a detainee. This does not, of course, impede the ability of the detaining force to take measures to secure the captured enemy and protect security interests. Accordingly, there is nothing inhumane about

[91] Humane treatment operates as a counterweight against the human instinct of revenge or retribution that is so easily evoked by participation in mortal combat. One of the most difficult challenges for any battlefield warrior is to overcome the natural aversion of civilized society to the killing of another human being. Because of this, professional armed forces have long understood that preparing warriors for battle requires the dehumanization of the enemy. An interesting pop culture illustration of this is seen in a movie about the Korean War, *Fixed Bayonets!* During one scene, a young soldier confronts his first opportunity to kill an enemy with direct fire from his rifle. He is incapable of pulling the trigger, and another soldier must then shoot the enemy. However, his Sergeant mistakenly believes that the soldier who froze was actually the one who killed the enemy, and the following dialogue ensues: "[A]ll you gotta remember is that you're not shooting at a man; you're shooting at an enemy. Once you remember this you are over the hump; you are a rifleman." This fictional moment reflects the reality that transforming a civilian into a warrior requires dehumanization of the enemy. As brutal as this may sound, it has become a core tenet of military training, particularly in response to empirical studies following World War II, which indicated that a large percentage of front-line soldiers, like the fictional soldier in this film, were unable to overcome their aversion to killing, and as a result never fired a shot. It is therefore no accident that soldiers train by shooting at "silhouettes," and that the enemy is referred to with negative characterizations. Fixed Bayonets! (Twentieth Century Fox Film Corporation 1951).

[92] Expert Report of Geoffrey Corn, *supra* note 89, at 8.

[93] Blank et al., *supra* note 36, at 585.

[94] Commentary, GC I, *supra* note 86, at 53.

following what are known in U.S. military practice as the five "S's": Secure, Search, Segregate, Safeguard, and Speed to the Rear.[95] Moreover, blindfolding a captured enemy is not considered inhumane, as long as there is a security-based justification.[96]

As the detainee progresses from the point of initial capture to more long-term detention facilities, the treatment standards should become more "mature" and less ad hoc.[97] Additional concerns arise at the established detention facility level. Although the humane treatment obligation does not result in the conclusion that detainees are to be treated analogously to individuals afforded special protections, such as POWs, some fundamental aspects of POW treatment do seem to fall under the rubric of humane treatment in all contexts. These include first and foremost the provision of basic needs of human existence: adequate food, shelter, clothing, and medical care.[98] In addition, the right to free exercise of religion, respect for religious and cultural meal preferences, and access to impartial humanitarian relief agencies also should fall within the definition of humane treatment. To this end, it is significant that all of these aspects of humane treatment are expressly provided for by Additional Protocol II, the treaty that supplemented Common Article 3. Although the United States is not a party to this treaty, these provisions should be treated as a reflection of customary international law, or at a minimum "best practices," and therefore provide important insight into the established minimum standard of detainee treatment.[99]

There are, however, several other analogies to the required treatment of POWs that would arguably fall under the humane treatment mandate. The most obvious yet still controversial of these is the obligation to provide notice to some third

---

[95] *See* U.S. Dep't of Army, Field Manual 5-170, Engineer Reconnaissance 7-11 (July 1998).

[96] The creation of the detainee category of "unlawful enemy combatant" was unfortunately used at certain points in time as a basis to "manipulate" the humane treatment standard. This is clearly reflected in President Bush's February 2002 memorandum where he indicates that captured al Qaida operatives are entitled to humane treatment as a matter of "policy" and subject to the dictates of military necessity. However, the basic components of the humane treatment obligation come into force not as a matter of policy, but as a matter of law in the context of the Transnational Armed Conflict (TAC). Corn & Jensen, *supra* note 83, at 27–28.

[97] Acknowledging the indelible nature of the specific prohibitions of Common Article 3 does not, however, resolve every question regarding detainee treatment. The combat environment is one of extreme uncertainty, and even the most comprehensive detainee treatment doctrine is susceptible to this uncertainty. However, as a general proposition, the humane treatment obligation can be effectively implemented by building detainee treatment on a three-pillar foundation. The first pillar is to ensure detaining forces recognize that once hors de combat, an enemy is no longer the permissible object of hostility. The second pillar is to comply with the express prohibitions contained in Common Article 3. The final pillar is to ensure that at a minimum, conditions for detainees are never worse than those for the detaining forces. This last pillar is the essential solution to the variables of the combat environment, for it ensures that "situational" application of the humane treatment mandate is linked to a standard of reasonableness. *Id.* at 28. For example, if rations are in short supply, they will be shared equally by detaining and detained forces; medical treatment will always be based on principles of triage applied equally to detaining and detained personnel; the shelter provided for detainees will mirror that provided for detaining forces, and so on.

[98] *Id.*

[99] *See* AP II, *supra* note 33, art. 5.

party of the fact of detention.[100] For POWs, this is a critical obligation, for this notice requires ultimate accountability for the POW by the detaining power. Because of this effect, this requirement provides perhaps the most meaningful safeguard against abusive treatment or even execution of POWs. It is therefore clear that providing analogous notice to the state of nationality or to the International Committee of the Red Cross of the existence of detention for detainees not entitled to special status serves as an equally critical safeguard against maltreatment.[101] Such notice provides the detainee with some minimal sense of protection derived from outside concern, and sends a powerful signal to both the detainee and the detaining power that there will be ultimate accountability for the whereabouts and the treatment of the detainee. The extent of access to communication with third parties is more problematic, but barring some imperative security concern, there seems to be little justification for excluding such access from the scope of the obligation. Indeed, the relationship between AP II and the principle of humane treatment reflected in Common Article 3 simply bolsters the conclusion that all individuals subject to detention must be "respected and protected" at all times.

As a matter of operational practice, the humane treatment obligation must be factored into all detention operations planning and execution. Operational orders related to a given mission should anticipate detention by including a detention operations annex. This annex should include not only the procedural framework for reviewing and validating detention, but also treatment standards (to include privileges provided to detainees and procedures for imposing discipline on detainees) applicable at every level of the detention continuum. These considerations must also be factored into planning for logistics, transportation, security, and medical activities. Incorporating detainee issues into every phase of the planning process will significantly mitigate the risk of deliberate or inadvertent violations of the humane treatment obligation. An example of implementing detainee treatment standards through operational plans and annexes is reflected in Appendix A.

V. Conclusion

Detention operations are an almost inevitable aspect of all ground operations. Recent conflicts in Iraq and Afghanistan have seen the emergence of a third category of detainees: unprivileged enemy belligerents. Unfortunately, legal advisors are handicapped by the lack of a comprehensive international legal regime applicable to all operational contexts. In response to this reality, the common practice of analogizing to the most comprehensively regulated context, that of

---

[100] Corn & Jensen, *supra* note 83, at 28.

[101] GC IV, *supra* note 5, at art. 136 (authorities shall inform the ICRC of any detained persons within the shortest possible time after the detained person has been held in custody for more than two weeks).

international armed conflict, provides a useful method to fill these gaps and ensure a fair balance of interests when detention is necessary.

The decade of experience in Afghanistan and Iraq provided U.S. forces an important opportunity to learn from both mistakes and positive decisions, and capture best practices for future operations. Relying on this experience, this chapter outlined the basic methodology utilized by operational legal advisors to ensure detention operations are conducted consistently with law and U.S. policy while meeting mission imperatives. The detainee review process implemented in Afghanistan in 2009 provided detainees in that conflict with numerous substantive rules and due process protections that did not exist in the early years of the conflict. Future developments in international law and military practice will certainly result in evolutions on the determination of "what right looks like," but ensuring compliance with the most basic obligations of international law will and should remain the touchstone of effective and legitimate operations.

Appendix A: Combined Joint Operations Area Afghanistan Detainee Treatment Annex

Paragraph 14.[102] (U) Standards of Treatment. Once in the custody of U.S. Forces, the standards set forth in this policy will apply, regardless of what unit or organization originally captured the individual and/or the involvement of a non-U.S. unit or organization in the previous detention or interrogation of the individual. At a minimum, U.S. Forces will, at all times, treat detainees humanely and with dignity and respect, in accordance with the References b, f, and g.[103] Pursuant to Common Article 3 to the Geneva Conventions, U.S. law, DOD Directives, and command guidance, all persons detained by U.S. Forces shall be treated according to the following rules:

- Detainees will be treated humanely without any adverse distinction based on race, color, religion or faith, gender, birth, wealth, or any similar criteria.
- Detainees must be protected from harm and must not be subjected to murder, mutilation, torture, or cruel treatment.
- Detainees will not be abused in any way. They will not be subject to physical abuse, humiliating or degrading treatment, public curiosity, or deprivation of food, sleep, or water.
- Detainees will be afforded adequate food, drinking water, shelter, clothing, and medical treatment.
- Detainees will be allowed to practice their religion to the maximum extent possible, subject to significant operational and security considerations. Muslim detainees will be shown the direction of Mecca and told when it is time for prayer.
- If necessary for purposes of operational security, darkened goggles and earmuffs may be placed on a detainee, unless units do not have darkened goggles, then blindfolds may be used. No other items may be used to block eyesight. In accordance with Reference h,[104] no form of sensory deprivation may be used as an interrogation technique, to punish a detainee, or to disorient a detainee.

---

[102] In 2012, the overall classification of the "U.S. Detention Operations Policy in Combined Joint Operations Area—Afghanistan (CJOA-A)" (Oct. 5 2012), was Secret//Rel to USA, ISAF, NATO, however, the entirety of Paragraph 14, Standards of Treat. (listed verbatim below) of the Policy is Unclassified. Paragraph 14 appears on pages 4–6 of the Policy. The twenty-four-page base document of the Policy is Unclassified, For Official Use Only when separated from the classified annexes. There are nineteen total annexes, with the last two being classified.

[103] Reference b: DOD Directive 2310.01E, DOD Detainee Program (Sept. 5, 2006); Reference f: Common Article 3 to the Geneva Conventions; Reference g: Detainee Treatment Act of 2005 (Jan. 6, 2006).

[104] Reference h: Dep't of the Army, Field Manual 2-22.3 Human Intelligence Collector Operations (Sept. 6, 2007).

- Restraints will be the minimum required by the tactical situation. Flex cuffs will be used only when a detained person is an imminent threat to Coalition Forces and will only be used for limited time.
- Detainee Photographs. Photographing or filming detainees as well as the possession, distribution, transfer, or posting, whether electronically or physically, of visual images depicting detainees is prohibited, except as required for official duties and as specifically authorized by Commander, CJIATF 435. Official photographs should be taken to document injuries, wounds, and distinctive marks during in-processing or for investigative purposes. The genitals will be covered in all photographs unless necessary to document an injury or identifying mark on the genitals themselves. Photographs shall be appropriately marked with classification markings (Reference i, do, and dp).[105]
- No dogs, to include Military Working Dogs (MWD) or contracted dogs, will be used as part of an interrogation purpose or approach nor to harass, intimidate, threaten, coerce, or frighten a detainee. See Reference h, U.S. Army Field Manual 2-22.3, Human Intelligence Collector Operations, 6 September 2006. This paragraph does not limit other uses of MWDs authorized by the Rules for the Use of Force (RUF) and DOD Regulations. See also Reference j, CJCS Standing Rules of Engagement, 13 June 2005. Use of MWDs in the vicinity of detainees for any purpose is prohibited with the prior approval of Commander, CJIATF 435.

[105] Reference i: USCENTCOM Regulation 380-14, Security Classification Guide. Reference do: USFOR-A FRAGO 11-282, Provides Policy on Unauthorized Photography, Videos, and Audio Visual Recordings (S//REL USA, ISAF, NATO) (Nov. 4, 2011); Reference dp: HQ ISAF FRAGO 269-2011, HQ ISAF Policy on Inappropriate Photography and Video (Nov. 4, 2011).

11 }

Multinational Operations

Richard C. Gross and Ian Henderson*

There is at least one thing worse than fighting with allies—and that is to fight without them.[1]

I. Introduction

As recent combat operations in Kosovo, Iraq, Afghanistan, Libya, and North Africa have shown, nations will rarely go to battle alone; multinational or coalition operations are much more likely. Multinational operations not only allow nations to share the costs and burdens of warfare, but they also may achieve greater effectiveness when pooling resources and capabilities while simultaneously promoting international legitimacy of the operation. In order to fight effectively together as members of a coalition, nations must strive for interoperability, defined as the "ability to operate in synergy in the execution of assigned tasks."[2]

This chapter deals with the legal issues, or issues that have a legal element, that arise uniquely in multinational military operations. Issues such as interoperability of equipment or language barriers do not have a legal element and are not discussed. Rather, the:

> . . . requirements for coalition interoperability may start with, but must ultimately transcend, the relatively simple questions of equipment commonality

---

* Brigadier General Richard C. "Rich" Gross, U.S. Army and Group Captain Ian Henderson, Royal Australian Air Force. BG Gross, an Army judge advocate with multiple combat deployments including as the Chief Legal Advisor for the International Security Assistance Force (ISAF) and SJA for U.S. Forces-Afghanistan (USFOR-A). He is currently serving as the Legal Counsel to the Chairman of the Joint Chiefs of Staff, the Pentagon, Washington, DC. The views expressed are those of Brigadier General Gross and do not reflect the official policy or position of the Department of Defense, the Joint Staff, the U.S. Army, or the U.S. government. This chapter was written in Group Captain Henderson's personal capacity and does not necessarily represent the views of the Australian Department of Defence or the Australian Defence Force.

[1] MILITARY Quotes, Sir Winston Churchill Quotes (2014), *available at* http://www.military-quotes.com/churchill.htm (last visited June 18, 2014).

[2] Joint Chiefs of Staff, Joint Publication 3-16, Joint Doctrine for Multinational Operations GL-8 (Mar. 7, 2007).

> and compatibility to include interoperability in the non-materiel realm.... Planning for and achieving maximum interoperability in the non-materiel aspects of military operations can and should be a key focus of multinational cooperation initiatives.[3]

A primary focus of nonmaterial interoperability should be on legal issues.

> Legal interoperability is, in many ways, similar to technological interoperability; it is required for nations to operate effectively in coalitions. However, legal interoperability is also in many ways more difficult to achieve.... [M]ilitary planners, with the assistance of their lawyers, must find a practical way to accommodate the various legal needs of their coalition partners while ensuring that operations are not compromised.[4]

Although nations come to the coalition sharing certain legal regimes, such as customary international law, the Geneva Conventions, and the United Nations charter, they also each have a unique set of legal obligations and responsibilities that may vary widely, to include their own domestic statutory law and policy, as well as judicial rulings from their domestic courts and regional human rights courts. Beyond domestic law, some nations in the coalition may be parties to various international treaties that other nations in the coalition are not, such as the 1977 Additional Protocols to the Geneva Conventions. Each nation will have a different set of legal obligations and responsibilities, which may create issues within the coalition.

Some of these issues are inherently legal in nature, such as a prohibition on a state that is a party to the Ottawa Convention to assist, encourage, or induce another state to use antipersonnel land mines.[5] Generally, these types of issues will also be subject to various forms of legal resolution. Other issues arise from having different parts of the multinational force governed by different legal systems, policies, and orders. For example, soldiers from one country may have different leave and relief-out-of-country entitlements than those from another. This difference in entitlements may cause morale issues and thereby require the attention of commanders, but any solutions are unlikely to be of a legal nature. As another example, some nations' service members will be subject to their country's military justice system for disciplinary infractions or criminal acts, while others may be subject to civilian criminal jurisdiction in their home country.

---

[3] Doctrine, Plans and Procedures Multinational Interoperability Working Group of the Multinational Interoperability Council, *The Lead Nation Concept in Coalition Operations* 3–4 (2000), *available at* http://www.aiai.ed.ac.uk/project/coalition/coax/demo/2002/mic/LeadNationConcept.pdf (last visited June 18, 2014).

[4] Vicki McConachie, *Coalition Operations: A Compromise or an Accommodation*, *in* M.D. Carsten, *International Law and Military Operations*, 84 Int'l L. Studies 235, 235–36 (2008).

[5] *See* Convention on the Prohibition of the Use, Stockpiling, Production and Transfer of Anti-Personnel Mines, Art. 1(c), opened for signature Dec. 3, 1997, 2056 UNTS 211 (entered into force Mar. 1, 1999) [hereinafter Ottawa Convention]. This general statement is subject to further explanation at the section dealing with *Weapons* below.

Despite there being a large number of potential legal issues that might, to a greater or lesser degree, affect interoperability, there are three key areas that commanders and their legal advisors must pay attention to in every operation, namely: coalition building, state responsibility for internationally wrongful acts, and the role and impact of national caveats on operations.

II. Coalition Building

Although building and maintaining a coalition is principally a political and diplomatic activity, many legal aspects of the operation will affect coalition building. Those legal issues can be strategic, operational, tactical, or a combination thereof. First, the political leadership of a state must decide whether the state will join the military coalition, and if it does, what type of military forces it will commit, and what roles/missions those forces will be authorized to undertake. These decisions are directly influenced by strategically significant legal issues, such as the legal basis for undertaking the military operation; the command and control relationship inside the coalition; the process for target approval; and detention operations.

If we use military detention operations as an example, a fundamental issue with detention operations is the ability to hand over a detainee from one state to another, as well as the procedures in place to facilitate that handover. Differences in legal obligations can frustrate reaching an agreement on these issues. The clearest example of legal interoperability for detainee issues is whether a state believes that its military has the authority to even conduct detention operations.[6] Another good example is the conditions of detention and, therefore, whether a state is a party to Additional Protocol I, and if not, whether it accepts Article 75[7] as reflecting customary international law.[8]

If issues such as command and control, targeting, and detention operations cannot be resolved in a mutually satisfactory manner, a state is either unlikely

---

[6] A. Cole, *Legal Issues in Forming the Coalition, in* The War in Afghanistan: A Legal Analysis, 85 Int'l L. Studies 141, 149–51 (Michael Schmitt ed., 2009).

[7] *See generally* Protocol Additional to the Geneva Conventions of 12 August 1949, and Relating to the Protection of Victims of International Armed Conflict (Protocol I) art. 75 June 8, 1977, 1125 U.N.T.S. 3 [hereinafter AP I] (Article 75 lists fundamental guarantees for those persons who are in the power of a party to a conflict).

[8] C. Garraway, *England Does Not Love Coalitions—Does Anything Change?, in* The Law of War in the 21st Century: Weaponry and the Use of Force, 82 Int'l L. Studies 233, 238 (A. Helm ed., 2006). Since Garraway's article appeared, the U.S. government has stated that it "will therefore choose out of a sense of legal obligation to treat the principles set forth in Article 75 as applicable to any individual it detains in an international armed conflict, and expects all other nations to adhere to these principles as well." *See* Fact Sheet: *New Actions on Guantanamo and Detainee Policy* (2011), *available at* http://www.whitehouse.gov/sites/default/files/Fact_Sheet_--_Guantanamo_and_Detainee_Policy.pdf (last visited June 17, 2014).

to commit forces to a coalition, or to commit forces in a very limited and tightly controlled manner, thereby making interoperability a challenge.

Once the broad framework for a coalition has been agreed upon, legal issues of operational significance that need to be worked through include: basing and status of forces agreements, intelligence-sharing arrangements, logistical arrangements, rules of engagement, and interoperability issues arising out of differing legal obligations concerning weapons (e.g., antipersonnel land mines). Whereas strategic legal issues will affect whether a state will join a coalition at all, operational legal issues are more likely to affect where and how a state commits its military forces. Of course, what for one state might be an operational issue might be a strategic issue for another. Part of building and maintaining a coalition is determining what are the true legal impediments versus what issues may be manageable through innovative policy solutions. Finally, other legal issues that may arise in the course of the military operation include: discipline and personnel policies, managing exchange personnel and liaison officers, investigations, and claims. Issues of this nature should be managed in-theater and generally by the coalition commander and the various senior national representatives.[9]

Having provided a broad overview of the legal issues that may arise in multinational operations, this chapter now examines what is perhaps the most fundamental of all questions to be resolved in a multinational operation: the legal basis for the use of force.

A. LEGAL BASIS FOR THE USE OF FORCE

In a coalition operation, there may be different understandings concerning the underlying legal basis for resorting to the use of force. To take but one example as to how this might manifest itself, one state may view "the operation as a police action, another as a non-international armed conflict and a third as an international armed conflict."[10]

Although it is not essential for each potential troop-contributing nation to have a common understanding of the legal basis for the operation, divergence of opinion on this point can frustrate the forming of a coalition. As Charles Garraway explains:

> A coalition, by my definition, is a "temporary combination for special ends between parties that retain distinctive principles." The problem is not so much in the "temporary combination" as in the "distinctive principles." For

[9] "In multinational operations, each participating nation will normally be represented by a national commander responsible for ensuring that full command can be exercised and that respective national law and policies are observed." Dieter Fleck, *Legal Issues of Multinational Military Units: Tasks and Missions, Stationing Law, Command and Control*, *in* International Law across the Spectrum of Conflict: Essays in Honour of Professor L.C. Green on the Occasion of His Eightieth Birthday 75 Int'l L. Studies 161, 171 (Michael Schmitt ed., 2000). The senior national representatives will usually fulfill the national commander role.

[10] *See* McConachie, *supra* note 4, at 236.

> a coalition to work, those "distinctive principles" must be at least similar. If there is no "coalescing" there, there can be no "coalition."[11]

Even if complete agreement cannot be achieved, it is important that each potential partner nation has a clear understanding of the position of the other potential partners. This becomes more important again at the multinational commander level, as understanding why a troop-contributing nation has adopted certain rules of engagement, and targeting and detention policies, and how those rules and policies will be interpreted, requires an understanding of the nation's national policy concerning the operation. There is no reason to expect each troop-contributing nation to have identical objectives. Rather, as Raydon Gates has pointed out:

> within the coalition force we immediately have the potential for a number of different military objectives, reflecting differing national political objectives. A tension is thus created within coalition structures, in my view that tension is an enduring feature of coalitions and therefore of the future war fighting landscape. It is up to military commanders to account for and manage national divergences so that unity of effort is maintained, within national constraints and in accordance with national priorities.[12]

That nation's understanding of the legal basis for the operation will significantly influence national policy. Where troop-contributing nations have significantly different views on the legal basis for an operation, the multinational commander will be presented with many challenges. A well-known issue for such a multinational commander is the appropriate assignment of troops to task based on the various rules of engagement (or legal positions) adopted by each troop-contributing nation. Michael Short gives an example from the NATO air campaign in Kosovo:

> In the case of the Canadians, there were targets I knew the Canadian F-18s were not allowed to attack. . . . So it was my job to assign those targets to a nation with less restrictive guidance. I could still use the Canadians in many roles. It is my job to fold all those capabilities together and produce a coherent war-making effort.[13]

Gates provides another example:

> It may be possible for a coalition commander to use the forces of another nation to undertake a task with more freedom of maneuver than would be available to their own forces. For example, I experienced this in the Red Sea

---

[11] *See* Garraway, *supra* note 8, at 234.

[12] *See* R. Gates, *Toward 2015, Challenges for a Medium Navy: An Australian Perspective*, *in* The Law of War in the 21st Century: Weaponry and the Use of Force 82 Int'l L. Studies 259, 260 (A. Helm ed., 2006).

[13] *See, e.g.*, M. Short, *Operation Allied Force from the Perspective of the NATO Air Commander*, *in* Legal and Ethical Lessons of NATO's Kosovo Campaign 78 Int'l L. Studies 19, 29 (A.E. Wall ed., 2002).

> in 1992/93 where Australian ROE gave our units greater freedom of action, in certain areas, when conducting maritime interception operations with coalition partners. This was an advantage to the US commander, who subsequently employed RAN units closest to the Straits of Tiran at the mouth of the Gulf of Aqaba to intercept "inspection runners" when required.[14]

Managing differing rules of engagement is discussed further in the section on "Rules of Engagement" below.

B. RESPONSIBILITY FOR INTERNATIONALLY WRONGFUL ACTS

The assignment of responsibility for internationally wrongful acts in multinational operations is a developing area of the law. In a typical state-on-state conflict, if a member of the armed forces of State A tortures and shoots a prisoner of war from State B, the legal analysis to determine whether State A is responsible for the act of torture and killing is relatively straightforward. However, to date this has not proven to easily be the case for multinational operations. There are two reasons for this. First, the inherent complexity of multinational operations means determining which state, states, or international organizations might incur international responsibility requires careful factual and legal analysis. In addition, the law itself on state (and international organization) responsibility, particularly in military operations, is not yet completely certain.

Determining which state has, or shares, legal responsibility for internationally wrongful acts that are committed in the complex command and control arrangements that typically arise in multinational operations is not straightforward.[15] One of the difficulties in providing a clear legal answer to such issues is that the role and responsibility of a coalition commander under international law is not as well developed as the doctrine of "command responsibility," which has historically been applied along national command lines. Note, the issue here is not about individual or command responsibility for war crimes or similar,[16] but rather the general notion of responsibility of a state or international organization for an internationally wrongful act.

Although it has been suggested that all members of a coalition should bear joint responsibility for the internationally wrongful acts of any other member,[17]

---

[14] *See* Gates, *supra* note 12, at 260.

[15] Indeed, "for the military lawyer, issues of State responsibility for the actions of others are some of the most complex that they encounter in coalition operations." Cole, *supra* note 6, at 148.

[16] On the potential for a coalition commander to be found liable under the doctrine of command responsibility for the actions of foreign coalition forces, see Christopher Hanna, *The Doctrine of Command Responsibility in Coalition Operations: Who's in Charge?* (2009) (masters Paper, University of Sydney) (on file with author).

[17] T. Stein, *Coalition Warfare and Differing Legal Obligations of Coalition Members under International Humanitarian Law*, *in* LEGAL AND ETHICAL LESSONS OF NATO'S KOSOVO CAMPAIGN, 78 INT'L L. STUDIES 317, 334 (A.E. Wall ed., 2002).

that is not the law.[18] At the simplest level, the international legal responsibilities of states vary. Also, the roles of coalition partners in operations are different. It would seem peculiar, for example, if in an operation led by the United States, and to which both Australia and New Zealand contribute forces, that New Zealand might attract international legal responsibility for an act committed by Australian forces during a mission authorized by an American commander and to which New Zealand had not participated in either the planning or execution.

Rather, to determine potential legal liability, one must examine the law that deals with the responsibility of states and international organizations. Accordingly, the following section will analyze the Articles on State Responsibility for internationally wrongful acts prepared by the International Law Commission,[19] along with the Draft Articles on the Responsibility of International Organizations.[20] Note that neither set of articles are treaties, and therefore they possess no independent force of law. However, in the case of the Articles on State Responsibility, they are potentially a useful black-letter expression of what may be customary international law.[21] The draft Articles on the Responsibility of International Organizations are yet to be finalised by the International Law Commission, so greater caution needs to be adopted when considering their status as reflective of customary international law.[22]

C. LAW COMMISSION ARTICLES ON STATE AND INTERNATIONAL ORGANIZATION RESPONSIBILITY

The Law Commission Articles establish five ways in which a state or international organization could attract international responsibility in a multinational operation.

---

[18] For example, the European Human Rights Court recently held that the United Nations had immunity and national courts had no jurisdiction over the United Nations in the "Mothers of Srebrenica" case against Dutch UN peacekeepers. *See Stitching Mothers of Srebrenica and others* v. *The Netherlands* (dec.), Application no. 65542/12, ECtHR, ¶ 156 (June 11, 2013).

[19] Responsibility of States for Internationally Wrongful Acts, G.A. Res. 56/83, Annex, U.N. Doc. A/RES/56/83 (Dec. 12, 2001) [hereinafter Articles on State Responsibility].

[20] *Responsibility of International Organizations: Texts and Titles of Draft Articles 1 to 67*, International Law Commission, work of Its Sixty-Third Session, U.N. Doc. A/CN.4/L.778 (2011), *available at* http://legal.un.org/ilc/texts/instruments/english/draft%20articles/9_11_2011.pdf (last visited June 18, 2014) [hereinafter Draft Articles on the Responsibility of International Organizations].

[21] *See* C. Bell, *Reassessing Multiple Attribution: The International Law Commission and the Behrami and Saramati Decision*, 42 N.Y.U. J. INT'L L. & POL. 501, 520–21 and the cases discussed therein.

[22] *See, e.g., Al-Jedda* v. *United Kingdom* [2011] ECtHR 1092, ¶ 56, 84 (July 7, 2011) [hereinafter *Al-Jedda*].

1. Article 4: Conduct of Organs of a State

First, and uncontroversially, Article 4 of the Articles on State Responsibility states that the actions of an organ of state "shall be considered an act of that State under international law" and "officers of the military are a *de jure* organ of the [State]."[23] In addition, a person or a group who is not otherwise a state organ may, in very limited circumstances, be equated with a state organ for the purposes of state responsibility. The International Court of Justice held that to:

> determine . . . whether or not the relationship of the *contras* to the United States Government was so much one of dependence on the one side and control on the other that it would be right to equate the *contras*, for legal purposes, with an organ of the United States Government, or as acting on behalf of that Government[.][24]

Further, in the *Bosnian Genocide Case*, the International Court of Justice held that:

> persons, groups of persons or entities may, for purposes of international responsibility, be equated with State organs even if that status does not follow from internal law, provided that in fact the persons, groups or entities act in "complete dependence" on the State, of which they are ultimately merely the instrument. In such a case, it is appropriate to look beyond legal status alone, in order to grasp the reality of the relationship between the person taking action, and the State to which he is so closely attached as to appear to be nothing more than its agent . . . .
>
> However, so to equate persons or entities with State organs when they do not have that status under internal law must be exceptional, for it requires proof of a particularly great degree of State control over them, a relationship which the Court's Judgment quoted above expressly described as "complete dependence" . . . it is only if this condition is met that they can be equated with organs of the Respondent for the purposes of its international responsibility.[25]

If the actions were not committed by an organ of the state, or an entity that is equated to being a state organ due to its "complete dependence," then further analysis under the Articles on State Responsibility is required. Four further

---

[23] *Case concerning the Application of the Convention on the Prevention and Punishment of the Crime of Genocide (Bosnia and Herzegovina v. Serbia and Montenegro) (Judgment)* I.C.J. 91, ¶ 388 (2007). [Hereinafter *Herzegovina v. Serbia and Montenegro*]. *See also Case concerning Armed Activities on the Territory of the Congo* (*Democratic Republic of the Congo* v *Uganda*) (Judgment) (2005) I.C.J. Rep. 168, ¶ 213–4 ("The conduct of individual soldiers and officers . . . is to be considered as the conduct of a State organ" and "a party to an armed conflict shall be responsible for all acts by persons forming part of its armed forces.").

[24] *Military and Paramilitary Activities in and against Nicaragua (Nicaragua v. United States of America) (Merits)*, 1986 I.C.J., Rep. 14, ¶ 109 [hereinafter *Nicaragua*].

[25] *Case concerning the Application of the Convention on the Prevention and Punishment of the Crime of Genocide (Bosnia and Herzegovina v. Serbia and Montenegro) (Judgment)*, 2007 I.C.J., ¶ 392–3 [hereinafter *Bosnian Genocide* case].

grounds for attributing state responsibility are particularly relevant to analyzing multinational operations.

2. Article 6: Conduct of Organs Placed at the Disposal of a State by Another State

Article 6 of the Articles on State Responsibility states that the conduct of an organ of State A that is placed at the disposal of State B shall be considered an act of State B under international law if the organ is acting in the exercise of elements of the governmental authority of State B.[26] Article 7 of the Draft Articles on the Responsibility of International Organizations provides for a similar result in the case of international organizations, although perhaps in clearer terms:

> The conduct of an organ of a State or an organ or agent of an international organization that is placed at the disposal of another international organization shall be considered under international law an act of the latter organization if the organization exercises effective control over that conduct.[27]

The key issue to determine is whether an organ of State A has been placed at the disposal of State B (or at the disposal of an international organization such as the United Nations). According to James Crawford, the issue is whether the organ of State A acts "with the consent, under the authority of and for the purposes of the receiving State."[28] This means the organ must be appointed to perform functions attaching to the state at whose disposal it is placed. The International Law Committee explained:

> The criterion for attribution of conduct either to the contributing State or organization or to the receiving organization is based . . . on the factual control that is exercised over the *specific conduct* taken by the organ or agent placed at the receiving organization's disposal.[29]

The International Court of Justice held in its 2007 decision in the *Bosnian Genocide* case that:

> It must however be shown that this "effective control" was exercised, or that the State's instructions were given, *in respect of each operation* in which the

---

[26] *See* Articles on State Responsibility, *supra* note 19, at art. 6.

[27] Draft Articles on the Responsibility of International Organizations, *supra* note 20, art. 7. In fact, notwithstanding dealing with conduct placed at the disposal of another state, art. 7 of the Draft Articles on the Responsibility of International Organizations is closer in wording to Article 8 of the Articles on State Responsibility dealing with the conduct of a person or group rather than an organ of state. Article 8 of the Articles on State Responsibility states: "The conduct of a person or group of persons shall be considered an act of a State under international law if the person or group of persons is in fact acting on the instructions of, or under the direction or control of, that State in carrying out the conduct." Articles on State Responsibility, *supra* note 19.

[28] James Crawford, The International Law Commission's Articles on State Responsibility: Introduction, Text and Commentaries 103 (2002).

[29] Report of the International Law Commission on the Work of Its Fifty-Sixth Session, U.N. GAOR, 59th Sess., Supp. No. 10, U.N. Doc. A/59/10 at 111 (2004) (emphasis added).

> alleged violations occurred, *not generally in respect of the overall actions* taken by the persons or groups of persons having committed the violations.[30]

Although other tests have been expounded, they have generally not found ongoing favor. For example, the International Court of Justice specifically rejected, in the 2007 *Bosnian Genocide* case, the argument that state responsibility might be incurred on the basis of "overall control."[31] Importantly, to the extent that the ICTY Appeals chamber had previously held otherwise in *Prosecutor v. Tadic*,[32] the ICJ disagreed with this previous ruling.[33]

The decisions of the European Court of Human Rights are helpful in understanding how these tests are to be applied. It is important to realize that the following discussion deals with attribution of responsibility between a state and the United Nations, and, therefore, is dealing with the Draft Articles on the Responsibility of International Organizations rather than the Articles on State Responsibility. In the *Behrami/Saramati* cases, the European Court of Human Rights indicated that the operative issue is which state exercised "ultimate authority and control" over the conduct of the operation.[34] However, in the subsequent 2011 decision in the *Al-Jedda* case, the European Court of Human Rights held:

> that the conduct of an organ of a State placed at the disposal of an international organisation should be attributable under international law to that organisation if the organisation exercises effective control over that conduct (see paragraphs 18 and 56 above). For the reasons set out above, the Court considers that the United Nations Security Council had neither effective control nor ultimate authority and control over the acts and omissions of troops within the Multi-National Force and that the applicant's detention was not, therefore, attributable to the United Nations.[35]

We have, therefore, a mixing of both the "effective control" and "ultimate authority and control" tests.

---

[30] *Bosnian Genocide* case, *supra* note 25, ¶ 400 (emphases added). *See also Mustafić-Mujić et al. v. The Netherlands*, Judgment (English translation), July 5, 2011, *available at* http://zoeken.rechtspraak.nl/detailpage.aspx?ljn=BR5386 & *Nuhanović v. The Netherlands*; Judgment (English translation), July 5, 2011, *available at* http://zoeken.rechtspraak.nl/detailpage.aspx?ljn=BR5388 [hereinafter *Mustafic/Nuhanovic cases*]; *Nicaragua*, *supra* note 24, ¶ 115 (noting that the term "effective control" may have different meanings depending upon whether the issue is one of state responsibility or command responsibility); Hanna, *supra* note 16, at 68–69); Draft Articles on the Responsibility of International Organizations, *supra* note 20, at art. 6; Bell, *supra* note 21, at 513–14.

[31] *Bosnian Genocide* case, *supra* note 25, ¶ 404.

[32] *Prosecutor v. Tadic*, (*Appeals Chamber*) IT-94-1-A, Judgment, ¶ 145 (July 15, 1999).

[33] *Bosnian Genocide* case, *supra* note 25, ¶¶ 404–406. *But see* dissenting opinions of Vice-President Al-Khasawneh, ¶¶ 37–39 and of judge *ad hoc* Mahiou, ¶¶ 112–117.

[34] *Behrami v. France; Saramati v. France* (Dec.), nos. 71412/01 and 78166/01, ECt.HR, ¶ 133 (2007), *available at* http://cmiskp.echr.coe.int/tkp197/search.asp [hereinafter *Behrami/Saramati cases*]

[35] *Al-Jedda*, *supra* note 22, ¶ 84.

Two relevant domestic court decisions are 2011 decisions of the Dutch Court of Appeal in the related *Mustafic/Nuhanovic* cases.[36] Although not referring to the 2007 decisions of the European Court of Human Rights in *Behrami/Saramati*,[37] the Dutch Court of Appeal stated, "the decisive criterion for attribution is not who exercised 'command and control', but who actually was in possession of 'effective control'."[38]

3. Article 16: Aid or Assistance in the Commission of an Internationally Wrongful Act

Article 16 of the Articles on State Responsibility states that where State A aids or assists State B in the commission of an internationally wrongful act by State B, State A is internationally responsible where State A acted with knowledge of the circumstances of the internationally wrongful act, and the act would have been internationally wrongful if committed by State A.[39] This is an example of separate liability. State B is responsible for its own unlawful act, and State A is responsible not as a joint actor but rather for its own unlawful act in aiding or assisting the perpetration of an act that was unlawful for both States A and B. Accordingly, State A is only responsible to the extent that its own conduct has contributed to the internationally wrongful act.[40] Also, it is only where the act of State B would have been unlawful if committed by State A that State A has international responsibility.[41] Where State A and State B's international legal responsibilities vary such that what would be an unlawful act for State B is not an unlawful act for State A,[42] State A does not attract liability under this article.

4. Article 17: Direction and Control Exercised Over the Commission of an Internationally Wrongful Act

Article 17 of the Articles on State Responsibility states that where State A directs or controls the commission of an internationally wrongful act by State B, State A is internationally responsible where State A acted with knowledge of the circumstances of the internationally wrongful act, and the act would have been an internationally wrongful act if committed by State A.[43] Similar to Article 16, to attract liability under Article 17, the act in question must have been wrongful for

---

[36] *Mustafic/Nuhanovic* cases, *supra* note 30.

[37] The judgments in the *Mustafic/Nuhanovic* cases were handed down just before the decision in Al-Jedda.

[38] *Mustafic/Nuhanovic* cases, *supra* note 30, at ¶ 5.7.

[39] For international organizations, see Draft Article on the Responsibility of International Organizations, *supra* note 20, at art. 14.

[40] This point is explained in more detail in Articles on State Responsibility, *supra* note 19.

[41] *Id.*

[42] For example, State B is a party to a treaty obligation that is not binding (either as a matter of treaty or customary international law) on State A.

[43] For international organizations, see Draft Articles on the Responsibility of International Organizations, *supra* note 20, art. 15. For entities not associated with another state, see also Article 8 of the *Draft Articles on State Responsibility*.

State A if committed directly by State A.[44] The mere ability or authority to be able to give direction or exercise control is not enough to attract liability under this article—actual direction or control must have been exercised with respect to the act of interest.[45] An interesting example is referred to by the International Law Committee of the responsibility of a military occupier who directs the operations of the occupied police force:

> [D]uring the belligerent occupation of Italy by Germany in the Second World War, it was generally acknowledged that the Italian police in Rome operated under the control of the occupying Power. Thus, the protest by the Holy See in respect of wrongful acts committed by Italian police who forcibly entered the Basilica of St. Paulin Rome in February 1944 asserted the responsibility of the German authorities. In such cases the occupying State is responsible for acts of the occupied State that it directs and controls.[46]

Notably though, the extent of liability under Articles 16 and 17 is different. While liability under Article 16 is limited to the extent of State A's aid or assistance to State B, under Article 17 State A's liability is for the entire internationally wrongful act of State B, due to direction and control exercised by State A.

5. Article 18: Coercion of Another State

Article 18 of the Articles on State Responsibility states that where State A coerces the commission of an internationally wrongful act by State B, State A is internationally responsible where State A acted with knowledge of the circumstances of the internationally wrongful act, and the act would, but for the coercion, have been an internationally wrongful act by State B.[47] In this case, State A is responsible not for the act of coercion per se, but for the internationally wrongful act that it coerced State B to commit. State B has no international responsibility because of the coercion. In this case, State A has responsibility even if the act committed does not breach an international obligation of State A.[48] Actual coercion (i.e., where State B had no effective choice but to comply) must have been exercised. The strong influence and guidance of a stronger state as part of a military alliance is not enough. For example, take the *Romano-Americana* case from WWI where in 1916 the Romanian government ordered the destruction of certain oil storage and other facilities owned by a U.S. company but located within Romanian territory. The destruction was ordered as Romania was then at war with the Germans, who were planning an invasion. The government of the United States originally commenced action against the British government on the basis that the British authorities had compelled the Romanian authorities to order the destruction, the British

---

[44] *See* U.N. Doc A/56/10, *supra* note 40, at 69.

[45] *Id.* at 68–69.

[46] *Id.* at 68 (internal footnote omitted).

[47] For international organizations, see Draft Articles on the Responsibility of International Organizations, *supra* note 20, art. 16.

[48] *See* U.N. Doc A/56/10, *supra* note 40, at 70.

government being the stronger ally in the alliance. The British government denied responsibility on the basis that it had simply urged and advised the Romanian government to take action on the basis of common sense and in furtherance of the common cause. After negotiations, America dropped its case against the United Kingdom and pursued action directly against the Romanian government.[49]

6. Article 47: Plurality of Responsible States

Finally, it is worth noting that it may also be possible for more than one entity to share legal responsibility. For example, Article 47 of the Articles on State Responsibility provides that "[w]here several States are responsible for the same internationally wrongful act, the responsibility of each State may be invoked in relation to that act."[50] Unlike the previously cited articles, this article does not deal with determining whether State A is internationally responsible for the acts of State B, but rather finds that both States A and B can be concurrently liable.[51]

The following section analyzes various operational scenarios to determine where international legal responsibility might lie.

D. COUNTER-PIRACY OPERATION

Operation SAFE SEAS is a hypothetical counter-piracy operation off the coast of Redland. The operation is conducted by a multinational (combined) naval task force (CTF 700).[52] Although the counter-piracy operation is supported by various UN Security Council resolutions, it is not directly authorized by any particular resolution, nor is it under UN command or control. Blueland has provided the task force commander (CCTF 700). Blackland has supplied naval assets (CTU 700.1.1).

A civilian commercial vessel (MT *Heart of Gold*, a Panaland flagged vessel) has been hijacked by "pirates" from Redland. A plan is devised and presented to

---

[49] *Id.;* Roberto Ago, Eighth Report on State Responsibility, Special Rapporteur—the Internationally Wrongful Act of the State, Source of International Responsibility 24 U.N. Doc A/CN.4/318 and Add.1 to 4.

[50] For international organizations, see Draft Articles on the Responsibility of International Organizations, *supra* note 20, art. 48.

[51] This issue is the main subject of discussion in the article by Bell, *supra* note 21. In *Behrami/Saramati*, the court did not specifically rule out joint or multiple responsibility; rather the court "found the conduct in question to be attributable to the UN and stopped its assessment there, dismissing on that basis the claim against the states. The Court thus failed to carry out the additional multiple attribution analysis . . . ." *Id.* at 515. *See also Mustafic/Nuhanovic, supra* note 30, at ¶ 5.9 (holding that the possibility that more than one party has effective control is generally accepted, so it cannot be ruled out that there can be attribution to more than one party).

[52] The usual nomenclature adopted by NATO and a number of other Western forces is, in descending order: Task Force (TF), Task Group (TG), Task Unit (TU), and Task Element (TE). With each subdivision, a decimal point and (usually) a single digit number is added (e.g., TF 633, TG 633.2, TU 633.1.3, TE 633.1.1.2). Where forces from two or more national services are working together, the word "joint: is added (e.g., Joint Task Force (JTF). Where forces from two or more states are working together, the word "combined" is added (e.g., Combined Task Force (CTF). And finally, a multinational, multiservice force would be a Combined Joint Task Force (CJTF).

CCTF 700 (Blueland) for a mission to be executed by CTU 700.1.1 (Blackland) to recapture the MT *Heart of Gold* and take the "pirates" into custody.

Presume that in the course of conducting the mission, an internationally wrongful act is committed by members of the naval forces of CTU 700.1.1 (Blackland). As a multinational headquarters (CTF 700 (Blueland) in this case) is unlikely to have a legal personality of its own,[53] there is a need to determine whether it is the state of Blueland, Blackland, both states, the United Nations, or all who might be liable for the alleged internationally wrongful act.

By approving an operation plan for the boarding of the MT *Heart of Gold*, it is *arguable* that CCTF 700 (Blueland) exercised effective command and control over the operation. In addition, as a senior naval officer of Blueland acted within the scope of his or her apparent authority, the actions of CCTF 700 (Blueland) will be attributed to Blueland.[54]

Alternatively, and probably the better argument, is whether CCTF 700 (Blueland) exercised effective command and control over the operation; this depends on the nature of the alleged internationally wrongful act. For example, if it is being argued that the mere boarding alone was an internationally wrongful act, then there is a strong argument that Blueland exercised effective control over the decision to conduct a boarding.

Another alternative is that the alleged internationally wrongful act was committed in the course of an otherwise lawful boarding; for example, excessive force is alleged to have been used by Blackland to restrain a member of the pirate's crew. In such a case, if CCTF 700 (Blueland) had signed an operation plan that provided merely for the conduct of boarding operations "pursuant to international law," then it could be argued that an excessive use of force by a member of the boarding party from CTU 700.1.1 (Blackland) is not attributable to Blueland.[55] Arguably, the mere approval of an operation plan does not invoke state responsibility under any of the draft articles. The most relevant article would be Article 17, which deals with the situation where State A directs or controls the commission of an internationally wrongful act by State B. However, the mere ability or authority to be able to give direction or exercise control is not enough to attract liability under this article—actual direction or control must have been exercised with respect to the act of interest.[56] In other words, it is not sufficient that CCTF 700 (Blueland) could have exercised effective control over the conduct of the boarding operation. Rather, to attract state liability for Blueland under Article 17, CCTF 700 (Blueland) must have actually exercised control over the boarding operation.

---

[53] Fleck, *supra* note 9, at 170.

[54] *See generally* Herzegovina v. Serbia and Montenegro, *supra* note 24.

[55] In the words of Cole, this approach to authorization or direction "does not presuppose an activity which the commander is not allowed to carry out himself." Cole, *supra* note 6, at 149.

[56] *See* U.N. Doc A/56/10, *supra* note 40, at 68–69; *Bosnian Genocide* case, *supra* note 25, ¶ 400.

Returning to the example of where it is alleged that the mere boarding alone was an internationally wrongful act, assume the boarding was conducted on the basis of receiving consent of the master of the ship. There are two opposing schools of thought as to whether a boarding on the high seas can be conducted on the basis of the master's consent. There is general agreement that states may board their own-state flagged vessels, board other-state flagged vessels under Article 110 of the United Nations Convention on the Law of the Sea,[57] and board other-state flagged vessels based on consent of the flagged state. However, there is a divergence of opinion among states on whether a state may, in the absence of other authority, board an other-state flagged commercial vessel in international waters based not on consent of the flagged state but only on the master's consent.[58] Assume for the purposes of this example that the MT *Heart of Gold* was boarded on the basis of the master's consent, and further assume that Panaland is now arguing that that is not a valid basis for boarding under international law. If the plan required CCTF 700 (Blueland) to personally give prior approval for any proposed boarding where the basis for the boarding would be the master's consent, then CCTF 700 (Blueland) would be exercising effective control over that particular operation. But if the plan stated that approval for any proposed boarding must be given by the appropriate senior national representative of a CTU, then CCTF 700 would not be exercising effective control over the particular operation. Rather, the role of CCTF 700 (Blueland) would be better thought of as coordinating, but not directing, the actions of the various CTUs.

Another example is if the government of Blueland characterized Operation SAFE SEAS as an "armed conflict" and stated that is would apply and comply with the law of armed conflict.[59] However, the government of Blackland stated that it believed Operation SAFE SEAS instead to be a law enforcement activity. As a result of the different characterizations of the military operation, the government of Blueland prohibited during planned operations against the pirates the use of bullets that expand or flatten easily in the human body, whereas the government of Blackland had authorized the use of such bullets. Generally, an appropriate approach for CCTF 700 would be to approve the plan for CTU 700.1.1 (Blackland) to undertake the recapture mission without the plan dealing with the type of ammunition to be used. In such circumstances, it would be arguable that the choice of

---

[57] *United Nations Convention on the Law of the Sea*, opened for signature Dec. 10, 1982, 1833 UNTS 3 (entered into force Nov. 16, 1994). In summary, a warship may exercise a right of boarding commercial vessels when there are reasonable grounds to suspect that: (a) the ship is engaged in piracy; (b) the ship is engaged in the slave trade; (c) the ship is engaged in unauthorized broadcasting and the flag State of the warship has jurisdiction under article 109; (d) the ship is without nationality; or (e) though flying a foreign flag or refusing to show its flag, the ship is, in reality, of the same nationality as the warship. *Id.*

[58] *See generally* D. Wilson, *Interdiction on the High Seas: The Role and Authority of a Master in the Boarding and Searching of His Ships by Foreign Warships*, 55 NAVAL L. REV. 157 (2008).

[59] The government of Blueland has not stated whether the conflict is an international or non-international armed conflict.

ammunition is a tactical decision and properly rests with CTU 700.1.1 (Blackland); and, therefore, is the national responsibility of Blackland.

Importantly, there is little to no likelihood that responsibility would attach to the United Nations. As held in *Al-Jedda*:

> The Court does not consider that, as a result of the authorisation contained in Resolution 1511, the acts of soldiers within the Multi-National Force became attributable to the United Nations or—more importantly, for the purposes of this case—ceased to be attributable to the troop-contributing nations . . . The unified command structure over the force, established from the start of the invasion by the United States and United Kingdom, was not changed as a result of Resolution 1511 . . . Although the United States was requested to report periodically to the Security Council about the activities of the Multi-National Force, the United Nations did not, thereby, assume any degree of control over either the force or any other of the executive functions of the Coalition Provisional Authority.[60]

E. MULTINATIONAL OPERATION TO ASSIST WITH SECURITY

A different example, with likely different outcomes for who has international legal responsibility during multinational operations, would be a UN security force established by resolution of the UN Security Council to assist with security in Redland after troubled elections.[61]

1. Force Is under UN Command and Control

Assume our hypothetical security force is titled "United Nations International Security Force-Redland" (UNISF-R). UNISF-R is a so-called "blue helmet" force (i.e., a force acting under the direct command and control of the United Nations). Blueland agrees to provide the commander for UNISF-R. Blackland contributes a military contingent, and assigns operational control[62] to Commander UNISF-R. As states will rarely, if ever, transfer full command to an officer of another state in an alliance or coalition,[63] Blackland has retained 'national command' for itself.[64]

Acting under a broad operational order to maintain security, military forces of Blackland detain a number of Redland citizens prior to a protest that had been organized. The Redland citizens allege a violation of their human rights for

---

[60] *Al-Jedda, supra* note 22, at ¶ 80; *see also Stichting Mothers of Srebrenica and others* v. *The Netherlands* (Dec.), Application no. 65542/12, ECtHR, ¶ 154 (June 11, 2013).

[61] *See generally* Behrami/Saramati, *supra* note 34; *Al-Jedda, supra* note 22, ¶ 83 (summarizing the *Behrami/Saramati* decision).

[62] NATO, Glossary of Terms and Definitions, 2-O-3 (2014), *available at* http://nsa.nato.int/nsa/zPublic/ap/aap6/AAP-6.pdf (last visited June 19, 2014).

[63] Fleck, *supra* note 9, at 171.

[64] The NATO glossary does not provide a useful contemporary definition for national command. In this context, national command means retaining the responsibility for discipline, as well as the authority to withdraw the forces or veto any assigned mission.

extrajudicial detention. Which party should be the "proper respondent" for the alleged wrongful detention? Analyzed under the Articles on State Responsibility and the decisions in *Behrami/Saramati* and *Al-Jedda*, it is clear that the mere retention of national command does not of itself result in international responsibility for wrongful acts. This is because retention of national command does not negate a force being placed at the disposal of another state or organization. Rather, the operative issue when determining whether a force has been placed at the disposal of another is determining which entity exercised effective control over the conduct of the operation?[65] Where the United Nations exercises operational command or control over assigned forces, then international responsibility will be attributed to the United Nations.[66] Whether or not Blueland and Blackland also share international responsibility under Article 47 of the Articles on State Responsibility will be fact specific, as shown by the cases of *Mustafic/Nuhanovic*.[67]

Importantly, Article 47 is not about assigning or determining state responsibility as such, but rather is a reminder that more than one state can be concurrently liable. Accordingly, for either Blueland or Blackland to share international responsibility with the United Nations pursuant to Article 6, one or both of those states must have also exercised effective control over the operation. This will not have occurred merely because a senior officer from Blueland was the commander of the security force, and Blackland was the military contingent that conducted the detention operation. Rather, more direct national involvement will have to have occurred in a manner similar to that in *Mustafic/Nuhanovic*. A key factor will be the level of discretion available in determining who is subject to detention, as this will be an indicator of who had the relevant effective control over the operation—recalling that mere "overall control' is not sufficient to attract state liability.[68] That discretion might be in relation to the "groups" that were subject to detention, or it might be in relation to whether a particular person came within the ambit of one of those groups.

2. Role of Multinational Force Commanders

A question that does not go directly to issues of state responsibility but nonetheless is an issue that arises in multinational operations is: What is the appropriate role for the multinational force commander in dealing with diverging national opinions on international legal obligations? To return to the earlier example of the boarding operation that was to be conducted as part of Operation SAFE SEAS, suppose the government of Blueland is of the view that under international law a consensual boarding requires explicit flag state consent and not just the master's consent, whereas the government of Blackland is of the opposite view.[69] The usual course would be for the government of Blueland to have directed its military, and particularly CCTF 700, not to engage in any decision-making concerning

---

[65] *See Mustafic/Nuhanovic* case, *supra* note 30, ¶ 5.7.

[66] *See Behrami/Saramati, supra* note 34, ¶¶ 139–141.

[67] *See generally Mustafic/Nuhanovic, supra* note 30.

[68] *See supra* note 31 and accompanying text.

[69] *See* Cole, *supra* note 6, at 149.

military action contrary to Blueland's international legal obligations. Clearly the best course of action for CCTF 700 in such circumstances is to be careful and to limit his or her role to merely approving a broad operation plan, as opposed to approving a particular execution of that plan.

3. Mentoring (aka "Train/Assist/Advise")

Another type of operational relationship warranting discussion is that of military mentor and liaison teams, sometimes referred to as "train/assist/advise (TAA) teams." Although the exact nature of any given mentor and liaison team may vary, for the purposes of discussion NATO provides a useful outline in a "fact sheet" dealing with operations in Afghanistan.[70] Based on the fact sheet, we see the role for a mentoring and liaison team is to provide training and mentoring to the military forces of another state, serve as a liaison capability between the military forces of the mentoring state (or an alliance/coalition) and the mentored state's military forces, coordinate the planning of operations, and ensure that the mentored units receive necessary enabling support (e.g., close air support and casualty/medical evacuation).[71] Now, suppose that the mentored forces commit an internationally wrongful act. For example, it is alleged that in two separate incidents, members of the Afghan Army under the training and mentorship of the Australian Defence Force torched houses, beat up several people in a remote northern area of Afghanistan, and killed a prisoner who was under arrest for suspicion of being an insurgent.[72]

Again, the analysis of whether the actions of a mentor and liaison team vis-à-vis the internationally wrongful act are such as to incur state liability will be fact specific; there is no presumption of state liability. Although mentor and liaison teams are tasked to assist with the development of a mentored state's armed forces, mentoring and liaison teams generally do not have a command relationship vis-à-vis the mentored forces. Mentoring and liaison teams are there to train, guide, and assist, not to direct and command. Of course, the exact command and control relationship in any specific case must be examined. Often, an important part of the mentoring is "teaching" the mentored armed forces relevant international legal obligations and operationally appropriate means and methods for conducting military operations in conformity with those obligations. In such an environment, the obligation on the mentoring state is to provide appropriate instruction, act as a role model for correct action, and not knowingly assist or direct the commission of an internationally wrongful act. A s a distinct rule, there is no legal obligation on the mentoring state to positively prevent the commission of internationally wrongful acts by the mentored armed forces, nor does the mentoring state assume or share liability if such acts are committed contrary to the training and mentoring being

---

[70] NATO, Fact Sheet: *NATO's Operational Mentor and Liaison Teams (OMLTs)* (2009), http://www.nato.int/isaf/topics/factsheets/omlt-factsheet.pdf (last visited June 17, 2014).

[71] *Id.*

[72] J. Kelly, *US Shift Leaves Diggers Exposed*, THE AUSTRALIAN, Feb. 19, 2011, *available at* http://www.theaustralian.com.au/national-affairs/us-shift-leaves-diggers-exposed/story-fn59niix-1226008394o.

provided. Rather, the mentoring state incurs state liability only pursuant to the legal principles discussed above.

The most relevant articles of the Articles on State Responsibility are likely to be Article 16 (aids or assists) or Article 17 (directs or controls). Both articles require knowledge of the circumstances of the internationally wrongful act.[73] Assume the above allegations occurred in the context of a planned cordon and search operation. Unless the mentor and liaison team provided assistance in the knowledge that houses would be burnt and people assaulted, liability will not be incurred under Article 16. Nor would it be sufficient that the mentor and liaison team had arranged logistical support (e.g., transport). Nor would liability be attracted under Article 17, even if the mentor and liaison team had assisted (or even agreed) to the operation plan for the cordon and search. State responsibility does not attach to the mentoring state if the mentored force *intentionally* commits wrongful acts contrary to the training and mentoring being provided.

There is, however, a situation in which arguably a mentoring force might attract liability. Where the mentoring force is aware of previous breaches, does nothing toward preventing further breaches,[74] and continues to assist the mentored force, then arguably liability might attach. The argument would be that if the mentored force had regularly and systematically engaged in internationally wrongful acts such that the mentoring team would have reasonable grounds to believe that an internationally wrongful act is likely to be committed if the mentoring team continued to provided assistance to the mentored force, then this would be no different from the situation of one state party providing assistance to another state party in the knowledge that the second state party would be using that assistance to commit internationally wrongful acts. Liability would be accruing not because of mentoring, per se, but rather because of assistance.[75]

The legal issues that may affect coalition forming and assignment of international legal responsibility are principally strategic issues. In this context, it is appropriate at this point to address one critical legal issue that should be dealt with prior to the conduct of operations, which is managing status-of-forces issues in a multinational context.

F. STATUS OF FORCES AGREEMENTS

Coalition operations raise some unique issues regarding status of forces. In general, a status-of- forces agreement is a bilateral agreement between the host nation and the sending nation. As a consequence, in a coalition operation, there will usually be

---

[73] See the wording of Articles on State Responsibility, *supra* note 19, arts. 16(a) and 17(a).

[74] For example, providing additional corrective training or reporting prior breaches to the mentored force's higher command for corrective action or punishment.

[75] For a discussion of this concept in the context of command responsibility, see *Prosecutor v. Hadžihasanović and Kubura (Trial Chamber)* Case No. IT-01-47-T, 89, 133 (Mar. 15, 2006). *See also Prosecutor v. Hadžihasanović and Kubura (Appeals Chamber)* Case No.IT-01-47-A (Apr. 22, 2008), ¶¶ 26–31.

a requirement for each sending nation to negotiate its own status-of-forces agreement with the host nation. This may well result in the various bilateral agreements having different terms. Note, however, that NATO often negotiates a status-of-forces agreement for its operations within the territory of a host nation (the NATO-ISAF Military Technical Agreement is an example of one such agreement).

Where the host nation is, in effect, a staging point for military operations in another state (or in international waters or airspace), the lack of commonality may be little more than an inconvenience. But where the host nation is also the site of military operations under the command of a coalition commander, the lack of commonality is yet another complication for the coalition commander to manage. Any differences in terms in the status-of-forces agreements are a potential source of logistical and administrative issues for coalition headquarters.

Take the example of an operation where a troop-contributing nation has a status-of-forces agreement that allows entry into the host nation upon production of military identification. The status-of-forces agreement also allows entry via a military airfield. Contrast this with the hypothetical status-of-forces agreement negotiated by a second troop-contributing nation that requires entry only upon a passport, with a valid visa, through normal immigration channels. The consequence would be that troops from the first nation could enter via military transport whereas troops from the second nation generally will have to use civil airlines. Not only would this affect arriving into the area of operations, it would also complicate intra-theater airlift. This is but one example of how differing status-of-forces arrangements on a bilateral basis can complicate coalition logistic operations, resulting in curtailed interoperability.

It is advisable, therefore, for these issues to be addressed, or at least recognized, during the formation (or any subsequent expansion) of the coalition. One way this can be achieved is for the lead nation, and other troop-contributing nations, to share information and work cooperatively when negotiating status-of-forces agreements.

Of course, some multinational operations do not have a sole lead nation for the duration of the operation. Also, many states consider their bilateral arrangements sensitive and confidential, and may not be prepared to share the text or even the key points of the discussion with other states. If complete cooperation and transparency are not feasible, or there is no single nation likely to be the lead nation for the duration of the operation, an alternative to various bilateral agreements is, paradoxically, the negotiation of yet a further agreement. This super-agreement would not be a state-to-state agreement but rather be between the host nation and the coalition force itself.[76] This can arise even where the coalition force does not have a legal personality, and in such circumstances it might be better termed an *arrangement* rather than an *agreement*. By entering into an agreement/arrangement with a coalition force that does not have a permanent

---

[76] A useful example is provided by the Military Technical Agreement between the International Security Assistance Force (ISAF) and the Interim Administration of Afghanistan (Interim Administration) of Jan. 4, 2002, *available at* http://www.operations.mod.uk/isafmta.pdf.

lead nation, not only can issues such as jurisdiction, entry, and exit arrangements be harmonized, but the overall mission, area of operations, locations for coalition facilities and bases, and relationship with host-nation agencies of the entire coalition can be determined. This is clearly a vital matter for a coalition commander, and is of particular importance where the lead nation may vary over time.

The foregoing discussion focused on some of the key strategic legal issues—namely the issues that affect (or should affect) the decision to participate in a multinational operation. The following discussion deals with legal issues that affect the conduct of multinational operations and, accordingly, are more operational in nature.

IV. The Impact of National Caveats on Operations

When a nation agrees to contribute forces to a multinational operation, it is quite common for that contribution to be made on specific terms. In particular, certain limitations may be imposed on how the force may be used,[77] where it may operate,[78] and so forth. There are many ways in which these limitations are implemented, but a common one is in the national rules of engagement.

A. RULES OF ENGAGEMENT

Rules of engagement (ROE) are broadly discussed earlier in this book. This chapter is concerned only with the affect of national ROE on multinational operations. In particular, the issue is where national ROE differ among the troop-contributing nations, and particularly from that of either the leading nation using force, or from the multinational rules. The operation of coalition (if any) and national ROE are a vital issue for a coalition commander. Rarely will two troop-contributing nations have similar national ROE, or even similar doctrinal approaches. Rules of engagement reflect not just legal and operational issues but also national policy positions.[79]

Although it is clearly desirable for a multinational force to "operate under coherent ROE arrangements,"[80] this may not always be possible. Even countries with similar legal systems and a long history of military cooperation may not be able to reach agreement. For example:

> There were also legal problems among members of the International Force East Timor (INTERFET) led by Australia. Australian planners confronted

---

[77] For example, whether a force is authorized to conduct offensive patrolling.

[78] For example, how close particular naval units may be allowed to approach or operate in disputed maritime zones.

[79] International Institute of Humanitarian Law, Sanremo Handbook on Rules of Engagement 2 ¶ 6 (2009) [hereinafter Sanremo Handbook].

[80] *Id.* ¶ 7.

> the dilemma of putting together rules of engagement that would meet with the approval of all INTERFET participants. One of the most contentious aspects of the mission concerned legal provisions for using lethal force in operations designed to defend property. Australia and the United States accepted such provisions, but Britain, New Zealand and Canada did not support the use of lethal force to defend property because of domestic legal considerations.[81]

Unsurprisingly, differences in legal and policy positions "can lead to different ROE among the members of a multinational force,"[82] "reflecting each nation's unique political and legal interests and its reason for entering the coalition."[83] These national differences are colloquially often referred to as "national caveats."

An important issue to determine is whether differences in ROE are due to varying policy positions or varying legal positions. The former may be subject to change, whereas the latter are less likely to be.[84] So, although a single set of multinational force ROE is desirable, often allowances for ROE differences will have to be made as part of forming the multinational force. Various options are available to accommodate varying national ROE. The three principle options are to have:

a. a single set of multinational ROE with national caveats,
b. multiple national ROE, or
c. both multinational ROE along with multiple national ROE.

So, how is this best managed in practice?

Practically speaking, merely having multinational ROE is unlikely to be achieved. Just about all states will want to issue their own national ROE, particularly regarding the right of self-defense. The authors have been involved in operations that had multiple national ROE, and this is achievable where the number of coalition partners is small, such as two or three nations. It is not, however, very practical as the number of troop-contributing nations increases. Accordingly, it is the view of the authors that, in general, the best approach is to have a single set of multinational ROE issued by the multinational force commander alongside the various national ROE. To the extent that any individual national ROE is more limited than the multinational ROE, these limitations can be thought of as national caveats. Where this solution is adopted, it is highly desirable to have a matrix produced at the multinational headquarters level indicating the differences between the various national ROE. This matrix is generally compiled,

---

[81] Michael Kelly, *Legal Factors in Military Planning for Coalition Warfare and Military Interoperability: Some Implications for the Australian Defence Force*, II AUSTRALIAN ARMY J. 2 at 161, 164 (2005).

[82] SANREMO HANDBOOK, *supra* note 79, at 2, 7.

[83] Doctrine, Plans and Procedures Multinational Interoperability Working Group of the Multinational Interoperability Council, *The Lead Nation Concept in Coalition Operations*, 3 (2000).

[84] N. Brown, *Issues Arising from Coalition Operations: An Operational Lawyer's Perspective*, *in* INTERNATIONAL LAW AND MILITARY OPERATIONS, 84 INT'L L. STUDIES 226, 231 (M.D. Carsten ed., 2008).

coordinated, and made available at the level of the multinational force headquarters. If for reasons of classification or restrictions on releasability the national ROE cannot be made available at the multinational force headquarters level, then so the matrix can still be completed the senior national representatives from each state needs to provide a clear explanation to the multinational force commander on the national caveats that apply to the multinational force ROE.

A very useful feature that can be identified at this point is whether national ROE can reduce the areas of apparent difference that might be found when looking solely at the law of armed conflict obligations of troop-contributing nations. For example, Australia, as a party to the Ottawa Convention, is under an international legal obligation not to use victim-activated antipersonnel land mines.[85] The United States, however, is under no such international legal obligation. However, in any particular armed conflict the United States may choose, for whatever reasons, to prohibit the use of victim-activated antipersonnel land mines in that particular conflict. The practical effect of this ROE restriction would be that the potential interoperability issue between Australia and the United States vis-à-vis victim-activated antipersonnel land mines would not exist.

Up until now, the discussion has been in terms of restrictions imposed by national caveats upon the multinational force ROE. What about the case where the national ROE are more liberal than the multinational force ROE? A question that is often asked is: Does a soldier from State A follow the ROE of State A, or the multinational ROE? Presume for the moment that the forces of State A are acting under the operational control of the multinational force commander. The simple answer is, subject to any contrary national command direction, to apply the more restrictive of the relevant ROE. So, for instance, if the multinational ROE allow the use of unobserved indirect-fire weapons, but the national ROE require indirect fire to be observed, soldiers from State A should participate only in observed indirect-fire support. Similarly if the multinational ROE prohibit pursuing opposing forces across a particular national boundary while the national rules permit cross-border pursuit operations, then soldiers from State A should not undertake cross-border pursuits while operating under the operational control of the multinational force commander.

B. INDIVIDUAL SELF-DEFENSE

National law and policy on individual self-defense poses similar issues to that of rules of engagement generally. Practice has shown that troop-contributing nations do have different approaches to when, where, and how their troops may exercise an individual right of self-defense. In the authors' experience, some states assert the right to limit individual self-defense for military members,

[85] Victim-activated antipersonnel land mines are land mines that are triggered by tripwire, pressure plate etc. Compare this to command-detonated land mines, which are activated by an operator choosing to detonate the land mine.

whereas others believe that it is an inherent right that cannot be modified by ROE or military orders. Whether a soldier is required to at least consider firing a warning shot has also proven to be an issue in multinational operations. As a consequence, the general approach that now seems to be adopted is to require forces to operate under multinational ROE, with the exception that issues pertaining to individual self-defense are reserved to national ROE.

C. TARGETING

The process for approving preplanned targets in a coalition may take one of three main forms. One option is to require every troop-contributing nation to agree to a target before it is placed on a target list. This was the approach adopted by NATO during Operation Allied Force.[86] Although this is sometimes put in terms of any coalition partner being able to exercise a veto over a target being attacked, that is not quite accurate. Rather than on occasion exercising a negative veto, each coalition partner is actually positively agreeing to a target being subject to attack. The importance and reason for this approach is explained by James E. Baker. In a "highly idiosyncratic campaign involving coalition warfare by nineteen democracies . . . some individual target decisions assumed strategic policy implications."[87] This type of target-approval process is more likely to arise where the formation and maintenance of the coalition has its own strategic importance beyond successful prosecution of the mission.[88]

The second approach is where a coalition partner indicates that it is not prepared to participate in conducting an attack on a particular target. The consequence of this type of arrangement is that the target may still be attacked, and the "veto" operates only with respect to using the military assets of the partner or partners who have not agreed to participate.[89] A subtly different version of this process is where the coalition partner whose assets might be used has to positively agree to (not just "not veto") the use of its assets. This is the process adopted by the International Security Assistance Force in Afghanistan.[90] A hybrid situation is also possible, in which the outcome of any targeting deliberations is merely a determination whether particular coalition partner assets may be used as part of an attack. However, coalition partners also reserve to themselves the right to veto the attack on a target by any coalition partner.

---

[86] J.E. Peters et al., *European Contributions to Operation Allied Force: Implications for Transatlantic Cooperation* 26 (RAND 2001). *See also* Short, *supra* note 13, at 26 (". . . the French exercised total veto over targets. They would take the position that not only would their aircraft not strike the 'Rock-and-roll Bridge,' no one could strike the 'Rock-and-roll Bridge.'").

[87] James Baker, *Judging Kosovo: The Legal Process, the Law of Armed Conflict, and the Commander In Chief*, *in* LEGAL AND ETHICAL LESSONS OF NATO'S KOSOVO CAMPAIGN, 78 INT'L L. STUDIES 7, 13 (A.E. Wall ed., 2002).

[88] *See generally* Short, *supra* note 13, at 24–25.

[89] *Id.* at 29.

[90] *See* Cole, *supra* note 6, at 146–47.

Regardless of what type of approval process is in place, a multinational force commander needs to ensure that the targeting process and information flow is set up to meet these requirements while concurrently ensuring mission effectiveness.

D. WEAPONS

The legal issues associated with certain weapon types have become particularly complex, especially with respect to antipersonnel land mines and cluster munitions.

Article 1. Of the *Ottawa Convention* provides that:

> 1. Each State Party undertakes never under any circumstances:
>   a) To use anti-personnel mines;
>   b) To develop, produce, otherwise acquire, stockpile, retain or transfer to anyone, directly or indirectly, anti-personnel mines;
>   c) To assist, encourage or induce, in any way, anyone to engage in any activity prohibited to a State Party under this Convention.[91]

With the exception of Article 1(c), there are no further specific interoperability provisions. As is common, a number of states made declarations upon signing the Ottawa Convention. To take an example that is relevant to the interoperability issue, Australia made the following declaration:

> It is the understanding of Australia that, in the context of operations, exercises or other military activity authorised by the United Nations or otherwise conducted in accordance with international law, the participation by the Australian Defence Force, individual Australian citizens or residents in such operations, exercises or activities in combination with the armed forces of States not party to the Convention which engage in activity prohibited under the Convention would not, by itself, be considered to be in violation of the Convention.[92]

In his 2005 article, Michael Kelly provides an operational example from 2003.

> Another legal issue that proved difficult in the context of coalition operations [during the 2003 Gulf War] was Australian and British adherence to the Ottawa Treaty prohibiting the use of antipersonnel mines. The Ottawa Treaty will be considered in further detail later in this article, but for the moment it is important to note that Australia was unable to refuel any US aircraft that was fitted with air-delivered anti-personnel mines such as the scatter-based and mixed munition GATORS system.[93]

---

[91] Ottawa Convention, *supra* note 5, art. 1.

[92] ICRC, *Treaties and States Parties to Such Treaties*, Convention on the Prohibition of the Use, Stockpiling, Production and Transfer of Anti-Personnel Mines and on Their Destruction, 18 September 1997, Australia, Declarations, *available at* http://www.icrc.org/applic/ihl/ihl.nsf/Notification.xsp?action=openDocument&documentId=C94AC352BD44A2494125658500442880 (last visited June 18, 2014).

[93] Kelly, *supra* note 81, at 165.

Kelly further explains that:

> In further declarations on use, assistance, encouragement and inducement, Australia has refined its approach. Australia believes that in the context of the Ottawa Treaty, "use" means the physical emplacement of anti-personnel mines and does not include any indirect or incidental benefit derived from these weapons when they are laid by another state. Furthermore, in the context of the Treaty, Australia interprets "assist" to mean direct physical participation in prohibited activity with respect to anti-personnel mines, but not indirect support (such as the provision of security for personnel engaging in those activities).
>
> Australia considers "encouragement" to mean a request for the commission of prohibited activity and "inducement" to imply active engagement in the offering of incentives to obtain the commission of a prohibited activity. Finally, in dealing with the need to de-mine territory under ADF jurisdiction or control, Australia has asserted that any interpretation should not include the temporary occupation of, or presence on, foreign territory where mines may have been laid.[94]

Notwithstanding these further declarations, difficult legal issues still arise. To return to the example of air-to-air refueling of U.S. aircraft carrying antipersonnel land mines, whether Australian forces are under an absolute prohibition to conduct air-to air-refueling is still a debated point. For example, it has been suggested that an "exception to the rule may be where the safety of the coalition aircraft needing to be refuelled is at risk."[95]

To further complicate matters, the interoperability provisions in different weapon prohibition treaties are not identical. The best example of this is the recent Dublin Convention banning cluster munitions.[96] Unlike the Ottawa Convention the Dublin Convention has a more detailed provision dealing with interoperability. Article 1 of the Dublin Convention is written in almost exactly the same terms as Article 1 of the Ottawa Convention except, of course, replacing references to antipersonnel land mines with a reference to cluster munitions. Importantly though it should also be noted that the words "in any way" that appear in Article 1(c) of the Ottawa Convention do not appear in Article 1(c) of the Dublin Convention. This leads us to Article 21 Relations with States not party to this Convention of the Dublin Convention, which states:

> 1. Each State Party shall encourage States not party to this Convention to ratify, accept, approve or accede to this Convention, with the goal of attracting the adherence of all States to this Convention.
> 2. Each State Party shall notify the governments of all States not party to this Convention, referred to in paragraph 3 of this Article, of its

---

[94] *Id.* at 169.

[95] McConachie, *supra* note 4, at 245.

[96] Convention on Cluster Munitions, opened for signature Dec. 3, 2008, 48 I.L.M. 357 (entered into force Aug. 1, 2010).

obligations under this Convention, shall promote the norms it establishes and shall make its best efforts to discourage States not party to this Convention from using cluster munitions.

3. Notwithstanding the provisions of Article 1 of this Convention and in accordance with international law, States Parties, their military personnel or nationals, may engage in military cooperation and operations with States not party to this Convention that might engage in activities prohibited to a State Party.
4. Nothing in paragraph 3 of this Article shall authorise a State Party:
   (a) To develop, produce or otherwise acquire cluster munitions;
   (b) To itself stockpile or transfer cluster munitions;
   (c) To itself use cluster munitions; or
   (d) To expressly request the use of cluster munitions in cases where the choice of munitions used is within its exclusive control.[97]

Compared to the Ottawa Convention, it is obvious that there is a greater scope for interoperability under the provisions of the Dublin Convention.

V. Conclusion

The purpose of this chapter was to identify the key legal issues that may arise in multinational operations. Although a number of particular issues were discussed, the three key areas include coalition building, state responsibility for internationally wrongful acts, and the role and impact of national caveats on operations.

Although building and maintaining a coalition is principally a political and diplomatic activity, there are numerous legal issues at the strategic, operational, and tactical levels that will affect coalition building. If these issues are not resolved in a mutually satisfactory manner, a state is either unlikely to commit forces to a coalition, or to commit forces in a very limited and tightly controlled manner, thereby making interoperability a challenge. Part of building and maintaining a coalition is determining what are the true legal "show-stoppers" versus what issues may be manageable through innovative policy solutions or, alternatively, can and should be managed in-theater by the coalition commander and the various senior national representatives.

Having agreed to commit forces to a multinational operation, states need to be conscious of the law concerning responsibility for internationally wrongful acts. Advising on this issue is likely to remain difficult for some time as not only is there the inherent factual and policy complexity of multinational operations, the law itself on state and international organization responsibility, particularly in military operations, remains unsettled. This is even more so when it comes to

[97] *Id.* art. 21.

the law concerning the role and responsibility of a coalition commander, which is underdeveloped when compared the traditional doctrine of command responsibility that is applied along state lines.

Regardless, a few broad conclusions can be drawn. First, it is currently not the law that states have joint responsibility for the internationally wrongful acts of any other member. Nor, in the authors' view, should that be the law. Simply put, the international legal responsibilities of states vary, and the roles of coalition partners in operations are different. Second, the Articles on State Responsibility (along with the Draft Articles on the Responsibility of International Organizations) prepared by the International Law Commission constitute a solid starting point for analyzing legal responsibility in a multinational operation. There are five main articles of relevance, although the applicability of Article 4, Conduct of Organs of a State, of the Articles on State Responsibility is relatively straightforward, noting that officers of the military are a de jure organ of the state. Of particular interest is the interpretation of Article 6, Conduct of Organs Placed at the Disposal of a State by Another State, of the Articles on State Responsibility. Although still not completely settled, the law has strongly moved toward the position that a state will be responsible for the conduct of a military component of another state where the first state possesses "effective control" over that military component.

Under Article 16, Aid or Assistance in the Commission of an Internationally Wrongful Act, of the Articles on State Responsibility, a state is responsible to the extent that its conduct has contributed to the internationally wrongful act of another state. However, it is only where the act committed by the aided/assisted state would have been unlawful if committed by the aiding/assisting state that the aiding/assisting state has international responsibility. Similarly, under Article 17, Direction and Control Exercised over the Commission of an Internationally Wrongful Act, of the Articles on State Responsibility, a directing/controlling state is only responsible if the act committed would have been internationally wrongful if committed by that state itself. Further, and unlike under Article 6, the mere ability or authority to be able to give direction or exercise control is not enough to attract liability under this article: actual direction or control must have been exercised with respect to the act of interest.

Conversely, under Article 18, Coercion of Another State, of the Articles on State Responsibility, a state is responsible for the coerced act if, but for the coercion, it would have been a wrongful act for the coerced state. It does not matter whether it would have been a wrongful act if committed directly by the coercing state. Importantly though, actual coercion must have been exercised. The strong influence and guidance of a stronger state as part of a military alliance is not enough.

Finally, it is important to remember that under Article 47, Plurality of Responsible States, of the *Articles on State Responsibility*, it is possible for more than one entity to share legal responsibility (concurrent liability). In this respect, it is important to note that a state that provides a military mentor and liaison team (sometimes referred to as a train/assist/advise team) does not ipso facto incur liability for the wrongful acts of the mentored military unit. Rather, liability must be analyzed per the grounds of liability discussed above.

The third key issue involves ROE and national caveats. Notwithstanding the desirability of having a single set of multinational force ROE, typically allowances for ROE differences will have to be made as part of forming the multinational force. Accordingly, the main focus will need to be on accommodating varying national ROE. Although there are a number of options, it is the view of the authors that, in general, the best approach is to have a single set of multinational ROE issued by the multinational force commander alongside the various national ROE. Then, to the extent that any individual national ROE is more limited than the multinational ROE, these limitations can be thought of as national caveats. Where this solution is adopted, it is highly desirable to have a matrix produced at the multinational headquarters level indicating the differences among the various national ROE. Although neither set of ROE have formal precedence, in any given situation, and subject to any national command direction to the contrary, the more restrictive of the relevant ROE will apply.

Although coalition, or multinational, operations present a host of interoperability issues, both in the physical as well as the legal domain, the benefits clearly outweigh the costs. Additionally, it is much less likely today that a single nation will enter combat operations alone, preferring instead to act as part of a coalition. The legal challenges are not insurmountable, but will require careful planning and diligence on the part of operational attorneys at the strategic, operational, and tactical levels, whether working as part of their national team or as part of the multinational headquarters.

12 }

Modern U.S. Military Operations and the International Committee of the Red Cross

THE DEPARTMENT OF DEFENSE'S UNIQUE RELATIONSHIP WITH THE GUARDIAN OF INTERNATIONAL HUMANITARIAN LAW

Rachel E. VanLandingham*

I. Introduction

People must be made to see . . . the cost in torment and in tears of the glory of the battlefield.

GENERAL GUILLAUME HENRI DUFOUR[1]

The Department of Defense's relationship with the International Committee of the Red Cross (ICRC), a private organization with an international legal mandate, is a fascinating one.[2] The ICRC "is an impartial, neutral and independent organization whose exclusively humanitarian mission is to protect the lives and

* Associate Professor of Law, Southwestern Law School, Lt Col., USAF, (ret). While an active duty Air Force Judge Advocate, Professor VanLandingham served in the position of Chief, International Law at U.S. Central Command from 2006 to 2010 and as U.S. Central Command Liaison to the International Committee of the Red Cross, among other assignments, and has written and lectured on the law of armed conflict.

[1] Henry Dunant, A Memory of Solferino 128 (ICRC trans., 1986).

[2] *See, e.g.*, Simon Bradley, *Geneva Convention Needs Updating, Says ICRC*, Swissinfo.ch, Aug. 12, 2009, http://www.swissinfo.ch/eng/specials/red_cross/news/Geneva_Conventions_need_updating,_says_ICRC.html?cid=225360 (describing the ICRC as a private organization, governed by a committee of between fifteen and twenty-five exclusively Swiss members). Though never a part of the Swiss government, the ICRC's failure during World War II to condemn the Nazi atrocities of the Holocaust was due in part to the ICRC's concern about such action's impact on neutral Switzerland. The ICRC finally obtained diplomatic status, such as that accorded United Nations organs, under Swiss law in 1991. *See Neutral in a Harsh World, A History of the ICFC*, Agence France-Presse, Feb. 13, 2013, *available at* http://www.globalpost.com/dispatch/news/afp/130210/neutral-harsh-world-the-history-the-icrc (discussing seminal moments in the history of the ICRC).

dignity of victims of armed conflict and other situations of violence and to provide them with assistance."[3] Its relationship with the United States government is much broader, and deeper, than the formal legal boundaries prescribed for it by law, and influences U.S. military operations in often surprising ways. The current alliance can be described at times as resembling a partnership, and represents both the U.S. government's enhanced appreciation of such a relationship since September 11, 2001, and philosophical changes in the ICRC's operating modalities, which have allowed it to seek closer ties with state militaries.[4]

Furthermore, the ICRC's unique mandate, roles, and modus operandi distinguish it from all other nongovernmental entities that deal with the U.S. government, and have contributed to its extensive influence both on the battlefield and beyond.[5] Its long-standing modalities of independence, neutrality, and impartiality, plus reliance on confidential dialogues, have led to its unprecedented access to top U.S. military and civilian defense leadership. The ICRC's delegates enjoy direct and regular access to the civilian leadership of the Department of Defense (DoD), combatant commanders and their staffs, and commanders and troops in forward-deployed battlefield areas. These links create a networked, symbiotic relationship between a federal entity and a private organization that is truly sui generis within the U.S. government, though one that entails sometimes conflicting interests.

In the words of the State Department's Legal Advisor in 2011, "[t]he ICRC's indispensable role as an independent and impartial intermediary and humanitarian partner has proven, time and again, absolutely critical to addressing complex and unpredictable conflict situations."[6] Despite this supposedly indispensable role, the U.S. military failed to systematically integrate coordination with the ICRC during combat operations until quite recently.[7] It was not until the Abu Ghraib detainee scandal in 2004, and the subsequent realization that proper attention to the ICRC's multiple warnings regarding the prison could have

---

[3] *See* ICRC, *The ICRC's Mandate and Mission* (Oct. 29, 2010), http://www.icrc.org/eng/who-we-are/mandate/overview-icrc-mandate-mission.htm.

[4] Pierre Gentile, *Humanitarian Organizations Involved in Protection Activities: A Story of Soul-Searching and Professionalization*, 93 Int'l Rev. Red Cross 1167 (2011) (discussing change in ICRC working modalities to work more closely with state actors when implementing protection strategies in a region).

[5] The ICRC also maintains contacts and engages in dialogues with other U.S. organizations, such as the Central Intelligence Agency and the U.S. Department of State, as evidenced by its reports on CIA detention activities. *See generally* ICRC, *ICRC Report on the Treatment of Fourteen "High Value Detainees" in CIA Custody* (Feb. 14, 2007) (detailing the treatment of several detainees held by the CIA).

[6] Harold Hongju Koh, Legal Advisor to the Department of State, *U.S. Reaffirms Its Deep and Abiding Commitment to International Humanitarian Law at ICRC Conference* (Nov. 28, 2011), http://geneva.usmission.gov/2011/11/28/icrc-conference/ [hereinafter Koh Statement].

[7] ICRC, *The International Committee of the Red Cross Relations with the U.S. Armed Forces: An Overview of the Past Five Years of Interaction* (2010), *available at* https://community.apan.org/cfs-file.ashx/__key/telligent-evolution-components-attachments/13-4923-00-00-00-06-04-29/ICRC-5-Years-of-Interaction-US-Forces.pdf [hereinafter ICRC Relations].

averted the crisis, that the DoD re-evaluated its relationship with the ICRC and built the institutional foundation for today's robust alliance. These institutional moves included the formation of a new office within the Office of the Secretary of Defense (OSD) specifically charged with maintaining a formal dialogue with the ICRC, as well as promulgation of OSD policy to coordinate the processing of ICRC communications with the Department.[8] This chapter describes these developments, as well as provides a glimpse into the day-to-day working relationships in the field and domestically.

The ICRC fulfills its traditional, central role of the protection of victims of armed conflict by interacting with the U.S. military and its civilian leadership across a wide-spectrum of military activities, most notably detention operations, but also regarding activities related to targeting and civilian casualty mitigation; collection, care, and treatment of the wounded and sick; and responsibilities during periods of belligerent occupation. Although the ICRC also influences the DoD's training programs regarding international humanitarian law (IHL, also referred to as the Law of Armed Conflict, or LOAC), today the ICRC's primary effect is felt operationally as the result of observance-based feedback provided to the U.S. military via multiple layers of dialogue throughout the military and civilian defense echelons.[9]

Although historically involved with providing services to both civilian and belligerent detainees, the ICRC's more recent involvement regarding incidents of alleged civilian casualties and other targeting issues has grown dramatically since 2008. This evolution of the ICRCs role is consistent with the evolution of "Geneva law" itself, which since the advent of the two Additional Protocols of 1977 has included important rules regulating the means and methods of warfare, and is no longer restricted to issues related to victims of war who are hors de combat. The ICRC refers to this latter scope of means and methods activities as the "conduct of hostilities," and its growing engagement in this arena represents one of the newer developments in the relationship between the ICRC and the United States military, as described later in this chapter in Part II.

Part I of this chapter overviews the ICRC's history, institutional structure, and operating modalities, highlighting the roles given to it by both the Geneva Conventions and customary international law. This lengthy section is warranted because the ICRC's current relationship with the DoD cannot be fully appreciated without a working knowledge of the ICRC's evolution, which is part of the larger evolution of the modern law of armed conflict itself. Part II outlines the formal and informal working relationships between the ICRC and the DoD, both on the civilian side of the house in the Pentagon and on the uniformed military side, with an emphasis on the operational components.

---

[8] *See* Memorandum, Sec'y of Def, SUBJECT: Handling of Reports from the International Committee of the Red Cross (July 14, 2004) [hereinafter DoD ICRC Memo].

[9] The ICRC has regular contact within DOD regarding the education and training of the law of armed conflict to service members at military schoolhouses and doctrinal centers, as well as during training exercises.

A. CAVEAT EMPTOR: THE ICRC'S ATTEMPTS TO MAKE LAW

Much of the ICRC's interaction with the U.S. military involves the ICRC's provision of tangible, protective measures to victims of armed conflict. These primarily treaty-based functions, such as facilitating communication between detainees and their family members via Red Cross Messages, are explicitly provided for in the 1949 Geneva Conventions and customary international law. However, it is important to highlight that the ICRC not only implements existing law by fulfilling its Geneva Conventions mandates, it simultaneously strives to actually *advance* international law regarding armed conflict. In its own words: "[t]he ICRC also endeavors to prevent suffering by promoting *and strengthening* humanitarian law and universal humanitarian principles."[10] Also according to the ICRC, "[t]he States gave the ICRC the responsibility of monitoring the faithful application of international humanitarian law. As the guardian of humanitarian law, the ICRC takes measures to ensure respect for, to promote, to reaffirm and *even to clarify and develop this body of law*."[11] The actual legal mandate for this and the other ICRC roles is assessed in Part I of this chapter.

Though the ICRC views its developmental efforts as evolving the law toward greater protection against suffering, it is important to note that the positions it stakes out are not always fully synchronized with the views of states regarding the balance the law of armed conflict must strike between military necessity and humanity—a balance that accounts for states' inherent right to take those measures not otherwise prohibited by international law to achieve military objectives.[12] The ICRC's efforts to change the *lex lata* (existing law) range from formal, transparent draftings of new or updated treaties at the bequest of the world community, to more subtle, less transparent efforts, typically in the form of pronouncements regarding what the law ostensibly means. Such pronouncements may obscure the fact that these legal interpretations are, at times, the ICRC's *lex feranda*, or desired version of the law, versus what the law actually is, or *lex lata*. These pronouncements take various forms, ranging from ICRC field delegates telling U.S. military commanders in deployed battlefield locations that their treatment, for example, of certain detainees violates customary international law (when the law itself is either unclear or blatantly not what the ICRC purports it being), to published accounts that purport to list customary international law precepts of IHL.[13]

---

[10] ICRC, *The International Committee of the Red Cross (ICRC): Its Mission and Work*, 91 INT'L REV. RED CROSS 400 (2009) (emphasis added) [hereinafter ICRC Mission].

[11] *Id.* at 402. It is interesting that the ICRC fails to cite where they find support for their claim that states have given the ICRC the responsibility of monitoring the application of the law of armed conflict; perhaps because states have never explicitly or even implicitly (at least not across the spectrum of conflict) done so.

[12] *See, e.g.*, YORAM DINSTEIN, THE CONDUCT OF HOSTILITIES UNDER THE LAW OF INTERNATIONAL ARMED CONFLICT 3–5 (2d ed., 2010) (discussing the balancing act of *jus in bello*).

[13] JEAN-MARIE HENCKAERTS & LOUISE DOSWALD-BECK, CUSTOMARY INTERNATIONAL HUMANITARIAN LAW VOLUME I: RULES (2005) [hereinafter ICRC CIL Study]. Since being published, the ICRC has placed the rules in an interactive website with updates. ICRC International Humanitarian Law Database, http://www.icrc.org/customary-ihl/eng/docs/home (last visited May 12, 2013).

The ICRC's legal interpretations provided via its delegates to U.S. military members in the field are, at times, problematic because the ICRC occasionally characterizes them as *lex lata* when they are better understood as the ICRC vision of what they want the law to be. Identifying the line between *lex lata* and *lex ferenda* is often complicated by the lack of comprehensive coordination between levels of U.S. military command. The ICRC is quite skilled at synchronizing its messages up, down, and across the various levels of dialogue they enjoy with the DoD (that is, their legal positions are fully coordinated at all levels of ICRC intervention). In contrast, the DoD is not as adept as the ICRC at communicating and synchronizing its nuanced legal interpretations of existing IHL—particularly between the OSD policy offices and the numerous uniformed military levels. Therefore, military commanders at lower levels may not realize, or communicate, to the ICRC that the ICRC's interpretation of the law is not consistent with the DoD's understanding—and may make operational changes based on ICRC legal interpretations that are not considered binding by higher levels of command.

Additionally, all ICRC reports (even those made orally) are collated and regularly shared with Congress; if the DoD is not consistent with their challenges to the ICRC's legal interpretations (which are also provided to Congress), there is increased risk that Congress may understand the ICRC's positions as a correct reading of the governing law. Although such dynamics seem to have the potential to promote positive humanitarian changes in the law (through the development of customary international law based on state practice and *opinio juris*), they may actually skew the core balance IHL strikes with military necessity, thus endangering future adherence to the law of armed conflict if the latter is seen, or actually is, unworkable by states.[14]

The concern that the ICRC's efforts may indicate a sub rosa objective to unilaterally change the law via interpretation has not gone unnoticed, at times prompting high-level reminders from the United States that the ICRC does not make international law: "[b]ecause customary law derives not from aspirational pronouncements, but from State practice, it remains important that the development of international humanitarian law should continue to be led by States."[15] The fact that the ICRC is consistently aggressive in its efforts to publish what are often referred to as authoritative treatises, as well as scholarly articles, on the law of armed conflict, contributes to both this concern and the ICRC's influence. The principal example of this phenomenon is the ICRC's Customary International Humanitarian Law study. Originally published in 2006 at the bequest of the international community and now available via an ICRC online database, this study purports to state what is in fact the customary law of armed conflict, despite not

[14] *See* Michael N. Schmitt, *The Interpretive Guidance on the Notion of Direct Participation in Hostilities: A Critical Analysis*, 1 HARV. NAT'L SEC. J. 5, 6 (2010) (describing this phenomena in relation to the ICRC's study on direct participation in hostilities).

[15] Koh Statement, *supra* note 6.

having secured agreement by states to these assertions, such as the United States, whose *opinio juris* is legally essential to such determinations.[16]

By working behind the scenes to urge states to follow certain practices, and then by consolidating its version of what constitutes customary international law in widely cited publications, the ICRC is a formidable shaper of the law of armed conflict.[17] This dynamic is best captured in the words of the ICRC's former president, Jakob Kellenberger, in his description of the ICRC's study on customary international humanitarian law:

> The ICRC believes that the study does indeed present an accurate assessment of the current state of customary international humanitarian law. It will therefore duly take the outcome of this study into account in its daily work, while being aware that the formation of customary international law is an ongoing process. The study should also serve as a basis for discussion with respect to the implementation, clarification and development of humanitarian law.[18]

II. Part I: ICRC Overview: History and Operating Modalities

A. ICRC ORGANIZATIONAL HISTORY

The genesis of the ICRC sprang from Swiss businessman Henry Dunant's horror at the suffering of soldiers wounded on the battlefield at Solferino, Italy in the mid-nineteenth century.[19] Haunted by this event, Dunant outlined in his book, *A Memory of Solferino*, proposals to alleviate battlefield suffering.[20] He suggested the creation of private, volunteer national relief societies to be organized prior

---

[16] *See* ICRC CIL Study, *supra* note 13. The ICRC compiled this study on customary international law in response to a task given to it by the members of the International Conference of the Red Cross in 1995. *See e.g., id.* at xvi (describing genesis of study).

[17] The closest mandate for the ICRC's role in the general development of international humanitarian law, in the sense of interpreting its meaning and thus potentially changing the law via such interpretation, is found in the ICRC "Statutes of the International Committee of the Red Cross." *See* ICRC, *Statutes of the International Committee of the Red Cross* (Aug. 5, 2003), http://www.icrc.org/eng/resources/documents/misc/icrc-statutes-080503.htm (tasking, in Article 4, the ICRC, inter alia, "to undertake the tasks incumbent upon it under the Geneva Conventions, to work for the faithful application of international humanitarian law applicable in armed conflicts and to take cognizance of any complaints based on alleged breaches of that law.") In order to work for the faithful application of the law, one has to have a clear understanding, or at least stated interpretive position, of what the law requires. However, the ICRC statutes, which were adopted at an International Conference of the Red Cross and Red Crescent (at which states party to the Geneva Convention participate), do not constitute binding international law, despite the ICRC's use of them as providing a mandate for ICRC activities, such as for its work in situations of internal domestic violence.

[18] *See* ICRC CIL Study, *supra* note 13, at xvii.

[19] ICRC Mission, *supra* note 10, at 399. *See also* CAROLINE MOOREHEAD, DUNANT'S DREAM: WAR, SWITZERLAND, AND THE HISTORY OF THE RED CROSS 50 (1998) (reviewing in detail Henry Dunant's experiences and the formation of the ICRC).

[20] "No quarter is given, it is sheer butchery . . . [o]aths of shrieks of rage, groans of anguish and despair, mingle with the whinnying of horses." DUNANT, *supra* note 1, at 19.

to the onset of war to supplement the military medical services once conflict erupted.[21] He also indicated the need for a foundational international principle, enshrined in a treaty, to outline and support the roles of such aid societies and treatment of the wounded.[22] Dunant envisioned that large groups of volunteers would be organized and trained during peacetime—and critically, that their battlefield function would be accepted by governments during peacetime—so that they would be utilized immediately once war broke out. Furthermore, these organized volunteers and their military medical counterparts would be granted neutral status by the opposing parties and therefore not harmed or captured.[23] The abysmal context for these suggestions cannot be overstated: the lack of neutrality given to medical personnel meant that military doctors either fled the nineteenth-century battlefield with their retreating forces or were captured or killed; similarly, civilians caught tending the wounded were often treated as the enemy and killed, thereby providing no incentive for those in the areas of battles to leave their homes to provide aid.[24]

Dunant's book was amazingly influential across Europe, and his proposals immediately began to take shape in his philanthropic, Calvinist hometown of Geneva. In 1863, five prominent Swiss men from Geneva, including a lawyer, several doctors, a retired general, and Dunant, established a permanent body to promote Dunant's ideas—and by doing so, they founded the ICRC.[25] That same year, this private "committee of five" sponsored an international conference in Geneva dedicated to promoting the ideas in Dunant's book.[26] Attended by fourteen states as well as by private individuals, the conference debated numerous committee proposals, including the establishment of national, voluntary medical relief societies, the neutrality of medical services, and the designation of a red cross on a white background as the emblem of medical neutrality.[27] The resolutions

---

[21] *See id.* at 115 (proposing permanent, volunteer relief societies).

[22] *See, e.g., id.* at 126 (proposing an international principle "inviolate in character" to serve as basis for relief societies' work during war).

[23] *See, e.g.*, ICRC Mission, *supra* note 10. *See also* François Bugnion, From Solferino to the Birth of Contemporary International Humanitarian Law 5–8 (Apr. 22, 2009) *available at* http://www.icrc.org/eng/assets/files/other/solferino-bugnion-icrc.pdf (describing the inability of nineteenth-century militaries to treat wounded soldiers because military doctors were not given neutral status, and civilians lending aid were often labeled as enemies).

[24] Bugnion, *supra* note 23, at 5–8.

[25] *See* ICRC Mission, *supra* note 10, at 399 (describing ICRC as founded in 1863). *See also* Dunant, *supra* note 1, at 129, 130 (describing events following publication of Dunant's seminal book). The original five Swiss men—a lawyer, a retired general, two doctors, and Dunant (the dreamer)—originally called themselves the "International Committee for Relief to the Wounded." Moorehead, *supra* note 19, at 17.

[26] *See* Bugnion, *supra* note 23, at 18–19 (highlighting the early onset of the hybrid public-private nature of the ICRC's work: the national societies it proposed were not meant to be governmental organs but by necessity needed access from and protection by respective governments in order to fulfill mandates on the battlefield).

[27] Dunant, *supra* note 1, at 130. *See also* Moorehead, *supra* note 19, at 18–21 (describing the 1863 conference). *See also* John S. Haller Jr., Farmcarts to Fords: A History of the Military

produced by this conference would serve as the basis of the National Red Cross and Red Crescent Societies for over sixty years.[28]

The following year, the Swiss government, at the committee's prompting, sponsored a diplomatic international conference in Geneva, at which twelve states formally adopted many of the 1863 proposals by signing the 1864 Geneva Convention for the Amelioration of the Condition of the Wounded in Armies in the Field.[29] This first Geneva Convention, composed of ten succinct articles, required states party to care for *all* wounded and sick on the battlefield,[30] expressly providing for the "relief to the wounded without any distinction as to nationality; neutrality (inviolability) of medical personnel and medical establishments and units; [and] the distinctive sign of the red cross on a white ground."[31]

Though the United States participated in the 1864 conference, with one of its two representatives quite influential in convincing participants of the utility of various wartime protocols,[32] the U.S. participation was expressly "informal."[33] This U.S. hesitancy to formally engage in the shaping of the treaty stemmed in

---

AMBULANCE, 1790–1925, 63 (1992) (detailing the proposals at the 1863 conference). The original committee inverted the colors of the Swiss flag to adopt the emblem of the ICRC, nodding at its Swiss beginnings. *See, e.g.*, MOOREHEAD, *supra* note 19, at 18. A common and uniform emblem to designate hospital areas and medical personnel was vital because up to that time each country used its own particular flag for its medical service. "In Austria it was white, in France red, in Spain yellow, and in other countries black or green. The soldiers knew only the hospital flag of their own country, and were ignorant of the others." MABEL THORP BOARDMAN, UNDER THE RED CROSS FLAG AT HOME AND ABROAD 37 (1915). *See also* BUGNION, *supra* note 23, at 11 (discussing the disuse, in 1863, of the ancient practice of making field hospitals immune via agreement between opposing generals immediately prior to battle, and highlighting the use of different flags for national medical units).

[28] *See* BUGNION, *supra* note 23, at 22 (stating that the 1863 resolutions provided the framework for the national Red Cross organizations until the Thirteenth International Conference of the Red Cross adopted the Statutes of the International Red Cross in 1928).

[29] *See, e.g.*, ICRC, *Introduction to the Convention for the Amelioration of the Condition of the Wounded in Armies in the Field. Geneva, 22 August 1864, available at* http://www.icrc.org/ihl/INTRO/120?OpenDocument (summarizing the genesis of 1864 Convention) [hereinafter "Red Cross Convention Introduction"]. *See also* D. SCHINDLER & J. TOMAN, THE LAWS OF ARMED CONFLICTS 280–81 (1988) (transcribing the text of the draft convention created at the Convention for the Amelioration of the Condition of the Wounded in Armies in the Field in Geneva on August 22, 1984) [hereinafter "Red Cross Convention"]. Although the Geneva proposals were the first to become codified as international humanitarian principles, Dunant and his original committee of fellow Swiss were not the first to articulate respect and neutrality for the wounded on the battlefield and their caregivers; *see* MOOREHEAD, *supra* note 19, at 23–50 (highlighting the earlier work by men such as Anatoli Demidov, Henri Arrault, and Ferdinano Palasciano, who had espoused earlier ideas regarding neutral treatment of the wounded, as well as leading humanitarians such as Florence Nightingale and Clara Barton, who both pushed for dramatic reorganizations of national militaries instead of a volunteer corps).

[30] Red Cross Convention, *supra* note 29, at art. 6.

[31] Red Cross Convention Introduction, *supra* note 29.

[32] *See* BOARDMAN, *supra* note 27, at 32–45 (discussing the U.S. representative Charles S.P. Bowles's impressions of the conference, which he described as greatly influenced by his descriptions of the U.S. Sanitary Commission during the Civil War).

[33] The United States allowed its Ambassador to Switzerland, George C. Fogg, as well as Bowles, European agent of the American Sanitary Commission, to informally attend. The U.S. Secretary of State's letter to Fogg regarding the conference stated that:

> [t]he object of the proposed congress is certainly laudable and important, and the Department sees no objection to your being present on the occasion. You are, therefore,

part from a desire to stay out of European affairs and to avoid any "entangling alliances";[34] it took almost twenty years for the United States to finally become a party to the convention.[35] The reluctance to sign the treaty was also partially attributable to an aversion to having "civilian volunteers interfering in military matters," a sentiment that this author heard echoed over 150 years later.[36] This isolationist tendency was finally overcome by the persistent efforts of American Clara Barton, who had already established the American Red Cross in 1881 after she was inspired by European Red Cross societies during travel through Europe.[37]

B. ICRC HISTORICAL DEVELOPMENT OF INTERNATIONAL HUMANITARIAN LAW

Since the development of the original 1864 Geneva Convention, in earlier times referred to as the "Red Cross Treaty," the ICRC has continued to fulfill its broad role as developer and guardian of international humanitarian law, which it now views as one of its primary responsibilities.[38] As described above,

---

> authorized to attend the meeting in an informal manner, for the purpose of giving or receiving such suggestions as you may think likely to promote the humane ends which have prompted it. It is hardly necessary to add that your presence at the congress would be improper if any of the insurgent emissaries of the United States in Europe should be permitted to take part in its proceedings.

BOARDMAN, *supra* note 27, at 43.

[34] JOHN F. HUTCHINSON, CHAMPIONS OF CHARITY: WAR AND THE RISE OF THE RED CROSS 45 (1996).

[35] *See* ICRC, *Treaties and States Parties to Such Treaties*, *available at* http://www.icrc.org/ihl.nsf/WebSign?ReadForm&id=120&ps=P (last visited June 4, 2015). The U.S. reluctance to sign the 1864 Convention was also partially motivated by a feeling that the United States had based on its Civil War experiences devised better ways to provide medical services on the battlefield. *See* MOOREHEAD, *supra* note 19, at 89–111 (describing the U.S. movement led by Clara Barton and others); *see also* WILLIAM HOWARD TAFT, SERVICE WITH FIGHTING MEN: AN ACCOUNT OF THE WORK OF THE AMERICAN YOUNG MEN'S CHRISTIAN ASSOCIATIONS IN THE WORLD WAR 46 (1922) (discussing American reluctance to get involved in European affairs).

[36] *See, e.g.* MOOREHEAD, *supra* note 19, at 92 (discussing American delay in signing 1864 treaty). *See also* HALLER, *supra* note 26, at 84 (citing the U.S. Army's aversion to aid from civilian volunteer charities). This author witnessed attitudes among some U.S. military personnel (from military police colonels to military attorneys) that belied a belief that the ICRC's suggestions were not informed by reality; that ICRC suggestions were based on human rights or other law, and not on military requirements or legally binding law of armed conflict obligations.

[37] *See, e.g.*, American Red Cross: Our History, http://www.redcross.org/about-us/history (last visited May 14, 2013). Clara Barton was asked by the ICRC to lobby the U.S. government to sign the convention. *See* MOOREHEAD, *supra* note 19, at 92, 94.

[38] *See, e.g.*, TAFT, *supra* note 35 (referring to 1864 Geneva Convention as the Red Cross Treaty). *See also* JEFFREY DUNOFF, STEVEN RATNER & DAVID WIPPMAN, INTERNATIONAL LAW: NORMS, ACTORS, PROCESS 499 (2010) (discussing ICRC's "key role in the development of draft conventions.") *See also* ICRC Mission, *supra* note 10, at 400 (describing the dual nature of the ICRC's work as both helping victims of armed conflict and other situations of violence and the developing and promoting of international humanitarian law and humanitarian principles.) This author believes that the ICRC role as "guardian of international humanitarian law" has reached the status of customary international law.

the ICRC designed the now long-standing template for the formal development of international humanitarian law when it drafted proposed articles for the first Geneva Convention, which were then modified and adopted by the diplomatic conference in 1864 convened (at the ICRC's request), by the Swiss government, and at which it was an active participant.[39] It followed this model when it wrote revisions and participated in another such conference in 1899 (at which its proposed changes to the 1864 Convention were not adopted), and similarly again in 1906, at which time its proposals to overhaul the first convention were adopted.[40]

The ICRC's initially informal role regarding the development of IHL became more formal in the initial decades following its inception. This transpired primarily through the establishment of regular international conferences that came to be known as the "International Conference of the Red Cross and Red Crescent,"[41] the first of which was held in Berlin in 1869.[42] Today International Conference attendees include all the states parties to the Geneva Conventions, plus representatives of the Red Cross Movement entities, which include the national Red Cross/Red Crescent Societies, the ICRC, and the International Federation.[43] The International Conferences continue today to provide mandates to the ICRC to draft specific IHL proposals. For example at the 1921 conference, conference participants, led by states, asked the ICRC to draft a separate convention for the treatment of prisoners of war, based on the experiences of World War I.[44] The resultant draft convention, written by the ICRC, was debated at an international diplomatic (that is, state) conference sponsored by the Swiss government (per the norm established in 1864), and signed by most states at that 1929 gathering.[45]

While early ICRC efforts focused on relief for the wounded, via creation of binding international norms of neutrality and of the establishment of volunteer national societies, these efforts were occurring within a context of the

---

[39] *See, e.g.*, Bugnion, *supra* note 23, at 17 (describing the committee's role prior to, and during, the 1864 conference).

[40] *See* ICRC Treaties and States Parties to Treaties, http://www.icrc.org/ihl/INTRO/180?OpenDocument (last visited June 4, 2015)(describing development and substance of 1906 Convention).

[41] *See, e.g.*, International Conference of The Red Cross and Red Crescent, (Sept. 11, 2011), *available at* http://www.icrc.org/eng/who-we-are/movement/international-conference/overview-international-conference-of-the-red-cross-and-red-crescent.htm (describing procedural and constitutive elements of such conferences).

[42] *See* Christina Grisewood, *Universal Values for a Changing World*, Red Cross Crescent Mag. (1995), http://www.redcross.int/EN/mag/magazine1995_3/2-6.html (tracing the history of the conferences and explaining their utility).

[43] Philippe Abplanalp, *The International Conferences of the Red Cross as a Factor for the Development of International Humanitarian Law and the Cohesion of the International Red Cross and Red Crescent Movement*, 35 Int'l Rev. Red Cross 520 (2011).

[44] *See* Schindler & Toman, *supra* note 29, at 341–64 (tracing the impetus and creation of the 1929 prisoner-of-war convention).

[45] *See* Convention for the Amelioration of the Condition of the Wounded and Sick in Armies in the Field, 118 L.N.T.S. 303 (1929) (listing signatories) [hereinafter 1929 Convention].

modernization and codification of the laws of war.[46] Specifically, the "Hague tradition" of the law of armed conflict resulted from international diplomatic conferences sponsored by the Russian monarch Tsar Alexander II in 1899 and 1907, which produced conventions focusing primarily on the means and methods of warfare.[47] These conventions differed from the ICRC's "Geneva tradition," which focused on alleviating suffering of the victims of armed conflict, and generally did not address how parties conducted hostilities. During the efforts to codify customs regarding means and methods, the ICRC successfully fought attempts to replace the Geneva Convention with more comprehensive law-of-war regulations, because the ICRC feared dilution of the protective measures.[48] The two strands of IHL finally merged in 1977 when two additional protocols to the 1949 Geneva Conventions were opened for signature following the ICRC's efforts to update these conventions, both of which included provisions addressing both the protection of war victims *and* the means and methods of warfare.[49]

A modern example of the ICRC's continuing role in this developmental process occurred when the participants of the 2011 International Conference passed a resolution that expressly recognized the ICRC's role in developing international humanitarian law,[50] and asked the ICRC to:

> [p]ursue further research, consultation and discussion in cooperation with States and, if appropriate, other relevant actors, including international and regional organizations, to identify and propose a range of options and its recommendations to: i) ensure that international humanitarian law remains practical and relevant in providing legal protection to all persons deprived of their liberty in relation to armed conflict; and ii) enhance and ensure the effectiveness of mechanisms of compliance with international humanitarian law. . . .[51]

---

[46] *See, e.g.*, Francis Lieber, General Orders No. 100: The Lieber Code art. 22, art. 15 (1863), *available at* http://avalon.law.yale.edu/19th_century/lieber.asp (the first national law-of-war manual, drafted by Sir Francis Lieber during the U.S. Civil War at the behest of the commanding Union general).

[47] *See, e.g.*, Int'l & Operational Law Dep't, The Judge Advocate General's Legal Ctr. & Sch., U.S. Army, Operational Law Handbook 14 (Major Sean Condron et al. eds., 2011) [hereinafter Oplaw Handbook] (discussing Hague versus Geneva traditions). *See also* Moorehead, *supra* note 19, at 125 (highlighting that Geneva tradition concerned victims of war while the Hague tradition dealt with the conduct of war.)

[48] *See, e.g.*, Moorehead, *supra* note 19, at 124 (discussing ICRC's battle against incorporation into general regulations).

[49] *See supra* Part I (describing the role of the ICRC in developing the Geneva Conventions).

[50] ICRC, *World's Largest Humanitarian Meeting Resolves to Strengthen IHL and Local Humanitarian Action* (Dec 12, 2011), http://www.icrc.org/eng/resources/documents/feature/2011/31-international-conference-feature-2011-12-20.htm.

[51] ICRC, *31st International Conference 2011: Resolution 1—Strengthening Legal Protection for Victims of Armed Conflicts* (Jan 12, 2011), http://www.icrc.org/eng/resources/documents /resolution/31-international-conference-resolution-1-2011.htm.

Notably, this mandate does not call on the ICRC to determine what the current law is, or to develop the law itself, but rather to propose options and recommendations to states. This contrasts with the 1995 International Conference, which did ask the ICRC to determine the exact constitution of customary international humanitarian law, which in large measure explains why the ICRC considers its CIL study reflective of the current state of the law.[52] However, states such as the United States have formally articulated their disagreement with various provisions of this report, and therefore ambiguity continues to surround the exact contours of numerous provisions of what the ICRC claims to constitute binding law.[53]

C. ICRC: MODERN MANDATES AND MODALITIES

1. From Ideas to Operations

As mentioned above, the ICRC pursues two primary lines of work. It continues to work toward the promotion and development of international humanitarian law.[54] However, as first exemplified by the original committee delegates, its primary mission is operational: to protect populations from the effects of armed conflicts and other situations of violence.[55] It is important to underscore that these two efforts complement each other, with the development of the law informed by delegates working within, and pushing the boundaries of, the law of armed conflict's framework.[56]

The original 1863 Swiss committee of five envisioned itself as a promoter of ideas only, with all operational activities assigned to what would become the national Red Cross and Red Crescent societies. During the first 1863 conference and subsequent period, the committee was viewed by itself, the nascent societies, and states as an entity that would cease to exist once national societies gained ground.[57] However, beginning with the short-lived fighting between Austria and Prussia in 1866, and the Franco-Prussian War in 1870, the ICRC began sending delegates to the battlefields.[58] The primary function of these delegates was to observe and report back on adherence to and implementation of the 1864

---

[52] *See* CIL Study, *supra* note 13, at xvii ("The ICRC believes that the study does indeed present an accurate assessment of the current state of customary international humanitarian law.")

[53] *See, e.g.*, John B. Bellinger III & William J. Haynes II, *A U.S. Government Response to the International Committee of the Red Cross Study Customary International Humanitarian Law*, 89 INT'L REV. RED CROSS 443 (2007).

[54] ICRC Mission, *supra* note 10, at 401.

[55] Gentile, *supra* note 4, at 1167. *See also* ICRC Mission, *supra* note 10, at 401.

[56] ICRC Mission, *supra* note 10, at 401.

[57] *See, e.g.*, BUGNION, *supra* note 23, at 19 (citing the Dutch representative's comment at the 1863 conference as evidence of the ICRC's temporary nature: "*[t]he provisional position of the Geneva Committee will cease when the committees in other countries have been formed."*) *See also* MOOREHEAD, *supra* note 19, at 58 (highlighting that the original five committee members never intended their group to be permanent).

[58] *See, e.g.*, MOOREHEAD, *supra* note 19, at 55–56 (recounting Dr. Appia's role as surgeon and observer in 1866 hostilities).

Convention, though they also took direct part in the relief of suffering.[59] These delegates laid the foundation for the active, operational role the ICRC now plays in contemporary conflicts.

In addition to monitoring battlefield activities and liaising among various national Red Cross groups, during the 1870 Franco-Prussian War the ICRC also began what would become standard protocol when it immediately contacted the opposing governments to remind them at the onset of hostilities of their 1864 treaty obligations.[60] During this conflict the ICRC inaugurated its practice of finding missing soldiers and relaying messages from them to their families; the ICRC also began formal visits to prisoners of war and utilized its services as a "neutral intermediary" to achieve, among other things, the repatriation of wounded soldiers.[61] During the war the committee also established the first "tracing agency," a bureau set up to collect and share information about soldiers during war.[62] Today the ICRC does all these things and more.[63]

A. FUNDAMENTAL PRINCIPLES AND APPROACHES

The ICRC's operational mission is informed by what the ICRC calls its seven "Fundamental Principles," of which impartiality, neutrality, and independence are the most referenced, the others being humanity, voluntary service, unity, and universality.[64] Neutrality dictates that the ICRC not take sides in a conflict or judge any side's particular *jus ad bellum* basis for conflict, or take sides in political, racial, religious, or ideological controversies.[65] This is sometimes difficult for U.S. military personnel to understand, given the atrocities often perpetrated by U.S. adversaries. The ICRC believes (and rightly so) that its access to the victims of violence depends on its neutrality. The ICRC's impartiality directs that the ICRC treat people equally according to needs versus nationality, etc.,[66] whereas the independence principle allows it to fully adhere to these earlier principles, based on the fact that the ICRC is "independent of national and international politics, interest groups, and any other entity that may have some connection

---

[59] *See, e.g.*, MOOREHEAD, *supra* note 19, at xxi (citing the ICRC as the guardian).

[60] *Id.* at 61. (stating that "the ICRC gained acceptance as a neutral humanitarian intermediary during the wars that flared up round Europe in the 1860s and 1870s.")

[61] *See, e.g.*, MOOREHEAD, *supra* note 19, at 63 (highlighting ICRC efforts during the Franco-Prussian War).

[62] *Id.*

[63] The ICRC is one component of the triad comprising the International Red Cross and Red Crescent Movement, which includes the ICRC, the Red Cross and Red Crescent Societies, and the International Federation of the Red Cross and Red Crescent. *See, e.g.*, ICRC, *Statutes of the International Committee of the Red Cross* (Aug. 5, 2003), http://www.icrc.org/eng/resources/documents/misc/icrc-statutes-080503.htm.

[64] *See, e.g.*, Claudia McGoldrick, *The Future of Humanitarian Action: An ICRC Perspective*, 93 INT'L REV. RED CROSS 965, 966 (2011). *See also* ICRC Mission, *supra* note 10, at 404. (describing mission and principles in detail).

[65] ICRC Mission, *supra* note 10, at 404.

[66] *Id.*

with a situation of violence."[67] Furthermore, the ICRC is structurally independent, given that its governing body, the Committee, is comprised solely of Swiss citizens chosen via co-option (not by the Swiss government); it also strengthened its formal independence from the Swiss government after its failure to publicly condemn the Holocaust was partially attributed to Swiss national interests.[68]

The ICRC principles complement its four primary approaches to fulfilling its mission, which consist of protection, assistance, cooperation, and prevention.[69] Of particular relevance for the ICRC's interaction with the U.S. military are the ICRC's protection, assistance, and prevention activities.[70] Protection focuses on efforts to ensure that the applicable actors are fulfilling their legal obligations, and attempts to prevent or end violations of international humanitarian law by communicating directly with those responsible for such violations, as well as with those who can influence them.[71] For example, the ICRC's work inside U.S. detention centers such as that at Guantanamo Bay, Cuba or at Bagram Airfield, Afghanistan would be considered protective in nature (described below in Part II.) Its newer history of providing allegations of allegedly U.S.-caused civilian casualties would also fall within this rubric. Assistance covers particular concrete measures such as helping communities adversely affected by armed conflict or other violence by providing medical care, responding to needs relating to water or shelter, etc.[72] As such work in an armed conflict context occurs within a battlefield commander's area of operation, the U.S. military must frequently interact with the ICRC regarding such measures (for example, the commander may want to seek advice from the ICRC regarding the community's needs prior to engaging in humanitarian assistance missions).

Finally, the ICRC's prevention approach focuses on "influencing those who have a direct or indirect impact on the fate if people affected" by violent situations.[73] This approach often couples with what the ICRC calls "humanitarian diplomacy" to influence the political choices of States, armed groups, and international organizations to "promote the ICRC's major objectives."[74] Such prevention efforts relating to the United States primarily emanate from the ICRC's offices in Washington, DC, which house the ICRC's Regional Delegation for the

---

[67] *Id.*

[68] *See Neutral in a Harsh World, A History of the ICFC*, AGENCE FRANCE-PRESSE (Feb. 13, 2013), *available at* http://www.globalpost.com/dispatch/news/afp/130210/neutral-harsh-world-the-history-the-icrc (discussing seminal moments in the history of the ICRC). The ICRC is funded by states that are parties to the Geneva Conventions. It also receives funding from national Red Cross and Red Crescent societies, private donations, as well as supranational organizations such as the European Commission. *See* ICRC, *Where Does Your Money Go* (Apr. 23, 2010) http://www.icrc.org/eng/donations/where-your-money-go/overview-where-does-your-money-go.htm.

[69] ICRC Mission, *supra* note 10, at 407.

[70] The fourth, cooperation, deals with the ICRC's work to enhance the capacities of the various national-level Red Cross and Red Crescent societies. *See, e.g.*, ICRC Mission, *supra* note 10, at 408.

[71] *Id.* at 407.

[72] *Id.* at 707.

[73] *Id.* at 708.

[74] *Id.* at 709.

United States and Canada, which opened in 1995.[75] This office, primarily through its chief delegate, maintains a robust and regular dialogue with officials not only within the DoD and U.S. military, but also with national security officials such as the National Security Council legal advisor, the Legal Advisor to the State Department, officials at the Department of Justice, and the Central Intelligence Agency.[76] In fact, the ICRC president recently met with President Barack Obama and high-level policy officials such as John Brennan.[77]

B. CONFIDENTIAL DIALOGUE

These conversations demonstrate the primary tool in the ICRC's arsenal for achieving its protective objective: that of confidential dialogue with various stakeholders. The ICRC enjoys a long history of confidential, one-on-one dialogue with governments, and the United States is no exception.[78] This modus operandi generally functions in the following manner: ICRC delegates observe, for example, U.S. military detention facilities and privately interview detainees, then discuss their observations with their ICRC hierarchy. Written reports detailing the observations and legal opinions of compliance/non-compliance with international humanitarian law, as well as human rights law,[79] are compiled and then provided to the local U.S. detention facility authorities. Subsequently, ICRC delegates raise the reports' main issues to DoD officials at the Pentagon and elsewhere (such as at a combatant command headquarters such as USCENTCOM in Tampa, Florida). These reports form the basis of a multi-tiered dialogue among the ICRC, the U.S. military, and DoD, starting at the field level and reinforced at the highest policy levels.[80]

The ICRC treats all their reports and communications with the United States (and all state parties to the Geneva Conventions) as confidential, and does not release their reports to third parties or to the media (on the U.S. side, DoD policy directs the U.S. military to treat all ICRC reports as classified at the secret level).[81]

---

[75] ICRC, *Delegation for the United States and Canada* (2013), *available at* http://www.icrc.org/eng/assets/files/other/icrc-fact-sheet-usa-canada.pdf (last visited Apr. 14, 2013).

[76] *Id.*

[77] *See* ICRC, *United States: ICRC President Completes Visit to Washington* (Apr. 11, 2013), http://www.icrc.org/eng/resources/documents/news-release/2013/04-11-us-president-obama-maurer.htm (describing visit). Prior to the meeting with President Obama, the ICRC last met with a sitting U.S. president in 2005, when then-ICRC President Jakob Kellenberger met with President George W. Bush. ICRC, *ICRC President Meets US President Bush* (Feb. 2, 2005), http://www.icrc.org/eng/resources/documents/misc/69lttv.htm.

[78] Gentile, *supra* note 4, at 1168.

[79] The ICRC often refers to human rights law when it finds international humanitarian law either inapplicable or ambiguous. This is often a source of tension with the United States, which views international humanitarian law as a *lex specialis* that replaces human rights law during armed conflict. *See* ICRC, *IHL and Human Rights Law* (Oct. 29, 2010), http://www.icrc.org/eng/war-and-law/ihl-other-legal-regmies/ihl-human-rights/overview-ihl-and-human-rights.htm.

[80] The DoD maintains policies directing that all ICRC communications be quickly disseminated to the respective combatant command and OSD staff; *see infra* Part II.

[81] Raymond F. DuBois, *Handling of Reports from the International Committee of the Red Cross* (July 14, 2004), *available at* http://library.rumsfeld.com/doclib/sp/3377/2004-07-08%20from%20Ray%20DuBois%20re%20Handling%20Reports%20from%20the%20Intl%20Committee%20of%20the%20Red%20Cross.pdf [hereinafter DoD ICRC Memo].

Typically, when the ICRC or the United States desires to provide information to the press, the ICRC and the United States coordinate their statements, ensuring that both sides are satisfied that equities are protected. The ICRC works very hard at maintaining its confidentiality,[82] which it views as paramount to continued and future access to situations of violence and to authorities—that is, confidentiality is paramount to its mission success.[83] This confidentiality applies to all governments; for example, if the United States desires information regarding ICRC observations of Afghan prisons, the United States must obtain such reports from the Afghan government, not from the ICRC.

2. 1949 Geneva Conventions: Treaty Basis for ICRC Roles

A. HISTORICAL BACKGROUND

The ICRC's international legal mandates for action have a long history. Article 5 of the seminal 1864 Geneva Convention laid the groundwork by both establishing the principle of neutrality (termed inviolability) of military medical personnel, hospitals, and ambulances as well as that for civilians (inhabitants) helping wounded soldiers on and around the battlefield.[84] Organized relief work regarding the care of wounded on the battlefield, though not specifically that of the ICRC, was first specifically mentioned in the 1906 Geneva Convention, which detailed state responsibilities for respecting the neutrality of voluntary aid societies while emphasizing that such organizations could only operate with state consent.[85] Critically, this treaty was the first to recognize not only national relief societies working with their respective militaries for the care of wounded soldiers, but relief societies from neutral nations offering their services to the wounded as well.[86]

---

[82] Leaks of ICRC reports occasionally happen, prompting considerable angst within the ICRC. This occurred when the ICRC's 2007 confidential report to the CIA regarding its black sites was leaked in 2009 to the media. *See, e.g.*, Joby Warrick, Peter Finn & Julie Tate, *Red Cross Described "Torture" at CIA Jails*, WASH. POST (Mar. 16, 2009), http://articles.washingtonpost.com/2009-03-16/news/36836881_1_cia-prisons-secret-prisons-cia-jails. This of course differs from a formal ICRC denunciation, which is an intentional breach by the ICRC of their confidentiality in order to bring attention to a humanitarian situation that other methods have failed to rectify. *See* ICRC Mission, *supra* note 10, at 410.

[83] To preserve this confidentiality, the ICRC gained immunity from testimony from the International Criminal Tribunal for the Former Yugoslavia, as well as successfully enshrined this privilege into the Rome Statue governing the International Criminal Court. *See* DUNOFF ET AL., *supra* note 38, at 14, 15; Gabor Rona, *The ICRC Privilege Not to Testify: Confidentiality in Action*, 84 INT'L REV. OF THE RED CROSS 207 (Mar. 3, 2002), *available at* http://www.icrc.org/eng/resources/documents/misc/59kcr4.htm). This immunity from testimony is likely also enshrined in the confidential headquarters agreement between the United States and the ICRC.

[84] Article 5 states that "[in]habitants of the country who may bring help to the wounded shall be respected, and shall remain free." *See also* Red Cross Convention, *supra* note 29, at art. 2 (establishing the neutrality of military medical personnel), and Article 1 (the same for hospitals and ambulances).

[85] *See* Convention for the Amelioration of the Condition of the Wounded and Sick in Armies in the Field, 11 L.N.T.S. 440 (1906) (showing that Articles 6–9 discuss the neutrality of national sanitary units, whereas Articles 10–14 authorize and protect voluntary relief societies, including those from neutral nations) [hereinafter 1906 Convention].

[86] *Id.* at art. 11.

Regarding relief work specifically aimed at prisoners of war, specific mention of relief societies in international treaty law was first made in the 1899 and 1907 Hague Regulations (after a failed attempt at inserting protective language into the 1864 Brussels Declaration).[87] Article 15 of the 1899 and 1907 Hague Regulations requires belligerent states to provide facilities to "relief societies" and to allow these groups into places of internment in order to distribute relief, though subject to military necessity and security-related regulations.[88] This article, which was mirrored in Article 78 of the 1929 Geneva Convention, "served during two world wars as a legal basis for the relief activities of charitable societies, particularly national Red Cross Societies and the International Committee of the Red Cross."[89] Regarding prisoners of war, Article 88 of the 1929 Geneva Conventions finally carved out a specific role for the ICRC: "[t]he foregoing provisions do not constitute any obstacle to the humanitarian work which the International Red Cross Committee may perform for the protection of prisoners of war with the consent of the belligerents concerned."[90]

B. ICRC ACTION DURING INTERNATIONAL ARMED CONFLICTS

Today the ICRC mandates, at least regarding international armed conflicts (referred to as Article 2 conflicts), are explicitly expressed in the 1949 Geneva Conventions. These four treaties include provisions recognizing the roles for the ICRC plus relief societies in general, and combine the relief work focused on the wounded with that regarding prisoners of war and civilian internees.[91] The

---

[87] *See, e.g.*, ICRC, *Commentary to Article 125 Convention Relative to the Treatment of Prisoners of War (Third Geneva Convention), Aug. 12, 1949*, 75 U.N.T.S. 135, *available at* http://www.icrc.org/ihl.nsf/COM/375-590150 (discussing the original, unsuccessful effort to enshrine relief work in the 1874 Brussels Declaration) [hereinafter Article 125 Commentary].

[88] Article 15 of both the 1899 and 1907 Hague Regulations provides:

> [r]elief societies for prisoners of war, which are regularly constituted in accordance with the law of the country with the object of serving as the intermediary for charity, shall receive from the belligerents for themselves and their duly accredited agents every facility, within the bounds of military requirements and administrative regulations, for the effective accomplishment of their humane task. Delegates of these societies may be admitted to the places of internment for the distribution of relief, as also to the halting places of repatriated prisoners, if furnished with a personal permit by the military authorities, and on giving an engagement in writing to comply with all their regulations for order and police as issued.

Convention (II) with Respect to the Laws and Customs of War on Land and its annex: Regulations concerning the Laws and Customs of War on Land. The Hague, 29 July 1899, http://www.icrc.org/ihl/WebART/150-110021. Similarly, Article 10 of the 1906 revision of the original 1864 Geneva Convention expressly recognizes volunteer aid societies and accords them neutral status. 1906 Convention, *supra* note 85.

[89] Article 125 Commentary, *supra* note 87.

[90] 1929 Convention, *supra* note 45, at art. 88.

[91] Geneva Convention for the Amelioration of the Condition of the Wounded and Sick in Armed Forces in the Field (First Geneva Convention), Aug. 12, 1949, 75 U.N.T.S. 31, *available at* http://www.unhcr.org/refworld/docid/3ae6b3694.html [hereinafter Geneva Convention I]; Geneva Convention for the Amelioration of the Condition of Wounded, Sick and Shipwrecked Members of

ICRC's formal role is articulated in Common Articles 9–11 of the four Geneva Conventions, as well as in Article 125, GC III, and Article 63, GC IV.[92] Common Article 9, which replaces 1929's Article 88, recognizes the ability of the ICRC to conduct humanitarian activities during international armed conflicts at the consent of the belligerent parties, though does not specify its tasks.[93] According to the commentaries, this provision highlights that the ICRC's "right of initiative," or right to offer its services, is not specifically relegated only to those provisions that explicitly list ICRC tasks.[94]

i. Individuals Subjected to Detention and Internment

As originally conceived, state parties to armed conflicts would agree on a Protecting Power—a neutral state whose diplomats would oversee compliance with the respective Geneva Conventions. Perhaps unsurprisingly, this method of

---

Armed Forces at Sea (Second Geneva Convention), Aug. 12, 1949, 75 U.N.T.S 85, *available at* http://www.unhcr.org/refworld/docid/3ae6b37927.html [hereinafter Geneva Convention II]; Geneva Convention Relative to the Treatment of Prisoners of War (Third Geneva Convention), Aug. 12, 1949, 75 U.N.T.S. 135, *available at* http://www.unhcr.org/refworld/docid/3ae6b36c8.html [hereinafter Geneva Convention III]; Geneva Convention Relative to the Protection of Civilian Persons in Time of War (Fourth Geneva Convention), Aug. 12, 1949, 75 U.N.T.S. 287, *available at* http://www.unhcr.org/refworld/docid/3ae6b36d2.html [hereinafter Geneva Convention IV]; Protocol Additional to the Geneva Conventions of 12 August 1949, and relating to the Protection of Victims of International Armed Conflicts (Protocol I), 8 June 1977, 1125 UNTS 3, art. 41, *available at* http://www.unhcr.org/refworld/docid/3ae6b36b4.html (last visited Dec. 20, 2012) [hereinafter Additional Protocol I]; Protocol Additional to the Geneva Conventions of 12 August 1949, and relating to the Protection of Victims of Non-international Armed Conflicts (Protocol II), June 8, 1977, 1125 U.N.T.S. 609, *available at* http://www.unhcr.org/refworld/docid/3ae6b37f40.html [hereinafter Additional Protocol II]; International Conferences (The Hague), Hague Convention (IV) Respecting the Laws and Customs of War on Land and Its Annex: Regulations Concerning the Laws and Customs of War on Land, 26 Stat. 2277, Oct. 18 1907, *available at*: http://www.unhcr.org/refworld/docid/4374cae64.html [hereinafter Hague Convention]; *see, e.g.*, Jean-Marie Henckaerts, *Study on Customary International Humanitarian Law: A Contribution to the Understanding and Respect for the Rule of Law in Armed Conflict*, 87 Int'l Rev. Red Cross 187 (2005), *available at* http://www.icrc.org/eng/assets/files/other/irrc_857_henckaerts.pdf, (highlighting that much of Additional Protocols I and II have attained the status of customary international law).

[92] *See* Geneva Convention III, *supra* note 91. Additionally, Article 63 of the Fourth Geneva Convention states:

> Subject to temporary and exceptional measures imposed for urgent reasons of security by the Occupying Power: (a) recognized National Red Cross (Red Crescent, Red Lion and Sun) Societies shall be able to pursue their activities in accordance with Red Cross principles, as defined by the International Red Cross Conferences. Other relief societies shall be permitted to continue their humanitarian activities under similar conditions; (b) the Occupying Power may not require any changes in the personnel or structure of these societies, which would prejudice the aforesaid activities. The same principles shall apply to the activities and personnel of special organizations of a non-military character, which already exist or which may be established, for the purpose of ensuring the living conditions of the civilian population by the maintenance of the essential public utility services, by the distribution of relief and by the organization of rescues.

Geneva Convention IV, *supra* note 91, art. 63.

[93] Geneva Convention I, *supra* note 91, at art. 9.

[94] 2 Jean Pictet, Commentary on the Geneva Conventions of 12 August 1949, at 67 (1960).

oversight never really functioned effectively, as parties to conflicts are rarely able to reach such agreement. [95] As a result, the ICRC's protection roles regarding prisoners of war and civilian internees complement those given in the Conventions to representatives of the "Protecting Powers." Applicable during an international armed conflict, Article 126 of the Geneva Convention Relative to the Treatment of Prisoners of War (GC III) specifically states that ICRC delegates *shall*: have access to all prisoners of war; be able to interview them without witnesses; and be allowed to both select the places they want to visit and to dictate the duration and frequency of their visits.[96] Visits may be denied only "as an exceptional and temporary measure" for "reasons of imperative military necessity."[97] What the United States defines as imperative military necessity, and how it construes "access to all premises occupied by prisoners of war" is situationally dependent, as discussed in Part II of this chapter. Contrasted with the ICRC's Article 9 right of initiative, which depends on state consent, state parties possess an obligation to facilitate these access and visitation rights.[98]

Article 125 of GC III speaks to the activities pertaining to prisoners of war of relief organizations in general, allowing the "Detaining Powers" to limit such activities based on security or other reasonable grounds.[99] Detaining Powers are to provide logistical and other support to relief agencies to support their relief work for prisoners of war, subject to the above restrictions; Article 125 further notes that "[t]he special position of the International Committee of the Red Cross in this field shall be recognized and respected at all times."[100]

In addition to mandating ICRC access to prisoners of war, GC III also requires states parties to the conflict to establish "Information Bureaus" to track information of "enemy persons" in its power, and to transmit this information "immediately" to the Central Agency organized by the ICRC per Article 123.[101] GC III furthermore gives the ICRC the job of proposing the establishment of a central tracing agency for prisoners of war, similar to the one it organically grew during the 1870 Franco-Prussian War.[102] Article 123, GC III, specifically provides that the ICRC shall "propose . . . the organization of such an Agency," which shall "collect all the information it may obtain through official or private channels respecting prisoners of war" and transmit this information to the prisoners' countries of origin.[103] Although the treaty language provides flexibility for a state party to operate such an agency in a neutral country, in reality the ICRC has operated

---

[95] *See* Oplaw Handbook, *supra* note 47, at 34.

[96] Geneva Convention III, *supra* note 91, at art. 126.

[97] *Id.*

[98] ICRC access to detainees, both civilian and military, in an international armed conflict has become customary international law. *See* ICRC CIL Study, *supra* note 13, at 442.

[99] Geneva Convention III, *supra* note 91, at art. 125.

[100] *Id.*

[101] *Id.* at art. 122, 123.

[102] *Id.* at art. 123.

[103] *Id.*

what is known as the Central Agency, tracing prisoners of war, detainees, and civilians, since World War II.[104] This agency receives compulsory information from the national bureaus and disseminates the information to the countries of origin or residence of those interned.

The ICRC plays a similar role vis-à-vis civilians who are interned for reasons of imperative security. The Geneva Convention Relative to the Protection of Civilian Persons in Time of War of August 12, 1949 (GC IV) mandates analogous ICRC to these civilians during international armed conflicts.[105] Article 143, similar to Article 126 in GC III, provides that the ICRC "shall" have the same prerogatives regarding access to internees as do representatives from Protecting Powers.[106] This includes the same access as described above for prisoners of war, including the right to select the places and times of visit, as well as private internee interviews, subject only to "reasons of imperative military necessity, and then only as an exceptional and temporary measure."[107] Parties to the conflict are required to establish information bureaus with the same responsibilities as regarding prisoners of war, and the ICRC likewise has assimilated its Central Information Agency for civilian internees into its Central Agency described above.[108] Additionally, Article 10 provides that "[t]he provisions of the present Convention constitute no obstacle to the humanitarian activities which the International Committee of the Red Cross or any other impartial humanitarian organization may, subject to the consent of the Parties to the conflict concerned, undertake for the protection of civilian persons and for their relief."[109]

C. ICRC ACTION DURING NON-INTERNATIONAL ARMED CONFLICTS

During non-international armed conflicts, Common Article 3 to the four Geneva Conventions is the only treaty provision binding on the United States regarding the ICRC functions and access (additional provisions apply to states bound by Additional Protocol II). This "humane treatment" article simply provides for the ICRC's right of initiative regarding such conflicts; that is, it authorizes the ICRC to offer its services to the belligerent parties.[110] In other words, there is no specific treaty mandate for access to detainees (civilian and belligerent) during such an Article 3 conflict or in those violent situations not even rising to the status of an armed conflict. However, the ICRC's study on customary international law, mentioned above, finds that "an ICRC offer to visit persons deprived of their liberty in the context of a non-international armed conflict must be examined in good faith and may not be refused arbitrarily."[111] United States Department of Defense policy reiterates Common Article 3's right of initiative, and hews to the position that

---

[104] *See* 3 JEAN PICTET, COMMENTARY ON THE GENEVA CONVENTIONS OF 12 AUGUST 1949, at 581 (1960) (discussing history of the Central Agency).

[105] Geneva Convention III, *supra* note 91, at art. 126.

[106] *Id.*

[107] *Id.*

[108] See *id.* at art. 138, 140 (outlining national and neutral tracing agency responsibilities).

[109] Geneva Convention IV, *supra* note 91, at art. 10.

[110] Geneva Convention I, *supra* note 91, at art. 3.

[111] ICRC CIL Study, *supra* note 13, at 445.

ICRC access is not legally required by international law in a non-international armed conflict.[112]

President Obama, in a 2009 Executive Order, mandated that all U.S. government agencies provide the ICRC with access and notification of all detentions:

> All departments and agencies of the Federal Government shall provide the International Committee of the Red Cross with notification of, and timely access to, any individual detained in any armed conflict in the custody or under the effective control of an officer, employee, or other agent of the United States Government or detained within a facility owned, operated, or controlled by a department or agency of the United States Government, consistent with Department of Defense regulations and policies.[113]

Although this remains policy and therefore subject to modification, it is interesting that this executive statement does not include a caveat indicating the U.S. government does not believe this is a binding legal obligation.[114] Hence, a statement such as this could be cited in the future as state practice to build an ICRC right of access to, and notification of, detainees as customary international law.[115]

Interestingly, the U.S. Congress passed legislation requiring ICRC access, subject to the imperative military necessity, to the U.S.-run Bagram Theater Internment Facility (BTIF) as part of the 2010 National Defense Authorization Act.[116] However, this legislation changed nothing on the ground, as the ICRC had already been provided regular access to detainees there since January 2002, based on U.S. policy allowing ICRC access to "theater internment facilities," such as Camp Bucca in Iraq, which housed detainees transferred from short-term holding facilities.[117] Regarding notification of detention to the ICRC, this occurred approximately at the time of transfer to the BTIF with assignment of an "Internment Serial Number," which was provided to the ICRC's Central Agency via the U.S. National Detainee Reporting Center, which is operated by the U.S. Army.[118]

---

[112] *See* Dep't of Defense Directive 2311.01E, DoD Law of War Program (Sept. 5, 2006) [hereinafter DODD 2310.01E]. Comment of John H. Bellinger III, Legal Advisor to the U.S. Dep't of State, *in* Yonah Alexander & Michael B. Kraft, Evolution of United States Counterterrorism Policy (2007) ("We do not think we are required to give the ICRC access" to detainees captured in the non-international armed conflict against al Qaida).

[113] Exec. Order No. 13491, 74 C.F.R. § 4893 (2009).

[114] The DoD even requires ICRC notification and access to individuals detained on suspicion of pirate activity and held on board U.S. Navy or other vessels longer than thirty days. *See* Email from Captain Errol Henriques, U.S. Navy, May 2013 (on file with author).

[115] Of course the second prong of *opinio juris* must be met as well.

[116] National Defense Authorization Act for Fiscal Year 2010, Pub. L. No. 111-84, 123 Stat. 2190 (2009).

[117] *See generally* ICRC, *Persons Detained by the US in Relation to Armed Conflict and the Fight against Terrorism—the Role of the ICRC* (Jan. 9, 2012), http://www.ikrk.org/eng /resources/documents/misc/united-states-detention.htm (highlighting that ICRC has had access to detainees at Bagram Air Base since January 2002) [hereinafter Role of the ICRC].

[118] Regarding information provided to the ICRC Central Agency, the DoD operates the National Detainee Reporting Center (NDRC), formerly called the National Prisoner of War Information

What the ICRC was not afforded for many years in Afghanistan (as well as in Iraq), and had complained about for the same period,[119] was the lack of access to and knowledge of U.S. conventional *temporary* field detention sites. These temporary sites typically held detainees for up to two weeks at a time, primarily to determine whether to transfer the detainee to the BTIF (or other relevant theater internment facility) or to release. Nor did the ICRC have access to, or official knowledge of, so-called special operations "black sites," including the facility at Bagram Air Base, Afghanistan (and analogous sites in Iraq), which were also ostensibly temporary sites (though occasionally not in practice).[120] However, the ICRC did eventually gain both access and knowledge of both conventional and "special" temporary sites. In 2008 the ICRC gained access to conventional field temporary detention facilities in Afghanistan, and the ICRC gained notification of detainees held by special forces units held longer than two weeks in Afghanistan in 2009, plus was finally granted regular access to the special forces' "black sites" in 2010.[121]

According to the ICRC,

> Since August 2009, the ICRC is notified of all persons detained by the US military in situations of armed conflict within 14 days of their capture. This helps the ICRC monitor the fate of those detained until they leave US custody, and to respond to queries by family seeking news of their relatives. The ICRC has a transparent relationship with the Department of Defense and is satisfied with progress made as regards access to detention facilities. The ICRC has access to internment, screening, and transit facilities under the control of the Department of Defense.[122]

As demonstrated by the above descriptions both of the ICRC's rich lineage and the international community's incorporation of the ICRC into international humanitarian law, the ICRC plays a pivotal role during armed conflicts and

---

Center. *See* DODD 2310.01E, *supra* note 112, at 5 (requiring the Department of the Army to operate a national-level detainee reporting center and subordinate theater elements). *See also* Memorandum for OPMG, Correction Branch, *available at* http://dspace.wrlc.org/doc/get/2041/78158/01010_030926.pdf (last visited Apr. 11, 2013) (discussing Reporting Center's name change). *See also* Army Regulation 190–8 at 3, ¶ 1-7 (outlining responsibilities of reporting center) [hereinafter AR 190-8].

[119] *See, e.g.*, Eric Schmitt, *U.S. Shifts, Giving Detainee Names to the Red Cross*, N.Y.TIMES (Aug. 23, 2009), http://www.nytimes.com/2009/08/23/world/middleeast/23detain.html (highlighting that the ICRC "has been lobbying for years for access to those held at the Special Operations camps, or least information about who is being detained in them); see also ICRC, *ICRC Visits to Detainees in Afghanistan* (Dec. 13 2012), http://www.icrc.org/eng/resources/documents/interview/afghanistan-interview-131207.htm. ("However, not all places of detention and detainees are notified to the ICRC. The organization can therefore not confirm that it has access to all detainees in Afghanistan.").

[120] Schmitt, *supra* note 119.

[121] *See* Schmitt, *supra* note 1 (ICRC granted notification of detainees held at special operations site at Bagram in 2009). The conclusion that the ICRC was eventually given access to this same facility is based on the ICRC's subsequent statements that it enjoyed access to all DoD detention facilities. *See generally* Role of the ICRC, *supra* note 117.

[122] Role of the ICRC, *supra* note 117.

other periods of violence. Therefore, states such as the United States have developed policies and procedures for managing their relationship with the ICRC, as detailed in the following section.

III. Part II: Snapshot of Current ICRC/DoD Relationship

A. THE FORMAL RELATIONSHIP WITH THE CIVILIAN SIDE OF THE HOUSE

The ICRC's legal relationship with the DoD occurs within the framework of a bilateral agreement between the ICRC and the U.S. government, which is typical of the ICRC's relations with states. The existing "headquarters agreement": provides the ICRC with diplomatic privileges and immunities such as the inviolability of its offices and chief delegates' homes; outlines U.S. consent to respect the ICRC's confidentiality; and provides ICRC delegates with certain evidentiary privileges.[123] The agreement's focus is on the ICRC's formal status within the United States, and therefore contains very little guidance regarding actual day-to-day management of the relationship. The result, one influenced by the ICRC's modus operandi of confidential dialogue (humanitarian diplomacy), is a fluid relationship largely shaped by personalities and events, such as changes of presidential administrations and the personality of the ICRC's chief delegate. However, the greatest influence on this long-standing relationship is war itself—periods of conflict naturally thrust the ICRC's traditional role of caring for the victims of conflict into the forefront, and individual incidents within conflicts, such as the Abu Ghraib scandal, further serve as a catalyst for both entities to pursue their respective and often overlapping interests.

The Department of Defense's formal relationship with the ICRC gradually transitioned from a "largely diplomatic relationship to an operational one" after the tragic events on September 11, 2001.[124] The current relationship formally centers on the Office of the Under Secretary of Defense for Policy (USD-P), which has primary responsibility for DoD detainee operations,[125] and specifically

---

[123] Rona, *supra* note 83, at 207 (outlining primary components of standard headquarters agreements). The U.S.-ICRC headquarters agreement is treated as a classified document and is not available for review or citation.

[124] ICRC, *Interview with Geoff Loane, Head of ICRC Regional Delegation for the United States and Canada* (Aug. 2009), http://archive.constantcontact.com/fs013/1102236947549/archive/1102640745856.html.

[125] DoD Directive 2310.01E, *supra* note 112. This department-wide regulation provides in relevant part that:

> The USD(P) shall: 5.1.1. Review, ensure coordination of, and approve all implementing policies or guidance to the DoD Detainee Program.... 5.1.3. Serve as the principal DoD interlocutor with the ICRC and develop policy and procedures to ensure the proper and timely reporting of ICRC communications to appropriate DoD and U.S. Government officials.

Id. at 4.

its subordinate office of the Office of the Deputy Secretary of Defense for the Rule of Law and Detainee Affairs (OSD-RDP).[126] The latter office was formally established in 2004 in the wake of the Abu Ghraib scandal to both oversee DoD detainee policies and to specifically serve as a focal point for ICRC communications.[127] Prior to this office's establishment, ICRC written reports, which typically result from ICRC visits to field detention sites or other combat activity spawning ICRC concerns, had remained either in the field or within the responsible combatant command. This undermined uniformity in the U.S. interaction with the ICRC, as well as the ability of DoD to react in a comprehensive and fully informed manner to ICRC interventions.

The lack of an overarching DoD policy to deal with ICRC communications came into sharp relief in 2004 with the discovery that numerous ICRC reports, detailing the worsening conditions at Abu Ghraib, had been given to U.S. military personnel in the field, yet never reached decision-makers in Tampa at U.S. Central Command or at the Pentagon.[128] Hence the new "DASD-D" office (as it was known for the first several years of its existence, standing for the Deputy Assistance Secretary of Defense for Detainee Affairs), was established and formally charged with handling ICRC reports on behalf of the DoD while serving as "the single focal point in communicating with the ICRC on DoD's behalf."[129]

At the same time the new DASD-D office was established, then-Secretary of Defense Donald Rumsfeld promulgated DoD-wide policy guidance regarding ICRC communications.[130] This policy memo, since replaced by a similar though less onerous policy in 2007 that has not been made public, required that all ICRC reports be disseminated within twenty-four hours to numerous levels of the recipient's chain of command, as well as to the new DASD-D office and other OSD offices such the Office of the General Counsel (OGC).[131] Furthermore, in a fit of piqued paternalism prompted by U.S. CENTCOM leadership's failure to both read and act on the earlier negative ICRC reports on Abu Ghraib, the Rumsfeld policy required that combatant commanders provide their "assessment" to the Office of the Secretary of Defense in response to all ICRC reports received within twenty-four hours of receipt—an effort designed to ensure such reports were actually being reviewed by responsible commanders.[132] At U.S. CENTCOM, this requirement was implemented by the Office of the Staff Judge Advocate (OSJA),

---

[126] Interview with Nicolas Nobbs, ICRC Delegate to the Armed Forces, Regional Delegation for the United States and Canada (Apr. 9, 2013) [hereinafter Nobbs Interview].

[127] Samantha L. Quigley, *DoD Creates Office of Detainee Affairs*, American Forces Press Service (July 16, 2004), http://www.defense.gov/news/newsarticle.aspx?id=25695.

[128] *See, e.g.*, Josh White & R. Jeffrey Smith, *House Panel Reviews Iraq Prison Reports*, Wash. Post, July 15, 2004, at A14.

[129] Quigley, *supra* note 127.

[130] DoD ICRC Memo, *supra* note 81.

[131] *Id.*

[132] *Id.* The policy required in relevant part that "Combatant Commanders shall provide their assessment of the ICRC reports they receive to the USD(P) through the Director, Joint Staff within 24 hours of receipt." *Id.*

who designated one attorney to summarize reports both received from the field and those received at the combatant command directly from the ICRC; such summaries were sent to the two-star Chief of Staff who signed on behalf of the command.[133] Notably, these summaries contained little to no actual assessments, given the short time frame, compounded by the fact that the OSJA office, at least until 2006, was not sufficiently knowledgeable of the daily detainee operations in the field to comment on or assess the ICRC reports.[134] Surprisingly, these summaries were not reviewed by the U.S. CENTCOM J-3 (operations) office responsible for detention operations before signature by the two-star general, thus initially undercutting the intent of the policy to force combatant commands to use ICRC reports as early warning mechanisms.[135]

B. THE FORMAL RELATIONSHIP WITH THE OPERATIONAL/UNIFORMED SIDE

The operational relationships extant between the ICRC and the uniform side of the DoD are of an ad hoc nature, usually driven by a particular exigency entailing the ICRC's involvement. As the DoD is functionally structured to manage military operations through six geographical combatant commands (as well as Special Operations Command (SOCOM) which is not geographically constrained),[136] the ICRC has developed ongoing relationships with these combatant commands headquarters elements based on activities within their respective areas of responsibility (AOR) or mission (for SOCOM).[137] Although these relationships are not enshrined in either joint doctrine or DoD-wide policy, they are critically important for both the ICRC and the DoD. They allow combatant command leadership to better understand the effects of military and other operations within their area of responsibility, unfiltered through the subordinate military chain of command. Additionally, such relationships allow the ICRC direct access to military decision-makers, contacts that enable the ICRC to push for policy-driven changes within particular regions. They further provide opportunities to explain ICRC positions, and for the ICRC to gain a better understanding driving regional policies and practices.

The specific relational link, or "in-point" for the ICRC at each of the combatant commands differs; while the OSJA typically is the lead host of ICRC visits in deployed locations (that is, in Iraq when the United States had troops there, plus

---

[133] Personal Experience of Rachel Vanlandingham, Author and Former Lt. Col., USAF (retired), gathered during assignment to U.S. Central Command OSJA from June 2006 to June 2010.

[134] *Id.*

[135] *Id.* Starting in early 2007, the U.S. Central Command designated the Office of the Staff Judge Advocate, and one judge advocate in particular, to act as the U.S. Central Command liaison with the ICRC. From that point forward, the U.S. Central Command relationship with the ICRC was coordinated and led by the Office of the Staff Judge Advocate.

[136] *See* Andrew Feickert, Cong. Research Serv., R42077, The Unified Command Plan and Combatant Commands: Background and Issues for Congress 2, 3 (Jan. 3, 2013).

[137] Nobbs Interview, *supra* note 126. *See also* ICRC Relations, *supra* note 7.

Afghanistan and Guantanamo Bay),[138] this is not the norm stateside. For example, the ICRC has maintained a dialogue with officials at SOUTHCOM for numerous years, primarily prompted by that command's responsibility for the detainees in DoD custody at Guantanamo Bay, Cuba. While the ICRC liaisons with the SOUTHCOM OSJA on detainee issues, it also interfaces with the SOUTHCOM J5 (strategic planning and policy) and J9 (pacific outreach) offices regarding human rights training being overseen by SOUTHCOM in Central America.[139] At NORTHCOM, the primary interface is the J9 (interagency partnering), with subsidiary contacts with the J5 (plans) office and the OSJA.[140] At both EUCOM and AFRICOM, dialogue is conducted primarily with the J5 and J9 offices, while at SOCOM the relationship has been directly with the COCOM Commander, with new contacts currently being established.[141] Although the ICRC has little regular contact with US PACOM elements, it occasionally liaisons with the J7 (training) directorate there, as well as their legal advisors, regarding ICRC participation in various in-theater multinational and bilateral military exercises.[142] As stated above, U.S. CENTCOM has designated its OSJA office as the lead liaison with the ICRC, though the ICRC also maintains a relationship with the so-called AfPakCA office that operates under the auspices of OSD-P.[143]

These informal, flexible, and ad hoc relationships are consistent with the classic ICRC modus operandi. When asked whether it would be beneficial to have such relationships institutionalized via DoD-wide policy, an ICRC representative hesitated, stating that this would be beneficial only if such institutionalization did not lead to specific offices in various commands becoming "gatekeepers" and preventing ICRC access to other important command players.[144] However, although gatekeeping was a stated concern, lack of continuity with various commands based on the transitory nature of commanders rotating in and out of leadership positions perhaps could lead to larger concerns. The ICRC stated that it was struggling with such a situation (in early 2013) regarding its relationship with U.S. SOCOM; it had enjoyed a robust relationship directly with Admiral Eric Olsen, the commander of U.S. SOCOM from 2006 to 2010, but saw this relationship degrade once he left command. Hence the careful cultivation of personal relationships with powerful military and civilian individuals at various levels of command, although extremely beneficial to the ICRC, also carries the risk of a degraded relationship once said individuals rotate to

---

[138] In fact, the Army has institutionalized the role of the judge advocate as ICRC liaison downrange in doctrine. *See* U.S. DEP'T OF ARMY, FIELD MANUEL 71-100-2: INFANTRY DIVISION OPERATIONS, TACTICS, TECHNIQUES, AND PROCEDURES ¶ 6-28 (1993). This lead role for the judge advocate dates back to the Vietnam War, in which judge advocates met with ICRC delegates. *See* Oplaw Handbook, *supra* note 47, at 35.

[139] Oplaw Handbook, *supra* note 47, at 35.

[140] *Id.*

[141] *Id.*

[142] *Id.*

[143] *Id.*

[144] *Id.*

other assignments, thus requiring new relationship-building and temporary loss of information and access.

Although the ICRC's relationship with OSD-RDP currently remains as the single formal, institutionalized linkage between it and the DoD, which is supplemented by the robust relationships with various combatant commands described above, there are other noteworthy linkages maintained between the two organizations. The ICRC's relationships with the military services themselves are primarily centered on the various services' education and training processes, as well as interaction with units about to deploy. For example, for the last decade the ICRC has focused on involvement in pre-deployment training for units taking over regional commands in Afghanistan, as well as providing speakers at the Army's two National Training Centers (NTCs).[145] The pre-deployment interaction has focused on familiarizing troops with the ICRC's role downrange, such as ICRC detention modalities, and not on training in international humanitarian law.[146] This is due to the ICRC's acknowledgment that the United States already operates a robust training program regarding LOAC.[147]

Regarding formal DoD schools, the ICRC continues its efforts to enhance U.S. military members' appreciation for the ICRC's roles by having its representatives participate in various formal DoD courses at institutions such as the National Defense University and its subordinate schools, the various service war colleges, the Army Military Police School, and other DoD-run places of higher education and training.[148] The ICRC also has been nurturing a growing link with the Army's school for training and educating its army lawyers, The Judge Advocate General's Legal Center and School (TJAGLCS); this relationship consists of regular presentations during law-of-war courses and other seminars as well as dialogue.[149]

C. ICRC'S EXPANDING ROLE REGARDING THE CONDUCT OF HOSTILITIES

The evolution of the relationship the DoD currently maintains with the ICRC has undergone three "revolutions" since the Persian Gulf War and Vietnam War era: the seminal events of September 11, 2001; the Abu Ghraib scandal in 2004, as discussed above, and the spike in civilian casualties in Afghanistan, epitomized by the Bala Baluk incident in May 2009.[150] Prior to the armed attacked by

---

[145] Nobbs Interview, *supra* note 126. *See also* ICRC Relations, *supra* note 7, at 3 (detailing the increasing number of pre-deployment training exercises and events in which the ICRC participates, such as U.S. Marine Corps I and II MEF training events.)

[146] ICRC Relations, *supra* note 7, at 3.

[147] Nobbs Interview, *supra* note 126.

[148] ICRC Relations, *supra* note 7, at 4.

[149] *Id.* Finally, the ICRC has sought to provide input directly into the DoD's development of doctrine, with varying levels of success. The ICRC lists numerous DoD publications, such as the counterinsurgency manual and joint publication, to which it provided comments. *See, e.g.*, *id.* at 5.

[150] Nobbs Interview, *supra* note 126. *See, e.g.*, Laura King, *Afghan Civilian Deaths: Who Is to Blame?*, L.A. Times (May 17, 2009), http://articles.latimes.com/2009/may/17/world/fg-afghan-deaths17 (describing civilian casualties emanating from Bala Baluk incident).

al Qaida against the United States in September 2001, the United States maintained relations with the ICRC via the latter's delegation to the United States and Canada, which was a relatively small staff headquartered in Washington DC. The immediate capturing of detainees in Afghanistan following the U.S. invasion in October 2001 put the ICRC back in its traditional role of detainee tracking and visiting. This immediately transformed the relationship, especially once regular ICRC visits to detainees began at both Bagram Air Base, Afghanistan and Guantanamo Bay, Cuba in January 2002;[151] the DoD's attention to the relationship was prompted by the need to facilitate detainee visits as well as to respond to ICRC criticisms. This growing relationship was subsequently adrenalized by the 2004 Abu Ghraib scandal, which promoted the above-mentioned institutionalization and formalization of the DoD's relationship with the ICRC at the OSD level.

The latest evolution in the relationship between the ICRC and the DoD, although not as public or as organizational as the first two, is important because it relates to the ICRC's role in influencing the development of international law, and demonstrates the ICRC's expansion beyond its Geneva Conventions-based mandate regarding those deprived of their liberty (prisoners and internees), and the wounded. As explained above, the ICRC's relationship with the United States, and particularly the DoD, has primarily centered on visitation of detainees in U.S. custody.[152] However, beginning in approximately 2008, the ICRC greatly broadened its discussions relating to what it refers to the "conduct of hostilities."[153] These discussions, stemming primarily from incidents involving alleged or actual civilian casualties in Afghanistan, were detailed in various ICRC reports, which up that point had, with only minor exception, detailed concerns emanating from ICRC visits to U.S. detention facilities. In 2008, military officials on the ground, and then the U.S. CENTCOM commander directly, began receiving reports from the ICRC that detailed situations in which the ICRC raised humanitarian concerns based on particular U.S. tactical methods (such as the so-called "night raids"), civilian casualties due to air strikes, and various other combat-related issues distinct from detainee ones.

In these reports and the ensuing dialogue, the ICRC was careful to emphasize that they did not and do not conduct investigations, and instead regularly asked the United States to investigate the ICRC's claims. Based on the averred lack of investigation by the ICRC, the credibility of their reports (were they based on deliberate Taliban disinformation?) was not always clear. Once in receipt of such reports, the commanders had to decide what resources to devote to investigating the ICRC's allegations, and this was based heavily on the advice they received

---

[151] *See* Role of the ICRC, *supra* note 117 (highlighting temporal scope of ICRC visits to U.S. detention facilities since 9/11).

[152] The United States has sought ICRC help in other matters, such as during the Cuban Missile Crises. *See generally* Thomas Fischer, *The ICRC and the 1962 Cuban Missile Crisis*, 83 INT'L REV. RED CROSS 287 (2001).

[153] Nobbs interview, *supra* note 126.

from their judge advocates. This was not an easy decision, given the reports' paucity (at times) of detailed information, and at times outrageous claims (the beheading of Afghan civilians by U.S. soldiers, as a hypothetical example). Given that DoD policy required and continues to require thorough investigations of all credible reports of law-of-war violations, these new types of reports by the ICRC prompted various levels of investigations at various levels of command regarding Afghanistan. The levels varied because an initial determination had to be made regarding the reports' credibility, which in itself required thorough legal analysis and inquiry to the units downrange responsible for operations in the alleged area.

IV. Conclusion

The continuously evolving relationship between the U.S. Department of Defense and the International Committee of the Red Cross is one shaped most dramatically by the nature of the armed conflict de jure. The intense level of interaction and dialogue that marks the current relationship will necessarily decrease as the current armed conflict winds down. Yet the institutionalized linkages, enshrined in DoD policy, will remain and serve the United States well when it inevitably enters into new armed conflicts in the future. In the interim, the United States would serve its interests, and those of the international community, by continuing to engage with the ICRC regarding the contours and requirements of international humanitarian law—to ensure that military necessity is not lost to humanitarian concerns, thus upsetting the delicate balance the law strives valiantly to strike.

13 }

Environmental Law in Military Operations

Mark P. Nevitt*

I. Introduction

Military commanders and their operational attorneys must be cognizant of the myriad environmental laws, treaties, associated regulations, international agreements, and policies that apply to military activities and operations within and outside the United States.[1] Deciphering applicable environmental considerations can quickly become complicated, and is dependent on numerous factors, including the nature of the operation, where it takes place, and the associated host nation's relevant environmental laws and regulations. Irrespective of the environmental legal drivers, respecting host-nation and global environmental norms

---

* Commander (CDR), United States Navy. CDR Mark P. Nevitt is an active duty Navy judge advocate. He obtained his JD and LLM at the Georgetown University Law Center, and his BSE from the University of Pennsylvania. A former Naval Flight Officer who has flown missions from aircraft carriers, CDR Nevitt is currently assigned as the Regional Environmental Counsel for the Mid-Atlantic Region in Norfolk, VA. The positions and opinions in this chapter are those of the author and do not represent the official views of the Department of Defense or the United States Navy. He would like to thank Captain (ret.) Jeffrey Luster, JAGC, USN; CDR Robert "Rock" Detolve, JAGC, USN; and Lieutenant Colonel Shane Reeves, USA for the help and edits with this book chapter, and Professors Geoffrey Corn and Rachel VanLandingham for the opportunity to write it.

[1] For purposes of the discussion within this chapter, the jurisdictional phrase "within the United States" mirrors the current DoD policy definition found in environmental policy documents, and includes "all states, territories, and possessions of the United States; and all waters and airspace subject to the territorial jurisdiction of the United States." *See* Dep't of Def. Inst. 6050.7, Environmental Effects Abroad of Major Department of Defense Actions, para 3.6 (Mar. 31, 1979) [hereinafter DoDD 6050.7]. Throughout this chapter I will use the term "military activities and operations" broadly to cover the full spectrum of military functions. This includes operations that have been historically described as "Military Operations Other Than War" (MOOTW), humanitarian assistance, disaster relief operations, and other military operations that take place outside an armed conflict. The term "environment" is also used broadly in this chapter to include protection of both natural and cultural resources, and is aligned with existing EPA definitions. *See* David E. Mosher et. al, *Green Warriors: Army Environmental Considerations for Contingency Operations from Contingency through Post-conflict*, Rand Corporation, 2 n.3 2008 [hereinafter *Green Warriors*].

is often inextricably linked to larger strategy and mission goals. Indeed, the failure to comply with non-prescriptive environmental standards and norms abroad can generate worldwide criticism that ultimately undermines the strategic goals of the larger military operation and can negatively affect the health and safety of service members.[2]

This chapter is intended as an operational environmental law overview and toolkit for use by military commanders and their lawyers in identifying and addressing environmental issues within the geographic locations and operational contexts in which they are likely to arise. Clear standards and definitive legal requirements for a large amount of military activities operations—to include contingency operations—at non-enduring military installations outside the United States can be particularly difficult to decipher.[3] And environmental considerations during military operations have taken on increased importance in recent years, with the proliferation of domestic environmental laws and an increasing international awareness of the environmental harm caused by military operations.[4]

This chapter addresses three different areas where myriad environmental laws and policies could feasibly apply to military operations. First, it briefly provides an overview of the Title 10 "man, train and equip" missions at U.S. installations within the jurisdiction of the United States.[5] Here, nearly the full menu

---

[2] *See generally* U.S. Dep't of Army, Field Manual 3-24/U.S. Marine Corps Warfighting Publication 3-33.5, Insurgencies and Countering Insurgencies, at 13-3 (June 2, 2014) [hereinafter FM 3-24] (discussing the importance of upholding the rule of law and applicable host-nation laws as part of a broader strategy to establish legitimacy and control in an operational environment); *see also* U.S. Dep't of Defense, Joint Pub. 4-04, Joint Doctrine for Civil Engineering Support, ch. VI (Sept. 27, 2001).

[3] Within DoD environmental guidance, installation is defined as "an *enduring location* consisting of a base, camp, post, station, yard, center, or other DoD activity under the operational control of the Secretary of a Military Department or the Secretary of Defense" (emphasis added). "Enduring location" is further defined as a location that is intended to be used for the foreseeable future and includes a (1) main operating base; (2) forward operating site; and (3) cooperative security location. *See* U.S. Dep't of Defense, Inst. 4715.05, Environmental Compliance at Installations outside the United States 22–23 (Nov. 1, 2013). Within the U.S. military, joint planning guidance defines "contingency" as "a situation requiring military operations in response to natural disasters, terrorists, subversives, or as otherwise directed by appropriate authority to protect U.S. interests." *See* JP 1-02, Dep't of Def. Dict. of Military and Associated Terms 53, Nov. 8, 2010 (as amended through Mar. 15, 2014). The term "armed conflict" is absent from the DoD dictionary but is defined in implementing environmental regulations. For example, the term "armed conflict" is defined as: "hostilities for which Congress has declared war or enacted a specific authorization for the use of armed forces; hostilities or situations for which a report is prescribed by sections 4(a)(1) of the War Powers Resolution . . . and other actions by the armed forces that involve defensive use or introduction of weapons in situations where hostilities occur or are expected. This exemption applies as long as the armed conflict continues." DoDD 6050.7, *supra* note 1, at E.2.3.3.1.3.

[4] *See, e.g.*, Winter v. Natural Res. Def. Council, 555 U.S. 7 (2008) (alleging environmental legal violations against the U.S. Navy, with litigants seeking injunctive relief against the U.S. Navy for its use of Mid-Frequency Acoustic Sonar (MFAS) off the coast of Southern California). One scholar has asserted that until the Vietnam War any environmental protection during wartime was entirely incidental. *See* Michael N. Schmitt, *Green War: An Assessment of the Environmental Law of International Armed Conflict*, 22 Yale J. Int'l L. 1 (1997).

[5] *See, e.g.*, 10 U.S.C. § 5013(b) (2014) (describing the role for the Secretary of the Navy in man, train, and equipping functions within the United States).

of domestic environmental laws applies to military activities. Indeed, failure to comply with environmental laws within the jurisdiction of the United States could lead to civil lawsuits and injunctions against the Department of Defense (DoD)[6] or a military service, or even criminal charges against the alleged wrongdoers.[7] Second, this chapter addresses military activities outside the United States at established and enduring DoD installations. Military bases outside the United States are largely governed by executive branch policy and DoD directives as most—but not all—U.S. domestic environmental laws lack a clear extraterritorial application that applies to military activities abroad. Third, this chapter addresses military activities and operations outside the United States where DoD directives and domestic environmental law have only limited application. This includes operations that take place in both international and non-international armed conflict,[8] contingency operations, and the large swath of other DoD activities abroad where DoD policies do not clearly apply.[9] Although this chapter addresses U.S. military operations, other nations also have domestic environmental laws that impact their individual militaries.[10] These foreign domestic laws remain particularly important for the U.S. military during multinational operations. Additionally, emerging international environmental law and Law of Armed Conflict (LOAC) principles increasingly inform environmental compliance for military operations, and will be discussed in the latter part of this chapter.

Within this general construct, a complete understanding of the intersection between the military and U.S. environmental laws and policies requires analysis of at least six relevant factors: (1) the plain meaning of the statutory language of the relevant environmental law; (2) the statutory language describing any national security exemptions; (3) the statutory language addressing its extraterritorial

---

[6] Environmental statutes apply to the Department of Defense and "to their commercial contractors operating defense facilities, and to industrial plants of every description." Stephen Dycus, National Defense and the Environment 39 (1996).

[7] *See, e.g.*, William D. Palmer, *Environmental Compliance: Implications for Senior Commanders*, Parameters 81 (Spr. 1993); *see also* United States v. Dee, 912 F.2d 741 (4th Cir. 1990) (holding Department of the Army civilian employees criminally responsible for environmental violations).

[8] Environmental regulations sometimes take care to describe when certain exemptions apply. For example, Executive Order 12,114 and its implementing regulations do *not* apply during "[a]ctions take by or pursuant to the direction of the President or a cabinet officer in the course of armed conflict." Exec. Order No. 12,114, 44 Fed. Reg. 1,957 (Jan. 4, 1979).

[9] *See generally Green Warriors, supra* note 1, at 27 (finding that few directives and regulations apply to military contingency operations). In addition, DoDD 6050.7 exempts all actions taken by the President in the course of armed conflict. *See* DoDD 6050.7, *supra* note 1, para. E.2.3.3.1.2.

[10] *See generally* Mark P. Nevitt, *Defending the Environment: A Mission for the World's Militaries*, 36 U. Haw. L. Rev. 27 (2014) (addressing the domestic environmental laws affecting the militaries of the United States, China, India, European Union, and Russia). In other developing nations where environmental laws and norms are still emerging, environmental laws are simply not applicable to the military. *Cf.* Nada Al-Duaij, Environmental Law of Armed Conflict 222 (Jan. 1, 2002) (unpublished SJD dissertation, Pace University School of Law), *available at* http://digitalcommons.pace.edu/lawdissertations/1/ (asserting that environmental laws often apply to civilian institutions and not military institutions in developing states).

application; (4) the practical implementation and application of environmental laws and regulations to the military via military instructions, directives, and regulations;[11] (5) international agreements to include host nation's laws and status-of-forces agreements (SOFAs); and (6) traditional LOAC treaties addressing environmental protections in armed conflict. These six factors are discussed in greater detail below.

II. Environmental Laws and DoD Policies within the United States

A. BROAD CONGRESSIONAL WAIVERS OF SOVEREIGN IMMUNITY REQUIRE THAT ALL FEDERAL AGENCIES—TO INCLUDE DOD—COMPLY WITH U.S. ENVIRONMENTAL LAWS

Within the United States, each military service has the responsibility for man, train, and equip missions and to prepare forces for operations by combatant commanders overseas.[12] Within the United States, the major federal environmental laws largely apply to the DoD as a federal agency via broad congressional waivers of sovereign immunity. Sovereign immunity is a common law doctrine[13] that effectively allows a lawsuit against the federal government and its agencies in limited circumstances.[14] Only Congress can waive sovereign immunity.[15] It cannot be waived by executive order or federal regulation, or by a military commander.[16] Within domestic U.S. environmental law, there is what may be described as vertical sovereign immunity whereby all federal agencies—to include DoD–are required to comply with not only federal environmental laws but also state and local environmental laws and regulations falling within the scope of the applicable waiver.[17] This vertical sovereign immunity is relatively unique to American

---

[11] *See, e.g.*, U.S. Dep't of Def. Dir. 6050.16, DoD Policy for Establishing and Implementing Environmental Standards at Overseas Installations (Sept. 20, 1991) [hereinafter DoDD 6050.16].

[12] *See, supra* note 5.

[13] It stems from the legal doctrine, predating the Constitution, that the "the king can do no wrong." Sovereign immunity is defined as "a government's immunity from being sued in its own courts without its consent; Congress has waived much of the federal government's sovereign immunity." Black's Law Dict. 297–98 (1996). The U.S. government is subject to a lawsuit only to the extent to which Congress has waived sovereign immunity. *See* United States v. Sherwood, 312 U.S. 584, 590 (1941) (stating that any waiver of sovereign immunity must be strictly interpreted, and waivers cannot be inferred).

[14] For a comprehensive critique of the doctrine of sovereign immunity, see Erwin Cheriminsky, *Against Sovereign Immunity*, 53 Stan. Law. Rev. 1201 (2001).

[15] *See, e.g.*, U.S. Dep't. of Energy v. Ohio, 112 S. Ct. 1627,1639 (1992).

[16] Further, congressional waivers must be "clear and unambiguous," and congressional legislative history has no bearing on a sovereign immunity legal analysis. *See* United States v. Nordic Village, Inc., 503 U.S. 30, 37 (1992).

[17] For example, the Clean Water Act states that each agency of the federal government is subject to and must comply with "all *Federal, State, interstate, and local* requirements, administrative authority, and process and sanctions respecting the control and abatement of water pollution in the same manner, and to the same extent as any nongovernmental entity . . ." 42 U.S.C. § 1323(a)

law, and gives state and local jurisdictions enormous authority over the actions of military installations in their respective jurisdiction. Accordingly, military installations within the United States must comply with *all* the environmental laws and regulations (federal, state, local) that are nested within each federal environmental statute's respective sovereign immunity waiver.

Related to the common law doctrine of sovereign immunity, all military aircraft and warships enjoy sovereign immunity from foreign environmental regulators in accordance with long-standing principles of international law.[18] Hence, foreign environmental regulators or inspectors are normally prohibited from exercising any governmental authority or accessing a military warship or aircraft for environmental inspection or examination.[19] Commanding officers and aircraft mission commanders can take steps to certify compliance with host-nation environmental requirements, but access to the warship or aircraft by foreign environmental regulators is not required absent a separate international agreement authorizing such access.[20] Nevertheless, a military warship operating in areas under the jurisdiction of a foreign state still must operate with due regard and respect for that nation's environmental and natural resource- related laws and regulations.[21]

B. KEY U.S. DOMESTIC ENVIRONMENTAL LAWS AND THEIR APPLICABILITY TO THE MILITARY

This section will address core domestic environmental laws with an additional focus on laws that apply to the military extraterritorially and their associated national security exemptions. As a general matter, there is not a separate or parallel environmental legal structure within U.S. law that applies only to the U.S. military. United States' environmental laws generally speak to "federal agencies," "federal departments," and "federal facilities" generally without carving out exceptions for military facilities or the DoD. And the Supreme Court has recently reaffirmed that military interests do not always trump environmental considerations.[22]

The discussion focuses on statutes that are routinely invoked in litigation against the DoD: (1) the National Environmental Policy Act (NEPA);[23] (2) the Federal Water Pollution Control Act ("Clean Water Act" or CWA);[24] (3) the

---

(2012) (emphasis added). Additionally, many environmental statutes empower state and local agencies to issue permits and collect fees or reasonable service charges from federal facilities related to the administration of state and local requirements. *See* Dep't of the Navy, Manual of the Judge Advocate General 13–14 (JAGINST 5800.7F) [hereinafter JAGMAN]; *see also* Nevitt, *supra* note 10.

[18] *See, e.g.*, JAGMAN, *supra* note 17, at 13-3.

[19] *Id.* at 13-3.

[20] *Id.* at 13-3.

[21] *See, e.g.*, U.S. Dep't of Navy Naval Warfare Publication (NWP) 4–11, Environmental Protection 1–4 (Mar. 1999) [hereinafter NWP 4–11].

[22] Winter v. Natural Res. Def. Council, 555 U.S. 7, 12 (2008).

[23] 42 U.S.C. §§ 4321–4347 (2012).

[24] 33 U.S.C. §§ 1251–1387 (2012).

Comprehensive Environmental Response, Compensation, and Liability Act (CERCLA);[25] (4) the Endangered Species Act (ESA);[26] (5) the National Historic Preservation Act (NHPA)[27] and the (6) Marine Mammal Protection Act (MMPA).[28] Absent, too, from most environmental statutes is an expression of its precise jurisdictional application overseas. The question of extraterritoriality of environmental statutes is particularly important for the U.S. military due to the large number of military installations and forces operating outside the United States.[29] In accordance with the "Foley doctrine," there is a presumption that domestic laws do not apply extraterritorially unless Congress expressly includes an extraterritorial provision in the statute.[30] Yet three statutes (the ESA, MMPA, and NHPA) have uncertain jurisdictional contours that could apply to military activities and operations outside the United States. Although the precise jurisdictional boundaries of these statues remain unclear,[31] in at least one case the NHPA has been held to apply to military activities within a sovereign nation.[32]

1. National Environmental Policy Act (NEPA)

The NEPA[33] requires all federal agencies to take environmental considerations into account during their project planning, through the publication of detailed environmental impact statements and environmental assessments.[34] As it fully applies to federal agencies and its actions, the U.S. military complies with NEPA for military activities with environmental impacts in the United States. The NEPA is essentially a procedural planning statute without any substantive requirements. It mandates that DoD "shall consult with and obtain the comments of any federal agency which has jurisdiction by law or special expertise with respect to any environmental impact involved."[35] It "has had an enormous influence on national security decision-making, not only by increasing the environmental sensitivity of government planners, but also by providing members

---

[25] 42 U.S.C. §§ 9601–9675 (2012).

[26] 16 U.S.C. §§ 1531–1544 (2012).

[27] 16 U.S.C. §§ 470–470x-6 (2012).

[28] 16 U.S.C. §§ 1361–1423(h) (2012).

[29] *See, e.g.*, Dycus, *supra* note 6, at 72 (noting that the U.S. military "has hundreds of operations in foreign countries and territories").

[30] Foley Bros., Inc. v. Filardo, 336 U.S. 281, 285 (1949); *see also* EEOC v. Arabian Am. Oil Co., 499 U.S. 244, 248 (1991).

[31] *See generally* Keith S. Gibel, *Defined by the Law of the Sea: "High Seas" in the Marine Mammal Protection Act and the Endangered Species Act*, 54 Naval L. Rev. 1 (2007) (discussing the continual jurisdictional uncertainty of both the Marine Mammal Protection Act and Endangered Species Act).

[32] Okinawa Dugong v. Gates, 543 F. Supp. 2d 1082, 1111 (N.D. Cal. 2008).

[33] For a more comprehensive discussion of environmental laws as domestically applied to other militaries of the world, *see* Nevitt, *supra* note 10, at 31–45.

[34] 42 U.S.C. §§ 4321–347 (2012). The NEPA requires the "federal government to plan ahead for the environmental consequences of its actions, and it sets out a procedural framework for doing so." Dycus, *supra* note 6, at 11. Professor Dycus also notes, however, that NEPA has historically been "less rigorously" applied to the defense establishment "especially when fear of foreign aggression has displaced worries about environmental consequences." *Id.*

[35] NEPA § 102(C)(v), 42 U.S.C. § 4332(C)(v) (2004).

of the public with a window into the [military] planning process."[36] Further, NEPA lacks an express citizen suit provision, but litigants may bring a lawsuit against DoD pursuant to the the Administrative Procedures Act (APA).[37]

Although NEPA may lack a specific statutory national defense exemption, the implementing regulations promulgated by the Council of Environmental Quality (CEQ) provide for emergency alternative arrangements that could be utilized by the military.[38] And on specified occasions, Congress has granted NEPA waivers in circumstances such "that a particular action is of such vital importance to the nation that its environmental consequences can be ignored."[39] But applying this standard is still subject to judicial review.[40]

The NEPA lacks an express extraterritorial provision mandating compliance at military activities outside the United States. And courts have generally followed the Foley doctrine in addressing NEPA's extraterritorial application to the military. For example, in *NEPA Coalition of Japan v. Aspin*, a federal court concluded that NEPA's procedural requirements did not specifically apply to a military activity in Japan.[41] Federal courts have applied NEPA's requirements outside the United States, but their circumstances have been unique: in *Environmental Defense Fund, Inc. v. Massey*, NEPA was held to apply to federal activities in Antarctica, a landmass without a sovereign government.[42]

But as discussed in more detail later, NEPA's procedural requirements largely apply to federal and DoD activities abroad via an executive order and a DoD implementing directive.[43] Despite the territorial limitations of NEPA as construed by federal courts, the DoD implements NEPA-type requirements as a matter of policy outside the United States.[44]

---

[36] DYCUS, *supra* note 6, at 11; For additional information on NEPA, *see* Nevitt, *supra* note 10, at 37–38.

[37] *See, e.g.*, Winter v. Natural Res. Def. Council, Inc., 555 U.S. 7 (2008).

[38] *See* 40 C.F.R. § 1506.11 (2014). This provision states:

> Where emergency circumstances make it necessary to take an action with significant environmental impact without observing the provisions of these regulations, the Federal agency taking the action should consult with the Council about alternative arrangements. Agencies and the Council will limit such arrangements to actions necessary to control the immediate impacts of the emergency. Other actions remain subject to NEPA review. *Id.*

[39] *See* DYCUS, *supra* note 6, at 21 (noting that Congress explicitly waived NEPA requirements for the closing of military installations during the 1988 Base Realignment and Closure Act).

[40] *See, e.g., Winter v, Natural Resources Defense Council, Inc.*, 555 U.S. 7 (2008).

[41] NEPA Coalition of Japan v. Aspin, 837 F. Supp. 466 (D.D.C. 1993).

[42] Envtl. Def. Fund, Inc. v. Massey, 986 F.2d 528, 529 (D.C. Cir. 1993) (applying NEPA's applicability in Antarctica); *see also* Center for Biological Diversity v. National Sci. Foundation, No. 02-5065, 2002 WL 31548073 (N.D. Cal 2002) (applying NEPA acoustical research conducted by the National Science Foundation in the Gulf of California with potential effects on Mexico's Exclusive Economic Zone).

[43] *See infra* Part II.

[44] *See, e.g.*, JAGMAN, *supra* note 17, at 5–7. In addition, within the Department of the Navy, there is an "At-Sea Policy" that appears to go beyond NEPA's strict legal requirements, requiring environmental analysis of testing and training beyond NEPA's three nautical mile requirement. *Id.* at 5–8;

2. Clean Water Act (CWA)

The CWA's waiver of sovereign immunity is broad and applies to the DoD as an agency of the federal government.[45] The CWA lacks an express extraterritorial application, but federal facilities (to include military installations) are subject to the CWA's requirements within the United States.[46] The CWA authorizes the President to exempt federal facilities if the activity is in the "paramount interest" of the United States.[47] In addition, there is a citizen suit provision[48] within the CWA as the CWA's reference to "person" has been construed to include governmental agencies.[49]

The CWA contains a section creating a process for a national uniform standard for discharges from vessels of the armed forces.[50] The CWA makes it unlawful for any vessel of the armed forces to "operate in the navigable waters of the United States or the waters of the contiguous zone" if the vessel lacks devices to meet the CWA's standards.[51] The CWA also permits states to limit discharges from military vessels while in port upon approval of the EPA Administrator.[52]

3. Comprehensive Environmental Responses, Compensation, and Liability Act (CERCLA)

CERCLA, often referred to as the "Superfund statute," governs the response to and cleanup of hazardous substances.[53] It is a statute of particular importance

---

see also Robert B. Pirie Jr., Memorandum for the Chief of Naval Operations Commandant of Marine Corps, Subject: Compliance with Environmental Requirements in the Conduct of Naval Exercises or Training at Sea, 2 n.1 (Dec. 28, 2000) [hereinafter At-Sea Policy].

[45] The CWA's waiver language follows many other domestic environmental laws and reads:

> Each department, agency, or instrumentality of the executive, legislative, and judicial branches of the Federal government (1) having jurisdiction over any property or facility, or (2) engaged in any activity resulting, or which may result, in the discharge or runoff of pollutants . . . shall be subject to, and comply with all Federal, State, interstate, and local requirements, administrative authority, and process and sanctions respecting the control and abatement of water pollution in the same manner, and to the same extent as any nongovernmental entity including the payment of reasonable service charges. The preceding sentence shall apply . . . to . . . any requirement whether substantive or procedural [.]

CWA § 313(a), 33 U.S.C. § 1323(a) (2012). This waiver language is mirrored in other statutes, including the Clean Air Act. *See, e.g.*, CAA § 118(a), 42 U.S.C. § 7418(a) (2012); Nevitt, *supra* note 10, at 40–41.

[46] *See* 33 U.S.C. § 1323 (1996).

[47] *Id.* § 1323(a) ("The President may exempt any effluent source of any department, agency, or instrumentality in the executive branch from compliance with any such a requirement if he determines it to be in the *paramount interest* of the United States to do so . . . ." (emphasis added)).

[48] *Id.* § 1365(a)(1) (1986).

[49] *Id.* § 1362(5).

[50] *Id.* § 1322(n).

[51] *Id.* § 1322(n)(8)(A).

[52] *Id.* § 1322(n)(7)(A)(i)(II).

[53] *See Federal Facilities and the Comprehensive Environmental Response, Compensation, and Liability Act (CERCLA)/Superfund*, U.S. Envtl. Protection Agency, http://www.epa.gov/compliance/federalfacilities/enforcement/civil/cercla.html (last visited Sept. 27, 2013); *see also* Nevitt, *supra* note 10, at 43.

to the U.S. military as it impacts the large number of military base closure and cleanup efforts. Under CERCLA's sovereign immunity waiver, it applies to military activities during peacetime,[54] and lawsuits have been filed against the DoD challenging the effectiveness of base cleanup mechanisms.[55] Although CERCLA does not contain a distinct citizen suit provision, suits can still be brought pursuant to the APA. It does contain a national security exemption, but this is limited to one year.[56]

The CERCLA has not been held to apply extraterritorially.[57] This is of critical importance for base cleanup efforts overseas when the United States transfers property back to the host nation. For example, in one recent case, *Arc Ecology v. United States Department of the Air Force*, citizens alleged that the DoD failed to properly clean up Clark Air Force Base in the Philippines following transfer to the Philippine government.[58] In *Arc Ecology,* the court expressly ruled that CERCLA had no extraterritorial effect.[59]

4. Environmental Statutes with an Extraterritorial Application: The Endangered Species Act (ESA), Marine Mammal Protection Act (MMPA), and National Historic Preservation Act (NHPA)

The ESA,[60] MMPA,[61] and NHPA[62] have extraterritorial provisions that apply, in part, to military operations outside the United States. The ESA was passed in 1973 to prevent the extinction of imperiled animal and plant species through the identification of threatened or endangered ones.[63] The ESA also protects critical habitats of threatened or endangered species from habitat loss—a primary threat to imperiled species.[64] Because of its broad application beyond merely federal actions and the broad prohibition of the "taking" of listed species, it is often

---

[54] CERCLA § 120, 42 U.S.C. § 9620(a) (2012).

[55] *See, e.g.*, New York v. United States, 620 F. Supp. 374 (E.D.N.Y. 1985) (denying the State of New York's claims against the DoD on a jurisdictional issue but acknowledging that the Air Force may have contaminated New York groundwater during a leak at a former Air Force base).

[56] 42 U.S.C. § 9620(j) (1986). One commentator has noted that this exemption has never been successfully applied. *See* Dycus, *supra* note 6, at 49 (stating that there has never been a CERCLA exemption for the military granted).

[57] *See* Arc Ecology v. U.S. Dep't of the Air Force, 411 F.3d 1092 (9th Cir. 2005) (denying CERLCA claims at an Air Force base overseas brought by appellant citizens of the Philippines because there was no evidence that Congress intended for CERCLA to apply extraterritorially to allow relief to foreign claimants).

[58] *Id.*

[59] *Id.* at 1094 (affirming the district court's dismissal of the case "because CERCLA [did] not provide for the extraterritorial application sought by the appellants").

[60] 16 U.S.C. §§ 1531–544 (2012).

[61] 16 U.S.C. § 1372 (2012).

[62] 16 U.S.C. §§ 470–470x-6 (2012). But the precise jurisdictional contours of the MMPA and ESA are still uncertain. For a discussion of this ongoing uncertainty, see generally Gibel, *supra* note 31.

[63] 16 U.S.C. §§ 1531–1544 (2012).

[64] *Id.*

referred to as the "pit bull" of environmental statutes.[65] The ESA applies to the military,[66] and there is a citizen suit provision embedded within ESA's statutory scheme.[67]

The ESA requires federal agencies, including the DoD, to ensure that their actions are not "likely to jeopardize the continued existence of any endangered or threatened species or result in the destruction or adverse modification" of their critical habitat.[68] The ESA is of particular importance to the DoD as military installations often have habitats that are conducive to threatened or endangered species.[69] It reflects a conscious decision by Congress to give endangered species priority over the "primary missions" of federal agencies.[70]

Today, the ESA's precise jurisdictional contours are unclear. Both Sections 8 and 9 of the ESA discuss both the "territorial sea" and the "high seas," suggesting some support that the ESA applies outside U.S. borders.[71] And one federal appellate court has found an extraterritorial application: in *Defenders of Wildlife, Friends of Animals v. Lujan (Defenders II)*, the Eighth Circuit stated that the ESA demonstrates clear "congressional commitment to worldwide conservation efforts."[72] On appeal, the Supreme Court reversed the Eighth Circuit on the narrow issue of standing without directly addressing the ESA's extraterritorial application.[73] Although courts have been reluctant to follow the Eighth Circuit's extraterritorial holding, operational lawyers should be aware that a violation of the ESA outside the United Stats may open the military to litigation, irrespective of location.

The MMPA was enacted in 1972 and prohibits, with certain limitations, the "taking" of marine mammals in U.S. waters and the high seas.[74] This includes harassing, hunting, capturing, or killing. Its application is of critical importance to the Navy, which operates on the high seas.[75] As a matter of policy, the Navy

---

[65] *See, e.g.*, James E. Landis, *The Domestic Implications of Environmental Stewardship at Overseas Installations: A Look at Domestic Questions Raised by the United States' Overseas Environmental Policies*, 49 Naval L. Rev. 99, 118 (2002).

[66] *See, e.g.*, Natural Res. Def. Council v. Evans, 279 F. Supp. 2d 1129, 1179–180 (N.D. Cal. 2003) (holding that the Navy failed to abide by the best available science requirement in 16 U.S.C. § 1536(a)(2) when considering sonar use during peacetime).

[67] ESA § 11(g), 16 U.S.C. § 1540(g) (2002).

[68] ESA § 7(a)(2), 16 U.S.C. § 1536(a)(2) (1998); *see also* Dycus, *supra* note 6, at 31.

[69] *See, e.g.*, L. Peter Boice, *Threatened and Endangered Species on DoD Lands*, Dep't of Def. Natural Res. (Jan. 2010), http://www.denix.osd.mil/nr/upload/T-E-s-fact-sheet-1-15-10-final.pdf (stating that DoD has the "highest density of species list as threatened or endangered species of any land management agency").

[70] Tenn. Valley Auth. v. Hill, 437 U.S. 153, 185 (1978).

[71] 16 U.S.C. §§ 1536–1538 (1988). In *Lujan v. Defenders of Wildlife*, the Supreme Court overturned a circuit court opinion applying the ESA overseas, but did not specifically address the jurisdictional issue. *See* Lujan v. Defenders of Wildlife, 504 U.S. 555 (1992).

[72] Defenders of Wildlife, Friends of Animals v. Lujan, 911 F.2d 117 (8th Cir. 1990).

[73] Defenders of Wildlife, Friends of Animals v. Lujan, 112 S. Ct. 2130 (1992). Justice John Paul Stevens, in a concurring opinion in dicta, stated that if the Court *had* considered the issue of extraterritoriality, then a clear congressional expression of extraterritoriality would not have been found.

[74] 16 U.S.C. § 1372 (2012).

[75] *See id.* § 1362(13), 1372(a).

applies both the MMPA and ESA to the high seas, but not in foreign Exclusive Economic Zones (EEZ).[76]

The NHPA, most closely associated with the protection of physical historical properties within the United States,[77] stands alone as the only environmental statute that has been interpreted to expressly apply in another sovereign nation.[78] It mandates that federal agencies—to include DoD—take into account prior to a federal undertaking the effect of their actions on properties listed on the World Heritage List or the nation's equivalent National Register.

Because there are thousands of DoD employees in numerous bases overseas, NHPA is of particular importance to military activities in light of a recent federal district court case. In *Okinawa Dugong v. Gates*, a federal district court ruled that the extraterritorial provision of the NHPA could be utilized to protect a marine mammal in Japan from the consequences of the construction of a new American military installation.[79] The ruling effectively thwarted the movement of a Marine Corps air station within Japan. In light of the ruling in *Dugong*, operational attorneys outside the United States should be familiar with the host nation's equivalent National Historic Register and what, exactly, it protects.[80]

5. Existing Exemptions within Environmental Laws

Major U.S. environmental statutes do not have a general exemption for military operations. Although environmental statutes do not address their applicability during armed conflict, military commanders do not interpret them to apply during times of armed conflict.[81] There may be a mechanism within each environmental

---

[76] *See* At Sea Policy, *supra* note 44.

[77] NHPA § 1(a), 16 U.S.C. § 470(a) (2012).

[78] *See* Okinawa Dugong v. Gates, 543 F. Supp. 2d 1082, 1111 (N.D. Cal. 2008) (holding that the DoD did not properly comply with the APA and section 402 of the NHPA when it failed to take into account the effects of an installation move on the Okinawa dugong).

[79] *Id.* at 1100.

[80] The NHPA lacks a blanket exemption during times of war or other military operation. There is an exemption procedure in place for the NHPA, but there is little evidence that it has been used much. *See* 16 U.S.C. § 470h-2(j)(2014) .

[81] *See, e.g.*, USCINCCENT Operation Enduring Freedom (OEF), Environmental Considerations, Annex L, para. 1(b)(2), (5) (Jan. 3, 2002) (reiterating that DoD environmental regulations exempt combat operations with the assumption that "threatened host nations will relax enforcement of their environmental laws throughout the duration of hostilities.") (on file with author) [hereinafter OEF Annex L]. There is some legal basis for this in what is known as "Law of the Flag," which states that nations that enter another nation by force are immune from host-nation law. *See, e.g., Green Warriors, supra* note 1, at 154–55. In response to the Green Warriors report, Central Command, the combatant command encompassing military activities in Afghanistan and Iraq, issued a new regulation with more definitive environmental guidance for contingency operations. *See* CENTCOM Contingency Environmental Guidance, Regulation 200–202 (Mar. 26, 2012) (on file with author) [hereinafter CENTCOM Guidance]. This guidance was first issued in September 2009 and was most recently updated on March 26, 2012. This contingency guidance is a positive step in attempting to fill the legal void discussed in the Green Warriors report. Under this guidance, it is CENTCOM policy to limit damage to the environment "caused during full spectrum operations wherever and whenever possible." *Id.* at 1–1.

statute to receive an exemption that could apply to military activities, but this is reserved to the very highest levels of U.S. government.[82] Further, the different exemption schemes require a finding that the military activity would be either in the "paramount interest"[83] of the United States or linked to a "national security interest."[84] Also lacking is clear statutory guidance addressing the threshold for what would entail a national security exemption or what is clearly in the "paramount interest." The exemption scheme is time-limited (in most circumstances one year), making the request for an exemption an administratively repetitive and arduous process.[85] Because of its time limits and the administrative burden, DoD does not often request exemptions, and these requests are seldom granted.[86] The exemption process has been a recent source of debate among DoD officials who view the current scheme as onerous and time-consuming due to the large number and complexity of ongoing military activities taking place at hundreds of military bases and the global commons throughout the world.[87]

Last, civilian and military DoD employees are largely subject to the criminal provisions within environmental statutes.[88] The major environmental statutes, including the CWA,[89] Clean Air Act (CAA),[90] Resource Conservation and Recovery Act (RCRA),[91] CERCLA,[92] and ESA,[93] have criminal provisions that apply to DoD employees. For example, the criminal provisions of RCRA have been used to prosecute civilian Department of the Army employees "for failing to properly identify, store, and dispose of hazardous wastes generated by their chemical weapons laboratory."[94] As this enforcement action shows, the doctrine

---

[82] *See, e.g.*, CAA § 118, 42 U.S.C. § 7418(b) (2012) ("The President may exempt any emission source of any department, agency, or instrumentality in the executive branch from compliance with such a requirement if he determines it to be in the *paramount interest* of the United States to do so . . . ." (emphasis added)).

[83] *Id.*

[84] *See, e.g.*, CERCLA § 120(j), 42 U.S.C. § 9620(j) (2012) ("The President may issue such orders regarding response actions at any specified site or facility of the Department of Energy or the Department of Defense as may be necessary to protect the national security interests of the United States at that site or facility.").

[85] *See* David Bearden, Cong. Research Serv., RS22149, Exemptions from Environmental Law for the Department of Defense: Background and Issues for Congress 1–2 (2007).

[86] *Cf. id.* at 2; *see also* Stephen Dycus, *Osama's Submarine: National Security and Environmental Protection after 9/11*, 30 Wm. & Mary Envtl. L. & Pol'y Rev. 1, 49 (2005) (discussing the absence of national security exemptions processed for CERCLA and RCRA).

[87] Bearden, *supra* note 85, at 1–2.

[88] *See, e.g.*, United States v. Dee, 912 F.2d 741, 744 (4th Cir. 1990); United States v. Curtis, 988 F.2d 946, 948 (9th Cir. 1993). Criminal liability could also extend to members of the Armed Forces. *See, e.g*, NWP 4-11, *supra* note 21, para. 1.1. *See also* Nevitt, *supra* note 10, at 44–45.

[89] CWA § 309(c), 33 U.S.C. § 1319(c) (2012).

[90] CAA § 113(c), 42 U.S.C. § 7413(c) (2012). This appears to exclude an employee carrying out normal activities who is not a part of senior management or a corporate officer. *See* 42 U.S.C. § 7413(h) (1990).

[91] RCRA § 6001(a), 42 U.S.C. § 6961(a) (2012).

[92] CERCLA § 103(b)(3), 42 U.S.C. § 9603(b)(3) (2012); *see also* United States v. Carr, 880 F.2d 1550, 1550–51 (2d Cir. 1989).

[93] ESA § 10(b), 16 U.S.C. § 1540(b) (2012).

[94] *See* Palmer, *supra* note 7; *see also* United States v. Dee, 912 F.2d 741 (4th Cir. 1990).

of sovereign immunity does not attach to DoD employees seeking to avoid criminal prosecution.[95]

III. Environmental Considerations outside the United States at Enduring Military Installation

Although many major environmental media statutes lack an extraterritorial application that would allow for a lawsuit in federal court, there are numerous DoD and executive branch policies applicable to military activities and operations outside the United States. They are discussed in greater detail below.

A. NEPA AND MILITARY POLICY: EXECUTIVE ORDERS 12,088, 12,114, AND DOD AND SERVICE ENVIRONMENTAL POLICIES

Irrespective of domestic environmental laws and regulations discussed earlier, executive orders, DoD environmental policies, and service-specific environmental policies *do* apply outside the United States. But these policies do not independently create a basis for a cause of action for a lawsuit in a U.S. court. First, Executive Order (E.O.) 12,088, titled "Federal Compliance with Pollution Control Standards," was signed in 1978 by President Jimmy Carter and should be read in conjunction with congressional waivers of sovereign immunity embedded within each environmental statute.[96] This E.O. applies to the head of each federal agency, to include the DoD. Each agency is responsible for the prevention, control, and abatement of pollution for federal activities under the direction of the agency.[97] Pursuant to this E.O., outside the United States the DoD must "ensure that such construction or operation complies with the environmental pollution control standards of general applicability in the host country or jurisdiction."[98]

Second, E.O. 12,114, titled "Environmental Effects Abroad of Major Federal Activities," was signed in 1979 and requires that each federal agency put procedures in place to effectively comply with the spirit and intent of NEPA outside the United States.[99] Also signed by President Carter, E.O. 12,114 mandates that each federal agency promulgate guidance to implement NEPA-type requirements outside the United States. The military implements E.O. 12,114 via DoD Directive (DoDD) 6050.7, titled "Environmental Effects Abroad of Major Department of

---

[95] *Dee*, 912 F.2d at 744. (ruling that sovereign immunity does not immunize DoD employees from individual criminal acts).

[96] Exec. Order No. 12,088, 43 Fed. Reg. 47,707 (Oct. 13, 1978).

[97] *Id.* para. 1–101.

[98] *Id.* para. 1–801.

[99] Exec. Order No. 12,114, 44 Fed. Reg. 1,957 (Jan. 4, 1979). *See also* Karen Fair, *Environmental Compliance in Contingency Operations: In Search of a Standard?*, 157 MIL. L. REV. 112, 117 (1998).

Defense Actions."[100] In addition, each service has amplifying instructions that describe its individual service obligations under this directive. Signed in 1979, DoDD 6050.7 ensures that federal agency actions undertake extensive environmental analysis for major federal actions outside the United States. It applies to U.S. actions in both foreign nations and the global commons placing NEPA-like requirements for activities outside the United States.[101] For such actions the action proponent should prepare a bilateral or multilateral environmental study (ES) or a concise environmental review (ER). The actions identified in DoDD 6050.7 "are the exclusive and complete requirement for taking account of environmental considerations with respect to DoD activities in the global commons."[102] But as discussed below, large swaths of military activities are effectively exempt from the requirements of DoDD 6050.7.[103]

Three terms are particularly important when determining the applicability of DoDD 6050.7: (1) "federal action," (2) "major action," and (3) "participating nation." First, "federal action" means an action that is "implemented or funded directly by the U.S. Government."[104] This encompasses actions that significantly harm the environment, to include projects that produce emissions or products strictly regulated by U.S. law, projects that are strictly regulated in the United States to protect the environment against radioactive substances, and actions that significantly harm resources designated for protection by the President.[105] Federal action does not include DoD actions taken overseas in an advisory, information-gathering, or diplomatic capacity.[106]

The second key term, "major action," is defined as:

> [A]n action of considerable importance involving substantial expenditures of time, money, and resources, that affects the environment on a large geographic scale or has substantial effects on a more limited geographical area, and that is substantially different or a significant departure from

---

[100] DoDD 6050.7, *supra* note 1. The DoD also has guidance on the return of overseas sites to host-nation control, but this does not apply to temporary DoD facilities or sites used during contingency operations. *See generally* DEP'T OF DEF. INST. 4165.69, REALIGNMENT OF DOD SITES OVERSEAS (Apr. 6, 2005).

[101] Global commons, within the meaning of DoDD 6050.7, are "geographical areas that are outside the jurisdiction of any nation, and include the oceans outside the territorial limits and Antarctica . . . [and] do not include contiguous zone and fisheries zones of foreign nations." DoDD 6050.7, *supra* note 6, para. E 3.5.

[102] *Id.* para. E1.1. Some commentators have highlighted that there is a large amount of discretion in its practical application. *See* Sarah Hilbert, *A Legislative Solution to Environmental Protection in Military Action Overseas*, 38 WM. & MARY ENVTL. L. & POL'Y REV. 263, 272 (2012).

[103] For example, ship and aircraft deployments are not considered major actions for purposes of DoDD 6050.7. *See* DoDD 6050.7, *supra* note 1, para. 3.5.

[104] DoDD 6050.7, *supra* note 1, para. 3.2.

[105] *Id.*

[106] *Id.* para. 3.2

other actions, previously analyzed with respect to environmental considerations and approved, with which the action under consideration may be associated.[107]

The definition of "major action" differs from "major federal action" within the meaning of NEPA and its associated federal regulations. Under NEPA, major federal actions include "actions with effects that may be major and which are potentially subject to federal control . . . [m]ajor reinforces but does not have a meaning independent of significantly."[108] Within DoD guidance, major federal actions do not include deployment of ships, aircraft, or other mobile equipment.[109]

Third, DoDD 6050.7 applies only to proposed actions in foreign nations when the host nation is *not participating* with the United States.[110] So major military actions outside the United States that significantly harm the environment do not need to follow E.O. 12,114 and DoDD 6050.7 when the host nation *is* participating. Determining whether the foreign nation is participating is crucial in determining whether the NEPA-like provisions of DoDD 6050.7 apply. Yet the term "participating" nation is not well defined—there is no case law—and is subject to a military commander's ongoing interpretation and discretion.[111] The U.S. military has utilized the participating nation exclusion in contingency operations in both Haiti and Bosnia where the host nation was involved in the military operation.[112]

During a contingency operation, a certain environmental-planning legal void may exist due to the vagueness of the "participating nation" term. The United States may enter a foreign nation via a fully permissive, semi-permissive, or a forced entry.[113] A permissive entry typically involves a participating (i.e. cooperating) nation where NEPA-like analysis would *not* apply. For a forced entry into a foreign nation, the U.S. military is clearly not participating with the host nation. But an exemption may still be sought under DoDD 6050.7.[114]

---

[107] *Id.* para. 3.5. Within this definition, DoD does not define "substantial expenditures," "substantial effects," "substantially different," and "significant departure."

[108] 40 C.F.R. § 1508.18 (2014).

[109] DoDD 6050.7, *supra* note 1, para. 3.5

[110] *Id.* para. E.1.1 (emphasis added).

[111] For example, although Status of Forces Agreements (SOFAs) often indicate some level of formal participation with the United States, their mere existence or absence is not dispositive in a "participating nation" analysis. *See* DoDD 6050.7, *supra* note 1 (describing the factors in a participating nation analysis). *See also* Int'l & Operational Law Dep't, The Judge Advocate General's Legal Ctr. & Sch., U.S. Army, Operational Law Handbook 324 (Maj. William Johnson ed. 2013) [hereinafter Oplaw Handbook].

[112] Oplaw Handbook, *supra* note 111, at 324, n.951. But the participating nation exclusion was not applied in Cuba during humanitarian relief operations for Cuban and Haitian migrants in Operation SEA SIGNAL and in Somalia during Operation RESTORE HOPE. Nevertheless, these operations were able to receive an exemption from DoDD 6050.7's requirements due to national security concerns.

[113] *See, e.g.* Oplaw Handbook, *supra* note 111, at 324.

[114] DoDD 6050.7, *supra* note 1, para. E2.3.3.2. (authorizing how exemptions may be sought on a case-by-case basis). The nature of the operation may dictate the application of the Law of the Flag for immunity from host-nation laws. The level of immunity appears to be in flux depending on how

In addition, environmental planning under DoDD 6050.7 and E.O. 12,114 is not required in certain circumstances. Beyond exempting all actions that do not significantly harm the environment or a designated resource of global importance, the DoD directive exempts actions taken by the President (such as signing treaties, and signing bills into law), actions taken by DoD in advising the President, actions taken by the President or cabinet officer in the course of armed conflict, and in disaster or emergency relief actions.[115] And the Secretary of Defense has the authority to categorically exclude actions that do not significantly harm the environment.[116]

B. OVERSEAS ENVIRONMENTAL BASELINE GUIDANCE DOCUMENT AND FOREIGN GOVERNING STANDARDS

The DoD designates a service Lead Environmental Component (LEC) for every nation where there is a permanent military installation. The LEC, in turn, promulgates an Overseas Baseline Guidance Document (OEBGD) that establishes basic criteria for environmental management practices.[117] The OEBGD applies to permanent military installations outside the United States "to support functions for U.S. military vessels and U.S. military aircraft provided by the DoD Components, including management or disposal of off-loaded waste or material."[118]

As the relationship between the U.S. military installation and the host nation matures, Foreign Governing Standards (FGS) will be issued. The FGS provide more substantive provisions, building off the previously established OEBGD. It includes an important fallback provision when reconciling DoD policy with host-nation law:

> Unless inconsistent with applicable host-nation law, base rights and/or status of forces agreements (SOFAs), or other international agreement, or

---

the force entered the nation. *See, e.g., Green Warriors, supra* note 1, at 154–55 (stating that entering a nation with its consent may no longer trigger Law of the Flag immunity for the foreign forces).

[115] *See* DoDD 6050.7, *supra* note 1, para. E2.3.3.1.2, E2.3.3.1.3, E2.3.3.1.8.

[116] *Id.* para. E2.3.4. This includes: (1) actions that the DoD determines do not do significant harm to the environment outside the United States, (2) actions taken by the President or members of his Cabinet, (3) DoD actions taken pursuant to the direction of the President (or Cabinet member) during an armed conflict, (4) actions taken pursuant to the direction of the President (or a Cabinet member) when national security interests are involved, (5) activities of the intelligence components, (6) actions with respect to arms transfers to foreign nations, (7) actions with respect to membership in international organizations, (8) disaster and emergency relief actions, (9) actions relating to nuclear activities and nuclear material. *Id. See also* Major Richard M. Whitaker, *Environmental Aspects of Overseas Operations*, The Army Lawyer 29 (Apr. 1995).

[117] Dep't of Defense, Dir. 4715.05-G, Overseas Envtl. Guidance Document 11–12 (May 1, 2007), *available at* http://www.dtic.mil/whs/directives/corres/pdf/471505g.pdf [hereinafter OEBGD].

The OEBGD: includes baseline standards for the protection of human health and the environment; considers generally accepted federal environmental standards; and incorporates requirements of U.S. law that have extraterritorial application to the DoD. *See* Oplaw Handbook, *supra* note 111, at 326. For further discussion of the OEBGD and FGS, see Nevitt, *supra* note 10, at 49–50.

[118] OEBGD, *supra* note 117, para. C1.3.3.

> practices established pursuant to such agreements, the baseline guidance shall be applied by the DoD Components stationed in foreign countries when host-nation environmental standards do not exist, are not applicable, or provide less protection to human health and the natural environment than the baseline guidance.[119]

But the OEBGD and FGS do not apply to off-installation operational and training deployments.[120] For operational deployments and situations of actual or threatened hostilities, environmental guidance and direction will normally be integrated into the military planning process and will be described in the operational annexes of the Joint Operational Planning and Execution System (JOPES).[121] For example, the "Environmental Considerations" annex utilized by Central Command during Operation Enduring Freedom stated that the applicable FGS and OPEBGD are to be utilized in establishing a baseline of environmental standards.[122]

Although the FGS and OEBGD do not create judicially enforceable causes of action, these guidelines may nevertheless be transmitted as lawful orders through the military chain of command. This creates a prescriptive duty to comply, potentially subjecting service member violators to disciplinary action under the Uniformed Code of Military Justice (UCMJ).[123]

C. ENVIRONMENTAL COMPLIANCE AND REMEDIATION OVERSEAS

DoD Instruction 4715.05, titled "Environmental Compliance at Installations outside the United States" was updated in 2013 and serves as the foundational DoD written environmental policy for DoD's compliance at established overseas military installations.[124] It applies to "actions of DoD components outside the United States on installations under DoD control."[125] Similar to other DoD environmental policy guidance, it does not apply to military vessels, ships, aircraft,

[119] DoDD 6050.16, *supra* note 11, para. 3.1.2. This fallback provision is reiterated within military department guidance. For example, within the U.S. Navy, facilities must comply with FGS requirements overseas. *See* JAGMAN, *supra* note 17, at 13–3; *see also* Nevitt, *supra* note 10, at 49–50.

[120] OEBGD, *supra* note 117, at C.1.2.

[121] Joint Chiefs of Staff, Staff Manual 3122.03C, Joint Operation Planning and Execution System Vol. II: (Planning Formats and Guidance), Enclosure C (Aug. 17, 2007), http://www.dtic.mil/doctrine/doctrine/other/jopes.pdf (last visited June 25, 2014) [hereinafter JOPES].

[122] OEF Annex L, *supra* note 81, para. 3(a)(3).

[123] *See* Richard Phelps, *Environmental Law for Overseas Installations*, 40 AF. L. Rev. 49, 61 (1996).

[124] U.S. Dep't of Defense, Inst. 4715.05, Environmental Compliance at Installations outside the United States (Nov. 1, 2013) [hereinafter DoDI 4715.05]. It is U.S. policy, to the maximum extent practicable, to dispose of hazardous waste in a manner to not retain future liability for the waste. *Id.* at 15.

[125] *Id.* para. 2(a)(1)(b). This includes a "base, camp, post, station, yard, center, or other activity under the jurisdiction of the Secretary of a Military Department that is located outside the United States and outside any territory, commonwealth, or possession of the United States." *Id.* at 23 (Glossary) (defining "enduring location" as a location where "DoD intends to maintain access and

and off-installation training,[126] and "contingency locations and associated operations."[127] This includes "contingency operations in hazardous areas, peacekeeping missions, or relief operations . . ."[128]

Hazardous waste generation is of critical importance to military operations and activities overseas. The DoD policy states that hazardous waste generated at overseas installations should not be disposed of in the host nation unless the disposal complies with baseline guidance, is in accordance with applicable international agreements, or has "otherwise received explicit or implicit concurrence of the appropriate host-nation authority."[129] Without an applicable agreement that grants disposal authority, DoD must obtain concurrence from the host nation prior to hazardous waste disposal.[130] If these conditions are not met, the hazardous waste should be disposed of in the United States or in another foreign country where satisfactory conditions can be met.[131] Any deviation from these procedures due to mission imperatives (e.g., force protection or significant threats) is subject to approval by senior military officers and State Department representatives, among others.[132]

Remediation of environmental contamination outside the United States is governed by another recently updated instruction, DoDD 4715.08, titled "Remediation of Environmental Contamination outside the United States."[133] Updated in 2013, it governs the cleanup of environmental contamination on DoD installations outside the United States and[134] reiterates DoD policy to not take action to "remediate environmental contamination resulting from armed conflict."[135] And DoD "takes no action outside of a DoD installation to remediate environmental contamination caused by the DoD actions or activities beyond that

---

use that location for the foreseeable future . . . [to include] main operating base, forward operating site, and cooperative security location.").

[126] *Id.* para 2(a)(2).

[127] *Id.* para. 2(c).

[128] *Id.* para. 2 (a)(2) (a)–(c). "Off installation operational deployments include contingency locations and associated operations and deployments, including cases of hostilities, contingency operations in hazardous areas, peacekeeping missions, or relief operations. These include U.S. forces operating as part of a multinational force not under full U.S. control." *Id.*

[129] DoDD 6050.16, *supra* note 11, para. 3.4.

[130] *Id.* at 14.

[131] *Id.* para. 3.4.1.

[132] *Id.* at 15.

[133] U.S. Dep't of Def. Inst. 4715.08, Remediation of Environmental Contamination outside the United States (Nov. 1, 2013) [hereinafter DoDI 4715.08].

[134] *Id.* Similar to other directives, it does not create any independent right or enforceable action against the DoD. *Id.* para 2(b)(c).

[135] *Id.* para. 3(c). The term "armed conflict" is absent from the DoD Dictionary of Military and Associated Terms but is defined in DoDD 6050.7. *See* DoDD 6050.7, *supra* note 1, at E.2.3.3.1.3 (defining "armed conflict" as "hostilities for which the Congress has declared war or enacted a specific authorization for the use of armed forces; hostilities or situations for which a report is prescribed by section 4(a)(1) of the War Powers Resolution, 50 U.S.C.A. § 1543(a)(1) (Supp. 1978); and other actions by the Armed Forces that involve defensive use or introduction of weapons in situations where hostilities occur or are expected.").

specifically required by applicable international agreement."[136] It is DoD policy to "identify host-nation national environmental standards, including those specifically delegated to regional or local governments for implementation, and determine their applicability to DoD operations at installations and facilities in that country."[137] Outside of any legal requirement in U.S. law or international agreement, it requires a "baseline guidance" document to be implemented at DoD installations and facilities outside U.S. territory. This serves as an important standard in countries that otherwise lack environmental standards.

Furthermore, each service (Army, Navy, and Air Force) has its own environmental guidance that builds upon the relevant DoD environmental directives. For example, the Navy's governing environmental policy document is titled the "Environmental Readiness Program Manual" and is regularly updated.[138] It applies to all "Navy commands, organizations, installations, personnel (civilian and Military), Navy contractors . . . within the Chief of Naval Operations chain of command."[139] The Army and Marine Corps have additional service guidance in Field Manual 3-34.5, entitled "Environmental Considerations," which amplifies the joint planning guidance[140] and adds force health protection as an important environmental consideration.[141] And Army Regulation 200-1, titled "Environmental Protection and Enhancement," "implements Federal, State, and local environmental laws and DOD policies for preserving, protecting, conserving, and restoring the quality of the environment."[142]

IV. Operational Environmental Considerations at Non-enduring Installations and during Armed Conflict

A. A LONG HISTORY OF ENVIRONMENTAL DAMAGE IN MILITARY OPERATIONS

Historically, it has been difficult to justify environmental and natural resource protections while people are struggling for their lives.[143] Yet attacks on the

---

[136] *Id.* para. 3(d).

[137] *Id.*

[138] U.S. Dep't of Navy, Sec'y of the Navy Instr. 5090.1D, Environmental Readiness Program Manual (Jan. 10, 2014).

[139] *Id.* at 1–4. At close to a thousand pages, the Navy's Environmental Readiness Program Manual consolidates the myriad environmental laws, regulations, directives, and instructions as applied to the Navy. *Id.* at 1–2.

[140] U.S. Dep't of Army, Field Manual 3-34.5, Environmental Considerations (Feb. 2010) [hereinafter FM 3-34.5].

[141] *Id.* at 1–2.

[142] U.S. Dep't of Army, Reg. 200–201, Environmental Protection and Enhancement para 1–1 (Dec. 13, 2007). The Air Force has environmental guidance at Air Force Handbook 10–222, Volume 4.

[143] *Cf.* Edith Brown Weiss et al., International Environmental Law and Policy 723 (Aspen 2d ed. 2007). Professor Weiss defines the measures or rules to protect the environment during armed conflict to encompass the protection of people, facilities, private and public property, and cultural heritage. This characterization is adopted here.

environment are not new: concern for the protection of the environment dates from biblical times. Indeed, in the Old Testament Moses stated,

> When you are trying to capture a city, do not cut down its fruit trees, even though the siege lasts a long time. Eat the fruit, but do not destroy the trees; the trees are not your enemies. You may cut down the other trees and use them in the siege mounts until the city is captured.[144]

At the end of the Third Punic War, Rome destroyed Carthage and salted the earth to prevent crops from growing and future generations of Carthaginians from becoming a threat. And in the American Civil War, General William Tecumseh Sherman's "March to the Sea" caused severe environmental destruction to the property, agriculture, and economic means of the American South.[145]

For military operations and activities that are not subject to domestic environmental statutes, executive branch, and DoD policy directives discussed above, it is more difficult to determine the applicable environmental laws and policies. Yet the large amount of military operations at non-enduring installations can clearly significantly affect the environment. And failure to respect the health of the human environment can negatively impact larger mission goals. This was recently reaffirmed in Army doctrine, which stated that local civilians are likely to support the larger military mission if there is a healthy, safe, and livable environment.[146] Nevertheless, there are few concrete laws, policies, and directives that apply to contingency operations in a foreign country. This is particularly true for the numerous operations that are not part of an armed conflict and fall outside core LOAC treaties addressing environmental considerations that are discussed below.[147] Nevertheless, environmental considerations are integrated into the military planning process, providing some level of procedural accountability and environmental stewardship.

Regardless of how the operation is actually classified, within the U.S. military, the DoD Law of War program mandates that all LOAC "reportable incidents" are promptly reported and investigated regardless of the characterization

---

[144] *Id.* at 730 (quoting DEUTERONOMY 20:19–20). Hugo Grotius also touched upon environmental considerations in warfare, stating "[i]f trees could speak they would cry out, and reproach us with [i]njustice, for making them suffer the Punishment of War, who were in no Occasion of it." HUGO GROTIUS, THE RIGHTS OF WAR AND PEACE, IN THREE BOOKS: WHEREIN ARE EXPLAINED, THE LAWS OF NATIONS, AND THE PRINCIPAL POINTS RELATING TO GOVERNMENT 651(1783).

[145] *See, e.g.*, WEISS ET AL., *supra* note 143, at 730. The Lieber Code, adopted during the Civil War, is silent on the term "environment." Yet it condemned the destruction of property in the absence of military necessity. *See* General Orders No. 100: The Lieber Code, http://avalon.law.yale.edu/19th_century/lieber.asp#sec1 (last visited June 25, 2014); WEISS ET AL., *supra* note 143, at 731.

[146] *See generally* FM 3–24, *supra* note 2, at 13–3 (discussing the importance of upholding the rule of law and applicable laws as part of a broader strategy to establish legitimacy and control in an operational environment); *see also Green Warriors, supra* note 1, at 119 (linking environmental problems and lack of respect for the Iraq environment to an increase in insurgency problems).

[147] Fair, *supra* note 99, at 127 (describing the lack of an environmental doctrine for military operations other than war (MOOTW)).

of the military operation.[148] "Reportable incident" is broadly defined under DoD regulations to reasonably include major environmental violations.[149] And reportable incidents must be "reported promptly, investigated thoroughly, and, where appropriate, remedied by corrective action."[150]

B. U.S. OPERATIONS AND THE JOINT PLANNING PROCESS

As discussed above, DoD directives and policy largely do not apply to military operations activities overseas at non-enduring installations, to include most contingency operations. Environmental considerations, however, are integrated via joint doctrine and environmental annexes to operation orders (OPORDs) and operational plans (OPLAN).[151] The operational planning process covers most military operations, regardless of their intensity or legal characterization of the operations.[152] The U.S. military utilizes the Joint Operational Planning Execution System (JOPES) with a specific planning annex—Annex L—devoted to environmental issues and considerations.[153] Although there is "little guidance available to guide the practitioner in advising the commander [on environmental considerations] in a deployed contingency operation,"[154] the U.S. military utilizes the joint planning process to incorporate environmental considerations into its operational planning.

Three joint publications are particularly important and provide an overview of the myriad environmental considerations that must take place throughout the operational planning process: Joint Publication 4-04, "Joint Doctrine for Civil Engineering Support;"[155] Joint Publication 3-34, "Joint Engineer Operations;"[156] and Joint Publication 3-60, "Joint Targeting."[157] For example, Joint Publication 4-04 addresses six elements of environmental planning, including solid waste

---

[148] *See* U.S. Dep't of Defense, Dir. 2311.01E, DoD Law of War Program, para. 4.4 (May 9, 2006) (Incorporating Change 1 of Nov. 15, 2010, certified current as of Feb. 22, 2011).

[149] "Reportable incident" includes "a possible, suspected, or alleged violation of the law of war, for which there is credible information, or conduct during military operations other than war that would constitute a violation of the law of war if it occurred during an armed conflict." *Id.* para. 3.2.

[150] *Id.* para. 4.4.

[151] *See, e.g.*, U.S. European Command Operational Plan 4000, Annex L Environmental Considerations (2002) (on file with author).

[152] *See, e.g., id.* para 1(a) (stating that the guidance protects the health and welfare of U.S. personnel and minimizes adverse impacts "during the conduct of operations . . ."). But federally mandated occupational safety and health standards do not clearly apply to overseas military operations, potentially exposing service members to increased occupational and environmental risk. *See Green Warriors*, *supra* note 1, at 150.

[153] Joint Chiefs of Staff, Staff Manual 3122.03C, Joint Operation Planning and Execution System Vol. II: (Planning Formats and Guidance), Enclosure C (Aug. 17, 2007) [hereinafter JOPES].

[154] Oplaw Handbook, *supra* note 111, at 326.

[155] JP 4–04, *supra* note 1, at VI-1.

[156] U.S. Dep't of Defense, Joint Pub. 3–34, Joint Engineer Operations, Appx. D. Environmental Considerations (June 30, 2011).

[157] U.S. Dep't of Defense, Joint Pub. 3–60, Joint Targeting (Jan. 31, 2013) [hereinafter JP 3–60].

management and the responsibilities to protect and preserve the environment during operations. Within the joint planning process, environmental considerations include "the spectrum of programs that may impact on or are affected by, the planning and execution of military operations."[158]

Additionally, warfare publications promulgated by the DoD and individual services offer additional guidance for military operations. For example, within the U.S. Navy, two warfare publications instruct operational commanders on how to protect the environment during naval operations: Naval Warfare Publication 1-14M: The Commander's Handbook on the Law of Naval Operations ("NWP 1-14M");[159] and Naval Warfare Publication (NWP) 4-11: Environmental Protection ("NWP 4-11").[160] In addressing environmental protection during naval operations, NWP 1-14M states:

> It is not unlawful to cause collateral damage to the natural environment during an attack upon a legitimate military objective. However, the commander has an affirmative obligation to avoid unnecessary damage to the environment *to the extent that it is practicable to do so consistent with mission accomplishment.* To that end, and as far as military requirements permit, methods or means of warfare should be employed with due regard to the protection and preservation of the natural environment. Destruction of the natural environment not necessitated by mission accomplishment and carried out wantonly is prohibited. Therefore, a commander should consider the environmental damage that will result from an attack on a legitimate military objective as one of the factors during targeting analysis.[161]

NWP 4-11 requires that environmental considerations be integrated into the operational planning process and that all military operation plans and orders must contain an environmental protection annex.[162]

As the military operation moves from the planning to the execution and conflict stage, the level of attention by military commanders to environmental considerations will adjust.[163] For example, as the conflict increases in intensity and enters the kinetic phase, the military force will inevitably afford less attention to the environment as it focuses on execution of the combat mission, saving lives, larger strategic objectives, and force protection.[164] But the LOAC treaties and

---

158 JP 4-04, *supra* note 1, at VI-1.

159 U.S. Dep't of Navy Naval Warfare Publication (NWP) 1-14M The Commander's Handbook on the Law of Naval Operations (July 2007) [hereinafter NWP 1-14M].

160 NWP 4-11, *supra* note 21.

161 NWP 1-14M, *supra* note 159, at 8-4 (emphasis added).

162 *Id.* at 3–8.

163 *See, e.g.*, OEF Annex L, *supra* note 81, para 1(b)–(c) (stating that "operational requirements of units in contact, including force protection . . . will supersede compliance with environmental regulations . . .").

164 Although domestic environmental laws do not have an automatic armed conflict exclusion that would suspend their applicability, most domestic laws lack an extraterritorial application. And different legal theories—such as Law of the Flag or force majeure—likely apply to the applicability or suspension of domestic laws and regulations during armed conflict. For example, during the oral

principles that serve to protect the environment will continue to apply.[165] And the principles of military necessity, unnecessary suffering, proportionality, and distinction as set forth in joint military planning doctrine continually apply to *all joint operations*, however the armed conflict is legally characterized.[166] This is reinforced in the U.S. Joint Targeting publication, which states:

> It is generally lawful under the laws of war to cause collateral damage to the environment during an attack on a legitimate military target. However, the commander has an affirmative obligation to avoid unnecessary damage to the environment to the extent that Legal Considerations in Targeting it is practical to do so consistent with mission accomplishment. To that end and as far as military requirements dictate, methods and means of attack should be employed with due regard to the protection and preservation of the natural environment. *Destruction of the environment not required by military necessity and carried out wantonly is prohibited.*[167]

In sum, regardless of the nature of the operation, the joint planning process reaffirms the general duty for the military to avoid unnecessary damage to the environment and a general prohibition of environmental destruction not required by military necessity.[168] Nevertheless, there is still a large amount of discretion left to operational commanders in complying with these policy directives.[169] Commentators, too, have critiqued the joint operational planning process, asserting it is "inadequate for environmental planning and execution."[170]

---

argument hearing in Winter v. Natural Res. Def. Council, Justice Stephen Breyer asked counsel for NRDC whether NEPA planning documentation is required prior to a "combat bombing mission." The counsel for NRDC effectively conceded that compliance with NEPA was not required during times of armed conflict to include the combat mission hypothetical asked by Justice Breyer:

> JUSTICE BREYER: How does the basic thing work? Because to a layperson, when I think of the armed forces preparing an environmental impact statement, I think, the whole point of the armed forces is to hurt the environment. I mean . . . I don't understand how it's supposed to work. Of course they are going to do something that is harmful. You go on a bombing mission, do they have to prepare an environmental impact statement first?
>
> MR. KENDALL [COUNSEL FOR NATURAL RESOURCES DEFENSE COUNCIL]: No . . . We have never, ever contended that any of our proposed restrictions should apply to combat at all, and it doesn't.

See Transcript of Oral Argument at 44–45, Winter v. Natural Res. Def. Council, 555 U.S. 7 (2008), *available at* http://www.oyez.org/cases/2000-2009/2008/2008_07_1239.

[165] *See* OPLAW HANDBOOK, *supra* note 111, at 328.

[166] JP 3-60, *supra* note 157, at APPX. A6–A7 (emphasis added). Under the "Application" section of the Joint Targeting Publication, it states, "[t]he guidance in this publication is authoritative; as such, this doctrine will be followed except when, in the judgment of the commander, exceptional circumstances dictate otherwise." *Id.* at i.

[167] JP 3-60, *supra* note 157, at APPX. A6–A7.

[168] *See id* (emphasis added).

[169] *See, e.g.*, OEF ANNEX L, *supra* note 81, para. 3(a)(1)(b). "To the greatest extent practical measures shall be taken to prevent pollution and to minimize adverse environmental impacts during all aspects of the operation." *Id.*

[170] *See, e.g.*, Fair, *supra* note 99, at 150.

Once the hostilities end and the operation enters the post-conflict stage, environmental considerations will once again take on renewed importance as reconstruction and remediation efforts become more prominent.[171] The post-conflict stage may also involve a base camp selection phase that takes into account environmental considerations.

C. MULTINATIONAL OPERATIONS

Military commanders must be particularly aware of their partner nations' environmental obligations during multinational operations. Multinational operations may incorporate environmental considerations into their military planning, similar to the U.S. joint planning process. For example, within the North Atlantic Treaty Organization (NATO), Standardization Agreement ("STANAG") No. 7141[172] effectively incorporates environmental concerns within NATO operations. It serves as NATO military doctrine in protecting the environment during NATO-led military activities.[173] The STANAG 7141 states that "NATO Forces should be committed to taking all reasonably achievable measures to protect the environment"[174] and that "[e]xercises under peacetime conditions should be conducted in a manner consistent with applicable environmental regulations."[175] Under this agreement, NATO military commanders are required to consider environmental protection during each phase of the military exercise, and must "balance environmental protection against risks to the forces and mission accomplishment."[176] There is an acknowledgment that NATO commanders "should be aware of differences in the priority given to environmental protection among nations."[177] Although NATO environmental guidelines inform decision-making for NATO operations, it stops short of requiring participating nations to fund or undertake specific actions that are not legally prescribed. Last, multinational forces have different environmental responsibilities based upon their respective treaty obligations, making it imperative that operational commanders and their attorneys are aware of their partner nations' legal obligations.

D. ENVIRONMENTAL CLAIMS

Environmental damages may also be sought for military operations pursuant to the Foreign Claims Act (FCA).[178] The FCA regulations prohibit claims from foreign

---

[171] *See, e.g.*, OPLAW HANDBOOK, *supra* note 111, at 328.

[172] NATO STANDARDIZATION AGREEMENT, STANAG 7141: JOINT NATO DOCTRINE FOR ENVIRONMENTAL PROTECTION DURING NATO LED MILITARY ACTIVITIES (Feb. 26, 2008), [hereinafter STANAG 7141] (on file with author). *See also* Nevitt, *supra* note 10, at 54–56 (discussing environmental planning for NATO activities).

[173] *See generally* Nevitt, *supra* note 10, at 54–56.

[174] *Id.* at A-1.

[175] *Id* at A-4. "The only exceptions to this requirement would be emergency situations that threaten human life or safety." *Id.*

[176] *Id.* at A-1.

[177] *Id.* at A-2.

[178] 10 U.S.C. §§ 2734–736 (2013).

military members for personal injuries arising incident to service, and under the "Feres doctrine," service members preclude members of the armed forces from bringing tort lawsuits against the military.[179] Yet a claim under the FCA could still be sought for real estate damage brought about by environmental damage.[180] The FCA allows claims for damage, loss of life, and injury to inhabitants of a foreign country for noncombatant activities caused by DoD employees.[181] Furthermore, the current U.S. Army claims manual acknowledges the possibility of environmental claims arising during military operations overseas, mandating reporting requirements for damage, injury, or death caused by toxic contamination in the air or ground.[182]

E. LOAC TREATIES AND ENVIRONMENTAL CONSIDERATIONS IN ARMED CONFLICT

During times of armed conflict operational attorneys must be aware of several LOAC treaties addressing environmental protection. The United States is bound by LOAC treaties to which it is a party, as well as by binding norms of customary international law.[183] As a general matter, military actions that inflict environmental damage during time of war can be divided into three categories: (1) collateral damage; (2) wanton, unnecessary impact; and (3) modification of the environment.[184] The core LOAC principles of necessity, proportionality, and distinction

---

[179] 32 C.F.R. § 536.138 (2014); Feres v. United States, 340 U.S 135 (1950). Under the FCA, claims are not payable for armed forces engaged in combat. 10 U.S.C. § 2734a(b) (2014).

> is brought by or on behalf of a member of a foreign military force for personal injury or death arising incident to service, or pursuant to combined military operations. Combined military operations include exercises and United Nations and North Atlantic Treaty Association (NATO) peacekeeping and humanitarian missions. Derivative claims arising from these incidents are also excluded.

Id.

[180] *See* Fair, *supra* note 99, at 160 n.181 (describing possible environmental claims that could be sought in military operations in Bosnia).

[181] *See* 10 U.S.C. § 2734(a) (2013).

[182] U.S. Dep't of Army Regulation (AR) 27-20, Claims 20 (Mar. 8, 2008) [hereinafter AR 27-20].

This is located in a section entitled "Unique Issues Related to Environmental Claims."

[183] *See, e.g.,* FM 3-24, *supra* note 2, at 13-2, 13-3. Determining what is customary international law is particularly difficult for operational law attorneys who must translate this legal doctrine into the military planning process. Nevertheless, an understanding of customary international law is important for discerning a state's obligations regarding the environment. *See generally* 1 Restatement (Third) of the Foreign Relations Law of the United States § 601 (Am, Law Inst. 1987). To give one prominent example announcing a customary international law principle of environmental law, the 1941 Trail Smelter case limited the ability of one nation to cause environmental injury to another nation: "[U]nder the principles of international law . . . no State has the right to use or permit the use of its territory in such a manner as to cause injury by fumes in or to the territory of another or the properties or persons therein, when the case is of serious consequence and the injury is established by clear and convincing evidence." Trail Smelter Case (U.S. v. Can.), 3 R. Int'l Arb. Awards 1905, 1965 (1941).

[184] For amplification of these categories, *see* Brigadier General Joseph G. Garrett III, *The Army and the Environment: Environmental Consideration during Army Operations*, 69 U.S. Naval War C. Int'l L. Stud. 42, 51–52 (1996).

are the guiding principles when ascertaining lawful actions affecting the environment. Environmental damage that conforms to these principles is largely permissible.

1. The Hague Conventions

The 1899 Hague Convention II with Respect to the Laws and Customs of War on Land ("Hague II")[185] and the 1907 Hague Convention IV Respecting the Laws and Customs of War on Land ("Hague IV")[186] are the first LOAC treaties that provide some measure of environmental protection. The Regulations Respecting the Laws and Customs of War on Land ("Hague Regulations") are annexed to both Hague II and Hague IV and are the focus of the discussion below.

Although the environment is not specifically mentioned in the Hague Regulations, several provisions effectively protect the human environment by requiring belligerents to comply with basic measures of environmental standards.[187] For example, Article 22 states that the "right of belligerents to adopt means of injuring the enemy is not unlimited."[188] Article 25 prohibits the employment of "poison or poisoned weapons"[189] and the "attack or bombardment, by whatever means, of towns, villages, habitations, or buildings which are not defended."[190] Additional articles of Hague IV limit the means of warfare that inflict unnecessary environmental harm; for example, Article 23 forbids the employment of "arms, projectiles, or material calculated to cause unnecessary suffering," and specifically prohibits the destruction of an enemy's property unless "imperatively demanded by the necessities of war."[191]

Article 55 of the Hague Regulations addresses the specific responsibilities of the "occupying State," affording wartime environmental protections:

> The occupying State shall only be regarded as administrator and usufructuary of the public buildings, real property, forests and agricultural works belonging to the hostile State, and situated in the occupied country. It must protect the capital of these properties, and administer it according to the rules of usufruct.[192]

---

[185] Hague Convention No. II, Respecting the Laws and Customs of War on Land, July 29, 1899, 32 Stat. 1803, T.S. 403, including the regulations thereto [hereinafter Hague II].

[186] Hague Convention No. IV, Respecting the Laws and Customs of War on Land, Oct. 18, 1907, 36 Stat. 2277, 205 Consol. T.S. 277, including the regulations thereto [hereinafter Hague IV].

[187] The term "environment" was absent from any LOAC treaty until 1977. *See* Fair, *supra* note 99, at 128 n.56.

[188] Hague IV, *supra* note 186, art. 22.

[189] *Id.* art. 23(a).

[190] *Id.* art. 25(e), (g).

[191] *Id.* art. 23 (g).

[192] *Id.* art. 55. "Usufruct" is defined as "[a] right to use and enjoy another's property without damaging or diminishing the property." Black's Law Dict. 651 (1996).

Although over a century old, this provision is of continual relevance—it served as the principle legal source to condemn Iraq's burning of Kuwaiti oil wells during the First Gulf War when the Iraqi armed forces occupied Kuwait.[193]

Unlike other LOAC treaties discussed below, the Hague Regulations apply throughout the conduct of hostilities, regardless of its particular phase. In contrast, the Fourth Geneva Convention of 1949[194] applies only during certain conditions (e.g., during occupation), whereas Hague IV applies "to all property, wherever located, and by whomever owned."[195] In addition, the Hague Regulations represent customary norms that are binding on all states.[196]

2. The 1949 Geneva Conventions and Additional Protocols I and II

The 1949 Geneva Conventions also addressed environmental protections during times of armed conflict. And it reaffirmed much of the earlier provisions in the Hague Regulations. For example, purposeful and wanton destruction of the environment that cannot be justified by military necessity violates the law of armed conflict as envisioned by both the Hague Conventions and the Fourth Geneva Convention.[197] Article 53 of the Fourth Geneva Convention forbids destruction of real property during occupation:

> Any destruction by the Occupying Power of real or personal property belonging individually or collectively to private persons, or to the State, or to other public authorities, or to social or co-operative organizations, is prohibited, except where such destruction is rendered absolutely necessary by military operations.[198]

Article 53 of the Fourth Geneva Convention applies to the "occupying power," prohibiting the destruction or damage of the environment "except where such destruction is rendered absolutely necessary by military operations."[199] And excessive destruction of property in the absence of military necessity is considered a "grave breach" triggering additional requirements.[200]

---

[193] *See* Weiss et al., *supra* note 144, at 738–39.

[194] The Geneva Convention Relative to the Protection of Civilian Persons in Time of War, Aug. 12, 1949 6 U.S.T. 3516, 75 U.N.T.S. 287 [hereinafter Geneva Convention IV].

[195] OPLAW Handbook, *supra* note 111, at 329.

[196] *See Treaties and State Parties to Such Treaties*, Int'l Comm. of the Red Cross (ICRC), http://www.icrc.org/ihl/INTRO/195 (last visited Aug. 1, 2014).

"The provisions of the two Conventions on land warfare, like most of the substantive provisions of the Hague Conventions of 1899 and 1907, are considered as embodying rules of customary international law. As such they are also binding on States which are not formally parties to them." *Id.*

[197] *See* Hague IV, *supra* note 186, at art. 55. "The occupying State shall be regarded only as administrator and usufructuary of public buildings, real estate, forests, and agricultural estates belonging to the hostile State, and situated in the occupied country. It must safeguard the capital of these properties, and administer them in accordance with the rules of usufruct." *Id.*

[198] Geneva Convention IV, *supra* note 194, art. 53.

[199] *Id.* art. 53.

[200] *Id.* art. 147. Operational attorneys must also be aware of the continual uncertainty regarding the definition of "property" and the extent to which this includes public goods, land, and

Additional Protocols I (AP I) and II (AP II) to the Geneva Conventions signify a trend for LOAC treaties to address environmental protections.[201] But the United States is not a party to these Protocols, and the environmental provisions in AP I and II are not customary international law that are binding on U.S. military operations.[202] Nevertheless, U.S. forces often operate as part of a multinational force or operate in nations who may fully comply with AP I's provisions. Hence, military attorneys must still be aware of these provisions and the evolving view on what articles represent customary international law and are therefore binding on the U.S. military.[203] Several are of particular importance and are discussed below. First, Article 35 (3) of AP I provides specific protections for the environment. It states:

> It is prohibited to employ methods or means of warfare, which are intended, or may be expected, to cause *widespread, long-term and severe damage* to the natural environment.[204]

Second, Article 54 protects objects indispensable to the survival of the civilian population to include drinking water installations, foodstuffs, and agricultural areas. Third, Article 55, found under the "Civilian Objects" chapter of AP I, states:

> 1. Care shall be taken in warfare to protect the natural environment against widespread, long-term and severe damage. This protection includes a prohibition of the use of methods or means of warfare which are intended or may be expected to cause such damage to the natural environment and thereby to prejudice the health or survival of the population.
> 2. Attacks against the natural environment by way of reprisals are prohibited.[205]

---

environmental resources. If property is construed broadly, this could trigger powerful environmental protections. *See, e.g.*, Meredith DuBarry Huston, *Wartime Environmental Damages: Financing the Cleanup*, 34 U. PA. J. INT'L ECON. L. 899, 904 (2002).

[201] Protocol Additional to the Geneva Conventions of 12 August 1949, and Relating to the Protection of Victims of International Armed Conflicts (Protocol I), *opened for signature* Dec. 12, 1977, 16 I.L.M. 1391, 1125 U.N.T.S. 3 [hereinafter Additional Protocol I]. Additional Protocol (AP) I applies to international armed conflicts. Many Additional Protocol (AP) II provisions mirror those found in AP I and apply to non-international armed conflicts. Protocol Additional to the Geneva Conventions of 12 August 1949, and Relating to the Protection of Victims of Non-International Armed Conflicts (Protocol II), 16 I.L.M. 1442 1125 U.N.T.S. 609 [hereinafter Additional Protocol II].

[202] Michael Matheson, U.S. Department of State Deputy Legal Advisor, presented an overview to a conference at American University in 1987 of the American position on the applicability of Additional Protocols I and II. For a summary of his comments, see Martin P. Dupuis, John Q. Heywood & Michele Y.F. Sarko, *The Sixth Annual American Red Cross-Washington College of Law Conference on International and the 1977 Protocols Additional to the 1949 Geneva Conventions*, 2 AM. U.J. INT'L. L. & POLICY 419 (1987).

[203] *See id.*

[204] Additional Protocol I, *supra* note 201, art. 35 (emphasis added).

[205] *Id.* art. 55.

Article 56 of AP I protects the environment through restrictions on the targeting of works or installations containing dangerous forces.[206] This protects dams, dykes, and nuclear electrical generation stations if such attack "may cause the release of dangerous forces and consequent severe losses among the civilian population."[207]

Last, Protocol III (Protocol III) on the Prohibitions or Restrictions on the Use of Incendiary Weapons of the 1980 Inhumane Weapons Protocol prohibits the targeting of forests or plant cover by incendiary weapons except in certain circumstances:

> It is prohibited to make forests or other types of plant cover the object of attack by incendiary weapons except when such natural elements are used to cover, conceal or camouflage combatants or other military objectives, or are themselves military objects.[208]

Protocol III was first adopted in 2005 and is only slowly gaining acceptance, with only twenty-eight signatory states at the time of this writing.[209]

F. LIMITATIONS ON THE USE OF CHEMICAL AND BIOLOGICAL WEAPONS

The United States believes that international law prohibits the use of both chemical weapons and biological weapons in armed conflict.[210] Further, the United States considers this prohibition on biological weapons to be customary international law and binding on all parties regardless of whether states are party to the 1925 Gas Protocol or the 1993 Chemical Weapons Convention.[211] Following the horrific use of chemical weapons in the First World War, the 1925 Geneva Gas Protocol banned the use of "asphyxiating, poisonous, or other gases, and all analogous liquids, materials or devices . . . [in war]."[212] It is of continual relevance today when analyzing the modern application of Riot Control Agents and herbicidal agents.[213]

---

206 *Id.* art. 56.

207 *Id.*

208 Protocol additional to the Geneva Conventions of 12 August 1949, and relating to the Adoption of an Additional Distinctive Emblem (Protocol III), art. 2, Dec. 8, 2005 1342 U.N.T.S. 171.

209 *Signatory States, Protocol Additional to the Geneva Conventions of 12 August 1949, and Relating to the Adoption of an Additional Distinctive Emblem (Protocol III), Dec. 8, 2005*, INT'L COMM. OF THE RED CROSS (ICRC), http://www.icrc.org/applic/ihl/ihl.nsf/States.xsp?xp_viewStates=XPages_NORMStatesSign&xp_treatySelected=615 (last visited Aug. 1, 2014).

210 *See, e.g.*, NWP 1–14M, *supra* note 159, at 10.3, 10.4.

211 *Id.* at 10.4.

212 The 1925 Geneva Protocol for the Prohibition of the Use of Asphyxiating, Poisonous, or Other Gases, and of Bacteriological Methods of Warfare, June 17, 1925, 26 U.S.T. 571, T.I.A.S, No. 8061 [hereinafter 1925 Gas Protocol].

213 Although the United States' position is that RCAs and herbicides do not meet the definition of "chemical," authorization for the use of RCAs and herbicides is still held at the highest levels of U.S. government. *See, e.g.*, NWP 1-14M, *supra* note 159, at 10.3 (stating that such use "may be

Both the 1993 Chemical Weapons Convention (CWC) and Executive Order 11,850[214] should be read in conjunction with the 1925 Geneva Gas Protocol. They serve to limit the U.S. use of herbicides and Riot Control Agents (RCAs) against combatants during offensive operations in an armed conflict.[215] The present U.S. position on the use of RCAs and herbicidal agents is outlined in Executive Order 11,850: the use of RCAs as a "method of warfare" is not permitted during an armed conflict.[216] Although the United States *does* authorize RCAs in armed conflict in defensive mode to save lives (as opposed to an offensive method of warfare), the President must approve such use.[217] Further, the U.S. position is that the 1925 Gas Protocol and 1993 Chemical Weapons Convention do not apply to military activities outside of an armed conflict, to include peacekeeping, disaster relief, and law enforcement operations.[218]

The United States views that the 1925 Gas Protocol and 1993 Chemical Weapons Convention does not prohibit the use of herbicidal agents in wartime.[219] Nevertheless, as a matter of U.S. military policy, the use of herbicidal agents during armed conflict requires higher-level approval[220] and the United States has renounced the *first* use of herbicides, except for limited circumstances.[221]

G. THE PROTECTION OF CULTURAL PROPERTY AND ENMOD

Environmental considerations also include protections for cultural property. The 1954 Hague Convention for the Protection of Cultural Property in the Event of Armed Conflict prohibits the use of cultural property "for purposes which are likely to expose it to destruction or damage in the event of armed conflict."[222]

---

authorized by the Secretary of Defense or in limited circumstances by the commanders of the combatant commands"). Herbicide agents are defined as "gases, liquids, and analogous substances that are designed to defoliate trees, bushes, or shrubs, or to kill long grasses and other vegetation that could shield the movement of enemy forces." *See, e.g., id.* at 10–4.

214 Exec. Order No. 11,850, 40 Fed. Reg. 16,187 (1975). This executive order "renounces, as a matter of national policy, first use of herbicides in war except under regulations applicable to their domestic use, for control of vegetation within U.S. bases and installations or around immediate defensive perimeters, and first use of riot control agents except in defensive modes to save lives . . ." *Id.*

215 *See* NWP 1-14M, *supra* note 159, at 10.3. Two treaties address, in part, the use of herbicides and riot control agents during warfare: The 1925 Geneva Gas Protocol for the Prohibition of the Use in War of Asphyxiating, Poisonous or Other Gases and of Bacteriological Methods of Warfare ("the 1925 Gas Protocol") and the 1993 Convention on the Prohibition of Development, Production, Stockpiling and Use of Chemical Weapons and on their Destruction (the "1993 Chemical Weapons Convention").

216 *Supra* note 214.

217 NWP 1-14M, *supra* note 159, at 10.3.

218 *Id.*

219 *See, e.g., id.* at 10–4.

220 *Id.*

221 *Id.* The United States will still utilize herbicides in limited circumstances to include the control of vegetation within U.S. bases. *Id.*

222 Convention for the Protection of Cultural Property in the Event of Armed Conflict, May 14, 1954, art. 4, S. Treaty Doc. No. 106–1, 249 U.N.T.S. 215 [hereinafter Cultural Property Convention].

It also ensures the immunity of cultural property under special protection by limiting the circumstances when an act of hostility could occur against the property.[223] The United States ratified this in 2008, and operational attorneys should be generally familiar with its provisions.

While the previous LOAC treaties placed limitations on weapons systems, the 1977 Convention on the Prohibition of Military or Any Other Hostile Use of Environmental Modification Techniques (ENMOD) bans the manipulation or use of the environment itself as a weapon.[224] It prohibits the hostile use of "environmental modification techniques having widespread, long-lasting or severe effects as the means of destruction, damage, or injury to any other State Party."[225]

Yet the standard for environmental modification as set forth in ENMOD is extremely high—ENMOD prohibits the wartime manipulation of the environment to include the dynamics, composition, or structure of the earth.[226] And ENMOD's illustrative examples include modification techniques such as earthquakes, tsunamis, and changes in the ozone layer.[227] Potential Examples that violate ENMOD include the destruction of the rainforests in the Amazon River Basin due to global climate change.[228] Despite being thirty-five-years old, it is difficult to imagine a scenario where ENMOD would clearly apply. As existing conventional warfare capabilities do not appear to trigger ENMOD, its application appears to be limited. Nevertheless, operational lawyers should be generally familiar with the provisions of ENMOD and be able to articulate the threshold for its application.

V. Environmental Law in Military Operations: Lessons Learned, Practical Concerns and Future Trends

A. RECENT OPERATIONS—LESSONS LEARNED

Recent military operations in Bosnia, Kosovo, Iraq, and Afghanistan have highlighted practical concerns associated with environmental cleanup and the applicability of U.S. and host-nation environmental law, and international environmental law in an operational environment. Furthermore, lessons from these conflicts reinforce the importance of respecting the host-nation's environment to ensure the overall integrity and success of the mission.[229]

---

[223] *Id.* art. 9, entitled "Immunity of Cultural Property under Special Protection."

[224] The Convention on the Prohibition of Military or Any Other Hostile Use of Environmental Modification Techniques, *opened for signature* May 18, 1977, 31 U.S.T. 333. 1108 U.N.T.S. 151 [hereinafter ENMOD].

[225] *Id.*

[226] *Id.* art. II.

[227] *See id.* art. II

[228] *See* YORAM DINSTEIN, THE CONDUCT OF HOSTILITIES UNDER THE LAW OF INTERNATIONAL ARMED CONFLICT 181 (2004).

[229] *Cf.* CTR. FOR LAW & MILITARY OPERATIONS, THE JUDGE ADVOCATE GEN.'S SCH., U.S. ARMY AFTER ACTION REPORT, LAW AND MILITARY OPERATIONS IN THE BALKANS 1995–1998, 167

Proper disposal of hazardous waste is a routine problem associated with military operations. And foreign claims may result from environmental damage inflicted in the absence of a clear governing environmental standard. For example, during Hurricane Mitch in 1998, the U.S. military deployed to Central America and confronted environmental legal issues associated with the disposal of medical and hazardous waste.[230] In Nicaragua, military officials were concerned about the handling of hazardous waste by local Nicaraguan contractors. To mitigate future foreign claims against the United States, military commanders chose to bring hazardous and medical waste back to the United States rather than risking improper disposal by a local contractor within Nicaragua.[231]

Although it is not a LOAC treaty per se, operational attorneys should be keenly aware of the Basel Convention on the Control of Transboundary Movements of Hazardous Wastes and Their Disposal (Basel Convention) as it can directly affect military operations.[232] The Basel Convention encourages the disposal of hazardous waste in the generating nation and prohibits the disposal or transport of hazardous waste from nonparties to parties without a separate arrangement.[233] The United States has signed but not ratified the treaty. Nevertheless, the Basel Convention is widely followed, and over 180 nations are party to this treaty.[234]

The Basel Convention took on critical importance in Operation Joint Endeavour in Bosnia, when the United States was part of a multinational force and needed to dispose of hazardous waste. Bosnia lacked meaningful environmental law and enforcement provisions, yet military personnel needed to establish baseline environmental standards to ensure the integrity of its mission and to prevent later claims against the U.S. government. In Bosnia, the U.S. Army initially hired a contractor to transport hazardous waste generated during the operation from Bosnia with ultimate disposal in Germany (a member of NATO).[235] This planned transit included movement through Croatia. But Croatia demanded a separate

---

available at http://www.loc.gov/rr/frd/Military_Law/pdf/Lessons-Learned_Balkans.pdf [hereinafter BALKANS LESSONS LEARNED] (highlighting an Army Order in Operation Joint Endeavour to respect the environment for the purposes of "maintaining the good name of U.S. Army environmental stewardship").

[230] *See* CTR. FOR LAW & MILITARY OPERATIONS, THE JUDGE ADVOCATE GEN.'S SCH., U.S. ARMY AFTER ACTION REPORT, LAW AND MILITARY OPERATIONS IN CENTRAL AMERICA: HURRICANE MITCH RELIEF EFFORTS 1998–1999, 109.

[231] *Id.*

[232] Basel Convention on the Control of Transboundary Movements of Hazardous Waste and Their Disposal, Mar. 22, 1989, U.N. Doc. UNEP/WG.1904/4, UNEP/IG.80/3 (1989), 28 I.L.M. 657. Basel's Protocol, titled "Protocol on Liability and Compensation for Damage Resulting from Transboundary Movements of Hazardous Waste and Their Disposal," limits liability if it can be proven that the damage was caused by "act of armed conflict, hostilities, civil war or insurrection." *Id.* at art. IV. 5(a).

[233] *Id.*

[234] *See Parties to the Basel Convention*, BASEL CONVENTION, http://www.basel.int/Countries/Statusofratifications/PartiesSignatories/tabid/1290/language/en-US/Default.aspx (last visited June 23, 2015) (listing the 181 parties to the Basel Convention).

[235] *See* Fair, *supra* note 99, at 136–38.

transit agreement in accordance with the Basel Convention.[236] In the interim, active-duty military transporters (not contractors) had to move the waste across international borders, diverting military forces from the ongoing peacekeeping mission. After lengthy negotiations over an eight-month period, a transit agreement was reached with all the affected parties to allow the contractors to proceed through Croatia.[237] A clearer understanding of Basel's application in Europe and the anticipation that a more formalized agreement with neighboring countries would be required could have mitigated the underlying delays and mission impacts.[238]

Some nations may lack the capacity to enforce their own environmental standards, resulting in situations where U.S. forces may have to take action to protect health and safety of its own service members.[239] For example, when the U.S. military deployed to Haiti as part of Operation Unified Response in 2010, the earthquake resulted in thousands of Haitian deaths and hasty burials in mass graves.[240]

The use of open-air burn pits is yet another example of the environmental impacts of military operations that impacts the host-nation environment as well as the health of service members. This became an increasing environmental concern in Iraq and Afghanistan as American troops utilized burn pits extensively to dispose of military items.[241] It also highlighted another potential legal void in military operations overseas. Afghanistan and Iraq lacked meaningful environmental protection and enforcement mechanisms, and the OEBGD, FGS, and related DoD Directives did not apply. U.S. Forces-Afghanistan (USFOR-A) environmental guidance stated, "open burning will not be the regular method of solid waste disposal." Nevertheless, open pit burning was still relied heavily upon in both Iraq and Afghanistan.[242] And its widespread usage put the DoD on the defensive as health issues from service members began to arise. The DoD recently issued open pit burning guidance in DoDI 4715.09, titled "Use of Open-Air Burn

---

[236] *See generally id.*

[237] *Id.*

[238] *Id.*

[239] *See* Center for Law and Military Operations, Tip of the Spear: After Action Reports from August 2009 –August 2010, 2010 Supplement to Forged in the Fire, Legal Lessons Learned during Military Operations 1994–2008, 87 (Sept. 2010) (on file with author) [hereinafter Tip of the Spear]. There are two source documents to identify lessons learned from rule of law operations in Afghanistan that are published by the Center for Law and Military Operations. The first is Tip of the Spear and the second is Forged in the Fire: Lessons Learned during Military Operations (1994–1998) (Sept. 2008) [hereinafter Forged in the Fire]. Tip of the Spear is on file with the author and is available through the Center for Law and Military Operations, based in Charlottesville, VA. Forged in the Fire is available online at http://www.loc.gov/rr/frd/Military_Law/CLAMO.html (last visited June 29, 2014).

[240] *Id.*

[241] *See generally* Hilbert, *supra* note 102 (discussing the American military's use of burn pits in Iraq and Afghanistan). The items burned included " . . . [p]lastic tires, Humvee doors, vehicles, [and] medical waste." *Id.* at 264. The dangers associated with the use of burn pits in Iraq and Afghanistan has been analogized to the use of Agent Orange in Vietnam. *Id.* at 268.

[242] *Id.*

Pits in Contingency Operations."[243] This instruction generally prohibits the use of open air burn pits "except in circumstances in which no alternative disposal method is feasible."[244]

When U.S. forces transitioned out of Iraq, the U.S. forces were nonetheless required to meet standards of environmental regulation as set forth by United States Forces-Iraq despite meaningful host-nation environmental regulations.[245] Redeploying forces in Iraq mitigated environmental impacts but did not remediate bases. Further, they did not comply with domestic U.S. environmental laws and regulations that lacked an extraterritorial application.[246]

Environmental considerations took on increased importance when the United States exited Iraq. The U.S.-Iraqi security agreement, under the "Protecting the Environment" section states:

> Both Parties shall implement this Agreement in a manner consistent with protecting the natural environment and human health and safety. The United States reaffirms its commitment to respecting applicable Iraqi environmental laws, regulations, and standards in the course of executing its policies for the purposes of implementing this Agreement.[247]

This provision took on importance as American troops began to withdraw from Iraq as U.S. forces had to comply with environmental standards pursuant to the security agreement.[248] And the actual execution of the return of property to Iraq was not entirely seamless.[249]

B. INTERNATIONAL AGREEMENTS AND EMERGING THEMES IN INTERNATIONAL ENVIRONMENTAL LAW

As international agreements increasingly inform environmental obligations for military forces overseas, military commanders and their lawyers must be aware of the international agreements that protect the environment.[250] For example,

---

[243] Dep't of Def. Inst. 4715.19, Use of Open-Air Burn Pits in Contingency Operations (Feb. 15, 2011).

[244] *Id.* para. 4(b).

[245] Hilbert, *supra* note 102, at 274.

[246] The general in charge of environmental remediation was careful to point out that installations in Iraq are not being returned in accordance with U.S. environmental regulations. "That would be unrealistic and impractical, and extremely costly," he said. *Id.*

[247] "Agreement between the United States of America and the Republic of Iraq on the Withdrawal of United States Forces from Iraq and the Organization of Their Activities during Their Temporary Presence in Iraq," *available at:* http://graphics8.nytimes.com/packages/pdf/world/20081119_SOFA_FINAL_AGREED_TEXT.pdf (last visited June 23, 2015) [hereinafter Iraqi-U.S. Security Agreement].

[248] *See* Tip of the Spear, *supra* note 239, at 86.

[249] One Judge Advocate commenting on the United States returning land previously used as a training range stated: "Overall, commands are not very effective at returning real estate." *See id.* at 86.

[250] *See, e.g.*, OEF Annex L, *supra* note 81, para 3(a)(1)(c) (stating that "U.S. Forces will comply with treaty obligations, and respect the sovereignty of other nations").

there are numerous treaties addressing naval vessels at sea. The United Nations Convention on the Law of the Sea (UNCLOS) has numerous provisions concerning preservation of the maritime environment.[251] Although the United States has not formally ratified UNCLOS, it complies with its substantive provisions that relate to both navigation and overflight.[252] In addition, international agreements may mandate obligations for military activities and operations overseas. For example, outside the United States, the London Dumping Convention governs disposal of wastes from ships, aircraft, and other man-made structures, and applies through a wide spectrum of both commercial and military operations.[253]

Status of Forces Agreements (SOFAs) between the United States and host nations have increasingly addressed environmental considerations. For example, while the NATO SOFA from 1951 places a general obligation on U.S. forces in a NATO host nation to respect the host nation's domestic laws,[254] the more recent NATO Supplementary Agreement (SA) with Germany places environmental protections within the agreement. Signed in 1993, it mandates that U.S. forces stationed on military installations in Germany comply with German law except in "matters which have no foreseeable effect on the rights of third parties or on adjoining communities."[255]

Although not yet customary international law that would bind military operations, the Rio Declaration on Environment and Development ("Rio Declaration") contains provisions representing what appears to be an emerging trend in international environmental law to protect the environment in wartime. Operational commanders and their attorneys should be generally familiar with these principles as they have begun to inform international environmental protections in armed conflict, and multinational partners may construe these principles as binding. For example, Principle 24 of the Rio Declaration states that "[w]arfare is inherently destructive of sustainable development. States shall therefore respect international law providing protection for the environment in times of armed conflict and cooperate in its further development, as necessary."[256]

In addition, Principle 25 of the Rio Declarations states, "Peace, development, and environmental protection are independent and indivisible."[257] Following the

---

[251] *See generally* United Nations Convention on the Law of the Sea, Dec. 10, 1982, U.N. Doc. A/CONF.62/122. 21 I.LM. 1261.

[252] *United States Oceans Policy, Statement of President Reagan, Mar. 10, 1983*, U.S. State Dep't, http://www.state.gov/documents/organization/143224.pdf (last visited Aug. 3, 2014).

[253] *See* Convention on the Prevention of Marine Pollution by Dumping of Waste and Other Matter, Dec. 29, 1972, 26 U.S.T. 2403. The United States has signed and ratified the London Dumping Convention.

[254] Agreement between the Parties to the North Atlantic Treaty Regarding the Status of Forces, 19 June 1951, 4 U.S.T. 1792, 199 U.N.T.S. 67 [hereinafter NATO SOFA].

[255] Phelps, *supra* note 123, at 53. *See also* Agreement to Supplement the Agreement between the Parties to the North Atlantic Treaty Regarding the Status of Their Forces with Respect to Foreign Forces Stationed in the Federal Republic of Germany, 18 Mar. 1993.

[256] United Nations Conference on Environment and Development: Rio Declaration on Environment and Development, princ. 24, June 13, 1992, 31 I.L.M. 874.

[257] *Id.* princ. 25.

massive environmental destruction caused by burning oil wells in Kuwait during the First Gulf War, the United Nations General Assembly adopted a resolution reaffirming the importance of environmental protections during armed conflict and urged states to better incorporate international law principles of environmental law into their respective military manuals.[258]

The importance of protecting the environment has further been reinforced by international tribunals. For example, in the International Court of Justice's (ICJ)'s Advisory Opinion on the *Legality of the Use by a State of Nuclear Weapons* addressed whether the threat or use of nuclear weapons is ever lawful under international law. In analyzing this question, the court reinforced the dangers to the environment posed by nuclear weapons: "The environment is not an abstraction but represents the living space, the quality of life and the very health of human beings, including generations unborn."[259] The court discussed the importance of taking environmental considerations into account in the context of proportionality:

> States must take environmental considerations into account when asserting what is necessary and proportionate in the pursuit of legitimate military objectives. Respect for the environment is one of the elements that go to assessing whether an action is in conformity with the principles of necessity and proportionality.[260]

Although the ICJ opinion is only advisory in nature and not binding on military operations, it does reinforce the unmistakable trend within international tribunals and international environmental law generally of requiring environmental protections during armed conflict.

VI. Conclusion

This analytical précis of environmental laws and regulations during operations is intended to emphasize not only the importance of environmental stewardship in achieving larger mission goals, but the relative complexity of determining which environmental laws and regulations apply throughout the sometimes extended duration of a military operation. Operational commanders and attorneys should at all times be aware of their operational environment and the applicable environmental laws and standards.

---

[258] *See* G.A. Res. 47/37, U.N. Doc. A/RES/47/37 (Nov. 25, 1992) (expressing its concern for the destruction of oil wells and release of crude oil into the sea, and urging states "to take steps to incorporate the provisions of international law applicable to the environment into their military manuals . . .").

[259] Advisory Opinion on *Legality of the Threat of Nuclear Weapons*, 1996, ICJ Rep. 226, 241 [hereinafter ICJ Nuclear]. *See also* DINSTEIN, *supra* note 228, at 176–77.

[260] ICJ Nuclear, *supra* note 259, at 242.

14 }

Soldiers in Combat and Military Justice

Charles N. Pede*

A grenade is thrown into the tent of sleeping 101st Airborne Division Soldiers on the eve of the invasion of Iraq in 2003. Sergeant Akbar is seen in the chaos shooting an officer in the back at almost point blank range. The brigade is pulled out of the line for 24 hours. Akbar is court-martialed, found guilty and sentenced to death.[1]

In the prison halls of Abu Ghraib, American military police (MPs) abuse Iraqi detainees and memorialize their deeds in searing photos of depravity. Their crimes are discovered and an international outcry ensues. Courts-martial and prison soon follow.[2]

An infantry Lieutenant is ordered to return a detainee to his village. The Iraqi is suspected to have planted an improvised explosive device (IED) against the Lieutenant's platoon, killing some of his Soldiers. The Lieutenant, frustrated by his view of a "catch and release" program, orders the unarmed,

---

* Brigadier General, Commander, United States Army Legal Services Agency and Chief Judge, U.S. Army Court of Criminal Appeals. Previous assignments include: Trial Defense Counsel, Mannheim Field Office, Germany; Chief, Criminal Law, and Chief, Administrative & International Law, 21st Theater Army Area Command, Mannheim, Germany and Army Forces-Turkey; Chief, Military Justice, 10th Mountain Division (Light Infantry), Fort Drum, New York and OPERATION RESTORE HOPE, Mogadishu, Somalia; Professor of Law, Criminal Law Department, The Judge Advocate General's Legal Center and School, Charlottesville, VA; Assignments Officer, Office of The Judge Advocate General (OTJAG); Assistant Executive Officer, OTJAG; Staff Judge Advocate, 10th Mountain Division (Light Infantry), Fort Drum, NY, and Joint Task Force Mountain and Combined Joint Task Force-180, OPERATION ENDURING FREEDOM, Afghanistan; Legislative Counsel, Office of the Chief of Legislative Liaison, Pentagon, Washington, DC; Chief, Criminal Law Division, OTJAG; Staff Judge Advocate, United States Forces Iraq, Baghdad, OPERATION IRAQI FREEDOM, Iraq; Chief, Criminal Law Division, OTJAG; and Executive Officer to The Judge Advocate General of the Army. DISCLAIMER: The views expressed in this chapter are those of the author alone, and do not represent the views of DoD, or the Army. Special thanks to Colonel George Smawley, U.S. Army, for his invaluable contributions.

[1] Manuel Roig-Franzia, *Army Soldier Is Convicted in Attack on Fellow Troops*, WASH. POST (Apr. 22, 2005), http://www.washingtonpost.com/wp-dyn/articles/A7210-2005Apr21.html.

[2] Abu Gharaib, N.Y. TIMES, http://topics.nytimes.com/top/news/international/countriesandterritories/iraq/abu_ghraib/index.html (last visited Aug. 15, 2014).

zip tied Iraqi into a culvert, questions him and then murders him. At his court-martial he is sentenced to 25 years in prison.[3]

A non-commissioned officer (NCO) leaves his outpost, enters 2 villages and murders 17 Afghans and injures many more. The court-martial sentences him to life in prison without the possibility of parole.[4]

I. Introduction

Wherefore[5] *a Separate System of Justice?*

Since Roman Legions marched with Caesar, and Napoleon and Wellington crossed the rivers of Spain in furtive parries, armies have struggled to balance fanning the violence held in the hands of youthful warriors to destroy the enemy with the ever-present danger that this same violence, if not properly contained, could spill over in myriad ways to the loss of innocent life and property.

This point of balance is one of the greatest challenges of a field commander. Although difficult in conventional wars[6] with uniformed enemies and linear battle lines, this balancing act is magnified and exacerbated by unseen enemies, nonlinear battlefields, and, in modern war, terror tactics.[7] The crimes sketched above freeze-frame this tense and unfortunate, and yes, inevitable point of departure. These particular cases may have mirror images in wars of old, but it is also the nature of our wars of the last decade that "magnify and exacerbate" the root causes of such crime.

The cases also express the essence of military justice at war and the persistently incontrovertible truth that crime, even in the most disciplined army, is inevitable, and that a readily available and tailored system of justice must be in

---

[3] Adam Kemp, *Michael Behenna Released from U.S. Disciplinary Barracks*, The Oklahoman (Mar. 14, 2014), http://newsok.com/michael-behenna-released-from-u.s.-disciplinary-barracks/article/3943282.

[4] Jack Healy, *Soldier Sentenced to Life without Parole for Killing 16 Afghans*, N.Y. Times (Aug. 23, 2013), http://www.nytimes.com/2013/08/24/us/soldier-gets-life-without-parole-in-deaths-of-afghan-civilians.html?_r=0.

[5] Merriam-Webster Dictionary, "for what reason or purpose, why." Definition of Wherefore, Merriam-Webster, http://www.merriam-webster.com/dictionary/wherefore (last visited Aug. 15, 2014) ("for what reason or purpose, why").

[6] *The Fifth Field*, by French L. MacLean (2013), in which the author tells the story of the ninety-six American soldiers sentenced to death and executed in Europe and North Africa in World War II. Crime against person and property, whether in conventional or unconventional war, abides.

[7] Vietnam was the American Army's most recent experience in nonlinear war. The last thirteen years of war and the phenomenon of triple or more deployments to war, if they show anything, demonstrate the terrible mental and physical costs on soldiers and the fabric of their family life. It also shows the immense resiliency and strength of the American Army. http://www.washingtonpost.com/sf/national/2014/03/29/a-legacy-of-pride-and-pain/ (last visited June 6, 2015) [terror acts in warfare and in politics have not been limited to the past thirteen years—see first-century C.E. and Sicarii Zealots, or even Jacobin Reign of Terror.]

place to address it. Despite hundreds of thousands of American soldiers manifesting American values daily in combat, crime is part of the American social and military fabric. The impact of military crime and indiscipline in Iraq and Afghanistan, especially affecting civilians, simply cannot be overstated.

These events also occupied the international and national media spin cycle, further magnifying, and in some cases distorting the conduct beyond its actual facts. Some critics have even erroneously applied the sobriquet "strategic corporal" regarding crimes committed by junior soldiers.[8] This moniker does not praise the strategic vision of the junior NCO; it instead expresses the potential strategic impact of the actions of the most junior soldier (or Marine) on the greater, theater-wide mission.[9] Indeed, a crime akin to desecrating corpses,[10] or murdering civilians during clearing operations[11] sets a military mission on its heels, potentially compromises the effectiveness of the unit, and jeopardizes relationships with host nations and allies.

For these powerful reasons the military justice system has operated with vigor and with unprecedented public scrutiny through the last decade and half of war. The military justice system continues to operate for many of the same reasons as it did for General George Washington and the countless field commanders through the generations that followed. At its core, the military justice system operates as a codification of evolving American principles of justice as America projects power around the world: respect for authority, respect for the value of life, and respect for property. These precepts are central to military law and are the spoken and unspoken code of American forces in the field. Although commanders today do not have the same concerns about desertion that George Washington labored under, the need to enforce basic discipline remains just as elemental to a field commander today, and is at the core of mission accomplishment. Basic discipline is required not only to ensure a disciplined force is ready to carry out orders, but to preserve our allies and host-nation support as we wage war.[12]

It would be the best sort of fiction to suggest that soldier crime in combat is no different than soldier crime in garrison (at home station in the continental United States). However, this sentiment, although attractive, ignores the intersection of

---

[8] General Charles Krulak, *The Strategic Corporal: Leadership in the Three Block War*, MARINES MAG., Jan. 1999, *available at* http://www.au.af.mil/au/awc/awcgate/usmc/strategic_corporal.htm. Krulak intended to invoke what he called "strategic corporals": low-level unit leaders able to take independent action and make major decisions. *Id.*

[9] *Id.*

[10] While an oddly explosive offense, this crime is not even an enumerated offense under the UCMJ.

[11] Bo Petersen, *Murder at Thar Thar*, THE POST AND COURIER (Mar. 22, 2009), http://www.postandcourier.com/article/20090621/PC1602/306219948.

[12] *See* Ken Burns, *Communicating the Experience of War, America's Civil War*, HISTORYNET.COM (Aug. 12, 2009), http://www.historynet.com/ken-burns-communicating-the-experience-of-war.htm (quoting Oliver Wendell Holmes during a speech and referring to his experience as a Union Soldier during the American Civil War: "We have shared the incommunicable experience of war. We have felt, we still feel, the passion of life to its top . . . .In our youths, our hearts were touched with fire.")

the war and all of its terrible pressures with human nature, and the inevitable collision with the rule of law. Crime in combat is different because it at times involves judgment of conduct that in the cold light of day makes those judging a bit uncomfortable, and frankly has no equivalent with that committed in downtown Cincinnati, or Fayetteville, or New York.

Was it really necessary to prosecute a soldier who executed a German machine-gunner who raised his hands in surrender after gunning down five Americans? Why would the military prosecute a soldier who shot a Korean who spat on him after the soldier survived thirty-plus days of constant combat and being overrun by the Chinese? By what right did the U.S. military fault a young soldier in Vietnam who, scared, sleepless, and under constant fire, killed a Vietcong fighter he pulled from a hole in the ground on a supply trail? Ought society to have imprisoned a soldier who shot an Iraqi he suspected killed his buddies with an IED? The intersection of war and justice is often vague, complicated by the circumstances in which violations of law occur and the inescapable value judgments of how the environment shapes the way men think when conditioned by the depravities of combat.

> *The fact of the matter is that war changes men's natures. The barbarities of war are seldom committed by abnormal men. The tragedy of war is that these horrors are committed by normal men in abnormal situations, situations in which the ebb and flow of everyday life have departed and have been replaced by a constant round of fear and anger, blood and death.*
>
> *Soldiers at war are not to be judged by civilian rules . . . even though they commit acts which, calmly viewed afterwards could only be seen as unchristian and brutal. . . . we cannot hope to judge such matters unless we ourselves have been submitted to the same pressures, the same provocations, as these men whose actions are on trial.*[13]

In *Breaker Morant*, perhaps the most powerful and timelessly relevant film on military crimes in combat, the besieged defense counsel *Major* James Francis *Thomas* paints an elegant Hobson's choice to the audience. The dramatization has Major Thomas imploring the jury that the brutal prisoner killings by his client, an English officer fighting the Boer guerrillas, were necessary and pursuant to orders. We learn that the officer, Lieutenant Morant, was ordered to execute captured Boers after this fate befell British prisoners and, in particular, his own beloved commander. In the movie's closing argument, Major Thomas theorized that conditions under which soldiers operated were so charged with peril that normal rules were suspended. For the uninitiated and even for those whose professional lives are spent in harm's way, the sentiment is deceptively attractive. For soldiers, however, this compelling argument fails, and indeed it must fail.

---

[13] *Breaker Morant* (1980), *available at* http://books.google.com/books/about/Breaker_Morant.html?id=GADsAAAAMAAJ (opening statement from the film).

Although the experience of war, as Justice Oliver Wendell Holmes said, is incommunicable,[14] at least to those who have not experienced it, it must nevertheless be judged. The motives for crimes during war and the pressures on the human spirit are indeed profoundly powerful. Nonetheless, for an Army to function it must control, and therefore judge, such behavior that not only falls outside our fundamental values, but intimately jeopardizes the fine line between a disciplined army and a ruthless mob. Impunity in the face of crime is not an option in organized civilized society, nor in one of its aspirationally virtuous sub-elements—the Armed Forces.

In the delicate balance of modern war in coalition and host-nation relationships, such behavior must also be judged to address the wrong in often highly visible ways. And so, the Armed Forces have, during our wars on terror, vigorously prosecuted theater crime. Most recently, trials in both Iraq and Afghanistan were common features of the operational landscape. A similarly large volume of criminal proceedings were returned to the United States for trial as units rotated out of theater. The delicate matters about which Major Thomas eloquently waxed were inevitably center stage in courtrooms charged with assessing guilt and punishment.

In the pages that follow, these and other current issues in military justice in combat are addressed.

II. Foundations—Visibile, Local, and Swift

Mindful that any effective system of discipline and justice must be responsive to the nature of the wrong perpetrated, the military justice system is a finely tuned, graduated set of applied tools. Indeed, these tools go well beyond the courtroom, and operate as the precursors to a trial with the design to promote order and discipline, as well as to correct the tendency to engage in criminal behavior early, in order to avoid the courtroom and get soldiers back to soldiering.

When a young 101st trooper struck an Afghan detainee on the head with a rifle barrel in 2003, there was a tool for dealing with this soldier. Article 15 of the Uniform Code of Military Justice (UCMJ) was the answer. This article of the UCMJ allows commanders to impose low-level punishments without resort to trial. With the trooper in question, the commander was able to swiftly address the wrong, visibly to the unit so as to discourage others and set an immediately visible standard of care that soldiers understood would cost them should they too violate the standard. The commander was able to reinforce basic rules about how American soldiers treat people in their care and custody. Thirteen years of war have also shown the significant utility of the full scope of the military justice system, from counseling sessions with young soldiers to improve treatment of villagers during operations, to nonjudicial summary courts for disrespect to a

[14] *See* Burns, *supra* note 12.

senior officer or petty larceny, to capital trials. It is a highly adaptive system, built on a graduated scale of commander-driven responses to misconduct at all levels.

The military justice system is animated by a set of fundamental principles that apply the right kind of tool to the specific wrong. Or, as Henry V purportedly said when faced with betrayal by some of his trusted knights upon his departure for France and fame at Agincourt:

> *If little faults, proceeding on distemper,*
> *Shall not be wink'd at, how shall we stretch our eye*
> *When capital crimes, chew'd, swallow'd and digested,*
> *Appear before us?*[15]

Like King Henry, the U.S. military must treat "little faults" differently from those "capital." Thus, the carefully calibrated system of military justice properly understood, whether in garrison or at war, has countless tools of increasing gravity to address indiscipline and crime: visibly, locally, and swiftly.

Indisputably, the military justice system, like any criminal justice system anywhere in the United States, is not perfect. It is a human system and therefore, subject to human failure both through omission and commission. A commander or prosecutor may fail to take appropriate action upon the report of a crime. In the eyes of critics leaders may take the wrong action, suggesting either a reluctance to address the crime, or worse, the application of a double standard. And of course, there is the timeless criticism that commanders take care of their own by not meting out discipline at all, or disparately.[16] This debate has raged and will continue to rage.

The American military justice system is certainly not immune from the realities about which its critics despair. However, as the last decade of conflict has clearly proven, it is the fairest, most earnest system in practice able to meet the special requirements of the modern military. The evils of which critics rail at are in this author's opinion rare, with many of the stated failures actually honest disagreements between reasonable professionals about what really is the correct disposition for a particular crime. In the end, the system, although not perfect, is about as good as any system of justice administered by humans can be given the nation's justifiable expectations for its military's inherent need for discipline and expeditionary capability.

Therefore, for what any soldier knows are countless indisputable reasons,[17] an army must be able to discipline itself. An army must and has always had the

---

[15] William Shakespeare, *Henry V*, Act 2, Scene 2, *available at* http://shakespeare.mit.edu/henryv/full.html. Southhampton, A Council Chamber. Henry had just proposed releasing a drunk from confinement who had assaulted him the day before. Three of his knights suggested that the man should be punished first. Knowing of the three knights' treachery on the eve of sailing for France and fame, Henry then spoke these words, knowing he would soon be sentencing each of the knights to death.

[16] The case of Lieutenant Colonol Allen West is a good example of arguments of double standard.

[17] I offer the qualifier "for what any soldier knows" because this axiom of armies has recently experienced attack from Congress in the arena of sexual assault offenses. To suggest that this criticism is fundamentally compromised by their lack of soldier experience is at once obvious, as it is simplistic and incomplete. One need not have cancer to know it is bad, or painful.

ability to punish transgressions within the ranks. George Washington attempted to curb his massive desertion problems with the lash. Zachary Taylor, commanding the American Army in the early stages of the War with Mexico, held a court-martial in almost permanent session for crimes ranging from theft of fruit from local villagers to murder. Both the ability to discipline and a soldier's sure knowledge that discipline will be meted out if a line is crossed is to armies as oil is to a motor engine. So it remains today.

This foundational bedrock remains a fixture of the U.S. armed forces. Although indiscipline in the form of purely military offenses, such as sleeping on guard duty and disrespect, as well as common law crimes such as rape and murder, remain relatively rare in the U.S. military, they each require a seasoned system of criminal justice to deal with them responsibly.

For this and many other reasons the military justice system is an essential element of a deployed army. It is not the center of the commander's attention. It is not the substance of the daily operations and intelligence briefing during the daily battle update. But like the communications systems, the fuel handler, the cook, and the supply trains, the ability to address indiscipline and criminal misconduct is one of the vital lifebloods of the military. Without the systems of punishment and rewards, discipline erodes. One knows these simple truths with children. Why would a nation ignore them in something as important as an army? Commanders' orders and directives would have no teeth in the face of a petulant or dangerous soldier. A commander who appears impotent in dealing with a soldier who drinks alcohol in violation of the General Order, deals in illegal drugs, or sexually assaults a fellow soldier on a small forward-operating base (FOB) in a combat zone will have his or her authority questioned in other venues. Every soldier on the FOB, in the tents, in the showers, on patrol would be more vulnerable, less confident in his own security, and less sure of the trust he places in his leadership.

III. In Brief: Sources of Authority[18]

The modern military justice system springs from the UCMJ, a comprehensive and visionary statute first passed by Congress in 1950 following the unsatisfactory experience of millions of Americans with the Articles of War (AW) during World War II.[19] To implement the UCMJ, judge advocates (uniformed military lawyers) look to the Manual for Courts-Martial (MCM)[20] and numerous regulations and

---

[18] The best comprehensive overview of the modern military justice system is LAWRENCE J. MORRIS, MILITARY JUSTICE, A GUIDE TO THE ISSUES (2010).

[19] The *UCMJ* was passed by Congress on May 5, 1950, and signed into law by President Harry S Truman the next day. It took effect on May 31, *1951*. *Military Justice Fact Sheets*, U.S. MARINE CORP, http://www.hqmc.marines.mil/Portals/135/MJFACTSHTS[1].html (last visited Sept. 6, 2014).

[20] *See* MANUAL FOR COURTS-MARTIAL, UNITED STATES (2012) [hereinafter MCM], *available at* http://www.apd.army.mil/pdffiles/mcm.pdf.

policies that set out for prosecutors and defense counsel everything from sex offender registration requirements, to how many copies of a record of trial must be prepared and when and where they are to be shipped. No detail escapes regulatory attention. After 239 years of the American military experience in promoting order, discipline, and meting out justice, the modern military justice system is, as one would expect, an extremely comprehensive system. It is as capable of trying capital murder cases as it is in ensuring pay is deducted from a soldier found guilty of disrespect.

Passed in 1950, the UCMJ is a comprehensive criminal code for the Army, Air Force, Navy, and Marine Corps as well as the Coast Guard.[21] This system of military justice, administered under the UCMJ, has been implemented through Executive Orders of the President of the United States pursuant to his authority under Article 36, UCMJ (10 U.S.C. § 836).[22] Those Executive Orders form a comprehensive volume of law compiled in the MCM. The Preamble to the MCM states: "[t]he purpose of military law is to promote justice, to assist in maintaining good order and discipline in the armed forces, to promote efficiency and effectiveness in the military establishment, and thereby to strengthen the national security of the United States."[23]

The UCMJ has worldwide application, and unlike most federal or state criminal statutes, applies extraterritorially to any uniformed member, wherever he or she may commit a crime. This long-arm reach of the military penal code allows commanders to convene criminal trials anywhere in the world, whether on a firebase in Vietnam, the sands of Kuwait at the start of the Persian Gulf War, or in a bombed-out airport in Kandahar, Afghanistan. The notion of a uniform code has nothing to do with the fact that soldiers wear uniforms. Neither does it mean that each armed service does everything the same. The point of uniformity was to establish basic criminal processes that ensured a common application of justice to any service member. Thus, all services are subject to Articles 31 and 37, and all service members benefit from Article 32,[24] although how the various services implement these statutory provisions by regulation differ slightly.

The UCMJ was enacted as a response to the perceived abuses by commanders of its predecessor, the Articles of War (AW).[25] On June 30, 1775, the Second Continental Congress established sixty-nine articles of war to govern the conduct of the Continental Army, adapting the British AW.[26] The Army and Navy used the AW from the Revolution onward without significant change through

---

[21] *See* UCMJ (2012), *available at* http://www.apd.army.mil/pdffiles/mcm.pdf.

[22] 10 U.S.C. § 836 (West Supp. 2014).

[23] MCM, *supra* note 20, at pt. 1, ¶ 3.

[24] The pretrial investigation at the heart of Article 32 was significantly altered in recent legislation. *See, e.g.*, Rear Admiral Sean Buck, *Changes to Article 32 Hearings and Other Victims' Rights: What You Need to Know*, Feb. 3, 2014, *available at* http://navylive.dodlive.mil/2014/02/03/changes-to-article-32-hearings-and-other-victims-rights-what-you-need-to-know/.

[25] *See, e.g.*, Articles of War (1912–1920), Loc.gov, *available at* http://www.loc.gov/rr/frd/Military_Law/AW-1912-1920.html (last visited June 8, 2014).

[26] *Id.*

World War II. Beginning in World War I and reaching a crescendo of criticism after World War II, the AW blossomed into the UCMJ. The AW were not sinister in their language or spirit, but in their application. Commanders, at least those commanders with a stunted sense of justice and fair play, used the AW to the obvious detriment of the soldier.[27] Examples include the courts-martial arising from the 1917 "Houston Mutiny," where thirteen African-American soldiers were convicted and executed within weeks of their sentence and denied any semblance of post-trial appellate review.[28] The increasing focus on military *justice* in the 1940s, as distinct from discipline, gave way to the review of the unfettered authority commanders had for imposing discipline. Following the war the result was an outcry over the greater than two million courts-martial in WW II, and some hundred capital executions, in a total force of some sixteen million,[29] and the abuse of authority by commanders. Commanders were appropriately criticized for sending sentences back to a military panel to be increased, for example. These abuses inspired the UCMJ and the focus on protections for the soldier.

The Code was progressive in its day and remains so today. Sixteen years before *Miranda* rights were recognized by the Supreme Court,[30] the UCMJ required police to read a soldier rights regarding self-incrimination upon suspicion of an offense (unlike the *Miranda* warnings, which require custodial interrogation). The UCMJ, recognizing the pressures of rank and command, deliberately codified that a custodial setting was not required. Even today, custody is not required for the protections to activate; differing from a civilian accused downtown, who must be informed of his rights only if he is in the custody of the police (or in a situation in which a person would reasonably believe she is in custody). This is

---

[27] History, however, is full of examples of vigilant, fastidious commanders with exacting standards and a ruthless and noble adherence to the law. Early examples are not hard to find. General Zachary Taylor was faced with a battalion of Irish deserters who with the promise of land in Mexico fled and fought with the Mexican Army at the start of the Mexican-American War. Upon capture, the Irishmen were court-martialed in courts that were in almost permanent session. They were convicted and sentenced to death. General Taylor commuted the death sentences, reasoning dispassionately that death was not an authorized punishment because at the time of their desertion, the United States had not yet declared war. General Taylor found there was no proof the Irishmen had deserted after the American declaration of war. Such adherence to the law was not a product of fear of appeals or reversals or media criticism—none of which were available at the time. The result speaks to Taylor's sense of fair play and sense of duty. *See generally* Robert Ryal Miller, Shamrock and Sword: The Saint Patrick's Battalion in the U.S.-Mexican War (1989).

[28] *United States v. Sgt. William C. Nesbit et al.* and *United States v. Cpl. Robert Tillman et al., cited in* Garna L. Christian, *The Houston Mutiny of 1917*, 18(1) Trotter Rev., art. 14 (2009), *available at* http://scholarworks.umb.edu/trotter_review/vol18/iss1/14/.

[29] *See* Major George S. Prugh Jr., *Observations of the Uniform Code of Military Justice: 1954 and 2000*, 165 Mil. L. Rev. 21 (2000), *available at* http://www.loc.gov/rr/frd/Military_Law/Military_Law_Review/pdf-files/276085~1.pdf; *see also Military Justice Fact Sheets,* U.S. Marine Corp, http://www.hqmc.marines.mil/Portals/135/MJFACTSHTS%5B1%5D.html (last visited Aug. 24, 2014).

[30] Miranda v. Arizona, 384 U.S. 436 (1966) (holding that statements obtained during custodial interrogation without a warning of his or her rights given to the defendant may not be admitted as evidence).

one of the numerous examples of the Code's progressive quality.[31] Others include the 1968 Amendments to the UCMJ establishing a civilian-styled independent trial judiciary, adoption of the Federal Rules of Evidence, and the 1980 creation of an independent criminal defense bar.

In keeping with this enlightened approach to criminal law, Congress amended Article 120 of the UCMJ in 2007. In so doing the Code acquired one of the most progressive sexual assault proscriptions in the nation, eliminating from the proof process the element that the victim did not consent, and instead causing the focus to shift to the behavior of the accused in using force to effect the crime.[32]

In its basic architecture the Code is simple. It is comprised of 146 Articles—or statutory provisions. It is divided roughly into procedural and substantive sections. The last half of the code contains the punitive articles, those articles that set out crimes and their elements. Supplementing the Code is the Manual for Courts-Martial, as mentioned above.[33] As the name implies, it is designed to inform the practitioner how to conduct a court-martial. Early versions of the MCM were truly hornbooks[34] designed to assist line officers who served as prosecutors. The MCM today is a robust and sophisticated fabric of rules and guidance for licensed uniformed attorneys.

The current MCM, now found in hard copy, and electronically available, is broken into three parts: (1) the Rules for Court-Martial, (2) the Rules of Evidence, and (3) the punitive articles. The law that constitutes the UCMJ empowers the President to make rules for implementing the UCMJ. This is often referred to as the President's rulemaking authority. Using this power the President regularly publishes changes to the MCM.[35]

IV. The Myths of Military Justice

Criminal trials are often the stuff of movies, and not surprisingly, movies are often how the public envisions military justice. In an early scene in *A Few Good Men*[36] Hollywood's fundamental ignorance of military justice is broadly displayed when we learn that the Navy Defense Attorney played by Tom Cruise is

---

[31] Although Article 32's adversarial pretrial hearing also demonstrated the Code's progressive quality, at least in the form of defense rights, this has been altered as mentioned in note 32.

[32] *See* MCM, *supra* note 20, at IV-68 (Uniform Code of Military Justice Article 120); *see also* Lisa M. Schenck, *Sex Offenses under Military Law: Will the Recent Changes in the Uniform of Military Justice (UCMJ) Re-traumatize Sexual Assault Survivors in the Courtroom?*, 11 Ohio St. J. Crim. L. 439 (2014).

[33] *See* MCM, *supra* note 20.

[34] Hornbooks typically provide a synopsis of a particular area of law, and require additional legal knowledge.

[35] *Military Justice Research Guide*, Rutgers Law Library, http://law-library.rutgers.edu/military-justice-research-guide (last visited Sept. 6, 2014).

[36] *A Few Good Men* (1992), IMDB.com, http://www.imdb.com/title/tt0104257/ (last visited June 8, 2014).

selected for a murder case, as he only "deals" (enters pleas of guilt in) his cases, has never seen the inside of a courtroom, and is therefore an "easy mark."[37]

Entertaining as the movie is, this movie's nakedly uninformed portrayal of military justice is profoundly wrong on almost every level of detail. First, military defense attorneys are not chosen by the prosecutor. Second, pleas are not rendered in some commander's office but in a proper courtroom with a military judge and jury. Like so much else in Hollywood or in print media, such "Picasso-like" portraits[38] of justice in the military slides right by the viewer or reader as wildly good entertainment—and unfortunately, over time—begins to root as the truth in the American mind. So the myths inevitably and unwittingly deepen.

Alternatively, media (mis)perception of the military justice system has been defined by big trials, the latest conviction, sentence, or acquittal. The summer of 2013 will be remembered as historic in military justice for many reasons—but primarily for the confluence of three enormously important and high profile trials. It is remarkable that each case—*United States v Hasan*, the Fort Hood shooter; *United States v Manning*; the Wikileaks leaker, and *United States v Bales*, the Afghan shooter—came to conclusion in the same week of August 2013. All three began at different times, and each had separate trial teams on both sides of the bar, and different military judges. The public was then later mesmerized by the tawdry details of a general officer trial in *United States v Sinclair*. A salacious expose on abuse of power and hubris played itself out in a courtroom on Fort Bragg, with the nation watching uncomfortably.

Of course each case is remembered popularly due to the media's chosen focus, not necessarily on the essence of the wrongs addressed at the criminal trials. For Hasan, instead of a focus on the tragic harm suffered, the media and certain politicians focused on his supposed affiliations with terror organizations, the need for Purple Hearts for the victims, and debates about workplace violence.[39] In *Manning*, the efforts of the government to prosecute massive leaks of classified information by abusing combat zone access by an intelligence analyst were criticized because certain aspects of the preliminary hearing and trial had to be closed due to classified evidence.[40] The critics, in their complaints, were unforgiving to the prosecutors who endeavored to minimize even greater, more disastrous disclosures of classified information. Yet, the public story of a high profile case often becomes what the media chooses to focus on. In *Manning*, the

---

[37] *Id.*

[38] Meant to evoke the contrast between extreme expressionism or cubism, and realism in painting. A self-coined phrase simply to denote that Picasso's paintings only in their most rudimentary sense depicted reality—unlike, for example the Hudson River School paintings that sought realism in their paintings of landscapes.

[39] U.S. Dep't of Def., Instr. 1438.06, DoD Workplace Violence Prevention and Response Policy (Jan. 16, 2014), *available at* http://www.dtic.mil/whs/directives/corres/pdf/143806p.pdf.

[40] *Bradley Manning Hearing—Wednesday 21 December*, The Guardian, http://www.theguardian.com/world/blog/2011/dec/21/bradley-manning-hearing-live-updates (last visited Sept. 6, 2014).

storyline migrated from "what is the government hiding," to the bizarre tale of a hapless, misguided young person grappling with transgender issues. The power of good public relations by defense counsel and a 24/7 media cycle can turn military justice and a national security crime and its aftermath into extraordinary theater.

In *United States v. Bales*, myths effectively propagated both early on and in the later stages that somehow Bales's murderous rampage was the result of multiple combat tours, or a malarial drug, which never materialized at trial.[41] Instead of a media focus on the heinousness of the crimes, its cold-blooded hate, and the despicable nature of the blood-soaked Afghan hovels, or even human interest stories on the impact on two Afghan villages and their families, or on the overall mission—the storyline was instead often cast in "DoD is culpable" hues and tints. It is this creatively written public record, propelled by an enormously powerful media, which may alter the factual reality to leave the public viewing military justice in combat in a certain myth-bound landscape. It is also true that in today's instant information-saturation culture, expecting Americans to wait for the story to be told in a courtroom may be asking too much.

It seems that Americans tend to try cases in the media spin cycle. The wife of an accused is interviewed shortly after the allegation of crime surfaces. Eyewitnesses to the crime are interviewed on TV. The case is effectively tried on stage, long before the real facts are tested in the crucible of the courtroom. Americans often forget in the media spin that fundamentally, as a society, they have placed trust in the truth-finding process of the courtroom, where those who may be deprived of their liberty or life are given the opportunity to confront witnesses and question them, and where the government—the people—must prove guilt beyond a reasonable doubt. These principles of balanced scales are the province of the American courtroom—not the interview of a CNN or Fox News reporter. This tension certainly places strains on any system of justice—and for many reasons already discussed, tends to perpetuate myths about military justice.

No doubt, the various and persistent myths of military justice come with the inherent goodness of the exercise of the First Amendment of the U.S. Constitution. And certainly no jurisdiction in the United States is immune from the scrutiny and lens the media and others apply. The point is that crime committed in overseas operations is unique, has both immediate and strategic impact potentially, and captures the public's attention in ways that are both important and profound in consequence.

---

[41] Mark Benjamin, *Robert Bales Charged: Military Works to Limit Malaria Drug in Midst of Afghanistan Nightmare*, Huffington Post (Mar. 25, 2012), http://www.huffingtonpost.com/2012/03/25/robert-bales-malaria-drug_n_1378671.html.

V. Persistent Issues In Deployed Justice

A. CIVILIAN CASUALTIES—THE DEFENSE LEGAL POLICY BOARD AND WINDS OF CHANGE

After a number of years of very public efforts to hold culpable Marines accountable, the Marine Corps announced in January 2012 the results in the last and final prosecution involving the deaths of Iraqi civilians at Haditha.[42] In November 2005, a Marine squad on a vehicle resupply mission hit an IED and sustained one killed and two injured Marines. The Command sent two quick reaction elements to help secure the site. After arrival, Marines cleared (neutralized threats, to include shooting to kill occupants) nearby houses from which, it was said, hostile fire had emanated. The resulting house clearing left twenty-four Iraqis dead. Multiple, lengthy investigations ensued.[43] An NCO would plead guilty to dereliction of duty.[44] For this the NCO was sentenced to ninety days of confinement, reduction to the lowest enlisted grade, and forfeiture of $984 for each of three months. Because of a pretrial agreement, the confinement was disapproved so the NCO would only be reduced in rank and forfeit his pay.[45] The media castigated this apparent meager trial result after six years of effort.[46]

Some leaders inside the Pentagon may have harbored the view that military justice failed to deliver justice regarding civilian deaths on the battlefield.[47] Six months after the conclusion of this case, on July 30, 2012, the Secretary of Defense Leon Panetta published his order to convene the Defense Legal Policy Board (DLPB).[48] Although "abuses have been rare among our professional fighting force," Panetta wrote, they became "huge flash points that threatened

---

[42] Charlene Savage, *An Iraqi Massacre, a Light Sentence and a Question of Military Justice*, N.Y. Times (Jan. 27, 2012), http://www.nytimes.com/2012/01/28/us/an-iraqi-massacre-a-light-sentence-and-a-question-of-military-justice.html?pagewanted=all&_r=0.

[43] Tim McGrick, *Collateral Damage or Civilian Massacre in Haditha?*, Time (Mar. 19, 2006), http://content.time.com/time/world/article/0,8599,1174649,00.html.

[44] The dereliction was cast as issuing an order to "shoot first and ask questions later." DLPB Report, App V, DLPB Case Studies at 162. The final judicial action was focused on the court-martial of Marine Sergeant Frank Wuterich.

[45] For a discussion of the Wuterich court-martial, see http://www.cnn.com/2012/01/24/justice/california-iraq-trial/ (last visited June 6, 2015).

[46] "It was the massacre which left 24 unarmed Iraqis dead and cast fresh shame on the American military, already reeling from Abu-Ghraib. But a military judge yesterday ruled that the final U.S. soldier to face charges over the notorious assault on Haditha will not be jailed." *See* http://www.dailymail.co.uk/news/article-2091333/Frank-Wuterich-trial-Stunning-denial-US-Marine-Haditha-massacre-court-martial.html (last visited June 6, 2015).

[47] Author's observation.

[48] *See* Establishment of the Defense Legal Policy Board, April 6, 2012, *available at*: https://www.federalregister.gov/articles/2012/04/06/2012-8251/establishment-of-the-defense-legal-policy-board ; *see also See* U.S. Dep't of Def., Report of the Subcommittee on Military Justice in Combat Zones, at 133 (May 30, 2013) [hereinafter DLPB Report], *available at* http://www.caaflog.com/wp-content/uploads/20130531-Subcommittee-Report-REPORT-OF-THE-SUBCOMMITTEE-ON-MILITARY-JUSTICE-IN-COMBAT-ZONES-31-May-13-2.pdf. (last viewed June 8, 2014).

to undermine our entire mission . . . . [I]t is critical that our system of military justice be efficient, fair, dependable, and credible. . . . we must get this right."[49] Panetta then appointed a distinguished group of Americans to evaluate and report to him on the ability of the military justice system to address the abuse, injury, or death of noncombatants in a combat zone.[50]

The DLPB's procedures included hearings with testimony from commanders, investigators, judge advocates, other experts, special interest groups, critics, and even parents of soldiers convicted for such crimes, including the parents of First Lieutenant Michael Behenna. The DLPB's yearlong effort generated a comprehensive, well-written, and forward-thinking report published in May 2013.[51] Its manifold recommendations affirmed the central role of the commander in establishing and maintaining discipline, stressed the need for improved administration of justice by a joint force commander, marked the necessity of trying cases forward, and called attention to the persistent and troubling critical seam in effective accountability over contractors, among other important findings.[52]

Indeed, the DLPB found serious flaws in deployed defense contractor accountability.[53] These flaws permitted crimes to go unpunished, resulting in strategic impact on the mission.[54] Perhaps most significant is that the DLPB was the first comprehensive, reflective report on the operations of military justice in theater. Although its aperture was limited to crimes involving civilian injury or death, the report is also important as its membership was a distinguished group of American policymakers and diplomats who rendered a holistic appraisal of a military criminal law in operation in combat—without bias or agenda.[55] The DLPB's comprehensive and authoritative imprimatur of a commander-centric military justice system makes it an enduring contribution to any serious student of the law, and military law in particular.

As succinctly stated by the DLPB in its May 2013 report,

> [s]ince the initiation of Operation Enduring Freedom in 2001, the Services have demonstrated increasing proficiency in the administration of military justice in the deployed environment. Between 2001 and 2011, the Army conducted over 800 courts-martial in the deployed environment. During that same time, the Navy and Marine Corps conducted eight courts-martial in Afghanistan and 34 in Iraq. The Air Force conducted ten courts-martial in Iraq and three in Afghanistan.[56]

---

[49] *See* DLPB Report, *supra* note 48, at 134–36.
[50] *Id.*
[51] *Id.*
[52] DLPB Report, Recommendations, *supra* note 48, at 144.
[53] DLPB Report, *supra* note 48, at 125–30.
[54] Notwithstanding the Alaa Ali case tried in 2008.
[55] DLPB Report, *supra* note 48, at i.
[56] *Id.* at 91–92.

Significantly, these numbers do not account for those cases that began in theater, but given late discovery of the offense, complexity, gravity, time, and unit rotations were tried at home station. There are many in the latter category. However, the Army does not maintain a central tracking system, and therefore the multitude of such cases is not known. The author's personal estimate would place that number at twice the number actually tried in theater.[57] Indeed, most of the high-profile cases highlighted in this chapter certainly began in the war zone, but for a host of sound reasons, were tried in garrison in the United States.

The unique nature of Army culture, and disparate concentration of land forces on twelve-to-eighteen-month deployment rotations, may explain the wide disparity between the military services. Many Army commanders, for example, take an intensely proprietary approach to command and inherent responsibility for unit discipline, and so are less willing to simply transition offending soldiers back home to be dealt with by another commander. The enduring nature of Army deployments, as well, afforded commanders and their judge advocates the opportunity to develop the physical and professional infrastructure (courts, judges, defense counsel, court reporters, etc.) required to administer military justice. The Air Force, Navy, and Marine Corps acknowledge their combat theater courtroom footprint during the past twelve years of war was small—favoring instead trial in the United States.[58] Consequently, the discussion below is Army-centric, but importantly represents the bulk of wartime courtroom activity for U.S. forces deployed to both theaters.

Day-to-day, military prosecutors, defense counsel, judges, staff judge advocates, and general court-martial convening authorities wrestled with the typical variety of misconduct, and handled much of it, indeed most of it outside the courtroom through lesser disciplinary measures such as counseling, reprimands, and Article 15, UCMJ. Drinking alcohol in violation of the punitive General Order or the accidental discharge of a weapon into a clearing barrel without injury were typically resolved through reprimands or Article 15. For those cases that impelled court-martial, commanders and their legal personnel were able to try cases at virtually any point throughout either theater of war, and did.

Very often serious cases including murder would be charged, the Article 32 investigation would be conducted in theater, and the case would return to home station for trial. Courtroom venues varied. The Army has always brought its justice system forward. Trials, the most visible manifestation of the system, found a home early in Afghanistan and Iraq in the most humble settings. Retrofitted conference rooms of old Russian HQ buildings on Bagram Airfield or rooms within the bombed-out Kandahar airfield were used early for trials. Later, large metal Conex shipping containers could be seen forming part of a courtroom, or entirely new buildings fabricated from countless sheets of plywood. The variety was as endless as the American soldier is creative, and in that trait there is truly no limit.

---

[57] Author's Note: this conclusion is based upon my observations during assignments with primary responsibilities that included, for four years, Army-wide management of the military justice function from 2002 to 2014.

[58] *See* DLPB Report, *supra* note 48, at 26.

B. SENIOR LEADER ACCOUNTABILITY

Throughout over a decade of war, persistent criticism has centered on the extent to which senior leaders are responsible for their own criminal acts, as well as the criminal acts of soldiers under their command and control. This notion saw its attention zenith after World War II, focusing on the Nuremburg trials and those of the Commissions in the Far East under General Douglas MacArthur.[59] Examples from the most current wars are plentiful. The most notorious cases centered on the abuse of detainees at the Abu Ghraib prison in Iraq from 2003 to 2004. When military police guards in the Abu Ghraib prison abused Iraqi detainees, there were vigorous and sustained calls in the media to hold senior leaders, including the Commander of the 525th Battlefield Surveillance Brigade, the Commanding General of the 800th MP Brigade, and even the Secretary of Defense, accountable for the criminal acts of military police on the graveyard shift. One investigation followed another until there was quite literally too many to count.[60] The most comprehensive report was, perhaps, the one published by the Senate Armed Services Committee in 2008.[61] Striking in its bipartisanship, the report echoed many of the Department of Defense (DoD) and other examinations of the issues surrounding detainee abuse. In the end, it seems the conclusions of any of these reports could never escape the terribly politicized nature of the war and its resulting confounding issues surrounding the policy and treatment of detainees in what was widely debated as a new paradigm of detainees who were considered neither civilians nor prisoners of war.[62]

Most recently, murder cases from Afghanistan in 2010 once again raised the issue of command responsibility. The 5-2 Stryker Brigade operated in the Maywand District of the Kandahar Province under the command of Colonel Harry Tunnell, an experienced combat leader who was seriously wounded in Iraq early in the war as a Battalion Commander.[63] Soldiers within his brigade began to deliberately kill innocent Afghans for sport and masked the killings to their immediate commanders as self-defense firefights. The Company and Battalion commanders received reports of these Afghan engagements and deaths, and upon query were told that the Afghans had opened fire on the U.S. forces, in response to which soldiers engaged and killed the Afghans. Members of this corrupt squad even left what were called "drop weapons" at the scene to convince

---

[59] Victor Hansen, *What's Good for the Goose Is Good for the Gander Lessons from Abu Ghraib: Time for the United States to Adopt a Standard of Command Responsibility towards Its Own*, 42 Gonz. L. Rev. 335 (2007).

[60] The essential question never really was answered: How did these soldiers lose their moral compass so completely?

[61] Staff of S. Comm. on Armed Services, 110th Congress, Inquiry into the Treatment of Detainees in U.S. Custody (Comm. Print 2008).

[62] *Id.* at 2.

[63] Rajiv Chandrasekaran, *Search and Destroy*, Slate, http://www.slate.com/articles/news_and_politics/foreigners/2012/06/the_war_in_afghanistan_and_harry_tunnell_s_stryker_battalion.html (last visited Sept. 6, 2014).

their superiors that the Afghan citizens had indeed been firing at the soldiers. The ruses apparently worked, for a time. [64]

The murders were concealed by an effective cone of silence within the squad until one junior soldier was found using marijuana on the Combat Outpost. While being interviewed for drug abuse charges, he implicated his squad members, and in particular his squad leader, Staff Sergeant Calvin Gibbs. Once the lid was off the story, a lengthy United States Army Criminal Investigation Command (CID) investigation followed and resulted in eleven courts-martial, all conducted at Joint Base Lewis McChord. At his court-martial, Gibbs was convicted of premeditated murder and given a life sentence for manufacturing three murders.[65]

Although the CID investigation implicated a squad-level[66] conspiracy, it was not long before critics began suggesting that responsibility for such crime could reasonably rest with the Brigade Commander. The question that burned like a brush fire in the media was how such a thing could happen without the leadership knowing.[67] Was the squad's cavalier, callous, and brutal approach to Afghans a product of a command climate that fostered a "mere Afghan" mentality? This same soldier dynamic of dehumanizing the enemy, common in many wars, especially unconventional war, resulted in such derogatory terms as "gook" in Vietnam, leading the Peers Inquiry to assess that dehumanization of an opponent, although natural, can lead to unintended consequences.[68] As is often the case, the command initiated its own investigation of the command climate to see what might have contributed to Staff Sergeant Gibbs and his soldiers' conduct.

The supposed nexus between command climate and criminal behavior was purportedly the Brigade Commander's vocal combat philosophy that on the surface appeared to place him at odds with the "Tactical Directive" governing counterinsurgency operations at the time in Afghanistan.[69] Colonel Tunnell's approach was often described as kinetic, to the detriment of capacity building.[70]

---

[64] *Id.*

[65] Patrick Oppmann, *Soldier Found Guilty of Murdering Afghans, Sentenced to Life*, CNN.com (Nov. 11, 2011), http://www.cnn.com/2011/11/10/justice/soldier-murder--rial/.

[66] Author's note: An Army squad typically consists of nine to ten soldiers, commanded by a sergeant or staff sergeant. A squad or section is the smallest element in the Army structure, and its size is dependent on its function. *See, e.g., U.S. Army Infantry Squad Organization*, America's Army, http://manual.americasarmy.com/index.php/U.S._Army_Infantry_Squad_Organization (last visited Sept. 6, 2014).

[67] Author's observation.

[68] The Peers Inquiry was the official U.S. Army investigation into the Army's massacre of civilians at My Lai during the conflict in Vietnam. *See* Robert Rielly, *The Inclination for War Crimes*, Military Rev. (May–June 2009), *available at* http://usacac.army.mil/CAC2/MilitaryReview/Archives/English/MilitaryReview_20090630_art006.pdf.

[69] N. Atl. Treaty Org. [NATO], *Tactical Directive* (July 6, 2009) [hereinafter *Tactical Directive*], *available at* http://www.nato.int/isaf/docu/official_texts/Tactical_Directive_090706.pdf.

[70] Sean D. Naylor, *Stryker Soldiers Say Commanders Failed Them*, Army Times (Dec. 21, 2009), http://www.armytimes.com/article/20091221/NEWS/912210313/Stryker-soldiers-say-commanders-failed-them.

The governing tactical directive's essential focus was on building relationships and capacity and minimizing kinetic operations.[71] This guidance reflected a concern that kintetic philosophies such as Colonel Tunnell's might operate on the squad-level soldier to such a degree that the soldier would begin to devalue and objectify Afghan life, thereby breaking down respect for civilians.[72]

However, the simple truth was that there was no evidence that the intellectual differences between the Brigade Commander and the Tactical Directive was connected to the deliberate, calculated, and methodical murders by a squad three echelons below this commander. More illuminating is that eleven criminal trials with multiple different defense attorneys and accused failed to develop any culpability on the part of senior leadership. However, the specter of command responsibility is so powerful that the matter still resonates with the media and critics.

C. CONTRACTORS

1. Jurisdictional Tools

During recent conflicts truly staggering number of contractors supported the military forces; in the case of Afghanistan in 2013, the United States employed over a hundred thousand contractors, or approximately 1.6 contractors for every American soldier.[73] Also staggering was the notion that no courts were capable of addressing the misdeeds of contractors. The Military Extraterritorial Jurisdiction Act (MEJA), passed in 2000, was not really viable until 2005 when implementing regulations were finally published.[74] Even after rules were established, prosecutions were rare. The MEJA allows federal prosecutors in the United States to prosecute contractors overseas who (1) work for or are in support of the DoD

---

[71] *Tactical Directive, supra* note 69.

[72] *Id.*

[73] *See, e.g.*, Kevin H. Govern & Eric C. Bales, *Taking Shots at Private Military Firms: International Law Misses Its Mark (Again)*, 32(1) FORDHAM INT'L LAW J. 55–95 (2008), *available at* http://papers.ssrn.com/sol3/papers.cfm?abstract_id=2070437 (last visited June 8, 2014); *see also* Aubrey Bloomfield, *108,000 Private Contractors Are in Afghanistan and We Have No Idea What They're Doing*, POLICYMIC.COM (June 5, 2013), *available at* http://www.policymic.com/articles/46621/108-000-private-contractors-are-in-afghanistan-and-we-have-no-idea-what-they-re-doing (last visited June 8, 2014):

> Two recently released reports, one by the Congressional Research Service (CRS) and one by the Government Accountability Office (GAO), show that not only is the number of private contractors in Afghanistan increasing, but the Pentagon is also unable to tell what they are even doing there. Citing the reports, David Francis of the *Fiscal Times* points out that there are now 108,000 private contractors in Afghanistan (over 30,000 of whom are Americans), far more than the 65,700 U.S. troops still there.

Id.

[74] 18 U.S.C. § 3261 (2010).

mission ,(2) if the offense is a felony crime, and (3) the accused is not a citizen of the host nation.[75]

With the debate continuing to rage over contractor accountability for crimes in 2005 and 2006 and the persistent paucity of trials, Senator Lindsay Graham inserted into the 2007 National Defense Authorization Act a potentially far-reaching provision under Article 2, UCMJ. His amendment added to the UCMJ a basis under Article 2 for commanders to prosecute at court-martial contractors who were serving with the armed forces in a contingency operation.[76] This is further evidence of the confidence some senior civilian leaders have in the capacity of the military to mete justice to the standard of American jurisprudence, and of the integral importance of its portability into combat and contingency operations.

Although the jurisdictional reach would excite any military prosecutor in a deployed environment, it was not long before process requirements published by DoD operated as de facto chilling measures on the reach of Article 2. In the eyes of some, it just became too hard. Nonetheless, in 2008, a contract interpreter for the Army named Alaa Ali stabbed a fellow interpreter and the first test case, and so far the last test case, began to take shape. Through sheer force of will and sense of right, and despite many obstacles and procedural setbacks, Ali was prosecuted at court-martial by the U.S. military command in Iraq. It became the necessary test case and is now historic in fact and in legal precedent.

In this case of *United States v Ali*, the Army prosecuted a Canadian-Iraqi dual national interpreter for aggravated assault against a fellow interpreter. The issues were abundant, from pretrial confinement to whether a defense of peaceful character required flying his wife into theater as a character witness.[77] In the end the case was tried; Ali was convicted and sentenced to five months of confinement. As the sentence length did not require a review by the Army Court of Criminal Appeals (ACCA), The Judge Advocate General certified the issue to ACCA for resolution.[78]

Both ACCA and later the United States Court of Appeals for the Armed Forces (CAAF) affirmed the Ali conviction and sentence. The U.S. Supreme Court denied certiorari in 2012.[79] Hence the Ali precedent likely means that the expanded Article 2 passes constitutional muster. No doubt there are unexplored corners of Ali regarding the trial of civilians accompanying the force. This is

---

[75] *Id.*

[76] Joint Chiefs of Staff, Joint Pub. 1-02, Department of Defense Dictionary of Military and Associated Terms, at 53 (Nov. 8, 2010), *available at* http://www.dtic.mil/doctrine/new_pubs/jp1_02.pdf.

> contingency operation—A military operation that is either designated by the Secretary of Defense as a contingency operation or becomes a contingency operation as a matter of law (Title 10, United States Code, Section 101[a][13]). See also contingency; operation. (JP 1).

Id.

[77] United States v. Ali, 71 M.J. 256 (C.A.A.F. 2012).

[78] *Id.*

[79] Ali v. United States, 133 S. Ct. 2338 (2013).

especially true in cases when the Department of Justice (DoJ) actually has jurisdiction under MEJA—which it did not possess in Ali. The contours remain somewhat gray—but well worth the next vanguard's exploration and lawmaking.

2. Blackwater, Nisour Square, and the Short Arm of the Law

On September 16, 2007, contractors working for the Department of State (DoS) shot and killed seventeen Iraqi civilians and injured another twenty in Nisour Square, Baghdad. Blackwater operated as a private security company in support of the DoS mission around Iraq. On that fateful day, a Personal Security Detail provided security for a convoy of DoS diplomats driving to a meeting in Baghdad with officials of the United States Agency for International Development. Their apparent indiscriminate killings and injuries outraged Iraqis and strained relations between Iraq and Washington.[80]

The Blackwater guards claimed they were ambushed and returned fire in self-defense. The Iraqi government found that the killings were unprovoked. The *Washington Post* cited a military report that appeared to agree with "the Iraqi government's contention that Blackwater was at fault."[81] The incident sparked at least five investigations. An FBI investigation found that at least fourteen of the fatalities were without cause.[82] In September 2008, the DoJ, not the military commander with operational control over Baghdad, charged five Blackwater guards with fourteen counts of manslaughter, twenty counts of attempted manslaughter, and a weapons violation.[83] However, a year later in December 2009, a U.S. district judge dismissed all charges on the grounds that the case against the Blackwater guards was built on immunized testimony. More outrage erupted in Iraq. Sixteen months later, in April 2011 a U.S. federal appeals court reinstated the manslaughter charges against some of the defendants. The proceedings against the four guards ultimately resulted in numerous convictions.[84]

There are several simple facts about current military jurisdictional shortcomings. Even as expansively written as it is, Article 2, UCMJ does not reach non-DoD U.S. agencies operating in the combat commanders' battle space. It should. The second simple fact is that the MEJA does not apply either. The MEJA

---

[80] James Glanz, *From Errand to Fatal Shot to Hail of Fire to 17 Deaths*, N.Y. Times (Oct. 3, 2007), http://www.nytimes.com/2007/10/03/world/middleeast/03firefight.html?pagewanted=all&_r=0.

[81] Sudarsan Raghavan et al., *Blackwater Faulted in Military Reports from Shooting Scene*, Wash. Post (Oct. 5, 2007), http://www.washingtonpost.com/wp-dyn/content/article/2007/10/04/AR2007100402654.html.

[82] David Johnston & John M. Broder, *F.B.I. Say Guards Killed 14 Iraqis without Cause*, N.Y. Times (Nov. 14, 2007), http://www.nytimes.com/2007/11/14/world/middleeast/14blackwater.html?pagewanted=all.

[83] Press Release, U.S. Dep't of Justice, Five Blackwater Employees Indicted on Manslaughter and Weapons Charges for Fatal Nisur Square Shooting in Iraq (Dec. 8, 2008), *available at* http://www.justice.gov/opa/pr/2008/December/08-nsd-1068.html.

[84] John Queally, *DOJ Brings Fresh Manslaughter Charges against Blackwater Mercenaries for Iraqi Massacre*, Common Dreams (Oct. 18, 2013), http://www.commondreams.org/news/2013/10/18/doj-brings-fresh-manslaughter-charges-against-blackwater-mercenaries-iraqi-massacre.

is limited to contractors working for DoD and those in support of the DoD mission. Blackwater worked for DoS, and DoS does not "work for" DoD. Hence the legal impediments are daunting. As a matter of legislation, this potential seam, like Article 2's limit, can be easily fixed (despite DoJ's successful convictions in the Blackwater incident, made quite difficult by the extraterritorial jurisdictions issues). That is, the events following the aftermath of Blackwater in Nisour Square are as significant for their loss of life as they are for placing into inescapable relief the fact that under current law contractors working for U.S. agencies outside of DoD could potentially operate with impunity, or at least federal prosecutors attempting to hold them accountable face difficult jurisdictional challenges. These challenges could be easily lessened with legislation.

VI. Is Justice Portable?

A. A MATTER OF WILL, NOT CAPABILITY OR CAPACITY

Since 1775 the Army has conducted courts-martial in the field of operations.[85] This facet of portable justice remains just as important today. Advances in telecommunications, high-speed scanners, and Tandberg VTCs[86] do not replicate the stark reality of being present when soldiers in open court face criminal justice. Whether it is for crimes against fellow soldiers, or crimes against local inhabitants, or crimes of indiscipline such as wrongful consumption of alcohol, the message is proximate, immediate, and unmistakable. Judge Wayne Alley opined about his time as a military judge in Vietnam that ". . . we should try cases forward . . . and they should be located in theater . . . . There's an atmosphere. When a case is a combat refusal, to join your unit in the line or refusal of an order in the field, . . . that is not a rear area case."[87]

In the conflicts in Iraq and Afghanistan the debate among judge advocates has been healthy and vigorous on the issue of whether the military can and should still deliver this important service to commanders in the forward areas. Two respected judge advocates set out both sides of the argument in compelling articles in recent years.[88] The upshot from the articles taken together is whether the

[85] *United States Court of Appeals for the Armed Forces*, USCourts.gov, http://www.armfor.uscourts.gov/newcaaf/about.htm (last visited Sept. 7, 2014).

[86] A Tandberg is a commercial product that is essentially a video teleconference device.

[87] Colonel George R. Smawley, *In Pursuit of Justice, a Life of Law and Public Service: United States District Court Judge and Brigadier General (Retired) Wayne E. Alley (U.S. Army 1952–1954, 1959–1981)*, 208 Mil. L. Rev. 213, 216 (2011), *available at* https://www.jagcnet.army.mil/DOCLIBS/MILITARYLAWREVIEW.NSF/20a66345129fe3d885256e5b00571830/eac4e29c03a4343b85257991004c3ddo/$FILE/Article%202%20-%20By%20COL%20George%20R.%20Smawley.pdf.

[88] *Compare* Major Franklin D. Rosenblatt, *Non-deployable: The Court- Martial System in Combat from 2001 to 2009*, Army Law. 12–34 (Sept. 2010) (arguing that courts-martial are difficult to conduct in a deployed environment, with substantial statistics supporting this point), *with* Major E. John Gregory, *The Deployed Court-Martial Experience in Iraq 2010: A Model for Success*, Army Law. 6–34 (Jan. 2012) (attempting to show that courts-martial can be successful in a deployed environment).

drive to ensure constitutional fairness during a criminal trial can be achieved in forward areas. Witness availability for the accused to mount his defense is often cited as the principle obstacle. Much like in the movie *Breaker Morant*, those witnesses who gave Lieutenant Morant the order to shoot prisoners were curiously all ordered to India prior to trial, and were ruled unavailable for Morant's trial. In modern American military courtrooms, such witnesses are often ordered produced, and the government must make a practical decision whether the production is worth the unit and institutional effort.[89]

At no time was this question more frequently asked than in 2011, the final year of America's foray into Iraq, during OPERATION NEW DAWN. During that year U.S. forces, principally the Army, repostured three Infantry division headquarters and a force of fifty thousand train-and-assist personnel out of Iraq. That final year was characterized by a worsening security situation, political uncertainty regarding an enduring American presence, a commitment to partnering and capacity building with Iraqi security forces, and the challenge of rapidly shrinking the U.S. footprint via base closures, transportation, and transfer of massive amounts of equipment, transitions to the Embassy, and the movement of forces out of the country after nine years of war.

It was in this environment that most Army commanders steadfastly decided to continue to underwrite the administration of military justice within their formations, rather than send the cases back to the United States for trial. Certainly, there were dramatic and complex cases clearly beyond the remit of a withdrawing force to properly adjudicate. One such example was that against Army Specialist Neftaly Platero, who was charged with premeditated murder for the September 23, 2010, shooting of three of his roommates at their base near Fallujah, in which two soldiers later died and the third was grievously injured. The case was ultimately tried at Platero's home station at Fort Stewart, Georgia, near Savannah, where he was sentenced to life in prison.

Importantly, however, the extensive Article 32, UCMJ, investigation leading up to the court-martial was conducted in Iraq where the soldier's unit was stationed. Platero was kept in pretrial confinement in Kuwait while the government and defense worked through pretrial hearings, leading up to a week-long investigative hearing by an officer who also happened to be a military judge (although that was not required). The hearing featured over forty witnesses from Platero's unit, and six different defense counsel, including two civilian attorneys and one civilian expert hired by the defendant and brought into Iraq from the United States. The entire hearing was conducted in Fallujah in the Spring of 2011, because that was where the crime occurred, where the military witnesses were assigned, and where the officers whose soldiers had been brutally murdered were in command. The trial itself did not occur until a year later on June 13, 2012, after

---

[89] *The Juice Iis Worth the Squeeze*, URBAN DICTIONARY, http://www.urbandictionary.com/define.php?term=The+juice+is+worth+the+squeeze (last visited Sept. 7, 2014) ("Knowing if something is worth the trouble of trying to get it, i.e. does the reward outweigh the punishment.").

U.S. forces had departed Iraq. But the unit's willingness to commit vast time and resources (such as helicopters and convoys from Baghdad to Fallujah) to facilitate the system of military justice through the Article 32 investigation speaks volumes to Army culture, and its commitment to the portability of the military justice system.

That commitment found expression in the dozens of cases conducted in Iraq in 2011, and the willingness of the Army judiciary to forward-deploy a military judge to the region to oversee them. One, in particular, merits mention for the way it epitomized the capacity of the Army to mete out justice in a collapsing theater of operations. In *United States v. Elliot Carrasquillo*,[90] the defendant was a New York National Guardsman assigned as a military policeman in Al Asad Airbase, a sprawling facility located in the western Al Anbar Province, Iraq. In the course of his police duties, Specialist Carrasquillo became aware that a local Iraqi businessman, Mr. Diia, who lived and worked on the base, maintained a large cache of American dollars used in his day- to-day transactions with U.S. personnel, principally related to maintenance work. On April 1, 2011, the day before Carrasquillo and his unit were due to return to the United States, he and two codefendants forcibly entered Mr. Diia's housing unit at gunpoint, tied him up, and robbed him of $380,000. The plan was to hide the money on the departing plane the next day, and divide the money upon their redeployment to the United States.

Within twenty-four hours the money was found and a fellow soldier, who had been approached about the conspiracy but declined, revealed the identity of the offenders. The question was how to handle the misconduct for soldiers in a National Guard unit that was redeploying and scheduled to demobilize, fewer than eight months prior to the complete cessation of U.S. operations in Iraq. In a bold move driven by the desire to ensure justice was done and, collaterally, to demonstrate to Iraqis that U.S. commanders took violence against civilians seriously, the chain of command decided to transfer the three defendants to the headquarters and headquarters battalion (HHBN) for the active-duty 25th Infantry Division (their higher command), thereby preserving jurisdiction over the soldiers while their unit redeployed back to New York. In so doing, the command and its judge advocates committed to achieving justice in a set of burglary and robbery cases involving an Iraqi civilian in theater, during the waning days of the operation.

Within ninety days, all three defendants had separate Article 32 hearings, each involving military defense counsel, military police investigators, the Iraqi victim, and a translator who traveled the 119 miles from Al Asad to Baghdad for testimony as required. Following a series of pretrial motions, Specialist Carrasquillo, the mastermind of the conspiracy and its most culpable member, was tried at

---

[90] United States v. Specialist Elliot Carrasquillo (ACCA, 2011), *available at* https://www.jagcnet.army.mil/Portals%5CFiles%5CACCAOther.nsf/OD/1B9FAC3AB8A6010985257C37004EE26D/$FILE/oc-carrasquillo,%20em.pdf.

a contested court-martial comprised of officers and enlisted panel members on August 17, 2011, at Camp Liberty, Iraq. He was sentenced to ten years confinement and a dishonorable discharge. His codefendant, Specialist Travis Jones, was tried by a officer and enlisted panel on August 9, 2011, at Camp Liberty, where he was sentenced to two years confinement and a bad conduct discharge.[91] The third defendant was returned to the United States for trial following prolonged plea negotiations involving civilian counsel. He was subsequently convicted by a court-martial and received a two-year sentence and a bad conduct discharge. All three cases survived various appellate reviews.

Following their respective courts-martial, both Carrasquillo and Jones were remanded to the provost martial with onward movement by HHBN to Kuwait, enroute to confinement in the United States. Army attorneys, paralegals, judges, and court reporters completed the record of trial in time for the commanding general for the 25th Infantry Division to take final action in both cases while still in theater on December 3, 2011, fourteen days before the division redeployed out of Iraq, essentially closing the theater of operations. The signed action and court record were hand delivered to Kuwait by a paralegal noncommissioned officer due to the absence of U.S. or military postal service. These two cases represent the type of felony-level misconduct many commanders faced in Iraq and Afghanistan, occasionally victimizing local civilians and deeply contrary to American values and the good order of the force. Although not as dramatic or complex as the *Manning* case, or *Akbar*, or those arising from Abu Gharaib, *Carrasquillo* and *Jones* represent the capacity of commanders and the UCMJ to mete out justice during operations in a timely, efficient, and highly responsible manner.

Thus, the root criticism in current discourse centers more on degrees of difficulty, not on impossibility. Difficulty is a question of will and thus, surmountable through leadership and good lawyering. However, an additional criticism centers on a supposed inability to project courtrooms to smaller operating bases. The argument suggests that the military can only do justice at those "bases with Burger Kings," military vernacular not just reflecting the fast-food choices available, but rather, larger bases with adequate transportation and larger populations to support the court-martial business, such as panel members.

Both criticisms are misplaced, and as the contrary view is exposited in Major E. John Gregory's article, obstacles to modern justice in the field is primarily a function of personal will, knowledge of the law, and experience in its application. Similarly, the DLPB examined these issues in detail and found in its extensive fact finding that not only did the Army effectively try cases in forward areas in the combat zone, but that the capacity to do so remains a critical feature of future combat and force projection.

---

[91] United States v. Travis Jones (CAAF, 2011), *available at* http://www.armfor.uscourts.gov/newcaaf/opinions/2013SepTerm/140071.pdf.

B. UNITARY JUSTICE

A curious permutation of conducting military justice in a deployed location is the notion that commanders who leave the Continental United States (CONUS) still maintain jurisdiction despite being thousands of miles away. In this scenario, the General Court-Martial Convening Authority continues to refer cases to trial at say, Fort Riley, Kansas, while he also refers cases to trial in Afghanistan or Iraq while he is deployed. Normally, a Commanding General "takes the flag" (deploys the command element) forward to the combat zone and leaves residual general court authority at home station to continue military justice operations. Such a commander desists thereupon in influencing the military justice process at home and leaves to his Rear Commander the responsibility for referring cases to trial upon the advice of the Staff Judge Advocate in garrison.

In 2010, the Commander of the 25th Infantry Division (25th ID) in Hawaii, and his Staff Judge Advocate challenged this time-honored paradigm. Facing enormous challenges of distance and communications, the vision of the Commander and Staff Judge Advocate of unitary justice operations succeeded. The able demonstration of this manpower and time-intensive groundbreaking venture is expertly captured and explained in a recent article by the Staff Judge Advocate responsible for its acknowledged success.[92]

Such an approach is rare, not least because it requires a commanding general indisputably dedicated to the proposition and a legal staff of immense capacity and endurance. The 25th ID had both, in abundance. Cautions abound however. What must be constantly assessed, of course, is whether there is a field skew to the cases taken and not taken to court in the rear given the thinner resources, or physical absence of senior leaders. This is no small reality as some units during twelve years of war lost much of their justice practice to local civilian prosecutors. Regardless, unitary justice is rare, and it should be, but is certainly doable, and something every commander and staff judge advocate should discuss prior to deployment.[93]

C. NOTEWORTHY CASES

Somewhat like certain combat events of the last twelve years of war (Tora Bora, the capture of Saddam Hussein, or the raid that killed Osama bin Laden), certain trials of these two wars have helped to define this epoch in military justice. These cases, although interesting in their own right, are also significant in their import. Each speaks volumes about the brutality and ugliness of war. Although such

---

[92] A great accomplishment, maybe even the first instance of this under the 1984 Manual for Courts-Martial, but not the first instance this has ever been done, especially under the 1951 and 1969 MCM. *See* Colonel George Smawley, *Making Justice Flat: A Challenge to the View That Deploying Commanders Must Relinquish Command and General Court-Martial Convening Authority over Non-deploying Forces*, ARMY LAW. (Jan. 2013), *available at* http://www.loc.gov/rr/frd/Military_Law/pdf/01-2013.pdf.

[93] Author's observation.

lessons are not new to any army, they do remind all that the human condition, in every age, is liable to such transgressions. High-profile cases tend to define periods of war. Certain particularly noteworthy cases occupy a special place in the history of military justice in the late wars. The Nuremburg Trials define a certain accounting for crimes following World War II.[94] The case of Second Lieutenant William Calley tends to define in the public mind the tensions of the Vietnam War.[95]

Although none of the trials outlined here were tried in theater, each represents that crime in combat remains a dramatically different sort of crime. Perhaps more important, each of these cases originated as the result of the leverage of the military justice system by commanders and the Judge Advocates supporting them at the tip of the proverbial spear. Accordingly, each represents the centrality of the portable military justice system to the effective response to allegations of battlefield misconduct. In this sense, these examples are truly illustrative, because for every high-profile case there were dozens more cases of misconduct addressed through the military justice system. Ultimately, these cases all highlight what commanders have always known: the importance of good order and discipline is indelibly linked to combat effectiveness, and a military justice system that is responsive to all acts of misconduct in all environs is an indispensable tool in the commander's arsenal for maintaining good order and discipline.

It began most visibly with *United States v. Akbar*, a soldier now awaiting appellate review of his trial and execution of his death sentence for murdering fellow soldiers on the eve of the start of the war.

1. Death and Fragging on the Berm—The Case of *United States v. Akbar*[96]

Just before the start of the U.S. invastion of Iraq on the early morning hours of March 23, 2003, at Camp Pennsylvania, Kuwait Sergeant Hasan Akbar threw four hand grenades into three tents in which fellow 101st Airborne Division soldiers were sleeping. Akbar carefully selected his targets to immobilize his unit, a brigade scheduled to launch an attack the next day. The first tent contained the brigade commander and his staff. Akbar then fired his rifle at fellow soldiers, in the ensuing chaos killing Captain Christopher S. Seifert who was shot in the back at a range of a few feet, and Major Gregory L. Stone who was injured by a grenade and bled to death. Fourteen other soldiers were wounded by Akbar, mostly from grenade shrapnel.[97]

---

[94] *Nuremberg Trials*, Library of Congress, http://www.loc.gov/rr/frd/Military_Law/Nuremberg_trials.html (last visited Sept. 6, 2014).

[95] *My Lai Massacre: Lt. William Calley Apologizes More than 40 Years after Vietnam*, The Telegraph (Aug. 22, 2009), http://www.telegraph.co.uk/news/worldnews/6072064/My-Lai-massacre-Lt-William-Calley-apologises-more-than-40-years-after-Vietnam.html.

[96] On appeal the Army Court of Criminal Appeals affirmed the sentence. A subsequent appeal is now pending before the United States Court of Appeals for the Armed Forces.

[97] Manuel Roig-Franzia, *Army Soldier Is Convicted in Attack on Fellow Troops*, Wash. Post (Apr. 22, 2005), http://www.washingtonpost.com/wp-dyn/articles/A7210-2005Apr21.html.

At trial in April 2005 Akbar was convicted and sentenced to death for the murders of Seifert and Stone. Akbar's military defense attorneys contended that Akbar had psychiatric problems, including paranoia, irrational behavior, insomnia, and other sleep disorders. The prosecution emphasized the calculated death and destruction planned and executed by Akbar, and the impact of his murders and grievous assaults to a brigade on the eve of battle. Worse than desertion in the face of the enemy, Akbar had literally aided the enemy by disabling an entire brigade of combat power.[98] The case captured the attention of the world and the Army. Akbar was the first soldier since the Vietnam War to be convicted for fragging fellow soldiers overseas during wartime. It remains a singular case of fragging in the U.S. Army's history, and the only one on record to earn a death sentence.[99]

2. Catch and Release? The Case of Lieutenant Michael Behenna

In April 2008, Behenna was a platoon leader in the 101st Airborne Division, operating in northern Iraq. During a typical convoy operation Behenna's unit was hit by an IED, killing two soldiers and seriously wounding others. The resulting chaos and carnage had an understandably significant impact on the young officer. Witnesses at the court-martial described Behennna breaking down in tears over the incident.[100]

In early May, Behenna received intelligence on a certain Ali Mansur, thought to be responsible for the April attack and working for al Qaida. Behenna's platoon quickly raided Mansur's house, and during the capture, Behenna beat Mansur. Mansur was then detained for questioning.[101] Less than two weeks later, deepening his frustration, Behenna was ordered to return Mansur to his village because the intelligence team simply could not develop the evidence necessary to hold Mansur any longer. On May 16, instead of returning Mansur to his home, Behenna stopped his convoy near a culvert, and directed Mansur, his NCO, and his interpreter "Harry" out of the vehicles. He told his NCO to bring a thermite grenade. They entered a culvert out of sight of the convoy.

"Harry" later testified that "Lieutenant Behenna started talking with Ali Mansur and his NCO followed them. Behenna and his NCO started taking off Ali Mansur's clothes with their knives. They then cut his handcuffs." Behenna then ordered the naked Mansur to sit. "He was anxious to get information from Mansur," Harry's testimony continued. Behenna wanted information on the IED attack in April. Behenna asked Mansur several times, "What do you know? You

---

[98] *Id.*

[99] *Id.*

[100] Joe Mozingo, *A Killing in the Desert: An Unlikely Witness Provides One Last Hope for Soldier in Murder Case*, L.A. Times, Sept. 14, 2009 (last visited May 12, 2010).

[101] Kali Borkoski, *The Story of Michael Behenna and Mad Dog 5: "Self Defense" in War*, Scotus Blog (May 29, 2013, 5:49 PM), http://www.scotusblog.com/2013/05/the-story-of-michael-behenna-and-mad-dog-5-self-defense-in-war/.

have to tell me." Harry then testified that "Ali Mansur said I will talk to you but Lieutenant Behenna pulled trigger and killed him." Behenna shot Mansur twice.

Harry also disclosed that "[b]efore we started the patrol, Lieutenant Behenna told Ali Mansur I will kill you." I thought Lieutenant Behenna was trying to scare him. I did not think he would go through (with it) . . . I was standing 10 metres (yards) back during the shooting—I could see everything even if it was getting dark—and [the NCO] was next to me." The NCO then "took the grenade from his pocket, pulled the safety ring, walked around and put the grenade under Ali Mansur's head. Then they hid his clothes, and Behenna and [the NCO] went back."

Following the discovery of the burned body, the Army's CID investigated. Behenna was later charged with murder. At his trial at Fort Campbell, Kentucky, Behenna's defense counsel argued their client was under an acute stress disorder as a result of the attacks on his platoon, and that during the shooting he had acted in self-defense. They claimed Behenna looked at "Harry" for a translation, and when he looked back the naked Mansur had thrown a piece of concrete at him and was reaching for his weapon. A panel of fellow officers discarded these defenses and convicted Behenna of unpremeditated murder, sentencing him to a Dismissal and confinement for twenty-five years.[102]

The case of Behenna is significant for even the most casual observer of military justice. It is noteworthy that a panel of experienced officers convicted Behenna on the evidence before them; neither pressures of combatnor the pervasive operator frustration with the dynamics of catching and then releasing suspected al Qaida operatives were legal justifications for Behenna's actions or defenses colorable under the UCMJ. However unpleasant, this was simply the accepted operating environment. The American soldier, and soldiers—most especially officers, must "embrace the suck."[103]

Even more important to potential critics of course is that the panel meted out a sentence of great weight: twenty-five years. Every soldier operating in Iraq or Afghanistan needed to abide by American law, regardless of the thankless and indeed dangerous tasks they faced, such as having to release a detainee who might set about the next day emplacing yet another IED. Such a release was not an unusual occurrence, and lawful orders must not be challenged via a personal vendetta to employ terror tactics, death threats, or unlawful lethal violence to those who would offer them up to soldiers if given the chance.

---

[102] Kemp, *supra* note 3. This sentence was later reduced by five years by the Commanding General, and another five years by the Army Clemency and Parole Board—remarkably, even before the Army Court of Criminal Appeals had rendered their review. The Court of Appeals for the Armed Forces affirmed the findings and sentence, and the Supreme Court denied certiorari. United States v. Behenna, 70 M.J. 521 (A. Ct. Crimm. App. 2011).

[103] A phrase that gained notoriety in the movie, *The Hurt Locker*, denoting the "unpleasantness" of war. *See The Hurt Locker* (2008) The Online Urban Dictionary adds that the phrase is "[o]ften used by NCO's in the military. The term would be used when an individual or a group must complete a task that is pointless, tiring, and/or lame."

D. CRITICISM'S CRESCENDO

Perhaps at no time since 1948–1950 and the hearings leading up the enactment of the UCMJ has military justice been so scrutinized as during the present. The efforts of the DLPB seem now to be merely an appetizer to a sustained feast to come over a number of years of impending evaluation and re-evaluation of the military justice system. The two-step review of how the UCMJ handles sexual assault mandated by Congress in late 2012 will by its own terms take upwards of thirty-six months or longer to complete. Victim advocate groups continue their admirable and well-intentioned effort to seek change in the military justice system.[104] And the media continues to exploit the issue of the day in an unforgiving 24/7 news cycle.

The year 2013's legislative cycle was momentous for military justice. Much of the focused changes in military justice centered on sexual assault litigation. But the changes ultimately wrought through a contentious cycle of hearings and debates are even now uncertain and formative. Although many statutory changes to the military's sexual assault statute were passed, the debates and the sentiments undergirding the debates raised more profound, fundamental questions about the role of the commander and the nature of our system of justice in uniform, and frankly, whether it would remain a commander's tool in the next overseas operation.

The debates between Senators Kirsten Gillibrand and Claire McCaskill highlight the issues most pointedly. Should commanders, advised by lawyers, remain in control of prosecution decisions? Or should lawyers make such decisions independent of the commander?

Perspectives of military justice are shared widely among current and former uniformed military leaders, lawyers, and commanders: the American armed forces are successful, not in spite of its system of justice, but because of it. The United States are different from our allies. Our allies' apparent vision in the modern world has, arguably, weakened them as martial forces. British soldiers must now worry, for example, about civil lawsuits when using force in war. From the individual soldier to the commander calling in artillery, mental hesitance now is rooted in the potential for personal civil suit. If America wants its Army to remain victorious on the battlefield, it must adamantly avoid such European tendencies, and more pointedly, embrace with pride what has made American forces unique, as well as so vital and so powerful on the battlefield.

VII. Conclusion

War is an ugly business. But American warriors are viewed as capable of accomplishing any mission, and continue to collectively exceed even the highest expectations of performance and professionalism. This is in large measure

---

[104] *See, e.g.*, *Support for Military Sexual Assault Victims and Family Members*, MilitaryFamily.org, http://www.militaryfamily.org/feature-articles/sexual-assault.html (last visited Sept. 7, 2014).

attributable to unique aspects of the U.S. military. The military justice system that is so central to establishing and maintaining good order and discipline is an inseparable part of that unique fabric. This is a criminal justice system that must be resilient in garrison and in the field, in peace and in war. Unlike any other American system of criminal justice, military justice must ultimately be responsive to the core mission of the U.S. military: close with and destroy the enemy.[105] This may sometimes appear sterile, as in the launch of a cruise missile, or an aircraft bombing a target in a foreign land far away. But if the last twelve-plus years demonstrate anything, closing with the enemy means in its purest form, a life-and-death struggle between two people, up close and personal.

Executing operations to subdue an enemy may require levels of violence most civilians can barely comprehend, violence that is often impossible to describe, but such conduct is necessary. "Boots on the ground" is the most recent windy phrase that illustrates the essential nature of war. It will always be true, and no trenchant argument or study or book can dispense with the reality of thousands of years of reproving this lesson: that to hold ground, to displace and destroy the enemy, troops must be physically present. There must be "boots on the ground." Like a sentry standing guard, or a platoon of soldiers patrolling, or a battalion conducting clearing operations to root out the enemy, the U.S. military justice system must likewise be there, wherever "there" is, to help the field commander manage this violence when it spills over the edges. The tools must be there to influence behavior before it happens. The consequence of a trial must be visible to the soldier after it happens. There is no substitute in human endeavors for visible consequences.

The years of warfare post 9/11 demonstrate that military justice in combat has been visible and effective. Whether it is manifest in the hundreds of trials conducted in theater, or the countless trials conducted at home station following a crime in theater, the message is unmistakable. The system, although not perfect, has performed well. Only time will tell if and how the system changes. The author only hopes that those with the power to change do not mistake success on the battlefield as independent of an effective justice system.

[105] Author's note: This phrase is a common inclusion in commanders' intent statements or in soldierly dialogue, but the DoD Mission Statement is "The *mission* of the *Department of Defense* is to provide the military forces needed to deter war and to protect the security of our country." *See About the Department of Defense*, DEFENSE.GOV, http://www.defense.gov/about/ (last visited Sept. 7, 2014).

15 }

Operational Claims

Jim Barkei*

I. Introduction

Military operations range from combat to humanitarian relief to training exercises to post-conflict stability, and involve vast numbers of personnel and equipment. As a result, people and property imminently suffer injury and damage despite any armed force's best efforts to avoid such harm. The nature of armed conflict creates a need for a program to compensate the innocent sufferers of the ill effects of military operations. In U.S. practice (and that of most modern militaries), implementing an operational claims program forms an essential component of mission accomplishment, provides a mechanism to mitigate civilian suffering, reinforces the humanitarian goals of the Law of Armed Conflict (LOAC), and girds support for a commander's objectives. Operational claims programs establish—often gratuitously—accountability for the actions of military forces through tort-type principles, and reflect an amalgamation of international legal principles, domestic law and policy, and the laws of the host nation. Mitigation of civilian suffering necessitates planning for and executing claims operations in almost every environment in which a military force operates. Ultimately, claims programs must address the full spectrum of military operations that result in cognizable claims, including vehicle accidents, personal injury and death, environmental damage (e.g., hazardous material spills), displacement, detention, and real and personal property damage. Although the scope of operational claims

---

* Lieutenant Colonel (LTC), U.S. Army. LTC Jim Barkei is an active duty Army Judge Advocate. He earned his JD at Chicago-Kent College of Law, and an LLM at The Judge Advocate General's Legal Center and School. LTC Barkei deployed in support of the 1st Infantry Division, International Security Assistance Force (ISAF) and United States Forces-Afghanistan in Iraq and Afghanistan, respectively. The positions and opinions in this chapter are those of the author and do not represent the official views of the Department of Defense, the United States Army, or other Department of Defense components. The author greatly appreciates the opportunity given by and assistance of Professor Geoffrey Corn, Professor Rachel VanLandingham, LTC Shane Reeves, and Major Evan Seamone in writing this chapter.

proves vast, this chapter focuses on operational claims in a combat or armed conflict environment.

Providing compensation for the ravages of military operations is not a new concept, although the scope and extent of this practice evolved over time. As early as 1784 the Continental Congress created the Board of Treasury to settle the numerous claims that arose from the Revolutionary War.[1] During the height of World War I, President Woodrow Wilson formulated a law to give indemnity for damages caused by U.S. forces overseas.[2] Today, U.S. policymakers and the international community expect the U.S. military to implement operational claims programs to facilitate victory by promoting justice and fairness within the afflicted population while protecting the individual members of its own armed forces.[3]

This chapter outlines the general principles that underlie the planning, execution, and oversight of an operational claims program. First, the chapter explains how domestic law and policy, and to a lesser extent international legal principles, form the basis for a claims program, including application of the doctrine of sovereign immunity. The chapter also describes the laws and policies that regulate U.S. military claims programs by assessing the strategic and tactical objectives and application of the laws that enable an armed force to implement a claims program. This portion of the chapter covers all aspects of a claims program framework, from the type of operation involved, to the status of both the aggrieved party and the member of the armed force, and even the location of the event that caused the harm and the consideration of the laws in place at that site. Claims are not the only method of addressing the harm suffered by the host-nation

---

[1] Floyd D. Shimamora, *The History of Claims against the United States*, 45 LA. L. REV. 625, 663–64 (1985). The Board of Treasury encountered mostly small claims such as requests for reimbursement for cattle procured for the Army, supplementation of pay affected by the depreciation of currency, and payment for property destroyed in order to prevent the enemy from benefitting from its use. *Id.* Earlier yet, the practice of war reparations extended back to at least the Punic Wars where Carthage succumbed to Rome. TITUS LIVY, THE EARLY HISTORY OF ROME (Penguin Classics 2002). Although operational claims differ from war reparations in that reparations bestowed payments by a defeated state or entity to the victor, the two concepts share the premise of compensating those who suffered the consequences of armed conflict, though the spoils of victory distinguish the systems. Thus, modern operational claims evolved in the opposite direction of reparations because often the victorious military uses a claims program to mitigate the suffering inflicted on the populace, in order to build favor and trust and promote the rule of law instead of exploiting the populace for its own benefit.

[2] An Act to Give Indemnity, ch. 57, 40 Stat. 535 (1918). This inaugural process mirrored the claims laws and policies of the state in which the claim arose; for example, if French armed forces would have a payable claim to a French citizen, U.S. armed forces would adopt a similar claim-payable posture.

[3] Claims programs facilitate military and political mission success by mitigating the suffering of the local population for harm suffered as a result of the military operation, with the goal of promoting civil support for the mission and preventing civil unrest or insurgency. Claims also promote the rule of law and provide a foundation for civil governance by establishing a process for citizens to resolve disputes. Last, an operational claims program also acts as a potential shield from individual liability for leaders and individual members of the armed forces.

population; thus, the chapter also explores the ways an armed force and its policymakers have established alternative programs to facilitate mission success. Next, the chapter follows with a brief examination of multinational claims policies and an overview of the challenges associated with implementing a coherent program in the context of a multinational military operation. Finally, the chapter concludes with a synopsis of how a military force applies claims laws and principles in the operational environment, ultimately establishing the benefit of such a program to both the armed forces implementing it and the host-nation citizens who benefit from it.

II. Foundations of Operational Claims Programs: Morality, Policy, and International Legal Principles

Every military must ensure respect for the LOAC principle of distinction[4] during the execution of combat operations; however, even strict adherence to this obligation cannot eliminate the nearly inevitable collateral damage and incidental injury to civilians and their property from armed conflict. When military activities produce such unfortunate consequences, an operational claims program contributes to the just mitigation of the harm. It also promotes dignity by addressing the need to provide a remedy for victims of such suffering. Then, it supports the rule of law by establishing a compensation system that does not require the local civilian to seek redress through local courts unlikely to have the requisite jurisdiction to adjudicate a claim. Moreover, not only does the citizen benefit, but, from the military commander's perspective, claims operations provide the armed force with a tactical program to promote public trust.[5] It is therefore not surprising that U.S. (and many international) commanders view claims programs as an essential combat multiplier when properly implemented.[6]

---

[4] *See* Protocol Additional to the Geneva Conventions of 12 August 1949, and Relating to the Protection of Victims of International Armed Conflict (Protocol I) art. 48, June 8, 1977, 1125 U.N.T.S. 3 [hereinafter API] (stating "the Parties to the conflict shall at all times distinguish between the civilian population and combatants and between civilian objects and military objectives . . .").

[5] As stated by an Iraqi citizen, Sheik Mohammed Iassim al Mashadani in Tarmiya, Iraq, the claims process helps "remove the hatred in the hearts of citizens who lost everything during the initial occupation of Iraq and never received any type of compensation." CAPTAIN EVAN SEAMONE, TAJI STANDING OPERATING PROCEDURE C-01, INTAKE, INVESTIGATION, PROCESSING, AND BUDGETING OF FOREIGN CLAIMS 4 (May 23, 2006).

[6] *See, e.g.*, CENTER FOR LAW AND MILITARY OPERATIONS, THE JUDGE ADVOCATE GENERAL'S SCHOOL, U.S. ARMY, LEGAL LESSONS LEARNED FROM AFGHANISTAN AND IRAQ: VOLUME I, MAJOR COMBAT OPERATIONS (11 September 2001—1May 2003) § F. Claims 175, 180–1, nn. 2–3 and 32–3. Though less common, when military forces do not implement a claims program, or do not adequately address the adverse effects of the conflict, sometimes the international community creates a relief system. Consider that the United Nations Security Council created the United Nations Compensation Commission in 1991 to resolve claims that resulted from Iraq's invasion of Kuwait. This body demonstrated the international community's effort to impose liability for violations of international humanitarian law when a state did not voluntarily implement a claims program.

Armed conflict compensation programs emanate from domestic laws and policies instead of international legal obligations. Thus, operational claims promote national plans for recovery with the motivating force of financing reconstruction and promoting justice via apportioning blame for combat damage.[7] However, although compensating sufferers of military operations remains commendable, and even vital to the success of a military operation, critics lament that international law provides no universal obligation to compensate those adversely affected by warfare.[8]

We recognize that claims programs involve a significant commitment of national financial resources, but they also implicate important principles of national sovereignty. Sovereign states engaged in military operations almost always shield themselves under the umbrella of sovereign immunity from a legal obligation to compensate for unavoidable battle damage.[9] Public international law application of sovereign immunity protects states and their governments from lawsuits in foreign courts without their consent, instead turning state-upon-state torts into matters of diplomacy, generally holding armed forces members accountable to their own laws rather than those of the nation in which the operation took place.[10] Accordingly, claims against a government and its agents require a waiver of sovereign immunity, albeit likely a very limited waiver, in the context of armed conflict.[11]

See Menno T. Kamminga, *Towards a Permanent International Claims Commission for Victims of Violations of International Humanitarian Law*, 25 WINDSOR Y.B. ACCESS JUST 23, 3 (2007).

[7] Quincy Wright, *War Claims: What of the Future?*, 16 LAW & CONTEMP. PROBS. 543, 550 (Summer 1951).

[8] Luke T. Lee, *Introduction* to INTERNATIONAL LAW ASSOCIATION, TORONTO CONFERENCE (2006) [hereinafter Toronto Conference]: COMPENSATION FOR VICTIMS OF WAR 2 (2006); Yaël Ronen, *Avoid or Compensate? Liability for Incidental Injury to Civilians Inflicted during Armed Conflict*, 42 VAND. J. TRANSNAT'L L. 181, 181 (2009).

[9] *See, e.g.*, Colonel Jody Prescott, *EBAO and NATO Operational Claims*, THE THREE SWORDS II (Oct. 10, 2007) (in Bosnia-Herzegovina operations, European Union and NATO forces declared several categories of claims as non-cognizable, including combat-related activities and those of operational necessity).

[10] IAN BROWNLIE, PRINCIPLES OF PUBLIC INTERNATIONAL LAW 325–26 (4th ed. 1990); LASSA OPPENHEIM, INTERNATIONAL LAW: A TREATISE 500 (2d ed. 1912) (1905).

[11] *See, e.g.*, Price v. United States, 174 U.S. 373 (1899). In Canada, see State Immunity Act of 1985 § 6; in the United Kingdom, see SIA § 5; and in Australia, see Foreign Sovereign Immunities Act of 1985 § 13. In the context of coalition and joint military operations conducted with the consent of the state where the operation occurs, or military operations conducted at the invitation by a host or "receiving state," participating nations often negotiate a limited waiver of sovereign immunity covering potential claims resulting from the activities of the armed forces involved in the operation. The most significant example of this joint waiver of sovereign immunity is the North Atlantic Treaty Organization (NATO) Status of Forces Agreement (SOFA). Pursuant to this treaty, each NATO member state waives claims of one contracting party against any other contracting party for damage to property owned by its armed forces, or for injury or death suffered by a member of its armed forces performing official duties. Agreement between the Parties to the North Atlantic Treaty regarding the Status of their Forces, London, art. VIII, June 19, 1951, 4 U.S.T. 1792, T.I.A.S. 2646 [hereinafter NATO SOFA].

In U.S. practice, several statutes pertaining to foreign claims, along with Department of Defense (DoD) directives and implementing regulations, provide limited waivers of sovereign immunity.[12] The most significant of these is the Foreign Claims Act (FCA), through which the U.S. government minimally waives its sovereign immunity by authorizing the settlement of claims by a foreign state or its inhabitants against the United States for personal injury, death, or property damage caused by military members or civilian employees, and claims that arise incident to noncombat activities of its armed forces.[13] Whether in the form of a specific waiver of sovereign immunity such as the FCA, or an implicit waiver resulting from the mere practice of compensating for harm resulting from military operations, all operational claims programs involve a prioritization of just compensation over sovereign prerogative.

Once the hurdle of sovereign immunity topples, operational claims for U.S. armed forces transition to a state policy decision to pay a claim without relation to the lawfulness of the operation or the act that caused the harm. Even though the 1907 Hague Convention introduced a state obligation to compensate another state for violations of the Convention itself as a consequence of armed conflict, the Convention did not open international law to individual claims against an armed force.[14] Courts in the United States support this interpretation.[15] Nonetheless, the United States often pays gratuitous claims regardless of whether the suffering or damage was foreseeable as collateral or wholly unanticipated, as claims programs offer the victims solace and manifest commitment to mitigate the suffering of war derived from the fundamental LOAC principle of humanity.[16]

---

[12] *See, e.g.*, Foreign Claims Act, 10 U.S.C. § 2734 (2006) (limited waiver permitting foreign citizens to make claims against the U.S. government for incidents arising in a foreign state); Military Claims Act, 10 U.S.C. § 2733 (2006) (limited waiver allowing claims against the U.S. government for damage or injury caused by military and DoD civilian personnel within the scope of their employment); Public Vessels Act, 46 U.S.C. § 31101 (2006) (limited waiver allowing claims against the U.S. government for damage caused by government vessels on the high seas).

[13] Foreign Claims Act, 10 U.S.C. § 2734 (1942).

[14] Hague Convention No. IV Respecting the Laws and Customs of War on Land, Oct. 18, 1907, 36 Stat. 2277, 205 C.T.S. 277, art. 3 (entered into force Jan. 26, 1910) [hereinafter Hague Regulations]. Despite increasing acknowledgment of individual rights under international law, both the lack of specific codification and the overwhelming consistent state interpretation of this provision do not support adoption of a customary international law norm. Rainier Hofmann, Toronto Conference, *supra* note 8, at 7–8. The only court to date to take a contrary stance is in Greece. *See* Court of First Instance of Leivadia of 30 October 1997, I. Bantekas, International Decisions: Prefecture of Voiotia v. Federal Republic of Germany, AM. J. INT'L L. 92, 765 (1998).

[15] Tel Oren v. Libyan Arab Republic, 726 F.2d 774 (D.C. Cir 1984); Leo Handel v. Artukovic, 601 F. Supp. 1421 (D.D.C. 1985); Goldstar (Panama) S.A. v. United States, 967 F.2d 965, 968 (4th Cir. 1972).

[16] Although most often referred to Toronto Conferencethe principle of unnecessary suffering, the same LOAC principle is also referred to as the principle of humanity when considered on a broad spectrum, focusing on the humanitarian goals behind the Geneva Convention "to limit the effects of war on the civilian population and property, and also serves as a counterbalance to the principle of military necessity." INTERNATIONAL AND OPERATIONAL LAW DEP'T, THE JUDGE ADVOCATE GENERAL'S LEGAL CENTER AND SCHOOL, OPERATIONAL LAW HANDBOOK 13 (2013) [hereinafter OPLAW Handbook].

As important as a system is that facilitates providing just compensation to mitigate the suffering of victims of harm associated with military operations, it does not require and rarely will provide compensation for all such harm. Several limitations on the extent of both state and personal liabilities establish the parameters within which a military balances the objectives furthered by an operational claims program with rational limits on compensable harm. For example, most armed forces exclude compensation for combat-related damage and injury, a concept central to the practice of U.S. armed forces and mandated by its statutory law.[17] Thus, remaining consistent with the principles of LOAC, an intentional attack that knowingly would result in harm to civilians is not one that spawns legal liability as long as it is a legitimate attack. Further, although commanders may feel an instinct to provide compensation for all claims resulting from the ravages of war, in the interest of establishing goodwill with a local population and contributing to ultimate mission success, doing so will quickly deplete the resources available for the commander, and could lead states to hesitate to participate in coalition operations. Nonetheless, as the following discussion of U.S. and coalition claims practice demonstrates, striking an operationally rational balance between compensable and non-compensable claims is an essential component of all military operations.

Aside from the interests of national-level armed forces, individual military members would face a significant risk in the absence of government sovereign immunity and combat exclusions. Without a government supporting the actions of its armed forces, individual members might find themselves subject to a liability suit for their actions during a military operation. If commonplace, it would paralyze operations because military commanders could not tolerate the common imposition of personal liability on their subordinates for executing their obligations. The inevitable fear of personal liability would inhibit tactical initiative, produce potentially mission-debilitating hesitation, and undermine the vital trust between commander and subordinate. Governments also cannot tolerate the threat of having their military members subject to the jurisdiction and legal sanctions of a foreign court, particularly one that could be hostile toward their armed forces. Thus, concepts such as legal immunity for combat activities and an alternative mechanism for providing just compensation form essential components of a military operation.

Developing and implementing an operational claims program, at least for U.S. armed forces, falls within the responsibility of commanders through their military attorneys (Judge Advocates or JAGs) and paralegals.[18] Despite the intimate legal administration of a claims program, the commander "owns" it due to its operational significance and direct link to mission accomplishment. Claims endow a commander with an operational tool to effectively carry out the mission,

---

[17] Foreign Claims Act, 10 U.S.C. § 2734 (1942).

[18] Although all military members should be aware of claims programs in theaters of operation, other key personnel to train, or at least become familiar with claims procedures, include engineers, civil affairs, and special forces personnel. Prescott, *supra* note 9.

assigning resources, establishing policies, and overseeing its successful employment. Hence, the degree of emphasis on an operational claims program and the measure of its effectiveness will inevitably reflect the commander's intent.

Military planners also include claims programs in the military decision-making process because they support the restoration of a stable society and legitimate governance at the termination of hostilities. Without a claims program, an occupying power, ruling party, or victorious state would likely find itself responsible for an aggrieved population in an economically depressed territory with damaged infrastructure and depleted resources; in other words, a burdened society unlikely to support governance. Mitigating the threat of a hostile populace during, and just as importantly after, hostilities is nearly as important as defeating the enemy during the focus of combat operations. Effective implementation of a military claims operation fosters civil support for the governing armed force or allied government. Operational claims dilute support for insurgent, resistance, terrorist, or other general efforts to thwart the controlling or occupying command from successfully governing the area.[19] This is a root principle of counterinsurgency operations. Claims operations also form a building block of force protection for friendly forces by implementing the rule of law and promoting fairness, garnering the respect and trust of the local populace by establishing a consistent and trustworthy process to right the wrongs of warfare upon the civilian populace to the extent possible. Additionally, a claims program can create or restore a relationship with a host government and offer a path to justice for local citizens while avoiding a potentially complicated, inaccessible, or dysfunctional local judicial system.[20] At a minimum, sometimes an aggrieved claimant simply wants the foreign armed forces to acknowledge the harm and provide closure, which can be readily and efficiently accomplished through a claims program. These benefits explain why the United States, and other countries, allocate significant resources to empower military commanders to implement operational claims programs.

For the U.S. military, commanders bear the responsibility of developing and implementing an operational claims program to meet the objectives of the mission discussed above. Judge Advocates, military attorneys, and paralegals provide the primary resourcing tool for commanders to carry out this aspect of the mission. Although the commander "owns" the program, legal personnel often take the lead in claims programs due to the legal foundation and intimate

---

[19] Vietnam exemplifies a military operation that required an effective claims program because of hostility toward the government on the part of some segments of the population, while other segments remained apathetic. U.S. Army Center for Military History, Vietnam War 80, http://www.history.army.mil/books/Vietnam/Law-War/law-05.htm (last visited Jan. 15, 2014).

[20] Claims emerge as a learning tool for a developing host nation through implementation of the rule of law, reflected by a respect for property rights. Courts adjudicating claims and property rights issues are a natural offspring of the principles that underpin claims, hearing cases that they might not have otherwise resolved. For example, the citizens of Vietnam rarely brought property rights and personal injury claims before courts because they either lacked sufficient money to see the process through or avoided hiring counsel. *Id.* at 79.

administration of the program, including protection of the military forces' personnel, judicial expenditure of the forces' resources (primarily money), and adjudicative responsibilities with respect to fault and liability involved in each citizen's request for redress. Claims operations empower a commander to employ a non-kinetic resource that meets both the strategic and tactical objectives of maintaining supportive relations with local citizens. Ultimately, the measure of success for a claims operation will depend upon the amount of resources dedicated to the mission and the emphasis the commander places upon it. Even though a commander and his legal team understand and accept the importance of claims to the overall mission through policy and military planning processes, the claims program itself must still be established in law.

III. Claims Laws of the United States

This section explains how the United States conducts operational claims. Although often implemented through command policies without any judicial intervention, U.S. operational claims programs are based in large measure on common law tort principles. The objective is to provide rational and factually justified monetary or in-kind compensation for civilians and friendly governments and their armed forces who suffer as a result of U.S. military activities. These programs are therefore based on the premise that U.S. armed forces bear a duty of care toward the host nation and its citizens and coalition partner forces.

A. FOREIGN CLAIMS ACT

Planning to implement a U.S. operational claims program begins with the FCA. Enacted in 1942, President Roosevelt proposed the FCA as part of a legislative agenda in response to the asserted national emergency created by the threat of German aggression following the Nazi conquest of Europe.[21] Considering the rapid and unprecedented expansion of U.S. military activities across the globe, the U.S. government designed the FCA to engender goodwill and promote friendly relations between its military and host nations.[22] As designed, the FCA covers damage to, or loss of, real property and personal injury or death of foreign governments or citizens, including land and maritime claims.[23] The damage, loss, personal injury, or death must occur outside the United States and must be

---

[21] U.S. Dep't of Army, Pam. 27–162, Claims Procedures para. 10–1a (Mar. 21, 2008) [hereinafter DA PAM 27–162].

[22] *Id.* para. 10–1a; *see also* 10 U.S.C. § 2734 (1942) (the FCA intends to "promote and to maintain friendly relations through the prompt settlement of meritorious claims").

[23] 10 U.S.C. § 2734 (1942). For domestic military operations, 10 U.S.C. § 2733 provides for similar claims incident to noncombat operations, although inhabitants of foreign states are not proper claimants under 10 U.S.C. § 2733. Niedbala v. United States, 37 Fed. Cl. 43 (1996).

incident to *noncombat* activities of the U.S. armed forces.[24] Further, when the claim presented involves actions of foreign nationals on behalf of the United States, an "in-scope of duty" limitation requires foreign nationals to show that they were working for the United States and were hired in the country where the incident occurred.[25]

Regarding timing, claimants must present their claims under the FCA within two years of the event causing loss to prevent an ongoing threat of liability for the state.[26] Further, a claimant must submit the claim as a request in local currency or the currency of the country in which the claimant was an inhabitant at the time of the loss.[27] This requirement supports the correct valuation of the claim and establishes the logical link to resolution under the local legal framework. Although claimants may initially present it verbally, they should reduce the claim to writing at some point.[28] During the process adjudicators (also known as commissioners) must make claimants aware that the FCA does not authorize compensation for punitive damages, court costs, filing costs, attorney's fees, or bailment, even when the claim is properly presented,[29] essentially placing a cap on the potential compensation exposure for the U.S. military command. Collectively, these seemingly minor implementation procedures greatly influence the manner in which the U.S. military conducts claims operations under the FCA.

Whenever a binding international agreement covers claims in the theater of operations, such as the NATO SOFA, the terms of the international agreement will trump the FCA and render it inapplicable.[30] In contrast, the lack of an international agreement with the United States as a party leaves the FCA as an exclusive claims authority. In a situation where joint multinational operations results in damage or injury caused by U.S. forces to the forces or property of a different nation, and claims were not already waived by agreement between the troop-contributing governments, a claim may be payable under the FCA because the coalition military members would likely be proper claimants. This results in an especially sensitive situation when the combined military forces are those of the sending state and the host nation.

Although the host nation may recognize that assuming responsibility to provide compensation will enhance its credibility in the eyes of the aggrieved claimant, circumstances may render it difficult for the nation to bear this compensation burden. As a result, the host nation will often seek financial assistance from other

---

[24] 10 U.S.C. § 2734 (1942). Noncombat activities means that the damage, loss, personal injury, or death cannot arise from "action by the enemy or result directly or indirectly from an act of the U.S. armed forces in combat." *Id.* The fact that the incident, injury, or damage occurred on a U.S. military installation in a foreign state does not prevent a valid claim under the FCA.

[25] OPLAW Handbook, *supra* note 16, at 301.

[26] U.S. Dep't of Army, Reg. 27–20, Claims para. 2–5 (Feb. 8, 2008) [hereinafter AR 27–20].

[27] *Id.* para. 10–9b.

[28] *Id.* para. 2–5.

[29] *Id.* para. 2–34e. Implementing regulations of the FCA also result in limiting the exposure of the U.S. government by deducting recovered insurance proceeds. 32 C.F.R. § 536.139 (c) (2006).

[30] OPLAW Handbook, *supra* note 16, at 302.

coalition armed forces, such as the United States, especially when the host nation is a less-developed state. Local law may also excuse or exempt injuries caused by the host nation's own armed forces, which could prevent compensation, leaving the victims of such harm to turn to other members of the coalition for relief. Although it may seem odd that coalition partners would assume responsibility for harm caused to local nationals by the host nation's own forces, when those forces are included within the broader coalition command, it will often be the case that their acts will be perceived as those of the coalition. Accordingly, coalition commanders may perceive an imperative to functionally subrogate claims attributable to the host nation's own forces.

One important limitation remains the inapplicability of the FCA to contractual claims in an operational setting. Generally, armed forces look to the laws of the host nation to provide the appropriate remedy for contractual agreements; failure to recognize the principle of contracts in the theater of operations would otherwise undermine the rule of law and effectiveness of the local court system upon which the other contracting party relies. Nonetheless, contractors may avail themselves of possible FCA redress when a contract with U.S. armed forces does not address damage or injury caused by U.S. government employees, apart from contractual performance. One example of this exception involves real estate claims, which can arise when U.S. forces require the use of real property in a foreign theater of operations as logistical hubs, command and control centers, transportation centers, and tactical positions of advantage. The FCA (and the Military Claims Act if a scope-of-employment question is at issue) covers claims for damage and use of real estate for thirty days or less.[31] For property a commander anticipates using more than thirty days, U.S. forces have the authority to enter into leases in foreign states, normally handled by a Contingency Real Estate Support Team (CREST) of the U.S. Army Corps of Engineers.[32] Real estate claims apply contract principles to resolve any subsequent lease dispute, and U.S. forces may use operations and maintenance (O&M) funds to settle the claims rather than the FCA. Tangentially, although rent is not payable under the FCA, a claimant may still recover for the loss of use or any damage to the property because the FCA makes business losses generally compensable as a tort.[33] Business losses might include damage or destruction of the physical facility, a loss of income, or occupation of the facility for the use of the armed forces. In all cases, armed

---

[31] Major Michael C. Evans, *Influencing the Center of Gravity in Counterinsurgency Operations: Contingency Leasing in Afghanistan*, ARMY LAW. 27 (Feb. 2012).

[32] *Id.*

[33] UNITED STATES ARMY IN EUROPE REAL ESTATE/OFFICE OF THE JUDGE ADVOCATE STANDARD OPERATING PROCEDURES FOR PROCESSING CLAIMS INVOLVING REAL ESTATE DURING CONTINGENCY OPERATIONS 4 (Aug. 20, 2002). One way to mitigate claims, particularly in the realm of property damage, is to enter into easement contracts for a right of use or entry. The cost of the easement contract may be less than a future claim. Coordination with local officials may also prevent claims issues; contact with the local mayor or a significant village elder or religious leader may calm fears and manage the expectations of the citizens, and even establish support for the operation.

forces must distinguish claims regarding use of property from those involving rent.[34]

Primary points of emphasis lie within the FCA's exclusions: the FCA does not apply in cases of combat losses, contracts, domestic obligations, and claims that are not in the U.S. interest to pay or are contrary to public policy.[35] Several policies under the FCA demonstrate the types of circumstances considered to undermine the military mission or be contrary to public policy. For example, the FCA prohibits payments not in the best interest of the United States (e.g., claims by the enemy or a subversive group or individual not identified as the enemy, but one that is undermining the U.S. role in the operation); subrogation claims; claims by insurers; claims from inhabitants of the United States or U.S. military and civilian component personnel (if in the foreign state where the damage or injury occurred incident to service); claims authorized under another compensation program, and claims barred by the statute of limitations (generally two years). Additionally, FCA claims adjudicators must determine whether the person presenting the claim is a national of a state at war with the United States, or of a state allied with a country at war with the United States.[36] If so, the claim is not cognizable. These policies ensure that allocation of claims-related U.S. resources will not jeopardize military efforts. Furthermore, in none of these situations will denial of a claim be inconsistent with LOAC obligations, such as compensating the enemy for conflict-related loss; claims will also not be allowed in situations in which an alternate method of compensation or claim may be available. Finally, when the policies of the FCA deem a claim unpayable or payable for a decreased

---

[34] One area that does not receive much coverage in claims guidance is post-conflict restitution for those persons displaced by the war. The restoration of property rights is critical to the rule of law in a recovering state, as it promotes peace and quells political discontent; however, U.S. claims policies have not established a regime for this specific category of post-conflict claims. The Pinhiero Principles provide a framework for a restitution program. *See* Megan J. Ballard, *Post-conflict Property Restitution: Flawed Legal and Theoretical Foundations*, 28 BERKELEY J. INT'L L. 462, 495 (2010).

[35] AR 27–20, *supra* note 26, para. 10–4. As an example, detention operations can generate claims issues. As military forces release detainees, the newly freed or transferred persons may have had property confiscated or suffered an injury at the time of detention. These claims may be proper, depending upon the nature of the detention operation, that is, whether the detention occurred during a combat operation. At a minimum, the military force may consider returning confiscated property that it stored or can reasonably locate (e.g., vehicles, a weapon, etc.). These considerations require thoughtful consideration of the U.S. policy that prohibits payments that are not in the United States' interest. Army Regulation 27–20 contains a list of claims not payable under the FCA: damage or suffering wholly from the negligent or wrongful act of the claimant; contractual claims; private or domestic obligations; solely for compassionate reasons; bastardy claim for child support expenses; anything that violates a Department of the Army or DoD policy; rent damage or other payments for real property or interests therein; when not in the best interest of the United States or against public policy; a claim presented by an entity of a country in armed conflict against the United States; a claim waived by international agreement; subrogation claims; claims covered by insurance; claims payable under the Military Claims Act or Personnel Claims Act; and, claims by or on behalf of a member of a foreign military force for personal injury or death incident to service or pursuant to combined military operations. *Id.* para. 10–4.

[36] DA PAM 27–162, *supra* note 21, para. 10–2a(3); OPLAW Handbook, *supra* note 16, at 301.

amount than requested, the claims commissioner will notify the claimant in writing of the decision and its basis.[37]

Last, understanding U.S. claims procedures under the FCA requires a brief explanation of a Foreign Claims Commission (FCC). Command authority to process and pay claims starts with a succession of authority delegations. For example, within the U.S. Army, the United States Army Claims Service (USARCS) appoints high echelon commands as Command Claims Services (CCS) (within the Army usually at the major command or Army command level). Normally, the CCS will then appoint FCCs to process claims, and in the absence of a CCS, the Service Claims department such as USARCS will appoint the FCCs. The FCC then acts not only as an adjudicator, investigator, and command communicator as described throughout this chapter, but also takes on the responsibilities of record custodian and answering to the Service Claims authorities. An FCC usually consists of one to three members, and when there is more than one member a person will be appointed president.[38] Although AR 27-20 contains numerous additional directives for an FCC, the primary purpose for this short overview is to emphasize that even though commanders own the claims program within their areas of responsibility, they do not execute the mission without support and guidance from service-level officials.

1. Contending with the Combat Activities Exclusion

The most controversial provision by far of the FCA states that "damages caused by enemy action, or by the U.S. armed services resisting or attacking an enemy or preparing for immediate combat with an enemy"[39] are not payable, because they arise directly or indirectly from combat activity. The U.S. District Court in *Koohi v. United States*, assessed this provision, noting that

> The combat activities exception applies whether U.S. military forces hit a prescribed or an unintended target, whether those selecting the target act wisely or foolishly, whether the missiles we employ turn out to be "smart" or dumb, whether the target we choose performs the function we believe it does or whether our choice of an object for destruction is a result of error or miscalculation.[40]

This expansive interpretation of the combat exclusion is consistent with the general implementation of the FCA, and indicates that any act in support of war or combat, regardless of intent or effect, falls outside the scope of FCA compensability. As a result, in the context of any armed conflict, the claims adjudicator faces a fact-dependent, case-by-case, and often difficult determination whether the damage, loss, or injury is attributable to combat activities.[41] This combat

[37] AR 27–20, *supra* note 26, para. 10–6.

[38] *Id.* para. 10–7.

[39] DA PAM 27–162, *supra* note 21, para. 10–3b.

[40] Koohi v. United States, 976 F.2d 1328 (9th Cir. 1992).

[41] DA PAM 27–162, *supra* note 21, para. 10–3b.

exclusion applies whether or not war is declared, and also applies to hostile actions against the United States during peacekeeping or humanitarian assistance missions involving de facto hostilities, which is a determination assigned to the appropriate operational commander.[42] Finally, the United States is not alone in maintaining this type of exclusion; many other states and joint forces refuse to provide compensation for combat-related damage.[43]

From a national policy level, this is a logical measure to protect the state from the potentially tremendous scope of liabilities that would result from any military action. Absent the limit, the potential liability could inhibit aggressive military action by commanders because of concerns related to the financial liability that may result. Thus, the fiscal risks of an operation could play such a key factor as to sacrifice the safety of troops or compromise the ultimate objective of victory in war.[44] However, at the operational level, commanders may also perceive this exclusion as an impediment to their efforts to establish goodwill with a local population by offsetting the negative impact of combat operations. Nonetheless, it is the national concern over excessive liability that has, to date, prevailed in this competition of interests.

One workaround to this operational constraint is to designate losses as a result of noncombat activities. The authority to designate loss that results from noncombat activities varies. Political leadership might establish a presumption that U.S. forces are not engaging in combat activities in a particular theater of operation, thus making this designation easier and facilitating access to FCA relief. Furthermore, even in the context of an armed conflict, an operational commander may decide that the armed forces are entering a phase of the operation that, based on conditions, indicates that combat activities are no longer taking place, thereby triggering a presumption of FCA claim viability. In some circumstances a claims adjudicator may even make the determination.[45] Another

---

[42] *Id.*

[43] In Bosnia-Herzegovina, the European Union Force and NATO Headquarters Sarajevo declared two categories of claims as non-cognizable: claims resulting from "Combat and Combat Related Activities" and claims from "Operational Necessity." These categories precluded payment for force protection, detention operations, riot control, and other actions in furtherance of the mandates. Prescott, *supra* note 9, at 17. Similarly, in Kosovo, in the 1999 Military Technical Agreement between the Kosovo Force (KFOR) and the Federal Republic of Yugoslavia, the NATO forces negotiated a waiver of liability "for any damages to private or public property that they may cause in the course of duties related to the implementation of this Agreement." *Id.* at I.b. However, several prominent military forces willingly compensate those who suffer harm from combat activities; for example, the German military paid the victims of an air strike in Kunduz, Afghanistan. *See* Matthias Gebauer, *Aftermath of an Afghan Tragedy: Germany to Pay $500,000 for Civilian Bombing Victims*, Spiegel Online (Aug. 6, 2010), *available at* http://www.spiegel.de/international/germany/aftermath-of-an-afghanistan-tragedy-germany-to-pay-500-000-for-civilian-bombing-victims-a-710439.html.

[44] The United States previously deviated from this policy: after OPERATION URGENT FURY in Grenada in 1983, the U.S. Department of State established a program to pay for combat-related death, injury, and property damage as an expressed exception to the combat activities exclusion under the FCA. The United States instituted this policy with the intention of maintaining the support of the citizens of Grenada, but after the conflict. OPLAW Handbook, *supra* note 16, at 308.

[45] An example of a combat activities adjudication: SFOR in Bosnia-Herzegovina received a claim from Vlatka Kupreskic, a man under indictment by the International Criminal Tribunal for former

workaround, as explained later in this chapter, includes creating an alternative compensation program to the traditional operational claims system, usually emanating from a special appropriation or funding source tailored to the specific military engagement. In all cases, the principle of humanity, concept of justice, command priorities, and intent of the FCA should guide the adjudication process toward fairness without undermining U.S. public policies or military objectives.

The combat activities exclusion, borderline cases of noncombat activity, and the constant pressure of local citizens' grievances add complexity to implementing a claims program. Further complications with implementation originate from the law of the country in which the claim arises, which dictates FCA claim adjudication for both liability and extent of damages and including comparative negligence and joint tortfeasors.[46] Failure to understand the local culture and customs forms a major impediment to an effective claims mission, which may also undermine the potential success of the overall military mission. Examples of this vital, yet delicate application include U.S. JAGs applying Sharia Law in an Islamic state or a tribal custom in an operation in Africa.[47] To avoid operating in a vacuum of knowledge, self-study, contacting a local consulate or embassy, seeking assistance from a coalition force, or even consulting and hiring local counsel are all options. Additionally, claims adjudicators commonly rely upon local interpreters, whose familiarity with local customs, true cost of goods and services, and simple ability to communicate effectively with the claimant

---

Yugoslavia in 1997 (SFOR apprehended Kupreskic after a gun battle, which damaged his house). Using the combat and combat-related activities and operational necessity analyses, the SFOR Legal Advisor opined that the exemptions barred payment. Three main factors supported the Legal Advisor's findings: that the SFOR troops complied with the rules of engagement, that the apprehension of an indicted person was lawful, and that Kupreskic should have known that he was indicted and had no legitimate right to resist arrest. Memorandum from Colonel Michael Neveu, SFOR Legal Advisor, Interpretation of SFOR Authority under Annex 1-A, GFAP, in Connection with Claim of Kupreskic, Vlatka, SFOR Claim No. C-4724 (Jan. 28, 1998).

[46] United States Army Regulation 27–20 directs the adjudication of claims under the law and custom of the host nation. AR 27-20, *supra* note 26, para. 10-5a (once a claim is deemed payable, application of the law and custom of the host nation determine which elements of damage are payable and which individuals are entitled to compensation). NATO also advises its forces to adjudicate claims as consistently as possible with host-nation laws and customs. Headquarters International Security Force, Standard Operating Procedures 1151, Claims against ISAF para. 5 (Oct. 21, 2009) [hereinafter HQISAF SOP 1151]. As an example, local laws may provide for excusal of injurious acts under certain circumstances present in the armed forces' activities. Iraqi Civil Code, Article 211, states, "A person who has established that the injury had arisen from a cause beyond his control such as by an act of God, and accident, a force majeure, by the act of a third party or the fault of the injured himself shall not be liable on damages unless there is a provision or an agreement otherwise." This would mean that in a combat situation, if the enemy caused the damage, not only would the military force be able to deny a claim based upon a combat exemption, but also based upon third-party liability. Iraqi Civil Code art. 211, *available at* http://gjpi.org/wp-content/uploads/2009/01/civilcode198-5011.pdf (last visited June 6, 2015).

[47] In contrast, an underdeveloped state may not have any substantial body of law upon which to base claims adjudications (e.g., Haiti in the 1990s). Center for Law and Military Operations, The Judge Advocate General's School, U.S. Army, Law and Military Operations in Haiti, 1994–1995—Lessons Learned for Judge Advocates 49 (1995).

prove invaluable.[48] Overall, claims personnel encounter a daunting challenge in researching, understanding, and implementing local laws in foreign states to the satisfaction of claimants, while complying with the limits of the U.S. FCA.

2. Addressing Acts by Non-military Personnel

Claims for damage caused by civilians employed by the military and accompanying the force are an increasingly common aspect of claims operations. Current military operations, at least for the United States, involve civilian members of the force and joint actions with other militaries. An effective claims operation must, therefore, account for potential liability for the acts of its civilian personnel and contractors, particularly in an era of increasing integration of civilians as supporting elements of military contingency forces.[49] Thus, the United States maintains laws to authorize settlement, adjudication, and cost sharing of claims arising out of the acts of either members of the armed forces or civilian employees who act within the scope of their duties and cause damage to another party in a foreign state.[50]

To illustrate, consider the example of a contractor transporting supplies from one forward operating base to another, when during transit the contractor suffers an accident. As a general proposition, the United States will not pay a claim by the persons harmed in the accident. However, three exceptions will result in the United States providing compensation when harm is caused by the act of a contractor: (1) if the item or service is deemed an inherently dangerous activity, (2) if the government has a nondelegable duty created by law, or (3) if the contractor maintains control of parts of the contract and fails to discharge those duties in a reasonable manner. One potential justification for these exceptions is that under an applicable international agreement (such as the NATO SOFA), a claim may only be payable for acts or damage caused by a member or employee of the armed services. Many states, including the United States, recognize the concept of employer liability for the acts of their employees, including contracted employees,[51] but often the status of the person as a contractor or the terms of the specific contract covering the activity in an operational theater will limit an aggrieved individual's ability to recover damages. As an example, NATO directs its participating nations to take responsibility for the acts of contractors working to support operations.[52] Moreover, claims programs normally impose limits

---

[48] Center for Law and Military Operations, The Judge Advocate General's School, U.S. Army, Legal Lessons Learned from Afghanistan and Iraq: Volume II, Full Spectrum Operations 191 (May 2003–30 June 2004). Civil affairs and public affairs officers may also be of substantial assistance.

[49] Including civilian employees of the military, contractors hired to perform specific duties, and civilians from other government agencies.

[50] International Agreement Claims Act, 10 U.S.C. § 2734a (2006). 10 U.S.C. § 2734b (1942) covers damage suffered by the other party to the international agreement in the United States.

[51] Consider the concept of statutory employees, who are not quite self-employed or completely independent for some purposes, including liability or taxation.

[52] HQISAF SOP 1151, *supra* note 46, at para. 5.

on liability for the actions of contractors; as such, the U.S. military will not pay claims caused by the acts of independent contractors. Ultimately, the matter of identifying the responsible party and determining whether the claim is payable will likely depend on the employment relationship and the mission, an often complex analysis.

Claims filed by nongovernmental organization (NGO) personnel add another level of complexity to the claims operation. The contemporary operational environment involves participation of multiple NGOs and associated personnel providing humanitarian, medical, media/journalistic, and a range of other services. These organizations and their personnel are generally eligible to file a claim on the same terms as host-nation victims of harm; however, it may be more complicated for these individuals because they do not have a tie to the host-nation processing office if one is used. As a result, many NGOs file directly with the sending state military force or international coalition command. In terms of harm caused by U.S. personnel, members of an NGO in a foreign theater of operations would likely qualify as eligible claimants under the FCA as it is an expansive coverage statute.

3. FCA Applications

Whenever a claim is presented to a U.S. operational command, the military claims adjudicator will apply a general analytical methodology to assess whether the claim is viable pursuant to the FCA. First, claimants must be proper: foreign nationals. In all cases, the claimant should provide identification, which is not always an easy standard procedure in less-developed states. Second, the cause of loss must be attributable to the United States or persons working as agents of the United States. Third, a determination of the nature of the loss (combat or noncombat activity) must be made. Fourth, the claim must be for a certain sum, and supported by evidence, even if that is nothing more than a statement. A thorough claimant interview will normally occur to establish as solid a record as possible for claim adjudication.[53] Throughout the process, the claims adjudicator will likely rely heavily on translation services, force protection and security, and possibly an expert in local laws.

If at this point the claim appears viable, the claims adjudicator then must consider the types of damages recoverable under U.S. laws, which include: pain and suffering, both past and future; physical disfigurement; mental or physical disability; loss of enjoyment of life; emotional distress; loss of consortium; and, survivors' mental anguish in wrongful death cases. Special damages may also be considered under a claims process, including: "past lost wages, loss of future income or earning capacity, past out-of pocket medical expenses, future medical expenses, loss of household services, and any loss stemming from a permanent disability."[54] In death cases, recoverable losses include: loss to beneficiaries,

---

[53] DA PAM 27-162, *supra* note 21, para. 2-53.

[54] *Id.* para. 2-54.

loss to estate, deceased's medical expenses before death and funeral expenses, deceased's pain and suffering before death, and mental anguish of survivors.[55] Under property loss considerations, factors that may be considered include: diminution in value, cost of repair, loss of use, and loss of business profit.[56] Finally, any calculation of these potential losses will also hinge upon a noncombat-related activities determination.

Damage and loss calculations often prove difficult for a claim's adjudicator. To illustrate, consider a common cause of asserted harm resulting from military operations: a dwelling search. Damage that may occur during the search, such as breaking a door or dumping foodstuffs to determine whether contraband was hidden within, may facially not be compensable because the damage logically flows from the combat operation of an entry-and-search mission. In contrast, if the troops take things too far and decide to act outside the scope of their duties, for example by bending the blades of a house fan upward to make them useless, or breaking off a faucet from a sink, such acts are not necessarily within the legitimate scope of the combat entry-and-search operation and therefore arguably should be classified as noncombat activities. If such damage is not deemed to be excluded by a combat-activities determination under the FCA, compensation would certainly mitigate the harm suffered and possibly promote the goodwill of the community. At that point, all the other complexities of assessing damages for such loss must be worked through to support the commander's objective.

The concept of comparative negligence further complicates operational claims. The initial difficulty centers on whether local law recognizes comparative negligence, both in the merits of the act itself and the award determination. Although claimant negligence does not necessarily bar an award, in many cases the injured or suffering party's comparative negligence may be considered by the claim's adjudicator, with adjustments on final awards.[57] The common scenario of vehicle accidents demonstrates the application of comparative fault during a military operation. In several states, particularly less-developed ones, driving motor vehicles in an aggressive or offensive manner constitutes the norm; the state may lack sophisticated traffic laws, may not require any formal training or certification to operate a vehicle, or simply may not enforce the rules that do exist. Local

---

[55] *Id.* para. 2-55.

[56] *Id.* para. 2-56. Under the FCA, the collateral source rule does not apply. In developed states where citizens or entities commonly have insurance for property or commercial interests, and possibly even personal insurance, insurance claims should take precedence over military claims, with the military payment being subordinate or secondary to the insurance. This does not stop an insurance company from filing a claim against the military force or its government; however, it is less likely that a military force will compensate an insurance company. The United States government is self-insured, as is NATO.

[57] For example, Article 120 of the Iraqi Civil Code recognizes the theory of comparative fault, which would be applied by a military force adjudicator during operations in Iraq. Under the Article, the court may reduce the sum of or refuse to adjudge payment of any compensation due to contributory fault or aggravating the injury or worsening the situation. Iraqi Civil Code art. 120, *available at* http://gjpi.org/wp-content/uploads/2009/01/civilcode198-5011.pdf (last visited June 6, 2015).

drivers may also not yield to a military vehicle or obey visual or verbal signals due to an inability to understand or read the intentions of the military member, causing difficult situations in which an armed force may take protective or even aggressive actions in response, including warning shots. Further, when considering the combat- activities exclusion, driving fast may be considered a unique military activity, for example, maintaining a certain speed during a convoy or patrol, but not necessarily a combat operation as it may be a relatively simple movement from one support area to another, and force protection necessitates the increased speed. Moreover, a vehicle that failed to pull over or tried to cut in front of the convoy may be comparatively negligent, which could reduce the amount of recovery.[58] All of these scenarios invite application of a comparative negligence analysis. On top of the comparative negligence challenge, a claims adjudicator will also have to weave through the maze of considerations of fault, local laws, damage, and the complex point of whether the activity was combat related.[59]

B. OTHER U.S. CLAIMS AUTHORITIES

The FCA remains the most prominent tool for U.S. armed forces to effectively implement a program that supports mitigating the suffering resulting from actions of U.S. military forces during foreign operations. It is not, however, the only tool in the operational claims arsenal. Other programs will contribute to this effort, and in many cases ameliorate the gaps in coverage inherent in FCA claims adjudication.

1. Military Claims Act

Although claims personnel will use the FCA for the vast majority of operational claims in a foreign theater of operations, other U.S. claims laws may apply periodically. Congress enacted the Military Claims Act (MCA) in 1943 to "establish a new system of compensation for both personal injuries and property losses caused by newly mobilized troops in civilian communities throughout the United States, its territories and possessions, and provided a corollary to the [FCA]."[60] It specifically covers activities essentially military in nature, such as firing weapons; field exercises and military maneuvers with aircraft and vehicles;

[58] This was often the case in Iraq using Article 210 of the Iraqi Civil Code, which would possibly reduce liability, but not necessarily bar all recovery. A second section of the Code, Article 227, may also be useful as it requires a reasonable degree of care on the roadway, which can be used to formulate a comparative negligence argument for the vehicle that tried to pass or pull out in front of or failed to pull over for a convoy. IRAQI CIVIL CODE arts. 210, 227, *available at* http://gjpi.org/wp-content/uploads/2009/01/civilcode198-5011.pdf (last visited June 6, 2015).

[59] Although uncommon, the United States could employ its affirmative claims authorities in a deployed environment for damage U.S. forces suffer as a result of intentional or tortious acts of a foreign party in a foreign state. The collection could be from the tortfeasor or the tortfeasor's insurance company. OPLAW Handbook, *supra* note 16, at 305.

[60] DA PAM 27-162, *supra* note 21, para. 3-1a.

use and occupancy of real estate; and, certain civilian activities such as engineering projects performed by the Corps of Engineers.[61] Under the MCA, residents of the United States may file a claim against the government for damage or injury caused by a negligent or wrongful act or omission, or an act that is otherwise the fault of military personnel acting within the scope of their employment, or for any damage or injury caused by their noncombat activities.[62]

Like the FCA, the MCA excludes harm caused by combat activities, whether in time of war or not. Further, in the context of a domestic operation within the United States, it does not cover damage or injury caused by military and civilian employees in connection with civil disturbances or disasters.[63] A critical distinction from other operational claims authorities is that only U.S. residents may invoke the MCA, such as members of the armed forces, federal civilian employees, family members, American NGOs, members of the media, and even tourists.[64] Although persons may file a claim for an act that occurs worldwide, the claim is subordinate to the Federal Tort Claims Act (FTCA) for incidents that occur in the United States; therefore, the claim must be barred under the FTCA before relief can be sought under the MCA. A typical example of overseas claims consists of family members, contractors, or members of the media seeking compensation for loss attributed to some U.S. military activity, while domestic claims examples would include vehicle movements during training and exercises.[65] Interested claimants should understand that if the FCA might apply, then the claimant should file his or her claim under the FCA.[66] Accordingly, the MCA plays a role in operational claims because it gives civilian employees who may accompany the force, or contractors performing duties for the U.S. military, an avenue for redress due to the negligent or wrongful acts of omission by U.S. service members. Thus, although minimal in use compared to the FCA, the MCA remains a claims tool that U.S. military forces must account for during operations.

2. Personnel Claims Act

During military operations, a state's armed forces may also suffer personal property losses. It is common for deployed military personnel to carry with them personal comfort items not issued by the government, or items of significant personal meaning. Furthermore, during the deployment family and friends will often send gifts, or military personnel may purchase personal items while in the

---

[61] Other activities at risk for damage include: illumination rounds, maneuvering equipment through villages, controlled detonations, and pedestrians who get too close to moving vehicles. Claims from unique activities such as these may not easily translate into a civil tort, and should be decided upon causation alone. *Id.* para. 3-3b(1).

[62] Military Claims Act, 10 U.S.C. § 2733 (2006).

[63] *Id.* para. 3-2c.

[64] *Id.* para. 3-4a(1).

[65] *See* U.S. Army Claims Service, Disaster Claims Handbook (Nov. 1998).

[66] 10 U.S.C. § 2733(b)(2) (1942); 10 U.S.C. § 2734 (1942).

operational area. Sometimes, military movements, extreme weather conditions, or simple accidents damage a service member's personal property, such as a personal computer used to communicate with home, a set of DVD movies used for entertainment during low tempo periods, or a guitar that might be used for anything from entertainment to learning a new skill.

In order to contribute to service member morale, the Personnel Claims Act (PCA) permits recovery for the losses to members' personal property that occur incident to service.[67] Similar to the MCA, the PCA applies anywhere the incident occurs. Two important principles dictate the viability of a PCA claim. First, if the claimant was negligent, then the claim is not recoverable. Second, U.S. military members may only recover for losses of personal items during a deployment if it was reasonable for a military member to possess the item during the operation.[68] This second principle curtails recovery for items that service members should have known would suffer damage during an operation, thus placing a reasonable limit on the scope of the government's extent of liability.[69] As the PCA in no way addresses losses suffered by nonmilitary personnel during an operation, it plays only a minimal role in the general objectives associated with operational claims.

3. Federal Tort Claims Act

The FTCA provides a limited waiver to the U.S. government's sovereign immunity by permitting persons harmed by government employees' acts or omissions to file a claim.[70] However, the FTCA also provides the authority for denying claims by U.S. service members against the government for injuries sustained while conducting military operations. Furthermore, because the FTCA does not cover acts that occur outside the United States, only domestic military operations, such as disaster response or homeland defense, will fall within its scope.[71]

With regard to potential claims during a military operation, the FTCA does not permit a "claim for the personal injury or death of, or the loss of or damage to property belonging to, a member of the Armed Forces of the United States that occurs incident to service," also known as the *Feres* Doctrine.[72] This exercise of sovereign immunity protects the government from the potentially infinite damage claims that service members could file as a result of injuries sustained

---

[67] Personnel Claims Act, 31 U.S.C. § 3721 (2006).

[68] *Id.* (loss, damage, or destruction of personal property of military personnel or civilian employees incident to their service); AR 27-20, *supra* note 26, para. 11-11d ("The type of property claimed and the amount or quantity claimed was reasonable or useful under the attendant circumstances for the claimant to have used or possessed incident to military service or employment.").

[69] Commanders will often publish policies on what is acceptable and reasonable to possess during an operation; a commander could limit the amount of DVDs a service member can possess, for example to twenty, which would limit a service member's ability to claim more than twenty DVDs should his or her personal property be lost or suffer damage.

[70] Federal Tort Claims Act, 28 U.S.C. §§ 2671–2680 (2006).

[71] 28 U.S.C. § 2680k (1988); Beattie v. United States, 756 F.2d 91 (D.C. Cir. 1984). The FTCA also excludes admiralty claims. 28 U.S.C. § 2671–680 (1988).

[72] Feres v. United States, 340 U.S. 135 (1950).

during training, deployment, or execution of military missions. The umbrella of federal benefits, such as medical care, disability, and retirement are considered to sufficiently substitute for the necessity of filing an FTCA claim, sue, or otherwise recover damages due to military-related service. Although the *Feres* Doctrine is subject to constant attack and critique,[73] it has survived for more than six decades, and although the FTCA's exclusion of incidents occurring outside the United States makes it relatively insignificant to operations in foreign states, it provides potentially important redress for U.S. residents who suffer harm during the execution of domestic military training and operations.

4. Maritime Claims

Damages caused by military operations do not always occur on land. The movement of personnel and equipment by sea, activities at a port, and the conduct of hostilities by a naval force may subject a military force to maritime claims. Often, in support of a contingency operation, the military force will move equipment and supplies by merchant vessel, and if the ship causes damage, a person may seek compensation for such damage.[74] Three statutes permit claims arising from maritime incidents involving torts: the Suits in Admiralty Act (SAA), 46 U.S.C. §§ 30901–30918; the Public Vessels Act (PVA), 46 U.S.C. §§ 31101–31113; and the Army Maritime Claims Settlement Act (AMCSA), 10 U.S.C. §§ 4801, 4802, and 4806. The SAA and PVA both provide waivers of sovereign immunity for property damage and personal injury caused by U.S. employees or vessels in the service of the United States on international waters or the waters of a foreign state.[75] Claims on the seas may include negligent maintenance or operation of vessels or aircraft, or towing or salvaging requirements that resulted from the damage.[76] Interestingly, a national of a foreign country may not bring an action under the PVA unless the government of that foreign national would, under similar circumstances, allow U.S. nationals to bring suit in its courts.[77] In contrast, the SAA facilitates claims by waiving U.S. government sovereign immunity for damage suffered as a result of government-owned merchant vessels.[78]

Next, the AMCSA establishes administrative settlement and compromise of admiralty and maritime claims both in favor of and against the United States

---

[73] *See, e.g.*, Andrew Cohen, *Quietly, U.S. Moves to Block Lawsuits by Military Families*, The Atlantic (Jan. 30, 2012), *available at* http://www.theatlantic.com/national/archive/2012/01/quietly-us-moves-to-block-lawsuits-by-military-families/252171/.

[74] *Id.*

[75] *See* 10 U.S.C. § 7622 (2006) and 32 C.F.R. § 752.1-752.5 (2012) for the Navy; 10 U.S.C. § 646 (2006) and 33 C.F.R. Part 25 (2012) for the Coast Guard; 10 U.S.C. §§ 4802-6 (2006) and 33 C.F.R. §§ 536.44-536.45 (2012) for the Army; 10 U.S.C. § 9802 (2006) and 32 C.F.R. Part 842 (2012) for the Air Force.

[76] 46 U.S.C. § 31101 (2006); OPLAW Handbook, *supra* note 16, at 303.

[77] 46 U.S.C. § 31111 (2006).

[78] 46 U.S.C. § 30903 (2006).

involving the Army.[79] All maritime claims statutes incorporate general maritime law and recognize the concept of proportional fault, which applies to claims against the U.S. government.[80] In addition to the three specialty maritime claims statutes, the FCA also recognizes maritime claims as cognizable if they arise on the high seas or in the territorial waters of foreign countries.[81] In addressing responses to maritime losses, many factors will influence the choice of the applicable claims statutes, including: the service involved (for example, the AMCSA); the location of the incident (triggering the FCA if the event occurs on the high seas or territorial waters of a foreign country); the type of U.S. vessel involved (applying the SAA if it involves a merchant vessel); and, the question whether the vessel was engaged in combat activities (negating application under the FCA). Maritime claims likely comprise a small fraction of the potential pool of claims events during an operation, but the U.S. military must be prepared to apply these maritime claims procedures.

5. International Agreements Claims Act

In 1954 Congress enacted the International Agreements Claims Act (IACA), authorizing payment of obligations under treaties and international agreements, primarily as a mechanism to permit claims payments under the NATO SOFA and subsequent agreements.[82] Increasing numbers of U.S. operations in partnership and coordination with friendly foreign forces necessitated a mechanism to soothe damage-related disputes that arose among allies. Section 2734a of the IACA authorizes the U.S. government to pay claims arising out of incidents caused by foreign forces within the United States, while section 2734b authorizes the U.S. government to reimburse foreign governments for the U.S. share of claims pursuant to a reciprocal claims agreement.

The IACA specifically covers: damage to, or loss of, real property of any foreign country or of any political subdivision or inhabitant of a foreign country, including damage or loss incident to use and occupancy; damage to, or loss of, personal property of any foreign country or of any political subdivision or inhabitant of a foreign country, including property bailed to the United States; or personal injury to, or death of, any inhabitant of a foreign country, as long as the damage, loss, or injury occurs outside the United States and is incident to noncombat activities and is caused by a military member or civilian employee of the armed forces. A two-year statute of limitations applies to claims under the IACA, and a commander or claims commission must deem the claimant friendly to the United States when the claim is filed by a citizen of a country at war with the United States or an ally of a state at war with the United States.

---

[79] Interestingly, the U.S. Army has more boats in its inventory than the U.S. Navy. Corporal Jeffrey Daniel, *Army's "Best Kept Secret" Floats*, WWW.ARMY.MIL (Jan. 26, 2012), http://www.army.mil/article/72469.

[80] DA PAM 27–162, *supra* note 16, para. 2-61e.

[81] *Id.* para. 10-2d.

[82] 10 U.S.C. §§ 2734a, 2734b (2006).

Finally, just like the FCA, the IACA does not apply to combat activities, with a notable declared exception for an accident or malfunction incident to the operation of an aircraft and its ordnance while preparing for, going to, or returning from a combat mission.[83]

In contrast to IACA, an international agreement may in some cases undermine state authority to pay claims. The June 1999 Military Technical Agreement between NATO-led Kosovo Forces (KFOR) and the Federal Republic of Yugoslavia is an example. That agreement declared that KFOR forces were not liable "for any damages to private or public property that they may cause in the course of duties related to the implementation of this Agreement."[84] This expansive provision covering the spectrum of activities during the military operation created an environment where U.S. and other KFOR forces could not pay claims as the international agreement subordinated the U.S. claims laws. This undermined the use of operational claims to contribute to efforts to mitigate harm suffered by the local populace as the consequence of KFOR activities, even when such harm was not directly the result of combat and KFOR was clearly at fault. The KFOR forces responded to this blanket claims prohibition by entering into a joint declaration between the United Nations and NATO forces indicating that troop-contributing nations would "establish procedures in order to address any third party claims for property loss or damage and personal injury caused by them or any of their personnel."[85] For U.S. forces the declaration provided a method to implement U.S. claims authorities without being limited by inconsistent international agreements. However, had this accommodation not been reached, all claims in Kosovo would have remained prohibited. The effort to redress this issue demonstrates the vital role compensation plays in establishing and maintaining a safe and secure environment during military operations.

C. CLAIMS ADJUDICATION PRINCIPLES

The previous sections examine and explain the United States' approach to operational claims, yet the process involves much more than knowledge of relevant legal authorities. It is inevitable that the operational claims context will involve limitless factual scenarios in which a claim must be adjudicated. Thus, commanders and claims officials require tools to implement the existing laws and policies effectively. These tools guide commanders and their claims adjudicators' decision-making processes to ensure claims contribute to mission accomplishment.

---

[83] *Id.*

[84] Military Technical Agreement between the International Security Force ("KFOR") and the Governments of the Federal Republic of Yugoslavia and the Republic of Serbia, Appendix B, para. 3 (June 9, 1999), *available at* http:/www.nato.int/Kosovo/docu/a990609a.htm.

[85] Joint Declaration, Commander, KFOR, UN SRSG, Kosovo (17 Aug. 2000) (classified NATO document).

The legal standard of proof for a claim is commonly a preponderance of the evidence, and the burden of proof lies on the claimant to prove the injury or damage.[86] As with traditional tort analysis, the military force must have had a duty of care, and the claimant must show a breach of the duty and proof of the damage or injury. The adjudicator must also consider actual and proximate cause—"but for" the acts or omissions of the military members, the damage or injury would not have occurred, and that the damage or injury was a foreseeable consequence of this cause when determining whether to compensate the claimant.

An operational claims program may also incorporate an appeals process. Where implemented, the applicable standard of appellate review will generally be whether the initial adjudication was "clearly erroneous" or resulted in "manifest injustice."[87] An appeals process is intended to provide the claimant with a greater sense of confidence in the claim adjudication. If nothing else, it endows the individual claimant with the knowledge that an authority higher in the military organization than the initial adjudicator or the commander of the unit in close proximity to the individual will consider that person's grievance. An appeals process also gives the higher headquarters of the operational command the opportunity to assist the adjudicator and commander closest to the event by imprinting its strategic objectives upon the process. Thus, in cases where the claim itself has failed to satisfy all the requisite elements at the intake level, the claimant may benefit from a strategic humanitarian view at the appellate level. The risk of an appeals process lies in the fact that the appellate adjudicator may have the most complete and advantageous viewpoint with an eye toward consistent application across a theater of operations, which could result in undermining the local area commander's objectives. In either event, the delicate and sometimes logistically difficult process of appeals adds one more potential benefit to the local citizens and support of the rule of law. Ultimately, commanders should always endeavor to incorporate an appeal and reconsideration process to both provide a "second look" at claims and to allow for presentation of new evidence. This latter aspect of a claims appeal is especially important, as it can be difficult for either the claimant or the armed force to have all of the facts at the moment a claim is submitted, a time often filled with turmoil.

The principles of speed, transparency, and accuracy also play integral roles in operational claims adjudication. Timely adjudication of claims helps aggrieved citizens cover medical expenses, funerals, or simply the cost of adequate food and shelter in extreme situations. Speed prevents both suffering and potential festering of grievances. Additionally, in the interest of force protection and establishing goodwill with the local populace, resolving claims quickly can avoid alienating the citizenry against the armed forces. Transparency promotes trust in the rule of law: when a claims adjudicator settles a claim among the populace for differing

---

[86] ISAF uses a balance of probabilities, or 51 percent. HQISAF SOP 1151, *supra* note 46, at Annex A, para. 5.

[87] NATO uses these two standards for appeals. *Id.* at 10.

amounts, whether the factual case presented is exactly the same or not, claimants inevitably communicate, compare, and eventually complain to the armed forces about perceived disparate treatment. To maintain good relations with the populace, transparency underscores a fair and just grievance system. Then, accuracy mitigates fraud, waste, and abuse involving claimants, for the benefit of the host- nation government and the military itself regarding stewardship of its resources. Accuracy depends upon armed forces' reporting of events that may result in claims with as much detail as possible. It also relies upon a comprehensive record-keeping system that can be searched to determine whether a similar claim had been filed by the same potential claimant or that the claim was in fact paid. Further, a file system also promotes transparency by giving the adjudicator a frame of reference to compare a similar previous claim. Finally, an adjudicator may deny a claim for any number of reasons to buttress accuracy, but the concept of spreading goodwill and justice should remain a part of the strategic approach, particularly in disputable, unclear, or close cases. Common criticisms of a claims program can often be traced back to deviation from these principles. Accordingly, constant emphasis on these principles of speed, transparency, and accuracy mitigates the frequency and viability of these criticisms.

The myriad of challenges routinely confronted by claims personnel quickly stack one upon another. When a claims official receives a claim during a contingency operation, the requested relief can range from provision of livestock to a loss of potential income. The claim may also originate from an unexpected source, possibly the individual harmed, a family member, a tribal representative, or even a political representative on behalf of the suffering party. Regarding who may file a claim, a claim for wrongful injury or death may be filed by or on behalf of a decedent's spouse, parent, child, or dependent relative. In some areas of the world, it would not be uncommon for the senior male in the family that suffered the harm to be a minor, and due to the cultural restrictions upon women conducting business or being seen with or conversing with non-family member males, a claims officer may encounter a young male child presenting a claim on behalf of his family.[88] Whenever possible, claims personnel should attempt to attribute the claim to the specific aggrieved person or appointed agent or appropriate family representative, and obtain substantial documentation regarding the authority of the individual filing the claim, in order to prevent future protests.

In the area of potential compensation, under the FCA or other applicable claims laws such as the maritime laws mentioned above, complex issues often

---

[88] Dealing with minors can be a sensitive matter because the child may not possess the maturity or requisite knowledge to understand the process or consequences of the transaction, or the adjudicator may simply be uncomfortable dealing with a child on such a serious matter. As claims officials apply local laws and customs to the extent practical, perverse interpretations and outcomes may result. For example, Article 97 of the Iraqi Civil Code states that a rational minor over the age of seven years can make decisions on the disposition of property, even over the objection of guardians, if the benefit of the disposition favors the minor. This could create an unusual circumstance when a claim is received from a minor. IRAQI CIVIL CODE art. 97, *available at* http://gjpi.org/wp-content/uploads/2009/01/civilcode198-5011.pdf (last visited June 6, 2015).

include verifying medical expenses, determining earning capacity, or valuing nurturing in an unfamiliar social setting. A hypothetical involving the loss of future earnings demonstrates some of the complexity:

> In a deployed environment, the armed force cut down trees and destroyed a crop near a forward operating base because they impaired the visual security of the base. The landowner, the head of a large family, files a claim for the value of the trees and crop, and the claims adjudicator approves a claim based upon the negotiated value. Several months later, a minor son of the now deceased landowner returns to file another claim for the value of another crop because he states that he will not be able to cultivate the land due to the continuing presence of the armed forces.

The scenario contains potential evidence of lost future earnings, but includes the difficulty of valuing the lost income and a timing factor. It is arguable that the claimant should have collected for future lost earnings at the time of the initial claim; however, theoretically the armed forces' presence is only temporary, and it is difficult to forecast the duration of the property loss. Finally, all claims are subject to the availability of funds; within the United States, this depends upon yearly congressional authorizations and appropriations. Forecasting too far in advance may therefore risk violation of fiscal legal restrictions prohibiting obligating funds that would have otherwise not been needed in the future due to a change in mission. This relatively minor element of a claim may have large repercussions for the landowner, local populace, and the ultimate effectiveness of the claims process.

D. CLAIMS ALTERNATIVES

Despite the maturity of U.S. operational claims missions, some settings nonetheless reveal gaps in the force's ability to effectively implement an operational claims program. Most notably, the FCA's combat activities exclusion creates an impediment to compensating victims for harm suffered when the victim was in no way at fault and the commander believes some compensation will contribute to the strategic end state. Although civilians' initial attempts to file claims after an incident in which they suffer harm may be denied, that is not always the end of the process.[89] In an effort to propagate the principle of humanity and build support for the military mission, U.S. and several other armed forces developed policies permitting goodwill, or ex gratia, payments to maintain good relations with

[89] In November 2004, an innocent Iraqi civilian was killed in the crossfire between American and anti-Iraqi forces. Subsequently, the victim's brother filed a claim against U.S. forces under the FCA, and although the JAG denied the claim using an incidental to combat exclusion, the JAG approved a condolence payment "as an expression of sympathy and good will and in the best interest of the US government." JONATHAN TRACY, COMPENSATING CIVILIAN CASUALTIES: "I AM SORRY FOR YOUR LOSS, AND I WISH YOU WELL IN A FREE IRAQ" 3 (2007), http://www.hks.harvard.edu/cchrp/Tracy%20Report%20Nov%203%202008.pdf.

the host nation and its citizens despite the absence of legal liability.[90] Generally, these payments are reserved for private property damages or personal injury, but not for host-nation government property or injury.

Ex gratia payments make an important contribution to force protection for deployed forces by mitigating the impact of their military operations upon the populace and thereby ameliorating potential ill will against the deployed forces. The maintenance of goodwill counteracts citizen discontent and any incentive to exact revenge upon friendly forces. Robust use of ex gratia payments can also contribute to the perceived legitimacy of the host-nation government, particularly if friendly forces participate in nation building to restore the function of the host-nation government. Although technically these payments serve to offset the harm caused by U.S. operations, the combined efforts of U.S. and host-nation authorities will often mean attribution for both harm and compensation will not be segregated by the local population. To support this objective, host-nation forces or authorities may also assist in the verification process.[91] In the context of a specific type of conflict, such as counterinsurgency, this alternative compensation procedure may be a vital tool for winning the hearts and minds of the civilian population, in turn generating support for the government and sending state forces rather than the insurgency.[92]

The United States often refers to its version of ex gratia payments as solatia. Solatia payments are not claims; rather, they are payments in money or in kind to a victim or victim's relative as an expression of sympathy or condolence, intended to offer relief immediately after an event to express sympathy in accordance with local custom.[93] United States' policy only authorizes solatia programs in geographic areas where such payments are widely recognized as custom or a cultural norm.[94] Hence, solatia payments provide a way to offset the impact of the FCA combat activities exclusion, allowing payments to individuals who suffer harm at the hands of U.S. forces during armed conflict. Although armed forces leaders

---

[90] For example, ISAF instituted a policy of goodwill payments for damage to privately owned property or individual suffering due to injury when the damage or injury was caused by ISAF forces. HQISAF SOP 1151, *supra* note 46, para. 2.

[91] John Ryan, *Condolence Payments to Afghans Total Millions*, ARMY TIMES (Jan. 23, 2012), *available at* http://www.armytimes.com/news/2012/01/military-afghanistan-condlence-payments-millions-012312w/.

[92] NATO Security Forces (SFOR) also used ex gratia payment procedures when claims were not cognizable. In 2002, the SFOR Commander authorized ex gratia payments to alleviate "personal wrongs" and to help citizens repair their village after SFOR troops caused property damage while searching for an indicted criminal. Prescott, *supra* note 9, at I.a. Armed forces may also use ex gratia payments to compensate survivors and surviving family members as a result of combat operations. For example, when U.S. forces in Afghanistan conducted an air strike in 2011 that killed several civilians, U.S. forces paid each survivor about \$2,900 and the families of the deceased about \$4,800. David S. Cloud, *High-Tech Tools and Human Errors*, L.A. TIMES, Apr. 10, 2011. Similarly, United Kingdom armed forces paid approximately £2,900 for civilian deaths in Afghanistan. Mark Townsend, *Nato Draws Up Payout Tariffs for Afghan Civilian Deaths*, THE OBSERVER, Feb. 27, 2010.

[93] OPLAW Handbook, *supra* note 16, at 305.

[94] DA PAM 27-162, *supra* note 21, para. 10-10.

need not make solatia payments, most seek to use this discretionary authority in order to maintain goodwill and demonstrate empathy in support of the mission.

Legally, these payments are not an admission of fault; claims payments under a U.S. statutory authority such as the FCA or an ex gratia payment under a claims alternative program are never an admission of fault. Instead, these "gratuitous" payments make a positive impression on the populace of the armed forces' compassion and understanding.[95] As a result of the gratuitous nature of solatia, funds come from the unit's O&M funds unless otherwise appropriated by Congress. This is an important distinction from payment of FCA claims, which are funded from dedicated claims appropriations. As a result, solatia payments consume finite resources relied upon by the commander to sustain operations and training. This demonstrates the interconnectedness of a claims program and solatia, as claims personnel must maintain awareness of both programs. Doing so ensures viable FCA claims are paid by dedicated claims funds that do not deplete O&M funds. Furthermore, if the adjudicator later awards a claim for the same event in which a solatia payment was made, the amount of the solatia payment should be deducted from the claim award. This prevents overpayment for an individual incident, and again promotes fairness when redressing the population's grievances. Finally, the armed force using solatia or ex gratia payments may not have caused the harm, yet they might find it in their strategic or operational interest to provide some form of compensation, such as in a case where insurgents cause the death of civilians or damage to their property.

During the most recent U.S. conflicts in Iraq and Afghanistan, the United States initially failed to implement solatia payments. This was based on a determination that solatia was not a customary practice in either country.[96] Unfortunately, this determination did not obviate the need for U.S. commanders to have access to some method for compensating victims of the conflicts in order to complete their mission, protect the force, and mitigate the suffering produced by the conflicts. Thus, beginning in Iraq, and later spreading to Afghanistan, the United States created a program called the Commander's Emergency Response Program (CERP) as an alternative to the statutory claims process.

The CERP program originated during Operation Iraqi Freedom to provide commanders with a compensation tool for the benefit of the Iraqi populace,

---

[95] Memorandum, Deputy Gen. Couns. (Int'l. Aff.), Dep't of Def. to Chairman, Joint Chiefs of Staff, subject: Solatia (Nov. 26, 2004).

[96] Even though the U.S. military did not immediately adopt solatia payment processes, other U.S. agencies implemented claims-like programs such as the Afghan Civil Assistance Program run by the United States Agency for International Development (USAID). This also demonstrates that other entities besides the armed force may be heavily involved in a claims operation. USAID Office of Inspector General, Audit of USAID/Afghanistan's Afghan Civilian Assistance Program, Audit Report No. 5-206-10-004-P (2009). Some posit that more effective claims programs will have military officers both control the process and make the payments because their interaction with civilians will enhance the goodwill of the compensation. Jonathan Tracey, *Responsibility to Pay: Compensating Civilian Casualties of War*, 15(1) Human Rights Brief 18 (2007).

sourced by seized funds of the Ba'athist Party.[97] This new program provided a speedy alternative to claims, and empowered commanders to exercise maximum initiative and flexibility in a range of stability and humanitarian operations.[98] In practice, these payments were similar to solatia. Authorized uses for CERP included: water and sanitation; food production and distribution; agriculture; electricity; healthcare; education; telecommunications; economic, financial and management improvements; transportation, rule of law and governance, irrigation; civic cleanup activities; civic support vehicles; repair of civic and cultural facilities; battle damage not compensable under the FCA; condolence payments to civilians for death, injury, or property damage; payments to individuals upon release from detention; protective measures to enhance the durability and survivability of a critical infrastructure site; and other urgent humanitarian or reconstruction projects.[99] Originally, CERP excluded payments to individuals, but eventually it morphed to cover "repair of damage that results from U.S., coalition, or supporting military operations and is not compensable under the [FCA];" and, "condolence payments to individual civilians for death, injury, or property damage resulting from U.S., coalition, or supporting military operations."[100] As commanders grew accustomed to CERP's flexibility, and the seized Iraqi funds began to dwindle, Congress appropriated funds for CERP, thus creating a supplemental account from U.S. claims appropriations through the defense budget.

The CERP program did not cure all claims ills during the Iraq campaign, or the campaign in Afghanistan when it spread to Operation Enduring Freedom in 2005. One significant difficulty surfaced in that little identifiable difference existed between what qualified for a FCA claim and a CERP-appropriate payment, except for the combat-activities limitation. If a claimant presented under the FCA (because most victims during operations received a claims card/notice) and the claim resulted in denial, then the claims official bore the responsibility of referring the rejected claimant to a commander's CERP program, often administered by a different officer in the command. This often caused confusion and a lack of compensation synchronization. The CERP program also lacked an

---

[97] The Coalition Provisional Authority received the charge from Congress to enable U.S. military commanders in Iraq to respond to urgent humanitarian relief and reconstruction requirements, resourcing the effort with the seized Iraqi assets. American soldiers discovered caches of U.S. currency throughout Iraq, including aluminum boxes with approximately $650 million in Baghdad, and $112 million in an animal kennel, along with other seizures. Lieutenant Colonel Mark Martins, *No Small Change of Soldiering: The Commander's Emergency Response Program (CERP) in Iraq and Afghanistan*, ARMY LAW. 12 (Feb. 2004). The overall CERP program also joined with Developmental Fund for Iraq of the United Nations to achieve humanitarian and reconstruction goals. *Id.*

[98] As a comparison to CERP, after OPERATION JUST CAUSE in Panama, the United States provided funds directly to the government of Panama to fund emergency needs, economic recovery, and development assistance. OPLAW Handbook, *supra* note 16, at 308.

[99] U.S. GEN. ACCT. OFF., MILITARY OPERATIONS: THE DEPARTMENT OF DEFENSE'S USE OF SOLATIA AND CONDOLENCE PAYMENTS IN IRAQ AND AFGHANISTAN 19 (2007), *available at* http://www.gao.gov/products/GAO-07-699.

[100] Memorandum, Under Secretary of Def. for Secretaries of the Military Departments, et al., subject: Commanders' Emergency Response Program (CERP) Guidance (July 27, 2009).

appellate process, transparency, and the formal adjudication process of a military claims program. In addition, as the CERP program provided speedier benefits, commanders often fell into the trap of addressing all claims issues using a CERP review, or confusing the process by making demands of a traditional claims officer or commission in furtherance of the CERP program.[101]

Ultimately, claims JAGs and command legal advisors experienced several obstacles when attempting to educate leaders and practice expectation management. Nonetheless, CERP definitively promoted community growth compared to the limitations of a traditional claims program and, when combined with a claims program, furthered the objective of humanitarian relief and just compensation for the adverse effects of combat. Unfortunately, CERP's limited duration and design specifically for the Iraq and Afghanistan theaters of operation means that U.S. commanders cannot count on its availability during future operations.

In contingencies where solatia is not authorized, and a claim is not cognizable under an existing law or policy, another approach for a military unit is to consider its capacity to repair damage, whether to roads, the natural environment, or a structure, using either their O&M funds or other fiscal authorization. Other fiscal authorizations could include humanitarian assistance funds authorized under the Foreign Assistance Act, or a specific DoD appropriation for humanitarian assistance may underwrite a project that benefits a community that otherwise suffered damage during an operation.[102] Humanitarian assistance funds, depending upon the specific authority, may fund repair of schools, hospitals, or roads, or underwrite other beneficial civic uses. These claims alternatives demonstrate that the U.S. military possesses several tools to implement an effective program to mitigate the harm it causes as a result of its operations.

IV. Multinational and NATO Claims Laws

Consistent with the view that international law does not create an obligation to compensate civilian victims of armed conflict or give individuals a mandated course of redress for violations of international humanitarian law, other states' courts cemented this position alongside the United States.[103] Whether as part of a coalition operation, forward-deployed stationing, or friendly training exercises, states regularly enter into agreements to frame their waivers of sovereign

---

[101] One method to avoid issues such as double payment is to put both a claims program and a solatia program under the responsibility of the servicing JAG; another, is to empower a specific officer or leader with the solatia authority and appoint a JAG officer as an advisor.

[102] *See* 22 U.S.C. § 2151 et seq. (2006); Humanitarian and Civic Assistance, 10 U.S.C. § 401 (2006); Foreign Disaster Assistance, Denton Transportation of Humanitarian Relief Supplies for NGOs, 10 U.S.C. § 402 (2006), 10 U.S.C. § 404 (2006); Humanitarian Demining Assistance, 10 U.S.C. § 407 (2006); Excess Nonlethal Supplies for Humanitarian Relief, 10 U.S.C. § 2557 (2006); Humanitarian Assistance, 10 U.S.C. § 2561 (2006).

[103] Rainer Hofmann, Toronto Conference, *supra* note 8, at 4, 9.

immunity and limit their exposure to foreign court adjudications involving their armed forces. Status of Forces Agreements (SOFAs) and other international agreements often define processes for resolution of claims issues between and among states during military operations.[104] Frequently, states will waive, or at least limit, claims between the parties for injury or damage to government property and personnel as long as the harm resulted from official activities within the scope of their official mission or purpose. The NATO SOFA implements this precise methodology, and includes other provisions that guide claims adjudication, covering both operational settings and the permanent and temporary stationing or training of forces in a host nation. Article VIII of the NATO SOFA states,

> Each Contracting Party waives all its claims against any other Contracting Party for damage to any property owned by it and used by its land; sea or air armed services, if such damage: was caused by a member or an employee of the armed services of the other Contracting Party in the execution of his duties in connection with the operation of the North Atlantic Treaty; or arose from the use of any vehicle, vessel or aircraft owned by the other Contracting Party and used by its armed services, provided either that the vehicle, vessel or aircraft causing the damage was being used in connection with the operation of the North Atlantic Treaty, or that the damage was caused to property being so used.[105]

The Contracting Parties also waived a category of private claim amounts, which for the United States is less than $1,400.[106]

Considering civilians, the NATO SOFA extends its protections beyond the members of the armed forces to include the civilian components of the armed forces, providing the same protections for acts within the scope of their official duties.[107] "Within the scope of official duties" is a crucial determination for the NATO claims process, much like a combat activities evaluation, because it will affect whether the damage or injury is recoverable. If the parties dispute whether the responsible individuals acted within the scope of their official duties, then the matter is subject to binding arbitration. The judgment regarding performance of official duties proves critical not only to potential claims for damage or harm to

---

[104] For example, damage or injury caused by ISAF members was covered by the Military Technical Agreement, later modified by an Exchange of Letters between the government of Afghanistan and the North Atlantic Treaty Organization (NATO) Secretary General. Military Technical Agreement between the International Security Assistance Force (ISAF) and the Interim Administration of Afghanistan ('Interim Administration') Annex A (4 Jan. 2002) [hereinafter ISAF MTA]; Exchange of Letters between the Islamic Republic of Afghanistan and the North Atlantic Treaty Organization Secretary General (5 Sep. 2004/22 Nov. 2004).

[105] NATO SOFA, *supra* note 11, art. VIII, para. 1. This covers government-owned military property and equipment; however, the NATO SOFA also covers other property by directing the use of an arbitrator if the Contracting Parties cannot agree on the liability or amount of damage. *Id.* art. VIII, para. 2.

[106] *Id.*

[107] *Id.* art. VIII, para. 5.

the Contracting Parties themselves, but also when members of the armed forces or civilian components cause harm to third parties, or persons or entities not a party to the NATO SOFA.

The NATO SOFA uses the ex gratia concept as a cornerstone for its compensation program, and for the United States, the FCA acknowledges ex gratia payments as a discretionary form of compensation.[108] However, the IACA, and not the FCA, provides statutory authority for U.S. payment of claims in states party to the NATO or Partnership for Peace SOFAs.[109] For both military and civilian components, the process starts when the harmed or injured person files the claim with the receiving state authorities; those authorities then investigate[110] and adjudicate the claim under their own laws, assess compensation, and finally deliver a report to the sending state of the responsible parties. Upon receipt of the report, the sending state will consider making an ex gratia payment in lieu of payment of an adjudicated claim, as the result of the general waiver of liability among the NATO members. If the responsible state offers an ex gratia payment, and the claimant accepts it as full compensation, then the matter closes; however, this process does not prevent the receiving state courts from entertaining a lawsuit against the sending state. Instead, it prevents the individual military or civilian member of the sending state armed force from being subject to the jurisdiction of the receiving state court.[111]

For harm caused by activities outside the scope of official duties, the NATO SOFA may also facilitate compensation. For example, where a U.S. service member maliciously injures a member of another contracting state's armed force in a fit of alcohol-induced rage, the act is unlikely to be considered to occur within the performance of official duties. As a result, the service member may well be personally liable for whatever damage or harm caused. Ultimately, a state or military command may still offer *ex gratia* payments as a way to soothe relations with the aggrieved party. The organization of NATO itself never accepts legal responsibility for damages or injury caused by military operations; thus, all NATO payments are ex gratia.

Once the parties determine responsibility and an award amount, the NATO SOFA also contains precise guidance on cost apportionment of claims among its parties.[112] Members of NATO share costs of claims under a framework based on which state, and how many states, bear responsibility for the harm. If one

---

[108] AR 27-20, *supra* note 26, at 107.

[109] The Partnership for Peace Status of Forces Agreement is a corollary of the NATO SOFA, and essentially similar, covering activities among the states that participate in the program. Agreement among the States Parties to the North Atlantic Treaty and Other States Participating in the Partnership for Peace regarding the Status of Their Forces, June 19, 1995, T.I.A.S. No. 12 [hereinafter PfP SOFA].

[110] Often the armed forces responsible for the incident will already have conducted an investigation, which may be shared with the receiving state authorities to assist in adjudication.

[111] NATO SOFA, *supra* note 11, art. VIII, para. 5.

[112] Whenever NATO member states operate within an environment that may give rise to claims, payment for loss of income is not authorized. HQISAF SOP 1151, *supra* note 46, at 7.

sending state alone bears responsibility, then the cost apportionment goes 25 percent to the receiving state and 75 percent to the sending state responsible for the damage or harm. When multiple states bear responsibility for the incident, then cost apportions are made equally, except when the receiving state is not a responsible party, in which case it shall contribute 50 percent of the amount of the other contributing states. Finally, where it is not possible to identify the responsible party, the NATO members share the cost equally, but again, if the receiving state forces are not involved, it pays only 50 percent of the other state parties' share.[113]

Claim settlement as a result of multinational or unilateral military operations must also take into consideration statutes of limitation. Although no international standard for statutes of limitation exists for claims, one practical limitation involves the issues of access to the armed force that caused the injury. Upon termination of the operation and departure of the armed forces from a foreign state, a potential claimant may no longer have access to the claims process except through a local court, which will rarely have the power to provide a meaningful remedy. Thus, during many military operations, armed forces establish a statute of limitations specific to the conflict. For example, in Afghanistan the International Security Assistance Force (ISAF) implemented a six-month statute of limitations from the period that the claimant suffered or could have reasonably discovered that he/she suffered harm or damage.[114] This framework provides some assurance for the state that when it commits its armed forces to an operation, a terminal date will exist to constrain the extent of its potential liabilities.

In a multinational operational environment, member states of a coalition may choose to make claims matters subject to national responsibility. That is, each troop-contributing nation will process claims in accordance with their own national policies and procedures when their forces are responsible for the damage or injury.[115] The participating members of NATO in Bosnia, Kosovo, and Afghanistan operations exercised this policy.[116] Alternatively, participating states may establish a common fund from which to settle claims.[117] Although NATO forces follow the ISAF procedure of national responsibility in Afghanistan, NATO also created a common fund (although small in comparison to national claims funds) from which to settle claims not attributable to a specific national force, or to cover those situations in which a responsible force cannot or will not settle the claim due to a contradiction with national policy or unavailability of funds.[118] This common fund developed from voluntary contributions of the ISAF troop-contributing nations.

---

[113] NATO SOFA, *supra* note 11, art. VIII, para. 5.

[114] *Id.* This policy applied to ISAF forces, but participating state national policies could have modified or extended this period.

[115] NATO, as an institution, does not have a policy in place to pay combat-related damages or injury or operational necessity, much like the prohibited claims under the U.S. FCA. *See* HQISAF SOP 1151, *supra* note 46.

[116] Major Sonya Vichnevestskaia, *ISAF Claims Process in a Nutshell*, ISAF Legal Gazette (Sept. 30, 2008).

[117] NATO SOFA, *supra* note 11; PfP SOFA, *supra* note 109.

[118] ISAF forces also follow this procedure, drawing from a common fund when a responsible ISAF force cannot be identified. Vichnevestskaia, *supra* note 116.

NATO's first experience involving significant claims operations was in Bosnia-Herzegovina, where it implemented a complicated claims system with host-nation participation, piggybacking on an inadequate United Nations claims mission.[119] This initial program used the Dayton Status of Forces Agreements and the General Framework Agreement for Peace as the legal foundations. These agreements made Bosnia-Herzegovina responsible for claims intake. No waivers among the participating states existed, but the agreements excluded combat-related damages.[120] Overall, the policy showed that a NATO headquarters may impose an obligation upon itself to pay claims and suggest its process as a model to participating states; however, states could follow their own laws and policies.[121]

This NATO claims system did not last long as the participating forces determined that Bosnia-Herzegovina could not process the claims effectively.[122] Troop-contributing nations then accepted responsibility for intake, processing, and adjudication of claims resulting from their own operations. If a claimant disagreed with the offered settlement, a NATO International Forces (IFOR) claims office mediated, and, if mediation was unsuccessful, a claims commission acted as the final arbiter.[123] The claims commission attempted to resolve disputes between the receiving state entity and the IFOR armed force, and had to reach a unanimous conclusion.[124] If this process failed, then the claim went before an Arbitration Tribunal, and finally, if the tribunal's order was not carried out, the matter went to NATO Headquarters for final disposition.[125] As some IFOR participating states experienced, claims commissions decisions could cause fiscal issues under domestic laws. For example, if a proposed paying state lacked representation on the commission itself, the state may lack authority to pay the claim because the commission was comprised of all foreign personnel.[126] Overall, the NATO experience in Bosnia-Herzegovina illustrates how significant a claims program can be during peacekeeping operations, having received and processed more than thirteen thousand claims and paying out more than 11 million Euros.[127]

---

[119] The Handbook of the Law of Visiting Forces 173–4 (Dieter Fleck ed., 2001).

[120] General Framework Agreement for Peace in Bosnia and Herzegovina, Annex 1-A, art. VI, para. 9(a) Dec. 14, 1995.

[121] NATO Claims Policy for Designated Crisis Response Situations, Annex 1, AC/119-N(2004)0058 (May 19, 2004).

[122] The Handbook of the Law of Visiting Forces, *supra* note 119, at 170.

[123] *Id.* at 171. The claims commission comprised of two IFOR and two receiving state representatives, all with legal qualifications. Prescott, *supra* note 9, at I.a.

[124] Prescott, *supra* note 9, at I.a.

[125] *Id.*

[126] NATO Legal Deskbook 273 (Sherrod L. Bumgardner et al. eds, 2d ed. 2010 [hereinafter NATO Legal Deskbook]. For the United States, representation on a claims commission was not a determining factor for payment; even if the United States had representation, if U.S. claims authorities disagreed with the Commission's decision, the United States still did not pay the claim. Prescott, *supra* note 9.

[127] NATO Legal Deskbook, *supra* note 126, at 274.

The existing NATO claims policy, adopted in 2010, makes no changes with respect to a troop-contributing nation's obligations, because the policy is non-binding. Nonetheless, the policy's most critical components outline the humanitarian aspects of operations and the suffering that civilians in the conflict area endure, and the policy ultimately urges proactive assistance to mitigate the harmful effects of combat.[128] Consistent with most national policies, NATO forces exclude combat-related and mission-necessity activities from their coalition claims programs, such as detention operations, riot control, force protection, and of course, combat.[129] In many operational environments, NATO forces also enjoy immunity, sometimes broad and close to absolute, from host-nation claims. As the Military Technical Agreement between ISAF and the interim Government of the Republic of Afghanistan states, "The ISAF and its personnel will not be liable for any damages to civilian or government property caused by any activity in pursuit of the ISAF Mission."[130] As combat operations accelerated and spread throughout the country, the need for an alternate claims program arose. Although legally immune, several NATO troop-contributing nations established the Post-Operational Humanitarian Relief Fund,[131] which applied to incidents not otherwise covered by existing claims policies. By 2003, ISAF itself implemented a policy of paying for mission-related damages caused by ISAF forces for force protection reasons.[132] For the United States, in light of its national laws and policies prohibiting compensation for combat-related damage, its armed forces could then use the solatia system (or CERP as described above).

Brief analysis of a September 2009 NATO air strike in Kunduz, Afghanistan highlights several challenges, including the intersection of claims adjudication principles and those of war crimes. The Taliban hijacked two tanker trucks, and NATO forces, in this case German forces, called for an air strike. The strike was effective; however, dozens of civilians may have also died from the it.[133] The aftermath spawned several investigations by NATO, German, and Afghan authorities, as well as NGOs, some occurring months after the event. Consequently, multiple investigations conducted by multinational entities and organizations with varying interests resulted in different findings and points of emphasis, and inconsistencies.[134] Moreover, security classification of information, which may

[128] Non-binding Guidelines for Payments in Combat-Related Cases of Civilian Casualties or Damage to Civilian Property, Annex to SG (2010)0377 (June 11, 2010), (on file with author).

[129] NATO Legal Deskbook, *supra* note 126, at 273.

[130] ISAF MTA, *supra* note 104, Annex A, para. 10.

[131] NATO Legal Deskbook, *supra* note 126, at 278.

[132] *Id.* at 276.

[133] Nichilas Kulish, *German General Quits over Airstrike*, The N.Y. Times (Nov. 27, 2009), *available at* http://www.nytimes.com/2009/11/27/world/europe/27germany.html?_r=2&pagewanted=pr.

[134] Events such as this led ISAF to adopt a strategy of initiating immediate investigations of civilian casualties, conducted by the nation whose armed forces were involved in the event. This policy has a positive impact of immediate response, but also receives criticism in allowing a nation whose armed forces were involved in the event to provide the narrative with the potential of a skewed version to promote national interests.

have included aircraft video, radio transmission recordings, or filed reports by troops involved, also inhibited all interested parties from sharing the same facts. Further, in some circumstances, nations may not make their personnel available to provide statements to other investigating entities, citing sovereign immunity or other agreements such as a SOFA that may provide protections to the operational forces. Another overarching challenge arises due to the nature of current military conflicts, specific to counter-insurgency (COIN) and other conflicts where terrorists, insurgents, or other irregular armed forces live and blend-in with the local populace, and that is identifying a combatant vice a civilian. Military leaders and operators face this challenge in the heat of the moment of use-of-force decision-making, and claims adjudicators must make a similar determination when assessing the status of claimants. In the end, the ability to obtain the most enhanced picture and details of what really happened is often hampered.

We return now to the Kunduz strike, where, ultimately, negotiations between lawyers for the victims' families and German officials resulted in German Bundeswehr application of an ex gratia claims payment for the victims of the air strike, determinedly avoiding admissions of guilt or recognizing legal liability.[135] The German government also officially declared its mission in Afghanistan to be a non-international armed conflict, which then encompassed the operation as part of war and invited the combat exclusion from a traditional claim and legal liability.[136] The German government became intimately involved in the process, over and above its armed force in Afghanistan, adding political complexities to the process.[137] The Kunduz air strike presents just one simplified example of military force that caused injuries to potentially unintended persons and the complications surrounding the events that eventually give rise to claims. Cooperation of interested parties and the ability to reconstruct an accurate accounting of military operations are just broad scope challenges to the claims process. Several more hurdles arise once the claims process begins.

V. Claims Challenges in Military Operations

A. ACCESS AND INFORMATION

Military forces encounter both legal and practical challenges to effectively implementing an operational claims program. These challenges often arise from a seemingly simple event. To illustrate, consider a typical claim in a modern operational environment arising from a road traffic accident. Quite often, claims adjudicators find it difficult to assess the damage because the accident occurred some distance away, or the initial claim lacks critical information necessary to resolve

---

[135] Gebauer, *supra* note 43 (the German government paid the victims about $5,000 each).

[136] *Id.*

[137] Although such a situation would not be impossible with U.S. forces, as the U.S. claims mission is commander centric, the threat of policymaker involvement is decreased.

the matter.[138] Upon intake, the official will seek more information in most cases; accordingly, claims personnel often have to gather information themselves, sometimes traveling to areas with risk of significant peril. Upon arrival, claims personnel often find the site unfamiliar, because the area does not look like it did at the time of the incident, and they may have concerns as to whether the people around (if any) are friendly, cautious, or hostile and whether they will be able to effectively communicate with the claimant or witnesses, as well as concerns for their own safety. A complex claim can require multiple trips, to the same site or others, and can take a significant length of time to develop into a full and accurate picture. This elapsed time may create a problem for the claimant in his or her anxiousness in getting satisfaction, and for a commander who views an unresolved claim as one more impediment to fulfilling the military mission.

As this illustration highlights, claims operations involve much more than simply reviewing files and are oftentimes military missions for the exclusive purpose of effective and efficient claim adjudication. These military missions are necessary as the reality that presentation of claims rarely includes detailed documentation of the incident or loss. Furthermore, such documentation is often difficult to acquire due to the chaotic nature of military operations or quite possibly the lack of law enforcement infrastructure to respond to incidents of loss or damage. The local populace may also expect in-person communications when they encounter the ill effects of military operations, while many armed forces establish high-tech communications and use intermediaries with the idea that they will be able to more effectively, and safely, communicate with the claimants.[139] However, these efforts often simply exacerbate existing suspicions and cultural differences.

Additional complexities lie in unperceived claimants' expectations. As an example, after U.S. forces conducted an errant raid that resulted in the deaths of several Afghan officials and civilians, senior officials held a council with local leaders at which U.S. forces brought sheep as a sign of goodwill.[140] However, the local elders were not only interested in compensation, but also wanted information regarding the intelligence that led to the raids, specifically the "spy" who led the Americans to the location of the raid.[141] Examples such as this demonstrate the interconnectedness of claims programs and the fundamental aspects of

[138] A claims officer will usually conduct some type of investigation. The scope of an investigation can range from simple document review, to interviews with the claimant and/or witnesses, to questioning of the military members allegedly involved in the incident, to site visits in order to assess the amount of damage from the road traffic accident. These missions often involve perils and require considerable resources to complete, while sometimes not resulting in any additional helpful information because the site conditions changed or witnesses are absent or unwilling to communicate.

[139] One practical step of requiring operational forces to carry claims forms in their vehicles to distribute to citizens involved in an automobile accident mitigates, but cannot eliminate, these cultural challenges. Forces in Afghanistan discovered that when they distributed claims forms at the site of an accident, it reduced the number of citizens who would follow the armed forces back to their operational bases, resulting in better force protection. *See* Prescott, *supra* note 9, at I.c.

[140] Julius Cavendish, *US Military Offers Sheep in Apology for Afghanistan Deaths*, THE CHRISTIAN SCIENCE MONITOR (Apr. 8, 2010).

[141] *Id.*

combat and military operations. These efforts provide benefits in the citizenry's perception of the military's willingness to be present and part of the process, as well as in enabling the claims team to obtain evidence independently and fashion their own impressions of the circumstances, damage, or injury. Although this will often result in significant security risks, commanders support these missions and accept this risk because they know effective claims operations may ultimately save lives by building trust with the local populace and contributing to a safe and secure environment.

B. REASON AND PERCEPTION

More challenges arise when considering negligence and the reasonableness of the actions of either the armed force's members or the claimant. Consider the case of a traffic control point, where a civilian vehicle approaches the armed force. A military member may fire upon the vehicle if he or she determines that the vehicle is approaching too quickly, but possibly the driver missed the warning signs or could not read them, or was distracted by music or other occupants in the vehicle. Getting to the truth in these situations is difficult, for the armed force, the victims and their families, and the JAG and commanders who are making the decision whether to apply a claim or condolence payment analysis to further their mission.

Looking at another example of how military operations impact the civil society: U.S. troops sought to expand a forward operating base in Afghanistan and seized the ground in the winter; however, the site for expansion also infringed upon the ancient tunnel and irrigation systems, known as karez, upon which the local community relied. When spring arrived authorities discovered that the seized land and planned operations would have destroyed the karez. A clash of propaganda efforts ensued, with the Taliban touting the harmful effects of the foreign invaders while U.S. forces struggled to communicate with local elders. Subsequently, the top U.S. commander sent a senior claims officer to the site to assess property lines and the extent of potential claims, while also assisting engineers in redesigning the base to mitigate any effects upon the karez and the community.[142]

C. CONSISTENCY AND SYNCHRONIZATION

An effective claims operation must also account for the importance of intra-force synchronization, both within a state's joint forces and among the armed forces of different states. A claimant may submit a claim at different claims offices or different operating bases (including civil-military outreach centers) in an attempt to collect multiple compensatory claims for the same damage. Compounding this

---

[142] Michael M. Phillips, *Learning a Hard History Lesson in "Talibanistan,"* The Wall Street Journal (May 14, 2009), *available at* http://online.wsj.com/news/articles/SB124224652409516525.

challenge is the lack of consistent forms of identification among less-developed states, which inhibits accurate accounting of claimants. Practice indicates that it is not uncommon for one claimant to change his name and present several claims for the same damage, and the sending state force may not have an effective manner in which to prevent such "double dipping." Sometimes, local nationals view the claims process as an opportunity to take advantage of the sending state forces, profiting through submission of a false claim. Then, claims adjudicators may experience a divergence in interpreting the language of claims agreements or laws, even among cooperating allies and the host nation. These interpretational challenges may dull in comparison to interpretations of third-country nationals and the claimants themselves, particularly when adjudicators may encounter multiple ethnic, tribal, or racial languages and customs within their area of responsibility.

Elaborating on just who is involved in a claims operation beyond the commander, JAG, and policymakers, claims officers generally do not operate independently. Many armed forces, including the United States, require a pay (finance) officer to actually effect payments in an operational environment.[143] The pay officer's duties mitigate the possibility of fraudulent actions on the part of the claims JAG, and act as an additional security buffer.[144] This raises another practical consideration for planning and implementing a claims mission—the number of personnel required. The complete resourcing of a claims mission also requires security for the operation of a claims intake center, security for any site visits, translation services, transportation, cultural advisors, and administrative personnel. Practical items needed include cameras, scanners, printers, computers, and an Internet connection to communicate with other claims offices or an approving headquarters. Another practical obstacle emerges from conversion from the host nation valuation and U.S. funding authorizations, with currency conversion for payment to the local nationals.[145] Last, claims personnel always face the challenge of managing the expectation of host-nation governments,

---

[143] U.S. Dep't of Def. Fin. Mgmt. Reg. 7000.14-R, vol. 5, ch. 2, para. 0206 (June 2011).

[144] Potential fraudulent actions include generation of false claims and payments, awarding non-meritorious claims, and inflating claims in order to generate a kickback. One method implemented within the U.S. Army to offer a claims JAG some assistance and ability to deal with the claimant at an arm's length is the appointment of a Foreign Claims Commission. *See* AR 27–20, *supra* note 26, at 20. A claims JAG must be wary of his ethical responsibilities to the government and his service. Although a claims JAG may provide advice on the claims process to a prospective or current claimant, the JAG should avoid providing advice about the merits or good judgment of filing a claim. In fact, federal law, 18 U.S.C. § 205, prevents attorneys from acting as an agent or an attorney in the prosecution of a claim against the government. 18 U.S.C. § 205 (2006).

[145] Until the Vietnam War, U.S. claims personnel usually paid claimants by check. Due to the practical difficulties Vietnamese claimants faced in cashing checks, the U.S. military implemented a process in which checks remained the payment method, but a team of pay agents (Class A Agents) would go to a village and negotiate or cash the check for the claimant. Checks remained a method for accounting rather than simply relying on a cash payment. U.S. Army Center for Military History, Vietnam War, 81, http://www.history.army.mil/books/Vietnam/Law-War/law-05.htm (last visited Jan. 12, 2014).

military leaders, interested NGOs, and the citizens affected by military operations regarding the extent of relief a claims program has to offer. The pressure for transparency surrounding a claims event, from investigation to claims settlement, is constant and widespread. In the end, claims personnel perform roles as trainers, educators, and the face of the armed force in public outreach, underscoring the delicate balance of humanitarian principles and promoting the sponsoring government's best interests.

Further complications lie in the fact that in joint operations, the United States assigns responsibility to implement a claims program to one of the participating troop-contributing military services (for example, the U.S. Army contingent or the U.S. Air Force contingent).[146] The service establishes the claims program, including appointment of claims commissions; implements adjudication policies; and processes appeals at higher levels.[147] The goals of this singular responsibility are efficiency, speed of implementation through early knowledge of the task, and consistency in application. Commanders, adjudicators, and claimants may experience friction in the varying procedural applications of the various claims statutes among the different services.[148]

Finally, some critics call for permanence when considering laws and regulations implementing operational claims programs, instead of the ad hoc approach used by most armed forces today. Each military operation an armed force encounters differs, from the type and intensity of the conflict, to the enemy faced, terrain, density of population and structures, and the comparative wealth of the citizenry. Thus, a permanent and inflexible system likely will not result in the humanitarian justice critics seek.

VI. Conclusion

Military operations at any level of intensity or duration expose both noncombatants and participants to the risks of harm and suffering. Armed forces implement operational claims programs to advance the restoration of peace and security. Operational claims therefore comprise a key element of a military's efforts to achieve mission success by alleviating suffering, promoting justice, supporting dignity, and advancing governance through the rule of law. Operational claims laws and policies also insulate individual members of the armed forces from exponential liabilities resulting from the performance of their duties.

---

[146] U.S. Dep't of Defense, Instr. 5515.08, Assignment of Claims Responsibility (Nov. 11, 2006). For example, the U.S. Army has single service claims responsibility for claims in Afghanistan.

[147] Responsibility is usually assigned by country of operation, and supports an effort to resolve claims efficiently and quickly by assigning an existing task that a service may plan for accordingly. *Id.*

[148] *See, e.g.*, U.S. Dep't Of Navy JAG Instr. 5890.1A, Administrative Processing and Consideration of Claims on behalf of and against the United States (June 18, 2005) (for the Navy); U.S. Dep't Of Air Force, Instr. 51-502, Personnel and Government Recovery Claims (Mar. 1, 1997) (for the Air Force).

Although operational claims programs emanate from noble grounds of equity and humanity, they remain bound by military, economic, political, cultural, and practical challenges. As a result, planning and education remain steadfast requirements of any military operational claims program. Judge Advocates and other leaders must train military personnel regarding the proper application of claims principles, practicing expectation management, while also explaining to the citizenry not only what the claims program can do for them, but what it cannot. Government and military leaders, such as commanders, can ensure the effective implementation of a claims program by sharing their visions with those charged to carry out the claims mission. Despite the limitations of compensatory claims, simple acts such as listening to an aggrieved citizen or establishing a place where he or she can air complaints still supports the overall military mission. The collection of all of these interests and obligations demonstrates the critical role of claims operations, which must be planned for, implemented, and concluded to the benefit of all concerned to ultimately result in peace, stability, and the rule of law.

16 }

Intelligence Law

Richard M. Whitaker*

I. Introduction

A. PURPOSE AND INTENT

The purpose of this chapter is to provide the reader with a solid legal and practical foundation upon which to build a deeper understanding and appreciation for the complex and nuanced nature of intelligence law. The chapter has a tripartite focus. First, it explains the various authorities that permit the conduct of intelligence activities and operations.[1] Second, it provides a discussion of the laws and executive orders, regulations, and directives that regulate the outer limits of those same activities and operations. Finally, it discusses the integration of the essential practice techniques and procedures that are necessary to balance and thereby

---

* Richard M. Whitaker serves as the Director of Sensitive Activities Oversight, United States Special Operations Command (USSOCOM). Additionally, he is a retired Colonel, United States Army, who served as the Staff Judge Advocate (General Counsel) of the USSOCOM from 2006 to 2010; the 101st Airborne Division (Air Assault) from 2003 to 2005; the First Calvary Division from 1998 to 1999; as an Assistant Professor of International and Operational Law at the United States Army Judge Advocate General's School and Legal Center from 1994 to1997, and in numerous other assignments over a nearly thirty-year military career. He was the architect of the Department of Defense's first Intelligence Law post-graduate course and annual workshop, and continues to speak at the United States Army Judge Advocate General's annual Intelligence Law course for practitioners. He holds a JD from the University of Tennessee College of Law, an LLM in International Law from the United States Army Judge Advocate's General's School, and a Masters of Strategic Studies from the United States Army War College. The positions and opinions in this chapter are those of the author and do not represent the official views of the Department of Defense, the United States Army, Air Force, or other Department of Defense component.

1 The terms "activities" and "operations" are used throughout this chapter in a more or less interchangeable manner. There is, however, a distinction between the two terms within the Department of Defense usage. An intelligence activity is the broader term, frequently used in law and national-level documents. It describes an entire host of actions taken to collect intelligence by almost any organization. An intelligence operation is the more narrow term, used to describe the actions of uniformed military formations or units under the overall command of a combatant commander.

operationalize these two separate bodies of intelligence law.[2] The goal is not to list and explain every nuance and element of relevant law. Instead, the intent is to explain the method of legal analysis that best facilitates effective understanding and legal review in this unique and rarely understood area of practice.

It is imperative to understand that intelligence activities are authorized, staffed, and executed across a wide enterprise of U.S. government organizations; however, this chapter will focus primarily upon the Department of Defense (DoD). Having made this clarification, it is important to note that many of the laws and regulations that regulate the DoD find their foundational sources in superior national-level laws and regulations that regulate the intelligence community.[3] Accordingly, the pages that follow provide frequent reference to these important sources of law and explain how they impact the DoD's intelligence activities.

Over the past two decades, practitioners who have spent a great deal of time working in this area of practice may have come across a number of the truly superior academic offerings that strive to explain how intelligence law works. Unfortunately, neither these offerings, nor any others adequately respond to the threshold imperatives that are listed or implied in the opening paragraph. Instead, public and private sector academics chartered to provide an article for publication on intelligence law almost invariably direct the reader's attention to the U.S. Code, and focus on the 3000 series of Title 50, with particular attention paid to Section 3093,[4] and thereafter continue with a discussion of Executive Order (EO) 12,333 (United States Intelligence Activities),[5] wading seriatim through the oversight provisions of that document. They then inform the reader as to recent cases, updates, and issues regarding the areas of practice that surround these two well-known sources of law (covert action and general intelligence oversight). When they have finished, they have provided a discussion of the Covert Action Statute and the law of intelligence oversight; they have not discussed what is best described as positive intelligence law: the body of law that provides authority for the execution of intelligence activities within the DoD.

The foregoing paragraph seems to place extreme emphasis on the necessity of understanding the structure and nature of intelligence law. This point is

---

[2] This is a relatively new way to look at this body of law. In essence, practitioners must balance the authorizing laws and instruments against the separate body of laws and regulations that serve as their regulatory counterweight. It is near impossible to understand the true range of the legally possible until the practitioner has considered both dimensions of intelligence law.

[3] For instance, DoD level practitioners enjoy extreme fluency with Department-level directives, regulations, and instructions that provide very good guidance in regard to the approval and execution of intelligence activities and operations. However, these Department-level instruments spring from federal statutes and executive orders, and as is typically the case in other areas of practice, it is difficult to interpret and apply the lower-level law without consideration of the superior law.

[4] National Security Act of 1947, 50 U.S.C. § 3093 (1947) [hereinafter Title 50]. This statute has recently been renumbered and was formerly known as 50 U.S.C. § 413b.

[5] Exec. Order No. (E.O.) 12,333, 46 F.R. 59941 (1981), *as amended by* Exec. Order No. 13470 (2008) [hereinafter EO 12,333].

intentionally stated and restated because it is an overwhelmingly important one. In fact, it is so critically important, it bears one last restatement: of the two broad categories of intelligence law described above, most scholarly legal offerings limit their scope to the regulatory law. These products are helpful for those conducting legal research into narrow questions of intelligence oversight, but do little to provide an explanation of how the law works and how it is put into actual practice. Within the DoD (and a number of other agencies within our government), where activities are conceived, planned, and approved, leaders and their lawyers must understand how they should go about the task of finding the positive law that serves as the cornerstone for their future actions. Moreover, they must understand how that law is interpreted, and how and when it should be applied. Within this chapter, the reader is offered a roadmap for the performance of these essential legal tasks.

The previous two paragraphs sound heretical, but there is almost no academic source or location where an intelligence law practitioner—and by implication an outside observer—might find an explanation of how the entire canvas of intelligence law is wired, structured, and painted. Moreover, there is little guidance to highlight why it is of vital importance to understand that structure, and how practitioners leverage the segments of this construct to develop rational legal opinions, track compliance, and negotiate solutions to all manner of problem-sets within and beyond their own outside agencies. These questions must be answered in order to develop rational and coherent legal opinions to ensure that intelligence activities and operations are properly authorized and conducted in accordance with law and policy. To rephrase and provide additional texture to this chapter's opening sentence, the purpose of this short effort is to provide an explanation for the structure of the authorities necessary for the conduct of intelligence activities and operations, and to the extent possible, describe those authorities and the actors involved in seeking their approval and execution. Finally, the chapter will also provide a thumbnail sketch of the overall U.S. intelligence oversight mechanism, with an explanation of how the components of that mechanism work in tandem. Given the realities and imperatives described above, this mechanism will not be discussed in depth; however, there are many other excellent resources already available that adequately service that need.[6]

B. SECURITY'S COST/BENEFIT RELATIONSHIP

It is appropriate at this juncture to identify and describe the rather large red elephant that stands before this chapter: the highly classified and sensitive nature of

---

[6] *See, e.g.*, THE INT'L & OPERATIONAL LAW DEP'T, THE JUDGE ADVOCATE GENERAL'S LEGAL CTR. & SCH., UNITED STATES ARMY, OPERATIONAL LAW HANDBOOK 105–08 (2012) [hereinafter OPLAW HANDBOOK]; STEPHEN DYCUS, ARTHUR L. BERNEY, WILLIAM C. BANKS & PETER RAVEN-HANSEN, NATIONAL SECURITY LAW, FIFTH EDITION, PART III (5th ed. 2011); AMERICAN BAR ASSOCIATION, THE U.S. INTELLIGENCE COMMUNITY LAW SOURCEBOOK: 2012 EDITION (Andrew M. Borene ed., ABA Standing Committee on Law and National Security 2013).

this subject matter. As those who have practiced in this field well know, the reason for the foregoing paradigm is that many of the really relevant ideas, authorities, restrictions, and the context to which they apply are extremely important components of the nation's national security complex. This makes intelligence law far and away the most difficult area of law to describe in a nonclassified, academic forum. Any detailed conversation, when held in an uncontrolled facility or medium, might well violate any number of security rules, some of which are criminal in nature. Consequently, the authors who have access to the information that might be harnessed to explain the positive law can only wheel out small bits of this information, which generally makes for a disjointed conversation.

The goal of this chapter is to provide an unclassified explanatory roadmap that addresses the essential subject matter set out above, remains coherent even though all classified details are intentionally left out, and provides significant assistance to even those who do not have access to the classified information. As for the need to follow these rules, no apology is made for acting in deference to this imperative; the disclosure restrictions exist for very good reasons, and whatever injury they cause to academic work is more than offset by the positive impact of protecting our nation's vital secrets.[7] It is important to note that this chapter has undergone a government security and policy review, and has been approved for formal academic release.

The first step in gaining a working comprehension of intelligence law is to understand the community to which it applies. The law cannot be read or applied in the absence of this understanding, because much of the law applies only to that community, and in many instances to only a segment of the community. The following discussion introduces that community and explains the commons errors that practitioners new to this field make in regard to applying the law to it.

II. The Intelligence Community and Intelligence Components

The abbreviation "IC" is perhaps the most frequently used term in almost any conversation regarding the staffing and approval of an intelligence activity. It is also one of the most confusing and misunderstood terms within this area of legal practice. This is because it is frequently misused, even by DoD insiders. The IC is the shorthand term for the United States Government Intelligence Community; it is not the shorthand for any other term within the intelligence lexicon. This is an exceedingly important point, and if not understood can lead to serious confusion in regard to which organizations within the DoD have the authority to

[7] For those in government service with an active security clearance, the chapter author plans to produce a classified version of this chapter in the near future that provides the granularity that was intentionally omitted because of the requirement to produce this chapter in an unclassified format. Within that revised and classified version, the author will discuss cover and cover support as well as special operations activities that are similar to intelligence and intelligence- related activities.

approve certain actions, as well as which oversight rules apply to various activities.[8] In this area of practice, as with most other areas of National Security Law, confusion leads to imprecision, which in turn leads to mistakes, both large and small. Such mistakes can lead to intelligence failures, the loss of tactical and strategic advantage, and great embarrassment for our nation. The following two sections provide the information necessary to avoid such mistakes.

A. THE INTELLIGENCE COMMUNITY (IC)

As explained above, the Intelligence Community is the official term for the group of organizations within the United States government (USG) that are chartered to perform one or more types of intelligence activities. In other words, the IC is the organizational structure for the USG intelligence establishment. It is an organization of sixteen executive branch agencies within the federal government that are responsible for carrying out the nation's intelligence activities. Congress has articulated the membership of the IC on a number of occasions. Most recently, it provided a definitive list within The Intelligence Reform and Terrorism Prevention Act of 2004 (IRTPA).[9] Section 1073 of IRTPA lists the sixteen members; the Department of Defense makes up eight of these members (which include the intelligence elements of the military departments: Army, Navy, Marine Corps, and Air Force). The IC is led by the Director of National Intelligence (DNI), who reports directly to the President. The IC members include the Central Intelligence Agency (CIA); DoD intelligence agencies; DOE's Office of Intelligence and Counterintelligence (OICI); DHS's Office of Intelligence and Analysis (I&A) and Coast Guard Intelligence (CGI); DOJ's FBI and Drug Enforcement Administration's Office of National Security Intelligence (DEA/ONSI); DOS's Bureau of Intelligence and Research (INR); and the Treasury's Office of Terrorism and Financial Intelligence (TFI). As the foregoing list indicates, most of these organizations have the word "intelligence" in their name, and their functions are largely intuitive.

The President provided the same list of IC members in Section 1.7 of Executive Order 12,333. Reading through this version of the list is extremely helpful in understanding the collective mission-set of the IC and the specific purpose of each member, as it provides context and explanation regarding the mission of each of these organizations.[10] It also serves as the authoritative headstream for

---

[8] *See* E.O. 12,333, *supra* note 5, §§ 1.4, 1.6, 1.7, & 2.3. In each of the foregoing sections, authorities and restriction on such authorities are prescribed and levied based on the prerequisite requirement of IC membership. Very frequently, attorneys read through these and similar provisions without realizing that they apply only to members of the IC.

[9] The Intelligence Reform and Terrorism Prevention Act, Pub L. No. 108-458, § 118, Stat. 3638 (2004).

[10] E.O. 12,333, *supra* note 5, §§ 1–7 enumerate the members of the IC and the authorities and roles of each member as described hereinafter: *Intelligence Community Elements*. Each element of the Intelligence Community shall have the duties and responsibilities specified below, in addition to those specified by law or elsewhere in this order. Intelligence Community elements within executive departments shall serve the information and intelligence needs of their respective heads of

much of the positive authority for the respective missions of each organization. Lawyers who practice in this field must always be on the trail of authorities for the proposed actions of their clients. All legal opinions regarding these types of activities and operations should begin in the same way, tracing the line of

---

departments and also shall operate as part of an integrated Intelligence Community, as provided in law or this order.

(a) **The Central Intelligence Agency**. The Director of the Central Intelligence Agency shall:
   (1) Collect (including through clandestine means), analyze, produce, and disseminate foreign intelligence and counterintelligence;
   (2) Conduct counterintelligence activities without assuming or performing any internal security functions within the United States;
   (3) Conduct administrative and technical support activities within and outside the United States as necessary for cover and proprietary arrangements;
   (4) Conduct covert action activities approved by the President. No agency except the Central Intelligence Agency (or the Armed Forces of the United States in time of war declared by the Congress or during any period covered by a report from the President to the Congress consistent with the War Powers Resolution, Public Law 93-148) may conduct any covert action activity unless the President determines that another agency is more likely to achieve a particular objective;
   (5) Conduct foreign intelligence liaison relationships with intelligence or security services of foreign governments or international organizations consistent with section 1.3(b)(4) of this order;
   (6) Under the direction and guidance of the Director, and in accordance with section 1.3(b)(4) of this order, coordinate the implementation of intelligence and counterintelligence relationships between elements of the Intelligence Community and the intelligence or security services of foreign governments or international organizations; and
   (7) Perform such other functions and duties related to intelligence as the Director may direct.

(b) **The Defense Intelligence Agency**. The Director of the Defense Intelligence Agency shall:
   (1) Collect (including through clandestine means), analyze, produce, and disseminate foreign intelligence and counterintelligence to support national and departmental missions;
   (2) Collect, analyze, produce, or, through tasking and coordination, provide defense and defense-related intelligence for the Secretary of Defense, the Chairman of the Joint Chiefs of Staff, combatant commanders, other Defense components, and non-Defense agencies;
   (3) Conduct counterintelligence activities;
   (4) Conduct administrative and technical support activities within and outside the United States as necessary for cover and proprietary arrangements;
   (5) Conduct foreign defense intelligence liaison relationships and defense intelligence exchange programs with foreign defense establishments, intelligence or security services of foreign governments, and international organizations in accordance with sections 1.3(b)(4), 1.7(a)(6), and 1.10(i) of this order;
   (6) Manage and coordinate all matters related to the Defense Attaché system; and
   (7) Provide foreign intelligence and counterintelligence staff support as directed by the Secretary of Defense.

(c) **The National Security Agency**. The Director of the National Security Agency shall:
   (1) Collect (including through clandestine means), process, analyze, produce, and disseminate signals intelligence information and data for foreign intelligence and counterintelligence purposes to support national and departmental missions;
   (2) Establish and operate an effective unified organization for signals intelligence activities, except for the delegation of operational control over certain operations that are conducted through other elements of the Intelligence Community. No

authority for the underlying actions through agency directives or military orders and to such statements as are found in the foregoing section of EO 12,333.

Understanding and correctly interpreting the foundational laws and policies regarding intelligence law requires intelligence lawyers to carefully study the scope and application paragraphs of these laws. This careful and detailed analysis

---

other department or agency may engage in signals intelligence activities except pursuant to a delegation by the Secretary of Defense, after coordination with the Director;

(3) Control signals intelligence collection and processing activities, including assignment of resources to an appropriate agent for such periods and tasks as required for the direct support of military commanders;

(4) Conduct administrative and technical support activities within and outside the United States as necessary for cover arrangements;

(5) Provide signals intelligence support for national and departmental requirements and for the conduct of military operations;

(6) Act as the National Manager for National Security Systems as established in law and policy, and in this capacity be responsible to the Secretary of Defense and to the Director;

(7) Prescribe, consistent with section 102A(g) of the Act, within its field of authorized operations, security regulations covering operating practices, including the transmission, handling, and distribution of signals intelligence and communications security material within and among the elements under control of the Director of the National Security Agency, and exercise the necessary supervisory control to ensure compliance with the regulations; and

(8) Conduct foreign cryptologic liaison relationships in accordance with sections 1.3(b)(4), 1.7(a)(6), and 1.10(i) of this order.

(d) **The National Reconnaissance Office**. The Director of the National Reconnaissance Office shall:

(1) Be responsible for research and development, acquisition, launch, deployment, and operation of overhead systems and related data processing facilities to collect intelligence and information to support national and departmental missions and other United States Government needs; and

(2) Conduct foreign liaison relationships relating to the above missions, in accordance with sections 1.3(b)(4), 1.7(a)(6), and 1.10(i) of this order.

(e) **The National Geospatial-Intelligence Agency**. The Director of the National Geospatial-Intelligence Agency shall:

(1) Collect, process, analyze, produce, and disseminate geospatial intelligence information and data for foreign intelligence and counterintelligence purposes to support national and departmental missions;

(2) Provide geospatial intelligence support for national and departmental requirements and for the conduct of military operations;

(3) Conduct administrative and technical support activities within and outside the United States as necessary for cover arrangements; and

(4) Conduct foreign geospatial intelligence liaison relationships, in accordance with sections 1.3(b)(4), 1.7(a)(6), and 1.10(i) of this order.

(f) **The Intelligence and Counterintelligence Elements of the Army, Navy, Air Force, and Marine Corps**. The Commanders and heads of the intelligence and counterintelligence elements of the Army, Navy, Air Force, and Marine Corps shall:

(1) Collect (including through clandestine means), produce, analyze, and disseminate defense and defense-related intelligence and counterintelligence to support departmental requirements, and, as appropriate, national requirements;

(2) Conduct counterintelligence activities;

(3) Monitor the development, procurement, and management of tactical intelligence systems and equipment and conduct related research, development, and test and evaluation activities; and

provides the foundation to make a deliberate determination in regard to whether the provisions apply to only members of the IC, to all government agencies and departments, or to a subset of one of these two larger groups. Executive Order 12,333 provides an excellent example of this reality. In almost every material

---

(4) Conduct military intelligence liaison relationships and military intelligence exchange programs with selected cooperative foreign defense establishments and international organizations in accordance with sections 1.3(b)(4), 1.7(a)(6), and 1.10(i) of this order.

(g) **Intelligence Elements of the Federal Bureau of Investigation**. Under the supervision of the Attorney General and pursuant to such regulations as the Attorney General may establish, the intelligence elements of the Federal Bureau of Investigation shall:
  (1) Collect (including through clandestine means), analyze, produce, and disseminate foreign intelligence and counterintelligence to support national and departmental missions, in accordance with procedural guidelines approved by the Attorney General, after consultation with the Director;
  (2) Conduct counterintelligence activities; and
  (3) Conduct foreign intelligence and counterintelligence liaison relationships with intelligence, security, and law enforcement services of foreign governments or international organizations in accordance with sections 1.3(b)(4) and 1.7(a)(6) of this order.

(h) **The Intelligence and Counterintelligence Elements of the Coast Guard**. The Commandant of the Coast Guard shall:
  (1) Collect (including through clandestine means), analyze, produce, and disseminate foreign intelligence and counterintelligence including defense and defense-related information and intelligence to support national and departmental missions;
  (2) Conduct counterintelligence activities;
  (3) Monitor the development, procurement, and management of tactical intelligence systems and equipment and conduct related research, development, and test and evaluation activities; and
  (4) Conduct foreign intelligence liaison relationships and intelligence exchange programs with foreign intelligence services, security services or international organizations in accordance with sections 1.3(b)(4), 1.7(a)(6), and, when operating as part of the Department of Defense, 1.10(i) of this order.

(i) **The Bureau of Intelligence and Research, Department of State; The Office of Intelligence and Analysis, Department of the Treasury; The Office of National Security Intelligence, Drug Enforcement Administration; The Office of Intelligence and Analysis, Department of Homeland Security; and The Office of Intelligence and Counterintelligence, Department of Energy. The heads of the Bureau of Intelligence and Research, Department of State; the Office of Intelligence and Analysis, Department of the Treasury; the Office of National Security Intelligence, Drug Enforcement Administration; the Office of Intelligence and Analysis, Department of Homeland Security; and the Office of Intelligence and Counterintelligence, Department of Energy** shall:
  (1) Collect (overtly or through publicly available sources), analyze, produce, and disseminate information, intelligence, and counterintelligence to support national and departmental missions; and
  (2) Conduct and participate in analytic or information exchanges with foreign partners and international organizations in accordance with sections 1.3(b)(4) and 1.7(a)(6) of this order.

(j) **The Office of the Director of National Intelligence**. The Director shall collect (overtly or through publicly available sources), analyze, produce, and disseminate information, intelligence, and counterintelligence to support the missions of the Office of the Director of National Intelligence, including the National Counterterrorism Center, and to support other national missions.

paragraph, the order provides guidance in regard to its scope. In many paragraphs, it explains that its application applies only to members of the IC, in others it expands its application to all parts of the USG, while still in others it narrows the scope of application to specific members of the IC.

B. THE INTELLIGENCE COMPONENTS

The Defense Department established the DoD Intelligence Components (there is no other group of intelligence components outside of the DoD) with the publication of its oversight directives, DoD Directive 5240.01[11] and DoD Regulation 5240.1-R,[12] which implement EO 12,333. There is significant confusion, even among those who participate in the staffing and coordination of USG intelligence activities, in regard to the abbreviation "IC." Does it stand for the term "intelligence community," or the term "intelligence component," or is it properly used interchangeably for both or either? And for that matter, should we understand "intelligence community" and "intelligence components" to be two interchangeable terms? As explained above, the answer to the first question is that the IC is the shorthand description for the intelligence community; it should not be confused with the DoD's intelligence components. Accordingly, the two terms are not interchangeable.

The significance of membership in the DoD Intelligence Components is twofold. First, the rules expressed in the various DoD intelligence directives, instructions, and regulations apply only to the Defense Intelligence Components. Second, the rules that apply to the members of the intelligence community may or may not apply to the components, because the components are not all members of the IC. For example, DoD's Combatant Commands (all operational forces of the military services are assigned to one of the unified or specified combatant commands, e.g., United States Central Command)[13] are not members of the IC; thus they do not fall under the immediate oversight provisions of those rules that

---

[11] U.S. DEP'T. OF DEF., DIR. 5240.01, DOD INTELLIGENCE ACTIVITIES (Aug. 27, 2007) [hereinafter DoDD 5240.01].

[12] U.S. DEP'T OF DEF., DIR. 5240.1-R, PROCEDURES GOVERNING THE ACTIVITIES OF DOD INTELLIGENCE COMPONENTS THAT AFFECT UNITED STATES PERSONS (Dec. 7, 1982) [hereinafter DoDR 5240.1-R].

[13] Goldwater-Nichols DoD Reorganizational Act of 1986, 10 U.S.C. §§ 161–166 (1986) [hereinafter Goldwater-Nichols Act]. Congress reorganized the Department of Defense in 1986 by directing the United States Army, Navy, Air Force, and Marine Corps to assign their forces to one of the newly formed Combatant Commands. These commands are frequently referred to as either "geographic combatant commands" or "functional combatant commands." Within the military community, the former are referred to as "GCCs." Each GCC exercises command responsibility over an area of responsibility or "AOR" that encompasses a large portion of the globe. The eight GCCs exercise responsibility over AORs that taken together include the entire world. For example, United States Southern Command (SOUTHCOM) has an AOR that includes all of South America and all of Central America (less Mexico). The four-star commanders of each of these GCC are responsible for all United States' military action that might occur within his AOR. This includes all military intelligence activities or operations.

are designed to regulate the IC. The combatant commands are, however, DoD intelligence components, and do fall under the directives and regulations that prescribe the conduct and restrictions for the DoD components. Failure to intellectually separate these two terms (Intelligence Community versus Intelligence Components) and apply the right rules to the right groups has led to flawed legal opinions. More frequently, outside journalists and academics misunderstand the nature of DoD organizations and misapply IC rules to such organizations, which has led to inaccurate articles and erroneous claims of abuse.[14]

Even more problematic, journalists (and others) have confused the role and authorities of special operation operatives, and misapplied various intelligence community requirements to these operatives. These personnel can and do work under various forms of authority, many of which cannot be disclosed in this forum. It is important, however, for lawyers to do two things whenever they try to understand what authority empowers the labors of a special operator. First, they must determine the legal and operative command and control status in which such units and individuals operate. For instance, are such special operators under the operational control (OPCON)[15] of a geographic combatant commander (such as United States Central Command)[16], the United States Special Operations Command (USSOCOM) or some other agency?[17] The Geographic Combatant Commanders and USSOCOM are military commands. Accordingly, the special operator(s) under their control must derive their authority from some form of military order, and their actions can be properly characterized as military activity. On the other hand, if the authority is derived from an agency external

---

[14] *See* Adam Serwer, *Obama Embraces Special Operations Forces*, MSNBC, National Security/Society, June 25, 2014, *available at* http://www.msnbc.com/msnbc/obama-embraces-special-operations-forces. In this and similar articles the author erroneously claims that although Congress has put laws into place to provide intelligence oversight limits on the Central Intelligence Agency, no such laws are in place for special operators, who operate in an environment free of restrictions and limits. In reality, the species of oversight rules varies by the type of activity and the authorities from which it springs, but oversight rules of some version apply in all cases.

[15] OPCON is the authority to perform those functions of command over subordinate forces involving organizing and employing commands and forces, assigning tasks, designating objectives, and giving authoritative direction necessary to accomplish the mission. *See* U.S. Joint Chiefs of Staff, Joint Pub. (JP) 1-02, Dep't. of Def. Dictionary of Military and Associated Terms 191 (Nov 8, 2012) (as amended through July 16, 2014) [hereinafter DOD Dictionary].

[16] United States Central Command (U.S.CENTCOM) has responsibility for the geographic region where many recent U.S. operations have occurred (Operations Desert Shield, Desert Storm, Restore Hope, Iraqi Freedom, and Enduring Freedom), and is well known to most government officials, members of the media, academics, and even most U.S. citizens.

[17] The United States Special Operations Command is the only military command in the U.S. military that was legislated into existence. Congress did this when it passed Section 167 of Title 10. *See* Unified Combatant Command for Special Operations, 10 U.S.C. §167 (2011). This law also specifies that "unless otherwise directed by the President or the Secretary of Defense, a special operations activity or mission shall be conducted under the command of the commander of the unified combatant commander whose geographic area the activity or mission is to be conducted." *Id.* at § 167(d). Accordingly, the law establishes the default setting for which entity typically enjoys operational control, but this default setting can be altered by direction of the President and by certain other mechanisms. *Id.*

to the DoD, this opens up an entirely different analytical set of questions for the supporting legal team.[18] However, the analysis follows the same path: the supporting lawyers must determine what the authorizing documents and directives direct and permit. After determining the status in which the proposed actors might operate, lawyers must gain access to and master all parts of the military order that authorizes the operator's actions. Although all military orders and mission directives will frequently have analogous provisions, the legal advisor must always assume that all orders are unique, and must carefully scrutinize each such document to avoid mistakes that might jeopardize the nation's security and reputation.

Once intelligence law practitioners gain a basic working knowledge of the intelligence community and those organizations that are in orbit just beyond that community, they must then work to understand how law and regulation applies to these various agencies, departments, and commands. To do this, they must work to grasp the basic structure of the law that they are charged to apply; the following section provides insight into that structure.

C. THE BASIC STRUCTURE OF INTELLIGENCE LAW

1. Permissive or Restrictive

There are two basic jurisprudential models: permissive and restrictive. American jurisprudence is primarily built upon a permissive framework, which means that the actor may safely assume that he or she is permitted to legally perform an act, unless that specific act is prohibited or restricted by a specific legal rule. Conversely, within a restrictive system, the actor may not perform an act unless there is a positive grant of authority that specifically permits the act.

Legal scholars and practitioners within the field of fiscal law nearly always hasten to point out that fiscal law is different from all other sources of law inasmuch as it is not a permissive area of the law: it is a restrictive area of the law. This means that in the absence of a positive grant of authority to act, the actor may not perform.[19] As described above, within American jurisprudence, almost all other

---

[18] In the aftermath of the May 1, 2011, raid to kill or capture Osama bin Laden, a number of very good academic articles surfaced in an attempt to explain the framework under which uniformed members of the military might operate under the authority of agencies beyond the DoD. One of the best of these articles was written by Lieutenant Colonel Joe Berger, United States Army Judge Advocate General's Corps. *See generally* Joseph Berger, *Covert Action: Title 10, Title 50, and the Chain of Command*, 67 JOINT FORCES Q. (4th Qtr—Oct. 2012).

[19] The United States Constitution is the source of this restriction. The Constitution grants the power to authorize the use of funds to the legislative branch, and it clearly asserts that no money may be spent without a specific appropriation. *See* U.S. Const., art. I, § 9, cl. 7. Accordingly, fiscal law demands that practitioners rest all actions on positive grants of fiscal authority that can be traced back to a congressional appropriation and authorization. Intelligence law is similar to fiscal law in this respect, in that it requires a positive grant of authority that can be traced back to some authoritative figure that has been granted authority by either Congress or the President.

areas of the law are permissive in nature, meaning that unless there is a rule of law that restricts or limits action, the actor is free to perform.

Within the foregoing framework, where is intelligence law positioned? Many scholars might quickly place it solidly within the permissive ranks but, although this response is understandable, it is incorrect.[20] Intelligence law is a "quasi-restrictive" area of law, which means that every intelligence activity or operation must be tied to an authority that can be traced to either Congress or the Commander in Chief. For unit-level actions, practitioners typically begin their authority analysis by asking if the unit "has the mission" to perform a proposed intelligence-based act. If the unit does indeed have the mission, this merely means that the unit is chartered and designed to execute these types of operations. The next question is: Does the unit have a specific grant of authority? As described elsewhere in this chapter, this means that a specific authorization has been granted by some proper statute, regulation, or superior command with the authority to do so. For a uniformed military unit, commanded and controlled by a uniformed officer, this means a superior officer from the chain of command (which begins with the President and runs down through the Secretary of Defense, to the four-star Combatant Commanders and on down to subordinate flag officers, colonels, captains, and so forth).

The bottom line is that the decision-maker and his or her lawyer need to understand from where the authority to act is derived and be positioned to articulate this lineage of authority when someone from the outside inquires concerning the activity's legal basis. Military practitioners are trained to always assume that something will go wrong and that the spotlight of public scrutiny will be shone across the avenues of their client's activities. They are further trained to always be positioned and prepared to defend their organization's actions by persuasive explanation of their robust authorities. These superb judge advocates, service-department level, and DoD level lawyers well understand that Murphy is alive and well and intervenes often. Accordingly, they draft their legal opinions with great care, have them reviewed by lawyers from above, and know to always have them ready.

2. Tracing the Positive Law

The practitioner should be able to trace and articulate the source of law that undergirds the intelligence activities and operations of his clients. If he cannot do this, and can merely assert that he could "find no prohibition to these

[20] Placing intelligence law in the permissive ranks is intuitive at first glance because unlike fiscal law, it has no restrictive charter etched in the U.S. Constitution or some other lofty superior law, other than E.O. 12,333. Instead, its restrictive nature is born in policy and practice. Generations of intelligence law practitioners have learned that "eventually all secrets become known, and when this occurs, those who labored under the shroud of those secrets must be found on the high ground, having worked with proper legal authority." Comment by Admiral Eric T. Olson, Commander of the United States Special Operations Command at the time of the comment, made in the context of giving guidance on a classified planning effort, May 11, 2009. At the time of this comment, Admiral Olson was pressing his lawyer to find and cite the authority for the execution of several elements of the operational plan, because he fully realized the restrictive nature of this arena.

activities," he has not served his client well. To demonstrate how military practitioners trace the source of their client's authorities, we will examine the Army's positive grant of authority to perform intelligence activities and operations.[21] In this example-based explanation, it is important to understand that the Army is merely used by way of example; the authorities that are discussed below are unique to the Army, and each organization has its own unique authorities and history. For lawyers within any particular organization this means that they might find the homework of the lawyers from other organizations interesting and useful, but they should never rely upon it as a replacement for their own research and analysis. (For example, Army authorities might be radically different from Navy authorities or those of the Defense Intelligence Agency).

The Army is a member of the intelligence community and is also a DoD intelligence component. Accordingly, it derives authorities from three independent sources. The positive grants of authority provided to members of the IC and the DoD intelligence components make up the first two sources, while the last source is derived from its assigned military missions. Fortunately, there are a wide variety of positive grants of authority available to the official actors within the IC. The nature and extent of these grants is tied to the identity, mission, and characteristics of each member of the IC. Importantly, each member of the IC has a charter that is based in law and regulation.[22]

In the case of the Army (or any other member of the IC), the best point of origin is with Articles I and II of the United States Constitution.[23] In regard to the Army, these two provisions specify the obligation for the Congress to raise and support the Army and the President to command it. The Constitution makes clear that the function of the Army is to provide for the common defense; from this, a number of implied authorities spring. These authorities rest first with the President and flow down through the Secretary of Defense, to the Under Secretary of Defense for Intelligence (USD(I)),[24] and to subordinate uniformed commanders and agency heads. Military judge advocates are fond of referring to these authorities

---

[21] There is no particular reason I chose the Army to demonstrate my point, other than I am quite fond of the Army, having spent a large portion of my adult life in its ranks.

[22] As before, the United States Constitution is the initial source of all of the authorities that undergird all intelligence activities. More specifically, the Constitution grants authorities for Congress to provide for the "Common Defence" of the nation and for the President to serve as the "Commander in Chief" of the armed forces. The statutes, which extend from the Congress, and executive orders and inherent command authorities, which extend from the President, all extend from this common point of legal origin. *See* U.S. Const., art. I, §§ 1, 8, &12; art. II, § 2, respectfully.

[23] It is not by happenstance that the very first document included in the Intelligence Community Legal Reference Book, an incredibly helpful product published by the Office of the Director of the National Intelligence, is the United States Constitution. Lawyers at all levels find themselves turning to the Constitution on a fairly frequent basis to begin the search for authorities for their client's proposed actions. *See* Office of the Director of National Security, Intelligence Community Legal Reference Book (2012).

[24] *See* 10 U.S.C. § 137 (2002) . The Congress created this position to serve as the primary actor with the Office of the Secretary of Defense for all intelligence matters. As such, the USDI enjoys the

as the "inherent authorities of the commander," as if they spring from thin air. In truth, however, they spring from the master law itself, the Constitution.

In tracing the Army's authority to conduct an intelligence operation, we discover the next link in the chain is found in a number of provisions within Title 10 of the U.S. Code, wherein, Congress expresses its intent

> to provide an Army that is capable . . . of preserving the peace and security and providing for the defense of the United States; as well as supporting . . . national policies [and] . . . implementing the national objectives; and overcoming any nations responsible for aggression . . . .[25]

Derived from these express statutory provisions is the inherent authority vested in Army commanders to execute activities that accomplish the foregoing tasks. In addition, Congress also recognized that the Secretary of Defense is vested with broad authorities to serve as the President's "principal assistant" in wielding the military arm of national power, and as such he acts with the President's constitutionally granted authorities to defend the nation; he may act through any instrument within the Department of Defense, to include its intelligence components, unless specifically prohibited by law.[26] Thus, the Secretary of Defense and the intelligence components within his Department enjoy a broad grant of constitutional authority to conduct intelligence activities and operations that are not otherwise prohibited or limited by law.

Congress has bestowed additional specific positive grants of authority upon the Secretary of Defense through Title 10 of the United States Code. For example, Title 10, Section 423 authorizes the Secretary to use proceeds from counterintelligence operations of the military departments (the Departments of Army, Navy,[27] and Air Force) "to offset necessary and reasonable expenses, not otherwise prohibited by law, incurred in operations . . . ."[28] Title 10, Section 424 empowers the Secretary to conceal and refrain from revealing the identity, purpose, number, salary, or titles of persons assigned to "covered" organizations, even when the source of such inquiry is another branch of government (it also protects the organizations and functions of these organizations).[29] Title 10, Section 431 grants the Secretary the authority to "engage in commercial activities as security for intelligence collection activities abroad." The list goes on and on, but suffice it to say that Congress has bestowed a treasure trove of important authorities upon the

delegation of many of the Secretary of Defense's authorities as they relate to the conduct of intelligence activities. Although technically no one stands between the Secretary of Defense and the combatant commanders within the chain of command, the USD(I) holds particular sway in regard to the planning, approval, and execution of intelligence activities. *See id.*

[25] 10 U.S.C. § 3062(a) (1950).

[26] 10 U.S.C. § 113 (1953).

[27] The United States Marine Corps is part of the Department of the Navy.

[28] 10 U.S.C. § 423 (2009)

[29] 10 U.S.C. § 424 (2014) .

Secretary in order to position him to conduct the type of intelligence activities that are necessary to keep the nation's military leadership informed.[30]

In addition to Congress' statutory endorsement of the Chief Executive's constitutional authority to conduct intelligence activities, the executive branch embraced its own empowerment through a number of critically important expressions of executive power. The instruments that document these Presidential authorities also serve to document the existence of the same or similar authorities within each of the members of the IC and/or Defense Intelligence Components. For example, Parts 1 and 2 of Executive Order 12,333 compliment the U.S. Code in providing authority for the conduct of intelligence activities. This is relevant to the question of Army authority because these presidential authorities serve as foundational authoritative sources for Army intelligence activities. Additionally, they line up perfectly with Congress' grant of similar authority to the Army, which bolsters the express and implied powers that flow from these symmetrical sources.[31]

It is beyond the scope and purpose of this chapter to trace the Army's authority to conduct every manner of intelligence operation or activity. The purpose of the foregoing example-based illustration is to express and describe the need for a clear understanding for a specific point of origin in regard to the authorities necessary to execute various activities. Although all Defense Department authorities share a common origin, the authorities for different actors vary dramatically based upon the actor and the activity. Laws and regulations address some organizations, activities, and even individual actors, providing specific authorities and imposing specific restrictions. Attorneys dealing with such organizations, capabilities, and individuals must understand these realities. Moreover, they must carefully trace the specific authorities that attach to their organization through the laws and regulations that apply to their specific organization or the proposed activity. Obviously, these laws and regulations sometimes serve to expand and sometimes act to limit the range of possible action.

Within the Defense Department's construct, the methodology of passing authorities down to the level of action takes on two distinct forms: one for traditional military formations, which are commanded by uniformed officers, and one for Defense agencies, which are supervised (not commanded) by either civilian or uniformed leaders. This is a critical distinction and must be understand because the final expression of authority differs based upon which of these two types of DoD entity is under discussion. Although both of these chains of authority have the same point of origin, the form taken on by the authorities change

[30] Congress has also bestowed significant authorities upon the Secretary of Defense to conduct a wide range of intelligence activities under Title 50. This is true, despite the fact that the federal government lexicon associates Title 50 with CIA-based authorities. Although it should come as no surprise that the Secretary of Defense might derive significant power from that portion of U.S. law entitled "War and National Defense."

[31] *See* E.O. 12,333, *supra* note 5, Part 1 and Part 2, §§ 2.1, 2.2, and 2.3. The order directly empowers agencies within the IC "to collect, retain, or disseminate information."

dramatically as they transverse from the Constitution and statute to regulations and directives and the ultimate end user.

Military units, whether they are platoon-sized or combatant commands, are commanded by uniformed officers who give authoritative direction in the format of orders. Accordingly, the authority to conduct intelligence operations is expressed and passed down the chain of command in the form of orders. Combatant Command Staff Judge Advocates (roughly equivalent to an organizational general counsel or senior legal advisor) frequently encounter competent staff officers who assert that this or that DoD directive provided authority for the execution of various types of military action. When making such a claim, these hard-working officers, although otherwise competent, are entirely off the mark. Such directives, in the context of military commanders and units, merely provide guidance and explain the left and right limits of how various actions might be carried out; they do not provide authority for military units to act, even when the wording in the directive might so indicate. In other words, there is no authority for a military commander to perform an operational act in the absence of an execute order, despite whatever language might be found in a DoD directive or manual.[32]

On the other hand, Defense agencies are not military units and do not operate as such; they do derive authority for action from law and regulation without the need of a military order. There are a number of classified DoD Directives that grant authority for the various agencies to conduct a wide range of intelligence activities. The operatives that take their directions from such agencies do not require an execute order, even if these actors are ultimately members of the armed forces.

3. The Importance of the Goldwater-Nichols Act

Most people might assume that leaders and organizations associated with the U.S. military would operate in a world that requires military orders, either written or verbal, in order to act, and these people would be exactly right. Military forces operating under the authorities of uniformed military commanders, to include those executing intelligence activities, are subject to this axiom. It is important to point this out, because a number of the classified manuals, instructions, and

---

[32] A historical example of this rule is the publication of the Lieber Code. In 1862, the early days of the American Civil War, a German-American jurist and scholar, Professor Francis Lieber, approached Major General Henry W. Halleck, the General-in-Chief of the Union Army in the West, and encouraged the adoption of a set of rules that might serve to regulate the conduct of Union soldiers. The rules were to be based on internationally recognized laws of war. President Abraham Lincoln thought this a splendid idea and approved the refined set of rules in the form of General Order No. 100, Instructions for the Government of Armies of the United States in the Field. The rules were issued in the form of an order, because military chains of command, commanders, officers, noncommissioned officers, and common soldiers look for their instructions in the form of orders. Placing directives in service regulations provides guidance and instruction, but authority passes exclusively in the form of military orders. *See* The Yale Law School Avalon Project Official Website, *available at* http://avalon.law.yale.edu /19th century/lieber.asp (last visited Feb. 14, 2013).

directives within the DoD intelligence arena seem to provide original authority for various types of intelligence activities. Despite whatever such a document professes to grant, the foregoing axiom is in no way diluted by these Departmental authorities. At the tip of the spear, the mission actor or unit must act based on a valid military order, issued by a person within the valid chain of command. Many of the foregoing regulations, instructions, or directives are approved and issued under the authority of various principal assistant or undersecretaries of defense. However, these officials, who are otherwise important political appointees charged with great responsibility, are not members of the chain of command, and cannot issue valid military orders.[33]

As described above, within the Department of Defense, the authorities to conduct the various types of intelligence activities either run to the defense agencies or down to military formations, through the chain of command. This chain of command was fundamentally reshaped, or reorganized, by the Department of Defense Reorganization Act of 1986, otherwise referred to as the Goldwater-Nichols Act.[34] The Goldwater-Nichols Act dramatically reformed the Department of Defense's structure to enhance joint interoperability by the various services, which was recognized as a necessity in order to facilitate the military's seminal Cold War Air-Land Battle Doctrine, which required the joint application of overwhelming combat power by all of the military services (Army, Navy, Marine Corps, and Air Force). To accomplish the efficient planning for and execution of this type of joint military arrangement, the Service Chiefs[35] were removed from the operational chain of command and almost all units and personnel were assigned directly to four-star combatant commanders. The Goldwater-Nichols Act resulted in revision of Title 10 of the United States Code by removing the word "operations" from wherever it appeared in relationship to a Service Secretary's authorities and responsibilities. The new chain of command continued to originate with the President, passing through to the Secretary of Defense, as was the previous case, but then passing directly to the Combatant Commanders. As a result, whenever an operational act is executed by U.S. forces, all units and personnel are directly assigned to one of the four-star combatant commanders, who report directly to the Secretary of Defense.[36]

The foregoing reorganization resulted in the rise of the Pentagon's modern Joint Staff (which works in direct support of the Chairman of the Joint Chiefs of Staff) and all the processes inherent in the joint staff process, most specifically the Joint Operation Planning and Execution System (JOPES). In a nutshell,

---

[33] This is true because the legal chain of command passes directly from the President to the Secretary of Defense and then to the four-star combatant command commanders. It does not include, as sometimes reported by the media, the Chairman of the Joint Chiefs of Staff or any other high-level Pentagon political appointee.

[34] *See* Goldwater-Nichols Act, *supra* note 13, at 10 U.S.C. §§ 161–166 (1956).

[35] The senior military officer from each of the military branches (Army, Navy, Marine Corps, and Air Force).

[36] *See* Goldwater-Nichols Act, *supra* note 13, at 10 U.S.C. § 162 (1996).

the JOPES model funnels authority that originates with the "National Command Authorities,"[37] invokes the joint planning processes, and terminates with a military order, typically an execute order (EXORD),[38] which is passed down to a named Combatant Commander to take action within his Area of Responsibility (AOR).[39]

This is all relevant because military intelligence operations fall within this Goldwater-Nichols command and control framework. Additionally, the properly authorized military order, whether it is an EXORD or deployment order (DEPORD),[40] is the single valid expression of authority for military intelligence activities and operations. Thus, although a grant of authority that is found in an authoritative manual, directive, or regulation of one of the members of the IC may well grant authority to actors within that agency, it does not extend authority to a uniformed formation or organization under the command of one of the combatant commands. Similarly, the directives, instructions, and regulations issued within the DoD do not bestow authority upon those within a combatant command to execute intelligence operations; such authority originates exclusively within the context of a valid military order.

This command and control paradigm is simple enough to explain, but in practice it is difficult for those unacquainted with military law and practice to understand and apply. It is difficult enough to grasp the seemingly counterintuitive rule that the General in charge of the Army or Admiral in charge of the Navy play simply no role whatsoever in the planning, execution, and oversight of military operations conducted by their forces. However, this intellectual challenge is substantially increased given the incredible complexity of modern martial operations and activities, wherein, military personnel and nonmilitary personnel from one or more government agencies work in tandem to execute common national

---

[37] Joint Doctrine that was written prior to the tenure of Secretary of Defense Donald Rumsfeld explains that the President and the Secretary of Defense comprise the two officials who wield national-level command authority, and were properly referred to as the National Command Authority (NCA). This model remained in place during the Rumsfeld tenure; however, he acted to discontinue the use of the term "NCA." A comparison of the current DoD Dictionary with earlier versions reveals the discontinuation of the term, *supra* note 15. Either of these command personalities may properly approve actions that require this level of authority, unless Congress has specifically designated the President as the sole approval authority. The JOPES Doctrine, written in the late 1980s and routinely updated, is an example of this rule. The U. S. Joint Chiefs of Staff, Joint Pub 5-03.1, Joint Operational Planning and Execution System, Vol. 1 (Planning Policies and Procedures) (Oct. 31, 2009)

[38] An EXORD is an order issued by the Chairman of the Joint Chiefs of Staff, at the direction of the Secretary of Defense, to implement a decision by the President to initiate military operations. *See DoD Dictionary, supra* note 15, at 100.

[39] An AOR is the geographical area associated with a combatant command within which a geographic combatant commander has authority to plan and conduct operations. *See* DoD Dictionary, *supra* note 15, at 19.

[40] A DEPORD is a planning directive from the Secretary of Defense, issued by the Chairman of the Joint Chiefs of Staff, which authorizes and directs the transfer of forces between combatant commands by reassignment and attachment. *See* DoD Dictionary, *supra* note 15, at 80.

security goals.[41] When these arrangements occur, and they occur frequently, commanders and their lawyers must clearly define lines of operational authority. More specifically, the lawyer must constantly ensure that he understands which organizational leader is being relied upon to provide the various authorities (in terms of statutory or executive grant) required to conduct necessary intelligence activities.

As the lawyers work their way through the foregoing analytical process, it is critical that they keep in mind that the "Valid Military Orders Rule" expressed above applies only to those forces, units, and organizations that fall under the command of a combatant commander. It does not apply to units or individuals—whether military or civilian—under the authority of a defense agency that is a member of the IC. For example, if a given defense agency directive purported to bestow authority to conduct a particular intelligence activity or intelligence-related activity to those within that agency who were not assigned to a combatant command, such an authoritative grant is valid. However, actors within a combatant command reading the same directive would not be able to rely upon the directive as authority to conduct the same activities. Instead, those who fall under the command authority of a combatant commander must submit plans through the JOPES process, which, if supported by all echelons of command, will produce a valid military order, signed by a military commander or member of the civilian leadership with the requisite command authority necessary to approve the proposed action. All military intelligence activities or operations executed by operational military commands must be based upon such a military order.

D. THE CORPUS

1. The General Construct

The body of intelligence law is broken into two grand divisions. The first is the positive law that authorizes the conduct of intelligence activities and operations. The second is the body of restrictive oversight rules that regulate and limit how those activities and operations are conducted, against whom and what they might be aimed, and what techniques and procedures may be utilized. Positive law is most frequently referred to as "authority," while the restrictive oversight rules are typically referred to as "intelligence oversight law."[42] Within the positive

---

[41] The most well-known recent example of military/interagency cooperation is the Osama bin Laden Raid of May 1, 2011. This successful operation was the fruit of various executive departments, which acted to provide legal authorities, vital intelligence, national assets, and international cooperation. *See generally* Scott Wilson, Craig Whitlock & William Branigin, *Osama bin Laden Killed in U.S. Raid, Buried at Sea*, The Wash. Post (May 2, 2011), *available at* http://www.washingtonpost.com/national/osama-bin-laden-killed-in-us-raid-buried-at-sea/2011/05/02/AFxoyAZF_story.html

[42] Although the positive law that authorizes the various intelligence activities springs from the National Security Act of 1947 (*see* Title 50, *supra* note 4), the oversight law springs initially from EO 12,333, *supra* note 5, and its implementing directives and regulations.

law, the numerous authoritative grants are further broken down into two additional categories. The first of these two categories is military orders. As discussed above, at the strategic level of the Joint Staff[43] and the Combatant Commands, these orders typically take the form of either EXORDS or DEPORDS. As this source of authority flows down to subordinate military formations, these orders are subsequently transformed into the form of operations orders (OPORDS). The EXORDS and DEPORDS are typically approved and signed by the Chairman of the Joint Chiefs of Staff, and provide detailed authority and guidance regarding decisions made by either the Secretary of Defense or the President. The OPORDS are approved and signed by the commander of the level of military headquarters from which they issue.[44]

The second of the two categories of positive intelligence law is agency directives, which are issued by the head of the issuing agency. It is important to note that whereas EXORDS and DEPORDS may serve as authority for both defense agencies and military units to act, agency directives may only provide authority for the subject agency to act. This is an important point, because a large number of departmental and agency directives and instructions exist that provide various authorities to engage in all manner of intelligence activities. Occasionally, uniformed intelligence professionals from a military service will view these instruments and rely upon them as authority to engage in the specified activities. As a general rule, these instruments do not extend authority to uniformed military units or personnel. Uniformed units and personnel may act only in response to a valid military order.[45] Although this point has been beaten to death, it deserves such punishment because it is very widely misunderstood, even by those within the Department of Defense.

In the case of a directive issued from the office of an Undersecretary of Defense, such as the Undersecretary of Defense for Intelligence, these directives may properly authorize all defense agencies to act. However, as before, the general rule permits military personnel and units to act only when directed by valid military orders. Accordingly, units and personnel assigned to one of the geographic combatant commanders or the United States Special Operations Command cannot rely upon a directive signed by an Undersecretary of Defense as authority to execute military operations, despite the high level of office this official

---

[43] Although many military organizations might have joint staffs, which merely means a staff made up from officers from multiple services, the "Joint Staff" is a term of art and refers to the staff that supports the Chairman of the Joint Chiefs of Staff and serves as the critical mechanism for the staffing of military taskings, plans, and orders within the highest reaches of the United States military.

[44] U.S. Army Doctrine Publication (ADP) 5-0, The Operations Process 1–4 (May 17, 2012).

[45] Of course, all general rules have exceptions. Military personnel or even whole units that are tasked or assigned to an agency for specific purposes may operate under such an agency's authorities. For example, the Secretary of Defense has certain authorities under the provisions of Title 50, United States Code. Commanders of military units do not share these authorities. However, if military personnel were to be assigned to a defense agency that exercises the Secretary of Defense Title 50 authorities through the written mandate of a agency directive, then these uniformed personnel could properly rely upon this authority.

might occupy. The reason for this rule is not complex. Only men and women in the chain of command may issue orders to military personnel and units. The President stands at the top of that chain.[46] The Secretary of Defense occupies the next rung down.[47] The next level of command is occupied by the Combatant Commanders.[48] Consequently, the collective group of Undersecretaries and Assistant Secretaries of Defense do not wield command authority and cannot issue valid military orders to uniformed personnel.[49] In the past, there has been confusion in regard to this rule, because in several instances the Secretary of Defense has issued official memorandums asserting that directives issued by an undersecretary or the director of a defense agency carry command authority. In doing so, he ratified the actions of his subordinates. In such a case, it is this act of ratification, by a valid member of the chain of command, which generates a valid military order, not the underlying agency directive. Described differently, the Secretary of Defense's letter converts the directive of his subordinate into a valid military order by the force of the Secretary's authority.[50]

2. The Intelligence Activities

Perhaps the best definition of intelligence is found within the Preamble to Executive Order 12,333. This premiere executive expression within the intelligence arena defines intelligence as "timely, accurate, and insightful information about the activities, capabilities, plans, and intentions of foreign powers, organizations, and persons, and their agents."[51] The operational utility of such information is obvious. The entire purpose for the body of rules commonly referred to as intelligence law is to balance this operational capability[52] against the protective principles upon which our nation was founded. Intelligence law does this by first providing an understanding of what activities are authorized under law and the source of such authority. It next separates intelligence activities from other similar activities that derive their authorities from separate discreet sources. Finally, it establishes limits, rules, and procedures for the execution of the various intelligence tasks.

A key component of our nation's military might is its ability to observe, analyze, and understand the actions of our enemies, both before and during conflict. Operational capacity takes on many forms or domains, one of which is the intelligence domain. Within this domain a number of activities are practiced that yield different operational products and advantages. These products and

---

[46] *See* U.S. Const. art. II, sec. 2., *supra* note 22 and Goldwater-Nichols Act, § 162(b), *supra* note 13.

[47] Goldwater-Nichols Act, § 162 (a) (4); (b), *supra* note 13.

[48] *Id.*

[49] *Id.*

[50] *Id.*

[51] *See* E.O. 12,333, *supra* note 5.

[52] Within this chapter I use the terms "operation," "operations," or "operational" in reference to military actions to gain a military advantage against a military enemy. Accordingly, the reader should always, upon reading this term, visualize a military setting or context in which our armed forces are working to understand, weaken, and/or destroy a military adversary.

advantages either deliver information or improve preparation for future military actions.[53] Understanding and quantifying the conceptual distance between these proper military purposes and the apparent purpose of the ultimate activity on the ground is critical in either correctly categorizing the type of intelligence activity, or potentially making a determination that the purpose is not an intelligence activity at all. In the latter case, a clear understanding of the nature of the activity might lead to a determination that it is some type of nonmilitary activity. Similarly, this type of careful and informed analysis might lead to a conclusion that the proposed actions represent military activity of an unconventional nature (doctrinally described as unconventional warfare), which would require different authoritative foundations.[54] Whatever the case, this determination always depends upon a clear understanding of the purpose and context of the intended activity.

Within the DoD, a wide range of intelligence activities and operations are approved and executed. Generally, these activities are broken down into two broad categories: strategic intelligence and tactical intelligence. In short, strategic intelligence is information required for the formulation of policy and military plans at the national and international levels, and is similarly tasked and approved at these levels.[55] In contrast, tactical intelligence is information that military commanders seek for the conduct of military operations and for force protection. Tactical intelligence activities—the collection, analysis, and dissemination of intelligence related to the tactical execution of authorized military actions—is an inherent element of command authority and military operations, and requires no express statutory or regulatory authorization.[56] Accordingly, if a commander is assigned a particular mission, he has the inherent authority to conduct tactical intelligence operations in order to execute his assigned mission

---

[53] There are dozens of doctrinal examples of these types of products, but perhaps the oldest and most frequently referred to product are those that spring from the formal process known as intelligence preparation of the battlefield (IPB) or intelligence preparation of the operational environment (IPE). This process results in the intelligence estimate, which informs the course of action development during the military and strategic planning processes. *See generally* Joint Chiefs of Staff, Joint Pub. (JP) 2-01.3, Joint Intelligence Preparation of the Operational Environment (June 16, 2009).

[54] For example, many of the operational tasks associated with intelligence activities, especially collection of intelligence through the actions of human beings placed around the globe, might be conducted as an element of unconventional warfare (UW). If conducted as an element of Human Intelligence (HUMINT), then the underlying activities must be authorized as a valid HUMINT activity and approved by the appropriate level leader within the IC. However, if that same or similar activity is conducted as a UW operation, the authorization for this operation would be handed down by a different chain of leadership, within the military chain of command.

[55] The Director of National Intelligence (DNI) is responsible for ensuring that the senior leaders within the Department of Defense receive relevant strategic intelligence. *See* 50 U.S.C § 3024(2014). However, the authority and responsibility to conduct required operational and tactical-level intelligence operations to satisfy requirements at the operational level fall clearly within the authorities of military commanders. *See generally* 10 U.S.C. § 164 (2008).

[56] *See* U.S. Dep't Army, Reg. 381-10, U.S. Army Intelligence Activities, para. 1-5 (May 3, 2007) [hereinafter AR 381-10], stating that "an Army unit must first have the mission and authority to conduct the intelligence activity."

and protect his force. The reasoning behind this authority is very simple: if the overall mission has been properly authorized, then all inherent elements of that same mission are also authorized, to include the conduct of implied intelligence operations.

There is, however (and perhaps unsurprisingly), a significant exception to this basic rule. A potentially significant component of tactical intelligence is battlefield human intelligence through interrogation and questioning. This source of intelligence is carefully regulated and authorized pursuant to specific requirements and theater-level approvals. For example, the United States Army Operational Law Handbook[57] details specific guidance that is based upon the Detainee Treatment Act of 2005[58] and United States Army Field Manual 2-22-3, Human Intelligence Collector Operations.[59] The bottom line is that this is a politically charged area; it rests upon specific mission-based approvals, and is controlled by a number of activity-based restrictions. Chief among these is that only trained and certified interrogators may engage in interrogation activities, although it should be noted that "tactical questioning"—conducted by military personnel at the point of capture or when dealing with other individuals in the battle space—is not considered interrogation, and is customarily performed by any member of the armed forces.[60]

As for the form that intelligence activities might take, there are seven broad categories, which are based upon the traditional intelligence disciplines:

(1) Human Intelligence (HUMINT)
(2) Signal Intelligence (SIGINT)
(3) Imagery Intelligence (IMINT)
(4) Measurement and Signature Intelligence (MASINT)
(5) Open-source Intelligence (OSINT)
(6) Technical Intelligence (TECINT)
(7) Counterintelligence (CI)

Each type of activity requires different training, skill sets, equipment, and authorities. Typically, these areas of collection are very complex and involve personnel who spend their entire professional careers working to master the science and art of their respective disciplines. The same is true of their supporting lawyers.

---

[57] *See* OPLAW HANDBOOK, *supra* note 6, at 108–10.

[58] Detainee Treatment Act of 2005, 10 U.S.C. § 801(1956).

[59] U.S. DEP'T OF ARMY, FIELD MANUAL 2-22.3, HUMAN INTELLIGENCE COLLECTOR OPERATIONS (Sept. 6, 2006) [hereinafter FM 2-22.3].

[60] Obviously, this turns on the definition of "Interrogation, which is defined in the Interrogation Field Manual as "the systematic effort to procure information to answer specific collection requirements by direct and indirect questioning techniques of a person who is in the custody of the forces conducting the questioning." *See id.* para. 1-20. Although this is a Department of the Army definition it is also the greater Department of Defense definition, as FM 2-22.3 serves as the common rulebook for all Department of Defense organizations and agencies. *See id. at* Preface.

3. Divining Which Is Which

The primary characteristics that define any given activity as a subset of one of the seven foregoing categories are the: purpose, context, essential legal elements, operational authority, and the fiscal authority to conduct the activity. For the untrained and perhaps even the trained eye, it is often quite difficult to draw distinctions between these different categories of intelligence activities as they unfold in an operational setting, and yet drawing such distinctions is essential to provide proper legal advice and required oversight. Like other areas of operational legal practice, this poses a tremendous challenge for the legal practitioner whose expertise in the law is simply no substitute for developing a genuine understanding of the client's business. This reality leads to one of the most important points in this chapter: unless the supporting lawyer understands the *purpose and authority* for the activity, she will be unable to properly characterize that activity and apply the proper legal and regulatory guidelines to its staffing and approval process. Finally, the simple assertion of the client that it intends to engage in a certain activity should not be taken at face value until the lawyer performs his or her own analysis. The client may understand the effect or result that the client intends, but may not understand the legal test for determining the characterization of that same activity.

An additional aspect of the foregoing imperative is that lawyers must do more than simply work to rapidly gain an understanding of the underlying activity: they must retain an open mind to the possibility that their initial assessment was flawed. Members of the legal community who work in support of intelligence practitioners occasionally opine that a particular activity is *not* proper or legal because specific measures have not been undertaken. In some of these instances, the lawyers might be correct in observing that oversight rules for a particular type of activity have not been observed, but because they had misjudged and erroneously categorized the activity, they failed to realize that such measures were never actually required. For example, assume that lawyers incorrectly interpret an activity to fall under the umbrella of the first category listed above (Human Intelligence). This initial determination would cause them to initiate the standard legal analysis associated with Human Intelligence (HUMINT). This process would necessarily involve an inquiry into the type of fiscal authority required. The next step would be a search for the official within or above the lawyers organization who possesses the authority to conduct the specific type of HUMINT intended, and an analysis of the conditions and limitations on that official's grant of authority. From there, the lawyers might work to understand the required oversight rules and mechanism and what limitations are associated with these rules. If, however, the activity is not HUMINT, but something less or different, all of this legal work would result in flawed foundational documents, which in turn would lead to significant man-hours spent on problems that never existed, and needless restrictions on imperative intelligence work.

4. The Relationship and Communication among Lawyers

An issue that is closely related to the legal analysis described in the previous section is the vital importance of open, continuous, and candid communication among the lawyers at all levels of the intelligence field. For example, the dangers of activity mischaracterization are fairly obvious, as described above. This challenge, however, is greatly magnified by the extremely complex nature of the law and associated policy, and requires consistent and meaningful communication among the members of this specialized legal community. The absence of this caliber of crosstalk leads lawyers to incorrectly focus on problems that do not exist to the detriment of problems that they fail to comprehend, because their energy and attention is focused elsewhere. Furthermore, the complexity of the assessment process (determining which type of intelligence activity is under review) has a significant impact at all levels of the legal community. Although it might be tempting to believe that mistakes occur only at low levels of command where relatively inexperienced lawyers labor, this is simply not the case: these mistakes can and do occur at about the same frequency at the highest levels of the DoD legal establishment as they do at the lower levels.

If the senior-most attorneys were offered an opportunity to comment on this assertion, they would agree and further explain that although the lawyers at the higher levels do possess an impressive degree of sophistication, they do not enjoy the same quality or quantity of information about the problem-set, and therein lays the problem. The most successful attorneys in the intelligence field have found that it is critical to keep the technical channels of communication between the lawyers closest to the proposed activity and those closest to the ultimate approval authorities open. Within such a relationship, the higher-level lawyers gain greater understanding of the facts, while the tactical-level lawyers gain greater sophistication and appreciation for legal nuances, and an understanding for the impact of policy considerations.

This last aspect of the legal advisory process, policy considerations, is worthy of additional comment. While attorneys at the ground and mid levels owe the higher-level attorneys a clear explanation of the facts and attending tactical circumstances, the higher-level attorneys owe subordinate lawyers a clear understanding of when policy decisions intervene and disrupt the approval of proposed activities that are perfectly legal. If this type of candid dialogue is inhibited or non-existent, attorneys at the tactical and operational levels may come to the false conclusion that their legal analysis was flawed, when in fact it was not. Instead, a proposed intelligence activity was prohibited simply because (as is often the case), leaders at the policy level simply made a choice to not employ the specific capability that was under consideration.[61] In such cases, the senior leaders understand that a proposed course of action may be legal, but choose not to approve that option because they find it less than fully acceptable for other reasons. When this happens, the leaders at the approval level need to ensure that the entire legal and operational chain understands upon what basis the decision was made.

---

[61] Within government practice circles, the term "policy level" refers to the very senior level of government leaders that are typically appointed by the President and the Senior Executive Service (SES) level employees that assist them to make policy decisions.

The full and accurate flow of information is critical in nearly all important enterprises where lawyers provide advice and work to mitigate mistakes, and this is especially true in the practice of intelligence law. The failure to effectively communicate described in the previous paragraphs conjures up images of frustration in the minds of almost any experienced lawyer, but unless such lawyers have practiced at the various levels of the federal government it would be difficult to fully appreciate the damaging effect of this failure. Uniformed judge advocates and civilian lawyers working at the various level of headquarters draw conclusions and establish office and command precedent when proposed actions are disapproved by policy-level decision- makers. These decisions might be based upon a temporary absence of funds, the temporary presence of an alternative course of action, or even the belief that one agency is more competent or better positioned for operational success than another. These reasons or any number of other temporary conditions have absolutely nothing to do with the legality or the soundness of the legal opinion that accompanied the recommended action as it moved through the hierarchy of headquarters. Unfortunately, false precedents and distrust spring from the belief that high-level disapprovals are driven by the perceived illegality of the requested action.

To make matters even more challenging for intelligence lawyers, the authorities and restrictions associated with each of the intelligence activities is further complicated by another division within the intelligence field. All activities belong to one of several categories: traditional intelligence activity, traditional counterintelligence activity, or traditional military activity. In short, nearly all of the seven intelligence activities can be further categorized and placed in one of these three grand conceptual and legal divisions. The analysis and resulting placement is significant in terms of required authorities, oversight, reporting, and any potential special measures required for actions that cross over into the covert activity arena.

5. Traditional Military Activities

As the name implies, traditional military activity (TMA) covers a broad category of martial activities in which the uniformed services of the United States have historically engaged during the preparation for, and execution of, armed conflict and other military operations.[62] Traditional military activity is frequently referred to within military circles as "Title 10 Activity," which refers to the basic statutory authority military commanders draw upon to prepare for, equip, and conduct military operations.[63] The determination that a particular activity is a version of TMA is absolutely critical in reaching a number of important legal

[62] The U.S. military has relied upon intelligence operations and unconventional warfare techniques from the earliest days of the Continental Army and George Washington's need for battlefield and strategic information regarding his British enemies. *See generally* Brian Kilmeade & Don Yeager, Washington's Secret Six: The Spy Ring That Saved the American Revolution (2013).

[63] *See generally* 10 U.S.C. §§ 101-3000 (1956) The foregoing sections make up Subtitle A of Title 10, which serves as the foundational authorities for the Department of Defense. Each Service Department derives its respective authorities from the remaining subtitles (Subtitle B: Army,

conclusions. For example, a TMA is frequently understood to spring from a properly missioned military commander's inherent authorities to accomplish his mission. Accordingly, in many instances no further authoritative grant is required.

Within the intelligence domain, a wide variety of activities fall within the TMA category. Military commanders have need of tactical intelligence in order to accomplish most military objectives, and tactical level counterintelligence to protect friendly forces from espionage and other clandestine hostile threats. This intelligence might be collected through several of the seven intelligence disciplines listed above. It is extremely important to understand that the TMA characterization is based on the nature and context of the military mission and the supporting intelligence activity. To demonstrate this point, let us assume a commander intends to rely upon HUMINT assets to collect tactical intelligence. Let us further assume that the armed forces of the United States have already conducted a forced entry into another nation's territory, and that the aforementioned commander requires HUMINT in order to plan for and execute a general assault on a fortified area. He inserts personnel into an area that is reportedly, based on strategic/national level intelligence, occupied by local citizens friendly to the United States. The U.S. personnel reach out to locals to develop an understanding of the scope and quality of enemy forces, the terrain, communication networks, and so forth. There is little doubt that this activity is TMA, and as such, no additional authorities are necessary to conduct these activities beyond the valid military orders to prepare for and conduct the assault. However, in other contexts that are different or removed from one in which the collection activities are executed in direct support of an immediate military action, such activities would trigger a requirement for independent authorization and much more complex oversight requirements.

Accordingly, changing the context changes the legal analysis. Assume that the facts remain constant, with the exception of the timing of the insertion of U.S. personnel. What happens to the analysis if the commander inserts his personnel a year prior to the planned assault, prior to the commander's receipt of his orders, and prior to the area's designation as a theater of operations? Obviously, even if relations between the United States and the other nation have deteriorated and tensions exist, there can be no TMA in regard to this nation, because the new facts do not assert that the United States has made a deliberate decision to employ military action. Accordingly, there is no valid military order that authorizes military activities. The absence of a valid military order eviscerates the possible use of the TMA rationale as a legal justification for the characterization of an intelligence operation without separate legal authority.[64]

Subtitle C: Navy and Marine Corps, Subtitle D: Air Force, Subtitle E: Reserve Components). The modern era warfighting authorities are found in 10 U.S.C. §§ 161-168 (1956), referred to as the "Combatant Command" statutes. It is within these last statutes where the unified (joint) and specified commands are established and empowered.

[64] This does not mean that separate legal authority might not be needed for other reasons. For example, some level of the U.S. government might have placed restrictions on activities within the targeted operational space. If this were the case, additional authorities would be required in order to conduct any operation in that space.

Altering the context a third time changes the analysis once more. Assume that the use of the HUMINT assets is directed against the territory of a nation-state sponsoring hostile actions against U.S. forces who are engaged in active operations. Further assume that the insertion timing remains fixed, and the United States is involved in limited hostilities with this other nation-state as it fights to neutralize the efforts of third-party proxies (nationals of this hostile nation state) who plant improvised explosive devices intended to harm U.S. forces and allies. Finally, further assume that there is a declared theater of operations.[65] However, in this scenario the commander desires to execute a HUMINT activity outside the theater of hostilities; in fact, he wants to conduct his intelligence activity in a different hemisphere. In this case, the physical change in location does impact the analysis, but does it alter the ultimate conclusion in regard to whether the HUMINT is TMA or not? Is this TMA or something else? Perhaps unsurprisingly, the only accurate response to this question is the client's most dreaded legal maxim: "it depends." It depends on the nature of the proposed intelligence operation, the nature of the targeted enemy activity, and the operational nexus of the enemy activity in the other hemisphere to the commander's aggressive action within the theater of operations. The greater the connection between the enemy's distant activity to the commander's aggressive action in the theater, the easier it is to justify the United States response as TMA. In other words, it is conceptual proximity that is relevant, not geographic proximity.

Whether intelligence activities are characterized as TMA is also dependent on whether U.S. forces are operating under the command and control of a U.S. uniformed commander. When this is the case, it creates a very strong argument that the underlying activity is TMA. Said in reverse, if the intelligence activity is not conducted under the command and control of a military commander, it cannot be characterized as TMA. Congress provided very good insight into its understanding and definition of TMA; perhaps the best sources are the United States House of Representatives Conference Reports for the 1991 Intelligence Authorization Act[66] and the Covert Action Statue.[67]

The foregoing rule seems obvious because it is often assumed that all U.S. military operations are conducted under a clear and visible uniformed chain of command. However, this assumption is complicated by the fact that although a

---

[65] This scenario replicates a fact pattern similar to that claimed by General David H. Petraeus when he described the continuous attacks upon U.S. Forces in Iraq, which were the result of Iranian planning and supplies, working by, through, and with disgruntled Iraqi nationals. *See* Lee Smith, *Losing Petraeus, Losing Iran*, TABLET MAG., Nov. 2012.

[66] H.R. Rep. No. 102-106, 102nd Cong., 1st Sess. (1991) [hereinafter 1991 Intelligence Authorization Act Conf. Rep].

[67] H.R. Rep. No. 102-1155898, 102nd Cong., 1st Sess. (1991) (Conf. Rep.) [hereinafter 1991 Covert Action Statute Conf. Rep.] The Conference Report to 50 U.S.C. 413 (recently renumbered and transferred as 50 U.S.C. 3093) is considered to be the single best explanation of Congress' legislative intent. The wording of the Report leaves absolutely no room for speculation in regard to the importance of the presence of military control to the issue of whether an activity is to be properly considered to be TMA or something else.

clear chain of command almost certainly exists, it might not be visible to those outside its control. Moreover, military chains of command are also often constructed in a manner that is less than standard. The bottom line is that all TMA must be exercised under a uniformed chain of command; the more definitive that control is the more definitively persuasive the legal argument becomes for TMA.

The final characteristic of TMA is whether the activity has been employed previously as a military activity. After all, there is a reason that Congress chose the word "traditional" when describing this category of activity. Lawyers might work with unit historians to determine if certain activities have been used in previous conflicts. If they can answer the question in the affirmative, then the "traditional" portion of the test is easier to hurdle. The previous and regular use of a technique or activity makes for a strong case of "traditional" use of the technique or activity.

The intent in providing these illustrations is to provide a glimpse into the complexity of the analysis that goes into determining the legality of these types of activities. The importance of understanding what is and what is not TMA is at the heart of several forms of this analysis. Most important, the art of discerning a TMA from other forms of U.S. activities is critical in the analysis behind determining what is and is not a covert activity, sometime referred to as the "Title 10 versus Title 50 discussion."

E. THE TITLE 10 VERSUS TITLE 50 DISCUSSION

On May 1, 2011, the United States conducted an operation to kill terrorist and mass-murderer Osama bin Laden. As America learned details of the operation during the first several days following its execution, it became apparent that the operation was conducted as some sort of partnership between the CIA and the DoD. In the days that followed, CIA Director Leon Panetta asserted that:

> [T]his was what's called a Title 50 operation, which is a covert operation, and it comes directly from the President of the United States, who made the decision to conduct this operation . . . I am, you know, the person who then commands the mission. But having said that, I have to tell you that the real commander was Admiral McRaven because he was on site, and he was actually in charge of the military operation that went in and got bin laden.[68]

Members of Congress, the media, and academia began to almost immediately ask whether this was some sort of CIA paramilitary activity, a traditional military operation, or some new variant that mixes the two species of operations under a

[68] Interview by Jim Lehrer with Leon Panetta, Director of Central Intelligence, on PBS Newshour, *CIA Chief Panetta: Obama Made "Gutsy" Decision on Bin Laden Raid* (May 3, 2011), *available at* http://video.pbs.org/video/1907800922/.

similar mix of authorities.[69] This appears to be an excellent recent example of an operation that might well be authorized as either a TMA or as a special activity approved by the President and executed by the CIA.

In addition to the sensationalized magazine articles, television commentary, and even major motion pictures about this topic, a few excellent academic articles were offered that explain that this type of operation could have been authorized under various legal authorities. Under each of these authorities, the armed forces could have played a major role, to include command and control of the entire tactical element of the operation.[70]

Within the outer rings of the Pentagon, there is much discussion about what operational acts might be approved using Title 10 as opposed to Title 50 authorities. Obviously, this involves Titles 10 and 50 of the United States Code, and the crux of the foregoing discussion always revolves around one of two potential issues: (1) should a specific activity be authorized under the provisions of Title 10 or Title 50 (the Secretary of Defense has specific powers under both titles), and (2) does a specific activity qualify as a covert activity, and thereby trigger the additional oversight, approval measures, and reporting required by those types of activities.[71]

The first of the foregoing issues is straightforward and involves the possible presence of two intelligence tools, rather than one tool. This is preferable, because it is always best to have the ability to perform an operational act based on more than one line of statutory authority and by varying operational capabilities or mechanisms. The second issue is more complex and involves more than one question. The first of these questions is determining who will take the lead for a necessary intelligence activity: the DoD or another agency, such as the CIA. Title 50, Section 3093 (formally Section 413), the "Covert Action Statute," and E.O. 12,333 instruct that any operation that is categorized as a covert activity should normally be orchestrated and executed by the CIA, instead of the DoD.[72]

---

[69] *See* Mark Ambinder, *The Secret Team that Killed bin Laden*, National J. Online (May 3, 2011), *available at* http://nationaljournal.com/whitehouse/the-secret-team-that-killed-bin-laden-20110502.

[70] *See generally* Berger, *supra* note 18 (offering a sophisticated and accurate insight into the complex laws and policies that permit America's national leaders to wield a flexible tool bag to combat her enemies).

[71] *See generally* 50 U.S.C. § 3093 (formerly § 413) (2014)

[72] *Id.* This section of Title 50 is generally described as the Covert Action Statute, as it defines the term, describes the requirements for the approval of the underlying activity, and then specifies the associated documentation and reporting requirements. E.O. 12,333 specifies that "no agency except the Central Intelligence Agency (or the Armed Forces of the United States in time of war declared by Congress or during any period covered by a report from the President to Congress consistent with the War Powers Resolution, Public Law 93-148) may conduct any covert activity unless the President determines that another agency is more likely to achieve a particular result." *See* E.O. 12,333, supra note 5, § 1.7 (a) (4). This provision illustrates the historical friction between the legislative and executive branches. While Congress defines and specifies the limits for covert action in 50 U.S.C. § 3093, the President (Ronald Reagan) acted to protect the executive prerogative to decide to use other departments or agencies, if in the judgment of the Chief Executive, another department or agency could better achieve the desired end state.

However, the executive branch retained its option to use covert activity when the President makes an election to do so.[73]

Section 3093 makes obvious the importance of its covert action definition and those activities exempted from the definition's general reach. Only the President may authorize a covert action by making a specific "finding" that "such an action is necessary to support identifiable foreign policy objectives of the United States and is important to the national security of the United States."[74] Moreover, once a covert action is approved it must be promptly reported to Congress.[75]

The Statute defines covert actions as those "activities of the United States Government to influence political, economic, or military conditions abroad, where it is intended that the role of the United States Government will not be apparent or acknowledged publicly."[76] However, the Statute goes on to exempt certain types of activity from the definition's general umbrella. In short, "traditional" diplomatic, military, intelligence collection, and counterintelligence activities are exempted. Thus, once again, the obvious importance of the TMA designation becomes apparent. In general, when the DoD claims that its activities are TMA, and this designation is approved by either the Secretary of Defense or the President, the requirements of the Covert Action Statute are inapplicable.

As many commentators have pointed out, there exists no statutory definition for TMA, but most lawyers with the DoD rely upon the description provided in the legislative history for the Covert Action Statute:

> It is the intent of the conferees that "traditional military activities" include activities by military personnel under the direction and control of a United States military commander (whether or not the U.S. sponsorship of such activities is apparent or later to be acknowledged) preceding and related to hostilities which are either anticipated (meaning approval has been given by the National Command Authorities for activities and for operational planning for hostilities) to involve U.S. military forces, or where such hostilities involving United States military forces are ongoing, and, where the fact of the U.S. role in the overall operation is apparent or to be acknowledged publicly.[77]

When lawyers and their clients attempt to determine if a specified activity satisfies the elemental requirements of a TMA, it makes perfect sense to look at whatever guidance Congress provided at the time it drafted the Covert Action Statute or thereafter. With this logic in mind, and the legislative history provided above, policymakers are given useful insight into the mindset and intent of Congress as it drafted the Statute. Accordingly, DoD decision-makers place great weight on two elements: (1) command and control by a uniformed commander, and (2) the

[73] *See* E.O. 12,333, §1.7 (a) (4).

[74] 50 U.S.C. § 3093(c) (2002)

[75] *Id.*

[76] 50 U.S.C. § 3093(e) (2014)

[77] *See* 1991 Intelligence Authorization Act Conf. Rep, *supra* note 66.

reasonableness of the assertion that hostilities are imminent. Congress clearly indicated that without these two elements there can be no TMA.[78]

As described above, many might suggest that the DoD clearly favors the characterization of its intelligence activities as TMA because such a characterization would make the approval, recordation, and reporting requirements much less onerous than a covert action designation. This is not, however, an entirely correct assertion. Even though the Covert Action Statute creates no specific legal burden for properly staffed TMA-type actions, it does necessitate second-order staffing requirements that result in very lengthy and complex authorization procedures.[79] This is largely the case because even a TMA characterization requires very high-level staffing and approval, if not Presidential approval and staffing. In such cases, it is likely that the President will make a written "finding" that the underlying activity is not covert activity and is instead TMA.[80]

The TMA designation is, however, vitally important to the DoD for two reasons. First, in accordance with the 10 U.S.C. § 3093(e)(2), DoD retains ownership and control for the execution of all TMA. In contrast, covert action typically falls under the authorities, policies, and control of the CIA.[81] Second, the staffing and approval processes for TMA remain with the DoD. Accordingly, the timetable for approval and execution of all TMA remain internal to the Department, which has tremendous value. This is not to say, however, that the approval process within the DoD does not involve obvious and abundant coordination with the CIA and other potentially interested and impacted agencies and departments.[82]

One might reasonably ask how such actions begin, how they reach the approval authority, and who influences them along the way. Such actions would typically originate in a theater military headquarters, such as a theater-level task force or a theater special operations command (TSOC). After significant development, coordination, and maturation the proposed action would then move up through the chain of command to the four-star headquarters of the combatant

---

[78] *See* 1991 Covert Statute Action Conf. Rep., *supra* note 67.

[79] "Staffing" requires detailed and lengthy analysis by scores of military headquarters, directorates, and offices within the upper reaches of the Defense Department, and can be a lengthy and frustrating process. For example, even an action as sensitive as a TMA with attributes of a potential covert action would require dozens of lawyers and senior directorate heads to study and make comment on it. This would happen on the uniformed-side of the Pentagon (the Joint Staff that works to advise the Chairman of the Joint Chiefs of Staff) and again on the civilian-side of the Pentagon, the Office of the Secretary of Defense. What is more, this accounts only for the staffing that would happen within the DoD, while an action of this sensitivity would be staffed far beyond the Pentagon.

[80] 50 U.S.C. § 3093 (a) and (e) (2014) Although the statute specifies only the requirement for a written finding for the conduct of a covert action, the better and historical practice is for a written finding for military operations that have some of the earmarks of a covert action, but fall under the TMA exception to the subsection (e) of Section 413.

[81] *See* 50 U.S.C. § 3093 (a)(3) (2014)

[82] The caveat here is that although TMA actions might be faster to staff, they would still require interagency staffing and potentially a Presidential decision to characterize the activity as TMA and specify the agencies and organizations that might be involved. *See* 50 U.S.C. § 3093 (a)(3) & (4); (e) (2014)

commander who exercises combatant command (COCOM)[83] and who owns the geographic area within which the operational activity is contemplated.

Given the construct of our DoD, the frequent point of departure for an idea that might get the ball rolling toward the production of a finished plan might be the COCOM commander or a member of his staff. In the alternative, and much less frequently, such an idea might originate within the Office of the Secretary of Defense or one of his principle undersecretaries.[84] Regardless of the level of command that conceives of such a mission, it would typically undergo initial staff scrutiny and development within a subordinate command headquarters[85] as described above and then move up the chain of command for senior staff review and coordination at the highest level of command in the U.S. military, the COCOM. Moreover, it is in the context of a COCOM staff where the question of whether the operational idea might be a valid TMA is initially asked and answered. Thereafter, such actions are passed up to the United States Joint Staff, where they undergo final staffing and coordination (which includes interagency coordination). It is at this level where the senior-most staff officers and lawyers within the DoD weigh the TMA issue and provide final advice to the Chairman of the Joint Chiefs of Staff and the Secretary of Defense.

One of the primary officers who weigh the question of TMA is the COCOM Staff Judge Advocate, the commander's senior lawyer and general counsel. In making his legal determination this officer considers a number of factors that spring from the Statute's definition of covert action. In short, the legal analysis follows the same process as described above in the TMA section of this chapter. In regard to the covert action determination, there is one additional issue that was not previously covered: that of acknowledgment. The Statute defines and explains that covert activity is different from clandestine activity. Both types of activity are designed to be concealed from the general public, but clandestine activity is intended to be publicly acknowledged once it is discovered.[86] This is

---

[83] *See* 10 U.S.C. § 164(2008)establishing the various combatant commands and the unique command and control exercised by their commanders (referred to as Combatant Command). Combatant Command is nontransferable command authority and includes both operational control and administrative control; it is only exercised by commanders of unified or specified combatant commands unless otherwise directed by the President or Secretary of Defense. *See* DoD Dictionary, *supra* note 15.

[84] In the case of an intelligence activity, one might assume such an action would originate from the Undersecretary of Defense for Intelligence.

[85] Typically the initial development of the mission concept will occur at the command level responsible for operational execution.

[86] *See* 1991 Intelligence Authorization Act Conf. Rep, *supra* note 66, at 29. The Congressional Conferees detail their understanding of the difference between clandestine and covert activities, asserting that the former employs low-visibility techniques and procedures, which once discovered will be acknowledged. Moreover, the Conferees explain that "United States government activities which are intended to mislead a potential adversary as to the true nature of United States military capabilities, intentions, or operations" do not fall under the definition of covert activity, as acknowledgment is the primary element of a truly covert activity. Conversely, the United States never intends the acknowledgment of covert activities; thus, those activities that it plans from the start to never acknowledge or admit, even after the passage of significant time, are within the definition of covert activity, as expressed in the statute.

not so with covert action. As the statute explains, "the role of the United States Government will not be apparent or publicly acknowledged."[87]

This necessitates that the Staff Judge Advocate and the Commander evaluate whether the underlying activity is of a nature that the President would be willing to acknowledge. Frankly, when such actions are staffed, legal/policy issues such as this are discussed up and down the legal chain in a simultaneous method versus a hierarchical one. Players along the entire policy and legal chain consider these issues in a dialogue that occurs at the same time as the associated tactical staff analysis and planning process. The ultimate question is whether the President would be willing to eventually permit public acknowledgment, if the operation were to be exposed. It is important to note that the Statute places no specific timing requirement on its description of acknowledgment; hence an activity that is intended for public acknowledgment (and is accordingly not covert in nature) might have the act of acknowledgment significantly delayed.[88] It is clear that such delays might involve commonsensical concerns of national security, but what is not as clear is how long this period of delay might run before it runs too long—indicating that the original analysis was flawed, because an overly long period of delayed acknowledgment is tantamount to an intention to not make public at all.

III. Intelligence oversight

A. HISTORY OF INTELLIGENCE OVERSIGHT

Although the history of intelligence oversight began far before the 1960s and 1970s, it underwent a massive evolution during this era, precipitated by actual or perceived abuses of power within the intelligence community. The abuses led to a number of investigations and culminated in formation of a Senate Committee, famously known as the Church Committee, after its chairman, Idaho senator Frank Church. The committee interviewed some eight hundred people, held hundreds of hearings, and produced a two-foot-thick final report in May 1976.[89]

The Church Committee's investigative process and resulting report initiated a government-wide reaction that encouraged Congress to pass the Intelligence Oversight Act of 1980, and Presidents Gerald Ford, Jimmy Carter, and Ronald Reagan to sign a number of executive orders to increase and enhance the oversight

---

[87] *See* 50 U.S.C. § 3093(e) (2014)

[88] For example, even "United States government activities taken to intentionally influence public opinion or government attitudes in foreign countries" are not considered covert in nature, if those activities are concurrently or even subsequently acknowledged, and even if the subsequent acknowledgment occurs a significant period of time after the fact. *See* 1991 Intelligence Authorization Act Conf. Rep, *supra* note 66, at 29.

[89] *See* United States Senate Official Website, Art & History Section, *available at* https://www.senate.gov/ artand history /history/minute/Church_Committee_Created.htm (last visited Aug. 30, 2014) [hereinafter Senate Church Site].

over intelligence activities.[90] The most meaningful of these orders was Executive Order 12,333, United States Intelligence Activities, signed by President Reagan in 1981.[91] The executive orders represented the executive branch's attempt to preempt Congress' effort to create statutory rules that might result in the compromise of critical national security information and practices. In short, Congress felt it had a legitimate need to know, and both branches of government were attempting to balance that valid need with the counterweight of national security.

One of the more important changes that took place after Executive Order 12,333 came into effect was the dramatic increase in the involvement of lawyers in the planning and execution of intelligence activities and operations. Insiders noted that "questions of legality were no longer ignored or left unresolved."[92] Moreover, oversight compliance was integrated into the normal routine of the various agency inspector generals.[93] This increase in legal involvement and oversight certainly extended to DoD, and as a result an entire generation of intelligence law experts now populates the various legal advisor billets throughout the Department and its many agencies and subordinate commands engaged in intelligence activities.[94]

Three primary positive changes that flowed from this trend within the DoD dramatically altered the oversight posture within the Department. First, the Department and its subordinate organizations established a number of oversight organizations.[95] Second, the leadership caused the formal articulation of

---

[90] Stephen B. Slick, The *2008 Amendments to Executive Order 12,333, United States Intelligence Activities*, 58 CIA: Studies in Intelligence 1–2, n.2 (2014).

[91] *See generally* E.O. 12,333, *supra* note 5.

[92] L. Britt Snider, *Recollections from the Church Committee's Investigation of NSA, available at*. https://www.cia.gov/library/center-for-the-study-of-intelligence/csi-publications/csi-studies/studies/winter99-00/art4.html (last visited June 8, 2015).

[93] *Id.*

[94] In recognition of the growing cadre of Intelligence Law practitioners from across the Army, Navy, Air Force, Marine Corps, and DoD agencies, the U.S. Army began to produce consolidated training and educational materials to prepare these attorneys to provide support to their clients. In furtherance of this effort, in 1995, The U.S. Army Judge Advocate General's School and Legal Center (JAG School), Department of International and Operational Law, planned for and then conducted the first week-long joint Intelligence course at Charlottesville, VA, as a continuing legal education (CLE) course. The JAG School produced a comprehensive textbook. *See* The International and Operational Law Department, The Judge Advocate General's School, United States Army, Cases and Materials on Intelligence Law (1995). For the first two years, the author planned, taught, and managed this course and served as the editor for the textbook, which was updated on an annual basis. Over the years the course has become more refined and continues to serve the same cadre of government practitioners. In addition to this course, a number of related CLE courses are offered by various agencies and organizations within the intelligence legal field.

[95] Within the Department of Defense, the Office of the Assistant to the Secretary of Defense for Intelligence Oversight (ATSD(IO)) stands at the apex of the intelligence oversight structure. *See generally* U.S. Dep't. of Def. Dir. 5148.11, Assistant to the Secretary of Defense for Intelligence Oversight (ATSD(IO)) (Apr. 24, 2013) [hereinafter DoDD 5148.11]. The various Department and Combatant Command inspector general's stand one tier below the ATSD(IO), who share independent oversight with the three judge advocate generals, the Staff Judge Advocate

intelligence oversight mandates within the charters of existing organizations (DoD, service, and component inspectors general).[96] Third, the Department of Defense formally and clearly articulated its oversight responsibilities at each relevant level within the military's chain of command.[97] The general purpose of these initiatives include: ensuring that oversight rules are issued and understood, providing decision-makers access to well-versed intelligence lawyers, creating reporting channels for allegations of improprieties, and ensuring leaders understand the requirements and utility of inspections, inquiries, and investigations.

B. DOD INTELLIGENCE OVERSIGHT ORGANIZATIONS

The senior actor within the Department for intelligence oversight is the Secretary of Defense, who is supported by the Assistant to the Secretary of Defense for Intelligence Oversight (ATSD(IO)) and his office.[98] The ATSD(IO) is a senior executive service employee who directly advises the Secretary of Defense and is also chartered to run the DoD Intelligence Oversight Program.[99] In this capacity he ensures that Department oversight directives and regulations are kept up to date, that DoD components understand and properly carry out their oversight roles, and that the various intelligence organizations undergo rigorous scrutiny by way of audits and inspections. He also ensures that reporting channels exist for the reporting of questionable or improper intelligence activities.[100] The ATSD(IO)'s full charter is found in DoD Directive 5148.11.[101] Importantly, he ensures proper and complete reporting of any potential violations and that investigative results and reports are provided to those with responsibility to take corrective action. He also serves as the DoD lead for any required reporting to the Intelligence Oversight Board (IOB) of the President's Intelligence Advisory Board (PIAB).[102] Finally, he ensures that any required congressional reporting of potential violations is accomplished to the satisfaction of Departmental leadership and Congress.[103]

---

to the Commandant of the U.S. Marine Corps, and the combatant command staff judge advocates. In addition to the independent oversight structure described herein, the senior intelligence officer (SIO) at each of these levels carried responsibility for functional intelligence oversight.

[96] At the Department of Defense level, DoDD 5240.01, *supra* note 11, and DoDR 5240.1-R, *supra* note 12, provide authoritative direction and guidance for intelligence oversight. Within the U.S. Army, AR 381-10, *supra* note 56, performs the identical role, passing on and implementing the authoritative direction of E.O. 12,333 and other executive orders and Directive 5240.01 and Regulation 5240.1-R. Each of the services and Combatant Commands have similar directives and regulations.

[97] *Id.*

[98] *See generally* DoDD 5148.11, *supra* note 95.

[99] *Id,* para. 3.

[100] *See* Assistant to the Secretary of Defense (Intelligence Oversight), Mission and History, *available from* http://atsdio.defense.gov/AboutDODSIOO/Organization,MissionandFunctions.aspx (last visited June 8, 2015).

[101] See DoDD 5148.11, *supra* note 95.

[102] *Id.* para. 3.d.

[103] *Id.* para. 3.

The DoD intelligence oversight constellation also includes a number of additional organizations chartered to ensure that DoD intelligence activities and operations are conducted in strict accordance with the rules. For example, the various Departmental Special Access Program Central Offices (SAPCOs) are chartered to protect the highly sensitive information found within their programs, but they are also chartered to ensure that program actors comply with intelligence oversight rules.[104] These organizations work closely with their servicing legal offices and inspector general offices, and directly liaise with the ATSD(IO) to make certain that they each share the same view of how the rules are intended to work, when investigations or inquiries are required, and who should take staff responsibility for such matters.

C. SHARED RESPONSIBILITY (FUNCTIONAL VERSUS INDEPENDENT OVERSIGHT)

The foregoing paragraph implies a close and continuing relationship among all organizations with an oversight mandate. These relationships are not just a good idea: they are required by policy and regulation.[105] For instance, at the DoD level the ATSD (IO) is chartered with responsibility for independent oversight for the collection of human intelligence.[106] This function is complimented by the Undersecretary of Defense for Intelligence (USDI), who has the responsibility for functional oversight over human intelligence.[107] The difference between these two types of oversight is very important. In functional oversight, the senior actor within a group is formally charged with ensuring that the group conducts itself in accordance with established protocols, procedures, and laws. He does this with the advantage of legal support from the servicing general counsel or staff judge advocate. In independent oversight, an officer from outside the acting group is charged with intervening for the specific purpose of providing unbiased additional oversight. Independent oversight actors report to an authority superior to the senior authority within the group being overseen.[108]

---

[104] *See* Dept. of Def. Dir. 5205.07, Special Access Program (SAP) Policy (July 1, 2010) [hereinafter DoDD 5205.07]. In addition, SAP policy ensures that even the most closely guarded of these sensitive programs is subject to congressional review and reporting, and sets out exactly how that reporting will occur. *Id.*

[105] *See* E.O 12,333, *supra* note 5, § 1.6(h). Section 1.6(h) also requires that agencies grant "inspectors general, general counsels, and agency officials responsible for privacy and civil liberties protection" unimpeded access to information and documents necessary to perform their oversight roles. *Id.*

[106] *See* DoDD 5148.11, *supra* note 95.

[107] ***See*** Dept. of Def. Inst. S-5200.42, Defense Human Intelligence (HUMINT) and Related Intelligence Activities (U) (Dec. 8, 2009), *available at* http://fas.org/irp/doddir/dod/is5200-42.pdf (last visited June 8, 2015).

[108] The ATSD(IO) is a very good example of an independent oversight authority. He or she provides oversight over the activities of the Undersecretary of Defense for Intelligence (the USDI) and all subordinate intelligence actors with the Department, but reports not to the USDI, but to his or her superior, the Secretary of Defense. *See* DoDD 5148.1, *supra* note 95, para 1.b.

This dual oversight model is redundant, and this redundancy is intentional. It is engineered to prevent violations that might otherwise occur because the functional oversight authority became too close to the underlying actors and actions. This is not unlike the phenomenon of a corporate counsel losing her ability to separate the interests of the CEO from the interests of the entity that is the client.

This dual oversight arrangement is also employed at the combatant command level, where proximity to the warfighter and the need for accurate and timely intelligence might generate subtle pressure to intentionally bend the rules. Dual oversight also serves to protect the senior staff directors and Commander from the much more likely trap, wherein groupthink causes hard-working counsel, striving to find a workable and legal solution, to lose their objectivity and subject their clients to unnecessary risk.

The foregoing problem is addressed at the United States Special Operations Command (USSOCOM) by formal recognition of functional and independent oversight authorities and specific enumeration of the responsibilities of each oversight official.[109] For instance, the Command J-2 is the senior intelligence officer and is chartered with responsibility for "functional" oversight of intelligence. The independent oversight function is performed by a trio of two senior military officers and a senior civilian: the Inspector General, the Staff Judge Advocate, and the Director of the Command Operations Review Board. It is important to note that each of these officers report directly to the four-star Commander. This close relationship provides them with sufficient gravity and influence to perform their oversight functions, and prevents other senior players within the Command organization from frustrating their efforts. Moreover, all three work in very close coordination with one another.[110]

So what is the quantitative difference between these unique oversight organizations? The uninitiated observer might comment that the apparent difference between functional and independent oversight is the intellectual distance the various oversight organizations and personalities enjoy from the operational planning process. However, this statement would be somewhat misleading in regard to the lawyers involved in the process, who work as closely to the problem-set as any other staff group. The true difference is intellectual perspective. While the lawyers work hard to find solutions to problems posed by other members of the staff, they carry a strategic and future-impact perspective, always mindful of what might happen if their client fails to comply with law and policy. They realize that the reversals and setbacks associated with these types of violations greatly outweigh any temporary gain made by stretching the rules.

---

[109] *See generally* U.S. Special Operations Command, Dir. 1-10, Oversight of Command Activities (Dec. 1, 2009).

[110] *Id.*

D. THE BASIC INTELLIGENCE OVERSIGHT MANDATE

The primary objective of this oversight regime, and E.O. 12,333, is to shield U.S. persons from becoming the object of unreasonable and improper collection efforts. The Department of Defense issued a directive and a companion regulation to implement the executive order's mandate (DoD Directive 5240.1 and DoD Regulation 5240.1-R).[111] Each of the military services and combatant commands has issued its own implementing regulation or directive, and each of these instruments is based upon DoD Regulation 5240.1-R. For example, the United States Army's implementing regulation is Army Regulation 381-10,[112] while the United States Special Operations Command's implementing directive is United Special Operations Command Directive 381-10.[113] Each of these instruments provides their service or command with specific guidance in regard to the collection, retention, and dissemination of information that regards or originates with U.S. persons. Moreover, they provide detailed guidance relative to what measures should be undertaken to inquire into and react to instances where these procedures and rules have been violated.

A U.S. person is defined as a U.S. citizen, a permanent resident alien, a corporation incorporated in the United States, or an association substantially composed of U.S. citizens or permanent resident aliens.[114] Furthermore, any person whose status cannot be positively established must be presumed a U.S. person. The bottom line is that a military organization or unit may only collect information about a U.S. person that fits the foregoing definition when such an organization has the mission and authority to collect such information. The implementing regulations of the services and combatant commands further refine and expand this requirement by inserting language that directs the military actor to collect against a U.S. person only through lawful means and only using the least intrusive method.[115] Accordingly, military organizations must first determine that they have the mission to collect the type of intelligence that is under consideration for collection. Second, they must determine that they have been authorized

---

[111] *See generally*, DODD 5240.1, *supra* note 11 and DODR 5240.1-R, *supra* note 12.

[112] *See* AR 381–10, *supra* note 56.

[113] *See generally* U.S. Special Operations Command (USSOCOM), Man. 381–10, Activities of United States Special Operations (USSOCOM) Intelligence That Affect United States Persons (Dec. 28, 2008) [hereinafter USSOCOM Manual 381–10]. Observers sometimes comment on the fact that USSOCOM uses the same nomenclature (381–10) for its regulation as that of the Army. The history of this similarity is traced to the founding days of USSOCOM in 1987. All the primary staff officers, to include the J2 and the Staff Judge Advocate, were Army officers, who were familiar with Army regulations. Colonel Albert E. Vernon III, the SJA at that time, proposed that the new command base its intelligence oversight regulation on the well-drafted Army version. Interview with Colonel (Retired) Albert E. Vernon, III, former USSOCOM Staff Judge Advocate (1987–1992) and former USSOCOM Director, Command Operations Review Board (1992–2011) (Mar. 21, 2014).

[114] *See* E.O. 12,333, *supra* note 5, Part 3, § 3.5(k).

[115] I have provided cites to the USSOCOM and Army regulations as examples of this restrictive directive, but each of the other regulations possess similar wording. *See* USSOCOM MAN. 381–10, *supra* note 113, at 3; AR 381–10, *supra* note 56, paras. 1–5 & 2–3.

by either military order (in the case of a military formation) or valid directive (in the case of a defense agency). Third, they must determine that the collection method is not otherwise prohibited by law. Fourth, they must further determine that the collection method is the least intrusive method available. Finally, they must determine that a logical link exists between their legal and authorized mission to collect and the U.S. person who is the proposed target of their collection efforts.

It is important to note that a decision to collect only from publicly available sources does not alleviate the need to follow the foregoing rules and procedures. Instead, it merely morphs the requirements. For instance, in such a case, the organization must determine that it has the mission and authority to collect information. Moreover, it must further determine that collection of publicly available information about the subject U.S. person is consistent with that mission and authorization. It is equally important to note that in addition to the foregoing requirements, the use of certain "special collection techniques," such as electronic surveillance, concealed monitoring, physical searches, physical surveillance, or undisclosed participation in organizations requires special associated authorities above and beyond those already mentioned. Moreover, the use of these techniques also requires rigid compliance with established procedures, which are expressed in the service, agency, or combatant command implementing directive for DoD Regulation 5240.1-R.

A great deal of legal analysis goes into the determination of whether certain actions constitute "collection," and if collection does occur, further analysis goes into determining whether collected information is "retained." None of the foregoing requirements exist if the specified information is never collected. Thus, military lawyers spend their time analyzing their facts against this question. Raw data or information is not considered collected until it has been received by an employee of a DoD Intelligence Component in the course of his or her official duties and has been processed into an intelligible form by intelligence professionals.[116] The need for this type of rule becomes obvious when one considers the vast quantum of data that might be downloaded from some electronic source, but cannot be adequately analyzed for some period of time because of the number of required man-hours needed to perform that task.

Once a determination is made that U.S. person information has been properly collected, the next question becomes whether that information might be retained. If the information was properly collected it may be retained. If it was not properly collected, because the proper collection analysis was not performed ahead of time, post-collection analysis should be performed. If the post-collection analysis confirms all the elements required for proper collection were present at the time when that analysis should have been performed, the information may be deemed properly collected and be retained. Finally, the collecting organization

---

[116] DoDR 5240.1-R, *supra* note 12, para. C2.2.1.

has up to ninety days to make the retainability determination.[117] In fact, this is called the "90 Day Rule" by military practitioners.

There are also rules that regulate the dissemination of information that has been properly collected and retained. DoD Regulation 5240.1-R governs the dissemination or transfer of information collected about U.S. persons. In short, a collecting organization or agency that collected and retained U.S. person information may only the information only with another agency or organization (to include those with the DoD) if the collecting agency has a reasonable basis to believe the receiving organization will use the information to perform an official and lawful governmental function. However, if a military organization shares information with a member of the Intelligence Community or with a DoD Intelligence Component, it need not perform this analysis. Instead, the receiving organization has the responsibility to perform and document the analysis.

E. REPORTING QUESTIONABLE ACTIVITIES

The most important goal of oversight is to prevent violations, mistakes, and abuse. A component of this goal is reporting events or activities that fall short of obvious compliance. Accordingly, each of the oversight directives or regulations provides specific instruction in regard to when such reporting is necessary and to whom these reports should be made.[118] Violations typically occur because of haste and good intentions gone awry. In most cases, rapid corrective action plus adequate reporting is the only required remedy. This is one of the many areas where overreporting is superior to underreporting.

As indicated above, there are specific legal thresholds for a reportable activity.[119] An activity that is "unlawful or contrary to executive order, Presidential directive, or applicable DoD policy"[120] is defined as a "Questionable Intelligence Activity"[121] and requires immediate reporting through a prescribed reporting chain. Additionally, an intelligence activity that "could impugn the reputation or integrity of the DoD Intelligence Community or otherwise call into question the propriety of an intelligence activity"[122] is referred to as "Significant or Highly Sensitive Matters" and also requires immediate reporting.[123]

---

[117] *Id.* para. C3.

[118] *See* DoDR 5240.1-R, *supra* note 12, ch. 15, and App. 1 to ch. 15. Chapter 15 introduces the term "questionable activity" and describes the reporting procedures for reporting such an event. Appendix 1 (Directive-Type Memorandum (DTM) 08-052, dated June 17, 2009)) to chapter 1 amends chapter 15 to expand the original term into two more specific categories: (1) questionable intelligence activities (QIA), and (2) significant or highly sensitive matters (SHSM). The DTM was signed by the Deputy Secretary of Defense on June 17, 2009, and added to DoDR 5240.1-R to provide additional guidance.

[119] DoDR 5240.1-R, *supra* note 12, ch. 15, and App. 1 to ch. 15.

[120] *See id.* attachment 2, para. 1.a.(1).

[121] *Id.*

[122] *See id.* attachment 2, para. 1.a.(2).

[123] *See id.* The DTM attached to DoDR 5240.1-R provides specific examples of matters that might reasonably be considered to be SHSM, to wit: those involving congressional inquiries or

A warning and practice tip to the effective practitioner: always err in favor of reporting. If there is the slightest doubt about whether one of the foregoing reporting thresholds has been reached, a report should be launched. Failure to report results in a demanding and painful series of additional reports and coordination events. Additionally, these reports are frequently accompanied by explanatory congressional engagements with multiple congressional committees and the Intelligence Oversight Board (IOB) of the President's Intelligence Advisory Board (PIAB).[124] Additionally, the prudent practitioner ensures the reports that are advanced in response to these reporting requirements provide all the bad news that is known. It is not sufficient to indicate that an investigation is pending, when sufficient information is available to indicate that the likely facts set the stage for various potential violations. The various oversight directives and regulations do not provide guidance for such generous reporting; however, the author has learned this lesson and desires to correct the record in terms of the expectation for reporting.[125] Do not get caught *over-lawyering* the reporting thresholds or in reliance upon one of the categories of events that does not require reporting (a mere security violation). If a question of reporting requires a significant investment of time and analysis, or if lawyers struggle with an answer in regard to this issue, the well-advised organization forwards a report that contains all that is known, even if certain elements of the report are missing. Overreporting is cost free; however, the reverse is certainly not true.

IV. Conclusion

The military practice of intelligence law has evolved a great deal over the past thirty years. When the current cadre of senior military judge advocates entered their respective services in the early 1980s, intelligence law was never mentioned during either the judge advocate basic or advanced courses.[126] It was not until

---

investigations, those that may result in adverse media coverage, those that may impact foreign relations, and those related to the unauthorized disclosure of classified or protected information.

[124] *See* DoDD 5148.11, *supra* note 95, at 2 & 5. Although the ATSD(IO) has responsibility for coordination and reporting to the IOB and Congress, it is the reporting organizations that carry the burden of meeting with and satisfying the requests for information from these entities.

[125] USSOCOM Manual 381–10, *supra* note 113, at 41. The USSOCOM Manual defines questionable activity similarly to DoDR 5240.1-R, and provides no additional guidance in regard to events that do not meet the reporting criteria. However, the Army Intelligence Oversight regulation, AR 381–10, *supra* note 56, provides specific guidance in regard to events that do not merit reporting. For example, events that appear to be merely security violations or acts of personal misconduct "normally dealt with through normal command actions" do not meet the questionable intelligence activity reporting criteria. *Id.* para. 15–5.

[126] The Judge Advocate General's School and Legal Center Basic Course is an intense eleven-week course wherein young lawyers new to the Corps receive information they will need to succeed in government practice. The Advanced Course (now referred to as the Graduate Course) is a year-long course directed toward the earning of a LLM in military law, with a specialty in some sub-area of military law such as international or intelligence law. The graduate course is designed for mid-career judge advocates.

the mid-1990s that the first one-hour block of instruction was added to the U.S. Army's Judge Advocate General's Corps mid-career graduate course. Obviously, this was a quantum step forward, but in the context of a year-long masters of law program, a one- hour block was hardly impressive. Accordingly, lawyers of this era learned intelligence law on the fly, made a lot of mistakes, and worked hard to not repeat those mistakes. We collectively applaud the efforts of past and present leaders to bring ever-increasing emphasis to this area of our practice, and we appreciate the growing legal sophistication that now exists in the military departments and services, the Defense Intelligence Agency, and most notably within the DoD General Counsel's Office.

Over the past ten years, an obvious and healthy debate has occurred in regard to all manner of legal issues in this arena, all of which directly and immediately impacted the warfighting client. Combatant command staff judge advocates now work closely with their DoD General Counsel peers and superiors to provide understanding of the ground-level facts and associated legal analysis. The Department of Defense has achieved a temporary plateau of excellence in this area of national security law practice. Military lawyers have impacted legislation, participated in the interpretation of law and policy, and given practical voice to modern tactics and techniques. Moreover, they have gained the ability, up and down the legal chain, to confidently identify the important intelligence law issues and provide accurate and timely advice in regard to these issues.

In regard to the content of this chapter, the intent was to hammer away at the twin imperatives: (1) understanding the importance of searching for legal authorities, where those authorities originate, and what form they might take, and (2) understanding that the trick is not to understand all the details (although, at some point this should become a secondary aspiration). The real trick is mastering the method of legal analysis and developing relationships with other intelligence law practitioners who hold the answers to questions that have not yet been considered

17 }

Legal Issues in Special Operations

Matthew R. Grant* and Todd C. Huntley**

I. Introduction

In the thirteen years since the attacks of 9/11 special operations have been garnering much media attention.[1] From the images of bearded U.S. special operation forces (SOF) on horseback in Afghanistan in 2001 to the killing of Osama bin Laden

* Colonel, U.S. Air Force, Judge Advocate General's Corps; Director of Legal Services, U.S. Air Forces in Europe—United Kingdom. BS Business Administration, California State Polytechnic University, Pomona, 1990; JD, University of Louisville Brandeis School of Law, 1998; LLM, The Judge Advocate General's Law Center and School, U.S. Army, Charlottesville, VA, 2005. Colonel Grant's prior special operations assignments include: Deputy Staff Judge Advocate, U.S. Special Operations Command, 2010–2013; Deputy Legal Advisor, Joint Special Operations Command, 2001–2004; and numerous deployments in support of special operations joint task forces in Iraq and Afghanistan between 2001 and 2009. Colonel Grant served in the U.S. Army and Army National Guard for ten years before joining the U.S. Air Force as a judge advocate in 1998, including four years on active duty as an Armor officer, 1990–1994 (3rd Battalion (Airborne), 73rd Armor, 82nd Airborne Division, 1991–1994).

** Captain, Judge Advocate General's Corps, U.S. Navy; Head, National Security Law Department, International and Operational Law Division, Office of the Navy Judge Advocate General and Adjunct Professor, Georgetown University Law Center. BA, University of Cincinnati, 1991; JD, University of Cincinnati, 1996; MA, Fletcher School of Law and Diplomacy, Tufts University, 2006; LLM Harvard Law School, 2009. Captain Huntley has extensive experience working with special operations legal issues from his previous assignments, which include Assistant Staff Judge Advocate, U.S. Special Operations Command, 2005–2008 and 2012–2014; Staff Judge Advocate for Special Operations Command Central/Combined Forces Special Operations Component Command, 2009–2011; and deployments as a legal advisor with a special operations joint task forces in Afghanistan in 2006 and 2013. The views and opinions expressed in this chapter are those of the authors and do not necessarily reflect the official policy or position of the Department of the Air Force, Department of the Navy, Department of Defense, or any agency of the U.S. government. The authors would like to thank Colonel Michael Smidt, Judge Advocate, U.S. Army for his advice and invaluable contributions to this chapter.

[1] Although the exploits of special operations have been the focus of both page and screen in the past, the number of books and movies about them seem to have only increased since the attacks of 9/11. *E.g.*, CAPTAIN PHILLIPS (Columbia Pictures 2013); ZERO DARK THIRTY (Sony Pictures 2012); ACT OF VALOR (Relativity Media 2012). There have been complaints from some corners that the increased media focus is ill-advised and may endanger future operations. *See* Huma Khan & Luis Martinez, *Navy SEAL Commander Advised to "Get the Hell Out of the Media,"* THE

by Navy SEALs, special operations continue to make headlines, and are unlikely to disappear from either the operational environment or the headlines anytime soon.[2] Since 9/11 U.S. SOF have experienced incredible growth with the number of personnel doubling, the budget tripling, and demand signal, as evidenced by deployment requirements, quadrupling.[3] United States' SOF are typically deployed to seventy-five or more countries at any given time, conducting operations with interagency and international partners.[4] In spite of current U.S. defense cutbacks, SOFs are scheduled to slightly increase in the coming years, signaling that political and military leaders will increasingly rely upon special operations in protecting the nation's national security interests.[5]

Advising SOF engaged in the conduct of special operations across the spectrum of armed conflict, from banditry and low-level insurgency, Cold War-style confrontation with militarily near-peer adversaries, to high-intensity regional warfare, is a specialized sub-practice of operational law within the U.S. armed forces' legal communities.[6] Before an operation is ever launched, these lawyers, along with the commanders and planners, spend countless hours analyzing, discussing, and coordinating with each other; the unit conducting the operation, and higher echelons of command to ensure that the operation is conducted in full compliance with U.S. domestic law and the law of armed conflict (LOAC).[7] Although there is no exception to the applicability of these laws to military special operations, the nature of special operations activities raises issues not often encountered by legal advisors supporting conventional forces conducting overt military operations.[8]

Note, ABC News Online (Feb. 7, 2012 3:42 pm), http://abcnews.go.com/blogs/politics/2012/02/navy-seal-commander-advised-to-get-the-hell-out-of-the-media/.

[2] *E.g.*, Mark Bowden, The Finish: The Killing of Osama Bin Laden (2012); Mark Owen, No Easy Day: The Firsthand Account of the Mission That Killed Osama bin Laden (2012); Doug Stanton, The Horse Soldiers: The Extraordinary Story of a Band of US Soldiers Who Rode to Victory in Afghanistan (2009); Sean Naylor, Not a Good Day to Die: The Untold Story of Operation Anaconda (2005). *See* Headquarters, Department of the Army, Army Doctrine Publication 3-05, Special Operations ("The future will likely increase SOF's role at not only the tactical level but also at the operational level as the requirement for long-term SOF campaigns grows.") [hereinafter ADP 3-05].

[3] *The Future of U.S. Special Operations Forces: Ten Years after 9/11 and Twenty-Five Years after Goldwater-Nichols: Hearing Before the Subcomm. on Emerging Threats and Capabilities of the H.Comm. on Armed Services,* 112th Cong. 6 (2011) (statement of ADM William H. McRaven, USN, Commander, U.S. Special Operations Command).

[4] Admiral William H. McRaven, USN, Commander, United States Special Operations Command Posture Statement, Before the 113th Congress Senate Armed Services Committee Emerging Threats and Capabilities Subcommittee 6 (Mar. 11, 2014).

[5] *Id.* ("[D]espite current fiscal austerity and force drawdown, the office of the Secretary of Defense has recommended that SOF grow to 69,700 from roughly 66,000 today."); Department of Defense Quadrennial Defense Review 2014 37 (Mar. 4, 2014).

[6] *See* ADP 3-05, *supra* note 2, at 6–7.

[7] *See* Department of Defense Directive 2311.01E, DoD Law of War Program (May 9, 2006, incorporating change 1, Nov. 15, 2010, certified current as of Feb. 22, 2011) [hereinafter DoDD 2311.01E].

[8] *See* Department of Defense Joint Publication 3-05 Special Operations IV-11 (July 16, 2014) [hereinafter Joint Pub. 3-05].

This chapter will briefly survey some of the domestic and international legal issues raised by the conduct of special operations, which differ from those found in conventional operations.[9] It will begin by defining special operations and describing those activities encompassed by this term, followed by an introduction and analysis of the domestic law considerations impacting special operations. The distinction between special operations and covert action/special activities is then clarified in order to provide a better understanding of the legal relationship between these factually-similar activities. Fiscal law issues and human rights requirements will also be discussed before concluding the section with an examination of the legal issues related to the conduct of special operations activities within the United States. The final section will focus on the application of LOAC to special operations, to include issues of distinction and ruses in warfare related to the wearing of civilian clothes and nonstandard uniforms, distinction in targeting of members of nonstate organized armed groups and civilians directly participating in hostilities, and the use of non-standard or specialized weapons.

II. Special Operations: Definition and Description

The U.S. military defines special operations as "[o]perations requiring unique modes of employment, tactical techniques, equipment and training often conducted in hostile, denied, or politically sensitive environments and characterized by one or more of the following: time sensitive, clandestine, low visibility, conducted with and/or through indigenous forces, requiring regional expertise, and/or a high degree of risk."[10] In identifying and developing a framework to analyze the legal issues raised by special operations, it is helpful to examine the specific underlying activities that comprise special operations rather than the above expansive and ambiguous definition. For U.S. special operations, those activities are set forth at 10 U.S.C. § 167(j) and include direct action, strategic reconnaissance, unconventional warfare, foreign internal defense, civil affairs, military information support operations, counterterrorism, humanitarian assistance, and theater search and rescue.[11] United States Department of Defense (DoD) doctrine

---

[9] An exhaustive and in-depth analysis of these broad and complex issues would fill an entire volume. Thus, the goal of the authors is to introduce those legal issues that attorneys reviewing special operations and advising special operations forces will most likely face, and to provide a framework for analyzing them. Given the authors' experience and knowledge, this review will focus on special operations conducted by U.S. military forces and the legal issues related to those operations. Although many of the international law issues are also relevant to special operations conducted by other nations, this chapter is written from a U.S. perspective.

[10] JOINT PUB. 3-05, *supra* note 8, at GL-11.

[11] Nunn-Cohen Amendment to the National Defense Authorization Act of 1987, Pub. L. No. 99-661, § 1311, 100 Stat. 3816 (1986) (codified at 10 U.S.C. § 167). The list of special operations activities is set forth at 10 U.S.C. § 167(j)(1)–(9). The President and Secretary of Defense are also granted the authority to specify additional activities as special operations. 10 U.S.C. § 167(j)(10) (2014). For definitions and more detailed descriptions of these activities *see* JOINT PUB. 3–05, *supra* note 8, at II-1 to II-18.

further elucidates these statutorily defined activities, referring to them as special operations core activities, and also includes countering weapons of mass destruction, security force assistance, hostage rescue and recovery, counterinsurgency, and foreign and humanitarian assistance.[12]

Although these statutory and doctrinal definitions and descriptions disaggregate special operations into distinct activities, in reality these activities are often conducted simultaneously or in conjunction with other such missions during an operation.[13] Reviewing U.S. Army special operations doctrine is helpful in illustrating the relationship between these different activities, as it discusses special operations forces as having two distinct critical capabilities: special warfare and surgical strike.[14] Special warfare includes those activities such as unconventional warfare, foreign internal defense, and security force assistance; it focuses on long-term operations conducted by, with, or through local security or nonstate forces. Surgical strike includes activities such as hostage rescue, direct action, and counterproliferation requiring the capability to conduct largely unilateral lethal operations.[15] This description is also helpful in characterizing special operations as it further describes who, or how, those activities will be conducted, with each raising related but distinct legal concerns.

As implied by these definitions, special operations are different from conventional operations in how, where, and in what manner those operations are conducted. Other key factors differentiating special operations from conventional operations are the usually small number of personnel involved, the type of target, and the high degree of risk normally associated with such operations. Thus, special operations is perhaps best described not by referring to a specific activity but rather by the operational flexibility that the specially trained forces bring to the fight, as reflected in the definition described above.[16] For the purposes of this chapter, military operations conducted by specially trained, equipped, and supported armed forces employing unconventional means and methods of warfare against a target or set of targets in a hostile or politically sensitive area, to achieve effects which are critical to accomplishing important national objectives, are referred to as "special operations."[17]

---

[12] Joint Pub. 3-05, *supra* note 8, at II-3. These activities, as well as those listed in 10 U.S.C. § 167(2014) , are described in more detail in Headquarters, Department of the Army, Army Doctrine Reference Publication 3-05, Special Operations (Aug. 2012) at 2-1 to 2-8 [hereinafter ADRP 3-05]. ADRP 3-05 also includes preparation of the environment as a core activity.

[13] Joint Pub. 3-05, *supra* note 8, at I-2 to I-3; ADP 3-05, *supra* note 2, at 6-7.

[14] ADP 3-05, *supra* note 2, at 8. Although Army doctrine applies specifically only to Army Special Operations, it heavily influences all U.S. DoD special operations as Army SOF make up the majority of all U.S. SOF. *Id.* at 1.

[15] *Id.* at 8.

[16] *See* Joint Pub. 3-05, *supra* note 8, at GL-11. *See also* ADP 3-05, *supra* note 2, at 12-16 (discussing Army SOF characteristics and imperatives).

[17] This definition borrows heavily from DoD doctrine and the writings of Admiral (retired) William H. McRaven, until 2014 the Commander of U.S. Special Operations Command. Admiral McRaven is the retired U.S. Navy SEAL officer widely credited with commanding the SOF mission that resulted in Osama bin Laden's death in Pakistan on May 1, 2013. *See generally* Joint Pub. 3-05, *supra* note 8, at I-1; William H. McRaven, Spec Ops: Case Studies in Special Operations

Examining the definition of special operations and the activities of which it consists is also helpful in highlighting the different legal issues that arise in such operations. Operations in denied or politically sensitive environments will often involve questions of sovereignty and intervention if conducted without the knowledge or consent of that country. Operations conducted by, with, or through indigenous forces will involve questions regarding the legal status of those individuals. Activities directed at nonstate actors will raise the issue of distinction in targeting. Methods employed in clandestine operations may also give rise to questions on the status of the SOF conducting them. The use of unique tactical techniques and equipment, particularly weapons, may require new or additional reviews to ensure that those comply with the LOAC.[18] A legal advisor working with SOF needs to be knowledgeable of the legal issues that arise during all of these activities because, as noted above, most special operation missions consist of several different activities.

For example, during the course of a deployment to Afghanistan, U.S. SOF conducting a foreign internal defense and counterinsurgency mission will have to incorporate civil affairs and military information support operations while simultaneously being prepared to conduct a counterterrorism or hostage rescue mission.[19] This integration of different activities into a special operation creates its own set of operational legal challenges.

III. U.S. Domestic Law and Special Operations

Most casual observers of military special operations, and even more than a few lawyers working in the armed forces, assume that a SOF legal advisor's primary legal domain is the LOAC, that *lex specialis* applicable to armed conflict by and between states.[20] The LOAC is certainly a major component of the operational activities of a SOF legal advisor, but typically the most vexing legal issues involve the applicability of, and limitations imposed by, domestic laws regarding current and anticipated special operations missions. The body of domestic law affecting

---

WARFARE THEORY AND PRACTICE (1996). Although the DoD definition is most suitable for doctrinal instruction and planning of special operations, it is verbose; Admiral McRaven's definition is focused and brief, but by its terms is limited only to a particular special operations activity: direct action. This proposed definition is neither as focused as the Admiral's or as precise and all-encompassing as the DoD's; it is sure to please no one, but suits our purposes in providing a concise definition for further discussion of SOF legal challenges.

[18] As can be seen from this wide range of activities that make up special operations, the legal issues raised are broad and could fill an entire volume. This chapter will focus primarily on those legal issues arising in the most common, or most well-known, special operations activities: counterterrorism, direct action, foreign internal defense, and unconventional warfare.

[19] For a further illustration of how special operations core activities may be coordinated within a mission, see JOINT PUB. 3–05, *supra* note 8, at II-04.

[20] DoDD 2311.01E, *supra* note 7, ¶ 3.1; International Committee of the Red Cross, *War and International Humanitarian Law* (Oct. 29, 2010), https://www.icrc.org/eng/war-and-law/overview-war-and-law.htm.

special operations rests upon the foundation built by Congress in 1987 with the establishment of the United States Special Operations Command (USSOCOM).

The long history of spectacular successes—and spectacular failures—of U.S. military special operations is beyond the scope of this chapter. Yet one special operations mission was the catalyst for both the creation of USSOCOM and the legislative foundation of modern U.S. special operations. Following the overthrow of the U.S.-supported Shah of Iran, the revolutionary Shi'ite Islamic government in Iran fomented the armed takeover of the U.S. Embassy in Tehran, Iran's capital city, and the capture of fifty-two U.S. civilian and military diplomats and diplomatic staff members on November 4, 1979. After a joint special operations task force's failed attempt to rescue the hostages on April 24, 1980, investigations of both the hostage rescue mission specifically, and U.S. special operations capabilities generally, recommended that a Counterterrorist Joint Task Force should be established to plan, train for, and conduct operations to counter terrorist activities directed against the United States.[21] The October 1983 invasion of Grenada highlighted continuing challenges in properly resourcing SOF, and the misuse of SOF by conventional force leaders, resulting in high SOF casualties, eventually led to the creation of USSOCOM in 1987.[22] Though the Goldwater-Nichols Department of Defense Reorganization Act of 1986[23] did not include provisions to reorganize U.S. SOF under a single authority, it was quickly amended by the Nunn-Cohen amendment to the National Defense Authorization Act (NDAA) for Fiscal Year 1987, which did.[24]

Section 1311 of the 1987 NDAA established a unified combatant command for special operations forces, to "prepare special operations forces to carry out assigned missions."[25] The amendment assigned all active and reserve special operations forces stationed in the United States to USSOCOM, and gave the USSOCOM commander broad authority to develop strategy, doctrine, and tactics; train SOF; and formulate and submit requirements for intelligence support.[26] The USSOCOM commander also possesses broad acquisition authorities, such as the authority to validate and prioritize SOF requirements; develop and acquire special operations-peculiar equipment, and acquire special operations-peculiar material, supplies, and services; and ensure the interoperability of each of the service's SOF and their equipment.[27] Historically, SOF officers faced difficult career choices in peacetime, including whether to remain in SOF (which was not endorsed or favored by conventionally minded military senior leaders), or return to the traditional military specialties. The 1987 NDAA gave the

---

[21] Special Operations Review Group Commissioned by the Chairman of the Joint Chiefs of Staff [Iran Hostage] Rescue Mission Report 61 (1980).

[22] U.S. Special Operations Command History 6–7 (2007).

[23] Goldwater-Nichols Department of Defense Reorganization Act of 1986, Pub. L. No. 99–433, 100 Stat. 992 (1986) [hereinafter Goldwater-Nichols Act].

[24] 10 U.S.C. § 167 (2014).

[25] 10 U.S.C. § 167(a) (1987).

[26] 10 U.S.C. § 167(b), (e), and (g) (2014).

[27] 10 U.S.C. § 167(e) (2013).

USSOCOM commander authority to monitor promotions, assignments, retention, and training and education of SOF officers.[28] These authorities, and the creation of a Major Force Program (MFP) category in the Department of Defense's (DoD) Five-Year Defense Plan, describe a unified combatant command that also performs service-like functions; it possesses some Military-Department-like responsibilities and authorities for "programming, budgeting, acquiring, organizing, training, equipment and providing combat ready-SOF for employment" by other combatant commanders.[29]

A. SPECIAL OPERATIONS, TRADITIONAL MILITARY ACTIVITIES, AND COVERT ACTION

Lodged within the Nunn-Cohen amendment was the hint of a long-standing and unresolved issue for the SOF community, DoD, the White House, and Congress: the circumstances under which military special operations activities would constitute intelligence activities or covert action, triggering notice and briefings to the congressional intelligence oversight committees and, potentially, a Presidential covert action finding. Section 167(g) states that:

> [10 U.S.C. § 167] does not constitute authority to conduct any activity which, if carried out as an intelligence activity by the Department of Defense, would require a notice to the Select Committee on Intelligence of the Senate and the Permanent Select Committee on Intelligence of the House of Representatives under title V of the National Security Act [50 U.S.C. § 3091 *et seq.*].[30]

Under 50 U.S.C. § 3091(a), the President is required to keep the congressional intelligence committees "fully and currently informed" of ongoing and planned intelligence activities.[31] Absent program-specific funding, or notification and regular updates on intelligence activities (including the intelligence activities of the Armed Forces), section 3094 prohibits the expenditure of appropriated funds for any intelligence activity, including covert action.[32]

Covert action is defined in statute as an activity or activities of the United States Government to "influence political, economic, or military conditions abroad, where it is intended that the role of the United States Government will not be apparent or acknowledged publicly."[33] Importantly, "traditional ... military activities or routine support to such activities" are outside the scope of "covert action."[34] Traditional military activities (TMA) are not otherwise defined in the 1991 law, though the conference committee report accompanying the final bill

---

[28] *Id.*

[29] 10 U.S.C. § 167 (2014); Joint Pub. 3-05, *supra* note 8, at I-3.

[30] 10 U.S.C. § 167(g) (2014) .

[31] 50 U.S.C. § 3091(a) (2002) .

[32] 50 U.S.C. § 3094 (2010).

[33] 50 U.S.C. § 3093(e) (2002) .

[34] 50 U.S.C. § 3093(e) (2002).

and the earlier Senate committee report frame the parameters of TMA. According to the conference committee report, TMA includes activities by military personnel under the direction and control of a U.S. military commander, preceding or related to hostilities that are either anticipated or ongoing, involving the employment of U.S. Armed Forces.[35] The earlier Senate intelligence committee report also clarified what was meant by the term "routine support," stating that:

> The committee considers as "routine support" unilateral U.S. activities to provide or arrange for logistical or other support for U.S. military forces in the event of a military operation that is publicly acknowledged. Examples include caching communications equipment or weapons, the lease or purchase from unwitting sources of residential or commercial property to support an aspect of an operation, or obtaining currency or documentation for possible operational uses, if the operation as a whole is to be publicly acknowledged.[36]

Activities that are not under the direction and control of a military commander, or are "other-than-routine," are not TMA and must be reported as intelligence activities, and, if covert, be subject to a preexisting Presidential finding.[37] For the SOF legal advisor, ensuring that proposed special operations missions constitute TMA requires early and regular involvement in operational planning, and continuing oversight of ongoing operations.

One particular special operations activity, Preparation of the Environment (PE), illustrates the challenge of determining when, and whether, a special operations activity may be considered a reportable intelligence activity or a TMA exception to the reporting requirements of 50 U.S.C. § 3091 *et seq*.[38] DoD defines PE as SOF

> actions to prepare the operational environment for potential operations. PE is conducted during the shape phase of an operation as well as for developing and preparing for the entry of forces and supporting agencies to resolve conflicts using either lethal or nonlethal actions.[39]

Unlike SOF Advance Force Operations (AFO), which prepare for near-term direct action against specific, identified targets, PE activities are undertaken in support of regional plans "to alter or shape the operational environment."[40] These

---

[35] H.R. Rep. No. 102–166, 102d Cong., 1st Sess., at 29–30 (1991).

[36] S. Rept. No. 102–85, 102d Cong., 1st Sess., at 47 (1991).

[37] *Id.* For an excellent, and more detailed, treatment of this issue, see Andru E. Wall, *Demystifying the Title 10—Title 50 Debate: Distinguishing Military Operations, Intelligence Activities & Covert Action*, 3 Harv. Nat'l Sec. J. 85 (2011). *See also* Robert Chesney, *Military—Intelligence Convergence and the Law of the Title 10/Title 50 Debate*, 5 J. Nat'l Sec. L. & Pol'y 539 (2012).

[38] Preparation of the environment (PE) is also often referred to as "Operational Preparation of the Environment" (OPE). *See* Joint Pub. 3–05, *supra* note 8, at GL-9.

[39] Joint Pub. 3–05, *supra* note 8, at II-4 to II-5.

[40] *Id.* at IV-4; U.S. Special Operations Command, Pub. 1, Doctrine for Special Operations 26 (2011) [hereinafter USSOCOM Pub. 1]. As the Permanent Select Committee on Intelligence of the

activities are accomplished by employing "cross-cultural insights, language capabilities, and relationships of SOF [to] provide access to and influence nations where the presence of conventional U.S. forces is not warranted."[41] In situations where conventional U.S. military action is neither imminent nor anticipated, above-defined clandestine PE seemingly appears to some stakeholders on Capitol Hill as an intelligence activity, and potentially a "covert action" under 50 U.S.C. § 3093:

> The [House Permanent Select Committee on Intelligence] notes with concern the blurred distinction between the intelligence-gathering activities carried out by the Central Intelligence Agency (CIA) and the clandestine operations of the Department of Defense (DOD).... In categorizing its clandestine activities, DOD frequently labels them as "Operational Preparation of the Environment" (OPE) to distinguish particular operations as traditional military activities and not as intelligence functions. The Committee observes, though, that overuse of this term has made the distinction all but meaningless.... Clandestine military intelligence-gathering operations, even those legitimately recognized as OPE, carry the same diplomatic and national security risks as traditional intelligence-gathering activities.... [T]hese activities often escape the scrutiny of the intelligence committees, and the congressional defense committees cannot be expected to exercise oversight outside of their jurisdiction.[42]

A 2013 Congressional Research Service (CRS) report posed several questions about DoD's apparently expansive use of the TMA exception to avoid intelligence oversight, including whether the post-9/11 environment in which U.S. military operations has changed sufficiently to warrant a review of the covert action statute.[43] An earlier 2010 CRS report, citing news reports of alleged CIA-led SOF covert action, questioned whether U.S. SOF were operating under CIA control to "get around restrictions placed on military operations," and what those restrictions might be.[44] Though the use of SOF under CIA control would fall outside of the TMA exception (as it would not be under the direction or control of a military commander), the authors of the 2010 CRS report recommended consideration

---

House of Representatives noted in 2010, "DOD has shown a propensity to apply the OPE label where the slightest nexus of a theoretical, distant military operation might one day exist." H.R. RPT. NO. 111–186, 111th Cong., 1st Sess., at 40.

[41] USSOCOM PUB. 1, *supra* note 40, at 26.

[42] H.R. RPT. NO. 111–186. *supra* note 40, at 48–9. The Committee went further, threatening new legislation to bring gray-area PE within its jurisdiction: "Based on recent discussions, the Committee is hopeful that DOD will be more fulsome in its reporting. In the future, if DOD does not meet its obligations to inform the Committee of intelligence activities, the Committee will consider legislative action clarifying the Department's obligation to do so." *Id.*

[43] MARSHALL CURTIS ERWIN, CONG. RESEARCH SERV., RL33715, COVERT ACTION: LEGISLATIVE BACKGROUND AND POSSIBLE POLICY QUESTIONS 9 (2013).

[44] ANDREW FEICKERT & THOMAS K. LIVINGSTON, CONG. RESEARCH SERV., RS21048, U.S. SPECIAL OPERATIONS FORCES (SOF): BACKGROUND AND ISSUES FOR CONGRESS 9–10 (2010).

of whether current law ensures that Congress knows when, and why, particular special operations activities are moved out from under the TMA framework and into CIA-led covert action authorities, and then back again.[45] Although the unclassified and publicly releasable document did not provide specific recommendations, the report prompted the House Permanent Select Committee's concern regarding PE, as expressed in the previous paragraph. The critical role of SOF legal advisors in identifying the legal authorities for SOF missions was also highlighted in the 2010 CRS report: "it is reported that in order to carry out counterterrorism operations, that U.S. SOF must 'shop around' to find circumstances (i.e., operating under CIA Title 50 authorities) conducive to mission accomplishment."[46]

The 2013 CRS report is not likely to steady the nerves or salve the concerns of the Senate intelligence committee's members. In reviewing proposed PE missions, SOF legal advisors in tactical units must be mindful of attempts to further expand the parameters of permissible by simply mimicking the (loose) terminology that statutorily bounds TMA. Further, they must carefully consider the relationship between SOF units and other government agencies to ensure that SOF PE activities remain under military command-and-control, and are intended to support readily identifiable military contingency plans. Close and continuous coordination with legal advisors at higher echelons of command is also essential to prevent any adverse impact to current TMA authorities and future congressional constraints.

B. FUNDING SPECIAL OPERATIONS: THE APPLICATION OF U.S. FISCAL LAW

One of the first questions a SOF legal advisor must answer is: What type of funds may be used to pay for the special operation and its attendant activities?[47] Funding special operations is theoretically no different than funding conventional operations. However, unique challenges arise during the conduct of special operations, particularly when dealing with clandestine operations or operations with a partner nation or indigenous forces. This section will briefly discuss a few of the more common fiscal law challenges present in such operations, highlighting the fiscal authorities commonly relied upon in their funding.

United States' fiscal law is fundamentally different from other fields of law as it is inherently restrictive, requiring an affirmative appropriation and authorization from Congress.[48] Funds for DoD operations are usually appropriated

---

45 *Id.* at 10.

46 *Id.*

47 *See* The Int'l & Operational Law Dep't, Judge Advocate Gen.'s Legal Ctr. & Sch., U.S. Army, Operational Law Handbook 217 (2014) [hereinafter Operational Law Handbook] ("Fiscal law touches everything we do, whether in garrison or in contingency operations.").

48 *See* U.S. Const., art. I, § 8, cl. 12 (Congress has power to "raise and support Armies."), art. I, § 8, cl. 13 (Congress has power to "provide and maintain a Navy."), art. I, § 9, cl. 7 ("[n]o Money shall be drawn from the Treasury, but in consequence of Appropriations made by Law . . . "). *See also* United

by Congress in the annual DoD Appropriations Act in the form of Operational and Maintenance (O&M) funds. As the name implies, this appropriation is the primary source of funding for operational expenses of the U.S. military.[49] The O&M funds are apportioned to the military services and defense agencies; they include funding for baseline, or normal day-to-day operations, as well as for overseas contingency operations (OCO), for operations that were not otherwise programmed, such as those in Afghanistan and Iraq during the decade-plus following September 11, 2001 (hereinafter 9/11).

Funds may only be spent for the purpose for which they were appropriated.[50] Given the wide range of activities required to keep the military functioning, it would be impossible to specify all possible authorized expenditures in the appropriation act. Expenditures may also be authorized if the purpose is necessarily incident to accomplishing that object and are not otherwise prohibited by law or provided for elsewhere.[51] Such authorizations and prohibitions may be found in the appropriation act itself or may be set forth elsewhere, such as in the annual NDAA or in a separate, stand-alone statute.[52] Untangling this web of fiscal authorities and prohibitions is often challenging in even the most conventional of situations. When dealing with special operations missions consisting of different activities with multiple purposes, conducted by, with, or through foreign security forces, nonstate groups, and other U.S. government agencies, the difficulty is compounded as it requires identifying various fiscal authorities to fund the disparate activities taking part within the overall operation.

A classic illustration of the funding purpose problem in combined operations of the type often conducted by SOF may be found in the 1984 U.S. General Accountability Office (GAO) review of the AHUAS TARA II joint combined exercise in Honduras.[53] During the course of the six-month exercise, U.S. military units constructed airstrips, barracks, a school, and other facilities, provided

---

States v. MacCollom, 426 U.S. 317, 321 (1976) ("The established rule is that the expenditure of public funds is proper only when authorized by Congress, not that public funds may be expended unless prohibited by Congress.").

[49] Operations and Maintenance "pay for the current operations of the force, and for the maintenance of all the Armed Services' equipment, including base maintenance services, vehicle maintenance services, civilian salaries, and all expenses requires to operate the force." Cont. & Fiscal L. Dep't, Judge Advoc. Gen.'s Legal Center. & Sch., U.S. Army, Fiscal Law Deskbook at 2–9 (2014) [hereinafter Fiscal Law Deskbook]. Congress grants separate appropriations to DoD for the purposes of Military Personnel (MILPER); Research, Development, Test, and Evaluation (RDT&E); Procurement; and Military Construction (MILCON). For a more in depth discussion, see *id.* at 2–9 to 2–12.

[50] 31 U.S.C. §1301(a) (1997), commonly referred to as the Purpose Statute, states "[a]ppropriations shall be applied only to the objects for which the appropriations were made except as otherwise provided by law."

[51] Major General Anton Stephan, Commanding Officer, District of Columbia Militia, Mar. 25, 1927, A-17671, 6 Comp. Gen. 619; U.S. Commodity Futures Trading Commission—Availability of the Customer Protection Fund, B-321788, 2011 WL 3510145 (Comp. Gen.) (2011).

[52] Fiscal Law Deskbook, *supra* note 49, at 2–20 to 2–21.

[53] The Honorable Bill Alexander, B-213137, 63 Comp. Gen. 422 (1984).

medical and veterinary assistance to Honduran civilians, and provided radar systems as well as artillery, infantry, and medical training to the Honduran military, most of which were paid for with DoD O&M funds.[54] In their opinion, GAO found that the use of O&M funds for the construction was impermissible as Congress had provided funding for facilities intended for use by U.S. forces via the Military Construction appropriation, and for facilities intended for use by foreign forces via the Security Assistance appropriation.[55] Similarly, the GAO found that use of O&M funds to conduct the training of Honduran military forces, given the cost and the length of that training, was also improper, and should have been funded with Security Assistance appropriations.[56]

Department of Defense O&M funds may be used to train foreign military forces when the purpose of that training is for familiarization and safety in order to enhance the interoperability of those foreign forces with U.S. forces. Thus, the purpose must not be to increase the capacity or capability of the foreign forces being trained, but rather to prepare them for combined operations with U.S. forces.[57] Although the foreign forces will receive a tangential benefit from the training, the real benefit accrues to the U.S. forces in the way of ensuring that the foreign forces may operate safely and effectively alongside U.S. forces.[58] Of course almost any training will also have an ancillary effect of improving the receiving unit's capability and capacity. In determining whether the planned training is appropriate under this authority, or whether it requires a specific security assistance authority, the factors to be considered are the number of personnel being used to conduct the training, the length of the training, and the cost of the training, and whether the training does improve the capability and capacity of the unit receiving the training.[59]

Legal advisors reviewing proposed interoperability, safety, and familiarization training must be vigilant as the use of this authority is rife with problems. As commanders may use their own O&M funds to conduct such training, it is often seen as the easy way to train or engage with a foreign partner force. Working with the planners, the legal advisor must ask the hard questions to ensure the appropriate funding source is utilized. In addition to the factors cited above, the

[54] *Id.* at 426.

[55] *Id.* at 432–37. The O&M funds may be used for minor MILCON in some limited circumstances. *See* 10 U.S.C. § 2805(c) (2011). *See also* Fiscal Law Deskbook, *supra* note 49, at 8–29 to 8–30.

[56] *Id.* at 440–43. Congress typically appropriates security assistance funds to the State Department for the training, equipping, and logistical support of foreign security forces. Given that DoD O&M funds, as discussed above, are appropriated to pay for U.S. military operations, using them to pay for training foreign security forces or to provide weapons and equipment to foreign security forces, absent some other authorization, would be unlawful.

[57] These operations need not be actual combat operations, but may also be to prepare the foreign forces for combined exercises with U.S. forces. *See id.*

[58] If the foreign forces require extensive training prior to being able to operate alongside U.S. forces, then the use of O&M funds to conduct that training would be inappropriate. *See id.*

[59] *Id.*

legal advisor should also confirm that such training is in support of a planned combined exercise or operation.

As a result of the AHUAS TARA II GAO review and the uncertainty over the use of O&M funds to train foreign forces, Congress enacted 10 U.S.C. § 2011.[60] Although it is appropriate to use O&M funds to pay for the training of U.S. military forces, the GAO AHUAS TARA II opinion raised questions as to whether the use of O&M funds was appropriate when such training consisted of SOF conducting training of foreign forces. 10 U.S.C. § 2011(a) specifically authorizes the use of O&M funds to pay for SOF to train and train with foreign security forces including, in some cases, paying for "incremental expenses" of those other forces to participate in the training.[61] The primary purpose of these activities, commonly referred to as Joint Combined Exchange Training (JCET), is to maintain SOF proficiency in a foreign language, cultural, and geographic awareness, and in training foreign forces, all skills required to conduct both their foreign internal defense and unconventional warfare missions.[62] The authority provided in 10 U.S.C. § 2011 recognizes that, although foreign security forces receive training during JCETs, the main purpose of this activity is to maintain SOF proficiency in their critical ability to work with foreign forces, and the use of O&M funds is appropriate.[63]

In the early stages of operations in Afghanistan after 9/11, U.S. SOF lacked an appropriation or authorization to purchase weapons, ammunition, and equipment for, or to pay for the operations of, their indigenous partner forces.[64] Small teams of SOF were inserted into Afghanistan in November 2001 and partnered with indigenous Afghan forces known as the Northern Alliance in a classic unconventional warfare mission. Operating alongside Northern Alliance forces, U.S. SOF were to use their indigenous partners' experience and knowledge of the local area to conduct operations that would lead to the downfall of the Taliban regime and defeat of Taliban forces and their al Qaida allies. Although the groups

---

[60] 10 U.S.C. § 2011 (2011) is one of the few SOF-specific authorities in U.S. domestic law. In the NDAA for fiscal year 2014, Congress extended a similar authority allowing conventional forces to train with foreign security forces, including the use of DoD O&M funds to pay the incremental expenses incurred by those foreign security forces. National Defense Authorization Act for Fiscal Year 2014, Pub. L. No. 113-66 § 1203, 127 Stat. 673, 894–95 (2013) [hereinafter § 1203 of the FY14 NDAA].

[61] "Incremental expenses" is defined here as "the reasonable and proper cost of rations, fuel, training ammunition, transportation, and other goods and services consumed by such country, except that the term does not include pay, allowances, and other normal costs of such country's personnel." 10 U.S.C. § 2011(d) (2011) . The same definition is found in § 1203 of the FY14 NDAA. Absent this specific authorization, use of O&M funds to pay for the operating and exercise costs of foreign security forces would be impermissible.

[62] GAO Report to Congressional Requesters, Military Training: Management and Oversight of Joint Combined Exchange Training 19 (July 1999).

[63] *Id.*

[64] Douglas Jehl & Eric Schmitt, *Law Gives Spending Power to Special Operations Forces*, N.Y. Times, Feb. 1, 2005, http://www.nytimes.com/2005/02/01/politics/01intel.html?pagewanted=print&position=&_r=0.

aligned as the Northern Alliance had been fighting the Taliban since the withdrawal of Soviet forces in 1989, they were on the brink of defeat, in control of only a small portion of northeastern Afghanistan. To go on the offensive with U.S. SOF the Northern Alliance needed equipment, arms, and ammunition as well as other financial support to pay their fighters. Lacking an appropriation or an authorization to expend O&M funds for this purpose, SOF initially had to rely on the CIA to make these payments under their covert action authority.[65]

Although the SOF were ultimately successful in their mission, this lack of fiscal authority was identified as a weakness in SOF's ability to perform its counterterrorism and unconventional warfare missions. In response, Congress added Section 1208 to the National Defense Authorization Act for 2005.[66] Section 1208 initially provided authority to expend $25 million "to provide support to foreign forces, irregular forces, groups, or individuals engaged in supporting or facilitating ongoing military operations by United States special operations forces to combat terrorism."[67] Originally set to expire in fiscal year 2007, this funding authority has been extended through fiscal year 2015 and increased to $50 million annually.[68] This is a particularly important development as prior to Congress granting Section 1208 authority, only the CIA had authority to fund surrogate counterterrorism operations.[69]

In light of U.S. operations in Iraq and Afghanistan, and in recognition of the importance of working by, with, and through partner forces, Congress has recently provided additional appropriations and authorization for the training, equipping, and support of security forces in Iraq, Afghanistan, and Pakistan, as well as authority to use DoD O&M funds to enhance the counterterrorism capability of foreign forces in the Horn of Africa and Yemen.[70] Section 1206 of the Fiscal Year 2006 NDAA, also referred to as the Global Train and Equip fund, authorizes the Secretary of Defense to expend funds to "conduct or support a program to build the capacity of a foreign country's national military forces

---

[65] *Id. See also* Gary Berntsen, Jawbreaker: The Attack on bin Laden and al Qaeda: A Personal Account by the CIA's Key Field Commander 109, 124, 192 (2005); Stanton, *supra* note 2, at 57.

[66] National Defense Authorization Act for Fiscal Year 2005, Pub. L. 108–375 § 1208, 18 Stat. 1811, 2086–2087 (2004) [hereinafter § 1208 of the FY05 NDAA].

[67] § 1208 of the FY05 NDAA, *supra* note 66. As in 10 U.S.C. § 167 and as discussed above, § 1208(e) also has a provision making clear that the authority contained therein "does not constitute authority to conduct a covert action."

[68] National Defense Authorization Act for Fiscal Year 2012, Pub. L. 112–81 § 1203, 125 Stat. 1298, 1621 (2011).

[69] Jehl & Schmitt, *supra* note 64.

[70] *See, e.g.*, National Defense Authorization Act for Fiscal Year 2013, Pub. L. 112–39 § 1203, 126 Stat. 1632, 1980–1981 (2013) (Authority to Build the Capacity of Certain Counterterrorism Forces in Yemen and East Africa); National Defense Authorization Act for Fiscal Year 2010, Pub. L. 111–84 § 1224 (Pakistani Counterinsurgency Fund) and § 1234 (Authority to Transfer Defense Articles and Provide Defense Services to the Military and Security Forces of Iraq and Afghanistan), 123 Stat. 2201, 2521–2523, 2535–2535 (2009). For other sources of authority to conduct training with or support operations of foreign security forces, see also Department of Defense Joint Publication 3–07, Stability Operations E-7 (Sept. 29, 2011)[hereinafter Joint Pub. 3–07].

in order for that country to conduct counterterrorist operations; or participate in or support military and stability operations in which the Armed Forces of the United States are participating."[71] More recently Congress authorized the Secretary of Defense, in coordination with the Secretary of State, "to provide assistance, including training, equipment, supplies, and sustainment, to appropriately vetted elements of the Syrian opposition and other appropriately vetted Syrian groups and individuals" in order to defend the Syrian people, the United States, and its allies from the threats posed by ISIL and terrorists in Syria.[72] Although not SOF-specific, these authorities have been relied upon heavily by SOF in order to conduct foreign internal defense, unconventional warfare, and counterterrorism missions in Iraq, Afghanistan, and elsewhere.

When advising on the legal aspects of special operations, it is imperative that a legal advisor know the various fiscal authorizations and their limitations. Appropriations and authorities may be included in a variety of statutes as either stand alone or as part of a broader law. These authorities may also be further amended in later authorization and appropriations, compounding the difficulty in finding and keeping track of current authorities. It is critical that the legal advisor be involved early in the planning process to ensure that an appropriate funding source is identified. A knowledge of the available funding authorities coupled with an understanding of the mission and commander's intent is key to providing the advice necessary to identify potential alternate funding sources that would allow the commander to conduct the mission and accomplish his intent. [73]

C. PROMOTING HUMAN RIGHTS: LEAHY VETTING FOR SOF ACTIVITIES WITH PARTNER FORCES

Allegations of human rights abuses committed by foreign security forces trained or advised by U.S. special operations forces in Central America and elsewhere not only have created negative headlines, they also led to greater congressional oversight. These allegations ultimately resulted in the restriction of U.S. assistance to foreign military and security forces implicated in human rights abuses.[74] The current restriction is found in two separate statutes. The term "Leahy Amendment"

---

[71] National Defense Authorization Act for Fiscal Year 2006, Pub. L. 109–63 § 1206, 119 Stat. 3136, 3456–58 (2006).

[72] Continuing Appropriations Resolution for Fiscal Year 2015, Pub. L. 113–64 § 149, 128 Stat. 1867, 1875–77 (2014).

[73] For a detailed discussion of fiscal law applicable to military operations, see FISCAL LAW DESKBOOK, CHAPTER 10, OPERATIONAL FUNDING, *supra* note 49.

[74] *See, e.g.*, Clifford Krauss, *How U.S. Actions Helped Hide Salvador Human Rights Abuses*, N.Y. TIMES, Mar. 21, 1993, http://www.nytimes.com/1993/03/21/world/how-us-actions-helped-hide-salvador-human-rights-abuses.html; JERRY M. LAURIENTI, THE U.S. MILITARY AND HUMAN RIGHTS PROMOTION 38–40 (2007); NINA M. SERAFINO ET AL., CONG. RESEARCH SERV. "LEAHY LAW" HUMAN RIGHTS PROVISIONS AND SECURITY ASSISTANCE: ISSUE OVERVIEW (Jan. 29, 2014) [hereinafter CRS Leahy Report].

is now generally used as shorthand to refer to both, which jointly prohibit assistance to foreign military and security units where there is "credible information that such unit has committed a gross violation of human rights."[75] Gross violations of international- recognized human rights include "torture or cruel, inhuman, or degrading treatment or punishment, prolonged detention without charges and trial, causing the disappearance of persons by the abduction and clandestine detention of these persons, and other flagrant denial of the rights to life, liberty, or the security of the person."[76]

Section 620M of the Foreign Assistance Act states "[n]o assistance shall be furnished . . . to any unit of the security forces of a foreign country if the Secretary of State has credible information that such unit has committed a gross violation of human rights" and applies to all assistance authorized by the Foreign Assistance Act (FAA) and Arms Export Control Act (AECA), including assistance provided to foreign security forces authorized by the FAA and the AECA. This includes Foreign Military Sales (FMS) and Foreign Military Financing (FMF), International Military Education and Training (IMET), and Peacekeeping Operations (PKO) assistance.[77] The FAA does allow the provision of assistance to a "tainted" foreign security force unit if the government of that unit is "taking effective steps to bring the responsible members of the security forces unit to justice."[78] What constitutes "effective steps" is not defined or described in the statute, but was discussed in the legislation's conference report; it stated that effective steps required the government to "carry out a credible investigation and that the individuals involved face appropriate disciplinary action or impartial prosecution in accordance with local law."[79] Although it would certainly include criminal prosecution of those members or turning them over to an international tribunal for prosecution, it is not clear if lesser measures, such as administrative punishment, removal from command, or separation from the military would constitute sufficient disciplinary action.

The DoD-funded training and assistance is also restricted by language that has been placed, in some format, in every DoD appropriations bill since 1999, including the current Consolidated Appropriations Act (CAA) for Fiscal Year 2014, which states "[n]one of the funds made available by this Act may be used for any training, equipment, or other assistance for the members of a unit of a foreign security force if the Secretary of Defense has credible information that the unit has committed a gross violation of human rights."[80] "Assistance" is not

---

[75] 22 U.S.C. § 2378d(a) (2014); Consolidated Appropriations Act for Fiscal Year 2014, Pub. L. 113–76 § 8057, H.R. 3547 115–14 (2014) [hereinafter § 8057 CAA].

[76] 22 U.S.C. § 2304(d) (2014) .

[77] 22 U.S.C. § 2378d(a) (2011); *see also* CRS Leahy Report, *supra* note 74, at 5.

[78] 22 U.S.C. § 2378d(b) (2011).

[79] Foreign Operations, Export Financing, and Related Programs Appropriations Act, Pub. L. 105–18; H. Rept. 105–401 (1998); *see also* GAO Report to Congressional Requesters, Human Rights: Additional Guidance, Monitoring, and Training Could Improve Implementation of the Leahy Laws 6 (Sept. 2013).

[80] § 8057 CAA. The provision contained in the CAA for Fiscal Year 2014 extended the scope of the DoD version of Leahy by including a prohibition on DoD assistance; previously it had applied only to training; *see* CRS Leahy Report, *supra* note 74, at 2.

defined by § 8057 CAA but has been determined to include counterdrug, counterterrorist, humanitarian demining training, and Joint Combined Exchange Training (JCET), assistance provided by the Combatant Commander's Initiative Fund (CCIF), and pursuant to the Building Partnership Capacity legislation (Section 1206) and the State-DoD Global Security Contingency Fund.[81] It does not apply to assistance provided by Section 1208, foreign disaster assistance, and humanitarian assistance.[82] This lack of a definition may complicate the efforts of legal advisors and commanders in determining whether the planned activity may take place absent human rights vetting or will be conducted with a unit that is known to have been involved in past credible incidents of human rights abuse.

Assistance under § 8057 CAA may be provided to "tainted" units if "all necessary corrective steps have been taken."[83] Although this provision would remediate a previously tainted unit and make it eligible to receive assistance under the CAA, what constitutes "all necessary corrective steps" is not defined or discussed in the statute.[84] This standard appears to be more forgiving than that found in the FAA in that it does not specifically mention bringing the alleged perpetrators to justice, so it would appear to include measures such as remedial training, removal of the perpetrators from the unit, and other measures short of criminal prosecution, provided that such measures will effectively end the abuses. Further, in extraordinary circumstances, the Secretary of Defense may waive the prohibition and allow the provision of assistance despite the allegations.[85] Restrictions pursuant to the FAA Leahy provision may not be waived.[86]

The FAA Leahy provision also contains an additional requirement not found in the DoD Leahy provision. In those cases where foreign assistance is being withheld based on the finding of credible information of gross human rights violations, this must be promptly communicated to the foreign government by the Secretary of State.[87] For special operations forces operating in the country the communication of this information may create a risk of a possible backlash from their partner security forces or others in the country. Those forces are, optimally, notified by the Country Team at the U.S. Embassy or through the chain of command prior to the notification being made.

Human rights vetting pursuant to the Leahy amendments is the responsibility of the U.S. State Department and is conducted by U.S. Embassy staffs overseas and the Bureau for Democracy, Human Rights, and Labor at the State Department in Washington, DC.[88] The process is coordinated with and receives information

---

[81] CRS Leahy Report *supra* note 74, at 5.

[82] *Id.*

[83] § 8057(b) CAA. Assistance may also be provided under this section "if the equipment or other assistance is necessary to assist in disaster relief operations or other humanitarian or national security emergencies."

[84] *Id.*

[85] § 8057(c) CAA.

[86] 22 U.S.C. § 2378d (2014); *see also* CRS Leahy Report, *supra* note 74, at 6.

[87] 22 U.S.C. § 2378d(c) (2014).

[88] CRS Leahy Report, *supra* note 74, at 9–11.

from other U.S. government agencies, including DoD and intelligence agencies.[89] Information may also be received from nongovernment organizations as well as media sources.[90]

Respect for human rights is a core U.S. national interest, and promotion of human rights is an integral component of all U.S. military operations. [91] This interest is especially important in foreign internal defense and counterinsurgency missions where building the integrity and legitimacy of the host-nation government and security forces is integral to mission success.[92] Protection and promotion of human rights is also an important aspect of unconventional warfare missions where U.S. special operations forces are working alongside nonstate armed groups. United States' military forces, including special operations forces, have a duty to report suspected human rights abuses as well as suspected violations of the law of armed conflict.[93] The SOF legal advisor should remain cognizant of human rights vetting and reporting requirements, and provide guidance to SOF who become aware of human rights violations.

D. "THE FINAL OPTION": SPECIAL OPERATIONS IN THE HOMELAND

The use of SOF to conduct counterterrorist operations within the United States, particularly countering weapons of mass destruction (CWMD) and hostage rescue missions, is one of the most sensitive and important issues on which a legal advisor might have to opine.[94] The Posse Comitatus Act (PCA) prohibits the employment of the Army and Air Force to execute or enforce the laws, except under express authorizations in the Constitution or by an Act of Congress. [95] Several provisions of law authorize the Secretary of Defense (SECDEF) to provide military equipment to any federal, state, or local law enforcement official for law enforcement purposes,[96] and make military personnel available to train those

---

[89] The DoD's role in the vetting process is typically limited to forwarding the names of those individuals and units who are nominees for security assistance and training. *Id.*

[90] *Id.*

[91] *See* 22 U.S.C. § 2304(a)(1) (2014).

[92] Department of Defense Joint Publication 3–22 Foreign Internal Defense VI-38 (July 13, 2010) [hereinafter Joint Pub. 3–22].

[93] Joint Pub. 3–22, *supra* note 92, at A-2; DoDD 2311.01E, *supra* note 7, at 4.4 and 4.5.

[94] The title of this section is borrowed from the U.S. title of a 1982 British film (titled "Who Dares Wins" in the United Kingdom) about a fictitious British Army Special Air Service (SAS) counterterrorist raid to rescue hostages in the U.S. Embassy in London. The movie is based upon the real-life SAS hostage rescue operation that successfully freed nineteen hostages in the Iranian Embassy in London in 1980. The TV images of black-clad SAS assaulters wearing gas masks, carrying submachine guns, and tossing flash-bank "stun" grenades through breached windows and doors before storming the Iranian Embassy was broadcast worldwide and remains the iconic image of a successful urban hostage rescue mission. *See In Depth: Iranian Embassy Siege, Six Days of Fear*, BBC News, http://news.bbc.co.uk/2/hi/in_depth/uk/2000/iranian_embassy_siege/703016.stm (last visited Oct. 28, 2014).

[95] 18 U.S.C. § 1385(1994).

[96] 10 U.S.C. § 372(1956).

officials in the operation and maintenance of that equipment.[97] The SECDEF may also provide expert advice to law enforcement officials on the use of military equipment and basic military training,[98] such as basic marksmanship, patrolling, advanced first aid and lifesaver training, mission planning, and survival skills.[99] With a few discrete exceptions, DoD policies prohibit training civilian law enforcement on advanced military subjects that focus on the "tactics, techniques, and procedures (TTPs) required to apprehend, arrest, detain, search for, or seize a criminal suspect when the potential for a violent confrontation exists."[100]

Although special operations forces maintain unique capabilities to interdict, disrupt, neutralize, or destroy a WMD threat, employment of these capabilities domestically is subject to a comprehensive statutory framework. [101] In matters related to WMD, federal law not only permits military assistance to law enforcement in the use of military equipment and training on basic military skills, but mandates SECDEF to develop specialized CWMD capabilities to support civilian law enforcement agencies in domestic crises. The SECDEF is required to "develop and maintain at least one domestic terrorist rapid response team" capable of aiding federal, state, and local officials in the "detection, neutralization, containment, dismantlement, and disposal of" WMD, including high-yield conventional explosives.[102] Upon the request of the Attorney General, the Secretary of Defense may provide assistance in an "emergency situation involving a weapon of mass destruction."[103] Assistance may include the provision and operation of DoD equipment to "monitor, contain, disable, or dispose of the weapon involved."[104] Military personnel are prohibited from any direct participation in an arrest, or the search for and seizure of evidence, and collection of intelligence for law enforcement purposes, unless "the action is considered necessary for the immediate protection of human life, and civilian law enforcement official are not capable of taking the action."[105] 18 U.S.C. § 831(e) is an explicit exception to the PCA and authorizes the use of the armed forces to enforce the statute that prohibits unauthorized transactions involving nuclear materials.[106]

---

[97] 10 U.S.C. § 373 (1995).

[98] *Id.*

[99] U.S. Dep't of Defense Instruction 3025.21, Defense Support of Civilian Law Enforcement Agencies 21–22 (Feb. 27, 2013).

[100] Memorandum from Deputy Secretary of Defense, to Secretaries of the Military Departments et al., Subject: DoD Training Support to U.S. Civilian Law Enforcement Agencies (June 29, 1996).

[101] USSOCOM Pub. 1, *supra* note 40, 25–6.

[102] 50 U.S.C. § 2314 (2006).

[103] 10 U.S.C. § 382(a) (1956). An "emergency situation involving a weapon of mass destruction" arises from a weapon of mass destruction which poses a serious threat to the interests of the United States, and in which civilian expertise and capabilities are not available to counter the immediate threat; special DoD capabilities and expertise are necessary to counter the threat; and enforcement of the laws relating to WMD would be seriously impaired without DoD assistance. 10 U.S.C. § 382(b) (1956).

[104] 10 U.S.C. 382(c) (1956).

[105] 10 U.S.C. 382(d)(B)(i) (1956) .

[106] (1) The Attorney General may . . . request assistance from the Secretary of Defense under this subsection in the enforcement of this section. Notwithstanding section 1385 of this title (Posse

Unlike the statutory WMD exceptions to the PCA in 10 U.S.C. § 831, employment of SOF for domestic hostage rescue operations is subject to the more general exceptions to the PCA found in the Insurrection Act. The Insurrection Act, which was first enacted in 1807, provides the broadest general authority to the President to employ federal military forces to enforce the laws whenever "unlawful obstructions, combinations, or assemblages, or rebellion against the authority of the United States, make it impracticable to enforce the laws . . . by ordinary course of judicial proceedings."[107] The President may also use the armed forces to "take such measures as he considers necessary to suppress . . . any insurrection, domestic violence, unlawful combination, or conspiracy, if it . . . opposes or obstructs the execution of the laws of the United States."[108] In executing federal law prohibiting hostage-taking, the President may determine in his or her reasonable discretion that the armed forces should be employed to suppress "domestic violence, unlawful combination, or conspiracy" that opposes or obstructs the execution of that law.[109] The most recent publicly acknowledged example of Presidential authorization to employ the armed forces, including SOF, was to suppress the 1987 Atlanta prison riots.

Comitatus Act) the Secretary of Defense may, in accordance with other applicable law, provide such assistance to the Attorney General if-

(A) an emergency situation exists (as jointly determined by the Attorney General and the Secretary of Defense in their discretion); and

(B) the provision of such assistance will not adversely affect the military preparedness of the United States (as determined by the Secretary of Defense in such Secretary's discretion).

(2) As used in this subsection, the term "emergency situation" means a circumstance—

(A) that poses a serious threat to the interests of the United States; and

(B) in which-

(i) enforcement of the law would be seriously impaired if the assistance were not provided; and

(ii) civilian law enforcement personnel are not capable of enforcing the law.

(3) Assistance under this section may include—

(A) use of personnel of the Department of Defense to arrest persons and conduct searches and seizures with respect to violations of this section; and

(B) such other activity as is incidental to the enforcement of this section, or to the protection of persons or property from conduct that violates this section.

18 U.S.C. § 831(e) (1948)

[107] 10 U.S.C. § 332 (1956).

[108] 10 U.S.C. § 333 (1956).

[109] After the Hurricane Katrina natural disaster in 2005, Congress amended 10 U.S.C. § 333 to explicitly authorize the President to employ the armed forces to "restore public order and enforce the laws . . . when, as a result of a . . . terrorist attack or incident . . . the President determines that . . . domestic violence has occurred to such an extent that the constituted authorities of the State or possession are incapable of maintaining public order; and . . .[the terrorist attack or incident] opposes or obstructs the execution of the laws . . . ." John Warner National Defense Authorization Act for Fiscal Year 2007, Pub. L. No. 109–364, § 1076(a)(1) (2006). In 2008 Congress revised 10 U.S.C. § 333 again, restoring most of the original language of section 333 before the 2006 amendments. National Defense Authorization Act for Fiscal Year 2008, Pub. L. No. 110-181, § 1068 (2008).

On November 26, 1987, following an uprising three days earlier by Cuban inmates holding ninety-four hostages at an Atlanta federal prison, approximately a hundred U.S. Army SOF experts were reported to have deployed to the prison scene to provide technical advice to the FBI dealing with the hostage situation.[110] According to the Special Agent-in-Charge (SAC) of the FBI's Atlanta office during the prison uprising, who was also the prison riot incident commander, U.S. Army SOF were actually deployed to Atlanta by order of the president to provide "backup" to the FBI's Special Weapons and Tactics (SWAT) teams, which were "stretched to the limit."[111] The FBI's premier Hostage Rescue Team was on-scene at a federal prison hostage-taking occurring simultaneously in Louisiana.[112] Army SOF demolition experts worked with FBI SWAT team members to prepare explosives for use to penetrate the prison walls, if necessary, while military snipers used their weapon systems to over-watch the prison and gather intelligence on the activities in areas under the hostage-takers' control.[113] The Army SOF snipers were under strict orders not to open fire unless authorized by the FBI SAC to save the life of a hostage.[114] Meanwhile, FBI SWAT teams and Army SOF teams rehearsed an immediate assault on the prison in case the rioters began killing hostages.[115]

Although the preparation of demolition explosives for use by FBI SWAT team breachers might be considered "military support to law enforcement" under 10 U.S.C. § 373, employment of military snipers and SOF assault teams for in extremis emergency assault to save hostages' lives and suppress domestic violence in the prison would clearly violate the PCA in the absence of a Presidential order under the Insurrection Acts. On December 8, 1987, Proclamation 5748[116] and accompanying Executive Order (E.O.) 12616[117] were filed with the Office of the Federal Register. Signed by President Reagan on November 24, 1987, the order authorized the Secretary of Defense to use the armed forces to suppress the violence and restore law and order at the Atlanta federal prison.[118] In a letter from the Executive Clerk of the White House to the Director of the Federal Register, the following statement was included with the text of E.O. 12616 and Proclamation 5748:

> The ... Proclamation and Executive Order were signed by the President because the possibility that existed on November 24, 1987, that the situation

---

[110] Robert Pear, *Military Hostage Specialists Sent to Help F.B.I. at Atlanta Prison*, N.Y. Times, Nov. 26, 1987, http://www.nytimes.com/1987/11/26/us/military-hostage-specialists-sent-to-help-fbi-at-atlanta-prison.html.

[111] Weldon L. Kennedy, On-Scene Commander: From Street Agent to Deputy Director of the FBI 151 (2007).

[112] *Id.*

[113] *Id.*

[114] *Id.*

[115] *Id.*

[116] Proclamation No. 5748, 3 C.F.R. Comp. 178 (1987), *and in* 101 Stat. 2238 (1987).

[117] Exec. Order No. 12,616, 3 C.F.R. Comp. 260–61 (1987).

[118] *Id.* at 261.

> at the Federal prison in Atlanta would deteriorate further and that the use of force to free the hostages would be necessary. That situation never arose, and a negotiated settlement was reached. Therefore, the use of units and members of the Armed Forces of the United States to suppress the violence described in the Proclamation and Executive Order was never required.[119]

Presidential proclamations or executive orders authorizing the use of the armed forces to execute the laws may not be issued prior to SOF units deploying to a hostage-rescue or CWMD crisis. This will present a challenge to the SOF legal advisor in advising the SOF commander. Of particular importance to the SOF commander are the rules for the use of force when the armed forces are employed pursuant to the Insurrection Act or any of the specific CWMD authorities described previously. Current Justice Department opinions would make Fourth Amendment prohibitions against unreasonable seizures in the context of the use of force, including deadly force, applicable to military forces called out to execute the laws.[120] The Standing Rules for the Use of Force for U.S. Forces (SRUF), applicable to armed forces engaged in military support to civilian law enforcement agencies, incorporate constitutional principles for the use of force in law enforcement.[121] Legal advisors should carefully review the SRUF's provisions for the use of force, including deadly force, which impose a minimum force standard, stating that "[d]eadly force is to be used only when all lesser means have failed or cannot be reasonably employed."[122] The minimum force standard is of particular concern for commanders where SOF assaulters will likely confront hostage-takers intermingled with (or shielded by) their hostages during aggressive and fast-moving room-to-room clearing operations. Vague directions to employ deadly force "*only* when lesser means have failed or cannot be reasonably employed" invite confusion and hesitation, with potentially deadly consequences for the hostages and their rescuers. The SOF legal advisors should consider whether to advise SOF commanders and planning staffs to request supplemental mission-accomplishment rules for the use of force without the minimum force provisions of the SRUF.[123]

---

[119] *Id., and in* 3 C.F.R. Comp. 178 (1987).

[120] Memorandum from U.S. Dep't of Justice O.L.C. to the files, Re: Oct 23, 2001 OLC Opinion Addressing the Domestic Use of Military Force to Combat Terrorist Activities (Oct 6, 2008), http://www.justice.gov/sites/default/files/olc/legacy/2009/08/24/memoolcopiniondomesticusemilitaryforce10062008.pdf (last visited Nov. 4, 2014).

[121] *See, e.g.*, Joint Chiefs of Staff, Chairman of the Joint Chiefs of Staff Instruction 3121.01B, Standing Rules of Engagement/Standing Rules for the Use of Force for U.S. Forces, Encl. L, para. 5.c. (June 13, 2005) (authorizing the use of deadly force when personnel "reasonably believe that a person poses an imminent threat of death or serious bodily harm . . . .") [hereinafter CJCSI 3121.01B].

[122] *Id.*

[123] Ctr. for Law & Military Operations, Domestic Operational Law Handbook for Judge Advocates 182 (2013).

IV. LOAC and Special Operations across the Spectrum of Conflict

Special operations activities are conducted across the spectrum of military operations and international relations, taking place in peacetime, periods of heightened tension, and civil unrest, as well as during non-international and international armed conflicts. In analyzing the particular issue raised, the legal advisor must determine the governing legal regime. Where the activity is to be conducted, who is conducting it, against whom is it directed, and the nature of the activity, as well as the overarching operational environment, will determine whether those activities are governed by the domestic law of the state where the activities are occurring, the domestic law of the sponsoring state, international human rights law, international criminal law, or LOAC.[124] The wide range of operational environments, activities, and personnel conducting these activities makes it difficult to provide a comprehensive analysis in a single chapter of the legal issues raised by all special operations activities. This section will attempt to shed light on a few of the more common, yet complicated, LOAC issues faced by SOF and their legal advisors.

A. PRINCIPLES OF LOAC

The law of armed conflict does not include a SOF exception to its proscriptions. United States' Armed Forces, including SOF, are required to "comply with the law of war during all armed conflicts, however such conflicts are characterized, and in all other military operations."[125] The principles of LOAC that apply to all SOF plans and tactics regardless of the legal character of the armed conflict, or military operation, are:

- *Military Necessity*: "Military necessity permits a belligerent, subject to the laws of war, to apply any amount and kind of force to compel the complete submission of the enemy with the least possible expenditure of time, life and money."[126] Destruction—of persons or property, merely for the sake of destruction itself, is a violation of LOAC.
- *Unnecessary Suffering:* Treaties and customary international law prohibit employment of weapons that are calculated to cause

---

[124] Although, strictly speaking, *jus in bello* would apply only to those activities conducted in an armed conflict, it is U.S. policy to apply the principles of the law of armed conflict to all military operations regardless of how they are characterized. Thus, U.S. SOF would have to comply with *jus in bello* principles even in operations that do not rise to the level of an armed conflict. DoDD 2311.01E, *supra* note 7, para. 4.1.

[125] *Id.*

[126] Trial of Wilhelm List and Others (The Hostages Trial), Case No. 47, Judgment (U.S. Mil. Trib., Nuremberg, Feb. 19, 1948), *reprinted in* 8 United Nations War Crimes Commission, Law Reports of Trials of War Criminals 66 (1949).

unnecessary suffering.[127] "[T]he act of combatants killing or wounding enemy combatants in combat is a legitimate act under the law of war."[128] This object "would be exceeded by the employment of arms which needlessly aggravate the sufferings of disabled men, or render their deaths inevitable."[129]

- *Distinction.* Combatants, nations, and their armed forces, must distinguish between military objectives and civilian objects, and only intentionally attack the former.[130] Belligerent armed forces must be distinguishable from civilian objects when in view of the enemy.[131]
- *Proportionality.* The LOAC principle of proportionality bridges the concepts described in the principles of military necessity and humanity by requiring that the "loss of life and damage to property incidental to attacks must not be excessive in relation to the concrete and direct military advantage expected to be gained."[132]

Although there are no special LOAC rules for SOF activities, the different means and methods in which they are conducted require LOAC application to situations not commonly found in conventional operations. The U.S. definition of special operations given above provides an illustration of how the application to SOF activities will present challenges to the conventional application of LOAC.[133] The use of unique weapons, equipment, and tactical techniques; the conduct of operations in hostile, denied, or politically sensitive areas; the clandestine nature of such operations; and the conduct of operations by, with, and through indigenous forces requires analysis of the above principles to situations generally not found in conventional operations.

B. WOUNDED AND DETAINED PERSONNEL

As discussed previously, many SOF missions will be conducted by a small number of forces operating in hostile, remote, and politically sensitive areas. Unlike conventional operations, there will likely be no detention or medical facilities available to provide support. The taking and safeguarding of prisoners or treatment of

---

[127] Convention (IV) Respecting the Laws and Customs of War on Land and Annex to the Convention: Regulations Respecting the Laws and Customs of War on Land, art. 23, Oct. 18, 1907, T.S. No. 539 [hereinafter 1907 Hague Regulations].

[128] W. Hays Parks, *Memorandum of Law—Sniper Use of Open-Tip Ammunition*, Army Law. 86, 87 (Feb. 1991).

[129] Declaration Renouncing the Use, in Time of War, of Certain Explosive Projectiles, Nov. 29 (Dec. 11), 1868, *reprinted in* Dietrich Schindler & Jill Toman, The Laws of Armed Conflicts 102 (1988) [hereinafter St. Petersburg Declaration].

[130] U.S. Dep't of Army, Field Manual 27-10, The Law of Land Warfare, ¶ 40 (July 18, 1956 & Change 1, July 15, 1976) [hereinafter FM 27-10].

[131] 1907 Hague Regulations, *supra* note 127, art. 1(2); Geneva Convention Relative to the Treatment of Prisoners of War of 12 August 1949, art. 4, 6 U.S.T. 3316, 75 U.N.T.S. 135 [hereinafter Third Geneva Convention]; FM 27-10, *supra* note 130, para. 74.

[132] FM 27-10, *supra* note 130, ¶ 41.

[133] Joint Pub. 3-05, *supra* note 8, at GL-11.

enemy wounded during a mission may very well put the mission, as well as the lives of the team members, at risk; this is exemplified by the incidents involving Bravo Two Zero of the British SAS in Iraq in 1991 and U.S. Navy SEALs in Afghanistan during Operation Red Wings in 2005.[134] Although the nature of the SOF missions, remote locations, and lack of resources may make it difficult to comply with LOAC provisions regarding prisoners and enemy wounded, violation of these protections are punishable under the Uniform Code of Military Justice.[135]

1. Treatment of Wounded Personnel

One of the most fundamental obligations of the LOAC is to care for and protect the wounded—enemy and friendly alike.[136] Wounded must be provided care, with the level of care distinguished only by medical necessity, not based on the uniform worn by the patient. The level of medical care required pursuant to this obligation is not absolute, but rather that which "to the fullest extent practicable and with the least possible delay" is required by the condition of the wounded.[137] The level of care provided must be the best within the circumstances, capabilities, and resources on hand at the time, but does not require evacuating and sending the wounded to the most advanced-care facility in the world.[138]

---

[134] Bravo Two Zero was the call sign of a British Special Air Service Team inserted behind Iraqi lines in January 1991 in the opening days of OPERATION DESERT STORM to conduct long-range reconnaissance and surveillance of Scud sites in western Iraq. Several days after being inserted they were discovered by Iraqi civilians, who ultimately alerted Iraqi forces. As the team attempted to evade and escape by heading toward the Syrian border, they became separated into two groups. Subsequently, several team members died, several were captured by Iraqi forces, and one managed to evade capture by traveling more than 150 miles to Syria. *See* MIKE COBURN, SOLDIER FIVE: THE REAL TRUTH ABOUT THE BRAVO TWO ZERO MISSION (2004); CHRIS RYAN, THE ONE THAT GOT AWAY: MY SAS MISSION BEHIND IRAQI LINES (2006). For a discussion on OPERATION RED WINGS, see *infra* Section III(B)2.

[135] FM 27-10, *supra* note 130, ¶ 506.

[136] *See, e.g.*, Geneva Convention (I) for the Amelioration of the Condition of the Wounded and Sick in Armed Forces in the Field of Aug. 12, 1949, art. 12, 6 U.S.T. 3114, 75 U.N.T.S. 31 [hereinafter First Geneva Convention]; Article 10, Protocol Additional to the Geneva Conventions of Aug. 12, 1949, and relating to the Protection of Victims of International Armed Conflict, June 8, 1977 (Protocol I) [hereinafter Protocol I]; Article 7, Protocol Additional to the Geneva Conventions of Aug. 12, 1949, and relating to the Protection of Victims of Non-International Armed Conflict, June 8, 1977 (Protocol II) [hereinafter Protocol II]. Although the United States is not a Party to Protocol I or Protocol II, it does consider some provisions as reflective of customary international law, including Article 10 of Protocol I and Article 7 of Protocol II. *See* MEMORANDUM FOR MR. JOHN H. MCNEILL, ASSISTANT GENERAL COUNSEL (INTERNATIONAL), OSD, SUBJECT: 1977 PROTOCOLS ADDITIONAL TO THE GENEVA CONVENTIONS: CUSTOMARY INTERNATIONAL LAW IMPLICATIONS (MAY 9, 1986), *reprinted in* THE INT'L & OPERATIONAL LAW DEP'T, JUDGE ADVOCATE GEN.'S LEGAL CTR. & SCH., U.S. ARMY, LAW OF ARMED CONFLICT DOCUMENTARY SUPPLEMENT 234–35 (2012) [hereinafter LOAC DOC. SUPP.].

[137] Protocol I, *supra* note 136, art. 10; Protocol II, *supra* note 136, art. 7.

[138] INTERNATIONAL COMMITTEE OF THE RED CROSS, COMMENTARY ON THE ADDITIONAL PROTOCOLS OF 8 JUNE 1977 TO THE GENEVA CONVENTIONS OF 12 AUGUST 1949 147 (Yves Sandez et al. eds., 1987) [hereinafter COMMENTARY ON THE ADDITIONAL PROTOCOLS].

> It is obvious that some wounded or sick persons could be saved, or at any rate be better cared for, in the clinics of wealthy countries which have the most advanced resources at

During most SOF missions, medical support will be very limited, usually consisting of a highly trained medic with a small amount of medical supplies.[139] Depending on the nature and location of the mission, medical evacuation (MEDEVAC) support in the form of helicopters or vehicles may be available to evacuate wounded personnel to trauma and care facilities of differing capabilities in different locations. In more remote locations and missions, medical care may be limited to that on hand in the unit. The realistic and reasonable standard of care required by LOAC would thus take into account the limited medical resources available during a SOF mission, and not require the commitment or use of additional resources that are not already available for the mission.

Whatever medical resources and care are available, however, must be made available to enemy wounded just as they would be for friendly forces. Although many would have difficulty treating enemy wounded ahead of one of their own, the SOF medic must be prepared to do so, discriminating based only on the nature of the medical condition itself, working to the utmost of his abilities and fully using the resources he has at hand. A more difficult situation presents itself when using those resources at hand is insufficient and the enemy wounded require MEDEVAC for further treatment. As discussed earlier, there is no requirement to send the wounded to the best treatment facility, however, the prohibition on discrimination in treatment would require evacuation of enemy wounded if that same standard of care was available for, and to be used on, friendly forces that are wounded. Of course, MEDEVAC assets are not always available and may be limited by a variety of factors, including higher priority needs elsewhere or the risk posed to MEDEVAC assets by enemy action in the area. All of these factors should be considered during the military planning process and discussed by the operators, medical planners, and legal advisor to ensure mission requirements are fully considered and are in compliance with LOAC.

2. Temporarily Detained Personnel

In spite of the clandestine nature of many activities SOF may be discovered by both civilians and enemy forces during a mission. During Operation Red Wings, a team of four U.S. Navy SEALs was discovered by three local, unarmed goatherds during a reconnaissance and surveillance mission.[140] The SEALs detained the goatherds and discussed whether they should be killed or released. The team realized that, if released, the goatherds would likely tell the local Taliban of the SEALs' location, resulting in mission failure and possible death. Although at least one team member supported killing the goatherds, the SEAL team leader made

> their disposal. However, the requirement imposed here relates to the material possibilities existing in the place and at the time that the wounded person is cared for. What is required is that everyone does his utmost.

Id.

[139] *See* Joint Pub. 3-05, *supra* note 8, at I-1.

[140] Marcus Luttrell with Patrick Robinson, Lone Survivor: The Eyewitness Account of Operation Redwing and the Lost Heroes of SEAL Team 10, 229–38 (2007).

the decision to release them.[141] A short time later a large group of Taliban attacked the team, killing three of them and seriously wounding the lone survivor who managed to escape and later be rescued.[142]

3. Temporary Detention of Enemy Combatants

The resources available to handle detainees in a SOF mission will be much more limited than those found in conventional operations.[143] There will be no military police or other conventional forces to whom detainees may be handed, and no detention facility in which to place them. In fact, it is likely that SOF conducting the mission will not be able to take or maintain control over detainees at all given the small numbers of personnel on the mission and the need for speed and secrecy in accomplishing the mission. In such cases, the available courses of action seem to be to either kill any detainees captured, or set them free. Although the first option is clearly unlawful, the second option is often almost certain to lead to mission failure and the possible death of those conducting the mission, making this one of the most difficult situations faced during a SOF mission. The better course of action, if permissible, would appear to be the temporary detention of those enemy and civilians encountered during a mission.[144]

The temporary detention of enemy and civilian personnel by SOF during a mission raises several related issues, the first of which is whether temporary detention is even permissible. It is without question that enemy personnel may be captured during military operations in an armed conflict and held until the end of hostilities.[145] This typically involves transporting captured personnel back to a secure location where they are handed over to military police for questioning and processing into long-term detention as prisoners of war or other category of combatant.[146] Although this chain of events is what commonly comes to mind when thinking of captured enemy personnel, it is not the only option available.

---

[141] According to the account of this incident there was no discussion of tying up the goatherds as "[w]e didn't have rope to bind them. Tying them up to give us more time to establish a new position wasn't an option." *Id.* at 236.

[142] *Id.* at 241–81.

[143] *See* JOINT PUB. 3-05, *supra* note 8, at I-1. A detainee is "[a]ny individual captured by, or transferred to the custody or control of, DoD personnel pursuant to the law of war." DEPARTMENT OF DEFENSE DIRECTIVE 2310.01E DOD DETAINEE PROGRAM (Aug. 19, 2014) [hereinafter DoDD 2310.01E].

[144] Discovery of SOF teams by local civilians or enemy forces is not uncommon. During the attempted rescue of the hostages being held at the U.S. Embassy in Tehran in 1979, a bus full of Iranian civilians who happened to be driving past the desert airfield as the U.S. SOF team was conducting its infiltration was stopped and detained. The bus and its occupants were held at the airfield and left there after U.S. forces were forced to abort the mission, although the original plan had been to fly any civilians encountered during the mission to Egypt where they would later by released. PAUL B. RYAN, THE IRANIAN RESCUE MISSION: WHY IT FAILED 79–80, 91 (1985).

[145] Third Geneva Convention, *supra* note 131, art. 118; DoDD 2310.01E, *supra* note 143, ¶ 3.f. For a full discussion of the status, treatment, and standard of care for detainees during armed conflicts, please see Chapters 9 and 10 of this book.

[146] *See* DoDD 2310.01E, *supra* note 143, ¶ 3.c.

There is no affirmative duty to take captured enemy soldiers into custody or place them into long-term detention as prisoners of war. The LOAC recognizes that the tactical situation on the battlefield may not permit securing and evacuating captured enemy personnel, and provides for their treatment as hors de combat. Article 41 of Additional Protocol I defines the term "hors de combat" and includes personnel who are in the power of an adverse party, clearly express an intention to surrender, or have been rendered unconscious or are otherwise incapacitated and incapable of defending themselves.[147] The inclusion of the hors de combat provisions was a recognition that there existed a gap in protection between the time a combatant lays down his arms and clearly expresses his intention to surrender, and the time when he becomes a prisoner of war, a point in time which may not always be clear.[148]

In addition to defining "hors de combat," Article 41 also addresses "unusual conditions of combat" and provides that persons entitled to protection as prisoners of war "shall be released and all feasible precautions shall be taken to ensure their safety" when conditions do not allow for their evacuation as provided for in the Third Geneva Convention.[149] The Commentary to Article 41 sheds further light on what might constitute these unusual conditions, referring to the report of the Rapporteur, which stated that this provision was intended to deal with "the situation of the long distance patrol which is not equipped to detain and evacuate prisoners."[150] The Commentary goes on to say that "[t]he requirement that all 'feasible precautions' be taken to ensure the safety of released prisoners was intended to emphasize that the detaining Power, even in those extraordinary circumstances, was expected to take all measures that were practicable in the light of the combat situation."[151] In a declaration made at the time of its signing of the Additional Protocol, the United Kingdom stated "that the word 'feasible' means that which is practicable or practically possible, taking into account all circumstances at the time including those relevant to the success of military operations."[152]

Taken together, the language of Article 41 along with the Commentary, Report of the Rapporteur, and the declaration of the United Kingdom recognizes that both the safety of the captured personnel as well as operational requirements may be considered when deciding whether those personnel will be evacuated or released, and, if so, what precautions are required. This provision should not be seen as a way to simply divest oneself of the burden of guarding and caring for detainees, but must be based on both humanitarian and operational

---

[147] Protocol I, art. 41, *supra* note 136.

[148] Commentary on the Additional Protocols, *supra* note 138, at 481. For a more detailed analysis of the treatment of individuals rendered hors de combat during SOF missions, see Commander Gregory Raymond Bart, U.S. Navy, *Special Operations Commando Raids and Enemy Hors de Combat*, Army Law. 33 (July 2007).

[149] Protocol I, art. 41, *supra* note 136.

[150] Commentary on the Additional Protocols, *supra* note 138, at 489.

[151] *Id.* at 489–90.

[152] *Id.* at 489 fn. 36.

considerations. Detainees must not be released in such a condition and into such a situation where there is almost no chance of survival. For example, detainees released in remote areas must be given sufficient food, water, and protection from the elements that would allow them to survive until they are rescued or return to their lines.

4. Temporary Detention of Civilians

As in Operation Red Wings, SOF may also encounter civilians on the battlefield who, if not detained, might present a risk to the security of the force and the success of the mission. Although civilians who are not directly participating in hostilities may not be detained as combatants, they need not be left to merely go on their way, free to alert the enemy. Article 27 of the Fourth Geneva Convention states "the Parties to the conflict may take such measures of control and security in regard to protected persons as may be necessary as a result of war."[153] These control measures may include registering and reporting to local authorities, carrying identification cards, denying access to certain places, restricting movement, assignment to a specific residence, or even internment.[154] While further restrictions are placed on the use of assigned residences and internment as measures of control, there is no further discussion of the use of denial of access or restriction of movement in the Convention or Commentary thereto.

Article 75 of Additional Protocol I addresses the protection to be afforded to those civilians detained and interned during an international armed conflict "for actions related to the armed conflict" but without specifically setting forth authority for this action.[155] Internment refers to the "deprivation of liberty ordered by the executive authorities when no specific criminal charge is made against the individual concerned" and may be for a variety of reasons, including security concerns.[156] Persons covered by this article must be "released with the minimum delay possible and . . . as soon as the circumstances justifying the arrest, detention or internment have ceased to exist."[157] Lesser measures, such as those mentioned in Article 27 of the Fourth Convention, are not mentioned.

Although the use of such measures is not specifically included in Additional Protocol II, several articles address protections for those who have been deprived of liberty as well as those whose liberty has been restricted for reasons related to the armed conflict.[158] These measures appear to have a wide application and "covers all detainees and persons whose liberty has been restricted for reasons

---

[153] Geneva Convention (IV) Relative to the Protection of Civilian Persons in Time of War of Aug. 12, 1949, art. 27, 6 U.S.T. 3516, 75 U.N.T.S. 287 [hereinafter the Fourth Geneva Convention].

[154] International Committee of the Red Cross, Commentary to the Geneva Convention (IV) Relative to the Protection of Civilian Personnel in Time of War, Aug, 12, 1949, 207 (1958) [hereinafter Commentary on the Fourth Geneva Convention].

[155] Protocol I, art. 75(3), *supra* note 136.

[156] Commentary on the Additional Protocols, *supra* note 138, at 875.

[157] Protocol I, art. 75(3), *supra* note 136.

[158] Protocol II, arts. 2, 4, 5, *supra* note 136.

related to the conflict."[159] This would also appear to include those whose liberty has been restricted for security and operational reasons. The Commentary further states "[t]his provision [Protocol II, art. 4 establishing fundamental guarantees] is aimed at ensuring reasonable living conditions to persons under house arrest or who live under surveillance in any other way."[160]

The permissibility of other restrictions on movement is also implied by the Commentary to Article 17. noting that Article 17 does not "restrict the right of civilians to move about freely within the country, subject to any restrictions that may be imposed by the circumstances . . . ."[161] Further, Article 17 provides an exception to the prohibition on forced displacement of the civilian population, specifically for security of the civilian population and for imperative military reasons.[162] Although the Commentary does not give any further examples of what would constitute military necessity, it refers to use of the same terms in Article 49 of the Fourth Geneva Convention, which deals with the deportation, transportation, and evacuation of protected persons in occupied areas and in which the same two exceptions to the prohibitions on such actions are given.[163] The Commentary to this Article provides more detail on when evacuation may be justified, including when "an area is in danger as a result of military operations or is liable to be subjected to intense bombing" or "when the presence of protected persons in an area hampers military operations."[164] It goes on to stress that evacuation in these cases would be justified only when overriding military considerations make it imperative.[165]

Imperative military necessity would certainly include those situations where, if released, the lives of the SOF would be placed at risk, as well as if their release would compromise the mission. Those personnel so detained must be released as soon as the reason for their temporary detention has ended. While being temporarily detained, personnel may be questioned for those same reasons listed above, that is, to determine whether there are other people in the area who might present a risk to the force, and to gather immediate information on conditions in the area of operations. As in the case of enemy detained personnel, civilians temporarily detained must be given sufficient food, water, and protection from the elements, and must not be released in such a condition and into such a situation where there is almost no chance of survival. Of course, if temporary detention is unnecessary, those personnel should be permitted to go on their way.

These LOAC provisions discussed above would allow for SOF to temporarily detain both civilians and enemy forces encountered during the course of a

---

[159] Commentary on the Additional Protocols, *supra* note 138, at 1384.
[160] *Id.* at 1393.
[161] *Id.* at 1472.
[162] Protocol II, art. 17(1), *supra* note 136.
[163] Commentary on the Additional Protocols, *supra* note 138, at 1472–73.
[164] Commentary on the Fourth Geneva Convention, *supra* note 154, at 280.
[165] *Id.*

mission if necessary to protect the individuals detained as well as for imperative military necessity. How this is accomplished will depend on the resources at hand, mission requirements, and operational environment at the time. Such considerations must be factored into the mission planning process so as to ensure that SOF conducting the mission are prepared for the difficult but necessary balancing of mission accomplishment, force protection, and the protection and care of those detained in a way that complies with the LOAC.

5. Treatment of Temporarily Detained Combatants and Civilians

Due to the nature of their missions and limited organic resources, SOF will typically not be conducting long-term detention operations or processing releases from long-term detention. The SOF interaction with detainees will generally be short-term and limited to the initial capture and tactical questioning on the battlefield or immediately thereafter. Even during this limited time, SOF must afford both temporarily detained enemy combatants and civilians, at a minimum, the level of treatment and protection afforded detainees under Common Article 3 of the Geneva Conventions.[166] As discussed in the section above, medical care must be provided to any wounded, injured, or sick detainees. Detainees must be treated humanely, protected from violence, and not be humiliated or degraded. They must be provided food, water, and protection from the elements as much as possible. Additionally, U.S. SOF must comply with the provisions of the Detainee Treatment Act (DTA) of 2005, which prohibits any cruel, inhuman, or degrading treatment or punishment, and limits the use of interrogation techniques to those contained in the U.S. Army Field Manual on Intelligence Interrogation.[167]

Due to the limited resources available to SOF on most missions, the means in which personnel may be temporarily detained will also be limited. Leaving personnel behind to guard and care for the detainees may not always be possible; thus, restraining and leaving the detainees where they will not immediately attract attention may be the only method available. If doing so would likely result in the death or injury of the detainees, due to extreme conditions, remote location, or intensity of surrounding military operations, another option must be found. Release of those temporarily detained must also be done safely and humanely and must be considered during the mission planning process, whether this is done by notifying other friendly, enemy, or local personnel of the detainees' location once the mission is completed; returning to their location upon mission completion; or leaving them in a location where it is known they will be found in a short period of time.

---

[166] First Geneva Convention, art. 3, *supra* note 136; Geneva Convention (II) for the Amelioration of the Condition of Wounded, Sick and Shipwrecked Members of the Armed Forces at Sea of Aug. 12, 1949, art. 3, 6 U.S.T. 3217, 75 U.N.T.S. 85 [hereinafter Second Geneva Convention]; Third Geneva Convention, art. 3, *supra* note 131; Fourth Geneva Convention, art. 3, *supra* note 154.

[167] Detainee Treatment Act of 2005, Department of Defense Appropriations Act of 2006 (2005). For a more detailed discussion of what standard of care must be provided to detainees, see Chapters 9 and 10 of this book.

C. MEANS AND METHODS OF WARFARE: SPECIAL PURPOSE WEAPONS

As stated at the beginning of this chapter, SOF are special trained *and equipped* to conduct their strategically sensitive missions. Technological superiority can be the critical enabler to SOF mission success, such as the reported employment of stealth helicopters to infiltrate and exfiltrate Pakistan during the successful mission to kill Osama bin Laden.[168] Exceptional circumstances requiring the use of controversial or otherwise prohibited weapons may also be critical to mission accomplishment. The SOF legal advisor must often look beyond the hornbook answer to understand the development of the rule in question, its relation to the LOAC principles the rule purports to uphold, and the circumstances in which an exception to the rule may be permissible (or even mandated). For illustrative purposes, we will consider the employment of expanding small arms ammunition for hostage rescue or CWMD missions.

At the 1899 International Peace Conference in The Hague, Netherlands, delegates adopted comprehensive international regulations for the conduct of war.[169] The regulations annexed to the 1899 Hague Convention with Respect to the Laws and Customs of War on Land declared that the "right of belligerents to adopt means of injuring the enemy is not unlimited."[170] Specifically, the regulations prohibited the employment of "arms, projectiles, or material of a nature to cause superfluous injury."[171] These regulations were annexed to the 1907 Hague Conventions substantially unchanged.[172] In a separate declaration made during the 1899 Conference, twenty-three states (but not the United States) agreed to "abstain from the use of bullets which expand or flatten easily in the human body, such as bullets with a hard envelope which does not entirely cover the core or is pierced with incisions."[173] Although the United States never acceded to the

---

[168] Sean D. Naylor, *Mission Helo Was Secret Stealth Black Hawk*, ARMY TIMES, May 4, 2011, http://www.armytimes.com/article/20110504/NEWS/105040314/Mission-helo-secret-stealth-Black-Hawk.

[169] Convention with Respect to the Laws and Customs of War on Land and its annex: Regulations Respecting the Laws and Customs of War on Land, July 29, 1899, T.S. No. 403 [hereinafter 1899 Hague Regulations].

[170] *Id.* art. 22.

[171] *Id.* art. 23(e).

[172] 1907 Hague Regulations, *supra* note 127. The official English translation of article 23(e) of the 1907 Hague Regulations changed the 1899 Hague Regulation, Article 23(e), phrase "of a nature to cause superfluous injury" to "calculated to cause unnecessary suffering." Article 35(2) in Protocol I to the Geneva Conventions resolved this apparent discrepancy: "It is prohibited to employ weapons, projectiles and material and methods of warfare of a nature to cause superfluous injury or unnecessary suffering." United States' officials have stated that article 35(2) is a codification of customary international law. W. Hays Parks, *Memorandum of Law—Review of Weapons in the Advanced Combat Rifle Program*, ARMY LAW. 18, 19 (July 1990).

[173] Declaration (IV, 3) concerning Expanding Bullets, July 29, 1899, *reprinted in* THE PROCEEDINGS OF THE HAGUE PEACE CONFERENCES: THE CONFERENCE OF 1899, 262–64 (James Brown Scott ed., 1920) [hereinafter Expanding Bullets Declaration]. Only thirty-two states are parties to the Declaration according to the International Committee of the Red Cross's (ICRC) unofficial count.

declaration, many commentators assert that the Expanding Bullets Declaration is customary international law, binding upon the United States, despite the small number of countries that have ratified or acceded to the declaration since 1899.[174]

The United States Department of Defense evaluates new weapons, including small arms bullets, to determine whether the weapon complies with the LOAC.[175] Specifically, the bullet's intended uses and its effects must not violate the 1907 Hague Regulations, Article 23(e), prohibition against "projectiles . . . calculated [or of a nature] to cause unnecessary suffering."[176] The evaluation of weapons systems against the Article 23(e) standard necessarily involves subjective assessments of what constitutes unnecessary suffering.[177] "What weapons cause 'unnecessary suffering' can only be determined in light of the practice of states in refraining from the use of a given weapon because it is believed to have that effect."[178] The United States takes a pragmatic approach, recognizing that the "necessity" of the suffering must be judged in relation to the military utility of the weapons.[179] The "inherent cruelness" of the weapon's effects must be measured against the anticipated military results to determine whether the weapon should be fielded or prohibited.[180]

Although not explicitly stated in the 1907 Hague Regulations, any evaluation of a projectile under Article 23(e) must also take into consideration the military necessity for employing the subject projectile:

> The fact that a weapon causes suffering does not lead to the conclusion that the weapon causes unnecessary suffering, or is illegal per se. Military

---

Int'l Comm. of Red Cross, *ICRC Databases on International Humanitarian Law, Treaty Database, States Parties and Signatories*, https://www.icrc.org/applic/ihl/ihl.nsf/Treaty.xsp?documentId=D528A73B322398B5C12563CD002D6716&action=openDocument (last visited June 11, 2015) [hereinafter *States Parties and Signatories*]. Of these, only four states have acceded to the Declaration since 1907, an underwhelming number when considering the explosion of new states since the United Nations was founded in 1945. *Id.* Fifty-one states are original member states of the United Nations; the United Nations now numbers 193 states. United Nations, *Growth in United Nations Membership, 1945-present*, http://www.un.org/en/members/growth.shtml (last visited June 11, 2015).

[174] *See, e.g.*, Eric Prokosch, Small-Calibre Weapon Systems: Bringing the Dum-Dum Ban Up to Date 1 (Human Rights Ctr., Papers in the Theory and Practice of Human Rights No. 11, 1995).

[175] U.S. Dep't of Defense, Dir. 5000.01, DOD The Defense Acquisition System para. E1.1.15 (May 12, 2003) [hereinafter DOD Dir. 5000.01]; U.S. Dep't of Army, Reg. 27–53, Review of Legality of Weapons under International Law para. 4.b (Jan. 1, 1979) [hereinafter AR 27-53]; U.S. Dep't of Air Force, Instr. 51–402, Legal Reviews of Weapons and Cyber Capabilities, para. 1.1 (July 27, 2011) [hereinafter AFI 51-402]; U.S. Dep't of Navy, Sec'y of the Navy Instr. 5000.2C, Implementation and Operation of the Defense Acquisition System and the Joint Capabilities and Development System encl. 2 para. 2.6 (Nov. 14, 2004) [hereinafter SECNAVINST 5000.2C].

[176] 1907 Hague Regulations, *supra* note 127. The practice of the United States is to interpret the 1907 art. 23(e) phrase "calculated to cause" in light of the statement of customary international law found in Protocol I, which adopts the 1899 Hague Regulations phrase "of a nature to cause." *See supra* note 128 accompanying note 37.

[177] Legal Regulation of Use of Force: The Laws of War: Methods of Warfare, 1974 Digest § 2, at 706 [hereinafter 1974 Digest].

[178] FM 27-10, *supra* note 130, para. 34b.

[179] 1974 Digest, *supra* note 177, at 707.

[180] *See id.*

> necessity dictates that weapons of war lead to death, injury, and destruction; the act of combatants killing or wounding enemy combatants in combat is a legitimate act under the law of war. In this regard, there is an incongruity in the law of war in that while it is legally permissible to kill an enemy combatant, incapacitation must not result inevitably in unnecessary suffering. What is prohibited is the design (or modification) and employment of a weapon for the purpose of increasing or causing suffering beyond that required by military necessity.[181]

The military necessity for employing the most efficacious small arms bullet is to "stop the stricken soldier and put him immediately *hors de combat*."[182] The mechanics of bullet injury dictate that large bullets fired at higher velocities are a more efficient means of rendering a combatant immediately hors de combat than small high-velocity bullets.[183]

Then-Professor Christopher Greenwood, currently serving as a judge on the International Court of Justice, in his 2001 keynote address to the Swiss-sponsored Third International Workshop on Wound Ballistics,[184] went a step further. In his address, Greenwood strongly suggested that the degree of permissible suffering may be greater when the state's intent is to limit the risk of injury to civilians trapped on the urban battlefield:

> It is possible to envisage a weapon which causes a more serious injury to the combatant than those caused by other equivalent weapons . . . but which has the advantage of being more precise and, therefore, capable of being used in a more discriminating fashion. Moreover, there are circumstances, particularly in street warfare and in counter terrorist operations where it may be necessary to make a trade, in effect, between the principle of the protection of civilian life and the principle of "unnecessary suffering" to combatants. What I would like to suggest is that where that trade has to be made—and I accept that it is not one which has to be made in all, or even most, types of combat—one cannot regard suffering as unnecessary if it is inflicted for the purpose of protecting the civilian population. In other words, if the civilian

---

[181] Parks, *supra* note 128, at 87.

[182] The International Peace Conference, The Hague, May 18–July 29, 1899 [The Netherlands] Ministry for Foreign Affairs (Martinus Nijhoff ed., 1907) *reprinted in* The Proceedings of the Hague Peace Conferences: The Conference of 1899, 276 (James Brown Scott ed., 1920).

[183] Several delegates to the 1899 Hague Conference accepted as fact that the larger bullets fired by earlier muskets were more effective at stopping a charging and determined enemy. *Id.* at 278. "Penetration must be sufficiently deep to reach and pass through vital organs, and the permanent cavity must be large enough to maximize tissue destruction and consequent hemorrhaging." Urey W. Patrick, Fed. Bureau of Investigation Academy Firearms Training Unit, Handgun Wounding Factors and Effectiveness 11 (July 14, 1989).

[184] Professor Christopher Greenwood, Legal Aspects of Current Regulations, Address before the Third International Workshop on Wound Ballistics (n.d.), *in* Gen. Staff of Swiss Armed Forces, Third International Workshop on Wound Ballistics, Thun, Switzerland, 28–29 March 2001.

> population's protection is enhanced by the use of a particular weapon, then the adverse effects of that weapon on combatants cannot properly be regarded as unnecessary.[185]

An underappreciated aspect of expanding bullets is its inherent lack of over-penetration; bullets that mushroom within the human body slow dramatically and are less likely to exit the body and strike an unintended victim (or WMD).[186] Use of expanding bullets in certain special operations missions, such as hostage rescue or counterproliferation, satisfies the military necessity to limit over-penetration and avoid injuring hostages or damaging sensitive weapons material.[187] United States' policy presently authorizes the use of expanding bullets by elements of its armed forces for law enforcement, counterterrorism and other special operations, and special security missions.[188] For some special operations missions, expanding bullets are authorized for use in international armed conflict.[189]

Because SOF may be called upon to conduct operations under geostrategic circumstances where anything less than complete mission accomplishment may constitute strategic failure (such as the failed Iran hostage rescue attempt in 1980), unconventional weapons and employment methods may be developed specifically for the mission, either as a one-off variant of existing weapons or a

---

[185] *Id.* at 6. For a thorough review of the history of the Expanding Bullets Declaration and cogent arguments against its purported status as customary international law, see Major Joshua F. Berry, *Hollow Point Bullets: How History Has Hijacked Their Use in Combat and Why It Is Time to Reexamine the 1899 Hague Declaration concerning Expanding Bullets*, 206 MIL. L. REV. 88–156 (2010).

[186] Parks, *supra* note 172, at 19 (citing an unpublished U.S. Army Judge Advocate General's legal review approving the use of expanding bullets during counterterrorist operations).

[187] *Id.*

[188] U.S. DEP'T OF NAVY, OFFICE OF THE CHIEF OF NAVAL OPERATIONS, THE COMMANDER'S HANDBOOK ON THE LAW OF NAVAL OPERATIONS, NWP 1-14M, ¶9.1.1 n.7 (July 2007) [hereinafter NWP 1-14M].

[189] *Id.* The International Committee of the Red Cross (ICRC), in its effort to identify and substantiate customary international humanitarian law (LOAC), asserts that the rule prohibiting the use of expanding bullets is a norm of customary international law applicable in international and non-international armed conflict. 2 JEAN-MARIE HENCKAERTS & LOUISE DOSWALD-BECK, CUSTOMARY INTERNATIONAL HUMANITARIAN LAW 268–69 (2005). Although the ICRC does not recognize the United States as a persistent objector, it does note that legal opinions issued by the U.S. Department of the Army in this area assert the lawful use of expanding bullets when "there is 'a clear showing of military necessity for its use.'" *Id.* at 269. In fact, the United States has objected to the prohibition on expanding bullets on a fairly consistent basis since the Expanding Bullets Declaration was first adopted at the 1899 Hague Peace Conference. Captain William Brozier, a U.S. military delegate to the 1899 Conference, summed up the U.S. objections to the Expanding Bullets Declaration:

> First, that it forbade the use of expanding bullets, notwithstanding the possibility that they might be made to expand in such regular manner as to assume simply the form of a larger caliber, which property it might be necessary to take advantage of, if it should in the future be found desirable to adopt a *musket of very much smaller caliber than any now actually in use.* Second, that by thus prohibiting what might be the most humane method of increasing the shocking power of a bullet and limiting the prohibition to expanding

technology that was not previously considered and evaluated for LOAC compliance by DoD or service lawyers when the original or base-model weapon was reviewed. The SOF legal advisors reviewing new weapons procurement initiatives, or proposed novel uses of existing weapons, must consider whether the new weapon—or new method of employing an existing weapon—violates specific arms prohibitions (such as the Expanding Bullets Declaration) as well as the general prohibition against indiscriminate and "uselessly cruel" weapons.

These legal advisors cannot operate in an academic vacuum; they must comb through the weapon's technical data, including its proving ground test reports, to apply the LOAC principles discussed earlier to the technical facts of the weapon's performance and intended employment to arrive at a legal review that answers the precise question: Is this weapon lawful for use in the manner intended (and reasonably anticipated, even if unintended) during the proposed special operation? The SOF legal advisors must apply the same level of rigor to improvised

---

> and flattening bullets, it might lead to the adoption of one of much more cruel character than that prohibited. Third, that it condemned by designed implication, without even the introduction of any evidence against it, the use of a bullet actually employed by the army of a civilized nation.

3 Charles Cheney Hyde, International Law: Chiefly as Interpreted and Applied by the United States 1817 (2d ed., 1951). While Professor Hyde argued that expanding bullets should be "looked upon with greatest disapproval," he also discussed the difficulty—in 1951—of finding a general agreement "denying to a belligerent the right to use particular types of bullets." *Id.* George B. Davis, an American delegate to the 1907 Hague Peace Conference, and former Army Judge Advocate General, emphatically stated in 1908 that the United States "declined to accept [the Expanding Bullets Declaration] and that that Government has never, by accession or adherence, become a party to its operation." George B. Davis, *The Amelioration of the Rules of War on Land*, 2 Am. J. Int'l L. 63, 75 (1908). The ICRC argues that U.S. practice in this area is ambiguous, and certain statements of purported U.S. policy would seem to underscore the ICRC's assertion. Although the 1956 U.S. Army LOAC field manual (FM 27-10, *supra* note 130) made no reference to the Expanding Bullets Declaration, the Army's 1962 pamphlet on International Law inartfully restated paragraph 34.b. of FM 27-10, which prohibits the use of "irregular-shaped bullets" and "the scoring or filing off of the ends of hard cases of bullets" as "an official prohibition of bullets [sic] which tear an unnecessarily large hole." U.S. Dep't of Army, Pam. 27-161-2, International Law Volume II, 45 (Oct. 23, 1962) [hereinafter DA Pam. 27-161-2]. The entire DA Pamphlet was rescinded in 1990, though it continued to be referenced in the American military law community for some time thereafter. U.S. Dep't of Army, Pam. 25–30, Consolidated Index of Army Publications and Blank Forms (June 1990). *See, e.g.*, W. Hays Parks, *Joint Service Combat Shotgun Program*, 1997 Army Law. 16, 23 n.3. In January, the Acting General Counsel of the Department of Defense, Leonard Niederlehner, replied to a letter from U.S. Congressman Donald M. Fraser regarding the use of the M-16 rifle in armed conflict. 1974 Digest § 2, *supra* note 177, at 706. In his letter to Congressman Fraser, Niederlehner said that the United States was not a party to the Expanding Bullets Convention, but that the United States had "acknowledged that it will abide by the terms of the agreement prohibiting expanding bullets." *Id.* The 1974 Digest provides no supporting documentation to substantiate Niederlehner's assertion, and his response to Congressman Fraser has not been cited in any subsequently published U.S. Department of Defense weapons review of expanding bullets. *See, e.g.*, Parks, *supra. See also* Parks, *supra* note 172, at 18; Parks, *supra* note 128. For further discussion of opinions of the Judge Advocates General of the United States armed forces, see U.S. Dep't of Navy, United States Naval War College, Annotated Supplement to the Commander's Handbook on the Law of Naval Operations, para. 9.1.1 n.7 (1997) [hereinafter Annotated Supplement to Commander's Handbook].

munitions proposed for inclusion in training programs for SOF-trained indigenous forces or insurgents in unconventional warfare. Although the LOAC does not prohibit the employment of booby traps, for example, international law prohibits the use of booby traps attached to or associated with: sick, wounded, or dead people; children's toys; food or drink; and religious and cultural objects, among other apparently harmless civilian objects.[190] A training syllabus that does not specifically highlight these prohibitions, or merely assumes that the trainees are familiar with LOAC and these prohibitions, may later expose the United States to allegations of complicity in, or state responsibility for, violation of these LOAC proscriptions.

D. THE PRINCIPLE OF DISTINCTION

Perhaps the most frequent, yet challenging, LOAC issue is the application of the principle of distinction to special operations. The principle of distinction consists of two separate but related duties. First, combatants must distinguish themselves from the civilian population so that opposing combatants know whom they may lawfully target.[191] In conventional operations this is accomplished primarily by combatants wearing uniforms and by separating military personnel and objects from the civilian population.[192] Second, combatants may only attack lawful military targets such as opposing combatants and military objectives.[193] Noncompliance with the first duty makes it infinitely more difficult for opposing forces to comply with the second duty, ultimately putting civilians at risk. In advising SOF, a legal advisor will face both sides of the distinction issue: whether SOF sufficiently distinguish themselves from the civilian population, and whether force may be used against groups and individuals who fail to distinguish themselves from the civilian population.

1. Distinction and Status of Personnel on the Battlefield

Historically, LOAC has separated those on the battlefield into two distinct groups: combatants privileged to engage in armed conflict, and civilians, including unprivileged combatants.[194] Combatants may directly participate in hostilities and may not be prosecuted or punished for their lawful use of force against

---

[190] Protocol on Prohibitions or Restrictions on the Use of Mines, Booby-Traps and Other Devices as Amended on May 3, 1996, art. 7. A "booby-trap" is defined as "any device or material which is designed, constructed or adapted to kill or injure, and which functions unexpectedly when a person disturbs or approaches an apparently harmless object or performs an apparently safe act." *Id.* art. 2.

[191] Protocol I, art. 44(3), *supra* note 136. *See also* NWP 1-14M, *supra* note 188, ¶ 5.3.2,

[192] *See* W. Hays Parks, *Special Forces' Wear of Non-Standard Uniforms*, 4 Chi. J. Int'l. Law 493, 514 (2003). Although wearing of uniforms is the typical means by which combatants distinguish themselves from the civilian population, it is not the only means. Combatants may also distinguish themselves through carrying arms openly and wearing a distinctive emblem or sign. *Id.* at 516–17. *See also* Operational Law Handbook, *supra* note 47, at 13.

[193] Protocol I, arts. 48, 50, 51, 52, *supra* note 136. *See also*, Parks, *supra* note 192, at 516–17.

[194] How to characterize those individuals who do not meet the criteria for treatment as prisoners of war, and whether there exists a category of persons referred to as unprivileged or unlawful

enemy forces; however, they may be targeted at any time.[195] If captured, combatants are entitled to prisoner-of-war status and may be held until the end of hostilities.[196] All others are considered to be civilians who may not be targeted or detained so long as they do not directly participate in hostilities.[197] Those civilians who do directly participate in hostilities may be targeted for so long as they are directly participating, and may also be detained if captured.[198] Additionally, they may be prosecuted for participating in the conflict.[199]

This structure works well in situations of international armed conflicts where combatants wear uniforms and are easily distinguished from the civilian population. This is not the situation though in many special operations missions. Instead, the special operations environment is filled with guerillas, insurgents, and terrorists in various manner of dress, including civilian clothing. The SOF themselves may also be wearing enemy or non-standard uniforms or even civilian clothing. Determining who is a combatant and who is a civilian in the foreign internal defense, unconventional warfare, and counterterrorism environments is much more complicated.

In analyzing the status of those encountered on the modern battlefield, the first step is determining whether the individual has a relationship to a state party to the

---

combatants under the LOAC, has been much discussed in the aftermath of 9/11 and the use of military commissions to try individuals for their attacks against the United States and U.S. forces. While combatants are defined as those individuals who meet the requirements set forth in Article 4 of the Third Geneva Convention, civilians are defined in the negative as being all those who do not qualify for treatment as a prisoner of war. Some international law scholars argue that no one on the battlefield exists outside the provisions of LOAC and, therefore, must fall into one of these two categories as there are no others established by any written international agreements. The United States, as is well known, has taken a different position. *See* Curtis A. Bradley, *The United States, Israel & Unlawful Combatants*, 12 GREEN BAG 397–411 (2009); Knut Dörman, *The Legal Situation of "Unlawful/Unprivileged Combatants"*, *in* 849 INTERNATIONAL REV. OF THE RED CROSS 45 (2003); Marco Sassòli, Query: Is There a Status of "Unlawful Combatant?," *in* ISSUES IN INTERNATIONAL LAW AND MILITARY OPERATIONS 57–67, INTERNATIONAL LAW STUDIES 80 (Richard B. Jaques ed., 2006); Third Geneva Convention, art. 4(A)(1),(2),(3), and (6), *supra* note 131; Protocol I, art. 50, *supra* note 136. *See also* FM 27-10 *supra* note 130, ¶ 60.

195 *See* OPERATIONAL LAW HANDBOOK, *supra* note 47, at 16–17.

196 Third Geneva Convention, art. 118, *supra* note 131; Protocol I, art. 44(1), *supra* note 136.

197 Protocol I, art. 51(3), *supra* note 136; Protocol II, art. 13(3), *supra* note 136.

198 Protocol I, arts. 45, 75, *supra* note 136. For a detailed discussion on what constitutes direct participation in hostilities and the targeting of individuals engaged in those acts, see INTERNATIONAL COMMITTEE OF THE RED CROSS, INTERPRETIVE GUIDANCE ON THE NOTION OF DIRECT PARTICIPATION IN HOSTILITIES UNDER INTERNATIONAL HUMANITARIAN LAW (2009) [hereinafter INTERPRETIVE GUIDANCE].There is much debate concerning what constitutes "a direct part in hostilities" and the ICRC Interpretive Guidance is only one side of the debate. *Compare* ICRC Interpretive Guidance at 5-6 ("The Interpretive Guidance provides a legal reading of the notion of 'direct participation in hostilities' with a view to strengthening the implementation of the principle of distinction.") *with* Kenneth Watkin, *Opportunity Lost: Organized Armed Groups and the ICRC "Direct Participation in Hostilities" Interpretive Guidance*, 42(3) N.Y.U. J. INT'L L. & POL. 641, 641 (2010) *and* Michael N. Schmitt, *The Interpretive Guidance on the Notion of Direct Participation in Hostilities: A Critical Analysis*, 1 HARV. NAT. SEC. J. 1, 5 (May 2010) (criticizing the Interpretive Guidance recommendations).

199 Protocol I, arts. 45, 75, *supra* note 136. *See also* FM 27-10, *supra* note 130, at 80–81.

conflict. Members of militia and other volunteer groups, including resistance movements, belonging to a party to the conflict are combatants pursuant to Article 4 of the Third Geneva Convention provided they meet four conditions: they are under responsible command, wear a distinctive emblem visible at a distance, carry their arms openly, and comply with the law of armed conflict.[200] The relationship of these groups to a state party to the conflict is a key element as it gives the group legitimacy, by requiring that it act responsibly, and that it is accountable should there be any serious violations of LOAC.[201] This point was stressed by law-of-war scholar W. Hays Parks, who wrote:

> Entitlement to lawful combatant and prisoner of war status for organizations other than the regular forces of a nation was provisional. It was dependent upon the forces acting under government authority and complying strictly with the four conditions listed . . . Individuals acting unilaterally outside an organization were not entitled to the combatant's privilege.[202]

Combatant status and protections were purportedly expanded by Additional Protocol I to the 1949 Geneva Conventions in 1977. Although combatant status for militia and other organized armed groups still required such groups to operate under the responsible command of a party to the conflict, be subject to an internal disciplinary system, and comply with LOAC, failing to wear a uniform or distinctive emblem would not deprive members of combatant or prisoner-of- war status.[203] Instead, carrying of arms openly while deploying to and during an attack would be sufficient for a member to retain his privileged combatant status.[204] In order to give effect to this principle, combatants are required to distinguish themselves while they are engaged in offensive military operations.[205] The main method in which combatants distinguish themselves is by wearing a uniform and carrying their weapons openly "during such time as he is visible to the adversary while he is engaging in a military deployment preceding the launching of an attack in which he is to participate."[206] Combatants include "members of the armed forces of a Party to

---

[200] Third Geneva Convention, art. 4, *supra* note 131; Protocol I, art. 43(1), *supra* note 136; FM 27-10, *supra* note 130, at 64.

[201] *See* Todd C. Huntley & Andrew D. Levitz, *Controlling the Use of Power in the Shadows: Challenges in the Application of* Jus in Bello *to Clandestine and Unconventional Warfare Activities*, 5 HARV. NAT'L SECURITY J. 461, 486 (2014).

[202] W. Hays Parks, *Combatants*, *in* THE WAR IN AFGHANISTAN: A LEGAL ANALYSIS, 85 INTERNATIONAL LAW STUDIES 265 (Michael N. Schmitt ed., 2009).

[203] Protocol I, arts. 43, 44, *supra* note 136.

[204] Protocol I, art. 44(3), *supra* note 136. The United States does not consider this provision reflective of customary international law insofar as it would bestow prisoner-of-war status on irregular forces who do not comply with the four provisions of Article 4 of the Third Geneva Convention. *See* Statement of Michael J. Matheson, Department of State Deputy Legal Advisor, *in Report of the Sixth Annual American Red Cross—Washington College of Law Conference on International Humanitarian Law: A Workshop on Customary International Law and the 1977 Protocols Additional to the 1949 Geneva Conventions*, 2 AM. U. J. INTL. L. & POL'Y 415, 425–26 (1987)[hereinafter Matheson *Additional Protocol I Statement*]; FM 27-10, *supra* note 130, at 80–81.

[205] Protocol I, art. 44(3), *supra* note 136.

[206] Protocol I, art. 44(3)(b), *supra* note 136.

the conflict, as well as members of militias or volunteer corps forming part of such armed forces."[207]

Members of nonstate organized armed groups meeting the criteria discussed above are not afforded privileged combatant status in a non-international armed conflict. A state fighting an insurgency within its borders will not recognize or give legitimacy to those groups who have taken up arms against the state. [208] Neither AP II nor Common Article 3 defines "combatant," and this problem is further complicated by the difficulty of determining who is a member of an organized armed group, and when those members may be attacked—a question that continues to be debated.[209] While Common Article 3 of the 1949 Geneva Conventions guarantees a minimum standard of treatment if captured, attacks by such groups against state and other opposing forces is unlawful and may be prosecuted under domestic criminal law.[210]

2. Non-standard Uniforms: Distinction and Status of State Special Operations Forces

In conducting operations in "hostile, denied or politically sensitive environments" SOF must first gain access to such areas and then be able to operate, alongside their partners, unnoticed by opposing forces. This is often accomplished by those forces wearing enemy or non-standard uniforms, or even civilian clothing, during operations in these areas. This does not mean, however, that SOF wearing such clothing are in violation of LOAC. Although the principle of distinction stands at the very heart of the law of armed conflict and appears, on its face, to be irreconcilable with this tactic, the standard is much more nuanced, and is supported by rich historical background.

During American military operations in Afghanistan immediately following the 9/11 terrorist attacks in the United States, U.S. SOF were criticized in the media and from within certain quarters of the U.S. Armed Forces for wearing indigenous Afghan attire while participating in combined operations with their Afghan counterparts against Taliban and al Qaida fighters.[211] Critics of U.S. SOF

---

[207] Third Geneva Convention, art. 4(a), *supra* note 131; Protocol I, art. 43(1), *supra* note 136.

[208] The exception being the customary international law provision of the recognition of belligerency by a state in a non-international armed conflict, thereby making the whole *jus in bello*, including the granting of prisoner-of-war status to captured members of a nonstate organized group, applicable in a non-international armed conflict. *See* Yoram Dinstein, *Concluding Remarks on Non-International Armed Conflicts*, *in* NON-INTERNATIONAL ARMED CONFLICT IN THE TWENTY-FIRST CENTURY 408–10, INTERNATIONAL LAW STUDIES 88 (Kenneth Watkin & Andrew J. Norris eds., 2012).

[209] *See* INTERPRETIVE GUIDANCE, *supra* note 198, at 31–36 and 71–73; Watkin, *supra* note 198, at 648–58.

[210] First Geneva Convention, art. 3, *supra* note 136; Second Geneva Convention, art. 3, *supra* note 166; Third Geneva Convention, art. 3, *supra* note 131; Fourth Geneva Convention, art. 3, *supra* note 154.

[211] *See, e.g.*, James Brooke, *Vigilance and Memory: Kandahar; Pentagon Tells Troops in Afghanistan: Shape Up and Dress Right*, N.Y. TIMES, Sept. 12, 2002, http://www.nytimes.com/2002/09/12/us/vigilance-memory-kandahar-pentagon-tells-troops-afghanistan-shape-up-dress-right.html.

in indigenous clothing point to the 1907 Hague Regulations and the 1949 Geneva Conventions, which require militias and other organized resistance movements belonging to a state party to an international armed conflict to wear a "fixed distinctive sign recognizable at a distance."[212] Given that the LOAC principle of distinction requires belligerents to distinguish themselves from civilian non-combatant populations, commentators argue that regularly constituted armed forces must be at least as distinguishable as militias belonging to a belligerent state.[213] Further, the Geneva Conventions permit the trial and punishment of spies, including soldiers captured in enemy territory while wearing a disguise to conceal their status as members of the opposing armed forces. For reasons of distinction, and to merit protections as a prisoner of war if captured, critics argue that armed forces, including SOF, must wear at least a distinctive sign, if not their country's uniform, when engaged in combat during international armed conflict.[214]

Legal advisors supporting U.S. SOF "non-standard" uniforms (indigenous attire that closely resembles the attire worn by their Afghan Northern Alliance and Southern Alliance militia co-belligerents), argue that state practice is not nearly as consistent with regard to the wearing of traditional uniforms as critics claim.[215] These commentators point to numerous historical examples of regular armed forces members belonging to major world powers, including the United Kingdom and the United States, wearing civilian clothing while attached to partisan or resistance groups, operating behind enemy lines.[216] While acknowledging the imperative to distinguish belligerents from civilian noncombatant populations, they argue that distinction may come in many forms, including those forms that would obtain prisoner-of-war status for militias and organized resistance groups belonging to a belligerent state.

As Parks, the former Special Assistant for International Law to The Judge Advocate General, U.S. Army, states in his article supporting the U.S. SOF conduct at issue in this case, the SOF legal advisor's analysis must be based upon the facts, including the specific circumstances and intent of the relevant commander in ordering the use of a non-standard uniform, and, the law that is applicable to the conflict. [217] The facts were, according to the SOF personnel Parks interviewed, that U.S. SOF dressed like their Afghan militia counterparts, and that the Taliban and al Qaida had "no difficulty in distinguishing Northern Alliance or Southern Alliance forces from the civilian population."[218] If true, than there would seem to be no reasonable basis to allege that U.S. SOF in those circumstances violated the

---

[212] *See, e.g.*, Major William H. Ferrell III, *No Shirt, No Shoes, No Status: Uniforms, Distinction, and Special Operations in International Armed Conflict*, 178 Mil. L. Rev. 94, 106–09 (2003).

[213] *Id.* at 108.

[214] *Id.* at 137–38.

[215] *See, e.g.*, Parks, *supra* note 192, at 525.

[216] *Id.* at 545–60.

[217] *Id.* at 513.

[218] *Id.* at 498.

LOAC principle of distinction. The law does not require that the belligerent must be able to identify the nationality of the enemy belligerent, only that the enemy belligerent is distinguishable from the civilian noncombatant population (and his own forces) "at a distance" as an enemy belligerent. Thus, by their conduct, the wearing of distinctive clothing by which the enemy could distinguish U.S. SOF from civilians, the carrying of arms openly, and their status as members of the U.S. military, U.S. SOF remained combatants pursuant to LOAC.

3. Civilian Clothes or Enemy Uniforms for Infiltration or Combat: Lawful Ruses, or Perfidy?

Although SOF must comply with LOAC during armed conflict, and in all other military operations, the nature of their operations—small teams operating in areas isolated from other conventional forces against targets of great value to the United States and (implicitly) to the enemy—require employment of unconventional methods to complete the mission. These methods of clandestine infiltration and exfiltration often raise legal issues that require the SOF legal advisor to distinguish between legitimate ruses on the one hand, and the war crimes of perfidy and treachery on the other.

Ruses are "those measures for mystifying or misleading the enemy against which the enemy ought to take measures to protect himself."[219] Ruses may be tactics, techniques, and procedures to hide the location of friendly forces from enemy observation, such as by the use of natural or artificial camouflage to conceal an ambush or river crossing. Ruses may deceive the enemy about the size, location, and intentions of friendly forces by broadcasting false information over radio frequencies used or monitored by the enemy. Ruses may be better understood when contrasted with perfidy and treachery.

Perfidy is a breach of faith by placing the enemy at a material disadvantage because of the enemy's compliance with LOAC. For example, approaching an enemy strongpoint by displaying a white flag of truce so that friendly forces can maneuver into an advantageous position to defeat the strongpoint is perfidy. Customary international law requires that belligerents respect a flag of truce and avoid targeting enemy forces displaying the flag.[220] The friendly force's conduct is treacherous if it then launches an attack against the enemy strongpoint having obtained an advantage because of the enemy's compliance with LOAC. The SOF legal advisors should apply the same analytical framework when considering the SOF operator's use of civilian clothing to portray himself as a civilian so as to close with and destroy the enemy during military operations subject to LOAC.[221]

---

[219] FM 27-10, *supra* note 130, ¶ 49.

[220] 1907 Hague Regulations, art. 23, *supra* note 127.

[221] *Cf.* Parks, *supra* note 192, at 518–19 (describing a similar scenario wherein the use of civilian clothing to approach the enemy, which is the "proximate cause of death or injury to others," as

After the Second World War, the Allied Powers tried dozens of Germany military officers for war crimes committed during the course of the war. Among those was the famous German special operations commander, Colonel Otto Skorzeny, and many of his officers. Skorzeny was accused of ordering his men to enter into combat while wearing American military uniforms, and that his men treacherously fired upon and killed U.S. soldiers while wearing American uniforms.[222] Skorzeny defended his actions, stating that his orders were to reach his unit's objectives (bridges behind American lines important to the German advance during the Battle of the Bulge) at night while in American uniforms, but to remove those uniforms upon being detected by enemy forces and to fight in German uniforms.[223] One American witness testified to engaging Skorzeny's forces while the Germans were wearing a mixed ensemble of American and German uniforms. One of Skorzeny's commandos admitted that he fired at an American soldier who detected the German's presence while the German was still wearing an American uniform.[224]

The law was, and is, uncertain as to the circumstances when belligerents may wear their enemy's uniform as a ruse. The Hague Regulations prohibit the *improper* use of enemy uniforms and insignia, and the Army law-of-war field manual prohibits the use of enemy uniforms during combat; their use during other times is not prohibited.[225] The war crimes tribunal surveyed the law on ruses involving the use of enemy uniforms other than in actual fighting, but could not find a consensus of opinion among learned international law commentators.[226] Skorzeny and his subordinate officers were acquitted on all charges related to the use of American uniforms during operations in the Battle of the Bulge, likely because the tribunal was not provided sufficient evidence that Skorzeny and his men engaged in perfidious or treacherous conduct.[227] Similarly, in the situation discussed above, U.S. SOF use of non-standard uniforms would not constitute perfidy, but must be carefully considered.

---

being "treacherous.") During other SOF military operations outside of international armed conflict or non-international armed conflict, such as a hostage rescue mission, LOAC applies as a matter of DoD policy but may be waived by the President or Secretary of Defense, for example, to allow SOF rescue forces to approach an airplane occupied by hostages and hostage-takers while wearing airplane mechanics uniforms. *See also* OPERATIONAL LAW HANDBOOK, *supra* note 47, at 15 for additional discussion on the applicability of LOAC to other military operations short of armed conflict.

[222] Trial of Otto Skorzeny and Others, Case No. 56, Outline of the Proceedings (Gen. Mil. Gov't Ct. of the U.S. Zone of Germany, Sept. 9, 1947), *reprinted in* 9 UNITED NATIONS WAR CRIMES COMMISSION, LAW REPORTS OF TRIALS OF WAR CRIMINALS 90 (1949) [hereinafter Skorzeny Trial].

[223] *Id.* at 92.

[224] *Id.* at 91.

[225] FM 27-10, *supra* note 130, ¶¶ at 52, 54; 1907 Hague Regulations IV, art. 23(f), *supra* note 127; Protocol I, art. 39, *supra* note 136 (prohibiting the use of enemy uniforms "while engaging in attacks or in order to shield, favour, protect or impede military operations"). *See also* NWP-14M, *supra* note 188, ¶¶ 12-2, 12-3 (it is "prohibited to kill, injure, or capture an adversary by feigning civilian or noncombatant status").

[226] Skorzeny Trial, *supra* note 222, at 92.

[227] *Id.*

E. DISTINCTION AND TARGETING

Unlike conventional conflicts of the past that pitted state armed forces against those armed forces of another state, military operations and conflicts today are marked by the use of force by nonstate actors. This is especially so for SOF who, in many operations, will be facing an adversary who uses the protected status of civilians to gain an advantage, and conducts attacks from within the civilian population. The difficulty in distinguishing the enemy from the local civilian population will likely be compounded in many of these operations where members of the civilian population assist or even participate in attacks against U.S. and partner forces. In such situations, who may be targeted and when? How are protected civilians distinguished from combatants? Just as in a conventional conflict, the answer will be determined by examining both the status and the conduct of the adversary.

1. Targeting: Civilians Directly Participating in Hostilities

Civilians are normally protected from attack; however, in exchange for this protected status they have the obligation to not participate in the hostilities.[228] If they do, they lose this protection "for such time as they take a direct part in hostilities."[229] The standard of direct participation in hostilities is a LOAC targeting provision that aims to help in the application of the principle of distinction regarding civilians who have become participants in the armed conflict. Although this standard does not apply uniquely to SOF, they are more likely to encounter civilians in the course of executing their foreign internal defense, unconventional warfare, and counterterrorism missions, and will have to determine whether such involvement in the hostilities constitutes direct participation.

Prior to targeting someone who would otherwise be a protected civilian, SOF must determine whether the conduct of the individual constitutes a hostile act, defined in the Commentary to Additional Protocol I as an act "which by [its] nature and purpose [is] intended to cause actual harm to the personnel and equipment of the armed forces."[230] The line between direct and indirect participation and support is unclear. Certainly some acts such as shooting at friendly forces and emplacing an IED would clearly constitute direct participation; however, acts need not cause the death or injury of military personnel or destruction

---

[228] Protocol I, art. 51(3) *supra* note 136; Protocol II, art. 13(3), *supra* note 136.

[229] Protocol I, art. 51(3), *supra* note 136; Protocol II, art. 13(3), *supra* note 136.

[230] COMMENTARY TO THE ADDITIONAL PROTOCOLS, *supra* note 138, at 618. The Commentary uses both "hostile acts" and "hostilities" interchangeably in this paragraph; however, these terms are explained further in the ICRC's report on direct participation in hostilities. *See* INTERPRETIVE GUIDANCE, *supra* note 198, at 44 n.88 ("the notion of 'hostile' act refers to a specific act qualifying as direct participation in hostilities," while "hostilities" includes the time a civilian is using and also carrying a weapon as well as when engaged in hostile acts without a weapon).

of military objects to meet this standard.[231] Electronic interference with military computer networks, clearing mines planted by the adversary, capturing military personnel and objects, transmitting tactical targeting information for an attack, and armed or unarmed activities that restrict or disrupt deployments, logistics, and communications are examples of acts that, although not rising to the level of a hostile act, would nonetheless be considered as adversely affecting the adversary's military operations or capacity.[232] Other acts by civilians that may support the overall conflict would not be sufficient to subject those engaged in such acts to attack. Disseminating propaganda; providing funding, training, and logistics support to opposition political parties and candidates; and other activities that undermine the opposing party's control and support of its civilian population would not generally rise to the level of direct participation.[233]

In the case of insurgencies and terrorist attacks, those carrying out such acts will often do so from the midst of a civilian population, or even direct those hostile acts toward the civilian population. In such cases waiting to use force until the attack begins places both the innocent civilians in the area, as well as SOF and friendly forces, at further risk. The Commentary to Additional Protocol I discusses the time period during which a civilian may lose his or her protected status, stating that it would appear that "for such time" includes "preparations for combat and the return from combat."[234] Military forces will want the broadest permissible time frame in which to use force so as to choose the time and place that will place friendly forces at the least possible risk, be most effective against the enemy, and protect civilian lives. Although not strictly limited to the time during which a hostile act is being committed, there is a temporal limitation as to when force may be used.[235] More important, however, is the causal relationship between the act and the likely harm resulting from it.[236]

Determination of whether a specific activity constitutes direct participation in hostilities is highly fact specific and requires a case-by-case analysis.[237] This approach gives little guidance to operators in the field, requiring them to make a "determination as to whether a particular person is or is not taking a direct part in hostilities based on the person's behavior, location and attire, and other information available at the time."[238] Ensuring that SOF are aware of, and given

---

[231] An in-depth discussion of what acts by a civilian would constitute direct participation in hostilities is beyond the scope of this chapter. There is a lack of consensus over where the boundaries of direct participation lie, as well as no commonly agreed upon standard to use when analyzing what constitutes direct participation. *See* Michael N. Schmitt, *Deconstructing Direct Participation in Hostilities: The Constitutive Elements*, 42 N.Y.U. J. Int'l L. & Pol. 697, 699 (2010); Huntley & Levitz, *supra* note 201, at 491–509.

[232] Interpretive Guidance, *supra* note 198, at 48. *See, e.g.*, Schmitt, *supra* note 231, at 716; Huntley & Levitz, *supra* note 201, at 491–509.

[233] *See, e.g.*, Interpretive Guidance, *supra* note 198, at 34, 51.

[234] Commentary to the Additional Protocols, *supra* note 138, at 618–19.

[235] Interpretive Guidance, *supra* note 198, at 17, 65–68.

[236] *See id.* at 55, 65–68.

[237] Schmitt, *supra* note 231, at 705; *NWP* 1-14M, *supra* note 188, ¶ 8.2.

[238] NWP 1-14M, *supra* note 188, ¶ 8.2

realistic training on applying, this standard in their use of force is a task in which the legal advisor must be engaged.

2. Targeting: Members of Nonstate Organized Armed Groups

For targeting purposes, LOAC has traditionally recognized two categories of individuals: combatants and civilians.[239] Members of state armed forces and other state-sponsored organized groups were categorized as combatants and could be targeted at any time and any place, limited only by the LOAC principles of military necessity, proportionality, and unnecessary suffering.[240] All others were to be considered civilians who, as discussed above, could not be targeted unless they were directly participating in the hostilities.[241] Due to the increasing presence of nonstate organized armed groups, the situation on the modern battlefield is not so clear.

Without some overarching organization that connects the various individuals taking part in the conflict, thus making them members of an armed force or other organized armed group, those individuals would be considered civilians and could only be targeted when directly participating in hostilities. Unlike state armed forces, where membership is determined by domestic law and identified by distinctive uniforms, nonstate armed groups lack any such concrete, objective characteristics.[242] The level of organization of terrorist and insurgent organizations varies over time and between organizations, often appearing to be amorphous groups of like-minded individuals rather than a well-organized structure. Membership in such groups is often informal and fluid, and lacks any external identifying characteristics, making distinguishing between members of such groups and civilians extremely difficult.[243]

Compounding the difficulty in identifying groups and their members is the fact that the term "nonstate organized armed group" is not defined in LOAC.[244]

---

[239] A discussion of the status of individuals captured on the battlefield is beyond the scope of this chapter. Once captured, such individuals will usually be turned over to conventional military forces for processing and detention. Thus the decision as to whether the captured individual will be categorized as a lawful combatant and thus given prisoner-of-war status and combatant immunity for his actions on the battlefield or be deemed an unlawful combatant and prosecuted, will not be made by SOF or their legal advisors. *See* Chapters 9 and 10of this volume for a fuller discussion. *See also* William J. Haynes II, General Counsel of the Department of Defense, Memorandum to Members of the ASIL-CFR Roundtable, Subject: Enemy Combatants (Dec. 12, 2002) ("Enemy combatant is a general category that subsumes two sub-categories: lawful and unlawful combatants. Lawful combatants receive prisoner of war (POW) and the protections of the Third Geneva Convention. Unlawful combatants do not receive POW status and do not receive the full protections of the Third Geneva Convention." (*Internal cites omitted*) http://www.cfr.org/international-law/enemy-combatants/p5312; NWP 1-14M, *supra* note 188, at ¶5.4.1.

[240] 1907 Hague Regulations, arts. 1-3, 22, *supra* note 127; Protocol I, arts. 43, 48, *supra* note 136. *See also*, NWP 1-14M, *supra* note 188, ¶ 5.3.

[241] Protocol I, arts. 48, 50(1), 51(3), *supra* note 136; Protocol II, art. 13(3), *supra* note 136. *See* discussion *infra* Section IV(E)1.

[242] Watkin, *supra* note 198, at 654.

[243] Interpretive Guidance, *supra* note 198, at 32–33.

[244] *Id.* at 27.

Although Article 1(1) of Additional Protocol II specifically includes organized armed groups that are neither a part of state armed forces nor dissident armed forces, there is no further definition or description of characteristics that would render a group as one whose members are to be considered targetable.[245] The criterion for when a group reaches a sufficient level of organization also continues to be debated but must include at least the capability of "planning and carrying out sustained and concerted military operations . . . ."[246] This would include having some structure so as to be able to exercise a measure of control over the members, such as the ability to "collect and share intelligence, communicate among members, deconflict operations and provide logistic support."[247]

Separating members of such groups from civilians is one of, if not the most, significant challenges on the modern battlefield. Failure to do so accurately will result in civilian deaths, erosion of support for the operation, and possible strategic failure. Overly restrictive targeting may give the adversary operating space in which to conduct more attacks, resulting in more civilian and friendly-force deaths. Some would argue that the principles of military necessity and distinction would permit targeting of these members of nonstate organized armed groups only for such time as they are directly participating in hostilities. This approach creates a perverse incentive, giving members of these groups the more protected status given to civilians for their failure to carry arms openly and otherwise distinguish themselves from the civilian population.[248]

Recognizing that applying this standard to nonstate organized armed groups in today's conflicts is not practical, the ICRC has stated that membership in these groups for distinction in targeting purposes may be based on a functional criterion, or what is termed as the continuous combatant function.[249] This continuous combatant function essentially states that those individuals who are integrated into an organized armed group "acting as the armed forces of a non-State party to an armed conflict" and performing acts that reach the level of direct participation in hostilities should be considered members of the group until "he or she ceases to exercise such function."[250]

Although the acknowledgment by the ICRC that these individuals may be targeted at times outside of direct participation is a welcome development, some

---

[245] Protocol II, art. 1(1), *supra* note 136.

[246] Commentary to Additional Protocols, *supra* note 138, at 1352.

[247] Michael N. Schmitt, *The Status of Opposition Fighters in a Non-International Armed Conflict*, *in* Non-International Armed Conflict in the Twenty-first Century 119, 129–30, International Law Studies 88 (Kenneth Watkin & Andrew J. Norris eds., 2012).

[248] Interpretive Guidance, *supra* note 198, at 22.

[249] *Id.* at 33–35; Watkin, *supra* note 198, at 655.

[250] *See* Interpretive Guidance, *supra* note 198, at 32–34. Individuals who are components of organized nonstate armed groups are unlawful combatants due to their functional membership through their "continuous combat function" for the group. "Membership must depend on whether the continuous function assumed by an individual corresponds to that collectively exercised by the group as a whole, namely conduct of hostilities on behalf of a non-State party to the conflict." *Id.* at 33. Members of nonstate armed groups do not have the privileges affiliated with combatant status and therefore should not be titled "combatants." *Id.*

critics maintain it is still overly restrictive.[251] These critics believe that a test that differentiates between membership in the state's armed forces and members of nonstate groups fails to recognize the reality of modern warfare. Applying such a standard affords too much protection to these groups in that it renders those individuals who provide vital combat support but do not directly participate in hostilities, such as trainers, logisticians, and some intelligence personnel, immune from attack.[252] Thus, in their view, the better approach is to target members of all organized armed groups—both state and nonstate –the same. Members in either organization involved in an armed conflict could be targeted at any time and at any place consistent with the other provisions of the LOAC.[253]

Even accepting a targeting standard that distinguishes based on membership alone, the difficulty remains in positively identifying an individual as a member of a nonstate organized armed group. This can often be accomplished only by examining the conduct of the individual; comparing that conduct against known tactics, techniques, and procedures employed by that group; and then making a determination as to whether the information is sufficient to identify that individual as a member. This approach does have an element of overlap with that of the ICRC in that the function of the individual is relied upon as an indicator of membership.[254]

A similar approach has been applied by U.S. federal courts in their habeas corpus analysis of Guantanamo detainees. In making a determination whether a detainee is a member of a group subject to LOAC detention pursuant to the Authorization for the Use of Military Force (AUMF),[255] the court has adopted a functional analysis of the individual's role in the group.[256] This analysis is based on the totality of the circumstances, which they have referred to as the mosaic approach, and have included such facts as whether the detainee had stayed at a known al Qaida guesthouse or received training at known al Qaida facilities, his associates, nicknames used, and even what model of watch he was wearing when captured. [257]

Of course, this approach is dependent on accurate and timely intelligence. It also does not account for the differences in opinion as to whether someone who is a member of a nonstate organized armed group, but only fills the role of

---

[251] Watkin, *supra* note 198, at 684–688; Schmitt, *supra* note 247, at 137.

[252] Schmitt, *supra* note 247, at 137; Watkin, *supra* note 198, at 689–90.

[253] Schmitt, *supra* note 247, at 137; Watkin, *supra* note 198, at 689–90.

[254] *See* Interpretive Guidance, *supra* note 198, at 32–34.

[255] Authorization for the Use of Military Force, Pub. L. 107–401, 15 Stat. 224 (Sept. 18, 2001).

[256] *See, e.g.*, Uthman v. Obama, 637 F.3d 400 (D.C. Cir. 2011), *cert. denied*, 132 S. Ct. 2739 (2012); Al-Adahi v. Obama, 613 F.3d 1102 (D.C. Cir. 2010), *cert denied*, 131 S. Ct. 1001 (2011); Bensayah v. Obama, 610 F.3d 718 (D.C. Cir 2010); Salahi v. Obama, 625 F.3d 745 (D.C. Cir. 2010). While these cases are reviewing status in order to determine whether an individual may be detained pursuant to LOAC and the AUMF, the cases are illustrative as an analytical framework that could be applied to determining whether an individual was a lawful military target based on membership in an organized armed group.

[257] *See, e.g.*, *Uthman*, 637 F.3d 400; *Al-Adahi*, 613 F.3d 1102; *Bensayah*, 610 F.3d 718; *Salahi*, 625 F.3d 745.

propagandist or logistician, may be targeted with military force. Although individuals filling these roles in the armed forces of a state could be targeted during an armed conflict, the concern is that members of nonstate groups fulfilling functions not constituting direct participation in hostilities are not sufficiently distinguishable from civilians performing similar functions, and would present too great a danger of mistakenly targeting civilians.[258]

V. Conclusion

Given the threats posed by nonstate organized armed groups, such as al Qaida and the Islamic State of Iraq and the Levant (ISIL), and the increasing use of irregular warfare by states, reliance on SOF in protecting and promoting U.S. national security interests will only increase in the coming years. Countering these threats will require operating in hostile and politically sensitive areas alongside foreign security forces and nonstate groups utilizing specialized weapons, tactics, techniques, and procedures. Such operations pose challenges not found in most conventional military operations, and require careful scrutiny to ensure that all activities comply with the LOAC.

To meet this challenge, SOF legal advisors must understand SOF capabilities and special operations activities, SOF domestic legal authorities, and the means and methods employed by SOF in the conduct of special operations activities, and must possess an intricate knowledge of the LOAC and its nuances. For SOF legal advisors, the public's interest in SOF operations can evolve into a critical review of the legal analyses and justifications for controversial SOF activities by national security lawyers, politicians, academics, and foreign and military affairs commentators. The use by the military of remotely piloted aircraft to conduct air strikes on terrorist targets outside of theaters of armed conflict, such as in Pakistan, Yemen, or Somalia, is just one example of such controversial military operations that are heavily scrutinized for compliance with both domestic and international law.

As stated at the beginning of this chapter, this cursory look at SOF-specific legal issues could easily have been expanded into a tome of its own. For SOF legal practitioners, this discussion hopefully provided a useful starting point for further consideration of the issues briefly surveyed, as it was written with the SOF legal advisor on her first tour with a special operations unit in mind. For the wider audience of national security lawyers, academics, and concerned citizens, the intent was merely to introduce just a few of the many fascinating and absorbing legal issues and challenges confronted by SOF legal advisors in support of the so-called "Quiet Professionals" who operate in the shadows to defend U.S. national security interests around the globe.

---

[258] INTERPRETIVE GUIDANCE, *supra* note 198, at 45.

18 }

Medical Operations

Geoffrey S. Corn*

I. Introduction

No U.S. military operation can occur without medical support. Integrating a medical operations capability into forces conducting such operations is therefore essential to mission accomplishment. These capabilities range from preventive medicine to search, rescue, and evacuation of casualties, to care and treatment of the wounded and sick, and even veterinary services. Although the primary mission of such assets is to provide for the collection and care of U.S. casualties, commanders routinely leverage military medical capabilities to contribute to the support of coalition partners, care and treatment of the local population, and capacity building in support of local medical infrastructure. Every aspect of these medical functions involves potentially complex legal issues, aspects of operational legal practice that are routinely overlooked or taken for granted by those unfamiliar with these facets of military operations. For the military legal adviser assigned to support a medical unit, however, familiarity with core law of armed conflict obligations related to the wounded and sick, and anticipation of common issues that medical personnel and commanders will encounter during operations, is vital to ensuring these capabilities are leveraged to maximum effect in support of the U.S. mission.

The Geneva Convention for the Amelioration of the Condition of the Wounded and Sick in the Field[1] (GWS) is the first of the four Geneva Conventions,[2] and the

* Presidential Professor of Law at South Texas College of Law, Lieutenant Colonel (Retired), U.S. Army. Former Special Assistant to the U.S. Army Judge Advocate General for Law of War Matters, and Chief of the Law of War Branch, U.S. Army Office of the Judge Advocate General International and Operational Law Division.

[1] *See generally* Geneva Convention for the Amelioration of the Condition of the Wounded and Sick in Armed Forces in the Field Aug. 12, 1949, 6 U.S.T. 3114, 75 U.N.T.S. 31 [hereinafter GWS].

[2] The other Geneva Conventions are: Geneva Convention for the Amelioration of the Condition of Wounded, Sick and Shipwrecked Members of Armed Forces at Sea, Aug. 12, 1949, 6 U.S.T. 3217, 75 U.N.T.S. 85 [hereinafter GC II]; Geneva Convention Relative to the Treatment of Prisoners of War,

seed from which the Geneva tradition of protecting victims of war blossomed. This tradition, which lies at the core of each of the four treaties and the broader "humanization of international humanitarian law,"[3] is in many ways founded upon the protection of the wounded and sick. Key operational principles derived from this treaty, such as equality of treatment[4] and the obligation to come to the aid of a wounded enemy,[5] in many ways provide the ultimate manifestation of the Geneva tradition: even your enemy may become a victim of war, and therefore the dictates of humanity require all parties to endeavor to mitigate the suffering of such victims.

The Geneva Convention for the Wounded (GWS) was developed to principally regulate inter-state hostilities. However, like the other three 1949 Geneva Conventions, Article 3 of the treaty applies to non-international armed conflicts, and includes an express obligation to collect and care for the wounded and sick.[6] Furthermore, many of the express obligations applicable as a matter of treaty obligation to international armed conflicts are widely considered to extend to non-international armed conflicts as a matter of customary international law.[7] In practice, U.S. medical operations rarely draw distinctions between these two types of armed conflict, and indeed extend these legal principles to operations in support of all missions, including Military Operations Other than War (such as peacekeeping operations). Nonetheless, an understanding the operational role of medical assets must begin with an understanding of the "black letter" law applicable to these two categories of armed conflicts.

Aug. 12, 1949, 6 U.S.T. 3316, 75 U.N.T.S. 135 [hereinafter GPW]; Geneva Convention Relative to the Protection of Civilian Persons in Time of War, Aug. 12, 1949, 6 U.S.T. 3516, 75 U.N.T.S. 287 [GC IV].

[3] *See* Yoram Dinstein, The Conduct of Hostilities under the Law of International Armed Conflict 5 (2d ed. 2010) (discussing the delicate balance between military necessity and humanity that underscores the law of armed conflict).

[4] The commentary to the GWS states:

> Accordingly there is nothing now which can justify a belligerent in making any adverse distinction between wounded or sick who require his attention, whether they be friend or foe. Both are on a footing of complete equality in the matter of their claims to protection, respect and care. Only grounds of medical urgency can justify priority in the order of treatment . . .

See Int'l Comm. of the Red Cross, Commentary on the Geneva Conventions of 12 August 1949, 138 (Jean S. Pictet et al. eds., 1952) [hereinafter Pictet], *available at* http://www.loc.gov/rr/frd/Military_Law/pdf/GC_1949-I.pdf.

[5] *See id.* at 135 (The GWS "imposed upon the enemy an obligation to come to his aid and give him such care as his condition required.").

[6] *See* Shane R. Reeves & David Lai, *A Broad Overview of the Law of Armed Conflict in the Age of Terror, in* The Fundamentals of Counterterrorism Law 139, 143–44 (Lynne Zusman ed., 2014) (discussing Common Article 3 of the Geneva Conventions).

[7] *See The Law of Armed Conflict: Non-international Armed Conflcit*, Int'l Comm. of the Red Cross (June 2002), http://www.icrc.org/eng/assets/files/other/law10_final.pdf [hereinafter *Non-international LOAC*].

II. Protecting the Wounded and Sick in Non-international Armed Conflicts

Common Article 3 of the GWS reinforces the broad humane treatment obligation applicable to any individual rendered hors de combat[8] in non-international armed conflicts. This category includes all persons taken out of the fight by "sickness, wounds, detention, or any other cause."[9] Common Article 3 imposes a humane treatment obligation for the protection of any such individual as well as "persons taking no active part in the hostilities, including members of armed forces who have laid down their arms."[10] Common Article 3 also prohibits any adverse distinction affecting treatment based on race, religion, sex, wealth, or nationality,[11] and prohibits any abusive treatment to any person who is hors de combat.[12] Perhaps most important for purposes of this chapter, Common Article 3 explicitly requires that "the wounded and sick be collected and cared for."[13]

Although Common Article 3 certainly provides important protections for the wounded and sick in non-international armed conflict, its provisions are meager compared to the comprehensive regulatory framework established by the GWS. In order to compensate for this minimalism, Additional Protocol II ("Protocol II"), the 1977 treaty supplementing the Geneva Conventions, substantially enhanced the rules related to the protection of the wounded and sick in non-international armed conflict.[14] Protocol II is far more modest than its international armed conflict counterparts in the scope of the regulation it provides. However, it represents a critical advancement in the regulation of internal (i.e., non-international)

---

[8] The Rules of Customary International Humanitarian Law define "hors de combat":

> A person hors de combat is:
>
> (a) anyone who is in the power of an adverse party;
> (b) anyone who is defenceless because of unconsciousness, shipwreck, wounds or sickness; or
> (c) anyone who clearly expresses an intention to surrender;
>
> provided he or she abstains from any hostile act and does not attempt to escape.

See Jean-Marie Henckaerts & Louise Doswald-Beck, Customary International Humanitarian Law: Rules 164 (2005) [hereinafter Customary IHL], *available at* http://www.icrc.org/eng/assets/files/other/customary-international-humanitarian-law-i-icrc-eng.pdf.

[9] GWS, *supra* note 1, at art. 3. Common Article 3 protections "have been recognized by the ICJ as an emanation of 'elementary considerations of humanity' constituting 'a minimum yardstick' applicable to all armed conflicts." Dieter Fleck, The Handbook of International Humanitarian Law 620 (2008) (citing Military and Paramilitary Activities in and against Nicaragua (Nicar v. U.S.), 1986 I.C.J. 113–14 (June 27)).

[10] GWS, *supra* note 1, at art. 3.

[11] *Id.*

[12] *Id.*

[13] *Id.*

[14] *See generally* Protocol Additional to the Geneva Conventions of August 1949, and Relating to the Protection of Victims of Non-international Armed Conflict (Protocol II), June 8, 1977, 1125 U.N.T.S. 609 [hereinafter Protocol II].

armed conflicts by extending to these conflicts the special protections for those devoted to the collection and care of the wounded and sick.[15]

Protocol II builds on the foundation laid by Common Article 3 for protecting victims of non-international armed conflicts by ameliorating their suffering once they are rendered hors de combat. To that end, it explicitly extends a number of core rules established for the regulation of international armed conflict to non-international armed conflicts. These include the obligation to respect and protect all wounded and sick, the equality of treatment rule; the obligation to respect and protect medical and religious personnel, the protection of medical transport equipment and medical facilities, the prohibition of attacking a medical facility being misused without first issuing a warning, and the protective effect of the distinctive emblem.[16] Finally, the treaty expressly acknowledges the role of relief organizations in aiding the wounded and sick, a role that is increasingly central to non-international armed conflicts:

> Relief societies located in the territory of the High Contracting Party, such as Red Cross (Red Crescent, Red Lion and Sun) organizations may offer their services for the performance of their traditional functions in relation to the victims of the armed conflict. The civilian population may, even on its own initiative, offer to collect and care for the wounded, sick and shipwrecked.[17]

Protocol II also establishes several additional important safeguards for medical personnel, safeguards considered necessary because of the non-international nature of the armed conflict. First, medical personnel may never be punished for carrying out their duties compatible with medical ethics, regardless of the beneficiary (effectively shielding such personnel from criminal prosecution by the state for activities in support of internal dissident forces).[18] Second, they may not be forced to perform acts contrary to the rules of medical ethics, nor may they be prevented from performing acts required by rules of medical ethics.[19] Finally, medical personnel may not be penalized for refusing to give information concerning any of the wounded and sick under their care, even when such information is considered essential to the internal security of the state.[20]

---

[15] *See* Int'l Comm. of the Red Cross, Commentary on the Additional Protocols of 8 June 1977 to the Geneva Conventions of 12 August 1949, 1403–04 (Yves Sandoz et al. eds., 1987) [hereinafter Sandoz].

[16] *See* Protocol II, *supra* note 14.

[17] *Id.* at art. 18(1). *See also* Sandoz, *supra* note 15, at 1467 ("Article 18 is aimed at permitting and facilitating humanitarian activities in non-international armed conflicts for the purpose of assisting victims wherever they are and assuring them the protection to which they are entitled").

[18] Protocol II, *supra* note 14, at art. 10(1). The definition is left intentionally broad to cover a wide variety of medical aid suppliers; aside from doctors, the article protects "any other persons professionally carrying out medical activities, such as nurses, midwives, pharmacists and medical students who have not yet qualified." Sandoz, *supra* note 15, at 1426.

[19] Protocol II, *supra* note 14, at art. 10(2).

[20] *Id.* at art 10(4).

III. Protecting the Wounded and Sick in International Armed Conflicts

A. DEFINITION AND CATEGORIES

Almost all U.S. military regulations, policies, and procedures related to medical operations in an international armed conflict[21] implement the legal framework established by the GWS. This include: defining categories of personnel; scope of permissible functions in the execution of medical functions; obligations related to friendly, enemy, and civilian wounded and sick; limitations on the use of ground and air transport utilized for the search for, collection, and evacuation of the wounded and sick; location of fixed and mobile medical facilities; repatriation of certain wounded and sick enemy prisoners of war and captured enemy medical personnel; and other aspects of medical activities.[22] Even a cursory review of these regulations and policies reveals how central this treaty is to the actual practice of military medical operations. The GWS of 1949 establishes a comprehensive framework for the protection of the wounded and sick and the respect for the deceased. The treaty establishes basic obligations, defines special protections for the wounded and sick and those exclusively engaged in their collection and care, and provides special protected status for equipment and facilities devoted to their care.[23]

The overarching purpose of the Wounded and Sick Convention is to facilitate the prompt collection of and effective care for the wounded and sick.[24] To this end, the GWS explicitly defines those individuals protected by the treaty. Any individual meeting this GWS definition is considered a "protected person," meaning that the individual qualifies for the protections provided by the treaty. This term is also critical for purposes of war crimes accountability, as each treaty

---

[21] Article 2 of the Geneva Convention defines "international armed conflict":

> . . . the present Convention shall apply to all cases of declared war or of any other armed conflict which may arise between two or more of the High Contracting Parties, even if the state of war is not recognized by one of them.
>
> The Convention shall also apply to all cases of partial or total occupation of the territory of a High Contracting Party, even if the said occupation meets with no armed resistance.

See GWS, *supra* note 1, at art. 2.

[22] *See, e.g.*, U.S. Dep't of Army, Field Manual 27-10, The Law of Land Warfare (July 1956), *available at* http://armypubs.army.mil/doctrine/DR_pubs/dr_a/pdf/fm27_10.pdf; U.S. Dep't of Army, Field Manual 4-02, Army Health System (Aug. 2013), *available at* http://armypubs.army.mil/doctrine/DR_pubs/dr_a/pdf/fm4_02.pdf; U.S. Dep't of Army, Field Manual 8-55, Planning for Health Service Support (Sept. 1994), *available at* http://armypubs.army.mil/doctrine/DR_pubs/dr_a/pdf/fm8_55.pdf.

[23] *See generally* GWS, *supra* note 1.

[24] *See* Pictet, *supra* note 4, at 19.

defines a "grave breach" (a violation triggering universal criminal jurisdiction) as a violation directed against a protected person.[25]

The Wounded and Sick Convention protects wounded and sick members of the armed forces and other associated forces who have fallen into enemy hands.[26] Throughout the Wounded and Sick Convention, the state controlling an armed force or militia is described as "the Party on which such persons depend."[27] This means simply the state on whose behalf the military force and the individuals therein operate, which is normally (but not necessarily) the state of the individual's nationality. It includes within the definition of protected persons the same categories of belligerents who qualify as prisoners of war pursuant to the Geneva Convention Relative to the Treatment of Prisoners of War ("Prisoner of War Convention").[28] These individuals retain their protected status until repatriation.[29]

Generally, any captured individual who is wounded or sick, and who also qualifies as a prisoner of war (POW) pursuant to the Third Geneva Convention will also qualify as a protected person within the meaning of the GWS. This includes members of the regular armed forces, associated militia and volunteer corps personnel who follow the rules for POW recognition, civilians associated with the armed forces, and several other categories.[30] The Wounded and Sick Convention is not, however, intended to provide for the protection of wounded and sick civilians. Accordingly, civilians are not included within the definition of persons protected by the treaty.[31] This does not mean that wounded and sick civilians are excluded from general LOAC protections. On the contrary, they benefit

---

[25] *See* GWS, *supra* note 1, at art. 50 ("Grave breaches to which the preceding Article relates shall be those involving any of the following acts, if committed against persons or property protected by the Convention . . . ").

[26] In addition to defining protections bestowed on protected persons, GWS also creates an absolute prohibition preventing protected persons from voluntarily relinquishing any of the protections bestowed upon them. *See* GWS, *supra* note 1, at art. 7 ("Wounded and sick, as well as members of the medical personnel and chaplains, may in no circumstances renounce in part or in entirety the rights secured to them by the present Convention and by any existing special agreements"). Pictet notes that in adopting this absolute prohibition of renunciation, the drafters of GWS did so "to safeguard the interests of the majority" instead of stating explicit exceptions for certain classes of individuals who may wish to renounce protection, and in doing so, "accepted the view that in wartime protected persons who fall into the hands of the enemy are not really in a sufficiently independent and objective moral position to realize fully the implications of a renunciation of their rights under the Convention." Pictet, *supra* note 4, at 81.

[27] *See* GWS, *supra* note 1, at art. 10.

[28] *Compare* GPW, *supra* note 2, at art 13 ("prisoners of war must at all times be protected") *with* GWS, *supra* note 1, at art 5 ("For the protected persons who have fallen into the hands of the enemy, the present Convention shall apply until their final repatriation.")

[29] GWS, *supra* note 1, at art. 5.

[30] Pictet explains that the Article 13 categories are more important to granting of POW rights under the Third Convention than the humanitarian aid rights under the GWS. He emphasizes that Article 13 "has its origin, and finds its real significance, in the Convention relative to the treatment of prisoners of war, the different categories which it enumerates cannot usefully be considered except in connection with the Third Convention." Pictet, *supra* note 4, at 146.

[31] *Contra* Protocol Additional to the Geneva Conventions of Aug. 12, 1949, and Relating to the Protection of Victims of International Armed Conflicts art. 8(a), June 8, 1977 [hereinafter Protocol I] (defining the wounded and sick as "persons, whether military *or civilian*, who, because of trauma, disease or other physical or mental disorder or disability, are in need of medical assistance or care

from a variety of LOAC provisions, including the humane treatment obligation reflected in Common Article 3 (which applies to any armed conflict as a matter of customary international law).[32] Nonetheless, this exclusion is operationally significant, as it draws a distinction between those who U.S. forces bear an obligation to collect and care for, and those for whom such care is often optional. This in turn impacts on force structure, medical logistics, and casualty evacuation planning, and rules related to who to aid and when to aid them.[33]

It is therefore clear that both international law and operational policy often reflect the reality that obligations are more extensive vis-à-vis captured enemy personnel than those applicable to civilians. This is the result of two considerations. First, the 1949 Wounded and Sick Convention evolved from a treaty premised on the expectation that civilians would rarely be casualties of war, whereas members of the armed forces were in dire need of protections.[34] Second, even during armed conflict, civilian services remain primarily responsible for the care of civilian wounded and sick (with the important exception of areas subject to belligerent occupation, where the responsibility imposed on the occupation commander is more significant).

This does not suggest that military commanders may ignore the plight of wounded and sick civilians. Instead, it reveals why military medical capabilities are traditionally tailored to respond to the needs of military casualties, both friendly and enemy. However, in an era of intense scrutiny on the treatment of the civilian population by armed forces, commanders ignore civilian suffering at great peril. Accordingly, even absent express treaty obligations, it is increasingly common for commanders to attempt to anticipate civilian medical needs and to assist in meeting those needs in a manner that does not compromise the capacity to meet the primary mission of caring for military casualties.[35] Furthermore, ignoring civilian casualties under certain circumstances would be considered by many as inconsistent with the customary humane treatment obligation.

---

and who refrain from any act of hostility") (emphasis added). Additional Protocol I was developed to update and supplement the humanitarian protections established in the four Geneva Conventions. This provision is a clear example of that effort. Recognizing that suffering associated with armed conflict is not restricted to combatants or other participants in hostilities, but will almost always extend to civilians, the Protocol expanded the definition of "wounded and sick" to include civilians. Although the United States is not a party to AP I, this provision is noncontroversial and was in no way associated with the U.S. decision not to join the treaty. Furthermore, in practice it is unlikely that military medical personnel would draw a distinction between civilian and combatant where care is urgently required.

[32] *See* Customary IHL, *supra* note 8, at xx.

[33] Medical logistical planning is a complex aspect of overall operational planning. During that process, medical logistics experts address questions related to numbers of medical personnel required, quantity of medical supplies, and casualty collection and transport resource requirements. These considerations may be significantly influenced by both the anticipated nature of the mission and legal obligation. Accordingly, because legal obligation extends primarily to the collection and care of enemy military personnel, it will be predictions of enemy casualties that will drive logistics planning. *See generally* Dep't of the Army, Field Manual 8-10-6, Medical Evacuation in a Theater of Operations: Tactics, Techniques, and Procedures (Apr. 14, 2000) [hereinafter FM 8-10-6].

[34] *See Non-international LOAC, supra* note 7.

[35] Joint Chiefs of Staff, Joint Pub. 4-02, Health Service Support, at V-5 (July 26, 2012), *available at* http://www.dtic.mil/doctrine/new_pubs/jp4_02.pdf.

Accordingly, what might best be described as medical care "rules of engagement" are a common feature of U.S. military operations.[36] These are command directives indicating how and when military resources will be devoted to the care of civilian wounded and sick. Common aspects of these directives include drawing a distinction between acute and chronic health issues (limiting intervention only to acute issues); authorizing essential care when necessary to save life, limb, or sight; sharing expertise and providing expert assistance in support of the efforts of civilian healthcare efforts; and coordinating the collective efforts of military and nongovernment organizations with the shared mission of enhancing civilian healthcare capacity. Ultimately, whereas intervening in extreme cases where failing to do so will result in loss of life, limb, or sight must almost always be an authorized action, assisting local and nongovernmental efforts to adequately provide for the civilian community is essential to husband military resources and capabilities so that they are available to meet the primary demand to which they are intended to respond.

B. HANDLING THE WOUNDED AND SICK

The Wounded and Sick Convention imposes two fundamental duties upon Parties in possession of wounded and sick: respect and protection.[37] The "respect" duty imposes an obligation of inaction: prohibiting any harmful action or attack directed against the wounded and sick.[38] The "protect" duty imposes an obligation of action: coming to the defense of the wounded and sick, regardless of their side in the conflict,[39] and once collected to care for the wounded and sick in need or defending them from further harm or victimization.[40]

---

[36] *See generally* FM 8-10-6. While FM 8-10-6 provides for comprehensive procedures in medical evacuation scenarios, it notes that "[t]he patient's medical condition is the overriding factor in determining the evacuation." *Id.* at ¶ 4–1(2).

[37] GWS, *supra* note 1, at art. 12 ("Members of the armed forces and other persons mentioned in the following Article who are wounded or sick, shall be respected and protected in all circumstances.") Pictet explains that the definitions adopted for respect and protect were, respectively, "to spare, not to attack" and "to come to someone's defence [sic], to lend help and support." Pictet, *supra* note 4, at 134–35. Furthermore, the use of these words was tailored to create dual obligations; the terms "made it unlawful for an enemy to attack, kill, illtreat or in any way harm a fallen and unarmed soldier, while it at the same time imposed upon the enemy an obligation to come to his aid and give him such care as his condition required." *Id.* at 135.

[38] There are many instances even in modern history of violations of the respect-and-protect principles. For example, North Vietnamese personnel shot wounded Americans on the Ia Drung Valley battlefield in November 1965. *See* Int'l & Operational Law Dep't, The Judge Advocate General's Legal Ctr. & Sch., U.S. Army, Law of War Deskbook E-5 (2006) (citation omitted) [hereinafter Law of War Deskbook].

[39] *See*, Robert Higginbotham, *Case Studies in the Law of Land Warfare II: The Campaign in the Falklands*, Military Review 52–53 (Oct 1984), noting that, "An excellent example of this concept occurred in the Falklands when a British soldier came upon a gravely wounded Argentine whose brains were leaking into to his helmet. The British soldier scooped the extruded material back into the soldier's skull and evacuated him. The Argentine survived." *Id.* at 50.

[40] Armed Forces field manuals have generally adopted the definitions of GWS Commentary in defining their obligations. *See* UK Ministry of Defense, The Manual for the Law of Armed Conflict, ¶ 7.3.1 [hereinafter UK Field Manual] ("The duty of respect means that the wounded and sick are not to be made the target of attack. The duty of protection imposes positive duties to assist them").

This fundamental obligation to care for the wounded and sick that have fallen into the hands of a Party must be executed in a nondiscriminatory manner.[41] Considerations must be made to ensure the continued protection of all wounded and sick, not simply those of one's own armed forces.[42] In no situation may the wounded and sick be subjected to reprisal. This prohibition extends not only to casualties, but also to personnel, facilities, and equipment exclusively devoted to the care of the wounded and sick.[43] These obligations are broad: it is "unlawful for an enemy to attack, kill, ill treat or in any way harm a fallen and unarmed soldier, while at the same time . . . the enemy [has] an obligation to come to his aid and give him such care as his condition require[s]."[44]

Article 12 of the Wounded and Sick Convention is perhaps the most important article in the treaty, and provides the foundation for the training of military medical personnel in relation to the treatment of enemy casualties. It establishes the requirements of care, and defines the standard as one of humane treatment: that "each belligerent must treat his fallen adversaries as he would the wounded of his own army."[45] Humane treatment prevents a Party in possession of wounded and sick from treating them adversely due to any "distinction founded on sex, race, nationality, religion, political opinions, or any other similar criteria."[46] Parties must safeguard the wounded and sick in their possession from any attempts on their lives, violence to their persons, and cruel punishment, including torture or biological experimentation.[47] The Party in possession must provide medical care to the wounded and sick, as well as shelter sufficient to prevent exposure to dangerous conditions, infection, or contagion.[48] Additionally, a wounded and sick captive is entitled to POW status and the benefits derived from the Third Geneva Convention.[49] While the captive is wounded, both Wounded and Sick Convention and the Prisoner of War Convention apply; after the soldier has recovered from his injuries, the Prisoner of War Convention is the exclusive source of status and rights.[50] In the event that a Party in possession of wounded and sick must abandon them to the enemy, the Party must leave medical personnel and material to

---

[41] GWS, *supra* note 1, at art. 12.

[42] *See, e.g., id.* (stating that humane treatment must be provided "without any adverse distinction founded on sex, race, nationality, religion, political opinions, or any other similar criteria" and that women among the wounded and sick population "shall be treated with all consideration due to their sex").

[43] GWS, *supra* note 1, at art. 46.

[44] Pictet, *supra* note 4, at 135.

[45] *Id.* at 137.

[46] GWS, *supra* note 1, at art. 46.

[47] *Id.*

[48] *Id.* A primary reason for these prohibitions arises out of practices during World War II, such as "the German . . . at their main aircrew interrogation center . . . [where] [t]hey frequently delayed medical treatment until after interrogation . . . [the Germans also] seal[ed] off Russian PW camps once typhus or tuberculosis was discovered." Law of War Deskbook, *supra* note 38, at E-6 (citations omitted). Under Article 46, these practices are now expressly forbidden.

[49] *See* GWS, *supra* note 1, at art. 14. *See generally* GPW, *supra* note 2.

[50] Law of War Deskbook, *supra* note 38, at E-8.

assist in caring for them.[51] However, the presence of personnel left behind does not obviate the adverse Party's duty to provide any additional assistance to the wounded and sick left behind.

One of the most important rules in the Wounded and Sick Convention is that determinations regarding the order of care must be made solely in terms of medical necessity and feasibility, a process called triage.[52] A commander may not prioritize allocation of medical care to his wounded soldiers above caring for captured enemy soldiers solely on the basis of the soldiers' national origins. Political and military considerations can play no role in determining priority of care; the determination must be made based on considering medical necessity and how best to allocate available medical supplies and services.[53] For example, a Party could provide the highest level of medical assets to those members of the enemy wounded and sick with significant injuries that might benefit from treatment and survive, while those who suffered mortal wounds and will die regardless of treatment may justifiably be given lesser priority. Although no adverse distinctions may be established in providing care, favorable distinctions may be made by taking certain attributes into account, such as age or pregnancy. Medical personnel

---

[51] GWS, *supra* note 1, at art. 12. The requirement to leave medical personnel and equipment with abandoned wounded and sick is constrained by the doctrine of military necessity. *See id.* As noted by the commentary to the 1929 Convention:

> This obligation, natural and necessary as it is, may be a heavy charge if, for example, a retreating belligerent is compelled to abandon several groups of wounded in turn, leaving medical personnel and equipment with them each time. He runs the risk in such a case of having no medical personnel or equipment left for those of his troops who are the last to fall. That cannot be helped. It is his duty to provide for present needs without keeping back the means of relieving future casualties. If as a result he has no more medical personnel or equipment for subsequent casualties, he will have to do all he can to ensure that they receive relief, even appealing, in such a case, to the charity of the inhabitants, as he is entitled to do under Article 5 [Article 18 in the 1949 Convention].

Paul des Gouttes, Commentaire de la Convention de Geneve, du 27 Juillet 1929 11 (Geneva 1930). However, although the general duty to leave personnel behind with abandoned wounded and sick "cannot . . . be considered imperative, it represents none the less a clear moral obligation which the responsible authority cannot evade except in cases of urgent necessity." Pictet, *supra* note 4, at 142.

[52] Triage principles are designed to "provide the greatest medical assets to those with significant injuries who may benefit from treatment, while those wounded who will die no matter what and those whose injuries are not serious are given lesser priority" Law of War Deskbook, *supra* note 38, at E-6. *See also* GWS, *supra* note 1, at art. 12 (stating "[o]nly urgent medical reasons will authorize priority in the order of treatment to be administered.") *See also* Pictet, *supra* note 4, at 139–40 (stating that the purpose of the triage principle is "to strengthen the principle of the equality of treatment of the wounded"). For a discussion of American military triage categories, *see* Law of War Deskbook, *supra* note 38, at E-7 (classifying triage categories into the order of immediate, delayed, minimal/ambulatory, and expectant, and providing examples of injuries fitting into each classification).

[53] For example, wounded Panamanian Defense Force personnel were provided the same medical care and evacuated on the same aircraft as wounded American personnel during Operation Just Cause. " *Id.* (citation omitted). Another example of fairly applied triage principles occurred during the Falklands conflict, and scholars note that "the quality of medical care provided by the British to the wounded, without distinction between British and Argentine, was remarkable. More than 300 major surgeries were performed, and 100 of these were on Argentine soldiers." *Id.* (citation omitted).

must make all decisions regarding priority on the basis of their expert knowledge and their medical ethics.[54]

C. CASUALTIES

The Wounded and Sick Convention also regulates the care and treatment of dead bodies. Parties to a conflict are required to "take all possible measures to search for and collect" both the wounded and sick and the dead.[55] The Convention suggests that the Parties should arrange "an armistice or a suspension of fire ... to permit the removal, exchange and transport of the wounded left on the battlefield ... [or] from a besieged or encircled area."[56] This search-and- collection mandate applies to both friendly and enemy casualties. However, it is critical to note that this search-and-collection obligation is qualified by feasibility considerations. Military personnel must assess the feasibility of search-and-collection efforts, and are not obligated to engage in those efforts when doing so will subject them to unnecessary risk.[57] Furthermore, the treaty drafters recognized that broad suspension-of-fire agreements to remove, transport, and exchange the wounded, sick, and dead are not always possible.[58] However, to offset these barriers to aiding the wounded and sick, the treaty sanctions "local arrangements": essentially ceasefires arranged by local commanders to accomplish the same search-and-collection function on a smaller scale.[59] Local arrangements also might provide for removing wounded and dead from a besieged or encircled area, or permitting medical and religious personnel and relief supplies to enter such an area.[60]

With specific regard to the dead, the GWS requires parties to take measures to aid in the identification of both the deceased and the cause of death, and in locating the remains interred during hostilities. These functions are performed by Graves Registration Units, normally associated with higher-echelon support units and experts in ensuring compliance with these obligations. Article

---

[54] *See* Protocol I, *supra* note 31, at art. 10.

[55] GWS, *supra* note 1, at art. 15. This requirement is active "[at] all times, and particularly after an engagement." *Id.* The Article seeks to prevent ill treatment of the wounded and sick, presumably due to bandits, exposure, or the risk of infection, and to prevent the dead from being despoiled. *See id.* With regards to the dead, they "must also be looked for and brought back behind the lines with as much care as the wounded." Pictet, *supra* note 4, at 151.

[56] *Id.*

[57] As military operations may render the search obligation impractical, the drafters left the decision of when to search up to the commander's discretion. Pictet, *supra* note 4, at 151. *See also* Law of War Deskbook, *supra* note 38, at E-7 ("By way of example, US policy during Operation DESERT STORM was not to search for casualties in Iraqi tanks or armored personnel carriers because of concern about unexploded ordnance").

[58] GWS, *supra* note 1, at art. 17.

[59] *Id.*

[60] *Id.* Local arrangements were used to allow medical supplies into Sarajevo during the siege in 1992. Sir Donald Acheson, *Conflict in Bosnia 1992-3*, BRITISH MED. J. (Dec. 18, 1999), http://www.ncbi.nlm.nih.gov/pmc/articles/PMC1127096/.

16 imposes a duty of examination of each body for the purpose of confirmation of death and identity as far as circumstances permit.[61] Parties must retain the following regarding the wounded, sick, and the dead: name, nationality, identification number, any particulars shown on the identity card or disc, date of birth, date and place of capture or death, and particulars concerning wounds, illness, or cause of death.[62] As soon as possible, the Party possessing the collected information should forward it to the Information Bureau (as described in Article 122 of the Prisoner of War Convention);[63] the Information Bureau then forwards that information to an appointed Protecting Power and the Central Prisoners of War Agency.[64] The final step is transfer of the information to the Party on which the wounded, sick, or dead person depends.[65] The Information Bureau also exchanges certificates of death or authenticated lists of the dead between the parties, as well as half of the double identity disk (or tag), wills, or other important documents, and all articles of intrinsic or sentimental value found on the dead.[66] The goal of Article 16 is the free flow of information concerning the wounded,

---

[61] GWS, *supra* note 1, at art. 17.

[62] GWS, *supra* note 1, at art. 16. Pictet notes that "[w]hen picking up the wounded and dead, care should be taken to collect all their belongings (which may be scattered about); for such objects may inter alia be of assistance in establishing their identity." Pictet, *supra* note 4, at 152.

[63] GPW states that "[u]pon the outbreak of a conflict and in all cases of occupation, each of the Parties to the conflict shall institute an official Information Bureau for prisoners of war who are in its power." GPW, *supra* note 2, at art. 122. A party must give its Information Bureau certain information, relating to identification, transfer, and health of POWs, in order for the Bureau to pass that information on to the party to whom the POW depends and his next-of-kin. *See id.* Each Information Bureau is "responsible for replying to all enquiries sent to it concerning prisoners of war, including those who have died in captivity," and is obligated to "make any enquiries necessary to obtain the information which is asked for if this is not in its possession." *Id.* Finally, each Bureau is charged with collecting personal valuables and documents important to the next-of-kin left by POWs no longer in the possession of the detaining party, and to forward those possessions to the party to whom the POW depended. *Id.* Pictet describes the general purpose of this article as "to centralize, not only the lists of prisoners taken, but also everything relating to them (such as movements, releases, illnesses or deaths)," and that creation of Information Bureaus by each belligerent party "was necessary both for administrative reasons and to enable particulars to be forwarded to the Power of Origin and to their families." Pictet, *supra* note 4, at 165.

[64] GWS, *supra* note 1, at art. 16. Defined in the GPW, the Central Prisoners of War Information Agency "shall be created in a neutral country"; its function is to "collect all the information it may obtain through official or private channels respecting prisoners of war, and to transmit it as rapidly as possible to the country of origin of the prisoners of war or to the Power on which they depend." GPW, *supra* note 2, at art. 123. Pictet thus summarizes the entire process of information transfer:

> The information is to be forwarded as soon as possible by the persons or authorities by whom it has been collected to the Information Bureau which the belligerent is required to open on his territory. The Information Bureau will transmit it to the Protecting Power and to the Central Prisoners of War Agency, and the Protecting Power and the Central Prisoners of War Agency will each pass it on to the Power to which the wounded, sick or dead in question belong. It thus travels by two different routes.

Pictet, *supra* note 4, at 165.

[65] GWS, *supra* note 1, at art. 16.

[66] *Id.*

sick, or dead between Parties to a conflict, and ultimately, when possible to give information and possessions to the next of kin.

The dead should be examined and preferably given a full medical examination to confirm death, determine causation of death, and assist in identification of the body.[67] Examination should be followed by burial or cremation.[68] Burial must be by honorable interment, preferably with individual graves, and should follow "the rites of the religion to which [the deceased] belonged"; graves should be grouped by nationality if possible, and must be marked and maintained so that they might be found.[69] Cremation should occur only for hygienic or religious reasons.[70] The exchange of grave locations and information regarding the occupants of the graves should occur "[as] soon as circumstances permit, and at latest at the end of hostilities."[71]

Civilians may assist in the collection and care of the wounded and sick.[72] A commander may request locals to do so, but civilian action must be voluntary. Such civilian support would, in practice, likely be coordinated through the civil affairs staff section of a command. Civilians are also permitted pursuant to the GWS to spontaneously provide care to the wounded and sick, without request from the military, although in practice such uncoordinated intervention may be discouraged if it will potentially interfere with the efficient execution of the military casualty collection mission.[73] At the same time, the military authority should grant civilians who have undertaken the task of caring for wounded and sick protection and facilities to aid in their efforts.[74] If U.S. forces take control of an area formerly under enemy control where such civilian activity was ongoing,

---

[67] GWS, *supra* note 1, at art. 17. These examinations should be carefully conducted, as a thorough examination and report can greatly assist in refuting allegations of war crimes. Further, "bodies must be examined twice over, even if they have to be placed in a common grave," first to determine that no trace of life remains and second to attempt to establish a time of death. Pictet, *supra* note 4, at 177.

[68] GWS, *supra* note 1, at art. 17.

[69] *Id.* In addition, half of the double identity disc, or the identity disc itself if it is a single disc, should remain on the body. *Id.*

[70] *Id.*

[71] GWS, *supra* note 1, at art. 17. Although individual burial is preferred, the military necessity exception permits mass graves if circumstances exist to necessitate it. *See* Pictet, *supra* note 4, at 177. Additionally, the individual inhumation or cremation was considered important because "the idea of a common grave conflicts with the sentiment of respect for the dead, in addition to making any subsequent exhumation impossible or very difficult." *Id.*

[72] GWS, *supra* note 1, at art. 18.

[73] *Id.* Three major changes to the rights of caring for the wounded made in the 1949 Convention are:

1. The protection and the facilities accorded to the inhabitants by a belligerent must also be accorded to them by the adverse Party.
2. The inhabitants [of the combat area] must be authorized spontaneously to care for the wounded.
3. The fact of having cared for enemy wounded is never a reprehensible act.

Pictet, *supra* note 4, at 185.

[74] GWS, *supra* note 1, at art. 18.

it must extend protection to civilians engaged in these activities.[75] Rapidly identifying civilian capabilities in such areas and encouraging them to continue to perform their humanitarian function is obviously in the interest of U.S. forces as it will reduce the burden on friendly medical capabilities. However, it must be noted that this civilian support is merely an augment to the military obligation imposed by the Wounded and Sick Convention. Accordingly, allowing and facilitating civilian care for the wounded and sick does not relieve the U.S. commander of her respect and protect obligations.[76]

The protection of the wounded and sick during international armed conflicts was augmented by provisions of The 1977 Additional Protocol I to the Geneva Conventions. Although the United States is not a party to this treaty, virtually all articles related to protection of the wounded and sick are considered customary international law and followed routinely in operational practice.[77] Additional Protocol I reinforces many of the protections established by the Wounded and Sick Convention,[78] and includes a number of important additions to the law. Perhaps most important, it expands the definition of the term "wounded and sick" to include many of the protected person classes enumerated by the Convention in Article 13.[79] Notably, civilians are expressly protected within the Additional Protocol I's definition of "wounded and sick,"[80] and the treaty further defines specifically what persons are entitled to protected person treatment as hors de combat and are no longer lawful targets of attack.[81] Overall, Additional

---

[75] *Id.* Under no circumstances should a civilian or medical care-provider be molested or convicted for giving aid to the wounded or sick. The Commentary to this article describes that during and after World War II, several countries imposed harsh penalties on civilians or members of a Red Cross Society who treated or cared for enemies, as "laws . . . treated any form of service in an enemy army as high treason, and [care-providers] were regarded purely and simply as individuals who had taken up arms against their country." *See* Pictet, *supra* note 4, at 192. Article 18 definitely states that "medical treatment, even where given to enemies, is always legitimate, and does not constitute a hostile act . . . This provision protects medical personnel in the strict sense of the word as well as civilians." *Id.* at 192–93.

[76] *See* GWS, *supra* note 1, at art. 18. In his commentaries, Pictet stated that an occupying power cannot use civilian care as a pretext for avoiding its responsibilities to care for the wounded and sick; civilian care is considered only incidental, and the party still has an "obligation to give both physical and moral care to the wounded and sick." Pictet, *supra* note 4, at 193.

[77] *See* Customary IHL, *supra* note 8, at 396–98.

[78] *See, e.g.*, Protocol I, *supra* note 31, at art. 17 (discussing the role of the civilian population in caring for the wounded and sick, and ensuring that civilians will not be punished for doing so).

[79] Protocol I, *supra* note 31, at art. 8(1) ("Persons, whether military or civilian, who, because of trauma, disease or other physical or mental disorder or disability, are in need of medical assistance or care and who refrain from any act of hostility").

[80] *See id.*

[81] A person is considered hors de combat if one of the following elements is met: (1) he is in the power of an adverse party; (2) he clearly expresses an intention to surrender; or (3) he has been rendered unconscious or is otherwise incapacitated by wounds or sickness, and therefore is incapable of defending himself. An additional requirement is that "in any of these cases he abstains from any hostile act and does not attempt to escape." Protocol I, *supra* note 31, at art. 41. *See also* Sandoz, *supra* note 15, at 224 ("It is a fundamental principle of the law of war that those who do not participate in the hostilities shall not be attacked. In this respect harmless civilians and soldiers 'hors de combat' are *a priori* on the same footing").

Protocol I reflects an attempt to address the needs of the wounded and sick more pragmatically with far less emphasis on limited categories of military wounded and sick, and is therefore an important source of authority providing for the protection of all war victims.[82]

D. STATUS AND PROTECTION: THE DISTINCTIVE EMBLEM

Implementing the objectives of the Wounded and Sick Convention requires the presence of personnel, equipment, and facilities devoted to that purpose in areas of armed hostilities. These human and material resources cannot be effective in their missions unless they are visibly distinguishable from combatant forces and equipment. It is therefore necessary to distinguish them in a manner that indicates to an opposing armed force that they are both inoffensive and engaged in activities serving the humanitarian interests of all parties to the conflict.

The Wounded and Sick Convention and Additional Protocol III to the Convention provide for this distinction in the form of special emblems of protection: the Red Cross, Red Crescent, and Red Square. Article 38 of the Wounded and Sick Convention describes the several recognized emblems that mark a person, vehicle, or facility as medical in nature.[83] U.S. forces utilize the Red Cross as the distinctive emblem indicating exclusive engagement in a medical function, although the enemy may use alternate emblems, to include the Red Crescent (used predominantly by Muslim nations), the Red Lion and Sun (formerly used by Persia/Iran, which now uses the Red Crescent), and the Red Crystal.[84] While the Red Star of David has been a controversial symbol,[85] it has nevertheless been respected even though it is not described in the treaty.[86] Additional Protocol III[87], which entered into force in 2005, provides for the use of a Red Square in lieu of the Star of David, resolving this uncertainty. Misuse of a distinctive emblem

---

[82] Additional Protocol I explicitly lists as noncombatants medical personnel and chaplains who are members of the armed services. Protocol I, *supra* note 31, at art. 43(2).

[83] GWS, *supra* note 1, at art. 38.

[84] *See* Pictet, *supra* note 4, at 297–300 (explaining the origin of the Red Cross symbol and discussing the ideological reasons that Turkey refused to use the Red Cross and adopted the Red Crescent, and Persia's desire to use the Red Lion).

[85] Pictet, *supra* note 4, at 301. Two major concerns arose with regard to allowing other emblems the same status as the Red Cross: (1) potential danger would arise from substituting national or religious symbols for a neutral emblem of international charity, and (2) the proliferation of symbols would degrade and undermine the universality of the Red Cross and diminish its protective value.

[86] *See* Law of War Deskbook, *supra* note 38, at E-22.

[87] *See generally* Protocol Additional to the Geneva Conventions of 12 August 1949, and relating to the Adoption of an Additional Distinctive Emblem, Dec. 8, 2005, *available at* http://www.icrc.org/ihl/INTRO/615?OpenDocument.

constitutes a war crime, and use of the emblem by medical personnel is subject to "competent military authority."[88]

Facilities, vehicles, and personnel must bear a distinctive medical emblem in order to be protected from attack; this emblem must also bear the stamp of the military authority.[89] Medical and religious personnel must wear one of the distinctive emblems on their left arms.[90] They must also carry an identity disk[91] and an identity card that also bears the distinctive emblem.[92] These identifying markers provide protection from intentional attack on the battlefield and indicate entitlement to retained person status (as opposed to prisoner-of-war status); personnel may not be deprived of either their insignia or their identity cards, and may not be prevented from wearing the armlet.[93]

Medical units and establishments must fly both the flag of the Red Cross (or other distinctive emblem) and the national flag of the Party that owns the facility.[94] If a facility is captured, the adverse party may not fly its flag; only the distinctive emblem flag may be flown.[95] Parties have an obligation to make the distinctive emblems clearly visible to enemy forces.[96] Neutral units assisting a Party to the conflict under Article 27 shall fly a flag bearing a descriptive emblem and the national flag of the belligerent Party they are assisting whenever

---

[88] GWS, *supra* note 1, at art. 39. Pictet emphasizes that a commander may give or withhold permission to use the emblem, and may order a medical unit or vehicle camouflaged. Pictet, *supra* note 4, at 308.

[89] *See* GWS, *supra* note 1, at art. 39. "What is above all essential is to ensure the 'bonafides' [sic] of the wearer: the armlet must only be worn by those who are entitled to do so under the Convention. The brassard is not in itself sufficient evidence ... The armlet will have no protective value, and cannot be lawfully worn, unless it has been stamped and issued by the military authority." Pictet, *supra* note 4, at 310–11.

[90] GWS, *supra* note 1, at art. 40.

[91] *See id.* at art. 16, 40.

[92] *Id.* at art. 40. The identification card must state the bearer's name, date of birth, rank, and service number; bear a photograph of the owner and his signature and/or fingerprints; bear the stamp of the issuing military authority; and "shall state in what capacity he is entitled to the protection of [GWS]." *Id.*

[93] *Id.*; *see also* Law of War Deskbook, *supra* note 38, at E-23. Confiscation of either the ID card or the armlet would render determination of retained person status difficult or impossible. *Id.* This provision against confiscation is a result of routine denial of RP protections during World War I and World War II. Pictet notes that "[i]n both World Wars medical personnel sometimes had their armlets and cards taken from them—a convenient way for the capturing State to evade its obligations. Such practices must be strictly forbidden; the special insignia and cards of medical personnel can only be withdrawn by the military authorities of their own armed forces." Pictet, *supra* note 4, at 316.

[94] GWS, *supra* note 1, at art. 42.

[95] *Id. See also* Pictet, *supra* note 4, at 321 ("There is no provision here for flying a national flag beside the red cross emblem, as there are objections to flying either the flag of the home country or that of the captor").

[96] GWS, *supra* note 1, at art. 42. The justification for the "clearly visible" requirement is because the distinctive emblem "is serving its most important purpose when it is displayed over mobile units and fixed establishments—particularly the latter. The large capacity of such buildings means that

that Party makes use of the neutral facility.[97] Neutral units may always fly their national flag, even if captured by an adverse Party.[98]

The United States has implemented its own policies with regard to use of the distinctive emblems: "[a]ll US medical facilities and units, except veterinary, display the distinctive flag of the Geneva Conventions."[99] However, FM 8-10-6 notes that camouflaging medical facilities is authorized "when the lack of camouflage might compromise tactical operations."[100] In such cases, camouflage of medical facilities may be ordered by commanders of at least brigade level, and the camouflage must only be temporary and local in nature; any camouflage order must be rescinded as soon as possible.[101]

> Few emblems carry more profound significance or demand more universal respect than these distinctive emblems. Indeed, if there is one LOAC principle that is understood well beyond the circles of professionals engaged in the study and implementation of the LOAC, it is almost certainly the principle of protection for individuals bearing these distinctive emblems. Each emblem, and the respect and protection they provide, is based on provisions of the Wounded and Sick Convention or the relatively new Additional Protocol III (developed to establish a distinctive emblem recognized by Israel and other nations that do not recognize the State of Israel). These treaties also define who may wear these emblems and what equipment and facilities may be marked with them. These definitions will be explained below. However, it is also important to note that in order to preserve the integrity of the protections accorded to persons, places, and things marked with these emblems, improper use of them is considered a war crime. Indeed, misuse of a protective distinctive emblem is one of the most serious violations of the LOAC, precisely because it compromises the trust and confidence afforded to other persons, places, or things properly marked.

---

the safety of a great many people is at stake. Precautions must, moreover, be taken against air raids." Pictet, *supra* note 4, at 321.

[97] GWS, *supra* note 1, at art. 43.

[98] *Id.* Pictet explains the reasoning allowing the neutral to fly its flag is subject only to certain limitations, but may not be arbitrarily denied:

> Unlike the solution adopted in the case of the national flag of the belligerent, this phrase does not mean that the belligerent can decide whether or not neutral units generally are to fly their own flags. It implies a restriction made, in particular cases and for a limited period only, for tactical reasons, such as the necessity for concealing medical units in forward areas.

Pictet, *supra* note 4, at 322.

[99] FM 8-10-6, *supra* note 36, at ¶ A-2(a).

[100] *Id.* at ¶ A-2(b).

[101] *Id.*

E. PERSONNEL AIDING THE WOUNDED AND SICK

Individuals authorized to wear the distinctive emblem of the Red Cross, Red Crescent, or Red Square are those exclusively engaged in the collection, evacuation, and care for the wounded and sick. The Wounded and Sick Convention establishes the rights and obligations of such personnel. Although they are normally members of the armed forces, according to the LOAC they are considered noncombatants because of their exclusive medical function.[102] This is a critical distinction. Although the term "noncombatant" is routinely used pragmatically as a designation for civilians, in fact civilians are a different category of individuals within the meaning of the LOAC. This special noncombatant status of members of the armed forces exclusively engaged in the protection of the wounded and sick was originally established by the Hague Regulations of 1899 and 1907, both of which indicated that "The armed forces of the belligerent parties may consist of combatants and non-combatants. In the case of capture by the enemy, both have a right to be treated as prisoners of war."[103] Thus, physicians, nurses, medics, and chaplains are in fact considered noncombatant members of the armed forces.

The protections provided by the Wounded and Sick Convention and the effective collection and care of the wounded and sick it seeks to facilitate turn in large measure on this special status. It would have been futile to cloak the wounded and sick with a respect-and-protect shield without allocating accordant protections to those responsible for their collection and care. Accordingly, Article 24 provides that:

> Medical personnel exclusively engaged in the search for, or the collection, transport or treatment of the wounded or sick, or in the prevention of disease, staff exclusively engaged in the administration of medical units and establishments, as well as chaplains attached to the armed forces, shall be respected and protected in all circumstances.[104]

---

[102] *See* CUSTOMARY IHL, *supra* note 8, at 13.

[103] Convention with Respect to the Laws and Customs of War on Land and its Annex: Regulations concerning the Laws and Customs of War on Land art. 3, July 29, 1899, *available at* http://www.icrc.org/ihl/INTRO/150? OpenDocument; Convention Respecting the Laws and Customs of War on Land and its Annex: Regulations concerning the Laws and Customs of War on Land art. 3, Oct. 18, 1907, 36 Stat. 2227, and Annex, 36 Stat. 2295.

[104] GWS, *supra* note 1, at art. 24. "Exclusively engaged" is interpreted to mean that a person's assignment to the medical service is permanent. *Compare* Pictet, *supra* note 4, at 219 *and* (discussing the nature of "exclusive engagement" and the grant of protection for exclusively engaged medical personnel at all times) *with id.* at 222.

Pictet states:

> ". . . auxiliary personnel are immune if they are carrying out their medical duties at the time when they come into contact with the enemy or fall into his hands," but cautioning that the interpretation of "carrying out medical duties" should not be be interpreted too literally and should extend, for example, to an auxiliary "detailed for medical duties but waiting his turn and not actually engaged in treating the wounded at the moment when his unit is captured."

Id. at 222.

The key to understanding this special status is the "exclusively engaged" requirement. In essence, the LOAC allows (or more appropriately encourages) parties to an armed conflict to field personnel, units, equipment, and facilities devoted exclusively to the amelioration of the suffering of the wounded and sick. Because Article 12 imposes an equality-of-care obligation for *all* wounded and sick irrespective of nationality, granting special status and protections to members of opposing armed forces exclusively engaged in the collection and care of casualties serves the interests of all parties to the conflict, for such personnel will act to protect all victims of the conflict. Accordingly, Article 24 status is contingent on the function assigned to a member of the armed forces: each member is categorized based upon the role he or she plays in medical or relief efforts, and is given rights accordingly. Medical personnel of the armed forces who are exclusively engaged in the practice of medicine receive the highest level of protection, along with chaplains and members of national relief organizations.

Again, medical personnel do not automatically lose their special protection merely by carrying weapons. Wounded and Sick Convention and Additional Protocol I both contemplate circumstances in which it is proper for a medical facility to have an escort or picket, and in which medical personnel may be armed to provide for defense of the wounded and sick under their care.[105] United States' policy entitles medical personnel to defend themselves and their patients with individual small arms.[106] Further, American medical personnel are restricted in when they can use their weapons; they may only fire "in their personal defense and for the protection of the wounded and sick in their charge against marauders and other persons violating the law of war."[107] Further, the American manual states that in event of evacuation, enemy POWs who are wounded or sick continue to receive the benefits of priority of care based on triage principles, and are evacuated from any combat zone as soon as their conditions permit.[108]

1. Exclusively-Engaged Medical Personnel and Staff of the Armed Forces, Chaplains, and Members of National Relief Organizations

As noted above, Article 24 describes the first category as permanent medical personnel: those exclusively engaged in the collection and care function. This category also includes staff of voluntary aid societies, such as national Red Cross, Red Crescent, or Red Frame groups, so long as members of those groups are employed in the same manner as medical personnel described in Article 24, and so long as

---

[105] *See* GWS, *supra* note 1, at art. xx; *See also* Protocol I, *supra* note 31, at art. xx.

[106] FM 8-10-6, *supra* note 36, at para. A-4. The Field Manual lists a number of offensive weapons that, if mounted on or used by dedicated medical vehicles, facilities, or aircraft, could jeopardize their protected status. These weapons include, but are not limited to: machine guns, grenade launchers, hand grenades, and light anti-tank weapons. *Id.* at para. A-4(a). The clear intent of allowing medical personnel to bear arms is for them to defend themselves against marauders or violations of the laws of war, not to make war upon the enemy in an offensive manner.

[107] *Id.* at ¶ A-4(b).

[108] *Id.* at ¶ A-5(a).

they are subject to military laws and regulations.[109] Permanent medical personnel as described by Articles 24 and 26 are entitled to full respect and protection at all times.[110] U.S. Army Regulation 190-8, which establishes the procedures for implementing obligations established by the Wounded and Sick Convention (and the other Geneva Conventions), provides the following categorization of captured individuals entitled to Retained Person (RP) status:

> b. Enemy personnel who fall within any of the following categories, are eligible to be certified as RP:
> (1) Medical personnel who are members of the medical service of their armed forces.
> (2) Medical personnel who are exclusively engaged in:
> (a) The search for or the collection, transport, or treatment of the wounded or sick.
> (b) The prevention of disease.
> (c) Staffs exclusively engaged in administering medical units and establishments.
> (3) Chaplains.
> (4) The staff of the National Red Cross, Red Crescent, and other voluntary aid organizations. These organizations must be duly recognized and authorized by their governments. The staff of these organizations may be employed on the same duties as persons in (2) above, if such organizations are subject to military laws and regulations.[111]

The most important aspect of this protection provided to RPs by the Wounded and Sick Convention is that they may not be made the deliberate object of attack, even when they are caring for enemy casualties. Furthermore, if captured, RPs are not classified as prisoners of war, but as *retained* personnel.[112] Although

---

[109] GWS, *supra* note 1, at art. 26. During either peacetime or upon the commencement of hostilities, all parties to the conflict must notify each other of which societies it has authorized to render assistance to the medical service of its armed forces. *Id.* This notification must occur before the party actually utilizes the services of one of these societies. *Id.* Pictet notes that a national Red Cross or similar society both be recognized and authorized by the government of its home country, and that "[r]ecognition alone is not sufficient [to assist the country's armed forces]. The Government must also authorize the society to lend its assistance to the Medical Service of the armed forces in time of war." Pictet, *supra* note 4, at 226. During the term of use, "the staff of voluntary aid societies are temporarily attached to the Medical Service, and are under its orders . . . [but are not considered] part of the armed forces [for purposes of treaties dealing solely with members of the armed forces]." *Id.* at 227.

[110] GWS, *supra* note 1, at art. 24.

[111] Dep't of the Army, Army Regulation 190–8: Enemy Prisoners of War, Retained Personnel, Civilian Internees and Other Detainees § 3–15(b) (Oct. 1, 1997) [hereinafter AR 190-8].

[112] *See* GWS, *supra* note 1, at art. 28. Retained personnel receive all of the benefits from the Prisoner of War Convention, including pay, monthly allowances, and correspondence privileges. *See* GPW, *supra* note 2, at Art's 49-57.

these personnel must be afforded all benefits provided by the Prisoner of War Convention for the duration of their captivity, unlike POWs they may only be retained "in so far as the state of health, the spiritual needs and the number of prisoners of war require."[113] In other words, captured personnel qualifying for RP (retained person) status pursuant to Articles 24 and 26 are retained for the exclusive purpose of providing for the care of wounded and sick POWs. This obligation is implemented for U.S. armed forces by AR 190-8:

> Retained medical personnel shall receive as a minimum the benefits and protection given to EPW and shall also be granted all facilities necessary to provide for the medical care of EPW. They shall continue to exercise their medical functions for the benefit of EPW, preferably those belonging to the armed forces upon which they depend, within the scope of the military laws and regulations of the United States Armed Forces. They shall be provided with necessary transport and allowed to periodically visit EPW situated in working detachments or in hospitals outside the EPW camp. Although subject to the internal discipline of the camp in which they are retained such personnel may not be compelled to carry out any work other than that concerned with their medical duties. The senior medical officer shall be responsible to the camp military authorities for everything connected with the activities of retained medical personnel.[114]

Retention is therefore an exception to the presumption of repatriation, and is justified for the exclusive purpose of providing for the care of captured enemy personnel. When retention is not indispensible for the health and spiritual needs of POWs, retained personnel must be repatriated.[115] Selection of personnel for return should be made irrespective of race, religion, or political opinion, and decisions are preferably made according to chronological order of capture.[116] This

---

[113] *See* GWS, *supra* note 1, at art. 28.

[114] AR 190-8, *supra* note 111, at § 1-5(f).

[115] *See* GWS, *supra* note 1, at art. 30; Pictet, *supra* note 4, at 260–61. Parties may enter into agreements determining the percentage of personnel to be retained in proportion to the number of POWs. GWS, *supra* note 1, at art. 31. Pictet further notes that the current treaty language was created in direct response to ambiguities in and shoddy application of the 1864 and 1906 Conventions during World War I, as well as the failure of the 1929 Convention to absolutely mandate a return of RPs at certain times. Pictet, *supra* note 4, at 236. The language of the 1864 and 1906 Conventions included that "medical personnel must be unconditionally repatriated . . . as soon as their presence was no longer considered indispensable to the wounded in their charge," while the 1929 language conferred an additional condition to the rule that members of the medical personnel were to be sent back to their own forces as soon as military considerations permitted, "by the use of the words 'in the absence of an agreement to the contrary.'" *Id.* The earlier ambiguity and the later conditionality gave the detaining power considerable leeway in determining when to repatriate RPs, under what conditions RPs could be held, and what work they could be forced to perform. *See id.* at 237 (noting that during World War II, the Germans retained large numbers of captured medical personnel in Germany and that "[m]edical personnel . . . were often employed on non-medical work. In defence [sic] of this measure it was alleged that a 'reserve' was essential if such eventualities as air raids, sudden influxes of prisoners, and epidemics in the camps were to be adequately dealt with"). *Id.* at 237.

[116] GWS, *supra* note 1, at art. 31.

is commonly called a first-in/first-out approach.[117] An example of the process for assessing when retention or repatriation is appropriate based on a POW-to-RP ratio is reflected in AR 190-8:

> RP [Retained Persons], who are members of the enemy's Armed Forces, will be assigned to EPW camps. If available, they will be assigned in the ratio of two physicians, two nurses, one chaplain, and seven enlisted medical personnel per 1,000 EPW. Economy of medical staffing may be achieved at higher levels per guidance from Commanding General, HSC [Health Services Command]. As much as possible, these RP will be assigned to camps containing EPW from the same Armed Forces upon which the RP depend.[118]

Thus, if there is no necessity for their services, the Wounded and Sick Convention obligates the retaining power to repatriate RPs.[119] In contrast, captured combatant members of the armed forces (POWs) are detained to prevent them for returning to hostilities, and therefore may be detained for the duration of the armed conflict.[120] Consistent with this special RP status, RPs (unlike POWs) may not be required to perform any work aside from their regular medical or religious duties, preferably ministering to the armed forces to which they themselves belong. Furthermore, they must be allowed to periodically visit and be transported to POWs in labor units or hospitals outside of the camp.[121] While in the camp, the senior medical officer and the chaplains must have direct access to the military and medical authorities overseeing the camp.[122]

2. Auxiliary Medical Support Personnel of the Armed Forces

The second category consists of auxiliary medical personnel: military personnel who have been specially trained in medical specialties, such as hospital orderlies, nurses, or auxiliary stretcher-bearers.[123] Typically, auxiliaries perform other military duties, and take up these medical duties only as the need arises.[124] When acting in a medical capacity, they are entitled to the same respect and protect

---

[117] *See* Law of War Deskbook, *supra* note 38, at E-13.

[118] AR 190-8, *supra* note 111, at § 1-5(k).

[119] Notably, this provision is one of the least honored. *See* Law of War Deskbook, *supra* note 38, at E-14 ("US medical personnel in Korea and Vietnam were not repatriated, but were also denied retained person status") (citation omitted).

[120] *See* GPW, *supra* note 2, at art. 118.

[121] *Id.* Article 24 or 26 personnel are still subject to the internal discipline procedures of the camp, but may not be forced to do labor aside from their medical or religious duties. *Id.* Medical personnel may only be retained to treat prisoners of war, though they may be required to treat POWs who are of different nationalities. Preferably, the retained persons will treat prisoners of war of their own nationality, but this is not a strict requirement, and as such, medical personnel may be retained to treat any POW. *See* GWS, *supra* note 1, at art. 30. Article 24 or 26 personnel may never be retained to treat enemy personnel. Pictet, *supra* note 4, at 241.

[122] GWS, *supra* note 1, at art. 28. The detaining party is still bound to provide any medical attention required by POWs in the camp. *Id.*

[123] GWS, *supra* note 1, at art. 25.

[124] *Id.*

requirements accorded to those meeting the qualification requirements of Article 24.[125] Auxiliary personnel must wear an armlet displaying a distinctive emblem in miniature, but only while carrying out medical duties, and their identification cards "should specify what special training they have received, the temporary character of the duties ... engaged upon, and their authority for wearing the armlet."[126]

Unlike dedicated medical or religious military personnel, or members of national aid societies, captured auxiliary medical personnel are considered POWs, not retained personnel.[127] Accordingly, the treatment of auxiliaries depends on the function they are providing at any given time, meaning they can effectively move back and forth between combatant and noncombatant status.

Because of the inherent uncertainty resulting from Article 26, the U.S. armed forces do not assert auxiliary status for its personnel.[128] Although there are some members of combatant forces who perform emergency medical support functions when needed (in the Army these personnel are routinely designated as "combat lifesavers"), they are considered combatants at all times and are not provided with the special insignia entitling them to Wounded and Sick Convention protections. Nonetheless, other armed forces may opt for a different approach to their auxiliary medical personnel. When this is the case, upon capture these auxiliaries are not RPs, but are instead POWs in accordance with the Prisoner of War Convention.[129] When not performing medical duties, they are treated as POWs in every manner.[130] When performing medical duties, they receive heightened benefits but are nevertheless not entitled to repatriation like their Article 24 qualified counterparts.

If captured, persons designated under Article 27 may not be detained, and must be allowed to return to their country or, if that is not possible, to territory of the party to the conflict whose service they were in at the time of capture.[131] United States Army Regulation 190-8 includes a formula for determining the ratio of POWs to Retained Personnel, and implements the repatriation obligation pursuant to this formula. Return to the party's territory may, of course, be

---

[125] *Id.*

[126] GWS, *supra* note 1, at art. 41. Notably, "if a military command should, without previous arrangement, send ordinary combatants to collect the wounded, it would be at their own risk" as such persons are not even considered auxiliary medical personnel and therefore are bestowed no protection under the GWS. Pictet, *supra* note 4, at 224.

[127] *See* GWS, *supra* note 1, at art. 29.

[128] *See* Law of War Deskbook, *supra* note 38, at E-15 ("The US Army does not have any personnel who officially fall into the category identified in Article 25 ... Air Force regulations do provide for these personnel") (citations omitted).

[129] *Id.* Further, auxiliary POWs shall be employed medically in the POW camp as the need arises. *Id.*

[130] "Members of the personnel designated in Article 25 who have fallen into the hands of the enemy, shall be prisoners of war." GWS, *supra* note 1, at art. 30.

[131] GWS, *supra* note 1, at art. 32. The explanation for the mandated return is that "[i]f [captured neutrals] cannot be retained, they cannot with even greater reason be regarded as prisoners of war; they should rather be treated as guests." Pictet, *supra* note 4, at 268.

difficult to implement in practice by military considerations.[132] United States' forces would likely request assistance from the International Committee of the Red Cross to facilitate such repatriation. Pending release, Retained Persons must be allowed to continue their work assisting the adverse party, preferably by caring for the wounded and sick of the Party whose service they were engaged in at the time of capture.[133]

F. MEDICAL UNITS, ESTABLISHMENTS, AND TRANSPORTATION

The protections provided for the wounded and sick and those who collect and care for them would be of little meaning if the facilities in which they work or the equipment they use to transport casualties were subject to attack like any other lawful target on the battlefield. It is therefore self-evident that the objectives of the Wounded and Sick Convention can only be achieved by extending special protections to these components of the collection and care function.

1. Facilities and Vehicles

Article 38 defines the status of fixed and mobile facilities established for medical use and marked with one of the distinctive emblems.[134] Such facilities are protected no differently than the wounded and sick they provide care for: they may not be attacked unless they abrogate their status.[135] This protection also

---

[132] GWS, *supra* note 1, at art. 32.

[133] *Id.*

[134] GWS, *supra* note 1, at art. 38. Pictet states that:

> Fixed establishments are, as their name indicates, permanent buildings used as hospitals or stores. Mobile units are defined as establishments which can move from place to place as circumstances require following the movement of the troops. It is field hospitals and ambulances which are in particular referred to, but it is not necessary for them to be accommodated in shelters or tents; an establishment in the open, however small, is a medical unit if its object is to collect the wounded.

Pictet, *supra* note 4, at 194–95. Pictet continues by noting that "it is not necessary for the wounded to be actually cared for in an establishment for the latter to be regarded as a medical unit. A post where they are collected before being evacuated will be protected, even if no dressings are kept there." *Id.* at 195.

[135] *Compare* GWS, *supra* note 1, at art. 19 (stating that fixed and mobile medical units owned by a medical service "may in no circumstances be attacked, but shall at all times be respected and protected by the Parties to the conflict," and emphasizing that if such a unit is captured, its "personnel shall be free to pursue their duties, as long as the capturing Power has not itself ensured the necessary care of the wounded and sick found in such establishments and units") *with id.* at art. 35 (stating that transports containing the wounded and sick or containing medical equipment must be "respected and protected in the same way as mobile medical units," and that if a medical transport is captured, it is subject to the laws of war "on condition that the Party to the conflict who captures them shall in all cases ensure the care of the wounded and sick they contain"). Additionally, there

extends to hospital ships covered by the Second Geneva Convention; such ships cannot be attacked from land.[136] However, in order to facilitate this protection, the Wounded and Sick Convention indicates that commanders should, when feasible, situate medical units away from potential military objectives to ensure their safety.[137] This can create significant operational challenges for U.S. forces. Establishing a mobile medical unit in an area isolated from other combat support and combat service support activities adds a logistics burden to the medical function and exposes the unit to potential risk. As a result, it is not uncommon to locate medical treatment facilities within "base clusters" in order to maximize force protection, even for medical personnel. This practice, however, obviously increases the risk that the mobile medical facility may be impacted by an otherwise lawful attack on the U.S. forces in close proximity. As a general rule, however, even in the context of contemporary U.S. military operations, large mobile medical units, such as Combat Support Hospitals (large mobile hospital facilities offering the full gamut of medical support) are established in areas somewhat attenuated from other U.S. forces, and protected by combat forces properly assigned to defend the unit against unlawful attack.

If captured, medical units and personnel assigned to them must be permitted to continue caring for the wounded and sick.[138] Allowing captured enemy medical personnel and units to continue their humanitarian function is operationally logical, and U.S. forces would likely rely on the senior U.S. medical officer to coordinate this continued function. This will facilitate treatment of captured wounded and sick enemy personnel, and enable the U.S. medical commander to leverage all available medical resources to execute the collection and

---

are examples of violations of this provision, notably during Soviet engagements in Afghanistan in the late 1970s and early 1980s, as well as during the Vietnam War:

> In Afghanistan, the Soviets engaged in a campaign to destroy hospitals and dispensaries operated by nongovernmental organizations (Medecins sans Frontieres, Medecins du Monde, Aide Medicale Internationale—all NGOs comprised of French doctors and nurses). In September of 1980, the Soviets sacked the hospital at Yakaolang, even destroying all medical supplies and equipment. In late 1981 the Soviets systematically bombed hospitals operated by French medical organizations. At least 8 hospitals of the three NGOs above were hit. One was rebuilt with a prominent red cross, but was still bombed again by Russian helicopters. In Vietnam during the 1968 Tet offensive, communist forces attacked the 45th MASH at Tay Ninh, killing one doctor and two medics.

Law of War Deskbook, *supra* note 38, at E-16 (citations omitted).

[136] GWS, *supra* note 1, at art. 20. Additionally, medical establishments ashore are protected by GWS and cannot be attacked from sea. GC II, *supra* note 2, at art. 23.

[137] *See* GWS, *supra* note 1, at art. 19. Under no circumstances should medical units be used to shield military objectives from attack. *See id.* at art. 12. The purpose of creating remoteness between military objectives and medical establishments is to protect the latter from attack against the former, and for medical units to be "situated [so] that attacks against military objectives cannot imperil their safety." Pictet, *supra* note 4, at 198. Although close proximity between a medical establishment and a lawful military target "would not weaken the legal protection enjoyed by a medical establishment . . . it would, in practice, endanger its security to some extent." *Id.* at 199.

[138] GWS, *supra* note 1, at art. 19.

care mission for all casualties. Of course, these personnel and facilities will be subjected to appropriate security measures, to included being located within a POW facility.

Under certain situations, a medical facility that would otherwise be protected from intentional attack may lose its protection. Protection is lost if the facility commits "acts harmful to the enemy," which fall outside the general humanitarian duties of the facility.[139] However, unlike any other potential object of attack, protection ceases only after a warning has been given and it remains unheeded after a reasonable amount of time to comply with it.[140] Some conditions that may be interpreted as "harmful to the enemy" in some manner nevertheless do not cause a medical facility to abrogate its protected status, for example retaining the arms and ammunition of casualties undergoing treatment in the hospital.[141]

The Wounded and Sick Convention enumerates the following as non-abrogating circumstances: (1) that personnel of the medical unit are armed and use their arms in their own defense or in the defense of the wounded and sick under their care; (2) in the absence of armed orderlies, the unit is protected by a picket, sentries, or an escort; (3) small arms and ammunition taken from the wounded and sick and not yet handed over to the proper service are founded in the unit; (4) personnel and material of veterinary services are found in the unit without forming an integral part of the unit; or (5) the humanitarian activities of the medical unit or its personnel extend to caring for civilian wounded and sick.[142]

In practice, this indicates that U.S. military medical personnel must not participate in actively defending their facilities or equipment from enemy capture, unless doing so is intended to protect the wounded and sick themselves from potential abuse (a genuine reality in our current era of conflict involving non-state groups who routinely violate the LOAC). If overrun by enemy forces and captured, mobile medical units need not be returned, but may only be used in continuing care for wounded and sick.[143] Fixed medical establishments, including the material therein, must be used to care for the wounded and sick so long as

---

[139] GWS, *supra* note 1, at art. 21. Pictet identified several possible examples of "harmful acts," such as using a hospital as a shelter for combatants, as an ammunition dump, or as an observation post. *See* Pictet, *supra* note 4, at 200–01.

[140] GWS, *supra* note 1, at art. 21. Reasonable times vary depending on the circumstances; for example, no time limit would be required if fire was currently being taken from a hospital. *See* Pictet, *supra* note 4, at 202.

[141] *See generally* GWS, *supra* note 1, at art. 22.

[142] *Id.* With specific regards to armed personnel in or around a medical unit, medical personnel may be armed with small arms, such as rifles or pistols, to defend against marauders or those violating the law of war, and a medical establishment may be protected with an armed picket or escort. Loss of protection would occur, however, if machine guns or artillery were placed around a medical unit, as these weapons are obviously not intended solely for the protection of the wounded and sick. *See* Pictet, *supra* note 4, at 202–06.

[143] GWS, *supra* note 1, at art. 33. This represents a departure from the 1929 Convention, which required mobile medical units to be returned. *See* Pictet, *supra* note 4, at 272.

a need exists.[144] An exception to this requirement is urgent military necessity, but the capturing party must ensure the continued welfare of any wounded and sick in a fixed medical establishment before converting it to another use.[145] It is also critical to distinguish captured medical supplies from other supplies captured from an enemy. Unlike the normal booty of war, under no circumstances may medical material and stores be intentionally destroyed.[146]

Vehicles devoted exclusively to medical purposes and properly marked with the distinctive emblem, such as ambulances, must be respected and protected in the same manner as mobile medical units.[147] Vehicles may be employed for medical duties either permanently or temporarily and need not be equipped specifically for medical purposes to be considered a medical vehicle.[148] If a vehicle is only temporarily employed as a medical vehicle, to ensure its protection it must display one of Article 38's distinctive emblems while engaged in the medical mission. Temporary medical employment and the importance of the distinctive emblem is explained in the following manner:

> As ambulances are not always available, any vehicles may be adapted and used temporarily for transport of the wounded. During that time they will be entitled to protection, subject to the display of the distinctive emblem. Thus military vehicles going up to the forward areas with ammunition may bring back the wounded, with the important reservation the emblem must be detachable, e.g., a flag, so that it may be flown on the downward journey. Conversely military vehicles may take down wounded and bring up military supplies on the return journey. The flag must then be removed on the return journey.[149]

It is not uncommon to use vehicles for a non-medical mission when traveling in one direction and for a medical mission when traveling in the other direction. For example, troops or supplies may be transported to the "front lines," while the same transport assets may be used to "back-haul" casualties to the rear area. It is essential that armed forces strictly comply with the obligation to remove the distinctive

---

[144] *Id.* First priority for captured medical material is treating the wounded and sick in the unit at the time of capture. If the captured unit has no patients, the captured material may be used on other patients. Pictet, *supra* note 4, at 274.

[145] GWS, *supra* note 1, at art. 33.

[146] *Id.* Not even military necessity justifies intentional destruction of medical material and stores. *See* Law of War Deskbook, *supra* note 38, at E-18.

[147] GWS, *supra* note 1, at art. 35.

[148] Pictet, *supra* note 4, at 281. In explanation for this absolute protection, Pictet states:

> [i]t is absolutely essential that the wounded should be transported to a hospital as quickly as possible. A motor ambulance of the Medical Service will not always be readily available and, as has often happened, any vehicle available will be used. It must not be possible for this to be used as a pretext for opening fire on the wounded.

Id.

[149] G.I.A.D. Draper, The Red Cross Conventions of 1949, 87 (1958).

emblem whenever the vehicle is not exclusively engaged in the medical function. Failing to do so will erode confidence in the effect of the emblem and invite attack on properly marked vehicles, and may also constitute the war crime of perfidy.[150]

If a medical vehicle is captured, the capturing party must ensure the care of any wounded and sick therein.[151] Upon capture, medical vehicles may be treated as booty of war. This means the captor may use them for any purpose, and is not obligated to use them for medical purposes. However, the capturing party is obligated to ensure that the wounded and sick in the vehicle are provided care and that any distinctive medical emblems have also been removed.[152]

The Wounded and Sick Convention does not require the use of the special emblem when transporting casualties. A party to the conflict may use whatever assets that are available to transport casualties. Indeed, it may be necessary to mix casualties and non-medical personnel and/or equipment in transport assets. When doing so, the transport may not be marked with the special emblem because it is not "exclusively engaged" in the medical transport function. Furthermore, tactical considerations may dictate the removal of special emblems.[153] For example, during an infiltration mission a commander may choose to remove or cover the Red Cross on a combat ambulance in order to mitigate the risk of enemy detection. However, it is important to note that whenever transport equipment is not marked, it will likely (and legitimately) be considered a lawful target by the enemy, even if it is in fact transporting the wounded and sick.

2. Medical Aircraft

Medical aircraft, defined as "aircraft exclusively employed for the removal of wounded and sick and for the transport of medical personnel and equipment,"[154] may not be attacked so long as they bear one of the appropriate distinctive emblems.[155] Like vehicles, aircraft may be permanently dedicated to medical use or may be assigned temporarily to such use. To remain protected during a relief mission, an aircraft must be used "exclusively" for medical purposes.[156]

---

150 *See* Protocol I, *supra* note 31, at art. 37(1)d.

151 GWS, *supra* note 1, at art. 35.

152 *See id.*

153 One tactical situation wherein a commander may order his medics not to wear the distinctive emblem is when the enemy makes a practice of *not* respecting the GWS's provisions protecting medical personnel and actually targets them. For example, during the Vietnam conflict,

> US soldiers claimed that the NVA and Vietcong targeted medical personnel because of their importance in maintaining morale. They'd shoot medics even if they were giving care. Consequently medics often avoided wearing armbands which acted as bulls-eyes. There were even reports that the Vietcong paid an incentive for killing medics.

Law of War Deskbook, *supra* note 38, at E-12. Under such circumstances, a commander might strongly consider ordering his medical personnel not to wear a distinctive emblem.

154 GWS, *supra* note 1, at art. 36.

155 *See id.* at art. 38.

156 Pictet states that exclusive engagement in medical operations means the aircraft must fly without any armament. *See* Pictet, *supra* note 4, at 289; *But see* Protocol I, *supra* note 31, at article

Unlike mobile or fixed units or vehicles, protection of medical aircraft is more dependent on agreements entered into by the belligerent parties to a conflict. These agreements are intended to provide notice to the parties regarding the routes and times of medical aircraft activity. Accordingly, the Wounded and Sick Convention requires parties to respect medical aircraft "while flying at heights, times and on routes specifically agreed upon between the belligerents concerned."[157] If no such agreement is in place, medical aircraft fly at their own risk.[158] Aircraft personnel may report information acquired incidentally to the aircraft's humanitarian mission; reporting such information does not cause the aircraft to lose its protection, and medical aircraft can search for the wounded and sick.[159] However, an aircraft on a humanitarian mission could not deviate from its mission so as to search for enemies.[160]

The only way that an adverse party can ensure that an aircraft bearing a distinctive medical emblem is not abusing the use of that emblem is by summoning the aircraft to land and inspecting its contents. Medical aircraft are obligated to obey any command to land.[161] The adverse party decides whether or not an aircraft is allowed to continue after summoning it to land and conducting an inspection.[162] In the event of an involuntary landing in enemy territory, the personnel aboard the aircraft, and any wounded and sick aboard, are treated as prisoners of war or retained personnel, depending on their status.[163] The adverse party retains

---

28(3) ("Medical aircraft shall not carry any armament except small arms and ammunition taken from the wounded, sick and shipwrecked on board ... and such light individual weapons as may be necessary to enable the medical personnel on board to defend themselves and the wounded, sick and shipwrecked in their charge.").

[157] *Id.* Professor Draper notes that "the speed of modern aircraft makes identification by colour or markings useless. Only previous agreement could afford any real safeguard." Draper, *supra* note 149, at 84.

[158] *See* Pictet, *supra* note 4, at 288. *See also* Law of War Deskbook, *supra* note 38, at E-20 (noting that, absent an agreement, medical aircraft fly at their own risk, and explaining "[t]his was certainly the case in Vietnam where 'any air ambulance pilot who served a full one year tour could expect to have his aircraft hit at least once by enemy fire.' 'Most of the Viet Cong and North Vietnamese clearly considered the air ambulances just another target.' ") (citations omitted).

[159] *Contra* Protocol I, *supra* note 31, at article 28(4) ("medical aircraft shall not, except by prior agreement with the adverse Party, be used to search for the wounded, sick and shipwrecked.")

[160] *See* Law of War Deskbook, *supra* note 38, at E-20–21, which discusses the occurrence of a medical aircraft, while working in furtherance of a humanitarian mission, gaining information that could be damaging to the enemy:

> Reporting information acquired incidentally to the aircraft's humanitarian mission does not cause the aircraft to lose its protection. Medical personnel are responsible for reporting information gained through casual observation of activities in plain view in the discharge of their duties. This does not violate the law of war or constitute grounds for loss of protected status ... For example, a Medevac aircraft could report the presence of an enemy patrol if the patrol was observed in the course of their regular mission and was not part of an information gathering mission outside their humanitarian duties.

[161] GWS, *supra* note 1, at art. 36.

[162] *See Id.*

[163] *See Id.*

the obligation to care for any wounded and sick aboard the aircraft.[164] Aircraft need not have been specially built for medical purposes to obtain protection as a medical aircraft; ordinary aircraft may be converted to medical use, and medical aircraft may be converted to other uses provided that the converted aircraft no longer bears distinctive medical emblems.[165]

The United States is obviously cautious whenever conducting air casualty search and evacuation missions. Because agreements to fly over enemy territory are almost never negotiated, such missions are conducted with full awareness of the risk of attack, but are nonetheless essential for prompt evacuation of friendly and captured enemy casualties. Flight over neutral airspace and landing on neutral territory in the case of necessity is generally permissible, although the aircraft may be subjected to identification and/or inspection requirements.[166] Aircraft flying above neutral territory should give notice of their passage and obey all commands to land, and will only be immune to attack if traveling on routes, at heights, and at times agreed upon between the parties to the conflict and the neutral.[167] Neutrals may place restrictions on medical aircraft, though the Wounded and Sick Convention advises that restrictions or conditions should apply to all parties to the conflict.[168] If any wounded and sick disembark into a neutral's territory, the neutral must detain the wounded and sick in a manner preventing them from taking part in the operation of war.[169]

Additional Protocol I included a number of provisions intended to update the law related to medical aircraft. The treaty added optional signals identifying medical aircraft,[170] and amended the right of a medical aircraft to fly over

---

[164] *See id.* at art. 12.

[165] *See* Dep't of the Army, Field Manual 27-10: The Law of Land Warfare ¶ 237(b) (July 1956) [hereinafter FM 27-10].

[166] GWS, *supra* note 1, at art. 37.

[167] *Id.* Though parties have a right to fly over neutral territory, they should always seek to establish an agreement with the neutral beforehand. This provision of Article 37 considers the competing interests at the time of drafting: "it did not seem possible to impose on a neutral State the duty of allowing the unconditional flight of aircraft over its territory. On the other hand, it did not seem feasible to leave neutral States at liberty to accord or refuse at will the access of medical aircraft to their territory." Pictet, *supra* note 4, at 295.

[168] GWS, *supra* note 1, at art. 37.

[169] *Id.*

[170] *See generally* Protocol I, *supra* note 31, at art. 18. In 1993, Annex I to Protocol I created a number of new signals to augment the distinctive emblems on an aircraft. These include the flashing blue light, radio signals, and use of a Secondary Surveillance Radar System, as well as special radio-communications signals and recognized international codes. *See* Annex I (to the Protocol I): Regulations Concerning Identification art. 6–12, Nov. 30, 1993, *available at* http://www.icrc.org/applic/ihl/ihl.nsf/Treaty.xsp?action=openDocument&documentId=A1D622EE77F6964A41256650004C9909. These markings "are merely intended to facilitate identification, and do not themselves confer protected status." Fleck, *supra* note 9, at 352. The Commentary to Protocol I states that the drafters recognized the limitations of pre-aircraft identification procedures, and stated that "adapting identification to modern combat techniques . . . was also of paramount importance, particularly for medical aircraft . . . Merely to have the emblem . . . painted on an aircraft seemed insufficient to ensure effective protection, having regard to modern means of warfare." Sandoz, *supra* note 15, at 224.

territory of a neutral power, requiring prior agreement to do so.[171] Additionally, it created three "overflight regimes" for medical aircraft, depending on the status of the terrain over which the aircraft is flying: friendly territory, a contact zone, or territory controlled by an adverse party.[172]

Article 25 covers land controlled by friendly forces and does not require agreement by the parties to the conflict.[173] However, agreement with or notice to an adverse party is encouraged, particularly if the flight plan brings medical aircraft into range of the adverse of party's surface-to-air weapons systems.[174]

Article 26 addresses medical aircraft in contact zones, especially areas "physically controlled by friendly forces and in and over those areas the physical control of which is not clearly established."[175] Article 26 emphasizes that aircraft safety can only be ensured by agreement between the parties.[176] If no agreement is made, the aircraft flies at its own risk.[177] Any party receiving a request for prior agreement must respond as rapidly as possible that the request and either agree, deny, or propose a

---

[171] *Compare* Protocol I, *supra* note 31, at art. 31(1) ("[e]xcept by prior agreement, medical aircraft shall not fly over or land on the territory of a neutral or other State not a Party to the conflict") *with* GWS, *supra* note 1, at art. 37 ("medical aircraft of Parties to the conflict may fly over the territory of neutral Powers, land on it in case of necessity, or use it as a port of call," subject to conditions or restrictions placed by the neutral powers).

[172] *See* Protocol I, *supra* note 31, at arts. 25–27.

[173] *See id.* at art. 25.

[174] *Id. See also* Sandoz, *supra* note 15, at 284 (noting that notification of status provides safety in and of itself, and is especially important when an aircraft enters the range of a surface-to-air weapon system).

[175] Protocol I, *supra* note 31, at art. 26(2). The Protocol defines "contact zone" as "any area on land where the forward elements of opposing forces are in contact with each other, especially where they are exposed to direct fire from the ground." *Id.* at art. 26(2). As noted in the commentary, the language of "in and above the contact zone" means that medical aircraft are protected both on the ground of a contact zone and when flying above a contact zone. *See* Sandoz, *supra* note 15, at 290. The forward zone is obviously more dangerous due to the presence of actual hostile contact between the parties and more limited mobility of the forces (compared to the rear zones of the battle area, which are less exposed to enemy contact and thus have greater freedom of movement). *See id.* at 288. The Commentary also notes that any portion of the contact zone controlled by enemy forces "is subject to the same rules as any area under the control of the adverse Party." *Id.* at 290.

[176] An agreement must state the proposed number of medical aircraft, their flight plans, and means of identification, and shall be understood to mean that every flight will be carried out in compliance with the restrictions on operations of medical aircraft in Article 28. *See* Protocol I, *supra* note 31, at art. 29. Sandoz notes that "[t]these three points 'must' be included in all notifications or requests for agreement although, as indicated in the commentary on Article 30 of the draft, this list is not exhaustive; the Parties sending the notification or the request for agreement may add other elements." Sandoz, *supra* note 15, at 309.

[177] Protocol I, *supra* note 31, at art. 26(1). However, medical aircraft operating in the absence of an agreement "shall nevertheless be respected after they have been recognized as such." *Id. See also* Sandoz, *supra* note 15, at 291. "Obviously there is a risk that members of the armed forces of the adverse Party might fire before recognizing that the aircraft are 'medical' aircraft, but as soon as they have recognized them as such, they are under a strict obligation to respect the aircraft . . . by violating this obligation, they would commit a grave breach." *Id.* Sandoz continues to note that in areas where control is not clearly established, the enemy may order the aircraft to land (so long as landing is actually possible in the area); if the aircraft refuses to comply with such an order, it loses the right to respect and may be targeted. *Id.* at 292.

reasonable alternative.[178] If the requesting party agrees to an alternative, it must give notice of its acceptance; upon acceptance of an agreement, both parties must disseminate the substance of the agreement to their military units and instruct those units about the means of identifying the medical aircraft in question.[179]

Article 27 states that medical aircraft flying over an area controlled by an adverse party are protected provided that prior agreements to medical flights have been properly obtained from the adverse party.[180] However, an aircraft that either flies over an adverse Party's territory without an agreement or deviates from the agreement must immediately attempt to identify itself and inform the adverse party of the circumstances, such as navigational error or emergency affecting the safety of the flight.[181] The adverse party must attempt to recognize the aircraft as medical in nature; after that has occurred, the party must either give the aircraft the order to land or take alternate measures that effectively protects the party's right to prevent use of its airspace without prior agreement.[182] In all circumstances, an aircraft identified as bearing a medical emblem should be given time to comply with any order given before the adverse party resorts to attack.[183]

In an effort to clarify rules related to air and missile warfare, the Program on Humanitarian Policy and Conflict Research at Harvard University convened a group of experts to develop The Air and Missile Warfare Manual (AMWM). This Manual is a "soft law" document that attempts to clarify the application of many of the rules related to medical aircraft.[184] Many of the AMWM's rules are applicable in both international armed conflict and non-international armed conflict situations.[185] Initially, the AMWM restates several other treaty provisions, including the requirement that weapons comply with the principle of distinction,[186] that weapons may not use bacterial, chemical, or poisonous components, lasers designed to inflict permanent blindness, or projectiles that produce fragments undetectable inside the human body.[187] Its major advancements are in the

---

[178] Protocol I, *supra* note 31, at art. 29.

[179] *Id.* There is a great concern for preserving the safety of medical aircraft in overflight zones. As such, prohibitions on medical aircraft flying over contact zones and areas controlled by an adverse party absent an explicit agreement are structured to minimize the dangers to medical aircraft. *See* Sandoz, *supra* note 15, at 294.

[180] Protocol I, *supra* note 31, at art. 27(1).

[181] *Id.* at art. 27(2).

[182] *Id.*

[183] *Id.* The purpose of Article 29(2) is "to prevent a tragic accident i.e., the shooting down of a medical aircraft, while taking into account the legitimate fears of the Parties to the conflict with regard to their security." Sandoz, *supra* note 15, at 296. Although Article 29 is designed to provide all possible measures and time to prevent such an attack, a party may resort to attack as a final solution to counter a perceived threat against its interests. *Id.*

[184] The Manual is available at http://www.ihlresearch.org/amw/manual/.

[185] Commentary to each AMWM Rule clarifies whether that Rule applies to international armed conflict or non-international armed conflicts.

[186] The principle of distinction requires that parties distinguish between military targets and the civilian population, and direct attacks only against military objectives. *See* Protocol I, *supra* note 31, at art. 48.

[187] *See* Harvard Program on Humanitarian Policy and Conflict Research, Manual on International Law Applicable to Air and Missile Warfare, With Commentary Rule 6 (2010) [hereinafter AMWM].

development of rules pertaining to aircraft; for instance, all civilian aircraft, even civilian aircraft belonging to the enemy, are entitled to protection from attack unless they constitute a military objective.[188] Although enemy nonmilitary aircraft may be protected from attack, they are still susceptible to non-attack interference, such as capture as a prize, interception, or inspection.

Medical aircraft, like medical personnel, transports, and facilities, are protected from attack "unless they commit or are used to commit, outside their humanitarian function, acts harmful to the enemy."[189] It is critically important for medical aircraft to be able to identify themselves as such in order to invoke their special protection. To facilitate identification, medical aircraft must bear both a distinctive emblem and appropriate national colors on upper, lower, and lateral surfaces.[190] Both the AMWM and Protocol I clarify that the presence of identifying markings does not confer protected status upon a medical aircraft; markings such as a distinctive emblem merely facilitate identification.[191] Protection is conveyed by status, and medical aircraft are protected even if they do not bear a distinctive emblem, so long as they can still be identified as medical in nature.[192]

The AMWM bestows specific protection from attack on medical aircraft, subject to the area-of-encounter rules described in Protocol I.[193] In and over areas controlled by the belligerent party that owns the medical aircraft or that party's allies, the protection accorded to medical aircraft is not dependent on enemy consent.[194]

However, over contact zones or enemy-controlled territory, prior express consent by the enemy is necessary to ensure full protection for the aircraft.[195] A request for consent should be accompanied by a flight plan to provide as much information as possible.[196] Should the enemy consent to the passage of a medical aircraft, the terms of consent must be strictly followed;[197] departure from the conditions means that the aircraft flies at its own risk.[198] If a medical aircraft flies

---

188 *Id.* at Rule 47. The Commentary to Rule 48 notes that during international armed conflicts, only the government's aircraft may be designated as military or state aircraft.

189 *Id.* at Rule 74. *Cf. id. with* Rule 83 ("Subject to Rule 74, a medical aircraft loses its specific protection from attack if it is engaged in acts harmful to the enemy.").

190 *Id.* at Rule 76. Medical aircraft should also employ additional methods of identification, whether from ad hoc agreements between the parties or utilizing the means described in Article 18(5) of Protocol I. *See id.* at Rule 76(b) cmt. 2.

191 *See id.* at Rule 76(d) ("[s]pecific protection must be conferred on a medical aircraft as soon as it is identified as such, even if the medical aircraft does not display the distinctive emblem and employs no additional means of identification.").

192 *Id.*

193 *See generally* Protocol I, *supra* note 31, at arts. 25–27.

194 AMWM, *supra* note 187, at Rule 77. Additionally, medical aircraft are protected whether in flight or on the ground. *See id.* at cmt. 5.

195 *Id.* at Rule 78.

196 *Id.* at Rule 78(b).

197 *Id.* at Rule 79. The Commentary notes that the AMWM's requirement to strictly follow all conditions for consent is a wider prohibition than Protocol I's that a medical aircraft will be protected so long as it does not engage in acts harmful to the enemy. *Id.* at Rule 79, cmt. 3. The Commentary emphasizes that "[e]ven . . . technical conditions must be adhered to." *Id.*

198 AMWM, *supra* note 187, at Rule 79 cmt. 2. Once identified as a medical aircraft, the aircraft must be respected by the enemy, even in the absence of an express agreement. *See id.* at Rule 78(a) cmts. 2–3.

over a contact zone or enemy territory without a prior agreement in place, the belligerent parties will not be held responsible if the aircraft is attacked by mistake.[199] If a medical aircraft deviates from the terms of an agreement or enters an area not covered by an agreement due to either navigational error or emergency, it must immediately attempt to identify itself and comply with any order given by enemy air traffic control; once identified as such, the medical aircraft cannot be attacked unless it fails to comply with orders given to it (i.e., orders to divert course or land) after a sufficient period of time to comply has elapsed.[200]

Even if the enemy consents to passage, it has the right to order medical aircraft to land for inspection.[201] Should it be confirmed that the aircraft has "engaged only in activities consistent with its medical status," the enemy must allow the aircraft to continue with its flight.[202] If inspection determines that the aircraft "engaged in activities inconsistent with its medical status, or if it has flown without or in breach of a prior agreement," then the enemy may seize the aircraft and treat anyone aboard in compliance with international armed conflict rules.[203] If an aircraft designated as a permanent medical aircraft is seized, the seizing party may only use that aircraft for medical purposes until the end of the armed conflict.[204] By contrast, aircraft designated as temporary medical aircraft may be repurposed so long as any distinctive emblems are removed and alternative means of identification, such as those outlined in Rule 76(b), are no longer utilized.[205]

Belligerent medical aircraft are prohibited from flying over the territory of a neutral absent a prior agreement with that neutral, unless the aircraft is exercising a right of transit passage "through straits used for international navigation or the right of archipelagic sea lanes passage."[206] In the absence of an agreement but in a situation of emergency or navigational error, the aircraft must attempt to identify

---

[199] *Id.* at Rule 78(a) cmt. 2. Notably, the medical aircraft does not lose its protected status; rather, the risk accrues because the medical aircraft may be fired upon before it can be identified as a medical aircraft. *Id.*

[200] *Id.* at cmt. 3.

[201] *Id.* at Rule 80(a). Orders to land must be obeyed, and aircraft may be ordered to land even if the parties have entered into an express agreement permitting passage of the aircraft. *See id.* at cmt. 2.

[202] *See id.* at Rule 80(a)–(b). Notably, this rule requires that a medical aircraft be allowed to continue its flight, while GWS merely states that the aircraft *may* be allowed to continue on. *Compare id.*, at Rule 80(b), *and* Protocol I, *supra* note 31, at art. 30(3) (stating that the medical aircraft *shall* be allowed to continue after being ordered to land, so long as the inspection reveals that the aircraft was not in violation of its role as a medical aircraft or any travel conditions) *with* GWS, *supra* note 1, at art. 36 (stating that the medical aircraft *may* be allowed to continue after landing, regardless of inspection).

[203] *See* AMWM, *supra* note 187, at Rule 80(c). The occupants are entitled to treatment as POWs and/or RPs, whichever is applicable, and the detaining party assumes responsibility for providing medical care to any wounded and sick aboard the aircraft. *Id.* at cmt. 3. The Commentary notes that if the detaining party is unable to care for wounded and sick on-board the aircraft, it may have to allow the aircraft to continue on its flight.

[204] *Id.* at Rule 80(d); *see also id.* at cmt. 2.

[205] *Id.* at cmt. 3.

[206] *Id.* at Rule 84.

itself; once it is identified as a medical aircraft, the aircraft may not be attacked by the neutral but the neutral may order the aircraft to land for inspection.[207]

The AMWM explicitly provides that a medical aircraft may be equipped with "deflective defenses" such as flares or chaff, but equipping a heavy weapon such as a machine gun (which could be used either offensively or defensively) could either cause complete forfeiture of protection or, at the least, erosion of the status of the protective emblem.[208] Although a medical aircraft may be equipped to send or receive encrypted information for navigation, identification, and communication purposes "consistent with the execution of its humanitarian mission," it may not mount or use equipment to collect or transfer intelligence harmful to the enemy, as this would remove it from the category of exclusive use as a medical transport.[209] Carrying or using any such equipment may cause the medical aircraft to lose its specific protection.[210]

Further, the AMWM draws a distinction between military-operated medical aircraft (engaged exclusively in the transport of the wounded and sick) and military search-and-rescue aircraft.[211] The former receive all the protection accorded the distinctive emblem, but the latter do not, and may not bear the distinctive emblem. Medical aircraft are also forbidden from acting as search-and-rescue aircraft in combat areas; if they do so, they are treated as unprotected and fly at their own risk.[212]

III. Conclusion

Protection of the wounded and sick is perhaps the most obvious manifestation of the principle of humanity. The history of warfare is replete with examples of

---

[207] *Id.* at Rule 85(a). This rule mirrors provisions made for aircraft operating in enemy territory during an emergency, including the provision requiring the detaining neutral to allow the aircraft to continue on once inspected and determined to be a medical aircraft. *Id.* If revealed not to be a medical aircraft, it may be seized and its occupants detained. *Id.* at (b). *See also* Protocol I, *supra* note 31, at art 31(3) (providing guidelines for inspection, and restating the continued obligation of a detaining neutral to provide for the care of any wounded and sick aboard a medical aircraft during the term of inspection).

[208] *See* AMWM, *supra* note 187, at Rule 82; *see also id.* at cmt. 1, 5.

[209] *See id.* at Rule 81; Protocol I, *supra* note 31, at art. 28(2) ("[m]edical aircraft shall not be used to collect or transmit intelligence data and shall not carry any equipment intended for such purposes"). The Commentary to the AMWM emphasizes that merely possessing equipment designed to collect or transmit intelligence harmful to the enemy is "prohibited because it is difficult to prove in practice that an aircraft actually collected or transmitted such information." AMWM, *supra* note 187, at Rule 81 cmt. 2.

[210] AMWM, *supra* note 187, at Rule 83.

[211] *Id.* at Rule 86. Military aircraft on search-and-rescue missions are deemed to be engaged in combat activities. *See id.* at Rule 86(a) cmts. 1–2. Civilian aircraft engaged in such activities are generally protected in the same manner as other civilian aircraft, and do not gain the specific manner of medical aircraft. *Id.* at cmt. 3.

[212] *Id.* at Rule 86(b); *see also* Protocol I, *supra* note 31, at art. 28(4). This rule is tempered by the parties' ability to commit to an agreement authorizing medical aircraft to conduct search-and-rescue functions without losing their protected status. *See id.*

the willingness of belligerents to come to the aid of their suffering comrades *and* enemies. The Wounded and Sick Convention establishes rules to facilitate this humanitarian action, rules that are among the most widely known and respected and deeply woven into the fabric of the LOAC. Indeed, attacking personnel, facilities, or equipment marked with the emblems of special protection established by the law would legitimately be considered *malum in se*, leaving virtually no room for doubt about the illegality of such attacks even for the most inexperienced soldier. The core of these protections applies today in all armed conflicts, and in many ways these protections establish an acceptable minimum, with parties often striving to enhance the protections for wounded and sick beyond that strictly required by the law.

It is therefore essential that military planners contemplate the scope of the obligations related to the wounded and sick, plan accordingly, and ensure personnel are properly trained and resourced to meet these obligations. Like so many other areas of the law, compliance will often become more challenging as operational situations mature. For the soldier on the front line, it is axiomatic that individuals marked with the Red Cross or similar protective emblem must not be subjected to attack. But issues related to collection, evacuation, interment, record-keeping, equality of care, location of facilities, air evacuation, or dual use of equipment present far more complex issues. Commanders and medical officers will therefore invariably turn to legal advisors to assist them in resolving these issues. Competence in the law that guides resolution is therefore equally essential to the JAG officer, for few LOAC violations will be more corrosive to the credibility of the operation than those that compromise the protections of the wounded and sick.

19 }

Belligerent Occupation

Marc Warren*

I. Introduction

This chapter outlines the legal framework applicable to modern belligerent occupation. It will then use examples from the occupation of Iraq in 2003–2004 to highlight some of the significant issues that arise during occupation, and the law related to resolution of such issues. The chapter concludes by examining the role of military legal advisors involved in the interagency (and frequently intergovernmental) process of planning and executing the administration of occupied territory.

The law of occupation applies when an invading army takes effective control of enemy territory. "Military occupation is a matter of fact." So observes the U.S. Army's classic Field Manual, The Law of War.[1] The short sentence was prescient, suggesting that occupation—and the law of occupation—is triggered by conditions on the ground that cannot be dismissed by politics or propaganda.[2]

---

* Marc Warren is a senior counsel in the Aviation and Administrative Law & Regulatory practice groups in Crowell & Moring's Washington, DC office. Prior to joining Crowell & Moring, Marc served as acting chief counsel of the Federal Aviation Administration (FAA). He served in the U.S. Army Judge Advocate General's Corps, from which he retired in 2007 after having been selected for promotion to brigadier general. Marc's military service included assignments as the senior legal officer for Multi-National Forces Iraq, V Corps, 101st Airborne Division (Air Assault), and Joint Special Operations Command. Marc received a BA and JD from the University of Florida; an LLM from The Judge Advocate General's School, U.S. Army; and a master of strategic studies (2002) from the U.S. Army War College; he is also an adjunct professor at The George Washington University Law School.

[1] U.S. Dep't of the Army, Field Manual 27–10: The Law of Land Warfare ¶ 355 (July 1, 1956 with change 1 July 15, 1976) [hereinafter Field Manual 27-10], *available at* http://Armypubs.army.mil/doctrine/Dr_Pubs/Dr_A/PDF/FM27_10.pdf.

[2] Dismissal or even denial of occupation has been an unintended consequence of the Fourth Geneva Convention, with occupiers seeking to evade the obligations imposed toward civilians by the Convention, as well as to avoid the political stigma associated with Israel's occupation of Palestine. Modern reluctance to acknowledge an occupation is in contrast to earlier concerns that "eager invaders would declare an area occupied prematurely" in order to exercise control over the enemy's strategic resources. *See* Eyal Bienvenisti & Guy Keinan, *The War in Iraq: A Legal Analysis;*

Occupation presupposes the existence of both an enemy state and a state of belligerency. There is no occupation unless the military forces of one state exercise effective control over the territory of a second state. Belligerent occupation must follow armed conflict, but may occur without actual combat as long as the presence of invading forces is against the will of the occupied state.[3]

Occupation is essentially provisional and does not imply a permanent transfer of sovereignty, but a temporary transfer of control; it is "invasion plus taking firm possession of enemy territory for the purpose of holding it."[4] In his authoritative book on belligerent occupation, Yoram Dinstein observes that "everything depends on whether or not (1) The contested area is solidly seized by the invader, and (2) The sovereign is actually displaced."[5]

The U.S. Military Tribunal at Nuremberg defined the threshold for belligerent occupation in the *Hostages* case:

> Whether an invasion has developed into an occupation is a question of fact. The term invasion implies a military operation while an occupation indicates the exercise of governmental authority to the exclusion of the established government. This presupposes the destruction of organized resistance and the establishment of an administration to preserve law and order. To the extent that the occupant's control is maintained and that of the civil government is eliminated, the area will be said to be occupied.[6]

In the first Gulf War against Iraq in 1990, the rapid pace and limited objectives of the Coalition invasion meant that there was little time to establish and maintain effective control of occupied territory. The presence of the invasion forces was too limited by time to exercise the authority of an occupier. In 2003, however, the situation was different. Coalition Forces invaded Iraq to accomplish "regime change" and displaced not only the authority of the enemy state but the enemy government in its entirety. Despite their reluctance to embrace the term "occupation," the United States and the United Kingdom were occupiers of Iraq as a matter of fact. As a result, the law of occupation imposed rights and responsibilities, supplemented by the authority of the United Nations, which serve as a primer on modern occupation practice.

---

ch. XIII The Occupation of Iraq: A Reassessment, 86 Int'l L. Studies 263, 264 (Raul "Pete" Pedrozo ed., 2010).

[3] Geneva Convention Relative to the Protection of Civilian Persons in Time of War, Aug. 12, 1949, 6 U.S.T. 3516, 75 U.N.T.S. 287, art. 2 [hereinafter GC IV].

[4] Field Manual 27-10, *supra* note 1, ¶ 352.

[5] Yoram Dinstein, The International Law of Belligerent Occupation 38 (2009).

[6] Hostages trial (List et al.), US Military Tribunal, Nuremberg, 8 LRTWC 34, 55 (1948).

II. The Law of Occupation

A. GENERAL OVERVIEW

The law of occupation is found in at least four sources: customary international law, the Hague Regulations, the Fourth Geneva Convention, and Additional Protocol I to the Geneva Conventions.[7] An emerging fifth source may very well be actions of the United Nations that modify traditional occupation law. The primary treaty law references for occupation are the Hague Regulations and the Fourth Geneva Convention. The Hague Regulations in particular presuppose the occupier as "trustee"[8] of property in occupied territory, and the Geneva Conventions impose upon the occupier the duty as protector of the civilians within that territory. Both treaties impose rights and responsibilities upon the occupier, the most important being the duty to restore security, stated in Article 43 of the Hague Regulations:

> The authority of the legitimate power having in fact passed into the hands of the occupant, the latter shall take all the measures in his power to restore, and ensure, as far as possible, public order and safety, while respecting, unless absolutely prevented, the laws in force in the country.[9]

The responsibility to establish security stems from historical experience establishing that lawlessness will occur as the lights go out and police leave their posts, and social order fractures when state authority and control are absent in the aftermath of combat.

The concept of occupier as "trustee" has changed over time. Originally, the occupier was to act as "administrator and usufructuary" for the property within the former enemy state, preserving the status quo ante in occupied territory as much as practicable, consistent with security.[10] With the emergence of "popular sovereignty," the occupier became a trustee for the people in the territory of the former enemy state rather than for the state itself. The change in the occupier's focus as trustee from "things" to "people" is demonstrated by the difference between the emphasis of the Hague Regulations on preserving institutions and of the Geneva Conventions on protecting persons.[11]

---

[7] Dinstein, *supra* note 5, at 4.

[8] *But see id.* at 36 (asserting that it is wrong to suggest that an occupier can or should administer an occupied territory as a trustee as there is no trust between an occupying army and the occupied population).

[9] Hague Convention No. IV Respecting the Laws and Customs of War on Land and its Annex: Regulations concerning the Laws and Customs of War on Land, Oct. 18, 1907, 36 Stat. 2277, 205 Consol. T.S. 277 [hereinafter HR IV].

[10] *Id.* art. 55.

[11] Put another way, the "Hague Tradition" focuses on regulating the means and methods of warfare (i.e., on targeting), and the "Geneva Tradition" focuses on protections for the victims of war. International and Operational Law Dep't, The Judge Advocate General's School, Law of War Deskbook 17, 18 (Jeff Bovarnick et al. eds., Jan. 2010).

As much as the emergence of popular sovereignty, the creation of the United Nations has impacted the traditional concept of the occupier as trustee. While the legal responsibilities of an occupier are triggered independent of any action of the United Nations, the rights of the occupier may be dramatically increased by the United Nations. In other words, the law of occupation applies regardless of whether a military action is authorized by the United Nations (and even regardless of whether the use of force precipitating the occupation is lawful under the United Nations Charter), but recent practice establishes that the United Nations can empower an occupier to act in a manner that would be considered ultra vires for an occupier acting as traditional conservator or trustee.[12] The United Nations may authorize an occupier to transform former enemy territory in a manner and to an extent that would not have been authorized by the historical application of occupation law.[13]

Occupation begins with effective control of former enemy territory. Surrender of the territory is not required. It is only necessary that the control of the former enemy state in the territory at issue has been effectively supplanted by the control of the invading state.[14] What constitutes "effective control" is a matter of debate and significance, because it triggers the application of the rights and responsibilities of occupation law.[15] Even before occupation law applies, the contested territory of the former enemy state is not in legal limbo. International humanitarian law protects persons and property in a combat zone regardless of whether the specific law of occupation has been triggered, but the *lex specialis* of occupation law imposes more specific standards and duties for the occupier (and greater protections and obligations for civilians in occupied territory) than does international humanitarian law generally.[16]

Just as an enemy state does not have to blanket its territory with security forces in order to assert sovereignty within its borders, so too an occupier need not have its invading army on every street corner in order to exercise effective control of former enemy territory. It is sufficient that the occupier is able to exercise active and effective control of territory where its actions have rendered the

---

[12] Departures from the conservationist principle should be viewed with caution, if not skepticism. Undertaken with U.N. authority in Iraq, unilateral transformative occupation cannot be undertaken by an occupier without running afoul of the law of occupation. *See* Gregory H. Fox, *Transformative Occupation and the Unilateralist Impulse*, 94 INT'L REV. OF THE RED CROSS 237 (Spring 2012).

[13] "Taken as a whole, the purposes of the occupation as outlined in [U.N. Security Council] Resolution 1483 went beyond the confines of the Hague Regulations and the Fourth Geneva Convention." Adam Roberts, *Transformative Military Occupation: Applying the Laws of War and Human Rights*, 100 A. J. INT'L L. 580, 613 (2006).

[14] "Territory is considered occupied when it is actually placed under the authority of the hostile army. The occupation extends only to the territory where such authority has been established and can be exercised." *Id.* art. 42.

[15] "[B]elligerent occupation must be both actual and effective, that is, the organized resistance must have been overcome and the force in possession must have taken measures to establish its authority." Field Manual 27-10, *supra* note 1, ¶ 356.

[16] "*Lex specialis*, thus, truly brings about specialization." DINSTEIN, *supra* note 5, at 88.

former enemy state unable to exercise control.[17] Essentially, where the invading army has created a vacuum of authority that it is capable of filling, it is under a legal duty to fill the vacuum with its own authority. The substantive law of occupation establishes the duty and, as augmented by the United Nations, establishes the scope of authority.

An invading army may be unable to exercise effective control because of the intensity of combat or because its forces are rapidly moving through the former enemy territory. Air and naval forces alone are unable to exercise effective control over territory.[18] In general, as long as invading forces remain in sustained combat with the military forces of the former enemy state, occupation law is not applicable in the zone of combat. Battle areas are not considered to be occupied territory.[19]

Occupation law may not be applicable in other areas as well. The invading army may be unable to exercise effective control over portions of former enemy territory where fighting has waned, because its attention and resources are devoted to prosecution of combat against enemy military forces in other areas. On the other hand, an invading army should not be able to avoid its status as an occupier simply by choosing to move its forces out of an area, particularly if it is able to reassert its control at any time, or by claiming to exercise control over former enemy territory but not authority over its population.[20]

The advent of highly mobile forces and sophisticated aerial surveillance and targeting platforms make it conceivable to have military supremacy over territory without exercising any authority over its people. This leaves the civilian population to fend for itself and is contrary to the implication of the Hague Regulations and the Fourth Geneva Convention that control over territory carries with it responsibility over the population.[21] Unfortunately, the issue has been clouded not only by emerging technology, but by the International Court of Justice (ICJ). In the *Armed Activities* case arising from Uganda's military operations in the Democratic Republic of the Congo (DRC), the ICJ held that Uganda did not occupy all of the DRC because it did not exercise "direct control" over parts of the population despite exercising military control over all of the territory.[22]

---

[17] "It is sufficient that the occupying force can, within a reasonable time, send detachments of troops to make its authority felt within the occupied district. It is immaterial whether the authority of the occupant is maintained by fixed garrisons or flying columns, whether by large or small forces, so long as the occupation is effective." Field Manual 27-10, *supra* note 1, ¶ 356.

[18] This is not to say that forces based on ships and moving by air could not maintain an effective occupation in some circumstances, but an occupation cannot be maintained by ships and aircraft. Air or maritime supremacy does not establish governmental authority over occupied territory. "[I]t is palpable that the Occupying Power must deploy 'boots' on the ground in or near the territory that is under occupation." Dinstein, *supra* note 5, at 44.

[19] *Prosecutor v. Naletilic & Martinovic*, Case No. IT-98-34-T, ICTY, Trial Chamber ¶ 217 (Mar. 31, 2003), *cited in* Dinstein, *supra* note 5, at 38.

[20] *See Case concerning Armed Activities on the Territory of the Congo (Congo, Uganda)*, 2005, 45 I.L.M. 271 (2006) [hereinafter Armed Activities case].

[21] Bienvenisti & Keinan, *supra* note 2, at 265.

[22] Armed Activities case, *supra* note 20.

The point in time where effective control has been established is imprecise, and practice has allowed for reasonable interpretation of what constitutes effective control. In general, once enemy military forces have been defeated and the enemy regime has been removed, occupation law applies presumptively. Even then, the occupier may be faced with continued resistance and hampered by the lack of sufficient planning and resources devoted to the occupation, although neither relieves the occupier of its legal obligations. An occupation continues despite an insurgency or resistance movement, as long as the invading army is not forcibly displaced from the former enemy territory for a significant period of time.[23]

Although not required to make an occupation legally effective, a Proclamation of Occupation may be used to announce the fact of occupation. A Proclamation clearly states who is in charge and what is expected of the civilian population. A Proclamation was prepared for use by Coalition Forces in Iraq in 2003, but never published.[24]

An occupier is under the legal duty to administer occupied territory in a manner that comports with The Hague Regulations and the Fourth Geneva Convention. Significant obligations are imposed on occupiers to:

1) Restore and maintain law and order, following to the extent practicable the laws that were in effect in the former enemy territory;
2) Protect civilians and property;
3) Provide essential governmental services necessary for the health and safety of the civilian population.

The occupier should set the conditions for a peaceful restoration of authority to a successor government at the end of a prolonged occupation.[25] The instrument by which an occupier administers occupied territory need not follow any particular form.[26] An occupation of short duration may require no more than

---

[23] Field Manual 27-10, *supra* note 1, ¶ 360.

[24] Instead, General Tommy Franks, Commander of Coalition Forces, issued a "Freedom Message" to the Iraqi people on April 16, 2003. The Message had characteristics of a Proclamation and announced the establishment of the "Coalition Provisional Authority to exercise powers of government temporarily, and as necessary, especially to provide security . . ." General Tommy R. Franks, American Soldier 528 (2004). However, the Message muddied the clear message of occupation by proclaiming that "Coalition forces have come as liberators . . . ."

[25] At the end of a short-term occupation, the occupying forces may simply leave former enemy territory, returning the territory to the control of the displaced sovereign. What to do when there is no apparent legitimate successor government is a difficult question, essentially triggering an examination of whether a transformative occupation is necessary to set the conditions for competent governance and respect for the human rights of the population. This conundrum, pitting the constraints of traditional occupation law against transformative occupation, was identified by Sir Adam Roberts (Roberts, *supra* note 13). From a military perspective, whether or not there is transformative occupation, there must be some form of transitional authority. *See* U.S. Dep't of the Army, Field Manual 3-07: Stability Operations ch. 5 (Oct. 6, 2008) [hereinafter Field Manual 3-07], *available at* http://armypubs.army.mil/doctrine/DR_pubs/dr_a/pdf/fm3_07.pdf.

[26] Dinstein, *supra* note 5, at 55.

the military forces present for the invasion; a long-term occupation will likely necessitate a military government, or what the U.S. Army's Stability Operations Field Manual euphemistically calls a "transitional military authority."[27] In Iraq, the Coalition Provisional Authority (CPA) served this purpose, although imperfectly.[28] Regardless of the title, the occupation administration will restore and maintain public order, ensure the safety and security of the local populace, and provide essential civil services.[29]

Obligations relating to security are the most difficult for the occupier because they relate not only to legal requirements, but to practical, even moral, duties. Although an occupying power is not a guarantor of public order and safety, it has a duty to protect civilians by restoring stability and security and, to the extent it is achievable, a sense of normalcy within the occupied territory. The Fourth Geneva Convention recites the duties of the occupier, as well as the protections to be accorded to the civilian population.[30]

In maintaining public order and safety, an occupier must respect, unless absolutely prevented, the civil and criminal laws of the occupied territory.[31] An occupier may suspend or terminate local laws if their continued effect would jeopardize the security of the occupation forces or create obstacles to the application of the Fourth Geneva Convention.[32] Where necessary to maintain public order and safety or to protect the occupation forces, an occupier may legislate by means of occupation ordinances or orders.[33] These penal provisions may address security-related offenses and prescribe punishments for their violation. Examples include criminalizing the possession of certain weapons and enhancing the punishment for specified criminal offenses. Penal provisions may not be retroactive, and must be published to the populace in the local language.[34] An occupier may also provide for adjudication of offenses, either by referral of offenses to local courts or by establishment of occupation courts, a form of military commission.[35]

---

[27] Field Manual 3-07, *supra* note 25.

[28] "When the CPA was established as a civilian entity, military commanders suffered a diminution of their authority to administer and exercise the rights of occupation, with no reduction in their legal responsibilities." Marc Warren, *The War in Iraq: A Legal Analysis; ch. X The"Fog of Law": The Law of Armed Conflict in Operation Iraqi Freedom*, 86 INT'L L. STUDIES 167, 187 (Raul "Pete" Pedrozo ed., 2010).

[29] Field Manual 3-07, *supra* note 25, ¶ 5–8.

[30] "The paramount purpose of the Convention was to provide this population [in occupied territory] with enhanced protection . . ." DINSTEIN, *supra* note 5, at 6.

[31] Hague IV, *supra* note 9, art. 43.

[32] GC IV, *supra* note 3, art. 64.

[33] The occupier has "the right to enact provisions necessary to maintain the orderly government of the territory in its capacity as the Power responsible for public law and order," as well as "penal provisions for its own protection." INT'L COMM. OF THE RED CROSS COMMENTARY, IV GENEVA CONVENTION RELATIVE TO THE PROTECTION OF CIVILIAN PERSONS IN TIME OF WAR 337 (Jean S. Pictet et al. eds., 1958) [hereinafter Pictet].

[34] GC IV, *supra* note 3, art. 65.

[35] Military commissions and tribunals were preserved when Congress passed the Uniform Code of Military Justice (UCMJ). *See* UCMJ, art. 21.

If required for imperative reasons of security, an occupier may assign civilians to specific residences or to internment camps.[36] Internment more typically occurs for individuals detained for "security offenses" committed against occupation forces.[37] Because internment could be misused as a means of arbitrary or indefinite extrajudicial detention, the Fourth Geneva Convention mandates reconsideration, review, and appeal processes.[38] Despite the process, internment is a difficult area, as demonstrated by the experiences of Coalition Forces in Iraq in 2003.[39]

When civilians in occupied territory take up arms against occupation forces, they may be prosecuted for violations of local law, as well as for violations of occupation ordinances or orders.[40] Because civilians in occupied territory have a duty to refrain from hostilities, those who participate in an insurgency are unlawful combatants and are therefore accorded no legal privilege (and, as a result, no legal immunity) for their warlike acts.[41] Although unlawful combatants, insurgents in occupied territory remain civilians.[42] Occupation forces may not impose any mass punishment on the civilian population because of an insurgency,[43] but may use force both in self-defense and to defeat the insurgency. The use of force against insurgents in occupied territory is complicated by the nuanced law on targeting civilians who are taking part in hostilities.[44]

---

[36] GC IV, *supra* note 3, art. 78.

[37] U.S. Army Regulation 190-8 prescribes procedures for internment, and states that it is only authorized when: "(1) Internment has been determined by competent U.S. Military authority to be necessary for imperative reasons of security to the United States Armed Forces in the occupied territory; (2) Internment has been directed by a properly constituted U.S. military court sitting in the occupied territory as the sentence for conviction of an offense in violation of penal provisions issued by the occupying U.S. ARMED FORCES." U.S. DEP'T OF ARMY, ARMY REGULATION 190–8: ENEMY PRISONERS OF WAR, RETAINED PERSONNEL, CIVILIAN INTERNEES AND OTHER DETAINEES (Oct. 1, 1997), para. 5-1b.

[38] The processes require reconsideration of internment actions as soon as possible by a court or board established for that purpose, and a defined procedure that includes a right of appeal and periodic review by a competent body, every six months if possible. GC IV, *supra* note 3, arts. 43, 78.

[39] *See* DONALD P. WRIGHT & TIMOTHY R. REESE, ON POINT II: TRANSITION TO THE NEW CAMPAIGN, THE UNITED STATES ARMY IN OPERATION IRAQI FREEDOM MAY 2003–JANUARY 2005 ch. 6 (2008) [hereinafter ON POINT II].

[40] GC IV, *supra* note 3, art. 64.

[41] *See, e.g.*, Richard R. Baxter, *So-Called "Unprivileged Belligerency": Spies, Guerillas, and Saboteurs*, 18 BRIT. Y.B. INT'L L. 323, 328, and 338 (1951).

[42] *See Public Committee against Torture in Israel v. Israel* (Supreme Court of Israel, sitting as the High Court of Justice, 2006) 46 I.L.M. 375 (2007).

[43] Hague IV, *supra* note 9, art. 50; GC IV, *supra* note 3, art. 33.

[44] Civilians directly participating in hostilities may be directly attacked. What constitutes direct (versus indirect) participation in hostilities, as well as the duration of the consequence for direct participation (i.e., whether a civilian who took part in hostilities remains lawfully targetable or regains his protection as a civilian when he ceases direct participation), are difficult issues in a counterinsurgency campaign unresolved by emerging law or ICRC guidance. *See* Protocol Additional to the Geneva Conventions of August 12, 1949, and Relating to the Protection of Victims of International Armed Conflicts, art. 51, June 8, 1977, 1125 U.N.T.S. 17512 [hereinafter AP I]; INT'L COMM. OF THE RED CROSS, COMMENTARY ON THE ADDITIONAL PROTOCOLS OF 8 JUNE 1977 TO THE GENEVA CONVENTIONS OF 12 AUGUST 1949 618 (Yves Sandoz et al. eds., 1987); INT'L COMM. OF THE RED CROSS, INTERPRETIVE GUIDANCE ON THE NOTION OF DIRECT PARTICIPATION IN HOSTILITIES

A. THE FOURTH GENEVA CONVENTION

Often called the "Civilians Convention" or the "Occupation Convention," the Fourth Geneva Convention had no predecessor in the 1929 Geneva Conventions. New in 1949, it was intended to supplement or "amplify" the Hague Regulations in order to address the horrific abuses of the civilian population during occupations in World War II.[45] As such, it should be read in concert with the Hague Regulations. The Convention applies in all cases of partial or total occupation of the territory of a High Contracting Party, even if the occupation meets with no armed resistance.[46]

The official text of the Convention is divided into parts, sections, and articles.[47] Margin notes identify the general topic of each article. More in-depth information about the Convention is contained in the Official Commentary, although practitioners in search of the answer to a specific question may be disappointed, because the Commentary is a conference history rather than an implementing manual.[48] With regard to manuals, the U.S., German and UK field manuals on the law of war are excellent references on occupation, even if they reflect different views on aspects of the Convention.[49] A pragmatic contemporary analysis of occupation law is contained in a recently published textbook, *The Law of Armed Conflict: An Operational Approach*.[50]

An occupier must safeguard civilians, restore security, and stabilize occupied territory. The significant articles of the Fourth Geneva Convention can be organized into four groups, three of which correspond to the occupier's essential tasks of Safeguard, Secure, and Stabilize. A fourth group, Supervise, includes articles that afford the means to oversee compliance with the Convention. Although there is considerable overlap among the groups, a practical organization affords a vehicle for comment. The following provides the pertinent text.

1. An Occupier Must Safeguard Civilians

- Article 4, Definition of Protected Persons. Although Article 4 does not use the word "civilian," it excludes persons protected by the other three Geneva Conventions, thus leaving only civilians within its scope. However, not all civilians are protected by the Convention in its entirety (nationals of an Occupying Power and nationals of a state which is

---

UNDER INTERNATIONAL HUMANITARIAN LAW (Nils Melzer ed., 2009), *available at* http://www.icrc.org/ eng/assets /files/other/icrc-002-0990.pdf [hereinafter ICRC INTERPRETIVE GUIDANCE].

[45] "At the end of the Second World War, unprecedented as it was in extent, the time had obviously come to revise the Geneva Conventions once more and extend them in the light of experience." Pictet, *supra* note 33, at 6.

[46] GC IV, *supra* note 3, art. 2.

[47] *Id.*, Section IV, Regulations for the Treatment of Internees, is further subdivided into chapters.

[48] *See generally* Pictet, *supra* note 33.

[49] *See, e.g.*, Bienvenisti & Keinan, *supra* note 2, at 265.

[50] *See generally* GEOFFREY S. CORN ET AL., THE LAW OF ARMED CONFLICT: AN OPERATIONAL APPROACH ch. 11 (2012).

not bound by the Convention are not protected, nor are nationals of neutral and co-belligerent states while their state has normal diplomatic relations with the state in whose hands they find themselves). Article 4 must be read in concert with Article 13, which affords the general protections of Part II of the Convention to "the whole of the populations of the countries in conflict . . . and are intended to alleviate the sufferings caused by war."[51] From a practical standpoint, almost all civilians in occupied territory should be presumed to be "protected persons" covered by the Convention.[52] An exception is the national of a country not party to the conflict who enters occupied territory to commit acts of terrorism or engage in hostilities. These "foreign fighters" are not covered by the Convention as protected persons, but are still civilians, albeit unlawful combatants, who must be treated humanely.[53]

- Article 31, Prohibition of Coercion. Article 31 prohibits "physical or moral coercion" against protected persons, in particular to obtain information from them or from third parties.[54] This Article is similar to Article 17 of the Third Geneva Convention, which prohibits coercion in the interrogation of prisoners of war, but has a much broader impact because it applies to circumstances outside of captivity.[55] Soldiers must be trained not to threaten or pressure civilians to obtain information about insurgents or terrorists. Prohibited coercion may be subtle, and can occur with a veiled threat that family members will not be released from detention unless cooperation or information is forthcoming.[56]
- Article 32, Prohibition of Corporal Punishment, Torture, etc. This Article prohibits "any measure of such a character as to cause the physical suffering or extermination of protected persons" and specifically proscribes "murder, torture, corporal punishment, mutilation and medical and scientific experiments not necessitated by the medical

[51] GC IV, *supra* note 3, art. 13.

[52] The first paragraph of GC Article 4 states: "Persons protected by the Convention are those who, at a given moment and in any manner whatsoever, find themselves, in case of a conflict or occupation, in the hands of a Party to the conflict or Occupying Power of which they are not nationals." The language is deliberately broad, and means that the protections of the Convention are triggered by a covered civilian's mere presence in occupied territory rather than by the civilian's detention or internment by the Occupying Power. *See Prosecutor v. Tadic*, Case No. IT-94-1-T (ICTY, Trial Chamber, May 7, 1997), 36 I.L.M. 908, 924 (2007).

[53] At a minimum, "foreign fighters" must be accorded the protections of Common Article 3 of the Geneva Conventions. *See infra* note 65 and accompanying text.

[54] GC IV, *supra* note 3, art. 31.

[55] However, "the prohibition only applies in so far as the other provisions of the Convention do not implicitly or explicitly authorize a resort to coercion. Thus, Article 31 is subject to the unspoken reservation that force is permitted whenever it is necessary to use it in the application of measures taken under the Convention. This power is embodied and expressed particularly in penal legislation and in the control and security regulations enacted by the belligerents and to which protected persons are subject." Pictet, *supra* note 33, at 220.

[56] Article 31 prohibits coercion, direct or indirect, for any purpose or reason, and the obtaining of information is only given as an example. Pictet, *supra* note 33, at 19, 220.

treatment of a protected person."[57] Significantly, it also prohibits "any other measures of brutality whether applied by military or civilian agents."[58] The last prohibition is an important and prescient catch-all because it includes detainee abuse that does not rise to the level of torture, as well as maltreatment by nonmilitary personnel such as contractors and local hires.[59]

2. An Occupier Must Restore Security
   - Article 5, Derogations. Article 5 is an extremely important provision because it pertains to security and forfeiture of protections. It must be read carefully, not only because of the general caution that should always apply to derogations, or exceptions, but because the language is misleading. The first paragraph would seem to authorize a party to the conflict the prerogative to deny the rights and privileges of the Convention to persons definitely suspected of or engaging in activities hostile to the security of the state.[60] The second paragraph contains a more modest derogation that allows an occupying power, in cases where absolute military security so requires, to deny rights of communication to a person detained as a "spy or saboteur" or under definite suspicion of activity hostile to the security of the occupying power[61] (in modern parlance, the category of "saboteur" includes a terrorist or guerilla.)[62] The distinction between the two paragraphs is best made by example. In the case of the Iraq war, the first paragraph would have applied to an Iraqi detained in the United States ("in the territory of a Party to the conflict"); the second paragraph would apply in Iraq ("in occupied territory"). As a practical matter, applying the derogation of the first paragraph in occupied territory would gut many of the Convention's protections for persons interned for security offenses. Regardless of the degree of derogation, the third paragraph of Article 5 reiterates that all persons "shall nevertheless be treated with humanity."[63] Of course, no person may ever be treated in a manner that

---

[57] GC IV, *supra* note 3, art. 32.

[58] *Id.*

[59] For example, the prisoners depicted in the infamous Abu Ghraib photos were common criminals held as "civilian detainees" for suspected violations of Iraqi law and not insurgents held as "security internees." Only security internees were interrogated. The practices that constituted the abuse "were not related to the process of managing the detainees for the interrogation mission." On Point II, *supra* note 39, at 257. Whether or not the abuse constituted torture, or coercion under GC IV Article 31, it was "brutality" under Article 32 and proscribed by the UCMJ (*supra* note 35).

[60] GC IV, *supra* note 3, art. 5.

[61] *Id.*

[62] Dinstein, *supra* note 5, at 63.

[63] GC IV, *supra* note 3, art. 5.

violates jus cogens.[64] In that regard, Common Article 3 of the Geneva Conventions, Article 27 of the Fourth Geneva Convention, and Article 51 of Additional Protocol (AP) I afford the minimum floor beneath which treatment may never descend.[65]

- Article 27, Treatment. Article 27 states the general requirement that protected persons shall be treated humanely and with respect.[66] The last paragraph of the Article should be read with caution. Although it states that "[T]he Parties to the conflict may take such measures of control and security in regard to protected persons as may be necessary as a result of the war,"[67] it is not a statement in derogation of Article 27. Rather, it reserves the right of an occupier to take necessary and lawful actions for reasons of control and security, making it clear that such measures would not violate Article 27 (or the Convention generally).
- Article 28, Danger Zones. The presence of a protected person may not be used to render certain points or areas immune from military operations.[68] In other words, military operations continue in occupied territory, subject to adherence to *jus in bellum*, despite the presence of civilians.
- Article 33, Individual Responsibility, Collective Penalties, Pillage, Reprisals. Article 33 prohibits collective penalties, reprisals and all measures of intimidation.[69] As in all military operations whether or not in occupied territory, care must be taken to ensure that the use of force is limited to lawful objects of attack, including insurgents and terrorists. Operations in occupied territory are particularly susceptible to excesses against the civilian population, and rules for the use of force and rules for detention should emphasize the importance of discipline and restraint. Excessive force and overly zealous detention fuel an insurgency and may violate Article 33, among other legal provisions.
- Article 34, Hostages. "The taking of hostages is prohibited."[70] This simple rule can be violated when soldiers detain civilians and inform family members or others that the detainee will be released when attacks

---

[64] *Jus cogens* are non-derogable fundamental and universal legal norms that are binding on all nations. Vienna Convention on the Law of Treaties, art. 53, 1155 U.N.T.S. 331, 8I.L.M. 679, May 23, 1969 (entered into force Jan. 27, 1980).

[65] The Supreme Court of the United States found that the humane treatment standards of Common Article 3 of the Geneva Conventions applied to al Qaida unlawful combatants; *see* Hamdan v. Rumsfeld, 548 U.S. 557 (2006), and shortly thereafter the United States Department of Defense (DoD) issued a memorandum mandating that all DoD personnel adhere to the treatment standards of Common Article 3. Department of Defense Memorandum, *Application of Common Article 3 of the Geneva Conventions to the Treatment of Detainees in the Department of Defense* (July 7, 2006).

[66] GC IV, *supra* note 3, art. 27.

[67] *Id.* para. 4.

[68] GC IV, *supra* art. 28.

[69] *Id.* art. 33.

[70] *Id.* art. 34.

against occupation forces cease, information is provided, or wanted insurgents surrender. As a practical matter, clear rules for the detention of civilians should be promulgated, and civilians should not ordinarily be detained simply because they may have information of value to the occupation forces. Such civilians may, of course, be subjected to tactical questioning.[71]

- Article 76, Treatment of Detainees. This Article requires that protected persons shall be detained and imprisoned in the occupied country.[72] They shall be separated from other detainees, if possible, and afforded food and hygiene to keep them in good health of a standard at least equal to those existing in prisons in the occupied country. Important requirements of Article 76 include provision of medical care and spiritual assistance; separation of male and female prisoners, with women held under the supervision of women guards; special treatment of minors; and the right of visitation by delegates of the Protecting Power and of the ICRC.[73]
- Article 77, Handing Over of Detainees at the Close of Occupation. Protected persons who have been accused or convicted of offenses shall be handed over to the authorities of the liberated country at the close of occupation, along with relevant records.[74]
- Article 78, Security Measures. This is among the most significant Articles in the Fourth Geneva Convention. It authorizes the Occupying Power to subject protected persons to assigned residence or internment where necessary for imperative reasons of security.[75] "Imperative reasons of security" is a term not defined in the Convention and, as discussed in the section of this chapter that covers Iraq, was a term neither evenly applied nor clearly understood. Article 78 mandates a regular procedure for making decisions on internment or assigned residence, for which there must be a right of appeal.[76] Appeals must be decided promptly. In cases where the appeal is denied, there must be a competent body that periodically reviews continued internment or assigned residence. If possible, the review should occur every six months.[77] Establishing and maintaining the process for "Article 78 reviews and appeals" is a huge task for an occupier.[78]

---

[71] "Tactical questioning is expedient initial questioning for information of immediate tactical value. Tactical questioning is generally performed by members of patrols . . ." U.S. DEP'T OFF THE ARMY, FIELD MANUAL 2-22.3 (FM 34-52): HUMAN INTELLIGENCE COLLECTOR OPERATIONS ¶ 1-17 (Sept. 2006), *available at* http://armypubs.army.mil/doctrine/DR_pubs/dr_a/pdf/fm2_22x3.pdf.

[72] GC IV, *supra* note 3, art. 76, para. 1.

[73] *Id.* paras. 2 through 6.

[74] *Id.* art. 77.

[75] *Id.* art. 78, para. 1.

[76] *Id.* para. 2.

[77] *Id.*

[78] *See* Brian J. Bill, *The War in Iraq: A Legal Analysis; ch. XVII Detention Operations in Iraq: A View from the Ground*, 86 INT'L L. STUDIES 411–56 (Raul "Pete" Pedrozo ed., 2010).

- Articles 79 through 141, Regulations for the Treatment of Internees. These Articles, collectively Section IV of Part III of the Fourth Geneva Convention, prescribe the conditions in places of internment, as well as the standards for treatment of internees.[79] Significant articles include Article 84, requiring the separation of internees from prisoners of war and persons deprived of their liberty for any other reason; Articles 85, 91 and 92, setting health and hygiene standards for internees; Article 86, mandating premises suitable for religious services "of whatever denomination"; and Article 97, requiring that valuables and personal effects may be taken from internees only in accordance with an established procedure and with a detailed receipt.

3. An Occupier Must Stabilize Occupied Territory.
    - Article 24, Measures Relating to Child Welfare. The Convention admonishes parties to the conflict to protect children under age fifteen, particularly those orphaned or separated from their families.[80] Article 50 more specifically addresses the obligations of the occupier with regard to the identification, maintenance, and education of children.[81] Occupiers should include child welfare, including dealing with juvenile offenders, in their occupation planning.
    - Article 25, Family News. This Article states the right of persons in occupied territory to send and receive family correspondence. The national postal service may be in disarray, and the Convention does not require that the occupier start delivering mail. However, the larger issue of communication and information flow, particularly about dispersed families (Article 26) and internees, will be a matter of concern raised to the occupier by the populace, the International Committee of the Red Cross (ICRC), non-governmental organizations, and any emerging indigenous government.[82]
    - Article 49, Deportations, Transfers, Evacuations. This Article prohibits individual or mass forcible transfers, as well as deportations of protected persons from occupied territory, regardless of motive.[83] The first paragraph of Article 49 states: "Individual or mass forcible transfers, as well as deportations of protected persons from occupied territory to the territory of the Occupying Power or to that of any other country, occupied or not, *are prohibited, regardless of motive*" (emphasis added).[84] This appears to be a total prohibition that is reinforced in the official

[79] GC IV, *supra* note 3, Part III, Status and Treatment of Protected Persons, Section IV, Regulations for the Treatment of Internees.

[80] *Id.* art. 24.

[81] *Id.* art. 50.

[82] *See generally*, On Point II, *supra* note 39, at 264.

[83] GC IV, *supra* note 3, art. 49.

[84] *Id.*

Commentary to the Fourth Geneva Convention: "The prohibition is absolute and allows of no exceptions . . ."[85] However, although there are no lawful exceptions to the rule against deportations and forcible transfers, persons may leave voluntarily or may be excluded.[86] Exclusions occur most prominently in the case of infiltrators, such as persons who had entered Iraq unlawfully to take part in a jihad against Coalition Forces. "Infiltrators are simply not shielded by the Convention as protected persons."[87] The prohibition against deportation can frustrate security and, in specific cases, complicate criminal accountability. Consider the case of Palestinian terrorist Abu Abbas, who hijacked the cruise ship *Achille Lauro* and murdered U.S. citizen Leon Klinghoffer in 1985. Abbas had been given sanctuary by Saddam Hussein and was living in Baghdad when captured by U.S. forces. He died of a heart attack while in U.S. custody in Iraq.[88] A strong argument can be made that Article 49 should not insulate a criminal such as Abbas from the process of law in the manner of an extradition, especially where the crime (1) was committed outside of the occupied territory, (2) before the occupation, (3) by a terrorist who was not a national of the occupied territory. However, any removal of a civilian, whether or not a protected person, is a matter necessitating caution, deliberation, and careful analysis. Unlawful deportation or transfer is a grave breach of the Convention.[89]

- Article 51, Enlistment, Labor. Occupiers may not compel protected persons to serve in its armed or auxiliary forces.[90] Although stated in the negative in the Article, an occupier may compel protected persons over eighteen years of age to work that is necessary for the needs of the army of occupation, for the public utility services, or for the feeding, sheltering, clothing, transportation, or health of the population of the occupied country.[91] Compelled work cannot include taking part in military operations or serving as security guards at facilities where protected persons are performing compulsory labor.[92] Compelled workers shall be kept in their usual place of employment, so far as practicable; paid a fair wage; and remain protected by the occupational safety and health, and employment, laws that were previously in force in the occupied country.[93] Article 51 is important because it is the legal authority to order

---

[85] Pictet, *supra* note 33, at 279

[86] Dinstein, *supra* note 5, at 160–68.

[87] *Id.* at 167.

[88] *See* "Terrorist Abu Abbas Dies in Iraq," Mar. 9, 2004, *available at* http://www.foxnews.com/story/2004/03/09/terrorist-abu-abbas-dies-in-iraq/.

[89] GC IV, *supra* note 3, art. 147.

[90] *Id.* art. 51, para. 1.

[91] *Id.* para. 2.

[92] *Id.*

[93] *Id.* art. 51, para. 3.

police officers, firefighters, public utility workers, sanitation workers, and other necessary civilians back to work so as to restore security and stability. In Iraq, Coalition Forces ordered civilians to return to work, and judges and court personnel were among the first so ordered.

- Article 54, Judges and Public Officials. Article 54 affords special protection to public officials and judges by prohibiting the imposition of sanctions or other coercive measures against judges who "abstain from fulfilling their functions for reasons of conscience."[94] However, Article 54 is tempered by its second paragraph reserving the right of the Occupying Power to remove public officials from their posts, and by its explicit reference to Article 51, which accords the Occupying Power the right to order adult public servants to return to work. Judges are among the "public officials" in Article 54 who may be removed from their posts.[95]
- Article 64, Penal Legislation. This very important Article elaborates on Hague Regulations Article 43 concerning respect for the laws in force and courts in occupied territory.[96] Article 43 states, in pertinent part, that the occupying power shall take measures to restore and ensure public order and safety "while respecting, unless absolutely prevented, the laws in force in the country."[97] Article 64 of the Fourth Geneva Convention states the same rule: "The penal laws of the occupied territory shall remain in force, with the exception that they may be repealed or suspended by the Occupying Power in cases where they constitute a threat to its security or an obstacle to the application of the present Convention."[98] In Iraq, CPA Order Number 7 suspended certain provisions of the 1969 Iraqi Penal Code "that the former regime used . . . as a tool of repression in violation of internationally recognized human rights standards" and suspended capital punishment.[99] Unless they would constitute a threat to security or an impediment to application of the Convention, Article 64 mandates that the tribunals of the occupied territory shall continue to function.[100] The second paragraph of Article 64 affords the occupier the right to impose penal legislation that is essential to fulfill its obligations under the Convention, maintain the orderly government of the occupied territory, and ensure the security of the occupier's forces, administration and property, including

---

[94] *Id.* art. 54

[95] Pictet, *supra* note 33, at 308.

[96] Hague IV, *supra* note 3, art. 43.

[97] *Id.*

[98] GC IV, *supra* note 3, art. 64.

[99] CPA Order 7, *Penal Code* (June 10, 2003), *available at* http://www.iraqcoalition.org/regulations/20030610_CPAORD_7_Penal_Code.pdf.

[100] GC IV, *supra* note 3, art. 64, para. 1.

establishments and lines of communication used by them.[101] This authority was used extensively by the CPA.

- Article 65, Publication. "The penal provisions enacted by the Occupying Power shall not come into force before they have been published and brought to the knowledge of the inhabitants in their own language. The effect of these penal provisions shall not be retroactive."[102] Implementation of this simple requirement can be difficult where decisions must be implemented quickly, and means of communications have been ravaged by war. In Iraq, most CPA Orders, including penal orders, did not comply with Article 65 because they entered into force on the date of signature by the Administrator. The CPA published Orders in a legal gazette and posted Orders in courthouses and other public buildings. Eventually, CPA Orders and Regulations were also posted online.[103]
- Article 66, Competent Courts. This Article allows the occupier to establish "properly constituted, non-political military courts" sitting in the occupied territory in order to try the penal provisions promulgated by it under the authority of Article 64 (and published as required by Article 65). Although convened after World War II and still authorized by the Uniform Code of Military Justice, military occupation courts or military commissions were not used to try civilians in Iraq. Rather, jurisdiction to try "occupation offenses" was given to Iraqi courts, including the Central Criminal Court of Iraq (CCCI) established by CPA Order.[104]
- Article 67, Applicable Provisions. Military occupation courts shall not apply ex post facto penal provisions, and penalties must be proportionate to the offense. Offenses and penalties must be "in accordance with general principles of law." Occupation courts shall take into consideration the fact that the accused is not a national of the Occupying Power.[105]
- Article 68, Penalties, Death Penalty. Military occupation courts may only sentence protected persons to internment or simple imprisonment for offenses intended to harm the Occupying Power, but which do not "constitute an attempt on the life or limb of members of the occupying forces or administration, nor a grave collective danger, nor seriously damage the property of the occupying forces or administration or the installations used by them."[106] The death penalty may be imposed on a protected person only "where the person is guilty of espionage,

---

[101] *Id.* para. 2.

[102] *Id.* art. 65.

[103] CPA official documents are still available at http://www.iraqcoalition.org/regulations/.

[104] CPA Order 13 (Revised) (Amended), *The Central Criminal Court of Iraq* (Apr. 22, 2004), *available at* http://www.iraqcoalition.org/regulations/20040422_CPAORD_13_Revised_Amended.pdf.

[105] GC IV, *supra* note 3, art. 67.

[106] *Id.* art. 68, para. 1.

of serious acts of sabotage against the military installations of the Occupying Power or of intentional offenses which have caused the death of one or more persons, provided that such offenses were punishable by death under the law of the occupied territory in force before the occupation began."[107] The United States has reserved the right to impose capital punishment for homicide regardless of whether the offense was previously punishable by death under the law of the occupied territory.[108] Regardless, the death penalty may not be pronounced against a protected person who was under eighteen years of age at the time of the offense.[109] Whether imposed by indigenous courts in accordance with preexisting local law or by occupation courts pursuant to Article 68, capital punishment is a potentially contentious issue among Coalition partners subject to a legal regime prohibiting the death penalty as a violation of human rights law. In Iraq, the occupying powers suspended the death penalty.[110]

- Article 70, Offenses Committed Before Occupation. The Occupying Power may not arrest, prosecute, or convict a protected person for acts committed or opinions expressed before the occupation, or during a temporary interruption of the occupation, "with the exception of breaches of the laws and customs of war."[111]
- Article 71, Penal Procedure, General Observations. This is the first of several "due process" articles. It provides for prompt notice of the charges against an accused in a language that the accused can understand, and regular trial as rapidly as possible by the "competent courts" of the Occupying Power.[112] Notice of proceedings that could result in imposition of the death penalty or imprisonment of two years or more shall be provided to the Protecting Power or the International Committee of the Red Cross (ICRC) in the absence of a Protecting Power, in a form specified in Article 71.
- Article 72, Right of Defense. An accused shall have the right to be represented by a counsel or advocate of his or her choice, to present a defense and call witnesses, and to have an interpreter during the preliminary investigation and at hearings. If the accused does not choose

[107] *Id.* para. 2.

[108] United States of America Reservation/Declaration Text to the Geneva Conventions of August 12, 1949, Final Record of Diplomatic Conference of Geneva of 1949, Vol. I, Federal Political Department, Berne, 346, *available at* http://www.icrc.org/ihl.nsf/NORM/D6B53F5B5D14F35AC1256402003F9920.

[109] GC IV, *supra* note 3, art. 68, para. 4.

[110] CPA Order 7, *supra* note 99; CPA Order 10, *Management of Detention and Prison Facilities* (June 5, 2003), *available at* http://www.iraqcoalition.org/regulations/20030605_CPAORD10_Management_of_Detention_and_Prison_Facilities.pdf.

[111] GC IV, *supra* note 3, art. 70, para. 1.

[112] *Id.* art. 71, para. 1.

an advocate or counsel, the Occupying Power is to provide representation to the accused in serious cases.[113]

- Article 73, Right of Appeal. A convicted person shall be afforded a right of appeal, and advised of the time limit within which an appeal must be filed. If there is no appellate right under the laws that applied to the court, there shall nonetheless be a right of appeal to the Occupying Power.[114]
- Article 74, Assistance by the Protecting Power (or the ICRC in the absence of a Protecting Power). The Protecting Power shall have the right to attend the trial of any protected person, unless held in camera as an exceptional security measure. Any judgment for a sentence of death or imprisonment for two years or more shall be communicated to the Protecting Power, along with a reference to the prior notification made under Article 71. The Occupying Power shall notify the Protecting Power where the sentence is to be served and keep a record of judgments open to inspection by the Protecting Power. No period of appeal in cases involving imposition of the death penalty or imprisonment for two years or more, shall run until notification of judgment has been received by the Protecting Power. [115]
- Article 75, Death Sentence. All persons condemned to death shall have the right to petition for pardon or reprieve. No death sentence shall be carried out until at least six months after the Protecting Power has received notification of the final judgment confirming the death sentence or of the order denying the pardon or reprieve. The six-month period may be reduced in individual cases where there is a "grave emergency involving an organized threat to the security of the Occupying Power or its forces."[116] In such cases, the Protecting Power must be notified and given time and opportunity to intervene on behalf of the convict sentenced to death.[117]

4. An Occupier (and High Contracting Parties) Must Provide for Mechanisms to Ensure Supervision and Implementation of the Convention

    - Article 143, Supervision. This Article is the authority for representatives or delegates of the Protecting Powers (and of the ICRC) to have generally unfettered access to internees. Access shall include the ability to interview internees without witnesses, personally or through an interpreter, and without restrictions on the duration and frequency of visits.[118] As an exceptional and temporary measure, visits may be

---

[113] *Id.* art. 72, para. 2.
[114] *Id.* art. 73, para. 2.
[115] *Id.* art. 74, para. 2.
[116] *Id.* art. 75, para. 3.
[117] *Id.*
[118] Id. art. 143, para. 1 and 2.

prohibited for reasons of "imperative military necessity."[119] Imposition of this measure on one occasion in Iraq caused considerable controversy and the authority of U.S. government personnel to deny ICRC access has been limited by order.[120]

- Article 144, Dissemination of the Convention. The High Contracting Parties shall widely disseminate the text of the Convention, and include the study of the Convention in military and civil instructional programs, so as to communicate its principles as widely as possible. Civilian, military, police, or other authorities who in time of war assume responsibilities for protected persons must be provided with the text of the Convention and specially instructed as to its provisions.[121]
- Article 146, Penal Sanctions. The High Contracting Parties agree to enact legislation necessary to provide effective penal sanctions for persons who commit, or who order others to commit, grave breaches of the Convention. (Grave breaches are defined in Article 147.)[122] The Parties agree to prosecute grave breaches or to hand over persons to other Parties for prosecution. Any prosecution shall at minimum meet the requirements of Articles 105 through 108 of the Third Geneva Convention.[123] The Parties also agree to "take measures necessary for the suppression of all acts contrary to the provisions of the present Convention other than . . . grave breaches."[124] These measures include disciplinary and remediation actions appropriate for a violation of the Convention not rising to a grave breach defined in Article 147.
- Article 147, Grave Breaches. Grave breaches of the Convention are the following acts committed against protected persons or property: willful killing; torture or inhuman treatment, including biological experiments; willfully causing great suffering or serious injury to body or health; unlawful deportation or transfer or unlawful confinement; compelled service in the forces of a hostile Power; willful deprivation of the rights of fair and regular trial as prescribed in the Convention; taking of hostages; and extensive unlawful and wanton destruction or appropriation of property.[125]
- Article 154, Relation with the Hague Conventions. The Fourth Geneva Convention is "supplementary" to sections II and III of the Hague Regulations annexed to the Hague Conventions of 1899 and 1907.[126] The

[119] *Id.* para. 3.

[120] *See* Exec. Order No. 13,491, *Ensuring Lawful Interrogation*, 74 Fed. Reg. 4893 (Jan. 22, 2009), at sec. 4(b).

[121] GC IV, *supra* note 3, art. 144, para. 2.

[122] *Id.* art. 146, para. 1.

[123] *Id.* para. 4.

[124] *Id.* para. 3.

[125] *Id.* art. 147.

[126] *Id.* art. 154.

cited sections of the Regulations are the important substantive provisions of "Hague Law."

- Annexes to the Convention. The most important is Annex III, the internment card. It serves to notify the ICRC of the fact and location of internment of identified persons. In Iraq, these cards were modified to differentiate between "civilian internees" and "security detainees." The key point is to account for persons under the control of occupation forces. When the ICRC is not present in occupied territory, as happened for several months in Iraq, the occupier must make arrangements to get the cards to the ICRC.

B. RIGHTS OF THE OCCUPIER

Occupation law governs in areas other than the protection of the civilian population. Although most modern commentators focus on their legal obligations, occupiers are accorded rights under occupation law. The occupier has the right to use the resources of the occupied territory, as well as the authority to levy taxes, to fund the costs of occupation.[127] The occupier may seize state property that may be used for military purposes, but may not confiscate private property.[128] Private property must be respected, as must family honor.[129]

C. TRANSFORMATIVE OCCUPATION

Where the strategic goal of the occupier is regime change and fundamental social, economic, and political reform, as was the case in Germany and Japan in World War II and in Iraq in 2003, an occupier will logically undertake the mission of nation-building and national transformation. The sweeping reforms made by the Allies in Germany and Japan far exceeded the authority accorded to them under traditional occupation law. However, the occupations of Germany and Japan followed unconditional surrenders, and the Allies took the position that they were not constrained by the limitations imposed by occupation law.[130]

Although the United Nations may not have expressly authorized the invasion of Iraq, it certainly recognized the subsequent occupation and authorized actions that would have been ultra vires for an occupier under the traditional

---

[127] Hague IV, *supra* note 9, arts. 48, 49.

[128] Private real property and private moveable property susceptible of direct military use may be requisitioned, with return and payment of compensation as soon as practicable. *Id.* arts. 46, 52, 53.

[129] *Id.* art. 46.

[130] *See* Dinstein, *supra* note 5, at 32, 33: "But, whatever legal theory is subscribed to, the facts speak for themselves: the victors introduced in occupied Germany sweeping institutional changes that were incompatible with the law of belligerent occupation ... By the same token, the Allied (in practice, American) occupation of Japan was intended to purge militarism and ultra-naturalism, dissolve ruling cliques and usher in land reform. The radical measures taken ... were brazenly inconsistent with the Hague Regulations. To use a popular idiom, the post-surrender occupations of Germany and Japan were 'transformative' in their nature."

law of occupation. Fundamental changes in the Iraqi government and economic reforms are examples of "transformative occupation" authorized by the United Nations that exceeded the historical authority of an occupier. It is an open question whether the acts of the United Nations concerning Iraq modified the customary law of occupation so as to generally expand the scope of authority of occupiers.[131] A cautious answer is that the United Nations can expand the scope of authority of occupiers when they act pursuant to the authorization of the Security Council.

Even where the strategic goal of an invasion is not regime change and fundamental reform, conditions may cause an occupier to consider transformative occupation. In some cases, there may be no successor government without transformative action by the occupier, and the absence of transformative action puts the civilian population at risk at the end of occupation. Where the former indigenous government has been removed or has ceased to exist, the occupier may be obligated to assist in the establishment of a functional successor government that affords relative security to its populace and respects human rights and the rule of law.[132] The successor government need not be a Western-style democracy at the end of occupation. Indeed, it may be unwise or impossible to establish a democracy in a country with significant ethnic, religious, and political differences between majority and minority populations. The successor government must be capable of exercising the role of a national government, even if still building its capabilities for governance. Although a prolonged occupation may help inculcate enduring democratic values and improve the efficacy of government, the law of occupation does not mandate a long-term commitment to nation-building or democratization as a prerequisite to the end of occupation. To the contrary, the traditional law of occupation limits the transformative powers of the occupier, so even a well-intended and necessary transformative occupation should be authorized by the United Nations.[133]

D. HUMAN RIGHTS LAW AND OCCUPATION

Expanding the body of law applicable to an occupation should be viewed with caution. The law of belligerent occupation is *lex specialis*, a defined body of law with specific application to the particular circumstances of occupation. As a component of international humanitarian law, it is known by military forces

---

[131] *See* David Scheffer, *The Security Council and International Law on Military Occupations*, *in* The United Nations Security Council and War: The Evolution of Thought and Practice since 1945 (Vaughan Lowe et al. eds., 2008); *see also* Nicholas F. Lancaster, *Occupation Law, Sovereignty, and Political Transformation: Should the Hague Regulations and the Fourth Geneva Convention Still Be Considered Customary International Law?*, 189 Mil. L. Rev. 51 (2006).

[132] Whether this obligation is moral or legal, or both, is a matter of debate and related to the emerging theory of *jus post bellum*, as well as the impact of human rights law. *See generally* Roberts, *supra* note 13. *Compare* Dinstein, *supra* note 5, at 272: an occupier may simply withdraw from the occupied territory, returning it to the displaced sovereign, if one exists.

[133] Fox, *supra* note 12.

charged with carrying out an occupation (even if not always consistently followed). International humanitarian law has developed over time for reasons of humanity and necessity and is grounded in pragmatism. Old law is still good law; the Geneva Conventions are neither quaint nor obsolete.[134] At a minimum, they can serve as guiding principles even when not applicable as a matter of law. When they do apply as a matter of law, as in Iraq, they have demonstrated their utility and ability to be meaningfully implemented in the new millennium.

There are continuing attempts to conflate international humanitarian law, particularly the law of belligerent occupation, with human rights law. These efforts should be viewed critically, as they dilute both and erode the clarity of the well-developed law of armed conflict on which commanders and soldiers are trained. Interjecting human rights law as a separate body of law into the wartime legal mix causes confusion. In the case of the Iraq occupation, both the United States and the United Kingdom flatly asserted that human rights law was not applicable during the occupation.[135]

This absolute position may be more appealing in theory than in practice. There are overlaps between human rights law and international humanitarian law, especially when including the aspects of Additional Protocol I that are customary international law.[136] The overlaps include those non-derogable human rights that are germane to wartime.[137] In those unusual cases where there are conflicts between overlapping human rights law and international humanitarian law, the latter must prevail under the *lex specialis* rule.[138] In even rarer and more sophisticated cases, there may be gaps between human rights law and international humanitarian law to which human rights law might apply.[139]

However, the application of human rights law as a separate body of law in wartime should be a clear exception, and only where justice necessitates that it address a gap such as when, for example, "the norms governing belligerent occupation are silent or incomplete."[140] Otherwise, applying human rights law in

---

[134] *See* Memorandum to the President from Alberto R. Gonzales, Subject: *Decision Re Application of the Geneva Convention on Prisoners of War to the Conflict with Al Qaeda and the Taliban*, Jan. 25, 2002. In fairness to Gonzales, his references to the Geneva Conventions having been rendered quaint and obsolete were made in the context of the "new paradigm" of the war against terrorism and applied to only certain aspects of the Conventions, not to the Conventions as a whole.

[135] Bienvenisti & Keinan, *supra* note 2, at 274.

[136] *See generally* JEAN-MARIE HENCKAERTS & LOUISE DOSWALD-BECK, CUSTOMARY INTERNATIONAL HUMANITARIAN LAW: RULES (2005). Although the United States is not a party to AP I, it regards many of its provisions as customary and binding international law. *See* Michael J. Matheson, *Session One: The United States Position on the Relation of Customary International Law to the 1977 Protocols Additional to the 1949 Geneva Convention*, 2 AM. U. J. INT'L L. & POL. 419, 425 (1987).

[137] DINSTEIN, *supra* note 5, at 81, 82.

[138] *Lex specialis derogate lex generali* ("The *Lex Specialis* Rule"). *Id.* at 85.

[139] For example, a national of the Occupying Power present in occupied territory is not a protected person under GC IV, but would be protected by at least core aspects of human rights law. *Id.* at 84, 85.

[140] *Id.* at 84.

wartime creates friction and uncertainty, while adding little. Many of the articles in the Fourth Geneva Convention already address and protect human rights, as did Article 46 of the earlier Hague Regulations.[141] The International Committee of the Red Cross observed that the Fourth Geneva Convention "aims at ensuring that, even in the midst of hostilities, the dignity of the human person, universally acknowledged in principle, shall be respected."[142]

Human rights law may find its way into occupied territory in the rucksacks of occupation troops. Despite the position on the non-applicability of human rights law asserted by the United Kingdom, its soldiers were held to account for violations of human rights law by courts in Europe.[143] Alleged human rights law violations may be a basis for civil lawsuits filed to obtain pecuniary damages and publicity.

Human rights law may be introduced into an occupation by the United Nations, and even by the Occupying Powers themselves. In Iraq, U.N. Security Council Resolution (UNSCR) 1483 requested the Secretary-General to appoint a Special Representative for Iraq whose responsibilities included "in coordination with the [Coalition Provisional] Authority ... promoting the protection of human rights."[144] Several CPA Orders referenced human rights.[145] To the extent that human rights laws are already in force in occupied territory, occupiers would be obligated to respect them as required generally by Article 43 of the Hague Regulations.

E. THE END OF OCCUPATION

Occupation ends when the occupier no longer maintains effective control over formerly occupied territory and no longer substitutes its authority for that of the indigenous government. Within occupied territory, the entire Fourth Geneva Convention applies for one year after the general close of military operations, and selected Articles of the Convention continue to apply for the duration of the occupation where the occupier exercises the functions of government.[146] The experience in Iraq illustrates the difficulty in applying the simple one-year rule: despite the overthrow of the regime, significant military operations continued through

---

[141] "Family honour and rights, the lives of persons, and private property, as well as religious convictions and practice must be respected." Hague IV, *supra* note 9, art. 46.

[142] International Committee of the Red Cross, The Geneva Conventions of August 12, 1949 (Reprint) 16 (Geneva: ICRC, 1983).

[143] *See, e.g.*, *Al-Skeini and others v. Secretary of State for Defence*, EWHC 2911 (2004), *cited in* Bienvenisti & Keinan, *supra* note 2, at 274, 284.

[144] S.C. Res. 1483, U.N. Doc. S/RES/1483 (May 22, 2003).

[145] *See, e.g.*, CPA Order 19, *Freedom of Assembly* (July 9, 2003), *available at* http://www.iraqcoalition.org/regulations/20030710_CPAORD_19_Freedom_of_Assembly_.pdf.

("to remove the unacceptable restrictions on human rights of the former ... regime."). *See also* CPA Order 60, *Establishing the Ministry of Human Rights* (Feb. 22, 2004), *available at* http://www.iraqcoalition.org/regulations/20040220_CPAORD60.pdf.

[146] GC IV, *supra* note 3, art. 6.

the occupation and even after the occupation. Coexistent occupation and combat in Iraq was not without historical precedent; it is the norm in much of the territory occupied by Israel, and occurred during the U.S. occupation of the Philippines after the Spanish-American War.[147]

III. Occupation Law and Issues in Iraq

The occupation of Iraq in 2003 and 2004 affords an excellent vehicle to explore occupation law and issues in a contemporary operational context. This section will highlight the role of military legal advisors (Judge Advocates) during the occupation. The war between the United States and the United Kingdom and Iraq was an international armed conflict under Common Article 2 of the Geneva Conventions, and the occupation that followed was a textbook case for the full application of the law of belligerent occupation. The transformative resolutions of the United Nations Security Council authorized the occupiers to take actions that clearly exceeded their authority under traditional occupation law.[148]

The effective occupation of Iraq was hampered by the lack of coherent and adequate planning. Although there could be no legal doubt that Coalition Forces entering Iraq and defeating Iraqi military forces for the purpose of regime change would be occupiers, practical aspects of the planning for the occupation were influenced by the inordinate emphasis on Coalition Forces as "liberators" rather than "occupiers." Before the invasion of Iraq, policy decisions were not timely made, and the requirements for occupation were not adequately resourced. Occupation is a fact, and the obligations of an occupier exist as a matter of law.[149] Using the euphemism of "liberator" or avoiding adequate planning alters neither the fact nor the legal obligations of occupation.

In the limited planning for the occupation of Iraq in 2003, Coalition Forces planners assumed that many Iraqi military forces would capitulate, that is surrender en masse without a fight, and would be available to serve as constabulary or security forces; that Iraq'd physical and social infrastructure would remain intact; and that a capable interim Iraqi government would quickly emerge. With regard to assumptions, it seems that planners assumed the worst about Iraq's capabilities and intentions in deciding whether to go to war, and assumed the best case as to what would happen once invasion forces crossed the Iraqi border.

The lack of planning was exposed once the invasion began on March 20, 2003. Coalition Forces had rapid military success. The regime of Saddam Hussein collapsed and, as should be expected to occur with the fall of a centralized

---

[147] Counterinsurgency and stability operations continued for thirteen years during the U.S. occupation of the Philippines. Many histories of the U.S. occupation are out of print, but the topic enjoyed a reprise in the new millennium. *See, e.g.*, Max Boot, The Savage Wars of Peace, Small Wars and the Rise of American Power (2002).

[148] *See* Fox, *supra* note 12, and Roberts, *supra* note 13.

[149] Field Manual 27-10, *supra* note 1.

totalitarian government, so did subordinate government institutions.[150] However, despite the reminder by the United Nations Security Council of the obligations of an occupier under the Fourth Geneva Convention and Hague Regulations,[151] the Coalition had not established any instrument to assume governmental authority, and commanders were given little guidance on how to administer occupied territory.

In the absence of guidance, Coalition military commanders issued orders in the March to Baghdad that addressed immediate security issues. These mandated warning procedures at checkpoints;[152] prescribed rules for cordon and search operations; authorized curfews; established weapons, explosives, and fuel possession controls; and provided guidance for the use of force against looters.[153] However, the orders were issued as necessary at the tactical level and not as part of any cohesive plan. Efforts to try to address the problem in a comprehensive way were thwarted by a lack of fundamental policy decisions at a higher level. For example, an Occupation Proclamation and orders to civilians had been staffed, drafted, printed, and pre-positioned, but no order was ever given to release them.[154]

In Baghdad, there was inadequate troop strength to effectively control the city. The U.S. Army's 3d Infantry Division, the lead division of the Coalition main effort, the U.S. Army's V Corps, had reached its culminating point. It had fought all the way to Baghdad and was exhausted; it had little energy left to detain looters or guard key infrastructure. Orders were issued to protect museums, courthouses, police stations, power and water plants, and public records holding areas,

---

[150] Saddam Hussein had ruled Iraq for twenty-four years and his "totalitarian rule eroded the civic infrastructure of Iraq as much as it damaged the physical infrastructure of the country." On Point II, *supra* note 39, at 402. "Coalition planners had not anticipated Iraq to be so void of basic, functioning systems." *Id.* at 385.

[151] *See* S.C. Res. 1472, U.N. Doc. S/RES/1472 (Mar. 28, 2003).

[152] Checkpoint shootings plagued Coalition Forces. Early in the war, an entire Iraqi family had been killed as their van approached a checkpoint without slowing down, despite warning shots. Deaths of civilians may be an inevitable collateral aspect of military operations, but they can undermine military success, particularly in an occupation or counterinsurgency campaign. "Success in operations and even major campaigns can be impacted by acts alleged to have been caused by U.S. forces, even if inaccurate or untrue. Therefore, how we respond to civilian casualties and the claims and allegations of civilian casualties must be a priority of mission planning, training and execution." Defense Legal Policy Board, *Final Report of the Subcommittee on Military Justice in Combat Zones*, 20 (May 30, 2013).

[153] On Point II, *supra* note 39, at 78.

[154] An Occupation Proclamation is declaratory only and not legally necessary. *See* Dinstein, *supra* note 5, at 48. In CPA Regulation 1, CPA announced that it "shall exercise powers of government temporarily . . . The CPA is vested with all executive, legislative, and judicial authority necessary to achieve its objectives." CPA Regulation 1, *The Coalition Provisional Authority* (May 16, 2003), *available at* http://www.iraqcoalition.org/regulations/20030516_CPAREG_1_The_Coalition_Provisional_Authority_.pdf.

but there were simply not enough troops.[155] Even when troops were available, they did not always follow through with their assigned security tasks.[156]

The period of lawlessness in Baghdad was unfortunate in a number of respects. First, it endangered civilians and led to substantial property damage and theft. Looting of government buildings and former regime property was extensive, and targeted theft of commercial and public property, including culturally and historically significant objects from museums,[157] was so widespread as to suggest the work of organized criminal elements. Second, it caused both innocent civilians and potential adversaries to question Coalition capability, resolve, and power. Third, it exposed a lack of planning by the Coalition. Looting and lawlessness should have been assumed as predictable consequences of combat consistent with the experience of U.S. forces in Grenada in 1983, Panama in 1989, and Kuwait in 1990.[158] Last, and most important, the tentative efforts of military forces to quickly establish security squandered a "golden window" of time during which the Coalition could have demonstrated its strength and set the conditions for an effective occupation.

By early May, more than a month after the start of the ground invasion, it was clear that the aspiration to quickly establish an indigenous Iraqi regime was unattainable. It was thus also clear that the United States and the United Kingdom had to establish a full-fledged occupation administration. Nevertheless, the occupying powers took only tentative and phased steps. On May 6, 2003, L. Paul Bremer was appointed U.S. Presidential Envoy to Iraq. Two days later, the U.S. and U.K. representatives to the United Nations acknowledged their obligations under The Hague Regulations and Geneva Conventions, but stopped short of acknowledging that their countries were Occupying Powers in Iraq.[159]

On May 13, 2003, the United States and United Kingdom announced that Envoy Bremer would also serve as the Administrator of the Coalition Provisional Authority (CPA), the occupation authority in Iraq. Initially the CPA was built on the Office of Reconstruction and Humanitarian Assistance (ORHA) that had been established only two months before the invasion.[160] The ORHA was designed for consequence management (reconstruction and humanitarian assistance), not for the administration of occupied territory.[161] It was under-resourced

---

[155] The Commanding General of the U.S. Army's 3d Infantry Division reported to his higher headquarters that he had too few troops to guard the specified facilities that he had been ordered to protect from looters. ON POINT II, *supra* note 39, at 148.

[156] In April and May 2003, the author would often travel into central Baghdad to key facilities, particularly courthouses and police stations. There would often be no soldiers there, despite orders having been issued to secure the buildings.

[157] *See* Convention for the Protection of Cultural Property in the Event of Armed Conflict, May 14, 1954, 249 U.N.T.S. 240, to which the United States was a signatory, but not a party, in 2003. (The United States ratified the Convention in 2009.)

[158] Limited looting by local nationals took place in Grenada, and widespread looting by Iraqi forces took place in Kuwait; the experience in Panama was the closest analogy to what occurred in Iraq. *See* ON POINT II, *supra* note 39, at 55.

[159] Bienvenisti & Keinan, *supra* note 2, at 266.

[160] ON POINT II, *supra* note 39, at 149–53.

[161] *Id.*

and unprepared to assume the functions of government for a country of 26 million people.

The CPA was significantly more robust. Larger and more capable than ORHA, it was specifically built to be the occupation authority in Iraq and staffed with military and civilian experts. On May 16, 2003, the CPA issued its Regulation 1, announcing its control, authority, and jurisdiction in Iraq:

> The CPA shall exercise powers of government temporarily in order to provide for the effective administration of Iraq during the period of transitional administration, to restore conditions of security and stability, to create conditions on which the Iraqi people can freely determine their own political future ... The CPA is vested with all executive, legislative and judicial authority necessary to achieve its objectives.[162]

In addition to vesting the powers of government in the CPA, Regulation 1 announced the applicable law in Iraq consistent with Article 64 of the Fourth Geneva Convention. It also established the system of orders, regulations, and memoranda to be promulgated by the CPA. CPA Regulation 1 is at Annex A to this chapter.

On May 22, 2003, UNSCR 1483 recognized the United States and United Kingdom as Occupying Powers in Iraq.[163] The Resolution authorized the Occupying Powers to take actions that exceeded the scope of occupation law in order to transform Iraq from a dictatorship to a democracy. Although the transformative nature of the Resolution is legally significant, it was also a significant fact that the regime of Saddam Hussein had ceased to exist, making it impossible for the occupiers to restore Iraq to its pre-war status quo ante.

UNSCR 1483 did not recognize "the Coalition" as the Occupying Power because occupation is a legal responsibility of individual accountable nations. The Resolution nonetheless acknowledged that the United States and United Kingdom would discharge their occupation responsibilities under "unified command," referring to the CPA. It also noted that "other States that are not occupying powers are working now or in the future may work under the Authority."[164]

Although Administrator Bremer initially reported to the U.S. Secretary of Defense,[165] his status as a civilian outside the military chain of command, and the vague relationship of the CPA to Coalition military forces, created friction between the CPA and the Coalition military headquarters, Combined Joint Task

---

[162] CPA Regulation 1, *supra* note 154.

[163] S.C. Res. 1483, *supra* note 144 ("Noting the letter of 8 May 2003 from the Permanent Representatives of the United States of America and the United Kingdom of Great Britain and Northern Ireland to the President of the Security Council (S/2003/538) and recognizing the specific authorities, responsibilities, and obligations under applicable international law of these states as occupying powers under unified command ... ").

[164] *Id.*

[165] The Administrator initially reported to the U.S. Secretary of Defense, but began reporting to the U.S. National Security Council in November 2003. *See* ON POINT II, *supra* note 39, at 181.

Force 7 (CJTF-7). The administration of occupied territory is an innately military mission.[166] Military forces in Iraq were placed in direct support, but not under the command, of the CPA. When the CPA was established as a civilian entity, military commanders suffered a diminution of their authority to administer and exercise the rights of occupation, with no reduction in their legal responsibilities. The military should be responsible for occupation and, if necessary, administer occupied territory through a military government. The three most important legal, moral, and military objectives in occupation are security, security, and security.[167] Civilian experts should augment military occupation forces as their expertise is required and as security conditions permit.

As a practical matter, placing CJTF-7 in direct support of the CPA violated the military maxims of unity of command and unity of effort.[168] It was not clear who was in charge in Iraq, nor was there clarity concerning the relative roles and responsibilities of the CPA and CJTF-7.[169] It was obvious that there was a diffusion of effort and the squandering of several golden months after a decisive military victory. This time was critical because the Iraqi population craved firm direction in the months after the invasion. It is possible that the insurgency may have been blunted had the military's decisions on de-Ba'athification and the dissolution of the Iraqi military not been overruled by the CPA.

From the beginning, the CPA took an active role in military matters. On the day CPA Administrator Bremer arrived in Iraq, he announced that U.S. forces would shoot to kill all looters.[170] This announcement was made without any coordination with the military in Iraq and no consideration of the military's rules of engagement (ROE), the military's rules for the use of force. The ROE did not allow the use of deadly force against looters, and considerable time and effort had to be expended to issue clarifying orders and guidance to troops in the field in order to counter the announcement.[171]

---

[166] Dinstein, *supra* note 5, at 56: "[T]he government of an occupied territory is military *per definitionem*."

[167] The point was made by Professor Yoram Dinstein at the U.S. Naval War College Conference on the Iraq War: "The three most important duties of the occupier are security, security, and security." U.S. Naval War College's 2009 International Law Conference, Newport, RI (notes on file with the author).

[168] The CJTF-7 mission statement read, in pertinent part: "Conduct offensive operations . . . in direct support of the Coalition Provisional Authority." On Point II, *supra* note 39, at 30.

[169] *Id.* at 153–56.

[170] Warren, *supra* note 28, at 188.

[171] Aside from the fact that most U.S. troopers simply would not shoot an unarmed civilian who was not threatening them, the Rules of Engagement (ROE) would not allow it. The Combined Forces Land Component Command (CFLCC) ROE allowed soldiers and marines to use deadly force to accomplish the mission against lawful targets (combatants), to protect themselves and others, and to protect designated property—but not to shoot a civilian walking down the street carrying a stolen TV set. CFLCC ROE Pocket Card, 252030 Nov 03, *id.* at 196.

The CPA's first exercise of legislative authority was to issue CPA Order Number 1, its de-Ba'athification policy.[172] Saddam Hussein exercised power through the Ba'ath Party in a manner similar to the way that Adolf Hitler used the Nazi Party to keep a political and economic stranglehold on German society. The CPA policy was intended to break the back of the Ba'ath Party. Instead, it took thousands of people out of the work force solely because of their level of membership in the Party, leaving them essentially unemployable and disaffected. Although there was a review mechanism for lower-level party members, it was centralized and slow to be implemented.[173]

The military had earlier recognized the importance of quickly addressing the issue of Ba'ath Party membership, which included most government workers, as well as teachers. The military advocated against adopting a status-based policy that would disqualify people from government (and Coalition Forces) employment simply because of their membership in the Ba'ath Party. It assessed that such a policy would cause massive practical problems and be counterproductive to efforts to quickly get the policeman back on the beat, the teacher back in the classroom, and the municipal worker back on the street. Instead, the military proposed a conduct-based policy that would not prohibit employment of persons solely based on their membership in the Ba'ath Party, but would bar only those persons who were suspected of crimes or other misconduct, including prominent members of the former regime or persons otherwise on a "black list."[174]

The conduct-based policy required Iraqi government workers to sign an "Agreement to Disavow Party Affiliation"[175] renouncing and denouncing the Ba'ath Party, Saddam Hussein, and his regime; promise to obey Iraqi law and military and CPA orders; and get back to work.[176] Vetting of employees would take place over time. Thousands of agreements were printed and distributed, and the policy was implemented. CPA Order Number 1 reversed the military's policy and sent a shock wave through Iraqi society. Of more practical importance, it excluded tens of thousands of government workers and teachers from employment when they were most sorely needed to restore security and normalcy to the civilian population.

CPA Order Number 2 dissolved the Iraqi military, cutting off at the knees the Coalition's plans to use Iraqi forces as security and constabulary forces.[177] Like CPA Order Number 1, it was implemented with no coordination with the commanders on the ground, and no consideration of what was already being done by the military—despite the fact that the policy would have a huge negative

---

[172] CPA Order 1, *De-Ba'athification of Iraqi Society and Government* (May 16, 2003), *available at* http://www.iraqcoalition.org/regulations/20030516_CPAORD_1_De-Ba_athification_of_Iraqi_Society_.pdf.

[173] ON POINT II, *supra* note 39, at 97.

[174] *Id.* at 93.

[175] *Id.*

[176] *Id.*

[177] *Id.* at 92, 93.

impact on law and order, security and stability, and reconciliation.[178] The dissolution order handicapped the CPA plans to rebuild the Iraqi police force and Army. CJTF-7 had to bolster the CPA effort and establish parallel training programs and organizations, such as the Iraqi Civil Defense Corps, in order to field Iraqi security forces.[179] The CPA and CJTF-7 expended enormous resources on rebuilding the security sector, especially the police.

After the missteps of CPA Orders 1 and 2, the CPA began issuing orders and regulations, some of which were punitive, that addressed security issues. These ranged from weapons possession controls to modifications to the Iraqi Penal Code. The modifications to the Penal Code increased jail sentences and denied bail for specified offenses related to security. (CPA Order 7, *Penal Code*, is at Annex B.) In furtherance of the decision to reinvigorate the Iraqi judicial system rather than to establish military occupation courts, CPA orders fielded a vetting mechanism for judges, gave support to the defense bar, modified the Iraqi Penal Code, promulgated security-related offenses and punishments, and even created a special Iraqi court of national jurisdiction to try significant security and corruption offenses.

Over time, the CPA's focus shifted from establishing its authority and restoring security to governmental transition and economic and societal transformation. The CPA created a body for Iraqi participation, the Iraqi Governing Council (IGC), which served as an indigenous partner in the remaking of Iraq. The CPA issued orders in "areas often untouched during occupation, such as trade law, company law, securities law, bankruptcy law, and even intellectual property and copyright laws."[180] The Iraqi government was reorganized, and new Ministries, including the Ministry of the Environment and the Ministry of Human Rights, were created. Although some of the orders were not consistent with traditional occupation law, they were lawful because they were authorized by the United Nations. Indeed, the preamble to many of the CPA's orders cited not only the authority of occupation law under Hague and Geneva, but the authority of the United Nations.[181]

Even as the CPA was broadly exercising its occupation authority, Coalition military forces were conducting extensive counterinsurgency and counterterrorism campaigns. The intensity of hostilities during the occupation caused

---

[178] When combined with the Order dissolving the Iraqi military (CPA Order 2, *Dissolution of Entities* (May 23, 2003), *available at* http://www.iraqcoalition.org/regulations/20030823_CPAORD_2_Dissolution_of_Entities_with_Annex_A.pdf, CPA's de-Ba'athification policy left hundreds of thousands of Sunni Arabs unemployed, while decapitating Iraq's governmental, security, and education infrastructure.

[179] On Point II, *supra* note 39, at ch. 11.

[180] Bienvenisti & Keinan, *supra* note 2, at 270.

[181] CPA used a "belt and suspenders" approach to citations of authority in the preambles of its publications, citing generally "the laws and usages of war" and specific UN Security Council Resolutions (UNSCR). Over time, these included S.C. Res. 1511, U.N. Doc. S/RES/1511 (Oct. 16, 2003) and S.C. Res. 1546, U.N. Doc. S/RES/1546 (June 8, 2004), which followed S.C. Res. 1483, *supra* note 144, that had recognized the United States and United Kingdom as occupying powers in Iraq.

U.S. forces to continue to use combat ROE. Thousands of captured insurgents and terrorists were held in military detention facilities, adding to the tens of thousands of common criminals held by Coalition Forces because Iraqi penal capability was inadequate or unavailable.[182]

Detention of prisoners was a monumental challenge for occupation forces in Iraq, closely tied to prosecuting the war effort and restoring security. At the start of the war, one of the first orders issued by the U.S. Army's V Corps dealt with prisoners and detainees.[183] The order cited the Third and Fourth Geneva Conventions and established a review and release mechanism for detainees that exceeded the requirements of the Fourth Geneva Convention; the order adopted best practices from U.S. operations in Haiti and Kosovo, and mandated a review by a Judge Advocate of all detentions of civilians.[184] However, the sheer number of detainees quickly overwhelmed the process.

Soon after closing on Baghdad in April 2003, Coalition Forces were deluged with prisoners. One of the first organizational tasks was to separate common criminals, prisoners of war, and persons who had attacked Coalition Forces during the occupation. In the crush of combat, prisoners had been commingled. Coalition Forces had not anticipated the impact of Saddam's General Amnesty, issued in November 2002.[185] The amnesty had emptied the prisons and jails of all prisoners except political ones.[186] Thousands of convicted criminals had been freed to prey upon the civilian population, and prisons and jails had been systematically looted, some to the extent that they had been reduced to their foundation. With few exceptions, Iraqi police and corrections personnel were unsuitable to perform law enforcement and confinement duties without significant training, close supervision, and continuous oversight.

Coalition troops not only captured prisoners of war and civilians who later would be called insurgents, but also detained thousands of common criminals. Some were detained in the act of committing violent crimes. Some were turned in after the acts by local civilians, some were convicted criminals who had been granted amnesty, some were probably innocent of any wrongdoing and unjustly accused, but the result was a huge influx of prisoners, later termed "criminal detainees," with precious few places to hold them, soldiers to guard them, or

---

[182] "The sheer volume of detainees generated by cordon and search and other operations became a formidable challenge." ON POINT II, *supra* note 39, at 247.

[183] Fragmentary Order (FRAGO) 007, *id.* at 249.

[184] Initially a five-day standard review of detentions by a Judge Advocate magistrate was accelerated to seventy-two hours in the summer of 2003. Neither standard was required by law and exceeded the standards imposed by Article 78 of the Fourth Geneva Convention, which requires only that decisions regarding internment shall be made according to a regular procedure that affords a right of appeal, to be decided with the least possible delay and, if denied, to be subject to periodic review conducted, if possible, every six months by a competent body. GC IV, *supra* note 3, art. 78. United States forces should have stressed that the reviews were neither required by law nor intended to be viewed as a right or as customary. The requirements of Article 78 were satisfied by the process specified in the "Mother of all FRAGOs." ON POINT II, *supra* note 39, at 249.

[185] *Id.* at 248.

[186] *Id.*

courts to try them. The problem was compounded by soldiers using prisoner-of-war capture tags to document the apprehension of these persons; there were tags with "murderer" or "rapist" written on them, and no more information upon which to form the basis for investigation and prosecution.

In May 2003, U.S. forces started using "CPA Apprehension Forms" that required soldiers to obtain sworn statements from witnesses about the circumstances of capture.[187] This helped ameliorate the situation and set conditions for future prosecutions. Prisoners were classified into two categories: security internee and criminal detainee. The former were those who had engaged in hostilities and who would be held until the conclusion of hostilities or otherwise earlier released, perhaps through a parole or release guarantor agreement;[188] the latter were criminals who were held for trial or other disposition by the emerging Iraqi criminal justice system. The ICRC modified its capture cards in Iraq to recognize the two categories of prisoner.

For those whose status was in doubt, U.S. forces conducted tribunals under Article 5 of the Third Geneva Convention.[189] Commencing in June 2003, tribunals were held for all of the High Value Detainees (HVD), prisoners such as Deputy Prime Minister Tariq Aziz. The tribunals consisted of three Judge Advocates who were to determine whether the prisoners were prisoners of war, security internees, or innocent civilians. None of the HVDs were deemed innocent civilians, but some were accorded prisoner-of-war status.

Despite these efforts, and the release of thousands of prisoners of war, the number of criminal detainees and security internees rose precipitously. In the late summer, Judge Advocates from commands all over the country came to Baghdad for Operation Clean Sweep.[190] Joined by a former Iraqi Judge, they reviewed the files on all criminal detainees to determine if they could be released outright or turned over to the emerging Iraqi courts for at least an investigative hearing. Nevertheless, the number of criminal detainees continued to grow. Iraqi courts were slow to open, and Iraqi judges were reluctant to release prisoners once detained by Coalition Forces. Transporting prisoners from U.S. detention

---

[187] *Available at* http://www.aclu.org/files/projects/foiasearch/pdf/DOD045972.pdf.

[188] Parole agreements and guarantor agreements were used with mixed success as a means to release internees who were thought to present a continuing, but manageable, threat. The former would be signed by the internee at release; the latter would be signed by a person who was willing to assume responsibility for the released internee, usually a tribal elder. Although many prominent Iraqis would advocate for an internee's release, few would be willing to serve as a guarantor. *See generally* On Point II, *supra* note 39, at 263; *see also* Coalition Provisional Authority, "Conditional Release Announcement," Jan. 7, 2004, 23, *available at* http://www.cpa-iraq.org/transcripts/Jan7Bremer_Conditional.htm.

[189] Article 5 of the Third Geneva Convention states, in pertinent part: "Should any doubt arise as to whether persons, having committed a belligerent act and having fallen into the hands of the enemy, belong to any of the categories enumerated in Article 4, such persons shall enjoy the protection of the present Convention until such time as their status has been determined by a competent tribunal." Geneva Convention Relative to the Treatment of Prisoners of War, Aug. 12, 1949, 6 U.S.T. 3316, 75 U.N.T.S. 135, art. 5 [hereinafter GC III].

[190] Warren, *supra* note 28, at 174.

facilities to Iraqi courthouses was a security, logistics, resource, and accountability nightmare. CJTF-7 began holding Criminal Detainee Review and Release Boards and simply released hundreds of prisoners, but most were bound over for disposition by the Iraqi criminal justice system.

One immediate issue was whether CPA should repeal the November 2002 General Amnesty, so that prisoners could be held under the authority of their prior convictions. Although this approach had practical logic, it would have been inconsistent with the requirement to respect the laws in force in Iraq. Instead, CPA issued a public notice that announced the enhancement of sentences for persons convicted of crimes after having been granted amnesty.[191]

In August 2003, CJTF-7 established a review and appeal board as required by Article 78 of the Fourth Geneva Convention.[192] The new Article 78 review and appeal board could not keep pace with the volume of prisoners. It began to meet more frequently and soon expanded in size, eventually to be composed of permanent members whose full-time duty was board service. Judge Advocates were assigned to serve internment orders and to ensure the processing of appeals and periodic reviews. Even when faced with a backlog of internees, the process exceeded the requirement of Article 78 for periodicity of reviews.[193]

Despite conducting timely reviews, the board struggled with commanders' opposition to release decisions and with its own uncertainty over the meaning of the "imperative reasons of security" standard for internment under Article 78.[194] Over the year of the occupation, the standard became more refined, and the board required more detailed information concerning the threat posed by the prisoner. Early on, an imperative threat was presumed if the prisoner had been identified in post-capture screening as possessing intelligence information of value to Coalition Forces, which under the rules of engagement was a basis for detention. The shortage of skilled interrogators meant that the prisoner could remain under "intelligence hold" for weeks or months awaiting meaningful interrogation.[195] Later, the "intelligence hold" was prohibited as a means to establish the "imperative reasons of security" standard. Nevertheless, pressure from commanders not to release prisoners continued. On the other hand, the

---

[191] CPA Public Notice, *Increased Sentences for Those Convicted of Crimes after Receiving Amnesty* (Dec. 19, 2003), *available at* http://www.iraqcoalition.org/regulations/20031228_Increased_Sentences_for_Persons_Convicted_of_Crimes.pdf.

[192] The FRAGO was issued on August 25, 2003; it replaced an earlier version issued on June 28, 2003. On Point II, *supra* note 39, at 248–49.

[193] GC IV Article 78 mandates a review of continued internment every six months, if possible. *See* GC IV, *supra* note 3, art. 78. The CJTF-7 review and appeal board conducted reviews every month.

[194] The "imperative reasons of security" standard is not elaborated upon or defined in the Article itself or in the official Commentary to the Fourth Geneva Convention. Pictet, *supra* note 33, at 367. *See also* Dinstein, *supra* note 5, at 172–76.

[195] The "intelligence hold" was not a category of detainee, but a descriptive term often used to satisfy the GC IV Article 78 "imperative reasons of security" requirement. Because of the accelerated pace of detentions and the shortage of interrogators, the number of detainees on intelligence hold grew from less than 100 in July 2003 to more than 1,200 in January 2004. *See* On Point II, *supra* note 39, at 208.

CPA frequently demanded the release of prisoners for political or public relations reasons, or based on anecdotal (and often inaccurate) humanitarian bases. The entire Article 78 review and appeal process was under constant strain.

Over the summer of 2003, it became clear that the Iraqi criminal justice system was making insufficient progress in increasing capacity (often referred to as through-put) to handle the number of criminal detainees who were in Iraqi or Coalition pretrial confinement awaiting adjudication. In the absence of occupation courts, all trials were held in Iraqi courts. Maneuver unit Judge Advocates, Civil Affairs Soldiers, and CPA civilian legal advisors went all over the country to meet with judges, coax them to the bench, re-establish regular court sessions, and increase the pace of cases moving through the criminal justice system.[196] This effort, a rudimentary rule-of-law program, was enthusiastically supported by commanders, who saw the reopening of the courts as an essential aspect of restoring security, stability, and public confidence.

Judge Advocates and CPA civilian attorneys routinely went to Iraqi courts, and even arranged for and executed payroll payments for judges and other Ministry of Justice personnel, and were under enemy fire on a number of occasions as they did it. Later, Judge Advocates at the Corps, division, and Brigade levels created and staffed Judicial Reconstruction Assistance Teams (called JRATs) and Ministry of Justice Offices (called MOJOs), and for almost a year managed the Baghdad and Mosul court dockets.

On the national level, CPA took action to reinvigorate the Iraqi judicial system. By Order establishing the Judicial Review Committee, CPA implemented a highly successful judicial vetting program that avoided the missteps of the de-Ba'athification Order.[197] Higher-level efforts concentrated on combating judicial corruption and improving the criminal justice system.[198] The CPA made enhancements to the Iraqi Penal Code that mandated rights advisements to suspects, funded civilian defense counsel, and made modifications to sentences and bail arrangements.[199] The enhancements necessitated training for police officers and judges. More fundamentally, CPA created two courts: the Central Criminal Court of Iraq (CCCI) and the Iraqi Special Tribunal (IST). The CCCI had nationwide jurisdiction to try significant security and corruption cases.[200] The IST had jurisdiction to try former regime members, and was the forum that convicted Saddam Hussein.[201] Although established by CPA Orders and supported by

---

[196] Warren, *supra* note 28, at 189.

[197] CPA Order 15, *Establishment of the Judicial Review Committee* (June 23, 2003), *available at* http://www.iraqcoalition.org/regulations/20030623_CPAORD_15_Establishment_of_the_Judicial_Reveiw_Committee.pdf.

[198] For an excellent primer on CPA's rule-of-law activities, see Daniel L. Rubini, *Justice in Waiting: Developing Rule of Law in Iraq*, THE OFFICER 45 (July–Aug. 2009).

[199] CPA Order 31, *Modifications of Penal Code and Criminal Proceedings Law* (Sept. 10, 2003), *available at* http://www.iraqcoalition.org/regulations/20030921_CPAORD31.pdf.

[200] CPA Order 13, *supra* note 104.

[201] CPA Order 48, *Delegation of Authority Regarding an Iraqi Special Tribunal* (Dec. 10, 2003), *available at* http://www.iraqcoalition.org/regulations/20031210_CPAORD_48_IST_and_Appendix_A.pdf.

Coalition investigators and attorney advisors, both courts were composed entirely of Iraqi judges.

The improvements to the Iraqi criminal justice did nothing to address the extrajudicial detention of captured insurgents. As the insurgency continued to strengthen, an increasing number of persons were interned for security offenses. Judge Advocates in Iraq envisioned and championed Operation Wolverine, which proposed the trial of captured Iraqi insurgents by military commission.[202] In October 2003, the proposal was modified to recommend a two-tiered approach, using the CCCI as the forum for most cases and General Courts-Martial where the cases involved attacks against U.S. victims.[203] The U.S. Secretary of Defense approved the plan in concept, but directed that all trials would be held in the CCCI. A CPA Order expanded the court's jurisdiction and established case referral procedures.[204]

Judge Advocates and detailed U.S. Department of Justice attorneys reviewed case files to identify cases amenable to prosecution. Many files were classified or incomplete. There was real difficulty in turning classified intelligence information into prosecutable evidence, and there was often a paucity of significant information in the first place. By November 2003, however, the process had begun, and convictions were eventually obtained for the murder of Coalition soldiers and Iraqi civilians.[205]

The determination that captured insurgents were unlawful combatants who could be held criminally accountable was misunderstood by some who confused the terms "unlawful combatant" and "enemy combatant." Ironically, this was a conclusion reached in the Schlesinger Report, commissioned by the U.S. Department of Defense (DoD), which found that CJTF-7 (and, impliedly, CPA and DOD) were acting "beyond the confines" of the Geneva Conventions because insurgents who were prosecuted in the CCCI were deemed "unlawful combatants" in the manner of the Guantanamo prisoners.[206] CJTF-7 never classified anyone

---

[202] The genesis was an incident in which two soldiers of the U.S. Army's 4th Infantry Division had been captured by insurgents at a checkpoint and then executed, their bodies dumped by the side of the road. The author flew to the scene with Lieutenant General Sanchez and there concluded that the command had to develop a legal process that could hold the perpetrators criminally accountable.

[203] Memorandum from CJTF-7 SJA through Commander, CJTF-7, to Commander, USCENTCOM, *Subject: Prosecuting Iraqis for Security Offenses against Coalition*, Oct. 21, 2003, Department of the Army, Preliminary Screening Inquiry Report, *Investigation of Legal Operations in CJTF-7* (Jan. 25, 2005) at exhibits D-20 and D-21, *available at* U.S. Army Office of The Judge Advocate, General Professional Responsibility Branch, 2200 Army Pentagon, Washington, DC 20310-2200 [hereinafter Preliminary Screening Inquiry Report].

[204] CPA Order 13, *supra* note 104. The revised amended order contains the following language at section 19(1): "Prior to 1 July 2004, the Administrator retains the authority to refer cases to the CCCI . . . Cases referred by the Administrator will have priority." *Id.*

[205] Court sessions began in the late fall of 2003, but were hampered by a shortage of resources available to review and process cases. The pace quickened with the arrival of attorneys, paralegals, and investigators of the Joint Services Law Enforcement Team (JSLET) in the spring of 2004. By July 2004, the CCCI had held thirty-seven trials for fifty-five defendants. On Point II, *supra* note 39, at 265.

[206] James R. Schlesinger, Chairman, *Final Report of the Independent Panel to Review DoD Detention Operations*, 82, 83 (Aug. 2004). The Schlesinger Report confused the term "unlawful

in the manner of the Guantanamo prisoners. It developed and fielded a means to hold insurgents criminally accountable for their warlike acts violating Iraqi law or CPA ordinances committed without benefit of combatant immunity. Those insurgents prosecuted were still "protected persons" under the Fourth Geneva Convention, but they could be prosecuted because they had committed criminal offenses and were not lawful or privileged combatants. They did not meet the criteria of Article 4 of the Third Geneva Convention.[207] This is a result not only clearly contemplated by international humanitarian law, but a result reached only by strict adherence to the Third and Fourth Geneva Conventions. Despite the finding of the Schlesinger Report, prosecution of insurgents as unlawful combatants continued in the CCCI, even after the end of occupation.

Accountability of prisoners and transparency of the detention and internment system were continuing issues, even with assistance from CPA.[208] In cooperation with the CPA Senior Advisor to the Iraqi Ministry of Justice, CJTF-7 provided Arabic lists of detainees and internees to Civil-Military Operations Centers and, in Baghdad, to courts and police stations.[209] Names of detainees and internees were provided to the ICRC through internment cards.[210] However, routine delivery of the cards, as well as frequent interaction with the ICRC, was suspended

---

combatant" used by CJTF-7 with the term "enemy combatant" used at Guantanamo. The Schlesinger Report is simply wrong when it states that "CJTF-7 concluded it had individuals in custody who met the criteria for unlawful combatants set out by the President and extended it in Iraq to those who were not protected as combatants under the Geneva Conventions, based on OLC opinions." *Id.* at 83.

[207] Article 4 of the Third Geneva Convention establishes the criteria for prisoner-of-war status. The portion of Article 4 relevant to operations in Iraq after May 2003 states that prisoners of war include:

> Members of other militias and members of other volunteer corps, including those of organized resistance movements, belonging to a Party to the conflict and operating in or outside their own territory, even if this territory is occupied, provided that such militias or volunteer corps, including such organized resistance movements, fulfill the following conditions:
>
> i. that of being commanded by a person responsible for his subordinates;
> ii. that of having a fixed distinctive sign recognizable at a distance;
> iii. that of carrying arms openly;
> iv. that of conducting their operations in accordance with the laws and customs of war.

GC III, *supra* note 189, art. 4.

[208] Although not understood (and largely not known) at the time was the impact of special operations and nonmilitary forces on detention operations. In hindsight, some of the record-keeping and accountability problems experienced by the 800th Military Police Brigade were probably caused by special operations and nonmilitary forces requesting that their prisoners held in conventional forces detention facilities be kept "off the books" and not reported to the ICRC. Some special operations forces not under the command and control of CJTF-7 had their own long-term detention facilities. *See* Eric Schmitt & Carolyn Marshall, *Task Force 6-26: Before and after Abu Ghraib, a U.S. Unit Abused Detainees*, N.Y. Times, Mar. 19, 2006, at A1.

[209] By February 2004, CPA had fielded an English and Arabic website, available to the public, which listed names and other key information pertaining to internees and detainees. On Point II, *supra* note 39, at 204.

[210] *See* GC IV, *supra* note 3, Annex III.

when the ICRC moved its operations to Jordan in response to safety concerns after the bombing of the U.N. headquarters building in Baghdad on August 19, 2003.[211]

ICRC Protection Delegates based in Jordan made periodic visits back to Iraq to visit internees as authorized under Article 143 of the Fourth Geneva Convention.[212] In January 2004, ICRC delegates visited the Baghdad Central Detention Facility at Abu Ghraib. Through the limited partial invocation of that portion of Article 143 pertaining to imperative military necessity, the ICRC was precluded from conducting private interviews of a small number of internees who were undergoing interrogation; however, the ICRC delegates were provided with the names of the internees and allowed to observe the internees and the conditions of their captivity.[213] Additionally, the ICRC was informed that their delegates would be free to hold private meetings with the internees on any future visit, including a surprise visit.[214] Even though the ICRC acknowledged the right of Coalition Forces to temporarily limit private interviews, this approach was characterized by some as a "new plan to restrict" ICRC access to Abu Ghraib.[215]

A unique prisoner issue was presented by the members of the Mujahedin-e Khalq (MEK), held at Camp Ashraf. The MEK was a military force of several thousand Iranians who had operated against Iran from bases in Iraq. The MEK were the only large scale capitulation of the war—and they were not even Iraqis! They were, however, on the U.S. list of designated foreign terrorist organizations[216] and CJTF-7 was directed not to process them under the Article 78 review and appeal process. After a year of interagency wrangling and debate concerning their status, the MEK were simply deemed "protected persons" under the Fourth Geneva Convention.[217]

---

[211] On Point II, *supra* note 39, at 33.

[212] Article 143 of the Fourth Geneva Convention provides that representatives or delegates of the Protecting Powers "shall have access to all premises occupied by protected persons and shall be able to interview the latter without witnesses, personally or through an interpreter. Such visits may not be prohibited except for reasons of imperative military necessity, and then only as an exceptional and temporary measure." GC IV, *supra* note 3, art. 143.

[213] Preliminary Inquiry Screening Report, *supra* note 203, at 8.

[214] The ICRC delegates accepted these conditions and made a return surprise visit in March 2004, when they were allowed to conduct private interviews with all of the detainees, except for one individual to whom access was erroneously denied. After the ICRC rightfully complained to the CJTF-7 SJA, the CJTF-7 C-2 directed that the ICRC be given unimpeded private access to the detainee. *Id.*

[215] Attachment A, paragraph (u) to Congressional Subpoena proposed by Senators Leahy and Feinstein, *Memorandum for MP and MI Personnel at Abu Ghraib from Colonel Marc Warren, the top legal advisor to Lt. General Ricardo Sanchez, New Plan to Restrict Access to Abu Ghraib, 2 January 2004*. (The subpoena was defeated by the Senate Judiciary Committee on June 17, 2004.) There was no such document. In fact, every effort was being made in January 2004 to support and enable the ICRC's pending visit to Abu Ghraib, after the disastrous visit in November 2003 (at which no Judge Advocates were present).

[216] The MEK was not delisted until September 28, 2012. *See* U.S. Department of State, *Designated Foreign Terrorist Organizations*, Sept. 28, 2012, at http://www.state.gov/j/ct/rls/other/des/123085.htm.

[217] On Point II, *supra* note 39, at 248.

Removal of prisoners from Iraq to other countries was an occasional, but significant, issue in Iraq. At least twice, the U.S. Central Command (USCENTCOM), the unified command that included Iraq within its area of operational responsibility, issued orders directing CJTF-7 to turn over non-Iraqi HVD for transport to locations outside Iraq. CJTF-7 insisted that Article 49 of the Fourth Geneva Convention generally prohibited removing prisoners from occupied territory.[218] Despite its inapplicability in an occupation regulated by the Geneva Conventions, USCENTCOM continued to invoke the "Global War on Terrorism Screening Criteria" as authority to classify prisoners and to remove them from Iraq.[219] The matter was not resolved until March 2004 when the U.S. Office of Legal Counsel (OLC) issued an opinion that led to the removal of a limited number of specified prisoners from Iraq. The opinion concluded that "operatives of the al Qaeda terrorist organization who were not Iraqi nationals or permanent residents of Iraq" were not protected persons within the meaning of the Fourth Geneva Convention.[220]

When Saddam Hussein was captured on December 13, 2003, he was accorded the status of prisoner of war, which meant, among other things, that the command was obligated to report his capture to the ICRC and allow the ICRC to visit him. This characterization was met with reluctance, if not resistance, at higher levels, at least in part because of the mistaken notion that his status as a prisoner of war might accord him immunity from prosecution for his pre-capture criminal offenses. Ultimately, Saddam's status as a prisoner of war was publicly acknowledged and the ICRC visited him in accordance with elaborate security precautions on numerous occasions, as did Judge Advocates.

---

[218] The first paragraph of GC IV Article 49 states: "Individual or mass forcible transfers, as well as deportations of protected persons from occupied territory to the territory of the Occupying Power or to that of any other country, occupied or not, are prohibited, regardless of motive." GC IV, *supra* note 3, art. 49. "The prohibition is absolute and allows of no exceptions . . . " Pictet, *supra* note 33, at 279.

[219] U.S. Deputy Secretary of Defense Memorandum, Global Screening Criteria for Detainees (Feb. 20, 2004), *available at* https://www.aclu.org/files/assets/2010_06_08_DOJ_Release.pdf. The memorandum includes an attachment dated August 22, 2003, which provides criteria and guidelines for screening and processing persons detained by the Department of Defense in connection with "Operation Enduring Freedom [Afghanistan] or other war-on-terrorism operations . . ."

[220] The interplay between derogations in GC Article 5 and "exclusions" from the definition of protected person under GC Article 4 is a dangerous area. The limited derogation of forfeiture of the rights of communication was used sparingly by U.S. forces in Iraq, and was subject to the admonitions and requirements of the third paragraph of GC IV Article 5. *See* GC IV, *supra* note 3, art. 5. *See also* Dinstein, *supra* note 5, at 63. A determination that civilians are not protected persons within the meaning of GC IV Article 4 is a decision of great significance that should be made at the national level. In Iraq, U.S. nationals, nationals of a state not bound by the Fourth Geneva Convention, nationals of a co-belligerent state, and operatives of the al Qaida terrorist organization who are not Iraqi nationals or permanent residents of Iraq were determined not to be "protected persons" within the meaning of GC IV Article 4. *See* Memorandum Opinion for the Counsel to the President, *"Protected Persons" Status in Occupied Iraq under the Fourth Geneva Convention* (Mar. 18, 2004), *available at* http://www2.gwu.edu/~nsarchiv/torturingdemocracy/documents/20040318.pdf.

Judge Advocates helped the command reconcile the juxtaposition of Saddam's status as a prisoner of war with his status as the war's most high-profile captive. He was segregated for his own safety and security (as were other HVD), but information about his capture, physical condition, and demeanor was released to the public. As had been done with the bodies of Saddam's sons Uday and Qusay on July 24, 2003, a small number of Iraqi political leaders were allowed to observe Saddam under controlled circumstances in order to corroborate his identity. The public and military advantage to be gained from the observation was weighed against the general admonition of Article 13 of the Third Geneva Convention not to expose prisoners of war to public curiosity.[221] The balance tipped in favor of the observation—if Saddam's identity had not been confirmed to the satisfaction of the Iraqi people, he would have continued to be a shadow rallying point for the insurgency, and his capture would have been dismissed as a hoax. Conversely, CPA's insistence that "foreign fighters" should be placed on public display was rebuffed as a violation of the principles of Article 13.[222]

Because the United Nations mandated its termination date, the occupation ended on July 1, 2004. With the occupiers unable to exercise the functions of government after that date, the United Nations was required to authorize an ambitious transformative occupation in order to rapidly create a successor Iraqi government. Thus, the duration of the Iraq occupation was not based on the achievement of security objectives or the attainment of conditions that would support the emergence of a capable indigenous government, but on an arbitrary date established by the United Nations.

IV. The Role of the Military Legal Advisor in Occupation

Occupation is a legally intensive environment where Judge Advocates play a key role along with civilian attorneys from various U.S. and foreign government agencies. Most Coalition members of a deploying military force of any significant size will have at least one legal advisor as part of their headquarters. The military government or occupation authority can be expected to have both Judge Advocates and civilian attorneys.

Identification and resolution of legal issues should begin during the planning phase for an occupation, and must be integrated into preparatory exercises and conferences. Military exercises must not end with the defeat of the enemy's military forces and intelligence preparation of the battlefield but must include an analysis of the capability of the systems of government and public administration, as well as the enemy's order of battle. As much intellectual effort must go

---

[221] GC III, *supra* note 189, art. 13.

[222] *But see* Dinstein, *supra* note 5, at 167 (stating "infiltrators are simply not shielded by the Convention as protected persons."). Moreover, the foreign fighters were not accorded prisoner-of-war status.

into planning for activities after decisive combat operations as is put into planning for fires and maneuver.

Judge Advocates are part of the commander's staff and generally participate as advisors in overall planning efforts. Occupation planning is comprehensive and interdisciplinary, and should involve intelligence, operations, medical, engineering, information, logistics, military police, and civil affairs functions. Planning must address the basic human needs of the civilian population, with immediate emphasis on restoring security and normalcy:

- When will the police and fire departments be back on duty?
- When will electricity and water be restored?
- When will trash collection resume?
- When will schools reopen?
- When will businesses, markets, banks, and gasoline stations reopen?
- How will medical care be provided?
- What restrictions on travel and movement will be imposed?
- Who is in charge of the neighborhoods, towns, and cities?

Legal advisors may consider the occupation planning checklist at Annex C.

Military legal advisors should be integrated into strategic- and operational-level interagency planning for occupation. As happened in Iraq, decisions made without an understanding of the conditions on the ground or an appreciation for how the policy will affect security can have deleterious consequences. Military legal advisors on planning staffs can provide insights on the legal and practical requirements of occupation law, and act in a representative capacity on behalf of the commander and military forces charged with maintaining security while administering the occupation.

Military legal advisors planning for an occupation should study not just occupation law, but occupation history, particularly the history of occupation in Germany and the Far East after World War II. These effective occupations demonstrate the importance of making a comprehensive plan and devoting adequate resources to its execution. Study of the U.S. and U.K. occupation of Iraq and the Israeli occupation of Gaza and the Golan Heights and West Bank will provide contemporary lessons in occupation, as well as an appreciation for the impact of human rights law. Past counterinsurgency and "nation-building" operations, such as the U.S. occupation of the Philippines after the Spanish-American War, British counterinsurgency operations in Malaysia, U.S. military operations generally in Central America in the last century, and British operations in Northern Ireland also afford valuable insights into issues likely encountered in an occupation.

Before the invasion, military legal advisors with Coalition Forces massed in Kuwait identified numerous issues and requirements pertaining to the potential occupation of Iraq. These included general questions concerning how occupation authority would be exercised and specific legal questions on the content of the Occupation Proclamation and ordinances, whether some

Iraqi judges should be removed from the bench,[223] whether occupation courts with military judges could be convened by commanders, and whether parts of the Iraqi Penal Code were to be suspended.[224] Unfortunately, the answer was that all of these matters were being addressed at "the National and Coalition level."

As in most modern military operations generally, legal advisors should deploy in sufficient numbers with the headquarters and operating forces in an occupation and advise occupation authorities, commanders, and staffs on applicable law and policy. Providing advice on international humanitarian law, including occupation law, is a solemn responsibility of Judge Advocates, involving issues of law, regulation, policy, discipline, humanity, politics, and treaty obligations on the part of the United States. In no small measure, Judge Advocates in the field are an affirmation of the nation's intent to follow and enforce international humanitarian law. Although the United States is not yet a party to Protocol I Additional to the Geneva Conventions, Judge Advocates provide a more comprehensive—and immediate—resource than was contemplated by Article 82 of the Protocol (mandating legal advisors for commanders).[225]

Military legal advisors deploying into occupied territory will find their attention immediately directed to the related activities of rule of law and restoration of security, with detention and internment to follow. In Iraq, Judge Advocates began efforts to restore Iraqi judicial capability almost as soon as Coalition Forces entered the country. Judge Advocates assigned to Civil Affairs units assessed courthouses in Basra and southern Iraq, and assessments continued as the war progressed northward.[226] Many court buildings had been looted. In some cases, however, judges and other court personnel had literally (and physically) protected their courthouses by remaining in the structures continuously.

In Baghdad, the V Corps Staff Judge Advocate (SJA) made radio broadcasts to order judges and court personnel to return to work. Judge Advocates unilaterally "deputized" court personnel as armed court police to guard many buildings and records.[227] Not all buildings could be protected. In the main public records repository building in Baghdad, where property and other records were stored, fires

[223] Sanctions or other coercive measures may not be imposed against public officials and judges who "abstain from fulfilling their functions for reasons of conscience." GC IV, *supra* note 3, art. 54. However, GC IV Article 54 acknowledges the right of the Occupying Power to remove public officials, including judges, from their posts. *See* Pictet, *supra* note 33, at 308.

[224] HR IV Article 43 states, in pertinent part, that the Occupying Power shall take measures to restore and ensure public order and safety "while respecting, unless absolutely prevented, the laws in force in the country." HR IV, *supra* note 9, art. 43. This rule is repeated in Article 64 of the Fourth Geneva Convention: "The penal laws of the occupied territory shall remain in force, with the exception that they may be repealed or suspended by the Occupying Power in cases where they constitute a threat to its security or an obstacle to the application of the present Convention." GC IV, *supra* note 3, art. 64. In CPA Order 7, *supra* note 99, the CPA suspended certain provisions of the 1969 Iraqi Penal Code "that the former regime used . . . as a tool of repression in violation of internationally recognized human rights standards" and suspended capital punishment.

[225] Marc Warren, *Operational Law—A Concept Matures*, 152 Mil. L. Rev. 33, 39 (1996).

[226] Warren, *supra* note 28, at 188.

[227] *Id.*

had been set in the document storage stacks. Courthouses, public records repositories, and police stations were prime targets for arsonists.

Modest rule-of-law activities are an essential and immediate instrument for the military to use to help re-establish security, order, and public confidence.[228] Rule of law requires clear definition, assignment of responsibility and resources, and establishment of objectives and performance measures. There is no simple template for rule-of-law activities; the objectives and performance measures must be relative to the history, culture, and reality on the ground.[229] The focus must be on the "Three Ps": Police, Prisons, and Prosecutors (courts).[230] In an occupation, the Fourth Geneva Convention properly limits the scope of rule-of-law activities. More transformative and sophisticated rule-of-law activities, such as judicial mentoring, building a public defender system, or helping to improve substantive law and procedure, should be delayed until security, legal, and practical conditions permit.[231]

The CPA and military attorneys expended Herculean effort and made progress, but synchronization of their efforts was uneven, and clear rule-of-law performance measures and objectives were not defined.[232] Directive authority for overall rule-of-law activities was not fixed, and SJAs and CPA attorneys engaged in the activities commanded no assets. In the first year in Iraq, there were four CPA Senior Advisors to the Iraqi Ministry of Justice, not counting acting advisors who filled the gaps. This meant new philosophies, new approaches, and redevelopment of personal bonds among all involved parties, including Iraqi ministers and judges.

In the summer and fall of 2003, troops dedicated to the detention and internment task were simply overwhelmed. The CJTF-7 SJA chaired a weekly meeting of Military Police, Military Intelligence, engineer, medical, legal, and CPA representatives that attempted to synchronize and improve detention activities.[233] Judge Advocates did everything in their power to ensure that all prisoners were treated humanely and in accordance with the law. In many cases, Judge Advocates personally intervened to ensure that military authorities provided prisoners with adequate food, water, hygiene, and shelter.[234]

---

[228] Rebuilding the rule of law is a task too enthusiastically embraced in the U.S. counterinsurgency Field Manual. *See generally* U.S. DEP'T OF ARMY, FIELD MANUAL 3-24/U.S. MARINE CORPS WARFIGHTING PUBLICATION 3-33.5: COUNTERINSURGENCY (Dec. 15, 2006). A more realistic view of rule-of-law activities is found in INT'L & OPERATIONAL LAW DEP'T, THE JUDGE ADVOCATE GENERAL'S LEGAL CTR. & SCH., U.S. ARMY THE RULE OF LAW HANDBOOK, A PRACTITIONER'S GUIDE FOR JUDGE ADVOCATES (2011).

[229] *See* Rosa Ehrenreich Brooks, *The New Imperialism: Violence, Norms, and the "Rule of Law,"* 101 MICH. L. REV. 2275 (2002–2003).

[230] The Three Ps are also termed the "Three Cs:" Cops, Courts, and Corrections.

[231] *See* Dan E. Stigall, *Comparative Law and State-Building: The "Organic Minimalist" Approach to Legal Reconstruction*, 29 LOY. L.A. INT'L & COMP. L. REV. 1, 30–31 (2007).

[232] Preliminary Screening Inquiry Report, *supra* note 203, at Tab 60 (End of Mission Report of Clint Williamson to the Administrator, CPA).

[233] ON POINT II, *supra* note 39, at 248.

[234] *Id.* at 244. Judge Advocates led the efforts to improve the Camp Cropper detention facility at the Baghdad International Airport and wrote orders to get tents, generators, and other equipment for detention facilities throughout Iraq. Warren, *supra* note 28, at 188.

Judge Advocates also helped occupation authorities reinforce discipline and restraint by drafting orders and command memoranda on adherence to the law of armed conflict. These documents were disseminated to troops in the field and formed the basis for training. The summary paragraph of a periodic memorandum from the Commander, CJTF-7 states a common message to subordinate commanders and their forces: "Respect for others, humane treatment of persons not taking part in hostilities, and adherence to the law of war and rules of engagement is a matter of discipline and values. It is what separates us from our enemies."[235]

Despite command emphasis on discipline, the stresses of a counterinsurgency campaign can lead to results that are counterproductive to an effective occupation. Commanders and their legal advisors should remain vigilant for signs of prisoner abuse, unlawful destruction of property, and use of excessive force. Frequent interaction with nongovernmental organizations, international and regional organizations, and public sector entities, including aspects of the civil society, will inform occupation authorities about problems and perceptions. Commanders and their staffs must pay attention to ICRC reports in particular.

A "rules of engagement working group" that is composed of operational, intelligence, and legal experts can help ensure that the rules for the use of force are properly adapted to the threat and the environment. Keeping a watchful eye over complaints by prisoners and civilians, and over claims by civilians for damage allegedly caused by occupation forces, can lead to the identification of trends suggesting breaches of discipline or insufficiency of training. That the demands of concurrent combat and occupation duty are neither insignificant nor novel is illustrated by the observation of The Judge Advocate General of the U.S. Army in his report on the court-martial of Major Edwin Glenn during the occupation of the Philippines:

> The situation thus presented was difficult and to the last degree exasperating, but it did not relieve the officers and men of the occupying forces of their obligation to adhere to the rules of war in the efforts put forth by them with a view to suppress the insurrection and restore public order . . .[236]

No discussion of discipline in an occupation is complete without mentioning the Abu Ghraib scandal. In Iraq, Abu Ghraib became synonymous with prisoner abuse. Ironically, the notorious prison had been chosen as a detention facility despite its awful history because it offered the only relatively safe location in the Baghdad area to house prisoners. It offered a vast improvement over the tents and open holding areas formed by concertina wire perimeters that had sprung up to serve as makeshift detention facilities. Nevertheless, the shocking abuses fueled

---

[235] Memorandum from CJTF-7 Commander to All Coalition Forces Personnel, *Subject: Proper Treatment of the Iraqi People during Combat Operations* (Oct. 5, 2003). On Point II, *supra* note 39, at 260.

[236] Court-Martial of Major Edwin F. Glenn, Samar, Philippine Islands, Apr. 1902, S. Doc. No. 213, 57th Cong. 20–28.

the insurgency and sapped public support for the war effort. Abu Ghraib serves as a searing reminder of the negative impact of indiscipline.

In that regard, legal advisors in an occupation must be aware that they are practicing law in a dangerous and politically charged environment. Despite talk of "winning hearts and minds," occupation is hard business maintained with the tip of the bayonet.[237] Administrator Bremer had a desktop sign in his office in Baghdad that read, "Success has a thousand fathers; failure is an orphan." There is a magnified and random spotlight of accountability for real and perceived failures in an occupation, and because an occupation is so legally intensive, the legal advisor is not likely to escape the light. Nor will the legal advisor be judged in the context of the danger, ambiguity, exigency, and imperfect information that define occupation. Rather, as U.S. Deputy Attorney General James B. Comey wrote, the legal advisor will be judged "in a quiet, dignified well-lit room" where his judgments will be "viewed with the perfect, and brutally unfair, vision of hindsight."[238]

Nevertheless, occupation is the ultimate environment for the practice of the professions of arms and law. It presents issues of international humanitarian law, policy, and public administration. When occupation is coincident with counterinsurgency, it stresses the law and the legal advisor. It is precisely when the operational environment presents its most difficult challenges that the law of occupation and the legal advisors who give it practical meaning are at their highest utility and greatest significance.

---

[237] The foundation of belligerent occupation is the "power of the bayonet." DINSTEIN, *supra* note 5, at 35.

[238] James B. Comey, *Intelligence under the Law*, 10 GREEN BAG 439, 443 (2007), *cited in* Jack Goldsmith, *Reflections on Government Lawyering*, 205 MIL. L. REV. 192, 201 (Fall 2010).

Annex A Coalition Provisional Authority Regulation Number 1

Pursuant to my authority as Administrator of the Coalition Provisional Authority (CPA), relevant U.N. Security Council resolutions, including Resolution 1483 (2003), and the laws and usages of war,

I hereby promulgate the following:

Section 1 The Coalition Provisional Authority

1) The CPA shall exercise powers of government temporarily in order to provide for the effective administration of Iraq during the period of transitional administration, to restore conditions of security and stability, to create conditions in which the Iraqi people can freely determine their own political future, including by advancing efforts to restore and establish national and local institutions for representative governance and facilitating economic recovery and sustainable reconstruction and development.
2) The CPA is vested with all executive, legislative and judicial authority necessary to achieve its objectives, to be exercised under relevant U.N. Security Council resolutions, including Resolution 1483 (2003), and the laws and usages of war. This authority shall be exercised by the CPA Administrator.
3) As the Commander of Coalition Forces, the Commander of U.S. Central Command shall directly support the CPA by deterring hostilities; maintaining Iraq's territorial integrity and security; searching for, securing and destroying weapons of mass destruction; and assisting in carrying out Coalition policy generally.

Section 2 The Applicable Law

Unless suspended or replaced by the CPA or superseded by legislation issued by democratic institutions of Iraq, laws in force in Iraq as of April 16, 2003 shall continue to apply in Iraq insofar as the laws do not prevent the CPA from exercising its rights and fulfilling its obligations, or conflict with the present or any other Regulation or Order issued by the CPA.

Section 3 Regulations and Orders issued by the CPA

1) In carrying out the authority and responsibility vested in the CPA, the Administrator will, as necessary, issue Regulations and Orders. Regulations shall be those instruments that define the institutions and authorities of the CPA. Orders are binding instructions issued

by the CPA. Regulations and Orders will remain in force until repealed by the Administrator or superseded by legislation issued by democratic institutions of Iraq. Regulations and Orders issued by the Administrator shall take precedence over all other laws and publications to the extent such other laws and publications are inconsistent. The Administrator may also from time to time issue Public Notices.

2) The promulgation of any CPA Regulation or Order requires the approval or signature of the Administrator. The Regulation or Order shall enter into force as specified therein, shall be promulgated in the relevant languages and shall be disseminated as widely as possible. In the case of divergence, the English text shall prevail.
3) CPA Regulations and orders shall bear the symbols CPA/REG/Date Month 2003/_ and CPA/ORD/Date Month 2003/_. A register of the Regulations and Orders shall indicate the date of entry into force, the subject matter and amendments or changes thereto, or the repeal or suspension thereof.

Section 4 Memoranda

1) The Administrator may issue Memoranda in relation to the interpretation and application of any Regulation or Order.
2) CPA Memoranda shall bear the symbols CPA/MEM/Date Month 2003/_. The provisions of Section 3 shall also apply to the promulgation of CPA Memoranda.

Section 5 Entry into Force

This Regulation shall enter into force on the date of signature.
L. Paul Bremer, Administrator
Coalition Provisional Authority

Annex B Coalition Provisional Authority Order Number 7 Penal Code

Pursuant to my authority as head of the Coalition Provisional Authority (CPA), relevant U.N. Security Council resolutions, including Resolution 1483 (2003), and the laws and usages of war,

Reconfirming the provisions of General Franks' Freedom Message to the Iraqi People of April 16, 2003,

Recognizing that the former regime used certain provisions of the penal code as a tool of repression in violation of internationally recognized human rights standards,

Acting on behalf, and for the benefit, of the Iraqi people,

I hereby promulgate the following:

Section 1 Judges, Police and Prosecutors

All judges, police and prosecutors shall perform their duties in accordance with CPA Regulation No. 1 (CPA/REG/23 May 2003/01) and in accordance with any other Regulations, Orders, Memoranda or instructions issued by the CPA.

Section 2 Suspension of Certain Provisions of Penal Code

1) Without prejudice to the continuing review of Iraqi laws, the Third Edition of the 1969 Iraqi Penal Code with amendments, registered in Baghdad on the fifth day of Jumada I 1389 or the nineteenth day of July 1969, shall apply, with the exception that i) Part Two, Chapter Two, Paragraph 200, and ii) Part Two, Chapter Three, Section One, paragraph 225 are hereby suspended.
2) Legal proceedings may be brought with respect to the following offenses only with the written permission of the Administrator of the CPA:
   a. Part One, Chapter Four, Paragraphs 81–84, publication offenses.
   b. Part Two, Chapter One, Paragraphs 156–189, offenses against the external security of the state.
   c. Part Two, Chapter Two, Paragraphs 190–195; 198–199; 201–219, offenses against the internal security of the state.
   d. Part Two, Chapter Three, Section One, Paragraphs 223–224; 226–228, offenses against public authorities.
   e. Part Two, Chapter Three, Section Two, Paragraph 229, offense of insulting a public official.

Section 3 Penalties

1) Capital punishment is suspended. In each case where the death penalty is the only available penalty prescribed for an offense, the court may substitute the lesser penalty of life imprisonment, or such other lesser penalty as provided for in the Penal Code.
2) Torture and cruel, degrading or inhuman treatment or punishment is prohibited.
3) No person will be prosecuted for aiding, assisting, associating with, or working for Coalition Forces or the CPA.

Section 4 Nondiscrimination

In exercising their official functions, all persons undertaking public duties or holding public office, including all police, prosecutors, and judges, must apply the law impartially. No person will be discriminated against on the basis of sex, race, color, language, religion, political opinion, national, ethnic or social origin, or birth.

Section 5 Delegation of Authority

The Administrator of the CPA may delegate his authority under this Order.

Section 6 Entry into Force

This Order shall enter into force on the date of signature.
L. Paul Bremer, Administrator, Coalition Provisional Authority

Annex C Occupation Planning Checklist for Legal Advisors (Organized using the pneumonic "LAST")

- LAW:
  - o Is there a clear understanding that occupation law applies?
  - o Is there any law supplementing occupation law?
    - Are there additional UN authorities?
    - Does the participation of Coalition partners present legal considerations that stem from the Additional Protocols, human rights law, or other sources (including national "red lines" that may constrain employment of the forces of Coalition partners)?
  - o What is the domestic law presently in force in the territory that will be occupied?
    - Should any parts of the law be suspended?
      - Political offenses?
      - Capital punishment?
- AUTHORITY:
  - o Will there be a Proclamation of Occupation and, if so, what is its content?
  - o Is there a need for occupation ordnances?
    - How will they be published and disseminated?
    - How will they be enforced?
  - o What is the instrument by which occupation authority will be exercised?
    - By local military commanders?
      - If so, what are the limits on their authority? (For example, may commanders appoint local officials or authorize elections?)
    - In collaboration with an existing or emerging domestic government?
    - Military government?
    - Occupation authority on the CPA model?
  - o What is the plan for governance by the occupation authority?
    - What orders and regulations may be necessary? (Review CPA orders and regulations as examples.)
    - How will the occupation be funded?
    - What are the requirements for fielding domestic police, security and military forces (security sector reform)?
      - May they be built on existing institutions?
      - How will their leadership be determined?
      - How will they be recruited, vetted, selected, housed, trained, equipped, led, paid and directed?
  - o What are the legal status and authorities for the use of force of contractors?

- o How will the occupation be funded?
  - Seized assets?
  - Taxes?
- SECURITY:
  - o How will immediate security issues be handled?
    - What are the rules of engagement for occupation forces?
    - Are curfews and exclusion zones necessary?
    - Should weapons possession by civilians be regulated?
    - Are other restrictions on civilians necessary? (For example, it may be appropriate to consider restrictions on freedom of movement and assembly; restrictions on possession of fuels, ammunition, explosives, and even on having excessive amounts of fertilizer, chemicals or other products that could be used to make bombs.)
    - Where will civilians arrested for security offenses and violations of domestic law be:
      - Detained?
      - Tried? (Is trial by domestic courts a realistic option or should there be a plan for occupation courts convened by commanders?)
  - o What is the status and capability of the civilian police and court system?
  - o What is the location and condition of police stations, courthouses, public records storage facilities, jails, prisons, hospitals, transportation infrastructure, and utilities?
    - Are they functional?
    - What plans and resources are required to safeguard them?
  - o Where are significant museums and cultural objects?
    - What plans and resources are required to safeguard them?
  - o How will public utilities and other public functions (schools, refuse collection, local governments, for example) remain operational?
    - Will it be necessary to order public officials to return to work? When and how will the order be given?
    - What is the vetting process to determine the reliability of public officials and workers?
    - How will public officials and workers be paid?
- TRANSITION:
  - o What are the goals and milestones for creating conditions for the successor domestic government?
    - What vehicle will be used for domestic interim government?
    - How will emerging leaders be vetted and developed?
    - What is the process by which leaders in developing ministries and departments are coached, mentored and trained?
    - What is the role of the courts and civil society (bar associations, e.g.), and how will they be supported?

- o How can intergovernmental organizations, international and regional organizations, non-governmental organizations, and private sector entities best work toward common goals? (Integration of activities may not be possible.)
- o What is the role of political subdivisions and how will the leaders of states or provinces, and cities and towns, be coached, mentored and trained?
- o When will elections be held?
- o Is there a role for Transitional Justice?
  - Is there a need to identify and detain former regime members and others who may be prosecuted for crimes committed before the occupation, and collect and preserve evidence for that purpose?
    - Should the occupation authority establish a special tribunal for this purpose?
  - Is there a need to resolve property claims (for example, where private property had been confiscated by the former regime)?
    - Should the occupation authority establish commissions for this purpose?
- o What is the duration of the occupation?
  - Is the end of occupation condition or time based?
  - Is there any residual role for military forces of the occupier after the end of occupation? If so:
    - Is there continuing UN authority for the forces to remain in formerly occupied territory?
    - What will govern the legal status and authority of the remaining military forces of the former occupier? (For example, is it necessary to conclude a Status of Forces Agreement with the successor government?)
    - What disposition will be made of detainees held by the occupation force

20 }

United Nations Peace Operations

CREATING SPACE FOR PEACE

Chris Jenks*

Peacekeeping is not a job for soldiers, but only a soldier can do it.[1]

DAG HAMMARSKJÖLD, *SECOND SECRETARY GENERAL OF THE UNITED NATIONS*

I. Introduction

In 2013, a hundred and twenty countries contributed over 118,000 military, police, civilian employees, and contractors[2] in support of sixteen different United Nations

* Assistant Professor of Law and Criminal Justice Clinic Director, SMU Dedman School of Law, Lieutenant Colonel (Retired), U.S. Army. Former Chief of the International Law Branch, U.S. Army Office of the Judge Advocate General International and Operational Law Division in the Pentagon and attorney advisor in the Office of the Legal Adviser at the Department of State. Prior to serving as a JAG, Jenks served as an infantry officer, including deploying to Bosnia as part of a multinational peacekeeping force. While at the Pentagon he served as the legal advisor to the U.S. Military Observers Group, which supports U.S. military personnel assigned to U.N. missions. While at the Department of State he briefly served at the U.S. Mission to the United Nations in New York where he represented the United States on cultural and humanitarian issues pending before the Third Committee. He has also served as the deputy course director of the Peace Operations course at the International Institute of Humanitarian Law in Sanremo, Italy.

[1] Dag Hammarskjöld quoted in U.S. DEP'T OF ARMY, FIELD MANUAL 100–23 PEACE OPERATIONS para. 1 (Dec. 30, 1994). Hammarskjöld is the only U.N. Secretary General to die in office. Hammarskjöld died in a plane crash in 1961 on the way to negotiate a ceasefire in what is now the Democratic Republic of the Congo.

[2] United Nations Peacekeeping Statistics, http://www.un.org/en/peacekeeping/resources/statistics/ (follow "Partnerships" hyperlink) (last visited Sept. 11, 2014) [hereinafter Peacekeeping Statistics]. When equipment and funds are factored in, all 193 U.N. member states support U.N. peacekeeping efforts, but to varied degrees. Technically under Article 17 of the U.N. Charter every member state is obligated to pay "their respective share towards peacekeeping" and does so through "a special scale of assessments under a complex formula that Member States have established." Financing Peacekeeping, http://www.un.org/en/peacekeeping/operations/financing.shtml (last visited Sept. 11, 2014) [hereinafter Financing Peacekeeping].

(UN) peace operations missions around the world.[3]Peacekeepers protected civilians, observed ceasefire compliance, monitored elections, trained military and police, cleared mines, and disarmed, demobilized, and reintegrated armed groups socially and economically into society.[4]Peacekeepers also conducted offensive operations using attack helicopters, artillery, and surveillance drones to neutralize recalcitrant warring factions.

Peace operations are a growth industry: since 2000 there has been a steady increase in the number of troops and equipment from around the world deployed as part of a U.N. peacekeeping mission.[5]The cost of these efforts for peace totaled $US 7.83 *billion* in 2013 alone. Of infinitely greater significance, 106 U.N. personnel were killed in 2013 while serving on a U.N. peacekeeping mission.[6]

Despite the number of missions, countries involved, and the cost (both financial and in human lives), not much is known about peace operations. Perhaps this is because for the First World, although peace operations are arguably how the international community endeavors to fulfill the charge of the U.N. Charter "to save succeeding generations from the scourge of war," those wars and associated

---

[3] The current U.N. peacekeeping missions include: United Nations Mission for the Referendum in Western Sahara (MINURSO), United Nations Multidimensional Integrated Stabilization Mission in Mali (MINUSMA), United Nations Stabilization Mission in Haiti (MINUSTAH), United Nations Organization Stabilization Mission in the Democratic Republic of the Congo (MONUSCO), African Union-United Nations Hybrid Operation in Darfur (UNAMID), United Nations Disengagement Observer Force (UNDOF), United Nations Peacekeeping Force in Cyprus (INFICYP), United Nations Interim Force in Lebanon (UNIFIL), United Nations Interim Security Force for Abeyei (UNISFA), United Nations Mission in the Republic of South Sudan (UNMISS), United Nations Operation in Cote d'Ivoire (UNOCI), United Nations Interim Administration Mission in Kosovo (UNMIK), Untied Nations Mission in Liberia (UNMIL), United Nations Military Observer Group in India and Pakistan (UNMOGIP), and United Nations Truce Supervision Organization (UNTSO). In 2014, the United Nations began its newest peacekeeping mission, United Nations Multidimensional Integrated Stabilization Mission in the Central African Republic (MINUSCA). In addition to those peacekeeping missions, the U.N.'s Department of Peace Keeping Operations directs one political mission, the United Nations Assistance Mission in Afghanistan.

[4] United Nations Peacekeeping Issues, http://www.un.org/en/peacekeeping/issues/.

[5] Peacekeeping Fact Sheet, http://www.un.org/en/peacekeeping/resources/statistics/factsheet.shtml (last visited Sept. 11, 2014) [herein after Peacekeeping Fact Sheet]. The logistics in supporting such missions involve 56 aircraft, 12 ships, 144 helicopters, over 34,000 vehicles, 30 hospitals, and 284 medical clinics. Peacekeeping Statistics, *supra* note 2. As referenced in the introduction and discussed later in this chapter, the United Nations also now employs attack helicopters, artillery, and even unmanned aerial systems, or "drones."

[6] United Nations Peacekeeping Fatalities by Year, http://www.un.org/en/peacekeeping/fatalities/documents/stats_1.pdf (last visited Sept. 11, 2014). Causes of death range from accident to illness but also malicious actions. And here the term "U.N. personnel" includes military members, military observers, police, international civilians, and local civilians working for the United Nations. In 2014, malicious acts claimed the lives of some thirty-nine U.N. personnel, the highest number in over twenty years. The sixty-nine peacekeeping missions the United Nations has undertaken since 1948 have claimed the lives of over 3,250 U.N. personnel. Peacekeeping Fact Sheet, *supra* note 5.

peace operations occur in the Third World.[7] And many U.N. peacekeepers are also from Third World countries, limiting the West, for the most part, to fund operations that, but for occasional media coverage, are out of sight and mind. This chapter seeks to alter, however slightly, the information deficit surrounding peace operations. Whether prompted by concern for the increased number of missions and what that suggests about the human condition, or concern about where and how money is being spent, today's global citizen should know something about U.N. peace operations.

II. U.N. Charter Foundation for Peace Operations

Peace operations "describes a very broad range of peace and security interventions in international conflict management."[8] Peace operations are "crisis response and limited contingency operations conducted by a combination of military forces and non military organizations."[9] The personnel involved range from military units, to individual military observers, to police, to international and local civilian U.N. workers, to contractors, to volunteers and aid organizations. This chapter follows the common practice of referring to the personnel, including civilian and military, assigned to and participating in any type of U.N. peace operation as peacekeepers.

There are a variety of types of peace operations, including peacekeeping, peace enforcement, peace building, peace making, and conflict prevention. A given mission may involve only one type of peace operation, but more often a mission involves multiple types, sometime occurring sequentially, sometimes in parallel. This chapter begins by explaining the U.N. Charter foundation for two types of peace operations: peacekeeping and peace enforcement. The chapter then explains the historical development of peace operations and their organizational structure. Next the chapter details some challenges in peace operations,

---

[7] Terms such as "First World" and "Third World" are defined in a variety of ways. This chapter uses "Third World" to refer to the bottom portion of the United Nations Human Development Index, which includes countries such as Pakistan, Ethiopia, Bangladesh, and Rwanda. United Nations Development Programme, Human Development Index and Its Components, https://data.undp.org/dataset/Table-1-Human-Development-Index-and-its-components/wxub-qc5k (last visited Sept. 11, 2014) [hereinafter Human Development Index]. These same countries represent four of the top five troop-contributing countries to U.N. peacekeeping missions. Ranking of Military and Police Contributions to U.N. Operations, https://data.undp.org/dataset/Table-1-Human-Development--and-its-components/wxub-qc5k (last visited Sept. 11, 2014) [hereinafter UN Troop-Contributing Countries].

[8] Corinna Kuhl, *The Evolution of Peace Operations, From Interposition to Integrated Missions*, Remarks at the 31st Roundtable on Current Problems of International Humanitarian Law, International Institute of Humanitarian Law, Sanremo, Italy, 70 (Sept. 4–6, 2008), *available at* https://www.icrc.org/eng/assets/files/other/sanremo-2008_peace_ops.pdf.

[9] Joint Chiefs of Staff, Joint Pub. 3-07.3 Peace Operations, vii (Oct. 17, 2007) [hereinafter Peace Operations].

including identifying the applicable law and accountability for peacekeeper misconduct. The chapter then utilizes the U.N. mission in the Democratic Republic of the Congo (DRC) as a case study to explore both how well the United Nations has implemented lessons learned and the ramifications of a peacekeeping force with a mandate to carry out offensive operations.

The international community established the United Nations on October 24, 1945, by ratifying the United Nations Charter.[10]The United Nation's formation followed two world wars that claimed millions of lives within twenty-five years of each other. Unsuccessful efforts to ensure peace following World War I included the League of Nations,[11] an intergovernmental organization designed to maintain world peace, and the Kellog-Briand Pact's idealistic ban on warfare.[12]Although the United Nation's formal establishment was not until the Charter's ratification after the conclusion of World War II, some fifty states signed the Charter in June 1945 when the war with Japan was still ongoing. In fact, China, the Soviet Union, the United Kingdom, and the United States developed the Charter the preceding summer, in 1944, roughly a year before the end of the war with Germany.

Lest their be any doubt as to the role Word War I and II, and the international communities inability to prevent them, on the development of the United Nations, the Charter begins with "we the peoples of the United Nations determined to save succeeding generations from the scourge of war, which twice in our lifetime has brought untold sorrow to mankind . . . ."[13]The stated purpose of the United Nations is "to maintain international peace and security and to that end to take effective collective measures for the prevention and removal of threats . . . . [and] for the suppression of acts of aggression."[14]

The U.N. Charter vests the U.N. Security Council (UNSC) with primary responsibility for maintaining international peace and security. The Security Council issues resolutions (UNSCR), which serve as the mandate for a peace operation. These resolutions specify, often in general terms, the operations size, length, and objectives.[15]But the United Nations has no dedicated military forces and depends on member countries to contribute troops, equipment, and funds.

---

[10] United Nations *Charter of the United Nations*, 24 October 1945, 1 UNTS XVI, *available at* http://www.un.org/en/documents/charter/ (last visited 11 Sept. 2014) [hereinafter U.N. Charter].

[11] League of Nations Covenant, *available at* http://avalon.law.yale.edu/20th_century/leagcov.asp (last visited 11 Sept. 2014). In the preamble, the high contracting parties to the Covenant agreed to accept the obligation not to resort to war.

[12] Under the pact, states agreed to not use war to settle "disputes or conflicts of whatever nature or of whatever origin they may be, which may arise among them." Kellog Briand Pact art. II, *available at* http://www.yale.edu/lawweb/avalon/imt/kbpact.htm (last visited Sept. 11, 2014).

[13] U.N. Charter, *supra* note 10.

[14] *Id.*, art. 1.

[15] Almost by definition, any region where a peace operation is needed is to varying degrees chaotic and confusing. As a result the UNSC resolutions authorizing a peace operation are generally not able to specify size of the force, objectives, and expected length. For example, in 1962 the UNSC issued a resolution authorizing a peacekeeping mission in Cyprus. The resolution left the composition and size of the force to the Secretary-General and stated that the objective of the force should be "in the interest of preserving international peace and security, to use its best efforts to prevent a recurrence of fighting and, as necessary, to contribute to the maintenance and restoration of law

Interestingly the U.N. Charter does not contain a single reference to any type of peace operations. Instead, the Charter authority for peace operations is inferred from Chapter VI for peacekeeping and Chapter VII for peace enforcement. The confusing results include peace operations that may be based on one or the other chapter without referring to either, and peace operations' mandates with aspects of both and the resulting concept of a "Chapter VI and a half" mission.[16]One reason for the lack of clarity in many UNSCR is that the resolutions are the result of a bureaucratic and highly politicized process. The proponents of a resolution lobby for not only what they feel is appropriate language, but language for which there can be sufficient agreement that the resolution passes.[17]Accordingly, strategic ambiguity sometimes plays a role in why UNSCRs often lack explicit reference to Chapter VI or VII.

A. CHAPTER VI AND PEACEKEEPING

Chapter VI of the Charter deals with pacific settlement of disputes and is associated with peacekeeping missions. Chapter VI requires that the parties to a dispute "[s]hall, first of all, seek a solution by negotiation, enquiry, mediation, conciliation, arbitration, judicial settlement, resort to regional agencies or arrangements, or other peaceful means of their own choice."[18]Where the parties have determined a peaceful means, a U.N. peacekeeping mission may then

---

and order and a return to normal conditions." Finally, the UNSC recommended that "the stationing of the Force shall be for a period of three months." S.C. Res. 186, ¶ 6, U.N. Doc. S/RES/186 (Mar. 4, 1964). As of this writing in 2015, the recommended three-month-long U.N. mission in Cyprus established in 1964 remains ongoing.

[16] For an example of a traditional Chapter VI mission that was not clearly stated as such for some time, consider the United Nations Mission for the Referendum in Western Sahara (MINURSO). The UNSC established MINURSO in 1991, "under its authority" while never specifying the authority. S.C. Res. 690, ¶ 4, U.N. Doc. S/RES/690 (Apr. 29, 1991). The role and mission of MINURSO in monitoring a ceasefire and with the consent of the former warring factions is very much aligned with Chapter VI. Yet it was not until 2003 that the UNSC issued a MINURSO resolution that clearly stated that it was "[a]cting under Chapter VI of the Charter of the United Nations." S.C. Res. 1495, preamble, U.N. Doc. S/RES/1495 (July 31, 2003). Although there have been any number of peace operations thought of as "Chapter VI" missions, it is rare for a UNSCR to identify Chapter VI as a stated basis of authority. Examples of a Chapter VII mission are easier to find and include the most recent U.N. peacekeeping mission in the Central African Republic, MINUSCA. The UNSCR establishing MINUSCA states the UNSC is "acting under Chapter VII of the Charter of the United Nations." S.C. Res. 2149, preamble, U.N. Doc. S/RES/2149 (Apr. 10, 2014). Additionally, UNSCR 2149 authorizes MINUSCA to "take all necessary means to carry out its mandate." *Id.* ¶ 29. For those resolutions, which, unlike 2149, lack a clear reference to Chapter VII, the use of "all necessary means" conveys that the mission is more properly thought of as a Chapter VII mission in which force may be more readily used other than in self-defense.

[17] Security Council decisions on other than procedural issues require affirmative votes by nine of the fifteen members, and the absence of a veto by any of the permanent members (China, France, Russia, the United Kingdom, and the United States). The Security Council is comprised of the five permanent members and ten representatives from other U.N. member states elected for two-year. *See* UN Charter, *supra* note 10, at art. 27.

[18] U.N. Charter, *supra* note 10, at art. 33.

assist in maintaining that peace. This is done through a UNSCR establishing the peacekeeping mission.[19]

Unhelpfully, such a resolution generally does not mention Chapter VI. As the United Nations reminds, "the Security Council need not refer to a specific Chapter of the Charter when passing a resolution authorizing the deployment of a UN peacekeeping operation and has never invoked Chapter VI."[20]For example, in 1993 the United Nations established a U.N. observer mission to verify the ceasefire between the Republic of Georgia and forces in Abkhazia.[21]Although this is a traditional peacekeeping mission whose authority derives from Chapter VI, the resolution makes no reference to that chapter.

Peacekeeping can and does take a variety of different forms. The United Nations categorizes peacekeeping missions as:

- Observer missions, consisting of unarmed officer observers who monitor the implementation of cease-fire agreements
- Peacekeeping forces, consisting of lightly armed troops generally organized on conventional unit lines and
- Combined observer/force missions[22]

More broadly, peacekeeping operations

> Consist of military operations undertaken with the consent of all major parties to a dispute, and are designed to monitor and facilitate implementation of an agreement to support diplomatic efforts to reach a long-term political settlement. *Before peacekeeping operations begin, a credible truce or cease fire must be in effect and the parties to the dispute must consent to the operation.* Peacekeeping operations take place following diplomatic negotiation and agreement among the parties to a dispute, the sponsoring organization, and the potential troop-contributing nations.[23]

On a traditional peacekeeping mission, peacekeepers may use force only in self-defense, of themselves and designated others. Observer and peacekeeping

---

[19] Although outside the scope of this chapter, there is a debate as to whether resolutions based on Chapter VI are legally binding. *See generally* HANS KÖCHLER, THE CONCEPT OF HUMANITARIAN INTERVENTION IN THE CONTEXT OF MODERN POWER (2001) (arguing that measures adopted under Chapter VI are nonbinding);*but see* Rossalyn Higgins, *The Advisory Opinion on Namibia*: Which UN Resolutions Are Binding under Article 25 of the Charter?*, 21 INT'L & COMP. L.Q. 270 (1972) (arguing that under Article 25 of the U.N. Charter, "[t]he Members of the United Nations agree to accept and carry out the decisions of the Security Council in accordance with the present Charter." Judge Higgins notes that Article 25 is not located in, and does not make any reference to, either Chapter VI or Chapter VII of the U.N. Charters, so member states are obligated to carry out the decisions of the Security Council period, regardless upon which Chapter they are acting).

[20] Mandates and the Legal Basis for Peacekeeping, http://www.un.org/en/peacekeeping/operations/pkmandates.shtml, (last visited Sept. 11, 2014).

[21] S.C. Res. 858, U.N. Doc. S/RES/858 (Aug. 24, 1993).

[22] United Nations Department of Peacekeeping Operations, United Nations Peacekeeping Training Manual, 15 (undated).

[23] PEACE OPERATIONS, *supra* note 9, at xi (emphasis added).

missions are difficult and risky endeavors performed by lightly armed U.N. personnel in relatively small numbers. The degree of difficulty and risk often depend on how much the reality on the ground corresponds with the definition of when peacekeeping operations are appropriate, notably a credible truce or cease fire and all major parties consenting to the presence and role of the United Nations. When there is not even a transitory peace to keep or consent of the parties, the United Nations turns to peace enforcement. Peace enforcement is a different kind of mission requiring different force size, equipment, and mandate.

B. CHAPTER VII AND PEACE ENFORCEMENT

Chapter VII addresses "action with respect to threats to the peace, breaches of the peace, and acts of aggression."[24] Chapter VII outlines the measures not involving the use of armed force, including "complete or partial interruption of economic relations and of rail, sea, air, postal, telegraphic, radio, and other means of communication, and the severance of diplomatic relations."[25] But Chapter VII also provides that if the Security Council considers those measures inadequate, the council "may take such action by air, sea, or land forces as may be necessary to maintain or restore international peace and security. Such action may include demonstrations, blockade, and other operations by air, sea, or land forces of Members of the United Nations."[26]

As with peacekeeping, a UNSCR initiates the operation and provides the mandate and objectives. Unlike peacekeeping, the UNSCR for contemporary peace enforcement missions generally *does* make specific reference to the U.N. Charter Chapter upon which the mission is based.[27] For example, the 2000 UNSCR expanding the U.N. mission in the DRC states that the United Nations was "[a]cting under Chapter VII of the Charter of the United Nations."[28] Another indication of whether a peace operation falls under Chapter VII is language authorizing the mission to use "all necessary means or measures." That is the most robust grant of authority the UNSCR can confer, and allows a U.N. mission to use force in situations other than in self-defense.

Peace Enforcement Operations (PEO)

> are generally coercive in nature and rely on the threat of or use of force; however, PEO may also be co-optive in nature, relying on the development of working relationships with locals. PEO may include the enforcement of sanctions and exclusion zones, protection of personnel conducting foreign

---

[24] U.N. Charter, *supra* note 10, at Chapter VII.

[25] *Id.* at art. 41.

[26] *Id.* at art. 42.

[27] As challenging as interpreting contemporary UNSCR is, their historical predecessors are even more perplexing. For example, in 1950 the UNSC authorized members states to respond to North Korea's invasion of South Korea, and while finding that North Korea had breached the peace, never mentioned Chapter VII. S.C. Res. 83, U.N. Doc. S/RES/1511 (June 27, 1950).

[28] S.C. Res. 1291, ¶ 8 U.N. Doc. S/RES/1291 (Feb. 24, 2000).

> humanitarian assistance missions, restoration of order, and forcible separation of belligerent parties or parties to a dispute. However, the impartiality with which the [peace operations] force treats all parties and the nature of its objectives separates PEO from major operations.[29]

An overarching challenge surrounding peace operations is while the Chapter VI/VII dichotomy is rigid, the operating environment tends to be fluid. Missions can and do morph, peace develops and erodes, and parties change alliances and withdraw previously provided consent. When the United Nations has encountered difficulties in peace operations, more often than not the problems stem from either misidentifying a peace enforcement mission as peacekeeping or failing to timely alter a mission that was at the outset peacekeeping but that has eroded to peace enforcement. As the history of U.N. peace operations demonstrates, there is nothing more damaging to the United Nation's credibility or dangerous to the lives of peacekeepers and civilians alike than calling and resourcing a peace enforcement mission as a peacekeeping operation.[30]

III. Historical Development of Peace Operations

The United Nation's first experience with peace operations came in 1948 with the United Nations Truce Supervision Organization (UNTSO), an unarmed observer mission initially established in order to supervise a truce between Israel and several Arab countries, and that subsequently supported the implementation of an armistice.[31]

The first armed U.N. peacekeeping force was the United Nations Emergency Force (UNEF), established in 1956 by the first emergency session of the U.N. General Assembly to "secure and supervise the cessation of hostilities, including the withdrawal of the armed forces of France, Israel and the United Kingdom from Egyptian territory and, after the withdrawal, to serve as a buffer between the Egyptian and Israeli forces"[32]

---

[29] PEACE OPERATIONS, *supra* note 9, at I-7.

[30] Some of the more glaring examples include U.N. efforts in Bosnia and Rwanda. Both are discussed later in this chapter. In each, there was a classic mismatch between reality on the ground and the type and kind of peace operations. The U.N. force, in size, equipment, and mandate, was based on the utterly flawed premise that there was peace to keep; there was not. In both Bosnia and Rwanda, thousands (in the case of Srebrenica) and hundreds of thousands (in the case of Rwanda) died with U.N. peacekeepers already deployed to the respective countries. The size, equipment, and mandate needed to enforce peace is exceedingly different than to keep peace that already exists.

[31] The Early Years, http://www.un.org/en/peacekeeping/operations/early.shtml (last visited Sept. 11, 2014). This first mission, begun in 1948, was followed in early 1949 by the U.N. Military Observer Group in India and Pakistan to supervise the ceasefire between those two countries. Both these missions have continued to present day.

[32] UNEF I Mandate, http://www.un.org/en/peacekeeping/missions/past/unef1mandate.html (last visited Sept. 11, 2014).

Both UNTSO and UNEF are examples of types of peacekeeping, unarmed military observers in UNTSO and an armed U.N. force in UNEF. But in each, the former warring factions had agreed to a ceasefire and to the presence and role of the United Nations. Arguably peacekeeping was the only peace operation the international community could agree on in the early days of the United Nations.

The start of the Cold War not long after the United Nation's founding resulted in the peace enforcement measures envisioned by the Charter being unrealized. Permanent members of the Security Council—the United States, France, Great Britain, China, and Russia—were unable to agree on issues, and each was able to veto any proposed action. [33]

Additionally, Chapter VII established a Military Staff Committee to "advise and assist the Security Council on all questions relating to the Security Council's military requirements for the maintenance of international peace and security, the employment and command of forces placed at its disposal, the regulation of armaments, and possible disarmament."[34]The committee, consisting of the military Chiefs of Staff of the permanent members of the Security Council, also proved ineffectual.[35]

The response to the seemingly intractable political problems flowing from the permanent members of the Security Council, according to the second U.N. Secretary-General (UNSG), Dag Hammarskjöldm, was an "alternative method of maintaining the peace" that fell under "Chapter VI and a half."[36]This theory was based on Language in Chapters V[37] and VII.[38]

---

[33] *See generally* Simon Chesterman, Thomas M. Franck & David M. Malone, Law and Practice of the United Nations Documents and Commentary (2008) (describing the legal, political, and institutional aspects of U.N. decision-making).

[34] U.N. Charter, *supra* note 10, at art. 47.

[35] The military staff committee does exist. Military representatives of each of the permanent Security Council members meet in New York every two weeks. But what if anything the committee accomplishes remains unclear. One commentator has labeled the military staff committee "a dead letter from the start." Council on Foreign Relations, *The Effectiveness of the UN Security Council: Online Debate* (Sept. 29, 2006), *available at* http://www.cfr.org/international-organizations-and-alliances/effectiveness-un-security-council/p11520 (quoting Joshua Muravchik of John Hopkins School of Advanced International Studies).

[36] *See* Henry Wiseman, *UN Peacekeeping: An Historical Overview*, *in* Peacekeeping: Appraisals and Proposals (Henry Wiseman ed., Pergamon 1983). Wiseman credits Hammarskjöldm with developing the term "Chapter VI and a half." Some contend that Hammarskjöldm was simply "referring to the absence of UN Charter references to armed peacekeeping missions rather than []inserting combat troops to impose international will on belligerents." David S. Alberts & Richard E. Hayes, Command Arrangements for Peace Operations (1995). Others are more critical, claiming that "[t]he popular phrase, 'Chapter VI and a half operation,' seemingly a cute way to note the clever ambiguity of international diplomacy, was in fact a recipe for disaster in which members of the international community inserted themselves into a conflict situation with the mindset, forces, and posture of a peacemaker." *Id.* (quoting from Center for Advance Command Concepts Workshop on Combined and Coalition Peace Operations).

[37] Chapter V of the U.N. Charter provides that the Security Council "may establish such subsidiary organs as it deems necessary for the performance of its functions." U.N. Charter, *supra* note 10, at art. 29.

[38] Chapter VII states that prior to resorting to enforcement, the Security Council may "call on the parties concerned to comply with such provisional measures as it deems necessary or desirable

This approach, termed the interposition model, is essentially peacekeeping, meaning that parties to the conflict must consent and cooperate with the UN's involvement.[39] And, of course, there must be a peace to keep. Under or through this approach, the majority of the peacekeeping operations the United Nations established during the Cold War were comprised of lightly or even unarmed military observers monitoring ceasefires.[40]

Although never saying "Chapter VI and a half" the United Nations has explained the area between Chapter VI and VII operations as:

> In certain volatile situations, the Security Council has given UN peacekeeping operations "robust" mandates authorizing them to "use all necessary means" to deter forceful attempts to disrupt the political process, protect civilians under imminent threat of physical attack, and/or assist the national authorities in maintaining law and order.
>
> Although on the ground they may sometimes appear similar, robust peacekeeping should not be confused with peace enforcement, as envisaged under Chapter VII of the United Nations Charter.
>
> - Robust peacekeeping involves the use of force at the tactical level with the authorization of the Security Council and consent of the host nation and/or the main parties to the conflict.
> - By contrast, peace enforcement does not require the consent of the main parties and may involve the use of military force at the strategic or international level, which is normally prohibited for Member States under Article 2(4) of the Charter, unless authorized by the Security Council.[41]

Despite the United Nation's inability to keep the peace, its early peacekeeping efforts were largely perceived as successful.[42]As the Cold War ended in 1989, that

---

. . . without prejudice to the rights, claims or position of the parties concerned." U.N. Charter, *supra* note 10, at art. 40.

[39] *See* Trevor Findlay, The Use of Force in UN Peace Operations (2002) (describing interpositional strategy or policy whereby U.N. peacekeepers literally interpose or insert themselves between former warring factions. This creates a much greater likelihood that the peacekeepers will subsequently be able to permissibly use force in self-defense, one of the few bases for doing so when not under Chapter VII or a peace enforcement mission).

[40] These early peacekeeping operations included deployments to India, Pakistan, Israel, Egypt, the Belgian Congo, Dominican Republic, New Guinea, Yemen, Cyprus, and Lebanon.

[41] Principles of UN Peacekeeping, http://www.un.org/en/peacekeeping/operations/principles.shtml (last visited Sept. 11, 2014).

[42] *See* 60 Ways the United Nations Makes a Difference, http://www.un.org/wcm/webdav/site/visitors/shared/documents/pdfs/Pub_United%20Nations_60%20ways.pdf (last visited Sept. 11, 2014). Under "Making Peace" the United Nations explains that "since 1945, the U.N. has assisted in negotiating more than 170 peace settlements that have ended regional conflicts. Examples including ending the Iran-Iraq war, facilitating the withdrawal of Soviet troops from Afghanistan and ending the civil wars in El Salvador and Guatemala. The United Nations has used quiet diplomacy to avert imminent wars." *Id.* at 7. Indeed the perception of the efficacy of the first forty years of UN

perception proved problematic as it fostered a belief that peacekeeping could be effective in resolving a widening array of conflicts. Dangerously, this included conflicts where there was no peace to keep, as the conflict was ongoing and the parties to the conflict not only did not cooperate but hindered and even targeted peacekeepers. Horrific U.N. failures in Somalia,[43] Bosnia,[44] and Rwanda[45] in the 1990s were the price of failing to recognize and align the reality in a conflict area with a corresponding peace operation's size, equipment, and mandate. But those same failures did prompt significant institutional reform in how the United Nations organizes peace operations.

---

peacekeeping led to the awarding of the Nobel Peace Prize in 1988 to "the peacekeeper." But as the United Nations itself notes, "[t]he general success of earlier missions raised expectations for UN Peacekeeping beyond its capacity to deliver." Post Cold-War Surge, http://www.un.org/en/peacekeeping/operations/surge.shtml (last visited Sept. 11, 2014).

[43] The United Nations established the first of two Somalia peacekeeping mission in 1992 to "monitor the ceasefire in Mogadishu and escort deliveries of humanitarian supplies to distribution centres in the city." United Nations Operation in Somalia I, http://www.un.org/en/peacekeeping/missions/past/unosomi.htm (last visited Sept. 11, 2014). Despite the deployment of over thirty thousand peacekeepers and close to $1.5 billion in funding, the missions were viewed as unsuccessful. U.N. Sec. Council, *Report of the Secretary-General on the Situation in Somalia*, ¶s 41,49 S/1995/231 (Mar. 28, 1995). United Nations' peacekeepers suffered one of the worst attacks in U.N. history in Somalia when in 1993 Somalia rebels killed twenty-three Pakistani peacekeepers and wounded some fifty-nine more. Michael R. Gordon, *U.S. Attacks Somalia Clan Chief Support U.N. Peacekeepers*, N.Y. TIMES, June 12, 1993, *available at* http://www.nytimes.com/1993/06/12/world/us-attacks-somali-clan-chief-to-support-un-peacekeepers.html?pagewanted=all&src=pm (last visited Sept. 11, 2014). That attack led to increased U.S. military involvement in Somalia in support of the United Nation's efforts, culminating in the deaths of eighteen U.S. service members in an incident referred to and depicted in the movie by the same name, "Black Hawk Down." Following the U.N. Missions in Somalia, the UNSG commented that there were lessons to be learned about the "theory and practice of multifunctional peacekeeping operations in conditions of civil war and chaos and especially about the clear line that needs to be drawn between peacekeeping and enforcement action". Somalia—UNOSOM II Background, http://www.un.org/en/peacekeeping/missions/past/unosom2backgr2.html#five (last visited Sept. 11, 2014). Although that is true, it is not clear how well those lessons have been learned or clear lines drawn in PSOs since Somalia.

[44] A 1995 attack of a U.N.-designated safe area, Srebencia, by the Army of Republika Srpska led to the mass murder of some eight thousand Bosniak. Then U.N. Secretary-General Kofi Anan labeled the attack the worst crime to be committed on European soil since World War II. *See* Press Release, United Nations, "May We All Learn and Act on the Lessons of Srebrenica", Says Secretary-General, in Message to Anniversary Ceremony, U.N. Doc. SG/SM/9993 (Nov. 7, 2005). The International Court of Justice later ruled the attack constituted genocide. Case concerning Application of the Convention on the Prevention and Punishment of the Crime of Genocide (Bosnia and Herzegovina v. Serbia and Montenegro), 2007 I.C.J. 43 (Feb. 26).

[45] The 1994 genocide in Rwanda claimed the lives of roughly a million people. And the massacres occurred with U.N. peacekeepers deployed to Rwanda, albeit far too few. As a UNSC press release accompanying the release of an independent inquiry into U.N. actions in Rwanda stated, "we failed." Press Release, Security Council, Chairman of Independent Inquiry into United Nations Actions during 1994 Rwanda Genocide Presents Report to Security Council Security Council U.N. Doc. SC/6843 (Apr. 14, 2000) and Letter from the Secretary-General to the President of the Security Council, U.N. Doc. S/1999/1257 (Dec. 16, 1999).

IV. Peace Operations Organizational Structure

United Nations Secretary-General Boutros Boutros-Ghali created the Department of Peace Keeping Operations (DPKO) in 1992.The DPKO

> provides political and executive direction to UN Peacekeeping operations around the world and maintains contact with the Security Council, troop and financial contributors, and parties to the conflict in the implementation of Security Council mandates. The Department works to integrate the efforts of UN, governmental and non-governmental entities in the context of peacekeeping operations. DPKO also provides guidance and support on military, police, mine action and other relevant issues to other UN political and peacebuilding missions.[46]

Four main offices make up DPKO: Office of Operations, Office of the Rule of Law and Security Institutions, Office of Military Affairs, and the Policy Evaluation and Training Division. Prior to DPKO, the United Nation's Office of Special Political Affairs coordinated peacekeeping missions. Establishing DPKO would ultimately prove a positive and significant step. But in the years immediately following DPKO's establishment the United Nation's failed efforts (notably Somalia, Bosnia, and Rwanda) called the concept of peacekeeping into question.

Following those failures, and likely because of them, the next most significant milestone came in 2000 when the UNSG appointed a panel to evaluate the U.N. peace operations system. The panel created what is known as the "Brahimi Report" named after Lakhdar Brahimi, an Algerian U.N. envoy who chaired the panel.[47] The report stated at the outset that between 1990 and 2000 the United Nations had "repeatedly failed" to meet the challenge of the U.N. Charter to "save succeeding generations from the scourge of war." The report also noted that

> There are many tasks which United Nations peacekeeping forces should not be asked to undertake and many places they should not go. But when the Untied Nations does send its forces to uphold the peace, they must be prepared to confront the lingering forces of war and violence, with the ability and determination to defeat them.[48]

The report reiterated that "[a]s the United Nations has bitterly and repeatedly discovered . . . no amount of good intentions can substitute for the fundamental ability to project credible force if complex peacekeeping in particular is to succeed."[49] To

---

[46] Department of Peacekeeping Operations, https://www.un.org/en/peacekeeping/about/dpko/ (last visited Sept. 11, 2014).

[47] Identical Letters dated 21 August 2000 from the Secretary General to the President of the General Assembly and the President of the Security Council, U.N. Doc. A/55/305—S/2000/809 (Aug. 21, 2000).

[48] *Id.* at viii.

[49] *Id.*

better ensure "clear, credible, and property resourced Security Council mandates," Brahimi called for:

- renewed political commitment on the part of Member States;
- significant institutional change;
- increased financial support.

One of the most significant aspects of the report was that its recommendations focused on concrete "operational and organizational areas of need" more than nebulous policy and strategy. This led to the United Nations increasing efforts to systematize and standardize a number of aspects of peacekeeping operations. This entailed adopting common terminology and understanding of what that terminology means. Numbers of troops or police or observers of course matter, but clarifying what activities they need to be able to perform and equipment they do or not need to bring (and whether that equipment will remain with the peace operation or return to the troop-contributing country) is equally or possibly more important. From there DPKO was able to develop reimbursement rates for troop-contributing countries and develop baseline standards for troops, police, and military observers.[50]

More recently, the UNSG restructured DPKO in 2007 to strengthen the United Nation's capacity to manage and sustain new peace operations.[51] This restructuring created the Department of Field Support (DFS), which is responsible for "for delivering dedicated support to United Nations field operations, including on personnel, finance, procurement, logistical, communications, information technology and other administrative and general management issues." The DFS is separate from DPKO, though as the organizational chart reflects, DFS shares capacities with DPKO. The organization chart also demonstrates the administrative complexity and challenges of peace operations.[52]

The DPKO continues to evolve, developing a capstone doctrine that provides peacekeeping principles and guidelines.[53] Far from the basic logistical problems that plagued early peace operations, the United Nations now seeks to identify capability gaps and improve its force generation process.[54] Nonetheless, peace operations encounter a wide range of challenges. Some are inherent in multinational operations, others brought on by the United Nation's increased assertiveness in how peace operations are conducted.

---

[50] Forming a New Operation, http://www.un.org/en/peacekeeping/operations/newoperation.shtml (last visited Sept. 11, 2014);*see also* Financing Peacekeeping, *supra* note 2.

[51] U.N. Sec. Gen., Comprehensive Report on Strengthening the Capacity of the United Nations to Manage and Sustain Peace Operations, U.N. Doc. A/61/858 (Apr. 13, 2007).

[52] United Nations Peacekeeping Group: Capacities to Ensure Integration http://www.un.org/en/peacekeeping/documents/dpkodfs_org_chart.pdf (last visited Sept. 11, 2014).

[53] United Nations Department of Peacekeeping Operations Department of Field Support, United Nations Peacekeeping Operations Principles and Guidelines (2008).

[54] Adam C. Smith & Arthur Boutellis, Rethinking Force Generation: Filling the Capability Gaps in UN Peacekekeeping Providing for Peacekeeping No. 2 (2013).

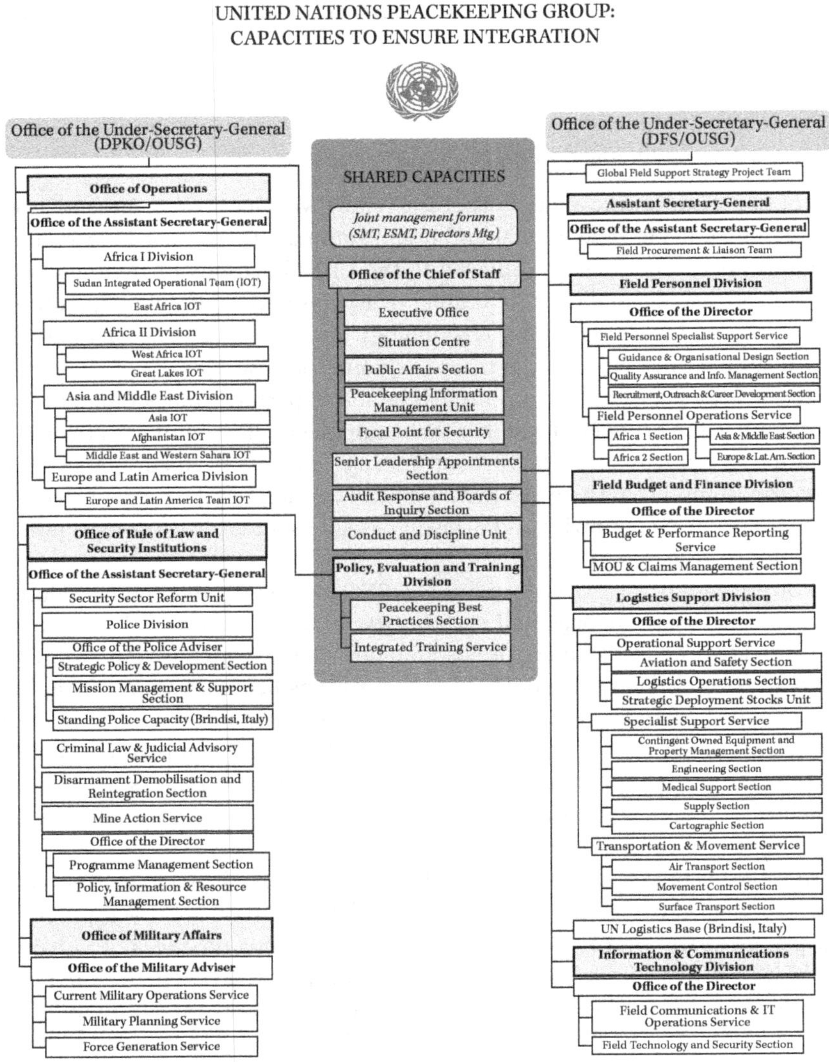

FIGURE 20.1 U.N. Peacekeeping Organizational Chart.

V. Peace Operations Challenges

A. WHAT LAW APPLIES?

An overarching question that has an unsatisfyingly vague answer is: What law applies during a peace operation? First, one must consider the range of options of possible law and legal relationships. There is the domestic law of the state in which the peace operation is occurring, and whether and to what extent it could or should apply to U.N. peacekeepers. As a general proposition, if there is a peace operation occurring in a state, its rule of law is either not well developed and/

or implemented. Hence a Status of Forces Agreement (SOFA) between the United Nations and the host country answers the question of relevant legal framework.

The SOFA is "one of the key documents that govern a U.N. peace operation."[55] The SOFA for a given peace operation derives from the model SOFA, which the UNSG developed in 1990 in response to a General Assembly request.[56] A SOFA is a "negotiated formal agreement between the UN and the host country that defines the legal status of both the peace keeping mission and the individual peace keeper .... [SOFAs] grant the facilities and rights, including privileges and immunities, required by peacekeepers to enable them to fulfill the peace operations mandate."[57]

Second is the extent that the law of armed conflict (LOAC) or international humanitarian law applies to peace operation. Imbedded in this question are several subordinate questions or issues, such as the triggering event for the LOAC to apply. The LOAC is triggered by armed conflict. The International Criminal Tribunal for the Former Yugoslavia defined when this threshold is reached as being when a state resorts to the use of armed force with another state, or when there is "protracted armed violence between governmental authorities and organized armed groups or between such groups in a State."[58]

So the first challenge is whether the threshold to trigger the application of the LOAC has been reached in a host country. Further complicating things is that there is different law for different types of armed conflict. So if there is a state-on-state conflict, this international armed conflict (IAC) triggers one body of law, notably the Hague and Geneva Conventions and their Protocols. Peace operations though tend to occur more often amid the other category of armed conflict, that is armed conflict not involving state against state. This non-international armed conflict (NIAC) could be in the form of government forces fighting one or more insurgent or rebel groups, or it could be various insurgent or rebel groups fighting other such groups.[59] Such NIACs draw from a subset of the Geneva Conventions and Additional Protocols.[60] Somewhat perversely although NIACs occur with far greater frequency than IACs, there is far less law applicable to NIAC than IAC.[61]

---

[55] Bruce Oswald, Helen Durham & Adrian Bates, Documents on the Law of UN Peace Operations 34 (2010) [hereinafter UN Documents].

[56] U.N. Sec. Gen., *Comprehensive Review of the Whole Question of Peace-Keeping Operations in All Their Aspects Model Status of Forces Agreement for Peace-Keeping Operations Report of the Secretary-General*, U.N. Doc. A/45/594 (Oct. 9, 1990).

[57] U.N. Documents, *supra* note 55, at 34. "The model SOFA develops the principles of law articled in 104 and 105 of the Charter of the United Nations.... These articles provide that the UN shall enjoy legal capacity, and such privileges and immunities in the territory of each of its Members as are necessary for the fulfillment of its purposes." *Id.*

[58] The Prosecutor v. Tadic, Decision on the Defence Motion for Interlocutory Appeal on Jurisdiction, IT-94-1-T, ¶ 70 (Oct. 2, 1995).

[59] *See* Yoram Dinstein, Non-International Armed Conflicts in International Law (2014).

[60] Article 3 of the 1949 Geneva Conventions applies to NIAC, and NIAC is the subject of Additional Protocol II.

[61] For example, according to the North Atlantic Treaty Organization (NATO), in 2000 there were twenty-five armed conflicts around the world. NATO Statistic on Armed Conflicts around

This discussion deals with the law applicable to the parties in different kinds of armed conflicts. Historically the United Nations was not thought of as a party to the conflict, but that view is changing.[62]And as discussed in this chapter, the U.N. force operating in the DRC is most certainly a party to that NIAC.[63]There the United Nations is allied with the DRC in fighting various militia groups, so even though the United Nations is a party to the armed conflict, its classification remains NIAC.[64]But under different circumstances, the United Nations as a party to a conflict could transform the classification from NIAC to IAC, and with it, the applicable laws governing the conduct of hostilities.[65]

In terms of legal analysis, the U.N. Charter recognizes the United Nations has legal capacity,[66] and the International Court of Justice has held that the United Nations is an "international person,"[67] meaning that it can be subject to international law, such as the LOAC. Indeed the United Nations has recognized as much and issued guidance as to the application of the LOAC to U.N. forces conducting

---

the World, http://nato.gov.si/eng/topic/threats-to-security/statistics/ (last visited Sept. 11, 2014). Of those, only one, the conflict between India and Pakistan, was of an international nature. *See also* Armed Conflict Database Armed Conflict by Type, 1946–2012, http://www.pcr.uu.se/digitalAssets/196/196093_conflict_types_2012.jpg (last visited Sept. 11, 2014).

[62] Tristan Ferraro, *The Applicability and Application of International Humanitarian Law to Multinational Forces*, 561 Int'l Rev. Red Cross 95 (2013)

(reiterating that "no IHL provisions preclude multinational forces from becoming a party to an armed conflict" and that "[t]he argument that multinational forces may not be deemed a party to an armed conflict . . . does not rest on any firm basis.") Ferraro goes on to quote from various military field manuals that "expressly qualify peace forces as a party to an armed conflict.").

[63] According to one noted commentator, referring to MONUSCO,

> whether a UN peacekeeping force engaged in armed conflict with opposing forces should be considered a party to the conflict (for the purposes of applying international law) has been controversial for a number of decades. The UN has never publicly admitted that its peacekeepers are parties to the conflicts in which they engage, notwithstanding the fact that on a number of occasions it has acknowledged that its peacekeeping forces have engaged in offensive operations against armed groups. As a matter of law, it is difficult to conclude that the Brigade would not be a party to the conflict in situations where it conducts offensive operations. As a party to the conflict, the Brigade would be required to abide by international humanitarian law.

Bruce Oswald, *The Security Council and the Intervention Brigade: Some Legal Issues*, 17 ASIL Insights 15 (2013), *available at* http://www.asil.org/insights/volume/17/issue/15/security-council-and-intervention-brigade-some-legal-issues.

[64] *See id.* and Ferraro, *supra* note 62.

[65] *Id.*

[66] U.N. Charter, *supra* note 10, at art. 104 (stating that "[t]he Organization shall enjoy in the territory of each of its Members such legal capacity as may be necessary for the exercise of its functions and the fulfillment of its purposes.").

[67] *See* Peter F. Chapman, *Ensuring Respect: United Nations Compliance with International Humanitarian Law*, 17 Hum. Rts. Brief 2 (2009) both generally and for citation to Interpretation of the Agreement of 25 March 1951 between the Who and Egypt, Advisory Opinion, 1980 I.C.J. 73, 89–90 (Dec. 20)(quoting that "[i]nternational organizations [such as the UN] are subjects of international law, and as such, are bound by any obligation incumbent upon them under general rules of international law.").

operations under U.N. command and control. That guidance, titled "Observance by United Nations forces of international humanitarian law" states that

> The fundamental principles and rules of [LOAC] set out in the present bulletin are applicable to United Nations forces when in situations of armed conflict they are actively engaged therein as combatants, to the extent and for the duration of their engagement. They are accordingly applicable in enforcement actions, or in peacekeeping operations when the use of force is permitted in self defense.[68]

The United Nation's guidance is then broken down in sections titled "Protection of the civilian population," "Means and methods of combat," "Treatment of civilians and persons hors de combat," "Treatment of detained persons," and "Protection of the wounded, the sick, and medical and relief personnel."[69]But the "UN has not clarified exactly what constitutes 'actively engaged' in combat or what applicable 'to the extent and for the duration of their engagement' means."[70]And the guidance recognizes that it does not "prejudice the application thereof, nor do they replace the national laws by which military personnel remain bound through the operation."[71]

The confusing result is that

> [d]ifferent instruments regulate each Member State of the UN, depending on the state's accession to different IHL instruments. Indeed, because the UN has not ratified any IHL instrument, the organization cannot clearly dictate what applies to its forces. While some Member States may be subject to additional regulations, the UN itself likely is subject to those provisions of IHL that are classified as customary law. [72]

This merely restarts the legal inquiry down another path without a definitive answer as to what part of LOAC is customary law. Different states/troop-contributing countries answer that question differently.[73]The end result is the very real possibility that different components of a U.N. peace operation would be subject to different legal regimes and restrictions, posing additional challenges for a U.N. force commander. [74] For example, such a commander may

---

[68] U.N. Sec. Gen, *Secretary General's Bulletin Observance United Nations Forces of International Humanitarian Law*, ¶1.1 U.N. Doc. ST/SGB/1999/13 (Aug. 6, 1999) [hereinafter UNSG's IHL Bulletin].

[69] *Id.*

[70] Chapman, *supra* note 67.

[71] UNSG's IHL Bulletin, *supra* note 68.

[72] Chapman, *supra* note 67, quoting Brian D. Tittemore, *Belligerents in Blue Helmets*, 33 Stan J. Int'l L. 61, 96–97 (1997).

[73] And although not definitive, the International Committee of the Red Cross provides its perspective on the portions of LOAC that may be customary international law. Jean-Marie Henckaerts & Louise Doswald-Beck, Customary International Humanitarian Law Volume I: Rules (2009).

[74] Arnaud De Borchgrave, *Commentary: NATO Caveats*, UPI, July 10, 2009, *available at* http://www.upi.com/Emerging_Threats/2009/07/10/Commentary-NATO-caveats/UPI-47311247244125/.

have one or more troop-contributing countries that have signed the Convention on Cluster Munitions participating in a peace operation with one or more countries that have not.[75] Hence the dilemma for the commander is whether that U.N. force can permissibly employ cluster munitions.[76]

Likewise, there is likely to be a difference in attitudes toward Additional Protocols I and II to the Geneva Conventions among troop-contributing countries. Additional Protocol I applies to IACs while AP II applies to NIAC in which the nonstate group controls territory, so regardless of which type of conflict the peace operation is occurring in, at least one of the protocols will be at issue. Here the analysis is even more convoluted than with the Convention on Cluster Munitions. With the Additional Protocols one has the first problem of whether a troop-contributing country has or has not ratified and is thus bound by the protocol. But even in peace operations in which all the troop-contributing countries are signatories to whichever of AP I and/or AP II was deemed to apply, the differences in the reservations, understandings, and declarations submitted by the various countries results in the protocols meaning something very different for each signatory.[77]

These legally based interoperability issues have not been a significant issue in U.N. peace operations. But that is only because the United Nations for the last several decades has not conducted offensive operations for a sustained period of time. As discussed later, that is changing. And with that change, the U.N. force commander may encounter similar frustrations akin to the NATO force commander in Afghanistan. In that conflict, different troop-contributing countries assert different national caveats or operational restrictions on the forces they provide NATO.[78] United States Army General John Craddock, former NATO

---

[75] Given that the Convention on Cluster Munitions has been signed by approximately 113 countries, and not signed by some 80 others, having troop-contributing countries with different legal obligations is quite possible, even likely. Particularly when one considers that none of the top four troop-contributing countries to U.N. peace operations are signatories (Pakistan, India, Ethiopia). *See* U.N. Troop- Contributing Countries, *supra* note 7, and United Nations Office at Geneva, Signatories and Ratifying States, http://www.unog.ch/80256EE600585943/(httpPages)/67DC5063EB530E02C12574F8002E9E49?OpenDocument (last visited Sept. 11, 2014). Other notable non-signatories include Brazil, China, Russia, and the United States.

[76] The answer may lie in the difference between can and should, or law and policy. A commander from a country that is not a signatory to the Convention on Cluster Munitions could lawfully order their use. But that would mean the other troop-contributing countries that are not members could no longer participate in the mission. And the United Nations itself, the originator of the Convention, would be very unlikely to approve such use.

[77] *See* Julie Gaudreau, *The Reservations to the Protocols Additional to the Geneva Conventions for the Protection of War Victims*, 849 Int'l Rev. of the Red Cross 143 (2003).

[78] *See* Stephen M. Saideman & David Auerswald, *NATO at War: Understanding the Challenges of Caveats in Afghanistan*, American Political Science Association 2009 Toronto Meeting Working Paper, *available at* http://papers.ssrn.com/sol3/papers.cfm?abstract_id=1450476 (last visited Sept. 11, 2014).

Indeed NATO proposed, and member states passed a resolution calling for the elimination of undeclared caveats and to minimize the use of declared caveats. NATO Parliamentary Assembly Resolution 336 on Reducing National Caveats, *available at* http://www.nato-pa.int/default.asp?SHORTCUT=828 (last visited November 15, 2005).The resolution is not binding.

Supreme Allied Commander Europe, once said he would gladly forgo additional NATO troops to fight the Taliban in Afghanistan if the troop-contributing countries dropped the caveats on the forces they provided to NATO.[79]Craddock contended that the caveats "increase the risk to every service member deployed in Afghanistan and bring increased risk to mission success." They are also "a detriment to effective command and control, unity of effort and . . . command."[80]

B. INHERENT DIFFICULTIES

Bureaucracy at the DPKO level, language, and culture differences among member states amplify problems such as determining the applicable law just discussed and the section that follows on accountability. They also stand alone as challenges in and of themselves. With any bureaucracy comes some degree of politics. The United Nations, being what it is, may be overly blessed with the widest range of inputs and interests from literally every country in the world. More specific to peace operations, as previously discussed affirmative votes by nine of the fifteen UNSC members and the absence of a veto by any of the five permanent members is required for a UNSCR authorizing an operation. The result is that the most important quality a resolution possesses is that it be worded in such a way as to allow for its passage. Similar to domestic legislation, this translates to wording that may not provide the peace operation the clearest or most coherent of mandate or guidance.

Consider for example the 2004 UNSCR establishing a U.N. force in Haiti. Among other mandates, the UNSC charged the force "to protect civilians under imminent threat of physical violence, within its capabilities and areas of deployment, without prejudice to the responsibilities of the Transitional Government and of police authorities."[81] What exactly does that mean to the force commander in Haiti? And how will a commander translate that into orders for subordinate peacekeepers? How imminent is imminent? What is the United Nation's understanding of the force's capabilities? And the last section is particularly opaque. While on patrol in Haiti, a group of U.N. peacekeepers encountered a group of Haitian police severely beating a person in the street. The peacekeepers' understanding of their mandate was that it was to be without prejudice to the responsibilities of the police. So the peacekeepers did not intercede, and instead watched (and were videotaped watching) the beating.[82]

---

[79] Borchgrave, *supra* note 74.

[80] *Id.*

[81] S.C. Res. 1542, ¶ 7I(f), U.N. Doc. S/RES/1542 (Apr. 30, 2004).

[82] *See* Victoria K. Holt & Tobias C. Berkman, The Impossible Mandate? Military Preparedness, the Responsibility to Protect and Modern Peace Operations (2006). Holt and Berkman describe how during the U.N. mission in Haiti (MINUSTAH) that "[t]he Brazilian contingent . . . appeared to view its role in MINUSTAH as a traditional peacekeeping mission where force is used only in self-defense, while the Chilean and Sri Lankan contingents have engaged in robust combined military/military police operations targeting criminal gangs in Cap Haitien and elsewhere." *Id.* at 96. And it was the Brazilian peacekeepers who observed but did not stop the beatings. The combination of the different approaches to the use of the force by

In terms of language, each U.N. peace operation designates one of the six U.N. official languages as the mission language, often English. But whatever the designated language is, there are a number of troop-contributing countries that do not primarily speak that language, and thus a wide range of language comprehension abilities exists within the same mission. Cultural differences also play a role, particularly in differing conceptions of what is considered criminal behavior and the corresponding punishment.

C. ACCOUNTABILITY

Given the difficulty in answering the question of what law applies, and adding language and cultural barriers, it likely comes as no surprise that the response to the question of what law applies to an individual peacekeeper is equally elusive.[83] What happens when a peacekeeper on a peace operation commits a crime in the host country? Accountability for peacekeeper misconduct while on a peace operation remains a challenge for the United Nations.

This question is an offshoot or legal progression of the earlier question asked in this chapter: What law applies collectively to a U.N. peace operation mission and the component troop-contributing country? But as discussed above, absent sustained U.N. combat operations, the broader questions of what applies to missions or countries is largely an abstraction. The question of individual peacekeeper liability, however, is both real and frequently asked. The issue is real in that there are actual victims of harm, whether victims peacekeepers have stolen from, assaulted, raped, or killed. And the issue is, unfortunately, the opposite of abstraction as peacekeeper misconduct occurs. These issues, combined with the inherent difficulty in effectively responding to peacekeeper misconduct committed outside the state in which the peacekeeper resides, yields one of the more contentious aspects of peace operations.

Modern concern for peacekeeper misconduct traces back to 2003, when the UNSG issued a bulletin on "[s]pecial measures for protection from sexual exploitation and sexual abuse."[84]This bulletin prohibited sexual abuse and exploitation,

---

different troop-contributing countries on the same U.N. mission led to the worst of both worlds, "MINUSTAH has been criticized both for being too passive—and failing to fulfill its mandate to protect civilians—and for being too aggressive in its actions and harming too many civilians." *Id.*

[83] This section focuses on individual peacekeeper misconduct and troop-contributing response (or lack thereof). Although outside the scope of this section and chapter, corruption at all levels of peace operations remains a problem for which accountability is often claimed to be lacking. A nongovernmental organization's 2013 report on transparency claimed the United Nations and its member states were not appropriately addressing corruption in the context of peace operations. Transparency International, *Corruption & Peacekeeping: Strengthening Peacekeeping and the UN* (Oct. 2013), *available at* http://www.ti-defence.org/publications/128-dsp-pubs-corruption-pk. The United Nations contends the report is systemically flawed. Rick Gladstone, *U.N. Questions Criticism of Its Peacekeepers*, N.Y. Times, Oct. 10, 2013, *available at* http://www.nytimes.com/2013/10/11/world/un-questions-criticism-of-its-peacekeepers.html?_r=0.

[84] U.N. Sec. Gen, *Secretary-General's Bulletin Special Measures for Protection from Sexual Exploitation and Sexual Abuse*, U.N. Doc. ST/SGB/2003/13 (Oct. 9, 2003). Some three years later, the United Nations grappled with the issue of making the SG's sexual exploitation and abuse

which the bulletin defined as including sexual activity with persons under the age of eighteen regardless of the local age of consent or majority, as well as any exchange of money, employment, goods, or services for sex.

In 2004, accusations arose of "sexual exploitation and abuse by a significant number of United Nations peacekeeping personnel in the Democratic Republic of the Congo"[85] This led the UNSG to review the nature and extent of peacekeeper sexual exploitation and abuse as well as measures taken in response. The SG asked Prince Zeid Ra'ad Zeid Al-Hussein of Jordan to prepare a comprehensive report on the problem and potential solutions.[86] The SG transmitted the result, commonly referred to as the Zeid report, to the United Nations in March 2005.[87] The Zeid report identified accountability gaps caused by the different categories of personnel who participate in a U.N. peace operation being governed by different rules.

The report focused on four areas of concern: the current rules on standards of conduct; the investigative process; organizational, managerial, and command responsibility; and individual disciplinary, financial, and criminal accountability. The report acknowledged that "troop-contributing countries are responsible for the conduct and discipline of their troops . . . ." and that "guidelines" and "codes of conduct" were not enforceable because "[r]ules can be made binding on military members of contingents only with the agreement of and action by the troop-contributing country concerned."[88]Ultimately, "[a] decision whether or not to prosecute is an act of sovereignty . . . ."that must come from the troop-contributing country.[89]

The report noted that the model U.N. SOFA "assumes that the Secretary-General will obtain formal assurances from a troop-contributing country that it will

---

bulletin binding. This yielded a sixteen-page report with four annexes, but the broader point is that UNSG bulletins, by themselves, are not binding on states. *See* U.N. Gen. Assembly, *Comprehensive Report Prepared Pursuant to General Assembly Resolution 58/526 on Sexual Exploitation and Sexual Abuse, including Policy Development, Implementation and Full Justification of Proposed Capacity on Personnel Conduct Issues*, U.N. Doc. A/60/862 (May 24, 2006). This is because while under the U.N. Charter, "[m]embers of the United Nations agree to accept and carry out the decisions of the Security Council," there is no such requirement in relation to the Secretary-General. U.N. charter, *supra* note 10, at art 25.

[85] U.N. Sec. Gen., *Comprehensive Review of the Whole Question of Peacekeeping Operations in All Their Aspects*, U.N. Doc A/59/710 (Mar. 24, 2005) [hereinafter Zeid Report]. The peacekeeper misconduct occurred in Bunia, a conflict-ravaged portion of eastern DRC. Among the accusations were that U.N. peacekeepers had sex with minors, bartered food and protection for sex, and had sex with prostitutes. Although the issue of peacekeeper offenses received increasing attention beginning in 2003, earlier reports of sexual abuse and exploitation date to the early 1990s and involve troops from over forty countries serving in peace operations in Bosnia, Cambodia, Haiti, and Southern Sudan. Olivera Simic, *Who Should Be a Peacekeeper?*, 21 PEACE REV. 396 (2009).

[86] Prince Zeid was a permanent Representative of Jordan to the United Nations. Jordan is a significant contributor of both troops and police to U.N. peace operations. Zeid himself served as a civilian peacekeeper on several occasions, including in the former Yugoslavia.

[87] Zeid Report, *supra* note 85.

[88] *Id.* at 12.

[89] *Id.* at 4 and 27.

exercise criminal jurisdiction over its troops in return for the immunity conferred upon them by the host State under the terms of the status-of-forces agreement" but that the United Nations was not obtaining such assurances.[90] The reasons the United Nations was not doing so are unclear. One likely reason is that with the increase of peace operations, the United Nations constantly struggles to secure enough troops from enough countries.[91] Furthermore, adding prerequisites, such as the assurances recommended by the report, only exacerbates the United Nation's force-generation problem.

In terms of the troop-contributing country, one reason for the lack of prosecution for peacekeeper misconduct is that the domestic law of that country has no extraterritorial application. So for example, in Bangladesh (the largest troop contributor to the United Nations), it is against Bangladeshi law for anyone to steal, to rape, or to murder within the territory of Bangladesh. But it is not against Bangladeshi law for a Bangladeshi peacekeeper to steal, to rape, or to murder while deployed on a U.N. peacekeeping mission in, say, Sierra Leone.[92] And Bangladesh is certainly not alone in not having extraterritorial application of its domestic law.[93]

The 6th Committee to the United Nations is the forum for legal considerations. A 2009 meeting of the 6th Committee on the topic of criminal accountability of U.N. personnel addressed whether various member states' domestic law did or did not have any extraterritorial application.[94] This question in essence asked "if a peacekeeper from your country commits a crime while on a peace operation in another country, would you possess jurisdiction to criminally prosecute him/her?" Several countries, after expressing "zero tolerance" for peacekeeper misconduct and stressing the need for accountability not impunity, acknowledged that their domestic law does not apply extraterritorially. This means they are unable to take criminal action against a peacekeeper from their country who commits a crime during a peace operation in another country.[95]

---

[90] *Id.* at 6.

[91] *See* Providing Peacekeepers: The Politics, Challenges and Future of United Nations Peacekeeping Contributions (Alex J. Bellamy & Paul D. Williams eds., 2013).

[92] American Civil Liberties Union, *Universal Jurisdiction: A Preliminary Study of Legislation around the World—2012, available at* http://www.amnesty.org/en/library/asset/IOR53/019/2012/en/2769ce03-16b7-4dd7-8ea3-95f4c64a522a/ior530192012en.pdf (last visited June 15, 2015)

(reporting that the Bangladeshi criminal code does not contain provisions criminalizing ordinary crimes committed outside Bangladesh).

[93] Indeed seven of the top ten troop-contributing countries have no extraterritorial application of their domestic criminal code for ordinary crimes (India, Nepal, Nigeria, Ghana, Senegal, and Egypt). *Id.*

[94] General Assembly of the United Nations Legal-Sixth Committee, Sixty-Fifth Session, The Scope and Application of the Principle of Universal Jurisdiction (Agenda Item 86), http://www.un.org/en/ga/sixth/65/ScopeAppUniJuri.shtml (last visited Sept. 11, 2014). Notably less than 25 percent of member states submitted replies.

[95] Which is not to say the troop-contributing country could not do anything, just that their actions would be limited to administrative ones, such as sending the offender home, fines, demotions, and/or administrative separation from the military.

And even where a troop-contributing state has extraterritorial application of its law, some of the "crimes" committed during a peace operation may not be a crime per the troop-contributing country's laws. For example, although the SG's directive banned sex with anyone under eighteen, in many countries the age of majority is under eighteen, meaning a seventeen-year-old could consent to sex. Although the directive notes that even where the age of majority is under eighteen sex is still forbidden, it is the sending state, and only the sending state, which may take criminal action. So if sex with a seventeen-year-old is not against say the law of the Dominican Republic, even if the U.N. directive applies to a Dominican Republic peacekeeper serving in Africa, there is little to nothing authorities from the Dominican Republic could do if one of its peacekeepers abides by its laws and not by the U.N. directive, at least in the criminal justice arena. A similar problem exists in those countries that do not criminalize prostitution.

Both the UNSC and General Assembly endorsed the Zeid report.[96] Endorsed, however, does not mean that U.N. member states agreed to implement the Zeid report's recommendations. But the report led to reforms and improvements, including mandatory pre-deployment training on the U.N.'s Code of Personal Conduct for Blue Helmets.[97]Additionally the United Nations established the Conduct and Discipline Unit (CDU) in 2007 to strengthen accountability.[98]

The CDU "maintains global oversight of the state of discipline in all peacekeeping operations and special political missions. It provides overall direction for conduct and discipline issues in field missions, including formulating policies, training and outreach activities and handling allegations of misconduct."[99]The CDU represents a substantial step forward for the United Nations in terms of accountability and transparency. Key to this is the statistics page, which provides quantitative data on investigations, allegations, and U.N. follow-up with troop- contributing countries.

For example, below are U.N. figures for allegations of sexual exploitation or abuse made against all categories of U.N. personnel on peace operations from 2007 through July 31, 2014:

The United Nations also tracks and reports the status of investigations into those allegations as substantiated, unsubstantiated, or pending.

But the last statistical category, U.N. follow-up, graphically demonstrates the U.N.'s limitations. The website displays the number of times the United Nations sent a "note verbale"[100]to a troop-contributing country requesting information

---

[96] Press Release, Security Council, Security Council Condemns "in the Strongest Terms" All Acts of Sexual Abuse, Exploitation by U.N. Peacekeeping Personnel, U.N. Doc. SC/8400 (May 31, 2005).

[97] United Nations Conduct and Discipline Unit, U.N. Standards of Conduct Code of Conduct, https://cdu.unlb.org/UNStrategy/Prevention.aspx (last visited Sept. 11, 2014). A copy of the code of personal conduct is included in Appendix 3.

[98] *See* United Nations Conduct and Discipline Unit, http://cdu.unlb.org/ (last visited Sept. 11, 2014).

[99] *Id.*

[100] A note verbale is a form of diplomatic communication. Generally a note verbale is written in the third person and is not signed. *See* Department of General Assembly Affairs and Conference Section, United Nations Correspondence Manual, A Guide to the Drafting, processing and Dispatch of Official United Nations Communications (2000).

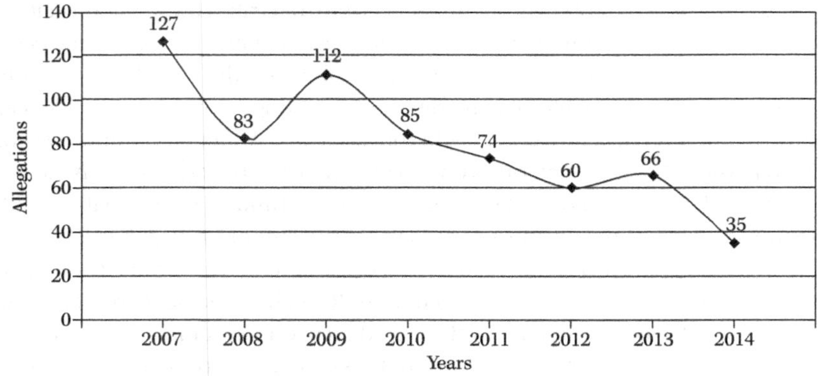

FIGURE 20.2 Allegations for All Categories of Personnel Per Year (Sexual Exploitation and Abuse) 2007–July 31, 2014.[101]

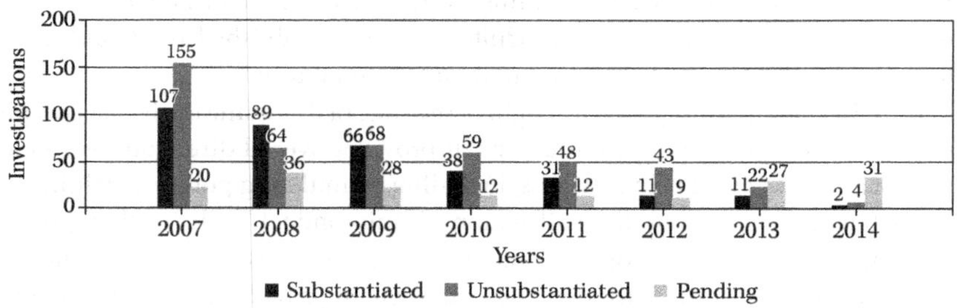

FIGURE 20.3 Status of Investigations (Sexual Exploitation and Abuse) 2007–Sept. 1, 2014.[102]

about disciplinary action the national authorities took following a substantiated allegation of misconduct by a peacekeeper from that country. Since 2007, the United Nations has sent some 520 notes verbale following substantiated allegations of sexual exploitation and abuse offenses. Troop-contributing countries responded to the United Nations only 223 times, approximately 43 percent.

Amazingly, the 43 percent response rate exceeds that for crimes not involving sexual exploitation and abuse. Since 2007, the United Nations sent 575 notes verbale to troop-contributing countries seeking information about disciplinary action taken in response to substantiated allegations of nonsexual offenses. States responded to the United Nations 241 times, approximately 40 percent.

[101] United Nations Conduct and Discipline Unit Statistics, https://cdu.unlb.org/Statistics/OverviewofStatistics.aspx (follow "statistics" tab, then follow "allegations by category of personnel (sexual exploitation and abuse)," then follow "allegations for all categories of personnel per year (sexual exploitation and abuse)" (last visited Sept 11, 2014).

[102] United Nations Conduct and Discipline Unit Statistics, https://cdu.unlb.org/Statistics/OverviewofStatistics.aspx (follow "statistics" tab, then follow "status of investigations (sexual exploitation and abuse)" (last visited Sept 11, 2014).

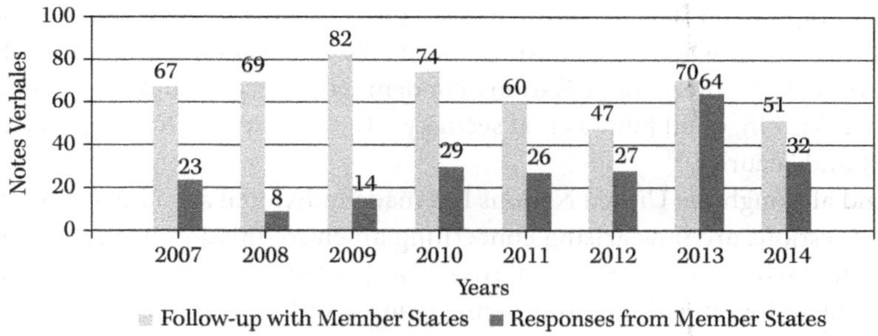

FIGURE 20.4 U.N. Follow-Up with Member States (Sexual Exploitation and Abuse) 2007–July 31, 2014.[103]

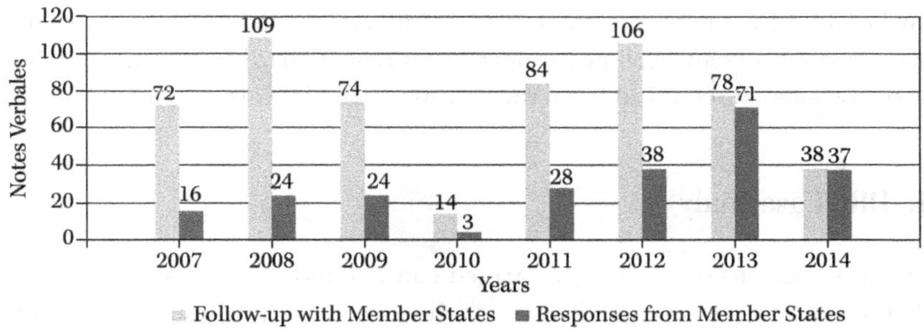

FIGURE 20.5 U.N. Follow-Up with Member States (Excluding Sexual Exploitation and Abuse) 2007–July 31, 2004.[104]

The Zeid report identified a number of deficiencies but also a corrective strategy. Although the United Nations has embraced the report and made progress toward improving peacekeeper accountability, ultimately there will only be as much accountability as member and troop- contributing states afford. Moreover, the United Nation's challenges regarding accountability and peacekeeping are not limited to lower-ranking soldiers but extend to those in leadership positions, and even questions at a normative level. For example, despite "credible evidence" that Rwandan military units under General Emmanuel Karenzi Karake committed "gross human rights violations" the United Nations selected Karake to serve as the deputy commander of the U.N. mission in Darfur.[105] A Fijian Army

[103] United Nations Conduct and Discipline Unit Statistics, https://cdu.unlb.org/Statistics/OverviewofStatistics.aspx (follow "statistics" tab, then follow "UN follow-up with member states (sexual exploitation and abuse) (last visited Sept 11, 2014).

[104] United Nations Conduct and Discipline Unit Statistics, https://cdu.unlb.org/Statistics/OverviewofStatistics.aspx (follow "statistics" tab, then follow "UN follow-up with member states (excluding sexual exploitation and abuse) (last visited Sept 11, 2014).

[105] Colum Lynch, *U.S. Backed U.N. General Despite Evidence of Abuse*, WASH. POST, Sept. 21, 2008, *available at* http://www.washingtonpost.com/wp-dyn/content/article/2008/09/20/AR2008092001801.html.

officer, Filipo Tarakinikini, commanded a peacekeeping force in Lebanon before returning to Fiji where he played a central role in a military coup of the Fijian government. [106] The United Nations condemned the coup, but later employed Tarakinikini in, of all jobs, a chief security advisor for the U.N.'s Department of Safety and Security.[107]

And although the United Nations has made individual accountability a focus area, questions are now arising concerning an entire mission, UNAMID, operating in Darfur. In the spring of 2014, *Foreign Policy* magazine published the results of an investigation into systemic failures, of UNAMID not even trying to protect civilians and systematically covering up incidents against both civilians and U.N. peacekeepers.[108] This in turn led the Prosecutor of the International Criminal Court to call on the UNSG to investigate UNAMID, which the United Nations agreed to do.[109] The UNAMID report which that investigation generates may herald the next set of strategic reforms at and within the United Nations. In terms of how current U.N. peace operations reflect changes in peacekeeping at the operational and tactical level, the mission in the DRC is instructive.

VI. DRC Case Study

Extending back to the mid 1990s, armed conflict and its destructive and destabilizing effects have ravaged the DRC.[110] The conflict, really a series of conflicts, are sometimes referred to as the First and Second Congo Wars or as Africa's first world war. The fighting, however styled, has claimed the lives of several million people[111] and displaced several million more, making it the deadliest conflict

---

[106] Jone Baledrokadroka, *The Unintended Consequences of Fiji's UN Peacekeeping Operations*, December 18, 2010, *available at* http://www.aspistrategist.org.au/the-unintended-consequences-of-fijis-un-peacekeeping-operations/

[107] *Former Fiji Army Spokesman Tarakinikini to Face Unspecified Charges*, Radio New Zealand International, July 2, 2004, *available at* http://www.radionz.co.nz/international/pacific-news/149448/former-fiji-army-spokesman-tarakinikini-to-face-unspecified-charges.

[108] Colum Lynch, *They Just Stood Watching*, Foreign Policy, Apr. 7, 2014, *available at* http://www.foreignpolicy.com/articles/2014/04/07/special_report_darfur_united_nations_peacekeeping_investigation.

[109] Colum Lynch, *Exclusive: ICC to UN: Investigate Your Alleged Coverups in Darfur*, Foreign Policy, June 17, 2014, *available at* http://thecable.foreignpolicy.com/posts/2014/06/16/icc_to_un_investigate_the_mess_you_made_in_darfurhttp://www.un.org/News/Press/docs/2014/sc11441.doc.htm.

[110] The origins of the conflicts are rooted in the genocide that occurred in neighboring Rwanda in 1994. After the genocide, over a million Rwandan Hutus fled to the DRC, then called Zaire. Tutsi forces, from Zaire as well as Rwanda and Uganda fought the Hutus and the military of Zaire across the country; captured the capital, Kinshasa; and renamed the country the Democratic Republic of the Congo. MONUSCO Background, http://www.un.org/en/peacekeeping/missions/monusco/background.shtml (last visited Sept. 11, 2014).

[111] According to the International Rescue Committee, "[l]ess than 10% of all deaths were due to violence, with most attributable to easily preventable and treatable conditions such as malaria, diarrhea, pneumonia, and malnutrition." International Rescue Committee, *Mortality in the Democratic Republic of the Congo: an Ongoing Crisis*, *available at* http://www.rescue.org/sites/default/files/

since World War II. The conflicts in the DRC have involved at least eight African countries and more than twenty armed groups with varying, and alternating, allegiances and backing.

In 1999 the UNSC established the United Nations Organization Mission in the Democratic Republic of the Congo or MONUC[112] to monitor the Lusaka ceasefire agreement[113] between the DRC and Angola, Namibia, Rwanda, Uganda, and Zimbabwe. The UNSCR establishing MONUC did not make specific reference to the legal basis for establishing the force. Rather the UNSCR noted the role the ceasefire agreement requested the United Nations play in implementing the agreement.

The role the agreement requested was that

> [t]he United Nations Security Council, acting under Chapter VII of the UN Charter ... constitute, facilitate and deploy an appropriate peacekeeping force in the DRC to ensure implementation of this Agreement; and taking into account the peculiar situation of the DRC, mandate the peacekeeping force to track down all armed groups in the DRC. In this respect, the UN Security Council shall provide the requisite mandate for the peace-keeping force.

The UNSC declined the request to provide a mandate for a force to track down armed groups, at least initially. As the Lusaka Agreement's attempt at ending the Second Congo War unraveled, the United Nation's role evolved and expanded from observer to enforcer of the peace.[114] By 2003 the UNSC issued resolution 1493, which specifically referenced Chapter VII of the U.N. Charter and authorized MONUC to use "all necessary means to fulfill its mandate in the Ituri district, and as it deems within its capabilities, in North and South Kivu."[115] Illustrating the significance of word choice, the proceeding paragraph authorized necessary measures (as opposed to all necessary measures) to accomplish other tasks.[116] The 1999 UNSCR establishing MONUC provided for "up to 500" U.N. military observers;[117] the 2003 Resolution authorized a U.N. military force of up to 10,800 personnel.[118]

---

migrated/resources/2007/2006-7_congomortalitysurvey.pdf (last visited June 21, 2015). *But see* Human Security Report Project, HUMAN SECURITY REPORT 2009/2010: THE CAUSES OF PEACE AND THE SHRINKING COSTS OF WAR (2011) (challenging the International Rescue Committee's mortality survey process and results for the DRC conflicts.) That debate though is on statistics and methodology.

[112] S.C. Res. 1279, U.N. Doc. S/RES/1279 (Nov. 30, 1999) [hereinafter UNSCR 1279].

[113] Letter dated 23 July 1999 from the Permanent Representative of Zambia to the United Nations Addressed to the President of the Security Council, U.N. Doc. S/1999/815 (July 23, 1999).

[114] Technically the UNSCR establishing MONUC did not assign the force the task of observing the ceasefire agreement. Rather, the Resolution assigned the task to "*plan* for the observation of the ceasefire and disengagement of force." UNSCR 1279, *supra* note 108, ¶ 5(d) (emphasis added).

[115] S.C. Res. 1493, ¶ 26, U.N. Doc. S/RES/1493 (July 28, 2003) [hereinafter UNSCR 1493]. The Ituri and North and South Kivu Regions, all in eastern DRC, were, and to a lesser extent remain, the epicenter of the conflicts.

[116] *Id.*¶ 25.

[117] *Id.*¶ 9.

[118] UNSCR 1493, *supra* note 111, ¶ 3.

In the fourteen years since the United Nations established MONUC (now called MONUSCO),[119] the U.N. force has grown to over twenty thousand uniformed members at a cost close to $US 1.5 billion a year.[120] In 2013 the UNSC issued another resolution concerning the DRC and the role of MONUSCO.[121] The resolution begins in typical U.N. fashion, recalling previous related resolutions. Interestingly, and maybe even contradictorily given the language that followed, the UNSCR "[r]eaffirms the basic principles of peacekeeping, including consent of the parties, impartiality, and non-use of force, expect in self defence and defence of the mandate."[122]

This may be contradictory because what follows in the resolution is anything but impartiality. Rather than protecting civilians under a self-defense concept, the resolution establishes an "Intervention Brigade" that is charged with the responsibility of "neutralizing armed groups" by carrying out "targeted offensive operations" in a "robust, highly mobile and versatile manner," either jointly with the Congolese Army or acting unilaterally.[123]

There is an argument to be made that the Intervention Brigade is much ado about, if not nothing, than little. This argument contends that prior to the UNSCR forming the Intervention Brigade, MONUSCO's mandate already included authority to take all necessary measures, the broadest grant of authority the United Nations may confer. Under this argument, authority to conduct offensive operations and neutralize armed groups was already extant, subsumed within the authority to take all necessary measures. Yet the Intervention Brigade resolution must add something, or why draft it at all? And functionally, there have been a number of U.N. peace operations under Chapter VII and "all necessary measures" authority, and they have looked and operated quite differently than the Intervention Brigade.

The brigade is comprised of three thousand soldiers from South Africa, Tanzania, and Malawi who form three infantry battalions, one field artillery

---

[119] United Nations Organization Stabilization Mission in the Democratic Republic of the Congo, *see* S.C. Res. 1925, ¶ 1, U.N. Doc. S/RES/1925 (May 28, 2010). UNSCR 1925 stated that "in view of the new phase that has been reached in the Democratic Republic of the Congo" the name of the U.N. Mission would be changed to reflect a mission to stabilize the relative peace. *Id.* Given what has unfortunately transpired in the DRC since the 2010 name change, including the U.N. peacekeepers assuming an offensive role in military operations, sadly "stabilization" remains tragically aspirational.

[120] MONUSCO Facts and Figures, http://www.un.org/en/peacekeeping/missions/monusco/facts.shtml (last visited Sept. 11, 2014). The U.N. force in the DRC has also suffered seventy-five fatalities: forty-five peacekeeping troops, four U.N. police officers, three military observers, twelve international civilian U.N. employees, and eleven local civilian employees. *Id.* Nine of the peacekeepers, all from Bangladesh, were killed in one incident in 2005 by members of an armed group commanded by Thomas Lubanga. That attack provided the catalyst for Lubanga's arrest and the first trial and conviction at the International Criminal Court, though for recruiting and employing child soldiers, not for attacking U.N. peacekeepers. *Prosecutor* v. *Thomas Lubanga Dyilo*, Judgment pursuant to Article 74 of the Statute, ICC-01/04-01/06-2842, T.Ch. I, 14 March 2012.

[121] S.C. Res. 209, U.N. Doc. S/RES/2098 (Mar. 28, 2013).

[122] *Id.* at preamble.

[123] *Id.* at 12(b).

battalion, and one special forces and reconnaissance company. Under the auspice of neutralize, "it is reasonable to assume that the Brigade is mandated to target armed groups with lethal force. In line with the usual concept of offensive operations, the Brigade would be able to conduct ambushes, deliberate attacks and hold ground against any armed group."[124]

All of which represents a "major departure from the often passive approach that has given peacekeepers a bad reputation."[125] Rather than using force only in self-defense, Lieutenant General Carlos Alberto dos Santos Cruz, the Brazilian Army General in command of MONUSCO's military force, claims that "[t]he posture now is to go and neutralize the threat . . . We go to where the threat is and we neutralize the threat . . . We need to take action. It's a different dynamic, a completely different idea."[126] The Intervention Brigade provided insight into what neutralize per the UNSCR means or looks like in August 2013, when the U.N. force fired artillery at rebels near the Congolese city of Goma.[127] The brigade has also employed attack helicopters, and, for the first time in U.N. peace operations, unarmed surveillance drones. [128]

One commentator claims that "[t]he deployment of drones in the DRC represents a defining moment in UN peacekeeping and aerial surveillance during ongoing conflict."[129] Hervé Ladsous, the head of DPKO, stated that the drones MONUSCO is using are "a very useful tool" that is changing peacekeeping."[130] Indeed Ladsousis advocating their use in other U.N. missions, including Mali, the Central African Republic, and South Sudan.[131]

---

[124] Oswald, *supra* note 63.

[125] Nicholas Kulish & Somini Sengupta, *New U.N. Brigade's Aggressive Stance Brings Success, and Risks*, N.Y. Times, Nov. 12, 2013, *available at* http://www.nytimes.com/2013/11/13/world/africa/new-un-brigades-aggressive-stance-in-africa-brings-success-and-risks.html?pagewanted=1.

[126] Jon Sawyer, *Congolese Army and Hardened UN Forces Make Gains against Rebels*, PBS Newshour, Oct. 30, 2013, *available at* http://www.pbs.org/newshour/updates/world/july-dec13/congo_10-30.html.

[127] Jonny Hogg, *U.N. Combat Brigade Fires on Congo Rebel Positions*, Reuters, Aug. 23, 2013, *available at* http://www.reuters.com/article/2013/08/23/us-congo-democratic-fighting-idUSBRE97MOJC20130823 It is unclear what "neutralize" means within the United Nations. In the U.S. military, the term is defined as "to render ineffective or unsable." Department of Defense Dictionary of Military Terms, http://www.dtic.mil/doctrine/dod_dictionary/data/n/5752.html (enter "neutralize" as search term) (last visited Sept. 11, 2014).

[128] Specifically, five unarmed Italian "Falco" unmanned aerial vehicles or drones. *Drones for Peace: Ladsous, Very Useful Tool for DPKO*, Onu Italia, May 15, 2014, *available at* http://www.onuitalia.org/drones-peace-ladsous-useful-tool-dpko/ [hereinafter Ladsous].

[129] Kasaija Phillip Apuuli, *The Use of Unmanned Aerial Vehicles (Drones) in United Nations Peacekeeping: The Case of the Democratic Republic of the Congo*, 18 ASIL Insight 13 (June 13, 2014).

[130] Ladsous, *supra* note 124.

[131] *Id. See also Ladsous and Haq: With UAV We Change Peacekeeping*, Onu Italia, May 28, 2014, *available at* http://www.onuitalia.org/ladsous-haq-uav-change-peacekeeping/. Ladsous notes the enormity of the challenge MONUSCO faces in the DRC, where there is "just one peacekeeper per 117 square kilometers." The drones are helping in a variety of ways, including spotting a capsized boat in Lake Kivu in the DRC, allowing MONUSCO to save fourteen passengers.

FIGURE 20.6 U.N. Armed Attack Helicopter in MONUSCO.[132]

FIGURE 20.7 U.N. Unarmed Unmanned Aerial Vehicle in MONUSCO.

[132] In another sign of the evolving nature of U.N. peace operations, the United Nations tweeted both photos and video links to the drone's first flight. UN Web TV, *UN Mission in DR Congo Launches the Inaugural Flight of Unarmed Unmanned Aerial Vehicles in Goma*, Dec. 3, 2013, *available at* http://webtv.un.org/watch/un-mission-in-dr-congo-launches-the-inaugural-flight-of-unarmed-unmanned-aerial-vehicles-in-goma/2889857885001/.

Although the United Nations is open about MONUSCO's drone use, other byproducts of the Intervention Brigade and its offensive mandate are not receiving attention.

One result of U.N. forces taking offensive action that has not been much discussed, at least publicly, is the issue of detention. If MONUSCO has the authority to kill members of armed groups, does it possess the authority to detain them?[133] With detention comes a legion of difficult issues and questions. Where will they will be detained? Who will fund the detention centers? Who will guard them? What would detention standards be? How would transfer, parole, or release work? Noted Australian commentator Bruce Oswald claims that the term "neutralize" may imply that the Brigade has the power to detain, and points to the U.N.'s Interim Standard Operating Procedures for Detention in United Nations Peace Operations for what U.N. detention would look like.[134] Oswald also contends that it is "reasonable to assume that, consistent with the UN's past practice, the Brigade will transfer the armed group members that they have captured to the DRC authorities. "Given the DRC's placement near the bottom of the human development index[135] and level of systemic human rights violations,[136] U.N. transfer of detainees to the DRC could result in charges of U.N. complicity and potential liability if (and more likely when) the Congolese mistreat the detainees.[137]

The longer the Intervention Brigade is taking offensive action, the more likely the issue of detention and other effects will be raised. And according to General Cruz, "[w]e are going to exercise our mandate to the maximum possible, not only against M23, against all the groups . . . When we finish one problem, we are in our heads thinking about the next step."[138] True to Cruz's word, the combined U.N. and DRC forces compelled the surrender of the M23 rebel group and are shifting their attention and offensive efforts to other armed groups.[139]

---

[133] The general answer is that detention is considered within the nature of, or inherent to, armed conflict and the LOAC reflects that in and for both international and non-international armed conflict. *See* Jelena Pejic, *The Protective Scope of Common Article 3: More than Meets the Eye*, 93 Int'l Rev. Red Cross 189, 207 (2011) (stating that "[i]n the ICRC's view, both treaty and customary [international humanitarian law] contain an inherent power to intern. . . .")

[134] Oswald, *supra* note 63. *See also* United Nations Department of Peacekeeping Operations Department of Field Support, *Interim Standard Operating Procedures Detention in United Nations Peace Operations* (2011).

[135] Human Development Index, *supra* note 7.

[136] Human Rights Watch, Human Rights in the Democratic Republic of the Congo, http://www.hrw.org/drc (last visited Sept. 11, 2014).

[137] One could imagine alleged U.N. detainee abuse or mistreatment playing out similarly to how allegations that U.N. peacekeepers brought cholera to earthquake ravaged Haiti—poorly. *See* Randal C. Archibold & Somini Sengupta, *U.N. Struggles to Stem Haiti Cholera Epidemic*, N.Y. Times, Apr. 19, 2014, *available at* http://www.nytimes.com/2014/04/20/world/americas/un-struggles-to-stem-haiti-cholera-epidemic.html and Rick Gladstone, *U.N. Chief Served Papers in Suit by Haitian Victims, Lawyers Say*, N.Y. Times, June 20, 2014, *available at* http://www.nytimes.com/2014/06/21/world/americas/un-chief-served-papers-in-suit-by-haitian-cholera-victims-lawyers-say.html (describing the United Nation's ongoing efforts to aid Haiti battle a deadly strain of cholera while avoiding discussing whether peacekeepers introduced the disease).

[138] Kulish, *supra* note 121.

[139] Somini Sengupta, *Peacekeepers in Congo to Focus on Another Rebel Group*, N.Y. Times, A7 Nov. 7, 2013.

VII. Intervention Brigade Effects, and Conclusion

Although the Intervention Brigade has been successful, there are negative consequences of MONUSCO undertaking offensive missions as well. "As a matter of law, it is difficult to conclude that the [Intervention] Brigade would not be a party to the conflict in situations where it conducts offensive operations."[140] As a party to the conflict, MONUSCO is seemingly not operating consistent with any of the three U.N. peacekeeping principles: consent of the parties, impartiality, and nonuse of force except in self-defense and defense of the mandate.

Beyond the doctrinal disconnect, the Intervention Brigade creates other issues, particularly for others operating in and around the peace operation as well as for peacekeepers themselves. Some are concerned that the use of the Intervention Brigade could "put [aid] workers at risk because armed groups will not distinguish between soldiers and those who feed, heal and house civilians in war."[141] A representative from Doctors Without Borders contended the issue is beyond a blurring of the lines, arguing that "[y]ou can have a helicopter one day used to deliver the Force Intervention Brigade troops to attack a village and next day to deliver aid to that same village."[142] He claimed that the presence of the Intervention Brigade "is a problem for all the humanitarian actors . . . [w]hen the population sees a white car, they don't differentiate between whether it is [Doctors Without Borders], the UN or [the Intervention Brigade. *It makes us military targets.*"[143]

In terms of peacekeepers, they are now "legitimate targets for the extent of their participation in accordance with international humanitarian law."[144] Prior to the employment of the Intervention Brigade, killing a member of MONUSCO was a war crime. Tragically that is what happened in May 2013 when assailants attacked a U.N. convoy in eastern DRC and killed a Pakistani peacekeeper. The UNSG "condemned the attack, saying that killing a peacekeeper was a 'war crime'."[145]

This is a reference to the Rome Statute of the International Criminal Court (ICC), which defines a war crime as "[i]ntentionally directing attacks against personnel, installations, material, units or vehicles involved in a humanitarian assistance or peacekeeping mission in accordance with the Charter of the United

---

[140] Oswald, *supra* note 63.

[141] Kulish, *supra* note 121.

[142] *Id.*

[143] Sudarsan Raghavan, *In Volatile Congo, a New U.N. Force with Teeth*, WASH. POST., Oct. 25, 2013, *available at* http://www.washingtonpost.com/world/africa/in-volatile-congo-a-new-un-force-with-teeth/2013/11/01/0cda650c-423f-11e3-b028-de922d7a3f47_story.html (emphasis added). Legally the Doctors Without Borders vehicle is not a permissible target. But one can see the makings of a possibly legitimate defense of mistaking the impermissible to target white vehicle (or blue-helmeted soldier) for the permissible to target white vehicle (or blue-helmeted soldier).

[144] Oswald, *supra* note 63.

[145] *Congo: Pakistani UN Peacekeeper Killed in Ambush*, BBC, May 8, 2013, *available at* http://www.bbc.co.uk/news/world-africa-22447390.

Nations, as long as they are entitled to the protection given to civilians or civilian objects under the international law of armed conflict."[146] And there is currently a case before the ICC involving just that—war crimes allegations based on attacking and killing U.N. peacekeepers (albeit in Sudan).[147]

But killing a peacekeeper is only a war crime if the peacekeeper was "entitled to the protection given to civilians or civilian objects under the international law of armed conflict."[148] A civilian who directly participated in hostilities by conducting offensive operations would not have protection from the law of war from being made the object of attack.[149] And neither will members of the Intervention Brigade.[150]

The Intervention Brigade's offensive actions also render the 1994 Convention on the Safety of United Nations and Associated Personnel void, at least in part. The Convention begins by stating "bearing in mind that attacks against, or other mistreatment of, personnel who act on behalf of the United Nations are unjustifiable and unacceptable by whomever committed."[151] The Convention claims that U.N. personnel shall not be made the object of attack and requires States to criminalize the intentional murder of U.N. peacekeepers.[152] This point is made clear in the UNSG's 1999 bulletin. While the bulletin refers to the protected status of members of peacekeeping operations under the 1994 Convention on the Safety of United Nations and Associated Personnel or their status as noncombatants, it qualifies the status as lasting "as long as [members of peacekeeping operations] are entitled to the protection given to civilians under the international law of armed conflict."[153] But again, the Intervention Brigade, in taking offensive action, is not entitled to the protection given to civilians, thus negating the basis the Convention on the Safety of United Nations and Associated Personnel claims for why, and when, killing a U.N. peacekeeper is illegal.

---

[146] Statute of the International Criminal Court, UN Doc. A/CONF.183/9 (1998) (last amended 2010), art 8(2)(b)(iii) [hereinafter Rome Statute].

[147] *Prosecutor v. Bahar Idriss Abu Garda*, ICC-02/05-02/09 (2009).

[148] Rome Statute, *supra* note 141.

[149] *See* Protocol Additional to the Geneva Conventions of 12 August 1949, and Relation to the Protection of Victims of international Armed Conflicts, art. 51, June 8, 1977, 1125 U.N.T.S. 17512.

[150] This is not to say that killing a member of the Intervention Brigade is not a crime; it is. But it is no longer an international or war crime. It would be a violation of the domestic criminal law of the DRC and possibly the country from which the slain peacekeeper originated. And given that the Intervention Brigade falls under the same command structure as the rest of MONUSCO, it is possible that all military members of MONUSCO are no longer immune from being made the object of attack. Moreover, to the extent MONUSCO employs civilian employees or contractors who are directly participating in hostilities by say operating drones or serving as targeting intelligence analysts for the Intervention Brigade, they too are no longer protected from being made the object of attack. *See* Ferraro, *supra* note 62 (stating that an intentional attack against U.N. forces and other associated personnel who are participating in the conflict "is not considered a crime under the Rome Statute. . . .). *See also* Apuuli, *supra* note 125 (stating that drone operators are directly participating in hostilities and thus "open to attack by enemy forces.").

[151] Office of Legal Affairs Codification Division, Convention on the Safety of United Nations and Associated Personnel, *available at* http://www.un.org/law/cod/safety.htm

[152] *Id.* at art 7.

[153] UNSG IHL Bulletin, *supra* note 68.

The United Nations has not publicly acknowledged that the Intervention Brigade's offensive nature renders its members the permissible object of attack under international law. Does or will DPKO inform members of the Intervention Brigade that targeting them may no longer be a war crime?[154] How will that impact a member state's willingness to contribute personnel, equipment, and funds in support of PSO? What of the irony that the United Nations through its actions has rendered partially null and void a Convention on the safety of U.N. personnel?

Regardless of these issues, the initial reaction to the Intervention Brigade's employment has been largely positive. The U.S. special envoy to the Great Lakes region of Africa claimed the brigade represented "a stronger approach that can give peacekeeping operations more strength in the future and help resolve knotty problems."[155]

But the envoy also acknowledged that the story of the Intervention Brigade, and its legacy, "has yet to be written . . ."[156] Therein lies the question, when the Intervention Brigade's legacy is determined, will it be one of effective incorporation of lessons learned and augur the future of U.N. peace operations? Or it will be viewed as a sui generis mission not able, or needed, to be repeated? More likely history will view the Intervention Brigade as successfully accomplishing some peacekeeping goals, but sacrificing or compromising others in the process. In the end, MONUSCO and the Intervention Brigade may well prove a bellwether.

---

[154] *See* Alex J. Bellamy, *Are New Robust Mandates Putting UN Peacekeepers More at Risk?*, IPI Global Observatory, May 29, 2014, *available at* http://theglobalobservatory.org/analysis/750-new-robust-mandates-putting-un-peacekeepers-at-risk.html.

[155] Kulish, *supra* note 121.

[156] *Id.* He added that "the first couple chapters are very good."

APPENDIXES

Appendix 1 Frequency of U.N. Peace Operations, 1991–2013

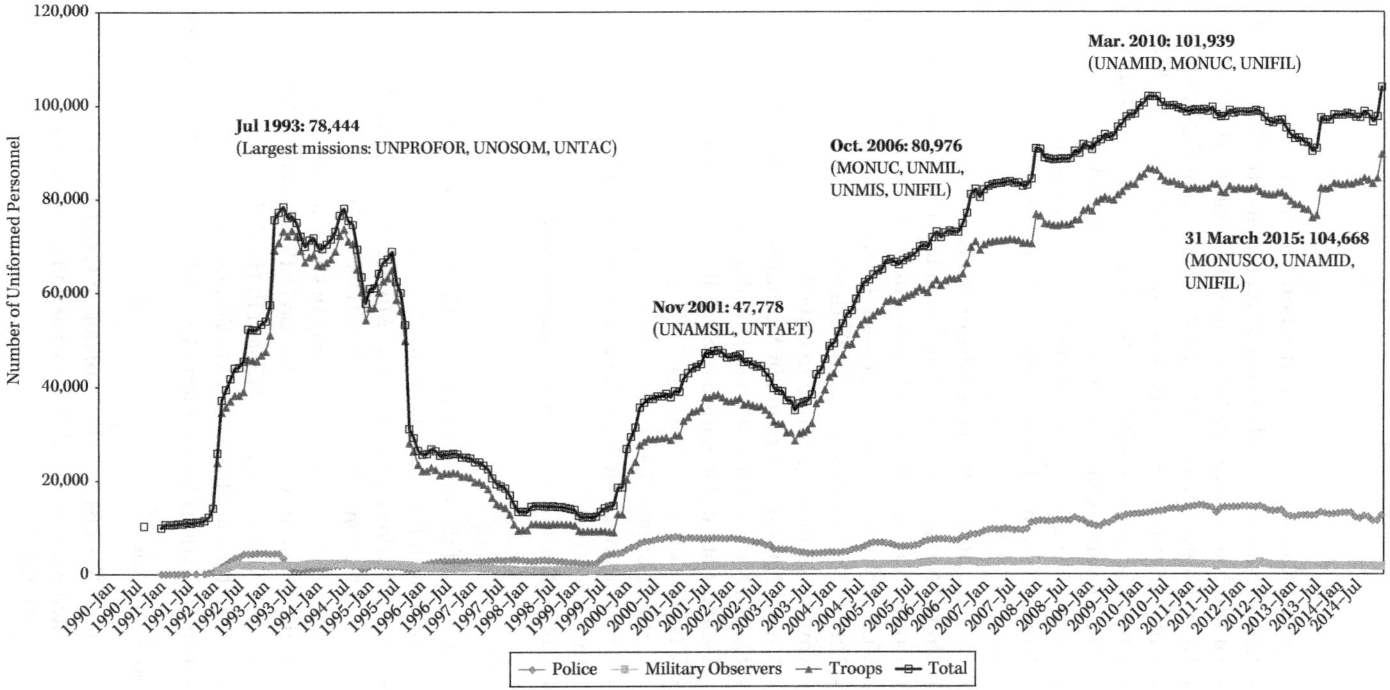

FIGURE 20.8 Surge in Uniformed UN Peacekeeping Personnel from 1991-Present.

Appendix 2 Past U.N. Peacekeeping Missions[157]

Africa

- United Nations Angola Verification Mission I (UNAVEM I)
- United Nations Angola Verification Mission II (UNAVEM II)
- United Nations Angola Verification Mission III (UNAVEM III)
- United Nations Aouzou Strip Observer Group (UNASOG)
- United Nations Assistance Mission for Rwanda (UNAMIR)
- United Nations Mission in Ethiopia and Eritrea (UNMEE)
- United Nations Mission in Sierra Leone (UNAMSIL)
- United Nations Mission in the Central African Republic (MINURCA)
- United Nations Mission in the Central African Republic and Chad (MINURCAT)
- United Nations Observer Mission in Angola (MONUA)
- United Nations Observer Mission in Liberia (UNOMIL)
- United Nations Observer Mission in Sierra Leone (UNOMSIL)
- United Nations Observer Mission Uganda-Rwanda (UNOMUR)
- United Nations Operation in Burundi (ONUB)
- United Nations Operation in Côte d'Ivoire (MINUCI)
- United Nations Operation in Mozambique (ONUMOZ)
- United Nations Operation in Somalia I (UNOSOM I)
- United Nations Operation in Somalia II (UNOSOM II)
- UN Mission in the Sudan (UNMIS)
- United Nations Operation in the Congo (ONUC)
- United Nations Organization Mission in the Democratic Republic of the Congo (MONUC)
- United Nations Transition Assistance Group (UNTAG)

Americas

- Mission of the Representative of the Secretary-General in the Dominican Republic (DOMREP)
- United Nations Civilian Police Mission in Haiti (MIPONUH)
- United Nations Mission in Haiti (UNMIH)
- United Nations Observer Group in Central America (ONUCA)
- United Nations Observer Mission in El Salvador (ONUSAL)
- United Nations Support Mission in Haiti (UNSMIH)
- United Nations Transition Mission in Haiti (UNTMIH)
- United Nations Verification Mission in Guatemala (MINUGUA)

Asia and the Pacific

- United Nations Advance Mission in Cambodia (UNAMIC)
- United Nations Good Offices Mission in Afghanistan and Pakistan (UNGOMAP)

[157] http://www.un.org/en/peacekeeping/operations/past.shtml

- United Nations India-Pakistan Observation Mission (UNIPOM)
- United Nations Mission of Observers in Tajikistan (UNMOT)
- United Nations Mission of Support in East Timor (UNMISET)
- United Nations Security Force in West New Guinea (UNSF)
- United Nations Transitional Administration in East Timor (UNTAET)
- United Nations Transitional Authority in Cambodia (UNTAC)
- UN Integrated Mission in Timor-Leste (UNMIT)

Europe

- United Nations Civilian Police Support Group (UNPSG)
- United Nations Confidence Restoration Operation in Croatia (UNCRO)
- United Nations Mission in Bosnia and Herzegovina (UNMIBH)
- United Nations Mission of Observers in Prevlaka (UNMOP)
- United Nations Observer Mission in Georgia (UNOMIG)
- United Nations Preventive Deployment Force (UNPREDEP)
- United Nations Protection Force (UNPROFOR)
- United Nations Transitional Administration for Eastern Slavonia, Baranja and Western Sirmium (UNTAES)

Middle East

- United Nations Emergency Force I (UNEF I)
- United Nations Emergency Force II (UNEF II)
- United Nations Iran-Iraq Military Observer Group (UNIIMOG)
- United Nations Iraq-Kuwait Observation Mission (UNIKOM)
- United Nations Observation Group in Lebanon (UNOGIL)
- United Nations Yemen Observation Mission (UNYOM)
- UN Supervision Mission in Syria (UNSMIS)

Appendix 3 United Nations Peacekeeper Code of Conduct

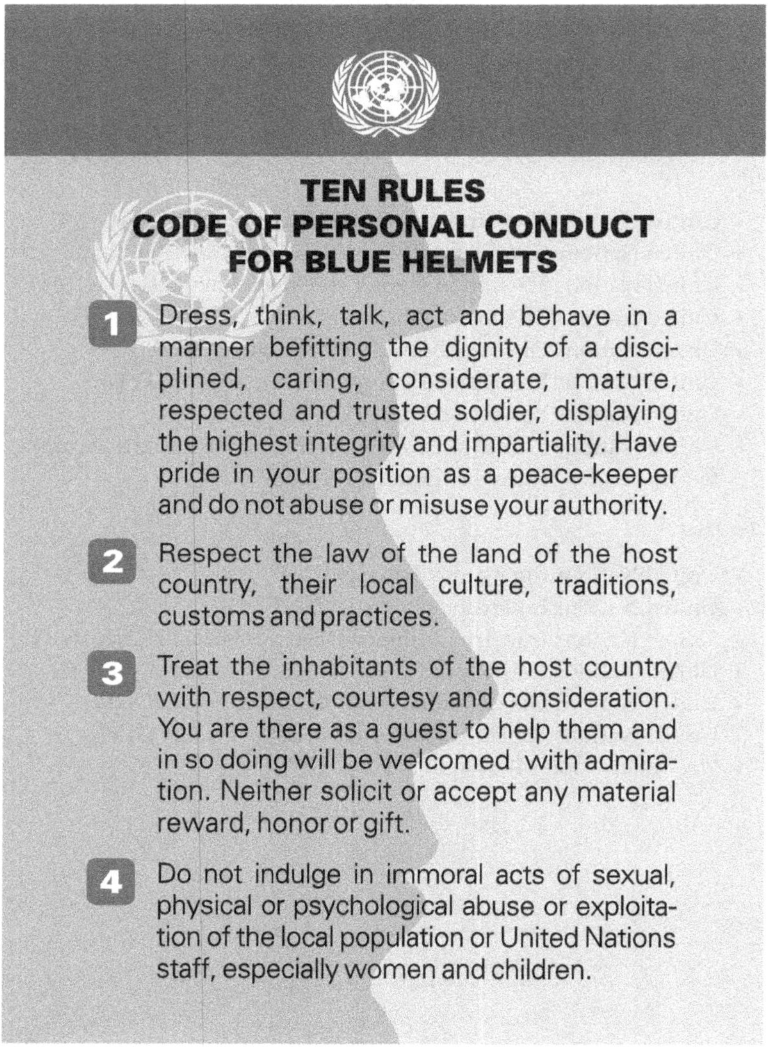

TEN RULES
CODE OF PERSONAL CONDUCT FOR BLUE HELMETS

1. Dress, think, talk, act and behave in a manner befitting the dignity of a disciplined, caring, considerate, mature, respected and trusted soldier, displaying the highest integrity and impartiality. Have pride in your position as a peace-keeper and do not abuse or misuse your authority.

2. Respect the law of the land of the host country, their local culture, traditions, customs and practices.

3. Treat the inhabitants of the host country with respect, courtesy and consideration. You are there as a guest to help them and in so doing will be welcomed with admiration. Neither solicit or accept any material reward, honor or gift.

4. Do not indulge in immoral acts of sexual, physical or psychological abuse or exploitation of the local population or United Nations staff, especially women and children.

FIGURE 20.9 UN Peacekeeper Code of Conduct.

21 }

Maritime Interdiction Operations

Stephanie M. Smart*

I. Introduction

In December 2002, a multinational coalition of ships patrolling the coast of Pakistan for terrorists fleeing Afghanistan began tracking the North Korean merchant vessel *So San* as United States intelligence revealed that it might be transporting ballistic missiles. The freighter was tracked for several days across the Indian Ocean and Arabian Sea. As the freighter approached Yemen, the United States asked Spain to stop and request to board the ship. Inspection of the ship uncovered fifteen Scud missiles, buried beneath sacks of cement, which the Yemeni government had purchased from North Korea.[1] The shipment was turned over to the U.S. Navy but ultimately was allowed to proceed for several reasons: the importation of the missiles did not violate any law, the U.S. alliance with Yemen in the war on terror was considered important and fragile, and the imported missile technology was so antiquated it presented only a very minimal threat to international security in the hands of the Yemeni government.[2]

---

* Stephanie M. Smart is a retired Navy Judge Advocate and currently Associate Deputy General Counsel (Intelligence), Department of Defense. She obtained her JD from George Washington University and LLM at the Georgetown University Law Center. While on active duty Stephanie commanded Naval Legal Service Office Southeast, served as Deputy Legal Counsel to the Chairman of the Joint Chiefs of Staff, and Fleet Judge Advocate to Commander, U.S. Seventh Fleet in Yokosuka, Japan. The positions and opinions in this chapter are those of the author and do not represent the official views of the Department of Defense or the United States Navy.

[1] Ian Patrick Barry, Note, *The Right of Visit, Search and Seizure of Foreign Flagged Vessels on the High Seas Pursuant to Customary International Law: A Defense of the Proliferation Security Initiative*, 33 HOFSTRA L. REV. 299, 299–300 (2004).

[2] In a statement by White House Spokesman, Ari Fleisher, the administration attributed the release of the shipment due to a failure of international law to prohibit Yemen from accepting delivery of the missile as neither Yemen nor North Korea were bound by the voluntary guidelines of the Missile Technology Control Regime. *See* David Sanger & Thom Shanker, *Threats and Responses: War Materiel; Reluctant U.S. Gives Assent for Missiles to Go to Yemen*, N.Y. TIMES, Dec 12, 2002, *available at* http://www.nytimes.com/2002/12/12/world/threats-responses-war-materiel-reluctant-us-gives-assent-for-missiles-go-yemen.html. However, other writers have attributed the release to the

The *So San* incident illustrates the ease of weapons proliferation or movement of other illicit cargo in the maritime environment and some of the difficulties states encounter when trying to prevent such proliferation using maritime interdiction. The ability to conduct effective maritime interdiction is complicated by the vastness of ocean space, the lack of "high seas" police, and the bedrock concept of flag state sovereignty over their vessels. This chapter will explore the role of the U.S. Navy in maritime interdiction operations, the legal basis and framework for unilateral and multilateral interdiction operations, and common legal issues encountered during execution of these operations.

II. What is MIO?

Interdiction Operations in general are operations to divert, disrupt, delay, or destroy an enemy's surface capabilities before they can be used effectively against friendly forces, or to otherwise achieve objectives.[3] When the threat emanates from the sea, a nation, at peace or at war, may conduct Maritime Interdiction Operations (MIO)[4] of vessels at sea to protect their national security from that threat. These operations can range from a bridge-to-bridge query of the master of the vessel through stopping, boarding, searching or seizing the cargo or vessel to an all-out blockade by a belligerent in war. It can be used to enforce sanctions or national policies imposed unilaterally, multinationally, or as directed by the United Nations or other intergovernmental organization or regional authority.

A. WHY IS MARITIME INTERDICTION IMPORTANT?

Maritime interdiction is extraordinarily important in the contemporary struggle against terrorism and particularly terrorist acts at sea. The U.S. Department of State defines "terrorism" as "premeditated, politically motivated violence perpetrated against noncombatant targets by subnational groups or clandestine agents."[5]

---

other rationales. *See* Andrew C. Winner, *PSI as Strategy*, 10 The Monitor 1 (Spring 2004), *available at* http://www.uga.edu/cits/documents/pdf/monitor/monitor_sp_2004.pdf.

[3] Joint Chiefs of Staff, Joint Publication 3-03, Joint Interdiction Operations I-1 (Oct. 14, 2011) [hereinafter JP 3-03].

[4] Maritime interception operations (as opposed to maritime interdiction operations) are a form or subset of interdiction used for sanction enforcement that are military or legal in nature, and serve both political and military purposes. Like the broader category of maritime interdiction operations, the political objective is to compel a country or group to conform to the objectives of the initiating body, while the military objective focuses on establishing a barrier that is selective, allowing only authorized goods or persons to enter or exit. *Id.* at II-6.

[5] 22 U.S.C. § 2656f(d)(2) (Dec 7 2011). The United Nations has not adopted an internationally binding definition of "terrorism" but the Security Council (UNSC) has stated in UNSC Resolution 1566, that it believes terrorism involves:

> "criminal acts, including against civilians, committed with the intent to cause death or serious bodily injury, or taking of hostages, with the purpose to provoke a state of terror

Maritime terrorism or terrorism at sea, therefore is a terrorist act that occurs at sea, or a terrorist act using vessels of the sea to perpetrate or facilitate terrorist activities on land.

Maritime terrorism is distinct from piracy: terrorism by definition is committed for political or ideological purpose, rather than for piracy's limited private ends. The piracy provisions of modern conventional international law define the offense of piracy as an illegal act of violence, detention, or depredation committed by the crew or passengers of a private ship for private ends committed on the high seas (or in a place outside the jurisdiction of any state) against another vessel.[6] This distinction was highlighted after the hijacking of the *Achille Lauro* in 1985 when the narrow definition of piracy limited the ability of the United States and Italy to hold and prosecute the hijackers and co-conspirators.[7] The prosecution of the crime of piracy, being one of the few crimes that international law has given the nations of the world universal jurisdiction to prevent and punish,[8] is much more readily prosecuted, largely due to international will, than ordinary crimes of assault, armed robbery, and kidnapping associated with terrorist hijackings.

B. THE THREAT

Although the security focus immediately after September 11th was directed at aviation and immigration, recently there has been an increasing focus on the threat from the sea.[9] Shipping is especially vulnerable to terrorism because the targets are slow-moving vessels with little maneuverability (especially when confronted by small fast-moving boats), plus in the course of international trade ships often travel through "choke points."

> These threats to security in the maritime domain are becoming increasingly important because the level of security there either directly or

in the general public or in a group of persons or particular persons, intimidate a population or compel a government or an international organization to do or to abstain from doing any act." S.C. Res. 1566, para 3, U.N. Doc S/RES/1566 (October 8, 2004).

[6] Geneva Convention on the High Seas, Apr. 29, 1958, 450 U.N.T.S 11, art. 15; United Nations Convention of the Law of the Sea, Dec. 10, 1982, S. Treaty Doc. No 103-39, 1833 U.N.T.S. 397, art. 101 (Although the United States has not ratified this convention, it is generally recognized to be a codification of customary international law) [hereinafter UNCLOS].

[7] Members of the Palestine Liberation Front hijacked the Italian passenger ship, *Achille Lauro*, on October 7, 1985. During the course of the hijacking, American passenger Leon Klinghoffer was killed. After negotiating their escape, an Egyptian commercial plane was taking the hijackers to Tunisia when it was intercepted by U.S. Navy fighters and forced to land in Sicily. The United States requested the extradition of the hijackers, but Italy refused to extradite them to a country that had the death penalty and promised to try them in Italy. However, the mastermind was released on furlough because of diplomatic immunity and remained at large until his capture by U.S. forces in Baghdad in 2003. Gerald P. McGinley, *The* Achille Lauro *Affair—Implications for International Law*, 52 TENN. L. REV. 691, 693–94 (1985).

[8] UNCLOS, *supra* note 6.

[9] U.S. Department of Homeland Security, The National Strategy for Maritime Security 3–6 (2005), https://www.hsdl.org/?collection&id=4.

> indirectly impacts an increasingly larger number of people around the globe. Currently, 2.2 billion people live within 100 kilometers of a coastline; the maritime domain is home to 50,000 large ships that carry about 80% of the world's trade; and each year about 1.9 billion tons of petroleum is shipped by maritime transportation—approximately 60% of all the petroleum produced. Shipping industries around the world are taking advantage of the booming economy in China—shipping tonnage can barely keep pace with demand as Chinese exports grew 37% in 2004. In addition, a record 10.5 million people embarked on cruise ships in 2004, an increase of about 10% over 2003. Cruise industry analysts predict more than 11 million cruise passengers for 2005.[10]

The dangers presented by terrorism at sea are varied and include: proliferation of weapons of mass destruction (WMD) and associated materials to rogue states or nonstate actors via the sea, terrorists hijacking or damaging ships carrying dangerous materials, intentional causing of environmental damage, or simply fear. An example of the latter was the October 2002 terrorist attack on the French supertanker *MT Limburg* that released ninety thousand gallons of oil into the Gulf of Aden.[11] The hijacking, sinking, and burning of one single oil tanker in a chokepoint such as the Strait of Malacca or Strait of Hormuz could block that sea lane, causing severe economic consequences by increasing oil and shipping costs globally.[12]

III. Overview of the Role of U.S. Navy Assets in MIOs

Maritime interdiction has been used by nations at war and during periods of tensions or hostilities not amounting to war to prevent enemies from moving forces or supplies, or engaging in commerce to fund their military efforts, or simply as a coercive measure to convince an adversary to change its policies. Both the Allies and the Central Powers in World War I used the belligerent act of blockade[13] to stem the flow of war supplies. Although the effectiveness of the Allies' blockade on Germany likely contributed to the outcome of the war, the well-known

---

[10] John Morgan Jr. & Charles Martoglio, *The 1,000 Ship Navy: Global Maritime Network* 14 (U.S. Naval Institute Proceedings, Nov. 2005).

[11] Elaine Sciolino, *Preliminary Investigation Indicates Oil Tanker Was Attacked*, N.Y. Times, Oct. 11, 2002, http://www.nytimes.com/2002/10/11/international/middleeast/11YEME.html.

[12] *See* Gail Luft & Anne Korin, *Terrorism Goes to Sea*, Foreign Affairs, Nov. /Dec. 2004, http://www.foreignaffairs.com/articles/60266/gal-luft-and-anne-korin/terrorism-goes-to-sea.

[13] The legal definition of "blockade" is a "belligerent's operation to prevent vessels and/or aircraft of all nations, enemy as well as neutral, from entering or exiting specified ports, airfields, or coastal areas belonging to, occupied by, or under the control of an enemy nation." Requirements of a legal blockade are that it be established and declared by a belligerent; that the blockading belligerent notify all affected nations of its establishment; that it must be effectively maintained by a surface, air, or subsurface force or other legitimate methods and means of warfare that is sufficient to render ingress or egress of the blockaded area dangerous; that it is applied impartially to the vessels and aircraft of all nations; and that it must not bar access to or departure from neutral ports and coasts

sinking of the *RMS Lusitania* enroute from the United States to England by a German U-boat is one of the more famous manifestations of Germany's maritime interdiction efforts during the war.[14]

The United States again used maritime interdiction to prevent the flow of Russian missiles into Cuba during the "Cuban Missile Crisis." The United States used the term "quarantine" to describe this peacetime action to prevent the movement of very specific materials into Cuba, de-escalate the situation, and return to the status quo ante.[15] This use of maritime interdiction in a situation short of full-scale war foreshadowed the modern use of maritime interdiction in the water space surrounding Iraq in the 1990s and in the war on terrorism thereafter, which will be the focus of this chapter. Other modern uses of maritime interdiction include protecting the homeland by preventing terrorists from traveling in the maritime environment, denying use of the maritime environment for proliferation of WMDs, and interdicting drug traffickers.

A. MARITIME NARCOTICS INTERDICTION

Counterdrug operations are perhaps one of the greatest examples of successful maritime interdiction through both multinational and interagency cooperation. The United States conducted the first maritime counterdrug operations in the early 1970s. This combined effort of the U.S. Coast Guard and Drug Enforcement Agency focused on areas along the coast of Florida and in the Gulf of Mexico where drugs most commonly arrived from South and Central America, and were successful due to the crude tactics employed by drug smugglers and the sheer number of assets dedicated to stop the smuggling.[16] As the smugglers' strategies became more sophisticated it became clear that more advanced tactics were required; DoD and international and cooperation would be required to execute more of a "choke point" strategy and expand operating areas.

In 1981, the United States and the United Kingdom reached a bilateral agreement to permit U.S. interdiction of British-flagged vessels suspected of drug

---

or be conducted for the sole purpose of starving the civilian population. COMMANDER'S HANDBOOK ON THE LAW OF NAVAL OPERATIONS NWP 1-14M, 7-9 to 7-10. (July 2007) [hereinafter NWP 1-14M].

[14] Douglas C. Peifer, *Maritime Commerce Warfare, The Coercive Response of the Weak*, 66(2) NAVAL WAR C. REV. 105–06 (Spring 2013).

[15] Quarantine is distinct from blockade. Quarantine is a measured response to a threat to national security or an international crisis whereas blockade is an act of war against an identified belligerent. Additionally, the goal of quarantine is de-escalation and return to the status quo ante or other stabilizing arrangement, whereas the goal of a blockade is denial and degradation of an enemy's capability, with the ultimate end state being capitulation in armed conflict. Finally, quarantine is a selective, proportional response to the threat, whereas a blockade requires impartial application to all nations—discrimination by a blockading belligerent renders the blockade legally invalid. NWP 1-14M, 4-9 to 4-10.

[16] Sterling W. Dawley, *A Task No Operational Commander Wants: Maritime Interception Operations (MIO) Are Not Going Away* 5–6 (unpublished M.S. paper, U.S. Naval War College, 1992) (on file with Naval War College).

trafficking in defined areas of the Caribbean and Gulf of Mexico. [17] This was the first of a web of international agreements that facilitated counterdrug interdictions. In the realm of drug trafficking agreements, the prior authorization for boarding has been established through a network of bilateral agreements. The multinational agreements such as the 1988 and 1995 agreements simply provide a framework for further agreements, and include provisions for prosecuting offenses.[18] In 1988, the United Nations Convention against Illicit Traffic in Narcotic Drugs and Psychotropic Substances was concluded; it entered into force in 1990.[19] Under the Convention, a state party may request permission to board a vessel of another state party operating beyond the territorial seas. This permission may be granted on an ad hoc basis or through agreements such as the one that existed between the United States and the United Kingdom. The web of agreements was further woven in 1995 when the Council of Europe Agreement on Illicit Traffic at Sea implemented Article 17 of the 1988 Convention. The Council of Europe agreement, like the 1988 Convention, requires flag state authorization before another state party can board one of its vessels suspected of drug trafficking.

While the United States strengthened bonds with partner nations to reduce the flow of illicit drugs, within the United States, DoD's role in counterdrug operations continued to expand. In 1989, DoD was assigned as the lead agency for all Detection and Monitoring of drug shipments into the United States.[20] Quite simply, DoD could bring a much larger number of assets and infrastructure to combat the growing operating areas. This was also the first year the President released a National Drug Control Strategy.[21] The United States' modern counterdrug campaign evolved into an international and multiagency effort led by Joint Interagency Task Force (JIATF) East and West, conducting operations targeted at various regions of the drug transit zone. The focused interagency efforts based on intelligence cuing forced smugglers to spend time and effort establishing new shipping routes while simultaneously spending money to develop advanced technology. Perhaps the greatest drug-smuggling innovation to develop during this period was the semisubmersible vessel.

---

[17] Agreement between the Government of the United States of America and the Government of the United Kingdom of Great Britain and Northern Ireland to Facilitate the Interdiction by the United States of Vessels of the United Kingdom Which Are Suspected of Being Engaged in Trafficking in Drugs (effected by exchange of notes at London), Nov. 13, 1981, 33 U.S.T. 4224, 1285 U.N.T.S. 197.

[18] A listing of U.S. bilateral agreements on Maritime Narcotics is available at http://www.state.gov/s/l/2005/87199.htm.

[19] *See* United Nations Convention against Illicit Traffic in Narcotic Drugs and Psychotropic Substances December 20, 1988 (entered into force Nov. 11, 1990), 1582 U.N.T.S. 165, *available at* http://www.unodc.org/pdf/convention_1988_en.pdf. A list of the 169 parties is *available at* https://treaties.un.org/doc/Publication/UNTS/Volume%201582/volume-1582-I-27627-English.pdf.

[20] Dawley, *supra* note 16, at 3.

[21] The White House, National Drug Control Strategy (1989), *available at* https://www.ncjrs.gov/pdffiles1/ondcp/119466.pdf.

The semisubmersible vessels allowed drug traffickers to increasingly avoid interdiction efforts as they are extremely difficult for even the most proficient and advanced intelligence, surveillance, and reconnaissance equipment to detect.[22] These vessels are powered by diesel engines and produce a very small radar signature; as one operator commented, it is like trying to find a Styrofoam cooler in the ocean. In addition to the interdiction challenge, there are associated legal challenges with interdicting these vessels if they are found. How does an interdicting nation determine intent? How does an interdicting nation stop or query the vessel without using deadly force? Is this a law enforcement effort, or a national security issue? It has been reported that terrorist organizations are building the semisubmersibles to fund their terrorist activities.[23] Is the next step for them to use the semisubmersibles to insert terrorist capabilities on U.S. shores?

B. MIO IN SUPPORT OF U.N. SECURITY COUNCIL RESOLUTIONS

Since 1990, U.S. forces have conducted MIO in support of the United Nations and national interests in the Adriatic against the former Republic of Yugoslavia, in the Red Sea and Persian Gulf against Iraq, and in the Caribbean against Haiti.[24] Today, MIO has been expanded to include Leadership Interception Operations (LIO) of individuals and shipping associated with al Qaida and the Taliban[25]; these operations are also called Expanded Maritime Interception Operations (EMIO).[26]

The United States has led the multinational forces conducting MIO in the northern Arabian Gulf since the United Nations passed United Nations Security Council Resolution (UNSCR) 661 and 665 in August 1990, imposing an economic embargo on Iraq.[27] This maritime interdiction took place in the Persian Gulf, during

---

[22] *Drug War at Sea: Rise of the Narco Subs*, THE DAILY BEAST, May 13, 2012, http://www.thedailybeast.com/articles/2012/05/13/the-drug-war-at-sea-rise-of-the-narco-subs.html.

[23] *Id.*

[24] WOLFF HEINTSCHEL VON HEINEGG ET AL., THE HANDBOOK OF THE INTERNATIONAL LAW OF MILITARY OPERATIONS 383 (Terry Gill & Dieter Fleck eds., 1st ed. 2010). For Yugoslavia, S.C. Res. 713, U.N. Doc. S/RES/713 (Sept. 25, 1991) and S.C. Res. 757, U.N. Doc S/RES/757 (May 30, 1992) pertain. For Iraq, S.C. Res 661, U.N. Doc S/RES/661 (Aug. 6, 1990) and S.C. Res. 665, U.N. Doc S/RES/665 (Aug. 25, 1990) pertain. For Haiti, S.C. Res. 841. U.N. Doc. S/RES/841 (June 16, 1993) pertains.

[25] Dawley, *supra* note 16, at 3.

[26] JP 3-03, *supra* note 3, at II-6. Further

> Expanded Maritime Interception Operations (EMIO) are operations authorized by the President and directed by the Secretary of Defense to deter, degrade, and/or disrupt or gather intelligence to prevent attacks against the US and its allies. EMIO involves interception of vessels identified to be transporting terrorists and/or terrorist-related materiel that pose an imminent threat to the United States and its allies. EMIO may be implemented without sanctions and may involve multinational forces or OGAs [other government agencies]. *Id.*

[27] Dawley, *supra* note 16, at 5.

Operation Southern Watch. These operations were conducted before Operation Desert Storm in 1991 and continued until the beginning of Operation Iraqi Freedom in 2003 to ensure Saddam Hussein was not smuggling his oil out of Iraq in violation of U.N. sanctions against Iraq. The operations involved stopping and boarding any and all ships transiting the Persian Gulf and the Strait of Hormuz to search them for oil, weapons, and certain fugitives from justice. During this twelve-year timespan, 42,000 ships were queried, 3,000 were boarded and 2,200 diverted.[28]

After 9/11, the United States went to war with the Taliban, and al Qaida and its associated forces.[29] This enemy looked and acted differently—it was not a nation with a navy and soldiers who wore uniforms. However, although it was an unconventional war against an unconventional enemy, the fight remained firmly rooted in conventional legal principles.[30] During Operation Iraqi Freedom alone, the United States and allies queried 5,000 ships, boarded 2,600 vessels, and diverted another 400.[31] Many of these operations were done with multinational forces, presenting another set of challenges that will be discussed later in this chapter.

IV. Legal Justifications for Conducting MIO

There are a number of legal bases available for conducting MIO, none of which are mutually exclusive. But in order to assess the legality of any maritime interdiction, one must understand international law as it applies to the law of the sea and who has authority to stop, board, and search vessels in different maritime zones.

A. THE LAW OF THE SEA

The international law of the sea is one of the most comprehensive and well-established bodies of international law, buttressed by long-standing international norms and formal legal agreements.[32] The principal resource on the topic is the United Nations Convention on the Law of Sea (UNCLOS), adopted in 1982, which entered into force in 1994.[33] Of the major maritime powers, only the United States has not ratified UNCLOS and therefore is not technically bound by its provisions.[34] However, the

---

[28] *Id.*

[29] Authorization for the Use of Military Force, Pub. L. 107–40, 115 Stat. 224 (2001) [hereinafter AUMF].

[30] *See* Jeh Johnson, General Counsel of the U.S. Department of Defense, *The Conflict against al Qaeda and Its Affiliates: How Will it End?* Speech at Oxford University (Nov. 30, 2012), *available at* http://www.lawfareblog.com/2012/11/jeh-johnson-speech-at-the-oxford-union/.

[31] Dawley, *supra* note 16, at 6.

[32] Devon Chaffee, *Freedom or Force on the High Seas? Arms Interdiction and International Law*, Nuclear Age Peace Foundation (Aug. 15, 2003), *available at* http://www.wagingpeace.org/freedom-or-force-on-the-high-seas-arms-interdiction-and-international-law/.

[33] UNCLOS, *supra* note 6.

[34] The United State's primary concern with UNCLOS was its opposition to the deep seabed mining provisions, but it otherwise reflected customary international law. In President Reagan's U.S. Oceans Policy statement in March 1983, he stated that the United States would act in accordance

United States recognizes that the major provisions of UNCLOS simply codify what the international community recognizes as customary international law.[35]

UNCLOS divides the Earth's waters into different maritime zones. States, individuals, and vessels have different duties, rights, and freedoms depending on the maritime zone in which they are operating. In general, coastal states have greater power to interdict a foreign vessel the closer the vessel is to the coastal state's shores. This authority diminishes in a state's territorial sea, and is virtually non-existent on the high seas.[36]

Additionally, all vessels have a nationality and must be registered by a nation. That nation is called the flag state.[37] Flag state responsibility is one of the most important means by which order is maintained at sea with the enforcement of international law, safety regulations, taxation, and insurance. Although UNCLOS gives some lip service to the concept that there must be a genuine link between the state and the ship,[38] that requirement has not been observed in practice, giving rise to several "flags of convenience." Generally these "flag of convenience" states require very little or no link to the ship and charge lower registry fees, have fewer safety standards, and are unwilling or unable to exercise effective jurisdiction over their ships to enforce pollution or safety standards, all resulting in a lower operating cost for ship owners.[39] In addition to international obligations, the flag state has sovereign rights over that vessel, subject only to limited conditions under international law, which will be discussed in more depth later in this chapter.

It is important to understand the legal character of the water in which a vessel is operating, in order to determine the extent of the flag state's and the coastal state's respective freedoms and sovereignty at any given time. UNCLOS guarantees freedom of navigation on the high seas, and protects the rights of

---

with the Convention's balance of interests relating to traditional uses of the oceans, with the exception of the deep seabed mining provisions contained in Part XI. President Ronald Reagan, Statement on United States Oceans Policy (Mar. 10, 1983), *available at* http://www.reagan.utexas.edu/archives/speeches/1983/31083c.htm. After Guyana became the sixtieth state to ratify UNCLOS in November 1993, and with its impending entry into force in November 1994, the United States was spurred to negotiate a Part XI Agreement modifying the deep seabed mining provisions to the satisfaction of President Clinton. Despite support by Presidents, all Secretaries of Defense, State, and Chairmen of the Joint Chiefs of Staff since the Part XI Agreement, Congress has failed to ratify the Convention. *See* John F. Turner, Assistant Secretary of State, Oceans and International Environmental and Scientific Affairs, *Accession to the 1982 Law of the Sea Convention Ratification of the 1994 Agreement Amending Part XI of the Law of the Sea Convention*, Testimony before the Senate Environmental and Public Works Committee (Mar. 23, 2004), *available at* http://2001-2009.state.gov/g/oes/rls/rm/2004/30723.htm.

[35] *Id.* One hundred and sixty nations are party to the Convention including most U.S. allies.

[36] *Supra* note 6, at Parts II, V, and VII.

[37] *Id.* at art. 91.

[38] *Id.*

[39] Examples of flags of convenience are Panama, Liberia, Cyprus, Bahamas, Malta, and the Marshall Islands. *See* R.R. CHURCHILL & A.V. LOWE, THE LAW OF THE SEA 258–59 (3d ed. 1999).

transit passage[40] and innocent passage[41] for vessels in international straits and the territorial waters[42] of other nations, respectively. These freedoms ensure a vessel's undisturbed movement through the seas, subject to only limited exceptions. Further, innocent passage through the territorial seas of other nations is inalienable "so long as it is not prejudicial to the peace, good order or security of the coastal state."[43] For the purposes of discussing maritime interdiction in this chapter, we will assume the vessels in question are in international waters, unless specified otherwise. Therefore, there must be some legal basis for a nation other than the flag state to interfere with the freedom of navigation of a vessel by conducting a maritime interdiction.

UNCLOS itself provides some legal bases for conducting a MIO. First, a state has authority to exercise jurisdiction over its own flagged vessels in its own waters (internal waters, including ports and territorial seas). Additionally, with few exceptions, the flag state has exclusive jurisdiction over its ships on the high seas.[44] Areas "beyond territorial seas of any other state" could, and most likely would, include portions of another state's contiguous zone (if declared) and exclusive economic zone (EEZ), which are considered international waters. To definitively determine the ability of a flag state to exercise jurisdiction over its vessels in these areas, the authority of the flag state and the rights of the coastal state in these waters must be explored.[45] Article 92 of UNCLOS gives the flag state exclusive jurisdiction over its vessels on the high seas, and by virtue of Article

[40] *See id.* at 104–10. Transit passage is continuous and expeditious transit incident to a vessel's normal mode of operation (submarines do not have to surface). Ships of all states have the right of transit passage in international straits, which are straits used for international navigation between one part of the high seas or exclusive economic zone (EEZ) or another part of the high seas or EEZ. *Id.*

[41] *Id.* at 81–91. Innocent passage is continuous and expeditious transit that is not prejudicial to the peace, good order, or security of the coastal state (submarines must surface and fly the flag of its nation during innocent passage). Ships of all states have the right of innocent passage in the territorial seas of all countries. *Id.*

[42] Territorial waters/sea are generally waters extending twelve miles from the lower low water line along a coastal state or a properly drawn baseline. UNCLOS, *supra* note 6, at art. 3.

[43] Andrew Prosser & Herbert Scoville, Jr., *The Proliferation Security Initiative in Perspective* 3 (June 16, 2004) (on file with author).

[44] UNCLOS, *supra* note 6, at arts. 87, 92; Convention on the High Seas, *supra* note 6. The high seas consist of all parts of the sea not included in the exclusive economic zone, territorial sea, or internal waters of a state or the archipelagic waters of an archipelagic state. All states have free use of the high seas, and as such can freely navigate, fish, lay submarine cables and pipelines, overfly, construct artificial islands, and conduct maritime research. *See generally id.*

[45] Although PSI Interdiction Principles do not specifically address this point, I assume territorial seas are meant not to include international straits, as the rights of vessels in these straits are more akin to high seas freedom. An international strait connects two parts of the high seas or EEZ, and is used for international navigation. UNCLOS, *supra* note 6, art. 37. Vessels have the right of "transit passage" in international straits. This includes freedom of navigation and overflight for the purpose of continuous and expeditious transit of the strait as long as the vessel transits in its "normal" mode (e.g., submarines can transit submerged, as opposed to innocent passage in territorial seas). *Id.*, art. 38.

58(2), Article 92 applies in the EEZ[46] to the extent that it is not incompatible with the coastal state's rights. In the EEZ, the coastal state has the sovereign right to explore, exploit, conserve and manage the living (fish) and nonliving natural resources (e.g., oil); conduct other activities for the economic exploitation/exploration of the zone; establish and use artificial islands, installations, structures (e.g., drilling platforms); conduct marine scientific research; and control pollution.[47] On the other hand, other states (including the flag state) enjoy the freedom of navigation and "other internationally lawful uses of the sea."[48] Therefore, in the case of transporting WMD or conducting other terror-related activities, as it seems that there is no coastal state right with which Article 92 is incompatible, then the flag state has exclusive jurisdiction over its vessels in another state's EEZ.[49]

Flag states may also give their consent for another nation to stop their ships. Similar to the network of agreements that have facilitated counterdrug interdiction, under the Proliferation Security Initiative (PSI)[50] the United States has negotiated a series of "boarding agreements" with other PSI participants. These agreements provide for U.S. boarding of these states' flag shipping vessels under defined circumstances and conditions. These agreements are often the first stop when confronted with the question of whether the United States can interdict a vessel of interest.[51] Although this may appear to be a simple approach, because the commercial maritime shipping industry often involves multiple layers of nationality in ownership, operating company, voyage contracting, leasing, and flagging, there are normally numerous countries that could be approached with a request to cooperate with WMD interdiction efforts.

In addition to flag state consent, the concept of master's consent may be used to conduct a MIO. The U.S. position is that if the master of the vessel in question provides consent, its forces may board (or visit) and conduct an inspection of portions of the ship agreed upon by the master.[52] However, some nations do not agree with the United State's position that master's consent is a valid legal basis for conducting anything more than a visit of the ship.

Stateless vessels, or ships of uncertain nationality, may be subject to boarding and searching by all nations' navies or coast guards. Stateless vessels are vessels

---

[46] The exclusive economic zone (EEZ) is a zone extending up to two hundred miles from a coastal state's baseline from which the breadth of the territorial sea is measured. Within the EEZ, the coastal state enjoys extensive rights in relation to its natural resources and other states enjoy the high seas' freedoms of navigation and overflight, among others. The EEZ is considered international waters. *See* UNCLOS, *supra* note 6, art. 55–58.

[47] UNCLOS, *supra* note 6, art. 56, 60, 246, Part VII (pollution control).

[48] *Id.*, art. 58.

[49] Churchill & Lowe, *supra* note 39, at 348.

[50] *See supra* note 45.

[51] Joint Chiefs of Staff, Joint Publication 3–40, Combating Weapons of Mass Destruction, B-6 (June 10, 2009) [hereinafter JP 3-40].

[52] Annotated Supplement to the Commander's Handbook on the Law of Naval Operations, Naval War College (1977) [hereinafter Annotated Supplement to NWP 1-14M] at 3-26.

that are not legitimately registered in any one state. They are not entitled to fly the flag of any nation, and are not entitled to the protection of any state's sovereignty.[53] Thus, if a suspect vessel is determined to be stateless on the high seas, a warship may visit and board the vessel without consent of the master.[54]

Naval forces or coast guard authorities may stop and search a flagged ship on the high seas when that ship is suspected of slave trading, piracy, illicit narcotics trafficking, and unauthorized broadcasting. These crimes are specifically enumerated in UNCLOS Article 110, and if there are reasonable grounds to believe that a ship is engaged in any of these crimes, personnel from a warship may board the suspect vessel on the high seas without the consent of the flag state or the master.[55]

Finally, a coastal state may impose any condition on ships entering its ports or internal waters, including a requirement that all ships (other than sovereign immune vessels) entering port will be subject to boarding and inspection.[56] In internal waters,[57] a coastal state has complete jurisdiction over vessels, with only two exceptions: foreign vessels with sovereign immunity (e.g., warships of other nations) and vessels in distress seeking safe harbor. A vessel intending to enter a nation's port or internal waters can therefore be boarded and searched without flag state consent provided the port state has on a nondiscriminatory basis imposed such a measure as a condition of port entry.[58] Such boardings and inspections can occur at any location once a ship enters the territorial sea if it has stated its intent to enter the coastal state's port or internal waters.[59]

B. BELLIGERENT'S RIGHTS TO CONDUCT MIO

Another category of legal bases for conducting a maritime interdiction can be founded on a belligerent's rights during an armed conflict. Interdiction in the maritime domain during an armed conflict is vitally important because it can isolate an enemy from outside support, halt undesired maritime activity, provide security for other naval operations, and ensure the availability of the sea lines of communication for friendly operations such as deployment of forces. However, if a nation is at war, a belligerent's rights under the law of armed conflict govern rather than the Law of the Sea.[60]

---

[53] *Molvan v. Attorney General for Palestine*, 81 Lloyd's List L. R. 277, United Kingdom: Judicial Committee of the Privy Council, 51 (Apr. 20, 1948) citing Lassa Oppenheim, 1 International Law 546 (H. Lauderpacht ed., 6th ed., June 1, 1940), *available at* http://www.unhcr.org/refworld/docid/3ae6b6544.html.

[54] UNCLOS, *supra* note 6, at art. 110.

[55] *Id.*

[56] NWP 1-14M, *supra* note 13, at 2-4.

[57] Internal waters are all waters landward of the lower low water line along a coast or a properly drawn baseline. *See* UNCLOS, *supra* note 6, at art. 8.

[58] *See* NWP 1-14M, *supra* note 13, at 4-7 to 4-8.

[59] *Id.*

[60] The law of armed conflict is considered *lex specialis* under the legal maxim "*lex specialis derogat legi generali*": a specific rule prevails over a general rule. *Legality of the Threat or Use of Nuclear*

The primary belligerent's rights implicated by maritime interdiction are the right to visit and search and the right to blockade. A belligerent's right to visit and search allows a belligerent to stop all enemy or neutral vessels from entering or exiting specific ports or coastal areas of an enemy nation, outside of neutral waters, to determine the true character of the vessels in order to interdict the flow of contraband goods.[61] This right does not permit the search and visit of warships.

A belligerent's blockade is intended to prevent vessels, regardless of their cargo, from crossing an established and publicized boundary separating the enemy from international waters and/or airspace. The legal definition of blockade is a "belligerent's operation to prevent vessels and/or aircraft of all nations, enemy as well as neutral, from entering or exiting specified ports, airfields, or coastal areas belonging to, occupied by, or under the control of an enemy nation." [62] Requirements of a legal blockade are that it be established and declared by a belligerent and that the blockading belligerent notify all affected nations of its establishment. It must also be effectively maintained by a surface, air, or subsurface force or other legitimate methods and means of warfare that are sufficient to render ingress or egress of the blockaded area dangerous; it must be applied impartially to the vessels and aircraft of all nations; and it must not prevent access to or departure from neutral ports and coasts or be conducted for the sole purpose of starving the civilian population.[63] Although modern weapons systems make close-in blockade impractical today, the blockade of Haiphong harbor during the Vietnam War demonstrated an effective use of naval mines to establish a blockade. Some theorists have said the blockade acted as a form of coercive diplomacy and forced North Vietnam to the negotiating table.[64] It is important to remember that, although these belligerent's rights regarding naval warfare exist, the overarching fundamental principles of lawful warfare must also be met—necessity, proportionality, and discrimination.

Since the signing of the U.N. Charter, which prohibits the threat and use of force in international conflicts,[65] wars declared formally in accordance with

---

Weapons, ICJ Reports 13–14 at para. 25 (1996); C.W. Jenks, *The Conflict of Law-Making Treaties*, 30 Brit. Y.B. Int'l L. 401, 446 (1953) ("A general type of lex specialis, constituting an exception to legal normality are the laws of war. It seems clear that, at least in the absence of evidence to the contrary, the laws of war must be regarded as leges speciales in relation to—and thus override—rules laying out the peace-time norms relating to the same subjects.").

[61] NWP 1-14M, *supra* note 13, at 7–8; International Institute of Humanitarian Law, San Remo Manual on International Law Applicable to Armed Conflicts at Sea 31–2 (Louise Doswald-Beck ed., 1995); International Peace Conference, Hague Convention XIII, Concerning the Rights and Duties of Neutral Powers in Naval War art. 2, Jan. 26, 1910, 36 Stat. 2415.

[62] See NWP 1-14M, *supra* note 13, at 7–9.

[63] *Id.* at 7–9 to 7–10.

[64] W.L. Greer, *The 1972 Mining of Haiphong Harbor: A Case Study in Naval Mining and Diplomacy*, Institute for Defense Analyses (Apr. 1997), *available* at http://www.dtic.mil/docs/citations/ADA355037.

[65] *See generally* UN Charter, art. 2(4) ("all members shall refrain in their international relations from the threat or use of force against the territorial integrity or political independence of any state.").

the Hague Convention[66] have become virtually obsolete. However, this has not prevented armed conflicts around the world, and thus it remains important to explore other legal bases for conducting maritime interdictions during peacetime and during conflicts that do not implicate the belligerent's rights discussed above.

C. MIO AS SELF-DEFENSE UNDER THE U.N. CHARTER

Article 51 of the U.N. Charter restates the inherent right of a state to defend itself from armed attack:

> Nothing in the present Charter shall impair the inherent right of individual or collective self-defense if an armed attack occurs against a Member of the United Nations, until the Security Council has taken measures necessary to maintain international peace and security.[67]

The use of force in self-defense requires necessity (force must be required under the circumstances) and proportionality (force must be limited to that which is clearly required).[68] Self-defense has been used by nations engaged in armed conflict as a legal basis to stop and search a foreign-flagged vessel suspected of carrying weapons to a party to the conflict, including when the United States and the United Kingdom embargoed Iraq in 1990 two weeks before the U.N. Security Council passed the resolution expressly permitting these interdictions and again after 9/11 to interdict fleeing terrorists.[69] In the case of the leadership interdictions or EMIO after 9/11, the United States specifically declared in a letter to the U.N. Security Council that it was acting under Article 51 of the Charter when it "initiated action in the exercise of its inherent right of individual and collective self-defense following the armed attacks that were carried out against the United States on September 11, 2001."[70] The United States considers itself to still be engaged in an armed conflict with the Taliban, al Qaida, and affiliates, and thus continues to conduct MIOs in furtherance of this armed conflict.[71] However, the United States does not purport to be at war with all terrorist groups worldwide; therefore, the MIOs conducted using self-defense as a legal basis must be limited

---

[66] *See* Hague Convention III Opening of Hostilities, Oct. 18, 1907, 36 Stat. 2259 (This convention sets out the accepted procedure for a state making a declaration of war).

[67] U.N. Charter, art. 51.

[68] Letter from Sec'y of State Daniel Webster, to Lord Ashburton (Apr. 24, 1841), *available at* http://avalon.law.yale.edu/19th_century/br-1842d.asp (last visited Mar. 15, 2014). *See also* David J. Harris, Cases and Materials on International Law 921-37 (6th ed. 2004). *Cf.* The Prize Cases, 67 U.S. 635 (1863).

[69] *See* Rear Admiral William L. Schachte Jr., Judge Advocate Generals Corps, U.S. Navy (retired), *Testimony Before the Senate Foreign Relations Committee* (Oct. 14, 2003), *available* at http://www.gpo.gov/fdsys/pkg/CHRG-108shrg99782/html/CHRG-108shrg99782.htm.

[70] Letter from Ambassador John Negroponte, Permanent Representative of the United States of America to the United Nations Addressed to the President of the Security Council, U.N. Doc. S/2001/946 (Oct. 7, 2001), *available at* http://www.usunnewyork.usmission.gov/s-2001-946.htm.

[71] *Supra* note 30.

to interdiction of Taliban, al Qaida, or affiliates, or those who may be supplying weapons for use in their armed conflict against the United States.

In both examples above, an armed attack had already occurred: the first against Kuwait and the second against the United States. However, Article 51 can also serve as the legal basis for maritime interdiction by nations who are not actively involved in armed conflict, under the legal concept of anticipatory self-defense. Anticipatory self-defense is invoked before an actual armed attack has occurred upon a nation but when an immediate military response is essential to national or unit security. Well before the Charter was penned, Daniel Webster articulated the framework for anticipatory self-defense in the international incident called the *Caroline* case. In the *Caroline* case, the American vessel *SS Caroline* aided Canadian rebels fighting Britain, which prompted the British to cross the border from Canada into the United States, seize the *Caroline*, set her on fire, and send her over Niagara Falls.[72] Although recognizing that force may be used in self-defense, the *Caroline* case doctrine stands for the proposition that anticipatory self-defense is authorized only when the "necessity of that self-defense is instant, overwhelming, and leaving no choice of means, and no moment for deliberation."[73]

It is conceivable to apply the legal basis of anticipatory self-defense to a maritime interdiction, where, for example intelligence indicates a ship is going to be detonated in a port by terrorists as a WMD or there are terrorists harbored on a ship who plan to carry out the attack when they arrive in port. Under this legal theory, conducting a non-consensual boarding of a vessel of another state in anticipatory self-defense does not depend on the consent of the flag state or master. Boarding a vessel, inspecting it, and perhaps collecting data from the crew and passengers could be a proportional response to this type of immediate threat.

D. MIO AND U.N. SECURITY COUNCIL RESOLUTIONS (UNSCR)

Many of the MIOs authorized under U.N. Security Council Resolutions (UNSCR) are also grounded in self-defense or collective self-defense. A UNSCR is the first place a practitioner should turn when faced with the question of whether a vessel can be interdicted. Therefore, when interpreting a UNSCR to determine whether a MIO is permitted, it is important to understand how the U.N. Security Council acts.

Chapter VII of the Charter of the United Nations allows the Security Council to "determine the existence of any threat to the peace, breach of the peace, or act of aggression" and to make recommendations or to resort to nonmilitary and military action to "maintain or restore international peace and security"[74].

---

[72] *See* Harris, *supra* note 68, at 921–37.

[73] *Supra* note 68.

[74] U.N. Charter, art. 39.

Article 41 of the Charter gives the Security Council the authority to use a variety of measures to enforce its decisions.

> The Security Council may decide what measures not involving the use of armed force are to be employed to give effect to its decisions, and it may call upon the Members of the United Nations to apply such measures. These may include complete or partial interruption of economic relations and of rail, sea, air, postal, telegraphic, radio, and other means of communication, and the severance of diplomatic relations.[75]

An important limitation within Article 41 is the reference to "measures not involving the use of armed force."[76] Therefore, when using a UNSCR as a legal basis for a maritime interdiction, the practitioner must be mindful that if it calls for measures under Article 41, the Security Council has not authorized the use of armed force in order to conduct that interdiction. This is contrasted with measures taken under Article 42 of the Charter when the Security Council determines that Article 41 measures would be or have been inadequate, wherein "it may take such action by air, sea, or land forces as may be necessary to maintain or restore international peace and security. Such action may include demonstrations, blockade, and other operations by air, sea, or land forces of Members of the United Nations."[77] The Security Council regularly creates subsidiary organs to support or implement these measures. Among the most common are those measures that are known as "sanctions," which are generally supported by a Committee, as well as Panels/Groups of Experts or other mechanisms to monitor implementation of the sanctions.[78]

As discussed above, there have been U.N. Security Council Resolutions that directly address and permit the interdiction or embargo of goods. These include UNSCR 661, which established comprehensive sanctions against Iraq, and authorized an open-ended arms embargo in August 1990 after Iraq invaded Kuwait. UNSCR 661, after affirming the inherent right of individual and collective self defense in accordance with Article 51 of the U.N. Charter, decided that states shall prevent "the sale or supply by their nationals or from their territories or using their flag vessels of any commodities or products, including weapons or any other military equipment, whether or not originating in their territories."[79]

The United Nations has used similar language (though without the reference to the inherent right of self-defense used in Resolution 661), in UNSCR 1718, condemning North Korea's testing of a nuclear weapon in 2006. In UNSCR 1718, the Security Council decided that "all member states shall prevent the direct or indirect supply, sale or transfer to the DPRK [North Korea], through their territories

---

[75] U.N. Charter, art. 41.

[76] *Id.*

[77] U.N. Charter, art. 42.

[78] A complete listing of U.N.-enforced sanctions regimes can be found at http://www.un.org/en/sc/repertoire/subsidiary_organs/sanctions_and_other_committees.shtml (last visited July 2, 2014).

[79] S.C. Res. 661, para. 3(c), U.N. Doc. S/RES/661 (Aug. 6, 1990).

or by their nationals, or using their flag vessels, and whether or not originating in their territories" prohibited items including weapons and goods that could contribute to DPRK's nuclear, ballistic missile, or other WMD-related programs.[80]

Similarly, in UNSCR 1737 of December 23, 2006, the Security Council established a Committee to oversee and monitor the implementation of the assets freeze, financial services restrictions, travel restrictions, and the embargo against Iran's proliferation of sensitive nuclear and ballistic missile technology.[81] The mandate of the Committee has since been expanded to apply also to the measures imposed in resolutions 1747 of March 24, 2007[82] and 1803 of March 3, 2008.[83] By resolution 1929 of June 9, 2010,[84] the Council established a Panel of Experts to assist the Committee in its work.

Most recently, in UNSCR 1973, the Security Council authorized MIO to enforce the arms embargo and support NATO operations in Libya by calling on member states to

> inspect in their territory, including seaports and airports, and on the high seas, vessels and aircraft bound to or from the Libyan Arab Jamahiriya, if the State concerned has information that provides reasonable grounds to believe that the cargo contains items the supply, sale, transfer or export of which is prohibited by . . . resolution 1970 . . . and authorizes Member States to use all measures commensurate to the specific circumstances to carry out such inspections.[85]

Because of the international legitimacy that a UNSCR carries, and the explicit authorization it may contain, a UNSCR is a valuable and often dispositive legal justification for MIO. However, obtaining the international consensus required to pass a UNSCR with teeth has become increasingly difficult due to the seemingly insurmountable political and diplomatic differences existing among the permanent members of the Security Council. Therefore, in the absence of a UNSCR many nations have sought to conclude international agreements outside of the Security Council to address the threat of maritime proliferation and terrorism.

V. Bilateral or Multilateral Agreements

As discussed relative to maritime narcotics interdiction above, bilateral or regional shipboarding agreements have also been used to conduct maritime interdiction. The most well-accepted and successful multinational efforts at providing legal authority for maritime interception has been the Proliferation

---

[80] S.C. Res. 1718, para. 8(a), U.N. Doc. S/RES/1718 (Oct. 14, 2006).

[81] S.C. Res. 1737, para. 18, U.N. Doc. S/RES/1737 (Dec. 23, 2006).

[82] S.C. Res. 1747, paras. 1–4, U.N. Doc. S/RES/1747 (Mar. 24, 2007).

[83] S.C. Res. 1803, paras. 1, 3–5, and 7, U.N. Doc. S/RES/1803 (Mar. 3, 2008).

[84] S.C. Res. 1929, para. 29, U.N. Doc. S/RES/1929 (June 9, 2010).

[85] *See* S.C. Res. 1973, para. 13, U.N. Doc. S/RES/1973 (Mar. 17, 2011).

Security Initiative and the 2005 Protocol to the Convention for the Suppression of Unlawful Acts against the Safety of Maritime Navigation (SUA).

A. PROLIFERATION SECURITY INITIATIVE

Post-September 11th and with the *So San* incident fresh in President George W. Bush's mind, the United States sought to formulate a strategy to prevent maritime terrorism, while

> preserving the freedom of the seas [as] a top national priority. The right of vessels to travel freely in international waters, engage in innocent and transit passage, and have access to ports is an essential element of national security. The free, continuing, unthreatened intercourse of nations is an essential global freedom and helps ensure the smooth operation of the world's economy.[86]

The greatest policy and legal concerns with any effort to prevent terrorism at sea are to ensure that tighter security and enforcement measures are undertaken without interfering with the efficient flow of international trade or state sovereignty in territorial seas and international waters. The first initiative that the Bush administration developed balancing these competing policy considerations was the Proliferation Security Initiative (PSI).

On May 31, 2004, in Krakow, Poland, President Bush announced PSI, a collective, consent-based effort to strengthen political commitment, capabilities, and the legal authorities necessary to stop, search, and possibly seize vessels and aircraft believed to be transporting WMD and related materials. In announcing PSI, a Bush administration official stated:

> We believe that the existing system of national export control systems [and] multilateral export control agreements were not completely effective because there's still a thriving black market in WMD components, technologies, and production materials. And what we wanted to do was to find more active ways of dealing with the ongoing trafficking in all of these WMD related materials, not to replace the export control regimes, but to do something that would be more effective in handling all of this trafficking.[87]

The Bush administration believed that "PSI is an activity and not an organization," and its "partners" are not bound by any legal agreement—they have simply agreed on a set of "interdiction principles" that were announced in September 2003.[88] The primary agreements are to exchange information and intelligence

---

[86] Nat. Strategy for Maritime Security 7 (Sept. 2005).

[87] Interview by Wade Boese with John Bolton, Under Sec. of State for Arms Control and Int'l Security, *The Proliferation Security Initiative*, Armed Control Today (Dec. 2003).

[88] Proliferation Security Initiative: Statement of Interdiction Principles, Fact Sheet, The White House, Office of the Press Secretary, Sept. 4, 2003, http://www.state.gov/t/isn/rls/fs/23764.htm.

concerning suspected proliferation by states or nonstate actors "of proliferation concern," to strengthen national and international laws to facilitate the interdiction of suspicious cargo, and to undertake specific interdiction measures.

> PSI participants . . . . call on all states concerned with this threat to international peace and security to join in similarly committing to:
>
> 1. Undertake effective measures, either alone or in concert with other states, for interdicting the transfer or transport of WMD, their delivery systems, and related materials to and from states and non-state actors of proliferation concern. "States or non-state actors of proliferation concern" generally refers to those countries or entities that . . . are engaged in proliferation through: (1) efforts to develop or acquire chemical, biological, or nuclear weapons and associated delivery systems; or (2) transfers . . . of WMD, their delivery systems, or related materials.
> 2. Adopt streamlined procedures for rapid exchange of relevant information concerning suspected proliferation activity . . . dedicate appropriate resources and efforts to interdiction operations and capabilities, and maximize coordination among participants in interdiction efforts.
> 3. Review and work to strengthen their relevant national legal authorities where necessary to accomplish these objectives, and work to strengthen when necessary relevant international law and frameworks in appropriate ways to support these commitments.
> 4. Take specific actions in support of interdiction efforts regarding cargoes of WMD, their delivery systems, or related materials, to the extent their national legal authorities permit and consistent with their obligations under international law and frameworks, to include:
>
> a. Not to transport or assist in the transport of any such cargoes . . . and not to allow any persons subject to their jurisdiction to do so.
>
> b. . . . to take action to board and search any vessel flying their flag in their internal waters or territorial seas, or areas beyond the territorial seas of any other state, that is reasonably suspected of transporting such cargoes . . . and to seize such cargoes that are identified.
>
> c. To seriously consider providing consent under the appropriate circumstances to the boarding and searching of its own flag vessels by other states, and to the seizure of such WMD-related cargoes in such vessels that may be identified by such states.
>
> d. To take appropriate actions to (1) stop and/or search in their internal waters, territorial seas, or contiguous zones (when declared) vessels that are reasonably suspected of carrying such cargoes to or from states or non-state actors of proliferation concern and to seize such cargoes that are identified; and (2) to enforce conditions on vessels entering or leaving their ports, internal waters or territorial seas that are reasonably suspected of carrying such cargoes, such as

> requiring that such vessels be subject to boarding, search, and seizure of such cargoes prior to entry.
>
> e. . . . [deals with aviation].
>
> f. If their ports, airfields, or other facilities are used as transshipment points for shipment of such cargoes . . . to inspect vessels, aircraft, or other modes of transport reasonably suspected of carrying such cargoes, and to seize such cargoes that are identified.[89]

The partnership originally included the United States and ten other major maritime allies and like-minded states on the issue of counterterrorism: Australia, France, Germany, Italy, Japan, the Netherlands, Poland, Portugal, Spain, and the United Kingdom. Since the rollout of the interdiction principles, Canada, Norway, Russia, Singapore, and Turkey have become partners. Approximately 104 other states have "endorsed" the PSI interdiction principles.[90] The success of PSI is not dependent solely on the *number* of countries that are partners or "agree to cooperate" but the *identity* of those countries. In order to make PSI as effective as possible, it is vital for the major flag states, coastal states, and states that operate large ports to participate in this interdiction regime. However, for many nations, going on record in support of PSI may be politically and economically unfeasible. For example South Korea's agreement to participate as an observer to a PSI exercise drew sharp criticism from the North, with one official calling it a "war crime" to "conspire with the U.S. in its moves for a war of aggression."[91]

At its core, PSI uses existing authorities—national and international—to put an end to WMD-related trafficking. The critics of PSI, however, have a long list of shortcomings of the interdiction regime.[92] One such criticism is that due to its nonbinding, informal structure, it provides no enforcement mechanism for states that fail to live up to their promises, and these promises could be pushed aside with a change in leadership of the partner states. Additionally, practical problems such as inadequate resources, lack of intelligence, and inability of the participant's armed forces or coast guards to cover the vast ocean geography are impediments to PSI's goal of interdicting weapons shipments.[93] Additionally, the interdiction principles do not explicitly state what constitutes a threat or establish a threshold of probable cause to suspect weapons trafficking; therefore

---

[89] *Id.*

[90] Department of State list of Proliferation Security Initiative Participants, http://www.state.gov/t/isn/c27732.htm (as of June 4, 2014).

[91] *South Korea's Participation in PSI Causes Controversy*, INT'L EXPORT CONTROL OBSERVER 14–15, Feb. 2006, *available at* http://cns.miis.edu/pubs/observer/pdfs/ieco _0602e.pdf.

[92] *See* Nigel Chamberlain, *Interdiction under the Proliferation Security Initiative : Counter-Proliferation or Counter-Productive?*, BASIC Briefing, Oct. 6, 2003 *available at* http://www.basicint.org/publications/nigel-chamberlain/2003/interdiction-under-proliferation-security-initiative-counter-pro (This briefing paper considers the origins of PSI, Britain's role, and questions whether PSI is in accordance with international law, noting concerns about the legality of stopping shipments in territorial waters or on the high seas and concerns that interdiction may be deemed an act of war under international law.)

[93] Prosser & Scoville, *supra* note 43.

it is up to each participant state to individually make this determination. This decision, in turn, may be influenced by economic, political, and other domestic considerations. [94]

PSI does not define what "reasonably suspected" means when it comes to suspecting a vessel of transporting dangerous cargo. Without a specific threshold or burden of proof, any state could attempt to interdict shipments for any subjective purpose and claim that it was acting in furtherance of PSI. Additionally, the lack of clear-cut standards could result in an unfounded or illegal interdiction being viewed as an act of aggression toward the flag state, and could prompt a military response by the flag state. Consider how this problem may present itself with respect to dual-use material. As there are widely divergent views of what constitutes dual-use material or technology,[95] differing interpretations between the interdicting state and the flag state could create a dicey international incident or at least slow the response to a vessel of interest. Although this criticism is valid, the vagueness also serves the purpose of not hamstringing legitimate interdictions with overly legalistic requirements.

The primary *legal* objection to PSI is that some of the interdictions proposed by the principles are contrary to international law.[96] Although PSI interdiction principles lack a great deal of specificity they specifically contemplate state action:

1) to board and search any vessel flying their flag in their internal waters or territorial seas, or areas beyond the territorial seas of any other state (e.g. international waters);[97]
2) to stop and/or search vessels in their internal waters, territorial seas, or contiguous zones (when declared)[98]; and
3) to enforce conditions on vessels entering or leaving their ports, internal waters or territorial seas.[99]

---

[94] *Id.*

[95] Nations rarely export or import turnkey weapons of mass destruction, so many of the parts that go into making a weapon may have a legitimate civilian use. For example, much of the nuclear weapon technology of concern can also be used for legitimate civilian nuclear power technology.

[96] *See, e.g.*, Chamberlain, *supra*, note 92, at 3–4; Samuel E. Logan, *The Proliferation Security Initiative: Navigating the Legal Challenges*, 14 J. Transnat'l & Pol'y 253, 257–69 (2005); Devon Chaffee, *Freedom or Force on the High Seas? Arms Interdiction and International Law*, Nuclear Age Peace Foundation, Aug. 15, 2003, *available at* http://www.wagingpeace.org/articles/2003/08/15_chaffee_freedom-of-force.htm; Fabrice Pothier, *The Proliferation Security Initiative: Towards a New Anti-Proliferation Consensus*, Nov. 18, 2004, *available* at http://www.basicint.org/sites/default/files/PUB181104.pdf; Michael A. Becker, *The Shifting Public Order of the Oceans: Freedom of Navigation and the Interdiction of Ships at Sea*, 46 Harv. Int'l L.J. 131, 134 (2005).

[97] *See supra* note 88 and accompanying text.

[98] Because a contiguous zone implies requirements by the coastal state to prevent violation of customs, fiscal, immigration, and sanitary regulations within the zone, states are not obliged to maintain these zones (unlike territorial seas). Just over one-third of coastal states have chosen to claim a contiguous zone. Churchill & Lowe, *supra* note 39, at 135–36. *See also supra* note 88 and accompanying text.

[99] *See* discussion *supra* part V(A).

Critics contend that taking these actions is contrary to international law. However, these criticisms are largely unfounded, as discussed below.

First, boarding and searching by a flag state of any vessel flying its flag in its internal waters or territorial seas, or areas beyond the territorial seas of any other state (e.g., international waters) contemplated in Interdiction Principle 4.b. is clearly legal, and is discussed earlier in the chapter as a legal basis for MIO.[100] Similarly, under UNCLOS, coastal states can enforce conditions on vessels entering or leaving their ports and internal waters.[101] Therefore, the action contemplated in Interdiction Principle 4.d(2) is also not unlawful. A coastal state has the right to impose some conditions on the actions conducted in its ports, internal waters, or territorial seas. It can impose sea lanes and traffic patterns, pollution controls, and port entry requirements. However, a coastal state cannot restrict innocent passage in territorial seas by imposing permission or notification requirements.[102]

Second, coastal-state action to stop and/or search vessels in its internal waters is certainly legal, and in some circumstances coastal states may be able to interdict vessels in their territorial seas or contiguous zones (when declared). The right of innocent passage is guaranteed in the territorial sea, and passage is considered innocent as long as it is not prejudicial to the peace, good order, or security of the coastal state.[103] Although UNCLOS does not prohibit the transport of WMD and/or related materials at sea,[104] coastal states may still legally be able to interdict vessels suspected of transporting WMD through these waters, given sufficient and reliable intelligence that these weapons are under the control of terrorists. Under those circumstances, it would be fairly straightforward to characterize WMD and WMD-related materials proliferation as a threat to the security of the coastal state and, consequently, for coastal states to overcome seagoing vessels' right of innocent passage through their territorial waters.[105] In a case in which the right of innocent passage has been deemed lost, seagoing vessels in the territorial sea are subject to the full jurisdiction, legislative and enforcement, of the coastal state.[106] However, in order to intercept a ship carrying WMD components in the *contiguous zone*, the coastal state must have enacted laws making an unauthorized cargo an infringement of its customs laws, and the cargo needs to be heading toward the mainland or must have originated on the mainland heading toward the high seas.[107] If a coastal state has not enacted such laws interdicting shipping in furtherance of this portion of Interdiction Principle 4.d(1), an interdiction could be a violation of international law.

---

[100] *See supra* Part IV(A).

[101] NWP 1-14M, *supra* note 13, at 2–4.

[102] UNCLOS, *supra* note 6, arts. 17–19.

[103] *See* Convention on the Territorial Sea and the Contiguous Zone, Apr. 29, 1958, 516 U.N.T.S. 205, art 14(4).

[104] *See infra* Part V(B) and accompanying notes.

[105] UNCLOS, *supra* note 6, arts. 19 and 25.

[106] *Id.*

[107] UNCLOS, *supra* note 6, art. 33.

The Interdiction Principles do not explicitly state that PSI partners will endeavor to interdict foreign flagged vessels on the high seas. However, Interdiction Principle 4.c.[108] indicates that such interdiction must be contemplated. As previously stated, foreign flagged vessels enjoy the freedom of navigation on the high seas, and flag states enjoy virtually exclusive jurisdiction over them.[109] The few exceptions to a flag state's exclusive jurisdiction are those in which a third state shares legislative or enforcement jurisdiction with the flag state (universal jurisdiction) with respect to piracy,[110] unauthorized broadcasting, and slave trading,[111] and over ships of uncertain or no apparent nationality. Additionally, certain special treaties such as the Vienna Convention against Illicit Traffic in Narcotic Drugs and Psychotropic Substances, grant treaty parties the right to visit and search ships of other parties to the treaties when a vessel is suspected of drug trafficking.[112] In fact, it is this multilateral, consent-based approach that provides the solution to closing the gap in international law that does not allow PSI partners to board foreign-flagged vessels on the high seas.

The best example of the influence that a PSI interdiction can have on proliferators' actions is the much-touted interception of the *BBC China* in October 2003. United States' and British intelligence indicated that the German-flagged freighter, *BBC China*, destined for Libya, was carrying thousands of parts for gas centrifuges, equipment used to enrich the uranium required in nuclear weapons.[113] The intelligence services alerted the German government (the ship's owner was based in Leer, Germany), and the owner diverted the ship to Taranto, Italy, where the cargo was inspected and seized.[114] Although Libya had been engaged in secret talks with the United States and the United Kingdom for several months before the interdiction, at the time the shipment was discovered, Libya had refused to set a date for the United States and the United Kingdom to visit its weapons sites. However, two weeks after the seizure, intelligence officials were allowed to inspect Libyan weapons laboratories and military factories.[115] By December, Libyan leader, Colonel Muammar el-Qaddafi announced that his country would disclose and dismantle its stocks of WMD, and abandon its nuclear program and quest to build nuclear and other WMD. Many speculate that the decision was influenced by the *BBC China* interdiction. However, Qaddafi cited his desire not to be driven from power like Saddam Hussein as his reason for getting out of the WMD business, and not the *BBC China* incident.[116]

---

[108] *Supra* Part V(A).

[109] *Supra*, Part IV(A).

[110] UNCLOS, *supra* note 6, art. 100.

[111] *Id.*, art. 110.

[112] *See generally* United Nations Convention against the Illicit Traffic in Narcotic Drugs and Psychotropic Substances, Dec. 20, 1988, 1992 U.K.T.S. 26.

[113] Editorial, *Progress on Proliferation*, WASH. TIMES, Jan. 3, 2005, *available at* http://www.washingtontimes.com/news/2005/jan/2/20050102-090728-1997r/print/.

[114] Douglas Frantz & Josh Meyer, *The Deal to Disarm Kadafi*, L.A. TIMES, Mar. 13, 2005, at 5.

[115] *Id.*

[116] *Id.*

B. 2005 PROTOCOL TO THE CONVENTION FOR THE SUPPRESSION OF UNLAWFUL ACTS AGAINST THE SAFETY OF MARITIME NAVIGATION (SUA)

The original SUA Convention[117] was adopted in 1988, after the hijacking of the Italian cruise ship *Achille Lauro* in October 1985, one of the first actual terrorist acts recorded in modern maritime history.[118] Following that incident, the U.N. General Assembly asked the International Maritime Organization (IMO) to study the problem of terrorism on board ships and make recommendations.[119] The IMO first adopted Resolution A.584(14) which included measures to prevent unlawful acts that threaten the safety of ships and the security of their passengers and crews, and eventually drafted the SUA Convention. The SUA Convention was designed to ensure that appropriate action was taken against persons committing unlawful acts such as the seizure of ships by force, acts of violence against persons on board ships, and the placing of devices on a ship likely to destroy or damage the ship. The Convention makes no distinction between piracy and terrorism when outlawing violence against mariners, and obliges state parties to either extradite or prosecute alleged offenders.[120] At the urging of the United States after September 11th, the

---

[117] Convention for the Suppression of Unlawful Acts against the Safety of Maritime Navigation, Mar. 10, 1988; 2005 Protocol to the Convention for the Suppression of Unlawful Acts against the Safety of Maritime Navigation (Oct. 14, 2005) 1678 UNTS 201 (hereinafter SUA). Entered into force July 28, 2010; seventeen Parties as of December 2, 2010. However, the following states are parties to the 1988 SUA and all but those with asterisks signed the Protocol at the Diplomatic Conference: Afghanistan, Albania, Algeria*, Argentina, Armenia, Australia, Austria, Azerbaijan, Bahamas, Bahrain, Bangladesh, Barbados, Belarus, Belgium, Bolivia, Bosnia & Herzegovina, Botswana, Brazil, Brunei Darussalam, Bulgaria, Burkina Faso, Canada, Cape Verde, Chile, China, Costa Rica, Croatia, Cuba, Cyprus, Czech Republic, Denmark, Dijibouti, Dominica, Ecuador, Egypt, El Salvador, Equatorial Guinea, Estonia, Ethiopia, Finland, France, Gambia*, Germany, Ghana, Greece, Grenada, Guinea, Guyana, Honduras, Hungary, Iceland, India, Ireland, Italy, Jamaica, Japan, Jordan, Kazakhstan, Kenya, Kiribati, Kuwait, Latvia, Lebanon, Liberia, Libya, Liechtenstein, Lithuania, Mali, Malta, Marshall Islands, Mauritius, Mexico, Micronesia*, Moldova, Monaco, Mongolia, Morocco, Mozambique, Myanmar, Namibia, Nauru, Netherlands, New Zealand, Nigeria*, Norway, Oman, Pakistan, Palau, Panama, Paraguay, Peru, Philippines, Poland, Portugal, Qatar, Republic of Korea, Romania, Russian Federation, Saint Kitts and Nevis*, Saint Lucia, St. Vincent & Grenadines, Samoa*, Saudi Arabia, Senegal, Serbia & Montenegro, Seychelles, Singapore*, Slovakia, Slovenia, South Africa, Spain, Sri Lanka*, Sudan, Swaziland, Sweden, Switzerland, Syria, Tajikistan, Togo, Tongo, Trinidad & Tobago, Tunisia, Turkey, Turkmenistan, Tuvalu*, Uganda*, Ukraine, UAE, UK, Tanzania*, United States, Uruguay, Uzbekistan, Vanuatu, Viet Nam, Yemen. *Available at* http://www.imo.org/includes/blastDataOnly.asp/data_id%3D14308/status.xls.

[118] *See supra* II(A) and accompanying note 7.

[119] Tullio Treves, *The Convention for the Suppression of Unlawful Acts Against the Safety of Maritime Navigation*, 2 Singapore J. Int'l & Comp. L. 541, 543 (1998).

[120] SUA, *supra* note 117.

United Nations adopted General Assembly Resolution 58/240,[121] and the IMO began reviewing the Convention in 2003 to address WMD proliferation.[122]

The 2005 Protocol to SUA was adopted on October 14, 2005, to complement PSI efforts by strengthening the tools available to respond to WMD trafficking, thus making it more difficult for terrorists to obtain such material. Specifically, the objectives of the 2005 Protocol were to criminalize the use of a ship to transport terrorists or as a weapon of terror, to provide broad legal authority and specific legal mechanisms to prevent proliferation and stop shipments of WMD and related materials, to detail the actions a boarding state can take to prevent or interrupt the commission of a SUA offense, and to establish WMD proliferation as an international crime for which parties are obligated to either extradite or prosecute.[123]

Article 3*bis* criminalizes the transfer and proliferation of WMD, delivery systems, and related materials consistent with the goal of interdicting the foregoing, establishes legal authority to prosecute those who use ships as weapons, and prohibits the transportation of terrorists. It enumerates prohibited items and requires proof of specific intent in order to protect legitimate trade and innocent seafarers.[124] This criminalization creates a basis for states to interdict foreign

---

[121] *See* G.A. Res. 58/240, U.N. GAOR, 58th Sess., U.N. Doc. A/Res/58/240 (2004) urging:

> all States, in cooperation with the International Maritime Organization, to combat piracy and armed robbery at sea by adopting measures, including those relating to assistance with capacity-building through training of seafarers, port staff and enforcement personnel in the prevention, reporting and investigation of incidents, bringing the alleged perpetrators to justice, in accordance with international law, and by adopting national legislation, as well as providing enforcement vessels and equipment and guarding against fraudulent ship registration; 37. Calls upon all States and relevant international bodies to cooperate in the prevention and combating of piracy and armed robbery at sea, and urges States to give urgent attention to promoting, concluding and implementing cooperation agreements, in particular at the regional level and in high-risk areas; 38. Urges States to become parties to the Convention for the Suppression of Unlawful Acts against the Safety of Maritime Navigation and its Protocol, invites States to participate in the review of those instruments by the Legal Committee of the International Maritime Organization to strengthen the means of combating such unlawful acts, including terrorist acts, and further urges States to take appropriate measures to ensure the effective implementation of those instruments, in particular through the adoption of legislation, where appropriate, aimed at ensuring that there is a proper framework for responses to incidents of armed robbery and terrorist acts at sea.

Id.

[122] Chris Trelawny, Maritime Security: Implementation of the ISPS Code, International Maritime Organization.

[123] International Conference on the Revision of the SUA Treaties, Submission by the United States, *Consideration of a Draft Protocol to the Convention for the Suppression of Unlawful Act against the Safety of Maritime Navigation, 1988 and a Draft Protocol to the Protocol for the Suppression of Unlawful Acts against the Safety of Fixed Platforms Located on the Continental Shelf*, 1988, para. 3, IMO Doc LEG/CONF.15/14 (Sept. 22, 2005), *available at* http://www.state.gov/t/isn/trty/58319.htm. Natalie Klein, *The Right of Visit and the 2005 Protocol on the Suppression of Unlawful Acts against the Safety of Maritime Navigation*, 35(2) Denv. J. Int'l L. & Pol'y 287–88.

[124] SUA, *supra* note 117, at 3*bis*.

flagged vessels in their territorial seas or contiguous zones that are suspected of proliferating WMD, a shortcoming of PSI discussed previously.

Article 8*bis* of the 2005 Protocol establishes the most comprehensive boarding regime in any international document.[125] The informal agreement to allow boarding by PSI partners, is just that—informal. The bilateral boarding agreements negotiated by the United States, discussed below, are also effective tools; however there have been only five agreements negotiated since 2005, with only eleven being negotiated thus far.[126] The regime in the SUA Protocol with potentially 125 states (based on the number of countries that signed the Protocol at the Diplomatic Conference) agreeing to procedures for boarding, respecting IMO involvement, and contained in one international agreement is landmark.[127] Prior to this Protocol there had been no single international legal standard that governed the conduct of boarding and searching a vessel at sea. The Protocol covers cooperation and procedures for a state to follow if it desires to board a foreign flagged ship of another state party "seaward of the requesting states territorial seas" (this would cover high seas and contiguous zone issues discussed previously) when the requesting state has reasonable grounds to suspect that the ship or a person on board the ship is, has been, or is about to be involved in, the commission of an offense under the Convention.[128] A state party has several options for allowing the boarding and searching of vessels flying its flag. On an ad hoc basis, it may either authorize the boarding by the requesting state, conduct the boarding and search itself, conduct the boarding and search with the requesting state, or decline to authorize a boarding.[129] Additionally, a state may file a blanket notification with the Secretary-General of the IMO that its non-response within four hours to a request to board and search a ship flying its flag would constitute authorization to board and search the ship's cargo and persons on board.[130]

The 2005 Protocol to SUA fundamentally transforms efforts to combat and prosecute WMD trafficking and proliferation at sea by providing, for the first time in a treaty, a framework for criminalizing the conduct of those who ship WMD, transport terrorists, or use a ship as a weapon and create international offenses for terrorist acts and maritime transport of WMD and related material. It provides treaty-based authority and procedures for boarding and searching vessels other than those of a country's own flag when in international waters, as opposed to the nonbinding agreement of PSI partners. This regime clarifies the questionable legality of some of the contemplated PSI interdictions by making it clear that state consent, whether a blanket-based consent or on an ad hoc basis,

---

[125] Klein, *supra* note 123, at 289.

[126] Antigua & Barbuda (Apr. 10), Bahamas (Aug. 08), Belize (Aug. 05), Croatia (June 05), Cyprus (July 05), Liberia (Feb. 04), Malta (Mar. 07), Marshall Islands (Aug. 04), Mongolia (Oct. 07), Panama (May 04), St. Vincent & The Grenadines (May 10). U.S. Department of State website, at http://www.state.gov/t/isn/c27733.htm (last visited, July 14, 2015).

[127] SUA *supra* note 117.

[128] SUA *supra* note 117, at 8*bis*, para 5.

[129] *Id.*, 8*bis*, para. 2.

[130] *Id.* para. 5(d).

is required before boarding a foreign flagged vessel outside of the territorial seas of another country.

However, the Protocol still leaves room for noncooperative nations, such as North Korea, to refuse to allow another state to board and search its ships—even if they are a party to the Protocol. It preserves this fundamental tenant of the law of the sea: flag state sovereignty over vessels on the high seas.[131] Like slavery and drug trafficking, the vilification of maritime proliferation and terrorism will take years, if not decades, to accomplish through a network of multilateral and bilateral treaties, state practice, and domestic legislation. In the meantime, there are still many more efforts to pursue in order to prevent maritime terrorism.

C. OTHER COMMON LEGAL AND PRACTICAL CHALLENGES ENCOUNTERED DURING MIOS

As previously discussed, modern MIOs are often joint (multi-service) and combined (multinational). Following 9/11, the United States had only thirty of the seventy ships involved in the leadership interdiction efforts searching the seas for escaping al Qaida. Coalition naval forces made up the majority of the effort.[132] These multinational operations carry with them additional challenges concerning information sharing and differing rules of engagement.

Successful multinational action requires the sharing of selected information and intelligence with international partners. The United States may desire to share information and intelligence to convince international partners that there is a reasonable suspicion that their vessel is carrying personnel or material in violation of law or treaty. Intelligence sharing is governed by specific regulations determining what intelligence will be shared, and with whom the United States will share it, requiring determination, on a case-by-case basis, of the risk to compromising intelligence sources and methods versus the expected gain.[133] The situation may be further complicated by the fact that the United States received intelligence from another international partner, who may not permit the United States to share the information further. The ability to share intelligence may prove to be the obstacle that cannot be overcome in a particular maritime interdiction effort.

Successful WMD interdiction also requires careful coordination and integration across all U.S. government agencies. Interagency coordination is vital to link the military, diplomatic, informational, and economic instruments of national power. The Maritime Operational Threat Response (MOTR) plan for the National Strategy for Maritime Security provides essential guidance for that

---

[131] Klein, *supra* note 123, at 290.

[132] Robert J. Schneller Jr., Naval Coalition Warfare, From the Napoleonic War to Operation Iraqi Freedom 198–202 (Bruce A. Elleman & S.C.M. Paine eds., 2008).

[133] Joint Chiefs of Staff, Joint Publication JP 3–16, Multinational Operations (July 16, 2013) III-13 to III-20.

coordination and integration.[134] The MOTR establishes an integrated network of existing, national-level, command or operations centers of the involved agencies to achieve coordinated, unified, timely, and effective planning and mission accomplishment. The MOTR addresses the full range of maritime security threats, including actionable knowledge of acts of terrorism, piracy, and other criminal or hostile acts committed by state and nonstate actors. In the maritime arena, the MOTR plan sets forth lead and supporting federal agency roles and responsibilities for MOTR, directs clear coordinating relationships and operational coordination requirements among the lead and supporting MOTR agencies, and includes protocols for interagency coordination, consultation, and assessment throughout MOTR execution.[135] The MOTR protocols and procedures allow rapid response to emerging threats.

The United States, and the world, continues to seek ways, domestically and internationally, to stem the threat of proliferators and terrorists who seek to use the sea as their means of delivering their payload. Although the world has made strides with multilateral agreements and arrangements confronting these issues, the bilateral agreements required to put teeth into the multilateral agreements have been slow to materialize. The United State's use of MOTR to internally coordinate responses to international threats is a model for leveraging all existing authorities: domestic, bilateral, and multilateral.

VI. Conclusion

Maritime interdiction operations are well founded in history and law as a means to counter threats from the sea. As threats have become more nuanced and sophisticated, MIO have similarly adapted to become more flexible and precise than the blunt instrument of blockade. Although the core emphasis in the law of the sea has always been the principle of freedom of the sea and respect for flag state authority, these interests may be shifting given the concerns surrounding maritime security. This raises the important question of whether there needs to be a paradigm shift to deal with the competing yet equally important interests: freedom of navigation and safety and security of the maritime environment. The intricate web of customary international law, multilateral and bilateral international agreements, and less formal cooperative efforts will continue to evolve. And the law governing MIO will increase in scope and complexity to meet the demands for safe international shipping.

---

[134] Scott Genovese, *The Maritime Operational Threat Response Plan*, The Coast Guard Journal of Safety and Security at Sea/ Proceedings of the Marine Safety & Security Council 56–57 (Spring 2012); Otto Kreisher, *Collaborative Approach*, Seapower 49 (May 2009).

[135] *Id.*

22 }

Weapons of Mass Destruction

ISSUES AND IMPLICATIONS FOR NATIONAL SECURITY LAWYERS

Todd W. Pennington*

I. Introduction

Weapons of mass destruction (WMD) present many diverse challenges for America's national leaders. The most challenging issues concern the moral and ethical implications of such weapons. Legal issues intermingle with questions of strategy and policy. The United States has entered treaties and conventions designed to limit the use and proliferation of WMD, even as the United States maintains a stockpile of deployed nuclear weapons. Arms control agreements bind U.S. military forces, who must adapt plans for deterrence and for warfighting to conform to the changing levels of authorized strategic weapons. For military forces, issues include operational considerations such as target planning, ensuring the reliability of means to deliver nuclear weapons, and preparing to operate in an environment contaminated by WMD. At a purely technical level there are many physical principles, engineering requirements, and safety considerations at issue in the production, deployment, and disablement of WMD. Counterproliferation, in particular, is fraught with legal and technical challenges

---

* Lieutenant Colonel (Lt Col), United States Air Force, Todd W. Pennington is an active duty judge advocate (JAG). He obtained his JD from the Cecil C. Humphreys School of Law at University of Memphis, and his BA from the University of Memphis. He was awarded a Certificate in WMD Studies from National Defense University. Lt Col Pennington is currently Deputy Legal Counsel to the Chairman of the Joint Chiefs of Staff. Prior to his current duty he was the Staff Judge Advocate for the 509th Bomb Wing, which operates America's fleet of B-2 stealth bombers, and served in several joint and Air Force special operations commands. The positions and opinions in this chapter are those of the author and do not represent the official views of the Department of Defense, the Joint Staff, or the United States Air Force. He would like to thank Wing Commander Ian Henderson, RAF Australia, and Captain Luke R. Nelson, United States Air Force, for invaluable editorial assistance with this chapter, and Professors Geoffrey Corn and Rachel VanLandingham for the opportunity to contribute to this work.

as it balances legitimate, peaceful use of technology against the risk of illicit weapons development.

Where WMD are concerned, there are often blurred or intersecting lines between the policy, strategic, operational, technological, and legal considerations presented in any given issue. This chapter will provide an overview of various legal issues raised by WMD, with special emphasis on providing background, context, and an appreciation of the legal implications of matters relevant to military legal practice. Where non-legal considerations are essential to understanding a legal or regulatory issue, a brief overview will be provided. However, further research into these non-legal considerations will in all cases enable a better understanding of the law.

A. DEFINING WEAPONS OF MASS DESTRUCTION

There is no consensus definition of the term "weapons of mass destruction."[1] The term is defined differently by various U.S. agencies and international regimes, and is sometimes used without definition. Even within a particular agency the term is not always applied consistently. Among the various definitions of weapons of mass destruction, some are surprisingly broad. For example, the Violent Crime Control and Law Enforcement Act of 1994 defines WMD as "any explosive . . . (i) bomb, (ii) grenade, . . . [or] (v) mine."[2] Bombs and grenades are common military ordnance, and few would consider their use in the course of military operations to amount to using WMD.

Other definitions are concise, although sometimes at the expense of clarity in application. The Weapons of Mass Destruction Control Act of 1992 defines WMD as "nuclear, biological, or chemical weapons."[3] Although this definition is intuitive and generally workable, it can present challenges in application. For example, former Russian intelligence officer Alexander Litvinenko was assassinated in London by surreptitious administration of a tiny amount of a radioactive isotope (^{210}PO).[4] Was this incident use of a weapon of mass destruction?

A workable middle ground in this range of definitions is found in the definition of WMD used in the Defense against Weapons of Mass Destruction Act of

---

[1] For a comprehensive survey of definitions of the term "Weapons of Mass Destruction" as used by elements of the U.S. government, see W. Seth Carus, *Defining "Weapons of Mass Destruction"* (National Defense University, Center for the Study of Weapons of Mass Destruction, Occasional Paper No. 8, Revised and Updated January 2012), *available at* http://wmdcenter.dodlive.mil/files/2006/01/OP8.pdf.

[2] 18 U.S.C. § 2332a (1994) (enacted as part of the Violent Crime Control and Law Enforcement Act of 1994, Pub. L. 103-322, Sept. 13, 1994). The quoted text technically comes from the definition of "destructive device" given in 18 U.S.C. § 921 (2010). Section 2332a(c)(2)(A) defines "weapon of mass destruction" to include any destructive device as defined in § 921.

[3] Title XV of the Defense Authorization Act of 1993, Pub. L. 102-484 (Oct. 23, 1992).

[4] Caroline DiCarlo, *Polonium-210 and the Assassination of Alexander Litvinenko*, FORENSIC MAGAZINE, June 1, 2009, http://www.forensicmag.com/article/polonium-210-and-assassination-alexander-litvinenko.

1996: "[a]ny weapon or device that is intended, or has the capability, to cause death or serious bodily injury to a significant number of people through the release, dissemination, or impact of (A) toxic or poisonous chemicals or their precursors, (B) a disease organism, or (C) radiation or radioactivity."[5] Unless otherwise noted, this is the definition of WMD used in this chapter.

Weapons producing effects through "toxic or poisonous chemicals or their precursors" are generally classified as chemical weapons.[6] Chemical weapons disperse toxic agents as a liquid, powder, or vapor. Toxic chemical agents are classified by their effect on the human body, and include choking agents (which cause a buildup of fluid in the lungs, resulting in suffocation; these include chlorine and phosgene), nerve agents (which interfere with the transmission of nerve impulses in the nervous system; these include Sarin or VX), blister agents (such as mustard gas), blood agents (which inhibit the ability of blood cells to utilize and transfer oxygen, effectively causing the body to suffocate; these include hydrogen cyanide), and psychotomimetic agents (which induce conditions similar to psychotic disorders and central nervous system impairment; LSD is a substance that produces psychotomimetic effects).[7]

Weapons producing effects through disease organisms are generally classified as biological weapons.[8] Biological weapons disperse pathogenic living organisms (bacteria such as anthrax) or replicating entities (viruses such as smallpox) to cause lethal or incapacitating disease against targeted individuals or populations. Toxin weapons occupy a curious middle ground between biological and chemical weapons: toxins are poisonous substances produced by living organisms, but are not themselves living or replicating entities. As discussed below,[9] toxins have been governed under both chemical and biological weapons regimes over time. Since ratification of the Biological Weapons Convention, toxins have been classified as biological weapons for most purposes.[10]

Weapons producing effects through radiation or radioactivity are either nuclear or radiological weapons. Nuclear weapons consist of devices containing highly unstable fissile material, designed to produce an uncontrolled, supercritical nuclear chain reaction in a very short span of time (fractions of a second).[11] This produces

---

[5] 50 U.S.C. § 2302 (1996) (enacted as part of the Defense against Weapons of Mass Destruction Act of 1996, Sept. 23 1996, Title XIV of the National Defense Authorization Act for Fiscal Year 1997, Pub. L. 104-201).

[6] 18 U.S.C. § 2332a(c)(2)(B) (2004)

[7] *See generally* Organization for the Prohibition of Chemical Weapons, *available at* http://www.opcw.org/about-chemical-weapons/types-of-chemical-agent/ (last visited July 30, 2014).

[8] The Biological Weapons Convention defines "biological weapons" as "microbial or other biological agents, or toxins whatever their method of production, of types and in quantities that have no justification for prophylactic, protective, or other peaceful purposes." Convention on the Prohibition of the Development, Production, and Stockpiling of Bacteriological (Biological) and Toxin Weapons and on Their Destruction, April 10, 1972, 26 U.S.T. 583, T.I.A.S. No. 8,062, 1015 U.N.T.S. 163 (1972) Article I (A).

[9] *Infra* notes 36–39, and accompanying text.

[10] *Supra* note 8.

[11] Generally only the ^{235}U isotope of Uranium and the ^{239}Pu isotope of Plutonium are suitable for use in nuclear weapons. Nuclear weapons achieve their effects through an uncontrolled,

effects, including heat and blast, far exceeding those that could be produced by a comparable volume of conventional high explosive. Nuclear weapons all work by changing, nearly instantaneously, a slightly subcritical mass of fissile material into a critical mass: a mass of fissile material large enough and dense enough to sustain an uncontrolled, supercritical chain reaction. Gun-type devices do this by slamming two subcritical masses into each other to rapidly form a single mass large and dense enough to sustain an uncontrolled, supercritical chain reaction. Implosion-type devices do this by imploding conventional high explosives around a slightly subcritical mass, thereby crushing it enough to increase its density into a mass large and dense enough to sustain an uncontrolled, supercritical chain reaction. Thermonuclear devices achieve exponentially larger heat and blast effects through the use of more complex nuclear reactions, details of which remain specially controlled.[12] Radiological weapons do not use fissile material to produce a nuclear chain reaction that generates heat or blast effects: rather, they kinetically disperse unstable radiological isotopes that are toxic to humans. These isotopes are inherently unstable at the molecular level, and through natural decay discharge particles and energy, tiny amounts of which can cause radiation poisoning (by inducing severe cell damage in live tissue).[13]

II. Weapons of Mass Destruction in Modern Warfare

The twentieth century saw a frightening trajectory of development, deployment, and use of WMD. Although Declaration II of 1899's Fourth Hague Convention purported to prohibit the use of "projectiles the object of which is the diffusion of asphyxiating or deleterious gases,"[14] chemical weapons were used by multiple armies in World War I. Germany first used chemical weapons (chlorine) successfully in 1914 at Ypres, where it released chlorine through stationary canisters, producing a toxic cloud.[15] Stationary canisters were used partly for operational

---

supercritical nuclear chain reaction. By comparison, nuclear power production facilities work through sustaining a controlled, critical nuclear chain reaction. The fissile materials in nuclear power reactor fuel and nuclear weapons is stored in a subcritical state. For an overview of nuclear physics relatively accessible to nonscientists, see Adam Bernstein, *A Presentation on the Production of Fissile Materials for Nuclear Weapons and Nuclear Power* (June 23, 2010), http://www.ornl.gov/sci/nsed/outreach/presentation/safeguards/2010/Bernstein%202010.pdf.

[12] *See infra* notes 58–80, and accompanying text.

[13] Medical Management of Radiological Casualties, Armed Forces Radiobiology Research Institute 7 (4th ed. July 2013).

[14] Hague Convention IV, Declaration II-Concerning the Prohibition of the Use of Projectiles Diffusing Asphyxiating Gases, July 29, 1899, 26 Martens Nouveau Recueil (ser. 2) 998, 187 Consol T.S. 453. The United States neither signed nor ratified this Declaration, although it was ratified by France and Germany in 1900 and by the United Kingdom in 1907.

[15] Jeffery K. Smart, *History of Chemical and Biological Warfare: An American Perspective*, *in* Medical Aspects of Chemical and Biological Warfare 14–15 (Frederick R. Sidell, Ernest T. Takafuji & David R. Franz eds., Office of the Surgeon General Department of the Army, United States of America 1997).

reasons and partly because Germany believed that this method exploited a loophole in Declaration II.[16] The Allies retaliated with chlorine use of their own; chemical warfare further escalated with the use of phosgene, diphosgene, and mustard gas.[17] In 1918, the United States began a formal biological and chemical weapons development program.[18]

Between WWI and WWII there was another unsuccessful attempt to prohibit the use of chemical and biological weapons. Commonly known as the "Geneva Protocol," the "Protocol for the Prohibition of the Use in War of Asphyxiating, Poisonous or other Gases, and of Bacteriological Methods of Warfare" opened for signature in 1925.[19] Several major powers, including France, the United Kingdom, and the Soviet Union ratified the treaty with reservations stipulating that the Protocol would cease to be binding on them if their enemies, or the allies of their enemies, failed to respect the prohibitions of the Protocol. The United States signed the treaty in 1925 with similar reservations but did not ratify it until 1975.[20] These reservations to the Protocol meant that for the greater part of the Cold War, most major powers were under no prohibition from developing chemical or biological weapons for retaliatory use. Indeed, chemical and biological weapons programs continued and expanded under this sweeping exception.

Conventional wisdom holds that the probability a type of weapon will be used increases with the weapon's prevalence and availability. However, history often confounds conventional wisdom, particularly with regard to WMD. Thus, despite greater availability of chemical weapons to a larger number of forces, the use of chemical weapons was more limited in the Second World War than in the First.[21] However, it was the Second World War that ushered in the atomic age with the development and employment of the first atomic weapons.

---

[16] Ground-based canisters are not "projectiles," which are technically what Declaration II proscribed. *Id.* at 14–15.

[17] *Id.* at 16.

[18] *Id.* at 22. It is not clear whether any rigorous law-of-war analysis preceded this U.S. parting with the Lieber Code's view that "Military necessity does not admit . . . of the use of poison in any way . . . " General Orders 100, Instructions for the Government of the Armies of the United States in the Field (the Lieber Code), Art. 16 (Apr. 24, 1863), *available at* http://avalon.law.yale.edu/19th_century/lieber.asp.

[19] Protocol for the Prohibition of the Use in War of Asphyxiating, Poisonous or other Gases, and of Bacteriological Methods of Warfare, 26 U.S.T. 571, T.I.A.S. No. 8061 (June 17, 1925) [hereinafter Geneva Protocol of 1925].

[20] Gerald R. Ford, President of the United States, Statement on the Geneva Protocol of 1925 and the Biological Weapons Convention, *The American Presidency Project*, compiled by Gerhard Peters and John T. Woolley (Jan. 22, 1975), http://www.presidency.ucsb.edu/ws/?pid=5049.

[21] No party to the conflict used chemical or biological weapons against U.S. forces, though Japan did use chemical and biological weapons in China. *See* Smart, *supra* note 15, at 37 regarding chemical weapons; regarding biological weapons, see Select Documents on Japanese War Crimes and Japanese Biological Warfare, 1934–2006 (William H. Cunliffe ed.), online by the U.S. National Archives at http://www.archives.gov/iwg/japanese-war-crimes/select-documents.pdf (last visited July 30, 2014).

Professor Albert Einstein identified the prospect of applying then-emerging developments in nuclear physics to weapons technologies in a letter, dated August 2, 1939, sent to President Franklin D. Roosevelt. The letter stated:

> Some recent work by E. Fermi and L. Szilard . . . leads me to expect that the element uranium may be turned into a new and important source of energy in the immediate future. Certain aspects of the situation which has arisen seem to call for watchfulness and, if necessary, quick action on the part of the Administration. I believe therefore that it is my duty to bring to your attention the following facts and recommendations: In the course of the last four months it has been made probable . . . that it may become possible to set up a nuclear chain reaction in a large mass of uranium, by which vast amounts of power and large quantities of new radium-like elements would be generated. Now it appears almost certain that this could be achieved in the immediate future. This new phenomenon would also lead to the construction of bombs, and it is conceivable—though much less certain—that extremely powerful bombs of a new type may thus be constructed.[22]

Einstein succeeded in getting President Roosevelt's attention. Following some internal deliberations, the Army was directed to establish the "Manhattan Engineer District" (better known today as the "Manhattan Project"). Its charter: to develop a bomb using the principles described in Einstein's letter. Under the overall leadership of Major General Leslie Groves and the scientific direction of Dr. J. Robert Oppenheimer, they succeeded. The first nuclear device—a plutonium-based, implosion-type device—was tested in the New Mexico desert on July 6, 1945.[23] The first nuclear weapon (nicknamed "Little Boy," a uranium-based, gun-type weapon) was detonated over Hiroshima, Japan on August 6, 1945.[24] The second use of a nuclear weapon in hostilities occurred three

---

[22] Letter from Albert Einstein to President Franklin D. Roosevelt (Aug. 2, 1939), online by the U.S. National Archives at http://research.archives.gov/description/593374.

[23] A nuclear "device" refers to a contrivance capable of producing an uncontrolled nuclear chain reaction; a nuclear "weapon" refers to a nuclear device when loaded onto a delivery system such as a missile or bomb. *See* P. Moorthy, Nuclear Weapon-Free Zone 68 (Concept Publishing Company 2006) (discussing "explosions of nuclear devices for peaceful purposes.").

[24] John Malik, Los Alamos National Laboratory, LA-8819, The Yields of the Hiroshima and Nagasaki Nuclear Explosions, (September 1985), 4 (The order to use the atomic bomb in combat stated:

> The 509 Composite Group, 20th Air Force, will deliver its first special bomb as soon as weather will permit visual bombing after about 3 August 1945 on one of the targets: Hiroshima, Kokura, Niigata and Nagasaki . . . . Additional bombs will be delivered on the above targets as soon as made ready by the project staff. Further instructions will be issued concerning targets other than those listed above.

Order from General Thomas T. Handy, Acting Army Chief of Staff to General Carl Spaatz, Commanding General, United States Army Strategic Air Forces (July 25, 1945) (Copy on display in the lobby of Headquarters, 509th Bomb Wing, Whiteman Air Force Base, Missouri).

days later, when a second device (nicknamed "Fat Man," a plutonium-based, implosion-type weapon) was detonated over Nagasaki, Japan.[25]

The detonation of two atomic bombs over Japan—the only operational use of nuclear weapons to date—was followed shortly by the general Japanese surrender in World War II.[26] However, America's nuclear monopoly was short-lived. The Soviet Union conducted its first successful nuclear weapons test on August 29, 1949, marking the beginning of the Cold War arms race.[27] Nuclear weapons development soon expanded to thermonuclear weapons: the "hydrogen bomb," so-called for its use of hydrogen fusion to produce massively more powerful nuclear yields. The "Little Boy" gun-type,^{235}U-based weapon produced a nuclear yield of approximately 15 kilotons, while the "Fat Man" implosion-type ^{239}Pu-based weapon produced a nuclear yield of approximately 21 kilotons.[28] The most powerful thermonuclear test conducted by the United States (the Bravo detonation, conducted on Bikini Island on February 28, 1954) produced a 15-megaton yield.[29] The largest yield yet produced by a nuclear weapon was the Soviet Union's "Tsar Bomba" test, which produced an assessed 58-megaton yield (equivalent to 58 million tons of TNT). This was assessed to be a scaled-down test of a weapon designed to produce up to 100 megatons of yield, had it entered production.[30]

During the Cold War, both the United States and Soviet Union developed a massive stockpile of nuclear, chemical, and biological weapons. At its height, the U.S. stockpile of WMD included large stockpiles of biological agents (including the bacteria causing anthrax, tularemia, brucellosis, Q fever, Venezuelan equine encephalitis, and two toxins: botulinum toxin and *Staphlococus* enterotoxin B) loaded onto bomblets, bombs, and spray tanks,[31] approximately thirty thousand tons of similarly weaponized chemical agents (including choking agents, blister

---

[25] *Supra* note 24, at 4.

[26] Historians disagree on the role the atomic bombs played in the Japanese surrender. For a review of historical works supporting, and questioning, the decision to drop the bomb, see Alonzo L. Hamby, *The Decision to Drop the Bomb*, 84(2) J. AM. HIST. (Sept. 1997), https://www.mtholyoke.edu/acad/intrel/hamby.htm.

[27] Harry S Truman, President of the United States, Statement by the President on Announcing the First Atomic Explosion in the U.S.S.R., *The American Presidency Project*, compiled by Gerhard Peters and John T. Woolley (Sept. 23, 1949), http://www.presidency.ucsb.edu/ws/?pid=13312.

[28] U.S. Department of Energy Nevada Operations, United States Nuclear Tests, July 1945–Sept. 1992 DOE/NV-209-REV 15 (2000), *available at* http://www.nv.doe.gov/library/publications/historical/DOENV_209_REV15.pdf. A kiloton denotes an explosive yield comparable to 1,000 tons of TNT; a megaton denotes an explosive yield comparable to 1,000,000 tons of TNT.

[29] *Id.* at 98–99.

[30] Central Intelligence Agency, *National Intelligence Estimate: The Soviet Atomic Energy Program*, 13 (NIE 11-2A-62, May 16, 1962), *available at* http://media.nara.gov/dc-metro/rg-263/6942952/Box-21-NIE-11-1-7-84-Nov-26/263-a1-29-Box-21-NIE-11-1-7-84-Nov-26.pdf (in redacted form from the CIA's online Freedom of Information Act Reading Room).

[31] Jonathan B. Tucker & Erin R. Mahan, *President Nixon's Decision to Renounce the U.S. Offensive Biological Weapons Program*, Ctr. for the Study of Weapons of Mass Destruction, National Defense University (Oct. 2009) (citing ED REGIS, THE BIOLOGY OF DOOM: THE HISTORY OF AMERICA'S SECRET GERM WARFARE PROJECT 210–11 (1990)).

agents, and nerve agents),[32] and 31,255 nuclear warheads loaded onto missiles, bombs, artillery shells, and other delivery systems.[33] The Soviet stockpile was similarly massive. Through deliberate transfer of weapons and technology, and through illicit proliferation, several other countries also developed these capabilities.[34] This terrifying expansion prompted renewed efforts not only to limit further proliferation of WMD, but to reverse it where possible.

III. Domestic and International Controls on Weapons of Mass Destruction

Despite a near-universal moral aversion to all forms of WMD, imposing a legal regime capable of controlling their use or proliferation has proven easier said than done. Some individual countries have forgone or renounced programs to develop and deploy WMD, but the success of international regimes conceived for this purpose has been constrained by several factors. First, despite the moral taboos involved, WMD do have military utility. They offer an asymmetric advantage over an enemy lacking them, and a claim to parity with adversaries armed with WMD. Second, possessing WMD (and the perceived political will to use them) provides a strategic deterrent—at least against an adversary that possesses resources it holds dear. Of course, the question of who is deterred by WMD and what they are deterred from doing is a subject of much debate and theorizing among strategists and policymakers. Third, much of the technology required to produce chemical, biological, or nuclear weapons is dual use, meaning it is used in legitimate peaceful activities such as industrial processes, medical research, and energy production, which are impacted by non-proliferation regulatory efforts. Finally, possessing WMD provides a hedge against an uncertain future in which technological breakthroughs may render current conventional military capabilities inadequate to meet security requirements. These issues form the backdrop against which nations have attempted to regulate WMD. This section will introduce several U.S. domestic and international legal regimes applicable to the various categories of WMD.

As the following discussion will show, particularly with regard to treaty-based controls on WMD, verification of compliance with agreed obligations is one of the most complex aspects of regulating WMD. Verification is inherently violative of national sovereignty. It is difficult to obtain broad acquiescence to a legal regime

---

[32] Press Release, U.S. Army Chemical Materials Agency, Army Agency Completes Mission to Destroy Chemical Weapons (Jan. 12, 2012), *available at* http://www.cma.army.mil/fndocumentviewer.aspx?DocID=003683880.

[33] Dep't of Def., *Fact Sheet, Increasing Transparency in the U.S. Nuclear Weapons Stockpile* (May 3, 2010), *available at* http://www.defense.gov/npr/docs/10-05-03_Fact_Sheet_US_Nuclear_Transparency__FINAL_w_Date.pdf.

[34] *See* Paul Kerr, Cong. Research Serv., RL30699, Nuclear, Biological, and Chemical Weapons and Missiles: Status and Trends (Feb. 20, 2008).

that includes intrusive verification protocols. However, the absence of verification procedures does not foster confidence in the efficacy of the legal regime. Compromise solutions may fail to address either concern, by failing to deter or detect violators, or by failing to provide adequate security assurance on the part of actors relying on the legal regime's success. Each of the WMD control frameworks discussed below wrestles with these competing values of national sovereignty, practical efficacy, and persuasive compliance. Success in balancing these values grows more complex the greater the number of parties to an agreement.

A. DOMESTIC AND INTERNATIONAL CONTROLS ON BIOLOGICAL AND CHEMICAL WEAPONS

The strands of the domestic and international legal regimes regulating biological and chemical weapons were woven together through related processes over many years. Early in the Cold War, the primary control on chemical and biological weapons was the 1925 Geneva Protocol.[35] States party to the Protocol retained the right to use chemical and biological weapons in retaliation if such weapons were first used against them. On that basis, most major powers maintained active chemical and biological weapons programs, at least in the early years of the Cold War. However, by the late 1960s, a time when chemical and biological weapons programs were still closely associated in the American public mind, a series of public mishaps involving chemical weapons programs prompted a review in 1969 of U.S. policies on the use of chemical and biological weapons.[36] On the basis of that review, President Richard Nixon signed National Security Decision Memorandum 35, renouncing all uses of biological weapons (but retaining an offensive chemical weapons capability) as a matter of U.S. national policy.[37] National Security Decision Memorandum 44 extended this policy to toxin-based weapons as well.[38] These decisions marked the first instance of a major power unilaterally abandoning an entire category of modern, fielded, operational weapons.[39]

---

[35] *See generally* Geneva Protocol of 1925, *supra* note 19.

[36] Tucker & Mahan, *supra* note 31, at 1–2.

[37] National Security Council, *National Security Decision Memorandum 35* (Nov. 25, 1969), *available at* http://nixon.archives.gov/virtuallibrary/documents/nsdm/nsdm_035.pdf. The policy review of chemical and biological weapons resulted in fractious and divided views. The strategic and military utility of chemical and biological weapons was endorsed by some—and questioned by others. Some views focused on the moral repugnance of such weapons; others focused on the collateral impact to overall deterrence of the Soviet Union. One issue was whether to treat biological and chemical weapons as a single category, or to regulate them separately. Chairman of the Joint Chiefs of Staff General Earle Wheeler supported retaining a full, offensive biological and chemical weapons program; however he was alone among National Security Council principals. Ultimately—and in large part to preserve the authority to maintain a chemical weapons capability for deterrence and retaliation—Wheeler joined the recommendation to renounce only an offensive biological weapons capability. *See* Tucker & Mahan, *supra* note 31, at 2–9.

[38] National Security Council, *National Security Decision Memorandum 44* (Feb. 20, 1970), *available at* http://nixon.archives.gov/virtuallibrary/documents/nsdm/nsdm_044.pdf.

[39] *See* Tucker & Mahan, *supra* note 31, at 17.

These U.S. policy decisions paved the way for negotiation of the 1972 Biological and Toxin Weapons Convention (BWC), which bans the development, production, stockpiling, or transfer of such weapons.[40] Although the BWC is comprehensive in its prohibition of the development or possession[41] of biological or toxin weapons, it does not establish any specific mechanisms for verification and compliance.[42] Article V of the BWC provides for consultation and cooperation regarding any problems arising from application of the convention, and Article VI provides for referral of suspected violations to the United Nations Security Council as the BWC's only enforcement mechanism. Prior to the BWC, chemical and biological weapons had traditionally been treated as a single category of weapons for legal purposes. The BWC marked the first division of these weapons into different categories under international law.[43]

The United States signed the BWC and submitted it for ratification along with the 1925 Geneva Protocol; the Senate ratified both in 1975.[44] The BWC entered force in 1975, and, together with the 1925 Geneva Protocol, it remains the overarching legal framework for the control of biological and toxin weapons today.[45]

---

[40] Convention on the Prohibition of the Development, Production, and Stockpiling of Bacteriological (Biological) and Toxin Weapons and on Their Destruction, April 10, 1972, 26 U.S.T. 583, T.I.A.S. No. 8,062, 1015 U.N.T.S. 163 (1972) [hereinafter Biological Weapons Convention].

[41] Curiously, the Biological Weapons Convention does not, by its terms, ban the "use" of biological or toxin weapons, other than by implication (as one cannot "use" a weapon without first "possessing" it). The Geneva Protocol of 1925 provides the international legal prohibition on use of biological weapons. *See* Geneva Protocol of 1925, *supra* note 19. By comparison, the Chemical Weapons Convention prohibits both use and possession of chemical weapons. *See* Chemical Weapons Convention, *infra* note 49, at Art 1.

[42] *See generally* Biological Weapons Convention, *supra* note 8. Unlike the regime applicable to chemical weapons, there is no meaningful organization or secretariat to oversee implementation of the BWC other than a three-person Implementation Support Unit established with limited authority—and a temporary mandate—at the U.N. Office in Geneva following the 2006 BWC Review Conference. A Verification Protocol to the BWC was negotiated in the 1990s, but never entered into force. The U.S. position is that the BWC is not susceptible to verification, as the line between legitimate medical research and illicit bioweapons development is solely a matter of intent. *See* Jonathan Tucker, Addressing the Spectrum of Biological Risks: A Policy Agenda for the United States, Testimony Before the House Committee on Foreign Affairs, Subcommittee on Terrorism, Nonproliferation, and Trade, National Strategy for Countering Biological Threats: Diplomacy and International Programs (Mar. 18, 2010), *available at* http://cns.miis.edu through the James Martin Center for Nonproliferation Studies, Monterey Institute of International Studies, Middlebury College.

[43] *See* Jez Littlewood, Managing the Biological Weapons Problem: From the Individual to the International, Weapons of Mass Destruction Commission paper no. 14, 18 (Aug. 2004), on file with author.

[44] Implementing legislation was not enacted until twenty-five years later. 18 U.S.C. § 175 (1989) (Biological Weapons Anti-Terrorism Act of 1989), Pub. L. 101-298, May 22, 1990).

[45] The United States ended its offensive biological weapons program in accordance with the President's direction in NSDM 35 and 44 and the BWC. Jonathan B. Tucker & Erin R. Mahan, *President Nixon's Decision to Renounce the U.S. Offensive Biological Weapons Program,* Ctr. for the Study of Weapons of Mass Destruction, National Defense University (Oct. 2009). However, the USSR continued a covert biological weapons program in willful violation of the BWC until as late as 1992, when Russian President Boris Yeltsin confirmed the existence of the program, and repudiated further violation of the BWC. Gulbarshyn Bozheyeva, Yerlan Kunakbayev, & Dastan Yeleukenov, *Former Soviet Biological Weapons Facilities in Kazakhstan: Past, Present, and Future* (Monterey

Concurrent with ratification of the Geneva Protocol, President Gerald Ford issued Executive Order 11850 regarding non-lethal herbicides and riot control agents. The order states:

> The United States renounces, as a matter of national policy, first use of herbicides in war except use, under regulations applicable to their domestic use, for control of vegetation within U.S. bases and installations or around their immediate defensive perimeters, and first use of riot control agents in war except in defensive military modes to save lives.[46]

The order gives several examples of "defensive military modes to save lives," including "riot control situations . . . to include rioting prisoners of war," "in situations in which civilians are used to mask or screen attacks and civilian casualties can be reduced or avoided," "rescue missions in remotely isolated areas, of downed aircrews and passengers, and escaping prisoners," and "to protect convoys from civil disturbances, terrorists, and paramilitary organizations."[47] These concepts continue to inform guidance for U.S. forces' use of riot control agents today. At the time, Executive Order 11850 reserved the right for use of herbicides or riot control agents in war in retaliation for use of either by an enemy, although as discussed below this option was later rescinded with ratification of the Chemical Weapons Convention.

The U.S. reservations to ratification of the 1925 Geneva Protocol preserved the option to develop and retain stockpiles of chemical weapons against a nonparty to—or a party in breach of—the 1925 Geneva Protocol. Indeed, the U.S. maintained, modernized, and improved stockpiles of chemical weapons as late as 1990. In that year, the United States and the Soviet Union signed an accord under which both parties committed to stop the production of chemical weapons and to draw down stockpiles to 5,000 metric agent tons.[48] Three years later the United States signed the Chemical Weapons Convention (CWC) and ratified it shortly before its entry into force in April 1997.[49]

The CWC obligates states party to not use, or prepare to use, chemical weapons, and to destroy their chemical weapons production facilities. The CWC also prohibits the use of riot control agents "as a method of warfare."[50] Nations have differed in their treatment of how to apply this provision. According to the

---

Institute of International Studies, Center for Non-Proliferation Studies, *available at* http://cns.miis.edu/opapers/op1/op1.pdf.

[46] Exec. Order No. 11850, 40 Fed. Reg. 16,187 (1975).

[47] *Id.*

[48] U.S.-Soviet Agreement on Destruction and Non-Production of Chemical Weapons and on Measures to Facilitate the Multilateral Chemical Weapons Convention, June 1, 1990, 29 I.L.M. 934, 1990, 56 Fed. Reg. 25,404 (1991). This agreement is generally referred to as the Bilateral Destruction Agreement.

[49] Convention on the Prohibition of the Development, Production, Stockpiling and Use of Chemical Weapons and on their Destruction, April 29, 1997, 1974 U.N.T.S. 45, 32 I.L.M. 800, S. Treaty Doc. No. 103-21 (1993) [hereinafter Chemical Weapons Convention].

[50] *Id.* at Article I.

Database of Customary International Humanitarian Law maintained by the International Committee of the Red Cross, "the vast majority of States are of the opinion that the Geneva Gas Protocol prohibits the use of all asphyxiating and poisonous gases and analogous materials, including riot control agents, and apply it as such."[51] However, the United States represents a "consistent minority view" that use of riot control agents in "defensive modes to save lives" does not constitute a "method of warfare," and is thus not barred by the Convention.[52] This exception is applied to U.S. forces through Executive Order 11850, as implemented through controlling Rules of Engagement.

Unlike the BWC, the CWC establishes verification and compliance procedures and establishes an international organization—the Organization for the Prohibition of Chemical Weapons—with a full-time, professional secretariat to implement verification and compliance. Verification procedures include accounting for national declarations, conducting on-site inspections, and investigating alleged prohibited usage of chemical weapons.[53] The CWC defines "chemical weapons" as:

> (a) Toxic chemicals and their precursors, except where intended for purposes not prohibited under this Convention, as long as the types and quantities are consistent with such purposes, (b) Munitions and devices, specifically designed to cause death or other harm through the toxic properties of those toxic chemicals specified in subparagraph (a), which would be released as a result of the employment of such munitions and devices; (c) Any equipment specifically designed for use directly in connection with the employment of munitions and devices specified in subparagraph (b).[54]

The definition of toxic chemicals also references the CWC's Annex on Chemicals, in which certain toxic chemicals are "identified for the application of verification measures" in one of three schedules. The schedules organize covered chemicals according to their potential for weaponization, and the nature and extent of permitted peaceful uses. The CWC also requires states parties to pursue national implementing legislation; the United States complied with this requirement in 1998 with the Chemical Weapons Convention Implementation Act.[55] The Act

---

[51] Database of Customary International Humanitarian Law, International Committee of the Red Cross, Rule 75, note 1 and accompanying text, http://www.icrc.org/customary-ihl/eng/docs/v1_rul_rule75 (last visited June 13, 2015).

[52] *Id.*

[53] The most recent report of verification activities is *Note by the Director General, Summary of Verification Activities in 2011*, Technical Secretariat, Verification Division, S/1042/2012/Rev.2 (Dec. 19, 2012), http://www.opcw.org/index/php=?eID=dam_frontend_push&docID=15822. Although the verification regime is robust in concept, "no challenge inspections (CIs) or investigations of alleged use (IAUs) were requested in 2011." *Id.*

[54] Chemical Weapons Convention, *supra* note 49, at Article II.

[55] 22 U.S.C. § 6701 *et seq.* (1998) (*Chemical Weapons Convention Implementation Act of 1998*, Pub. L. 105-277 (Oct. 21, 1998)).

establishes requirements for reporting of CWC-covered facilities, and procedures for coordinating and conducting verification and compliance inspections.

Legal controls on chemical and biological weapons originated from common prohibitions founded in international law. Though later divided into separate domestic and international legal regimes, the widespread adoption of both the BWC and CWC reflect international legal norms against the use of biological or chemical weapons, and a broad consensus that neither chemical nor biological weapons are permitted under modern *jus in bello*. One of the most infamous recent uses of chemical weapons was Iraq's of mustard gas, Tabun, Sarin, and VX against civilians in the Kurdish town of Halabja in 1988. Several Iraqi officials—including Ali Hassan al-Majid (aka "Chemical Ali")—were ultimately convicted of genocide and crimes against humanity and subsequently executed for their role in authorizing the attack.[56] Although the fact of a norm against use of chemical and biological weapons is clear, it is less clear whether this norm is due to these weapons' inability to be employed in accordance with the law-of-war requirement to distinguish between lawful combatants and protected persons—or because these weapons are thought to cause unnecessary suffering. The distinction matters because new developments in chemical engineering, life sciences, military capability, and doctrine may one day produce agents with conceptual similarities to those prohibited as weapons under the BWC and CWC, but that fall outside their strict terms of reference, and that are susceptible to use in a discriminate manner against lawful military targets, without causing unnecessary suffering to the targeted force. It is difficult to imagine any such use garnering any meaningful legal imprimatur in the near future, but the continually evolving technology of chemical and life sciences may eventually present unforeseen challenges in the application of *jus in bello*.

B. DOMESTIC CONTROLS ON NUCLEAR WEAPONS

Although laws and norms governing chemical and biological weapons developed in closely intertwined processes, the legal framework applicable to nuclear weapons (and nuclear energy) developed on a wholly separate path. For U.S. national security lawyers, there are two main bodies of law applicable to nuclear power: domestic U.S. law establishing responsibilities and authorities for control of nuclear energy, and an international arms control and non-proliferation regime designed to minimize the prevalence and proliferation of nuclear arms.

The U.S. nuclear enterprise began as a classified project within the U.S. Army Corps of Engineers. The Manhattan Engineer District (better known today as the Manhattan Project) was established by general order in April 1942.[57] Its task—to develop the atomic bomb—was so novel that no special legal framework applied

---

[56] *See "Chemical Ali" Executed in Iraq after Halabja Ruling*, BBC NEWS, Jan. 25, 2010, http://news.bbc.co.uk/2/hi/middle_east/8479115.stm.

[57] *See* F.G. Gosling, *The Manhattan Project: Making the Atomic Bomb* 15, U.S. Dep't of Energy, Office of History and Heritage Resources (Oct. 2005).

to it. At the time, there was no law unique to atomic energy. From the project's origins through the atomic detonation over Hiroshima, all that distinguished the Manhattan Project from other U.S. wartime activities was the project's incredible secrecy. The Hiroshima and Nagasaki detonations in August 1945 brought the atomic bomb into the public sphere, where the debate quickly came to focus on control and regulation of this new and remarkable power.

1. The Atomic Energy Act and the Domestic Nuclear Regulation Enterprise

After the war, Congress enacted the first public law governing nuclear energy—the Atomic Energy Act of 1946.[58] The Act's "Findings and Declaration" states:

> The significance of the atomic bomb for military purposes is evident. The effect of the use of atomic energy for civilian purposes upon the social, economic, and political structures of today cannot now be determined . . . It is reasonable to anticipate, however, that tapping this new source of energy will cause profound changes in our present way of life.[59]

The Atomic Energy Act (as amended) remains the foundation of the domestic legal framework governing nuclear energy today.

The Act established the Atomic Energy Commission (AEC) as an agency of the U.S. government, with the exclusive rights to own and operate facilities for the production of fissile material (other than small-scale research or medical facilities) and to own and regulate the possession of fissionable material.[60] The functions of the AEC were later dispersed across other U.S. government entities; a brief summary is in order to understand the progression of these changes. The Energy Reorganization Act of 1974 dissolved the AEC and bifurcated its responsibilities between two newly created agencies. The Nuclear Regulatory Commission (NRC), an independent agency of the U.S. government, was established to oversee the commercial nuclear power industry.[61] The remainder of the AEC's responsibilities—energy research, development of nuclear weapons, and naval power reactors—were assumed by the newly established Energy Research and Development Administration (ERDA).[62] In 1977, ERDA combined with the Federal Energy Administration, established earlier that decade in response to the oil crisis of the early 1970s,[63] to form the Department of Energy.[64] The last major

---

[58] *The Atomic Energy Act of 1946*, Pub. L. 79-585, 60 Stat. 755 (Aug. 1, 1946). (Formerly codified at 42 U.S.C. 1801–19.)

[59] *Id.*

[60] *Id.*

[61] *See* 42 U.S.C. ch. 73, subch. II, § 5841–5853 (1974) (enacted as part of the *Energy Reorganization Act of 1974*, Pub. L. 93-438 (Oct. 11, 1974)).

[62] *See* 42 U.S.C. ch. 73, subch. I, § 5811–5821 (1974) (enacted as part of the *Energy Reorganization Act of 1974*, Pub. L. 93-438 (Oct. 11, 1974)).

[63] *See* 15 U.S.C. ch. 16B, subch. I, § 761–788 (1974) (enacted as part of the *Federal Energy Administration Act of 1974*, Pub. L. 93-275 (May 7, 1974)); *see also* Exec. Order No. 11790, 39 Fed. Reg. 23,185 (1974).

[64] *See* 42 U.S.C. ch. 84, § 7101–7384 (1974) (*The Department of Energy Organization Act of 1977*, Pub. L. 95-91 (Aug. 4, 1977)).

reorganization of the nuclear enterprise occurred in 1999, with the responsibility for the military applications of nuclear power (primarily development and stewardship of nuclear weapons, and naval power reactors) being vested in the National Nuclear Security Administration, a subagency of the Department of Energy.[65]

The Department of Defense's legal authority to exercise custody of nuclear weapons similarly evolved over time. Initially, nuclear weapons remained in AEC custody, unless temporarily transferred to the Department of Defense for limited purposes. These temporary transfers were conducted under the authority of the 1946 Atomic Energy Act, which provided that the "President may from time to time direct the (AEC) to deliver such quantities of fissionable materials or weapons to the armed forces for such use as he deems necessary in the interest of national defense."[66] Later the AEC and the Department of Defense separately exercised physical control and legal custody of nuclear weapons and nuclear weapon components in accordance with detailed AEC-Department of Defense agreements regarding custody. Ultimately in 1967 the President concurred with an AEC-Department of Defense agreement under which most operationally deployed nuclear weapons would be transferred to Department of Defense custody and control.[67] Since that time, the Department of Defense has exercised custody and control of operationally deployed nuclear weapons.

Today, domestic controls on atomic energy and nuclear weapons are promulgated and administered by the agencies described above. The NRC regulates civilian nuclear power programs and U.S. government programs to dispose of radiological waste. Although these are non-weapons programs, they protect sensitive materials and technology for both public safety and counterproliferation purposes. The Department of Energy, through the National Nuclear Security Administration, operates the National Laboratories and other facilities that provide research and technical services essential to maintaining the U.S. nuclear weapons stockpile. The Department of Defense protects and maintains fielded nuclear weapons and the means to deliver them.[68]

---

[65] *See* 50 U.S.C. ch. 41, subch. I, § 2401–2484 (1999) (*The National Nuclear Security Administration Act*, enacted as part of the *National Defense Authorization Act for Fiscal Year 2000*, Pub. L. 106-65 (Oct. 5, 1999)).

[66] *The Atomic Energy Act of 1946*, Pub. L. 79-585, 60 Stat. 755 (Aug. 1, 1946) (Formerly codified at 42 U.S.C. 1801–1819).

[67] *See* Office of the Assistant to the Sec'y of Defense (Atomic Energy), History of the Custody and Deployment of Nuclear Weapons, July 1945–Sept. 1977, 113 (1978).

[68] A much more detailed survey of the laws and regulations currently applicable to the nuclear enterprise is available from NUREG-0980, a publication of the Nuclear Regulatory Commission General Counsel, which compiles Nuclear Regulatory Legislation from the Atomic Energy Act through the present. NUREG-0980 is available at http://www.nrc.gov/reading-rm/doc-collections/nuregs/staff/sr0980/ (last visited August 18, 2014).

2. Controlling Nuclear Information

The Atomic Energy Act of 1946 provided that information pertaining to the production of fissile material or the development of nuclear weapons was "Restricted Data," a novel concept (discussed in greater detail below) in which information pertaining to nuclear energy is subject to government protection and control merely by virtue of the nature of the information. "Restricted Data" is thus said to be "born secret."[69] A substantial modification of the Atomic Energy Act in 1954 provided authority for private companies to possess Restricted Data essential to civilian production of nuclear energy, removed prohibitions against patenting processes for generating nuclear energy or fissile materials, and authorized certain international exchanges of information related to atomic energy.[70]

In addition to the automatic classification of restricted data, a robust legal and regulatory classification scheme protects information relevant to nuclear weapons. Restricted data includes information pertaining to the design, manufacture, or utilization of atomic weapons; the production of Special Nuclear Material such as Uranium and Plutonium; or the use of Special Nuclear Material in the production of energy. This restricted data is controlled by the Department of Energy.[71] In addition to the statutory controls on Restricted Data, Department of Defense policy is to treat all such data as Classified Secret.[72] Severe penalties attach to the unauthorized possession or transfer of Restricted Data.[73]

The term "Formerly Restricted Data" refers to data that the Departments of Energy and Defense have jointly determined relates primarily to military utilization of atomic weapons. "Formerly Restricted Data" does not mean that the information is no longer protected: it merely denotes that the information falls under a different classification system.[74] Restricted Data and Formerly Restricted Data are subdivided into more discrete subcategories known as "Sigmas." Each Sigma has a number to provide an unclassified mechanism to reference a given

---

[69] *See generally* Howard Morland, *Born Secret*, 26(4) CARDOZO L. REV. 1401 (2005). By contrast, other forms of classified information result from an affirmative decision, made by an authorized government official designated under Executive Order 13526, to classify the information. *See infra* note 74.

[70] 42 U.S.C. ch. 23, § 2011–2297 (1954) (*The Atomic Energy Act of 1954*, Pub. L. 83-703, 60 Stat. 755 (Aug. 1, 1946, as amended)). The total prohibition on international transfer of atomic energy information in the original Atomic Energy Act was particularly galling to the United Kingdom, whose own nuclear weapons program (Tube Alloys) predated and was later formally merged into the U.S. Manhattan Project. Eric Ridge, *Completing the Transatlantic Nuclear Bridge: A U.S. View, in* U.S.-U.K. NUCLEAR COOPERATION AFTER 50 YEARS, 62 (Jenifer Mackby & Paul Cornish eds., Center for Strategic and International Studies 2008).

[71] *See* 42 U.S.C. § 2016 (1946).

[72] U.S. DEP'T OF DEF., DIRECTIVE 5210.02, ACCESS TO AND DISSEMINATION OF RESTRICTED DATA AND FORMERLY RESTRICTED DATA ¶ 4 (Mar. 4, 2005).

[73] *See generally* 42 U.S.C. § 2271–2284 (2005).

[74] *See generally* Exec. Order 13,526, 75 Fed. Reg. 31,425 (2009); U.S. DEP'T OF DEF., DIRECTIVE 5210.02, ACCESS TO AND DISSEMINATION OF RESTRICTED DATA AND FORMERLY RESTRICTED DATA (June 3, 2011); U.S. DEP'T OF DEF., MANUAL 5200.1, DOD INFORMATION SECURITY PROGRAM: OVERVIEW, CLASSIFICATION, AND DECLASSIFICATION (Vol. 1) (Feb. 24, 2012) [hereinafter DOD INFORMATION SECURITY PROGRAM].

category of information and to promulgate information protection rules at lower protection levels than the information to be protected. Most Restricted Data and Formerly Restricted Data are subject to controls or protocols over and above that applicable to collateral Secret information. For example, information protected in Sigmas 15, 14, or 20 may not be processed on the SIPRnet.[75] Information caveated as Critical Nuclear Weapons Design Information (CNWDI) or Nuclear Command and Control—Extremely Sensitive Information (NC2-ESI) is subject to additional special marking and handling controls.[76] Information marked ATOMAL or ATOMIC has been shared with cleared officials of NATO or the United Kingdom, respectively.[77] Personnel requiring access to nuclear weapons in the course of their duties must meet exacting citizenship, medical, psychological, and personal conduct requirements.[78]

Even certain unclassified information may be subject to special protections when it pertains to the nuclear enterprise. "Unclassified Controlled Nuclear Information" (UCNI) includes information on security measures (including security plans, procedures, and equipment) for the physical protection of Special Nuclear Material equipment or facilities. Certain officials, including military installation commanders and officials in charge of installation protection, are designated UCNI officials and are authorized to designate and grant access to UCNI. The UCNI must be marked as such and safeguarded, transmitted, and destroyed in a way that prevents inadvertent disclosure.[79] The UCNI may be transmitted via NIPRnet only when the material is encrypted, digitally signed, and the recipient has a ".mil" or ".gov" address extension.[80]

---

[75] *See* U.S. Dep't of Def., Directive 5210.02, Access to and Dissemination of Restricted Data and Formerly Restricted Data, ¶ 2(d)(6) (June 3, 2011). The SIPRnet is the Secure Internet Protocol Router, the U.S. government's network for processing normal classified information.

[76] *See* DoD Information Security Program, *supra* note 75, at Volume 1, DoD Information Security Program: Overview, Classification, and Declassification ¶ 12.f; U.S. Dep't of Def., Chairman of the Joint Chiefs of Staff Instruction 3231.01B, Safeguarding Nuclear Command and Control Extremely Sensitive Information, *Enclosure A* (June 21, 2006) (CJCSI 3231.01B is For Official Use Only. *Available at* https://ca.dtic.mil/cjcs_directives.index.htm to authorized recipients).

[77] *See* DoD Information Security Program, *supra* note 75, at Volume 2, DoD Information Security Program: Marking of Classified Information Part II, Definitions.

[78] For information about DoD's Personnel Reliability Program, see generally U.S. Dep't of Def., Directive 5210.42-R, Nuclear Weapons Personnel Reliability Program (PRP) Regulation (June 2006). For information about the DoE's Human Reliability Program, see generally 10 C.F.R. Part 712, Human Reliability Program.

[79] *See generally* U.S. Dep't of Def., Directive 5210.83, DoD Unclassified Controlled Nuclear Information (UCNI) (July 2012).

[80] *See generally* U.S. Dep't of Def., Directive 5210.83, Identification and Protection of Unclassified Controlled Nuclear Information: Unclassified Controlled Nuclear Information (UCNI), 10 CFR Part 1017 (July 12, 2012); U.S. Dep't of Energy, Order 471.1B, Identification and Protection of Unclassified Controlled Nuclear Information (Mar. 1, 2010), *available at* https://www.directives.doe.gov/directives/0471.1-BOrder-b/view. The NIPRnet is the Non-secure Internet Protocol Router, the U.S. government's network for processing unclassified information.

C. INTERNATIONAL CONTROLS ON NUCLEAR WEAPONS

The capstone structures of the international nuclear arms control regime include the International Atomic Energy Agency (IAEA) and the Treaty on the Non-proliferation of Nuclear Weapons, better known as the Nuclear Non-proliferation Treaty (NPT). However, the greatest reduction in the global number of total nuclear weapons is attributable to bilaterally negotiated agreements between the United States and the Soviet Union (later, Russia). These and other related matters are discussed in the following paragraphs.

1. International Atomic Energy Agency

The IAEA traces its origin to a proposal made by President Dwight D. Eisenhower in a December 8, 1953, speech before the United Nations General Assembly. As part of the United States' "Atoms for Peace" initiative, he proposed an international atomic energy agency "to which the governments principally involved would make joint contributions from their stockpiles of fissile material and natural uranium."[81] This international bank for nuclear materials would exist to "take this weapon out of the hands of soldiers" and put it "into the hands of those who will know . . . how to adapt it to the arts of peace."[82] The 1954 amendments to the Atomic Energy Act authorized greater transparency and information regarding peaceful uses of nuclear energy, in part to enable the purposes of Atoms for Peace.[83]

As U.S., Soviet, and other interested parties negotiated the framework for the proposed agency, they rapidly encountered a proliferation conundrum that remains unresolved today: "The problem was that international promotion and control of atomic energy were contradictory; the success of one tended to hurt the cause of the other."[84] The technical challenges involved with dual-use technology (coupled with collective mistrust regarding others' intentions) hobbled the effort, and Eisenhower's original proposal for an international bank to control all nuclear materials was first downgraded to a proposed clearinghouse, then ultimately to an almost aspirational charter to "minimize . . . the proliferation of nuclear weapons around the world."[85] This inability to accommodate the competing values of national sovereignty, practical efficacy, and persuasive compliance hampered early nuclear arms control efforts for decades.

The IAEA Statute, when finally approved in 1957, specified several functions of the Agency to promote safe, peaceful use of nuclear energy. Most relevant for lawyers in national security or nuclear energy practice, the IAEA is chartered to

> Establish and administer safeguards designed to ensure that special fissionable and other materials, services, equipment, facilities, and information

---

[81] David Fischer, History of the IAEA: The First Forty Years 9 (1997)

[82] *Id.*

[83] *Id.* at 29.

[84] *Id.* at 33 (citing R.G. Hewlett & J.M. Holl, Atoms for Peace and War 307 (1989).

[85] *Id.* at 34 (quoting R.G. Hewlett & J.M. Holl, Atoms for Peace and War 318 (1989).

> ... are not used in such a way as to further any military purpose, and to apply safeguards, at the request of the parties, to any bilateral or multilateral arrangement, or at the request of a State, to any of that State's activities in the field of atomic energy.[86]

The United States entered into a safeguards agreement with the IAEA effective on December 9, 1980.[87]

2. Nuclear Non-proliferation Treaty

Born in the turmoil of the Cold War nuclear arms race, the IAEA remained "essentially irrelevant" for many years.[88] However, in 1970 the IAEA's role as the guarantor of peaceful uses of atomic energy was enhanced substantially by the entry into force of the NPT.[89] States joining the NPT agreed to accept IAEA safeguards, thus providing the legal basis for IAEA oversight, inspections, and reporting that was absent from the IAEA statute itself.

Several factors drove support for the NPT. Nuclear-weapons states desired to limit further proliferation; non-nuclear-weapons states wanted legal assurances of access to peaceful uses of nuclear energy and to prevent their nonnuclear adversaries from acquiring the strategic advantage of nuclear weapons.[90] A common desire to reduce catastrophe induced by miscalculation (particularly in the wake of the Cuban Missile Crisis of 1963) also played a role. Further, global commons treaties and the Treaty of Tlatelolco (both discussed in more detail below) provided a model for regional efforts to limit the spread of nuclear weapons. Ultimately, a framework establishing the "central bargain" of the NPT was reached: "[T]he NPT non-nuclear-weapon states agree never to acquire nuclear weapons and the NPT nuclear-weapon states in exchange agree to share the benefits of peaceful nuclear technology and to pursue nuclear disarmament aimed at the ultimate elimination of their nuclear arsenals."[91]

In the NPT, those states parties already possessing nuclear weapons at the time of its entry into force—that is, the United States, the Soviet Union/Russia, the United Kingdom, France, and China, collectively the "nuclear-weapon states"[92]—agreed to not transfer nuclear weapons, directly or indirectly, or to "assist, encourage, or induce" any non-nuclear-weapon state to manufacture or

---

[86] International Atomic Energy Agency Statute, 8 U.S.T. 1093, T.I.A.S. No. 3873, 276 U.N.T.S. 3, Art. III (Oct. 23, 1956).

[87] *See* Agreement between the United States of America and the International Atomic Energy Agency for the Application of Safeguards in the United States (and Protocol Thereto), 32 U.S.T. 3059, T.I.A.S. No. 9889 (Nov. 18, 1977).

[88] Fischer, *supra* note 81, at 10.

[89] Treaty on the Non-Proliferation of Nuclear Weapons, July 1, 1968, 21 U.S.T. 483; T.I.A.S. No. 6839; 729 U.N.T.S. 161 [hereinafter Nuclear Non-Proliferation Treaty].

[90] Fischer, *supra* note 81, at 95.

[91] Ambassador Thomas Graham Jr., Address at Chatham House (Nov. 5, 2004), transcript *available at* http://www.gsinstitute.org/bsg/archives/000285.html.

[92] Perhaps not coincidentally, also the five permanent members of the United Nations Security Council.

acquire nuclear weapons.[93] Non-nuclear-weapons states parties agreed to not receive, manufacture, or otherwise acquire nuclear weapons. Further, all states party to the NPT agreed to accept safeguards implemented by the IAEA to prevent "diversion of nuclear energy from peaceful uses to nuclear weapons."[94] Finally, all states parties committed to "pursue negotiations in good faith on effective measures relating to cessation of the nuclear arms race at an early date and to nuclear disarmament, and on a treaty on general and complete disarmament under strict and effective international control."[95]

Since its entry into force in 1970, most states have ratified or acceded to the NPT. However, India, Pakistan, and Israel never signed the NPT; India and Pakistan have subsequently developed nuclear weapons (conducting initial nuclear weapons tests in, respectively, 1974[96] and 1998[97]). Many media reports and expert assessments indicate that Israel also possesses a nuclear weapons capability, though neither Israel nor the United States has ever officially confirmed this.[98] North Korea became a non-nuclear-weapons state party to the NPT in 1985, but subsequently maintained an illicit nuclear weapons program. It withdrew from the NPT in 2003,[99] and in 2006 successfully tested its first nuclear device.[100] The full significance of North Korea's nascent nuclear weapons capability remains to be seen.

Several nations including Argentina, Brazil, Iran, Iraq, Libya, South Africa, South Korea, Sweden, and Taiwan had nuclear weapons programs at some point. Of these, only South Africa succeeded in building functioning nuclear warheads—which it later dismantled, becoming the only nation to renounce a successful internal nuclear weapons program.[101]

Iran—a non-nuclear-weapons state party to the NPT—is suspected of maintaining an illicit nuclear weapons program. The IAEA has reported "many failures and breaches of [Iran's] obligations to comply with its NPT Safeguards Agreement," amounting to noncompliance with IAEA safeguards.[102] The IAEA's

---

[93] Nuclear Non-Proliferation Treaty, *supra* note 89, at Article I.

[94] *Id.* at Articles II and III.

[95] *Id.* at Article VI.

[96] Fischer, *supra* note 81, at 96.

[97] *See* Paul Kerr & Mary Beth Nikitin, Cong. Research Serv., RL34248, Pakistan's Nuclear Weapons: Proliferation and Security Issues 4 (Mar. 19, 2013).

[98] Casey L. Addis, Cong. Research Serv., RL33476, Israel: Background and U.S. Relations 36 (Feb. 14, 2011).

[99] For a concise legal assessment of North Korea's withdrawal from the NPT, see Frederick Kirgis, *North Korea's Withdrawal from the Nuclear Non-proliferation Treaty*, Am. Soc'y Int'l L. (Jan. 2003), *available at* http://www.asil.org/insigh96.cfm.

[100] *See* Emma Chanlett-Avery & Ian E. Rinehart, Cong. Research Serv., R41259, North Korea: U.S. Relations, Nuclear Diplomacy, and Internal Situation 10 (Jan. 15, 2014).

[101] *See* Mary Beth Nikitin, Paul K. Kerr & Steven A. Hildreth, Cong. Research Serv., RL31559, Proliferation Control Regimes: Background and Status 8 (Oct. 25, 2012).

[102] Implementation of the NPT Safeguards Agreement in the Islamic Republic of Iran, IAEA Board of Governors Resolution, GOV/2005/77 (Sept. 24, 2005).

concerns were subsequently reported to the United Nations Security Council.[103] The threat posed by an Iranian nuclear weapons program remains one of the most serious proliferation problems today.

The NPT's disarmament provisions from Article VI (to undertake negotiations on general disarmament measures) and Article VII (the authority to conclude regional treaties to limit nuclear weapons) are the foundation of most regional or bilateral nuclear arms control initiatives.

3. Nuclear Weapon-Free Zones

"Nuclear weapon-free zones" as conceived in NPT Article VII have been established through a series of regional treaties and declarations regarding areas free of nuclear weapons. The U.N. Office of Disarmament Affairs tracks nine nuclear weapon-free zones,[104] discussed in turn below. As will be seen, the concept of a "nuclear weapon-free zone" has been implemented differently in different regions.

The Treaty of Tlatelolco established a nuclear weapon-free zone in the Caribbean and Central and South America.[105] It entered force in 1969, predating the NPT by a year. The United States ratified a protocol regarding its territories in the region, and all NPT nuclear weapon states have ratified a protocol promising respect for this area's nuclear weapon-free status.[106] Cuba became the last state in the region to become a state party, ratifying the treaty in 2002.[107] Tlatelolco does not restrict the transit or visit of ships with nuclear propulsion systems. Likewise, it does not prohibit ships and aircraft of nonmember nations visiting their ports and airfields, or to transit through their territorial seas or airspace, while armed with nuclear weapons.[108]

The Treaty of Rarotonga established a nuclear weapon-free zone in the South Pacific—historically an area used for many U.S. and U.K. nuclear weapons tests.[109] There are three protocols pertaining to nuclear weapons states with territories in the treaty's zone of applicability; the United States has signed but not ratified each of them. The text of the treaty does not prohibit temporary presence

---

[103] Implementation of the NPT Safeguards Agreement in the Islamic Republic of Iran, IAEA Board of Governors, Resolution GOV/2006/14 (Feb. 4, 2006).

[104] *See* website of the United Nations Office of Disarmament Affairs, http://www.un.org/disarmament/WMD/ Nuclear/NWFZ.shtm (last visited Aug. 18, 2014).

[105] *See* Treaty for the Prohibition of Nuclear Weapons in Latin America, Feb. 14, 1967, 22 U.S.T. 762, T.I.A.S. No. 7137, 634 U.N.T.S. 281.

[106] *See* Additional Protocol II to the Treaty for the Prohibition of Nuclear Weapons in Latin America, Feb. 14, 1967, 22 U.S.T. 754, T.I.A.S. No. 7137, 634 U.N.T.S. 364.

[107] *Status of the Member States and Signatories to the Treaty of Tlatelolco* (June 10, 2007), *available at* http://www.opanal.org/Docs/t_tlatelolco/States_en.pdf (OPANAL, Organismo para la Proscription de las Armas Nuclearas en la America Latina el Caribe, is the organization established to implement Tlatelolco).

[108] *See* Commander's Handbook on the Law of Naval Operations NWP 1-14M, ¶ 10.2.2.4. (July 2007).

[109] *See generally* South Pacific Nuclear Free Zone Treaty, Aug. 6, 1985, 1445 U.N.T.S. 177.

of state-owned nuclear-powered or nuclear-armed ships or aircraft; however Article 5 provides that:

> Each Party . . . remains free to decide for itself whether to allow visits by foreign ships and aircraft to its ports and airfields, transit of its airspace by foreign aircraft, and navigation by foreign ships in its territorial sea or archipelagic waters in a manner not covered by the rights of innocent passage, archipelagic sea lane passage or transit passage of straits.[110]

Two states party to Rarotonga are also parties to a U.S. mutual defense treaty: the Australia, New Zealand, United States Security Treaty (commonly known as ANZUS).[111] Australia has not prohibited transit of nuclear-powered or nuclear-armed U.S. ships, but New Zealand has.[112] New Zealand's decision prompted the United States and New Zealand to suspend their obligations toward each other under ANZUS,[113] although the ANZUS remains applicable between the United States and Australia and between Australia and New Zealand.[114]

The Southeast Asia Nuclear Weapon-Free Zone Treaty (also known as the Treaty of Bangkok) establishes a nuclear weapon-free zone among the ten nations that are members of the Association of Southeast Asian Nations (ASEAN).[115] Each ASEAN member state has ratified the treaty. The treaty obligates member states to not possess or acquire nuclear weapons, to not permit their stationing within its territory, to not transfer fissionable material or related equipment to any nonnuclear weapon state, and to only provide such materials to nuclear weapon states in accordance with IAEA safeguards.[116] A protocol to the treaty is open for signature by nuclear weapon states; it would expand the zone of application to continental shelves and exclusive economic zones of member states, and would provide negative security assurances—specifically, the commitment to not use nuclear weapons against any state party or protocol party within the zone of application.[117] To date, no nuclear weapon state has signed the protocol.[118]

---

[110] *Id.* at Article 5.

[111] *See* Security Treaty (ANZUS Pact), U.S.-Austl.-N.Z., Sept. 1, 1951, 3 U.S.T. 3420, T.I.A.S. No. 2493, 131 U.N.T.S. 83.

[112] Initially, New Zealand's decision consisted only in the denial of a requested port call by a U.S. ship. *See* Amy L. Catalinac, *Why New Zealand Took Itself out of ANZUS: Observing "Opposition for Autonomy" in Asymmetric Alliances*, 6 Foreign Policy Analysis 318 (2010). Following suspension of U.S.-New Zealand assurances under ANZUS, New Zealand codified this position. *See* The New Zealand Nuclear Free Zone, Disarmament, and Arms Control Act 1987, Pub. Act 1987 No. 86 (June 8, 1987).

[113] *Id.* at 317–19.

[114] *See* U.S. Dep't of State, Treaties In Force, 354–55 (Jan. 1, 2011).

[115] Southeast Asia Nuclear Weapon-Free Zone Treaty, December 15, 1995, 1981 U.N.T.S. 130.

[116] *Id.*

[117] *Southeast Asia Nuclear-Weapon-Free Zone Treaty (Treaty of Bangkok)*, (March 1, 2013), James Martin Center for Nonproliferation Studies, Monterey Institute of International Studies, http://cns.miis.edu/inventory/pdfs/seanwfz.pdf (last viewed Aug. 19, 2014).

[118] *See* Peter Crail & Xiaodon Liang, *Southeast Asia Nuclear Weapon-Free Zone and the Nuclear-Weapon States*, Asia Pacific Bulletin, No. 148, 1 (Feb. 7, 2012).

The Treaty of Pelindaba (concluded at the site of South Africa's nuclear research facility), establishes Africa as a nuclear weapon-free zone.[119] To date, fifty-one of fifty-three African Union member states have signed the treaty; of these, thirty have ratified it.[120] Additional protocols to the Treaty, open to nuclear weapon states, prohibit use of nuclear weapons against any state party or against any protocol party in the zone of application.[121] All NPT nuclear weapons states have signed and ratified the additional protocols for which their responsibilities on the African continent make them eligible, except for the United States (which has signed, but not ratified, Protocols I and II).[122]

The Treaty on a Nuclear Weapon-Free-Zone in Central Asia establishes Kazakhstan, Kyrgyzstan, Tajikistan, Turkmenistan, and Uzbekistan, each of whom has ratified it, as a nuclear weapon-free zone.[123] The treaty prohibits the development or stationing of nuclear weapons in its territory. It defers to state parties questions regarding temporary transit of nuclear weapons aboard other states ships or aircraft.[124] A protocol to this treaty, providing assurances of no use of nuclear weapons against parties to the treaty, was signed by each of the NPT nuclear weapon states in May 2014.[125]

By domestic legislation, Mongolia declared itself a nuclear weapon-free zone. Its domestic legislation prohibits use, testing, storage, stationing, or transporting of nuclear weapons, or nuclear weapons-related waste or materials, within the territory or airspace of Mongolia.[126]

Finally, three treaties establish nuclear weapons-free zones in areas reserved as global commons.[127] The Antarctica Treaty prohibits testing or placement of

---

[119] African Nuclear Weapon-Free Zone Treaty, Apr. 11, 1996, 35 I.L.M. 698.

[120] *African Union List of Countries Which Have Signed, Ratified/Acceded to the African Nuclear Weapon-Free Zone Treaty (The Treaty of Pelindaba)*, (Aug. 27, 2010), African Union, http://www.africa-union.org/root/au/documents /treaties/List/Pelindaba%20Treaty.pdf. Morocco (the only African state not in the African Union) has also signed, but not ratified, the treaty. *See* U.S. Dep't of State, Treaty of Pelindaba, http://www.state.gov/t/isn/4699.htm#signatory (last visited Oct. 8, 2012).

[121] *African Nuclear Weapon Free Zone Treaty (Treaty of Pelindaba)*, United Nations Office for Disarmament Affairs, http://disarmament.un.org/treaties/t/pelindaba (April 11, 2006) (last visited Aug. 19, 2014).

[122] *Id.*

[123] *Treaty on a Nuclear-Weapon-Free Zone in Central Asia (CANWFZ)* (September 8, 2006), United Nations Office for Disarmament Affairs, http://disarmament.un.org/treaties/t/canwfz (last visited Aug. 19, 2014).

[124] *Id.* at Article 4.

[125] *United States Signs Protocol to Central Asian Nuclear-Weapon Free Zone Treaty* (May 6, 2014), United States Department of State, http://www.state.gov/r/pa/prs/ps/2014/05/225681.htm (last visited Aug. 19, 2014).

[126] The "Law of Mongolia on its nuclear weapon-free status," adopted on Feb. 3, 2000 was forwarded to the U.N. General Assembly by Mongolia's Ambassador to the United Nations. It was subsequently distributed as U.N. General Assembly, 55th Session, *General and Complete Disarmament: Mongolia's International Security and Nuclear Weapon-Free Status* (A/55/56) (New York, 2000).

[127] Though two of these treaties predate the Nuclear Non-Proliferation Treaty, which entered force in 1970, their provisions are consistent with the nuclear weapons-free zone concept found at Article VII of that treaty.

nuclear weapons in Antarctica. Article 5 prohibits nuclear weapons specifically; Article 1 restricts use of Antarctica for "peaceful purposes only," with "military activity, such as weapons testing" specifically prohibited, and presumptively banning nonnuclear WMD and other offensive weapons as well.[128] The Seabed Arms Control Treaty prohibits placement of nuclear weapons or other "weapons of mass destruction" (not defined in the treaty) on the international seabed.[129] The Outer Space Treaty, specifically Article IV, prohibits parties from placing nuclear weapons or any other kinds of WMD either in orbit around the Earth, elsewhere in outer space, or on celestial bodies to include the Moon.[130] The United States is a party to each of these treaties.

4. Bilateral U.S.-Soviet/Russian Nuclear Arms Control Agreements

Since the NPT's entry into force, the United States and the Soviet Union (later Russia), the two nations responsible for the vast majority of the world's nuclear weapons, have concluded a series of bilateral arms control agreements. Strategic Arms Limitation Talks in the early 1970s resulted in two agreements in 1972: an Interim Agreement on Offensive Arms (commonly known as SALT I),[131] and the Anti-Ballistic Missile Treaty (ABM Treaty).[132] The ABM Treaty limited each side to two ABM systems—limited in range and capability—one protecting each party's national capital, and one protecting another site.[133] The ABM Treaty was a "cornerstone of the Cold War policy of 'mutually assured destruction,' an understanding that without ABM defenses neither side would risk starting a nuclear war because it knew the other side would massively retaliate, thus ensuring the widespread destruction of both nations."[134]

SALT I froze authorized numbers of inter-continental ballistic missile (ICBM) launchers (1,054 for the United States and 1,618 for the Soviet Union) and permitted deployment of up to 710 submarine-launched ballistic missile

---

[128] Antarctic Treaty, Dec. 1, 1959, 12 U.S.T. 794, T.I.A.S. No. 4780, 402 U.N.T.S. 71.

[129] Treaty on the Prohibition of the Emplacement of Nuclear Weapons and other Weapons of Mass Destruction on the Sea-Bed and the Ocean Floor and in the Subsoil Thereof, Feb. 7, 1971, 23 U.S.T. 701, T.I.A.S. No. 7337, 955 U.N.T.S. 115.

[130] Treaty on Principles Governing the Activities of States in the Exploration and Use of Outer Space, Including the Moon and Other Celestial Bodies, Jan. 27, 1967, 18 U.S.T. 2410, T.I.A.S. No. 6347, 610 U.N.T.S. 205.

[131] Interim Agreement between the United States of America and the Union of Soviet Socialist Republics on Certain Measures with Respect to the Limitation of Strategic Offensive Arms, U.S.-Russ., May 27, 1972, 23 U.S.T. 3462, 7504, 94 U.N.T.S. 3.

[132] Treaty on the Limitation of Anti-Ballistic Missile Systems, May 26, U.S.-Russ., 1972, 23 U.S.T. 3435, T.IA.S. No. 7503, 944 U.N.T.S. 13.

[133] *Id.*, Art. III.

[134] Kucinich v. Bush, 236 F. Supp. 2d 1, 16 (D.D.C. 2002). The quoted background on the ABM Treaty is taken from a memorandum opinion by Judge John D. Bates dismissing a legal challenge to President Bush's 2002 withdrawal of the United States from the ABM Treaty. Thirty-two members of the U.S. House of Representatives challenged the President's authority to withdraw from the treaty without the same advice and consent of the Senate that had been required to enter it. Judge Bates dismissed the petition as raising a nonjusticiable political question.

(SLBM) launchers on forty-four U.S. submarines, and up to 950 SLBM launchers on sixty-two Soviet submarines.[135] SALT II, negotiated in June 1979, would have limited the U.S. and Soviet nuclear forces to 2,250 total delivery vehicles (ICBM silos, SLBM launch tubes, or heavy bombers) each; however, after the Soviet invasion of Afghanistan in December 1979, President Jimmy Carter declined to submit the agreement to Congress for ratification.[136]

Bilateral discussions continued after the failure of SALT II, and in the 1987 Intermediate-Range Nuclear Forces (INF) Treaty, the United States and Soviet Union agreed to destroy all intermediate-range and shorter-range ballistic missiles (and ground-launched cruise missiles).[137] The INF treaty marked two significant milestones in arms control history: first, it established an intrusive verification regime—including short-notice, on-site inspections, and second, it eliminated entire classes of modern and effective weapons.[138]

Further negotiations on strategic nuclear weapons continued and culminated in 1991's Strategic Arms Reduction Treaty (START), which continued the multi-faceted verification regime first implemented in INF and established new limits on both delivery systems (each side limited to 1,600 strategic nuclear delivery vehicles and 6,000 total warheads), with a complex "attribution" system in which some delivery systems had a specified number of warheads attributed to them, regardless of the actual loadout.[139] Both sides reached their agreed START limits by 2001,[140] although the 1991 breakup of the Soviet Union presented an intervening international legal challenge: about 30 percent of the Soviet nuclear weapons force was deployed under Soviet (later Russian) control in the territories of what became Kazakhstan, Ukraine, and Belarus. In May 1992, the United States signed a protocol with Russia, Kazakhstan, Ukraine, and Belarus making them all states parties to START. The leaders of Kazakhstan, Ukraine, and Belarus agreed to eliminate nuclear weapons from their territory (accomplished by 1996) and by 1994, all had joined the NPT as non-nuclear weapons states.[141]

In November 2001, President George W. Bush announced that the United States would unilaterally reduce its nuclear force to between 1,700 and 2,200 "operationally

---

[135] Interim Agreement between the United States of America and the Union of Soviet Socialist Republics on Certain Measures with Respect to the Limitation of Strategic Offensive Arms, U.S.-Russ., May 27, 1972, 23 U.S.T. 3462, 7504, 94 U.N.T.S. 3.

[136] *See* Amy Woolf, Mary Beth Nikitin & Paul Kerr, Cong. Research Serv., RL33865, Arms Control and Nonproliferation: A Catalog of Treaties and Agreements 6 (July 21, 2014).

[137] *See generally* Treaty on the Elimination of their Intermediate-Range and Shorter-Range Missiles, with Memorandum of Understanding and Protocols, U.S.-Russ., Dec. 8, 1987, 1657 U.N.T.S. 2.

[138] Woolf et al., *supra* note 136, at 7.

[139] Amy Woolf, Cong. Research Serv., R41219, The New START Treaty: Central Limits and Key Provisions 3 (Apr. 8, 2014).

[140] Colin Powell, U.S. Sec'y of State, Statement on the Achievement of the Final Reductions under the START Treaty (Dec. 5, 2001), http://2001-2009.state.gov/secretary/former/powell/remarks/2001/dec/6674.htm.

[141] *Id.* at 8.

deployed" nuclear warheads.[142] A similar commitment was later codified in the 2002 Strategic Offensive Reductions Treaty (SORT), which imposed a limit between 1,700 and 2,200 "strategic nuclear warheads," without elaboration of counting rules or verification protocols.[143]

Before START entered force on December 5, 1994, the United States and Russia were already negotiating START II, which would have (among other things) limited both sides to 3,000–3,500 warheads, banned all ICBMs with multiple re-entry vehicles, and limited each side to 1,750 warheads on SLBMs. START II was signed in January 1993 and ratified by the United States in January 1996. However, separate negotiations on the future of the ABM treaty held up ratification by the Russian Duma.[144] Ultimately, President George W. Bush withdrew the United States from the ABM Treaty in 2002. Administration statements at the time defended the withdrawal from the ABM treaty by arguing that in the three decades since START, the strategic relationship with Russia had become cooperative rather than adversarial and that threats from regional powers armed with WMD necessitated developing an ABM system.[145] Since the U.S. withdrawal from the ABM Treaty, the United States has begun testing and fielding systems to defend against the ballistic missile threat presented by regional and theater actors (primarily Iran and North Korea).[146] However, regaining the ability to develop ABM systems came at a cost to the arms control framework: after the U.S. withdrawal from the ABM treaty in June 2002, Russia withdrew from START II, and the treaty never entered into force.[147]

START expired on December 5, 2009, as U.S. and Russian negotiators continued meetings toward what became the current U.S.–Russian nuclear arms control treaty: "New START" was ultimately signed in April 2010, and entered into force on February 5, 2011.[148] New START contains three principal limits on strategic nuclear forces. First, each side may have no more than 800 nuclear weapon delivery vehicles: ICBMs, SLBM launchers, and heavy bombers capable of delivering nuclear weapons. Second, of these, only 700 such launchers may be deployed (i.e., not a test platform and not "located at a repair facility or production facility").

---

[142] Amy Woolf, Cong. Research Serv., R40084, Strategic Arms Control after START: Issues and Options, 9–10 (Mar. 4, 2010).

[143] Treaty between the Russian Federation and the United States of America on Strategic Offensive Reductions, U.S.-Russ., May 24, 2002, 41 I.L.M. 700 (2002).

[144] Amy Woolf, Cong. Research Serv., IB98030, Nuclear Arms Control: The U.S.-Russian Agenda 5–6 (Jan. 3, 2006).

[145] Richard Boucher, State Department Spokesman, Statement Releasing Text of Diplomatic Notes Sent to Russia, Belarus, Kazakhstan and the Ukraine (Dec. 14, 2001), *available at* http://www.acq.osd.mil/tc/treaties/abm/ABMdipnotes1.htm.

[146] *See* U.S. Dep't of Def., Ballistic Missile Defense Review Report, 15–28 (Feb. 2010), *available at* http://www.defense.gov/bmdr/.

[147] *See Treaty with Russia on Measures for Further Reduction and Limitation of Strategic Offensive Arms (The New START Treaty)*, Exec. Rept. 111-6, 49, U.S. Senate, 111th Congress, 2d Session, Oct. 1, 2010.

[148] Measures for the Further Reduction and Limitation of Strategic Offensive Arms, U.S.-Russ., April 8, 2010, S. Treaty Doc. No. 111-5, 2010 WL 2568202.

TABLE 22.1 } U.S. and Russian Nuclear Force Levels

	Nuclear Force Levels as of July 1, 2009[1]		New START limits	Nuclear Force Levels as of March 1, 2015[2]	
	US	Russia	Both	US	Russia
Total delivery vehicles	–	–	800	898	890
Deployed delivery vehicles	1,188	809	700	785	515
Total Attributed Warheads	5,916	3,897	1,500	1,597	1,582

[1] U.S. Dep't of State, Fact Sheet—START Aggregate Numbers of Strategic Offensive Arms, Bureau of Arms Control, Verification and Compliance (Apr. 6, 2012), http://www.state.gov/documents/organization/130361.pdf. Note this data does not include total versus deployed launchers (these were not distinguished under START), and the warhead totals are those attributed under START's counting rules. "Delivery vehicles" is here defined as ICBMs, SLBMs, and heavy bombers equipped to carry nuclear weapons. *Id.*

[2] U.S. Dep't of State, Fact Sheet—New START Treaty Aggregate Numbers of Strategic Offensive Arms, Bureau of Arms Control, Verification and Compliance (Apr. 1, 2015), http://www.state.gov/documents/organization/240274.pdf.

Finally, each side may deploy no more than 1,550 nuclear warheads.[149] Under New START counting rules, each warhead deployed on an ICBM or SLBM is counted, while each bomber equipped for carrying and delivering nuclear weapons counts as one warhead.[150] New START also provides an extensive verification regime, including short-notice on-site inspections. Table 22.1 summarizes U.S. and Russian attributed nuclear force levels under New START, based on data provided national disclosures filed pursuant to New START. The 2009 data was filed at New START's entry into force; the 2015 data reflects the most current national disclosures.

5. Other International Legal Controls

Two other treaty regimes warrant brief mention here. First, the Treaty on Open Skies provides for states parties to the treaty to conduct unarmed aerial observation flights, using commercially available imaging technology, over the territory of other states parties to monitor and verify arms control treaty obligations.[151] Prior coordination with the state to be observed (at least seventy-two hours in advance) is required before flights under the treaty. Observation flights are allocated among states parties, and no state may fly more than one-half of its allocated quota over any other single state party.[152] The United States, Russia,

[149] *Id.*

[150] Amy Woolf, Cong. Research Serv., R41219, The New START Treaty: Central Limits and Key Provisions 4–13 (Apr. 8, 2014). Woolf cites administration officials who assert that this "discounting" of nuclear weapons attributed to heavy bombers enhances strategic stability, as bombers are viewed as less destabilizing than ballistic missiles. *Id.* at 28.

[151] *See generally* Treaty on Open Skies, March 24, 1992, S. Treaty Doc. 102.37 (1992).

[152] *Id.* Annex A. The quotas for the Nuclear Non-Proliferation Treaty Nuclear Weapons States are: United States – 42; Russia; 42; France – 12; United Kingdom – 12. China is not a state party to the Treaty on Open Skies, nor are India, Pakistan, Israel, North Korea, or Iran.

and several European nations are states parties to the treaty. The U.S. Air Force and the Defense Threat Reduction Agency conduct treaty monitoring aboard the OC-135B "Open Skies" aircraft.[153] Between entry into force and December 2011, over 835 observation flights have been conducted under the treaty, including 92 flown by U.S. observers over Russia and 31 flown by Russian observers over the United States.[154]

Second, the Comprehensive Nuclear Test Ban Treaty bans all nuclear explosions, for test purposes or otherwise.[155] The treaty was ratified by Russia and many other states, but cannot enter force unless also ratified by all states that operated nuclear reactors as of 1996.[156] Entry into force is therefore contingent on China, North Korea, Egypt, Iran, Israel, Pakistan, and the United States ratifying the treaty; this has not yet happened.[157] Under President Bill Clinton, the United States signed the treaty and submitted it for ratification; however, the Senate voted against ratification.[158] Opponents of ratification noted at the time that "we may find at some future time that we cannot diagnose or remedy a problem in a warhead critical to the U.S. nuclear deterrent without conducting a nuclear test."[159] Nevertheless, the United States has observed a voluntary nuclear test moratorium since 1993.[160]

IV. Responding to WMD-Related Incidents

In addition to the danger posed by state actors deliberately using WMD, the very existence of such weapons presents the risk that dangerous forces will be released by accident or sabotage (such as a terrorist attack). Most of the guidance regarding WMD incidents pertains to nuclear weapons, as the U.S. chemical and biological weapons capabilities are limited to non-lethal riot control agents and to WMD defense programs. However, the guidance regarding nuclear weapons incidents—particularly with regard to the legal issues involved—can generally

---

[153] AIR COMBAT COMMAND, OC-135 OPEN SKIES FACT SHEET, http://www.af.mil/AboutUs/FactSheets/Display/tabid/224/Article/104496/oc-135b-open-skies.aspx (last visited Aug. 19, 2014).

[154] Open Skies Treaty Observation Flights, Open Skies Consultative Commission, U.S. Delegation, OSCC.DEL/5/12/Corr.1 (Feb. 24, 2012), http://www.osce.org/secretariat/68315.

[155] Comprehensive Nuclear Test-Ban Treaty, opened for signature Sept. 24, 1996, 35 I.L.M. 1439 (1996), Art. I.

[156] *See id.*, Art. XIV.

[157] *See Comprehensive Test Ban Treaty Organization Preparatory Commission*, http://www.ctbto.org/the-treaty/status-of-signature-and-ratification/ (last visited Aug. 19, 2014). The United States is a signatory to the treaty, but the Senate rejected ratification on October 13, 1999. *See* U.S. Senate, *U.S. Senate Roll Call Votes 106th Congress, 1st Session*, http://www.senate.gov/legislative/LIS/roll_call_lists/roll_call_vote_cfm.cfm?congress=106&session=1&vote=00325 (last visited Aug. 19, 2014).

[158] *See* JONATHAN MEDALIA, CONG. RESEARCH SERV., RL34394, COMPREHENSIVE NUCLEAR-TEST-BAN TREATY: BACKGROUND AND CURRENT DEVELOPMENTS 3 (Feb. 28, 2008).

[159] *Id.* at 4 (quoting a letter from Condoleeza Rice, Secretary of State, to Honorable Pete Domenici, United States Senate (June 25, 2007)).

[160] *Id.* at 2.

be applied to chemical or biological-related incidents in the absence of other guidance. In concert with various federal agencies, the Department of Defense maintains Nuclear Weapon Accident Response Procedures (DoD NARP), which provide detailed guidance for responding to this unique crisis situation.[161] Some of the legal issues associated with implementing DoD NARP are discussed below.

A "nuclear weapon incident" is "a nuclear weapon accident or an intentional hostile event involving a nuclear weapon, facility, or component."[162] Department of Defense guidance is to treat all U.S. nuclear weapon incidents as the result of a hostile act unless and until an incident is determined to be an "accident."[163] The immediate objectives when responding to a possibly hostile nuclear weapons incident are to recover the weapon (if physical control of the weapon was compromised), to secure the weapon from further interference, and to minimize the risk of releasing dangerous forces. Protocols and authorities, the details of which are sensitive information, exist to accomplish these vital objectives.

While treating a nuclear weapons incident as hostile until proven otherwise is operationally necessary, it quickly presents a legal issue: a hostile act—such as attempted sabotage or theft—involving a U.S. nuclear weapon (or any attempted or completed use of any weapon of mass destruction within the United States without proper authority) is a federal crime for which the Federal Bureau of Investigation (FBI) exercises primary investigative jurisdiction.[164] In addition to the other challenges that this situation presents, legal advisors should advise responsible officials that the incident site should be treated as a crime scene and (to the extent operationally feasible) preserved for forensic analysis. The on-scene commander should anticipate the need to work closely with FBI officials to provide FBI access to the incident site, while ensuring the safety and security of nuclear materials. [165] The Posse Comitatus Act generally prohibits the use of U.S. armed forces for law enforcement purposes.[166] However, there are several exceptions to the Act. Of relevance here, the Attorney General is authorized to

---

[161] *See generally* U.S. Dep't of Def., Department of Defense Manual 3150.08-M, Nuclear Weapon Accident Response Procedures (Aug. 22, 2013).

[162] U.S. Dep't of Def., Department of Defense Instruction 3150.10, Response to U.S. Nuclear Weapon Incidents 17 (July 7, 2010).

[163] *Id.* at ¶ 4.b. A nuclear weapon "accident" refers to a technical or mechanical mishap that could potentially damage a nuclear weapon. A nuclear weapon "incident" is a broader term for any situation in which a nuclear weapon could be lost, damaged, or detonated without authority. An "incident" could refer to an accident, but could also refer to a hostile attempt to steal, sabotage, or detonate a nuclear weapon. The "incident first" presumption means that U.S. forces will respond to a crisis involving a nuclear weapon as if the crisis was the result of a hostile act, unless and until they confirm otherwise. *Id.*

[164] *See* 18 U.S.C. § 832, (2004) (Participation in Nuclear and Weapons of Mass Destruction Threats to the United States).

[165] *See generally* U.S. Dep't of Just. Office of the Inspector General, Audit Division, The Federal Bureau of Investigation's Weapons of Mass Destruction Program, Audit Report 09-36 (Sept. 2009).

[166] *See* 18 U.S.C. § 1385 (1878) (Use of Army and Air Force as posse comitatus).

request military support to law enforcement efforts to respond to and investigate crimes involving special nuclear materials or WMD.[167]

Although policy dictates an "incident-first" approach to a nuclear incident response, to date all serious mishaps concerning U.S. nuclear weapons have been the result of accidents.[168] Most military accidents—including those involving nuclear weapons or chemical or biological agents—have the potential to raise legal issues, including three issues selected for discussion below.

First, to the extent sensitive information or material important to national security is compromised off-base within the United States, it may be necessary to declare a National Defense Area. A National Defense Area is an emergency extension of a commander's authority (including the authority to deny access to an area) onto nonmilitary property.[169] To the extent possible, requirements for securing an accident site should be negotiated with affected landowners and be enforced by civilian law enforcement authorities. However, it may be necessary to establish a National Defense Area unilaterally and to secure and enforce the area with the use of force—including lethal force—if required. The Rules for Use of Force applicable to domestic operations, including enforcement of a National Defense Area, are addressed in the Standing Rules of Engagement/Rules for Use of Force for U.S. Forces.[170]

Second, damage to private property or injury to civilian personnel resulting from a military accident may result in claims against the government.[171] Prompt payment of reasonable claims can assist commanders in maintaining public trust and confidence in the government's response to the mishap. Finally, WMD-related accidents may involve dispersal of radiological hazards or chemical or biological agents, with resulting public health and environmental consequences. Depending

---

[167] 18 U.S.C. § 831 (1982) (Prohibited transactions involving nuclear materials); 10 U.S.C § 382 (1996) (Emergency situations involving weapons of mass destruction). For procedures on how DoD support is requested, see generally U.S. Dep't of Def., Department of Defense Directive 3025.21, Defense Support of Civilian Law Enforcement Agencies (Feb. 27, 2013).

[168] Most U.S. nuclear weapons incidents involved aviation mishaps with nuclear weapons on-board the mishap aircraft. The great majority of such incidents occurred during Cold War-era airborne alert flights. *See generally* U.S. Dep't of Def., Department of Defense Narrative Summaries of Accidents Involving U.S. Nuclear Weapons 1950–1980 (April 1981), *available at* http://www.dod.mil/pubs/foi/operation_and_plans/NuclearChemicalBiologicalMatters/635.pdf (Department of Defense online Freedom of Information Act reading room).

[169] *See* 50 U.S.C. § 797 (Penalty for violation of security regulations and orders). *See also* U.S. Dep't of Def., Instruction 5200.08, Sec'y of DoD Installations and Resources (Dec. 10, 2005). Because 50 U.S.C. § 797 does not apply extraterritorially, National Defense Areas may not be established overseas.

[170] *See generally* Joint Chiefs of Staff, Instr. 3121.01B, The Standing Rules of Engagement/Standing Rules for the Use of Force for U.S. Forces (June 13, 2005) [hereinafter SROE], and this book's chapter on Rules of Engagement.

[171] Depending on the circumstances, claims may be styled under one of several claims authorities, including 8 U.S.C. §§ 1346(b), 2401, 2671–2680 (2013) (Federal Tort Claims Act), 10 U.S.C. § 2733 (1996) (Military Claims Act), 10 U.S.C. § 2734 (2006) (Foreign Claims Act), 10 U.S.C. § 2734(a)–(b) (2006) (International Agreements Claims Act), and possibly (though not likely) 31 U.S.C. § 3721 (1996) (Personnel Claims Act).

on the nature and location of the damage, there may be reporting and/or remediation requirements.[172]

V. Weapons of Mass Destruction in U.S. Military Operations

The preceding discussion has largely provided background and context for the WMD-related legal issues of special relevance for U.S. military operations, which will be addressed below.

A. SPECIAL AND CONVENTIONAL OPERATIONS TO COUNTER PROLIFERATION

Weapons of mass destruction in the hands of an adversary are a threat to be defeated or mitigated. Common to all types of hostile threats involving WMD is the possibility that national leaders will direct that military operations be part of the national response. In theory, any element of the U.S. armed forces could be given a mission designed to counter a WMD threat. In practice, however, unit capability and national policy limits certain types of counter-WMD missions to designated special purpose forces.

Historical examples of operations conducted to counter threats involving WMD span the spectrum of conflict and the range of military capabilities. At the high end, it can include major theater war, such as the 2003 Iraq war.[173] Operations to counter WMD threats may include more limited raids and strikes, such as Israel's 1980 bombing of Iraq's nuclear reactor site at Osirak[174] and of Syria's nuclear reactor site at Dair Alzour in 2007.[175] Both sites were destroyed before the reactors—believed

---

[172] *See generally* DEP'T OF DEF., DEPARTMENT OF DEFENSE INSTRUCTION 4715.6, ENVIRONMENTAL COMPLIANCE (Apr. 24, 1996).

[173] Detailed discussion of the international legal basis for the Iraq War is beyond the scope of this chapter. Relevant here is that several U.N. Security Council Resolutions applicable at the time (including UNSCRs 687, 707, 715, 986, 1284, and 1441) called on Iraq to cease all chemical and biological weapons programs and to permit inspections by IAEA and U.N. Special Commission—UNSCOM (later U.N. Monitoring, Verification and Inspection Commission—UNMOVIC) officials. As late as February 2003, in UNMOVIC's last report to the Security Council before the war began, inspectors had not yet verified several WMD and missile program disarmament requirements, and lamented:

> During the period of time covered by the present report, Iraq could have made greater efforts to find any remaining proscribed items or provide credible evidence showing the absence of such items. The results in terms of disarmament have been very limited so far.... It is hard to understand why a number of the measures, which are now being taken, could not have been initiated earlier. If they had been taken earlier, they might have borne fruit by now.

Twelfth Quarterly Report of the Executive Chairman of the United Nations Monitoring, Verification and Inspection Commission in accordance with paragraph 12 of Security Council resolution 1284 (1999), U.N. Sec'y Council, Annex, at ¶ 73 S/2003/232 (Feb. 28, 2003).

[174] *See generally* ROGER CLAIRE, RAID ON THE SUN (2005).

[175] International Atomic Energy Agency, *Implementation of the NPT Safeguards Agreement in the Syrian Arab Republic*, ¶ 2, GOV/2012/42 (Aug. 30, 2012).

to be associated with nuclear weapons programs—became operational. At the low end, countering WMD may include targeting of individual key personnel associated with nuclear weapons programs,[176] or covert action to disrupt or sabotage such programs. Operations like these could be conducted under very different operational authorities and rules of engagement. However, identifying the issues raised by a counterproliferation mission requires basic familiarity with the international WMD legal regimes discussed above.

B. ENSURING LAW OF WAR AND TREATY COMPLIANCE

Attorneys for the armed forces play a key role in ensuring compliance with the law of war and with arms-control treaties to which the United States is a party. The Department of Defense requires all weapons procured for U.S. armed forces to receive a legal review for compliance with the law of war.[177] The required echelon for legal review is normally reserved to high levels within a military service, but varies depending on the type of weapon, whether the weapon is part of a Special Access Program, and various service-specific delegations of authority.[178] Some service guidance prompts reviewers to consider specific WMD-related arms-control treaties. Whether required by service regulations or not, a thorough law-of-war legal review should consider whether a weapon's attributes may cause it to amount to a nuclear, radiological, chemical, or biological weapon. This aspect of a law-of-war compliance review may be very straightforward for a new rifle or new high-explosive bomb; it may be more nuanced for weapons incorporating high-energy lasers, directed energy, nanotechnology, or physical materials developed through breakthroughs in chemistry, physics, or the natural sciences. New technologies may blur the lines between categories of legacy weapon systems and present issues not foreseen in current arms-control treaties. Issues with

---

[176] Several scientists associated with Iran's nuclear program have been killed in recent years. *See, e.g.*, Farnaz Fassihi & Jay Solomon, *Scientist Killing Stokes U.S.-Iran Tensions*, WALL ST. J., Jan. 12, 2012, *available at* http://online.wsj.com/article/SB10001424052970204257504577153980963513686.html.

[177] *See* Protocol Additional to the Geneva Conventions of 12 August 1949, and Relating to the Protection of Victims of International Armed Conflict (Protocol I) Art. 36, June 8, 1977, 1125 U.N.T.S. 3. Article 36 states:

> In the study, development, acquisition or adoption of a new weapon, means or method of warfare, a High Contracting Party is under an obligation to determine whether its employment would, in some or all circumstances, be prohibited by this Protocol or by any other rule of international law applicable to the High Contracting Party.

Id.

[178] *See generally* U.S. DEP'T OF DEF., DEPARTMENT OF DEFENSE DIRECTIVE 5000.01, THE DEFENSE ACQUISITION SYSTEM (May 12, 2003); U.S. DEP'T OF DEF., ARMY REGULATION 27-53, REVIEW OF LEGALITY OF WEAPONS UNDER INTERNATIONAL LAW (Jan. 1, 1979); U.S. DEP'T OF DEF., SECRETARY OF THE NAVY INSTRUCTION 5000.2E, IMPLEMENTATION AND OPERATION OF THE DEFENSE ACQUISITION SYSTEM AND THE JOINT CAPABILITIES INTEGRATION AND DEVELOPMENT SYSTEM (Sept. 1, 2011); U.S. DEP'T OF DEF., AIR FORCE INSTRUCTION 51-402, LEGAL REVIEWS OF WEAPONS AND CYBER CAPABILITIES (July 27, 2011).

the potential to raise novel legal or national policy challenges should be identified as early as possible in the legal review process.

Additionally, many military organizations (and Department of Defense contractor-operated facilities) are subject to inspection under various WMD-related arms-control treaties. Within the U.S. government, the Department of State (more specifically, its Bureau of Arms Control, Verification, and Compliance) is the lead agency for coordinating treaty compliance activities.[179] The Defense Threat Reduction Agency (DTRA) serves as the Department of Defense lead for implementation of inspection, escort, and monitoring provisions of arms-control agreements applicable to the Department of Defense.[180] Inspection and monitoring requirements and protocols vary by treaty. For example, within one hour of designating a site for a New START compliance inspection, "pre-inspection restrictions" take effect, effectively halting many operations and maintenance activities at the inspected site until the inspection is complete.[181] Legal advisors to affected organizations should be prepared to advise their supporting Treaty Compliance Office on the applicability of arms-control treaty compliance and verification requirements to unit activities. Additionally, in the absence of a dedicated Treaty Compliance Office, inspection coordination responsibilities may fall in part to the supporting legal advisor.

Arms-control treaty compliance issues can arise outside the verification inspection context as well. To address matters that may arise this way, the Department of Defense established a Compliance Review Group under the general supervision of the Under Secretary of Defense for Acquisition, Technology, and Logistics for most arms control treaties.[182] "Any action, including but not limited to research, tests, development, exercises and operations that reasonably raise an issue of DoD compliance with an arms control agreement" should be coordinated in advance with the appropriate Compliance Review Group.[183] For example, a unit seeking to purchase certain general-purpose laboratory equipment for the purpose of testing methods of disabling an adversary chemical weapons laboratory in a non-permissive environment may find that the purchase raises an issue of compliance with the Chemical Weapons Convention. Prior coordination of such matters through the appropriate Compliance Review

---

[179] U.S. Senate, *National Security Bureaucracy for Arms Control, Counterproliferation, and Nonproliferation: The Role of the Department of State—Parts I and II*, May 15 and June 6, 2008, (S. Hrg. 110-679) Washington: Government Printing Office (2008).

[180] U.S. Dep't of Def., Department of Defense Directive 5105.62, Defense Threat Reduction Agency ¶ 5.3.2 (Nov. 28, 2005).

[181] *See* Annex on Inspection Activities to the Protocol to the Treaty between the United States of America and the Russian Federal on Measures for the Further Reduction and Limitation of Strategic Offensive Arms, Part Six, sect. I, ¶ 1(c), *available at* http://www.acq.osd.mil/tc/treaties/NST/Protocol/Annexes/NST_Protocol_Inspection_Annex.htm (last visited Aug. 19, 2014).

[182] *See* U.S. Dep't of Def., Department of Defense Directive 2060.1, Implementation of, and Compliance with, Arms Control Agreements ¶ 4.1.5. (Jan. 9, 2001).

[183] *Id.* at ¶ 4.6.7.

Group ensures that Department-level equities are accounted for, and enables full accounting of matters that may implicate national quantity or volume limits.

As a final note regarding law-of-war compliance and WMD, practitioners should bear in mind that any violation of the law of war—including proscribed use of WMD—must be reported.[184] Combatant commands normally promulgate detailed guidance for how such reports should be forwarded; in all cases, reports are ultimately forwarded to the Secretary of the Army as Executive Agent for both investigating reportable incidents committed against U.S. personnel and for collecting, recording, and reporting information concerning all reportable incidents related to enemy violations of the law of war.[185]

C. RIOT CONTROL AGENTS

Although the United States works to counter the threat of WMD proliferation, it also maintains a stockpile of operational nuclear weapons (discussed below) and fields Riot Control Agents, which are covered by the Chemical Weapons Convention (CWC). Riot Control Agents are defined in the CWC as "any chemical not listed in a Schedule, which can produce rapidly in humans sensory irritation or disabling physical effects which disappear within a short time following termination of exposure."[186]

In 1975—over twenty years before ratification of the CWC—by Executive Order the United States renounced "first use" of Riot Control Agents (and chemical herbicides) as methods of warfare, but reserved the right for retaliatory use of either.[187] Upon ratification in 1997, the CWC forbade any use of Riot Control Agents (and herbicides) "as a method of warfare."[188] The CWC does not specify what uses of Riot Control Agents do not amount to a "method of warfare."[189] However, the examples of "use in war ... in defensive military modes" given in Executive Order 11850 illuminate the circumstances in which Riot Control

---

[184] *See* U.S. Dep't of Def., Department of Defense Directive 2311.01E, DoD Law of War Program ¶¶ 3.2 and 5.8 (May 9, 2006) ("Forward all reports of reportable incidents against U.S. personnel to the Secretary of the Army ..." "Reportable incident: A possible, suspected, or alleged violation of the law of war, for which there is credible information, or conduct during military operations other than war that would constitute a violation of the law of war if it occurred during an armed conflict.")

[185] *Id.* at ¶ 5.9.1.

[186] Convention on the Prohibition of the Development, Production, Stockpiling and Use of Chemical Weapons and on their Destruction, with Annexes, Jan. 13, 1993, 1974 U.N.T.S. 317, at art. II, ¶ 7.

[187] Exec. Order No. 11,850, 40 Fed. Reg. 16,187 (1975).

[188] Convention on the Prohibition of the Development, Production, Stockpiling and Use of Chemical Weapons and on their Destruction, with Annexes, Jan.13, 1993, 1974 U.N.T.S. 317, at art. I, ¶ d.5.

[189] For a survey of Riot Control Agent employment tactics predating EO 11850 and the Chemical Weapons Convention, see Lieutenant Colonel Rufus T. Brown, *U.S. Policy and the Uncertain State of Military Usage of Riot Control Agents*, U.S. Army War College (1998), *available at* http://www.dtic.mil/dtic/tr/fulltext/u2/a345882.pdf (last visited Aug. 19, 2014).

Agents could be authorized in war. These include use in areas under "direct and distinct" U.S. control (including controlling rioting prisoners of war); use to disperse civilians being used to mask or screen an attack; use during missions to rescue downed aircrew, passengers, or escaping prisoners in remotely isolated areas; and use in rear areas to protect convoys from civil disturbances, terrorists, and paramilitary organizations.[190] The CWC's prohibition against the use of Riot Control Agents "as a method of warfare" does not foreclose use in operations other than war (such as peacekeeping or counterterrorism operations) in which Riot Control Agents could be authorized.[191] Given the political sensitivity involved, and the probability that U.S. decisions in this area may affect coalition partners' legal and policy analysis, practitioners should anticipate that the scope and limits of any authorization for use of Riot Control Agents in a particular

---

[190] Exec. Order No. 11,850, 40 Fed. Reg. 16,187 (1975).

[191] This authority was addressed more fully during ratification of the Chemical Weapons Convention and was subject to twenty-eight specified conditions. *See* S. Res. 75, 105th Congress, 1st Session (Apr. 24, 1997) (enacted). Condition 26, regarding riot control agents, stated:

> Permitted Uses—Prior to the deposit of the United States instrument of ratification, the President shall certify to Congress that the United States is not restricted by the Convention in its use of riot control agents, including the use against combatants who are parties to a conflict, in any of the following cases: (i) United States not a party. — The conduct of peacetime military operations within an area of ongoing armed conflict when the United States is not a party to the conflict (such as recent use of the United States Armed Forces in Somalia, Bosnia, and Rwanda). (ii) Consensual peacekeeping. — Consensual peacekeeping operations when the use of force is authorized by the receiving state, including operations pursuant to Chapter VI of the United Nations Charter. (iii) Chapter vii peacekeeping. —Peacekeeping operations when force is authorized by the Security Council under Chapter VII of the United Nations Charter.

Id. The President provided the required certifications the following day, in his "Message to the Congress on the Chemical Weapons Convention," April 25, 1997, which stated in relevant part:

> The United States is not restricted by the Convention in its use of riot control agents, including the use against combatants who are parties to a conflict, in any of the following cases: (i) the conduct of peacetime military operations within an area of ongoing armed conflict when the United States is not a party to the conflict (such as recent use of the United States Armed Forces in Somalia, Bosnia, and Rwanda); (ii) consensual peacekeeping operations when the use of force is authorized by the receiving state, including operations pursuant to Chapter VI of the United Nations Charter, and (iii) peacekeeping operations when force is authorized by the Security Council under Chapter VII of the United Nations Charter.... I have certified that the United States is not restricted by the Convention in its use of riot control agents in various peacetime and peacekeeping operations. These are situations in which the United States is not engaged in a use of force of a scope, duration, and intensity that would trigger the laws of war with respect to U.S. forces.

Public Papers of the Presidents of the United States: Williams J. Clinton 495–97 (Book 1) (Government Printing Office 1997). This certification is fairly sweeping, given that "peacetime military operations within an area of ongoing armed conflict when the United States is not a party to the conflict" may include operations such as counter-piracy, noncombatant evacuation, and counterterrorism that may, from time to time, involve use of force that would likely be deemed to implicate the law of war for most other purposes.

operation would be addressed in Rules of Engagement promulgated supplemental to the Standing Rules of Engagement for U.S. Forces.[192] Non-international armed conflicts raise a special challenge in applying the CWC: When does a use of Riot Control Agents to quell a public disturbance end, and offensive action against an enemy of the state begin? It may be very difficult to ascertain and characterize the facts in this situation.[193]

D. THE U.S. DEPARTMENT OF DEFENSE NUCLEAR WEAPONS ENTERPRISE

Nuclear weapons have not been used in anger since World War II. Although providing a powerful deterrent against existential threats, the existence of nuclear weapons also entails significant risks, which have come to be acknowledged by the leaders responsible for them. Despite spearheading the Atoms for Peace initiative that birthed the IAEA, in 1953 President Eisenhower stated: "In the event of hostilities, the United States will consider nuclear weapons to be as available for use as other munitions."[194] However in 1964, in the wake of the Cuban missile crisis, President Johnson announced a much more limited policy: "There is no such thing as a conventional nuclear weapon. For 19 peril-filled years no nation has loosed the atom against another. To do so now is a political decision of the highest order."[195] In his 1984 State of the Union Address, President Reagan said (to the people of the Soviet Union): "A nuclear war cannot be won and must never be fought. The only value in our two nations possessing nuclear weapons is to make sure they will never be used."[196]

United States' nuclear weapons policy under President Obama is to "seek the peace and security of a world without nuclear weapons,"[197] while recognizing that "as long as these weapons exist, the United States will maintain a safe, secure, and effective arsenal to deter any adversary, and guarantee that defense to our allies."[198] Today's military challenge—maintaining a fielded force of operational

---

[192] *See generally* SROE, *supra* note 170; U.S. Dep't of Def., Chairman of the Joint Chiefs of Staff Instruction 3110.07D, Guidance concerning Employment of Riot Control Agents and Herbicides (U) (Jan. 31, 2011). The existence, designation/title, and classification level of each of these references is unclassified, although the text of the actual references are classified. *See Current List of CJCSG/I/M/Ns* (July 8, 2012), http://www.dtic.mil/cjcs_directives/support/cjcs/cjcscurrent.pdf.

[193] *Manual on the Law of Non-international Armed Conflict, With Commentary*, International Institute of Humanitarian Law, 34 (San Remo, 2006).

[194] Thomas C. Shelling, *The Nuclear Taboo*, 9 MIT Int'l Rev. 9 (Spring 2007).

[195] *Id.*

[196] Ronald Reagan, President of the United States, Address Before a Joint Session of the Congress on the State of the Union (Jan. 25, 1984), *available at* http://www.presidency.ucsb.edu/ws/index.php?pid=40205.

[197] U.S. Dep't of Def., Nuclear Posture Review Report 1 (Apr. 2010).

[198] Barack Obama, President of the United States, Remarks by President Barack Obama, Hradcany Square, Prague, Czech Republic (Apr. 5, 2009), *available at* http://www.whitehouse.gov/the_press_office/Remarks-By-President-Barack-Obama-In-Prague-As-Delivered.

nuclear weapons to deter our enemies and assure our allies—is a significant national undertaking.

The U.S. nuclear force currently consists of 76 nuclear-capable B-52H bombers, 18 nuclear-capable B-2 stealth bombers, 450 Minuteman III ICBMs (all capable of fitting with multiple independently targetable re-entry vehicles, but programmed to be fitted only with single warheads), 14 SSBN[199] Ohio-class submarines armed with Trident II SLBMs, and a limited number of non-strategic nuclear weapons, capable of delivery by fighter-type aircraft, forward deployed in Europe.[200] The Navy's nuclear-armed submarines are under the day-to-day administrative control of U.S. Fleet Forces Command (Atlantic SSBNs) and U.S. Pacific Fleet (Pacific SSBNs).[201] The Air Force's ICBMs are under the day-to-day administrative control of 20th Air Force (Air Force Global Strike Command); Air Force nuclear-capable bombers and their associated weapons are under the day-to-day administrative control of 8th Air Force (Air Force Global Strike Command); Air Force nuclear-capable fighters, and their associated weapons, forward deployed in Europe are under the day-to-day administrative control of United States Air Force Europe (USAFE).[202] United States Strategic Command provides operational control of the strategic nuclear force: Atlantic SSBNs are organized as Task Force 144, Pacific SSBNs are organized as Task Force 134, heavy bombers are organized as Task Force 204, and ICBMs are organized as Task Force 214.[203] Operational control of USAFE's nuclear capabilities is provided by U.S. European Command.[204]

This framework, particularly the Air Force ICBM and bomber components, reflects a relatively recent reorganization driven in part by two incidents highlighting "unacceptable practices in the handling of nuclear weapons and nuclear weapons-related materiel within the U.S. Air Force."[205] Specifically, on two occasions in 2006, sensitive missile components used on the Minuteman III ICBM were mistakenly sent to Taiwan (in shipments intended to fulfill a foreign military sales order for helicopter batteries). Subsequently, there was an improper weapons transfer from Minot AFB, North Dakota to Barksdale AFB, Louisiana, in

---

[199] SSBN is the U.S. Navy hull classification symbol for a nuclear-powered, ballistic missile-carrying submarine. U.S. Dep't of the Navy, Secretary of the Navy Instruction 5030.8A, General Guidance for the Classification of Naval Vessels and Battle Force Ship Counting, Enclosure 1 ¶ 1.c. (Feb. 8, 2011).

[200] U.S. Dep't of Def., Nuclear Posture Review Report 22–27 (Apr. 2010).

[201] *See* U.S. Dep't of Def., Report of the Secretary of Defense Task Force on DoD Nuclear Weapons Management, Phase II, 39–40 (Dec. 2008) [hereinafter *Schlesinger Report, Phase II*].

[202] *See* U.S. Air Force, Reinvigorating the Air Force Nuclear Enterprise 68 (Oct. 24, 2008).

[203] U.S. Strategic Command, USSTRATCOM OPLAN 8010-12, Strategic Deterrence and Force Employment, Annex J, Command Relationships, ¶ 1 (July 30, 2012) (The overall plan is classified, but the plan designation and title, and ¶ 1 of Annex J are unclassified.)

[204] *See Schlesinger Report, Phase II, supra* note 201, at 40.

[205] U.S. Dep't of Def., Report of the Secretary of Defense Task Force on DoD Nuclear Weapons Management, Phase I, 13 (Sept. 2008).

August 2007 in which a B-52 aircraft ferried live nuclear weapons cross-country without following proper procedures.[206] In response, Secretary of Defense Robert Gates removed Air Force Secretary Michael W. Wynne and Air Force Chief of Staff T. Michael Moseley because "the focus of the Air Force leadership has drifted with respect to perhaps its most sensitive mission."[207] A task force led by Dr. James Schlesinger[208] was commissioned to review and make recommendations for improvements in the nuclear enterprise. The task force's reports led to the total reorganization of the Air Force nuclear enterprise, including the formation of Air Force Global Strike Command, which assumed responsibility for 8th Air Force on December 1, 2009, and 20th Air Force on February 1, 2010.[209]

The firings highlighted one of the core realities of the nuclear enterprise: accountability. Secretary Gates said of his decision: "I believe that we needed a change of leadership to bring a new perspective and to especially underscore the importance of accountability in dealing with these kinds of problems."[210] Enforcement of a rigorous standard of accountability continued after the shakeup in service leadership, as the wing commanders of the 5th Bomb Wing and the 91st Missile Wing (both at Minot AFB, North Dakota), along with several subordinate commanders, were relieved of command in October 2009 following poor performance in two separate nuclear surety inspections.[211] Actions that cause leaders to lose confidence in their subordinates often involve an investigation to establish a record on which to base accountability decisions, and in some cases may involve misconduct warranting disciplinary action. In both

---

[206] *Id.*

[207] News Transcript, *DoD News Briefing with Secretary Gates from the Pentagon*, June 5, 2008, *available at* http://www.defense.gov/transcripts/transcript.aspx?transcriptid=4236.

[208] Former Secretary of Defense, Secretary of Energy, and Director of the CIA.

[209] The original home for nuclear weapons in the Air Force had been Strategic Air Command (SAC). SAC's mission had been a major factor in the formation of the Air Force as an independent military service: SAC itself was established in 1946, a year before the Air Force became a separate service. In 1992, a year after the dissolution of the Soviet Union, SAC too was disestablished: its responsibilities and assets were divided among Air Combat Command (bombers), Air Mobility Command (tankers), and U.S. Strategic Command (a unified command assuming the combatant command responsibilities SAC had previously exercised as a specified command). The SAC's ICBMs originally transferred to Air Combat Command before later being transferred to Air Force Space Command. Munitions maintenance responsibilities for nuclear weapons were transferred to Air Force Materiel Command. *See* Michelle Spencer, Aadina Ludin & Heather Nelson, *The Unauthorized Movement of Nuclear Weapons and Mistaken Shipment of Classified Missile Components: An Assessment*, Counterproliferation Papers Future Warfare Series, 31, 68, No. 56, USAF, Counterproliferation Ctr. (Jan. 2012). All of these functions have subsequently been reconsolidated in Air Force Global Strike Command, the latest function to transfer being nuclear munitions maintenance (transferred Dec. 1, 2011). *See generally* U.S. Dep't of Def., Deputy Inspector General for Intelligence and Social Program Assessments, Assessment of Air Force Global Strike Command Organizational Structures, Roles and Responsibilities, Report No. DODIG-2012-113 (July 20, 2012), *available at* http://www.dodig.mil/lr/reports/DODIG-2012-113.pdf.

[210] News Transcript, DoD News Briefing with Secretary Gates from the Pentagon, June 5, 2008, http://www.defense.gov/transcripts/transcript.aspx?transcriptid=4236.

[211] Eloise Ogden, *Commander Relieved of Duties*, Minot Daily News (Oct. 31, 2009), http://www.minot dailynews. com/page/content.detail/id/533661.html.

cases (investigations and disciplinary actions), legal advisors play a key role in enforcing the uniquely demanding level of good order and discipline required in the nuclear weapons enterprise. In the words of 8th Air Force commander Major General Floyd Carpenter: "Perfection is the standard. We will continue to demand exacting focus, attention to detail, discipline and dedication to the highest principles and standards for all activities surrounding the nuclear enterprise."[212] Shortly after assuming responsibility as Chief of Staff of the Air Force in August 2012, General Mark Welsh announced that "stewardship of a safe, secure, and effective nuclear deterrent remains the #1 Air Force priority."[213]

Most nuclear-weapon-related legal issues are centered on complying with arms-control treaties, maintaining the security of the weapons and the means to deliver them, assisting commanders in maintaining a highly disciplined force, and responding to nuclear weapons incidents. However, employing nuclear weapons also invokes the law of war. There is no customary international law or treaty-based prohibition on the use of nuclear weapons. The question, "Is the threat or use of nuclear weapons in any circumstance permitted under international law?" was certified by the U.N. General Assembly to the International Court of Justice in 1994. The Court rendered an advisory opinion, in which it concluded, "There is in neither customary nor conventional international law any specific authorization on the threat or use of nuclear weapons," nor "any comprehensive and universal prohibition of the threat or use of nuclear weapons as such."[214] However, the use of any weapon (including nuclear weapons)

---

[212] Minot Wing Commander Relieved of Duties, AIR FORCE NEWS SERVICE, Oct. 30, 2009, http://www.af.mil/news/story.asp?id=123175455.

[213] General Mark A. Welsh III, USAF, *Message to the Airmen of the United States Air Force Nuclear Force* (Sept. 27, 2012) (on file with author).

[214] Legality of the Threat or Use of Nuclear Weapons, Advisory Opinion, 1996 I.J.C. 226 (July 1996). The former ruling was a unanimous advisory opinion of the court; the latter reflected an eleven-to-three majority. The court further advised (unanimously) that:

> A threat or use of force by means of nuclear weapons that is contrary to Article 2, paragraph 4 of the United Nations Charter and that fails to meet all the requirements of Article 51, is unlawful. A threat or use of nuclear weapons should also be compatible with the requirements of the international law applicable in armed conflict, particularly those of the principles and rules of international humanitarian law, as well as with specific obligations under treaties and other undertakings which expressly deal with nuclear weapons, [and] [t]here exists an obligation to pursue in good faith and bring to a conclusion negotiations leading to nuclear disarmament in all its aspects under strict and effective international control.

Id. The court opined seven-to-seven but with the President's casting vote earning its inclusion in the opinion,

> The threat or use of nuclear weapons would generally be contrary to the rules of international law applicable in armed conflict, and in particular the principles and rules of humanitarian law. However in view of the current state of international law, and of the elements of fact at its disposal, the Court cannot conclude definitively whether the threat or use of nuclear weapons would be lawful or unlawful in extreme circumstances of self-defence, in which the very survival of a State would be at stake.

Id.

in hostilities must comply with the fundamental legal principles of the law of war: targets must be based on military necessity, military forces must use proportional force and attempt to avoid unnecessary suffering, and all parties affected by a conflict must respect principles of humanity in war. Nuclear weapons differ from other weapons only in their capability to generate significant levels of civilian casualties, collateral damage, and environmental damage.[215] The United States has deliberately avoided committing to any legal position that would categorically preclude the use of nuclear weapons. However, should a President ever find him- or herself considering making the "political decision of the highest order," the absence of a categorical legal prohibition on the use of nuclear weapons will surely be cold comfort.

VI. Conclusion

Weapons of mass destruction present unique legal challenges for the foreseeable future. Legal regimes to contain proliferation and curtail use of nuclear, chemical, and biological weapons have matured in recent decades. However, WMD cannot be "un-invented," and as such will always present an opportunity for some . . . and a threat to all. Efforts to counter the proliferation of WMD require unique levels of mutual trust and confidence. The legally compliant but strategically unwary may find their good faith exploited by those willing to hide behind a pretense of legality to buy time in order to establish, maintain, expand, or conceal programs to develop and deploy WMD. The legal structures to regulate WMD and counter their proliferation are only as good as the strategy, capability, and political will to enforce them.

---

[215] Air Force Global Strike Command, AFGSC Supporting Plan 8010-09, Volume 2, Strategic Deterrence and Global Strike Support, Basic Plan, ¶ 1.j. (The overall plan is classified, but the plan designation and title, and paragraph 1.j. of the Basic Plan are unclassified.)

23 }

Defense Support of Civil Authorities Responding to Natural and Man-Made Disasters

Kevin H. Govern*

I. Introduction

The Department of Defense (DoD) released in 2013 some of its most significant policies regarding defense support to civilian authorities, reflecting past operational engagement, present emergencies and disasters, and future anticipated political, fiscal, and security realities. Specifically, DOD Instruction 3025.21 "Defense Support of Civilian Law Enforcement Agencies," was issued on February 27, 2013, supplementing DoD Directive (DoDD) Number 3025.18, Defense Support of Civil Authorities (DSCA).[1] It replaced several older DoD issuances[2] on military

---

* Associate Professor of Law at Ave Maria School of Law, and Executive Board Member at the University of Pennsylvania Law School's Center for Ethics and the Rule of Law. He began his legal career as a U.S. Army Judge Advocate, serving twenty years at every echelon during peacetime and war, including as the Joint Task Force (JTF) 140 Operation Hawkeye Judge Advocate for Humanitarian Assistance/Civil Disturbance operations after Hurricane Hugo in St. Croix, USVI in 1989. He has also served as an Assistant Professor of Law at the United States Military Academy and has taught at California University of Pennsylvania and John Jay College. Portions of this chapter have appeared previously under rights reserved by the author in *Defense Support of Civil Authorities—Dealing with Natural and Man-Made Disasters©*, The Officer 40–46 (Sept.–Oct. 2013).

[1] Department of Defense Instruction (DoDI) 3025.21, Defense Support of Civilian Law Enforcement Agencies (Feb. 27, 2013), http://www.dtic.mil/whs/directives/corres/pdf/302521p.pdf (last visited Aug. 29, 2014), published in the 78 Fed. Reg. 71 (to be codified at 2 CFR pt. 182), http://www.fas.org/sgp/news/2013/04/dsclea.pdf (last visited Aug. 29, 2014). It is important to note that Department of Defense Directive (DoDD) 3025.18 is also still in effect. *See* Department of Defense Directive (DoDD) 3025.18, Defense Support of Civil Authorities (DSCA) (Dec. 29, 2010) (incorporating Change 1, Sept. 21, 2012) [hereinafter DSCA December 29, 2010] http://www.dtic.mil/whs/directives/corres/pdf/302518p.pdf (last visited Aug. 29, 2014).

[2] *See, e.g.*, DoD Issuances and OSD Administrative Instructions, Washington Headquarters Services, last updated 2013, http://biotech.law.lsu.edu/blaw/dodd/general.html (last visited August 29, 2014) ("A [DoD Instruction] is a DoD issuance that implements the policy, or prescribes the manner or a specific plan of action for carrying out the policy, operating a program

assistance to civilian law enforcement and civil disturbances, and affects the way in which Active and Reserve Component forces implement nearly fifty-year-old civil disturbance contingency plans in the twenty-first century. Months after the disastrous effects of the October 2012 Superstorm Sandy,[3] and weeks prior to the devastating April 15, 2013, Boston Marathon bombings,[4] the May 20th El Reno tornado in Oklahoma,[5] and the Summer 2013 wildfires in both Arizona[6] and Colorado,[7] the DoD issued an instruction clarifying the rules for the involvement of military forces in civilian law enforcement. The instruction establishes DoD policy, assigns responsibilities, and provides procedures for DoD support to federal, state, tribal, and local civilian law enforcement agencies, including responses to civil disturbances within the United States.

The defense support instruction requires that senior DoD officials develop "procedures and issue appropriate direction as necessary for defense support of civilian law enforcement agencies in coordination with the General Counsel of the Department of Defense, and in consultation with the Attorney General of the United States," including "tasking the DOD Components to plan for and to commit DOD resources in response to requests from civil authorities for [civil disturbance operations]."[8] Military officials are to coordinate with "civilian law enforcement agencies on policies to further DOD cooperation with civilian law enforcement agencies," and the heads of the combatant commands are instructed to issue procedures for "establishing local contact points in subordinate commands for purposes of coordination with Federal, State, tribal, and local civilian law enforcement officials."[9] This is especially important in the realm of so-called complex catastrophes that would overwhelm local and state agencies individually and require federal agency involvement with the DoD supporting an overall effort.[10]

Also in February 2013, Deputy Secretary of Defense Ashton Carter issued a memorandum to define complex catastrophe as:

---

or activity, and assigning responsibilities." "A Regulation is a document of general application designed to implement, interpret, or prescribe procedural requirements.").

[3] *See, e.g.*, *Superstorm Sandy: Before, during and Beyond*, NPR.org., July 2, 2013, http://www.npr.org/series/164212970/full-coverage-superstorm-sandy (last visited Aug. 29, 2014).

[4] *See, e.g.*, *Boston Marathon Terror Attach Fast Facts*, CNN.com, June 9, 2013, http://www.cnn.com/2013/06/03/us/boston-marathon-terror-attack-fast-facts (last visited Aug. 29, 2014).

[5] *See, e.g.*, Kendis Gibson, *Oklahoma Tornado 2013: Death Toll Rises to 18*, June 3, 2013, http://www.wjla.com/articles/2013/06/oklahoma-tornado-2013-death-toll-rises-to-12-89611.html (last visited Aug, 29, 2014).

[6] *See, e.g.*, *Arizona Wildfires*, KPHO.com, updated July 2, 2013, http://www.kpho.com/category/213479/arizona-wildfires (last visited Aug. 29, 2014).

[7] *See, e.g.*, *Colorado Wildfires*, The Denver Post, updated July 2, 2013, http://www.denverpost.com/wildfires (last visited Aug. 29, 2014).

[8] *Id.* at 1.

[9] DoDI 3025.21, *supra* note 1, 12.

[10] *See* Christopher DeHart, *Army North Hosts Northern Command Complex Catastrophe Session*, U.S. Northern Command Public Affairs, June 14, 2013 (*quoting* Major Chris Byrd, civil support planner with the Army North Operations Section), http://www.jbsa.af.mil/shared/media/document/AFD-130614-066.pdf (last visited June 22, 2015).

> Any natural or man-made incident, including cyberspace attack, power grid failure, and terrorism, which results in cascading failures of multiple, interdependent, critical, life-sustaining infrastructure sectors and causes extraordinary levels of mass casualties, damage, or disruption severely affecting the population, environment, economy, public health, national morale, response efforts, and/or government functions.[11]

This was especially significant to enable the DoD to "assess a broader range of forces, defense installations assets, and other DoD capabilities that could aid in response to complex catastrophes,"[12] as well as align DoD efforts with the 2011 Presidential Policy Directive 8, "National Preparedness,"[13] and other key sources of policy and strategic guidance, and prioritize strategy, policy and planning, and preparedness.

At nearly the same time, DoD issued its Strategy for Homeland Defense and Defense Support of Civil Authorities to address the range of "current and emerging threats to the homeland and natural and manmade hazards inside the United States for the period 2012–2020, and it is in keeping with current fiscal realities."[14]

Part 1 of this chapter overviews the historic laws and policies that are the foundations for defense support to civilian authorities. This sets the stage for a non-exhaustive historical assessment in Part 2 of twentieth- and twenty-first-century examples of defense support to civil authorities, broken down into the eras of: the early to mid-twentieth century; mid to late-twentieth century; the late 1970s through early 1990s and the so-called "Garden Plot" civil disturbance plan being revisited in real-world application; and the early 2000s through 2010s, putting the federal government's National Response Plan (NRP)

---

[11] *Definition of Complex Catastrophe*, DoD Dictionary of Military and Associated Terms, https://definedterm.com/complex_catastrophe (last visited June 22, 2015).

[12] *Id.*

[13] Presidential Policy Directive / PPD-8: *National Preparedness*, Mar. 30, 2011, http://www.dhs.gov/presidential-policy-directive-8-national-preparedness (last visited Aug. 29, 2014). In this PPD, the President:

> [D]irect[ed] the development of a national preparedness goal that identifies the core capabilities necessary for preparedness and a national preparedness system to guide activities that will enable the Nation to achieve the goal. The system will allow the Nation to track the progress of our ability to build and improve the capabilities necessary to prevent, protect against, mitigate the effects of, respond to, and recover from those threats that pose the greatest risk to the security of the Nation.
>
> The Assistant to the President for Homeland Security and Counterterrorism shall coordinate the interagency development of an implementation plan for completing the national preparedness goal and national preparedness system. The implementation plan shall be submitted to me within 60 days from the date of this directive, and shall assign departmental responsibilities and delivery timelines for the development of thenational planning frameworks and associated interagency operational plans described below.

Id.

[14] DoD, *Strategy for Homeland Defense and Defense Support of Civil Authorities*, Feb. 2013, foreword, http://www.defense.gov/news/Homelanddefensestrategy.pdf (last visited Aug. 29, 2014).

(later called National Response Framework—NRF) to test in contemporary operations, including those ongoing at the time of this chapter's writing. This will set the stage for the way ahead described in Part 3, considering the current framework for future national response to disasters and emergencies.

II. Part 1: Historic Laws as the Foundations for Defense Support

Defense support of civil authorities policy changes must be read in light of an evolution, rather than revolution, involving over a century of federal troop deployments and two-hundred-plus years of legal precedent, starting with the U.S. Constitution. Article I, Section 8 is the wellspring from which military support to civil authorities draws sustenance. Specifically, "Congress shall have power . . . to provide for calling forth the Militia to execute laws of the Union, suppress Insurrections, and repel Invasions."[15] In conjunction with this congressional authority, each President ". . . shall take care that the Laws be faithfully executed" consistent with Article II, Section 3.[16] Read in conjunction with those provisions, the basis for federal government support, including DoD assistance, to state and local authorities arises under the Tenth Amendment, inasmuch as "[t]he powers not delegated to the United States by the Constitution, nor prohibited by it, are reserved to the States respectively."[17]

President George Washington found need to issue a proclamation in 1794 summoning the militia to act against the Whiskey Rebellion in Pennsylvania. Subsequent legislation empowered the President to use regular military forces as well, and laws passed during the Civil War and Reconstruction periods further strengthened the executive's use of federal troops, as well as setting forth limitations on its use.[18]

---

[15] U.S. CONST. art. I, § 8.

[16] *Id.* art. I, § 3.

[17] *Id.* amend. X, § 3.

[18] Presidential emergency power was established in six statutes in 1792, 1795, 1807, 1871, and 1878: the Calling Forth Act of 1792, ch. 28, 1 Stat. 264 (repealed 1795); the Militia Act of 1795, ch. 36, 1 Stat. 424 (repealed in part 1861 and current version at 10 U.S.C. §§ 331–335 (2013)); the Insurrection Act of 1807, ch. 39, 2 Stat. 443 (current version at 10 U.S.C. §§ 331–335 (2013)); the Suppression of the Rebellion Act of 1861, ch. 25, 12 Stat. 281 (current version at 10 U.S.C. §§ 331–335 (2013)); specific parts of the Ku Klux Klan (Civil Rights) Act of 1871, ch. 22, §§ 3–4, 17 Stat. 13, 14–15 (expired in part 1873 and current version at 10 U.S.C. § 333 (2012), and; the Posse Comitatus Act of 1878 (current version at 18 USC §1385 (2013). *See, e.g.*, Stephen I. Vladeck, *Emergency Power and the Militia Acts*, 114 YALE L.J. 149 (2004), http://www.learningace.com/doc/388182/2c11e52d849cf642c5582cce2ccd5dd2/vladeck_final-pdf (last visited Aug. 29, 2014) (discussing the first five statutes); PAUL J. SCHEIPS, The Role of Federal Military Forces in Domestic Disorders 1945–1992, 449–52 (Washington, DC, Center of Military History—United States Army, 2012), http://www.history.army.mil/html/books/030/30-20/CMH_Pub_30-20.pdf (last visited Aug. 29, 2014). Troop presence in the South for supposedly partisan political ends led to the Posse Comitatus Act of 1878, "restoring an earlier national consensus that military intervention in civil affairs should occur only when specifically authorized in the law." *Id.*

The Insurrection Act of 1807 was one of the first, and most important of, U.S. laws still in force on this subject, and was followed some seventy-one years later by the Posse Comitatus Act of 1878, which continues to limit executive authority to conduct military law enforcement on U.S. soil. Each of those and other civil support laws has evolved over time—consistent with the times and the popular will expressed through Congress. The Insurrection Act (codified, as amended, at 10 U.S.C. § 331–335) has changed from its 1807 inception many times, with most notable alterations in the mid-twentieth century. This succinct law has consistently exempted federal (and federalized troops) from legal prohibitions on employment and deployment on U.S. soil in the following instances:

> § 331. Federal aid for State governments
> Whenever there is an insurrections (*sic*) in any State against its government, the President may, upon the request of its legislature or of its governor if the legislature number requested by that State, and use such of the armed forces, as he considers necessary to suppress the insurrection.
>
> § 332. Use of militia and armed forces to enforce Federal authority
> Whenever the President considers that unlawful obstructions, combinations, or assemblages, or rebellion against the authority of the United States, make it impracticable to enforce the laws of the United States in any State or Territory by the ordinary course of judicial proceedings, he may call into Federal service such of the militia of any State, and use such of the armed forces, as he considers necessary to enforce those laws or to suppress the rebellion.
>
> § 333. Interference with State and Federal law
> The President, by using the militia or the armed forces, or both, or by any other means, shall take such measures as he considers necessary to suppress, in a State, any insurrection, domestic violence, unlawful combination, or conspiracy, if it—
>
> (1) so hinders the execution of the laws of that State, and of the United States within the State, that any part or class of its people is deprived of a right, privilege, immunity, or protection named in the Constitution and secured by law, and the constituted authorities of that State are unable, fail, or refuse to protect that right, privilege, or immunity, or to give that protection; or
> (2) opposes or obstructs the execution of the laws of the United States or impedes the course of justice under those laws.
>
> In any situation covered by clause (1), the State shall be considered to have denied the equal protection of the laws secured by the Constitution.

§ 334. Proclamation to disperse
Whenever the President considers it necessary to use the militia or the armed forces under this chapter, he shall, by proclamation, immediately order the insurgents to disperse and retire peaceably to their abodes within a limited time.

§ 335. Guam and Virgin Islands included as "State"
For purposes of this chapter, the term "State" includes the unincorporated territories of Guam and the Virgin Islands.[19]

For a brief year, the Insurrection Act was expanded under the 2007 John M. Warner Defense Authorization Act, then the long-standing language was returned in the subsequent fiscal year.[20] In 2011, President Obama signed the National Defense Authorization Act for Fiscal Year 2012 into law, in which Section 1031, Clause "b", Article 2 defines a "covered person," that is, someone possibly subject to martial law, as the following:

> A person who was a part of or substantially supported al-Qaeda, the Taliban, or associated forces that are engaged in hostilities against the United States or its coalition partners, including any person who has committed a belligerent act or has directly supported such hostilities in aid of such enemy forces.[21]

---

[19] 10 U.S.C. § 331–335 (2012), http://www.law.cornell.edu/uscode/text/10/subtitle-A/part-I/chapter-15 (last visited Aug. 29, 2014). *See also* John Brinkerhoff, *The Role of Federal Military Forces in Domestic Law Enforcement*, Center for Army Lessons Learned (CALL) Newsletter 10-16 (Ft. Leavenworth: CALL, Dec. 2009), http://usacac.army.mil/cac2/call/docs/10-16/ch_11.asp (last visited Aug. 29, 2014). Title 10, Section 331 was enacted in 1792 in response to challenges to the taxing power of the federal government. It allows the President, at the request of a governor or state legislature, to put down an insurrection by calling into federal service sufficient militia to "suppress the insurrection." Title 10, Section 332 was enacted in 1861 at the outset of the Civil War. It allows the President to use the armed forces to enforce the laws or suppress a rebellion whenever, in his opinion, unlawful obstructions, combinations, or assemblages or rebellion against the authority of the United States make it impractical to enforce the laws using the course of judicial proceedings. Title 10, Section 333 was enacted in 1869 during the Reconstruction Era. It allows the President to use the armed forces or militia to respond to insurrection, domestic violence, unlawful combination, or conspiracies that prevent a state government from enforcing the laws. Title 10, Section 334 was enacted in 1861. It prescribes that the President shall issue a proclamation calling on insurgents to disperse before using the militia or armed forces to enforce the law.

[20] On September 30, 2006, Congress modified the Insurrection Act as part of the 2007 Defense Authorization Bill (repealed as of 2008). The so-called "Insurrection Act Rider," Section 1076 of the law, changed Section 333 of the Insurrection Act, and widened the President's ability to deploy troops within the United States to enforce the laws. Under this act, the President could also deploy troops as a police force during a natural disaster, epidemic, serious public health emergency, terrorist attack, or other condition, when the President determines that the authorities of the state are incapable of maintaining public order. The bill also modified Section 334 of the Insurrection Act, giving the President authority to order the dispersal of either insurgents or "those obstructing the enforcement of the laws." The law changed the name of the chapter from "Insurrection" to "Enforcement of the Laws to Restore Public Order." The 2008 Defense Authorization Bill repealed the changes made in the 2007 bill. *See, e.g.*, Kevin Govern, *Making Martial Law Easier in the U.S*, 1 HOMELAND SEC. REV. 221–30 (Fall 2007), http://ssrn.com/abstract=2251998 (last visited Aug. 29, 2014).

[21] *Id. (citing* National Defense Authorization Act for Fiscal Year 2012, P.L. 112–81 (Dec. 31, 2011), http://www.treasury.gov/resource-center/sanctions/Programs/ Documents/ndaa_publaw.pdf (last visited Aug. 29, 2014).

The so-called Posse Comitatus Act (codified, as amended, at 18 U.S.C. § 1385) uses a Latin term found in sixteenth-century English law meaning "to have the right to an armed retinue."[22] The Posse Comitatus Act passed on June 18, 1878, prohibiting federal troops from supervising Confederate state elections in the latter portion of the Reconstruction Era.[23] It originally applied only to the U.S. Army, but was amended after the U.S. Air Force was created to include those forces in 1956, then has applied by DoD regulation to include U.S. Navy and U.S. Marine Corps forces as well. The Posse Comitatus Act reads now, as follows:

> Whoever, except in cases and under circumstances expressly authorized by the Constitution or Act of Congress, willfully uses any part of the Army or the Air Force as a posse comitatus or otherwise to execute the laws shall be fined under this title or imprisoned not more than two years, or both.[24]

Further, 6 U.S.C. § 466 is an unusual codification of a "sense of Congress reaffirming the continued importance and applicability of the Posse Comitatus Act," in particular the following subsections providing for exceptions and exemptions:

> (4) Nevertheless, by its express terms, the Posse Comitatus Act is not a complete barrier to the use of the Armed Forces for a range of domestic purposes, including law enforcement functions, when the use of the Armed Forces is authorized by Act of Congress or the President determines that the use of the Armed Forces is required to fulfill the President's obligations under the Constitution to respond promptly in time of war, insurrection, or other serious emergency.
>
> (5) Existing laws, including chapter 15 of Title 10 (commonly known as the "Insurrection Act"), and the Robert T. Stafford Disaster Relief and Emergency Assistance Act (42 U.S.C. 5121 et seq.), grant the President broad powers that may be invoked in the event of domestic emergencies, including an attack against the Nation using weapons of mass destruction, and these laws specifically authorize the President to use the Armed Forces to help restore public order.[25]

The Posse Comitatus Act has long prohibited troops under federal authority (that is Title 10 Active Component troops and "federalized" Title 32 National Guard troops) from generally conducting law enforcement duties on U.S. soil absent congressionally legislated or constitutionally enumerated authority or

---

[22] *See, e.g.*, Charles Holloway, *Posse Comitatus*, Millnet.co.uk, July 4, 2012, http://blog.millnet.co.uk/index.php/2012/07/posse-comitatus/ (last visited Aug. 29, 2014).

[23] Kevin Govern, *Lawful Military Support to Civil Authorities in Times of Crisis*, JURIST.ORG, May 2, 2013, http://jurist.org/forum/2013/05/kevin-govern-posse-comitatus.php (last visited Aug. 29, 2014).

[24] 18 U.S.C § 1385 (2012), http://www.law.cornell.edu/uscode/text/18/1385 (last visited Aug. 29, 2014).

[25] 6 U.S.C. § 466 (2006), http://www.law.cornell.edu/uscode/text/6/466 (last visited Aug. 29, 2014).

exception. By comparison and contrast, the Reserve components of the Armed Forces are: The Army National Guard of the United States, The Army Reserve, The Navy Reserve, The Marine Corps Reserve, The Air National Guard of the United States, The Air Force Reserve, and The Coast Guard Reserve (10 U.S.C. § 10101).[26] Federal troop use exceptions to the Insurrection Act and Posse Comitatus Act would be intelligence, military equipment, training, advice or facilities usage, among other matters, in support of civilian law enforcement under 10 U.S.C. § 381,[27] or troop employment and deployment during a biological, radiological, or nuclear event under 18 U.S.C. § 382.[28] Also § 1004 of the National Defense Authorization Act for Fiscal Year 1991, as amended,[29]

> allowed the Secretary of Defense to provide support for the counterdrug activities of any other department or agency of the federal government or of any state, local, or foreign law enforcement agency if certain criteria, set out in the statute [were] met.[30]

Under that authority, in September 2011, the Government Accountability Office (GAO) reported $1.35 billion in costs for DoD support to the Department of Homeland Security (DHS) in two separate coun-ternarcotics border operations in four border states—Operation Jump Start and Operation Phalanx—conducted by National Guard forces in Title 32 status from June 2006 to July 2008 and from June 2010 through September 30, 2011, respectively.[31] The GAO further noted that between 1989 and 2011, the DoD "estimate[d] the cost of using active duty Title 10

---

[26] 10 U.S.C. §10101(2011), http://www.law.cornell.edu/uscode/text/10/10101 (last visited Aug. 29, 2014). *See, e.g.*, Thesis, John H. Ebbighausen, *Unity of Command for Homeland Security: Title 32, Title 10, or a Combination*, 7–81, Ft. Leavenworth, KS, U.S. Army Command and General Staff College (2006), http://www.dtic.mil/cgi-bin/GetTRDoc?AD=ADA451789 (last visited Aug. 29, 2014). For a history of the National Guard, see also NCC Staff, *An Important Landmark Anniversary for the National Guard*, CONSTITUTIONCENTER.ORG, http://blog.constitutioncenter.org/2014/06/an-important-landmark-anniversary-for-the-national-guard/ (last visited Aug. 29, 2014), *citing with authority* The National Defense Act, Pub.L. 64–85, 39 Stat. 166, enacted June 3, 1916:

> On June 3, 1916, the National Defense Act made the use of the term "National Guard" mandatory for state militias, and the act gave the President the authority to mobilize the Guard during war or national emergencies here, for service or in different parts of the world, for the duration of the event that caused the mobilization.

[27] 18 U.S.C. § 381 (1948), http://www.law.cornell.edu/uscode/text/10/381 (last visited Aug. 29, 2014).

[28] 18 U.S.C. § 382 (1948), http://www.law.cornell.edu/uscode/text/10/382 (last visited Aug. 29, 2014).

[29] H.R. 4739 (101st): National Defense Authorization Act for Fiscal Year 1991 (Pub. L. 101–510.), https://www.govtrack.us/congress/bills/101/hr4739 (last visited Aug. 29, 2014).

[30] Memorandum, Government Accountability Office (GAO), September 11, 2011, subject, Observations on the Costs and Benefits of an Increased Department of Defense Role in Helping to Secure the Southwest Land Border 8, http://www.gao.gov/assets/100/97733.pdf (last visited Aug. 29, 2014), *citing with authority id.*

[31] *Id.* at 3. Missions "included aviation, engineering, entry identification teams (EIT), among others, according to National Guard officials." *Id.*

forces nationwide in support of drug law enforcement agencies (with additional operational costs borne by the military services) at about $10 million annually."[32]

The 1988 Robert T. Stafford Disaster Relief and Emergency Assistance Act (42 U.S.C. §§ 5121–5207) authorizes the President to release federal funds and assistance to states for use in disaster response, and declare an emergency or major disaster at the request of a state (or U.S. territory) governor, as well as the mayor of Washington, DC.[33] What the Stafford Act does not authorize is the use of the military to perform law enforcement functions ordinarily prohibited by the Posse Comitatus Act.

An "emergency" under the Stafford Act is "any occasion or instance for which . . . Federal assistance is needed to supplement State and local efforts and capabilities . . . or to lessen or avert the threat of a catastrophe."[34] A "major disaster" is defined as "any natural catastrophe (including any hurricane, tornado, storm, high water, winddriven water, tidal wave, tsunami, earthquake, volcanic eruption, landslide, mudslide, snowstorm, or drought), or, regardless of cause, any fire, flood, or explosion."[35]

Upon the request of the governor, the President may task the DoD to provide any emergency work the President deems essential for the preservation of life and property in the immediate aftermath up to ten days prior to a Presidential declaration of an emergency or major disaster.[36] Emergency work can include the clearance and removal of debris and wreckage and the restoration of essential public facilities and services.[37]

The declaration of an emergency under the Stafford Act requires that the governor of the affected state first make a determination that the situation is of such severity and magnitude that the state is unable to respond effectively without federal assistance, which determination must include a detailed definition of the type and amount of federal aid required, except where the President determines that a disaster implicates preeminently federal interests.[38]

---

[32] *Id.* at 3.

[33] 42 U.S.C. §§ 5121–5207 (2006), http://www.law.cornell.edu/uscode/text/42/chapter-68 (last visited Aug. 29, 2014).

[34] *Id.* § 5122.

[35] *Id.*

[36] *Id.* § 5170b. *See* Jennifer Elsea & R. Chuck Mason, Cong. Research Serv., 7-5000, *The Use of Federal Troops for Disaster Assistance: Legal Issues* 4-5 (Nov. 28, 2008), http://www.fas.org/sgp/crs/natsec/RS22266.pdf (last visited Aug. 29, 2014).

> The prerequisites for a major disaster declaration are similar to those for an emergency, 42 U.S.C. § 5170. The governor must first execute the state's emergency plan and make a determination that state capabilities are insufficient to deal with the circumstances. However, the governor need not specify which forms of assistance are needed. The governor must provide information regarding the resources that have been committed and certify that the state will comply with cost sharing provisions under the Stafford Act.

Id.

[37] *Id.*

[38] *Id.* § 5191.

Finally, DoD policy under color of the Stafford Act allows commanders to provide immediate response in the guise of resources and assistance to civil authorities prior to, or in the absence of, a declaration if disaster overwhelms the capabilities of local authorities and necessitates immediate action "to save lives, prevent human suffering, or mitigate great property damage within the United States," but "does not permit actions that would subject civilians to the use of military power that is regulatory, prescriptive, or compulsory."[39]

Aside from the Stafford Act basis for support, Section 1208 of the 1990 National Defense Authorization Act (NDAA) has allowed the Secretary of Defense to

> transfer to Federal and State agencies personal property of the Department of Defense, including small arms and ammunition, that the Secretary determines is—(A) suitable for use by such agencies in counter-drug activities; and (B) excess to the needs of the Department of Defense.[40]

In 1996, Congress replaced Section 1208 with Section 1033, which subsequently became Section 2576a.[41] The Defense Logistics Agency (DLA) notes that "[s]ince its inception, the 1033 program has transferred more than $5.1 billion worth of property. In 2013 alone, $449,309,003.71 worth of property was transferred to law enforcement."[42] As part of its outreach to civilian agencies, the DLA predicted that "[i]f your law enforcement agency chooses to participate, it may become one of the more than 8,000 participating agencies to increase its capabilities, expand

---

[39] DSCA, *supra* note 1, § 4g. *See also* Elsea & Mason, *supra* note 36, at 5 (*citing* Jim Winthorp, *The Oklahoma City Bombing: Immediate Response Authority and Other Military Assistance to Civil Authority (MACA)*, Army Lawyer 3–15 (July 1997), http://www.loc.gov/rr/frd/Military_Law/pdf/07-1997.pdf (last visited Aug. 29, 2014):

> The immediate response authority is not provided for in any statute, but is said to have deep historical roots. The 1906 San Francisco earthquake is a noted example. The commanding general of the Pacific Division, on his own initiative, deployed troops to assist civil authorities to stop looting, protect federal buildings, and to assist firefighters.

Id.

[40] 14 U.S.C. § 1 (1949), http://www.law.cornell.edu/uscode/text/14/1 (last visited Aug. 29, 2014). The law further provided that:

> 2) The Secretary shall carry out this section in consultation with the Attorney General and the Director of National Drug Control Policy.
>
> (b) Conditions for Transfer.—The Secretary of Defense may transfer personal property under this section only if—
>
> (1) the property is drawn from existing stocks of the Department of Defense;
> (2) the recipient accepts the property on an as-is, where-is basis;
> (3) the transfer is made without the expenditure of any funds available to the Department of Defense for the procurement of defense equipment; and
> (4) all costs incurred subsequent to the transfer of the property are borne or reimbursed by the recipient.

Id.

[41] 10 U.S.C. §2576a (2012), http://uscode.house.gov/view.xhtml?req=granuleid:USC-prelim-title10-section2576a&num=0&edition=prelim (last visited Aug. 29, 2014).

[42] Defense Logistics Agency, *The Law Enforcement Support Office—About the 1033 Program*, DLA.mil, http://www.dispositionservices.dla.mil/leso/Pages/default.aspx (last visited Aug. 29, 2014).

its patrol coverage, reduce response times, and save the American taxpayer's investment."[43] Critics of the program, such as the American Civil Liberties Union (ACLU), claimed "a disturbing range of military gear [is] being transferred to civilian police departments nationwide" and allege "one-third of all war materiel parceled out to state, local, and tribal police agencies is brand new."[44]

As "one of the five armed forces within the United States and the only military organization within the [DHS]," the U.S. Coast Guard (USCG), under 14 U.S.C. § 1-894, is the "[N]ation's leading maritime *law enforcement* agency" with "broad, multi-faceted jurisdictional authority" limited neither by the Insurrection Act nor the Posse Comitatus Act.[45] However, under 14 U.S.C. § 3 as amended by Section 211 of the Coast Guard and Maritime Transportation Act of 2006 (Pub. L. 109-241), the USCG operates as a service in the Department of the Navy upon the declaration of war and when Congress so directs in a declaration, or when the President so directs.[46]

President George W. Bush signed The Homeland Security Act of 2002 (Pub. L. No. 107-296) into law on November 25, 2002,[47] creating the DHS as an organization to "lead the unified national effort to secure America, ... prevent and deter terrorist attacks and protect against and respond to threats and hazards to the Nation, [and] ensure safe and secure borders, welcome lawful immigrants and visitors, and promote the free-flow of commerce."[48]

Empowering DHS to take a "nationwide approach for Federal, State, and local governments to work effectively and efficiently together to prepare for, respond to, and recover from domestic incidents, regardless of cause, size, or complexity," President Bush then issued Homeland Security Presidential Directive (HSPD-5), assigning the responsibility of developing a National Incident Management System (NIMS) to the DHS secretary, including a mandate for an NRP (later

---

[43] *Id*

[44] *See, e.g.*, Matthew Harwood, *To Terrify and Occupy*, ACLU.ORG (Aug. 14, 2014), https://www.aclu.org/blog/criminal-law-reform-free-speech/terrify-and-occupy (last visited Aug. 29, 2014), *citing with authority War Comes Home—The Excessive Militarization of American Policing*, ACLU.ORG (June 2014), https://www.aclu.org/sites/default/files/ assets/jus14-warcomeshome-report-web-rel1.pdf (last visited Aug. 29, 2014). *See also* Taylor Wofford, *How America's Police Became an Army: The 1033 Program*, NEWSWEEK.COM, http://www.newsweek.com/how-americas-police-became-army-1033-program-264537 (last visited Aug. 29, 2014), *and see* Julie Bosman & Matt Apuzzo, *In Wake of Clashes, Calls to Demilitarize Police*, NYTIMES.COM, 14 (Aug. 2014), http://www.nytimes.com/2014/08/15/us/ferguson-missouri-in-wake-of-clashes-calls-to-demilitarize-police.html?_r=0 (last visited Aug. 29, 2014).

[45] USCG, Office of Law Enforcement (CG-MLE) Mission, last modified Mar. 20, 2014, http://www.uscg.mil/top/about/ (last visited Aug. 29, 2014); for legal authority, *see also* 14 U.S.C. §1-894 (1949), http://www.law.cornell.edu/uscode/text/14/1 (last visited Aug. 29, 2014).

[46] *Id.* § 3. *See also* USCG, About Us—Overview of the United States Coast Guard, last modified June 12, 2013, http://www.uscg.mil/hq/cg5/cg531/ (last visited Aug. 29, 2014).

[47] P.L. 107-296, http://www.dhs.gov/xlibrary/assets/hr_5005_enr.pdf (last visited Aug. 29, 2014).

[48] DHS, *Securing Our Homeland—U.S. Department of Homeland Security Strategic Plan*, 4 (Aug. 4, 2003), https://www.hsdl.org/?view&did=712147 (last visited Aug. 29, 2014). *See also* FEMA, *FY 2011-2014 Strategic Plan, FEMA P-806, 1-30* (Feb. 2011), http://www.fema.gov/pdf/about/strategic_plan11.pdf (last visited Aug. 29, 2014).

called NRF).[49] The following four HSPD-5 criteria define when the DHS shall assume overall federal incident management coordination responsibilities:

> (1) A Federal department or agency acting under its own authority has requested DHS assistance,
> (2) The resources of State and local authorities are overwhelmed and Federal assistance has been requested,
> (3) More than one Federal department or agency has become substantially involved in responding to the incident, or
> (4) The Secretary has been directed by the President to assume incident management responsibilities.[50]

The NRP authorized "immediate action to save lives, prevent human suffering, or mitigate property damage," and a pre-approved authority under in extremis "Immediate Response" conditions. The DoD considers imminently serious conditions resulting from any civil emergency those where time does not permit approval from higher headquarters. Local military commanders and responsible officials from DoD components and agencies are authorized by DoD directive and pre-approval by the Secretary of Defense, subject to any supplemental direction that may be provided by their DoD component, to take necessary action to respond to requests of civil authorities consistent with the Posse Comitatus Act (18 U.S.C. § 1385).[51]

---

[49] White House, Homeland Security Presidential Directive/HSPD-5-*Management of Domestic Incidents* (Feb. 28, 2003), http://www.gpo.gov/fdsys/pkg/PPP-2003-book1/pdf/PPP-2003-book1-doc-pg229.pdf (last visited Aug. 29, 2014). In addition to Presidential Policy Directive / PPD-8, see *supra* note 13, additional HSPDs and Presidential Policy Directives (PPDs) regarding military support to civil authorities include, but are not limited, to the following: HSPD 7: Critical Infrastructure Identification, Prioritization, and Protection; HSPD 9: Defense of United States Agriculture and Food; HSPD 10: Biodefense for the 21st Century; HSPD 18: Medical Countermeasures against Weapons of Mass Destruction; HSPD 21: Public Health and Medical Preparedness, and; HSPD 22: Domestic Chemical Defense; *Laws and Regulations*, Homeland Security, DHS.GOV, https://www.dhs.gov/laws-regulations (last visited Aug. 29, 2014).

[50] *Id.*

[51] *The Department of Defense (DOD) Role in Incident Response*, Center for Army Lessons Learned (CALL) Handbook, ch. 3 at 06-08 (May 2006), http://usacac.army.mil/cac2/call/docs/06-08/ch-3.asp (last visited Aug. 29, 2014). Examples of such immediate response measures have included, but were not limited to: Air compression chambers for trapped miners (Various); Aerial Evacuation (fixed wing) to critical care patients (Hurricane Isadore) (2002); Medical support to 40 nursing home patients at Keesler AFB, MS (Hurricane Ivan) (2004); Helicopter water bucket operations (California Fires) (Various); Fire fighting trucks and equipment responding off post to protect threatened structures (Various); Transportation support to move disaster relief supplies (Various); Hazardous materials (HAZMAT) Teams responding to chemical spill resulting from a train derailment (Various). *See* PowerPoint Briefing, Edwin Hurston, *Defense Support of Civil Authorities*, Sept. 21, 2012, http://www.google.com/url?sa=t&rct=j&q=&esrc=s&source=web&cd=1&ved=0CB0QFjAA&url=http%3A%2F%2Fwww.millersville.edu%2Fcdre%2Ffiles%2FVirtual%2520Seminar%2520Series%2520Presentations%2FEd%2520Hurstin_Defense%2520Support%2520of%2520Civil%2520Authorities%2520v.2.ppt&ei=hBntUX4D9LesATwzYDgDQ&usg=AFQjCNElwYaEYwBfHxTbZr0TVKUmB13pQA&bvm=bv.72938740,d.cWc&cad=rja (last visited Aug. 29, 2014).

III. Part 2: Twentieth- and Twenty-First-Century Examples of Defense Support to Civil Authorities

In recent U.S. history, there have been many instances and exemptions whereby federal (or federalized) troops were called upon to conduct brief operations other than training on U.S. soil in accordance with an Executive Order or Proclamation under the Insurrection Act or some other exemption to the Posse Comitatus Act, the most salient of which will be discussed below.

A. EARLY TO MID-TWENTIETH CENTURY

In 1919, President Woodrow Wilson called out federal troops to quell race riots in twenty cities across the United States, commencing first in Chicago, ostensibly arising from postwar social tensions related to demobilizing World War I veterans, and competition for jobs among ethnicities.[52] In 1932, President Herbert Hoover called upon General Douglas MacArthur, with the aid of his staff officers Majors George Patton and Dwight D. Eisenhower, to send U.S. troops to displace and disperse a group of twenty thousand aggrieved WWI veterans (the so-called "Bonus Marchers") encamped on or near the Washington Mall; this infamous incident involved the first instance of MacArthur ignoring presidential directive, when he pursued veterans and families across the Anacostia River despite Hoover's orders to stand down.[53]

On Labor Day in 1934, textile workers in the northeast and southeastern United States began a strike against their treatment by employers at the mills.[54] In response to the strike, Georgia governor Eugene Talmadge declared martial law, and arrested strikers who continued their protests.[55] The first arrests, including many women workers, were from the Sargent and East Newnan Cotton Mills; carried out by bayonet-armed Georgia National Guardsmen, the strikers were transported by military trucks to Fort McPherson in Atlanta,[56] where the workers were incarcerated in outdoor holding cells formerly occupied by German prisoners of war during World War I.[57] Those arrested were held there until the

---

[52] Brinkerhoff, *supra* note 19.

[53] American Experience, *MacArthur, People and Events: The Bonus* March (May–July, 1932), PBS.ORG, 1999, http://www.pbs.org/wgbh/amex/macarthur/peopleevents/ pandeAMEX89.html (last visited Aug. 29, 2014).

[54] *General Textile Strike of 1934*, Digital Public Library of America, http://dp.la/item/1b7d6c9e6152da9c1896b0fccfaabb7d?back_uri=http%3A%2F%2Fdp.la%2Fsearch%3Fpartner%255B%255D%3DDigital%2BLibrary%2Bof%2BGeorgia%26place%255B%255D%3DNewnan%2B%28Ga.%29%26subject%255B%255D%3DFort%2BMcPherson%2B%28Ga.%29 (last visited Aug. 29, 2014).

[55] *Labor Unrest—Textile Industry*, The New Georgia Encyclopedia, updated Feb. 2, 2012, http://www.georgiaencyclopedia.org/nge/ArticlePrintable.jsp?id=h-2606 (last visited Aug. 29, 2014).

[56] *Redevelopment in Our Own Backyard*, Advantage Building Contractors, Inc., June 17, 2013, http://advantagebuildingcontractors.com/redevelopment-in-our-own-backyard/ (last visited Aug. 29, 2014).

[57] *Id.*

strike ended three weeks later, after the United Textile Workers (UTW) union received government assurances that the problems at southern textile mills would be investigated.[58]

During 1946, President Harry S Truman sent out federal troops against eight hundred thousand striking railroad workers—the largest strike in America's history—and Truman proposed legislation (which failed to pass) to draft striking workers into the Armed Forces.[59]

B. MID TO LATE-TWENTIETH CENTURY

In 1957 President Eisenhower federalized Arkansas National Guard troops and sent Active Component troops under Executive Order 10730[60] to Little Rock, Arkansas, to counter desegregation violence in the aftermath of the landmark *Brown v. Topeka Board of Education* case in which the U.S. Supreme Court ruled that segregated schools were "inherently unequal" and ordered that U.S. public schools be desegregated "with all deliberate speed."[61] In 1962, President John F. Kennedy sent sixteen thousand federal troops under the XVIII Airborne Corps[62] to Mississippi to quell the so-called "Ole Miss Riot," in conjunction with 123 Deputy Federal Marshals, 316 U.S. Border Patrolmen, and 97 federal prison guards protecting James Meredith, an African American blocked from registering at the university.[63] The task force arrested two hundred persons, including the arrest for insurrection of a retired Major General, Edwin A. Walker, who resigned his commission after reprimand for political activity.[64] In 1963 and 1965, forces also deployed to Tuscaloosa, Tuskegee, and Selma, Alabama, to counter racial violence as a result of the forced enrollment of African-American students and civil rights marches,[65] and in 1967 to Detroit to suppress riots there.[66]

---

[58] *Id.* Instead, seventy-two thousand southern textile workers were blacklisted from the mills, but the strike did lead to the formation of the Textile Workers Union of America (TWUA) in 1939. Labor Unrest, *supra* note 55.

[59] *American Experience, Truman, General Article: Domestic Policy*, PBS.ORG. (1997), http://www.pbs.org/wgbh/americanexperience/features/general-article/truman-domestic/ (last visited Aug. 29, 2014).

[60] Exec. Order No. 10,730, 22 FR 7628 (Sept. 25, 1957), http://www.ourdocuments.gov/doc.php?doc=89 (last visited Aug. 29, 2014).

[61] 347 U.S. 483 (1954).

[62] *XVIII Airborne Corps History*, BRAGG.ARMY.MIL, http://www.bragg.army.mil/18abc/Pages/XVIIIAbnCorpsHistory.aspx (last visited Aug, 29, 2014).

[63] *See, e.g.*, Harvey Gantt and the Desegregation of Clemson University, Clemson University Office of Institutional Research, an exhibit presented by the Library in conjunction with "Integration with Dignity: A Celebration of 40 Years" (Jan. 28, 2003), http://www.clemson.edu/oirweb1/FB/OIRWebpage/Integration.htm (last visited Aug. 29, 2014).

[64] For an interesting perspective on the diversity defamation case instituted by Walker involving this matter, see Walker v. The Pulitzer Publishing Co., 394 F.2d 800 (8th Cir. 1968), https://bulk.resource.org/courts.gov/c/F2/394/394.F2d.800.18994_1.html (last visited Aug. 29, 2014).

[65] Scheips, *supra* note 18, 159–64.

[66] XVIII Airborne Corps, *supra* note 62.

The increasing number of domestic disturbances and anticipated threats to security gave rise in 1965 to the U.S. Army Intelligence Command (USAINTC), the Army counterintelligence element conducting operations in the continental United States, utilizing 300 field and residents offices across the nation organized into seven Military Intelligence groups.[67] After the August 1965 Los Angeles Watts rioting, USAINTC provided crisis support and contingency planning for collecting domestic intelligence under the Steep Hill contingency plan to be implemented in the event of deployment of federal troops.[68] That plan, redesigned Garden Plot in 1967 (and still extant today) proved to be inadequate with respect to aiding Army commanders in civil disturbance situations;[69] thus, subsequent collection plans (e.g., Punch Block, Lantern Spike), with respect to military counterintelligence collection and analysis, were separate from any federal or local law enforcement capabilities.[70]

The years of 1967 and 1968 were especially significant, and tragic, with respect to military support to civilian authorities. The Newark, New Jersey, riot response involved elements of the Army's 108th Military Intelligence Group at Ft. Devens, Massachusetts. With the Army largely "limited to observing events, the whole burden fell upon the police and the National Guard, which reached a peak strength of 5,367 in Newark on 17 July [1967]."[71] The Detroit Riots of 1967 involved five thousand federal troops and seventeen thousand law enforcement officers quelling one of the deadliest and most destructive riots in U.S. history; reaction to a police raid of an unlicensed after-hours bar escalated to a loss of 43 lives, 467 injuries, 7,200 arrests, and the destruction of 2,000 buildings.[72] The October 1967 March on the Pentagon was the first national protest against the Vietnam Conflict, during which approximately six thousand armed Army troops deferred to three hundred U.S. Deputy Marshals to deal with thirty-five thousand protesters, and ultimately to arrest eighty-two.[73] Race riots in 110 cities across America ensued following the April 1968 assassination of the Reverend Dr. Martin Luther King Jr.,[74] most critically affecting Washington DC. In the largest federal occupation on U.S. soil since the Civil War, the White House dispatched some 13,600 federal troops, including the 3rd Infantry Division (Old Guard), and 1,750 federalized DC National Guard troops to augment civilian law enforcement and quell disturbances across the capital city.[75] Rioting spread to Chicago, Baltimore, and

---

[67] *See* John P. Finnegan, *Military Intelligence* 159, 161–63 (Washington, DC: Center of Military History—United States Army, 1997), https://www.hsdl.org/?view&did=437576 (last visited Aug. 29, 2014).

[68] Scheips, *supra* note 18, 161.

[69] *Id.* At 143.

[70] Finnegan, *supra* note 67, at 155.

[71] Scheips, *supra* note 18, at 174.

[72] *Id.* at 177–204.

[73] *Id.* at 231–66. The so-called "Spring Mobilization to End the War in Vietnam," which became the "National Mobilization Committee to End the War in Vietnam," was a coalition of antiwar activists formed in 1967 to organize large demonstrations in opposition to the Vietnam War.

[74] Finnegan, *supra* note 67, at 156.

[75] Scheips, *supra* note 18, at 267.

other cities across the nation as the "last of the great racial disturbances of the 1960s."[76]

On April 1968, Under Secretary McGiffert took charge of the Department of Defense Civil Disturbance Steering Committee, with the U.S. Deputy Attorney General as a member.[77] The committee's job was to advise the Secretary of the Army in his capacity as the executive agent in dealing with civil disturbances or other lawlessness prejudicial to public order—all of which was soon to be formally authorized by DoD Directive 3025.12, June 8, 1968.[78]

The year 1970 saw the peaceful as well as lethal use of military force to deal with civil disturbance. The Postal Strike of that year involved over 200,000 workers in over 30 cities,[79] in response to which President Richard Nixon ordered 18,500 troops into New York City under the DoD Postal Augmentation Plan, aka Operation Graphic Hand, ostensibly to sort mail, but with follow-on efforts of up to 115,000 troops to deploy to 35 cities if the strike continued.[80] Although Graphic Hand troops avoided confrontation, as did those who responded to the May 1970 New Haven demonstrations, the Ohio National Guard killed four unarmed students, with twenty-eight guardsmen acknowledging having fired live rounds during the Kent State campus protests.[81]

In a matter reflecting a nineteenth-century incident repeating itself in the late twentieth century, President Nixon sent federal troops to Wounded Knee, SD, in 1973 during a seventy-one-day siege of properties occupied by American Indian Movement activists, with the Federal Bureau of Investigation (FBI) cordoning off the area by using U.S. Marshals and later National Guard units.[82]

---

[76] *Id.* at 335.

[77] *Id.* at 342.

[78] The current version of this directive is DoD Dir. 3025.12, Military Assistance for Civil Disturbances (MACDIS) (1994), http://www.au.af.mil/au/awc/awcgate/ dod/d302512p.txt (last visited Aug. 29, 2014).

[79] American Postal Workers Union, AFL-CIO, "APWU History," APWU.org, last updated 2012, http://www.apwu.org/about/history.htm (last visited Aug. 29, 2014).

[80] For more information on Graphic Hand, see Mason R. Schaefer, *Operation Graphic Hand, 1970: The Army Moves the Mail*, presented at 2004 Conference of Army Historians, July 13–15, 2004, copy in Historian's files, CMH. For post-strike Graphic Hand activity of the civil disturbance directorate and its successor, the Directorate of Military Support, see DCDPO Historical Summary, 22–23, July 1969–June 1970, and DOMS Historical Summary, 9, 17, 21, July 1970–June 1971 (*cited in* Scheips, *supra* note 18, at 433).

[81] Scheips, *supra* note 18, at 406.

[82] *Id.* at 434–38 (*citing with authority* Fredrick S. Calhoun, The Lawmen: United States Marshals and Their Deputies, 1789–1989, 297–301 (1990)):

> Although National Guard troops under state control could not legally conduct operations on the reservation, the state called over 400 guardsmen to active duty to ensure that the disturbance was confined to the reservation. In addition, the state police established roadblocks around the disputed area. At peak strength about 350 federal, state, and local law enforcement officers were on the scene.

C. THE LATE 1970S THROUGH EARLY 1990S: GARDEN PLOT REVISITED

President Jimmy Carter established the Federal Emergency Management Agency (FEMA) under the 1978 Reorganization Plan No. 3, and activated it on April 1, 1979, by Executive Order 12127.[83] Executive Order 12148 shifted disaster relief efforts to the new federal-level agency, and FEMA gained responsibility from DoD for the nation's civil defense.[84]

In September 1989, President George H.W. Bush sent Active Component and federalized National Guard forces under Executive Order 12690[85] to St. Croix, U.S. Virgin Islands, ostensibly at the request of the Territorial Governor, to quell civil disturbance and provide disaster assistance to over fifty thousand inhabitants after Hurricane Hugo damaged or destroyed over 90 percent of the island's structures and created a significant number of hazardous oil spills.[86] Under the 1967 Garden Plot contingency plan, Joint Task Force (JTF) 140 brought together Army, Navy, and Coast Guard elements, with a contingent from the U.S. Marshals Service and the FBI, for Operation Hawkeye, FEMA's first major test of disaster relief capabilities.[87] Military Police, augmented by medical, engineer, legal, and other support personnel, enforced a dusk-to-dawn curfew, but not martial law. They patrolled the island for two months, securing key installations; worked with the FBI and the U.S. Marshals to apprehend several hundred escaped prisoners; intercepted air-dropped bundles of cocaine valued at over $50 million; and carried out extensive training for the Virgin Island National Guard, and conducted joint patrols with the St. Croix Police Department.[88]

Six days in early May 1992 were filled with rioting, arson, murder, and mayhem on the streets of Los Angeles following the controversial acquitting of officers involved in the Rodney King beating.[89] Garden Plot yet again became

---

[83] Exec. Order No. 12127, 44 FR 19367 (Mar. 31, 1979), http://www.archives.gov/federal-register/codification/executive-order/12127.html (last visited Aug. 29, 2014).

[84] Exec. Order No. 12148, 44 FR 43123 (July 20, 1979), http://www.archives.gov/federal-register/codification/executive-order/12148.html (last visited Aug. 29, 2014). Among other agencies, FEMA absorbed: the Federal Insurance Administration; the National Fire Prevention and Control Administration; the National Weather Service Community Preparedness Program; the Federal Preparedness Agency of the General Services Administration; the Federal Disaster Assistance Administration activities from HUD. Civil defense responsibilities were also transferred to the new agency from the Defense Department's Defense Civil Preparedness Agency. *Id*

[85] Exec. Order No. 12690, 54 FR 39153, Sept. 20, 1989, http://www.presidency.ucsb.edu/ws/?pid=60452 (last visited Aug. 29, 2014).

[86] William Branigin, *Hurricane Hugo Haunts Virgin Islands*, Wash. Post, Oct. 31, 1989, at A1, http://www.washingtonpost.com/wp-srv/national/longterm/hurricane/archives/hugo89a.htm (last visited Aug. 29, 2014).

[87] Michael Sullivan, Monograph, *The National and International Implications of U.S. Army Military Police* 8–12 (Carlisle, PA: U.S. Army War College, 1992), http://www.dtic.mil/cgi-bin/GetTRDoc?AD=ADA255620 (last visited Aug. 29, 2014).

[88] *Id. See also* Frederic L. Borch, Judge Advocates in Combat—Army Lawyers in Military Operations from Vietnam to Haiti 276–78 (2001).

[89] Scheips, *supra* note 18, at 441–49.

the contingency plan under which some 10,000 activated California National Guard troops served alongside 2,500 Active Component troops and 1,700 federal law-enforcement officers from different agencies from across the state to put down disturbances.

In August 1992, FEMA's second major test came as Hurricane Andrew struck the Florida and Louisiana coasts with 165 mph winds, making 250,000 people homeless in the affected areas. Within five days, some 20,000 National Guard and 16,000 XVIII Airborne Corps troops[90] deployed yet again under the Garden Plot contingency plan and FEMA's oversight, and by October, all disaster relief functions were eventually turned over to civilian contractors, so Corps units returned to Ft. Bragg.[91] In its February 1993 report, "Coping with Catastrophe," the National Academy of Public Administration (NAPA) found that "major changes were needed—in the White House, in Congress, in FEMA, in other federal agencies, and in the states and localities."[92] NAPA identified several basic paradigms in preparedness for national security emergencies and domestic civilian emergency preparedness and response that were causes of the failed response, and proposed a "comprehensive set of recommendations to address the causes of the nation's inadequate response to . . . catastrophic events."[93]

D. THE EARLY 2000S THROUGH THE 2010S—PUTTING THE NATIONAL RESPONSE PLAN (FRAMEWORK) TO TEST

Following the September 11, 2001, terrorist attacks, the 2002 Unified Command Plan (UCP)[94] established U.S. Northern Command (NORTHCOM) to plan, organize, and execute homeland defense and civil support missions—marking the first time these missions fell under the direction of a single unified command.[95] NORTHCOM's region of responsibility includes the continental United States, Alaska, Canada, and Mexico, including the Gulf of Mexico and Straits of Florida, as well as water space extending to approximately five hundred nautical miles from the coast.[96] United States Army North/Fifth Army (USARNORTH), at Fort Sam Houston, TX, is both the joint forces land component command

---

[90] XVIII Airborne Corps, *supra* note 62.

[91] *Id.*

[92] NAPA, *Coping with Catastrophe—Building and Emergency Management System to Meet People's Needs in Natural and Manmade Disasters* (Feb. 1993), http://www.fas.org/irp/agency/dhs/fema/coping.pdf (last visited Aug. 29, 2014).

[93] *Id.*

[94] *See, e.g., News Release No. 188-02—Unified Command Plan* (Apr. 2, 2002), http://www.au.af.mil/au/awc/awcgate/unified/ucp17apr.htm (last visited Aug. 29, 2014); MCM 0016-03, Subject: *Promulgation of Unified Command Plan 2002 (with Change-1 and Change-2 incorporated)* (Feb. 4, 2003), http://www.bits.de/NRANEU/others/strategy/UCP-1-2003.pdf (last visited Aug. 29, 2014).

[95] *Special Briefing on the Unified Command Plan, Presenter: Secretary of Defense Donald Rumsfeld*, Apr. 17, 2002, http://www.fas.org/irp/news/2002/04/dod041702b.html (last visited Aug. 29, 2014).

[96] *Id.*

(JFLCC) and the Army service component command (ASCC) to NORTHCOM.[97] Most relevant to military support to civil authorities, USARNORTH's responsibilities are to:

- Execute DoD's homeland defense and civil support operations in the land domain.
- Further develop, organize and integrate DoD CBRNE response capabilities and operations.
- Build the capability to perform the Joint Force Land Component Command and the Army Service Component Command functions.
- Secure land approaches to the homeland.
- Continue to build a highly competent, disciplined workforce in a world class organization.[98]

USARNORTH appointed Defense Coordinating Officers, to be assigned to all ten FEMA regional offices, to more effectively coordinate the availability and employment of DoD resources.[99]

Notwithstanding the realignment of FEMA under the new DHS, and the lessons that should have been learned during Hurricane Andrew and prior troop deployments, federal and state response plans were not adequately revised or rehearsed before the fateful natural disasters to come. Those events were the August–September 2005 disasters of Hurricanes Katrina and Rita, the first and ninth most costly and devastating Atlantic hurricanes ever recorded.[100] Within the United States, and as delineated in the then-extant NRP, disaster response and planning was first and foremost a local government responsibility. States had the option of receiving disaster assistance in accordance with numerous inter-jurisdictional mutual aid agreements, such as the Emergency Management Assistance Compact (EMAC),[101] under which 20,000 civilians and 46,500 Active and National Guard personnel were deployed to the Gulf Coast region to respond to these disasters.[102]

Aside from an estimated $200 billion cleanup cost,[103] the Inspector General of the DHS said his office "received accusations of fraud and waste in the

---

[97] Christine Le Jeune, *Consequence Management: Steps in the Right Direction?*, National Security Watch NSW 10–2, Sept. 8, 2010, at 3, http://www.ausa.org/publications/ilw/Documents/NSW%20 10-2%20v4.pdf (last visited Aug. 29, 2014).

[98] *Mission Statement, Army North*, http://www.arnorth.army.mil/ (last visited Aug. 29, 2014). Note: CBRNE is the abbreviation for chemical, biological, radiological, nuclear and high-yield explosive. *Id.*

[99] Consequence Management, *supra* note 97, at 4.

[100] *See, e.g.*, Special Report of the Committee on Homeland Security and Governmental Affairs, S. Rep. No. 109-322, at 1–737 (2006), http://www.gpo.gov/fdsys/pkg/CRPT-109srpt322/pdf/CRPT-109srpt322.pdf (last visited Aug. 29, 2014).

[101] *Id.* at 10, 99.

[102] U.S. Gov't Accountability Office, GAO-07-854, Emergency Management Assistance Compact: Enhancing EMAC's Collaborative and Administrative Capacity Should Improve National Disaster Response (Aug. 30, 2007), http://www.gao.gov/assets/270/263302.html (last visited Aug. 29, 2014).

[103] *See, e.g.*, *Ocean Facts*, National Ocean Service, NOAA.gov (*revised* Jan. 11, 2013), http://oceanservice.noaa.gov/facts/coastalthreat.html (last visited Aug. 29, 2014).

multibillion-dollar relief programs linked to Hurricane Katrina."[104] Many agencies, including the military, sought the opportunity, and resources, to "get well" and become fully equipped and ready to deploy instantly in a crisis. For instance, the then-Chief of the National Guard Bureau testified to a congressional committee in September 2005 that $1.3 billion was needed immediately, part of $7 billion for "radios, trucks, construction machinery, and medical gear" needed for the National Guard alone.[105]

On September 14, 2007, the DoD's Joint Staff produced overarching guidelines and principles to assist commanders and their staffs in planning, conducting, and assessing DSCA, in the guise of Joint Publication (JP) 3-28, Civil Support.[106] In February 2013, JP 3-28 was supplemented by a Multi-Service Tactics, Techniques, And Procedures (MTTP) publication for DSCA regarding national guard civil support,[107] and the 2007 version of JP 3-28 was superseded by, and updated through, the July 31, 2013, issuance of JP 3-28, Defense Support of Civil Authorities (DSCA) which provides the doctrinal basis for interagency coordination during DSCA operations.[108]

The 2010 Quadrennial Defense Review (QDR) acknowledged the increasing importance of DoD in assisting civil authorities and defending the nation from direct attacks, stating "when responding to an event within the United States, the

---

[104] Philip Shenon, *Official Vows Investigation of No-Bid Relief Contracts*, NYTimes.com, Sept. 14, 2005, http://www.nytimes.com/2005/09/14/national/ nationalspecial/14spend.html?_r=0 (last visited Aug. 29, 2014).

[105] Scott Shane, *At Hearings, Stats and National Guard Make Appeals for Aid*, N.Y. Times.com, Sept. 29, 2005, http://www.nytimes.com/2005/09/29/national/ nationalspecial/29guard.html (last visited Aug. 29, 2014):

> General Blum said the problem had become acute as Guard units had deployed to Iraq and Afghanistan, taking the newest equipment with them and then leaving it there for replacement soldiers to use. That practice was wise, he said, but left the home front with an outdated and dwindling supply of gear, at best about 34 percent of what was needed . . . But, he said, the terrorist attacks of Sept. 11, 2001, and Hurricane Katrina showed the need for the Guard to be fully equipped and ready to deploy instantly in a crisis.

[106] Joint Chiefs of Staff, Joint Publication (JP) *3-28*, Civil Support, Sept. 14, 2007, http://fas.org/irp/doddir/dod/jp3-28.pdf (last visited Aug. 29, 2014).

[107] Army, Marine Corps, Navy, Air Force, DSCA Multi-Service Tactics, Techniques, and Procedures for Defense Support of Civil Authorities and Integrating with National Guard Civil Support, ATP 3.28.1 (FM 3-28.1) (MCWP 3-36.2) (NTTP 3-57.2) (AFTTP 3-2.67) Feb. 2013, http://armypubs.army.mil/ doctrine/DRpubs/dr_a/pdf/atp3_28x1.pdf (last visited Aug. 29, 2014). Individual service component (e.g., Army, Marine Corps) issuances also exist to further guide doctrinal implementation, including but not limited to: Department of Army, Army Doctrine Publication (ADP) 3-28, Defense Support of Civil Authorities, July 2012, http://armypubs.army.mil/doctrine/DR_pubs/dra/pdf/adp3_28.pdf (last visited Aug. 29, 2014); US Marine Corps, MARADMINS Active Number: 589/05, USMC Roles and Missions in Homeland Defense and Defense Support of Civil Authorities, Dec. 13, 2005, http://www.marines.mil/News/ Messages/ MessagesDisplay/tabid/13286/ Article/117580/usmc-roles-and-missions-in-homeland-defense-and-defense-support-of-civil-author.aspx (last visited Aug. 29, 2014).

[108] Joint Chiefs of Staff, Joint Publication (JP) 3-28, Defense Support of Civil Authorities (July 31, 2013), http://www.dtic.mil/doctrine/new_pubs/jp3_28.pdf (last visited Aug. 29, 2014).

Department of Defense will almost always be in a supporting role."[109] To confront these security challenges, DoD, as stated in the 2010 QDR, intended to reorganize its domestic CBRNE consequence management enterprise primarily within state National Guard forces. As part of this initiative, DoD has been working to create Homeland Response Forces (HRFs) tailored to deal with CBRNE incidents yet to come in America's future.[110]

A significant change to the law came on December 31, 2011, with the amendment of Title 10 (specifically 10 U.S.C. § 12304a) ordering the Army Reserve, Navy Reserve, Marine Corps Reserve, and Air Force Reserve to active duty to provide assistance in response to a major disaster or emergency. When a governor requests federal assistance in responding to a major disaster or emergency, to respond to the governor's request the Secretary of Defense may, without the consent of the member affected, order any unit and any member of the Army Reserve, Navy Reserve, Marine Corps Reserve, and Air Force Reserve to active duty for a continuous period of not more than 120 days.[111]

The revisions that resulted in the NRF were put to the test during Fall 2012, when Hurricane Sandy and the northeaster that swept through the Mid-Atlantic and Northeastern United States required that the DoD provide emergency temporary power and pumping capability, and to distribute fuel, food, cold-weather clothing,

---

[109] U.S. Dep't of Def. Quadrennial Defense Review Report 19, Feb. 2010, http://www.defense.gov/qdr/images/QDR_as_of_12Feb10_1000.pdf (last visited Aug. 29, 2014). The DoD states that:

> The Quadrennial Defense Review (QDR) is a legislatively-mandated review of Department of Defense strategy and priorities. The QDR will set a long-term course for DoD as it assesses the threats and challenges that the nation faces and re-balances DoD's strategies, capabilities, and forces to address today's conflicts and tomorrow's threats.

[110] *Id.* Christine Le Jeune of the Institute of Land Warfare, Association of the United States Army (AUSA) noted that:

> Several states have already announced plans for development of HRFs for each FEMA region: Ohio and Washington will launch units by October 2011, and California, Georgia, Massachusetts, Missouri, New York, Pennsylvania, Texas and Utah will follow suit in 2012. Each unit will focus on planning, training and exercising at the regional level when not engaged in consequence management operations. If necessary, HRFs will function alongside other National Guard-sourced CBRNE consequence management forces that are employed by the governors. These forces include 57 weapons of mass destruction civil support teams (WMD-CSTs) and 17 CBRNE enhanced response force packages (CERFPs), as well as federally-controlled elements such as defense CBRNE response forces (DCRFs) and two consequence management command and control elements for follow-on forces. Current thought within the National Guard Bureau is that this new construct is more responsive with a better match of lifesaving capabilities and allows for an improved balance between state and federal control.

See Consequence Management, *supra* note 97, at 4.

[111] 10 U.S.C. § 12304a (2013), http://www.law.cornell.edu/uscode/text/10/12304a (last visited Aug. 29, 2014).

and other comfort items as requested by civil authorities.[112] Some 4,000 Active Component NORTHCOM personnel supported Hurricane Sandy relief operations in the affected area, alongside 6,618 National Guard personnel from New York, New Jersey, Connecticut, and West Virginia assisting in response and recovery efforts across their affected states.[113]

In May 2013, NORTHCOM coordinated DoD-provided support to the FEMA and state and local response activities in response to tornado-devastated areas in Oklahoma.[114] The command activated the Region VI Defense Coordinating Officer, and the Defense Coordinating Element to Moore, OK, to validate, plan and coordinate potential DoD support of FEMA's disaster response operations. It also deployed search-and-rescue coordinators as part of the Federal Search and Rescue Coordination Group (FSARCG), and to facilitate DoD's support of potential life-saving and response operations. DoD will provide regional knowledge, requirements validation, and liaison support to the affected areas.[115]

Natural disasters continued during the summer of 2013, especially in the guise of wildfires. Personnel and equipment from Colorado-based military installations assisted local, state, and federal authorities in battling the June 2013 Black Forest Fire in the southern part of Colorado.[116] Support was provided through several authorities, NORTHCOM officials said, including mission assignments, immediate response authority, and mutual aid agreements. [117] At least 150 Colorado National Guard troops, along with their equipment, were employed to contain 65 percent of blazes, affecting a twenty-two-square-mile area with at least two fatalities and the destruction of nearly five hundred homes,[118] with the mission complete by June 22, 2013.[119] *Arizona National* Guardsmen along with California and North Carolina Air National Guard tankers and crewmembers joined the response to *wildfires* that killed nineteen civilian firefighters in the first week of July 2013.[120]

---

[112] Department of Defense Office of the Ass't Sec. of Def. (Public Affairs), News Release No. 879-12, *Update on the DoD and National Guard Response to Hurricane Sandy*, Nov. 7, 2012, http://www.defense.gov/releases/release.aspx?releaseid=15665 (last visited Aug. 29, 2014).

[113] *Id.*

[114] *U.S. NORTHCOM Aids Oklahoma Tornado Disaster Relief Efforts*, Af.mil, May 22, 2013, http://www.af.mil/news/story.asp?id=123349626 (updated May 23, 2013) (last visited Aug. 29, 2014).

[115] *Id.*

[116] U.S. Northern Command News Release, *Military Bases Support Colorado Firefighting Effort*, Defense.gov, June 14, 2013, http://www.defense.gov/News/newsarticle.aspx?ID=120290 (last visited Aug. 29, 2014).

[117] *Id.*

[118] Jecca Geffre, *Guard Members Man Colorado Fire Lines on Father's Day*, Army.mil (June 17, 2013), http://www.army.mil/article/105709/ (last visited Aug. 29, 2014).

[119] Colorado National Guard Press Release, *Colo. National Guard Black Forest Fire Security Mission Complete*, co.ng.mil (June 22, 2013), http://co.ng.mil/media/releases/Pages/130619-bffire14.aspx (last visited Aug. 29, 2014).

[120] *See* Video, *National Guard Responds to Arizona Wildfires*, Dvidshub.net (July 2, 2013), http://www.dvidshub.net/video/295286/national-guard-responds-arizona-wildfires#.UdiPo1OHRmE (last visited Aug. 29, 2014); Tony Perry, *2 California Air National Guard Tankers to Fight Arizona Blaze*, L.A. Times, July 2, 2013, http://www.latimes.com/local/lanow/la-me-ln-air-national-guard-tankers-arizona-fire-20130702,0,6370548.story (last visited Aug. 29, 2014); *Charlotte National Guard*

Towards the end of predicting future natural disasters on the basis of past patterns, the National Geospatial-Intelligence Agency (NGA—formerly NGIC) began in Fall 2013 to create a global geographic intelligence database that can "anticipate future world trouble spots and humanitarian crises by combining detailed mapping with information about trends, demographics, and weather patterns in those areas."[121] The NGA publicly discloses it is "[a]n agency of the U.S. Department of Defense that manages and provides imagery and geospatial information for diverse *military*, civil, and international needs," and among its many missions, that it "assists humanitarian and disaster relief efforts by working directly with the lead federal agencies responding to fires, floods, earthquakes, landslides, hurricanes or other natural or manmade disasters."[122] Such a geospatial database may prove useful, if not indispensible in dealing with both foreign and domestic natural and man-made disasters.

During the spring of 2014, another series of domestic natural disasters included deadly and severe storms, tornadoes and flooding from April 28 through May 3, 2014. In the aftermath of destruction, National Guard members worked "in coordinated efforts with civilian agencies . . . responding to communities in several states across the south."[123]

Furthermore, in that same period at least sixty-two thousand unaccompanied children from Central America came across the U.S.-Mexico border from the fall of 2013 up through the time of this writing, more than twice the number that came the previous year; they were, in the estimation of NORTHCOM Commander General Jacoby, fleeing gang activity, hence seeking legal entry to the United States.[124] General Jacoby said the lawlessness in Central America could spawn hybrid organizations that deal in terrorism, posing a threat to U.S. national security.[125] In defense support to the Department of Health and Human Services (HHS), NORTHCOM established a temporary housing facility at Joint Base San Antonio-Lackland, Texas, for the unaccompanied children stopped by U.S. Border Patrol; they were later cared for by the HHS Administration for Children and Families (ACF).[126]

Team to Fight Wildfires in Arizona, WSOCTV.COM, July 5, 2013, http://www.wsoctv.com/news/news/local/charlotte-national-guard-team-fight-wildfires-ariz/nYfPs/ (last visited Aug. 29, 2014).

[121] Ray Locker, *Military Maps to Focus on Natural Disasters, Analysis*, USATODAY.COM (Nov. 19, 2013), http://www.usatoday.com/story/nation/2013/11/19/nga-geoanalytics-map-natural-disasters/3628911/ (last visited Aug. 29, 2014).

[122] *About NGA*, NGA.MIL https://www.nga.mil/About/Pages/default.aspx (last visited Aug. 29, 2014).

[123] American Forces Press Service, *National Guard Coordinates Storm Response with Civilian Agencies*, DEFENSE.GOV (Apr. 29, 2014), http://www.defense.gov/news/newsarticle.aspx?id=122145 (last visited Aug. 29, 2014).

[124] Michael De Yoanna, *Top U.S. General Says Border Kids Fleeing Gangs* CPR.ORG (Aug. 6, 2014). http://www.cpr.org/news/story/top-us-general-says-border-kids-fleeing-gangs#sthash.8yvdB79H.dpuf (last visited Aug. 29, 2014).

[125] *Id.*

[126] NORAD and USNORTHCOM Public Affairs Press Release, USNORTHCOM Supports Health and Human Services, NORTHCOM.MIL (May 17, 2014), http://www.northcom.mil/Newsroom/tabid/3104/Article/3065/usnorthcom-supports-health-and-human-services.aspx (last visited Aug. 29, 2014).

On July 21, 2014, the rapid influx of those so-called "border kids" across the Mexico-U.S. border prompted Texas governor Rick Perry to controversially deploy one thousand Title 32 National Guard troops along the 1,254-mile border as part of the ongoing Operation Strong Safety.[127] That multiagency law enforcement initiative, first launched in Fall 2013, was intended "to address three public safety issues identified in the region: 1) significant criminal activity; 2) significant number of commercial vehicles on the roadways; and 3) unsafe driving practices."[128] Governor Perry "guaranteed that the National Guard w[ould] remain on the border at least for . . . three months, which is the time that the $36 million in the state budget that can be used to pay for them w[ould] last."[129] Prior to that deployment, Lieutenant General (retired) H. Steven Blum, former Chief of the National Guard Bureau from 2003 to 2009, told the media that

> There may be many other organizations that might more appropriately be called upon. If you're talking about search and rescue, maintaining the rule of law or restoring conditions back to normal after a natural disaster or a catastrophe, the [National] Guard is superbly suited to that. I'm not so sure that what we're dealing with in scope and causation right now would make it the ideal choice.[130]

The deployment became a political campaign matter as well, with Democratic Texas gubernatorial candidate Wendy Davis "question[ing] the deployment of . . . troops on the border with Mexico to curtail illegal immigration and [promising], if elected, that she will study withdrawing them."[131]

The previously discussed 1033 program, as well as the National Guard deployment in Ferguson, MO, became the subject of critical media focus in the wake of police response to riots in August 2014 following the police shooting of crime suspect Mike Brown.[132] In response to calls for "demilitarization" of the police, Attorney General Eric H. Holder Jr. said "[a]t a time when we must seek to rebuild

---

[127] Leigh Ann Caldwell, Perry Sending National Guard Troops to Border, CNN.COM (July 21, 2014), http://www.cnn.com/2014/07/21/politics/perry-national-guard-border/ (last visited Aug. 29, 2014).

[128] News Release, Texas Department of Public Safety, *Operation Strong Safety Targets Crime, Takes Back Border*, TXDPS.STATE.TX.US (Oct. 24, 2013), http://www.txdps.state.tx.us/director_staff/media_and_communications/pr102413.htm (last visited Aug. 29, 2014).

[129] *Wendy Davis Says She May Withdraw Texas National Guard from Border if Elected Governor*, FOXNEWSLATINO.COM (Aug. 8, 2014), http://latino.foxnews.com/latino/politics/2014/08/07/wendy-davis-questions-deployment-national-guard-on-southern-border/ (last visited Aug. 29, 2014).

[130] Greg Sargent, *Sending in the National Guard Iisn't the Answer*, WASHINGTON POST.COM (July 15, 2014), http://www.washingtonpost.com/blogs/plum-line/wp/2014/07/15/sending-in-the-national-guard-isnt-the-answer/ (last visited Aug. 29, 2014).

[131] *Wendy Davis*, *supra* note 129.

[132] Bosman & Apuzzo, *supra* note 44. At least one media report disputes that the equipment worn or used by law enforcement responding to riots in Ferguson was obtained through the "1033 Program." *See, e.g.*, Jason Leopold, *Mittens, Not M4s: What Ferguson Police Really Got from the Pentagon's 1033 Program*, VICE.COM (Aug. 26, 2014), https://news.vice.com/article/mittens-not-m4s-what-ferguson-police-really-got-from-the-pentagons-1033-program (last visited Aug. 29, 2014).

trust between law enforcement and the local community . . . I am deeply concerned that the deployment of military equipment and vehicles sends a conflicting message."[133] On Friday, August 15, 2014, Senate Armed Services Chair Carl Levin (D-MI) called for a review of the so-called 1033 program, saying:

> Congress established this program out of real concern that local law enforcement agencies were literally outgunned by drug criminals. We intended this equipment to keep police officers and their communities safe from heavily armed drug gangs and terrorist incidents. Before the defense authorization bill comes to the Senate floor, we will review this program to determine if equipment provided by the Defense Department is being used as intended.[134]

Missouri Democratic senator Claire McCaskill, the chairman of the Subcommittee on Financial & Contracting Oversight, also announced she will lead a hearing on the program, observing that:

> We need to de-militarize this situation—this kind of response by the police has become the problem instead of the solution. I obviously respect law enforcement's work to provide public safety, but my constituents are allowed to have peaceful protests, and the police need to respect that right and protect that right. Today is going to be a new start, we can and need to do better.[135]

Shortly thereafter, President Obama ordered a "comprehensive review of the government's decade-old strategy of outfitting local police departments with military-grade body armor, mine-resistant trucks, silencers and automatic rifles," according to media interviews of senior officials.[136] This is, in no small part, due to accountability problems surfacing regarding the 184 state and local police agencies reportedly suspended from the "1033 Program" for losing weapons or failing

---

[133] Bosman & Apuzzo, *supra* note 44.

[134] Sahil Kapur, *Senate Will Review Military Transfers to Local Police, Key Senator Says*, TALKINGPOINTSMEMO.COM (Aug. 15, 2014), http://talkingpointsmemo.com/ livewire/carl-levin-senate-review-military-transfers-1033 (last visited Aug. 29, 2014).

[135] Caroline May, *McCaskill Announces Hearing on Police Militarization*, BREITBART.COM (Aug. 22, 2014), http://www.breitbart.com/Big-Government/2014/ 08/22/McCaskill-Announces-Hearing-on-Police-Militarization (last visited Aug. 29, 2014). By contrast, police associations are "beginning a major lobbying push to protect their access to the military equipment [and] are gearing up for a fight with lawmakers and the Obama administration over whether it should be continued." '"We are the most vigorous law enforcement advocacy group, and we intend to be at our most vigorous on this issue,' said Jim Pasco, the executive director of the Fraternal Order of Police, the largest police organization in the country." *See* Megan R. Wilson, *Police Lobby Fights to Keep Gear*, THEHILL.COM (Aug. 28, 2014), http://thehill.com/business-a-lobbying/business-a-lobbying/216127-law-enforcement-lobbies-to-keep-gear#ixzz3BpVgEXum (last visited Aug. 29, 2014).

[136] Matt Apuzzo & Michael S. Schmidt, *In Washington, Second Thoughts on Arming Police*, NYTIMES.COM (Aug. 23, 2014), http://www.nytimes.com/2014/08/24/us/in-washington-second-thoughts-on-arming-police.html?_r=0 (last visited Aug. 29, 2014).

to comply with other stipulations.[137] Notably, the nationally known sheriff of Maricopa County, Joe Arpaio, admitted that his department had been suspended from the program and was missing nine firearms (eight .45-caliber pistols and one M-16 rifle) issued to the agency out of two hundred weapons from the surplus program.[138] Some twenty to twenty-two weapons were unaccounted for over the years, but roughly half were recovered from retired or current deputies who, incredibly, had brought them home.[139] Under the 1033 Program, the Maricopa County Sheriff's Office amassed an arsenal of "a Hummer, a tank, 90 M-16 rifles, 116 .45-caliber pistols, 34 M-14 rifles and three helicopters."[140]

By way of partial closure regarding the Ferguson incidents, Missouri governor Jay Nixon announced early on August 21, 2014, that the National Guard, which was brought in to provide security for the police command center, would be withdrawn from Ferguson; this withdrawal began the next day, some five days after being dispatched to help "quell the unrest."[141]

IV. Part 3: The Framework for Future National Response to Disasters and Emergencies

The second edition of the NRF, updated in May 2013, provides context for how the whole community works together, and how response efforts under the myriad of documents cited up to this point relate to all other parts of national preparedness.[142] The NRF remains the primary instrument for applying federal capabilities during disaster response.[143] It is one of the five documents of a set of National Planning Frameworks, with each covering one preparedness mission area: Prevention, Protection, Mitigation, Response, or Recovery. Replacing the 2008 NRF, which superseded the corresponding sections of the NRP (2004, with 2006 revisions), it presents the principles guiding DHS that "enable the whole community to work together to prevent, protect against, mitigate, respond to, and recover from the effects of incidents regardless of cause, size, location, or

---

[137] Daniel Rivero & Jorge Rivas, *How Did America's Police Departments Lose Loads of Military-Issued Weapons?*, FUSION.NET (Aug. 27, 2014), http://fusion.net/leadership/story/americas-police-departments-lose-loads-military-issued-weapons-984250 (Aug. 29, 2014).

[138] Megan Cassidy, *MCSO Missing Nine Weapons from Pentagon's 1033 Program*, *AZcentral.com* (Aug. 27, 2014), http://www.azcentral.com/story/news/local/phoenix/2014/08/26/mcso-weapons-pentagon-suspension-1033/14659089/ (last visited Aug. 29, 2014).

[139] *Id.*

[140] *Id.*

[141] Campbell Robertson & Marc Santora, *National Guard Troops Begin to Leave Ferguson*, NYTIMES.COM (Aug. 22, 2014), http://www.nytimes.com/2014/08/23/us/ ferguson-missouri-protests.html?_r=0 (last visited Aug. 29, 2014).

[142] DHS, *National Response Framework, Second Edition* (May 2013), http://www.fema.gov/library/file;jsessionid=A834E1F9044051183C2A93744784ABA6.Worker2Public2?type=publishedFile&file=final_national_response_framework_20130501.pdf&fileid=caae7ee0-b35d-11e2-a3a3-001cc456982e (last visited Aug. 29, 2014).

[143] Strategy for Homeland Defense, *supra* note 14, at 8.

complexity."[144] In its most current iteration, the NRF establishes a comprehensive, national, all-hazards approach to domestic incident response. When federal military and civilian personnel and resources are authorized to support civil authorities, command of those forces will remain with the Secretary of Defense. DoD elements in the incident area of operations and National Guard forces under the command of a governor will coordinate closely with response organizations at all levels.[145]

The U.S. government has an inherent emergency power, in addition to those powers specifically set forth in law, as well as executive order, and policy. In addition to the Posse Comitatus Act, The Insurrection Act, and the Stafford Act, Executive Order 12630 provides for governmental actions and interference with constitutionally protected property rights.[146] Department of Defense regulations assert another exception that does not rest on statutory authority, but is available in very limited circumstances and covers:

> Actions that are taken under the inherent right of the U.S. Government . . . to ensure the preservation of public order and to carry out governmental operations within its territorial limits, or otherwise in accordance with applicable law, by force, if necessary.[147]

The emergency power, according to DoD directives, is available to protect federal property and functions, and to authorize

> prompt and vigorous Federal action, including use of military forces, to prevent loss of life or wanton destruction of property and to restore governmental functioning and public order when sudden and unexpected civil disturbances, disaster, or calamities seriously endanger life and property and disrupt normal governmental functions to such an extent that duly constituted local authorities are unable to control the situation.[148]

When employed or deployed after civil disturbances or natural disasters, federal troops from the DoD would and will receive direction from FEMA, in accordance with the NRF, to work solo or in concert with other federal agencies to

---

[144] *Id.* at 3.

[145] *Id.* DoD is a supporting agency for each of the fifteen Emergency Support Functions (ESFs) and each of the six Incident Annexes of the NRF. *See, e.g.*, Ass't. Sec. Def. for Homeland Def. and America's Sec. Aff., *Frequently Asked Questions*, http://policy.defense.gov/OUSDPOffices/ASDforHomelandDefenseAmericasSecurityAffa/faqs.aspx (last updated July 2013). For explanation of the fifteen ESFs, and the six Incident Annexes of the NRF, see National Response Framework, *supra* note 142, at 32–36 and 37–38, respectively.

[146] Exec. Order No. 12360, 53 FR 8859 (Mar. 15, 1988), http://www.archives.gov/federal-register/codification/executive-order/12630.html (Aug. 29, 2014).

[147] *See* Elsea & Mason, *supra* note 36, at 3 (*citing* Department of Defense Directive (DoDD) 5525.5, DoD Cooperation with Civilian Law Enforcement Officials Encl. 4, § E4.1.2.3 (January 15, 1986) (Administrative reissuance incorporating change 1, Dec. 20, 1989) http://www.fas.org/irp/doddir/dod/d5525_5.pdf, (last visited Aug. 29, 2014).

[148] *Id.* at 3.

provide personnel, equipment, supplies, facilities, and managerial, technical, and advisory services. Support scenarios could include: a Presidential Declaration of a Major Disaster,[149] an Order to Perform Emergency Work Essential for the Preservation of Life and Property,[150] and, a Presidential Declaration of an Emergency.[151]

In all but the instance of a Presidential Declaration of Emergency, the governor of an affected state or territory must request assistance regardless of any state or local capacity to render disaster assistance.[152] The NRF allows DHS to coordinate federal agencies that work alongside state and local agencies. In the words of past DHS Secretary Michael Chertoff, these scenarios do not "supersede

---

[149] *See, e.g., Disaster Declarations*, FEMA.GOV, http://www.fema.gov/disasters (last updated July 2, 2013) (last visited Aug. 29, 2014).

[150] *See, e.g., Federal Response Plan Basic Plan* (Jan. 2003), http://www.au.af.mil/au/awc/awcgate/frp/frpbasic.pdf (last visited Aug. 29, 2014).

[151] 50 U.S.C. § 1621 (2014), http://www.law.cornell.edu/uscode/text/50/1621 (last visited Aug. 29, 2014). This declaration under congressional statutory and Article II constitutional authority provides that:

> (a) With respect to Acts of Congress authorizing the exercise, during the period of a national emergency, of any special or extraordinary power, the President is authorized to declare such national emergency. Such proclamation shall immediately be transmitted to the Congress and published in the Federal Register.
> (b) Any provisions of law conferring powers and authorities to be exercised during a national emergency shall be effective and remain in effect
>   (1) only when the President (in accordance with subsection (a) of this section), specifically declares a national emergency, and
>   (2) only in accordance with this chapter. No law enacted after September 14, 1976, shall supersede this subchapter unless it does so in specific terms, referring to this subchapter, and declaring that the new law supersedes the provisions of this subchapter.

Id. In addition to such immediate response authority, military installations may have concluded mutual aid agreements with local agencies based on pre-coordinated conditions regarding fire, emergency medical services, hazardous materials, and public safety, and may also receive requests for assistance via an action required form in a mission assignment process. *See* Hurston, *supra* note 51, at slide 26 (*citing* DEPARTMENT OF DEFENSE INSTRUCTION 6055.17, DOD INSTALLATION EMERGENCY MANAGEMENT (IEM) PROGRAM (Jan. 13, 2009) (incorporating Change 1 (Nov. 19, 2010), http://www.dtic.mil/whs/directives/corres/pdf/ 605517p.pdf (last visited Aug. 29, 2014). With regards to response for all-hazards incidents, see DEPARTMENT OF DEFENSE INSTRUCTION 3020.40, DOD POLICY AND RESPONSIBILITY FOR CRITICAL INFRASTRUCTURE, Jan. 14, 2010, incorporating Change 2, Sept. 21, 2012, http://www.fas.org/irp/doddir/dod/d3020_40.pdf (last visited Aug. 29, 2014); DEPARTMENT OF DEFENSE INSTRUCTION 3020.45, DEFENSE CRITICAL INFRASTRUCTURE PROGRAM (DCIP) MANAGEMENT (21 Apr. 2008), 6, 2014); DEPARTMENT OF DEFENSE INSTRUCTION 3020.52, DOD INSTALLATION CHEMICAL, BIOLOGICAL, RADIOLOGICAL, NUCLEAR, AND HIGH-YIELD EXPLOSIVE (CBRNE) PREPAREDNESS STANDARDS (May 18, 2012), http://www.dtic.mil/whs/directives/corres/pdf/302052p.pdf (last visited Aug. 29, 2014); DEPARTMENT OF DEFENSE INSTRUCTION 6440.03, and; DEPARTMENT OF DEFENSE INSTRUCTION 6440.03, DOD LABORATORY NETWORK (DLN) (June 10, 2011), <http://www.dtic.mil/whs/directives/corres/pdf/644003p.pdf (last visited Aug. 29, 2014).

[152] *See, e.g., Federal Authorities for Disaster Response*, CSIS—Arnold & Porter LLP, http://csis.org/files/media/csis/events/051128_rolesauthorities.pdf (last visited Aug. 29, 2014).

the state and local government," but "fit with the state and local government in a comprehensive response plan."[153]

Plans are only useful if reviewed, rehearsed, and effectively implemented when contingencies arise. Toward that end, the DHS exhorts that effective preparedness is a critical precondition for successful response, and encourages a "higher level of readiness" of "engaged partnerships with elected and appointed officials, dedicated emergency management practitioners, nongovernmental organizations, and the private sector, "by drawing a sharper focus on the value of the following preparedness activities: planning, organizing, training, equipping, exercising, and applying lessons learned."[154] For end users of the NRF, preserving, and protecting private and public assets, the "[m]astery of these key functions supports unity of effort, and thus [the] ability to save lives, protect property, and meet basic human needs."[155]

The future is unpredictable, so in conjunction with state and federal plans, cities across the United States are taking steps to be in a better position to respond to disasters. *USA Today* reported that many local preparedness plans focus on how to protect critical infrastructure and how to keep critical systems functioning during and after a natural and man-made disaster.[156] The Rockefeller Foundation announced in May 2013 that it would fund "Chief Resilience Officer" (CRO) positions in a hundred cities, on six continents in twenty countries for five years.[157] In April 2014, San Francisco became the first city to benefit from a CRO; Patrick Otellini brings to the CRO role a background in public policy, private sector dealings with complex planning, building and fire code issues, and experience as San Francisco's Director of Earthquake Safety.[158] The CROs will have a wide range of duties, including developing a communications system that can reach anyone during a storm, or a transportation system to get people to safety in the event of a hurricane or weather-related disaster.[159] These CROs will

---

[153] *Federal Officials Hold News Conference on Katrina Response*, CNN.com, (Aug. 15, 2005) http://transcripts.cnn.com/TRANSCRIPTS/0508/31/lol.01.html (last visited Aug. 29, 2014).

[154] FEMA, *NRF Fact Sheet—Federal Emergency Management Agency* (2014), http://www.fema.gov/pdf/emergency/nrf/NRFOnePageFactSheet.pdf (last visited Aug. 29, 2014).

[155] Sarah Twombly, *Q&A With The World's First Chief Resilience Officer*, ROCKEFELLERFOUNDATION.ORG, 9 April 2014, http://www.rockefellerfoundation.org/ blog/q-with-worlds-first-chief-resilience (last visited Aug. 29, 2014). By June 4, 2014, the world's second CRO had been appointed, outside the United States in Medellin, Colombia; *see, e.g.*, Sarah Twombly, *Introducing Medellin's Chief Resilience Officer*, ROCKEFELLERFOUNDATION.ORG (June 4, 2014), http://www.rockefellerfoundation.org/ blog/ introducing-medellins-chief-resilience (last visited Aug. 29, 2014).

[156] Greg Toppo, *Cities Step Up Disaster-Response Planning*, USA TODAY, June 9, 2013, http://www.usatoday.com/story/news/nation/2013/06/09/cities-resilience-officer/2373911/ (last visited Aug. 29, 2014).

[157] *Id.* CROs will work to ensure cities will "emerge even stronger from these kinds of shocks and stresses," as Rockefeller president Judith Rodin told *USA Today.* Rodin further said "[w]e can't predict everything, but we can prepare for many things and prepare our capacity to rebound more effectively when they hit." *Id.*

[158] *Id.*

[159] *U.S. Cities Preparing for Disasters*, HOMELANDSECURITYNEWSWIRE.COM, June 13, 2013, http://www.homelandsecuritynewswire.com/dr20130613-u-s-cities-preparing-for-disasters (last visited Aug. 29, 2014).

necessarily need to closely coordinate for DoD support and operate in a complex interagency-public-private partnership with FEMA, in accordance with city, state, corporate, and NRF guidelines.[160]

In a so-called mega-catastrophe, however, when the status of every state's stability is uncertain, that willingness to share breaks down.[161] In cases such as these, the resources and competencies of the DoD will be in great need. In planning for such complex catastrophes, military leaders at all levels and federal partners from FEMA met on June 5, 2013, to participate in a one-day tabletop exercise hosted by USARNORTH to tackle different complex catastrophe scenarios that comprised the most serious crises imaginable, in a whole-of-government response to them.[162] The elaborate scenario "started with a massive earthquake rumbling throughout Southern California [with] cascading effects that followed included mudslides, broken dams, fires, flooding and massive property damage, not to mention the potential loss of life, and turned a very bad situation into a worst-case scenario."[163] Among the many lessons relearned or real-world experiences validated, the exercise demonstrated that after state and local authorities had reached their capacity in dealing with previous disasters, additional federal authorities, such as the Department of Justice, may have to assist local authorities with response to civil unrest and other challenges.[164]

The FBI has aptly observed that "[t]here's no room for failure—when it comes to weapons of mass destruction, even a single incident could be catastrophic."[165] A "second nuclear age" is one in which the threat of attack by various weapons of mass destruction always looms large over the United States and beyond.[166]

---

[160] *Id.* At the time of this writing, Berkeley, CA, had become the next city to appoint a Chief Resilience Officer, Timothy Burroughs. *See, e.g.*, Charles Siler, *Berkeley Appoints First "Chief Resilience Officer,"* BERKELEYSIDE.COM, Aug. 7, 2014, http://www.berkeleyside.com/2014/08/07/berkeley-appoints-first-chief-resilience-officer/ (Aug. 29, 2014). A week after that appointment, Oakland, CA, hired Victoria Salinas as their Chief Resilience Officer. *See* Will Doig, *Oakland Hires Its First "Chief Resilience Officer,"* PUBLICCEO.COM, Aug. 14, 2014, http://www.publicceo.com/2014/08/oakland-hires-its-first-chief-resilience-officer/ (last visited Aug. 29, 2014).

[161] PAUL STOCKTON, DOD AND THE PROBLEM OF MEGA-CATASTROPHES, THREATS AT OUR THRESHOLD HOMELAND DEFENSE AND HOMELAND SECURITY IN THE NEW CENTURY 30, Carlisle, PA, U.S. Army War College (Bert Tussing ed., 2007), http://www.csl.army.mil/usacsl/Publications/Threats%20at%20Our%20Threshold/Chap%201%20-%20Mega-Catastrophes.pdf (last visited Aug. 29, 2014).

[162] Army North, *supra* note 10.

[163] *Id.*

[164] *Id.*

[165] FBI—Weapons of Mass Destruction Directorate (WMDD), *There's No Room for Failure—When It Comes to Weapons of Mass Destruction, Even a Single Incident Could Be Catastrophic*, FBI.GOV, http://www.fbi.gov/about-us/investigate/terrorism/wmd (last visited Aug. 29, 2014).

[166] *See, e.g.*, Paul Bracken, *Biological Weapons as a Strategic Threat*, 116 PUB. HEALTH REP., 2001 SUPP. 2 at 5–8, http://www.publichealthreports.org/issueopen.cfm?articleID=1037 (last visited Aug. 29, 2014); Kevin H. Govern. *Agroterrorism and Ecoterrorism: A Survey of Indo-American Approaches under Law and Policy to Prevent and Defend Against the Potential Threats Ahead*, 10 FLA. COASTAL L. REV. 223–61 (2009), http://works.bepress.com/kevin_govern/4 (last visited Aug. 29, 2014).

In accordance with direction from the Chairman of the Joint Chiefs of Staff, the Army provides the bulk of the Defense Chemical, Biological, Radiological, and Nuclear Response Force for Fiscal Year [FY] 2013 and beyond. According to the National Guard Posture Statement, some "97% of America lives within a five-hour response of a National Guard Homeland Response Force or Chemical, Biological Radiological, Nuclear (CBRN) Enhanced Response Force Package."[167] If weapons of mass destruction are ever used on U.S. soil, the Army Reserve's consequence management capabilities, in particular, will prove indispensible in providing mission-ready soldiers and equipment.[168] Toward that end of readiness, "[s]pecialized units like the National Guard's Weapons of Mass Destruction Civil Support Teams conducted 1,720 response, standby, and assist missions in FY12."[169]

Former Secretary of Defense Leon Panetta warned the nation in 2012 of a potential coming "cyber Pearl Harbor; an attack that would cause physical destruction and the loss of life . . . [that] would paralyze and shock the nation and create a new, profound sense of vulnerability."[170] Beyond the realms of four-dimensional operations on land, in and below the seas, and in the air and space, is a so-called "fifth domain"[171] or "fifth dimension" of warfare.[172] In an era where the keyboard and mouse have become weapons of conflict as well as tools for peace, DoD will continue to use its significant capability and expertise in support of a whole-of-government approach to protect the nation. The policy and legal authorities governing DoD's domestic activities—such as Defense Support to Civil Authorities—extend to cyber operations, as they would in any other domain. DoD will continue to work closely with its interagency partners,

---

[167] National Guard Bureau, *2014 National Guard Posture Statement—Sustaining an Operational Force*, 4-38, http://www.arng.army.mil/News/publications/ ApostureStatements/2014/Posture%20 Statement%20FINAL%20hires.pdf (last visited Aug. 29, 2014).

[168] National Guard Bureau, *National Guard and Reserve Equipment Report for Fiscal Year 2013 (NGRER FY 2014)*, 2–5, http://ra.defense.gov/documents/publications/ NGRER%20FY2014.pdf (last visited Aug. 29, 2014).

[169] 2014 National Guard Posture Statement, *supra* note 167, at 27. Toward that end, "Lifesaving Capabilities" include:

- 10 Homeland Response Forces, totaling 5,660 Guard members.
- 17 Chemical, Biological, Radiological, Nuclear (CBRN) Enhanced Response Force Packages, called CERFPs, totaling 3,332 Guard members.
- 57 Weapons of Mass Destruction Civil Support Teams (WMD-CSTs), each with 22 full-time National Guard members, conducted in excess of 1,720 response, standby, and assist missions in FY12.

[170] Leon E. Panetta, U.S. Sec'y of Defense, Remarks on Cybersecurity to the Business Executives for National Security, New York City (Oct. 11, 2012), http://www.defense.gov/transcripts/transcript.aspx?transcriptid=5136 (last visited Aug. 29, 2014).

[171] *War in the Fifth Domain*, ECONOMIST.COM (July 1, 2010), http://www.economist.com/node/16478792 (last visited Aug. 29, 2014).

[172] *Fighting in the Fifth Dimension*, ALJAZEERA.COM (Feb. 19, 2012), http://www.aljazeera.com/programmes/aljazeeraworld/2011/10/2011101916939402528.html (Aug. 29, 2014).

including the Departments of Justice and Homeland Security, to address threats to the United States from wherever they originate.[173]

V. Conclusion

Past is certain to be prologue when it comes to both causes and effects of natural and man-made disasters. As then-Lieutenant Colonel Michael L. Sullivan, one of Operation Hawkeye's key Military Police commanders noted in the aftermath of Hurricane Hugo, military forces have tremendous capabilities to "restore public order and essential services following a natural disaster, to train local law enforcement personnel to improve services, and to operate in a complex cultural and political setting."[174] Still, in keeping with the nation's great traditions of our military forces being subject to civilian control, Lieutenant General Perry Wiggins, commanding general, USARNORTH has noted that:

> In 99 percent of the cases [in providing support to civil authorities], the DoD will be supporting another principal fellow agency in the response ... and that's important to understand in the difference of operating in the homeland. In the homeland, the strength of our nation resides in our ability to respond at all levels—local, state and federal. It's that synergy that creates the solution to the things in the homeland that challenge us in addressing our threats.[175]

The day after the tragic Boston Marathon bombings, Secretary of Defense Chuck Hagel pledged to provide any support from DoD that law enforcement agencies deem necessary as they investigated "this cruel act of terror,"[176] and Chairman of the Joint Chiefs of Staff Martin Dempsey told Members of Congress that DoD officials were in constant contact with state and federal agencies.[177] In the words of the NORTHCOM Commander,

> The commands' approach is to defend the homeland "forward" and in-depth through trusted partnerships with fellow combatant commands, our hemispheric neighbors, and the interagency community. We carry out our

---

[173] DEPARTMENT OF DEFENSE CYBERSPACE POLICY REPORT—A REPORT TO CONGRESS PURSUANT TO THE NATIONAL DEFENSE AUTHORIZATION ACT FOR FISCAL YEAR 2011, § 934 2 (Nov. 2011), http://www.defense.gov/home/features/2011/0411_cyberstrategy/docs/ NDAA%20Section%20934%20Report_For%20webpage.pdf (last visited Aug. 29, 2014).

[174] Michael Sullivan, *supra* note 87, at 36.

[175] Christopher DeHart, *Army North CG Leads Panel on North American Security, Missions at AUSA Conference*, ARNORTH.ARMY.MIL (Nov. 4, 2013), http://www.arnorth.army.mil/news/army-north-cg-leads-panel-on-north-american-securi.aspx (last visited Aug. 29, 2014).

[176] Jim Garamone, *Hagel Says DoD Will Provide Support after Cruel Act of Terror*, ARMED FORCES PRESS SERVICE (Apr. 16, 2013), http://www.defense.gov/news/ newsarticle.aspx?id=119782 (last Aug. 29, 2014).

[177] *Id.*

primary missions of homeland defense, security cooperation, and civil support with a focus on preparation, partnerships, and vigilance.[178]

The 207-year history of the Insurrection Act, the 136-year-old Posse Comitatus Act, and other current and future laws, defense policies, and regulations will continue to strictly delineate the limits to the military's role in cooperating with civil authorities when future domestic disasters strike.[179]

---

[178] House Armed Services Committee, *Statement of General Charles H. Jacoby, Jr., United States Army, Commander, United States Northern Command and North American Aerospace Defense Command Before The House Armed Services Committee, Guard* (Feb. 26, 2014) http://www.northcom.mil/Portals/28/Documents/2014%20NC% 20Posture%20Statement_Final_HASC.pdf (last visited Aug. 29, 2014).

[179] For an excellent yet brief commentary on the role of the military in dealing with international natural and man-made disasters, see Elizabeth Ferris, Future directions in Civil-Military Responses to Natural Disasters, Paper 05/2012 1-10, Brookings.edu, http://www.brookings.edu/research/papers/2012/05/civ-mil-disasters-ferris (last visited Aug. 29, 2014). Ferris notes that "[o]ver the last ten years natural disasters affected more than 2.4 billion people—the equivalent of one-third of the earth's population—and they have wrought over $910 billion in damages—equivalent to approximately 18 percent of global GDP." *Id.* at 1, 3–6. Ferris also makes five observations regarding civil-military relations in international natural disaster response:

1. The military will increasingly be called to respond to sudden-onset natural disasters, both at home and abroad
2. Generally there are fewer political tensions in civil-military relations at times of natural disaster compared with in conflict settings
3. International actors, military or civilian, simply are not—and perhaps cannot be—fast enough in immediate response
4. In the three phases of disaster management—prevention, response and recovery—the military's role is most needed and accepted in the response phase and least in the recovery phase
5. The military generally has more experience in preparedness activities hence an importance area of preparedness concerns developing more effective civil-military coordination mechanisms

Id. at 1, 3–6.

INDEX

(Note: "*n*" represents footnotes and "*f*" represents figures)